# McGraw-Hill/Irwin Series
# Operations and Decision Sciences

## Business Statistics

Aczel and Sounderpandian
**Complete Business Statistics**
*Fifth Edition*

ALEKS Corporation
**ALEKS for Business Statistics**
*First Edition*

Alwan
**Statistical Process Analysis**
*First Edition*

Bowerman and O'Connell
**Business Statistics in Practice**
*Third Edition*

Bowerman, O'Connell, and Orris
**Essentials of Business Statistics**
*First Edition*

*Bryant and Smith
**Practical Data Analysis: Case Studies in Business Statistics, Volumes I and II,** *Second Edition;* **Volume III,** *First Edition*

Cooper and Schindler
**Business Research Methods**
*Eighth Edition*

Delurgio
**Forecasting Principles and Applications**
*First Edition*

Doane
**Learning Statistics**
*First Edition, 1.2*

Doane, Mathieson, and Tracy
**Visual Statistics**
*Second Edition, 2.0*

Gitlow, Oppenheim, and Oppenheim
**Quality Management: Tools and Methods for Improvement**
*Second Edition*

Lind, Marchal, and Wathen
**Basic Statistics for Business and Economics**
*Fourth Edition*

Lind, Marchal, and Wathen
**Statistical Techniques in Business and Economics**
*Twelfth Edition*

Merchant, Goffinet, and Koehler
**Basic Statistics Using Excel for Office 2000**
*Third Edition*

Merchant, Goffinet, and Koehler
**Basic Statistics Using Excel for Office XP**
*Fourth Edition*

Neter, Kutner, Nachtsheim, and Wasserman
**Applied Linear Statistical Models**
*Fourth Edition*

Kutner, Nachtsheim, and Neter
**Applied Linear Regression Models**
*Fourth Edition*

Sahai and Khurshid
**Pocket Dictionary of Statistics**
*First Edition*

Siegel
**Practical Business Statistics**
*Fifth Edition*

Webster
**Applied Statistics for Business and Economics: An Essentials Version**
*Third Edition*

Wilson, Keating, and John Galt Solutions
**Business Forecasting with Excel Based Forecast X Software**
*Fourth Edition*

## Quantitative Methods and Management Science

Bonini, Hausman, and Bierman
**Quantitative Analysis for Business Decisions**
*Ninth Edition*

Hillier and Hillier
**Introduction to Management Science: A Modeling and Case Studies Approach with Spreadsheets**
*Second Edition*

*Available only through McGraw-Hill's Primis Digital Assets Library.

# Preface

The objective of *Statistical Techniques in Business and Economics* is to provide students majoring in management, marketing, finance, accounting, economics, and other fields of business administration with an introductory survey of the many applications of descriptive and inferential statistics. While we focus on business applications, we also use many problems and examples that are student oriented and do not require previous courses.

The first edition of this text was published in 1967. At that time locating relevant business data was difficult. That has changed! Today locating data is not a problem. The number of items you purchase at the grocery store is automatically recorded at the checkout counter. Phone companies track the time of our calls, the length of calls, and the number of the person called. Credit card companies maintain information on the number, time and date, and amount of our purchases. Medical devices automatically monitor our heart rate, blood pressure, and temperature. A large amount of business information is recorded and reported almost instantly. CNN, *USA Today*, and MSNBC, for example, all have websites where you can track stock prices with a delay of less than twenty minutes.

Today, skills are needed to deal with the large volume of numerical information. First, we need to be critical consumers of information presented by others. Second, we need to be able to reduce large amounts of information into a concise and meaningful form to enable us to make effective interpretations, judgments, and decisions.

All students have calculators and most have either personal computers or access to personal computers in a campus lab. Statistical software, such as Microsoft Excel and MINITAB, is available on these computers. The commands necessary to achieve the software results are available in a special section at the end of each chapter. We use screen captures within the chapters, so the student becomes familiar with the nature of the software output. Because of the availability of computers and software it is no longer necessary to dwell on calculations. We have replaced many of the calculation examples with interpretative ones, to assist the student in understanding and interpreting the statistical results. In addition we now place more emphasis on the conceptual nature of the statistical topics. While making these changes, we have not moved away from presenting, as best we can, the key concepts, along with supporting examples.

The twelfth edition of *Statistical Techniques in Business and Economics* is the product of many people: students, colleagues, reviewers, and the staff at McGraw-Hill/Irwin. We thank them all. We wish to express our sincere gratitude to the reviewers:

Wynn Abranovic
*University of Massachusetts—Amherst*

Mostafa Aminzadeh
*Towson University*

Lari Arjomand
*Clayton University*

J. R. Brey
*Cardinal Stritch University*

Nancy Brooks
*University of Vermont—Burlington*

Giorgio Canarella
*California State University—Los Angeles*

Chia-Shin Chung
*Cleveland State University*

Anne Davey
*Northeastern State University*

Nirmil Devi
*Embry Riddle University*

Casey DiRienzo
*Elon University*

Mark Eakin
*University of Texas at Arlington*

Joseph Fuhr
*Widener University*

Jonathan Furdek
*Purdue University—Calumet*

Joel Goldstein
*Western Connecticut State University*

Alison Kelly Hawke
*Suffolk University*

Clifford Hawley
*West Virginia University*

Gary Kettlitz
*Ramapo College*

Marcia Lambert
*Pittsburgh Community College*

Christopher Lowery
*Georgia College and State University*

Robert Lynch
*University of Northern Colorado*

Elaine McGivern
*Duquesne University*

Daniel Mihalko
*Western Michigan University—Kalamazoo*

Tracy Miller
*Grove City College*

Abdel-Aziz Mohamed
*California State University—Northridge*

Lee Neidleman
*San Jose State University*

Cliff Nowell
*Weber State University*

J. G. Patankar
*University of Akron*

James Payne
*Eastern Kentucky University*

Joseph A. Petry
*University of Illinois Champaign—Urbana*

Anastasia Pikas
*Niagara University*

Ali Rassui
*Purdue University—Fort Wayne*

Harriet Rojas
*Indiana Wesleyan University*

Christopher Rogers
*Miami Dade Community College*

Robert K. Smidt
*California Polytechnic University*

Gary Smith
*Florida State University*

Tara Sudderth
*Birmingham—Southern College*

Their suggestions and thorough review of the previous edition and the manuscript of this edition make this a better text.

Special thanks go to a number of people. Dr. Leonard Presby of William Paterson University, Dr. Julia Norton of California State University—Hayward, and Dr. Mary Elizabeth Camp of Indiana University reviewed the manuscript and checked exercises for accuracy. Professor Walter Lange, of the University of Toledo, prepared the study guide. Dr. Rick Cornack, of Coastal Carolina University, and Dr. Temoleon Rousos checked the study guide for accuracy. Dr. Samuel Wathen, of Coastal Carolina University, prepared the test bank. Professor Joyce Keller, of St. Edward's University, prepared the PowerPoint Presentation. Ms. Denise Heban and the authors prepared the Instructor's Manual.

We also wish to thank the staff at McGraw-Hill/Irwin. This includes Richard T. Hercher, Jr., Executive Editor; Christina Sanders, Developmental Editor; Douglas Reiner, Marketing Manager; James Labeots, Project Manager, and others we do not know personally, but who made valuable contributions.

# Brief Contents

# Contents

**Contents**

Chapter

# 4 Describing Data: Displaying and Exploring Data   96

Chapter

# 5 A Survey of Probability Concepts   139

Chapter

# 9 Estimation and Confidence Intervals 282

Chapter

# 10 One-Sample Tests of Hypothesis 316

Chapter

# 11 Two-Sample Tests of Hypothesis 355

Chapter

## 12 Analysis of Variance   386

Chapter

## 13 Linear Regression and Correlation   428

Chapter

## 14 Multiple Regression and Correlation Analysis   474

**Contents**

Chapter

# 15 Nonparametric Methods: Chi-Square Applications   522

Chapter

# 16 Nonparametric Methods: Analysis of Ranked Data   546

Chapter

# 17 Statistical Quality Control   586

# What Is Statistics?

## GOALS

*When you have completed this chapter you will be able to:*

1 Understand why we study statistics.

2 Explain what is meant by *descriptive statistics* and *inferential statistics.*

3 Distinguish between a *qualitative variable* and a *quantitative variable.*

4 Distinguish between a *discrete variable* and a *continuous variable.*

5 Distinguish among the *nominal, ordinal, interval,* and *ratio* levels of measurement.

6 Define the terms *mutually exclusive* and *exhaustive.*

High speed conveyor belts and state-of-the-art technology efficiently move merchandise through Wal-Mart's distribution centers to keep its nearly 3,000 stores in stock.

In 2003, the four largest American companies ranked by sales were Wal-Mart, Exxon Mobil, General Motors, and Ford Motor Company. (See Goal 5 and Statistics in Action box, page 4.)

# Introduction

More than 100 years ago H. G. Wells, an English author and historian, suggested that one day quantitative reasoning will be as necessary for effective citizenship as the ability to read. He made no mention of business because the Industrial Revolution was just beginning. Mr. Wells could not have been more correct. While "business experience," some "thoughtful guesswork," and "intuition" are key attributes of successful managers, today's business problems tend to be too complex for this type of decision making alone.

Fortunately, business managers of the twenty-first century have access to large amounts of information. Well known for his ability to analyze economic data, Alan Greenspan, Chairman of the Federal Reserve, knows the importance of statistical tools and techniques to provide accurate and timely information to make public statements that have the power to move global stock markets and influence political thinking. Dr. Greenspan, speaking before a National Skills Summit, stated: "Workers must be equipped not simply with technical know-how, but also with the ability to create, analyze, and transform information and to interact effectively with others. That is, separate the facts from opinions, and then organize these facts in an appropriate manner and analyze the information."

One of the tools used to understand information is statistics. Statistics is used not only by business people; we all also apply statistical concepts in our lives. For example, to start the day you turn on the shower and let it run for a few moments. Then you put your hand in the shower to sample the temperature and decide to add more hot water or more cold water, or you conclude that the temperature is just right and enter the shower. As a second example, suppose you are at the grocery store and wish to buy a frozen pizza. One of the pizza makers has a stand, and they offer a small wedge of their pizza. After sampling the pizza, you decide whether to purchase the pizza or not. In both the shower and pizza examples, you make a decision and select a course of action based on a sample.

Businesses face similar situations. The Kellogg Company must ensure that the mean amount of Raisin Bran in the 25.5-gram box meets label specifications. To do so, they might set a "target" weight somewhat higher than the amount specified on the label. Each box is then weighed after it is filled. The weighing machine reports a distribution of the content weights for each hour as well as the number "kicked-out" for being under the label specification during the hour. The Quality Inspection Department also randomly selects samples from the production line and checks the quality of the product and the weight of the box. If the mean product weight differs significantly from the target weight or the percent of kick-outs is too large, the process is adjusted.

On a national level, a candidate for the office of President of the United States wants to know what percent of the voters in Illinois will support him in the upcoming election. There are several ways he could go about answering this question. He could have his staff call all those people in Illinois who plan to vote in the upcoming election and ask for whom they plan to vote. He could go out on a street in Chicago, stop 10 people who look to be of voting age, and ask them for whom they plan to vote. He could select a random sample of about 2,000 voters from the state, contact these voters, and, on the basis of this information, make an estimate of the percent who will vote for him in the upcoming election. In this text we will show you why the third choice is the best course of action.

# Why Study Statistics?

If you look through your university catalog, you will find that statistics is required for many college programs. Why is this so? What are the differences in the statistics courses taught in the Engineering College, Psychology or Sociology Departments in the Liberal Arts College, and the College of Business? The biggest difference is the examples used. The course content is basically the same. In the College of Business we are interested in such things as profits, hours worked, and wages. In the Psychology Department they are interested in test scores, and in Engineering they may be interested in how many units are manufactured on a particular machine. However, all three are interested in what is a typical value and how much variation there is in the data. There may also be a difference in the level of mathematics required. An engineering statistics course usually requires calculus. Statistics courses in colleges of business and education usually teach the course at a more applied level. You should be able to handle the mathematics in this text if you have completed high school algebra.

So why is statistics required in so many majors? The first reason is that numerical information is everywhere. Look in the newspapers (*USA Today*), news magazines (*Time, Newsweek, U.S. News and World Report*), business magazines (*Business Week, Forbes*), or general interest magazines (*People*), women's magazines (*Home and Garden*), or sports magazines (*Sports Illustrated, ESPN The Magazine*), and you will be bombarded with numerical information.

Here are some examples:

*Examples of why we study statistics*

- In 2001 the typical household income in the United States was $42,228. For households in the Northeast the typical income was $45,716, $43,834 in the Midwest, $38,904 in the South, and $45,087 in the West. You can check the latest information by going to http://www.census.gov/hhes/income and then search among the choices and select income01 and inctab1.html.
- In 2002 the average amount of turkey consumed per person was 17.3 pounds, with 32 percent of the consumption over the Holidays. In the 1970s more than 50 percent of the consumption was over the Holidays. You can find similar information by going to http://www.usatoday.com/ and click on Snapshots.
- About 77 percent of the golfers in the United States attended college, their average household income is more than $70,000 per year, 60 percent own home computers, 45 percent have investments in stocks and bonds, and they spend $6.2 billion annually on golf equipment and apparel. You can find additional information at http://www.fcon.com/golfing/demographics.htm.
- The National Coffee Association found 54 percent of the adult population drinks coffee every day. Men drink an average of 1.9 cups per day and women 1.4. Americans spend $9.2 billion in the retail sector of the economy and $8.7 billion in the food service sector each year on coffee. Additional information is available at http://coffeeresearch/market/usa.htm.

How are we to determine if the conclusions reported are reasonable? Was the sample large enough? How were the sampled units selected? To be an educated consumer of this information, we need to be able to read the charts and graphs and understand the discussion of the numerical information. An understanding of the concepts of basic statistics will be a big help.

A second reason for taking a statistics course is that statistical techniques are used to make decisions that affect our daily lives. That is, they affect our personal welfare. Here are a few examples:

- Insurance companies use statistical analysis to set rates for home, automobile, life, and health insurance. Tables are available that summarize the probability that a 25-year-old woman will survive the next year. On the basis of these probabilities,

life insurance premiums can be established. These tables are available at http://www.budgetrates.com/mortality.htm.
- The Environmental Protection Agency is interested in the water quality of Lake Erie. They periodically take water samples to establish the level of contamination and maintain the level of quality.
- Medical researchers study the cure rates for diseases using different drugs and different forms of treatment. For example, what is the effect of treating a certain type of knee injury surgically or with physical therapy? If you take an aspirin each day, does that reduce your risk of a heart attack?

A third reason for taking a statistics course is that the knowledge of statistical methods will help you understand how decisions are made and give you a better understanding of how they affect you.

No matter what line of work you select, you will find yourself faced with decisions where an understanding of data analysis is helpful. In order to make an informed decision, you will need to be able to:

1  Determine whether the existing information is adequate or additional information is required.
2. Gather additional information, if it is needed, in such a way that it does not provide misleading results.
3. Summarize the information in a useful and informative manner.
4. Analyze the available information.
5. Draw conclusions and make inferences while assessing the risk of an incorrect conclusion.

The statistical methods presented in the text will provide you with a framework for the decision-making process.

In summary, there are at least three reasons for studying statistics: (1) data are everywhere, (2) statistical techniques are used to make many decisions that affect our lives, and (3) no matter what your career, you will make professional decisions that involve data. An understanding of statistical methods will help you make these decisions more effectively.

## What Is Meant by Statistics?

How do we define the word *statistics*? We encounter it frequently in our everyday language. It really has two meanings. In the more common usage, statistics refers to numerical information. Examples include the average starting salary of college graduates, the number of deaths due to alcoholism last year, the change in the Dow Jones Industrial Average from yesterday to today, and the number of home runs hit by the Chicago Cubs during the 2003 season. In these examples statistics are a value or a percentage. Other examples include:

- The typical automobile in the United States travels 11,099 miles per year, the typical bus 9,353 miles per year, and the typical truck 13,942 miles per year. In Canada the corresponding information is 10,371 miles for automobiles, 19,823 miles for buses, and 7,001 miles for trucks.
- The mean time waiting for technical support is 17 minutes.
- The mean length of the business cycle since 1945 is 61 months.

The above are all examples of **statistics.** A collection of numerical information is called **statistics** (plural).

We often present statistical information in a graphical form. A graph is often useful for capturing reader attention and to portray a large amount of information. For example, Chart 1–1 shows Frito-Lay volume and market share for the major snack and potato chip categories in supermarkets in the United States. It requires only a quick glance to discover there were nearly 800 million pounds of potato chips sold and that Frito-Lay sold 64 percent of that total. Also note that Frito-Lay has 82 percent of the corn chip market.

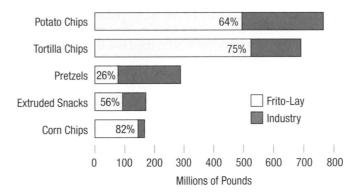

**CHART 1–1** Frito-Lay Volume and Share of Major Snack Chip Categories in U.S. Supermarkets

The subject of statistics, as we will explore it in this text, has a much broader meaning than just collecting and publishing numerical information. We define statistics as:

> **STATISTICS** The science of collecting, organizing, presenting, analyzing, and interpreting data to assist in making more effective decisions.

As the definition suggests, the first step in investigating a problem is to collect relevant data. It must be organized in some way and perhaps presented in a chart, such as Chart 1–1. Only after the data have been organized are we then able to analyze and interpret it. Here are some examples of the need for data collection.

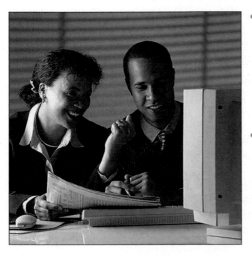

- Research analysts for Merrill Lynch evaluate many facets of a particular stock before making a "buy" or "sell" recommendation. They collect the past sales data of the company and estimate future earnings. Other factors, such as the projected worldwide demand for the company's products, the strength of the competition, and the effect of the new union-management contract, are also considered before making a recommendation.
- The marketing department at Colgate-Palmolive Co., a manufacturer of soap products, has the responsibility of making recommendations regarding the potential profitability of a newly developed group of face soaps having fruit smells, such as grape, orange, and pineapple. Before making a final decision, they will test it in several markets. That is, they may advertise and sell it in Topeka, Kansas, and Tampa, Florida. On the basis of test marketing in these two regions, Colgate-Palmolive will make a decision whether to market the soaps in the entire country.
- The United States government is concerned with the present condition of our economy and with predicting future economic trends. The government conducts a large number of surveys to determine consumer confidence and the outlook of management regarding sales and production for the next 12 months. Indexes, such as the Consumer Price Index, are constructed each month to assess inflation. Information on department store sales, housing starts, money turnover, and

industrial production are just a few of the hundreds of items used to form the basis of the projections. These evaluations are used by banks to decide their prime lending rate and by the Federal Reserve Board to decide the level of control to place on the money supply.

- Management must make decisions on the quality of production. For example, automatic drill presses do not produce a perfect hole that is always 1.30 inches in diameter each time the hole is drilled (because of drill wear, vibration of the machine, and other factors). Slight tolerances are permitted, but when the hole is too small or too large, these products are defective and cannot be used. The Quality Assurance Department is charged with continually monitoring production by using sampling techniques to ensure that outgoing production meets standards.

# Types of Statistics

## Descriptive Statistics

The study of statistics is usually divided into two categories: descriptive statistics and inferential statistics. The definition of statistics given earlier referred to "organizing, presenting, analyzing . . . data." This facet of statistics is usually referred to as **descriptive statistics.**

---

**DESCRIPTIVE STATISTICS** Methods of organizing, summarizing, and presenting data in an informative way.

---

For instance, the United States government reports the population of the United States was 179,323,000 in 1960, 203,302,000 in 1970, 226,542,000 in 1980, 248,709,000 in 1990, and 265,000,000 in 2000. This information is descriptive statistics. It is descriptive statistics if we calculate the percentage growth from one decade to the next. However, it would **not** be descriptive statistics if we used these to estimate the population of the United States in the year 2010 or the percentage growth from 2000 to 2010. Why? Because these statistics are not being used to summarize past populations but to estimate future populations. The following are some other examples of descriptive statistics.

- There are a total of 42,796 miles of interstate highways in the United States. The interstate system represents only 1 percent of the nation's total roads but carries more than 20 percent of the traffic. The longest is I-90, which stretches from Boston to Seattle, a distance of 3,081 miles. The shortest is I-878 in New York City, which is 0.70 of a mile in length. Alaska does not have any interstate highways, Texas has the most interstate miles at 3,232, and New York has the most interstate routes with 28.
- According to the *Bureau of Labor Statistics,* the average hourly earnings of production workers were $15.16 (a preliminary figure) for March 2003. You can review the latest information on wages and productivity of American workers by going to the Bureau of Labor Statistics website at: http://www.bls.gov/home.htm and select Average hourly earnings.

Masses of unorganized data—such as the census of population, the weekly earnings of thousands of computer programmers, and the individual responses of 2,000 registered voters regarding their choice for President of the United States—are of little value as is. However, statistical techniques are available to organize this type of data into a meaningful form. Some data can be organized into a **frequency distribution.** (This procedure is covered in Chapter 2.) Various **charts** may be used to describe data; several basic chart forms are also presented in Chapter 4.

Specific measures of central location, such as the mean, describe the central value of a group of numerical data. A number of statistical measures are used to describe how closely the data cluster about an average. These measures of central tendency and dispersion are discussed in Chapter 3.

# Inferential Statistics

Another facet of statistics is **inferential statistics**—also called **statistical inference** and **inductive statistics.** Our main concern regarding inferential statistics is finding something about a population from a sample taken from that population. For example, a recent survey showed only 46 percent of high school seniors can solve problems involving fractions, decimals, and percentages. And only 77 percent of high school seniors correctly totaled the cost of soup, a burger, fries, and a cola on a restaurant menu. Since these are inferences about a population (all high school seniors) based on sample data, we refer to them as inferential statistics.

> **INFERENTIAL STATISTICS** The methods used to determine something about a population on the basis of a sample.

Note the words *population* and *sample* in the definition of inferential statistics. We often make reference to the population living in the United States or the 1.29 billion population of China. However, in statistics the word *population* has a broader meaning. A *population* may consist of *individuals*—such as all the students enrolled at Utah State University, all the students in Accounting 201, or all the CEOs from the Fortune 500 companies. A population may also consist of *objects,* such as all the XB-70 tires produced at Cooper Tire and Rubber Company in the Findlay, Ohio, plant; the accounts receivable at the end of October for Lorrange Plastics, Inc.; or auto claims filed in the first quarter of 2003 at the Northeast Regional Office of State Farm Insurance. The *measurement* of interest might be the scores on the first examination of all students in Accounting 201, the wall thickness of the Cooper Tires, the dollar amount of Lorrange Plastics accounts receivable, or the amount of auto insurance claims at State Farm. Thus, a population in the statistical sense does not always refer to people.

> **POPULATION** The entire set of individuals or objects of interest or the measurements obtained from all individuals or objects of interest.

To infer something about a population, we usually take a **sample** from the population.

> **SAMPLE** A portion, or part, of the population of interest.

Reasons for sampling

Why take a sample instead of studying every member of the population? A sample of registered voters is necessary because of the prohibitive cost of contacting millions of voters before an election. Testing wheat for moisture content destroys the wheat, thus making a sample imperative. If the wine tasters tested all the wine, none would be available for sale. It would be physically impossible for a few marine biologists to capture and tag all the seals in the ocean. (These and other reasons for sampling are discussed in Chapter 8.)

As noted, using a sample to learn something about a population is done extensively in business, agriculture, politics, and government, as cited in the following examples:

- Television networks constantly monitor the popularity of their programs by hiring Nielsen and other organizations to sample the preferences of TV viewers. For example, in a sample of 800 prime-time viewers, 320 or 40 percent indicated they watched *CSI (Crime Scene Investigation)* on CBS last week. These program ratings are used to set advertising rates or to cancel programs.

- Gamous and Associates, a public accounting firm, is conducting an audit of Pronto Printing Company. To begin, the accounting firm selects a random sample of 100 invoices and checks each invoice for accuracy. There is at least one error on five of the invoices; hence the accounting firm estimates that 5 percent of the population of invoices contain at least one error.
- A random sample of 1,260 accounting graduates from four-year schools showed their mean starting salary was $42,694. We therefore estimate the mean starting salary for all accounting graduates of four-year institutions to be $42,694.

The relationship between a sample and a population is portrayed below. For example, we wish to estimate the mean miles per gallon of SUVs. Six SUVs are selected from the population. The mean MPG of the six is used to estimate MPG for the population.

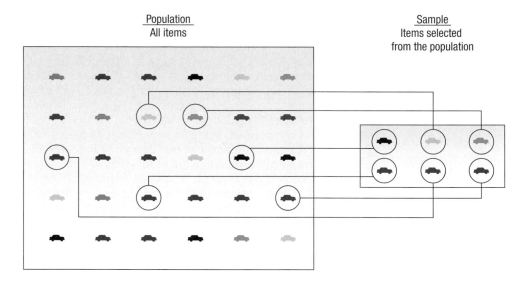

We strongly suggest you do the Self-Review exercises.

*Following is a self-review problem. There are a number of them interspersed throughout each chapter. They test your comprehension of the preceding material. The answer and method of solution are given at the end of the chapter. You can find the answer to the following Self-Review on page 22. We recommend that you solve each one and then check your answer.*

---

**Self-Review 1–1**

*The answers are at the end of the chapter.*
Chicago-based Market Facts asked a sample of 1,960 consumers to try a newly developed chicken dinner by Boston Market. Of the 1,960 sampled, 1,176 said they would purchase the dinner if it is marketed.
(a)  What could Market Facts report to Boston Market regarding acceptance of the chicken dinner in the population?
(b)  Is this an example of descriptive statistics or inferential statistics? Explain.

---

# Types of Variables

Qualitative variable

There are two basic types of variables: (1) qualitative and (2) quantitative (see Chart 1–2). When the characteristic being studied is nonnumeric, it is called a **qualitative variable** or an **attribute.** Examples of qualitative variables are gender, religious affiliation, type of automobile owned, state of birth, and eye color. When the data are qualitative, we are usually interested in how many or what proportion fall in each category. For example, what percent of the population has blue eyes? How many Catholics and how many Protestants are there in the United States? What percent of the total number of cars sold last month were SUVs? Qualitative data are often summarized in charts and bar graphs (Chapter 2).

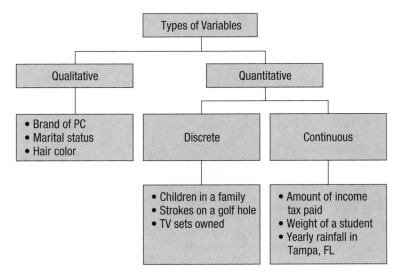

**CHART 1–2** Summary of the Types of Variables

When the variable studied can be reported numerically, the variable is called a **quantitative variable.** Examples of quantitative variables are the balance in your checking account, the ages of company presidents, the life of an automobile battery (such as 42 months), and the number of children in a family.

Quantitative variables are either discrete or continuous. **Discrete variables** can assume only certain values, and there are usually "gaps" between the values. Examples of discrete variables are the number of bedrooms in a house (1, 2, 3, 4, etc.), the number of cars arriving at Exit 25 on I-4 in Florida near Walt Disney World in an hour (326, 421, etc.), and the number of students in each section of a statistics course (25 in section A, 42 in section B, and 18 in section C). We count, for example, the number of cars arriving at Exit 25 on I-4, and we count the number of statistics students in each section. Notice that a home can have 3 or 4 bedrooms, but it cannot have 3.56 bedrooms. Thus, there is a "gap" between possible values. Typically, discrete variables result from counting.

Observations of a **continuous variable** can assume any value within a specific range. Examples of continuous variables are the air pressure in a tire and the weight of a shipment of tomatoes. Other examples are the amount of raisin bran in a box and the duration of flights from Orlando to San Diego. Typically, continuous variables result from measuring.

# Levels of Measurement

Data can be classified according to levels of measurement. The level of measurement of the data often dictates the calculations that can be done to summarize and present the data. It will also determine the statistical tests that should be performed. For example, there are six colors of candies in a bag of M&M's candies. Suppose we assign brown a value of 1, yellow 2, blue 3, orange 4, green 5, and red 6. From a bag of candies, we add the assigned color values and divide by the number of candies and report that the mean color is 3.56. Does this mean that the average color is blue or

**Statistics in Action**

Where did statistics get its start? In 1662 John Graunt published an article called "Natural and Political Observations Made upon Bills of Mortality." The author's "observations" were the result of a study and analysis of a weekly church publication called "Bill of Mortality," which listed births, christenings, and deaths and their causes. Graunt realized that the Bills of Mortality represented only a fraction of all births and deaths in London. However, he used the data to reach broad conclusions about the impact of disease, such as the plague, on the general population. His logic is an example of statistical inference. His analysis and interpretation of the data are thought to mark the start of statistics.

orange? Of course not! As a second example, in a high school track meet there are eight competitors in the 400 meter run. We report the order of finish and that the mean finish is 4.5. What does the mean finish tell us? Nothing! In both of these instances, we have not properly used the level of measurement.

There are actually four levels of measurement: nominal, ordinal, interval, and ratio. The lowest, or the most primitive, measurement is the nominal level. The highest, or the level that gives us the most information about the observation, is the ratio level of measurement.

## Nominal-Level Data

For the **nominal level** of measurement observations of a qualitative variable can only be classified and counted. There is no particular order to the labels. The classification of the six colors of M&M's milk chocolate candies is an example of the nominal level of measurement. We simply classify the candies by color. There is no natural order. That is, we could report the brown candies first, the orange first, or any of the colors first. Gender is another example of the nominal level of measurement. Suppose we count the number of students entering a football game with a student ID and report how many are men and how many are women. We could report either the men or the women first. For the nominal level the only measurement involved consists of counts. Table 1–1 shows a breakdown of the sources of world oil supply. The variable of interest is the country or region. This is a nominal-level variable because we record the information by country or region and there is no natural order. We could have reported the United States last instead of first. Do not be distracted by the fact that we summarize the variable by reporting the number of barrels produced per day.

**TABLE 1–1**  World Oil Supply by Country or Region

| Country or Region | Millions of Barrels per Day | Percent |
|---|---|---|
| United States | 9.05 | 12 |
| Persian Gulf | 18.84 | 25 |
| OAPEC | 19.50 | 26 |
| OPEC | 28.00 | 37 |
| Total | 75.39 | 100 |

Note: You can check the most recent information and find the countries included in the various groups by going to http://www.eia.doe.gov/emeu/ipsr/appa.html.

Table 1–1 shows the essential feature of the nominal scale of measurement: there is no particular order to the categories.

The categories in the previous example are **mutually exclusive,** meaning, for example, that a particular barrel of oil cannot be produced by the United States and the Persian Gulf Region at the same time.

> **MUTUALLY EXCLUSIVE** A property of a set of categories such that an individual or object is included in only one category.

The categories in Table 1–1 are also **exhaustive,** meaning that every member of the population or sample must appear in one of the categories. So the categories include all oil producing nations.

> **EXHAUSTIVE** A property of a set of categories such that each individual or object must appear in a category.

In order to process data on oil production, gender, employment by industry, and so forth, the categories are often numerically coded 1, 2, 3, and so on, with 1 representing the United States, 2 representing Persian Gulf, for example. This facilitates counting by the computer. However, because we have assigned numbers to the various categories, this does not give us license to manipulate the numbers. For example, 1 + 2 does not equal 3, that is, United States + Persian Gulf does not equal OAPEC. To summarize, the nominal-level data have the following properties:

1.  Data categories are mutually exclusive and exhaustive.
2.  Data categories have no logical order.

## Ordinal-Level Data

The next higher level of data is the **ordinal level.** Table 1–2 lists the student ratings of Professor James Brunner in an Introduction to Finance course. Each student in the class answered the question "Overall how did you rate the instructor in this class?" The variable rating illustrates the use of the ordinal scale of measurement. One classification is "higher" or "better" than the next one. That is, "Superior" is better than "Good," "Good" is better than "Average," and so on. However, we are not able to distinguish the magnitude of the differences between groups. Is the difference between "Superior" and "Good" the same as the difference between "Poor" and "Inferior"? We cannot tell. If we substitute a 5 for "Superior" and a 4 for "Good," we can conclude that the rating of "Superior" is better than the rating of "Good," but we cannot add a ranking of "Superior" and a ranking of "Good," with the result being meaningful. Further we cannot conclude that a rating of "Good" (rating is 4) is necessarily twice as high as a "Poor" (rating is 2). We can only conclude that a rating of "Good" is better than a rating of "Poor." We cannot conclude how much better the rating is.

**TABLE 1–2** Rating of a Finance Professor

| Rating | Frequency |
|---|---|
| Superior | 6 |
| Good | 28 |
| Average | 25 |
| Poor | 12 |
| Inferior | 3 |

Another example of ordinal-level data is the Homeland Security Advisory System. The Department of Homeland Security publishes this information regarding the risk of terrorist activity to federal, state, and local authorities and to the American people. The five risk levels from lowest to highest including a description and color codes are:

| Risk Level | Description | Color |
|------------|-------------|-------|
| Low | Low risk of terrorist attack | Green |
| Guarded | General risk of terrorist attack | Blue |
| Elevated | Significant risk of terrorist attack | Yellow |
| High | High risk of terrorist attack | Orange |
| Severe | Severe risk of terrorist attack | Red |

This is ordinal scale data because we know the order or ranks of the risk levels—that is, orange is higher than yellow—but the amount of the difference between each of the levels is not necessarily the same. You can check the current status by going to http://www.whitehouse.gov/homeland.

In summary, the properties of ordinal-level data are:

1. The data classifications are mutually exclusive and exhaustive.
2. Data classifications are ranked or ordered according to the particular trait they possess.

## Interval-Level Data

The **interval level** of measurement is the next highest level. It includes all the characteristics of the ordinal level, but in addition, the difference between values is a constant size. An example of the interval level of measurement is temperature. Suppose the high temperatures on three consecutive winter days in Boston are 28, 31, and 20 degrees Fahrenheit. These temperatures can be easily ranked, but we can also determine the difference between temperatures. This is possible because 1 degree Fahrenheit represents a constant unit of measurement. Equal differences between two temperatures are the same, regardless of their position on the scale. That is, the difference between 10 degrees Fahrenheit and 15 degrees is 5, the difference between 50 and 55 degrees is also 5 degrees. It is also important to note that 0 is just a point on the scale. It does not represent the absence of the condition. Zero degrees Fahrenheit does not represent the absence of heat, just that it is cold! In fact 0 degrees Fahrenheit is about $-18$ degrees on the Celsius scale.

The properties of the interval-level data are:

1. Data classifications are mutually exclusive and exhaustive.
2. Data classifications are ordered according to the amount of the characteristic they possess.
3. Equal differences in the characteristic are represented by equal differences in the measurements.

There are few examples of the interval scale of measurement. Temperature, which was just cited, is one example. Others are shoe size and IQ scores.

## Ratio-Level Data

Practically all quantitative data are the ratio level of measurement. The **ratio level** is the "highest" level of measurement. It has all the characteristics of the interval level, but in addition, the 0 point is meaningful and the ratio between two numbers is meaningful. Examples of the ratio scale of measurement include: wages, units of production, weight, changes in stock prices, distance between branch offices, and height. Money is a good illustration. If you have zero dollars, then you have no money. Weight is another example. If the dial on the scale of a correctly calibrated device is at zero, then there is a complete absence of weight. The ratio of two numbers is also meaningful. If Jim earns $40,000 per year selling insurance and Rob earns $80,000 per year selling cars, then Rob earns twice as much as Jim.

In summary, the properties of the ratio-level data are:

1. Data classifications are mutually exclusive and exhaustive.
2. Data classifications are ordered according to the amount of the characteristics they possess.
3. Equal differences in the characteristic are represented by equal differences in the numbers assigned to the classifications.
4. The zero point is the absence of the characteristic.

Table 1–3 illustrates the use of the ratio scale of measurement. It shows the incomes of four father and son combinations.

**TABLE 1–3** Father–Son Income Combinations

| Name | Father | Son |
|------|--------|-----|
| Lahey | $80,000 | $ 40,000 |
| Nale | 90,000 | 30,000 |
| Rho | 60,000 | 120,000 |
| Steele | 75,000 | 130,000 |

Observe that the senior Lahey earns twice as much as his son. In the Rho family the son makes twice as much as the father.

Chart 1–3 summarizes the major characteristics of the various levels of measurement.

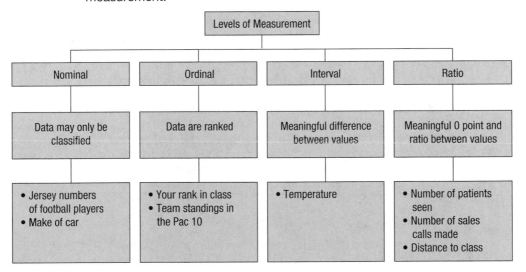

**CHART 1–3** Summary of the Characteristics for Levels of Measurement

**Self-Review 1–2**

What is the level of measurement reflected by the following data?

(a) The age of each person in a sample of 50 adults who listen to one of the 1,230 talk radio stations in the United States is:

| 35 | 29 | 41 | 34 | 44 | 46 | 42 | 42 | 37 | 47 |
| 30 | 36 | 41 | 39 | 44 | 39 | 43 | 43 | 44 | 40 |
| 47 | 37 | 41 | 27 | 33 | 33 | 39 | 38 | 43 | 22 |
| 44 | 39 | 35 | 35 | 41 | 42 | 37 | 42 | 38 | 43 |
| 35 | 37 | 38 | 43 | 40 | 48 | 42 | 31 | 51 | 34 |

(b) In a survey of 200 luxury-car owners, 100 were from California, 50 from New York, 30 from Illinois, and 20 from Ohio.

# Exercises

*The answers to the odd-numbered exercises are at the end of the book.*

1. What is the level of measurement for each of the following variables?
   a. Student IQ ratings.
   b. Distance students travel to class.
   c. Student scores on the first statistics test.
   d. A classification of students by state of birth.
   e. A ranking of students by freshman, sophomore, junior, and senior.
   f. Number of hours students study per week.
2. What is the level of measurement for these items related to the newspaper business?
   a. The number of papers sold each Sunday during 2004.
   b. The departments, such as editorial, advertising, sports, etc.
   c. A summary of the number of papers sold by county.
   d. The number of years with the paper for each employee.
3. Look in the latest edition of *USA Today* or your local newspaper and find examples of each level of measurement. Write a brief memo summarizing your findings.
4. For each of the following, determine whether the group is a sample or a population.
   a. The participants in a study of a new cholesterol drug.
   b. The drivers who received a speeding ticket in Kansas City last month.
   c. Those on welfare in Cook County (Chicago), Illinois.
   d. The 30 stocks reported as a part of the Dow Jones Industrial Average.

# Statistics, Graphics, and Ethics

You have probably heard the old saying that there are three kinds of lies: lies, damn lies, and statistics. This saying is attributable to Benjamin Disraeli and is over a century old. It has also been said that "figures don't lie: liars figure." Both of these statements refer to the abuses of statistics in which data are presented in ways that are misleading. Many abusers of statistics are simply ignorant or careless, while others have an objective to mislead the reader by emphasizing data that support their position while leaving out data that may be detrimental to their position. One of our major goals in this text is to make you a more critical consumer of information. When you see charts or data in a newspaper, in a magazine, or on TV, always ask yourself: What is the person trying to tell me? Does that person have an agenda? Following are several examples of the abuses of statistical analysis.

## Misleading Statistics

Several years ago, a series of TV advertisements reported that "2 out of 3 dentists surveyed indicated they would recommend Brand X toothpaste to their patients." The implication is that 67 percent of all dentists would recommend the product to their patients. What if they surveyed only three dentists? It would certainly not be a true representation of the real situation. The trick is that the manufacturer of the toothpaste could take *many* surveys of three dentists and report *only* the surveys of three dentists in which two dentists indicated they would recommend Brand X. This is concealing the information to mislead the public. Further, a survey of more than three dentists is needed, and it must be unbiased and representative of the population of all dentists. We discuss sampling methods in Chapter 8.

An average may not be representative of all the data.

The term *average* refers to several different measures of central location that we discuss in Chapter 3. To most people, an average is found by adding the values involved and dividing by the number of values. So if a real estate developer tells a client

**Statistics in Action**

There are about 700,000 physicians in the United States. Each year, according to the U.S. Dept. of Health and Human Services, there are 120,000 accidental deaths caused by physicians. In other words, there are 0.171 accidental deaths per physician, found by 120,000/700,000. Also in the United States, there are 80,000,000 gun owners and 1,500 accidental gun deaths per yer (all age groups). The number of accidental deaths per gun owner is 0.0000188, found by 1,500/80,000,000. Statistically, doctors are approximately 9,000 times more dangerous than gun owners. Are doctors more dangerous than gun owners? FACT: Not everyone has a gun, but everyone has at least one doctor. This is an example of the abuse of statistics.

that the average home in a particular subdivision sold for $150,000, we assume that $150,000 is a representative selling price for all the homes. But suppose there are only five homes in the subdivision and they sold for $50,000, $50,000, $60,000, $90,000, and $500,000. We can correctly claim that the average selling price is $150,000, but does $150,000 really seem like a "typical" selling price? Would you like to also know that the same number of homes sold for more than $60,000 as less than $60,000? Or that $50,000 is the selling price that occurred most frequently? So what selling price really is the most "typical"? This example illustrates that a reported average can be misleading, because it can be one of several numbers that could be used to represent the data. There is really no objective set of criteria that states what average should be reported on each occasion. We want to educate you as a consumer of data about how a person or group might report one value that favors their position and exclude other values. We will discuss averages, or measures of central location, in Chapter 3.

Sometimes numbers themselves can be deceptive. The mean price of homes sold last month in the Tampa, Florida, area was $134,891.58. This sounds like a very precise value and may instill a high degree of confidence in its accuracy. To report that the mean selling price was $135,000 doesn't convey the same precision and accuracy. However, a statistic that is very precise and carries 5 or even 10 decimal places is not necessarily accurate.

## Association Does Not Necessarily Imply Causation

Another area where there can be a misrepresentation of data is the association between variables. In statistical analysis often we find there is a strong *association* between variables. We find there is a strong negative association between outside work and grade point average. The more outside work a student is engaged in, the lower will be his or her grade point average. Does it mean that more outside work causes a lower grade point average? Not necessarily. It is also possible that the lower grade point average does not make the student eligible for a scholarship and therefore the student is required to engage in outside work to finance his or her education. Alternatively, both outside work and lower GPA could be a result of the social circumstances of the student. Unless we have used an experimental design that has successfully controlled the influence of all other factors on grade point average except the outside work, or vice versa, we are not justified in establishing any causation between variables based on statistical evidence alone. In general, *association based on observational (non-experimental) data is neutral with regard to causation.* We study the association between variables in Chapters 13 and 14.

## Graphs Can Be Misleading

Today in business, graphics are used as a visual aid for an easy interpretation. However, if they are not drawn carefully, they can lead to misinterpretation of information.

As either the preparer or the consumer of such graphics, it is useful to remember that the intention is to communicate an objective and accurate representation of reality. Really, neither sender nor receiver will benefit by intentional or sloppy distortions.

**Examples**     Suppose school taxes for the Corry Area Exempted School District increased from $100 in 2000 to $200 in the year 2004 (see Chart 1–4). That is, the taxes doubled during the 4-year period. To show this change, the dollar sign on the right is twice as tall as the one on the left. However, it is also twice as wide! Therefore the area of the dollar sign on the right is 4 times (not twice) that on the left.

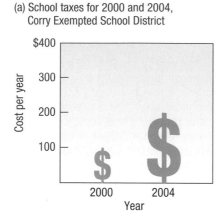

(a) School taxes for 2000 and 2004, Corry Exempted School District

(b) Full economy standards for autos set by Congress and supplemented by the Transportation Department. In miles per gallon.

This line, representing 18 miles per gallon in 1978, is 0.6 inches long.

This line, representing 27.5 miles per gallon in 1985, is 5.3 inches long.

**CHART 1–4**

Chart 1–4 is misleading because visually the increase is much larger than it really is. In Chart 1–4b, the line representing 27.5 miles per gallon in 1985 was 5.3 inches long and the line for 18 miles per gallon only 0.6 inches long in the original presentation.

Edward R. Tufte, in his book *The Visual Display of Qualitative Information* (Cheshire, CT: Graphics Press, 1983) has given many examples of how to recognize misleading graphs and how to construct a good graph. In his book, Tufte introduces a concept called the **"lie factor."** It can be defined as the percentage change in the graphic elements divided by the percentage change in the actual quantities represented by those graphic elements. By this definition, the value of the lie factor should equal 1 for an accurate and informative graph. In Chart 1–4b, the lie factor can be calculated as $\dfrac{(5.3 - 0.6)/0.6}{(27.5 - 18)/18} = 14.8$. Thus, the lie factor is 14.8!

*Graphs and charts of data,* such as histograms, line charts, and bar charts, can also be misleading if they are not drawn appropriately. We cover these graphs and charts in detail in the next chapter. A misleading visual interpretation in the context of charts arises often due to a presentation of only part of the data, or using the horizontal and/or vertical axis inappropriately.

Chart 1–5 is designed to show a relationship between unemployment rate (in percent) and crime rate (in thousands, per year) in Canada in three different ways based on the same data. In Chart 1–5a, we have broken the vertical axis at 2000, and thus show a strong relation between unemployment rate and crime. In Chart 1–5b, we have broken the horizontal axis at a 7-percent rate of unemployment.

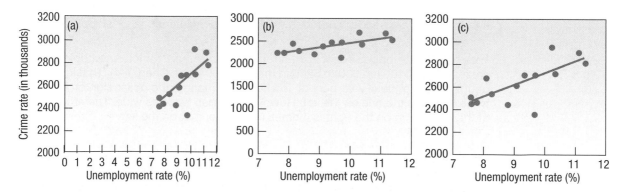

**CHART 1–5** Unemployment Rate and Crime Rate in Canada

In this graph, we get an impression of a weaker relation between unemployment rate and crime. A more accurate depiction of the relationship can be obtained by using values near the minimum values of the variables as starting points on each axis. Thus, a break on the vertical axis at 2000 and on the horizontal axis at 7 percent will give you a more accurate picture of the relationship as shown in Chart 1–5c.

There are many graphing techniques, but there are no hard and fast rules about drawing a graph. It is therefore both a science and an art. Your aim should always be a truthful representation of the data. The objectives and the assumptions underlying the data must be kept in mind and mentioned briefly along with graphs. The visual impressions conveyed by the graphs must correspond to the underlying data. The graphs should reveal as much information as possible with the greatest precision and accuracy. *Graphical excellence is achieved when a viewer can get the most accurate and comprehensive picture of the situation underlying the data set in the shortest possible time.* In brief, a graph should act like a mirror between the numerical data and the viewer. According to a popular saying, *"Numbers speak for themselves."* This is true for small data sets. For large data sets, it may be difficult to discern any patterns by looking at numbers alone. We therefore *need accurate portrayal of data through graphs that can speak for numbers,* and can give a quick overview of the data. We discuss graphic techniques in detail in Chapters 2 and 4.

## Become a Better Consumer and a Better Producer of Information

There are many other ways that statistical information can be deceiving. It may be because (1) The data are not representative of the population; (2) Appropriate statistics have not been used; (3) The data do not satisfy the assumptions required for inferences; (4) The prediction is too far out from the range of observed data; (5) Policy analysis does not meet the requirements of either data or theory or both; (6) Ignorance and/or carelessness on the part of the investigator; (7) A deliberate attempt to introduce bias has been made to mislead the consumer of information.

Entire books have been written about the subject. The most famous of these is *How to Lie with Statistics* by Darrell Huff. Understanding the art and science of statistics will make you both a better consumer of information as well as a better producer of information (statistician).

## Ethics

Aside from the ethical issues raised in recent years with financial reporting from companies such as Enron, professional practices with statistical research and reporting is strongly encouraged by the American Statistical Association. In 1999 the ASA provided written guidelines and suggestions (see http://www.amstat.org) for professionalism and the responsibilities that apply to researchers and consultants using or conducting statistical analysis. As the guidelines state, "Clients, employers, researchers, policy makers, journalists, and the public should be urged to expect that statistical practice will be conducted in accordance with these guidelines and to object when it is not. While learning how to apply statistical theory to problems, students should be encouraged to use these guidelines whether or not their target professional specialty will be 'statistician.' "

## Computer Applications

Computers are now available to students at most colleges and universities. Spreadsheets, such as Microsoft Excel, and statistical software packages, such as MINITAB, are available in most computer labs. The Microsoft Excel package is bundled with many home computers. In this text we used both Excel and MINITAB for the applications. We also use an Excel add-in called MegaStat. This add-in gives Excel the capability to produce additional statistical reports.

The following example shows the application of computers in statistical analysis. In Chapters 2, 3, and 4 we illustrate methods for summarizing and describing data. An example used in those chapters refers to the price reported in thousands of dollars of 80 vehicles sold last month at Whitner Autoplex. The following Excel output reveals, among other things, that (1) 80 vehicles were sold last month, (2) the mean (average) selling price was $23,218, and (3) the selling prices ranged from a minimum of $15,546 to a maximum of $35,925.

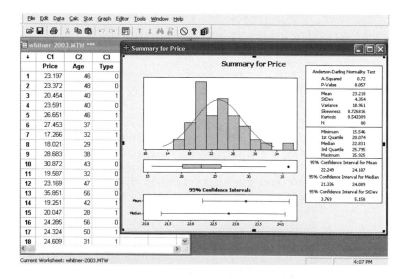

The following output is from the MINITAB system. It contains much of the same information.

Had we used a calculator to arrive at these measures and others needed to fully analyze the selling prices, hours of calculation would have been required. The likelihood of an error in arithmetic is high when a large number of values are concerned. On the other hand, statistical software packages and spreadsheets can provide accurate information in seconds.

At the option of your instructor, and depending on the software system available, we urge you to apply a computer package to the exercises in the **Dataset Exercises** section in each chapter. It will relieve you of the tedious calculations and allow you to concentrate on data analysis.

# Chapter Outline

I. Statistics is the science of collecting, organizing, presenting, analyzing, and interpreting data to assist in making more effective decisions.

II. There are two types of statistics.
    **A.** Descriptive statistics are procedures used to organize and summarize data.
    **B.** Inferential statistics involve taking a sample from a population and making estimates about a population based on the sample results.
        **1.** A population is an entire set of individuals or objects of interest or the measurements obtained from all individuals or objects of interest.
        **2.** A sample is a part of the population.

III. There are two types of variables.
    **A.** A qualitative variable is nonnumeric.
        **1.** Usually we are interested in the number or percent of the observations in each category.
        **2.** Qualitative data are usually summarized in graphs and bar charts.
    **B.** There are two types of quantitative variables and they are usually reported numerically.
        **1.** Discrete variables can assume only certain values, and there are usually gaps between values.
        **2.** A continuous variable can assume any value within a specified range.

IV. There are four levels of measurement.
    **A.** With the nominal level, the data are sorted into categories with no particular order to the categories.
        **1.** The categories are mutually exclusive. An individual or object appears in only one category.
        **2.** The categories are exhaustive. An individual or object appears in at least one of the categories.
    **B.** The ordinal level of measurement presumes that one classification is ranked higher than another.
    **C.** The interval level of measurement has the ranking characteristic of the ordinal level of measurement plus the characteristic that the distance between values is a constant size.
    **D.** The ratio level of measurement has all the characteristics of the interval level, plus there is a zero point and the ratio of two values is meaningful.

# Chapter Exercises

**5.** Explain the difference between *qualitative* and *quantitative* variables. Give an example of qualitative and quantitative variables.
**6.** Explain the difference between a sample and a population.
**7.** List the four levels of measurement and give an example (different from those used in the book) of each level of measurement.
**8.** Define the term *mutually exclusive.*
**9.** Define the term *exhaustive.*
**10.** Using data from such publications as the *Statistical Abstract of the United States,* the *World Almanac, Forbes,* or your local newspaper, give examples of the nominal, ordinal, interval, and ratio levels of measurement.
**11.** The Struthers Wells Corporation employs more than 10,000 white collar workers in its sales offices and manufacturing facilities in the United States, Europe, and Asia. A sample of 300 of these workers revealed 120 would accept a transfer to a location outside the United States. On the basis of these findings, write a brief memo to Ms. Wanda Carter, Vice-President of Human Services, regarding all white collar workers in the firm and their willingness to relocate.

12. AVX Stereo Equipment, Inc. recently began a "no-hassles" return policy. A sample of 500 customers who had recently returned items showed 400 thought the policy was fair, 32 thought it took too long to complete the transaction, and the remainder had no opinion. On the basis of these findings, make an inference about the reaction of all customers to the new policy.

13. Explain the difference between a discrete and a continuous variable. Give an example of each not included in the text.

14. The following chart depicts the sales, in thousands, of manufactured homes sold in the United States from 1990 to 2001.

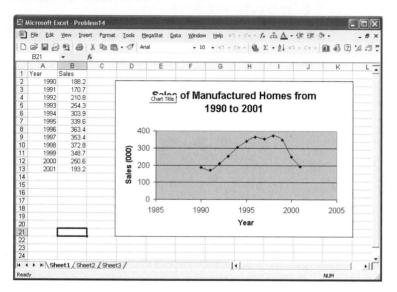

Write a brief analysis of the information. Did sales increase over the period? What was the trend of sales?

# exercises.com

These exercises use the World Wide Web, a rich and growing source of up-to-date information. Because of the changing nature and the continuous revision of websites, you may well see different menus, and the exact addresses, or URLs, may change. When you visit a page, be prepared to search the link.

15. Suppose you recently opened an account with AmeriTrade, Inc., an on-line broker. You have decided to purchase shares of either Johnson and Johnson (a pharmaceutical company) or Pepsico (the parent company of Pepsi and Frito Lay). For a comparison of the two companies go to http://finance.yahoo.com and in the space where it says "Get Quote" enter the letters JNJ and PEP, which are the respective symbols for the two companies. Click on GO and you should receive some current information about the selling price of the two stocks. To the right of this information click on More Info and then click on Research. Here you will find information from stock analysts evaluating these stocks. Brokers rate the stock a 1 if it is a strong buy and a 5 if it is a strong sell. What level of measurement is this information? Which of the stocks would you recommend?

# Dataset Exercises

16. Refer to the Real Estate data at the back of the text, which reports information on homes sold in the Denver, Colorado, area last year. Consider the following variables: selling price, number of bedrooms, township, and distance from the center of the city.
    **a.** Which of the variables are qualitative and which are quantitative?
    **b.** Determine the level of measurement for each of the variables.

17. Refer to the Baseball 2002 data, which reports information on the 30 Major League Baseball teams for the 2002 season. Consider the following variables: number of wins, team salary, season attendance, whether the team played its home games on a grass field or an artificial surface, and the number of home runs hit.

    **a.** Which of these variables are quantitative and which are qualitative?

    **b.** Determine the level of measurement for each of the variables.

**18.** Refer to the Wage data, which reports information on annual wages for a sample of 100 workers. Also included are variables relating to industry, years of education, and gender for each worker.

    **a.** Which of the 12 variables are qualitative and which are quantitative?

    **b.** Determine the level of measurement for each variable.

**19.** Refer to the CIA data, which reports demographic and economic information on 46 countries.

    **a.** Which of the variables are quantitative and which are qualitative?

    **b.** Determine the level of measurement for each of the variables.

# Chapter 1  Answers to Self-Review

**1–1**  **a.** On the basis of the sample of 1,960 consumers, we estimate that, if it is marketed, 60 percent of all consumers will purchase the chicken dinner (1,176/1,960) $\times$ 100 = 60 percent.

**b.** Inferential statistics, because a sample was used to draw a conclusion about how all consumers in the population would react if the chicken dinner were marketed.

**1–2**  **a.** Age is a ratio scale variable. A 40-year-old is twice as old as someone 20 years old.

**b.** Nominal scale. We could arrange the states in any order.

# Describing Data:

## Frequency Distributions and Graphic Presentation

## GOALS

*When you have completed this chapter, you will be able to:*

1 Organize data into a *frequency distribution.*

2 Portray a frequency distribution in a *histogram, frequency polygon,* and *cumulative frequency polygon.*

3 Present data using such graphical techniques as *line charts, bar charts,* and *pie charts.*

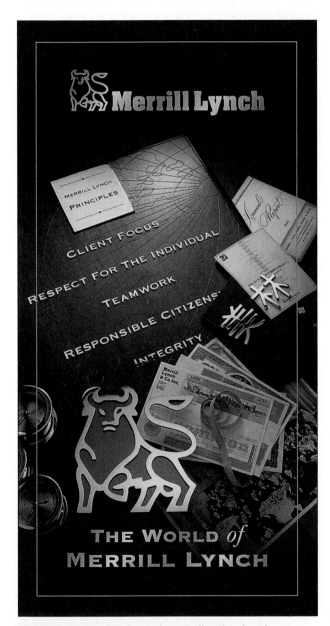

Merrill Lynch completed a study regarding the size of investment portfolios for a sample of clients in the 40- to 50-year-old age group. Create a frequency distribution and a histogram based on the sample. (See Goal 2 and Exercise 35.)

# Introduction

The highly competitive automotive retailing business has changed significantly over the past 5 years, due in part to consolidation by large, publicly owned dealership groups. Traditionally, a local family owned and operated the community dealership, which might have included one or two manufacturers, like Pontiac and GMC Trucks or Chrysler and the popular Jeep line. Recently, however, skillfully managed and well-financed companies have been acquiring local dealerships across large regions of the country. As these groups acquire the local dealerships, they often bring standard selling practices, common software and hardware technology platforms, and management reporting techniques. The goal is to provide an improved buying experience for the consumer, while increasing the profitability of the larger dealership organization. In many cases, in addition to reaping the financial benefits of selling the dealership, the family is asked to continue running the dealership on a daily basis. Today, it is common for these megadealerships to employ over 10,000 people, generate several billion dollars in annual sales, own more than 100 franchises, and be traded on the New York Stock Exchange or NASDAQ.

The consolidation has not come without challenges. With the acquisition of dealerships across the country, AutoUSA, one of the new megadealerships, now sells the inexpensive Korean import brands Kia and Hyundai, the high-line BMW and Mercedes Benz sedans, and a full line of Ford and Chevrolet cars and trucks.

Ms. Kathryn Ball is a member of the senior management team at AutoUSA. She is responsible for tracking and analyzing vehicle selling prices for AutoUSA. Kathryn would like to summarize vehicle selling prices with charts and graphs that she could review monthly. From these tables and charts, she wants to know the typical selling price as well as the lowest and highest prices. She is also interested in describing the demographics of the buyers. What are their ages? How many vehicles do they own? Do they want to buy or lease the vehicle?

Whitner Autoplex, which is located in Raytown, Missouri, is one of the AutoUSA dealerships. Whitner Autoplex includes Pontiac, GMC, and Buick franchises as well as a BMW store. General Motors is actively working with its dealer body to combine at one location several of its franchises, such as Chevrolet, Pontiac, or Cadillac. Combining franchises improves the floor traffic and a dealership has product offerings for all demographics. BMW, with its premium brand and image, wants to move away from calling its locations dealerships, instead calling them stores. In keeping with the "Nordstrom's" experience, BMW wants its consumers to feel a shopping/ownership experience closer to a Nordstrom's shopping trip, not the image of a trip to the dealership often creates.

Ms. Ball decided to collect data on three variables at Whitner Autoplex: selling price ($000), buyer's age, and car type (domestic, coded as 1, or foreign, coded as 0). A portion of the data set is shown in the adjacent Excel output. The entire data set is available on the student CD (included with the book), at the McGraw-Hill website, and in Appendix O at the end of the text.

| | B | C | D | E |
|---|---|---|---|---|
| 1 | Price($000) | Age | Type | |
| 2 | 23.197 | 46 | 0 | |
| 3 | 23.372 | 48 | 0 | |
| 4 | 20.454 | 40 | 1 | |
| 5 | 23.591 | 40 | 0 | |
| 6 | 26.651 | 46 | 1 | |
| 7 | 27.453 | 37 | 1 | |
| 8 | 17.266 | 32 | 1 | |
| 9 | 18.021 | 29 | 1 | |
| 10 | 26.683 | 38 | 1 | |
| 11 | 30.872 | 43 | 0 | |
| 12 | 19.587 | 32 | 0 | |
| 13 | 23.169 | 47 | 0 | |
| 14 | 35.851 | 56 | 0 | |
| 15 | 19.251 | 42 | 1 | |
| 16 | 20.047 | 28 | 1 | |
| 17 | 24.285 | 56 | 0 | |
| 18 | 24.324 | 50 | 1 | |
| 19 | 24.609 | 31 | 1 | |
| 20 | 28.67 | 51 | 1 | |
| 21 | 15.546 | 26 | 1 | |
| 22 | 15.935 | 25 | 1 | |
| 23 | 19.873 | 45 | 1 | |
| 24 | 25.251 | 56 | 1 | |

# Constructing a Frequency Distribution

Recall from Chapter 1 that we refer to techniques used to describe a set of data as *descriptive statistics.* To put it another way, we use descriptive statistics to organize data in various ways to point out where the data values tend to concentrate and help distinguish the largest and the smallest values. The first procedure we use to describe a set of data is a **frequency distribution.**

> **FREQUENCY DISTRIBUTION** A grouping of data into mutually exclusive classes showing the number of observations in each.

How do we develop a frequency distribution? The first step is to tally the data into a table that shows the classes and the number of observations in each class. The steps in constructing a frequency distribution are best described by using an example. Remember, our goal is to construct tables, charts, and graphs that will quickly reveal the shape of the data.

**EXAMPLE**

In the Introduction we described a situation where Ms. Kathryn Ball of AutoUSA wanted to develop some tables, charts, and graphs to show the typical selling price on various dealer lots. Table 2–1 reports only the price of the 80 vehicles sold last month at Whitner Autoplex. What is the *typical* selling price? What is the *highest* selling price? What is the *lowest* selling price? Around what value do the selling prices tend to cluster?

**TABLE 2–1** Prices of Vehicles Sold Last Month at Whitner Autoplex

Lowest

| | | | | | | |
|---|---|---|---|---|---|---|
| $23,197 | $23,372 | $20,454 | $23,591 | $26,651 | $27,453 | $17,266 |
| 18,021 | 28,683 | 30,872 | 19,587 | 23,169 | 35,851 | 19,251 |
| 20,047 | 24,285 | 24,324 | 24,609 | 28,670 | 15,546 | 15,935 |
| 19,873 | 25,251 | 25,277 | 28,034 | 24,533 | 27,443 | 19,889 |
| 20,004 | 17,357 | 20,155 | 19,688 | 23,657 | 26,613 | 20,895 |
| 20,203 | 23,765 | 25,783 | 26,661 | 32,277 | 20,642 | 21,981 |
| 24,052 | 25,799 | 15,794 | 18,263 | 35,925 | 17,399 | 17,968 |
| 20,356 | 21,442 | 21,722 | 19,331 | 22,817 | 19,766 | 20,633 |
| 20,962 | 22,845 | 26,285 | 27,896 | 29,076 | 32,492 | 18,890 |
| 21,740 | 22,374 | 24,571 | 25,449 | 28,337 | 20,642 | 23,613 |
| 24,220 | 30,655 | 22,442 | 17,891 | 20,818 | 26,237 | 20,445 |
| 21,556 | 21,639 | 24,296 | | | | |

Highest

**SOLUTION**

We refer to the unorganized information in Table 2–1 as **raw data** or **ungrouped data.** With a little searching, we can find the lowest selling price ($15,546) and the highest selling price ($35,925), but that is about all. It is difficult to determine a typical selling price. It is also difficult to visualize where the selling prices tend to cluster. The raw data are more easily interpreted if organized into a frequency distribution.

The steps for organizing data into a frequency distribution.

**Step 1: Decide on the number of classes.** The goal is to use just enough groupings or **classes** to reveal the shape of the distribution. Some judgment is needed here. Too many classes or too few classes might not reveal the basic shape of the data set. In the vehicle selling price example, three classes would not give much insight into the pattern of the data (see Table 2–2).

A useful recipe to determine the number of classes (*k*) is the "2 to the *k* rule." This guide suggests you select the smallest number (*k*) for the

**TABLE 2–2** An Example of Too Few Classes

| Vehicle Selling Price ($) | Number of Vehicles |
|---|---|
| 15,000 up to 24,000 | 48 |
| 24,000 up to 33,000 | 30 |
| 33,000 up to 42,000 | 2 |
| Total | 80 |

number of classes such that $2^k$ (in words, 2 raised to the power of $k$) is greater than the number of observations ($n$).

In the Whitner Autoplex example, there were 80 vehicles sold. So $n = 80$. If we try $k = 6$, which means we would use 6 classes, then $2^6 = 64$, somewhat less than 80. Hence, 6 is not enough classes. If we let $k = 7$, then $2^7 = 128$, which is greater than 80. So the recommended number of classes is 7.

**Step 2: Determine the class interval or width.** Generally the **class interval** or width should be the same for all classes. The classes all taken together must cover at least the distance from the lowest value in the raw data up to the highest value. Expressing these words in a formula:

$$i \geq \frac{H - L}{k}$$

where $i$ is the class interval, $H$ is the highest observed value, $L$ is the lowest observed value, and $k$ is the number of classes.

In the Whitner Autoplex case, the lowest value is $15,546 and the highest value is $35,925. If we need 7 classes, the interval should be at least ($35,925 − $15,546)/7 = $2,911. In practice this interval size is usually rounded up to some convenient number, such as a multiple of 10 or 100. The value of $3,000 might readily be used in this case.

Unequal class intervals present problems in graphically portraying the distribution and in doing some of the computations which we will see in later chapters. Unequal class intervals, however, may be necessary in certain situations to avoid a large number of empty, or almost empty, classes. Such is the case in Table 2–3. The Internal Revenue Service used unequal-sized class intervals to report the adjusted gross income on individual tax returns. Had they used an equal-sized interval of, say, $1,000, more than 1,000 classes would have been required to describe all the incomes. A frequency distribution with 1,000 classes would be difficult to interpret. In this case the distribution is easier to understand in spite of the unequal classes. Note also that the number of income tax returns or "frequencies" is reported in thousands in this particular table. This also makes the information easier to understand.

**Step 3: Set the individual class limits.** State clear class limits so you can put each observation into only one category. This means you must avoid overlapping or unclear class limits. For example, classes such as $1,300–$1,400 and $1,400–$1,500 should not be used because it is not clear whether the value $1,400 is in the first or second class. Classes stated as $1,300–$1,400 and $1,500–$1,600 are frequently used, but may also be confusing without the additional common convention of rounding all data at or above $1,450 up to the second class and data below $1,450 down to the first class. In this text we will generally use the format $1,300 up to $1,400 and $1,400 up to $1,500 and so on. With this format it is clear that $1,399 goes into the first class and $1,400 in the second.

Because we round the class interval up to get a convenient class size, we cover a larger than necessary range. For example, 7 classes of width $3,000 in the Whitner Autoplex case result in a range of 7($3,000) = $21,000. The actual range is $20,379, found by

**TABLE 2–3** Adjusted Gross Income for Individuals Filing Income Tax Returns

| Adjusted Gross Income | | | Number of Returns (in thousands) |
|---|---|---|---|
| No adjusted gross income | | | 178.2 |
| $        1 up to | $ | 5,000 | 1,204.6 |
| 5,000 up to | | 10,000 | 2,595.5 |
| 10,000 up to | | 15,000 | 3,142.0 |
| 15,000 up to | | 20,000 | 3,191.7 |
| 20,000 up to | | 25,000 | 2,501.4 |
| 25,000 up to | | 30,000 | 1,901.6 |
| 30,000 up to | | 40,000 | 2,502.3 |
| 40,000 up to | | 50,000 | 1,426.8 |
| 50,000 up to | | 75,000 | 1,476.3 |
| 75,000 up to | | 100,000 | 338.8 |
| 100,000 up to | | 200,000 | 223.3 |
| 200,000 up to | | 500,000 | 55.2 |
| 500,000 up to | | 1,000,000 | 12.0 |
| 1,000,000 up to | | 2,000,000 | 5.1 |
| 2,000,000 up to | | 10,000,000 | 3.4 |
| 10,000,000 or more | | | 0.6 |

$35,925 − $15,546. Comparing that value to $21,000 we have an excess of $621. Because we need to cover only the distance ($H − L$), it is natural to put approximately equal amounts of the excess in each of the two tails. Of course, we should also select convenient class limits. A guideline is to make the lower limit of the first class a multiple of the class interval. Sometimes this is not possible, but the lower limit should at least be rounded. So here are the classes we could use for this data.

| |
|---|
| $15,000 up to 18,000 |
| 18,000 up to 21,000 |
| 21,000 up to 24,000 |
| 24,000 up to 27,000 |
| 27,000 up to 30,000 |
| 30,000 up to 33,000 |
| 33,000 up to 36,000 |

**Step 4: Tally the vehicle selling prices into the classes.** To begin, the selling price of the first vehicle in Table 2–1 is $23,197. It is tallied in the $21,000 up to $24,000 class. The second selling price in the first column of Table 2–1 is $18,021. It is tallied in the $18,000 up to $21,000 class. The other selling prices are tallied in a similar manner. When all the selling prices are tallied, the table would appear as:

| Class | Tallies |
|---|---|
| $15,000 up to $18,000 | JHf III |
| $18,000 up to $21,000 | JHf JHf JHf JHf III |
| $21,000 up to $24,000 | JHf JHf JHf II |
| $24,000 up to $27,000 | JHf JHf JHf III |
| $27,000 up to $30,000 | JHf III |
| $30,000 up to $33,000 | IIII |
| $33,000 up to $36,000 | II |

**Step 5: Count the number of items in each class.** The number of observations in each class is called the **class frequency.** In the $15,000 up to $18,000 class there are 8 observations, and in the $18,000 up to $21,000 class there are 23 observations. Therefore, the class frequency in the first class

is 8 and the class frequency in the second class is 23. There is a total of 80 observations or frequencies in the entire set of data.

Often it is useful to express the data in thousands, or some convenient units, rather than the actual data. Table 2–4, for example, reports the vehicle selling prices in thousands of dollars, rather than dollars.

**TABLE 2–4** Frequency Distribution of Selling Prices at Whitner Autoplex Last Month

| Selling Prices ($ thousands) | Frequency |
|---|---|
| 15 up to 18 | 8 |
| 18 up to 21 | 23 |
| 21 up to 24 | 17 |
| 24 up to 27 | 18 |
| 27 up to 30 | 8 |
| 30 up to 33 | 4 |
| 33 up to 36 | 2 |
| Total | 80 |

Now that we have organized the data into a frequency distribution, we can summarize the pattern in the selling prices of the vehicles for the AutoUSA lot of Whitner Autoplex in Raytown, Missouri. Observe the following:

1. The selling prices ranged from about $15,000 up to about $36,000.
2. The selling prices are concentrated between $18,000 and $27,000. A total of 58, or 72.5 percent, of the vehicles sold within this range.
3. The largest concentration, or highest frequency, is in the $18,000 up to $21,000 class. The middle of this class is $19,500. So we say that a typical selling price is $19,500.
4. Two of the vehicles sold for $33,000 or more, and 8 sold for less than $18,000.

By presenting this information to Ms. Ball, we give her a clear picture of the distribution of selling prices for last month.

We admit that arranging the information on selling prices into a frequency distribution does result in the loss of some detailed information. That is, by organizing the data into a frequency distribution, we cannot pinpoint the exact selling price, such as $23,197 or $26,372. Further, we cannot tell that the actual selling price for the least expensive vehicle was $15,546 and for the most expensive $35,925. However, the lower limit of the first class and the upper limit of the largest class convey essentially the same meaning. Likely, Ms. Ball will make the same judgment if she knows the lowest price is about $15,000 that she will if she knows the exact price is $15,546. The advantages of condensing the data into a more understandable and organized form more than offset this disadvantage.

**Self-Review 2–1**

*The answers are at the end of the chapter.*
The commissions earned for the first quarter of last year by the 11 members of the sales staff at Master Chemical Company are:

| $1,650 | $1,475 | $1,510 | $1,670 | $1,595 | $1,760 | $1,540 | $1,495 | $1,590 | $1,625 | $1,510 |
|---|---|---|---|---|---|---|---|---|---|---|

(a) What are the values such as $1,650 and $1,475 called?
(b) Using $1,400 up to $1,500 as the first class, $1,500 up to $1,600 as the second class, and so forth, organize the quarterly commissions into a frequency distribution.
(c) What are the numbers in the right column of your frequency distribution called?
(d) Describe the distribution of quarterly commissions, based on the frequency distribution. What is the largest amount of commission earned? What is the smallest? What is the typical amount earned?

## Class Intervals and Class Midpoints

We will use two other terms frequently: **class midpoint** and **class interval.** The midpoint is halfway between the lower limits of two consecutive classes. It is computed by adding the lower limits of consecutive classes and dividing the result by 2. Referring to Table 2–4, for the first class the lower class limit is $15,000 and the next limit is $18,000. The class midpoint is $16,500, found by ($15,000 + $18,000)/2. The midpoint of $16,500 best represents, or is typical of, the selling price of the vehicles in that class.

To determine the class interval, subtract the lower limit of the class from the lower limit of the next class. The class interval of the vehicle selling price data is $3,000, which we find by subtracting the lower limit of the first class, $15,000, from the lower limit of the next class; that is, $18,000 − $15,000 = $3,000. You can also determine the class interval by finding the difference between consecutive midpoints. The midpoint of the first class is $16,500 and the midpoint of the second class is $19,500. The difference is $3,000.

# A Software Example

As we mentioned in Chapter 1, there are many software packages that perform statistical calculations and output the results. Throughout this text we will show the output from Microsoft Excel; from MegaStat, which is an add-in to Microsoft Excel; and from MINITAB. The commands necessary to generate the outputs are given in the **Software Commands** section at the end of each chapter.

The following is a frequency distribution, produced by MegaStat, showing the prices of the 80 vehicles sold last month at the Whitner Autoplex lot in Raytown, Missouri. The form of the output is somewhat different than the frequency distribution of Table 2–4, but the overall conclusions are the same.

**Self-Review 2–2** Barry Bonds of the San Francisco Giants established a new single season home run record by hitting 73 home runs during the 2001 season. The longest of these home runs traveled 488 feet and the shortest 320 feet. You need to construct a frequency distribution of these home run lengths.
(a) How many classes would you use?
(b) What class interval would you suggest?
(c) What actual classes would you suggest?

# Relative Frequency Distribution

*A relative frequency distribution converts the frequency to a percent.*

It may be desirable to convert class frequencies to **relative class frequencies** to show the fraction of the total number of observations in each class. In our vehicle sales example, we may want to know what percent of the vehicle prices are in the $21,000 up to $24,000 class. In another study, we may want to know what percent of the employees used 5 up to 10 personal leave days last year.

To convert a frequency distribution to a *relative* frequency distribution, each of the class frequencies is divided by the total number of observations. From the distribution of vehicle selling prices (Table 2–4, where the selling price is reported in thousands of dollars), the relative frequency for the $15,000 up to $18,000 class is 0.10, found by dividing 8 by 80. That is, the price of 10 percent of the vehicles sold at Whitner Autoplex is between $15,000 and $18,000. The relative frequencies for the remaining classes are shown in Table 2–5.

**TABLE 2–5** Relative Frequency Distribution of the Prices of Vehicles Sold Last Month at Whitner Autoplex

| Selling Price ($ thousands) | Frequency | Relative Frequency | Found by |
|---|---|---|---|
| 15 up to 18 | 8 | 0.1000 ← | 8/80 |
| 18 up to 21 | 23 | 0.2875 | 23/80 |
| 21 up to 24 | 17 | 0.2125 | 17/80 |
| 24 up to 27 | 18 | 0.2250 | 18/80 |
| 27 up to 30 | 8 | 0.1000 | 8/80 |
| 30 up to 33 | 4 | 0.0500 | 4/80 |
| 33 up to 36 | 2 | 0.0250 | 2/80 |
| Total | 80 | 1.0000 | |

---

**Self-Review 2–3**

Refer to Table 2–5, which shows the relative frequency distribution for the vehicles sold last month at Whitner Autoplex.
(a)  How many vehicles sold for $18,000 up to $21,000?
(b)  What percent of the vehicles sold for a price between $18,000 and $21,000?
(c)  What percent of the vehicles sold for $30,000 or more?

---

# Exercises

*The answers to the odd-numbered exercises are at the end of the book.*

1.  A set of data consists of 38 observations. How many classes would you recommend for the frequency distribution?
2.  A set of data consists of 45 observations between $0 and $29. What size would you recommend for the class interval?
3.  A set of data consists of 230 observations between $235 and $567. What class interval would you recommend?
4.  A set of data contains 53 observations. The lowest value is 42 and the largest is 129. The data are to be organized into a frequency distribution.
    **a.** How many classes would you suggest?
    **b.** What would you suggest as the lower limit of the first class?
5.  Wachesaw Manufacturing, Inc. produced the following number of units the last 16 days.

| | | | | | | | |
|---|---|---|---|---|---|---|---|
| 27 | 27 | 27 | 28 | 27 | 25 | 25 | 28 |
| 26 | 28 | 26 | 28 | 31 | 30 | 26 | 26 |

The information is to be organized into a frequency distribution.
   **a.** How many classes would you recommend?
   **b.** What class interval would you suggest?
   **c.** What lower limit would you recommend for the first class?
   **d.** Organize the information into a frequency distribution and determine the relative frequency distribution.
   **e.** Comment on the shape of the distribution.

**6.** The Quick Change Oil Company has a number of outlets in the metropolitan Seattle area. The numbers of oil changes at the Oak Street outlet in the past 20 days are:

| | | | | | | | | | |
|---|---|---|---|---|---|---|---|---|---|
| 65 | 98 | 55 | 62 | 79 | 59 | 51 | 90 | 72 | 56 |
| 70 | 62 | 66 | 80 | 94 | 79 | 63 | 73 | 71 | 85 |

The data are to be organized into a frequency distribution.
   **a.** How many classes would you recommend?
   **b.** What class interval would you suggest?
   **c.** What lower limit would you recommend for the first class?
   **d.** Organize the number of oil changes into a frequency distribution.
   **e.** Comment on the shape of the frequency distribution. Also determine the relative frequency distribution.

**7.** The manager of the BiLo Supermarket in Mt. Pleasant, Rhode Island, gathered the following information on the number of times a customer visits the store during a month. The responses of 51 customers were:

| | | | | | | | | | | | | | | |
|---|---|---|---|---|---|---|---|---|---|---|---|---|---|---|
| 5 | 3 | 3 | 1 | 4 | 4 | 5 | 6 | 4 | 2 | 6 | 6 | 6 | 7 | 1 |
| 1 | 14 | 1 | 2 | 4 | 4 | 4 | 5 | 6 | 3 | 5 | 3 | 4 | 5 | 6 |
| 8 | 4 | 7 | 6 | 5 | 9 | 11 | 3 | 12 | 4 | 7 | 6 | 5 | 15 | 1 |
| 1 | 10 | 8 | 9 | 2 | 12 | | | | | | | | | |

   **a.** Starting with 0 as the lower limit of the first class and using a class interval of 3, organize the data into a frequency distribution.
   **b.** Describe the distribution. Where do the data tend to cluster?
   **c.** Convert the distribution to a relative frequency distribution.

**8.** The food services division of Cedar River Amusement Park, Inc. is studying the amount families who visit the amusement park spend per day on food and drink. A sample of 40 families who visited the park yesterday revealed they spent the following amounts.

| | | | | | | | | | | | | | | |
|---|---|---|---|---|---|---|---|---|---|---|---|---|---|---|
| $77 | $18 | $63 | $84 | $38 | $54 | $50 | $59 | $54 | $56 | $36 | $26 | $50 | $34 | $44 |
| 41 | 58 | 58 | 53 | 51 | 62 | 43 | 52 | 53 | 63 | 62 | 62 | 65 | 61 | 52 |
| 60 | 60 | 45 | 66 | 83 | 71 | 63 | 58 | 61 | 71 | | | | | |

   **a.** Organize the data into a frequency distribution, using seven classes and 15 as the lower limit of the first class. What class interval did you select?
   **b.** Where do the data tend to cluster?
   **c.** Describe the distribution.
   **d.** Determine the relative frequency distribution.

# Graphic Presentation of a Frequency Distribution

Sales managers, stock analysts, hospital administrators, and other busy executives often need a quick picture of the trends in sales, stock prices, or hospital costs. These trends can often be depicted by the use of charts and graphs. Three charts that will help portray a frequency distribution graphically are the histogram, the frequency polygon, and the cumulative frequency polygon.

# Histogram

One of the most common ways to portray a frequency distribution is a **histogram.**

> **HISTOGRAM** A graph in which the classes are marked on the horizontal axis and the class frequencies on the vertical axis. The class frequencies are represented by the heights of the bars, and the bars are drawn adjacent to each other.

Thus, a histogram describes a frequency distribution using a series of adjacent rectangles, where the height of each rectangle is proportional to the frequency the class represents. The construction of a histogram is best illustrated by reintroducing the prices of the 80 vehicles sold last month at Whitner Autoplex.

**EXAMPLE**

Below is the frequency distribution.

| Selling Prices ($ thousands) | Frequency |
|---|---|
| 15 up to 18 | 8 |
| 18 up to 21 | 23 |
| 21 up to 24 | 17 |
| 24 up to 27 | 18 |
| 27 up to 30 | 8 |
| 30 up to 33 | 4 |
| 33 up to 36 | 2 |
| Total | 80 |

Construct a histogram. What conclusions can you reach based on the information presented in the histogram?

**SOLUTION**

The class frequencies are scaled along the vertical axis ($Y$-axis) and either the class limits or the class midpoints along the horizontal axis. To illustrate the construction of the histogram, the first three classes are shown in Chart 2–1.

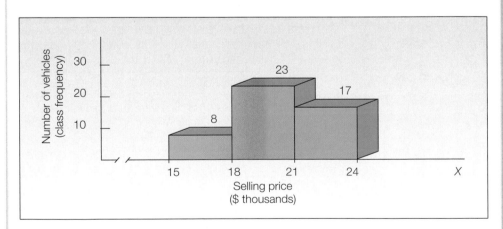

**CHART 2–1** Construction of a Histogram

From Chart 2–1 we note that there are eight vehicles in the $15,000 up to $18,000 class. Therefore, the height of the column for that class is 8. There are 23 vehicles in the $18,000 up to $21,000 class. So, logically, the height of that column is 23. The height of the bar represents the number of observations in the class.

This procedure is continued for all classes. The complete histogram is shown in Chart 2–2. Note that there is no space between the bars. This is a feature of the histogram. Why is this so? Because the variable plotted on the horizontal axis is quantitative and of the interval, or in this case the ratio, scale of measurement. In bar charts, which are described in a later section, the vertical bars are separated.

**CHART 2–2** Histogram of the Selling Prices of 80 Vehicles at Whitner Autoplex

From the histogram in Chart 2–2, we conclude:

1. The lowest selling price is about $15,000, and the highest is about $36,000.
2. The largest class frequency is the $18,000 up to $21,000 class. A total of 23 of the 80 vehicles sold are within this price range.
3. Fifty-eight of the vehicles, or 72.5 percent, had a selling price between $18,000 and $27,000.

Thus, the histogram provides an easily interpreted visual representation of a frequency distribution. We should also point out that we would have reached the same conclusions and the shape of the histogram would have been the same had we used a relative frequency distribution instead of the actual frequencies. That is, if we had used the relative frequencies of Table 2–5, found on page 30, we would have had a histogram of the same shape as Chart 2–2. The only difference is that the vertical axis would have been reported in percent of vehicles instead of the number of vehicles.

We used the Microsoft Excel system to produce the histogram for the Whitner Autoplex vehicle sales data (which is shown on page 25). Note that class midpoints are used as the labels for the classes. The software commands to create this output are given in the **Software Commands** section at the end of the chapter.

## Frequency Polygon

In a frequency polygon the class midpoints are connected with a line segment.

A **frequency polygon** is similar to a histogram. It consists of line segments connecting the points formed by the intersections of the class midpoints and the class frequencies. The construction of a frequency polygon is illustrated in Chart 2–3 (on page 35). We use the vehicle prices for the cars sold last month at Whitner Autoplex. The midpoint of each class is scaled on the X-axis and the class frequencies on the Y-axis. Recall that the class midpoint is the value at the center of a class and

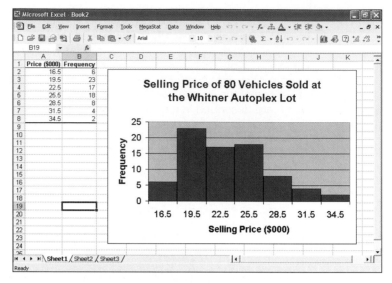

represents the values in that class. The class frequency is the number of observations in a particular class. The vehicle selling prices at Whitner Autoplex are:

| Selling Price ($ thousands) | Midpoint | Frequency |
|---|---|---|
| 15 up to 18 | 16.5 | 8 |
| 18 up to 21 | 19.5 | 23 |
| 21 up to 24 | 22.5 | 17 |
| 24 up to 27 | 25.5 | 18 |
| 27 up to 30 | 28.5 | 8 |
| 30 up to 33 | 31.5 | 4 |
| 33 up to 36 | 34.5 | 2 |
| Total | | 80 |

### Statistics in Action

Florence Nightingale is known as the founder of the nursing profession. However, she also saved many lives by using statistical analysis. When she encountered an unsanitary condition or an undersupplied hospital, she improved the conditions and then used statistical data to document the improvement. Thus, she was able to convince others of the need for medical reform, particularly in the area of sanitation. She developed original graphs to demonstrate that, during the Crimean War, more soldiers died from unsanitary conditions than were killed in combat. The adjacent graph by Nightingale is a polar-area graph showing the relative monthly proportions of causes of death from April 1854 to March 1855.

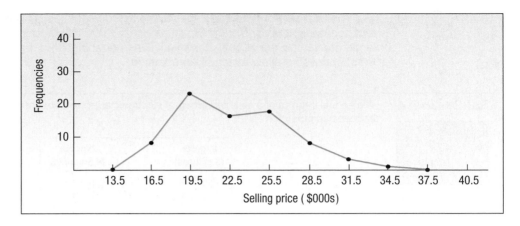

**CHART 2–3** Frequency Polygon of the Selling Prices of 80 Vehicles at Whitner Autoplex

As noted previously, the $15,000 up to $18,000 class is represented by the midpoint $16,500. To construct a frequency polygon, move horizontally on the graph to the midpoint, $16.5, and then vertically to 8, the class frequency, and place a dot. The X and the Y values of this point are called the *coordinates.* The coordinates of the next point are X = $19.5 and Y = 23. The process is continued for all classes. Then the points are connected in order. That is, the point representing the lowest class is joined to the one representing the second class and so on.

Note in Chart 2–3 that, to complete the frequency polygon, midpoints of $13.5 and $37.5 are added to the X-axis to "anchor" the polygon at zero frequencies. These two values, $13.5 and $37.5, were derived by subtracting the class interval of $3.0 from the lowest midpoint ($16.5) and by adding $3.0 to the highest midpoint ($34.5) in the frequency distribution.

Both the histogram and the frequency polygon allow us to get a quick picture of the main characteristics of the data (highs, lows, points of concentration, etc.). Although the two representations are similar in purpose, the histogram has the advantage of depicting each class as a rectangle, with the height of the rectangular bar representing the number in each class. The frequency polygon, in turn, has an advantage over the histogram. It allows us to compare directly two or more frequency distributions. Suppose Ms. Ball of AutoUSA wants to compare the Whitner Autoplex lot in Raytown, Missouri, with a similar lot, Fowler Auto Mall in Grayling, Michigan. To do this, two frequency polygons are constructed, one on top of the other, as in Chart 2–4. It is clear from Chart 2–4 that the typical vehicle selling price is higher at the lot in Grayling, Michigan.

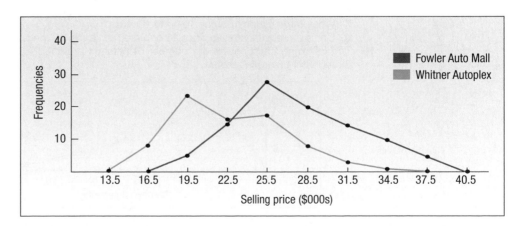

**CHART 2–4** Distribution of Vehicle Selling Prices at Whitner Autoplex and Fowler Auto Mall

The total number of frequencies at the two dealerships is about the same, so a direct comparison is possible. If the difference in the total number of frequencies is quite large, converting the frequencies to relative frequencies and then plotting the two distributions would allow a clearer comparison.

---

**Self-Review 2–4**

The annual imports of a selected group of electronic suppliers are shown in the following frequency distribution.

| Imports ($ millions) | Number of Suppliers |
|---|---|
| 2 up to 5 | 6 |
| 5 up to 8 | 13 |
| 8 up to 11 | 20 |
| 11 up to 14 | 10 |
| 14 up to 17 | 1 |

(a) Portray the imports as a histogram.
(b) Portray the imports as a relative frequency polygon.
(c) Summarize the important facets of the distribution (such as classes with the highest and lowest frequencies).

---

# Exercises

**9.** Molly's Candle Shop has several retail stores in the coastal areas of North and South Carolina. Many of Molly's customers ask her to ship their purchases. The following chart shows the number of packages shipped per day for the last 100 days.

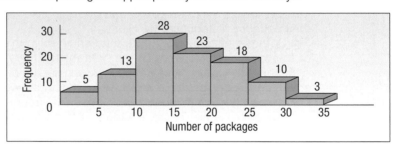

a. What is this chart called?
b. What is the total number of frequencies?
c. What is the class interval?
d. What is the class frequency for the 10 up to 15 class?
e. What is the relative frequency of the 10 up to 15 class?
f. What is the midpoint of the 10 up to 15 class?
g. On how many days were there 25 or more packages shipped?

**10.** The following chart shows the number of patients admitted daily to Memorial Hospital through the emergency room.

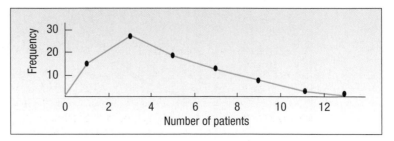

    **a.** What is the midpoint of the 2 up to 4 class?
    **b.** How many days were 2 up to 4 patients admitted?
    **c.** Approximately how many days were studied?
    **d.** What is the class interval?
    **e.** What is this chart called?

**11.** The following frequency distribution reports the number of frequent flier miles, reported in thousands, for employees of Brumley Statistical Consulting, Inc. during the first quarter of 2004.

| Frequent Flier Miles (000) | Number of Employees |
|---|---|
| 0 up to 3 | 5 |
| 3 up to 6 | 12 |
| 6 up to 9 | 23 |
| 9 up to 12 | 8 |
| 12 up to 15 | 2 |
| Total | 50 |

    **a.** How many employees were studied?
    **b.** What is the midpoint of the first class?
    **c.** Construct a histogram.
    **d.** A frequency polygon is to be drawn. What are the coordinates of the plot for the first class?
    **e.** Construct a frequency polygon.
    **f.** Interpret the frequent flier miles accumulated using the two charts.

**12.** Ecommerce.com, a large Internet retailer, is studying the lead time (elapsed time between when an order is placed and when it is filled) for a sample of recent orders. The lead times are reported in days.

| Lead Time (days) | Frequency |
|---|---|
| 0 up to 5 | 6 |
| 5 up to 10 | 7 |
| 10 up to 15 | 12 |
| 15 up to 20 | 8 |
| 20 up to 25 | 7 |
| Total | 40 |

    **a.** How many orders were studied?
    **b.** What is the midpoint of the first class?
    **c.** What are the coordinates of the first class for a frequency polygon?
    **d.** Draw a histogram.
    **e.** Draw a frequency polygon.
    **f.** Interpret the lead times using the two charts.

# Cumulative Frequency Distributions

Consider once again the distribution of the selling prices of vehicles at Whitner Autoplex. Suppose we were interested in the number of vehicles that sold for less than $21,000, or the value below which 40 percent of the vehicles sold. These numbers can be approximated by developing a **cumulative frequency distribution** and portraying it graphically in a **cumulative frequency polygon.**

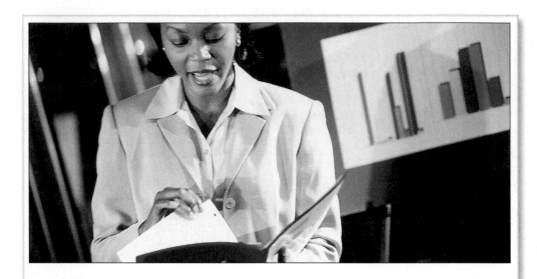

**EXAMPLE**

The frequency distribution of the vehicle selling prices at Whitner Autoplex is repeated from Table 2–4.

| Selling Price ($ thousands) | Frequency |
|---|---|
| 15 up to 18 | 8 |
| 18 up to 21 | 23 |
| 21 up to 24 | 17 |
| 24 up to 27 | 18 |
| 27 up to 30 | 8 |
| 30 up to 33 | 4 |
| 33 up to 36 | 2 |
| Total | 80 |

Construct a cumulative frequency polygon. Fifty percent of the vehicles were sold for less than what amount? Twenty-five of the vehicles were sold for less than what amount?

**SOLUTION**

As the name implies, a cumulative frequency distribution and a cumulative frequency polygon require *cumulative frequencies*. To construct a cumulative frequency distribution, refer to the preceding table and note that there were eight vehicles sold for less than $18,000. Those 8 vehicles, plus the 23 in the next higher class, for a total of 31, were sold for less than $21,000. The cumulative frequency for the next higher class is 48, found by 8 + 23 + 17. This process is continued for all the classes. All the vehicles were sold for less than $36,000. (See Table 2–6.)

**TABLE 2–6** Cumulative Frequency Distribution for Vehicle Selling Price

| Selling Price ($ thousands) | Frequency | Cumulative Frequency | Found by |
|---|---|---|---|
| 15 up to 18 | 8 | 8 | |
| 18 up to 21 | 23 | 31 ← | 8 + 23 |
| 21 up to 24 | 17 | 48 | 8 + 23 + 17 |
| 24 up to 27 | 18 | 66 | 8 + 23 + 17 + 18 |
| 27 up to 30 | 8 | 74 | |
| 30 up to 33 | 4 | 78 | |
| 33 up to 36 | 2 | 80 | |
| Total | 80 | | |

To plot a cumulative frequency distribution, scale the upper limit of each class along the X-axis and the corresponding cumulative frequencies along the Y-axis. To provide additional information, you can label the vertical axis on the left in units and the vertical axis on the right in percent. In the Whitner Autoplex example, the vertical axis on the left is labeled from 0 to 80 and on the right from 0 to 100 percent. The value of 50 percent corresponds to 40 vehicles sold.

To begin the plotting, 8 vehicles sold for less than $18,000, so the first plot is at X = 18 and Y = 8. The coordinates for the next plot are X = 21 and Y = 31. The rest of the points are plotted and then the dots connected to form the chart (see Chart 2–5).

**CHART 2–5** Cumulative Frequency Distribution for Vehicle Selling Price

To find the selling price below which half the cars sold, we draw a horizontal line from the 50 percent mark on the right-hand vertical axis over to the polygon, then drop down to the X-axis and read the selling price. The value on the X-axis is about 22.5, so we estimate that 50 percent of the vehicles sold for less than $22,500.

To find the price below which 25 of the vehicles sold, we locate the value of 25 on the left-hand vertical axis. Next, we draw a horizontal line from the value of 25 to the polygon, and then drop down to the X-axis and read the price. It is about 20.5, so we estimate that 25 of the vehicles sold for less than $20,500. We can also make estimates of the percent of vehicles that sold for less than a particular amount. To explain, suppose we want to estimate the percent of vehicles that sold for less than $28,500. We begin by locating the value of 28.5 on the X-axis, move vertically to the polygon, and then horizontally to the vertical axis on the right. The value is about 87 percent, so we conclude that 87 percent of the vehicles sold for less than $28,500.

---

**Self-Review 2–5**

A sample of the hourly wages of 15 employees at the Home Depot in Brunswick, Georgia, was organized into the following table.

| Hourly Wages | Number of Employees |
|---|---|
| $ 8 up to $10 | 3 |
| 10 up to 12 | 7 |
| 12 up to 14 | 4 |
| 14 up to 16 | 1 |

(a) What is the table called?
(b) Develop a cumulative frequency distribution and portray the distribution in a cumulative frequency polygon.
(c) On the basis of the cumulative frequency polygon, how many employees earn $11 an hour or less? Half of the employees earn an hourly wage of how much or more? Four employees earn how much or less?

# Exercises

**13.** The following chart shows the hourly wages of a sample of certified welders in the Atlanta, Georgia, area.

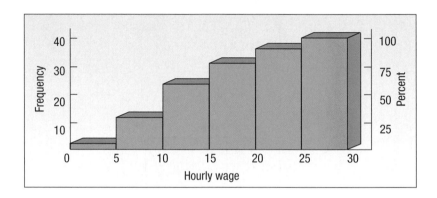

**a.** How many welders were studied?
**b.** What is the class interval?
**c.** About how many welders earn less than $10.00 per hour?
**d.** About 75 percent of the welders make less than what amount?
**e.** Ten of the welders studied made less than what amount?
**f.** What percent of the welders make less than $20.00 per hour?

**14.** The following chart shows the selling price ($000) of houses sold in the Billings, Montana, area.

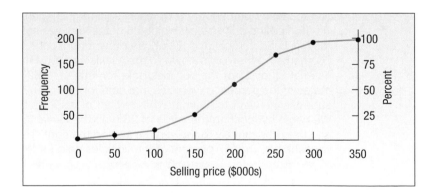

**a.** How many homes were studied?
**b.** What is the class interval?
**c.** One hundred homes sold for less than what amount?
**d.** About 75 percent of the homes sold for less than what amount?
**e.** Estimate the number of homes in the $150,000 up to $200,000 class.
**f.** About how many homes sold for less than $225,000?

**15.** The frequency distribution representing the number of frequent flier miles accumulated by employees at Brumley Statistical Consulting Company is repeated from Exercise 11.

| Frequent Flier Miles (000) | Frequency |
|---|---|
| 0 up to 3 | 5 |
| 3 up to 6 | 12 |
| 6 up to 9 | 23 |
| 9 up to 12 | 8 |
| 12 up to 15 | 2 |
| Total | 50 |

   a. How many employees accumulated less than 3,000 miles?
   b. Convert the frequency distribution to a cumulative frequency distribution.
   c. Portray the cumulative distribution in the form of a cumulative frequency polygon.
   d. Based on the cumulative frequency polygon, about 75 percent of the employees accumulated how many miles or less?

16. The frequency distribution of order lead time at Ecommerce.com from Exercise 12 is repeated below.

| Lead Time (days) | Frequency |
|---|---|
| 0 up to 5 | 6 |
| 5 up to 10 | 7 |
| 10 up to 15 | 12 |
| 15 up to 20 | 8 |
| 20 up to 25 | 7 |
| Total | 40 |

   a. How many orders were filled in less than 10 days? In less than 15 days?
   b. Convert the frequency distribution to a cumulative frequency distribution.
   c. Develop a cumulative frequency polygon.
   d. About 60 percent of the orders were filled in less than how many days?

# Other Graphic Presentations of Data

The histogram, the frequency polygon, and the cumulative frequency polygon all have strong visual appeal. That is, they are designed to capture the attention of the reader. In this section we will examine some other graphical forms, namely the line chart, the bar chart, and the pie chart. These charts are seen extensively in *USA Today, U.S. News and World Report, Business Week,* and other newspapers, magazines, and government reports.

## Line Graphs

Charts 2–6 and 2–7 are examples of **line charts.** Line charts are particularly effective for business and economic data because we can show the change or trends in a variable over time. The variable of interest, such as the number of units sold or the total value of sales, is scaled along the vertical axis and time along the horizontal axis. Chart 2–6 shows the Dow Jones Industrial Average and the NASDAQ, the two most widely reported measures of stock activity. The time of the day, beginning with the opening bell at 9:30 is shown along the horizontal axis and the value of the Dow on the vertical axis. For this day the Dow was at 8,790.44, up 5.55 points, at 12:08 PM. The NASDAQ was at 1,447.67, down .05 points, as of 12:08 PM. Line graphs are widely used by investors to support decisions to buy and sell stocks and bonds.

   Chart 2–7 is also a line chart. It shows the jobless rates for African-American males over the age of 16 from 1992 until 2002. Note at the start of the period the jobless rate was about 15 percent, the rate declined to about 8 percent in 2000, but it increased in the new decade to 12 percent in 2002.

**CHART 2–6** Line Chart for the Dow Jones Industrial Average and the NASDAQ

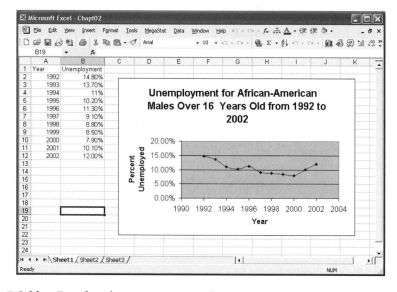

**CHART 2–7** Jobless Rate for African-American Males over 16 from 1992 to 2002

Quite often two or more series of data are plotted on the same line chart. Thus one chart can show the trend of several different variables. This allows for a comparison of several series over the same period of time. Chart 2–8 shows the domestic and international sales (in billions of dollars) for Johnson and Johnson, Inc., for the years 1992 to 2002. We can see that the sales of both segments are growing, but the domestic sales are growing more rapidly.

## Bar Charts

A **bar chart** can be used to depict any of the levels of measurement—nominal, ordinal, interval, or ratio. (Recall, we discussed the levels of measurement beginning on page 9 in Chapter 1.) From the Census Bureau *Current Population Reports*, the typical annual earnings for someone over the age of 18 are $22,895 if a high school diploma is the highest degree earned. With a bachelor's degree the typical earnings increase to $40,478, and with a professional or master's degree the typical amount increases to $73,165. This information is summarized in Chart 2–9. With this chart it is easy to see that a person with a bachelor's degree can expect to earn almost twice as much in a year as someone with a high school diploma. The expected earnings of someone with a master's or professional degree are nearly twice as much as someone with a bachelor's degree and three times that of someone with a high school diploma.

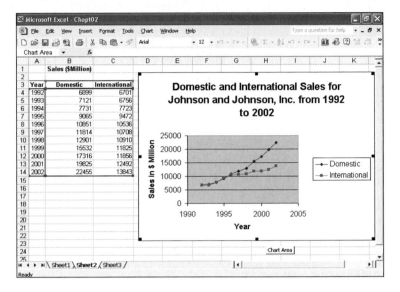

**CHART 2–8** Domestic and International Sales for Johnson and Johnson, Inc., 1992 to 2002

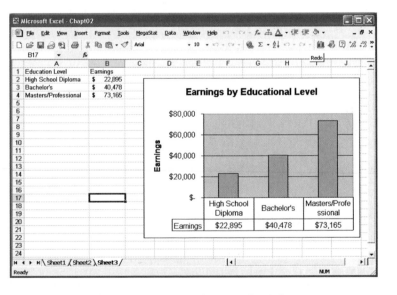

**CHART 2–9** Typical Annual Earnings Based on Educational Level

# Pie Charts

A **pie chart** is especially useful for illustrating nominal level data. We explain the details of constructing a pie chart using the information in Table 2–7, which shows a breakdown of the expenses of the Ohio State Lottery for 2002.

**TABLE 2–7** Ohio State Lottery Expenses in 2002

| Use of Sales | Amount ($ million) | Percent of Share |
|---|---|---|
| Prizes | 1,148.1 | 57 |
| Payments to Education | 635.2 | 32 |
| Bonuses/Commissions | 126.6 | 6 |
| Operating Expenses | 103.3 | 5 |
| Total | 2,013.2 | 100 |

The first step is to record the percentages 0, 5, 10, 15, and so on evenly around the circumference of a circle. To plot the 57 percent share awarded for prizes, draw a line from the center of the circle to 0 and another line from the center of the circle to 57 percent. The area in this "slice" represents the lottery proceeds that were awarded in prizes. Next, add the 57 percent of expenses awarded in prizes to the 32 percent payments to education; the result is 89 percent. Draw a line from the center of the circle to 89 percent, so the area between 57 percent and 89 percent depicts the payments made to education. Continuing, add the 6 percent for bonuses and commissions, which gives us a total of 95 percent. Draw a line from the center of the circle to 95, so the "slice" between 89 percent and 95 percent represents the payment of bonuses and commissions. The remaining 5 percent is for operating expenses.

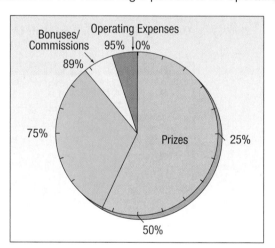

Because the area of the pie represents the relative share of each component, we can easily compare them:

- The largest expense of the Ohio Lottery is for prizes.
- About one-third of the proceeds are transferred to education.
- Operating expenses account for only 5 percent of the proceeds.

The Excel system will develop a pie chart and output the result. See the following chart for the information in Table 2–7.

**Self-Review 2–6** The Clayton County Commissioners want to show taxpayers attending the forthcoming meeting what happens to their tax dollars. The total amount of taxes collected is $2 million. Expenditures are: $440,000 for schools, $1,160,000 for roads, $320,000 for administration, and $80,000 for supplies. A pie chart seems ideal to show the portion of each tax dollar going for schools, roads, administration, and supplies. Convert the dollar amounts to percents of the total and portray the percents in the form of a pie chart.

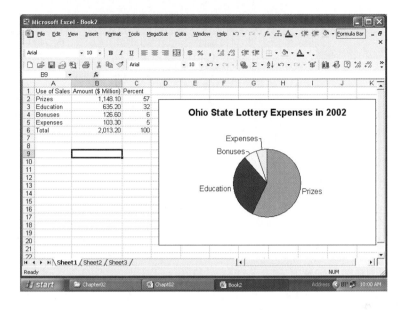

# Exercises

**17.** A small business consultant is investigating the performance of several companies. The sales in 2003 (in thousands of dollars) for the selected companies were:

| Corporation | Fourth-Quarter Sales ($ thousands) |
| --- | --- |
| Hoden Building Products | $ 1,645.2 |
| J & R Printing, Inc. | 4,757.0 |
| Long Bay Concrete Construction | 8,913.0 |
| Mancell Electric and Plumbing | 627.1 |
| Maxwell Heating and Air Conditioning | 24,612.0 |
| Mizelle Roofing & Sheet Metals | 191.9 |

The consultant wants to include a chart in his report comparing the sales of the six companies. Use a bar chart to compare the fourth quarter sales of these corporations and write a brief report summarizing the bar chart.

**18.** The Blair Corporation, located in Warren, Pennsylvania, sells fashion apparel for men and women plus a broad range of home products (http://www.blair.com). It services its customers by mail. Listed below are the net sales for Blair from 1997 through 2002. Draw a line chart depicting the net sales over the time period and write a brief report.

| Year | Net Sales ($ millions) |
| --- | --- |
| 1997 | 486.6 |
| 1998 | 506.8 |
| 1999 | 522.2 |
| 2000 | 574.6 |
| 2001 | 580.7 |
| 2002 | 568.5 |

**19.** A headline in a Toledo, Ohio, newspaper reported that crime was on the decline. Listed below are the number of homicides from 1986 to 2002. Draw a line chart to summarize the data and write a brief summary of the homicide rates for the last 17 years.

| Year | Homicides | Year | Homicides |
|------|-----------|------|-----------|
| 1986 | 21 | 1995 | 35 |
| 1987 | 34 | 1996 | 30 |
| 1988 | 26 | 1997 | 28 |
| 1989 | 42 | 1998 | 25 |
| 1990 | 37 | 1999 | 21 |
| 1991 | 37 | 2000 | 19 |
| 1992 | 44 | 2001 | 23 |
| 1993 | 45 | 2002 | 27 |
| 1994 | 40 | | |

**20.** A report prepared for the governor of a western state indicated that 56 percent of the state's tax revenue went to education, 23 percent to the general fund, 10 percent to the counties, 9 percent to senior programs, and the remainder to other social programs. Develop a pie chart to show the breakdown of the budget.

**21.** The following table, in millions, shows the population of the United States in 5-year intervals from 1950 to 2000. Develop a line chart depicting the population growth and write a brief report summarizing your findings.

| Year | Population (millions) | Year | Population (millions) |
|------|-----------------------|------|-----------------------|
| 1950 | 152.3 | 1980 | 227.7 |
| 1955 | 165.9 | 1985 | 238.5 |
| 1960 | 180.7 | 1990 | 249.9 |
| 1965 | 194.3 | 1995 | 263.0 |
| 1970 | 205.1 | 2000 | 281.4 |
| 1975 | 216.0 | | |

**22.** Shown below are the military and civilian personnel expenditures for the eight largest military locations in the United States. Develop a bar chart and summarize the results in a brief report.

| Location | Amount Spent (millions) | Location | Amount Spent (millions) |
|----------|-------------------------|----------|-------------------------|
| St. Louis, MO | $6,087 | Norfolk, VA | $3,228 |
| San Diego, CA | 4,747 | Marietta, GA | 2,828 |
| Pico Rivera, CA | 3,272 | Fort Worth, TX | 2,492 |
| Arlington, VA | 3,284 | Washington, DC | 2,347 |

# Chapter Outline

**I.** A frequency distribution is a grouping of data into mutually exclusive classes showing the number of observations in each class.
  **A.** The steps in constructing a frequency distribution are:
    **1.** Decide how many classes you wish.
    **2.** Determine the class interval or width.
    **3.** Set the individual class limits.
    **4.** Tally the raw data into the classes.
    **5.** Count the number of tallies in each class.
  **B.** The class frequency is the number of observations in each class.
  **C.** The class interval is the difference between the limits of two consecutive classes.
  **D.** The class midpoint is halfway between the limits of two consecutive classes.

II. A relative frequency distribution shows the percent of the observations in each class.

III. There are three methods for graphically portraying a frequency distribution.

    A. A histogram portrays the number of frequencies in each class in the form of rectangles.

    B. A frequency polygon consists of line segments connecting the points formed by the intersections of the class midpoints and the class frequencies.

    C. A cumulative frequency polygon shows the number of observations below a certain value.

IV. There are many charts used in newspapers and magazines.

    A. A line chart is ideal for showing the trend of a variable such as sales or income over time.

    B. Bar charts are similar to line charts and are useful for showing changes in nominal scale data.

    C. Pie charts are useful for showing the percent that various components are of the total.

# Chapter Exercises

**23.** A data set consists of 83 observations. How many classes would you recommend for a frequency distribution?

**24.** A data set consists of 145 observations that range from 56 to 490. What size class interval would you recommend?

**25.** The following is the number of minutes to commute from home to work for a group of automobile executives.

| 28 | 25 | 48 | 37 | 41 | 19 | 32 | 26 | 16 | 23 | 23 | 29 | 36 |
|----|----|----|----|----|----|----|----|----|----|----|----|----|
| 31 | 26 | 21 | 32 | 25 | 31 | 43 | 35 | 42 | 38 | 33 | 28 |    |

    a. How many classes would you recommend?

    b. What class interval would you suggest?

    c. What would you recommend as the lower limit of the first class?

    d. Organize the data into a frequency distribution.

    e. Comment on the shape of the frequency distribution.

**26.** The following data give the weekly amounts spent on groceries for a sample of households.

| $271 | $363 | $159 | $ 76 | $227 | $337 | $295 | $319 | $250 |
|------|------|------|------|------|------|------|------|------|
| 279  | 205  | 279  | 266  | 199  | 177  | 162  | 232  | 303  |
| 192  | 181  | 321  | 309  | 246  | 278  | 50   | 41   | 335  |
| 116  | 100  | 151  | 240  | 474  | 297  | 170  | 188  | 320  |
| 429  | 294  | 570  | 342  | 279  | 235  | 434  | 123  | 325  |

    a. How many classes would you recommend?

    b. What class interval would you suggest?

    c. What would you recommend as the lower limit of the first class?

    d. Organize the data into a frequency distribution.

**27.** The following histogram shows the scores on the first statistics exam.

    a. How many students took the exam?

    b. What is the class interval?

    c. What is the class midpoint for the first class?

    d. How many students earned a score of less than 70?

**28.** The following chart summarizes the selling price of homes sold last month in the Sarasota, Florida, area.

a. What is the chart called?
b. How many homes were sold during the last month?
c. What is the class interval?
d. About 75 percent of the houses sold for less than what amount?
e. One hundred seventy-five of the homes sold for less than what amount?

**29.** A chain of sport shops catering to beginning skiers, headquartered in Aspen, Colorado, plans to conduct a study of how much a beginning skier spends on his or her initial purchase of equipment and supplies. Based on these figures, they want to explore the possibility of offering combinations, such as a pair of boots and a pair of skis, to induce customers to buy more. A sample of their cash register receipts revealed these initial purchases:

| $140 | $ 82 | $265 | $168 | $ 90 | $114 | $172 | $230 | $142 |
|------|------|------|------|------|------|------|------|------|
| 86   | 125  | 235  | 212  | 171  | 149  | 156  | 162  | 118  |
| 139  | 149  | 132  | 105  | 162  | 126  | 216  | 195  | 127  |
| 161  | 135  | 172  | 220  | 229  | 129  | 87   | 128  | 126  |
| 175  | 127  | 149  | 126  | 121  | 118  | 172  | 126  |      |

a. Arrive at a suggested class interval. Use five classes, and let the lower limit of the first class be $80.
b. What would be a better class interval?
c. Organize the data into a frequency distribution using a lower limit of $80.
d. Interpret your findings.

**30.** The numbers of shareholders for a selected group of large companies (in thousands) are:

| Company | Number of Shareholders (thousands) | Company | Number of Shareholders (thousands) |
|---------|-----------------------------------|---------|-----------------------------------|
| Southwest Airlines | 144 | Standard Oil (Indiana) | 173 |
| General Public Utilities | 177 | Home Depot | 195 |
| Occidental Petroleum | 266 | Detroit Edison | 220 |
| Middle South Utilities | 133 | Eastman Kodak | 251 |
| DaimlerChrysler | 209 | Dow Chemical | 137 |
| Standard Oil of California | 264 | Pennsylvania Power | 150 |
| Bethlehem Steel | 160 | American Electric Power | 262 |
| Long Island Lighting | 143 | Ohio Edison | 158 |
| RCA | 246 | Transamerica Corporation | 162 |
| Greyhound Corporation | 151 | Columbia Gas System | 165 |
| Pacific Gas & Electric | 239 | International Telephone & | |
| Niagara Mohawk Power | 204 | Telegraph | 223 |
| E. I. du Pont de Nemours | 204 | Union Electric | 158 |
| Westinghouse Electric | 195 | Virginia Electric and Power | 162 |
| Union Carbide | 176 | Public Service Electric & Gas | 225 |
| BankAmerica | 175 | Consumers Power | 161 |
| Northeast Utilities | 200 | | |

The numbers of shareholders are to be organized into a frequency distribution and several graphs drawn to portray the distribution.
a. Using seven classes and a lower limit of 130, construct a frequency distribution.
b. Portray the distribution as a frequency polygon.
c. Portray the distribution in a cumulative frequency polygon.

**d.** According to the polygon, three out of four (75 percent) of the companies have how many shareholders or less?

**e.** Write a brief analysis of the number of shareholders based on the frequency distribution and graphs.

**31.** A recent survey showed that the typical American car owner spends $2,950 per year on operating expenses. Below is a breakdown of the various expenditure items. Draw an appropriate chart to portray the data and summarize your findings in a brief report.

| Expenditure Item | Amount |
|---|---|
| Fuel | $ 603 |
| Interest on car loan | 279 |
| Repairs | 930 |
| Insurance and license | 646 |
| Depreciation | 492 |
| Total | $2,950 |

**32.** The Midland National Bank selected a sample of 40 student checking accounts. Below are their end-of-the-month balances.

| $404 | $74 | $234 | $149 | $279 | $215 | $123 | $55 | $43 | $321 |
|---|---|---|---|---|---|---|---|---|---|
| 87 | 234 | 68 | 489 | 57 | 185 | 141 | 758 | 72 | 863 |
| 703 | 125 | 350 | 440 | 37 | 252 | 27 | 521 | 302 | 127 |
| 968 | 712 | 503 | 489 | 327 | 608 | 358 | 425 | 303 | 203 |

**a.** Tally the data into a frequency distribution using $100 as a class interval and $0 as the starting point.

**b.** Draw a cumulative frequency polygon.

**c.** The bank considers any student with an ending balance of $400 or more a "preferred customer." Estimate the percentage of preferred customers.

**d.** The bank is also considering a service charge to the lowest 10 percent of the ending balances. What would you recommend as the cutoff point between those who have to pay a service charge and those who do not?

**33.** Residents of the state of South Carolina earned a total of $69.5 billion in 2002 in adjusted gross income. Seventy-three percent of the total was in wages and salaries; 11 percent in dividends, interest, and capital gains; 8 percent in IRAs and taxable pensions; 3 percent in business income pensions; 2 percent in social security, and the remaining 3 percent was from other sources. Develop a pie chart depicting the breakdown of adjusted gross income. Write a paragraph summarizing the information.

**34.** A recent study of home technologies reported the number of hours of personal computer usage per week for a sample of 60 persons. Excluded from the study were people who worked out of their home and used the computer as a part of their work.

| 9.3 | 5.3 | 6.3 | 8.8 | 6.5 | 0.6 | 5.2 | 6.6 | 9.3 | 4.3 |
|---|---|---|---|---|---|---|---|---|---|
| 6.3 | 2.1 | 2.7 | 0.4 | 3.7 | 3.3 | 1.1 | 2.7 | 6.7 | 6.5 |
| 4.3 | 9.7 | 7.7 | 5.2 | 1.7 | 8.5 | 4.2 | 5.5 | 5.1 | 5.6 |
| 5.4 | 4.8 | 2.1 | 10.1 | 1.3 | 5.6 | 2.4 | 2.4 | 4.7 | 1.7 |
| 2.0 | 6.7 | 1.1 | 6.7 | 2.2 | 2.6 | 9.8 | 6.4 | 4.9 | 5.2 |
| 4.5 | 9.3 | 7.9 | 4.6 | 4.3 | 4.5 | 9.2 | 8.5 | 6.0 | 8.1 |

**a.** Organize the data into a frequency distribution. How many classes would you suggest? What value would you suggest for a class interval?

**b.** Draw a histogram. Interpret your result.

**35.** Merrill Lynch recently completed a study regarding the size of on-line investment portfolios (stocks, bonds, mutual funds, and certificates of deposit) for a sample of clients in the 40- to 50-year-old age group. Listed below is the value of all the investments in $000 for the 70 participants in the study.

| $669.9 | $   7.5 | $ 77.2 | $   7.5 | $125.7 | $516.9 | $219.9 | $645.2 |
|--------|---------|--------|---------|--------|--------|--------|--------|
| 301.9  | 235.4   | 716.4  | 145.3   | 26.6   | 187.2  | 315.5  | 89.2   |
| 136.4  | 616.9   | 440.6  | 408.2   | 34.4   | 296.1  | 185.4  | 526.3  |
| 380.7  | 3.3     | 363.2  | 51.9    | 52.2   | 107.5  | 82.9   | 63.0   |
| 228.6  | 308.7   | 126.7  | 430.3   | 82.0   | 227.0  | 321.1  | 403.4  |
| 39.5   | 124.3   | 118.1  | 23.9    | 352.8  | 156.7  | 276.3  | 23.5   |
| 31.3   | 301.2   | 35.7   | 154.9   | 174.3  | 100.6  | 236.7  | 171.9  |
| 221.1  | 43.4    | 212.3  | 243.3   | 315.4  | 5.9    | 1002.2 | 171.7  |
| 295.7  | 437.0   | 87.8   | 302.1   | 268.1  | 899.5  |        |        |

    **a.** Organize the data into a frequency distribution. How many classes would you suggest? What value would you suggest for a class interval?

    **b.** Draw a histogram. Interpret your result.

**36.** In early 2003, twenty percent of the Prime Time TV viewing audience watched shows on ABC, 25 percent on CBS, 16 percent on Fox, 24 percent on NBC, 8 percent on Warner Brothers, and 7 percent on UPN. You can find the latest information on TV viewing from the following website: http://tv.zap2it.com/news/ratings/. Develop a pie chart or a bar chart to depict this information. Write a paragraph summarizing the information.

**37.** The American Heart Association reported the following percentage breakdown of expenses. Draw a pie chart depicting the information. Interpret.

| Category | Percent |
|----------|---------|
| Research | 32.3 |
| Public Health Education | 23.5 |
| Community Service | 12.6 |
| Fund Raising | 12.1 |
| Professional and Educational Training | 10.9 |
| Management and General | 8.6 |

**38.** In their 2002 annual report Schering-Plough Corporation reported their income, in millions of dollars, for the years 1997 to 2002 as follows. Develop a line chart depicting the results and comment on your findings.

| Year | Income ($ million) |
|------|--------------------|
| 1997 | 1,444 |
| 1998 | 1,756 |
| 1999 | 2,110 |
| 2000 | 2,423 |
| 2001 | 1,943 |
| 2002 | 1,974 |

**39.** Annual revenues, by type of tax, for the state of Georgia are as follows. Develop an appropriate chart or graph and write a brief report summarizing the information.

| Type of Tax | Amount (000) |
|-------------|--------------|
| Sales | $2,812,473 |
| Income (Individual) | 2,732,045 |
| License | 185,198 |
| Corporate | 525,015 |
| Property | 22,647 |
| Death and Gift | 37,326 |
| Total | $6,314,704 |

**40.** Annual imports from selected Canadian trading partners are listed below for the year 2002. Develop an appropriate chart or graph and write a brief report summarizing the information.

| Partner | Annual Imports (million) |
|---|---|
| Japan | $9,550 |
| United Kingdom | 4,556 |
| South Korea | 2,441 |
| China | 1,182 |
| Australia | 618 |

**41.** Farming has changed from the early 1900s. In the early 20th century, machinery gradually replaced animal power. For example, in 1910 U.S. farms used 24.2 million horses and mules and only about 1,000 tractors. By 1960, 4.6 million tractors were used and only 3.2 million horses and mules. In 1920 there were over 6 million farms in the United States. Today there are less than 2 million. Listed below is the number of farms, in thousands, for each of the 50 states. Write a paragraph summarizing your findings.

| | | | | | | | | | |
|---|---|---|---|---|---|---|---|---|---|
| 47 | 1 | 8 | 46 | 76 | 26 | 4 | 3 | 39 | 45 |
| 4 | 21 | 80 | 63 | 100 | 65 | 91 | 29 | 7 | 15 |
| 7 | 52 | 87 | 39 | 106 | 25 | 55 | 2 | 3 | 8 |
| 14 | 38 | 59 | 33 | 76 | 71 | 37 | 51 | 1 | 24 |
| 35 | 86 | 185 | 13 | 7 | 43 | 36 | 20 | 79 | 9 |

**42.** One of the most popular candies in the United States is M&M's, which are produced by the Mars Company. In the beginning M&M's were all brown; more recently they were produced in red, green, blue, orange, brown, and yellow. You can read about the history of the product, find ideas for baking, purchase the candies in the colors of your school or favorite team, and learn the percent of each color in the standard bags at http://global.mms.com/us/about/products/milkchocolate.jsp. Recently the purchase of a 14-ounce bag of M&M's Plain had 444 candies with the following breakdown by color: 130 brown, 98 yellow, 96 red, 35 orange, 52 blue, and 33 green. Develop a chart depicting this information and write a paragraph summarizing the results.

**43.** The following graph compares the average selling prices of the Ford Taurus and the Toyota Camry from 1994 to 2002. Write a brief report summarizing the information in the graph. Be sure to include the selling price of the two cars, the change in the selling price, and the direction of the change in the 8-year period.

# exercises.com

**44.** Monthly and year-to-date truck sales are available at the website: http://www.pickup-truck.com. Go to this site and search under **News** to obtain the most recent information. Make a pie chart or a bar chart showing the most recent information. What is the best selling truck? What are the four or five best selling trucks? What is their market share? You may wish to group some of the trucks into a category called "Other" to get a better picture of market share. Comment on your findings.

**45.** The following graph shows the total wages paid by software and aircraft companies in the state of Washington from 1994 until 2002. Write a brief report summarizing this information.

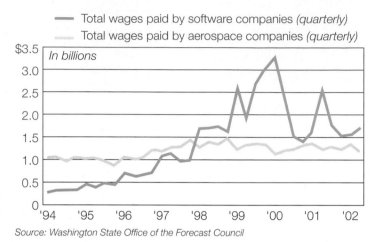

Source: *Washington State Office of the Forecast Council*

**46.** A pie chart shows the market shares of Cola products. The "slice" for Pepsi-Cola has a central angle of 90 degrees. What is their market share?

# Dataset Exercises

**47.** Refer to the Real Estate data, which reports information on homes sold in the Denver, Colorado, area during the last year.
   **a.** Select an appropriate class interval and organize the selling prices into a frequency distribution.
      **1.** Around what values do the data tend to cluster?
      **2.** What is the largest selling price? What is the smallest selling price?
   **b.** Draw a cumulative frequency distribution based on the frequency distribution developed in part (a).
      **1.** How many homes sold for less than $200,000?
      **2.** Estimate the percent of the homes that sold for more than $220,000.
      **3.** What percent of the homes sold for less than $125,000?
   **c.** Write a report summarizing the selling prices of the homes.
**48.** Refer to the Baseball 2002 data, which reports information on the 30 Major League Baseball teams for the 2002 season.
   **a.** Organize the information on the team salaries into a frequency distribution. Select an appropriate class interval.
      **1.** What is a typical team salary? What is the range of salaries?
      **2.** Comment on the shape of the distribution. Does it appear that any of the team salaries are out of line with the others?
   **b.** Draw a cumulative frequency distribution based on the frequency distribution developed in part (a).
      **1.** Forty percent of the teams are paying less than what amount in total team salary?
      **2.** About how many teams have total salaries of less than $80,000,000?
      **3.** Below what amount do the lowest five teams pay in total salary?
   **c.** Organize the information on the size of the various stadiums into a frequency distribution.
      **1.** What is a typical stadium size? Where do the stadium sizes tend to cluster?
      **2.** Comment on the shape of the distribution. Does it appear that any of the stadium sizes are out of line with the others?
   **d.** Organize the information on the year in which the 30 major league stadiums were built into a frequency distribution. (You could also create a new variable called AGE by subtracting the year in which the stadium was built from the current year.)
      **1.** What is the year in which the typical stadium was built? Where do these years tend to cluster?
      **2.** Comment on the shape of the distribution. Does it appear that any of the stadium ages are out of line with the others? If so, which ones?

49. Refer to the Wage data, which reports information on annual wages for a sample of 100 workers. Also included are variables relating to industry, years of education, and gender for each worker. Draw a bar chart of the variable occupation. Write a brief report summarizing your findings.
50. Refer to the CIA data, which reports demographic and economic information on 46 countries. Develop a frequency distribution for the variable GNP per capita. Summarize your findings. What is the shape of the distribution?

# Software Commands

1. The MegaStat commands for the frequency distribution on page 29 are:
   a. Open Excel and from the CD provided, select **Go to the Data Sets,** and select the Excel format; go to Chapter 2, and select **Table 2–1.** Click on **MegaStat, Frequency Distribution,** and select **Quantitative.**
   b. In the dialog box, input the range from *A1:A81,* select **Equal width intervals,** use *3,000* as the interval width, *15,000* as the lower boundary of the first interval, select **Histogram,** and then click **OK.**

2. The Excel commands for the histogram on page 34 are:
   a. In cell A1 indicate that the column of data is the selling price and in B1 that it is the frequency. In columns A2 to A8 insert the midpoints of the selling prices in $000. In B2 to B8 record the class frequencies.
   b. With your mouse arrow on A1, click and drag to highlight the cells A1:B8.
   c. From the **Tool bar** select **Chart Wizard,** under **Chart type** select **Column,** under **Chart subtype** select the vertical bars in the upper left corner, and finally click on **Next** in the lower right corner.
   d. At the top select the **Series** tab. Under the Series list box, **Price** is highlighted. Select **Remove.** (We do not want Price to be a part of the values.) At the bottom, in the **Category (X)** axis labels text box, click the icon at the far right. Put your cursor on cell A2, click and drag to cell A8. There will be a running box around cells A2 to A8. Touch the **Enter** key. This identifies the column of **Prices** as the *X*-axis labels. Click on **Next.**
   e. At the top of the dialog box click on **Titles.** Click on the **Chart title** box and key in *Selling Price of 80 Vehicles Sold at Whitner Autoplex.* Tab to the **Category (X)** axis box and key in the label *Selling Price in ($000).* Tab to the **Category (Y)** axis box and key in *Frequency.* At the top select **Legend** and remove the check from the **Show legend** box. Click **Finish.**
   f. To make the chart larger, click on the middle handle of the top line and drag the line to row 1. Make sure the handles show on the chart box. With your right mouse button, click on one of the columns. Select **Format Data Series.** At the top select the **Options** tab. In the **Gap width** text box, click the down arrow until the gap width reads 0, and click **OK.**

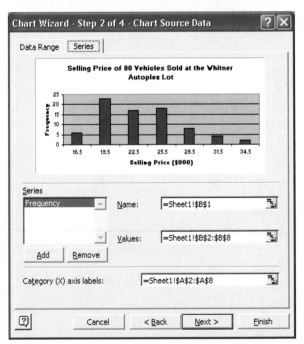

3. The Excel commands for the pie chart on page 45 are:
   a. Set cell *A1* as the active cell and type the words *Use of Sales*. In cells *A2* through *A5* type *Prizes, Education, Bonuses,* and *Expense.*
   b. Set *B1* as the active cell and type *Amount ($ Millions)* and in cells *B2* through *B5* enter the data.
   c. From the **Tool Bar** select **Chart Wizard.** Select **Pie** as the type of chart, select the chart type in the upper left corner, and then click on **Next.**
   d. For the **Data Range** type *A1:B5,* indicate that the data are in **Columns,** and then click on **Next.**
   e. Click on the chart title area and type *Ohio Lottery Expenses 2002*. Then click **Finish.**

# Chapter 2 Answers to Self-Review

**2–1**   **a.** The raw data or ungrouped data.

**b.**

| Commission | Number of Salespeople |
|---|---|
| $1,400 up to $1,500 | 2 |
| 1,500 up to 1,600 | 5 |
| 1,600 up to 1,700 | 3 |
| 1,700 up to 1,800 | 1 |
| Total | 11 |

    **c.** Class frequencies.

    **d.** The largest concentration of commissions is $1,500 up to $1,600. The smallest commission is about $1,400 and the largest is about $1,800.

**2–2**   **a.** $2^6 = 64 < 73 < 128 = 2^7$. So 7 classes are recommended.

    **b.** The interval width should be at least $(488 - 320)/7 = 24$. Class intervals of 25 or 30 feet are both reasonable.

    **c.** If we use a class interval of 25 feet and begin with a lower limit of 300 feet, eight classes would be necessary. A class interval of 30 feet beginning with 300 feet is also reasonable. This alternative requires only seven classes.

**2–3**   **a.** 23

    **b.** 28.75%, found by $(23/80) \times 100$

    **c.** 7.5%, found by $(6/80) \times 100$

**2–4**   **a.**

    **b.**

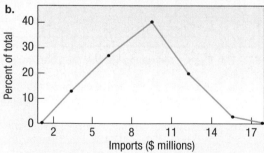

The plots are: (3.5, 12), (6.5, 26), (9.5, 40), (12.5, 20), and (15.5, 2).

    **c.** The smallest annual sales volume of imports by a supplier is about $2 million, the largest about $17 million. The highest frequency is between $8 million and $11 million.

**2–5**   **a.** A frequency distribution.

    **b.**

| Hourly Wages | Cumulative Number |
|---|---|
| Less than $8 | 0 |
| Less than $10 | 3 |
| Less than $12 | 10 |
| Less than $14 | 14 |
| Less than $16 | 15 |

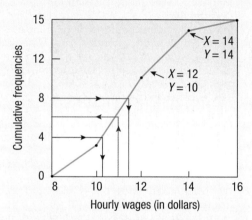

    **c.** About seven employees earn $11.00 or less. About half the employees earn $11.25 or more. About four employees earn $10.25 or less.

**2–6**

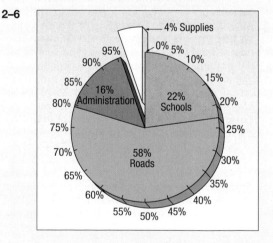

# Describing Data:

## Numerical Measures

The weights (in pounds) of a sample of five boxes being shipped to Texas using UPS are:

12, 6, 7, 3, and 10. Compute the standard deviation. (See Goal 4 and Exercise 72.)

## GOALS

*When you have completed this chapter you will be able to:*

1 Calculate the *arithmetic mean, weighted mean, median, mode,* and *geometric mean.*

2 Explain the characteristics, uses, advantages, and disadvantages of each *measure of location.*

3 Identify the position of the mean, median, and mode for both *symmetric* and *skewed distributions.*

4 Compute and interpret the *range, mean deviation, variance,* and *standard deviation.*

5 Understand the characteristics, uses, advantages, and disadvantages of each *measure of dispersion.*

6 Understand *Chebyshev's theorem* and the *Empirical Rule* as they relate to a set of observations.

**Statistics in Action**

Did you ever meet the "average" American? Well, his name is Robert (that is the nominal level of measurement), he is 31 years old (that is the ratio level), he is 69.5 inches tall (again the ratio level of measurement), weighs 172 pounds, wears a size 9½ shoe, has a 34-inch waist, and wears a size 40 suit. In addition, the average man eats 4 pounds of potato chips, watches 2,567 hours of TV, eats 26 pounds of bananas each year, and also, he sleeps 7.7 hours per night.

The average American woman is 5′4″ tall and weighs 140 pounds, while the average American model is 5′11″ tall and weighs 117 pounds. Most fashion models are thinner than 98% of American women. Four out of five American women say they're dissatisfied with the way they look. On any given day, almost half of the women in the United States are on a diet. Idolized in the 1950s, Marilyn Monroe would be considered overweight by today's standards. She fluctuated between a size 14 and 18 dress, and was a healthy and attractive woman.

# Introduction

Chapter 2 began our study of descriptive statistics. To transform a mass of raw data into a meaningful form, we organized it into a frequency distribution and portrayed it graphically in a histogram or a frequency polygon. We also looked at other graphical techniques such as line charts and pie charts.

This chapter is concerned with two numerical ways of describing data, namely, **measures of location** and **measures of dispersion.** Measures of location are often referred to as **averages.** The purpose of a measure of location is to pinpoint the center of a set of values.

You are familiar with the concept of an average. An average is a measure of location that shows the central value of the data. Averages appear daily on TV, in the newspaper, and in news magazines. Here are some examples:

- The average U.S. home changes ownership every 11.8 years.
- The average price of a gallon of gasoline last week in South Carolina was $1.43, according to a study by the American Automobile Association.
- The average cost to drive a private automobile is 55.8 cents per mile in Los Angeles, 49.8 cents per mile in Boston, 49.0 cents per mile in Philadelphia.
- An American receives an average of 568 pieces of mail per year.
- The average starting salary for a business school graduate last year was $36,357. For a graduate with a Liberal Arts major it was $31,599.
- There are 26.4 million golfers over the age of 12 in the United States. Approximately 6.1 million are avid golfers; that is, they play an average of 25 rounds a year. Some additional information on golfers and golfing: the median cost of a round of golf on an 18-hole course at a municipal course in the United States is $30. Today's typical golfer is male, 40 years old, has a household income of $68,209, and plays 21.3 rounds per year.
- In Chicago the mean high temperature is 84 degrees in July and 31 degrees in January. The mean amount of precipitation is 3.80 inches in July and 1.90 inches in January.

If we consider only the measures of location in a set of data, or if we compare several sets of data using central values, we may draw an erroneous conclusion. In addition to the measures of location, we should consider the **dispersion**—often called the *variation* or the *spread*—in the data. As an illustration, suppose the average annual income of executives for Internet-related companies is $80,000, and the average income for executives in pharmaceutical firms is also $80,000. If we looked only at the average incomes, we might wrongly conclude that the two salary distributions are identical or nearly identical. A look at the salary ranges indicates that this conclusion is not correct. The salaries for the executives in the Internet firms range from $70,000 to $90,000, but salaries for the marketing executives in pharmaceuticals range from $40,000 to $120,000. Thus, we conclude that although the average salaries are the same for the two industries, there is much more spread or dispersion in salaries for the pharmaceutical executives. To evaluate the dispersion we will consider the range, the mean deviation, the variance, and the standard deviation.

We begin by discussing measures of location. There is not just one measure of location; in fact, there are many. We will consider five: the arithmetic mean, the weighted mean, the median, the mode, and the geometric mean. The arithmetic mean is the most widely used and widely reported measure of location. We study the mean as both a population parameter and a sample statistic.

# The Population Mean

Many studies involve all the values in a population. For example, there are 39 exits on I-75 through the state of Kentucky. The mean distance between these state exits is 4.76 miles. This is an example of a population parameter because we have studied the distance between *all* the exits. There are 12 sales associates employed at the Reynolds Road outlet of Carpets by Otto. The mean amount of commission they earned last month was $1,345. This is a population value because we considered the commission of *all* the sales associates. Other examples of a population mean would be: the mean closing price for Johnson and Johnson stock for the last 5 days is $48.75; the mean annual rate of return for the last 10 years for Berger Funds is 8.67 percent; and the mean number of hours of overtime worked last week by the six welders in the welding department of Butts Welding, Inc., is 6.45 hours.

For raw data, that is, data that has not been grouped in a frequency distribution, the population mean is the sum of all the values in the population divided by the number of values in the population. To find the population mean, we use the following formula.

$$\text{Population mean} = \frac{\text{Sum of all the values in the population}}{\text{Number of values in the population}}$$

Instead of writing out in words the full directions for computing the population mean (or any other measure), it is more convenient to use the shorthand symbols of mathematics. The mean of a population using mathematical symbols is:

| | | |
|---|---|---|
| **POPULATION MEAN** | $\mu = \dfrac{\Sigma X}{N}$ | **[3–1]** |

where:

  $\mu$ represents the population mean. It is the Greek lowercase letter "mu."
  $N$ is the number of values in the population.
  $X$ represents any particular value.
  $\Sigma$ is the Greek capital letter "sigma" and indicates the operation of adding.
  $\Sigma X$ is the sum of the $X$ values in the population.

Any measurable characteristic of a population is called a **parameter.** The mean of a population is a parameter.

| |
|---|
| **PARAMETER**  A characteristic of a population. |

**EXAMPLE**

There are 12 automobile manufacturing companies in the United States. Listed below is the number of patents granted by the United States government to each company in a recent year.

| Company | Number of Patents Granted | Company | Number of Patents Granted |
|---|---|---|---|
| General Motors | 511 | Mazda | 210 |
| Nissan | 385 | Chrysler | 97 |
| DaimlerChrysler | 275 | Porsche | 50 |
| Toyota | 257 | Mitsubishi | 36 |
| Honda | 249 | Volvo | 23 |
| Ford | 234 | BMW | 13 |

Is this information a sample or a population? What is the arithmetic mean number of patents granted?

This is a population because we are considering all the automobile manufacturing companies obtaining patents. We add the number of patents for each of the 12 companies. The total number of patents for the 12 companies is 2,340. To find the arithmetic mean, we divide this total by 12. So the arithmetic mean is 195, found by 2340/12. From formula (3–1):

$$\mu = \frac{511 + 385 + \cdots + 13}{12} = \frac{2340}{12} = 195$$

How do we interpret the value of 195? The typical number of patents received by an automobile manufacturing company is 195. Because we considered all the companies receiving patents, this value is a population parameter.

# The Sample Mean

As explained in Chapter 1, we often select a sample from the population to find something about a specific characteristic of the population. The quality assurance department, for example, needs to be assured that the ball bearings being produced have an acceptable outside diameter. It would be very expensive and time consuming to check the outside diameter of all the bearings produced. Therefore, a sample of five bearings is selected and the mean outside diameter of the five bearings is calculated to estimate the mean diameter of all the bearings.

For raw data, that is, ungrouped data, *the mean is the sum of all the sampled values divided by the total number of sampled values.* To find the mean for a sample:

Mean of ungrouped sample data

$$\text{Sample mean} = \frac{\text{Sum of all the values in the sample}}{\text{Number of values in the sample}}$$

The mean of a sample and the mean of a population are computed in the same way, but the shorthand notation used is different. The formula for the mean of a *sample* is:

| SAMPLE MEAN | $\bar{X} = \dfrac{\Sigma X}{n}$ | [3–2] |
|---|---|---|

where:

$\bar{X}$ is the sample mean. It is read "X bar."
$n$ is the number of values in the sample.

The mean of a sample, or any other measure based on sample data, is called a **statistic.** If the mean outside diameter of a sample of five ball bearings is 0.625 inches, this is an example of a statistic.

STATISTIC  A characteristic of a sample.

SunCom is studying the number of minutes used monthly by clients in a particular cell phone rate plan. A random sample of 12 clients showed the following number of minutes used last month.

| 90 | 77 | 94 | 89 | 119 | 112 |
|----|----|----|----|-----|-----|
| 91 | 110 | 92 | 100 | 113 | 83 |

**SOLUTION**

What is the arithmetic mean number of minutes used?

Using formula (3–2), the sample mean is:

$$\text{Sample mean} = \frac{\text{Sum of all values in the sample}}{\text{Number of values in the sample}}$$

$$\bar{X} = \frac{\Sigma X}{n} = \frac{90 + 77 + \cdots + 83}{12} = \frac{1170}{12} = 97.5$$

The arithmetic mean number of minutes used last month by the sample of cell phone users is 97.5 minutes.

# Properties of the Arithmetic Mean

The arithmetic mean is a widely used measure of location. It has several important properties:

1.  Every set of interval- or ratio-level data has a mean. Recall from Chapter 1 that ratio-level data include such data as ages, incomes, and weights, with the distance between numbers being constant.
2.  All the values are included in computing the mean.
3.  A set of data has only one mean. The mean is unique. Later in the chapter we will discover an average that might appear twice, or more than twice, in a set of data.
4.  The *sum of the deviations of each value from the mean will always be zero.* Expressed symbolically:

$$\Sigma(X - \bar{X}) = 0$$

As an example, the mean of 3, 8, and 4 is 5. Then:

$$\Sigma(X - \bar{X}) = (3 - 5) + (8 - 5) + (4 - 5)$$
$$= -2 + 3 - 1$$
$$= 0$$

Mean as a balance point

Thus, we can consider the mean as a balance point for a set of data. To illustrate, we have a long board with the numbers 1, 2, 3, . . . , $n$ evenly spaced on it. Suppose three bars of equal weight were placed on the board at numbers 3, 4, and 8, and the balance point was set at 5, the mean of the three numbers. We would find that the board is balanced perfectly! The deviations below the mean (−3) are equal to the deviations above the mean (+3). Shown schematically:

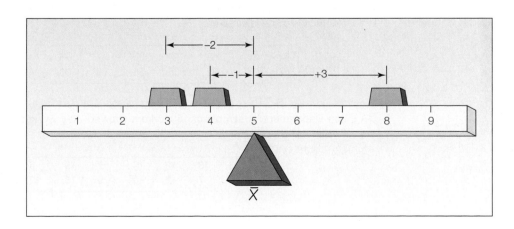

Mean unduly affected by unusually large or small values

The mean does have a weakness. Recall that the mean uses the value of every item in a sample, or population, in its computation. If one or two of these values are either extremely large or extremely small compared to the majority of data, the mean might not be an appropriate average to represent the data. For example, suppose the annual incomes of a small group of stockbrokers at Merrill Lynch are $62,900, $61,600, $62,500, $60,800, and $1,200,000. The mean income is $289,560. Obviously, it is not representative of this group, because all but one broker has an income in the $60,000 to $63,000 range. One income ($1.2 million) is unduly affecting the mean.

---

**Self-Review 3–1**

1.  The annual incomes of a sample of middle-management employees at Westinghouse are: $62,900, $69,100, $58,300, and $76,800.
    (a)  Give the formula for the sample mean.
    (b)  Find the sample mean.
    (c)  Is the mean you computed in (b) a statistic or a parameter? Why?
    (d)  What is your best estimate of the population mean?
2.  All the students in advanced Computer Science 411 are a population. Their course grades are 92, 96, 61, 86, 79, and 84.
    (a)  Give the formula for the population mean.
    (b)  Compute the mean course grade.
    (c)  Is the mean you computed in (b) a statistic or a parameter? Why?

---

# Exercises

*The answers to the odd-numbered exercises are at the end of the book.*

1.  Compute the mean of the following population values: 6, 3, 5, 7, 6.
2.  Compute the mean of the following population values: 7, 5, 7, 3, 7, 4.
3.  **a.** Compute the mean of the following sample values: 5, 9, 4, 10.
    **b.** Show that $\Sigma(X - \bar{X}) = 0$.
4.  **a.** Compute the mean of the following sample values: 1.3, 7.0, 3.6, 4.1, 5.0.
    **b.** Show that $\Sigma(X - \bar{X}) = 0$.
5.  Compute the mean of the following sample values: 16.25, 12.91, 14.58.
6.  Compute the mean hourly wage paid to carpenters who earned the following wages: $15.40, $20.10, $18.75, $22.76, $30.67, $18.00.

For Exercises 7–10, (a) compute the arithmetic mean and (b) indicate whether it is a statistic or a parameter.

7.  There are 10 salespeople employed by Midtown Ford. The numbers of new cars sold last month by the respective salespeople were: 15, 23, 4, 19, 18, 10, 10, 8, 28, 19.
8.  The accounting department at a mail-order company counted the following numbers of incoming calls per day to the company's toll-free number during the first 7 days in May 2003: 14, 24, 19, 31, 36, 26, 17.
9.  The Cambridge Power and Light Company selected a random sample of 20 residential customers. Following are the amounts, to the nearest dollar, the customers were charged for electrical service last month:

| 54 | 48 | 58 | 50 | 25 | 47 | 75 | 46 | 60 | 70 |
|----|----|----|----|----|----|----|----|----|----|
| 67 | 68 | 39 | 35 | 56 | 66 | 33 | 62 | 65 | 67 |

10. The Human Relations Director at Ford began a study of the overtime hours in the Inspection Department. A sample of 15 workers showed they worked the following number of overtime hours last month.

| 13 | 13 | 12 | 15 | 7 | 15 | 5 | 12 |
|----|----|----|----|---|----|----|----|
| 6  | 7  | 12 | 10 | 9 | 13 | 12 |    |

# The Weighted Mean

The weighted mean is a special case of the arithmetic mean. It occurs when there are several observations of the same value. To explain, suppose the nearby Wendy's Restaurant sold medium, large, and Biggie-sized soft drinks for $.90, $1.25, and $1.50, respectively. Of the last 10 drinks sold, 3 were medium, 4 were large, and 3 were Biggie-sized. To find the mean price of the last 10 drinks sold, we could use formula (3–2).

$$\bar{X} = \frac{\$.90 + \$.90 + \$.90 + \$1.25 + \$1.25 + \$1.25 + \$1.25 + \$1.50 + \$1.50 + \$1.50}{10}$$

$$\bar{X} = \frac{\$12.20}{10} = \$1.22$$

The mean selling price of the last 10 drinks is $1.22.

An easier way to find the mean selling price is to determine the weighted mean. That is, we multiply each observation by the number of times it happens. We will refer to the weighted mean as $\bar{X}_w$. This is read "X bar sub w."

$$\bar{X}_w = \frac{3(\$0.90) + 4(\$1.25) + 3(\$1.50)}{10} = \frac{\$12.20}{10} = \$1.22$$

In this case the weights are frequency counts. However, any measure of importance could be used as a weight. In general the weighted mean of a set of numbers designated $X_1, X_2, X_3, \ldots, X_n$ with the corresponding weights $w_1, w_2, w_3, \ldots, w_n$ is computed by:

| | | |
|---|---|---|
| **WEIGHTED MEAN** | $\bar{X}_w = \dfrac{w_1 X_1 + w_2 X_2 + w_3 X_3 + \cdots + w_n X_n}{w_1 + w_2 + w_3 + \cdots + w_n}$ | **[3–3]** |

This may be shortened to:

$$\bar{X}_w = \frac{\Sigma(wX)}{\Sigma w}$$

**EXAMPLE**

The Carter Construction Company pays its hourly employees $16.50, $17.50, or $18.50 per hour. There are 26 hourly employees, 14 are paid at the $16.50 rate, 10 at the $17.50 rate, and 2 at the $18.50 rate. What is the mean hourly rate paid the 26 employees?

**SOLUTION**

To find the mean hourly rate, we multiply each of the hourly rates by the number of employees earning that rate. From formula (3–3), the mean hourly rate is

$$\bar{X}_w = \frac{14(\$16.50) + 10(\$17.50) + 2(\$18.50)}{14 + 10 + 2} = \frac{\$443.00}{26} = \$17.038$$

The weighted mean hourly wage is rounded to $17.04.

**Self-Review 3–2**

Springers sold 95 Antonelli men's suits for the regular price of $400. For the spring sale the suits were reduced to $200 and 126 were sold. At the final clearance, the price was reduced to $100 and the remaining 79 suits were sold.
(a)  What was the weighted mean price of an Antonelli suit?
(b)  Springers paid $200 a suit for the 300 suits. Comment on the store's profit per suit if a salesperson receives a $25 commission for each one sold.

# Exercises

11. In June an investor purchased 300 shares of Oracle (an information technology company) stock at $20 per share. In August she purchased an additional 400 shares at $25 per share. In November she purchased an additional 400 shares, but the stock declined to $23 per share. What is the weighted mean price per share?

12. The Bookstall, Inc., is a specialty bookstore concentrating on used books sold via the Internet. Paperbacks are $1.00 each, and hardcover books are $3.50. Of the 50 books sold last Tuesday morning, 40 were paperback and the rest were hardcover. What was the weighted mean price of a book?

13. The Loris Healthcare System employs 200 persons on the nursing staff. Fifty are nurse's aides, 50 are practical nurses, and 100 are registered nurses. Nurse's aides receive $8 an hour, practical nurses $15 an hour, and registered nurses $24 an hour. What is the weighted mean hourly wage?

14. Andrews and Associates specialize in corporate law. They charge $100 an hour for researching a case, $75 an hour for consultations, and $200 an hour for writing a brief. Last week one of the associates spent 10 hours consulting with her client, 10 hours researching the case, and 20 hours writing the brief. What was the weighted mean hourly charge for her legal services?

# The Median

We have stressed that for data containing one or two very large or very small values, the arithmetic mean may not be representative. The center for such data can be better described by a measure of location called the **median.**

To illustrate the need for a measure of location other than the arithmetic mean, suppose you are seeking to buy a condominium in Palm Aire. Your real estate agent says that the average price of the units currently available is $110,000. Would you still want to look? If you had budgeted your maximum purchase price at $75,000, you might think they are out of your price range. However, checking the individual prices of the units might change your mind. They are $60,000, $65,000, $70,000, $80,000, and a superdeluxe penthouse costs $275,000. The arithmetic mean price is $110,000, as the real estate agent reported, but one price ($275,000) is pulling the arithmetic mean upward, causing it to be an unrepresentative average. It does seem that a price around $70,000 is a more typical or representative average, and it is. In cases such as this, the median provides a more valid measure of location.

> **MEDIAN** The midpoint of the values after they have been ordered from the smallest to the largest, or the largest to the smallest.

The data must be at least ordinal level of measurement. The median price of the units available is $70,000. To determine this, we ordered the prices from low ($60,000) to high ($275,000) and selected the middle value ($70,000).

| Prices Ordered from Low to High | | Prices Ordered from High to Low |
|---|---|---|
| $ 60,000 | | $275,000 |
| 65,000 | | 80,000 |
| 70,000 | ← Median → | 70,000 |
| 80,000 | | 65,000 |
| 275,000 | | 60,000 |

Median unaffected by extreme values

Note that there is the same number of prices below the median of $70,000 as above it. There are as many values below the median as above. The median is, therefore, unaffected by extremely low or high prices. Had the highest price been $90,000, or $300,000, or even $1 million, the median price would still be $70,000. Likewise, had the lowest price been $20,000 or $50,000, the median price would still be $70,000.

In the previous illustration there is an *odd* number of observations (five). How is the median determined for an *even* number of observations? As before, the observations are ordered. Then by convention to obtain a unique value we calculate the mean of the two middle observations. So for an even number of observations, the median may not be one of the given values.

**EXAMPLE**

**SOLUTION**

The five-year annualized total returns of the six top-performing stock mutual funds with emphasis on aggressive growth are listed below. What is the median annualized return?

| Name of Fund | Annualized Total Return |
| --- | --- |
| PBHG Growth | 28.5% |
| Dean Witter Developing Growth | 17.2 |
| AIM Aggressive Growth | 25.4 |
| Twentieth Century Giftrust | 28.6 |
| Robertson Stevens Emerging Growth | 22.6 |
| Seligman Frontier A | 21.0 |

Note that the number of returns is *even* (6). As before, the returns are first ordered from low to high. Then the two middle returns are identified. The arithmetic mean of the two middle observations gives us the median return. Arranging from low to high:

17.2%
21.0
22.6
25.4     48.0/2 = 24.0 percent, the median return
28.5
28.6

Notice that the median is not one of the values. Also, half of the returns are below the median and half are above it.

The major properties of the median are:

1. The median is unique; that is, like the mean, there is only one median for a set of data.
2. It is not affected by extremely large or small values and is therefore a valuable measure of location when such values do occur.

Median can be determined for all levels of data except nominal

3. It can be computed for ratio-level, interval-level, and ordinal-level data. Recall from Chapter 1 that ordinal-level data can be ranked from low to high—such as the responses "excellent," "very good," "good," "fair," and "poor" to a question on a marketing survey. To use a simple illustration, suppose five people rated a new fudge bar. One person thought it was excellent, one rated it very good, one called it good, one rated it fair, and one considered it poor. The median response is "good." Half of the responses are above "good"; the other half are below it.

# The Mode

The **mode** is another measure of location.

> **MODE** The value of the observation that appears most frequently.

The mode is especially useful in describing nominal and ordinal levels of measurement. As an example of its use for nominal-level data, a company has developed five bath oils. Chart 3–1 shows the results of a marketing survey designed to find which bath oil consumers prefer. The largest number of respondents favored Lamoure, as evidenced by the highest bar. Thus, Lamoure is the mode.

**CHART 3–1**  Number of Respondents Favoring Various Bath Oils

**EXAMPLE**

The annual salaries of quality-control managers in selected states are shown below. What is the modal annual salary?

| State | Salary | State | Salary | State | Salary |
|-------|--------|-------|--------|-------|--------|
| Arizona | $35,000 | Illinois | $58,000 | Ohio | $50,000 |
| California | 49,100 | Louisiana | 60,000 | Tennessee | 60,000 |
| Colorado | 60,000 | Maryland | 60,000 | Texas | 71,400 |
| Florida | 60,000 | Massachusetts | 40,000 | West Virginia | 60,000 |
| Idaho | 40,000 | New Jersey | 65,000 | Wyoming | 55,000 |

**SOLUTION**

A perusal of the salaries reveals that the annual salary of $60,000 appears more often (six times) than any other salary. The mode is, therefore, $60,000.

In summary, we can determine the mode for all levels of data—nominal, ordinal, interval, and ratio. The mode also has the advantage of not being affected by extremely high or low values.

Disadvantages of the mode

The mode does have disadvantages, however, that cause it to be used less frequently than the mean or median. For many sets of data, there is no mode because no value appears more than once. For example, there is no mode for this set of price data: $19, $21, $23, $20, and $18. Since every value is different, however, it could be argued that every value is the mode. Conversely, for some data sets there is more than one mode. Suppose the ages of the individuals in a stock investment club are 22, 26, 27, 27, 31, 35, and 35. Both the ages 27 and 35 are modes. Thus, this grouping of ages is referred to as *bimodal* (having two modes). One would question the use of two modes to represent the location of this set of age data.

| | |
|---|---|
| **Self-Review 3–3**  | 1. A sample of single persons in Towson, Texas, receiving Social Security payments revealed these monthly benefits: $426, $299, $290, $687, $480, $439, and $565.<br>(a) What is the median monthly benefit?<br>(b) How many observations are below the median? Above it?<br>2. The numbers of work stoppages in the automobile industry for selected months are 6, 0, 10, 14, 8, and 0.<br>(a) What is the median number of stoppages?<br>(b) How many observations are below the median? Above it?<br>(c) What is the modal number of work stoppages? |

## Exercises

**15.** What would you report as the modal value for a set of observations if there were a total of:
   **a.** 10 observations and no two values were the same?
   **b.** 6 observations and they were all the same?
   **c.** 6 observations and the values were 1, 2, 3, 3, 4, and 4?

For Exercises 16–19, (a) determine the median and (b) the mode.

**16.** The following is the number of oil changes for the last 7 days at the Jiffy Lube located at the corner of Elm Street and Pennsylvania Ave.

| 41 | 15 | 39 | 54 | 31 | 15 | 33 |
|---|---|---|---|---|---|---|

**17.** The following is the percent change in net income from 2002 to 2003 for a sample of 12 construction companies in Denver.

| 5 | 1 | −10 | −6 | 5 | 12 | 7 | 8 | 2 | 5 | −1 | 11 |
|---|---|---|---|---|---|---|---|---|---|---|---|

**18.** The following are the ages of the 10 people in the video arcade at the Southwyck Shopping Mall at 10 A.M. this morning.

| 12 | 8 | 17 | 6 | 11 | 14 | 8 | 17 | 10 | 8 |
|---|---|---|---|---|---|---|---|---|---|

**19.** Listed below are several indicators of long-term economic growth in the United States. The projections are through the year 2008.

| Economic Indicator | Percent Change | Economic Indicator | Percent Change |
|---|---|---|---|
| Inflation | 4.5 | Real GNP | 2.9 |
| Exports | 4.7 | Investment (residential) | 3.6 |
| Imports | 2.3 | Investment (nonresidential) | 2.1 |
| Real disposable income | 2.9 | Productivity (total) | 1.4 |
| Consumption | 2.7 | Productivity (manufacturing) | 5.2 |

   **a.** What is the median percent change?
   **b.** What is the modal percent change?

**20.** Listed below are the total automobile sales (in millions) in the United States for the last 14 years. During this period, what was the median number of automobiles sold? What is the mode?

| 9.0 | 8.5 | 8.0 | 9.1 | 10.3 | 11.0 | 11.5 | 10.3 | 10.5 | 9.8 | 9.3 | 8.2 | 8.2 | 8.5 |
|---|---|---|---|---|---|---|---|---|---|---|---|---|---|

# Software Solution

We can use a statistical software package to find many measures of location.

**EXAMPLE**

Table 2–1 on page 25 shows the prices of the 80 vehicles sold last month at Whitner Autoplex in Raytown, Missouri. Determine the mean and the median selling price.

**SOLUTION**

The mean and the median selling prices are reported in the following Excel output. (Remember: The instructions to create the output appear in the **Software Commands** section at the end of the chapter.) There are 80 vehicles in the study, so the calculations with a calculator would be tedious and prone to error.

| | A | B | C | D | E | F | G | H | I | J |
|---|---|---|---|---|---|---|---|---|---|---|
| 1 | Price | Price($000) | Age | Type | | | Price | | | |
| 2 | 23197 | 23.197 | 46 | 0 | | | | | | |
| 3 | 23372 | 23.372 | 48 | 0 | | Mean | 23218.1625 | | | |
| 4 | 20454 | 20.454 | 40 | 1 | | Standard Error | 486.8409474 | | | |
| 5 | 23591 | 23.591 | 40 | 0 | | Median | 22831 | | | |
| 6 | 26651 | 26.651 | 46 | 1 | | Mode | 20642 | | | |
| 7 | 27453 | 27.453 | 37 | 1 | | Standard Deviation | 4354.43781 | | | |
| 8 | 17266 | 17.266 | 32 | 1 | | Sample Variance | 18961128.64 | | | |
| 9 | 18021 | 18.021 | 29 | 1 | | Kurtosis | 0.5433087 | | | |
| 10 | 28683 | 28.683 | 38 | 1 | | Skewness | 0.72681585 | | | |
| 11 | 30872 | 30.872 | 43 | 0 | | Range | 20379 | | | |
| 12 | 19587 | 19.587 | 32 | 0 | | Minimum | 15546 | | | |
| 13 | 23169 | 23.169 | 47 | 0 | | Maximum | 35925 | | | |
| 14 | 35851 | 35.851 | 56 | 0 | | Sum | 1857453 | | | |
| 15 | 19251 | 19.251 | 42 | 1 | | Count | 80 | | | |
| 16 | 20047 | 20.047 | 28 | 1 | | | | | | |
| 17 | 24285 | 24.285 | 56 | 0 | | | | | | |
| 18 | 24324 | 24.324 | 50 | 1 | | | | | | |
| 19 | 24609 | 24.609 | 31 | 1 | | | | | | |
| 20 | 28670 | 28.67 | 51 | 1 | | | | | | |
| 21 | 15546 | 15.546 | 26 | 1 | | | | | | |
| 22 | 15935 | 15.935 | 25 | 1 | | | | | | |
| 23 | 19873 | 19.873 | 45 | 1 | | | | | | |
| 24 | 25251 | 25.251 | 56 | 1 | | | | | | |

The mean selling price is $23,218 and the median is $22,831. These two values are less than $400 apart. So either value is reasonable. We can also see from the Excel output that there were 80 vehicles sold and their total price is $1,857,453. We will describe the meaning of standard error, standard deviation, and other measures later.

What can we conclude? The typical vehicle sold for about $23,000. Ms. Ball of Auto USA might use this value in her revenue projections. For example, if the dealership could increase the number sold in a month from 80 to 90, this would result in an additional estimated $230,000 of revenue, found by 10 × $23,000.

# The Relative Positions of the Mean, Median, and Mode

For a symmetric, mound-shaped distribution, mean, median, and mode are equal.

Refer to the histogram in Chart 3–2. It is a symmetric distribution, which is also mound-shaped. This distribution *has the same shape on either side of the center.* If the polygon were folded in half, the two halves would be identical. For this symmetric distribution, the mode, median, and mean are located at the center and are always equal. They are all equal to 20 years in Chart 3–2. We should point out that there are symmetric distributions that are not mound-shaped.

The number of years corresponding to the highest point of the curve is the *mode* (20 years). Because the distribution is symmetrical, the *median* corresponds to the point where the distribution is cut in half (20 years). The total number of frequencies

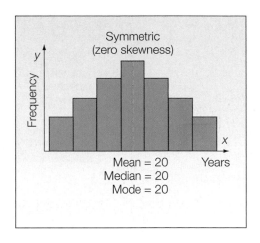

**CHART 3–2** A Symmetric Distribution

representing many years is offset by the total number representing few years, resulting in an *arithmetic mean* of 20 years. Logically, any of the three measures would be appropriate to represent the distribution's center.

A skewed distribution is not symmetrical.

If a distribution is nonsymmetrical, or **skewed,** the relationship among the three measures changes. In a **positively skewed distribution,** the arithmetic mean is the largest of the three measures. Why? Because the mean is influenced more than the median or mode by a few extremely high values. The median is generally the next largest measure in a positively skewed frequency distribution. The mode is the smallest of the three measures.

If the distribution is highly skewed, such as the weekly incomes in Chart 3–3, the mean would not be a good measure to use. The median and mode would be more representative.

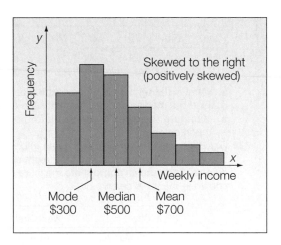

**CHART 3–3** A Positively Skewed Distribution

Conversely, if a distribution is **negatively skewed,** the mean is the lowest of the three measures. The mean is, of course, influenced by a few extremely low observations. The median is greater than the arithmetic mean, and the modal value is the largest of the three measures. Again, if the distribution is highly skewed, such as the distribution of tensile strengths shown in Chart 3–4, the mean should not be used to represent the data.

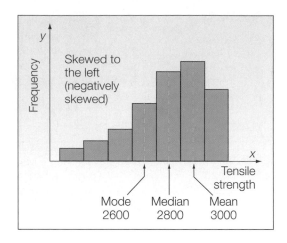

**CHART 3–4** A Negatively Skewed Distribution

**Self-Review 3–4**

The weekly sales from a sample of Hi-Tec electronic supply stores were organized into a frequency distribution. The mean of weekly sales was computed to be $105,900, the median $105,000, and the mode $104,500.
(a)  Sketch the sales in the form of a smoothed frequency polygon. Note the location of the mean, median, and mode on the X-axis.
(b)  Is the distribution symmetrical, positively skewed, or negatively skewed? Explain.

# Exercises

**21.** The unemployment rate in the state of Alaska for the 12 months of 2002 is given in the table below:

| Jan | Feb | Mar | Apr | May | Jun | Jul | Aug | Sep | Oct | Nov | Dec |
|-----|-----|-----|-----|-----|-----|-----|-----|-----|-----|-----|-----|
| 8.6 | 8.8 | 8.4 | 7.8 | 7.2 | 7.4 | 6.9 | 6.8 | 7.1 | 7.5 | 7.9 | 8.6 |

   **a.** What is the arithmetic mean of the Alaskan unemployment rates?
   **b.** Find the median and the mode for the unemployment rates.
   **c.** Compute the arithmetic mean and median for just the winter (Dec–Mar) months. Is it much different?
**22.** Big Orange Trucking is designing an information system for use on "in-cab" communications. It must summarize data from eight sites throughout a region to describe typical conditions. Compute an appropriate measure of central location for each of the three variables shown in the table below:

| City | Wind Direction | Temperature | Pavement |
|------|----------------|-------------|----------|
| Anniston, AL | West | 89 | Dry |
| Atlanta, GA | Northwest | 86 | Wet |
| Augusta, GA | Southwest | 92 | Wet |
| Birmingham, AL | South | 91 | Dry |
| Jackson, MS | Southwest | 92 | Dry |
| Meridian, MS | South | 92 | Trace |
| Monroe, LA | Southwest | 93 | Wet |
| Tuscaloosa, AL | Southwest | 93 | Trace |

# The Geometric Mean

The geometric mean is never greater than the arithmetic mean.

The geometric mean is useful in finding the average of percentages, ratios, indexes, or growth rates. It has a wide application in business and economics because we are often interested in finding the percentage changes in sales, salaries, or economic figures, such as the Gross Domestic Product, which compound or build on each other. The geometric mean of a set of $n$ positive numbers is defined as the $n$th root of the product of $n$ values. The formula for the geometric mean is written:

| | | |
|---|---|---|
| **GEOMETRIC MEAN** | $GM = \sqrt[n]{(X_1)(X_2) \cdots (X_n)}$ | **[3–4]** |

The geometric mean will always be less than or equal to (never more than) the arithmetic mean. Also all the data values must be positive.

As an example of the geometric mean, suppose you receive a 5 percent increase in salary this year and a 15 percent increase next year. The average annual percent increase is 9.886, not 10.0. Why is this so? We begin by calculating the geometric mean. Recall, for example, that a 5 percent increase in salary is 105 percent. We will write it as 1.05.

$$GM = \sqrt{(1.05)(1.15)} = 1.09886$$

This can be verified by assuming that your monthly earning was $3,000 to start and you received two increases of 5 percent and 15 percent.

Raise 1 = $3,000 (.05) = $150.00

Raise 2 = $3,150 (.15) =   472.50

Total                       $622.50

Your total salary increase is $622.50. This is equivalent to:

$3,000.00 (.09886) = $296.58

$3,296.58 (.09886) =   325.90

$622.48 is about $622.50

The following example shows the geometric mean of several percentages.

**EXAMPLE**

The return on investment earned by Atkins Construction Company for four successive years was: 30 percent, 20 percent, −40 percent, and 200 percent. What is the geometric mean rate of return on investment?

**SOLUTION**

The number 1.3 represents the 30 percent return on investment, which is the "original" investment of 1.0 plus the "return" of 0.3. The number 0.6 represents the loss of 40 percent, which is the original investment of 1.0 less the loss of 0.4. This calculation assumes the total return each period is reinvested or becomes the base for the next period. In other words, the base for the second period is 1.3 and the base for the third period is (1.3)(1.2) and so forth.

Then the geometric mean rate of return is 29.4 percent, found by

$$GM = \sqrt[n]{(X_1)(X_2) \cdots (X_n)} = \sqrt[4]{(1.3)(1.2)(0.6)(3.0)} = 1.294$$

The geometric mean is the fourth root of 2.808. So, the average rate of return (compound annual growth rate) is 29.4 percent.

Notice also that if you compute the arithmetic mean [(30 + 20 − 40 + 200)/4 = 52.5], you would have a much larger number, which would overstate the true rate of return!

A second application of the geometric mean is to find an average percent increase over a period of time. For example, if you earned $30,000 in 1995 and $50,000 in 2005, what is your annual rate of increase over the period? The rate of increase is determined from the following formula.

| AVERAGE PERCENT INCREASE OVER TIME | $GM = \sqrt[n]{\dfrac{\text{Value at end of period}}{\text{Value at start of period}}} - 1$ | [3–5] |

In the above box $n$ is the number of periods. An example will show the details of finding the average annual percent increase.

**EXAMPLE**

During the decade of the 1990s, Las Vegas, Nevada, was the fastest-growing metropolitan area in the United States. The population increased from 852,737 in 1990 to 1,563,282 in 2000. This is an increase of 710,545 people or an 83 percent increase over the 10-year period. What is the average *annual* increase?

**SOLUTION**

There are 10 years between 1990 and 2000 so $n = 10$. Then formula (3–5) for the geometric mean as applied to this type of problem is:

$$GM = \sqrt[n]{\frac{\text{Value at end of period}}{\text{Value at start of period}}} - 1.0 = \sqrt[10]{\frac{1,563,282}{852,737}} - 1.0 = 1.0625 - 1.0 = .0625$$

The value of .0625 indicates that the average annual growth over the 10-year period was 6.25 percent. To put it another way, the population of Las Vegas increased at a rate of 6.25 percent per year from 1990 to 2000.

---

**Self-Review 3–5**

1.  The percent increase in sales for the last 4 years at Combs Cosmetics were: 4.91, 5.75, 8.12, and 21.60.
    (a)  Find the geometric mean percent increase.
    (b)  Find the arithmetic mean percent increase.
    (c)  Is the arithmetic mean equal to or greater than the geometric mean?
2.  Production of Cablos trucks increased from 23,000 units in 1984 to 120,520 units in 2004. Find the geometric mean annual percent increase.

## Exercises

23.  Compute the geometric mean of the following percent increases: 8, 12, 14, 26, and 5.
24.  Compute the geometric mean of the following percent increases: 2, 8, 6, 4, 10, 6, 8, and 4.
25.  Listed below is the percent increase in sales for the MG Corporation over the last 5 years. Determine the geometric mean percent increase in sales over the period.

| 9.4 | 13.8 | 11.7 | 11.9 | 14.7 |

26.  In 1996 a total of 14,968,000 taxpayers in the United States filed their individual tax returns electronically. By the year 2002 the number increased to 46,282,200. What is the geometric mean annual increase for the period?
27.  The Consumer Price Index is reported monthly by the U.S. Bureau of Labor Statistics. It reports the change in prices for a market basket of goods from one period to another. The index for 1992 was 140.3, by 2002 it increased to 179.9. What was the geometric mean annual increase for the period?
28.  In 1976 the nationwide average price of a gallon of unleaded gasoline at a self-serve pump was $0.605. By 2003 the average price had increased to $1.394. What was the geometric mean annual increase for the period?
29.  In 1999 there were 42.0 million pager subscribers. By 2004 the number of subscribers increased to 70.0 million. What is the geometric mean annual increase for the period?

**30.** The information below shows the cost for a year of college in public and private colleges in 1992 and 2003. What is the geometric mean annual increase for the period for the two types of colleges? Compare the rates of increase.

| Type of College | 1992 | 2003 |
|---|---|---|
| Public | $ 4,975 | $ 8,954 |
| Private | 12,284 | 22,608 |

The average is not representative because of the large spread.

# Why Study Dispersion?

A measure of location, such as the mean or the median, only describes the center of the data. It is valuable from that standpoint, but it does not tell us anything about the spread of the data. For example, if your nature guide told you that the river ahead averaged 3 feet in depth, would you want to wade across on foot without additional information? Probably not. You would want to know something about the variation in the depth. Is the maximum depth of the river 3.25 feet and the minimum 2.75 feet? If that is the case, you would probably agree to cross. What if you learned the river depth ranged from 0.50 feet to 5.5 feet? Your decision would probably be not to cross. Before making a decision about crossing the river, you want information on both the typical depth and the dispersion in the depth of the river.

A small value for a measure of dispersion indicates that the data are clustered closely, say, around the arithmetic mean. The mean is therefore considered representative of the data. Conversely, a large measure of dispersion indicates that the mean is not reliable. Refer to Chart 3–5. The 100 employees of Hammond Iron Works, Inc., a steel fabricating company, are organized into a histogram based on the number of years of employment with the company. The mean is 4.9 years, but the spread of the data is from 6 months to 16.8 years. The mean of 4.9 years is not very representative of all the employees.

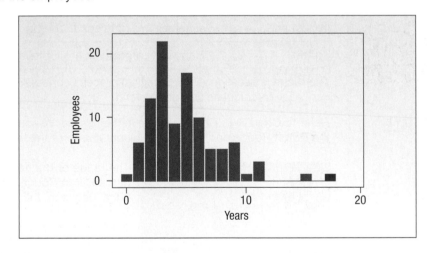

**CHART 3–5** Histogram of Years of Employment at Hammond Iron Works, Inc.

A second reason for studying the dispersion in a set of data is to compare the spread in two or more distributions. Suppose, for example, that the new PDM/3 computer is assembled in Baton Rouge and also in Tucson. The arithmetic mean hourly output in both the Baton Rouge plant and the Tucson plant is 50. Based on the two means, one might conclude that the distributions of the hourly outputs are identical. Production records for 9 hours at the two plants, however, reveal that this conclusion is not correct (see Chart 3–6). Baton Rouge production varies from 48 to 52 assemblies per hour. Production at the Tucson plant is more erratic, ranging from 40 to 60 per hour. Therefore, the hourly output for Baton Rouge is clustered near the mean of 50; the hourly output for Tucson is more dispersed.

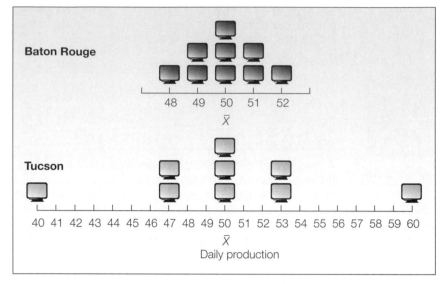

**CHART 3–6** Hourly Production of Computers at the Baton Rouge and Tucson Plants

A measure of dispersion can be used to evaluate the reliability of two or more measures of location.

# Measures of Dispersion

We will consider several measures of dispersion. The range is based on the largest and the smallest values in the data set. The mean deviation, the variance, and the standard deviation are all based on deviations from the arithmetic mean.

## Range

The simplest measure of dispersion is the **range.** It is the difference between the largest and the smallest values in a data set. In the form of an equation:

| RANGE | Range = Largest value − Smallest value | [3–6] |
|---|---|---|

The range is widely used in statistical process control (SPC) applications because it is very easy to calculate and understand.

**EXAMPLE**

Refer to Chart 3–6. Find the range in the number of computers produced per hour for the Baton Rouge and the Tucson plants. Interpret the two ranges.

**SOLUTION**

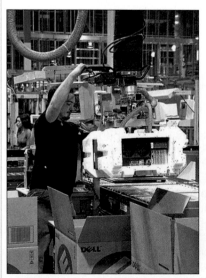

The range of the hourly production of computers at the Baton Rouge plant is 4, found by the difference between the largest hourly production of 52 and the smallest of 48. The range in the hourly production for the Tucson plant is 20 computers, found by 60 − 40. We therefore conclude that (1) there is less dispersion in the hourly production in the Baton Rouge plant than in the Tucson plant because the range of 4 computers is less than a range of 20 computers, and (2) the production is clustered more closely around the mean of 50 at the Baton Rouge plant than at the Tucson plant (because a range of 4 is less than a range of 20). Thus, the mean production in the Baton Rouge plant (50 computers) is a more representative measure of location than the mean of 50 computers for the Tucson plant.

# Mean Deviation

A defect of the range is that it is based on only two values, the highest and the lowest; it does not take into consideration all of the values. The **mean deviation** does. It measures the mean amount by which the values in a population, or sample, vary from their mean. In terms of a definition:

> **MEAN DEVIATION** The arithmetic mean of the absolute values of the deviations from the arithmetic mean.

In terms of a formula, the mean deviation, designated *MD,* is computed for a sample by:

| MEAN DEVIATION | $MD = \dfrac{\Sigma\lvert X - \bar{X}\rvert}{n}$ | [3–7] |
|---|---|---|

where:

$X$ is the value of each observation.
$\bar{X}$ is the arithmetic mean of the values.
$n$ is the number of observations in the sample.
$\lvert\ \rvert$ indicates the absolute value.

Why do we ignore the signs of the deviations from the mean? If we didn't, the positive and negative deviations from the mean would exactly offset each other, and the mean deviation would always be zero. Such a measure (zero) would be a useless statistic.

**EXAMPLE**

The number of cappuccinos sold at the Starbucks location in the Orange County Airport between 4 and 7 P.M. for a sample of 5 days last year were: 103, 97, 101, 106, and 103. Determine the mean deviation and interpret.

**SOLUTION**

The mean deviation is the mean of the amounts that individual observations differ from the arithmetic mean. To find the mean deviation of a set of data, we begin by finding the arithmetic mean. The mean number of cappuccinos sold is 102, found by (103 + 97 + 101 + 106 + 103)/5. Next we find the amount by which each observation differs from the mean. Then we sum these differences, ignoring the signs, and divide the sum by the number of observations. The result is the mean amount the observations differ from the mean. A small value for the mean deviation indicates that the data are clustered near the mean, whereas a large value for the mean deviation indicates greater dispersion in the data. Here are the details of the calculations using formula (3–7).

| Number of Cappuccinos Sold | $(X - \bar{X})$ | Absolute Deviation |
|---|---|---|
| 103 | (103 − 102) =   1 | 1 |
| 97 | (97 − 102) = −5 | 5 |
| 101 | (101 − 102) = −1 | 1 |
| 106 | (106 − 102) =   4 | 4 |
| 103 | (103 − 102) =   1 | 1 |
| | Total | 12 |

$$MD = \frac{\Sigma\lvert X - \bar{X}\rvert}{n} = \frac{12}{5} = 2.4$$

The mean deviation is 2.4 cappuccinos per day. The number of cappuccinos deviates, on average, by 2.4 cappuccinos from the mean of 102 cappuccinos per day.

Advantages of mean
deviation

The mean deviation has two advantages. First, it uses all the values in the computation. Recall that the range uses only the highest and the lowest values. Second, it is easy to understand—it is the average amount by which values deviate from the mean. However, its drawback is the use of absolute values. Generally, absolute values are difficult to work with, so the mean deviation is not used as frequently as other measures of dispersion, such as the standard deviation.

---

**Self-Review 3–6**

The weights of containers being shipped to Ireland are (in thousands of pounds):

| 95 | 103 | 105 | 110 | 104 | 105 | 112 | 90 |

(a) What is the range of the weights?
(b) Compute the arithmetic mean weight.
(c) Compute the mean deviation of the weights.

---

# Exercises

For Exercises 31–36, calculate the (a) range, (b) arithmetic mean, and (c) mean deviation, and (d) interpret the range and the mean deviation.

**31.** There were five customer service representatives on duty at the Electronic Super Store during last weekend's sale. The numbers of HDTVs these representatives sold are: 5, 8, 4, 10, and 3.
**32.** The Department of Statistics at Western State University offers eight sections of basic statistics. Following are the numbers of students enrolled in these sections: 34, 46, 52, 29, 41, 38, 36, and 28.
**33.** Dave's Automatic Door installs automatic garage door openers. The following list indicates the number of minutes needed to install a sample of 10 door openers: 28, 32, 24, 46, 44, 40, 54, 38, 32, and 42.
**34.** A sample of eight companies in the aerospace industry was surveyed as to their return on investment last year. The results are (in percent): 10.6, 12.6, 14.8, 18.2, 12.0, 14.8, 12.2, and 15.6.
**35.** Ten experts rated the taste of a newly developed sushi pizza topped with tuna, rice, and kelp on a scale of 1 to 50. The ratings were: 34, 35, 41, 28, 26, 29, 32, 36, 38, and 40.
**36.** A sample of the personnel files of eight employees at Acme Carpet Cleaners, Inc., revealed that, during a six-month period, they lost the following numbers of days due to illness: 2, 0, 6, 3, 10, 4, 1, and 2.

# Variance and Standard Deviation

Variance and standard
deviation are based on
squared deviations from
the mean.

The **variance** and **standard deviation** are also based on the deviations from the mean. However, instead of using the absolute value of the deviations, the variance, and the standard deviation square the deviations.

---

**VARIANCE** The arithmetic mean of the squared deviations from the mean.

---

The variance is nonnegative and is zero only if all observations are the same.

---

**STANDARD DEVIATION** The square root of the variance.

---

**Population Variance**    The formulas for the population variance and the sample variance are slightly different. The population variance is considered first. (Recall that a population is the totality of all observations being studied.) The **population variance** is found by:

| POPULATION VARIANCE | $\sigma^2 = \dfrac{\Sigma(X - \mu)^2}{N}$ | [3–8] |
|---|---|---|

where:

$\sigma^2$ is the symbol for the population variance ($\sigma$ is the lowercase Greek letter sigma). It is usually referred to as "sigma squared."

$X$ is the value of an observation in the population.

$\mu$ is the arithmetic mean of the population.

$N$ is the number of observations in the population.

Note the process of computing the variance.

- We begin by finding the mean.
- Next we find the difference between each observation and the mean and square that difference.
- Then we sum all the squared differences.
- And finally we divide the sum of the squared differences by the number of items in the population.

So you might think of the population variance as the mean of the squared difference between each value and the mean. For populations whose values are near the mean, the variance will be small. For populations whose values are dispersed from the mean, the population variance will be large.

The variance overcomes the problem of the range by using all the values in the population, whereas the range uses only the largest and the smallest. We overcome the issue where $\Sigma(X - \mu) = 0$ by squaring the differences, instead of using the absolute value. Squaring the differences will always result in non-negative values.

**EXAMPLE**

The number of traffic citations issued during the last five months in Beaufort County, South Carolina, is: 38, 26, 13, 41, and 22. What is the population variance?

**SOLUTION**

| Number (X) | $X - \mu$ | $(X - \mu)^2$ | | |
|---|---|---|---|---|
| 38 | +10 | 100 | | |
| 26 | −2 | 4 | | |
| 13 | −15 | 225 | $\mu = \dfrac{\Sigma X}{N} = \dfrac{140}{5} = 28$ | |
| 41 | +13 | 169 | | |
| 22 | −6 | 36 | | |
| 140 | 0* | 534 | $\sigma^2 = \dfrac{\Sigma(X - \mu)^2}{N} = \dfrac{534}{5} = 106.8$ | |

*Sum of the deviations from mean must equal zero.

Like the range and the mean deviation, the variance can be used to compare the dispersion in two or more sets of observations. For example, the variance for the number of citations issued in Beaufort County was just computed to be 106.8. If the variance in the number of citations issued in Marlboro County, South Carolina, is 342.9, we conclude that (1) there is less dispersion in the distribution of the number of citations issued in Beaufort County than in Marlboro County (because 106.8 is less than 342.9); and (2) the number of citations in Beaufort County is more closely clustered around the mean of 28 than for the number of citations issued in Marlboro County. Thus the mean number of citations issued in Beaufort County is a more representative measure of location than the mean number of citations in Marlboro County.

Variance is difficult to interpret because the units are squared.

**Population Standard Deviation**    Both the range and the mean deviation are easy to interpret. The range is the difference between the high and low values of a set of data, and the mean deviation is the mean of the deviations from the mean. However, the variance is difficult to interpret for a single set of observations. The variance of 106.8 for the number of traffic citations issued in Marlboro County is not in terms of citations, but rather "citations squared."

Standard deviation is in the same units as the data.

There is a way out of this dilemma. By taking the square root of the population variance, we can transform it to the same unit of measurement used for the original data. The square root of 106.8 citations-squared is 10.3 years. The square root of the population variance is called the **population standard deviation.**

| POPULATION STANDARD DEVIATION | $\sigma = \sqrt{\dfrac{\Sigma(X - \mu)^2}{N}}$ | [3–9] |
|---|---|---|

**Self-Review 3–7**

The Philadelphia office of Price Waterhouse Coopers LLP hired five accounting trainees this year. Their monthly starting salaries were: $3,536; $3,173; $3,448; $3,121; and $3,622.
(a)  Compute the population mean.
(b)  Compute the population variance.
(c)  Compute the population standard deviation.
(d)  The Pittsburgh office hired six trainees. Their mean monthly salary was $3,550, and the standard deviation was $250. Compare the two groups.

## Exercises

**37.**  Consider these five values a population: 8, 3, 7, 3, and 4.
   **a.** Determine the mean of the population.
   **b.** Determine the variance.
**38.**  Consider these six values a population: 13, 3, 8, 10, 8, and 6.
   **a.** Determine the mean of the population.
   **b.** Determine the variance.
**39.**  The annual report of Dennis Industries cited these primary earnings per common share for the past 5 years: $2.68, $1.03, $2.26, $4.30, and $3.58. If we assume these are population values, what is:
   **a.** The arithmetic mean primary earnings per share of common stock?
   **b.** The variance?
**40.**  Referring to Exercise 39, the annual report of Dennis Industries also gave these returns on stockholder equity for the same five-year period (in percent): 13.2, 5.0, 10.2, 17.5, and 12.9.
   **a.** What is the arithmetic mean return?
   **b.** What is the variance?
**41.**  Plywood, Inc. reported these returns on stockholder equity for the past 5 years: 4.3, 4.9, 7.2, 6.7, and 11.6. Consider these as population values.
   **a.** Compute the range, the arithmetic mean, the variance, and the standard deviation.
   **b.** Compare the return on stockholder equity for Plywood, Inc. with that for Dennis Industries cited in Exercise 40.
**42.**  The annual incomes of the five vice presidents of TMV Industries are: $125,000; $128,000; $122,000; $133,000; and $140,000. Consider this a population.
   **a.** What is the range?
   **b.** What is the arithmetic mean income?
   **c.** What is the population variance? The standard deviation?
   **d.** The annual incomes of officers of another firm similar to TMV Industries were also studied. The mean was $129,000 and the standard deviation $8,612. Compare the means and dispersions in the two firms.

**Sample Variance**    The formula for the population mean is $\mu = \Sigma X/N$. We just changed the symbols for the sample mean; that is $\overline{X} = \Sigma X/n$. Unfortunately, the conversion from the population variance to the sample variance is not as direct. It requires a change in the denominator. Instead of substituting $n$ (number in the sample) for $N$ (number in the population), the denominator is $n - 1$. Thus the formula for the **sample variance** is:

| SAMPLE VARIANCE | $s^2 = \dfrac{\Sigma(X - \bar{X})^2}{n - 1}$ | [3–10] |
|---|---|---|

where:

$s^2$ is the sample variance.
$X$ is the value of each observation in the sample.
$\bar{X}$ is the mean of the sample.
$n$ is the number of observations in the sample.

Why is this change made in the denominator? Although the use of $n$ is logical, it tends to underestimate the population variance, $\sigma^2$. The use of $(n - 1)$ in the denominator provides the appropriate correction for this tendency. Because the primary use of sample statistics like $s^2$ is to estimate population parameters like $\sigma^2$, $(n - 1)$ is preferred to $n$ in defining the sample variance. We will also use this convention when computing the sample standard deviation.

**EXAMPLE**

The hourly wages for a sample of part-time employees at Fruit Packers, Inc. are: $12, $20, $16, $18, and $19. What is the sample variance?

**SOLUTION**

The sample variance is computed by using formula (3–10).

$$\bar{X} = \frac{\Sigma X}{n} = \frac{\$85}{5} = \$17$$

| Hourly Wage (X) | $X - \bar{X}$ | $(X - \bar{X})^2$ |
|---|---|---|
| $12 | −$5 | 25 |
| 20 | 3 | 9 |
| 16 | −1 | 1 |
| 18 | 1 | 1 |
| 19 | 2 | 4 |
| $85 | 0 | 40 |

$$s^2 = \frac{\Sigma(X - \bar{X})^2}{n - 1} = \frac{40}{5 - 1}$$
$$= 10 \text{ in dollars squared}$$

**Sample Standard Deviation**   The sample standard deviation is used as an estimator of the population standard deviation. As noted previously, the population standard deviation is the square root of the population variance. Likewise, the *sample standard deviation is the square root of the sample variance.* The sample standard deviation is most easily determined by:

| STANDARD DEVIATION | $s = \sqrt{\dfrac{\Sigma(X - \bar{X})^2}{n - 1}}$ | [3–11] |
|---|---|---|

**EXAMPLE**

The sample variance in the previous example involving hourly wages was computed to be 10. What is the sample standard deviation?

**SOLUTION**

The sample standard deviation is $3.16, found by $\sqrt{10}$. Note again that the sample variance is in terms of dollars squared, but taking the square root of 10 gives us $3.16, which is in the same units (dollars) as the original data.

## Software Solution

On page 66 we used Excel to determine the mean and median of the Whitner Autoplex sales data. You will also note that it outputs the sample standard deviation. Excel, like most other statistical software, assumes the data are from a sample.

Another software package that we will use in this text is MINITAB. This package uses a spreadsheet format, much like Excel, but produces a wider variety of statistical output. The information for the Whitner Autoplex selling prices follows. Note that a histogram (although the default is to use a class interval of $2,000 and 11 classes) is included as well as the mean, median, and sample standard deviation. The mean and standard deviation are reported in thousands of dollars.

**Self-Review 3–8**

The weights of the contents of several small aspirin bottles are (in grams): 4, 2, 5, 4, 5, 2, and 6. What is the sample variance? Compute the sample standard deviation.

## Exercises

For Exercises 43–48, do the following:

a. Compute the sample variance.
b. Determine the sample standard deviation.

**43.** Consider these values a sample: 7, 2, 6, 2, and 3.
**44.** The following five values are a sample: 11, 6, 10, 6, and 7.
**45.** Dave's Automatic Door, referred to in Exercise 33, installs automatic garage door openers. Based on a sample, following are the times, in minutes, required to install 10 door openers: 28, 32, 24, 46, 44, 40, 54, 38, 32, and 42.

**46.** The sample of eight companies in the aerospace industry, referred to in Exercise 34, was surveyed as to their return on investment last year. The results are: 10.6, 12.6, 14.8, 18.2, 12.0, 14.8, 12.2, and 15.6.

**47.** The Houston, Texas, Motel Owner Association conducted a survey regarding weekday motel rates in the area. Listed below is the room rate for business class guests for a sample of 10 motels.

| $101 | $97 | $103 | $110 | $78 | $87 | $101 | $80 | $106 | $88 |

**48.** A consumer watchdog organization is concerned about credit card debt. A survey of 10 young adults with credit card debt of more than $2,000 showed they paid an average of just over $100 per month. Listed below is the amounts each young adult paid last month against their balances.

| $110 | $126 | $103 | $93 | $99 | $113 | $87 | $101 | $109 | $100 |

# Interpretation and Uses of the Standard Deviation

The standard deviation is commonly used as a measure to compare the spread in two or more sets of observations. For example, the standard deviation of the biweekly amounts invested in the Dupree Paint Company profit-sharing plan is computed to be $7.51. Suppose these employees are located in Georgia. If the standard deviation for a group of employees in Texas is $10.47, and the means are about the same, it indicates that the amounts invested by the Georgia employees are not dispersed as much as those in Texas (because $7.51 < $10.47). Since the amounts invested by the Georgia employees are clustered more closely about the mean, the mean for the Georgia employees is a more reliable measure than the mean for the Texas group.

## Chebyshev's Theorem

We have stressed that a small standard deviation for a set of values indicates that these values are located close to the mean. Conversely, a large standard deviation reveals that the observations are widely scattered about the mean. The Russian mathematician P. L. Chebyshev (1821–1894) developed a theorem that allows us to determine the minimum proportion of the values that lie within a specified number of standard deviations of the mean. For example, according to **Chebyshev's theorem,** at least three of four values, or 75 percent, must lie between the mean plus two standard deviations and the mean minus two standard deviations. This relationship applies regardless of the shape of the distribution. Further, at least eight of nine values, or 88.9 percent, will lie between plus three standard deviations and minus three standard deviations of the mean. At least 24 of 25 values, or 96 percent, will lie between plus and minus five standard deviations of the mean.

Chebyshev's theorem states:

> **CHEBYSHEV'S THEOREM** For any set of observations (sample or population), the proportion of the values that lie within $k$ standard deviations of the mean is at least $1 - 1/k^2$, where $k$ is any constant greater than 1.

**EXAMPLE**

The arithmetic mean biweekly amount contributed by the Dupree Paint employees to the company's profit-sharing plan was $51.54, and the standard deviation is $7.51. At least what percent of the contributions lie within plus 3.5 standard deviations and minus 3.5 standard deviations of the mean?

**SOLUTION**

1. About 68 percent are between $480 and $520, found by $\overline{X} \pm 1s = \$500 \pm 1(\$20)$.
2. About 95 percent are between $460 and $540, found by $\overline{X} \pm 2s = \$500 \pm 2(\$20)$.
3. Almost all (99.7 percent) are between $440 and $560, found by $\overline{X} \pm 3s = \$500 \pm 3(\$20)$.

---

**Self-Review 3–9**

The Pitney Pipe Company is one of several domestic manufacturers of PVC pipe. The quality control department sampled 600 10-foot lengths. At a point 1 foot from the end of the pipe they measured the outside diameter. The mean was 14.0 inches and the standard deviation 0.1 inches.

(a) If the shape of the distribution is not known, at least what percent of the observations will be between 13.85 inches and 14.15 inches?

(b) If we assume that the distribution of diameters is symmetrical and bell-shaped, about 95 percent of the observations will be between what two values?

## Exercises

49. According to Chebyshev's theorem, at least what percent of any set of observations will be within 1.8 standard deviations of the mean?

50. The mean income of a group of sample observations is $500; the standard deviation is $40. According to Chebyshev's theorem, at least what percent of the incomes will lie between $400 and $600?

51. The distribution of the weights of a sample of 1,400 cargo containers is symmetric and bell-shaped. According to the Empirical Rule, what percent of the weights will lie:
    a. Between $\overline{X} - 2s$ and $\overline{X} + 2s$?
    b. Between $\overline{X}$ and $\overline{X} + 2s$? Below $\overline{X} - 2s$?

52. The following graph portrays the distribution of the number of Biggie-sized soft drinks sold at the nearby Wendy's for the last 141 days. The mean number of drinks sold per day is 91.9 and the standard deviation is 4.67.

If we use the Empirical Rule, sales will be between what two values on 68 percent of the days? Sales will be between what two values on 95 percent of the days?

# The Mean and Standard Deviation of Grouped Data

In most instances measures of location, such as the mean, and measures of dispersion, such as the standard deviation, are determined by using the individual values. Statistical software packages make it easy to calculate these values, even for large data sets. However, sometimes we are given only the frequency distribution and wish to estimate the mean or standard deviation. In the following discussion we show how we can estimate the mean and standard deviation from data organized into a frequency distribution. We should stress that a mean or a standard deviation from grouped data is an *estimate* of the corresponding actual values.

**Statistics in Action**

Albert Pujols of the St. Louis Cardinals had the highest batting average at .359 during the 2003 season. Tony Gwynn hit .394 in the strike-shortened season of 1994, and Ted Williams hit .406 in 1941. No one has hit over .400 since 1941. The mean batting average has remained constant at about .260 for more than 100 years, but the standard deviation declined from .049 to .031. This indicates less dispersion in the batting averages today and helps explain the lack of any .400 hitters in recent times.

# The Arithmetic Mean

To approximate the arithmetic mean of data organized into a frequency distribution, we begin by assuming the observations in each class are represented by the *midpoint* of the class. The mean of a sample of data organized in a frequency distribution is computed by:

| ARITHMETIC MEAN OF GROUPED DATA | $\overline{X} = \dfrac{\Sigma fM}{n}$ | [3–12] |
|---|---|---|

where:

$\overline{X}$ is the designation for the sample mean.
$M$ is the midpoint of each class.
$f$ is the frequency in each class.
$fM$ is the frequency in each class times the midpoint of the class.
$\Sigma fM$ is the sum of these products.
$n$ is the total number of frequencies.

**EXAMPLE**

The computations for the arithmetic mean of data grouped into a frequency distribution will be shown based on the Whitner Autoplex data. Recall in Chapter 2, in Table 2–4 on page 28 we constructed a frequency distribution for the vehicle selling prices. The information is repeated below. Determine the arithmetic mean vehicle selling price.

| Selling Price ($ thousands) | Frequency |
|---|---|
| 15 up to 18 | 8 |
| 18 up to 21 | 23 |
| 21 up to 24 | 17 |
| 24 up to 27 | 18 |
| 27 up to 30 | 8 |
| 30 up to 33 | 4 |
| 33 up to 36 | 2 |
| Total | 80 |

**SOLUTION**

The mean vehicle selling price can be estimated from data grouped into a frequency distribution. To find the estimated mean, assume the midpoint of each class is representative of the data values in that class. Recall that the midpoint of a class is halfway between the upper and the lower class limits. To find the midpoint of a particular class, we add the upper and the lower class limits and divide by 2. Hence, the midpoint of the first class is $16.5, found by ($15 + $18)/2. We assume that the value of $16.5 is representative of the eight values in that class. To put it another way, we assume the sum of the eight values in this class is $132, found by 8($16.5). We continue the process of multiplying the class midpoint by the class frequency for each class and then sum these products. The results are summarized in Table 3–1.

**TABLE 3–1** Price of 80 New Vehicles Sold Last Month at Whitner Autoplex Lot

| Selling Price ($ thousands) | Frequency (f) | Midpoint (M) | fM |
|---|---|---|---|
| 15 up to 18 | 8 | $16.5 | $ 132.0 |
| 18 up to 21 | 23 | 19.5 | 448.5 |
| 21 up to 24 | 17 | 22.5 | 382.5 |
| 24 up to 27 | 18 | 25.5 | 459.0 |
| 27 up to 30 | 8 | 28.5 | 228.0 |
| 30 up to 33 | 4 | 31.5 | 126.0 |
| 33 up to 36 | 2 | 34.5 | 69.0 |
| Total | 80 | | $1,845.0 |

Solving for the arithmetic mean using formula (3–12), we get:

$$\bar{X} = \frac{\Sigma fM}{n} = \frac{\$1,845}{80} = \$23.1 \text{ (thousands)}$$

So we conclude that the mean vehicle selling price is about $23,100.

## Standard Deviation

To calculate the standard deviation of data grouped into a frequency distribution, we need to adjust formula (3–11) slightly. We weight each of the squared differences by the number of frequencies in each class. The formula is:

| STANDARD DEVIATION, GROUPED DATA | $s = \sqrt{\dfrac{\Sigma f(M - \bar{X})^2}{n - 1}}$ | [3–13] |
|---|---|---|

where:

  $s$ is the symbol for the sample standard deviation.
  $M$ is the midpoint of the class.
  $f$ is the class frequency.
  $n$ is the number of observations in the sample.

**EXAMPLE**

Refer to the frequency distribution for the Whitner Autoplex reported in Table 3–1. Compute the standard deviation of the vehicle selling prices.

**SOLUTION**

Following the same practice used earlier for computing the mean of data grouped into a frequency distribution, $f$ is the class frequency, $M$ the class midpoint, and $n$ the number of observations.

| Selling Price ($ thousands) | Frequency ($f$) | Midpoint ($M$) | $(M - \bar{X})$ | $(M - \bar{X})^2$ | $f(M - \bar{X})^2$ |
|---|---|---|---|---|---|
| 15.0 up to 18.0 | 8 | 16.5 | −6.6 | 43.56 | 348.48 |
| 18.0 up to 21.0 | 23 | 19.5 | −3.6 | 12.96 | 298.08 |
| 21.0 up to 24.0 | 17 | 22.5 | −0.6 | 0.36 | 6.12 |
| 24.0 up to 27.0 | 18 | 25.5 | 2.4 | 5.76 | 103.68 |
| 27.0 up to 30.0 | 8 | 28.5 | 5.4 | 29.16 | 233.28 |
| 30.0 up to 33.0 | 4 | 31.5 | 8.4 | 70.56 | 282.24 |
| 33.0 up to 36.0 | 2 | 34.5 | 11.4 | 129.96 | 259.92 |
| | 80 | | | | 1,531.80 |

To find the standard deviation:

**Step 1:** Subtract the mean from the class midpoint. That is, find $(M - \bar{X})$. For the first class $(16.5 - 23.1 = -6.6)$, for the second class $(19.5 - 23.1 = -3.6)$, and so on.

**Step 2:** Square the difference between the class midpoint and the mean. For the first class it would be $(16.5 - 23.1)^2 = (-6.6)^2 = 43.56$, for the second class $(19.5 - 23.1)^2 = (-3.6)^2 = 12.96$, and so on.

**Step 3:** Multiply the squared difference between the class midpoint and the mean by the class frequency. For the first class the value is $8(16.5 - 23.1)^2 = 348.48$, for the second $23(19.5 - 21.3)^2 = 298.08$, and so on.

**Step 4:** Sum the $f(M - X)^2$. The total is 1,531.8.

To find the standard deviation we insert these values in formula (3-13).

$$s = \sqrt{\frac{\Sigma f(M - \bar{X})^2}{n - 1}} = \sqrt{\frac{1531.8}{80 - 1}} = 4.403$$

The mean and the standard deviation calculated from the data grouped into a frequency distribution are usually close to the values calculated from raw data. The grouped data result in some loss of information. For the vehicle selling price problem the mean selling price reported in the Excel output on page 66 is $23,218 and the standard deviation is $4,354. The respective values estimated from data grouped into a frequency distribution are $23,100 and $4,403. The difference in the means is $118 or about 0.58 percent. The standard deviations differ by $49 or 1.1 percent. Based on the percentage difference, the estimates are very close to the actual values.

**Self-Review 3–10**

The net incomes of a sample of large importers of antiques were organized into the following table:

| Net Income ($ millions) | Number of Importers |
|---|---|
| 2 up to 6 | 1 |
| 6 up to 10 | 4 |
| 10 up to 14 | 10 |
| 14 up to 18 | 3 |
| 18 up to 22 | 2 |

(a) What is the table called?
(b) Based on the distribution, what is the estimate of the arithmetic mean net income?
(c) Based on the distribution, what is the estimate of the standard deviation?

# Exercises

53. When we compute the mean of a frequency distribution, why do we refer to this as an *estimated* mean?
54. Determine the mean and the standard deviation of the following frequency distribution.

| Class | Frequency |
|---|---|
| 0 up to 5 | 2 |
| 5 up to 10 | 7 |
| 10 up to 15 | 12 |
| 15 up to 20 | 6 |
| 20 up to 25 | 3 |

55. Determine the mean and the standard deviation of the following frequency distribution.

| Class | Frequency |
|---|---|
| 20 up to 30 | 7 |
| 30 up to 40 | 12 |
| 40 up to 50 | 21 |
| 50 up to 60 | 18 |
| 60 up to 70 | 12 |

**56.** SCCoast, an Internet provider in the Southeast, developed the following frequency distribution on the age of Internet users. Find the mean and the standard deviation.

| Age (years) | Frequency |
|---|---|
| 10 up to 20 | 3 |
| 20 up to 30 | 7 |
| 30 up to 40 | 18 |
| 40 up to 50 | 20 |
| 50 up to 60 | 12 |

**57.** The IRS was interested in the number of individual tax forms prepared by small accounting firms. The IRS randomly sampled 50 public accounting firms with 10 or fewer employees in the Dallas–Fort Worth area. The following frequency table reports the results of the study. Estimate the mean and the standard deviation.

| Number of Clients | Frequency |
|---|---|
| 20 up to 30 | 1 |
| 30 up to 40 | 15 |
| 40 up to 50 | 22 |
| 50 up to 60 | 8 |
| 60 up to 70 | 4 |

**58.** Advertising expenses are a significant component of the cost of goods sold. Listed below is a frequency distribution showing the advertising expenditures for 60 manufacturing companies located in the Southwest. Estimate the mean and the standard deviation of advertising expense.

| Advertising Expenditure ($ millions) | Number of Companies |
|---|---|
| 25 up to 35 | 5 |
| 35 up to 45 | 10 |
| 45 up to 55 | 21 |
| 55 up to 65 | 16 |
| 65 up to 75 | 8 |
| Total | 60 |

# Chapter Outline

I. A measure of location is a value used to describe the center of a set of data.
    **A.** The arithmetic mean is the most widely reported measure of location.
        **1.** It is calculated by adding the values of the observations and dividing by the total number of observations.
            **a.** The formula for a population mean of ungrouped or raw data is

$$\mu = \frac{\Sigma X}{N}$$ [3–1]

            **b.** The formula for the mean of a sample is

$$\bar{X} = \frac{\Sigma X}{n}$$ [3–2]

            **c.** The formula for the sample mean of data in a frequency distribution is

$$\bar{X} = \frac{\Sigma fM}{n}$$ [3–12]

2. The major characteristics of the arithmetic mean are:
   a. At least the interval scale of measurement is required.
   b. All the data values are used in the calculation.
   c. A set of data has only one mean. That is, it is unique.
   d. The sum of the deviations from the mean equals 0.
B. The weighted mean is found by multiplying each observation by its corresponding weight.
   1. The formula for determining the weighted mean is

$$\bar{X}_w = \frac{w_1X_1 + w_2X_2 + w_3X_3 + \cdots + w_nX_n}{w_1 + w_2 + w_3 + \cdots + w_n}$$   [3–3]

   2. It is a special case of the arithmetic mean.
C. The median is the value in the middle of a set of ordered data.
   1. To find the median, sort the observations from smallest to largest and identify the middle value.
   2. The major characteristics of the median are:
      a. At least the ordinal scale of measurement is required.
      b. It is not influenced by extreme values.
      c. Fifty percent of the observations are larger than the median.
      d. It is unique to a set of data.
D. The mode is the value that occurs most often in a set of data.
   1. The mode can be found for nominal-level data.
   2. A set of data can have more than one mode.
E. The geometric mean is the *n*th root of the product of *n* values.
   1. The formula for the geometric mean is

$$GM = \sqrt[n]{(X_1)(X_2)(X_3) \cdots (X_n)}$$   [3–4]

   2. The geometric mean is also used to find the rate of change from one period to another.

$$GM = \sqrt[n]{\frac{\text{Value at end of period}}{\text{Value at beginning of period}}} - 1$$   [3–5]

   3. The geometric mean is always equal to or less than the arithmetic mean.
II. The dispersion is the variation or spread in a set of data.
A. The range is the difference between the largest and the smallest value in a set of data.
   1. The formula for the range is

$$\text{Range} = \text{Largest value} - \text{Smallest value}$$   [3–6]

   2. The major characteristics of the range are:
      a. Only two values are used in its calculation.
      b. It is influenced by extreme values.
      c. It is easy to compute and to understand.
B. The mean absolute deviation is the sum of the absolute values of the deviations from the mean divided by the number of observations.
   1. The formula for computing the mean absolute deviation is

$$MD = \frac{\Sigma|X - \bar{X}|}{n}$$   [3–7]

   2. The major characteristics of the mean absolute deviation are:
      a. It is not unduly influenced by large or small values.
      b. All observations are used in the calculation.
      c. The absolute values are somewhat difficult to work with.
C. The variance is the mean of the squared deviations from the arithmetic mean.
   1. The formula for the population variance is

$$\sigma^2 = \frac{\Sigma(X - \mu)^2}{N}$$   [3–8]

   2. The formula for the sample variance is

$$s^2 = \frac{\Sigma(X - \bar{X})^2}{n - 1}$$   [3–10]

3. The major characteristics of the variance are:
   a. All observations are used in the calculation.
   b. It is not unduly influenced by extreme observations.
   c. The units are somewhat difficult to work with; they are the original units squared.
D. The standard deviation is the square root of the variance.
   1. The major characteristics of the standard deviation are:
      a. It is in the same units as the original data.
      b. It is the square root of the average squared distance from the mean.
      c. It cannot be negative.
      d. It is the most widely reported measure of dispersion.
   2. The formula for the sample standard deviation is

$$s = \sqrt{\frac{\Sigma(X - \overline{X})^2}{n - 1}}$$ [3–11]

   3. The formula for the standard deviation of grouped data is

$$s = \sqrt{\frac{\Sigma f(M - \overline{X})^2}{n - 1}}$$ [3–13]

III. We interpret the standard deviation using two measures.
   A. Chebyshev's theorem states that regardless of the shape of the distribution, at least $1 - 1/k^2$ of the observations will be within $k$ standard deviations of the mean, where $k$ is greater than 1.
   B. The Empirical Rule states that for a bell-shaped distribution about 68 percent of the values will be within one standard deviation of the mean, 95 percent within two, and virtually all within three.

# Pronunciation Key

| SYMBOL | MEANING | PRONUNCIATION |
|---|---|---|
| $\mu$ | Population mean | *mu* |
| $\Sigma$ | Operation of adding | *sigma* |
| $\Sigma X$ | Adding a group of values | *sigma X* |
| $\overline{X}$ | Sample mean | *X bar* |
| $\overline{X}_w$ | Weighted mean | *X bar sub w* |
| GM | Geometric mean | *G M* |
| $\Sigma fM$ | Adding the product of the frequencies and the class midpoints | *sigma f M* |
| $\sigma^2$ | Population variance | *sigma squared* |
| $\sigma$ | Population standard deviation | *sigma* |

# Chapter Exercises

59. The accounting firm of Crawford and Associates has five senior partners. Yesterday the senior partners saw six, four, three, seven, and five clients, respectively.
    a. Compute the mean number and median number of clients seen by a partner.
    b. Is the mean a sample mean or a population mean?
    c. Verify that $\Sigma(X - \mu) = 0$.
60. Owens Orchards sells apples in a large bag by weight. A sample of seven bags contained the following numbers of apples: 23, 19, 26, 17, 21, 24, 22.
    a. Compute the mean number and median number of apples in a bag.
    b. Verify that $\Sigma(X - \overline{X}) = 0$.
61. A sample of households that subscribe to the United Bell Phone Company revealed the following numbers of calls received last week. Determine the mean and the median number of calls received.

| 52 | 43 | 30 | 38 | 30 | 42 | 12 | 46 | 39 | 37 |
|----|----|----|----|----|----|----|----|----|----|
| 34 | 46 | 32 | 18 | 41 | 5  |    |    |    |    |

62. The Citizens Banking Company is studying the number of times the ATM located in a Loblaws Supermarket at the foot of Market Street is used per day. Following are the numbers of times the machine was used over each of the last 30 days. Determine the mean number of times the machine was used per day.

| | | | | | | | | | |
|---|---|---|---|---|---|---|---|---|---|
| 83 | 64 | 84 | 76 | 84 | 54 | 75 | 59 | 70 | 61 |
| 63 | 80 | 84 | 73 | 68 | 52 | 65 | 90 | 52 | 77 |
| 95 | 36 | 78 | 61 | 59 | 84 | 95 | 47 | 87 | 60 |

63. Listed below is the number of lampshades produced during the last 50 days at the American Lampshade Company in Rockville, GA. Compute the mean.

| | | | | | | | | | |
|---|---|---|---|---|---|---|---|---|---|
| 348 | 371 | 360 | 369 | 376 | 397 | 368 | 361 | 374 |
| 410 | 374 | 377 | 335 | 356 | 322 | 344 | 399 | 362 |
| 384 | 365 | 380 | 349 | 358 | 343 | 432 | 376 | 347 |
| 385 | 399 | 400 | 359 | 329 | 370 | 398 | 352 | 396 |
| 366 | 392 | 375 | 379 | 389 | 390 | 386 | 341 | 351 |
| 354 | 395 | 338 | 390 | 333 | | | | |

64. Trudy Green works for the True-Green Lawn Company. Her job is to solicit lawn-care business via the telephone. Listed below are the numbers of appointments she made in each of the last 25 hours of calling. What is the arithmetic mean number of appointments she made per hour? What is the median number of appointments per hour? Write a brief report summarizing the findings.

| | | | | | | | | | | | | |
|---|---|---|---|---|---|---|---|---|---|---|---|---|
| 9 | 5 | 2 | 6 | 5 | 6 | 4 | 4 | 7 | 2 | 3 | 6 | 3 |
| 4 | 4 | 7 | 8 | 4 | 4 | 5 | 5 | 4 | 8 | 3 | 3 | |

65. The Split-A-Rail Fence Company sells three types of fence to homeowners in suburban Seattle, Washington. Grade A costs $5.00 per running foot to install, Grade B costs $6.50 per running foot, and Grade C, the premium quality, costs $8.00 per running foot. Yesterday, Split-A-Rail installed 270 feet of Grade A, 300 feet of Grade B, and 100 feet of Grade C. What was the mean cost per foot of fence installed?

66. Rolland Poust is a sophomore in the College of Business at Scandia Tech. Last semester he took courses in statistics and accounting, 3 hours each, and earned an A in both. He earned a B in a five-hour history course and a B in a two-hour history of jazz course. In addition, he took a one-hour course dealing with the rules of basketball so he could get his license to officiate high school basketball games. He got an A in this course. What was his GPA for the semester? Assume that he receives 4 points for an A, 3 for a B, and so on. What measure of location did you just calculate?

67. The table below shows the percent of the labor force that is unemployed and the size of the labor force for three counties in Northwest Ohio. Jon Elsas is the Regional Director of Economic Development. He must present a report to several companies that are considering locating in Northwest Ohio. What would be an appropriate unemployment rate to show for the entire region?

| County | Percent Unemployed | Size of Workforce |
|---|---|---|
| Wood | 4.5 | 15,300 |
| Ottawa | 3.0 | 10,400 |
| Lucas | 10.2 | 150,600 |

68. The American Automobile Association checks the prices of gasoline before many holiday weekends. Listed below are the self-service prices for a sample of 15 retail outlets during the May 2003 Memorial Day weekend in the Detroit, Michigan, area.

| | | | | | | | |
|---|---|---|---|---|---|---|---|
| 1.44 | 1.42 | 1.35 | 1.39 | 1.49 | 1.49 | 1.41 | 1.46 |
| 1.41 | 1.49 | 1.45 | 1.48 | 1.39 | 1.46 | 1.44 | |

    **a.** What is the arithmetic mean selling price?
    **b.** What is the median selling price?
    **c.** What is the modal selling price?

**69.** The metropolitan area of Los Angeles–Long Beach, California, is the area expected to show the largest increase in the number of jobs between 1989 and 2010. The number of jobs is expected to increase from 5,164,900 to 6,286,800. What is the geometric mean expected yearly rate of increase?

**70.** A recent article suggested that if you earn $25,000 a year today and the inflation rate continues at 3 percent per year, you'll need to make $33,598 in 10 years to have the same buying power. You would need to make $44,771 if the inflation rate jumped to 6 percent. Confirm that these statements are accurate by finding the geometric mean rate of increase.

**71.** The ages of a sample of Canadian tourists flying from Toronto to Hong Kong were: 32, 21, 60, 47, 54, 17, 72, 55, 33, and 41.
    **a.** Compute the range.
    **b.** Compute the mean deviation.
    **c.** Compute the standard deviation.

**72.** The weights (in pounds) of a sample of five boxes being sent by UPS are: 12, 6, 7, 3, and 10.
    **a.** Compute the range.
    **b.** Compute the mean deviation.
    **c.** Compute the standard deviation.

**73.** A southern state has seven state universities in its system. The numbers of volumes (in thousands) held in their libraries are 83, 510, 33, 256, 401, 47, and 23.
    **a.** Is this a sample or a population?
    **b.** Compute the standard deviation.

**74.** Health issues are a concern of managers, especially as they evaluate the cost of medical insurance. A recent survey of 150 executives at Elvers Industries, a large insurance and financial firm located in the Southwest, reported the number of pounds by which the executives were overweight. Compute the mean and the standard deviation.

| Pounds Overweight | Frequency |
|:-----------------:|:---------:|
| 0 up to  6 | 14 |
| 6 up to 12 | 42 |
| 12 up to 18 | 58 |
| 18 up to 24 | 28 |
| 24 up to 30 | 8 |

**75.** The Apollo space program lasted from 1967 until 1972 and included 13 missions. The missions lasted from as little as 7 hours to as long as 301 hours. The duration of each flight is listed below.

| | | | | | | | | | |
|---|---|---|---|---|---|---|---|---|---|
| 9 | 195 | 241 | 301 | 216 | 260 | 7 | 244 | 192 | 147 |
| 10 | 295 | 142 | | | | | | | |

    **a.** Explain why the flight times are a population.
    **b.** Find the mean and median of the flight times.
    **c.** Find the range and the standard deviation of the flight times.

**76.** Creek Ratz is a very popular restaurant located along the coast of northern Florida. They serve a variety of steak and seafood dinners. During the summer beach season, they do not take reservations or accept "call ahead" seating. Management of the restaurant is concerned with the time a patron must wait before being seated for dinner. Listed below is the wait time, in minutes, for the 25 tables seated last Saturday night.

| | | | | | | | | | |
|---|---|---|---|---|---|---|---|---|---|
| 28 | 39 | 23 | 67 | 37 | 28 | 56 | 40 | 28 | 50 |
| 51 | 45 | 44 | 65 | 61 | 27 | 24 | 61 | 34 | 44 |
| 64 | 25 | 24 | 27 | 29 | | | | | |

a. Explain why the times are a population.
b. Find the mean and median of the times.
c. Find the range and the standard deviation of the times.

77. The manager of the local Wal-Mart Super Store is studying the number of items purchased by customers in the evening hours. Listed below is the number of items for a sample of 30 customers.

| 15 | 8 | 6 | 9 | 9 | 4 | 18 | 10 | 10 | 12 |
|---|---|---|---|---|---|---|---|---|---|
| 12 | 4 | 7 | 8 | 12 | 10 | 10 | 11 | 9 | 13 |
| 5 | 6 | 11 | 14 | 5 | 6 | 6 | 5 | 13 | 5 |

a. Find the mean and the median of the number of items.
b. Find the range and the standard deviation of the number of items.
c. Organize the number of items into a frequency distribution. You may want to review the guidelines in Chapter 2 for establishing the class interval and the number of classes.
d. Find the mean and the standard deviation of the data organized into a frequency distribution. Compare these values with those computed in part a. Why are they different?

78. The following frequency distribution reports the electricity cost for a sample of 50 two-bedroom apartments in Albuquerque, New Mexico, during the month of May of last year.

| Electricity Cost | Frequency |
|---|---|
| $ 80 up to $100 | 3 |
| 100 up to 120 | 8 |
| 120 up to 140 | 12 |
| 140 up to 160 | 16 |
| 160 up to 180 | 7 |
| 180 up to 200 | 4 |
| Total | 50 |

a. Estimate the mean cost.
b. Estimate the standard deviation.
c. Use the Empirical Rule to estimate the proportion of costs within two standard deviations of the mean. What are these limits?

79. Bidwell Electronics, Inc., recently surveyed a sample of employees to determine how far they lived from corporate headquarters. The results are shown below. Compute the mean and the standard deviation.

| Distance (miles) | Frequency | M |
|---|---|---|
| 0 up to 5 | 4 | 2.5 |
| 5 up to 10 | 15 | 7.5 |
| 10 up to 15 | 27 | 12.5 |
| 15 up to 20 | 18 | 17.5 |
| 20 up to 25 | 6 | 22.5 |

# exercises.com

80. The National Center for Health Statistics maintains a website at: http://www.cdc.gov/nchs. Under the section labeled **Tabulated State Data,** click on **Births.** Go to that page and locate the table "Live Births by Race and Hispanic Origin of Mother: U.S., Each State, Puerto Rico, Virgin Islands, and Guam." Suppose you are interested in birth rates for the 50 states. Compute the mean, median, and standard deviation. Write a brief report summarizing the data.

81. There are many financial websites that provide information on stocks by industry. For example, go to http://biz.yahoo.com and select **Stock Research;** under **Analyst Research**

select **Sector/Industry.** There are many choices available here such as **Energy, Financial, and Healthcare.** Select one of these sectors, such as **Healthcare.** Another list of choices is now available; select one such as **Major Drug.** A list of companies in that industry will appear. Select one of the variables available, such as the price to earnings ratio, listed as P/E. This variable is the ratio of the selling price of a share of the company's common stock to the earnings per share of common stock. Download this information into Excel and find the mean, median, and standard deviation. Go back to **Sector/Industry** and choose another **Sector** and **Industry.** You might want to select **Energy** and then **Coal.** A list of companies will appear. Select the same variable as before. Download the information to Excel and find the mean, median, and standard deviation for this industry. Compare the information on the two sectors. Write a brief report summarizing your findings. Are the means different? Is there more variability in one industry than another?

**82.** One of the most famous averages, the Dow Jones Industrial Average (DJIA), is not really an average. The following is a listing of the 30 companies whose stock prices make up the DJIA, their symbol, their current weight, and the closing value on April 24, 2003. Use a software package to find the mean of the 30 stocks. The DJIA closed at 8440.04. Is this the value you found for the average of the 30 stocks?

| Company | Symbol | Weight | Close $ |
|---|---|---|---|
| 3M Co. | MMM | 10.4312 | 125.72 |
| Alcoa Inc. | AA | 1.8262 | 22.01 |
| Altria Group Inc. | MO | 2.7298 | 32.90 |
| American Express Co. | AXP | 3.0741 | 37.05 |
| AT&T Corp. | T | 1.3715 | 16.53 |
| Boeing Co. | BA | 2.2925 | 27.63 |
| Caterpillar Inc. | CAT | 4.3768 | 52.75 |
| Citigroup Inc. | C | 3.2508 | 39.18 |
| Coca-Cola Co. | KO | 3.3114 | 39.91 |
| E.I. DuPont de Nemours & Co. | DD | 3.4724 | 41.85 |
| Eastman Kodak Co. | EK | 2.4809 | 29.90 |
| Exxon Mobil Corp. | XOM | 2.9148 | 35.13 |
| General Electric Co. | GE | 2.4145 | 29.10 |
| General Motors Corp. | GM | 3.0417 | 36.66 |
| Hewlett-Packard Co. | HPQ | 1.311 | 15.80 |
| Home Depot Inc. | HD | 2.2942 | 27.65 |
| Honeywell International Inc. | HON | 1.9233 | 23.18 |
| Intel Corp. | INTC | 1.5723 | 18.95 |
| IBM | IBM | 7.07 | 85.21 |
| International Paper Co. | IP | 2.9372 | 35.40 |
| J.P. Morgan Chase & Co. | JPM | 2.3697 | 28.56 |
| Johnson & Johnson | JNJ | 4.7709 | 57.50 |
| McDonald's Corp. | MCD | 1.3209 | 15.92 |
| Merck & Co. Inc. | MRK | 4.8372 | 58.30 |
| Microsoft Corp. | MSFT | 2.115 | 25.49 |
| Procter & Gamble Co. | PG | 7.4567 | 89.87 |
| SBC Communications Inc. | SBC | 1.8685 | 22.52 |
| United Technologies Corp. | UTX | 5.0447 | 60.80 |
| Wal-Mart Stores Inc. | WMT | 4.5726 | 55.11 |
| Walt Disney Co. | DIS | 1.5474 | 18.65 |

You may read about the history of the DJIA by going to http://www.djindexes.com and clicking on **About the Dow.** This will explain why it is not really an average. There are many sites you can visit to check the current value of the DJIA, http://www.cnnfn.com, http://www.foxnews.com/news/features/dow, and http://www.usatoday.com are three of the many sources. To find a list of the actual stocks that make up the average go to http://www.bloomberg.com. On the toolbar, click on **Market Data,** then down the left side of the screen select **Stocks,** and then select **Dow.** You should now have available a listing of the current selling price of 30 stocks that make up the DJIA.

# Dataset Exercises

**83.** Refer to the Real Estate data, which reports information on homes sold in the Denver, Colorado, area last year.

    **a.** Select the variable selling price.

        **1.** Find the mean, median, and the standard deviation.

        **2.** Write a brief summary of the distribution of selling prices.

    **b.** Select the variable referring to the area of the home in square feet.

        **1.** Find the mean, median, and the standard deviation.

        **2.** Write a brief summary of the distribution of the area of homes.

**84.** Refer to the Baseball 2003 data, which reports information on the 30 major league teams for the 2003 baseball season.

    **a.** Select the variable team salary and find the mean, median, and the standard deviation.

    **b.** Select the variable that refers to the year in which the stadium was built. (Hint: Subtract the current year from the year in which the stadium was built to find the stadium age and work with that variable.) Find the mean, median, and the standard deviation.

    **c.** Select the variable that refers to the seating capacity of the stadium. Find the mean, median, and the standard deviation.

**85.** Refer to the CIA data, which reports demographic and economic information on 46 countries.

    **a.** Select the variable Life Expectancy.

        **1.** Find the mean, median, and the standard deviation.

        **2.** Write a brief summary of the distribution of life expectancy.

    **b.** Select the variable GDP/cap.

        **1.** Find the mean, median, and the standard deviation.

        **2.** Write a brief summary of the distribution GDP/cap.

# Software Commands

**1.** The Excel Commands for the descriptive statistics on page 66 are:

    **a.** From the CD retrieve the Whitner data file, which is called **Table2–1.**

    **b.** From the menu bar select **Tools** and then **Data Analysis.** Select **Descriptive Statistics** and then click **OK.**

    **c.** For the **Input Range,** type *A1:A81,* indicate that the data are grouped by column and that the labels are in the first row. Click on **Output Range,** indicate that the output should go in D1 (or any place you wish), click on **Summary statistics,** then click **OK.**

    **d.** After you get your results, double-check the count in the output to be sure it contains the correct number of items.

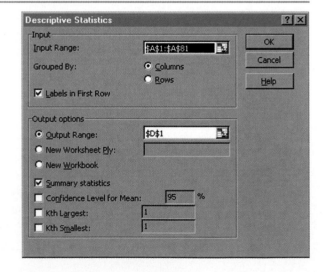

**2.** The MINITAB commands for the descriptive summary on page 78 are:

   **a.** From the CD retrieve the Whitner data, which is called **Table2–1.**

   **b.** Select **Stat**, **Basic Statistics**, and then **Display Descriptive Statistics**. In the dialog box select *Price* as the variable and then click on **Graphs** in the lower right-hand corner. Within the dialog box select **Histogram of data, with normal curve** and click **OK**. Click **OK** in the next dialog box.

# Chapter 3 Answers to Self-Review

**3–1** 1. **a.** $\bar{X} = \dfrac{\Sigma X}{n}$

**b.** $\bar{X} = \dfrac{\$267,100}{4} = \$66,775$

**c.** Statistic, because it is a sample value.

**d.** $66,775. The sample mean is our best estimate of the population mean.

2. **a.** $\mu = \dfrac{\Sigma X}{N}$

**b.** $\mu = \dfrac{498}{6} = 83$

**c.** Parameter, because it was computed using all the population values.

**3–2** **a.** $237, found by:

$$\dfrac{(95 \times \$400) + (126 \times \$200) + (79 \times \$100)}{95 + 126 + 79} = \$237.00$$

**b.** The profit per suit is $12, found by $237 − $200 cost − $25 commission. The total profit for the 300 suits is $3,600, found by $300 \times \$12$.

**3–3** 1. **a.** $439

**b.** 3, 3

2. **a.** 7, found by (6 + 8)/2 = 7

**b.** 3, 3

**c.** 0

**3–4** **a.**

Weekly sales ($000)

**b.** Positively skewed, because the mean is the largest average and the mode is the smallest.

**3–5** 1. **a.** About 9.9 percent, found by $\sqrt[4]{1.458602236}$, then $1.099 − 1.00 = .099$

**b.** About 10.095 percent

**c.** Greater than, because $10.095 > 8.39$

2. 8.63 percent, found by $\sqrt[20]{\dfrac{120,520}{23,000}} - 1 =$

$1.0863 − 1$

**3–6** **a.** 22 thousands of pounds, found by $112 − 90$

**b.** $\bar{X} = \dfrac{824}{8} = 103$ thousands of pounds

**c.**

| X | $\lvert X - \bar{X} \rvert$ | Absolute Deviation |
|---|---|---|
| 95 | $\lvert -8 \rvert$ | 8 |
| 103 | $\lvert 0 \rvert$ | 0 |
| 105 | $\lvert +2 \rvert$ | 2 |
| 110 | $\lvert +7 \rvert$ | 7 |
| 104 | $\lvert +1 \rvert$ | 1 |
| 105 | $\lvert +2 \rvert$ | 2 |
| 112 | $\lvert +9 \rvert$ | 9 |
| 90 | $\lvert -13 \rvert$ | 13 |
| | | Total 42 |

$$MD = \dfrac{42}{8} = 5.25 \text{ thousands of pounds}$$

**3–7** **a.** $\mu = \dfrac{\$16,900}{5} = \$3,380$

**b.** $\sigma^2 = \dfrac{(3536 - 3380)^2 + \cdots + (3622 - 3380)^2}{5}$

$$= \dfrac{\begin{array}{c}(156)^2 + (-207)^2 + (68)^2 \\ + (-259)^2 + (242)^2\end{array}}{5}$$

$$= \dfrac{197,454}{5} = 39,490.8$$

**c.** $\sigma = \sqrt{39,490.8} = 198.72$

**d.** There is more variation in the Pittsburgh office because the standard deviation is larger. The mean is also larger in the Pittsburgh office.

**3–8** 2.33, found by:

$$\bar{X} = \dfrac{\Sigma X}{n} = \dfrac{28}{7} = 4$$

| X | $X - \bar{X}$ | $(X - \bar{X})^2$ |
|---|---|---|
| 4 | 0 | 0 |
| 2 | −2 | 4 |
| 5 | 1 | 1 |
| 4 | 0 | 0 |
| 5 | 1 | 1 |
| 2 | −2 | 4 |
| 6 | 2 | 4 |
| 28 | 0 | 14 |

$$s^2 = \frac{\Sigma(X - \bar{X})^2}{n - 1}$$

$$= \frac{14}{7 - 1}$$

$$= 2.33$$

$$s = \sqrt{2.33} = 1.53$$

**3–9  a.** $k = \dfrac{14.15 - 14.00}{.10} = 1.5$

$1 - \dfrac{1}{(1.5)^2} = 1 - .44 = .56$

**b.** 13.8 and 14.2

**3–10  a.** Frequency distribution.

**b.**

| f | M | fM | (M − X̄) | f(M − X̄)² |
|---|---|-----|-----------|-------------|
| 1 | 4 | 4 | −8.2 | 67.24 |
| 4 | 8 | 32 | −4.2 | 70.56 |
| 10 | 12 | 120 | −0.2 | 0.40 |
| 3 | 16 | 48 | 3.8 | 43.32 |
| 2 | 20 | 40 | 7.8 | 121.68 |
| 20 | | 244 | | 303.20 |

$$\bar{X} = \frac{\Sigma fM}{M} = \frac{\$244}{20} = \$12.20$$

**c.** $s = \sqrt{\dfrac{303.20}{20 - 1}} = \$3.99$

# 4

# Describing Data
## Displaying and Exploring Data

A major airline wanted information on those enrolled in their "frequent flyer" program. A sample of 48 members resulted in data illustrating the number of miles flown last year by each participant. Check the data and develop a box plot for the information. (See Goal 4 and Exercise 41.)

# Introduction

Chapter 2 began our study of descriptive statistics. In order to transform raw or ungrouped data into a meaningful form, we organized the data into a frequency distribution. We presented the frequency distribution in graphic form as a histogram or a frequency polygon. This allowed us to visualize where the data tended to cluster, the largest and the smallest values, and the general shape of the data.

In Chapter 3 we first computed several measures of location, such as the mean and the median. These measures of location allow us to report a typical value in the set of observations. We also computed several measures of dispersion, such as the range and the standard deviation. These measures of dispersion allow us to describe the variation or the spread in a set of observations.

We continue our study of descriptive statistics in this chapter. We begin with dot plots and box plots. Both of these charts give us additional insight into where the values are concentrated and dispersed and the general shape of the data. Next we present some other measurers of dispersion, such as quartiles and percentiles. Finally we consider bivariate data. In bivariate data we observe two variables for each individual or observation selected. Examples include: a student's age and class rank, whether a sampled product is acceptable or not and the shift on which it is manufactured, and the amount of electricity used in a month by a homeowner and the mean daily high temperature in the region for the month.

# Dot Plots

A histogram groups data into classes. Recall in the Whitner Autoplex data from Table 2–1 that 80 observations were condensed into seven classes. When we organized the data into the seven classes we lost the exact value of the observations. A **dot plot,** on the other hand, groups the data as little as possible and we do not lose the identity of an individual observation. To develop a dot plot we simply display a dot for each observation along a horizontal number line indicating the possible values of the data. If there are identical observations or the observations are too close to be shown individually, the dots are "piled" on top of each other. This allows us to see the shape of the distribution, the value about which the data tend to cluster, and the largest and smallest observations. Dot plots are most useful for smaller data sets, whereas histograms tend to be most useful for large data sets. An example will show how to construct and interpret dot plots.

**EXAMPLE**

Recall in Table 2–1 on page 25 we presented data on the selling price of 80 vehicles sold last month at Whitner Autoplex in Raytown, Missouri. Whitner is one of the many dealerships owned by AutoUSA. AutoUSA has many other dealerships located in small towns throughout the United States. Reported below are the number of vehicles sold in the last 24 months at Smith Ford Mercury Jeep, Inc., in Kane, Pennsylvania, and Brophy Honda Volkswagen in Greenville, Ohio. Construct dot plots and report summary statistics for the two small town AutoUSA lots.

| Smith Ford Mercury Jeep, Inc. | | | | | | | | | |
|---|---|---|---|---|---|---|---|---|---|
| 23 | 27 | 30 | 27 | 32 | 31 | 32 | 32 | 35 | 33 |
| 28 | 39 | 32 | 29 | 35 | 36 | 33 | 25 | 35 | 37 |
| 26 | 28 | 36 | 30 | | | | | | |

| Brophy Honda Volkswagen | | | | | | | | | |
|---|---|---|---|---|---|---|---|---|---|
| 31 | 44 | 30 | 36 | 37 | 34 | 43 | 38 | 37 | 35 |
| 36 | 34 | 31 | 32 | 40 | 36 | 31 | 44 | 26 | 30 |
| 37 | 43 | 42 | 33 | | | | | | |

**SOLUTION**

The MINITAB system provides a dot plot and calculates the mean, median, maximum, and minimum values, and the standard deviation for the number of cars sold at each of the dealerships over the last 24 months.

**MINITAB**

From the descriptive statistics we see that Brophy sold an average of 35.83 vehicles per month and Smith an average of 31.29. So Brophy sells an average of 4.54 more vehicles per month. There is also more dispersion or variation in the monthly Brophy sales than in the Smith sales. How do we know this? The standard deviation is larger at Brophy (4.96 cars per month) than at Smith (4.11 cars per month).

The dot plot, shown in the lower right of the software output, shows the distributions for both dealerships. The plots show the difference in the location and dispersion of the observations. By looking at the plots, we can see that Brophy's sales are more widely dispersed and have a larger mean than Smith's sales. Several other features of the monthly sales are apparent:

- Smith sold the fewest cars in any month, 23.
- Brophy sold 26 cars in their lowest month which is 4 cars less than the next lowest month.
- Smith sold exactly 32 cars in four different months.
- The monthly sales cluster around 32 for Smith and 36 for Brophy.

# Stem-and-Leaf Displays

In Chapter 2, we showed how to organize data into a frequency distribution so we could summarize the raw data into a meaningful form. The major advantage to organizing the data into a frequency distribution is that we get a quick visual picture of the shape of the distribution without doing any further calculation. That is, we can see where the data are concentrated and also determine whether there are any extremely large or small values. There are two disadvantages, however, to organizing the data into a frequency distribution: (1) we lose the exact identity of each value and (2) we are not sure how the values within each class are distributed. To explain, the following frequency distribution shows the number of advertising spots purchased by the 45 members of the Greater Buffalo Automobile Dealers Association in the year 2003. We observe that 7 of the 45 dealers purchased 90 but less than 100 spots. However, is the number of spots purchased within this class clustered about 90, spread evenly throughout the class, or clustered near 99? We cannot tell.

| Number of Spots Purchased | Frequency |
|---|---|
| 80 up to 90 | 2 |
| 90 up to 100 | 7 |
| 100 up to 110 | 6 |
| 110 up to 120 | 9 |
| 120 up to 130 | 8 |
| 130 up to 140 | 7 |
| 140 up to 150 | 3 |
| 150 up to 160 | 3 |
| Total | 45 |

**Statistics in Action**

John W. Tukey (1915–2000) received a Ph.D. in mathematics from Princeton in 1939. However, when he joined the Fire Control Research Office during World War II, his interest in abstract mathematics shifted to applied statistics. He developed effective numerical and graphical methods for studying patterns in data. Among the graphics he developed are the stem-and-leaf diagram and the box-and-whisker plot or box plot. From 1960 to 1980, Tukey headed the statistical division of NBC's election night vote projection team. He became renowned in 1960 for preventing an early call of victory for Richard Nixon in the presidential election won by John F. Kennedy.

One technique that is used to display quantitative information in a condensed form is the **stem-and-leaf display.** An advantage of the stem-and-leaf display over a frequency distribution is that we do not lose the identity of each observation. In the above example, we would not know the identity of the values in the 90 up to 100 class. To illustrate the construction of a stem-and-leaf display using the number of advertising spots purchased, suppose the seven observations in the 90 up to 100 class are: 96, 94, 93, 94, 95, 96, and 97. The **stem** value is the leading digit or digits, in this case 9. The **leaves** are the trailing digits. The stem is placed to the left of a vertical line and the leaf values to the right.

The values in the 90 up to 100 class would appear as follows:

| 9 | 6 4 3 4 5 6 7 |
|---|---|

Finally, we sort the values within each stem from smallest to largest. Thus, the second row of the stem-and-leaf display would appear as follows:

| 9 | 3 4 4 5 6 6 7 |
|---|---|

With the stem-and-leaf display, we can quickly observe that there were two dealers that purchased 94 spots and that the number of spots purchased ranged from 93 to 97. A stem-and-leaf display is similar to a frequency distribution with more information, that is, the identity of the observations is preserved.

> **STEM-AND-LEAF DISPLAY** A statistical technique to present a set of data. Each numerical value is divided into two parts. The leading digit(s) becomes the stem and the trailing digit the leaf. The stems are located along the vertical axis, and the leaf values are stacked against each other along the horizontal axis.

The following example will explain the details of developing a stem-and-leaf display.

**EXAMPLE**

Listed in Table 4–1 is the number of 30-second radio advertising spots purchased by each of the 45 members of the Greater Buffalo Automobile Dealers Association last year. Organize the data into a stem-and-leaf display. Around what values do the number of advertising spots tend to cluster? What is the fewest number of spots purchased by a dealer? The largest number purchased?

**TABLE 4–1** Number of Advertising Spots Purchased by Members of the Greater Buffalo Automobile Dealers Association

| 96  | 93  | 88  | 117 | 127 | 95  | 113 | 96  | 108 | 94  | 148 | 156 |
| 139 | 142 | 94  | 107 | 125 | 155 | 155 | 103 | 112 | 127 | 117 | 120 |
| 112 | 135 | 132 | 111 | 125 | 104 | 106 | 139 | 134 | 119 | 97  | 89  |
| 118 | 136 | 125 | 143 | 120 | 103 | 113 | 124 | 138 |     |     |     |

**SOLUTION**

From the data in Table 4–1 we note that the smallest number of spots purchased is 88. So we will make the first stem value 8. The largest number is 156, so we will have the stem values begin at 8 and continue to 15. The first number in Table 4–1 is 96, which will have a stem value of 9 and a leaf value of 6. Moving across the top row, the second value is 93 and the third is 88. After the first 3 data values are considered, your chart is as follows.

| Stem | Leaf |
|------|------|
| 8    | 8    |
| 9    | 6 3  |
| 10   |      |
| 11   |      |
| 12   |      |
| 13   |      |
| 14   |      |
| 15   |      |

Organizing all the data, the stem-and-leaf chart looks as follows.

| Stem | Leaf              |
|------|-------------------|
| 8    | 8 9               |
| 9    | 6 3 5 6 4 4 7     |
| 10   | 8 7 3 4 6 3       |
| 11   | 7 3 2 7 2 1 9 8 3 |
| 12   | 7 5 7 0 5 5 0 4   |
| 13   | 9 5 2 9 4 6 8     |
| 14   | 8 2 3             |
| 15   | 6 5 5             |

The usual procedure is to sort the leaf values from the smallest to largest. The last line, the row referring to the values in the 150s, would appear as:

| 15 | 5   5   6 |
|----|-----------|

The final table would appear as follows, where we have sorted all of the leaf values.

| Stem | Leaf |
|------|------|
| 8 | 8 9 |
| 9 | 3 4 4 5 6 6 7 |
| 10 | 3 3 4 6 7 8 |
| 11 | 1 2 2 3 3 7 7 8 9 |
| 12 | 0 0 4 5 5 5 7 7 |
| 13 | 2 4 5 6 8 9 9 |
| 14 | 2 3 8 |
| 15 | 5 5 6 |

You can draw several conclusions from the stem-and-leaf display. First the minimum number of spots purchased is 88 and the maximum is 156. Two dealers purchased less than 90 spots, and three purchased 150 or more. You can observe, for example, that the three dealers who purchased more than 150 spots actually purchased 155, 155, and 156 spots. The concentration of the number of spots is between 110 and 130. There were nine dealers who purchased between 110 and 119 spots and eight who purchased between 120 and 129 spots. We can also tell that within the 120 to 129 group the actual number of spots purchased was spread evenly throughout. That is, two dealers purchased 120 spots, one dealer purchased 124 spots, three dealers purchased 125 spots, and two purchased 127 spots.

We can also generate this information on the MINITAB software system. We have named the variable *Spots.* The MINITAB output is below. You can find the MINITAB commands that will produce this output at the end of the chapter.

The MINITAB solution provides some additional information regarding cumulative totals. In the column to the left of the stem values are numbers such as 2, 9, 15, and so on. The number 9 indicates that there are 9 observations that have occurred before the value of 100. The number 15 indicates that 15 observations have occurred prior to 110. About halfway down the column the number 9 appears in parentheses. The parentheses indicate that the middle value or median appears in that row and that there are nine values in this group. In this case, we describe the middle value as the value below which half of the observations occur. There are a total of 45 observations, so the middle value, if the data were arranged from smallest to largest, would be the

23rd observation; its value is 118. After the median, the values begin to decline. These values represent the "more than" cumulative totals. There are 21 observations of 120 or more, 13 of 130 or more, and so on. The number 9 in parentheses also tells you there are 9 observations in the middle row.

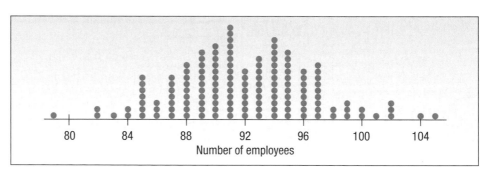

1.  The number of employees at each of the 142 Home Depot Stores in the Southeast region is shown in the following dot plot.

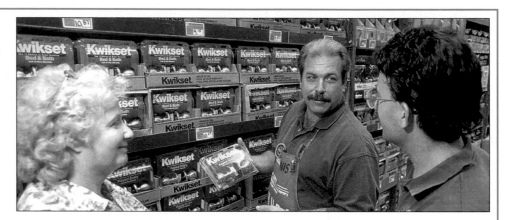

Number of employees

Answer the following questions.
(a)  What are the maximum and minimum numbers of employees per store?
(b)  How many stores employ 91 people?
(c)  Around what values does the number of employees per store tend to cluster?
2.  The price-earnings ratios for 21 stocks in the retail trade category are:

| 8.3 | 9.6 | 9.5 | 9.1 | 8.8 | 11.2 | 7.7 | 10.1 | 9.9 | 10.8 | |
| 10.2 | 8.0 | 8.4 | 8.1 | 11.6 | 9.6 | 8.8 | 8.0 | 10.4 | 9.8 | 9.2 |

Organize this information into a stem-and-leaf display.
(a)  How many values are less than 9.0?
(b)  List the values in the 10.0 up to 11.0 category.
(c)  What is the median value?
(d)  What are the maximum and the minimum price-earnings ratios?

# Exercises

1. Describe the differences between a histogram and a dot plot. When might a dot plot be better than a histogram?
2. Describe the differences between a histogram and a stem-and-leaf display.
3. Consider the following chart.

   a. What is this chart called?
   b. How many observations are in the study?
   c. What are the maximum and the minimum values?
   d. Around what values do the observations tend to cluster?
4. The following chart reports the number of clocks sold each day at Shaver Clocks for the last 26 days.

   a. What are the maximum and the minimum number of clocks sold in a day?
   b. What is a typical number of clocks sold?
5. The first row of a stem-and-leaf chart appears as follows: 62 | 1 3 3 7 9. Assume whole number values.
   a. What is the "possible range" of the values in this row?
   b. How many data values are in this row?
   c. List the actual values in this row of data.
6. The third row of a stem-and-leaf chart appears as follows: 21 | 0 1 3 5 7 9. Assume whole number values.
   a. What is the "possible range" of the values in this row?
   b. How many data values are in this row?
   c. List the actual values in this row of data.
7. The following stem-and-leaf chart from the MINITAB software shows the number of units produced per day in a factory.

| 1   | 3  | 8       |
|-----|----|---------|
| 1   | 4  |         |
| 2   | 5  | 6       |
| 9   | 6  | 0133559 |
| (7) | 7  | 0236778 |
| 9   | 8  | 59      |
| 7   | 9  | 00156   |
| 2   | 10 | 36      |

   a. How many days were studied?
   b. How many observations are in the first class?
   c. What are the minimum value and the maximum value?
   d. List the actual values in the fourth row.
   e. List the actual values in the second row.
   f. How many values are less than 70?
   g. How many values are 80 or more?
   h. What is the median?
   i. How many values are between 60 and 89, inclusive?

**8.** The following stem-and-leaf chart reports the number of movies rented per day at Video Connection on the corner of Fourth and Main Streets.

| | | |
|---|---|---|
| 3 | 12 | 689 |
| 6 | 13 | 123 |
| 10 | 14 | 6889 |
| 13 | 15 | 589 |
| 15 | 16 | 35 |
| 20 | 17 | 24568 |
| 23 | 18 | 268 |
| (5) | 19 | 13456 |
| 22 | 20 | 034679 |
| 16 | 21 | 2239 |
| 12 | 22 | 789 |
| 9 | 23 | 00179 |
| 4 | 24 | 8 |
| 3 | 25 | 13 |
| 1 | 26 | |
| 1 | 27 | 0 |

   **a.** How many days were studied?
   **b.** How many observations are in the last class?
   **c.** What are the maximum and the minimum values in the entire set of data?
   **d.** List the actual values in the fourth row.
   **e.** List the actual values in the next to the last row.
   **f.** On how many days were less than 160 movies rented?
   **g.** On how many days were 220 or more movies rented?
   **h.** What is the middle value?
   **i.** On how many days were between 170 and 210 movies rented?

**9.** A survey of the number of calls received by a sample of Southern Phone Company subscribers last week revealed the following information. Develop a stem-and-leaf chart. How many calls did a typical subscriber receive? What were the maximum and the minimum number of calls received?

| | | | | | | | | |
|---|---|---|---|---|---|---|---|---|
| 52 | 43 | 30 | 38 | 30 | 42 | 12 | 46 | 39 |
| 37 | 34 | 46 | 32 | 18 | 41 | 5 | | |

**10.** The Aloha Banking Co. is studying ATM use in suburban Honolulu. A sample of 30 ATMs showed they were used the following number of times yesterday. Develop a stem-and-leaf chart. Summarize the number of times each ATM was used: What was the typical, minimum, and maximum number of times each ATM was used?

| | | | | | | | | |
|---|---|---|---|---|---|---|---|---|
| 83 | 64 | 84 | 76 | 84 | 54 | 75 | 59 | 70 | 61 |
| 63 | 80 | 84 | 73 | 68 | 52 | 65 | 90 | 52 | 77 |
| 95 | 36 | 78 | 61 | 59 | 84 | 95 | 47 | 87 | 60 |

# Other Measures of Dispersion

The standard deviation is the most widely used measure of dispersion. However, there are other ways of describing the variation or spread in a set of data. One method is to determine the *location* of values that divide a set of observations into equal parts. These measures include *quartiles, deciles,* and *percentiles.*

Quartiles divide a set of observations into four equal parts. To explain further, think of any set of values arranged from smallest to largest. In Chapter 3 we called the middle value of a set of data arranged from smallest to largest the median. That is, 50 percent of the observations are larger than the median and 50 percent are smaller. The median is a measure of location because it pinpoints the center of the data. In a similar fashion quartiles divide a set of observations into four equal parts. The first quartile, usually labeled $Q_1$, is the value below which 25 percent of the observations occur, and the third quartile, usually labeled $Q_3$, is the value below which 75 percent of the observations occur. Logically, $Q_2$ is the median. The values corresponding to $Q_1$, $Q_2$, and $Q_3$ divide a set of data into four equal parts. $Q_1$ can be thought of as the "median" of the lower half of the data and $Q_3$ the "median" of the upper half of the data.

In a similar fashion deciles divide a set of observations into 10 equal parts and percentiles into 100 equal parts. So if you found that your GPA was in the 8th decile at your university, you could conclude that 80 percent of the students had a GPA lower than yours and 20 percent had a higher GPA. A GPA in the 33rd percentile means that 33 percent of the students have a lower GPA and 67 percent have a higher GPA. Percentile scores are frequently used to report results on such national standardized tests as the SAT, ACT, GMAT (used to judge entry into many Master of Business Administration programs), and LSAT (used to judge entry into law school).

## Quartiles, Deciles, and Percentiles

To formalize the computational procedure, let $L_p$ refer to the location of a desired percentile. So if we wanted to find the 33rd percentile we would use $L_{33}$ and if we wanted the median, the 50th percentile, then $L_{50}$. The number of observations is $n$, so if we want to locate the median, its position is at $(n + 1)/2$, or we could write this as $(n + 1)(P/100)$, where $P$ is the desired percentile.

| | | |
|---|---|---|
| **LOCATION OF A PERCENTILE** | $$L_p = (n + 1)\frac{P}{100}$$ | **[4–1]** |

An example will help to explain further.

**EXAMPLE**

Listed below are the commissions earned last month by a sample of 15 brokers at Salomon Smith Barney's Oakland, California, office. Salomon Smith Barney is an investment company with offices located throughout the United States.

| $2,038 | $1,758 | $1,721 | $1,637 | $2,097 | $2,047 | $2,205 | $1,787 | $2,287 |
|---|---|---|---|---|---|---|---|---|
| 1,940 | 2,311 | 2,054 | 2,406 | 1,471 | 1,460 | | | |

Locate the median, the first quartile, and the third quartile for the commissions earned.

**SOLUTION**

The first step is to organize the data from the smallest commission to the largest.

| $1,460 | $1,471 | $1,637 | $1,721 | $1,758 | $1,787 | $1,940 | $2,038 |
|---|---|---|---|---|---|---|---|
| 2,047 | 2,054 | 2,097 | 2,205 | 2,287 | 2,311 | 2,406 | |

The median value is the observation in the center. The center value or $L_{50}$ is located at $(n + 1)$ (50/100), where $n$ is the number of observations. In this case that is position number 8, found by $(15 + 1)(50/100)$. The eighth largest commission is $2,038. So we conclude this is the median and that half the brokers earned commissions more than $2,038 and half earned less than $2,038.

Recall the definition of a quartile. Quartiles divide a set of observations into four equal parts. Hence 25 percent of the observations will be less than the first quartile. Seventy-five percent of the observations will be less than the third quartile. To locate the first quartile, we use formula (4–1), where $n = 15$ and $P = 25$:

$$L_{25} = (n + 1) \frac{P}{100} = (15 + 1) \frac{25}{100} = 4$$

and to locate the third quartile, $n = 15$ and $P = 75$:

$$L_{75} = (n + 1) \frac{P}{100} = (15 + 1) \frac{75}{100} = 12$$

Therefore, the first and third quartile values are located at positions 4 and 12. The fourth value in the ordered array is $1,721 and the twelfth is $2,205. These are the first and third quartiles, respectively.

In the above example the location formula yielded a whole number result. That is, we wanted to find the first quartile and there were 15 observations, so the location formula indicated we should find the fourth ordered value. What if there were 20 observations in the sample, that is $n = 20$, and we wanted to locate the first quartile? From the location formula (4–1):

$$L_{25} = (n + 1) \frac{P}{100} = (20 + 1) \frac{25}{100} = 5.25$$

We would locate the fifth value in the ordered array and then move .25 of the distance between the fifth and sixth values and report that as the first quartile. Like the median, the quartile does not need to be one of the actual values in the data set.

To explain further, suppose a data set contained the six values: 91, 75, 61, 101, 43, and 104. We want to locate the first quartile. We order the values from smallest to largest: 43, 61, 75, 91, 101, and 104. The first quartile is located at

$$L_{25} = (n + 1) \frac{P}{100} = (6 + 1) \frac{25}{100} = 1.75$$

The position formula tells us that the first quartile is located between the first and the second value and that it is .75 of the distance between the first and the second values. The first value is 43 and the second is 61. So the distance between these two values is 18. To locate the first quartile, we need to move .75 of the distance between the first and second values, so .75(18) = 13.5. To complete the procedure, we add 13.5 to the first value and report that the first quartile is 56.5.

We can extend the idea to include both deciles and percentiles. If we wanted to locate the 23rd percentile in a sample of 80 observations, we would look for the 18.63 position.

$$L_{23} = (n + 1) \frac{P}{100} = (80 + 1) \frac{23}{100} = 18.63$$

To find the value corresponding to the 23rd percentile, we would locate the 18th value and the 19th value and determine the distance between the two values. Next, we would multiply this difference by 0.63 and add the result to the smaller value. The result would be the 23rd percentile.

With a statistical software package, it is quite easy to sort the data from smallest to largest and to locate percentiles and deciles. Both MINITAB and Excel output summary statistics. Listed below is the MINITAB output. The data are reported in $000. It includes the first and third quartiles, as well as the mean, median, and standard deviation for the Whitner Autoplex data (see Table 2–1). We conclude that 25 percent of the vehicles sold for less than $20,074 and that 75 percent sold for less than $25,795.

The following Excel output includes the same information regarding the mean, median, and standard deviation. It will also output the quartiles, but the method of calculation is not as precise. To find the quartiles, we multiply the sample size by the desired percentile and report the integer of that value. To explain, in the Whitner Autoplex data there are 80 observations, and we wish to locate the 25th percentile. We multiply $n + 1 = 80 + 1 = 81$ by .25; the result is 20.25. Excel will not allow us to enter a fractional value, so we use 20 and request the location of the largest 20 values and the smallest 20 values. The result is a good approximation of the 25th and 75th percentiles.

**Self-Review 4–2**

The quality control department of the Plainsville Peanut Company is responsible for checking the weight of the 8-ounce jar of peanut butter. The weights of a sample of nine jars produced last hour are:

| 7.69 | 7.72 | 7.8 | 7.86 | 7.90 | 7.94 | 7.97 | 8.06 | 8.09 |

(a) What is the median weight?
(b) Determine the weights corresponding to the first and third quartiles.

# Exercises

**11.** Determine the median and the values corresponding to the first and third quartiles in the following data.

| 46 | 47 | 49 | 49 | 51 | 53 | 54 | 54 | 55 | 55 | 59 |

**12.** Determine the median and the values corresponding to the first and third quartiles in the following data.

| 5.24 | 6.02 | 6.67 | 7.30 | 7.59 | 7.99 | 8.03 | 8.35 | 8.81 | 9.45 |
| 9.61 | 10.37 | 10.39 | 11.86 | 12.22 | 12.71 | 13.07 | 13.59 | 13.89 | 15.42 |

**13.** The Thomas Supply Company, Inc. is a distributor of small electrical motors. As with any business, the length of time customers take to pay their invoices is important. Listed below, arranged from smallest to largest, is the time, in days, for a sample of The Thomas Supply Company, Inc. invoices.

| 13 | 13 | 13 | 20 | 26 | 27 | 31 | 34 | 34 | 34 | 35 | 35 | 36 | 37 | 38 |
| 41 | 41 | 41 | 45 | 47 | 47 | 47 | 50 | 51 | 53 | 54 | 56 | 62 | 67 | 82 |

    **a.** Determine the first and third quartiles.
    **b.** Determine the second decile and the eighth decile.
    **c.** Determine the 67th percentile.

**14.** Kevin Horn is the national sales manager for National Textbooks, Inc. He has a sales staff of 40 who visit college professors all over the United States. Each Saturday morning he requires his sales staff to send him a report. This report includes, among other things, the number of professors visited during the previous week. Listed below, ordered from smallest to largest, are the number of visits last week.

| 38 | 40 | 41 | 45 | 48 | 48 | 50 | 50 | 51 | 51 | 52 | 52 | 53 | 54 | 55 | 55 | 55 | 56 | 56 | 57 |
| 59 | 59 | 59 | 62 | 62 | 62 | 63 | 64 | 65 | 66 | 66 | 67 | 67 | 69 | 69 | 71 | 77 | 78 | 79 | 79 |

    **a.** Determine the median number of calls.
    **b.** Determine the first and third quartiles.
    **c.** Determine the first decile and the ninth decile.
    **d.** Determine the 33rd percentile.

## Box Plots

A **box plot** is a graphical display, based on quartiles, that helps us picture a set of data. To construct a box plot, we need only five statistics: the minimum value, $Q_1$ (the first quartile), the median, $Q_3$ (the third quartile), and the maximum value. An example will help to explain.

**EXAMPLE**

Alexander's Pizza offers free delivery of its pizza within 15 miles. Alex, the owner, wants some information on the time it takes for delivery. How long does a typical delivery take? Within what range of times will most deliveries be completed? For a sample of 20 deliveries, he determined the following information:

$$\text{Minimum value} = 13 \text{ minutes}$$

$$Q_1 = 15 \text{ minutes}$$

$$\text{Median} = 18 \text{ minutes}$$

$$Q_3 = 22 \text{ minutes}$$

$$\text{Maximum value} = 30 \text{ minutes}$$

Develop a box plot for the delivery times. What conclusions can you make about the delivery times?

**SOLUTION**

The first step in drawing a box plot is to create an appropriate scale along the horizontal axis. Next, we draw a box that starts at $Q_1$ (15 minutes) and ends at $Q_3$ (22 minutes). Inside the box we place a vertical line to represent the median (18 minutes). Finally, we extend horizontal lines from the box out to the minimum value (13 minutes) and the maximum value (30 minutes). These horizontal lines outside of the box are sometimes called "whiskers" because they look a bit like a cat's whiskers.

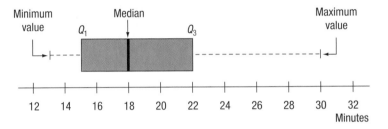

The box plot shows that the middle 50 percent of the deliveries take between 15 minutes and 22 minutes. The distance between the ends of the box, 7 minutes, is the **interquartile range.** The interquartile range is the distance between the first and the third quartile. It shows the spread or dispersion of the majority of deliveries.

The box plot also reveals that the distribution of delivery times is positively skewed. How do we know this? In this case there are actually two pieces of information that suggest that the distribution is positively skewed. First, the dashed line to the right of the box from 22 minutes ($Q_3$) to the maximum time of 30 minutes is longer than the dashed line from the left of 15 minutes ($Q_1$) to the minimum value of 13 minutes. To put it another way, the 25 percent of the data larger than the third quartile is more spread out than the 25 percent less than the first quartile. A second indication of positive skewness is that the median is not in the center of the box. The distance from the first quartile to the median is smaller than the distance from the median to the third quartile. We know that the number of delivery times between 15 minutes and 18 minutes is the same as the number of delivery times between 18 minutes and 22 minutes.

**EXAMPLE**

Refer to the Whitner Autoplex data in Table 2–1. Develop a box plot of the data. What can we conclude about the distribution of the vehicle selling prices?

SOLUTION

The MINITAB statistical software system was used to develop the following chart.

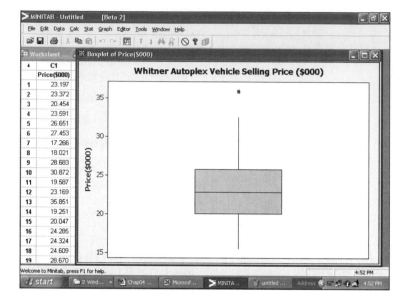

We conclude that the median vehicle selling price is about $23,000, that about 25 percent of the vehicles sell for less than $20,000, and that about 25 percent sell for more than $26,000. About 50 percent of the vehicles sell for between $20,000 and $26,000. The distribution is positively skewed because the solid line above $26,000 is somewhat longer than the line below $20,000.

There is an asterisk (*) above the $35,000 selling price. An asterisk indicates an outlier. An **outlier** is a value that is inconsistent with the rest of the data. The standard definition of an outlier is a value that is more than 1.5 times the interquartile range smaller than $Q_1$ or larger than $Q_3$. In this example, an outlier would be a value larger than $35,000, found by

$$\text{Outlier} > Q_3 + 1.5(Q_3 - Q_1) = \$26{,}000 + 1.5(\$26{,}000 - \$20{,}000) = \$35{,}000$$

A value less than $11,000 is also an outlier.

$$\text{Outlier} < Q_1 - 1.5(Q_3 - Q_1) = \$20{,}000 - 1.5(\$26{,}000 - \$20{,}000) = \$11{,}000$$

The MINITAB box plot indicates that there is only one value larger than $35,000. However, if you look at the actual data in Table 2–1 on page 25 you will notice that there are actually two values ($35,851 and $35,925). The software was not able to graph two data points so close together, so it shows only one asterisk.

---

**Self-Review 4–3**

The following box plot is given.

What are the median, the largest and smallest values, and the first and third quartiles? Would you agree that the distribution is symmetrical?

# Exercises

**15.** Refer to the box plot below.

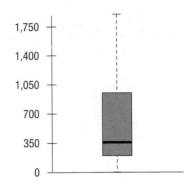

  **a.** Estimate the median.
  **b.** Estimate the first and third quartiles.
  **c.** Determine the interquartile range.
  **d.** Beyond what point is a value considered an outlier?
  **e.** Identify any outliers and estimate their value.
  **f.** Is the distribution symmetrical or positively or negatively skewed?

**16.** Refer to the following box plot.

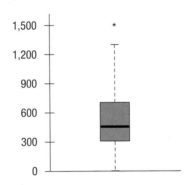

  **a.** Estimate the median.
  **b.** Estimate the first and third quartiles.
  **c.** Determine the interquartile range.
  **d.** Beyond what point is a value considered an outlier?
  **e.** Identify any outliers and estimate their value.
  **f.** Is the distribution symmetrical or positively or negatively skewed?

**17.** In a study of the gasoline mileage of model year 2004 automobiles, the mean miles per gallon was 27.5 and the median was 26.8. The smallest value in the study was 12.70 miles per gallon, and the largest was 50.20. The first and third quartiles were 17.95 and 35.45 miles per gallon, respectively. Develop a box plot and comment on the distribution. Is it a symmetric distribution?

**18.** A sample of 28 time shares in Florida revealed the following daily charges for a one-bedroom suite. For convenience the data are ordered from smallest to largest. Construct a box plot to represent the data. Comment on the distribution. Be sure to identify the first and third quartiles and the median.

| | | | | | | |
|---|---|---|---|---|---|---|
| $116 | $121 | $157 | $192 | $207 | $209 | $209 |
| 229 | 232 | 236 | 236 | 239 | 243 | 246 |
| 260 | 264 | 276 | 281 | 283 | 289 | 296 |
| 307 | 309 | 312 | 317 | 324 | 341 | 353 |

# Relative Dispersion

A direct comparison of two or more measures of dispersion—say, the standard devi-

ation for a distribution of annual incomes and the standard deviation of a distribution of absenteeism for this same group of employees—is impossible. Can we say that the standard deviation of $1,200 for the income distribution is greater than the standard deviation of 4.5 days for the distribution of absenteeism? Obviously not, because we cannot directly compare dollars and days absent from work. In order to make a meaningful comparison of the dispersion in incomes and absenteeism, we need to convert each of these measures to a *relative value*—that is, a percent. Karl Pearson (1857–1936), pictured here, who contributed significantly to the science of statistics, developed a relative measure called the **coefficient of variation** (CV). It is a very useful measure when:

When to use CV

1. The data are in different units (such as dollars and days absent).
2. The data are in the same units, but the means are far apart (such as the incomes of the top executives and the incomes of the unskilled employees).

| **COEFFICIENT OF VARIATION** The ratio of the standard deviation to the arithmetic mean, expressed as a percent. |
|---|

In terms of a formula for a sample:

| **COEFFICIENT OF VARIATION** | $CV = \dfrac{s}{\bar{X}}(100)$ ← Multiplying by 100 converts the decimal to a percent | [4–2] |
|---|---|---|

**EXAMPLE**

A study of the amount of bonus paid per year and the years of service of employees at Sea Pro Marine, Inc. of Newberry, South Carolina, resulted in these statistics: The mean bonus paid was $2,000; the standard deviation was $400. The mean number of years of service was 20 years; the standard deviation was 2 years. Compare the relative dispersion in the two distributions using the coefficient of variation.

**SOLUTION**

The distributions are in different units (dollars and years of service). Therefore, they are converted to coefficients of variation.

For the bonus paid:

$$CV = \frac{s}{\bar{X}}(100)$$
$$= \frac{\$400}{\$2000}(100)$$
$$= 20 \text{ percent}$$

For years of service:

$$CV = \frac{s}{\bar{X}}(100)$$
$$= \frac{2}{20}(100)$$
$$= 10 \text{ percent}$$

Interpreting, there is more dispersion relative to the mean in the distribution of bonus paid compared with the distribution of years of service (because 20 percent > 10 percent).

The same procedure is used when the data are in the same units but the means are far apart. See the following example.

**EXAMPLE**

The variation in the annual incomes of executives at Nash-Rambler Products, Inc. is to be compared with the variation in incomes of unskilled employees. For a sample of executives, $\overline{X} = \$500,000$ and $s = \$50,000$. For a sample of unskilled employees, $\overline{X} = \$32,000$ and $s = \$3,200$. We are tempted to say that there is more dispersion in the annual incomes of the executives because $\$50,000 > \$3,200$. The means are so far apart, however, that we need to convert the statistics to coefficients of variation to make a meaningful comparison of the variations in annual incomes.

**SOLUTION**

For the executives:

$$CV = \frac{s}{\overline{X}}(100)$$

$$= \frac{\$50,000}{\$500,000}(100)$$

$$= 10 \text{ percent}$$

For the unskilled employees:

$$CV = \frac{s}{\overline{X}}(100)$$

$$= \frac{\$3,200}{\$32,000}(100)$$

$$= 10 \text{ percent}$$

There is no difference in the relative dispersion of the two groups.

---

**Self-Review 4–4**

A large group of Air Force inductees was given two experimental tests—a mechanical aptitude test and a finger dexterity test. The arithmetic mean score on the mechanical aptitude test was 200, with a standard deviation of 10. The mean and standard deviation for the finger dexterity test were: $\overline{X} = 30$, $s = 6$. Compare the relative dispersion in the two groups.

# Exercises

**19.** For a sample of students in the College of Business Administration at Mid-Atlantic University, the mean grade point average is 3.10 with a standard deviation of 0.25. Compute the coefficient of variation.

**20.** Southwest Airlines is studying the weight of luggage for each passenger. For a large group of domestic passengers, the mean is 47 pounds with a standard deviation of 10 pounds. For a large group of overseas passengers, the mean is 78 pounds and the standard deviation is 15 pounds. Compute the relative dispersion of each group. Comment on the difference in relative dispersion.

**21.** The research analyst for the Sidde Financial stock brokerage firm wants to compare the dispersion in the price-earnings ratios for a group of common stocks with the dispersion of their return on investment. For the price-earnings ratios, the mean is 10.9 and the standard deviation 1.8. The mean return on investment is 25 percent and the standard deviation 5.2 percent.
   **a.** Why should the coefficient of variation be used to compare the dispersion?
   **b.** Compare the relative dispersion for the price-earnings ratios and return on investment.

**22.** The spread in the annual prices of stocks selling for under $10 and the spread in prices of those selling for over $60 are to be compared. The mean price of the stocks selling for under $10 is $5.25 and the standard deviation $1.52. The mean price of those stocks selling for over $60 is $92.50 and the standard deviation $5.28.

**a.** Why should the coefficient of variation be used to compare the dispersion in the prices?

**b.** Compute the coefficients of variation. What is your conclusion?

**Statistics in Action**

The late Stephen Jay Gould (1941–2002) was a professor of zoology and professor of geology at Harvard University. In 1982, he was diagnosed with cancer and had an expected survival time of eight months. However, never to be discouraged, his research showed that the distribution of survival time is dramatically skewed to the right and showed that not only do 50% of similar cancer patients survive more than 8 months, but that the survival time could be years rather than months! Based on his experience, he wrote a widely published essay titled, "The Median is not the Message."

# Skewness

In Chapter 3 we have described measures of central location for a set of observations by reporting the mean, median, and mode. We have also described measures that show the amount of spread or variation in a set of data, such as the range and the standard deviation.

Another characteristic of a set of data is the shape. There are four shapes commonly observed: symmetric, positively skewed, negatively skewed, and bimodal. In a **symmetric** set of observations the mean and median are equal and the data values are evenly spread around these values. The data values below the mean and median are a mirror image of those above. A set of values is **skewed to the right** or **positively skewed** if there is a single peak and the values extend much further to the right of the peak than to the left of the peak. In this case the mean is larger than the median. In a **negatively skewed** distribution there is a single peak but the observations extend further to the left, in the negative direction, than to the right. In a negatively skewed distribution the mean is smaller than the median. Positively skewed distributions are more common. Salaries often follow this pattern. Think of the salaries of those employed in a small company of about 100 people. The president and a few top executives would have very large salaries relative to the other workers and hence the distribution of salaries would exhibit positive skewness. A **bimodal distribution** will have two or more peaks. This is often the case when the values are from two or more populations. This information is summarized in Chart 4–1.

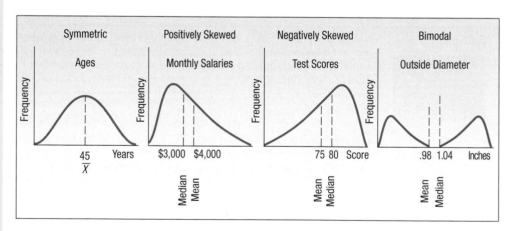

**CHART 4–1** Shapes of Frequency Polygons

There are several formulas in the statistical literature used to calculate skewness. The simplest, developed by Professor Karl Pearson, is based on the difference between the mean and the median.

| PEARSON'S COEFFICIENT OF SKEWNESS | $sk = \dfrac{3(\overline{X} - \text{Median})}{s}$ | [4–3] |

Using this relationship the coefficient of skewness can range from $-3$ up to 3. A value near $-3$, such as $-2.57$, indicates considerable negative skewness. A value such as 1.63 indicates moderate positive skewness. A value of 0, which will occur when the mean and median are equal, indicates the distribution is symmetrical and that there is no skewness present.

In this text we present output from the statistical software packages MINITAB and Excel. Both of these software packages compute a value for the coefficient of skewness that is based on the cubed deviations from the mean. The formula is:

$$\text{SOFTWARE COEFFICIENT OF SKEWNESS} \quad sk = \frac{n}{(n-1)(n-2)}\left[\sum\left(\frac{X-\bar{X}}{s}\right)^3\right] \quad \textbf{[4–4]}$$

Formula (4–4) offers an insight into skewness. The right-hand side of the formula is the difference between each value and the mean, divided by the standard deviation. That is the portion $(X - \bar{X})/s$ of the formula. This idea is called **standardizing.** We will discuss the idea of standardizing a value in more detail in Chapter 7 when we describe the normal probability distribution. At this point, observe that the result is to report the difference between each value and the mean in units of the standard deviation. If this difference is positive, the particular value is larger than the mean; if it is negative, it is smaller than the mean. When we cube these values, we retain the information on the direction of the difference. Recall that in the formula for the standard deviation [see formula (3–11)] we squared the difference between each value and the mean, so that the result was all non-negative values.

If the set of data values under consideration is symmetric, when we cube the standardized values and sum over all the values the result would be near zero. If there are several large values, clearly separate from the others, the sum of the cubed differences would be a large positive value. Several values much smaller will result in a negative cubed sum.

An example will illustrate the idea of skewness.

**EXAMPLE**

Following are the earnings per share for a sample of 15 software companies for the year 2003. The earnings per share are arranged from smallest to largest.

| $0.09 | $0.13 | $0.41 | $0.51 | $ 1.12 | $ 1.20 | $ 1.49 | $3.18 |
|-------|-------|-------|-------|--------|--------|--------|-------|
| 3.50 | 6.36 | 7.83 | 8.92 | 10.13 | 12.99 | 16.40 | |

Compute the mean, median, and standard deviation. Find the coefficient of skewness using Pearson's estimate and the software methods. What is your conclusion regarding the shape of the distribution?

**SOLUTION**

These are sample data, so we use formula (3–2) to determine the mean

$$\bar{X} = \frac{\sum X}{n} = \frac{\$74.26}{15} = \$4.95$$

The median is the middle value in a set of data, arranged from smallest to largest. In this case the middle value is $3.18, so the median earnings per share is $3.18.

We use formula (3–11) on page 77 to determine the sample standard deviation.

$$s = \sqrt{\frac{\sum(X-\bar{X})^2}{n-1}} = \sqrt{\frac{(\$0.09 - \$4.95)^2 + \cdots + (\$16.40 - \$4.95)^2}{15 - 1}} = \$5.22$$

Pearson's coefficient of skewness is 1.017, found by

$$sk = \frac{3(\bar{X} - \text{Median})}{s} = \frac{3(\$4.95 - \$3.18)}{\$5.22} = 1.017$$

This indicates there is moderate positive skewness in the earnings per share data.

We obtain a similar, but not exactly the same, value from the software method. The details of the calculations are shown in Table 4–2. To begin we find the difference between each earnings per share value and the mean and divide this result by the standard deviation. Recall that we referred to this as standardizing. Next, we cube, that is, raise it to the third power, the result of the first step. Finally, we sum the cubed values. The details of the first row, that is, the company with an earnings per share of $0.09, are:

$$\left(\frac{X - \bar{X}}{s}\right)^3 = \left(\frac{0.09 - 4.95}{5.22}\right)^3 = (-0.9310)^3 = -0.8070$$

When we sum the 15 cubed values, the result is 11.8274. That is, the term $\Sigma[(X - \bar{X})/s]^3 = 11.8274$. To find the coefficient of skewness, we use formula (4–4), with $n = 15$.

$$sk = \frac{n}{(n-1)(n-2)} \Sigma\left(\frac{X - \bar{X}}{s}\right)^3 = \frac{15}{(15-1)(15-2)}(11.8274) = 0.975$$

**TABLE 4–2** Calculation of the Coefficient of Skewness

| Earnings per Share | $\dfrac{(X - \bar{X})}{s}$ | $\left(\dfrac{X - \bar{X}}{s}\right)^3$ |
|---|---|---|
| 0.09 | −0.9310 | −0.8070 |
| 0.13 | −0.9234 | −0.7873 |
| 0.41 | −0.8697 | −0.6579 |
| 0.51 | −0.8506 | −0.6154 |
| 1.12 | −0.7337 | −0.3950 |
| 1.20 | −0.7184 | −0.3708 |
| 1.49 | −0.6628 | −0.2912 |
| 3.18 | −0.3391 | −0.0390 |
| 3.50 | −0.2778 | −0.0214 |
| 6.36 | 0.2701 | 0.0197 |
| 7.83 | 0.5517 | 0.1679 |
| 8.92 | 0.7605 | 0.4399 |
| 10.13 | 0.9923 | 0.9772 |
| 12.99 | 1.5402 | 3.6539 |
| 16.40 | 2.1935 | 10.5537 |
| | | 11.8274 |

We conclude that the earnings per share values are somewhat positively skewed. The following chart, from MINITAB, reports the descriptive measures, such as the mean, median, and standard deviation of the earnings per share data. Also included are the coefficient of skewness and a histogram with a bell-shaped curve superimposed.

**Self-Review 4–5**    A sample of five data entry clerks employed in the Horry County Tax Office revised the
following number of tax records last hour: 73, 98, 60, 92, and 84.
(a)   Find the mean, median, and the standard deviation.
(b)   Compute the coefficient of skewness using Pearson's method.
(c)   Calculate the coefficient of skewness using the software method.
(d)   What is your conclusion regarding the skewness of the data?

# Exercises

For Exercises 23–26, do the following:

**a.**   Determine the mean, median, and the standard deviation.
**b.**   Determine the coefficient of skewness using Pearson's method.
**c.**   Determine the coefficient of skewness using the software method.

**23.**   The following values are the starting salaries, in $000, for a sample of five accounting grad-
uates who accepted positions in public accounting last year.

| | | | | |
|---|---|---|---|---|
| 36.0 | 26.0 | 33.0 | 28.0 | 31.0 |

**24.**   Listed below are the salaries, in $000, for a sample of 15 chief financial officers in the elec-
tronics industry.

| | | | | | |
|---|---|---|---|---|---|
| $516.0 | $548.0 | $566.0 | $534.0 | $586.0 | $529.0 |
| 546.0 | 523.0 | 538.0 | 523.0 | 551.0 | 552.0 |
| 486.0 | 558.0 | 574.0 | | | |

**25.**   Listed below are the commissions earned ($000) last year by the sales representatives at
the Furniture Patch, Inc.

| | | | | | | | | |
|---|---|---|---|---|---|---|---|---|
| $ 3.9 | $ 5.7 | $ 7.3 | $10.6 | $13.0 | $13.6 | $15.1 | $15.8 | $17.1 |
| 17.4 | 17.6 | 22.3 | 38.6 | 43.2 | 87.7 | | | |

**26.**   Listed below are the salaries for the New York Yankees for the year 2000. The salary information is reported in millions of dollars.

| $9.86 | $9.50 | $8.25 | $6.25 | $6.00 | $5.95 |
|-------|-------|-------|-------|-------|-------|
| 5.25 | 5.00 | 4.33 | 4.30 | 4.25 | 3.40 |
| 3.13 | 2.02 | 2.00 | 1.90 | 1.85 | 1.82 |
| 0.80 | 0.38 | 0.35 | 0.35 | 0.20 | 0.20 |
| 0.20 | 0.20 | 0.20 | 0.20 | 0.20 | |

# Describing the Relationship Between Two Variables

In Chapter 2 and the first section of this chapter we presented graphical techniques to summarize the distribution of a single variable. We used a histogram in Chapter 2 to summarize the prices of vehicles sold at Whitner Autoplex. Earlier in this chapter we used dot plots and stem-and-leaf displays to visually summarize a set of data. Because we are studying a single variable we refer to this as **univariate** data.

There are situations where we wish to study and visually portray the relationship between two variables. When we study the relationship between two variables we refer to the data as **bivariate**. Data analysts frequently wish to understand the relationship between two variables. Here are some examples:

- Tybo and Associates is a law firm that advertises extensively on local TV. The partners are considering increasing their advertising budget. Before doing so, they would like to know the relationship between the amount spent per month on advertising and the total amount of billings. To put it another way, will increasing the amount spent on advertising result in an increase in billings?
- Coastal Realty is studying the selling prices of homes. What variables seem to be related to the selling price of homes? For example, do larger homes sell for more than smaller ones? Probably. So Coastal might study the relationship between the area in square feet and the selling price.
- Dr. Stephen Givens is an expert in human development. He is studying the relationship between the height of fathers and the height of their sons. That is, do tall fathers tend to have tall children? Would you expect Shaquille O'Neal, the 7'1", 335-pound professional basketball player, to have relatively tall sons?

One graphical technique we use to show the relationship between variables is called a **scatter diagram**.

To draw a scatter diagram we need two variables. We scale one variable along the horizontal axis (*X*-axis) of a graph and the other variable along the vertical axis (*Y*-axis). Usually one variable depends to some degree on the other. In the third example above, the height of the son *depends* on the height of the father. So we scale the height of the father on the horizontal axis and that of the son on the vertical axis.

We can use statistical software, such as Excel, to perform the plotting function for us. *Caution:* you should always be careful of the scale. By changing the scale of either the vertical or the horizontal axis, you can affect the apparent visual strength of the relationship.

**EXAMPLE**

In the Introduction to Chapter 2 we presented data from AutoUSA. In this case the information concerned the prices of 80 vehicles sold last month at the Whitner Autoplex lot in Raytown, Missouri. The data shown on page 119 include the selling price of the vehicle as well as the age of the purchaser. Is there a relationship between the selling price of a vehicle and the age of the purchaser? Would it be reasonable to conclude that the more expensive vehicles are purchased by older buyers?

**SOLUTION**

We can investigate the relationship between vehicle selling price and the age of the buyer with a scatter diagram. We scale age on the horizontal, or *X*-axis, and the selling price on the vertical, or *Y*-axis. We use Microsoft Excel to develop the scatter diagram. The Excel commands necessary for the output are shown in the **Software Commands** section at the end of the chapter.

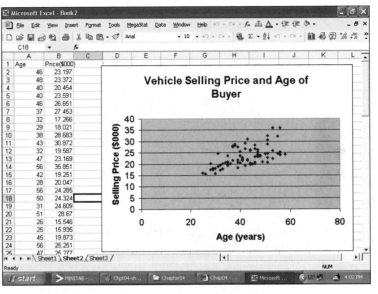

The scatter diagram shows a positive relationship between the variables. In fact, older buyers tend to buy more expensive cars. In Chapter 13 we will study the relationship between variables more extensively, even calculating several numerical measures to express the relationship between variables.

In the Whitner Autoplex example there is a positive or direct relationship between the variables. That is, as age increased the vehicle selling price also increased. There are, however, many instances where there is a relationship between the variables, but that relationship is inverse or negative. For example:

- The value of a vehicle and the number of miles driven. As the number of miles increases, the value of the vehicle decreases.
- The premium for auto insurance and the age of the driver. Auto rates tend to be the highest for young adults and less for older people.
- For many law enforcement personnel as the number of years on the job increases the number of traffic citations decreases. This may be because personnel become more liberal in their interpretations or they may be in supervisor positions and not in a position to issue as many citations. But in any event as age increases the number of citations decreases.

A scatter diagram requires that both of the variables be at least interval scale. In the Whitner Autoplex example both age and selling price are ratio scale variables. Height is also ratio scale as used in the discussion of the relationship between the height of fathers and the height of their sons. What if we wish to study the relationship between two variables when one or both are nominal or ordinal scale? In this case we tally the results into a **contingency table**.

---

**CONTINGENCY TABLE** A table used to classify observations according to two identifiable characteristics.

---

A contingency table is a cross tabulation that simultaneously summarizes two variables of interest. For example:

- Students at a university are classified by gender and class rank.
- A product is classified as acceptable or unacceptable and by the shift (day, afternoon, or night) on which it is manufactured.
- A voter in a school bond referendum is classified as to party affiliation (Democrat, Republican, other) and the number of children attending school in the district (0, 1, 2, etc.).

**EXAMPLE**

A manufacturer of preassembled windows produced 50 windows yesterday. This morning the quality assurance inspector reviewed each window for all quality aspects. Each was classified as acceptable or unacceptable and by the shift on which it was produced. Thus we reported two variables on a single item. The two variables are shift and quality. The results are reported in the following table.

|  | Shift | | | |
|---|---|---|---|---|
|  | Day | Afternoon | Night | Total |
| Defective | 3 | 2 | 1 | 6 |
| Acceptable | 17 | 13 | 14 | 44 |
| Total | 20 | 15 | 15 | 50 |

Compare the quality levels on each shift.

**SOLUTION**

The level of measurement for both variables is nominal. That is, the variables shift and quality are such that a particular unit can only be classified or assigned into groups. By organizing the information into a contingency table we can compare the quality on the three shifts. For example, on the day shift, 3 out of 20 windows or 15 percent are defective. On the afternoon shift, 2 of 15 or 13 percent are defective and on the night shift 1 out of 15 or 7 percent are defective. Overall 12 percent of the windows are defective. Observe also that 40 percent of the windows are produced on the day shift, found by (20/50)(100). We will return to the study of contingency tables in Chapter 5 during the study of probability and in Chapter 15 during the study of nonparametric methods of analysis.

**Self-Review 4–6**

The following chart shows the relationship between concert seating capacity (00) and revenue in $000 for a sample of concerts.

(a)  What is the above diagram called?
(b)  How many concerts were studied?
(c)  Estimate the revenue for the concert with the largest seating capacity.
(d)  How would you characterize the relationship between revenue and seating capacity? Is it strong or weak, direct or inverse?

# Exercises

**27.** Develop a scatter diagram for the following sample data. How would you describe the relationship between the values?

| X-Value | Y-Value |
|---------|---------|
| 10 | 6 |
| 8 | 2 |
| 9 | 6 |
| 11 | 5 |
| 13 | 7 |
| 11 | 6 |
| 10 | 5 |
| 7 | 2 |
| 7 | 3 |
| 11 | 7 |

**28.** Silver Springs Moving and Storage, Inc. is studying the relationship between the number of rooms in a move and the number of labor hours required. As part of the analysis the CFO of Silver Springs developed the following scatter diagram.

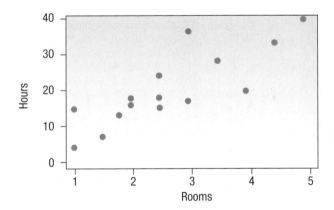

**a.** How many moves are in the sample?
**b.** Does it appear that more labor hours are required as the number of rooms increases, or does labor hours decrease as the number of rooms increases?

**29.** The manager of a restaurant wishes to study the relationship between the gender of a guest and whether the guest orders dessert. To investigate the relationship the manager collected the following information on 200 recent customers.

| Dessert ordered | Gender | | Total |
|-----------------|--------|--------|-------|
| | **Male** | **Female** | |
| Yes | 32 | 15 | 47 |
| No | 68 | 85 | 153 |
| Total | 100 | 100 | 200 |

**a.** What is the level of measurement of the two variables?
**b.** What is the above table called?
**c.** Does the evidence in the table suggest men are more likely to order dessert than women? Explain why.

**30.** A corporation is evaluating a proposed merger. The Board of Directors surveyed 50 stock-holders concerning their position on the merger. The results are reported below.

|  | Opinion | | | |
| --- | --- | --- | --- | --- |
| Number of shares held | Favor | Opposed | Undecided | Total |
| Under 200 | 8 | 6 | 2 | 16 |
| 200 up to 1,000 | 6 | 8 | 1 | 15 |
| Over 1,000 | 6 | 12 | 1 | 19 |
| Total | 20 | 26 | 4 | 50 |

**a.** What level of measurement is used in this table?
**b.** What is this table called?
**c.** What group seems most strongly opposed to the merger?

# Chapter Outline

**I.** A dot plot shows the range of values on the horizontal axis and a dot is placed above each of the values.
   **A.** Dot plots report the details of each observation.
   **B.** They are useful for comparing two or more data sets.
**II.** A stem-and-leaf display is an alternative to a histogram.
   **A.** The leading digit is the stem and the trailing digit the leaf.
   **B.** The advantages of a stem-and-leaf display over a histogram include:
      **1.** The identity of each observation is not lost.
      **2.** The digits themselves give a picture of the distribution.
      **3.** The cumulative frequencies are also shown.
**III.** Measures of location also describe the shape of a set of observations.
   **A.** Quartiles divide a set of observations into four equal parts.
      **1.** Twenty-five percent of the observations are less than the first quartile, 50 percent are less than the second quartile, and 75 percent are less than the third quartile.
      **2.** The interquartile range is the difference between the third and the first quartile.
   **B.** Deciles divide a set of observations in ten equal parts and percentiles into 100 equal parts.
   **C.** A box plot is a graphic display of a set of data.
      **1.** A box is drawn enclosing the regions between the first and third quartiles.
         **a.** A line is drawn inside the box at the median value.
         **b.** Dotted line segments are drawn from the third quartile to the largest value to show the highest 25 percent of the values and the first quartile and the smallest value to show the lowest 25 percent of the values.
      **2.** A box plot is based on five statistics: the maximum and minimum observations, the first and third quartiles, and the median.
**IV.** The coefficient of variation is a measure of relative dispersion.
   **A.** The formula for the coefficient of variation is:

$$CV = \frac{s}{\bar{X}}(100) \qquad \text{[4–2]}$$

   **B.** It reports the variation relative to the mean.
   **C.** It is useful for comparing distributions measured in different units and distributions whose means are far apart.
**V.** The coefficient of skewness is a measure of the symmetry of a distribution.
   **A.** There are two formulas for the coefficient of skewness.
      **1.** The formula developed by Pearson is:

$$sk = \frac{3(\bar{X} - \text{Median})}{s} \qquad \text{[4–3]}$$

**2.** The coefficient of skewness computed by statistical software is:

$$sk = \frac{n}{(n-1)(n-2)}\left[\sum\left(\frac{X-\bar{X}}{s}\right)^3\right] \qquad \textbf{[4–4]}$$

**VI.** A scatter diagram is a graphic tool to portray the relationship between two variables.
    **A.** Both variables are measured with interval or ratio scales.
    **B.** If the scatter of points moves from the lower left to the upper right the variables under consideration are directly or positively related.
    **C.** If the scatter of points moves from upper left to the lower right the variables are inversely or negatively related.
**VII.** A contingency table is used to classify nominal scale observations according to two characteristics.

# Pronunciation Key

| SYMBOL | MEANING | PRONUNCIATION |
|--------|---------|---------------|
| $L_p$ | Location of percentile | L sub p |
| $Q_1$ | First quartile | Q sub 1 |
| $Q_3$ | Third quartile | Q sub 3 |

# Chapter Exercises

**31.** A sample of students attending Southeast Florida University is asked the number of social activities in which they participated last week. The chart below was prepared from the sample data.

    **a.** What is the name given to this chart?
    **b.** How many students were in the study?
    **c.** How many students reported attending no social activities?

**32.** Doctor's Care is a walk-in clinic, with locations in Georgetown, Monks Corners, and Aynor, at which patients may receive treatment for minor injuries, colds, and flu, as well as physical examinations. The following charts report the number of patients treated in each of the three locations last month.

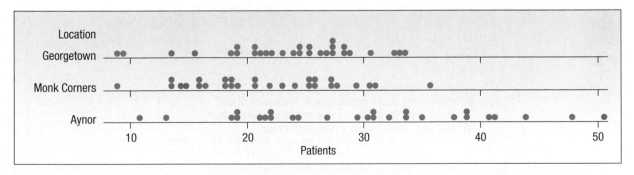

Describe the number of patients served at the three locations each day. What are the maximum and minimum numbers of patients served at each of the locations?

**33.** The following stem-and-leaf display shows the number of minutes of daytime TV viewing for a sample of college students.

| | | |
|---|---|---|
| 2 | 0 | 05 |
| 3 | 1 | 0 |
| 6 | 2 | 137 |
| 10 | 3 | 0029 |
| 13 | 4 | 499 |
| 24 | 5 | 00155667799 |
| 30 | 6 | 023468 |
| (7) | 7 | 1366789 |
| 33 | 8 | 01558 |
| 28 | 9 | 1122379 |
| 21 | 10 | 022367899 |
| 12 | 11 | 2457 |
| 8 | 12 | 4668 |
| 4 | 13 | 249 |
| 1 | 14 | 5 |

  **a.** How many college students were studied?
  **b.** How many observations are in the second class?
  **c.** What are the smallest value and the largest value?
  **d.** List the actual values in the fourth row.
  **e.** How many students watched less than 60 minutes of TV?
  **f.** How many students watched 100 minutes or more of TV?
  **g.** What is the median value?
  **h.** How many students watched at least 60 minutes but less than 100 minutes?

**34.** The following stem-and-leaf display reports the number of orders received per day by a mail-order firm.

| | | |
|---|---|---|
| 1 | 9 | 1 |
| 2 | 10 | 2 |
| 5 | 11 | 235 |
| 7 | 12 | 69 |
| 8 | 13 | 2 |
| 11 | 14 | 135 |
| 15 | 15 | 1229 |
| 22 | 16 | 2266778 |
| 27 | 17 | 01599 |
| (11) | 18 | 00013346799 |
| 17 | 19 | 03346 |
| 12 | 20 | 4679 |
| 8 | 21 | 0177 |
| 4 | 22 | 45 |
| 2 | 23 | 17 |

  **a.** How many days were studied?
  **b.** How many observations are in the fourth class?
  **c.** What are the smallest value and the largest value?
  **d.** List the actual values in the sixth class.
  **e.** How many days did the firm receive less than 140 orders?
  **f.** How many days did the firm receive 200 or more orders?
  **g.** On how many days did the firm receive 180 orders?
  **h.** What is the median value?

**35.** In the early 2000s interest rates were low so many homeowners refinanced their home mortgages. Linda Lahey is a mortgage officer at Down River Federal Savings and Loan. Below is the amount refinanced for twenty loans she processed last week. The data are reported in thousands of dollars and arranged from smallest to largest.

| | | | | | | | | |
|------|------|------|------|------|------|------|------|------|
| 59.2 | 59.5 | 61.6 | 65.5 | 66.6 | 72.9 | 74.8 | 77.3 | 79.2 |
| 83.7 | 85.6 | 85.8 | 86.6 | 87.0 | 87.1 | 90.2 | 93.3 | 98.6 |
| 100.2 | 100.7 | | | | | | | |

**a.** Find the median, first quartile, and third quartile.
**b.** Find the 26th and 83rd percentiles.
**c.** Draw a box plot of the data.

**36.** A study is made by the recording industry in the United States of the number of music CDs owned by senior citizens and young adults. The information is reported below.

| **Seniors** | | | | | | | | | |
|------|------|------|------|------|------|------|------|------|------|
| 28 | 35 | 41 | 48 | 52 | 81 | 97 | 98 | 98 | 99 |
| 118 | 132 | 133 | 140 | 145 | 147 | 153 | 158 | 162 | 174 |
| 177 | 180 | 180 | 187 | 188 | | | | | |

| **Young Adults** | | | | | | | | | |
|------|------|------|------|------|------|------|------|------|------|
| 81 | 107 | 113 | 147 | 147 | 175 | 183 | 192 | 202 | 209 |
| 233 | 251 | 254 | 266 | 283 | 284 | 284 | 316 | 372 | 401 |
| 417 | 423 | 490 | 500 | 507 | 518 | 550 | 557 | 590 | 594 |

**a.** Find the median and the first and third quartiles for the number of CDs owned by senior citizens. Develop a box plot for the information.
**b.** Find the median and the first and third quartiles for the number of CDs owned by young adults. Develop a box plot for the information.
**c.** Compare the number of CDs owned by the two groups.

**37.** The corporate headquarters of *Bank.com*, a new Internet company that performs all banking transactions via the Internet, is located in downtown Philadelphia. The director of human resources is making a study of the time it takes employees to get to work. The city is planning to offer incentives to each downtown employer if they will encourage their employees to use public transportation. Below is a listing of the time to get to work this morning according to whether the employee used public transportation or drove a car.

| **Public Transportation** | | | | | | | | | |
|------|------|------|------|------|------|------|------|------|------|
| 23 | 25 | 25 | 30 | 31 | 31 | 32 | 33 | 35 | 36 |
| 37 | 42 | | | | | | | | |

| **Private** | | | | | | | | | |
|------|------|------|------|------|------|------|------|------|------|
| 32 | 32 | 33 | 34 | 37 | 37 | 38 | 38 | 38 | 39 |
| 40 | 44 | | | | | | | | |

**a.** Find the median and the first and third quartiles for the time it took employees using public transportation. Develop a box plot for the information.
**b.** Find the median and the first and third quartiles for the time it took employees who drove their own vehicle. Develop a box plot for the information.
**c.** Compare the times of the two groups.

**38.** The following box plot shows the number of daily newspapers published in each state and the District of Columbia. Write a brief report summarizing the number published. Be sure to include information on the values of the first and third quartiles, the median, and whether there is any skewness. If there are any outliers, estimate their value.

Number of newspapers

**39.** The Walter Gogel Company is an industrial supplier of fasteners, tools, and springs. The amounts of their invoices vary widely, from less than $20.00 to over $400.00. During the month of January they sent out 80 invoices. Here is a box plot of these invoices. Write a brief report summarizing the amounts of their invoices. Be sure to include information on the values of the first and third quartiles, the median, and whether there is any skewness. If there are any outliers, approximate the value of these invoices.

Invoice amount

**40.** The National Muffler Company claims they will change your muffler in less than 30 minutes. An investigative reporter for WTOL Channel 11 monitored 30 consecutive muffler changes at the National outlet on Liberty Street. The number of minutes to perform changes is reported below.

| 44 | 12 | 22 | 31 | 26 | 22 | 30 | 26 | 18 | 28 | 12 |
| 40 | 17 | 13 | 14 | 17 | 25 | 29 | 15 | 30 | 10 | 28 |
| 16 | 33 | 24 | 20 | 29 | 34 | 23 | 13 |    |    |    |

**a.** Develop a box plot for the time to change a muffler.
**b.** Does the distribution show any outliers?
**c.** Summarize your findings in a brief report.

**41.** A major airline wanted some information on those enrolled in their "frequent flyer" program. A sample of 48 members resulted in the following number of miles flown last year, to the nearest 1,000 miles, by each participant.

| 22 | 29 | 32 | 38 | 39 | 41 | 42 | 43 | 43 | 43 | 44 | 44 |
| 45 | 45 | 46 | 46 | 46 | 47 | 50 | 51 | 52 | 54 | 54 | 55 |
| 56 | 57 | 58 | 59 | 60 | 61 | 61 | 63 | 63 | 64 | 64 | 67 |
| 69 | 70 | 70 | 70 | 71 | 71 | 72 | 73 | 74 | 76 | 78 | 88 |

**a.** Develop a box plot for the information.
**b.** Does the distribution show any outliers?
**c.** Summarize your findings in a brief report.

**42.** Listed below is the amount of commissions earned last month for the eight members of the sales staff at Best Electronics. Calculate the coefficient of skewness using both methods. *Hint:* Use of a spreadsheet will expedite the calculations.

| 980.9 | 1036.5 | 1099.5 | 1153.9 | 1409.0 | 1456.4 | 1718.4 | 1721.2 |

**43.** Listed below is the number of car thefts in a large city over the last week. Calculate the coefficient of skewness using both methods. *Hint:* Use of a spreadsheet will expedite the calculations.

| 3 | 12 | 13 | 7 | 8 | 3 | 8 |
|---|----|----|---|---|---|---|

**44.** The manager of Information Services at Wilkin Investigations, a private investigation firm, is studying the relationship between the age (in months) of a combination printer, copy, and fax machine and its monthly maintenance cost. For a sample of 15 machines the manager developed the following chart. What can the manager conclude about the relationship between the variables?

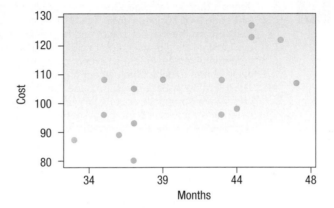

**45.** An auto insurance company reported the following information regarding the age of a driver and the number of accidents reported last year. Develop a scatter diagram for the data and write a brief summary.

| Age | Accidents |
|-----|-----------|
| 16  | 4         |
| 24  | 2         |
| 18  | 5         |
| 17  | 4         |
| 23  | 0         |
| 27  | 1         |
| 32  | 1         |
| 22  | 3         |

**46.** Wendy's offers eight different condiments (mustard, catsup, onion, mayonnaise, pickle, lettuce, tomato, and relish) on hamburgers. A store manager collected the following information on the number of condiments ordered and the age group of the customer. What can you conclude regarding the information? Who tends to order the most or least number of condiments?

| Number of condiments | Age | | | |
|----------------------|----------|-------------|-------------|-------------|
|                      | Under 18 | 18 up to 40 | 40 up to 60 | 60 or older |
| 0                    | 12       | 18          | 24          | 52          |
| 1                    | 21       | 76          | 50          | 30          |
| 2                    | 39       | 52          | 40          | 12          |
| 3 or more            | 71       | 87          | 47          | 28          |

**47.** A nationwide poll of adults asked if they favor gun control, oppose it, or have no opinion, as well as their preferred political party. The results are reported in the following table.

| Party Affiliation | Opinion on Gun Control | | | Total |
| | Favor | Oppose | No Opinion | |
| --- | --- | --- | --- | --- |
| Democrat | 88 | 96 | 36 | 220 |
| Republican | 64 | 96 | 20 | 180 |
| Total | 152 | 192 | 56 | 400 |

Analyze the information in the table. Who is more likely to favor gun control?

# exercises.com

**48.** Refer to Exercise 82 on page 91, which suggests websites to find information on the Dow Jones Industrial Average. One of the websites suggested is Bloomberg, which is an excellent source of business data. The Bloomberg website is: http://bloomberg.com. Click on **Markets** on the tool bar select and then select **Stocks in the Dow.** You should now have available a listing of the current selling price of the 30 stocks that make up the Dow Jones Industrial Average. Find the percent change from yesterday for each of the 30 stocks. Develop charts to depict the percent change.

**49.** The following website gives the Super Bowl results since the game was first played in 1967: http://www.superbowl.com/history/recaps. Download the scores for each Super Bowl and determine the winning margin. What was the typical margin? What are the first and third quartiles? Are there any games that were outliers?

# Dataset Exercises

**50.** Refer to the Real Estate Data, which reports information on homes sold in the Denver, Colorado, area last year. Select the variable selling price.
   **a.** Develop a box plot. Estimate the first and the third quartiles. Are there any outliers?
   **b.** Develop a scatter diagram with price on the vertical axis and the size of the home on the horizontal. Does there seem to be a relationship between these variables? Is the relationship direct or inverse?
   **c.** Develop a scatter diagram with price on the vertical axis and distance from the center of the city on the horizontal axis. Does there seem to be a relationship between these variables? Is the relationship direct or inverse?

**51.** Refer to the Baseball 2002 data, which reports information on the 30 major league baseball teams for the 2002 season.
   **a.** Select the variable that refers to the year in which the stadium was built. (*Hint:* Subtract the year in which the stadium was built from the current year to find the age of the stadium and work with this variable.) Develop a box plot. Are there any outliers?
   **b.** Select the variable team salary and draw a box plot. Are there any outliers? What are the quartiles? Write a brief summary of your analysis. How do the salaries of the New York Yankees and the Montreal Expos compare with the other teams?
   **c.** Draw a scatter diagram with the number of games won on the vertical axis and the team salary on the horizontal axis. What are your conclusions?
   **d.** Select the variable wins. Draw a dot plot. What can you conclude from this plot?

**52.** Refer to the Wage data, which reports information on annual wages for a sample of 100 workers. Also included are variables relating to industry, years of education, and gender for each worker.
   **a.** Develop a stem-and-leaf chart for the variable annual wage. Are there any outliers? Write a brief summary of your findings.
   **b.** Develop a stem-and-leaf chart for the variable years of education. Are there any outliers? Write a brief summary of your findings.
   **c.** Draw a bar chart of the variable occupation. Write a brief report summarizing your findings.

**53.** Refer to the CIA data, which reports demographic and economic information on 46 countries.
   **a.** Select the variable life expectancy. Develop a box plot. Find the first and third quartiles. Are there any outliers? Is the distribution skewed or symmetric? Write a paragraph summarizing your findings.
   **b.** Select the variable GDP/cap. Develop a box plot. Find the first and third quartiles. Are there any outliers? Is the distribution skewed or symmetric? Write a paragraph summarizing your findings.
   **c.** Develop a stem-and-leaf chart for the variable referring to the number of cell phones. Summarize your findings.

# Software Commands

1. The MINITAB commands for the dot plot on page 98 are:
   a. Enter the vehicles sold at Smith Ford Mercury Jeep in column C1 and Brophy Honda Volkswagen in C2. Name the variables accordingly.
   b. Select **Graph** and **Dot Plot**. In the first dialog box select **Simple** in the upper left corner and click **OK**. In the next dialog box select **Smith** and **Brophy** as the variables to **Graph**, click on **Labels** and write an appropriate title, click on **Multiple Graphs**, select **Options** and select the option **In separate panels on the same page** and click **OK** in the various dialog boxes.
   c. To calculate the descriptive statistics shown in the output select **Stat**, **Basic statistics**, and then **Display Descriptive statistics**. In the dialog box select Smith and Brophy as the **Variables**, click on **Statistics** and select the desired statistics to be output, and finally click **OK** twice.

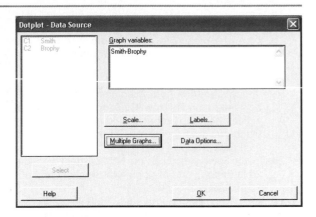

2. The MINITAB commands for the stem-and-leaf display on page 101 are:
   a. Import the data from the CD. The file name is **Table4–1**.
   b. Select **Graph**, and click on **Stem-and-Leaf**.
   c. Select the variable **Spots**, enter *10* for the **Increment**, and then click OK.

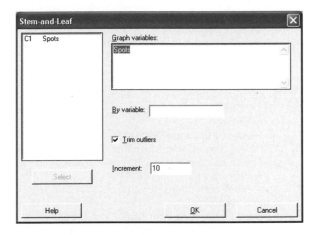

3. The MINITAB commands for the descriptive summary on page 107 are:

   a. Import the Whitner Autoplex data from the CD. The file name is **Table2–1**. Select the variable Price.
   b. From the tool bar select **Stat**, **Basic Statistics**, and **Display Descriptive Statistics**. In the dialog box select **Price** as the **Variable,** in the lower right zclick on **Graphs**. In this box select **Graphs**, click on **Histogram of data, with normal curve**, and then click **OK** twice.

4. The Excel Commands for the descriptive statistics on page 107 are:
   a. From the CD retrieve the Whitner Autoplex data file, which is Table2–1.
   b. From the menu bar select **Tools**, and the **Data Analysis**. Select **Descriptive Statistics** and then click **OK.**
   c. For the **Input Range**, type *B1:B81*, indicate that the data are grouped by column and that the labels are in the first row. Click on **Output Range**, indicate that the output should go into D1 (or any place you wish), click on **Summary Statistics**, then click **OK.**
   d. In the lower left click on **Kth Largest** and put *20* in the box and click on **Kth Smallest** and put *20* in that box.
   e. After you get your results, double-check the count in the output to be sure it contains the correct number of values.

5. The MINITAB commands for the box plot on page 110 are:
   a. Import the data from the CD. The file name is Table2–1.
   b. Select **Graph** and then **Boxplot**. In the dialog box select **Simple** in the upper left corner and click **OK**. Select **Price** as the **Graph variable**, click on **Labels** and include an appropriate heading, and then click **OK**.

6. The MINITAB commands for the descriptive summary on page 117 are:
   a. Retrieve the data from **Table4–1** on the **CD**.
   b. Select **Stat**, **Basic Statistics**, and then click on **Graphical Summary**. Select **Earnings** as the variable, and then click **OK**.

7. The Excel commands for the scatter diagram on page 119 are:
   a. Retrieve the data from **Table2–1** on the **CD**.
   b. You will need to copy the variables to other columns on the spreadsheet with age in a column and price in the next column. This will allow you to place price on the vertical axis and age on the horizontal axis.
   c. Click on **Chart Wizard**, select **XY (Scatter)** and the sub-type in the top left, and then click on next.
   d. Select or highlight the variables age followed by price.
   e. Type in a title for the chart and a name for the two variables. In the final dialog box select a location for the charts.

# Chapter 4 Answers to Self-Review

**4–1** **1. a.** 79, 105
     **b.** 15
     **c.** Between 89 and 91 accounts for 33 stores and 93 and 95 for 34 stores.

    **2.**

| 7 | 7 |
|---|---|
| 8 | 0013488 |
| 9 | 1256689 |
| 10 | 1248 |
| 11 | 26 |

     **a.** 8
     **b.** 10.1, 10.2, 10.4, 10.8
     **c.** 9.5
     **d.** 7.7, 11.6

**4–2** **a.** 7.9
    **b.** $Q_1 = 7.76$, $Q_3 = 8.015$

**4–3** The smallest value is 10 and the largest 85; the first quartile is 25 and the third 60. About 50 percent of the values are between 25 and 60. The median value is 40. The distribution is positively skewed.

**4–4** *CV* for mechanical is 5 percent, found by (10/200)(100). For finger dexterity *CV* is 20 percent, found by (6/30)(100). Thus, relative dispersion in finger dexterity scores is greater than relative dispersion in mechanical, because 20 percent is greater than 5 percent.

**4–5** **a.** $\bar{X} = \dfrac{407}{5} = 81.4$, Median = 84

     $s = \sqrt{\dfrac{923.2}{5-1}} = 15.19$

    **b.** $sk = \dfrac{3(81.4 - 84.0)}{15.19} = -0.51$

**c.**

| $X$ | $\dfrac{X - \bar{X}}{s}$ | $\left[\dfrac{(X - \bar{X})^3}{s}\right]$ |
|---|---|---|
| 73 | −0.5530 | −0.1691 |
| 98 | 1.0928 | 1.3051 |
| 60 | −1.4088 | −2.7962 |
| 92 | 0.6978 | 0.3398 |
| 84 | 0.1712 | 0.0050 |
| | | −1.3154 |

$$sk = \frac{5}{(4)(3)}[-1.3154]$$
$$= -0.5481$$

**d.** The distribution is somewhat negatively skewed.

**4–6** **a.** Scatter diagram
    **b.** 16
    **c.** $7,500
    **d.** Strong and positive

# A Review of Chapters 1–4

This section is a review of the major concepts and terms introduced in Chapters 1–4. Chapter 1 began by describing the meaning and purpose of statistics. Next we described the different types of variables and the four levels of measurement. Chapter 2 was concerned with describing a set of observations by organizing it into a frequency distribution and then portraying the frequency distribution as a histogram or a frequency polygon. Chapter 3 began by describing measures of location, such as the mean, weighted mean, median, geometric mean, and mode. This chapter also included measures of dispersion, or spread. Discussed in this section were the range, mean deviation, variance, and standard deviation. Chapter 4 included several graphing techniques such as dot plots, box plots, and scatter diagrams. We also discussed the coefficient of skewness, which reports the lack of symmetry in a set of data.

Throughout this section we stressed the importance of statistical software, such as Excel and MINITAB. Many computer outputs in these chapters demonstrated how quickly and effectively a large dataset can be organized into a frequency distribution, several of the measures of location or measures or variation calculated, and the information presented in graphical form.

## Glossary

### Chapter 1

**Descriptive statistics**   The techniques used to describe the important characteristics of a set of data. These may include organizing the values into a frequency distribution and computing measures of location and measures of dispersion and skewness.

**Exhaustive**   Each observation must fall into one of the categories.

**Inferential statistics,** also called **statistical inference** or **inductive statistics**   This facet of statistics deals with estimating a population parameter-based on a sample statistic. For example, if 2 out of the 10 hand calculators sampled are defective, we might infer that 20 percent of the production is defective.

**Interval measurement**   If one observation is greater than another by a certain amount, and the zero point is arbitrary, the measurement is on an interval scale. For example, the difference between temperatures of 70 degrees and 80 degrees is 10 degrees. Likewise, a temperature of 90 degrees is 10 degrees more than a temperature of 80 degrees, and so on.

**Mutually exclusive**   A property of a set of categories such that an individual, object, or measurement is included in only one category.

**Nominal measurement**   The "lowest" level of measurement. If data are classified into categories and the order of those categories is not important, it is the nominal level of measurement. Examples are gender (male, female) and political affiliation (Republican, Democrat, Independent, all others). If it makes no difference whether male or female is listed first, the data are nominal level.

**Ordinal measurement**   Data that can be logically ranked are referred to as ordinal measures. For example, consumer response to the sound of a new speaker might be excellent, very good, fair, or poor.

**Population**   The collection, or set, of all individuals, objects, or measurements whose properties are being studied.

**Ratio measurement**   If the distances between numbers are of a known constant size and *there is a true zero point,* and the ratio of two values is meaningful, the measurement is ratio scale. For example, the distance between $200 and $300 is $100, and in the case of money there is a true zero point. If you have zero dollars, there is an absence of money (you have none). Also the ratio between $200 and $300 is meaningful.

**Sample**   A portion, or subset, of the population being studied.

**Statistics**   The science of collecting, organizing, analyzing, and interpreting numerical data for the purpose of making more effective decisions.

### Chapter 2

**Charts**   Special graphical formats used to portray a frequency distribution, including histograms, frequency polygons, and cumulative frequency polygons. Other graphical devices used to portray data are line charts, bar charts, and pie charts. They are very useful, for example, for depicting the trend in long-term debt or percent changes in profit from last year to this year.

**Class**   The interval in which the data are tallied. For example, $4 up to $7 is a class; $7 up to $11 is another class.

**Class frequency**   The number of observations in each class. If there are 16 observations in the "$4 up to $6" class, 16 is the class frequency.

**Frequency distribution**   A grouping of data into classes showing the number of observations in each of the mutually exclusive classes. For example, data are organized into classes such as $1,000 up to $2,000, $2,000 up to $3,000, and so on to summarize the information.

**Histogram**   A graphical display of a frequency or relative frequency distribution. The horizontal axis shows the classes. The vertical height of adjacent bars shows the frequency or relative frequency of each class.

**Midpoint**   The value that divides the class into two equal parts. For the classes $10 up to $20 and $20 up to $30, the midpoints are $15 and $25, respectively.

**Relative frequency distribution**   A frequency distribution that shows the fraction or proportion of the total observations in each class.

## Chapter 3

**Arithmetic mean**   The sum of the values divided by the number of values. The symbol for the mean of a sample is $\bar{X}$ and the symbol for a population mean is $\mu$.

**Dispersion or spread**   A measure of central location pinpoints a single value that is typical of the data. A measure of dispersion indicates how close or far apart the values are from the mean or other measure of central tendency.

**Geometric mean**   The $n$th root of the product of all the values. It is especially useful for averaging rates of change and index numbers. It minimizes the importance of extreme values. A second use of the geometric mean is to find the mean annual percent change over a period of time. For example, if gross sales were $245 million in 1985 and $692 million in 2000, what is the average annual percent increase?

**Mean deviation**   The mean of the deviations from the mean, disregarding signs. It is abbreviated as *MD*.

**Measure of dispersion**   A number that shows the spread of a data set. The range, variance, and standard deviation are measures of dispersion.

**Measure of location**   A number that pinpoints a single value that is typical of the data. It pinpoints the center of a distribution. The arithmetic mean, weighted mean, median, mode, and geometric mean are measures of central location.

**Median**   The value of the middle observation after all the observations have been arranged from low to high. For example, if observations 6, 9, 4 are rearranged to read 4, 6, 9, the middle value is 6, the median.

**Mode**   The value that appears most frequently in a set of data. For grouped data, it is the *midpoint* of the class containing the largest number of values.

**Range**   A measure of dispersion computed as the maximum value minus the minimum value.

**Standard deviation**   The square root of the variance.

**Variance**   A measure of dispersion based on the average squared differences from the arithmetic mean.

**Weighted mean**   Each value is weighted according to its relative importance. For example, if 5 shirts cost $10 each and 20 shirts cost $8 each, the weighted mean price is $8.40: $[(5 \times \$10) + (20 \times \$8)]/25 = \$210/25 = \$8.40$.

## Chapter 4

**Box plot**   A graphic display that shows the general shape of a variable's distribution. It is based on five descriptive statistics: the maximum and minimum values, the first and third quartiles, and the median.

**Coefficient of skewness**   A measure of the lack of symmetry in a distribution. For a symmetric distribution there is no skewness, so the coefficient of skewness is zero. Otherwise, it is either positive or negative, with the limits of $\pm 3.0$.

**Coefficient of variation**   The standard deviation divided by the mean, expressed as a percent. It is especially useful for comparing the relative dispersion in two or more sets of data where (1) they are in different units or (2) one mean is much larger than the other mean.

**Contingency table**   A table used to classify observations according to two or more nominal characteristics.

**Deciles**   Values of an ordered (minimum to maximum) data set that divide the data into ten intervals of approximately equal frequencies.

**Dot plot**   A dot plot summarizes the distribution of one variable by stacking dots at points on a number line that shows the values of the variable. A dot plot uses all values.

**Interquartile range**   The absolute numerical difference between the first and third quartiles. Fifty percent of a distribution's values occur in this range.

**Percentiles**   Values of an ordered (minimum to maximum) dataset that divide the data into one hundred intervals of approximately equal frequencies.

**Quartiles**   Values of an ordered (minimum to maximum) dataset that divide the data into four intervals of approximately equal frequencies.

**Scatter diagram**   Graphical technique used to show the relationship between two variables measured with interval or ratio scales.

**Stem and leaf display**   A method to display a variable's distribution using every value. Values are classified by the data's leading digit. For example, if a dataset contains values between 13 and 84, eight classes based on the 10s digit would be used for the stems. The 1s digits would be the leaves.

## Exercises

### Part I—Multiple Choice

1. Employees who completed a training course were asked to rate it as either outstanding, very good, good, fair, or poor. The level of measurement is
   a. Nominal
   b. Ordinal
   c. Interval
   d. Ratio
2. A sample of new college graduates shows their mean starting salary is $29,000. $29,000 represents
   a. The population mean
   b. The sample median
   c. The sample mean
   d. The population mode

3. A sample of new college graduates shows that the standard deviation of their starting salary is $5,000. $5,000 represents
   a. The range of the starting salaries
   b. The variance
   c. 95% of all starting salaries
   d. The dispersion of starting salary around the mean
4. A useful measure to compare the relative dispersion in two or more distributions, if they are in different units, is the
   a. Coefficient of skewness
   b. Coefficient of variation
   c. Range
   d. Standard deviation
5. For a set of observations we have the following information: mean = 100, median = 100, mode = 100, and standard deviation = 4. The distribution is
   a. Symmetric
   b. Positively skewed
   c. Negatively skewed
   d. Nominal
6. For a set of observations we have the following information: mean = 100, median = 100, mode = 100, and standard deviation = 4. About 95 percent of the values lie between
   a. 92 and 108
   b. 96 and 104
   c. ±4
   d. 95 and 105
7. Fine Furniture Products, Inc. produced 2,460 desks in 1993 and 6,520 in 2003. To find the average annual percent increase in production, which statistic should be used?
   a. Arithmetic mean
   b. Median
   c. Mode
   d. Geometric mean

Refer to the following graph to answer questions 8 through 10.

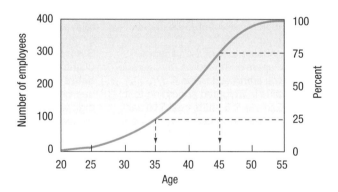

8. The graph is called a
   a. Frequency distribution
   b. Cumulative frequency distribution
   c. Frequency polygon
   d. Histogram
9. The interquartile range is
   a. 5
   b. 10
   c. 15
   d. 35
10. Which of the following statements is true?
    a. About 300 employees are younger than 30.
    b. 25 percent of the employees are older than 45.
    c. The interquartile range represents 60 percent of the employees.
    d. 75 percent of the employees are younger than 35.

11. A graph that shows the relationship between two interval or ratio variables is called a
    a. Scatter diagram
    b. Box plot
    c. Dot plot
    d. Stem-and-leaf display
12. A summary of data measured with two nominal variables is called
    a. Scatter diagram
    b. Contingency table
    c. Frequency distribution
    d. Histogram

## Part II—Problems
The answers to the odd-numbered exercises are at the end of the book.

13. A small number of employees were selected from all the employees at NED Electronics and their hourly rates recorded. The rates were: $9.50, $9.00, $11.70, $14.80, and $13.00.
    a. Are the hourly rates a sample or a population?
    b. What is the level of measurement?
    c. What is the arithmetic mean hourly rate?
    d. What is the median hourly rate? Interpret.
    e. What is the variance?
    f. What is the coefficient of skewness? Interpret.
14. The weekly overtime hours worked by all the employees at the Publix Market are: 1, 4, 6, 12, 5, and 2.
    a. Is this a sample or a population?
    b. What is the mean number of overtime hours worked?
    c. What is the median? Interpret.
    d. What is the mode?
    e. What is the mean deviation?
    f. What is the standard deviation?
    g. What is the coefficient of variation?
15. The Tourist Bureau of St. Thomas surveyed a sample of tourists as they left to return to the United States. One of the questions was: How many rolls of film did you expose when visiting our island? The responses were:

| 8 | 6 | 3 | 11 | 14 | 8 | 9 | 16 | 9 | 10 |
|---|---|---|----|----|----|---|----|----|---|
| 5 | 11 | 7 | 8 | 8 | 10 | 9 | 12 | 13 | 9 |

    a. Using five classes, organize the sample data into a frequency distribution.
    b. Portray the distribution in the form of a frequency polygon.
    c. What is the mean number of rolls exposed? Use the actual raw data.
    d. What is the median? Use the actual raw data.
    e. What is the mode? Use the actual raw data.
    f. What is the range? Use the actual raw data.
    g. What is the sample variance? Use the actual raw data.
    h. What is the sample standard deviation? Use the actual raw data.
    i. Assuming that the distribution is symmetrical and bell-shaped, about 95 percent of the tourists exposed between _____ and _____ rolls.
16. The annual amounts spent on research and development for a sample of electronic component manufacturers are (in $ millions):

| 8 | 34 | 15 | 24 | 15 | 28 | 12 | 20 | 22 | 23 |
|---|----|----|----|----|----|----|----|----|----|
| 14 | 26 | 18 | 23 | 10 | 21 | 16 | 17 | 22 | 31 |
| 13 | 25 | 20 | 28 | 6 | 20 | 19 | 27 | 16 | 22 |

    a. What is the level of measurement?
    b. Using six classes, organize the expenditures into a frequency distribution.
    c. Portray the distribution in the form of a histogram.
    d. Portray the distribution in the form of a cumulative frequency distribution.

**e.** Based on the cumulative frequency distribution, what is the *estimated* median amount spent on research and development? Interpret.

**f.** What is the mean amount spent on research and development?

**g.** Based on the cumulative frequency distribution, what is the interquartile range?

**17.** The rates of growth of Bardeen Chemicals for the past five years are 5.2 percent, 8.7 percent, 3.9 percent, 6.8 percent, and 19.5 percent.

**a.** What is the arithmetic mean annual growth rate?

**b.** What is the geometric mean annual growth rate?

**c.** Should the arithmetic mean or geometric mean be used to represent the average annual growth rate? Why?

**18.** The Currin Manufacturing Co. noted in its 2003 second-quarter report that as of June 30, 2003, notes payable amounted to $284.0 million. For the same date in 1993, they were $113.0 million. What is the geometric mean yearly percent increase (June to June) from June 1993 to June 2003?

**19.** BFI in its annual report revealed that working capital was (in billions) $4.4, $3.4, $3.0, $4.8, $7.8, and $8.3 consecutively for the years 1998–2003. Present these figures in either a simple line chart or a simple bar chart.

**20.** Refer to the following diagram.

**a.** What is the graph called?

**b.** What are the median, and first and third quartile values?

**c.** Is the distribution positively skewed? Tell how you know.

**d.** Are there any outliers? If yes, estimate these values.

**e.** Can you determine the number of observations in the study?

**21.** A sample of the funds deposited in First Federal Savings Bank's MCA (miniature checking account) revealed the following amounts.

| | | | | | | | | | |
|---|---|---|---|---|---|---|---|---|---|
| $124 | $14 | $150 | $289 | $52 | $156 | $203 | $82 | $27 | $248 |
| 39 | 52 | 103 | 58 | 136 | 249 | 110 | 298 | 251 | 157 |
| 186 | 107 | 142 | 185 | 75 | 202 | 119 | 219 | 156 | 78 |
| 116 | 152 | 206 | 117 | 52 | 299 | 58 | 153 | 219 | 148 |
| 145 | 187 | 165 | 147 | 158 | 146 | 185 | 186 | 149 | 140 |

Using the preceding raw data and a statistical package (such as MINITAB):

**a.** Organize the data into a frequency distribution.

**b.** Calculate the mean, median, and other descriptive measures. Include a dot plot, stem-and-leaf display, and a box plot. You decide on the class interval.

**c.** Interpret the computer output; that is, describe the central tendency, spread, skewness, and other measures.

**22.** A sample of 12 homes sold last week in St. Paul, Minnesota, revealed the following information. Draw a scatter diagram. Can we conclude that as the size of the home (reported below in thousands of square feet) increases, the selling price (reported in $ thousands) also increases?

| Home Size (thousands of square feet) | Selling Price ($ thousands) | Home Size (thousands of square feet) | Selling Price ($ thousands) |
|---|---|---|---|
| 1.4 | 100 | 1.3 | 110 |
| 1.3 | 110 | 0.8 | 85 |
| 1.2 | 105 | 1.2 | 105 |
| 1.1 | 120 | 0.9 | 75 |
| 1.4 | 80 | 1.1 | 70 |
| 1.0 | 105 | 1.1 | 95 |

**23.** Between 1789 and 2003, 89 judges served as associate justices of the Supreme Court of the United States. Their lengths of service are given below. Analyze the data.
   **a.** What is the typical length of service?
   **b.** What is the variation in the lengths of service?
   **c.** Is the distribution skewed?
   **d.** Develop a stem-and-leaf chart.

| 8 | 1 | 20 | 5 | 9 | 0 | 13 | 15 | 30 | 3 | 30 | 16 | 18 | 23 | 33 |
|---|---|----|---|---|---|----|----|----|---|----|----|----|----|----|
| 20 | 2 | 31 | 14 | 32 | 4 | 28 | 14 | 18 | 27 | 5 | 23 | 5 | 8 | 23 |
| 18 | 28 | 14 | 34 | 10 | 21 | 9 | 33 | 6 | 7 | 20 | 11 | 5 | 20 | 15 |
| 10 | 2 | 16 | 13 | 26 | 29 | 19 | 3 | 4 | 5 | 26 | 4 | 10 | 26 | 22 |
| 5 | 15 | 16 | 7 | 16 | 15 | 6 | 34 | 19 | 23 | 36 | 9 | 1 | 13 | 6 |
| 13 | 17 | 7 | 16 | 33 | 5 | 23 | 31 | 2 | 3 | 24 | 24 | 15 | 14 | |

**24.** The per capita personal income by state (including the District of Columbia), in thousands of dollars, follows.
   **a.** Organize these data into a frequency distribution.
   **b.** What is a "typical" per capita income for a state?
   **c.** How much variation in the income data is there?
   **d.** Is the distribution symmetrical?
   **e.** Summarize your findings.

| 11.1 | 17.7 | 13.2 | 10.7 | 16.8 | 15.1 | 19.2 | 15.1 |
|------|------|------|------|------|------|------|------|
| 18.9 | 14.3 | 13.2 | 14.7 | 11.4 | 15.4 | 12.9 | 13.2 |
| 14.4 | 11.1 | 11.2 | 12.7 | 16.6 | 17.5 | 14.1 | 14.7 |
| 9.5 | 13.6 | 11.9 | 13.8 | 15.1 | 15.9 | 18.3 | 11.1 |
| 17.1 | 12.2 | 12.3 | 13.7 | 12.4 | 12.2 | 13.9 | 14.7 |
| 11.1 | 11.9 | 11.8 | 13.5 | 10.7 | 12.8 | 15.4 | 14.5 |
| 10.5 | 13.8 | 13.2 | | | | | |

**25.** Following are the ages when the 43 U.S. presidents began their terms in office. Organize the data into a stem-and-leaf chart. Also construct a dot plot. Determine a typical age at the time of inauguration. Comment on the variation in age.

| 57 | 61 | 57 | 57 | 58 | 57 | 61 | 54 | 68 | 51 |
|----|----|----|----|----|----|----|----|----|----|
| 49 | 64 | 50 | 48 | 65 | 52 | 56 | 46 | 54 | 49 |
| 50 | 47 | 55 | 55 | 54 | 42 | 51 | 56 | 55 | 51 |
| 54 | 51 | 60 | 62 | 43 | 55 | 56 | 61 | 52 | 69 |
| 65 | 46 | 54 | | | | | | | |

# Cases

## A. Century National Bank

*The following case will appear in the review sections. Assume that you work in the Planning Department of the Century National Bank and report to Ms. Lamberg. You will need to do some data analysis and prepare a short written report. Remember, Mr. Selig is the president of the bank, so you will want to ensure that your report is complete and accurate. A copy of the data appears in Appendix N.*

The Century National Bank has offices in several cities in the Midwest and the southeastern part of the United States. Mr. Dan Selig, president and CEO, would like to know the characteristics of his checking account customers. What is the balance of a typical customer?

How many other bank services do the checking account customers use? Do the customers use the ATM service and, if so, how often? What about debit cards? Who uses them, and how often are they used?

To better understand the customers, Mr. Selig asked Ms. Wendy Lamberg, Director of Planning, to select a sample of customers and prepare a report. To begin, she has appointed a team from her staff. You are the head of the team and responsible for preparing the report. You select a random sample of 60 customers. In addition to the balance in each account at the end of last month, you determine: (1) the number of ATM (automatic teller machine) transactions in the last month; (2) the number of other bank services (a savings account, a certificate of deposit, etc.) the customer uses; (3) whether the customer has a debit card (this is a relatively new bank service in which charges are made directly to the customer's account); and (4) whether or not interest is paid on the checking account. The sample includes customers from the branches in Cincinnati, Ohio; Atlanta, Georgia; Louisville, Kentucky; and Erie, Pennsylvania.

1. Develop a graph or table that portrays the checking balances. What is the balance of a typical customer? Do many customers have more than $2,000 in their accounts? Does it appear that there is a difference in the distribution of the accounts among the four branches? Around what value do the account balances tend to cluster?

2. Determine the mean and median of the checking account balances. Compare the mean and the median balances for the four branches. Is there a difference among the branches? Be sure to explain the difference between the mean and the median in your report.

3. Determine the range and the standard deviation of the checking account balances. What do the first and third quartiles show? Determine the coefficient of skewness and indicate what it shows. Because Mr. Selig does not deal with statistics daily, include a brief description and interpretation of the standard deviation and other measures.

## B. Wildcat Plumbing Supply, Inc.: Do We Have Gender Differences?

Wildcat Plumbing Supply has served the plumbing needs of Southwest Arizona for more than 40 years. The company was founded by Mr. Terrence St. Julian and is run today by his son Cory. The company has grown from a handful of employees to more than 500 today. Cory is concerned about several positions within the company where he has men and women doing essentially the same job but at different pay. To investigate, he collected the information below. Suppose you are a student intern in the Accounting Department and have been given the task to write a report summarizing the situation.

| Yearly Salary ($000) | Women | Men |
|---|---|---|
| Less than 30 | 2 | 0 |
| 30 up to 40 | 3 | 1 |
| 40 up to 50 | 17 | 4 |
| 50 up to 60 | 17 | 24 |
| 60 up to 70 | 8 | 21 |
| 70 up to 80 | 3 | 7 |
| 80 or more | 0 | 3 |

To kick off the project, Mr. Cory St. Julian held a meeting with his staff and you were invited. At this meeting it was suggested that you calculate several measures of location, draw charts, such as a cumulative frequency distribution, and determine the quartiles for both men and women. Develop the charts and write the report summarizing the yearly salaries of employees at Wildcat Plumbing Supply. Does it appear that there are pay differences based on gender?

## C. Kimble Products: Is There a Difference In the Commissions?

At the January national sales meeting, the CEO of Kimble Products was questioned extensively regarding the company policy for paying commissions to its sales representatives. The company sells sporting goods to two major markets. There are 40 sales representatives who call directly on large volume customers, such as the athletic departments at major colleges and universities and professional sports franchises. There are 30 sales representatives who represent the company to retail stores located in shopping malls and large discounters such as Kmart and Target.

Upon his return to corporate headquarters, the CEO asked the sales manager for a report comparing the commissions earned last year by the two parts of the sales team. The information is reported on the right. Write a brief report. Would you conclude that there is a difference? Be sure to include information in the report on both the central tendency and dispersion of the two groups.

**Commissions Earned by Sales Representatives Calling on Athletic Departments ($)**

| | | | | | | | | | |
|---|---|---|---|---|---|---|---|---|---|
| 354 | 87 | 1,676 | 1,187 | 69 | 3,202 | 680 | 39 | 1,683 | 1,106 |
| 883 | 3,140 | 299 | 2,197 | 175 | 159 | 1,105 | 434 | 615 | 149 |
| 1,168 | 278 | 579 | 7 | 357 | 252 | 1,602 | 2,321 | 4 | 392 |
| 416 | 427 | 1,738 | 526 | 13 | 1,604 | 249 | 557 | 635 | 527 |

**Commissions Earned by Sales Representatives Calling on Large Retailers ($)**

| | | | | | | | | | |
|---|---|---|---|---|---|---|---|---|---|
| 1,116 | 681 | 1,294 | 12 | 754 | 1,206 | 1,448 | 870 | 944 | 1,255 |
| 1,213 | 1,291 | 719 | 934 | 1,313 | 1,083 | 899 | 850 | 886 | 1,556 |
| 886 | 1,315 | 1,858 | 1,262 | 1,338 | 1,066 | 807 | 1,244 | 758 | 918 |

# A Survey of Probability Concepts

Wendy's offers a choice of eight condiments on its hamburger. How many different ways are there to enjoy your hamburger? (See Goal 3 and Exercise 73.)

# Introduction

The emphasis in Chapters 2, 3, and 4 is on descriptive statistics. In Chapter 2 we organize the prices of 80 vehicles sold last month at the Whitner Autoplex location of Auto USA into a frequency distribution. This frequency distribution shows the lowest and the highest selling prices and where the largest concentration of data occurs. In Chapter 3 we use measures of location and dispersion to locate a typical selling price and to examine the spread in the data. We describe the spread in the selling prices with such measures of dispersion as the range and the standard deviation. In Chapter 4 we develop charts and graphs, such as a scatter diagram, to further describe the data.

Descriptive statistics is concerned with summarizing data collected from past events. For example, we described the vehicle selling prices last month at Whitner Autoplex. We now turn to the second facet of statistics, namely, *computing the chance that something will occur in the future.* This facet of statistics is called **statistical inference** or **inferential statistics.**

Seldom does a decision maker have complete information from which to make a decision. For example:

- Toys and Things, a toy and puzzle manufacturer, recently developed a new game based on sports trivia. They want to know whether sports buffs will purchase the game. "Slam Dunk" and "Home Run" are two of the names under consideration. One way to minimize the risk of making a wrong decision is to hire a market research firm to take a sample of, say, 2,000 consumers from the population and ask each respondent for a reaction to the new game and its proposed titles. Using the sample results the company can estimate the proportion of the population that will purchase the game.
- The quality assurance department of a Bethlehem Steel mill must assure management that the quarter-inch wire being produced has an acceptable tensile strength. Obviously, not all the wire produced can be tested for tensile strength

because testing requires the wire to be stretched until it breaks—thus destroying it. So a random sample of 10 pieces is selected and tested. Based on the test results, all the wire produced is deemed to be either satisfactory or unsatisfactory.
- Other questions involving uncertainty are: Should the daytime drama *Days of Our Lives* be discontinued immediately? Will a newly developed mint-flavored cereal be profitable if marketed? Will Charles Linden be elected to county auditor in Batavia County?

Statistical inference deals with conclusions about a population based on a sample taken from that population. (The populations for the preceding illustrations are: all consumers who like sports trivia games, all the quarter-inch steel wire produced, all television viewers who watch soaps, all who purchase breakfast cereal, and so on.)

Because there is uncertainty in decision making, it is important that all the known risks involved be scientifically evaluated. Helpful in this evaluation is *probability theory,* which has often been referred to as the science of uncertainty. The use of probability theory allows the decision maker with only limited information to analyze the risks and minimize the gamble inherent, for example, in marketing a new product or accepting an incoming shipment possibly containing defective parts.

Because probability concepts are so important in the field of statistical inference (to be discussed starting with Chapter 8), this chapter introduces the basic language of probability, including such terms as *experiment, event, subjective probability,* and *addition* and *multiplication rules.*

# What Is a Probability?

No doubt you are familiar with terms such as *probability, chance,* and *likelihood.* They are often used interchangeably. The weather forecaster announces that there is a 70 percent chance of rain for Super Bowl Sunday. Based on a survey of consumers who tested a newly developed pickle with a banana taste, the probability is .03 that, if marketed, it will be a financial success. (This means that the chance of the banana-flavor pickle being accepted by the public is rather remote.) What is a probability? In general, it is a number that describes the chance that something will happen.

> **PROBABILITY** A value between zero and one, inclusive, describing the relative possibility (chance or likelihood) an event will occur.

A probability is frequently expressed as a decimal, such as .70, .27, or .50. However, it may be given as a fraction such as 7/10, 27/100, or 1/2. It can assume any number from 0 to 1, inclusive. If a company has only five sales regions, and each region's name or number is written on a slip of paper and the slips put in a hat, the probability of selecting one of the five regions is 1. The probability of selecting from the hat a slip of paper that reads "Pittsburgh Steelers" is 0. Thus, the probability of 1 represents something that is certain to happen, and the probability of 0 represents something that cannot happen.

The closer a probability is to 0, the more improbable it is the event will happen. The closer the probability is to 1, the more sure we are it will happen. The relationship is shown in the following diagram along with a few of our personal beliefs. You might, however, select a different probability for Slo Poke's chances to win the Kentucky Derby or for an increase in federal taxes.

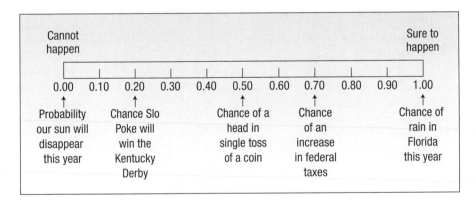

Three key words are used in the study of probability: **experiment, outcome,** and **event.** These terms are used in our everyday language, but in statistics they have specific meanings.

> **EXPERIMENT** A process that leads to the occurrence of one and only one of several possible observations.

This definition is more general than the one used in the physical sciences, where we picture someone manipulating test tubes or microscopes. In reference to probability, an experiment has two or more possible results, and it is uncertain which will occur.

> **OUTCOME** A particular result of an experiment.

For example, the tossing of a coin is an experiment. You may observe the toss of the coin, but you are unsure whether it will come up "heads" or "tails." Similarly, asking 500 college students whether they would purchase a new Dell computer system at a particular price is an experiment. If the coin is tossed, one particular outcome is a "head." The alternative outcome is a "tail." In the computer purchasing experiment, one possible outcome is that 273 students indicate they would purchase the computer. Another outcome is that 317 students would purchase the computer. Still another outcome is that 423 students indicate that they would purchase it. When one or more of the experiment's outcomes are observed, we call this an event.

> **EVENT**  A collection of one or more outcomes of an experiment.

Examples to clarify the definitions of the terms *experiment, outcome,* and *event* are presented in the following figure.

In the die-rolling experiment there are six possible outcomes, but there are many possible events. When counting the number of members of the board of directors for Fortune 500 companies over 60 years of age, the number of possible outcomes can be anywhere from zero to the total number of members. There are an even larger number of possible events in this experiment.

|  |  |  |
|---|---|---|
| Experiment | Roll a die | Count the number of members of the board of directors for Fortune 500 companies who are over 60 years of age |
| All possible outcomes | Observe a 1<br>Observe a 2<br>Observe a 3<br>Observe a 4<br>Observe a 5<br>Observe a 6 | None are over 60<br>One is over 60<br>Two are over 60<br>...<br>29 are over 60<br>...<br>...<br>48 are over 60<br>... |
| Some possible events | Observe an even number<br>Observe a number greater than 4<br>Observe a number 3 or less | More than 13 are over 60<br>Fewer than 20 are over 60 |

**Self-Review 5–1**

Video Games, Inc. recently developed a new video game. Its market potential is to be tested by 80 veteran game players.
(a)  What is the experiment?
(b)  What is one possible outcome?
(c)  Suppose 65 players tried the new game and said they liked it. Is 65 a probability?
(d)  The probability that the new game will be a success is computed to be −1.0. Comment.
(e)  Specify one possible event.

# Approaches to Assigning Probabilities

Two approaches to assigning probabilities will be discussed, namely, the *objective* and the *subjective* viewpoints. **Objective probability** is subdivided into (1) *classical probability* and (2) *empirical probability*.

## Classical Probability

**Classical probability** is based on the assumption that the outcomes of an experiment are *equally likely.* Using the classical viewpoint, the probability of an event happening is computed by dividing the number of favorable outcomes by the number of possible outcomes:

| DEFINITION OF CLASSICAL PROBABILITY | Probability of an event | $=\dfrac{\text{Number of favorable outcomes}}{\text{Total number of possible outcomes}}$ | [5–1] |
|---|---|---|---|

**EXAMPLE**

Consider an experiment of rolling a six-sided die. What is the probability of the event "an even number of spots appear face up"?

**SOLUTION**

The possible outcomes are:

There are three "favorable" outcomes (a two, a four, and a six) in the collection of six equally likely possible outcomes. Therefore:

$$\text{Probability of an even number} = \frac{3}{6} \begin{array}{l} \leftarrow \\ \leftarrow \end{array} \boxed{\begin{array}{l}\text{Number of favorable outcomes} \\ \text{Total number of possible outcomes}\end{array}}$$

$$= .5$$

The mutually exclusive concept appeared earlier in our study of frequency distributions in Chapter 2. Recall that we create classes so that a particular event is included in only one of the classes and there is no overlap between classes. Thus, only one of several events can occur at a particular time.

> **MUTUALLY EXCLUSIVE** The occurrence of one event means that none of the other events can occur at the same time.

The variable "gender" presents mutually exclusive outcomes, male and female. An employee selected at random is either male or female but cannot be both. A manufactured part is acceptable or unacceptable. The part cannot be both acceptable and unacceptable at the same time. In a sample of manufactured parts, the event of selecting an unacceptable part and the event of selecting an acceptable part are mutually exclusive.

If an experiment has a set of events that includes every possible outcome, such as the events "an even number" and "an odd number" in the die-tossing experiment, then the set of events is **collectively exhaustive.** For the die-tossing experiment, every outcome will be either even or odd. So the set is collectively exhaustive.

> **COLLECTIVELY EXHAUSTIVE** At least one of the events must occur when an experiment is conducted.

Sum of probabilities = 1

If the set of events is collectively exhaustive and the events are mutually exclusive, the sum of the probabilities is 1. Historically, the classical approach to probability was developed and applied in the 17th and 18th centuries to games of chance, such as cards and dice. It is unnecessary to do an experiment to determine the probability of an event occurring using the classical approach because the total number of outcomes is known before the experiment. The flip of a coin has two possible outcomes; the roll of a die has six possible outcomes. We can logically arrive at the probability of getting a tail on the toss of one coin or three heads on the toss of three coins.

The classical approach to probability can also be applied to lotteries. In South Carolina, one of the games of the Education Lottery is "Pick 3." A person buys a lottery ticket and selects three numbers between 0 and 9. Once per week, the three numbers are randomly selected from a machine that tumbles three containers each with balls numbered 0 through 9. One way to win is to match the numbers and the order of the numbers. Given that 1,000 possible outcomes exist (000 through 999), the probability of winning with any three-digit number is 0.001, or 1 in 1,000.

## Empirical Probability

Another way to define probability is based on **relative frequencies.** The probability of an event happening is determined by observing what fraction of the time similar events happened in the past. In terms of a formula:

$$\text{Probability of event happening} = \frac{\text{Number of times event occurred in past}}{\text{Total number of observations}}$$

The empirical concept is illustrated with the following example.

**EXAMPLE**

On February 1, 2003, the space shuttle Columbia exploded. This was the second disaster in 113 space missions for NASA. On the basis of this information, what is the probability that a future mission is successfully completed?

**SOLUTION**

To simplify, letters or numbers may be used. $P$ stands for probability, and in this case $P(A)$ stands for the probability a future mission is successfully completed.

$$\text{Probability of a successful flight} = \frac{\text{Number of successful flights}}{\text{Total number of flights}}$$

$$P(A) = \frac{111}{113} = .98$$

We can use this as an estimate of probability. In other words, based on past experience, the probability is .98 that a future space shuttle mission will be successfully completed.

# Subjective Probability

If there is little or no past experience or information on which to base a probability, it may be arrived at subjectively. Essentially, this means an individual evaluates the available opinions and other information and then estimates or assigns the probability. This probability is aptly called a **subjective probability.**

> **SUBJECTIVE CONCEPT OF PROBABILITY** The likelihood (probability) of a particular event happening that is assigned by an individual based on whatever information is available.

Illustrations of subjective probability are:

1. Estimating the likelihood the New England Patriots will play in the Super Bowl next year.
2. Estimating the probability General Motors Corp. will lose its number 1 ranking in total units sold to Ford Motor Co. or DaimlerChrysler within 2 years.
3. Estimating the likelihood you will earn an *A* in this course.

The types of probability are summarized in Chart 5–1. A probability statement always assigns a likelihood of an event that has not yet occurred. There is, of course, a considerable latitude in the degree of uncertainty that surrounds this probability, based primarily on the knowledge possessed by the individual concerning the underlying process. The individual possesses a great deal of knowledge about the toss of a die and can state that the probability that a one-spot will appear face up on the toss of a true die is one-sixth. But we know very little concerning the acceptance in the marketplace of a new and untested product. For example, even though a market research director tests a newly developed product in 40 retail stores and states that there is a 70 percent chance that the product will have sales of more than 1 million units, she still has little knowledge of how consumers will react when it is marketed nationally. In both cases (the case of the person rolling a die and the testing of a new product) the individual is assigning a probability value to an event of interest, and a difference exists only in the predictor's confidence in the precision of the estimate. However, regardless of the viewpoint, the same laws of probability (presented in the following sections) will be applied.

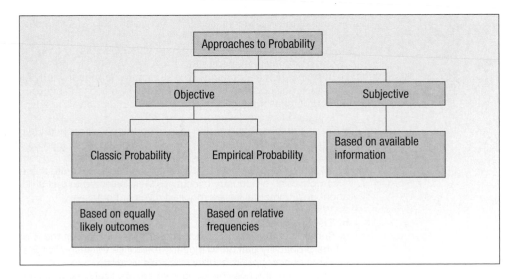

**CHART 5–1** Summary of Approaches to Probability

**Self-Review 5–2**

1. One card will be randomly selected from a standard 52-card deck. What is the probability the card will be a queen? Which approach to probability did you use to answer this question?
2. The Center for Child Care reports on the parental status of 539 children. There are 333 married, 182 divorced, and 24 widowed. What is the probability a particular child chosen at random will have a parent who is divorced? Which approach did you use?
3. What is the probability that the Dow Jones Industrial Average will exceed 12,000 during the next 12 months? Which approach to probability did you use to answer this question?

# Exercises

1. Some people are in favor of reducing federal taxes to increase consumer spending and others are against it. Two persons are selected and their opinions are recorded. List the possible outcomes.
2. A quality control inspector selects a part to be tested. The part is then declared acceptable, repairable, or scrapped. Then another part is tested. List the possible outcomes of this experiment regarding two parts.
3. A survey of 34 students at the Wall College of Business showed the following majors:

| | |
|---|---|
| Accounting | 10 |
| Finance | 5 |
| Info. Systems | 3 |
| Management | 6 |
| Marketing | 10 |

   Suppose you select a student and observe his or her major.
   a. What is the probability he or she is a management major?
   b. Which concept of probability did you use to make this estimate?
4. A large company that must hire a new president prepares a final list of five candidates, all of whom are qualified. Two of these candidates are members of a minority group. To avoid bias in the selection of the candidate, the company decides to select the president by lottery.
   a. What is the probability one of the minority candidates is hired?
   b. Which concept of probability did you use to make this estimate?
5. In each of the following cases, indicate whether classical, empirical, or subjective probability is used.
   a. A basketball player makes 30 out of 50 foul shots. The probability is .6 that she makes the next foul shot attempted.
   b. A seven-member committee of students is formed to study environmental issues. What is the likelihood that any one of the seven is chosen as the spokesperson?
   c. You purchase one of 5 million tickets sold for Lotto Canada. What is the likelihood you win the $1 million jackpot?
   d. The probability of an earthquake in northern California in the next 10 years is .80.
6. A firm will promote two employees out of a group of six men and three women.
   a. List the outcomes of this experiment if there is particular concern about gender equity.
   b. Which concept of probability would you use to estimate these probabilities?
7. A sample of 40 oil industry executives were selected to test a questionnaire. One question about environmental issues required a yes or no answer.
   a. What is the experiment?
   b. List one possible event.
   c. Ten of the 40 executives responded "yes." Based on these sample responses, what is the probability that an oil industry executive will respond "yes"?
   d. What concept of probability does this illustrate?
   e. Are each of the possible outcomes equally likely and mutually exclusive?

**8.** A sample of 2,000 licensed drivers revealed the following number of speeding violations.

| Number of Violations | Number of Drivers |
|---|---|
| 0 | 1,910 |
| 1 | 46 |
| 2 | 18 |
| 3 | 12 |
| 4 | 9 |
| 5 or more | 5 |
| Total | 2,000 |

    **a.** What is the experiment?
    **b.** List one possible event.
    **c.** What is the probability that a particular driver had exactly two speeding violations?
    **d.** What concept of probability does this illustrate?
**9.** Bank of America customers select their own three-digit personal identification number (PIN) for use at ATMs.
    **a.** Think of this as an experiment and list four possible outcomes.
    **b.** What is the probability Mr. Jones and Mrs. Smith select the same PIN?
    **c.** Which concept of probability did you use to answer b?
**10.** An investor buys 100 shares of AT&T stock and records its price change daily.
    **a.** List several possible events for this experiment.
    **b.** Estimate the probability for each event you described in a.
    **c.** Which concept of probability did you use in b?

# Some Rules for Computing Probabilities

Now that we have defined probability and described the different approaches to probability, we turn our attention to computing the probability of two or more events by applying rules of addition and multiplication.

## Rules of Addition

**Mutually exclusive events cannot both happen.**

**Special Rule of Addition**    To apply the **special rule of addition,** the events must be mutually exclusive. Recall that *mutually exclusive* means that when one event occurs, none of the other events can occur at the same time. An illustration of mutually exclusive events in the die-tossing experiment is the events "a number 4 or larger" and "a number 2 or smaller." If the outcome is in the first group {4, 5, and 6}, then it cannot also be in the second group {1 and 2}. Another illustration is a product coming off the assembly line cannot be defective and satisfactory at the same time.

    If two events *A* and *B* are mutually exclusive, the special rule of addition states that the probability of one *or* the other event's occurring equals the sum of their probabilities. This rule is expressed in the following formula:

| SPECIAL RULE OF ADDITION | $P(A \text{ or } B) = P(A) + P(B)$ | **[5–2]** |
|---|---|---|

For three mutually exclusive events designated *A, B,* and *C,* the rule is written:

$$P(A \text{ or } B \text{ or } C) = P(A) + P(B) + P(C)$$

An example will help to show the details.

148        Chapter 5

**EXAMPLE**

An automatic Shaw machine fills plastic bags with a mixture of beans, broccoli, and other vegetables. Most of the bags contain the correct weight, but because of the variation in the size of the beans and other vegetables, a package might be underweight or overweight. A check of 4,000 packages filled in the past month revealed:

| Weight | Event | Number of Packages | Probability of Occurrence | |
|---|---|---|---|---|
| Underweight | A | 100 | .025 | ← $\frac{100}{4,000}$ |
| Satisfactory | B | 3,600 | .900 | |
| Overweight | C | 300 | .075 | |
| | | 4,000 | 1.000 | |

What is the probability that a particular package will be either underweight or overweight?

**SOLUTION**

The outcome "underweight" is the event A. The outcome "overweight" is the event C. Applying the special rule of addition:

$$P(A \text{ or } C) = P(A) + P(C) = .025 + .075 = .10$$

Note that the events are mutually exclusive, meaning that a package of mixed vegetables cannot be underweight, satisfactory, and overweight at the same time. They are also collectively exhaustive; that is, a selected package must be either underweight, satisfactory, or overweight.

English logician J. Venn (1835–1888) developed a diagram to portray graphically the outcome of an experiment. The *mutually exclusive* concept and various other rules for combining probabilities can be illustrated using this device. To construct a Venn diagram, a space is first enclosed representing the total of all possible outcomes. This space is usually in the form of a rectangle. An event is then represented by a circular area which is drawn inside the rectangle proportional to the probability of the event. The following Venn diagram represents the *mutually exclusive* concept. There is no overlapping of events, meaning that the events are mutually exclusive.

*A Venn diagram is a useful tool to depict addition or multiplication rules.*

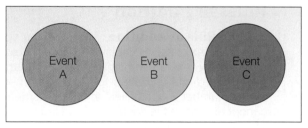

The probability that a bag of mixed vegetables selected is underweight, $P(A)$, plus the probability that it is not an underweight bag, written $P(\sim A)$ and read "not A," must logically equal 1. This is written:

$$P(A) + P(\sim A) = 1$$

This can be revised to read:

**COMPLEMENT RULE**        $P(A) = 1 - P(\sim A)$        [5–3]

This is the **complement rule.** It is used to determine the probability of an event occurring by subtracting the probability of the event not occurring from 1. This rule is useful because sometimes it is easier to calculate the probability of an event happening by determining the probability of it not happening and subtracting the result from

1. Notice that the events $A$ and $\sim A$ are mutually exclusive and collectively exhaustive. Therefore, the probabilities of $A$ and $\sim A$ sum to 1. A Venn diagram illustrating the complement rule is shown as:

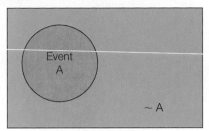

**EXAMPLE**

Recall the probability a bag of mixed vegetables is underweight is .025 and the probability of an overweight bag is .075. Use the complement rule to show the probability of a satisfactory bag is .900. Show the solution using a Venn diagram.

**SOLUTION**

The probability the bag is unsatisfactory equals the probability the bag is overweight plus the probability it is underweight. That is, $P(A \text{ or } C) = P(A) + P(C) = .025 + .075 = .100$. The bag is satisfactory if it is not underweight or overweight, so $P(B) = 1 - [P(A) + P(C)] = 1 - [.025 + .075] = 0.900$. The Venn diagram portraying this situation is:

**Self-Review 5–3**

A sample of employees of Worldwide Enterprises is to be surveyed about a new pension plan. The employees are classified as follows:

| Classification | Event | Number of Employees |
|----------------|-------|---------------------|
| Supervisors | $A$ | 120 |
| Maintenance | $B$ | 50 |
| Production | $C$ | 1,460 |
| Management | $D$ | 302 |
| Secretarial | $E$ | 68 |

(a) What is the probability that the first person selected is:
    (i) either in maintenance or a secretary?
    (ii) not in management?
(b) Draw a Venn diagram illustrating your answers to part (a).
(c) Are the events in part (a)(i) complementary or mutually exclusive or both?

**The General Rule of Addition** The outcomes of an experiment may not be mutually exclusive. Suppose, for illustration, that the Florida Tourist Commission selected

**Statistics in Action**

If you wish to get some attention at the next gathering you attend, announce that you believe that at least two people present were born on the same date—that is, the same day of the year but not necessarily the same year. If there are 30 people in the room, the probability of a duplicate is .706. If there are 60 people in the room, the probability is .994 that at least two people share the same birthday. With as few as 23 people the chances are even, that is .50, that at least two people share the same birthday. Hint: To compute this, find the probability everyone was born on a different day and use the complement rule.

a sample of 200 tourists who visited the state during the year. The survey revealed that 120 tourists went to Disney World and 100 went to Busch Gardens near Tampa. What is the probability that a person selected visited either Disney World or Busch Gardens? If the special rule of addition is used, the probability of selecting a tourist who went to Disney World is .60, found by 120/200. Similarly, the probability of a tourist going to Busch Gardens is .50. The sum of these probabilities is 1.10. We know, however, that this probability cannot be greater than 1. The explanation is that many tourists visited both attractions and are being counted twice! A check of the survey responses revealed that 60 out of 200 sampled did, in fact, visit both attractions.

To answer our question, "What is the probability a selected person visited either Disney World or Busch Gardens?" (1) add the probability that a tourist visited Disney World and the probability he/she visited Busch Gardens, and (2) subtract the probability of visiting both. Thus:

$$P(\text{Disney or Busch}) = P(\text{Disney}) + P(\text{Busch}) - P(\text{both Disney and Busch})$$

$$= .60 + .50 - .30 = .80$$

When two events both occur, the probability is called a **joint probability.** The probability that a tourist visits both attractions (.30) is an example of a joint probability.

The following Venn diagram shows two events that are not mutually exclusive. The two events overlap to illustrate the joint event that some people have visited both attractions.

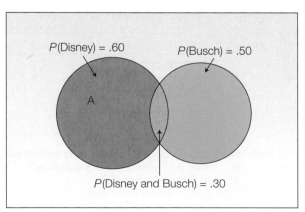

$P(\text{Disney}) = .60$

$P(\text{Busch}) = .50$

A

$P(\text{Disney and Busch}) = .30$

---

**JOINT PROBABILITY** A probability that measures the likelihood two or more events will happen concurrently.

This rule for two events designated *A* and *B* is written:

| GENERAL RULE OF ADDITION | $P(A \text{ or } B) = P(A) + P(B) - P(A \text{ and } B)$ | [5–4] |
|---|---|---|

For the expression $P(A \text{ or } B)$, the word *or* suggests that *A* may occur or *B* may occur. This also includes the possibility that *A* and *B* may occur. This use of *or* is sometimes called an **inclusive.** You could also write $P(A \text{ or } B \text{ or both})$ to emphasize that the union of the events includes the intersection of *A* and *B*.

If we compare the general and specific rules of addition, the important difference is determining if the events are mutually exclusive. If the events *are* mutually exclusive, then the joint probability $P(A \text{ and } B)$, is 0 and we could use the special rule of addition. Otherwise we must account for the joint probability and use the general rule of addition.

**EXAMPLE**

What is the probability that a card chosen at random from a standard deck of cards will be either a king or a heart?

**SOLUTION**

We may be inclined to add the probability of a king and the probability of a heart. But this creates a problem. If we do that, the king of hearts is counted with the kings and also with the hearts. So, if we simply add the probability of a king (there are 4 in a deck of 52 cards) to the probability of a heart (there are 13 in a deck of 52 cards) and report that 17 out of 52 cards meet the requirement, we have counted the king of hearts twice. We need to subtract 1 card from the 17 so the king of hearts is counted only once. Thus, there are 16 cards that are either hearts or kings. So the probability is $16/52 = .3077$.

| Card | Probability | | Explanation |
|---|---|---|---|
| King | $P(A)$ | $= 4/52$ | 4 kings in a deck of 52 cards |
| Heart | $P(B)$ | $= 13/52$ | 13 hearts in a deck of 52 cards |
| King of hearts | $P(A \text{ and } B) =$ | $1/52$ | 1 king of hearts in a deck of 52 cards |

From formula (5–4):

$$P(A \text{ or } B) = P(A) + P(B) - P(A \text{ and } B)$$

$$= 4/52 + 13/52 - 1/52$$

$$= 16/52, \text{ or } .3077$$

A Venn diagram portrays these outcomes, which are not mutually exclusive.

| Self-Review 5–4  | Routine physical examinations are conducted annually as part of a health service program for General Concrete, Inc., employees. It was discovered that 8 percent of the employees need corrective shoes, 15 percent need major dental work, and 3 percent need both corrective shoes and major dental work. <br> (a)   What is the probability that an employee selected at random will need either corrective shoes or major dental work? <br> (b)   Show this situation in the form of a Venn diagram. |
|---|---|

# Exercises

**11.** The events *A* and *B* are mutually exclusive. Suppose *P*(*A*) = .30 and *P*(*B*) = .20. What is the probability of either *A* or *B* occurring? What is the probability that neither *A* nor *B* will happen?

**12.** The events *X* and *Y* are mutually exclusive. Suppose *P*(*X*) = .05 and *P*(*Y*) = .02. What is the probability of either *X* or *Y* occurring? What is the probability that neither *X* nor *Y* will happen?

**13.** A study of 200 grocery chains revealed these incomes after taxes:

| Income after Taxes | Number of Firms |
|---|---|
| Under $1 million | 102 |
| $1 million to $20 million | 61 |
| $20 million or more | 37 |

  **a.** What is the probability a particular chain has under $1 million in income after taxes?

  **b.** What is the probability a grocery chain selected at random has either an income between $1 million and $20 million, or an income of $20 million or more? What rule of probability was applied?

**14.** The chair of the board of directors says, "There is a 50 percent chance this company will earn a profit, a 30 percent chance it will break even, and a 20 percent chance it will lose money next quarter."

  **a.** Use an addition rule to find the probability they will not lose money next quarter.

  **b.** Use the complement rule to find the probability they will not lose money next quarter.

**15.** Suppose the probability you will get a grade of A in this class is .25 and the probability you will get a B is .50. What is the probability your grade will be above a C?

**16.** Two coins are tossed. If *A* is the event "two heads" and *B* is the event "two tails," are *A* and *B* mutually exclusive? Are they complements?

**17.** The probabilities of the events *A* and *B* are .20 and .30, respectively. The probability that both *A* and *B* occur is .15. What is the probability of either *A* or *B* occurring?

**18.** Let *P*(*X*) = .55 and *P*(*Y*) = .35. Assume the probability that they both occur is .20. What is the probability of either *X* or *Y* occurring?

**19.** Suppose the two events *A* and *B* are mutually exclusive. What is the probability of their joint occurrence?

**20.** A student is taking two courses, history and math. The probability the student will pass the history course is .60, and the probability of passing the math course is .70. The probability of passing both is .50. What is the probability of passing at least one?

**21.** A survey of top executives revealed that 35 percent of them regularly read *Time* magazine, 20 percent read *Newsweek,* and 40 percent read *U.S. News and World Report.* Ten percent read both *Time* and *U.S. News and World Report.*

  **a.** What is the probability that a particular top executive reads either *Time* or *U.S. News and World Report* regularly?

  **b.** What is the probability .10 called?

  **c.** Are the events mutually exclusive? Explain.

**22.** A study by the National Park Service revealed that 50 percent of vacationers going to the Rocky Mountain region visit Yellowstone Park, 40 percent visit the Tetons, and 35 percent visit both.

  **a.** What is the probability a vacationer will visit at least one of these attractions?

  **b.** What is the probability .35 called?

  **c.** Are the events mutually exclusive? Explain.

# Rules of Multiplication

When we use the rules of addition we find the likelihood of combining two events. Venn diagrams illustrate this as the "union" of two events. In this section we find the likelihood that two events both happen. For example, a marketing firm may want to estimate the likelihood that a person is 21 years old or older *and* buys a Hummer. Venn diagrams illustrate this as the intersection of two events. To find the likelihood of two events happening we use the rules of multiplication. There are two rules of multiplication, the Special Rule and the General Rule.

**Special Rule of Multiplication**     The special rule of multiplication requires that two events *A* and *B* are independent. Two events are independent if the occurrence of one event does not alter the probability of the occurrence of the other event.

> **INDEPENDENCE** The occurrence of one event has no effect on the probability of the occurrence of another event.

One way to think about independence is to assume that events *A* and *B* occur at different times. For example, when event *B* occurs after event *A* occurs, does *A* have any effect on the likelihood that event *B* occurs? If the answer is no, then *A* and *B* are independent events. To illustrate independence, suppose two coins are tossed. The outcome of a coin toss (head or tail) is unaffected by the outcome of any other prior coin toss (head or tail).

For two independent events *A* and *B*, the probability that *A* and *B* will both occur is found by multiplying the two probabilities. This is the **special rule of multiplication** and is written symbolically as:

> **SPECIAL RULE OF MULTIPLICATION**     $P(A \text{ and } B) = P(A)P(B)$     **[5–5]**

For three independent events, *A*, *B*, and *C*, the special rule of multiplication used to determine the probability that all three events will occur is:

$$P(A \text{ and } B \text{ and } C) = P(A)P(B)P(C)$$

**EXAMPLE**

A survey by the American Automobile Association (AAA) revealed 60 percent of its members made airline reservations last year. Two members are selected at random. What is the probability both made airline reservations last year?

**SOLUTION**

The probability the first member made an airline reservation last year is .60, written $P(R_1) = .60$, where $R_1$ refers to the fact that the first member made a reservation. The probability that the second member selected made a reservation is also .60, so $P(R_2) = .60$. Since the number of AAA members is very large, you may assume that $R_1$ and $R_2$ are independent. Consequently, using formula (5–5), the probability they both make a reservation is .36, found by:

$$P(R_1 \text{ and } R_2) = P(R_1)P(R_2) = (.60)(.60) = .36$$

All possible outcomes can be shown as follows. *R* means a reservation is made, and *NR* means no reservation was made.

With the probabilities and the complement rule, we can compute the joint probability of each outcome. For example, the probability that neither member makes a reservation is .16. Further, the probability of the first or the second member (special addition rule) making a reservation is .48 (.24 + .24). You can also observe that the outcomes are mutually exclusive and collectively exhaustive. Therefore, the probabilities sum to 1.00.

| Outcomes | Joint Probability | |
|---|---|---|
| $R_1$  $R_2$ | (.60)(.60) = | .36 |
| $R_1$  NR | (.60)(.40) = | .24 |
| NR  $R_2$ | (.40)(.60) = | .24 |
| NR  NR | (.40)(.40) = | .16 |
| Total | | 1.00 |

**Self-Review 5–5**  From experience, Teton Tire knows the probability is .80 that their XB-70 will last 60,000 miles before it becomes bald or fails. An adjustment is made on any tire that does not last 60,000 miles. You purchase four XB-70s. What is the probability all four tires will last at least 60,000 miles?

If two events are not independent, they are referred to as **dependent.** To illustrate dependency, suppose there are 10 rolls of film in a box, and it is known that 3 are defective. A roll of film is selected from the box. The probability of selecting a defective roll is 3/10, and the probability of selecting a good roll is 7/10. Then a second roll is selected from the box without the first one being returned to the box. The probability this second roll is defective *depends* on whether the first roll selected was defective or good. The probability that the second roll is defective is:

   2/9, if the first roll was defective. (Only two defective rolls remain in the box containing nine rolls.)
   3/9, if the first roll selected as good. (All three defective rolls are still in the box containing nine rolls.)

The fraction 2/9 (or 3/9) is aptly called a **conditional probability** because its value is conditional on (dependent on) whether a defective or a good roll of film is chosen in the first selection from the box.

> **CONDITIONAL PROBABILITY**  The probability of a particular event occurring, given that another event has occurred.

**General Rule of Multiplication**   We use the general rule of multiplication to find the joint probability of two events when the events are not independent. For example, when event *B* occurs after event *A* occurs, and *A* has an effect on the likelihood that event *B* occurs, then *A* and *B* are not independent. To illustrate, suppose there are 10 rolls of film in a box, and it is known that 3 are defective. A roll of film is selected from the box. The probability of selecting a defective roll is 3/10, and the probability of selecting a good roll is 7/10. Then a second roll is selected from the box without returning the first one to the box. The probability that the second roll is defective is affected by the prior event that the first roll was defective or good. The probability that the second roll is defective is either:

   *P*(second roll is defective | first roll was defective) is 2/9. (Only two defective rolls remain in the box that now contains nine rolls.)
   *P*(second roll is defective | first roll was good) is 3/9. (All three defective rolls are still in the box that now contains nine rolls.)

The general rule of multiplication states that for two events, *A* and *B*, the joint probability that both events will happen is found by multiplying the probability event *A* will happen by the conditional probability of event *B* occurring given that *A* has occurred. Symbolically, the joint probability, *P*(A and B), is found by:

> **GENERAL RULE OF MULTIPLICATION**      $P(A \text{ and } B) = P(A)P(B|A)$      **[5–6]**

**EXAMPLE**

To illustrate the formula, let's use the problem with 10 rolls of film in a box, 3 of which are defective. Two rolls are to be selected, one after the other. What is the probability of selecting a defective roll followed by another defective roll?

**SOLUTION**

The first roll of film selected from the box being found defective is event $D_1$, $P(D_1) = 3/10$ because 3 out of the 10 are defective. The second roll selected being found defective is event $D_2$. Therefore, $P(D_2 \mid D_1) = 2/9$, because after the first selection was found to be defective, only 2 defective rolls of film remained in the box containing 9 rolls. Determining the probability of two defectives [see formula (5–6)]:

$$P(D_1 \text{ and } D_2) = P(D_1)P(D_2 \mid D_1) = \left(\frac{3}{10}\right)\left(\frac{2}{9}\right) = \frac{6}{90}, \text{ or about } .07$$

Incidentally, it is assumed that this experiment was conducted *without replacement*—that is, the first defective roll of film was not thrown back in the box before the next roll was selected. It should also be noted that the general rule of multiplication can be extended to more than two events. For three events, $A$, $B$, and $C$, the formula would be:

$$P(A \text{ and } B \text{ and } C) = P(A)P(B \mid A)P(C \mid A \text{ and } B)$$

For illustration, the probability the first three rolls chosen from the box will all be defective is .00833, found by:

$$P(D_1 \text{ and } D_2 \text{ and } D_3) = P(D_1)P(D_2 \mid D_1)P(D_3 \mid D_1 \text{ and } D_2)$$

$$= \left(\frac{3}{10}\right)\left(\frac{2}{9}\right)\left(\frac{1}{8}\right) = \frac{6}{720} = .00833$$

---

**Self-Review 5–6**

The board of directors of Tarbell Industries consists of eight men and four women. A four-member search committee is to be chosen at random to conduct a nationwide search for a new company president.
(a)   What is the probability all four members of the search committee will be women?
(b)   What is the probability all four members will be men?
(c)   Does the sum of the probabilities for the events described in parts (a) and (b) equal 1? Explain.

---

# Contingency Tables

Often we tally the results of a survey into a two-way table and use these results of this tally to determine various probabilities. We described this idea beginning on page 119 in Chapter 4. To review, we refer to a two-way table as a contingency table.

> **CONTINGENCY TABLE** A table used to classify sample observations according to two or more identifiable characteristics.

A contingency table is a cross tabulation that simultaneously summarizes two variables of interest and their relationship. The level of measurement can be nominal. Below are several examples.

- A survey of 150 adults classified each as to gender and the number of movies attended last month. Each respondent is classified according to two criteria—the number of movies attended and gender.

| Movies Attended | Gender | | Total |
|---|---|---|---|
| | Men | Women | |
| 0 | 20 | 40 | 60 |
| 1 | 40 | 30 | 70 |
| 2 or more | 10 | 10 | 20 |
| Total | 70 | 80 | 150 |

- The American Coffee Producers Association reports the following information on age and the amount of coffee consumed in a month.

| Age (Years) | Coffee Consumption | | | Total |
|---|---|---|---|---|
| | Low | Moderate | High | |
| Under 30 | 36 | 32 | 24 | 92 |
| 30 up to 40 | 18 | 30 | 27 | 75 |
| 40 up to 50 | 10 | 24 | 20 | 54 |
| 50 and over | 26 | 24 | 29 | 79 |
| Total | 90 | 110 | 100 | 300 |

According to this table each of the 300 respondents is classified according to two criteria: (1) age and (2) the amount of coffee consumed.

The following example shows how the rules of addition and multiplication are used when we employ contingency tables.

**EXAMPLE**

A sample of executives were surveyed about their loyalty to the company. One of the questions was, "If you were given an offer by another company equal to or slightly better than your present position, would you remain with the company or take the other position?" The responses of the 200 executives in the survey were cross-classified with their length of service with the company. (See Table 5–1.)

**TABLE 5–1** Loyalty of Executives and Length of Service with Company

| Loyalty | Length of Service | | | | Total |
|---|---|---|---|---|---|
| | Less than 1 Year $B_1$ | 1–5 Years $B_2$ | 6–10 Years $B_3$ | More than 10 Years $B_4$ | |
| Would remain, $A_1$ | 10 | 30 | 5 | 75 | 120 |
| Would not remain, $\sim A$ | 25 | 15 | 10 | 30 | 80 |
| | 35 | 45 | 15 | 105 | 200 |

What is the probability of randomly selecting an executive who is loyal to the company (would remain) and who has more than 10 years of service?

**SOLUTION**

Note that two events occur at the same time—the executive would remain with the company, and he or she has more than 10 years of service.

1. Event $A_1$ happens if a randomly selected executive will remain with the company despite an equal or slightly better offer from another company. To find the probability that event $A_1$ will happen, refer to Table 5–1. Note there are 120 executives out of the 200 in the survey who would remain with the company, so $P(A_1) = 120/200$, or .60.

2. Event $B_4$ happens if a randomly selected executive has more than 10 years of service with the company. Thus, $P(B_4|A_1)$ is the conditional probability that an executive with more than 10 years of service would remain with the company despite an equal or slightly better offer from another company. Referring to the contingency table, Table 5–1, 75 of the 120 executives who would remain have more than 10 years of service, so $P(B_4|A_1) = 75/120$.

Solving for the probability that an executive randomly selected will be one who would remain with the company and who has more than 10 years of service with the company, using the general rule of multiplication in formula (5–6), gives:

$$P(A_1 \text{ and } B_4) = P(A_1)P(B_4|A_1) = \left(\frac{120}{200}\right)\left(\frac{75}{120}\right) = \frac{9,000}{24,000} = .375$$

To find the probability of selecting an executive who would remain with the company *or* has less than 1 year of experience we use the general rule of addition, formula (5–4).

1. Event $A_1$ refers to executives that would remain with the company. So $P(A_1) = 120/200 = .60$.

2. Event $B_1$ refers to executives that have been with the company less than 1 year. The probability of $B_1$ is $P(B_1) = 35/200 = .175$.

3. The events $A_1$ and $B_1$ are not mutually exclusive. That is, an executive can both be willing to remain with the company and have less than 1 year of experience. We write this probability, which is called the joint probability, as $P(A_1 \text{ and } B_1)$. There are 10 executives who would both stay with the company and have less than 1 year of service, so $P(A_1 \text{ and } B_1) = 10/200 = .05$. These 10 people are in both groups, those who would remain with the company and those with less than 1 year with the company. They are actually being counted twice, so we need to subtract out this value.

4. We insert these values in formula (5–4) and the result is as follows.

$$P(A_1 \text{ or } B_1) = P(A_1) + P(B_1) - P(A_1 \text{ and } B_1)$$
$$= .60 + .175 - .05 = .725$$

So the likelihood that a selected executive would either remain with the company or has been with the company less than 1 year is .725.

---

**Self-Review 5–7**

Refer to Table 5–1 to find the following probabilities.
(a) What is the probability of selecting an executive with more than 10 years of service?
(b) What is the probability of selecting an executive who would not remain with the company, given that he or she has more than 10 years of service?
(c) What is the probability of selecting an executive with more than 10 years of service or one who would not remain with the company?

# Tree Diagrams

The **tree diagram** is a graph that is helpful in organizing calculations that involve several stages. Each segment in the tree is one stage of the problem. The branches of a tree diagram are weighted by probabilities. We will use the data in Table 5–1 to show the construction of a tree diagram.

*Steps in constructing a tree diagram*

1. To construct a tree diagram, we begin by drawing a heavy dot on the left to represent the root of the tree (see Chart 5–2).

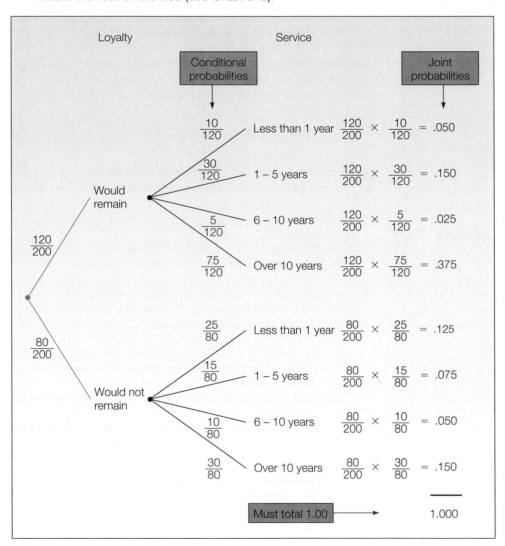

**Chart 5–2  Tree Diagram Showing Loyalty and Length of Service**

2. For this problem, two main branches go out from the root, the upper one representing "would remain" and the lower one "would not remain." Their probabilities are written on the branches, namely, 120/200 and 80/200. These probabilities could also be denoted $P(A)$ and $P(\sim A)$.

3. Four branches "grow" out of each of the two main branches. These branches represent the length of service—less than 1 year, 1–5 years, 6–10 years, and more than 10 years. The conditional probabilities for the upper branch of the tree, 10/120, 30/120, 5/120, and so on are written on the appropriate branches. These are $P(B_1|A_1)$, $P(B_2|A_1)$, $P(B_3|A_1)$, and $P(B_4|A_1)$, where $B_1$ refers to less than 1 year of service, $B_2$ 1 to 5 years, $B_3$ 6 to 10 years, and $B_4$ more than 10 years. Next, write the conditional probabilities for the lower branch.

4. Finally, joint probabilities, that the events $A_1$ and $B_i$ or the events $\sim A$ and $B_i$ will occur together, are shown on the right side. For example, the joint probability of randomly selecting an executive who would remain with the company and who has less than 1 year of service, from formula (5–6), is:

$$P(A_1 \text{ and } B_1) = P(A_1)P(B_1|A_1) = \left(\frac{120}{200}\right)\left(\frac{10}{120}\right) = .05$$

Because the joint probabilities represent all possible outcomes (would remain, 6–10 years service; would not remain, more than 10 years of service; etc.), they must sum to 1.00 (see Chart 5–2).

---

**Self-Review 5–8**

Consumers were surveyed on the relative number of visits to a Circuit City store (often, occasionally, and never) and if the store was conveniently located (yes and no). When variables are measured nominally, such as convenient location, or ordinally, such as visitation, the data can be presented and summarized in a two-way frequency or contingency table.

| | Convenient | | |
|---|---|---|---|
| Visits | Yes | No | Total |
| Often | 60 | 20 | 80 |
| Occasional | 25 | 35 | 60 |
| Never | 5 | 50 | 55 |
| | 90 | 105 | 195 |

(a) What is this table called?
(b) Are visits and convenience independent? Why? Interpret your conclusion.
(c) Draw a tree diagram and determine the joint probabilities.

---

# Exercises

**23.** Suppose $P(A) = .40$ and $P(B|A) = .30$. What is the joint probability of $A$ and $B$?
**24.** Suppose $P(X_1) = .75$ and $P(Y_2|X_1) = .40$. What is the joint probability of $X_1$ and $Y_2$?
**25.** A local bank reports that 80 percent of its customers maintain a checking account, 60 percent have a savings account, and 50 percent have both. If a customer is chosen at random, what is the probability the customer has either a checking or a savings account? What is the probability the customer does not have either a checking or a savings account?

**26.** All Seasons Plumbing has two service trucks which frequently break down. If the probability the first truck is available is .75, the probability the second truck is available is .50, and the probability that both trucks are available is .30, what is the probability neither truck is available?

**27.** Refer to the following table.

|              | First Event |     |     |       |
| Second Event | $A_1$ | $A_2$ | $A_3$ | Total |
| --- | --- | --- | --- | --- |
| $B_1$ | 2 | 1 | 3 | 6 |
| $B_2$ | 1 | 2 | 1 | 4 |
| Total | 3 | 3 | 4 | 10 |

  **a.** Determine $P(A_1)$.
  **b.** Determine $P(B_1 | A_2)$.
  **c.** Determine $P(B_2$ and $A_3)$.

**28.** Three defective electric toothbrushes were accidentally shipped to a drugstore by Cleanbrush Products along with 17 nondefective ones.
  **a.** What is the probability the first two electric toothbrushes sold will be returned to the drugstore because they are defective?
  **b.** What is the probability the first two electric toothbrushes sold will not be defective?

**29.** Each salesperson at Stiles-Compton is rated either below average, average, or above average with respect to sales ability. Each salesperson is also rated with respect to his or her potential for advancement—either fair, good, or excellent. These traits for the 500 salespeople were cross-classified into the following table.

|               | Potential for Advancement | | |
| Sales Ability | Fair | Good | Excellent |
| --- | --- | --- | --- |
| Below average | 16 | 12 | 22 |
| Average | 45 | 60 | 45 |
| Above average | 93 | 72 | 135 |

  **a.** What is this table called?
  **b.** What is the probability a salesperson selected at random will have above average sales ability and excellent potential for advancement?
  **c.** Construct a tree diagram showing all the probabilities, conditional probabilities, and joint probabilities.

**30.** An investor owns three common stocks. Each stock, independent of the others, has equally likely chances of (1) increasing in value, (2) decreasing in value, or (3) remaining the same value. List the possible outcomes of this experiment. Estimate the probability at least two of the stocks increase in value.

**31.** The board of directors of a small company consists of five people. Three of those are "strong leaders." If they buy an idea, the entire board will agree. The other "weak" members have no influence. Three salesmen are scheduled, one after the other, to make sales presentations to a board member of the salesman's choice. The salesmen are convincing but do not know who the "strong leaders" are. However, they will know who the previous salesmen spoke to. The first salesman to find a strong leader will win the account. Do the three salesmen have the same chance of winning the account? If not, find their respective probabilities of winning.

**32.** If you ask three strangers about their birthdays, what is the probability: (a) All were born on Wednesday? (b) All were born on different days of the week? (c) None were born on Saturday?

# Bayes' Theorem

In the 18th century Reverend Thomas Bayes, an English Presbyterian minister, pondered this question: Does God really exist? Being interested in mathematics, he attempted to develop a formula to arrive at the probability God does exist based on evidence available to him on earth. Later Laplace refined Bayes' work and gave it the name "Bayes' theorem." In a workable form, **Bayes' theorem** is:

| BAYES' THEOREM | $$P(A_i \mid B) = \frac{P(A_i)P(B \mid A_i)}{P(A_1)P(B \mid A_1) + P(A_2)P(B \mid A_2)}$$ | [5–7] |

Assume in formula 5–7 that the events $A_1$ and $A_2$ are mutually exclusive and collectively exhaustive, and $A_i$ refers to either event $A_1$ or $A_2$. The meaning of the symbols used is illustrated by the following example.

Suppose 5 percent of the population of Umen, a fictional Third World country, have a disease that is peculiar to that country. We will let $A_1$ refer to the event "has the disease" and $A_2$ refer to the event "does not have the disease." Thus, we know that if we select a person from Umen at random, the probability the individual chosen has the disease is .05, or $P(A_1) = .05$. This probability, $P(A_1) = P(\text{has the disease}) = .05$, is called the **prior probability.** It is given this name because the probability is assigned before any empirical data are obtained.

> **PRIOR PROBABILITY** The initial probability based on the present level of information.

The prior probability a person is not afflicted with the disease is therefore .95, or $P(A_2) = .95$, found by $1 - .05$.

There is a diagnostic technique to detect the disease, but it is not very accurate. Let $B$ denote the event "test shows the disease is present." Assume that historical evidence shows that if a person actually has the disease, the probability that the test will indicate the presence of the disease is .90. Using the conditional probability definitions developed earlier in this chapter, this statement is written as:

$$P(B \mid A_1) = .90$$

Assume the probability is .15 that for a person who actually does not have the disease the test will indicate the disease is present.

$$P(B \mid A_2) = .15$$

Let's randomly select a person from Umen and perform the test. The test results indicate the disease is present. What is the probability the person actually has the disease? In symbolic form, we want to know $P(A_1 \mid B)$, which is interpreted as: $P(\text{has the disease} \mid \text{the test results are positive})$. The probability $P(A_1 \mid B)$ is called a **posterior probability.**

> **POSTERIOR PROBABILITY** A revised probability based on additional information.

With the help of Bayes' theorem, formula (5–7), we can determine the posterior probability.

$$P(A_1 \mid B) = \frac{P(A_1)P(B \mid A_1)}{P(A_1)P(B \mid A_1) + P(A_2)P(B \mid A_2)}$$

$$= \frac{(.05)(.90)}{(.05)(.90) + (.95)(.15)} = \frac{.0450}{.1875} = .24$$

So the probability that a person has the disease, given that he or she tested positive, is .24. How is the result interpreted? If a person is selected at random from the population, the probability that he or she has the disease is .05. If the person is tested and the test result is positive, the probability that the person actually has the disease is increased about fivefold, from .05 to .24.

In the preceding problem we had only two mutually exclusive and collectively exhaustive events $A_1$ and $A_2$. If there are $n$ such events, $A_1, A_2, \ldots , A_n$, Bayes' theorem, formula (5–7), becomes

$$P(A_i|B) = \frac{P(A_i)P(B|A_i)}{P(A_1)P(B|A_1) + P(A_2)P(B|A_2) + \cdots + P(A_n)P(B|A_n)}$$

With the preceding notation, the calculations for the Umen problem are summarized in the following table.

| Event, $A_i$ | Prior Probability, $P(A_i)$ | Conditional Probability, $P(B|A_i)$ | Joint Probability, $P(A_i \text{ and } B)$ | Posterior Probability, $P(A_i|B)$ |
|---|---|---|---|---|
| Disease, $A_1$ | .05 | .90 | .0450 | .0450/.1875 = .24 |
| No disease, $A_2$ | .95 | .15 | .1425 | .1425/.1875 = .76 |
| | | | $P(B) = .1875$ | 1.00 |

Another illustration of Bayes' theorem follows.

**EXAMPLE**

A manufacturer of VCRs purchases a particular microchip, called the LS-24, from three suppliers: Hall Electronics, Schuller Sales, and Crawford Components. Thirty percent of the LS-24 chips are purchased from Hall Electronics, 20 percent from Schuller Sales, and the remaining 50 percent from Crawford Components. The manufacturer has extensive histories on the three suppliers and knows that 3 percent of the LS-24 chips from Hall Electronics are defective, 5 percent of chips from Schuller Sales are defective, and 4 percent of the chips purchased from Crawford Components are defective.

When the LS-24 chips arrive at the manufacturer, they are placed directly in a bin and not inspected or otherwise identified by supplier. A worker selects a chip for installation in a VCR and finds it defective. What is the probability that it was manufactured by Schuller Sales?

**SOLUTION**

As a first step, let's summarize some of the information given in the problem statement.

- There are three mutually exclusive and collectively exhaustive events, that is, three suppliers.

    $A_1$  The LS-24 was purchased from Hall Electronics
    $A_2$  The LS-24 was purchased from Schuller Sales
    $A_3$  The LS-24 was purchased from Crawford Components

- The prior probabilities are:

  $P(A_1) = .30$   The probability the LS-24 was manufactured by Hall Electronics
  $P(A_2) = .20$   The probability the LS-24 was manufactured by Schuller Sales
  $P(A_3) = .50$   The probability the LS-24 was manufactured by Crawford Components

- The additional information can be either:

  $B_1$   The LS-24 appears defective, or
  $B_2$   The LS-24 appears not to be defective.

- The following conditional probabilities are given.

  $P(B_1|A_1) = .03$   The probability that an LS-24 chip produced by Hall Electronics is defective
  $P(B_1|A_2) = .05$   The probability that an LS-24 chip produced by Schuller Sales is defective
  $P(B_1|A_3) = .04$   The probability that an LS-24 chip produced by Crawford Components is defective

- A chip is selected from the bin. Because the chips are not identified by supplier, we are not certain which supplier manufactured the chip. We want to determine the probability that the defective chip was purchased from Schuller Sales. The probability is written $P(A_2 \mid B_1)$.

Look at Schuller's quality record. It is the worst of the three suppliers. Now that we have found a defective LS-24 chip, we suspect that $P(A_2 \mid B_1)$ is greater than $P(A_2)$. That is, we expect the revised probability to be greater than .20. But how much greater? Bayes' theorem can give us the answer. As a first step, consider the tree diagram in Chart 5–3 on the next page.

The events are dependent, so the prior probability in the first branch is multiplied by the conditional probability in the second branch to obtain the joint probability. The joint probability is reported in the last column of Chart 5–3. To construct the tree diagram of Chart 5–3, we used a time sequence that moved from the supplier to the determination of whether the chip was acceptable or unacceptable.

What we need to do is reverse the time process. That is, instead of moving from left to right in Chart 5–3, we need to move from right to left. We have a defective chip, and we want to determine the likelihood that it was purchased from Schuller Sales. How is that accomplished? We first look at the joint probabilities as relative frequencies out of 1,000 cases. For example, the likelihood of a defective LS-24 chip that was produced by Hall Electronics is .009. So of 1,000 cases we would expect to find 9 defective chips produced by Hall Electronics. We observe that in 39 of 1,000 cases the LS-24 chip selected for assembly will be defective, found by 9 + 10 + 20. Of these 39 defective chips, 10 were produced by Schuller Sales. Thus, the probability that the defective LS-24 chip was purchased from Schuller Sales is 10/39 = .2564. We have now determined the revised probability of $P(A_2 \mid B_1)$. Before we found the defective chip, the likelihood that it was purchased from Schuller Sales was .20. This likelihood has been increased to .2564.

This information is summarized in the following table.

| Event, $A_i$ | Prior Probability, $P(A_i)$ | Conditional Probability, $P(B_1|A_i)$ | Joint Probability, $P(A_i$ and $B_1)$ | Posterior Probability, $P(A_i|B_1)$ |
|---|---|---|---|---|
| Hall | .30 | .03 | .009 | .009/.039 = .2308 |
| Schuller | .20 | .05 | .010 | .010/.039 = .2564 |
| Crawford | .50 | .04 | .020 | .020/.039 = .5128 |
| | | | $P(B_1) = .039$ | 1.0000 |

**CHART 5–3** Tree Diagram of VCR Manufacturing Problem

The probability the defective LS-24 chip came from Schuller Sales can be formally found by using Bayes' theorem. We compute $P(A_2|B_1)$, where $A_2$ refers to Schuller Sales and $B_1$ to the fact that the selected LS-24 chip was defective.

$$P(A_2|B_1) = \frac{P(A_2)P(B_1|A_2)}{P(A_1)P(B_1|A_1) + P(A_2)P(B_1|A_2) + P(A_3)P(B_1|A_3)}$$

$$= \frac{(.20)(.05)}{(.30)(.03) + (.20)(.05) + (.50)(.04)} = \frac{.010}{.039} = .2564$$

This is the same result obtained from Chart 5–3 and from the conditional probability table.

**Self-Review 5–9**    Refer to the preceding example and solution.
(a) Design a formula to find the probability the part selected came from Crawford Components, given that it was a good chip.
(b) Compute the probability using Bayes' theorem.

## Exercises

**33.** $P(A_1) = .60$, $P(A_2) = .40$, $P(B_1|A_1) = .05$, and $P(B_1|A_2) = .10$. Use Bayes' theorem to determine $P(A_1|B_1)$.

**34.** $P(A_1) = .20$, $P(A_2) = .40$, and $P(A_3) = .40$. $P(B_1|A_1) = .25$. $P(B_1|A_2) = .05$, and $P(B_1|A_3) = .10$. Use Bayes' theorem to determine $P(A_3|B_1)$.

**35.** The Ludlow Wildcats baseball team, a minor league team in the Cleveland Indians organization, plays 70 percent of their games at night and 30 percent during the day. The team wins 50 percent of their night games and 90 percent of their day games. According to today's newspaper, they won yesterday. What is the probability the game was played at night?

**36.** Dr. Stallter has been teaching basic statistics for many years. She knows that 80 percent of the students will complete the assigned problems. She has also determined that among those who do their assignments, 90 percent will pass the course. Among those students who do not do their homework, 60 percent will pass. Mike Fishbaugh took statistics last semester from Dr. Stallter and received a passing grade. What is the probability that he completed the assignments?

**37.** The credit department of Lion's Department Store in Anaheim, California, reported that 30 percent of their sales are cash, 30 percent are paid for by check at the time of the purchase, and 40 percent are charged. Twenty percent of the cash purchases, 90 percent of the checks, and 60 percent of the charges are for more than $50. Ms. Tina Stevens just purchased a new dress that cost $120. What is the probability that she paid cash?

**38.** One-fourth of the residents of the Burning Ridge Estates leave their garage doors open when they are away from home. The local chief of police estimates that 5 percent of the garages with open doors will have something stolen, but only 1 percent of those closed will have something stolen. If a garage is robbed, what is the probability the doors were left open?

# Principles of Counting

If the number of possible outcomes in an experiment is small, it is relatively easy to count them. There are six possible outcomes, for example, resulting from the roll of a die, namely:

If, however, there are a large number of possible outcomes, such as the number of heads and tails for an experiment with 10 tosses, it would be tedious to count all the possibilities. They could have all heads, one head and nine tails, two heads and eight tails, and so on. To facilitate counting, three counting formulas will be examined: the **multiplication formula** (not to be confused with the multiplication *rule* described earlier in the chapter), the **permutation formula,** and the **combination formula.**

## The Multiplication Formula

> **MULTIPLICATION FORMULA** If there are *m* ways of doing one thing and *n* ways of doing another thing, there are *m* × *n* ways of doing both.

In terms of a formula:

| MULTIPLICATION FORMULA | Total number of arrangements = $(m)(n)$ | **[5–8]** |
|---|---|---|

This can be extended to more than two events. For three events *m, n,* and *o*:

$$\text{Total number of arrangements} = (m)(n)(o)$$

**EXAMPLE**

An automobile dealer wants to advertise that for $29,999 you can buy a convertible, a two-door, or a four-door model with your choice of either wire wheel covers or solid wheel covers. How many different arrangements of models and wheel covers can the dealer offer?

SOLUTION

Of course the dealer could determine the total number of arrangements by picturing and counting them. There are six.

Convertible with wire wheels

Convertible with solid wheels

Two-door with wire wheels

Two-door with solid wheels

Four-door with wire wheels

Four-door with solid wheels

We can employ the multiplication formula as a check (where $m$ is the number of models and $n$ the wheel cover type). From formula (5–8):

$$\text{Total possible arrangements} = (m)(n) = (3)(2) = 6$$

It was not difficult to count all the possible model and wheel cover combinations in this example. Suppose, however, that the dealer decided to offer eight models and six types of wheel covers. It would be tedious to picture and count all the possible alternatives. Instead, the multiplication formula can be used. In this case, there are $(m)(n) = (8)(6) = 48$ possible arrangements.

Note in the preceding applications of the multiplication formula that there were *two or more groupings from which you made selections.* The automobile dealer, for example, offered a choice of models and a choice of wheel covers. If a home builder offered you four different exterior styles of a home to choose from and three interior floor plans, the multiplication formula would be used to find how many different arrangements were possible. The answer is there are 12 possibilities.

---

**Self-Review 5–10**

1. An Internet clothing retailer offers sweaters and slacks for women. The sweaters and slacks are offered in coordinating colors. If sweaters are available in five colors and the slacks are available in four colors, how many different outfits can be advertised?
2. Pioneer manufactures three models of stereo receivers, two cassette decks, four speakers, and three CD carousels. When the four types of components are sold together, they form a "system." How many different systems can the electronics firm offer?

---

## The Permutation Formula

As noted, the multiplication formula is applied to find the number of possible arrangements for two or more groups. The **permutation formula** is applied to find the possible number of arrangements when there is only *one* group of objects. As illustrations of this type of problem:

- Three electronic parts are to be assembled into a plug-in unit for a television set. The parts can be assembled in any order. The question involving counting is: In how many different ways can the three parts be assembled?
- A machine operator must make four safety checks before starting his machine. It does not matter in which order the checks are made. In how many different ways can the operator make the checks?

One order for the first illustration might be: the transistor first, the LEDs second, and the synthesizer third. This arrangement is called a **permutation.**

> **PERMUTATION** Any arrangement of $r$ objects selected from a single group of $n$ possible objects.

Note that the arrangements $a\ b\ c$ and $b\ a\ c$ are different permutations. The formula to count the total number of different permutations is:

| PERMUTATION FORMULA | $_nP_r = \dfrac{n!}{(n-r)!}$ | [5–9] |

where:

  $n$ is the total number of objects.
  $r$ is the number of objects selected.

Before we solve the two problems illustrated, note that permutations and combinations (to be discussed shortly) use a notation called $n$ *factorial.* It is written $n!$ and means the product of $n(n-1)(n-2)(n-3)\cdots(1)$. For instance, $5! = 5\cdot4\cdot3\cdot2\cdot1 = 120$.

As shown below, numbers can be canceled when the same numbers are included in the numerator and denominator.

$$\frac{6!3!}{4!} = \frac{6\cdot5\cdot\cancel{4}\cdot\cancel{3}\cdot\cancel{2}\cdot\cancel{1}(3\cdot2\cdot1)}{\cancel{4}\cdot\cancel{3}\cdot\cancel{2}\cdot\cancel{1}} = 180$$

By definition, zero factorial, written 0!, is 1. That is, $0! = 1$.

**EXAMPLE**

Referring to the group of three electronic parts that are to be assembled in any order, in how many different ways can they be assembled?

**SOLUTION**

There are three electronic parts to be assembled, so $n = 3$. Because all three are to be inserted in the plug-in unit, $r = 3$. Solving using formula (5–9) gives:

$$_nP_r = \frac{n!}{(n-r)!} = \frac{3!}{(3-3)!} = \frac{3!}{0!} = \frac{3!}{1} = 6$$

We can check the number of permutations arrived at by using the permutation formula. We determine how many "spaces" have to be filled and the possibilities for each "space." In the problem involving three electronic parts, there are three locations in the plug-in unit for the three parts. There are three possibilities for the first place, two for the second (one has been used up), and one for the third, as follows:

$$(3)(2)(1) = 6 \text{ permutations}$$

The six ways in which the three electronic parts, lettered $A$, $B$, $C$, can be arranged are:

| ABC | BAC | CAB | ACB | BCA | CBA |

In the previous example we selected and arranged all the objects, that is $n = r$. In many cases, only some objects are selected and arranged from the $n$ possible objects. We explain the details of this application in the following example.

**EXAMPLE**

The Betts Machine Shop, Inc., has eight screw machines but only three spaces available in the production area for the machines. In how many different ways can the eight machines be arranged in the three spaces available?

**SOLUTION**

There are eight possibilities for the first available space in the production area, seven for the second space (one has been used up), and six for the third space. Thus:

$$(8)(7)(6) = 336,$$

that is, there are a total of 336 different possible arrangements. This could also be found by using formula (5–9). If $n = 8$ machines, and $r = 3$ spaces available, the formula leads to

$$_nP_r = \frac{n!}{(n-r)!} = \frac{8!}{(8-3)!} = \frac{8!}{5!} = \frac{(8)(7)(6)5!}{5!} = 336$$

## The Combination Formula

If the order of the selected objects is *not* important, any selection is called a **combination.** The formula to count the number of $r$ object combinations from a set of $n$ objects is:

| COMBINATION FORMULA | $_nC_r = \dfrac{n!}{r!(n-r)!}$ | [5–10] |
|---|---|---|

For example, if executives Able, Baker, and Chauncy are to be chosen as a committee to negotiate a merger, there is only one possible combination of these three; the committee of Able, Baker, and Chauncy is the same as the committee of Baker, Chauncy, and Able. Using the combination formula:

$$_nC_r = \frac{n!}{r!(n-r)!} = \frac{3 \cdot 2 \cdot 1}{3 \cdot 2 \cdot 1(1)} = 1$$

**EXAMPLE**

The marketing department has been given the assignment of designing color codes for the 42 different lines of compact discs sold by Goody Records. Three colors are to be used on each CD, but a combination of three colors used for one CD cannot be rearranged and used to identify a different CD. This means that if green, yellow, and violet were used to identify one line, then yellow, green, and violet (or any other combination of these three colors) cannot be used to identify another line. Would seven colors taken three at a time be adequate to color code the 42 lines?

**SOLUTION**

According to formula (5–10), there are 35 combinations, found by

$$_7C_3 = \frac{n!}{r!(n-r)!} = \frac{7!}{3!(7-3)!} = \frac{7!}{3!4!} = 35$$

The seven colors taken three at a time (i.e., three colors to a line) would not be adequate to color-code the 42 different lines because they would provide only 35 combinations. Eight colors taken three at a time would give 56 different combinations. This would be more than adequate to color-code the 42 different lines.

When the number of permutations or combinations is large, the calculations are tedious. Computer software and handheld calculators have "functions" to compute these numbers. The Excel output for the location of the eight screw machines in the production area of Betts Machine Shop, Inc. is shown below. There are a total of 336 arrangements.

Below is the output for the color codes at Goody Records, Inc. Three colors are chosen from among seven possible. The number of combinations possible is 35.

Self-Review 5–11

1. A musician wants to write a score based on only five chords: B-flat, C, D, E, and G. However, only three chords out of the five will be used in succession, such as C, B-flat, and E. Repetitions, such as B-flat, B-flat, and E, will not be permitted.
   (a) How many permutations of the five chords, taken three at a time, are possible?
   (b) Using formula (5–9), how many permutations are possible?
2. A machine operator must make four safety checks before starting to machine a part. It does not matter in which order the checks are made. In how many different ways can the operator make the checks?
3. The 10 numbers 0 through 9 are to be used in code groups of four to identify an item of clothing. Code 1083 might identify a blue blouse, size medium; the code group 2031 might identify a pair of pants, size 18; and so on. Repetitions of numbers are not permitted. That is, the same number cannot be used twice (or more) in a total sequence. For example, 2256, 2562, or 5559 would not be permitted. How many different code groups can be designed?
4. In the above example involving Goody Records, we said that eight colors taken three at a time would give 56 different combinations.
   (a) Use formula (5–10) to show this is true.
   (b) As an alternative plan for color coding the 42 different lines, it has been suggested that only two colors be placed on a disc. Would 10 colors be adequate to color code the 42 different lines? (Again, a combination of two colors could be used only once—that is, if pink and blue were coded for one line, blue and pink could not be used to identify a different line.)
5. In a lottery game, three numbers are randomly selected from a tumbler of balls numbered 1 through 50.
   (a) How many permutations are possible?
   (b) How many combinations are possible?

# Exercises

**39.** Solve the following:
   **a.** 40!/35!
   **b.** $_7P_4$
   **c.** $_5C_2$

**40.** Solve the following:
   **a.** 20!/17!
   **b.** $_9P_3$
   **c.** $_7C_2$

**41.** A pollster randomly selected 4 of 10 available people. How many different groups of 4 are possible?

**42.** A telephone number consists of seven digits, the first three representing the exchange. How many different telephone numbers are possible within the 537 exchange?

**43.** An overnight express company must include five cities on its route. How many different routes are possible, assuming that it does not matter in which order the cities are included in the routing?

**44.** A representative of the Environmental Protection Agency (EPA) wants to select samples from 10 landfills. The director has 15 landfills from which she can collect samples. How many different samples are possible?

**45.** A national pollster has developed 15 questions designed to rate the performance of the President of the United States. The pollster will select 10 of these questions. How many different arrangements are there for the order of the 10 selected questions?

**46.** A company is creating three new divisions and seven managers are eligible to be appointed head of a division. How many different ways could the three new heads be appointed?

# Chapter Outline

**I.** A probability is a value between 0 and 1 inclusive that represents the likelihood a particular event will happen.

   **A.** An experiment is the observation of some activity or the act of taking some measurement.

   **B.** An outcome is a particular result of an experiment.

   **C.** An event is the collection of one or more outcomes of an experiment.

**II.** There are three definitions of probability.

   **A.** The classical definition applies when there are *n* equally likely outcomes to an experiment.

   **B.** The empirical definition occurs when the number of times an event happens is divided by the number of observations.

   **C.** A subjective probability is based on whatever information is available.

**III.** Two events are mutually exclusive if by virtue of one event happening the other cannot happen.

**IV.** Events are independent if the occurrence of one event does not affect the occurrence of another event.

**V.** The rules of addition refer to the union of events.

   **A.** The special rule of addition is used when events are mutually exclusive.

$$P(A \text{ or } B) = P(A) + P(B) \qquad \text{[5–2]}$$

   **B.** The general rule of addition is used when the events are not mutually exclusive.

$$P(A \text{ or } B) = P(A) + P(B) - P(A \text{ and } B) \qquad \text{[5–4]}$$

   **C.** The complement rule is used to determine the probability of an event happening by subtracting the probability of the event not happening from 1.

$$P(A) = 1 - P(\sim A) \qquad \text{[5–3]}$$

**VI.** The rules of multiplication refer to the product of events.

**A.** The special rule of multiplication refers to events that are independent.

$$P(A \text{ and } B) = P(A)P(B) \qquad \textbf{[5–5]}$$

**B.** The general rule of multiplication refers to events that are not independent.

$$P(A \text{ and } B) = P(A)P(B \mid A) \qquad \textbf{[5–6]}$$

**C.** A joint probability is the likelihood that two or more events will happen at the same time.

**D.** A conditional probability is the likelihood that an event will happen, given that another event has already happened.

**E.** Bayes' theorem is a method of revising a probability, given that additional information is obtained. For two mutually exclusive and collectively exhaustive events:

$$P(A_1 \mid B) = \frac{P(A_1)P(B \mid A_1)}{P(A_1)P(B \mid A_1) + P(A_2)P(B \mid A_2)} \qquad \textbf{[5–7]}$$

**VII.** There are three counting rules that are useful in determining the number of outcomes in an experiment.

**A.** The multiplication rule states that if there are $m$ ways one event can happen and $n$ ways another event can happen, then there are $mn$ ways the two events can happen.

$$\text{Number of arrangements} = (m)(n) \qquad \textbf{[5–8]}$$

**B.** A permutation is an arrangement in which the order of the objects selected from a specific pool of objects is important.

$$_nP_r = \frac{n!}{(n-r)!} \qquad \textbf{[5–9]}$$

**C.** A combination is an arrangement where the order of the objects selected from a specific pool of objects is not important.

$$_nC_r = \frac{n!}{r!(n-r)!} \qquad \textbf{[5–10]}$$

# Pronunciation Key

| SYMBOL | MEANING | PRONUNCIATION |
|---|---|---|
| $P(A)$ | Probability of $A$ | $P$ of $A$ |
| $P(\sim A)$ | Probability of not $A$ | $P$ of not $A$ |
| $P(A \text{ and } B)$ | Probability of $A$ and $B$ | $P$ of $A$ and $B$ |
| $P(A \text{ or } B)$ | Probability of $A$ or $B$ | $P$ of $A$ or $B$ |
| $P(A \mid B)$ | Probability of $A$ given $B$ has happened | $P$ of $A$ given $B$ |
| $_nP_r$ | Permutation of $n$ items selected $r$ at a time | Pnr |
| $_nC_r$ | Combination of $n$ items selected $r$ at a time | Cnr |

# Chapter Exercises

**47.** The marketing research department at Vernors plans to survey teenagers about a newly developed soft drink. Each will be asked to compare it with his or her favorite soft drink.
 **a.** What is the experiment?
 **b.** What is one possible event?

**48.** The number of times a particular event occurred in the past is divided by the number of occurrences. What is this approach to probability called?

**49.** The probability that the cause and the cure for all cancers will be discovered before the year 2010 is .20. What viewpoint of probability does this statement illustrate?

**50.** Berdine's Chicken Factory has several stores in the Hilton Head, South Carolina, area. When interviewing applicants for server positions, the owner would like to include information on the amount of tip a server can expect to earn per check (or bill). A study of 500 recent checks indicated the server earned the following tip.

| Amount of Tip | Number |
|---|---|
| $ 0 up to $ 5 | 200 |
| 5 up to  10 | 100 |
| 10 up to  20 | 75 |
| 20 up to  50 | 75 |
| 50 or more | 50 |
| Total | 500 |

    **a.** What is the probability of a tip of $50 or more?

    **b.** Are the categories "$0 up to $5," "$5 up to $10," and so on considered mutually exclusive?

    **c.** If the probabilities associated with each outcome were totaled, what would that total be?

    **d.** What is the probability of a tip of up to $10?

    **e.** What is the probability of a tip of less than $50?

**51.** Define each of these items:

    **a.** Conditional probability

    **b.** Event

    **c.** Joint probability

**52.** The first card selected from a standard 52-card deck was a king.

    **a.** If it is returned to the deck, what is the probability that a king will be drawn on the second selection?

    **b.** If the king is not replaced, what is the probability that a king will be drawn on the second selection?

    **c.** What is the probability that a king will be selected on the first draw from the deck and another king on the second draw (assuming that the first king was not replaced)?

**53.** Armco, a manufacturer of traffic light systems, found that under accelerated-life tests, 95 percent of the newly developed systems lasted 3 years before failing to change signals properly.

    **a.** If a city purchased four of these systems, what is the probability all four systems would operate properly for at least 3 years?

    **b.** Which rule of probability does this illustrate?

    **c.** Using letters to represent the four systems, write an equation to show how you arrived at the answer to part a.

**54.** Refer to the following picture.

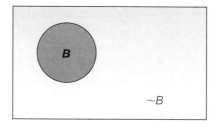

    **a.** What is the picture called?

    **b.** What rule of probability is illustrated?

    **c.** $B$ represents the event of choosing a family that receives welfare payments. What does $P(B) + P(\sim B)$ equal?

**55.** In a management trainee program at Claremont Enterprises, 80 percent of the trainees are female and 20 percent male. Ninety percent of the females attended college, and 78 percent of the males attended college.

    **a.** A management trainee is selected at random. What is the probability that the person selected is a female who did not attend college?

    **b.** Are gender and attending college independent? Why?

    **c.** Construct a tree diagram showing all the probabilities, conditional probabilities, and joint probabilities.

    **d.** Do the joint probabilities total 1.00? Why?

**56.** Assume the likelihood that any flight on Northwest Airlines arrives within 15 minutes of the scheduled time is .90. We select four flights from yesterday for study.
   **a.** What is the likelihood all four of the selected flights arrived within 15 minutes of the scheduled time?
   **b.** What is the likelihood that none of the selected flights arrived within 15 minutes of the scheduled time?
   **c.** What is the likelihood at least one of the selected flights did not arrive within 15 minutes of the scheduled time?

**57.** There are 100 employees at Kiddie Carts International. Fifty-seven of the employees are production workers, 40 are supervisors, 2 are secretaries, and the remaining employee is the president. Suppose an employee is selected:
   **a.** What is the probability the selected employee is a production worker?
   **b.** What is the probability the selected employee is either a production worker or a supervisor?
   **c.** Refer to part b. Are these events mutually exclusive?
   **d.** What is the probability the selected employee is neither a production worker nor a supervisor?

**58.** Barry Bonds of the San Francisco Giants had the highest batting average in the 2002 Major League Baseball season. His average was .370. So assume the probability of getting a hit is .370 for each time he batted. In a particular game assume he batted three times.
   **a.** This is an example of what type of probability?
   **b.** What is the probability of getting three hits in a particular game?
   **c.** What is the probability of not getting any hits in a game?
   **d.** What is the probability of getting at least one hit?

**59.** The probability that a bomber hits its target on any particular mission is .80. Four bombers are sent after the same target. What is the probability:
   **a.** They all hit the target?
   **b.** None hit the target?
   **c.** At least one hits the target?

**60.** Ninety students will graduate from Lima Shawnee High School this spring. Of the 90 students, 50 are planning to attend college. Two students are to be picked at random to carry flags at the graduation.
   **a.** What is the probability both of the selected students plan to attend college?
   **b.** What is the probability one of the two selected students plans to attend college?

**61.** Brooks Insurance, Inc. wishes to offer life insurance to men age 60 via the Internet. Mortality tables indicate the likelihood of a 60-year-old man surviving another year is .98. If the policy is offered to five men age 60:
   **a.** What is the probability all five men survive the year?
   **b.** What is the probability at least one does not survive?

**62.** Forty percent of the homes constructed in the Quail Creek area include a security system. Three homes are selected at random:
   **a.** What is the probability all three of the selected homes have a security system?
   **b.** What is the probability none of the three selected homes have a security system?
   **c.** What is the probability at least one of the selected homes has a security system?
   **d.** Did you assume the events to be dependent or independent?

**63.** Refer to Exercise 62, but assume there are 10 homes in the Quail Creek area and four of them have a security system. Three homes are selected at random:
   **a.** What is the probability all three of the selected homes have a security system?
   **b.** What is the probability none of the three selected homes have a security system?
   **c.** What is the probability at least one of the selected homes has a security system?
   **d.** Did you assume the events to be dependent or independent?

**64.** A juggler has a bag containing four blue balls, three green balls, two yellow balls, and one red ball. The juggler picks a ball at random. Then, without replacing it, he chooses a second ball. What is the probability the juggler first draws a yellow ball followed by a blue ball?

**65.** The board of directors of Saner Automatic Door Company consists of 12 members, 3 of whom are women. A new policy and procedures manual is to be written for the company. A committee of 3 is randomly selected from the board to do the writing.
   **a.** What is the probability that all members of the committee are men?
   **b.** What is the probability that at least 1 member of the committee is a woman?

**66.** A survey of undergraduate students in the School of Business at Northern University revealed the following regarding the gender and majors of the students:

| Gender | Major | | | Total |
|--------|-------|---|---|-------|
| | Accounting | Management | Finance | |
| Male | 100 | 150 | 50 | 300 |
| Female | 100 | 50 | 50 | 200 |
| Total | 200 | 200 | 100 | 500 |

  a. What is the probability of selecting a female student?
  b. What is the probability of selecting a finance or accounting major?
  c. What is the probability of selecting a female or an accounting major? Which rule of addition did you apply?
  d. Are gender and major independent? Why?
  e. What is the probability of selecting an accounting major, given that the person selected is a male?
  f. Suppose two students are selected randomly to attend a lunch with the president of the university. What is the probability that both of those selected are accounting majors?

67. The Wood County sheriff classifies crimes by age (in years) of the criminal and whether the crime is violent or nonviolent. As shown below, a total of 150 crimes were reported by the sheriff last year.

| Type of Crime | Age (in years) | | | Total |
|---------------|----------------|---|---|-------|
| | Under 20 | 20 to 40 | Over 40 | |
| Violent | 27 | 41 | 14 | 82 |
| Nonviolent | 12 | 34 | 22 | 68 |
| Total | 39 | 75 | 36 | 150 |

  a. What is the probability of selecting a case to analyze and finding it involved a violent crime?
  b. What is the probability of selecting a case to analyze and finding the crime was committed by someone less than 40 years old?
  c. What is the probability of selecting a case that involved a violent crime or an offender less than 20 years old? Which rule of addition did you apply?
  d. Given that a violent crime is selected for analysis, what is the probability the crime was committed by a person under 20 years old?
  e. Two crimes are selected for review by Judge Tybo. What is the probability that both are violent crimes?

68. An investor purchased 100 shares of 5/3 Bank stock and 100 shares of Santee Cooper Electric stock. The probability the bank stock will appreciate over a year is .70. The probability the electric utility will increase over the same period is .60.
  a. What is the probability both stocks appreciate during the period?
  b. What is the probability the bank stock appreciates but the utility does not?
  c. What is the probability at least one of the stocks appreciates?

69. Flashner Marketing Research, Inc. specializes in providing assessments of the prospects for women's apparel shops in shopping malls. Al Flashner, president, reports that he assesses the prospects as good, fair, or poor. Records from previous assessments show that 60 percent of the time the prospects were rated as good, 30 percent of the time fair, and 10 percent of the time poor. Of those rated good, 80 percent made a profit the first year; of those rated fair, 60 percent made a profit the first year; and of those rated poor, 20 percent made a profit the first year. Connie's Apparel was one of Flashner's clients. Connie's Apparel made a profit last year. What is the probability that it was given an original rating of poor?

70. Two boxes of men's Old Navy shirts were received from the factory. Box 1 contained 25 mesh polo shirts and 15 Super-T shirts. Box 2 contained 30 mesh polo shirts and 10 Super-T shirts. One of the boxes was selected at random, and a shirt was chosen at random from that box to be inspected. The shirt was a mesh polo shirt. Given this information, what is the probability that the mesh polo shirt came from box 1?

71. With each purchase of a large pizza at Tony's Pizza, the customer receives a coupon that can be scratched to see if a prize will be awarded. The odds of winning a free soft drink are

1 in 10, and the odds of winning a free large pizza are 1 in 50. You plan to eat lunch tomorrow at Tony's. What is the probability:
   **a.** That you will win either a large pizza or a soft drink?
   **b.** That you will not win a prize?
   **c.** That you will not win a prize on three consecutive visits to Tony's?
   **d.** That you will win at least one prize on one of your next three visits to Tony's?

72. For the daily lottery game in Illinois, participants select three numbers between 0 and 9. A number cannot be selected more than once, so a winning ticket could be, say, 307. Purchasing one ticket allows you to select one set of numbers. The winning numbers are announced on TV each night.
   **a.** How many different outcomes (three-digit numbers) are possible?
   **b.** If you purchase a ticket for the game tonight, what is the likelihood you will win?
   **c.** Suppose you purchase three tickets for tonight's drawing and select a different number for each ticket. What is the probability that you will not win with any of the tickets?

73. Several years ago Wendy's Hamburgers advertised that there are 256 different ways to order your hamburger. You may choose to have, or omit, any combination of the following on your hamburger: mustard, ketchup, onion, pickle, tomato, relish, mayonnaise, and lettuce. Is the advertisement correct? Show how you arrive at your answer.

74. It was found that 60 percent of the tourists to China visited the Forbidden City, the Temple of Heaven, the Great Wall, and other historical sites in or near Beijing. Forty percent visited Xi'an with its magnificent terracotta soldiers, horses, and chariots, which lay buried for over 2,000 years. Thirty percent of the tourists went to both Beijing and Xi'an. What is the probability that a tourist visited at least one of these places?

75. A new chewing gum has been developed that is helpful to those who want to stop smoking. If 60 percent of those people chewing the gum are successful in stopping smoking, what is the probability that in a group of four smokers using the gum at least one quits smoking?

76. Reynolds Construction Company has agreed not to erect all "look-alike" homes in a new subdivision. Five exterior designs are offered to potential home buyers. The builder has standardized three interior plans that can be incorporated in any of the five exteriors. How many different ways can the exterior and interior plans be offered to potential home buyers?

77. A new sports car model has defective brakes 15 percent of the time and a defective steering mechanism 5 percent of the time. Let's assume (and hope) that these problems occur independently. If one or the other of these problems is present, the car is called a "lemon." If both of these problems are present, the car is a "hazard." Your instructor purchased one of these cars yesterday. What is the probability it is:
   **a.** A lemon?
   **b.** A hazard?

78. The state of Maryland has license plates with three numbers followed by three letters. How many different license plates are possible?

79. There are four people being considered for the position of chief executive officer of Dalton Enterprises. Three of the applicants are over 60 years of age. Two are female, of which only one is over 60.
   **a.** What is the probability that a candidate is over 60 and female?
   **b.** Given that the candidate is male, what is the probability he is less than 60?
   **c.** Given that the person is over 60, what is the probability the person is female?

80. Tim Bleckie is the owner of Bleckie Investment and Real Estate Company. The company recently purchased four tracts of land in Holly Farms Estates and six tracts in Newburg Woods. The tracts are all equally desirable and sell for about the same amount.
   **a.** What is the probability that the next two tracts sold will be in Newburg Woods?
   **b.** What is the probability that of the next four sold at least one will be in Holly Farms?
   **c.** Are these events independent or dependent?

81. A computer password consists of four characters. The characters can be one of the 26 letters of the alphabet. Each character may be used more than once. How many different passwords are possible?

82. A case of 24 cans contains 1 can that is contaminated. Three cans are to be chosen randomly for testing.
   **a.** How many different combinations of 3 cans could be selected?
   **b.** What is the probability that the contaminated can is selected for testing?

83. A puzzle in the newspaper presents a matching problem. The names of 10 U.S. presidents are listed in one column, and their vice presidents are listed in random order in the second column. The puzzle asks the reader to match each president with his vice president. If you

make the matches randomly, how many matches are possible? What is the probability all 10 of your matches are correct?

**84.** The following diagram represents a system of two components, A and B, which are in series. (Being in series means that for the system to operate, both components A and B must work.) Assume the two components are independent. What is the probability the system works under these conditions? The probability A works is .90 and the probability B functions is also .90.

**85.** Horwege Electronics, Inc. purchases TV picture tubes from four different suppliers. Tyson Wholesale supplies 20 percent of the tubes, Fuji Importers 30 percent, Kirkpatricks 25 percent, and Parts, Inc. 25 percent. Tyson Wholesale tends to have the best quality, as only 3 percent of their tubes arrive defective. Fuji Importers tubes are 4 percent defective, Kirkpatricks 7 percent, and Parts, Inc. 6.5 percent defective.
   **a.** What is the overall percent defective?
   **b.** A defective picture tube was discovered in the latest shipment. What is the probability that it came from Tyson Wholesale?

**86.** ABC Auto Insurance classifies drivers as good, medium, or poor risks. Drivers who apply to them for insurance fall into these three groups in the proportions: 30 percent, 50 percent, and 20 percent, respectively. The probability a "good" driver will have an accident is .01, the probability a "medium" risk driver will have an accident is .03, and the probability a "poor" driver will have an accident is .10. The company sells Mr. Brophy an insurance policy and he has an accident. What is the probability Mr. Brophy is:
   **a.** A "good" driver?     **b.** A "medium" risk driver?     **c.** A "poor" driver?

# exercises.com

**87.** During the 1970s the game show *Let's Make a Deal* had a long run on TV. In the show a contestant was given a choice of three doors, behind one of which was a prize. The other two doors contained a gag gift of some type. After the contestant selected a door, the host of the show then revealed to them one of the doors from among the two not selected. The host asked the contestant if they wished to switch doors to one of those not chosen. Should the contestant switch? Are the odds of winning increased by switching doors?

Go to the following website, which is administered by the Department of Statistics at the University of South Carolina, and try your strategy: http://www.stat.sc.edu/~west/applets/ LetsMakeaDeal.html; Go to the following website and read about the odds for the game: http://www.stat.sc.edu/~west/javahtml/LetsMakeaDeal.html. Was your strategy correct?

# Dataset Exercises

**88.** Refer to the Real Estate data, which reports information on homes sold in the Denver, Colorado, area during the last year.
   **a.** Sort the data into a table that shows the number of homes that have a pool versus the number that don't have a pool in each of the five townships. If a home is selected at random, compute the following probabilities.
      **(1)** The home is in Township 1 or has a pool.
      **(2)** Given that it is in Township 3, that it has a pool.
      **(3)** Has a pool and is in Township 3.
   **b.** Sort the data into a table that shows the number of homes that have a garage versus those that don't have a garage in each of the five townships. If a home is selected at random, compute the following probabilities:
      **(1)** The home has a garage.
      **(2)** Given that it is in Township 5, that it does not have a garage.
      **(3)** The home has a garage and is in Township 3.
      **(4)** Does not have a garage or is in Township 2.

**89.** Refer to the Baseball 2002 data, which reports information on the 30 Major League Baseball teams for the 2002 season. Set up a variable that divides the teams into two groups, those that had a winning season and those that did not. That is, create a variable to count the teams that won 81 games or more, and those that won 80 or less. Next create a new variable for attendance, using three categories: attendance less than 2.0 million, attendance of 2.0 million up to 3.0 million, and attendance of 3.0 million or more.

**a.** Create a table that shows the number of teams with a winning season versus those with a losing season by the three categories of attendance. If a team is selected at random, compute the following probabilities:

**(1)** Having a winning season.

**(2)** Having a winning season or attendance of more than 3.0 million.

**(3)** Given attendance of more than 3.0 million, having a winning season.

**(4)** Having a losing season and drawing less than 2.0 million.

**b.** Create a table that shows the number of teams that play on artificial surfaces and natural surfaces by winning and losing records. If a team is selected at random, compute the following probabilities:

**(1)** Selecting a team with a home field that has a natural surface.

**(2)** Is the likelihood of selecting a team with a winning record larger for teams with natural or artificial surfaces?

**(3)** Having a winning record or playing on an artificial surface.

**90.** Refer to the wage data set, which reports information on annual wages for a sample of 100 workers. Also included are variables relating to industry, years of education, and gender for each worker. Develop a table showing the industry of employment by gender. A worker is randomly selected; compute the probability the person selected is:

**a.** Female.

**b.** Female or in manufacturing.

**c.** Female given that the selected person is in manufacturing.

**d.** Female and in manufacturing.

# Software Commands

1. The Excel commands to determine the number of permutations shown on page 169 are:
   **a.** Click on **Insert** on the toolbar, then select the $f_x$ **function** and click **OK**.
   **b.** In the **Paste Function** box select **Statistical** and in the **Function name** column scroll down to **PERMUT** and click **OK**.
   **c.** In the **PERMUT** box after **Number** enter 8 and in the **Number_chosen** box enter 3. The correct answer of 336 appears twice in the box.

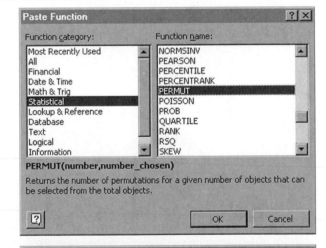

2. The Excel commands to determine the number of combinations shown on page 169 are:
   **a.** Click on **Insert** on the toolbar, then select the $f_x$ **function** and click **OK**.
   **b.** In the **Paste Function** box select **Math & Trig** and in the Function name column scroll down to **COMBIN** and click **OK**.
   **c.** In the **COMBIN** box after **Number** enter 7 and in the **Number_chosen** box enter 3. The correct answer 35 appears twice in the box.

# Chapter 5 Answers to Self-Review

**5–1** **a.** Testing of the new computer game.
   **b.** Seventy-three players liked the game.
   **c.** No. Probability cannot be greater than 1. The probability that the game, if put on the market, will be successful is 65/80, or .8125.
   **d.** Cannot be less than 0. Perhaps a mistake in arithmetic.
   **e.** More than half of the persons testing the game liked it. (Of course, other answers are possible.)

**5–2** **1.** $\dfrac{4 \text{ queens in deck}}{52 \text{ cards total}} = \dfrac{4}{52} = .0769$
   Classical.

   **2.** $\dfrac{182}{539} = .338$   Empirical.

   **3.** The author's view when writing the text of the chance that the DJIA will climb to 12,000 is .25. You may be more optimistic or less optimistic. Subjective.

**5–3** **a.** **i.** $\dfrac{(50 + 68)}{2,000} = .059$

   **ii.** $1 - \dfrac{302}{2,000} = .849$

   **b.**

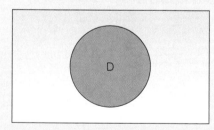

   **c.** They are not complementary, but are mutually exclusive.

**5–4** **a.** Need for corrective shoes is event $A$. Need for major dental work is event $B$.

   $P(A \text{ or } B) = P(A) + P(B) - P(A \text{ and } B)$

   $= .08 + .15 - .03$

   $= .20$

   **b.** One possibility is:

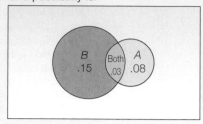

**5–5** $(.80)(.80)(.80)(.80) = .4096.$

**5–6** **a.** .002, found by:

   $\left(\dfrac{4}{12}\right)\left(\dfrac{3}{11}\right)\left(\dfrac{2}{10}\right)\left(\dfrac{1}{9}\right) = \dfrac{24}{11,880} = .002$

   **b.** .14, found by:

   $\left(\dfrac{8}{12}\right)\left(\dfrac{7}{11}\right)\left(\dfrac{6}{10}\right)\left(\dfrac{5}{9}\right) = \dfrac{1,680}{11,880} = .1414$

   **c.** No, because there are other possibilities, such as three women and one man.

**5–7** **a.** $P(B_4) = \dfrac{105}{200} = .525$

   **b.** $P(A_2 \mid B_4) = \dfrac{30}{105} = .286$

   **c.** $P(A_2 \text{ or } B_4) = \dfrac{80}{200} + \dfrac{105}{200} - \dfrac{30}{200} = \dfrac{155}{200} = .775$

**5–8** **a.** Contingency table
   **b.** Independence requires that $P(A \mid B) = P(A)$. One possibility is:

   $P(\text{visit often} \mid \text{yes convenient location}) = P(\text{visit often})$

   Does 60/90 = 80/195? No, the two variables are *not* independent.
   Therefore, any joint probability in the table must be computed by using the general rule of multiplication.

**c.**

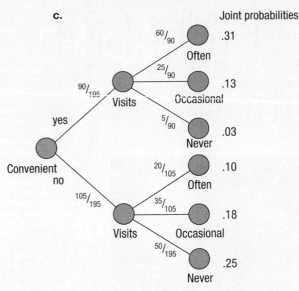

Joint probabilities

Often .31

Occasional .13

Never .03

Often .10

Occasional .18

Never .25

**5–9** **a.** $P(A_3|B_2) = \dfrac{P(A_3)P(B_2|A_3)}{P(A_1)P(B_2|A_1) + P(A_2)P(B_2|A_2) + P(A_3)P(B_2|A_3)}$

  **b.** $= \dfrac{.50(.96)}{(.30)(.97) + (.20)(.95) + (.50)(.96)}$

  $= \dfrac{.480}{.961} = .499$

**5–10** **a.** $(5)(4) = 20$

  **b.** $(3)(2)(4)(3) = 72$

**5–11** **1.** **a.** 60, found by (5)(4)(3).

  **b.** 60, found by:

  $$\frac{5!}{(5-3)!} = \frac{5 \cdot 4 \cdot 3 \cdot 2 \cdot 1}{2 \cdot 1}$$

  **2.** 24, found by:

  $$\frac{4!}{(4-4)!} = \frac{4!}{0!} = \frac{4!}{1} = \frac{4 \cdot 3 \cdot 2 \cdot 1}{1}$$

  **3.** 5,040, found by:

  $$\frac{10!}{(10-4)!} = \frac{10 \cdot 9 \cdot 8 \cdot 7 \cdot 6 \cdot 5 \cdot 4 \cdot 3 \cdot 2 \cdot 1}{6 \cdot 5 \cdot 4 \cdot 3 \cdot 2 \cdot 1}$$

  **4.** **a.** 56 is correct, found by:

  $$_8C_3 = \frac{n!}{r!(n-r)!} = \frac{8!}{3!(8-3)!} = 56$$

  **b.** Yes. There are 45 combinations, found by:

  $$_{10}C_2 = \frac{n!}{r!(n-r)!} = \frac{10!}{2!(10-2)!} = 45$$

  **5.** **a.** $_{50}P_3 = \dfrac{50!}{3!(50-3)!} = 117{,}600$

  **b.** $_{50}C_3 = \dfrac{50!}{3!(50-3)!} = 19{,}600$

# 6

# Discrete Probability Distributions

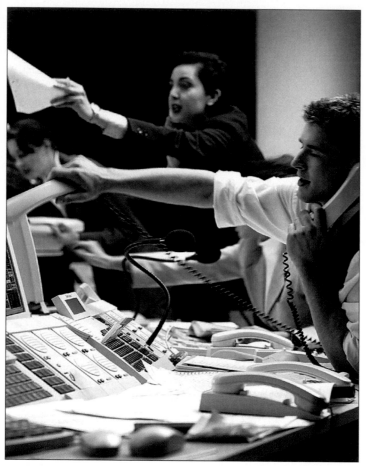

An American Society of Investors survey found 30 percent of individual investors have used a discount broker. In a random sample of nine individuals, what is the probability that exactly two of the sampled individuals have used a discount broker? (See Goal 4 and Exercise 13.)

# Introduction

Chapters 2 through 4 are devoted to descriptive statistics. We describe raw data by organizing it into a frequency distribution and portraying the distribution in tables, graphs, and charts. Also, we compute a measure of location—such as the arithmetic mean, median, or mode—to locate a typical value near the center of the distribution. The range and the standard deviation are used to describe the spread in the data. These chapters focus on describing *something that has already happened.*

Starting with Chapter 5, the emphasis changes—we begin examining *something that would probably happen.* We note that this facet of statistics is called *statistical inference.* The objective is to make inferences (statements) about a population based on a number of observations, called a sample, selected from the population. In Chapter 5, we state that a probability is a value between 0 and 1 inclusive, and we examine how probabilities can be combined using rules of addition and multiplication.

This chapter will begin the study of **probability distributions.** A probability distribution gives the entire range of values that can occur based on an experiment. A probability distribution is similar to a relative frequency distribution. However, instead of describing the past, it describes how likely some future event is. For example, a drug manufacturer may claim a treatment will cause weight loss for 80 percent of the population. A consumer protection agency may test the treatment on a sample of six people. If the manufacturer's claim is true, it is *almost impossible* to have an outcome where no one in the sample loses weight and it is *most likely* that 5 out of the 6 do lose weight.

In this chapter we discuss the mean, variance, and standard deviation of a probability distribution. We also discuss three frequently occurring probability distributions: the binomial, hypergeometric, and Poisson.

# What Is a Probability Distribution?

A probability distribution shows the possible outcomes of an experiment and the probability of each of these outcomes.

> **PROBABILITY DISTRIBUTION** A listing of all the outcomes of an experiment and the probability associated with each outcome.

How can we generate a probability distribution?

**EXAMPLE**

Suppose we are interested in the number of heads showing face up on three tosses of a coin. This is the experiment. The possible results are: zero heads, one head, two heads, and three heads. What is the probability distribution for the number of heads?

**SOLUTION**

There are eight possible outcomes. A tail might appear face up on the first toss, another tail on the second toss, and another tail on the third toss of the coin. Or we might get a tail, tail, and head, in that order. We use the multiplication formula for counting outcomes (5–8). There are (2)(2)(2) or 8 possible results. These results are listed below.

| Possible Result | Coin Toss | | | Number of Heads |
|---|---|---|---|---|
| | First | Second | Third | |
| 1 | T | T | T | 0 |
| 2 | T | T | H | 1 |
| 3 | T | H | T | 1 |
| 4 | T | H | H | 2 |
| 5 | H | T | T | 1 |
| 6 | H | T | H | 2 |
| 7 | H | H | T | 2 |
| 8 | H | H | H | 3 |

Note that the outcome "zero heads" occurred only once, "one head" occurred three times, "two heads" occurred three times, and the outcome "three heads" occurred only once. That is, "zero heads" happened one out of eight times. Thus, the probability of zero heads is one eighth, the probability of one head is three eighths, and so on. The probability distribution is shown in Table 6–1. Note that, since one of these outcomes must happen, the total of the probabilities of all possible events is 1.000. This is always true. The same information is shown in Chart 6–1.

**TABLE 6–1** Probability Distribution for the Events of Zero, One, Two, and Three Heads Showing Face Up on Three Tosses of a Coin

| Number of Heads, $x$ | Probability of Outcome, $P(x)$ |
|:---:|:---:|
| 0 | $\frac{1}{8} = .125$ |
| 1 | $\frac{3}{8} = .375$ |
| 2 | $\frac{3}{8} = .375$ |
| 3 | $\frac{1}{8} = .125$ |
| Total | $\frac{8}{8} = 1.000$ |

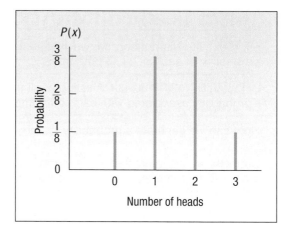

**CHART 6–1** Graphical Presentation of the Number of Heads Resulting from Three Tosses of a Coin and the Corresponding Probability

Characteristics of a probability distribution

Before continuing, we should note two important characteristics of a probability distribution.

1. The probability of a particular outcome is between 0 and 1, inclusive. [The probabilities of $x$, written $P(x)$ in the coin tossing example, were $P(0 \text{ head}) = 0.125$, $P(1 \text{ head}) = 0.375$, etc.]
2. The sum of the probabilities of all mutually exclusive events is 1.000. (Referring to Table 6–1, $.125 + .375 + .375 + .125 = 1.000$.)

**Self-Review 6–1**   The possible outcomes of an experiment involving the roll of a six-sided die are: a one-spot, a two-spot, a three-spot, a four-spot, a five-spot, and a six-spot.
(a)   Develop a probability distribution for the number of possible spots.
(b)   Portray the probability distribution graphically.
(c)   What is the sum of the probabilities?

# Random Variables

In any experiment of chance, the outcomes occur randomly. So it is often called a *random variable.* For example, rolling a single die is an experiment: any one of six possible outcomes can occur. Some experiments result in outcomes that are quantitative (such as dollars, weight, or number of children), and others result in qualitative outcomes (such as color or religious preference). A few examples will further illustrate what is meant by a **random variable.**

- If we count the number of employees absent from the day shift on Monday, the number might be 0, 1, 2, 3, . . . . The number absent is the random variable.
- If we weigh four steel ingots, the weights might be 2,492 pounds, 2,497 pounds, 2,506 pounds, and so on. The weight is the random variable.
- If we toss two coins and count the number of heads, there could be zero, one, or two heads. Because the number of heads resulting from this experiment is due to chance, the number of heads appearing is the random variable.
- Other random variables might be: the number of defective light bulbs produced during the week, the heights of the members of the girls' basketball team, the number of runners in the Boston Marathon for each of the last 20 years, and the daily number of drivers charged with driving under the influence of alcohol in Texas.

> **RANDOM VARIABLE**  A quantity resulting from an experiment that, by chance, can assume different values.

The following diagram illustrates the terms *experiment, outcome, event,* and *random variable.* First, for the experiment where a coin is tossed three times, there are eight possible outcomes. In this experiment, we are interested in the event that one head occurs in the three tosses. The random variable is the number of heads. In terms of probability, we want to know the probability of the event that the random variable equals 1. The result is $P$(1 head in 3 tosses) = 0.375.

Possible *outcomes* for three coin tosses

The *event* {one head} occurs and the *random variable x* = 1.

A random variable may be either *discrete* or *continuous.*

## Discrete Random Variable

A discrete random variable can assume only a certain number of separated values. If there are 100 employees, then the count of the number absent on Monday can only be 0, 1, 2, 3, . . . , 100. A discrete random variable is usually the result of counting something. By way of definition:

> **DISCRETE RANDOM VARIABLE** A random variable that can assume only certain clearly separated values.

A discrete random variable can, in some cases, assume fractional or decimal values. These values must be separated, that is, have distance between them. As an example, the scores awarded by judges for technical competence and artistic form in figure skating are decimal values, such as 7.2, 8.9, and 9.7. Such values are discrete because there is distance between scores of, say, 8.3 and 8.4. A score cannot be 8.34 or 8.347, for example.

## Continuous Random Variable

On the other hand, if the random variable is continuous, then the distribution is a continuous probability distribution. If we measure something such as the width of a room, the height of a person, or the pressure in an automobile tire, the variable is a *continuous random variable.* It can assume one of an infinitely large number of values, within certain limitations. As examples:

- The times of commercial flights between Atlanta and Los Angeles are 4.67 hours, 5.13 hours, and so on. The random variable is the number of hours.
- Tire pressure, measured in pounds per square inch (psi), for a new Chevy Trailblazer might be 32.78 psi, 31.62 psi, 33.07 psi, and so on. In other words, any values between 28 and 35 could reasonably occur. The random variable is the tire pressure.

Logically, if we organize a set of possible values of a discrete random variable in a probability distribution, the distribution is a **discrete probability distribution.**

The tools used, as well as the probability interpretations, are different for discrete and continuous random variables. This chapter is limited to discrete probability distributions. The next chapter will address two continuous probability distributions.

# The Mean, Variance, and Standard Deviation of a Probability Distribution

In Chapter 3 we discussed measures of location and variation for a frequency distribution. The mean reports the central location of the data, and the variance describes the spread in the data. In a similar fashion, a probability distribution is summarized by its mean and variance. We identify the mean of a probability distribution by the lowercase Greek letter mu ($\mu$) and the standard deviation by the lower-case Greek letter sigma ($\sigma$).

## Mean

The mean is a typical value used to represent the central location of a probability distribution. It also is the long-run average value of the random variable. The mean of a probability distribution is also referred to as its **expected value.** It is a weighted average where the possible values of a random variable are weighted by their corresponding probabilities of occurrence.

The mean of a discrete probability distribution is computed by the formula:

| MEAN OF A PROBABILITY DISTRIBUTION | $\mu = \Sigma[xP(x)]$ | [6–1] |
|---|---|---|

where $P(x)$ is the probability of a particular value $x$. In other words, multiply each $x$ value by its probability of occurrence, and then add these products.

## Variance and Standard Deviation

As noted, the mean is a typical value used to summarize a discrete probability distribution. However, it does not describe the amount of spread (variation) in a distribution. The variance does this. The formula for the variance of a probability distribution is:

| VARIANCE OF A PROBABILITY DISTRIBUTION | $\sigma^2 = \Sigma[(x - \mu)^2 P(x)]$ | [6–2] |
|---|---|---|

The computational steps are:

1. Subtract the mean from each value, and square this difference.
2. Multiply each squared difference by its probability.
3. Sum the resulting products to arrive at the variance.

The standard deviation, $\sigma$, is found by taking the positive square root of $\sigma^2$; that is, $\sigma = \sqrt{\sigma^2}$.

**EXAMPLE**

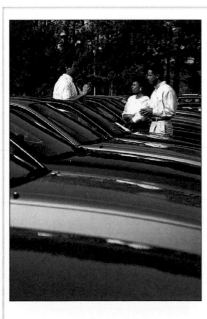

John Ragsdale sells new cars for Pelican Ford. John usually sells the largest number of cars on Saturday. He has the following probability distribution for the number of cars he expects to sell on a particular Saturday.

| Number of Cars Sold, x | Probability, P(x) |
|---|---|
| 0 | .1 |
| 1 | .2 |
| 2 | .3 |
| 3 | .3 |
| 4 | .1 |
| Total | 1.0 |

1. What type of distribution is this?
2. On a typical Saturday, how many cars does John expect to sell?
3. What is the variance of the distribution?

**SOLUTION**

1. This is a discrete probability distribution for the random variable called "number of cars sold." Note that John expects to sell only within a certain range of cars; he does not expect to sell 5 cars or 50 cars. Further, he cannot sell half a car. He can sell only 0, 1, 2, 3, or 4 cars. Also, the outcomes are mutually exclusive—he cannot sell a total of both 3 and 4 cars on the same Saturday.

2. The mean number of cars sold is computed by weighting the number of cars sold by the probability of selling that number and adding or summing the products, using formula (6–1):

$$\mu = \Sigma[xP(x)]$$
$$= 0(.10) + 1(.20) + 2(.30) + 3(.30) + 4(.10)$$
$$= 2.1$$

These calculations are summarized in the following table.

| Number of Cars Sold, x | Probability, P(x) | x · P(x) |
|---|---|---|
| 0 | .10 | 0.00 |
| 1 | .20 | 0.20 |
| 2 | .30 | 0.60 |
| 3 | .30 | 0.90 |
| 4 | .10 | 0.40 |
| Total | 1.00 | μ = 2.10 |

How do we interpret a mean of 2.1? This value indicates that, over a large number of Saturdays, John Ragsdale expects to sell a mean of 2.1 cars a day. Of course, it is not possible for him to sell *exactly* 2.1 cars on any particular Saturday. However, the expected value can be used to predict the arithmetic mean number of cars sold on Saturdays in the long run. For example, if John works 50 Saturdays during a year, he can expect to sell (50)(2.1) or 105 cars just on Saturdays. Thus, the mean is sometimes called the expected value.

3. Again, a table is useful for systemizing the computations for the variance, which is 1.290.

| Number of Cars Sold, x | Probability, P(x) | $(x-\mu)$ | $(x-\mu)^2$ | $(x-\mu)^2 P(x)$ |
|---|---|---|---|---|
| 0 | .10 | 0 − 2.1 | 4.41 | 0.441 |
| 1 | .20 | 1 − 2.1 | 1.21 | 0.242 |
| 2 | .30 | 2 − 2.1 | 0.01 | 0.003 |
| 3 | .30 | 3 − 2.1 | 0.81 | 0.243 |
| 4 | .10 | 4 − 2.1 | 3.61 | 0.361 |
| | | | | $\sigma^2 = 1.290$ |

Recall that the standard deviation, σ, is the positive square root of the variance. In this example, $\sqrt{\sigma^2} = \sqrt{1.290} = 1.136$ cars. How do we interpret a standard deviation of 1.136 cars? If salesperson Rita Kirsch also sold a mean of 2.1 cars on Saturdays, and the standard deviation in her sales was 1.91 cars, we would conclude that there is more variability in the Saturday sales of Ms. Kirsch than in those of Mr. Ragsdale (because 1.91 > 1.136).

**Self-Review 6–2**

The Pizza Palace offers three sizes of cola—small, medium, and large—to go with its pizza. The colas are sold for $0.80, $0.90, and $1.20, respectively. Thirty percent of the orders are for small, 50 percent are for medium, and 20 percent are for the large sizes. Organize the size of the colas and the probability of a sale into a probability distribution.
(a) Is this a discrete probability distribution? Indicate why or why not.
(b) Compute the mean amount charged for a cola.
(c) What is the variance in the amount charged for a cola? The standard deviation?

# Exercises

**1.** Compute the mean and variance of the following discrete probability distribution.

| x | P(x) |
|---|------|
| 0 | .2 |
| 1 | .4 |
| 2 | .3 |
| 3 | .1 |

**2.** Compute the mean and variance of the following discrete probability distribution.

| x | P(x) |
|---|------|
| 2 | .5 |
| 8 | .3 |
| 10 | .2 |

**3.** Three tables listed below show "random variables" and their "probabilities." However, only one of these is actually a probability distribution.
   **a.** Which is it?

| x | P(x) | | x | P(x) | | x | P(x) |
|---|------|---|---|------|---|---|------|
| 5 | .3 | | 5 | .1 | | 5 | .5 |
| 10 | .3 | | 10 | .3 | | 10 | .3 |
| 15 | .2 | | 15 | .2 | | 15 | −.2 |
| 20 | .4 | | 20 | .4 | | 20 | .4 |

   **b.** Using the correct probability distribution, find the probability that x is:
      **(1)** Exactly 15.      **(2)** No more than 10.      **(3)** More than 5.
   **c.** Compute the mean, variance, and standard deviation of this distribution.
**4.** Which of these variables are discrete and which are continuous random variables?
   **a.** The number of new accounts established by a salesperson in a year.
   **b.** The time between customer arrivals to a bank ATM.
   **c.** The number of customers in Big Nick's barber shop.
   **d.** The amount of fuel in your car's gas tank.
   **e.** The number of minorities on a jury.
   **f.** The outside temperature today.
**5.** Dan Woodward is the owner and manager of Dan's Truck Stop. Dan offers free refills on all coffee orders. He gathered the following information on coffee refills. Compute the mean, variance, and standard deviation for the distribution of number of refills.

| Refills | Percent |
|---------|---------|
| 0 | 30 |
| 1 | 40 |
| 2 | 20 |
| 3 | 10 |

**6.** The director of admissions at Kinzua University in Nova Scotia estimated the distribution of student admissions for the fall semester on the basis of past experience. What is the expected number of admissions for the fall semester? Compute the variance and the standard deviation of the number of admissions.

| Admissions | Probability |
|------------|-------------|
| 1,000 | .6 |
| 1,200 | .3 |
| 1,500 | .1 |

**7.** The following table lists the probability distribution for cash prizes in a lottery conducted at Lawson's Department Store.

| Prize ($) | Probability |
|---|---|
| 0 | .45 |
| 10 | .30 |
| 100 | .20 |
| 500 | .05 |

If you buy a single ticket, what is the probability that you win:
**a.** Exactly $100?     **b.** At least $10?     **c.** No more than $100?
**d.** Compute the mean, variance, and standard deviation of this distribution.

**8.** You are asked to match three songs with the performers who made those songs famous. If you guess, the probability distribution for the number of correct matches is:

| Probability | .333 | .500 | 0 | .167 |
|---|---|---|---|---|
| Number correct | 0 | 1 | 2 | 3 |

What is the probability you get:
**a.** Exactly one correct?     **b.** At least one correct?     **c.** Exactly two correct?
**d.** Compute the mean, variance, and standard deviation of this distribution.

# Binomial Probability Distribution

The **binomial probability distribution** is a widely occurring discrete probability distribution. One characteristic of a binomial distribution is that there are only two possible

outcomes on a particular trial of an experiment. For example, the statement in a true/false question is either true or false. The outcomes are mutually exclusive, meaning that the answer to a true/false question cannot be both true and false at the same time. As other examples, a product is classified as either acceptable or not acceptable by the quality control department, a worker is classified as employed or unemployed, and a sales call results in the customer either purchasing the product or not purchasing the product. Frequently, we classify the two possible outcomes as "success" and "failure." However, this classification does *not* imply that one outcome is good and the other is bad.

Another characteristic of the binomial distribution is that the random variable is the result of counts. That is, we count the number of successes in the total number of trials. We flip a fair coin five times and count the number of times a head appears; we select 10 workers and count the number who are over 50 years of age, or we select 20 boxes of Kellogg's Raisin Bran and count the number that weigh more than the amount indicated on the package.

A third characteristic of a binomial distribution is that the probability of a success remains the same from one trial to another. Two examples are:

• The probability you will guess the first question of a true/false test correctly (a success) is one half. This is the first "trial." The probability that you will guess correctly on the second question (the second trial) is also one half, the probability of success on the third trial is one half, and so on.

- If past experience revealed the swing bridge over the Intracoastal Waterway in Socastee was raised one out of every 20 times you approach it, then the probability is one-twentieth that it will be raised (a "success") the next time you approach it, one-twentieth the following time, and so on.

The final characteristic of a binomial probability distribution is that each trial is *independent* of any other trial. Independent means that there is no pattern to the trials. The outcome of a particular trial does not affect the outcome of any other trial.

Characteristics of a binomial distribution

> **BINOMIAL PROBABILITY DISTRIBUTION**
> 1. An outcome on each trial of an experiment is classified into one of two mutually exclusive categories—a success or a failure.
> 2. The random variable counts the number of successes in a fixed number of trials.
> 3. The probability of success and failure stay the same for each trial.
> 4. The trials are independent, meaning that the outcome of one trial does not affect the outcome of any other trial.

## How Is a Binomial Probability Distribution Computed?

To construct a particular binomial probability distribution, we use (1) the number of trials and (2) the probability of success on each trial. For example, if an examination at the conclusion of a management seminar consists of 20 multiple-choice questions, the number of trials is 20. If each question has five choices and only one choice is correct, the probability of success on each trial is .20. Thus, the probability is .20 that a person with no knowledge of the subject matter will guess the answer to a question correctly. So the conditions of the binomial distribution just noted are met.

The binomial probability distribution is computed by the formula:

> **BINOMIAL PROBABILITY DISTRIBUTION** $\qquad P(x) = {}_nC_x\,\pi^x(1 - \pi)^{n - x}$ $\qquad$ **[6–3]**

where:

$\qquad$ $C$ denotes a combination.
$\qquad$ $n$ is the number of trials.
$\qquad$ $x$ is the random variable defined as the number of successes.
$\qquad$ $\pi$ is the probability of a success on each trial.

We use the Greek letter $\pi$ (pi) to denote a binomial population parameter. Do not confuse it with the mathematical constant 3.1416.

**EXAMPLE**

There are five flights daily from Pittsburgh via US Airways into the Bradford, Pennsylvania Regional Airport. Suppose the probability that any flight arrives late is .20. What is the probability that none of the flights are late today? What is the probability that exactly one of the flights is late today?

**SOLUTION**

We can use Formula (6–3). The probability that a particular flight is late is .20, so let $\pi$ = .20. There are five flights, so $n$ = 5, and $x$, the random variable, refers to the number of successes. In this case a "success" is a plane that arrives late. Because there are no late arrivals $x = 0$.

$$P(0) = {}_nC_x(\pi)^x(1 - \pi)^{n - x}$$
$$= {}_5C_0(.20)^0(1 - .20)^{5 - 0} = (1)(1)(.3277) = .3277$$

The probability that exactly one of the five flights will arrive late today is .4096, found by

$$P(1) = {}_nC_x(\pi)^x(1 - \pi)^{n - x}$$
$$= {}_5C_1(.20)^1(1 - .20)^{5 - 1} = (5)(.20)(.4096) = .4096$$

The entire probability distribution is shown in Table 6–2.

**TABLE 6–2** Binomial Probability Distribution for $n = 5$, $\pi = .20$

| Number of Late Flights | Probability |
|:---:|:---:|
| 0 | .3277 |
| 1 | .4096 |
| 2 | .2048 |
| 3 | .0512 |
| 4 | .0064 |
| 5 | .0003 |
| Total | 1.0000 |

The random variable in Table 6–2 is plotted in Chart 6–2. Note that the distribution of the number of late arriving flights is positively skewed.

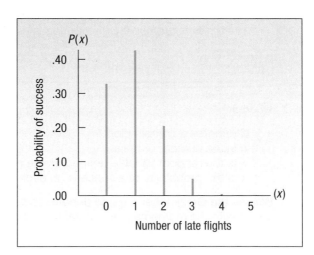

**CHART 6–2** Binomial Probability Distribution for $n = 5$, $\pi = .20$

The mean ($\mu$) and the variance ($\sigma^2$) of a binomial distribution can be computed in a "shortcut" fashion by:

| MEAN OF A BINOMIAL DISTRIBUTION | $\mu = n\pi$ | [6–4] |
|:---|:---:|---:|

| VARIANCE OF A BINOMIAL DISTRIBUTION | $\sigma^2 = n\pi(1 - \pi)$ | **[6–5]** |
|---|---|---|

For the example regarding the number of late flights, recall that $\pi = .20$ and $n = 5$. Hence:

$$\mu = n\pi = (5)(.20) = 1.0$$

$$\sigma^2 = n\pi(1 - \pi) = 5(.20)(1 - .20) = .80$$

The mean of 1.0 and the variance of .80 can be verified from formulas (6–1) and (6–2). The probability distribution from Table 6–2 and detailed calculations are shown below.

| Number of Late Flights, $x$ | $P(x)$ | $xP(x)$ | $x - \mu$ | $(x - \mu)^2$ | $(x - \mu)^2 P(x)$ |
|---|---|---|---|---|---|
| 0 | 0.3277 | 0.0000 | −1 | 1 | 0.3277 |
| 1 | 0.4096 | 0.4096 | 0 | 0 | 0 |
| 2 | 0.2048 | 0.4096 | 1 | 1 | 0.2048 |
| 3 | 0.0512 | 0.1536 | 2 | 4 | 0.2048 |
| 4 | 0.0064 | 0.0256 | 3 | 9 | 0.0576 |
| 5 | 0.0003 | 0.0015 | 4 | 16 | 0.0048 |
| | | $\mu = 1.0000$ | | | $\sigma^2 = 0.7997$ |

## Binomial Probability Tables

Formula (6–3) can be used to build a binomial probability distribution for any value of $n$ and $\pi$. However, for larger $n$, the calculations take more time. For convenience, the tables in Appendix A show the result of using the formula for various values of $n$ and $\pi$. Table 6–3 shows part of Appendix A for $n = 6$ and various values of $\pi$.

**TABLE 6–3** Binomial Probabilities for $n = 6$ and Selected Values of $\pi$

| $x\backslash\pi$ | .05 | .1 | .2 | .3 | .4 | .5 | .6 | .7 | .8 | .9 | .95 |
|---|---|---|---|---|---|---|---|---|---|---|---|
| 0 | .735 | .531 | .262 | .118 | .047 | .016 | .004 | .001 | .000 | .000 | .000 |
| 1 | .232 | .354 | .393 | .303 | .187 | .094 | .037 | .010 | .002 | .000 | .000 |
| 2 | .031 | .098 | .246 | .324 | .311 | .234 | .138 | .060 | .015 | .001 | .000 |
| 3 | .002 | .015 | .082 | .185 | .276 | .313 | .276 | .185 | .082 | .015 | .002 |
| 4 | .000 | .001 | .015 | .060 | .138 | .234 | .311 | .324 | .246 | .098 | .031 |
| 5 | .000 | .000 | .002 | .010 | .037 | .094 | .187 | .303 | .393 | .354 | .232 |
| 6 | .000 | .000 | .000 | .001 | .004 | .016 | .047 | .118 | .262 | .531 | .735 |

**EXAMPLE**

Five percent of the worm gears produced by an automatic, high-speed Carter-Bell milling machine are defective. What is the probability that out of six gears selected at random none will be defective? Exactly one? Exactly two? Exactly three? Exactly four? Exactly five? Exactly six out of six?

**SOLUTION**

The binomial conditions are met: (a) there are only two possible outcomes (a particular gear is either defective or acceptable), (b) there is a fixed number of trials (6), (c) There is a constant probability of success (.05), and (d) the trials are independent.

Refer to Table 6–3 for the probability of exactly zero defective gears. Go down the left margin to an $x$ of 0. Now move horizontally to the column headed by a $\pi$ of .05 to find the probability. It is .735.

The probability of exactly one defective in a sample of six worm gears is .232. The complete binomial probability distribution for $n = 6$ and $\pi = .05$ is:

| Number of Defective Gears, $x$ | Probability of Occurrence, $P(x)$ | Number of Defective Gears, $x$ | Probability of Occurrence, $P(x)$ |
|---|---|---|---|
| 0 | .735 | 4 | .000 |
| 1 | .232 | 5 | .000 |
| 2 | .031 | 6 | .000 |
| 3 | .002 | | |

Of course, there is a slight chance of getting exactly five defective gears out of six random selections. It is .00000178, found by inserting the appropriate values in the binomial formula:

$$P(5) = {_6}C_5(.05)^5(.95)^1 = (6)(.05)^5(.95) = .00000178$$

For six out of the six, the exact probability is .000000016. Thus, the probability is very small that five or six defective gears will be selected in a sample of six.

We can compute the mean or expected value of the distribution of the number defective:

$$\mu = n\pi = (6)(.05) = 0.30$$

$$\sigma^2 = n\pi(1 - \pi) = 6(.05)(.95) = 0.285$$

The MegaStat software will also compute the probabilities for a binomial distribution. Below is the output for the previous example. In MegaStat $p$ is used to represent the probability of success rather than $\pi$. The cumulative probability, expected value, variance, and standard deviation are also reported.

**Self-Review 6–3**

Eighty percent of the employees at the General Mills plant on Laskey Rd. have their bimonthly wages sent directly to their bank by electronic funds transfer. This is also called direct deposit. Suppose we select a random sample of seven recipients.

(a) Does this situation fit the assumptions of the binomial distribution?

(b) What is the probability that all seven employees use direct deposit?

(c) Use formula (6–3) to determine the exact probability that four of the seven sampled employees use direct deposit.

(d) Use Appendix A to verify your answers to parts (b) and (c).

Appendix A is limited. It gives probabilities for $n$ values from 1 to 15 and $\pi$ values of .05, .10, . . . , .90, and .95. A software program can generate the probabilities for a specified number of successes, given $n$ and $\pi$. The Excel output below shows the probability when $n = 40$ and $\pi = .09$. Note that the number of successes stops at 15 because the probabilities for 16 to 40 are very close to 0.

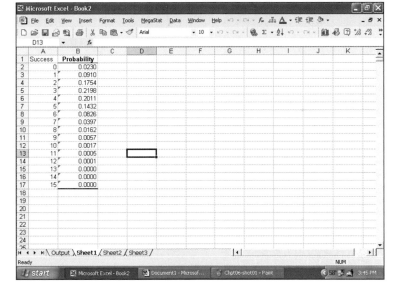

Several additional points should be made regarding the binomial probability distribution.

1.   If $n$ remains the same but $\pi$ increases from .05 to .95, the shape of the distribution changes. Look at Table 6–4 and Chart 6–3. The probabilities for a $\pi$ of .05 are

**TABLE 6–4** Probability of 0, 1, 2, . . . Successes for a $\pi$ of .05, .10, .20, .50, and .70 and an $n$ of 10

| $x \backslash \pi$ | .05 | .1 | .2 | .3 | .4 | .5 | .6 | .7 | .8 | .9 | .95 |
|---|---|---|---|---|---|---|---|---|---|---|---|
| 0 | .599 | .349 | .107 | .028 | .006 | .001 | .000 | .000 | .000 | .000 | .000 |
| 1 | .315 | .387 | .268 | .121 | .040 | .010 | .002 | .000 | .000 | .000 | .000 |
| 2 | .075 | .194 | .302 | .233 | .121 | .044 | .011 | .001 | .000 | .000 | .000 |
| 3 | .010 | .057 | .201 | .267 | .215 | .117 | .042 | .009 | .001 | .000 | .000 |
| 4 | .001 | .011 | .088 | .200 | .251 | .205 | .111 | .037 | .006 | .000 | .000 |
| 5 | .000 | .001 | .026 | .103 | .201 | .246 | .201 | .103 | .026 | .001 | .000 |
| 6 | .000 | .000 | .006 | .037 | .111 | .205 | .251 | .200 | .088 | .011 | .001 |
| 7 | .000 | .000 | .001 | .009 | .042 | .117 | .215 | .267 | .201 | .057 | .010 |
| 8 | .000 | .000 | .000 | .001 | .011 | .044 | .121 | .233 | .302 | .194 | .075 |
| 9 | .000 | .000 | .000 | .000 | .002 | .010 | .040 | .121 | .268 | .387 | .315 |
| 10 | .000 | .000 | .000 | .000 | .000 | .001 | .006 | .028 | .107 | .349 | .599 |

positively skewed. As π approaches .50, the distribution becomes symmetrical. As π goes beyond .50 and moves toward .95, the probability distribution becomes negatively skewed. Table 6–4 highlights probabilities for $n = 10$ and π of .05, .10, .20, .50, and .70. The graphs of these probability distributions are shown in Chart 6–3.

**CHART 6–3** Graphing the Binomial Probability Distribution for a π of .05, .10, .20, .50, and .70 and an $n$ of 10

2. If π, the probability of success, remains the same but $n$ becomes larger, the shape of the binomial distribution becomes more symmetrical. Chart 6–4 shows a situation where π remains constant at .10 but $n$ increases from 7 to 40.

**CHART 6–4** Chart Representing the Binomial Probability Distribution for a π of .10 and an $n$ of 7, 12, 20, and 40

# Exercises

9. In a binomial situation $n = 4$ and $\pi = .25$. Determine the probabilities of the following events using the binomial formula.
   **a.** $x = 2$
   **b.** $x = 3$
10. In a binomial situation $n = 5$ and $\pi = .40$. Determine the probabilities of the following events using the binomial formula.
    **a.** $x = 1$
    **b.** $x = 2$
11. Assume a binomial distribution where $n = 3$ and $\pi = .60$.
    **a.** Refer to Appendix A, and list the probabilities for values of $x$ from 0 to 3.
    **b.** Determine the mean and standard deviation of the distribution from the general definitions given in formulas (6–1) and (6–2).
12. Assume a binomial distribution where $n = 5$ and $\pi = .30$.
    **a.** Refer to Appendix A, and list the probabilities for values of $x$ from 0 to 5.
    **b.** Determine the mean and standard deviation of the distribution from the general definitions given in formulas (6–1) and (6–2).
13. An American Society of Investors survey found 30 percent of individual investors have used a discount broker. In a random sample of nine individuals, what is the probability:
    **a.** Exactly two of the sampled individuals have used a discount broker?
    **b.** Exactly four of them have used a discount broker?
    **c.** None of them have used a discount broker?
14. The United States Postal Service reports 95 percent of first class mail within the same city is delivered within two days of the time of mailing. Six letters are randomly sent to different locations.
    **a.** What is the probability that all six arrive within two days?
    **b.** What is the probability that exactly five arrive within two days?
    **c.** Find the mean number of letters that will arrive within two days.
    **d.** Compute the variance and standard deviation of the number that will arrive within two days.
15. The industry standards suggest that 10 percent of new vehicles require warranty service within the first year. Jones Nissan in Sumter, South Carolina, sold 12 Nissans yesterday.
    **a.** What is the probability that none of these vehicles requires warranty service?
    **b.** What is the probability exactly one of these vehicles requires warranty service?
    **c.** Determine the probability that exactly two of these vehicles require warranty service.
    **d.** Compute the mean and standard deviation of this probability distribution.
16. A telemarketer makes six phone calls per hour and is able to make a sale on 30 percent of these contacts. During the next two hours, find:
    **a.** The probability of making exactly four sales.
    **b.** The probability of making no sales.
    **c.** The probability of making exactly two sales.
    **d.** The mean number of sales in the two-hour period.
17. A recent survey by the American Accounting Association revealed 23 percent of students graduating with a major in accounting select public accounting. Suppose we select a sample of 15 recent graduates.
    **a.** What is the probability two select public accounting?
    **b.** What is the probability five select public accounting?
    **c.** How many graduates would you expect to select public accounting?
18. Suppose 60 percent of all people prefer Coke to Pepsi. We select 18 people for further study.
    **a.** How many would you expect to prefer Coke?
    **b.** What is the probability 10 of those surveyed will prefer Coke?
    **c.** What is the probability 15 prefer Coke?

## Cumulative Binomial Probability Distributions

We may wish to know the probability of correctly guessing the answers to 6 *or more* true/false questions out of 10. Or we may be interested in the probability of *selecting less than two* defectives at random from production during the previous hour. In these cases we need cumulative frequency distributions similar to the ones developed in Chapter 2. See page 37. The following example will illustrate.

**EXAMPLE**

A recent study by the American Highway Patrolman's Association revealed that 60 percent of American drivers use their seat belts. A sample of 10 drivers on the Florida Turnpike is selected.

1. What is the probability that exactly 7 are wearing seat belts?
2. What is the probability that 7 or fewer of the drivers are wearing seat belts?

**SOLUTION**

This situation meets the binomial requirements, namely:

- A particular driver either is wearing a seat belt or is not. There are only two possible outcomes.
- There is a fixed number of trials—10 in this case, because 10 drivers are checked.
- The probability of "success" (wearing a seat belt) is the same from driver to driver: 60 percent.
- The trials are independent. If the fourth driver selected in the sample is wearing a seat belt, for example, it has no effect on whether the fifth driver selected is wearing a seat belt.

1. To find the likelihood of *exactly* 7 drivers, we use Appendix A. Locate the page for $n = 10$. Next find the column for $\pi = .60$ and the row for $x = 7$. The value is .215. Thus, the probability of finding 7 out of 10 drivers in the sample wearing their seat belts is .215. This is often written as follows:

$$P(x = 7 \mid n = 10 \text{ and } \pi = .60) = .215$$

where $x$ refers to the number of successes, $n$ the number of trials, and $\pi$ the probability of a success. The bar "|" means "given that."

2. To find the probability that 7 or fewer of the drivers will be wearing seat belts, we apply the special rule of addition, formula (5–2), from Chapter 5. Because the events are mutually exclusive, we determine the probability that of the 10 drivers stopped, none was wearing a seat belt, 1 was wearing a seat belt, 2 were wearing a seat belt, and so on up to 7 drivers. The probabilities of the eight possible outcomes are then totaled. From Appendix A, $n = 10$, and $\pi = .60$.

$$P(x \le 7 \mid n = 10 \text{ and } \pi = .60) = P(x = 0) + P(x = 1) + P(x = 2) + P(x = 3)$$
$$+ P(x = 4) + P(x = 5) + P(x = 6) + P(x = 7)$$
$$= .000 + .002 + .011 + .042 + .111 + .201$$
$$+ .251 + .215$$
$$= .833$$

So the probability of stopping 10 cars at random and finding 7 or fewer of the drivers wearing their seat belts is .833.

This value may also be determined, with less computation, using the complement rule. First, find $P(x > 7)$ given that $n = 10$ and $\pi = .60$. This probability is .167, found by $P(x = 8) + P(x = 9) + P(x = 10) = .121 + .040 + .006$. The probability that $x \le 7$ is equal to $1 - P(x > 7)$, so $P(x \le 7) = 1 - .167 = .833$, the same as computed above.

---

**Self-Review 6–4**

For a case where $n = 4$ and $\pi = .60$, determine the probability that:
(a) $x = 2$.
(b) $x \le 2$.
(c) $x > 2$.

# Exercises

**19.** In a binomial distribution $n = 8$ and $\pi = .30$. Find the probabilities of the following events.
   **a.** $x = 2$.
   **b.** $x \leq 2$ (the probability that $x$ is equal to or less than 2).
   **c.** $x \geq 3$ (the probability that $x$ is equal to or greater than 3).
**20.** In a binomial distribution $n = 12$ and $\pi = .60$. Find the following probabilities.
   **a.** $x = 5$.
   **b.** $x \leq 5$.
   **c.** $x \geq 6$.
**21.** In a recent study 90 percent of the homes in the United States were found to have large-screen TVs. In a sample of nine homes, what is the probability that:
   **a.** All nine have large-screen TVs?
   **b.** Less than five have large-screen TVs?
   **c.** More than five have large-screen TVs?
   **d.** At least seven homes have large-screen TVs?
**22.** A manufacturer of window frames knows from long experience that 5 percent of the production will have some type of minor defect that will require an adjustment. What is the probability that in a sample of 20 window frames:
   **a.** None will need adjustment?
   **b.** At least one will need adjustment?
   **c.** More than two will need adjustment?
**23.** The speed with which utility companies can resolve problems is very important. GTC, the Georgetown Telephone Company, reports they can resolve customer problems the same day they are reported in 70 percent of the cases. Suppose the 15 cases reported today are representative of all complaints.
   **a.** How many of the problems would you expect to be resolved today? What is the standard deviation?
   **b.** What is the probability 10 of the problems can be resolved today?
   **c.** What is the probability 10 or 11 of the problems can be resolved today?
   **d.** What is the probability more than 10 of the problems can be resolved today?
**24.** Steele Electronics, Inc. sells expensive brands of stereo equipment in several shopping malls throughout the northwest section of the United States. The Marketing Research Department of Steele reports that 30 percent of the customers entering the store that indicate they are browsing will, in the end, make a purchase. Let the last 20 customers who enter the store be a sample.
   **a.** How many of these customers would you expect to make a purchase?
   **b.** What is the probability that exactly five of these customers make a purchase?
   **c.** What is the probability ten or more make a purchase?
   **d.** Does it seem likely at least one will make a purchase?

# Hypergeometric Probability Distribution

For the binomial distribution to be applied, the probability of a success must stay the same for each trial. For example, the probability of guessing the correct answer to a true/false question is .50. This probability remains the same for each question on an examination. Likewise, suppose that 40 percent of the registered voters in a precinct are Republicans. If 27 registered voters are to be selected at random, the probability of choosing a Republican on the first selection is .40. The chance of choosing a Republican on the next selection is also .40, assuming that the sampling is done *with replacement,* meaning that the person selected is put back in the population before the next person is selected.

Most sampling, however, is done *without replacement.* Thus, if the population is small, the probability for each observation will change. For example, if the population consists of 20 items, the probability of selecting a particular item from that population is 1/20. If the sampling is done without replacement, after the first selection there are only 19 items remaining; the probability of selecting a particular item on the second selection is only 1/19. For the third selection, the probability is 1/18, and so on. This assumes that the population is **finite**—that is, the number in the population is known and relatively small in number. Examples of a finite population are 2,842 Republicans in the precinct, 9,241 applications for medical school, and the 18 Pontiac Vibes currently in stock at North Charleston Pontiac.

Recall that one of the criteria for the binomial distribution is that the probability of success remain the same from trial to trial. Since the probability of success does not remain the same from trial to trial when sampling is from a relatively small population without replacement, the binomial distribution should not be used. Instead, the **hypergeometric distribution** should be applied. Therefore, (1) if a sample is selected from a finite population without replacement and (2) if the size of the sample $n$ is more than 5 percent of the size of the population $N$, then the hypergeometric distribution is used to determine the probability of a specified number of successes or failures. It is especially appropriate when the size of the population is small.

The formula for the hypergeometric distribution is:

| **HYPERGEOMETRIC DISTRIBUTION** | $P(x) = \dfrac{(_sC_x)(_{N-s}C_{n-x})}{_NC_n}$ | **[6–6]** |
|---|---|---|

where:

$N$ is the size of the population.
$S$ is the number of successes in the population.
$x$ is the number of successes in the sample. It may be 0, 1, 2, 3, . . . .
$n$ is the size of the sample or the number of trials.
$C$ is the symbol for a combination.

In summary, a hypergeometric probability distribution has these characteristics:

---

**HYPERGEOMETRIC PROBABILITY DISTRIBUTION**
1. An outcome on each trial of an experiment is classified into one of two mutually exclusive categories—a success or a failure.
2. The random variable is the number of successes in a fixed number of trials.
3. The trials are *not independent*.
4. We assume that we sample from a finite population without replacement. So, the probability of a success *changes* for each trial.

---

The following example illustrates the details of determining a probability using the hypergeometric distribution.

**EXAMPLE**

PlayTime Toys, Inc. employs 50 people in the Assembly Department. Forty of the employees belong to a union and ten do not. Five employees are selected at random to form a committee to meet with management regarding shift starting times. What is the probability that four of the five selected for the committee belong to a union?

**SOLUTION**

The population in this case is the 50 Assembly Department employees. An employee can be selected for the committee only once. Hence, the sampling is done without replacement. Thus, the probability of selecting a union employee, for example, changes from one trial to the next. The hypergeometric distribution is appropriate for determining the probability. In this problem,

$N$ is 50, the number of employees.
$S$ is 40, the number of union employees.
$x$ is 4, the number of union employees selected.
$n$ is 5, the number of employees selected.

We wish to find the probability 4 of the 5 committee members belong to a union. Inserting these values into formula (6–6):

$$P(4) = \frac{(_{40}C_4)(_{50-40}C_{5-4})}{_{50}C_5} = \frac{\left(\dfrac{40!}{4!36!}\right)\left(\dfrac{10!}{1!9!}\right)}{\dfrac{50!}{5!45!}} = \frac{(91{,}390)(10)}{2{,}118{,}760} = .431$$

Thus, the probability of selecting 5 assembly workers at random from the 50 workers and finding 4 of the 5 are union members is .431.

Table 6–5 shows the hypergeometric probabilities of finding 0, 1, 2, 3, 4, and 5 union members on the committee.

**TABLE 6–5** Hypergeometric Probabilities ($n = 5$, $N = 50$, and $S = 40$) for the Number of Union Members on the Committee

| Union Members | Probability |
|---------------|-------------|
| 0 | .000 |
| 1 | .004 |
| 2 | .044 |
| 3 | .210 |
| 4 | .431 |
| 5 | .311 |
| | 1.000 |

In order for you to compare the two probability distributions, Table 6–6 shows the hypergeometric and binomial probabilities for the PlayTime Toys, Inc. example. Because 40 of the 50 Assembly Department employees belong to the union, we let $\pi = .80$ for the binomial distribution. The binomial probabilities for Table 6–6 come from the binomial distribution with $n = 5$ and $\pi = .80$.

**TABLE 6–6** Hypergeometric and Binomial Probabilities for Playtime Toys, Inc. Assembly Department

| Number of Union Members on Committee | Hypergeometric Probability, $P(x)$ | Binomial Probability ($n = 5$ and $\pi = .80$) |
|---|---|---|
| 0 | .000 | .000 |
| 1 | .004 | .006 |
| 2 | .044 | .051 |
| 3 | .210 | .205 |
| 4 | .431 | .410 |
| 5 | .311 | .328 |
| | 1.000 | 1.000 |

When the binomial requirement of a constant probability of success cannot be met, the hypergeometric distribution should be used. However, as Table 6–6 shows, under certain conditions the results of the binomial distribution can be used to approximate the hypergeometric. This leads to a rule of thumb:

If selected items are not returned to the population, the binomial distribution can be used to closely approximate the hypergeometric distribution when $n < .05N$. In words, the binomial will suffice if the sample size is less than 5 percent of the population.

A hypergeometric distribution can be created using Excel. See the following output. The necessary steps are given in the Software Commands section.

**Self-Review 6–5**   Horwege Discount Brokers plans to hire 5 new financial analysts this year. There is a pool of 12 approved applicants, and George Horwege, the owner, decides to randomly select those who will be hired. There are 8 men and 4 women among the approved applicants. What is the probability that 3 of the 5 hired are men?

# Exercises

25. A population consists of ten items, six of which are defective. In a sample of three items, what is the probability that exactly two are defective? Assume the samples are drawn without replacement.

26. A population consists of 15 items, 10 of which are acceptable. In a sample of 4 items, what is the probability that exactly 3 are acceptable? Assume the samples are drawn without replacement.

27. Kolzak Appliance Outlet just received a shipment of ten DVD players. Shortly after they were received, the manufacturer called to report that he had inadvertently shipped three defective units. Ms. Kolzak, the owner of the outlet, decided to test two of the ten DVD players she received. What is the probability that neither of the two DVD players tested is defective? Assume the samples are drawn without replacement.

28. The Computer Systems Department has eight faculty, six of whom are tenured. Dr. Vonder, the chairman, wants to establish a committee of three department faculty members to review the curriculum. If she selects the committee at random:
    a. What is the probability all members of the committee are tenured?
    b. What is the probability that at least one member is not tenured? (Hint: For this question, use the complement rule.)

29. Keith's Florists has 15 delivery trucks, used mainly to deliver flowers and flower arrangements in the Greenville, South Carolina, area. Of these 15 trucks, 6 have brake problems. A sample of 5 trucks is randomly selected. What is the probability that 2 of those tested have defective brakes?

30. Professor Jon Hammer has a pool of 15 multiple-choice questions regarding probability distributions. Four of these questions involve the hypergeometric distribution. What is the probability at least one of these hypergeometric questions will appear on the five-question quiz on Monday?

# Poisson Probability Distribution

The **Poisson probability distribution** describes the number of times some event occurs during a specified interval. The interval may be time, distance, area, or volume.

The distribution is based on two assumptions. The first assumption is that the probability is proportional to the length of the interval. The second assumption is that the intervals are independent. To put it another way, the longer the interval the larger the probability, and the number of occurrences in one interval does not affect the other intervals. This distribution is also a limiting form of the binomial distribution when the probability of a success is very small and $n$ is large. It is often referred to as the "law of improbable events," meaning that the probability, $\pi$, of a particular event's happening is quite small. The Poisson distribution is a discrete probability distribution because it is formed by counting.

In summary, a Poisson probability distribution has these characteristics:

---

**POISSON PROBABILITY DISTRIBUTION**
1. The random variable is the number of times some event occurs during a defined interval.
2. The probability of the event is proportional to the size of the interval.
3. The intervals which do not overlap and are independent.

---

This distribution has many applications. It is used as a model to describe the distribution of errors in data entry, the number of scratches and other imperfections in newly painted car panels, the number of defective parts in outgoing shipments, the number of customers waiting to be served at a restaurant or waiting to get into an attraction at Disney World, and the number of accidents on I–75 during a three-month period.

The Poisson distribution can be described mathematically by the formula:

---

**POISSON DISTRIBUTION** $$P(x) = \frac{\mu^x e^{-\mu}}{x!}$$ **[6–7]**

---

where:

$\mu$ (mu) is the mean number of occurrences (successes) in a particular interval.
$e$ is the constant 2.71828 (base of the Naperian logarithmic system).
$x$ is the number of occurrences (successes).
$P(x)$ is the probability for a specified value of $x$.

The mean number of successes, $\mu$, can be determined by $n\pi$, where $n$ is the total number of trials and $\pi$ the probability of success.

---

**MEAN OF A POISSON DISTRIBUTION** $$\mu = n\pi$$ **[6–8]**

---

The variance of the Poisson is also equal to its mean. If, for example, the probability that a check cashed by a bank will bounce is .0003, and 10,000 checks are cashed, the mean and the variance for the number of bad checks is 3.0, found by $\mu = n\pi = 10,000(.0003) = 3.0$.

Recall that for a binomial distribution there is a fixed number of trials. For example, for a four-question multiple-choice test there can only be zero, one, two, three, or four successes (correct answers). The random variable, $x$, for a Poisson distribution, however, can assume an *infinite number of values*—that is, 0, 1, 2, 3, 4, 5, . . . . However, *the probabilities become very small after the first few occurrences* (successes).

To illustrate the Poisson probability computation, assume baggage is rarely lost by Northwest Airlines. Most flights do not experience any mishandled bags; some have one bag lost; a few have two bags lost; rarely a flight will have three lost bags; and so on. Suppose a random sample of 1,000 flights shows a total of 300 bags were lost. Thus, the arithmetic mean number of lost bags per flight is 0.3, found by 300/1,000. If the number of lost bags per flight follows a Poisson distribution with $\mu = 0.3$, we can compute the various probabilities using formula (6–7):

$$P(x) = \frac{\mu^x e^{-\mu}}{x!}$$

For example, the probability of not losing any bags is:

$$P(0) = \frac{(0.3)^0 (e^{-0.3})}{0!} = 0.7408$$

In other words, 74 percent of the flights will have no lost baggage. The probability of exactly one lost bag is:

$$P(1) = \frac{(0.3)^1 (e^{-0.3})}{1!} = 0.2222$$

Thus, we would expect to find exactly one lost bag on 22 percent of the flights.
Poisson probabilities can also be found in the table in Appendix C.

**EXAMPLE**

Recall from the previous illustration that the number of lost bags follows a Poisson distribution with a mean of 0.3. Use Appendix C to find the probability that no bags will be lost on a particular flight. What is the probability exactly one bag will be lost on a particular flight? When should the supervisor become suspicious that a flight is having too many lost bags?

**SOLUTION**

Part of Appendix C is repeated as Table 6–7. To find the probability of no lost bags, locate the column headed "0.3" and read down that column to the row labeled "0." The probability is .7408. That is the probability of no lost bags. The probability of one lost bag is .2222, which is in the next row of the table, in the same column. The probability of two lost bags is .0333, in the row below; for three lost bags it is .0033; and for four lost bags it is .0003. Thus, a supervisor should not be surprised to find one lost bag but should expect to see more than one lost bag infrequently.

**TABLE 6–7** Poisson Table for Various Values of $\mu$ (from Appendix C)

| x | 0.1 | 0.2 | 0.3 | 0.4 | 0.5 | 0.6 | 0.7 | 0.8 | 0.9 |
|---|------|------|------|------|------|------|------|------|------|
| 0 | 0.9048 | 0.8187 | 0.7408 | 0.6703 | 0.6065 | 0.5488 | 0.4966 | 0.4493 | 0.4066 |
| 1 | 0.0905 | 0.1637 | 0.2222 | 0.2681 | 0.3033 | 0.3293 | 0.3476 | 0.3595 | 0.3659 |
| 2 | 0.0045 | 0.0164 | 0.0333 | 0.0536 | 0.0758 | 0.0988 | 0.1217 | 0.1438 | 0.1647 |
| 3 | 0.0002 | 0.0011 | 0.0033 | 0.0072 | 0.0126 | 0.0198 | 0.0284 | 0.0383 | 0.0494 |
| 4 | 0.0000 | 0.0001 | 0.0003 | 0.0007 | 0.0016 | 0.0030 | 0.0050 | 0.0077 | 0.0111 |
| 5 | 0.0000 | 0.0000 | 0.0000 | 0.0001 | 0.0002 | 0.0004 | 0.0007 | 0.0012 | 0.0020 |
| 6 | 0.0000 | 0.0000 | 0.0000 | 0.0000 | 0.0000 | 0.0000 | 0.0001 | 0.0002 | 0.0003 |
| 7 | 0.0000 | 0.0000 | 0.0000 | 0.0000 | 0.0000 | 0.0000 | 0.0000 | 0.0000 | 0.0000 |

These probabilities can also be found using the MINITAB system. The commands necessary are reported at the end of the chapter.

The Poisson probability distribution is always positively skewed. Also, the Poisson random variable has no specific upper limit. The Poisson distribution for the lost bags illustration, where $\mu = 0.3$, is highly skewed. As $\mu$ becomes larger, the Poisson distribution becomes more symmetrical. For example, Chart 6–5 shows the distributions of the number of transmission services, muffler replacements, and oil changes per day at Avellino's Auto Shop. They follow Poisson distributions with means of 0.7, 2.0, and 6.0, respectively.

**CHART 6–5** Poisson Probability Distributions for Means of 0.7, 2.0, and 6.0

Only $\mu$ needed to construct Poisson

In summary, the Poisson distribution is actually a family of discrete distributions. All that is needed to construct a Poisson probability distribution is the mean number of defects, errors, and so on—designated as $\mu$.

**Self-Review 6–6**

From actuary tables the Washington Insurance Company determined the likelihood that a man age 25 will die within the next year is .0002. If Washington Insurance sells 4,000 policies to 25-year-old men this year, what is the probability they will pay on exactly one policy?

# Exercises

31. In a Poisson distribution $\mu = 0.4$.
    a. What is the probability that $x = 0$?
    b. What is the probability that $x > 0$?
32. In a Poisson distribution $\mu = 4$.
    a. What is the probability that $x = 2$?
    b. What is the probability that $x \leq 2$?
    c. What is the probability that $x > 2$?
33. Ms. Bergen is a loan officer at Coast Bank and Trust. From her years of experience, she estimates that the probability is .025 that an applicant will not be able to repay his or her installment loan. Last month she made 40 loans.
    a. What is the probability that 3 loans will be defaulted?
    b. What is the probability that at least 3 loans will be defaulted?
34. Automobiles arrive at the Elkhart exit of the Indiana Toll Road at the rate of two per minute. The distribution of arrivals approximates a Poisson distribution.
    a. What is the probability that no automobiles arrive in a particular minute?
    b. What is the probability that at least one automobile arrives during a particular minute?
35. It is estimated that 0.5 percent of the callers to the Customer Service department of Dell, Inc. will receive a busy signal. What is the probability that of today's 1,200 callers at least 5 received a busy signal?
36. Textbook authors and publishers work very hard to minimize the number of errors in a text. However, some errors are unavoidable. Mr. J. A. Carmen, statistics editor, reports that the mean number of errors per chapter is 0.8. What is the probability that there are less than 2 errors in a particular chapter?

# Chapter Outline

I. A random variable is a numerical value determined by the outcome of an experiment.

II. A probability distribution is a listing of all possible outcomes of an experiment and the probability associated with each outcome.

   A. A discrete probability distribution can assume only certain values. The main features are:

   1. The sum of the probabilities is 1.00.

   2. The probability of a particular outcome is between 0.00 and 1.00.

   3. The outcomes are mutually exclusive.

   B. A continuous distribution can assume an infinite number of values within a specific range.

III. The mean and variance of a probability distribution are computed as follows.

   A. The mean is equal to:

$$\mu = \Sigma[xP(x)] \qquad\qquad \text{[6–1]}$$

   B. The variance is equal to:

$$\sigma^2 = \Sigma[(x - \mu)^2 P(x)] \qquad\qquad \text{[6–2]}$$

IV. The binomial distribution has the following characteristics.

   A. Each outcome is classified into one of two mutually exclusive categories.

   B. The distribution results from a count of the number of successes in a fixed number of trials.

   C. The probability of a success remains the same from trial to trial.

   D. Each trial is independent.

   E. A binomial probability is determined as follows:

$$P(x) = {}_nC_x\, \pi^x\, (1 - \pi)^{n - x} \qquad\qquad \text{[6–3]}$$

   F. The mean is computed as:

$$\mu = n\pi \qquad\qquad \text{[6–4]}$$

   G. The variance is

$$\sigma^2 = n\pi(1 - \pi) \qquad\qquad \text{[6–5]}$$

V. The hypergeometric distribution has the following characteristics.

   A. There are only two possible outcomes.

   B. The probability of a success is not the same on each trial.

   C. The distribution results from a count of the number of successes in a fixed number of trials.

   D. Used when sampling without replacement from a finite population.

   E. A hypergeometric probability is computed from the following equation.

$$P(x) = \frac{({}_sC_x)({}_{N-s}C_{n-x})}{({}_NC_n)} \qquad\qquad \text{[6–6]}$$

VI. The Poisson distribution has the following characteristics.

   A. It describes the number of times some event occurs during a specified interval.

   B. The probability of a "success" is proportional to the length of the interval.

   C. Nonoverlapping intervals are independent.

   D. It is a limiting form of the binomial distribution when $n$ is large and $\pi$ is small.

   E. Used when the sample size is more than 5 percent of the population size.

   F. A Poisson probability is determined from the following equation:

$$P(x) = \frac{\mu^x e^{-\mu}}{x!} \qquad\qquad \text{[6–7]}$$

   G. The mean and the variance are:

$$\mu = n\pi$$
$$\sigma^2 = n\pi \qquad\qquad \text{[6–8]}$$

# Chapter Exercises

**37.** What is the difference between a random variable and a probability distribution?

**38.** For each of the following indicate whether the random variable is discrete or continuous.
   **a.** The length of time to get a haircut.
   **b.** The number of cars a jogger passes each morning while running.
   **c.** The number of hits for a team in a high school girls' softball game.
   **d.** The number of patients treated at the South Strand Medical Center between 6 and 10 P.M. each night.
   **e.** The number of miles your car traveled on the last fill-up.
   **f.** The number of customers at the Oak Street Wendy's who used the drive-through facility.
   **g.** The distance between Gainesville, Florida, and all Florida cities with a population of at least 50,000.

**39.** What are the requirements for the binomial distribution?

**40.** Under what conditions will the binomial and the Poisson distributions give roughly the same results?

**41.** Samson Apartments, Inc. has a large number of units available to rent each month. A concern of management is the number of vacant apartments each month. A recent study revealed the percent of the time that a given number of apartments are vacant. Compute the mean and standard deviation of the number of vacant apartments.

| Number of Vacant Units | Probability |
|:---:|:---:|
| 0 | .1 |
| 1 | .2 |
| 2 | .3 |
| 3 | .4 |

**42.** An investment will be worth $1,000, $2,000, or $5,000 at the end of the year. The probabilities of these values are .25, .60, and .15, respectively. Determine the mean and variance of the worth of the investment.

**43.** The personnel manager of the Cumberland Pig Iron Company is studying the number of on-the-job accidents over a period of one month. He developed the following probability distribution. Compute the mean, variance, and standard deviation of the number of accidents in a month.

| Number of Accidents | Probability |
|:---:|:---:|
| 0 | .40 |
| 1 | .20 |
| 2 | .20 |
| 3 | .10 |
| 4 | .10 |

**44.** Croissant Bakery, Inc. offers special decorated cakes for birthdays, weddings, and other occasions. They also have regular cakes available in their bakery. The following table gives the total number of cakes sold per day and the corresponding probability. Compute the mean, variance, and standard deviation of the number of cakes sold per day.

| Number of Cakes Sold in a Day | Probability |
|:---:|:---:|
| 12 | .25 |
| 13 | .40 |
| 14 | .25 |
| 15 | .10 |

**45.** A Tamiami shearing machine is producing 10 percent defective pieces, which is abnormally high. The quality control engineer has been checking the output by almost continuous sampling since the abnormal condition began. What is the probability that in a sample of 10 pieces:

    **a.** Exactly 5 will be defective?

    **b.** 5 or more will be defective?

**46.** Thirty percent of the population in a southwestern community are Spanish-speaking Americans. A Spanish-speaking person is accused of killing a non-Spanish-speaking American. Of the first 12 potential jurors, only 2 are Spanish-speaking Americans, and 10 are not. The defendant's lawyer challenges the jury selection, claiming bias against her client. The government lawyer disagrees, saying that the probability of this particular jury composition is common. What do you think?

**47.** An auditor for Health Maintenance Services of Georgia reports 40 percent of the policyholders 55 years or older submit a claim during the year. Fifteen policyholders are randomly selected for company records.

    **a.** How many of the policyholders would you expect to have filed a claim within the last year?

    **b.** What is the probability that ten of the selected policyholders submitted a claim last year?

    **c.** What is the probability that ten or more of the selected policyholders submitted a claim last year?

    **d.** What is the probability that more than ten of the selected policyholders submitted a claim last year?

**48.** Tire and Auto Supply is considering a 2-for-1 stock split. Before the transaction is finalized, at least two-thirds of the 1,200 company stockholders must approve the proposal. To evaluate the likelihood the proposal will be approved, the director of finance selected a sample of 18 stockholders. He contacted each and found 14 approved of the proposed split. What is the likelihood of this event, assuming two-thirds of the stockholders approve?

**49.** A federal study reported that 7.5 percent of the U.S. workforce has a drug problem. A drug enforcement official for the State of Indiana wished to investigate this statement. In his sample of 20 employed workers:

    **a.** How many would you expect to have a drug problem? What is the standard deviation?

    **b.** What is the likelihood that *none* of the workers sampled has a drug problem?

    **c.** What is the likelihood *at least one* has a drug problem?

**50.** The Bank of Hawaii reports that 7 percent of its credit card holders will default at some time in their life. The Hilo branch just mailed out 12 new cards today.

    **a.** How many of these new cardholders would you expect to default? What is the standard deviation?

    **b.** What is the likelihood that *none* of the cardholders will default?

    **c.** What is the likelihood *at least one* will default?

**51.** Recent statistics suggest that 15 percent of those who visit a retail site on the World Wide Web make a purchase. A local retailer wished to verify this claim. To do so, she selected a sample of 16 "hits" to her site and found that 4 had actually made a purchase.

    **a.** What is the likelihood of exactly four purchases?

    **b.** How many purchases should she expect?

    **c.** What is the likelihood that four or more "hits" result in a purchase?

**52.** In Chapter 17 we discuss the *acceptance sample.* Acceptance sampling is used to monitor the quality of incoming raw materials. Suppose a purchaser of electronic components allows 1 percent of the components to be defective. To ensure the quality of incoming parts, they normally sample 20 parts and allow 1 defect.

    **a.** What is the likelihood of accepting a lot that is 1 percent defective?

    **b.** If the quality of the incoming lot was actually 2 percent, what is the likelihood of accepting it?

    **c.** If the quality of the incoming lot was actually 5 percent, what is the likelihood of accepting it?

**53.** Colgate-Palmolive, Inc. recently developed a new toothpaste flavored with honey. They tested a group of ten people. Six of the group said they liked the new flavor, and the remaining four indicated they definitely did not. Four of the ten are selected to participate in an in-depth interview. What is the probability that of those selected for the in-depth interview two liked the new flavor and two did not?

**54.** Dr. Richmond, a psychologist, is studying the daytime television viewing habits of college students. She believes 45 percent of college students watch soap operas during the afternoon. To further investigate, she selects a sample of 10.

    **a.** Develop a probability distribution for the number of students in the sample who watch soap operas.

    **b.** Find the mean and the standard deviation of this distribution.

    **c.** What is the probability of finding exactly four watch soap operas?

    **d.** What is the probability less than half of the students selected watch soap operas?

**55.** A recent study conducted by Penn, Shone, and Borland, on behalf of LastMinute.com, revealed that 52 percent of business travelers plan their trips less than two weeks before departure. The study is to be replicated in the tri-state area with a sample of 12 frequent business travelers.
   **a.** Develop a probability distribution for the number of travelers who plan their trips within two weeks of departure.
   **b.** Find the mean and the standard deviation of this distribution.
   **c.** What is the probability exactly 5 of the 12 selected business travelers plan their trips within two weeks of departure?
   **d.** What is the probability 5 or fewer of the 12 selected business travelers plan their trips within two weeks of departure?

**56.** Suppose 5 of 25 Ford subcompact automobiles require adjustment of some kind. Four subcompacts are selected at random. We are interested in the probability that exactly one will require adjustment.
   **a.** Solve the problem assuming that of the 25 subcompacts, the samples are drawn without replacement.
   **b.** Solve the problem assuming the sampling is done with replacement.
   **c.** Assuming replacement, work the problem using the Poisson distribution.
   **d.** Compare the results in parts a, b, and c. Comment on your findings.

**57.** The law firm of Hagel and Hagel is located in downtown Cincinnati. There are ten partners in the firm; seven live in Ohio and three in northern Kentucky. Ms. Wendy Hagel, the managing partner, wants to appoint a committee of three partners to look into moving the firm to northern Kentucky. If the committee is selected at random from the ten partners, what is the probability that:
   **a.** One member of the committee lives in northern Kentucky and the others live in Ohio?
   **b.** At least one member of the committee lives in northern Kentucky?

**58.** Recent information published by the U.S. Environmental Protection Agency indicates that Honda is the manufacturer of four of the top nine vehicles in terms of fuel economy.
   **a.** Determine the probability distribution for the number of Hondas in a sample of three cars chosen from the top nine.
   **b.** What is the likelihood that in the sample of three at least one Honda is included?

**59.** The position of chief of police in the city of Corry, Pennsylvania, is vacant. A search committee of Corry residents is charged with the responsibility of recommending a new chief to the city council. There are 12 applicants, 4 of which are either female or members of a minority. The search committee decides to interview all 12 of the applicants. To begin, they randomly select four applicants to be interviewed on the first day, and none of the four is female or a member of a minority. The local newspaper, the Corry *Press,* suggests discrimination in an editorial. What is the likelihood of this occurrence?

**60.** A box of six electric hair trimmers includes two that do not operate properly. Three trimmers are selected from the box.
   **a.** What is the probability that one does not operate properly?
   **b.** What is the probability that two trimmers of the three selected do not operate properly?

**61.** The sales of Lexus automobiles in the Detroit area follow a Poisson distribution with a mean of 3 per day.
   **a.** What is the probability that no Lexus is sold on a particular day?
   **b.** What is the probability that for five consecutive days at least one Lexus is sold?

**62.** Suppose 1.5 percent of the antennas on new Nokia cell phones are defective. For a random sample of 200 antennas, find the probability that:
   **a.** None of the antennas is defective.
   **b.** Three or more of the antennas are defective.

**63.** A study of the checkout lines at the Safeway Supermarket in the South Strand area revealed that between 4 and 7 P.M. on weekdays there is an average of four customers waiting in line. What is the probability that you visit Safeway today during this period and find:
   **a.** No customers are waiting?
   **b.** Four customers are waiting?
   **c.** Four or fewer are waiting?
   **d.** Four or more are waiting?

**64.** An internal study at Lahey Electronics, a large software development company, revealed the mean time for an internal e-mail message to arrive at its destination was 2 seconds. Further, the distribution of the arrival times followed the Poisson distribution.
   **a.** What is the probability a message takes exactly 1 second to arrive at its destination?
   **b.** What is the probability it takes more than 4 seconds to arrive at its destination?
   **c.** What is the probability it takes virtually no time, i.e., "zero" seconds?

**65.** Recent crime reports indicate that 3.1 motor vehicle thefts occur each minute in the United States. Assume that the distribution of thefts per minute can be approximated by the Poisson probability distribution.
   **a.** Calculate the probability exactly *four* thefts occur in a minute.
   **b.** What is the probability there are *no* thefts in a minute?
   **c.** What is the probability there is *at least one* theft in a minute?

**66.** New Process, Inc., a large mail-order supplier of women's fashions, advertises same-day service on every order. Recently the movement of orders has not gone as planned, and there were a large number of complaints. Bud Owens, director of customer service, has completely redone the method of order handling. The goal is to have fewer than five unfilled orders on hand at the end of 95 percent of the working days. Frequent checks of the unfilled orders at the end of the day revealed that the distribution of the unfilled orders follows a Poisson distribution with a mean of two orders.
   **a.** Has New Process, Inc. lived up to its internal goal? Cite evidence.
   **b.** Draw a histogram representing the Poisson probability distribution of unfilled orders.

**67.** The National Aeronautics and Space Administration (NASA) has experienced two disasters. The *Challenger* exploded over the Atlantic Ocean in 1986 and the *Columbia* exploded over East Texas in 2003. There have been a total of 113 space missions. Use the Poisson distribution to estimate the probability of exactly two failures. What is the probability of no failures?

**68.** According to the "January theory," if the stock market is up for the month of January, it will be up for the year. If it is down in January, it will be down for the year. According to an article in *The Wall Street Journal,* this theory held for 29 out of the last 34 years. Suppose there is no truth to this theory. What is the probability this could occur by chance? (You will probably need a software package such as Excel or MINITAB.)

**69.** During the second round of the 1989 U.S. Open golf tournament, four golfers scored a hole in one on the sixth hole. The odds of a professional golfer making a hole in one are estimated to be 3,708 to 1, so the probability is 1/3,709. There were 155 golfers participating in the second round that day. Estimate the probability that four golfers would score a hole in one on the sixth hole.

**70.** On September 18, 2003, hurricane Isabel struck the North Carolina Coast causing extensive damage. For several days prior to reaching land the National Hurricane Center had been predicting the hurricane would come on shore between Cape Fear, North Carolina, and the North Carolina-Virginia border. It was estimated that the probability the hurricane would actually strike in this area was .95. In fact, the hurricane did come on shore almost exactly as forecast and was almost in the center of the strike area.

**STORM CONTINUES NORTHWEST**
Position : **27.8 N, 71.4 W**
Movement: **NNW at 8 mph**
Sustained winds: **105 mph**
*As of 11 p.m. EDT Tuesday*

Suppose the National Hurricane Center forecasts that hurricanes will hit the strike area with a .95 probability. Answer the following questions:
**a.** What probability distribution does this follow?
**b.** What is the probability that 10 hurricanes reach landfall in the strike area?
**c.** What is the probability at least one of 10 hurricanes reaches land outside the strike area?

**71.** A recent CBS News survey reported that 67 percent of adults felt the U.S. Treasury should continue making pennies.

Suppose we select a sample of fifteen adults.
**a.** How many of the fifteen would we expect to indicate that the Treasury should continue making pennies? What is the standard deviation?
**b.** What is the likelihood that exactly 8 adults would indicate the Treasury should continue making pennies?
**c.** What is the likelihood at least 8 adults would indicate the Treasury should continue making pennies?

# Dataset Exercises

**72.** Refer to the Real Estate data, which reports information on homes sold in the Denver, Colorado, area last year.
**a.** Create a probability distribution for the number of bedrooms. Compute the mean and the standard deviation of this distribution.
**b.** Create a probability distribution for the number of bathrooms. Compute the mean and the standard deviation of this distribution.

**73.** Refer to the Baseball 2002 data, which contain information on the 2002 Major League Baseball season. There are 30 teams in the major leagues, and 5 of them have home fields with artificial playing surfaces. As part of the negotiations with the players' union, a study regarding injuries on grass versus artificial surfaces will be conducted. Five teams will be selected to participate in the study, and the teams will be selected at random. What is the likelihood that two of the five teams selected for study play their home games on artificial surfaces?

# Software Commands

**1.** The MegaStat commands to create the binomial probability distribution on page 192 are:
**a.** Select the **MegaStat** option on the toolbar, click on **Probability**, and **Discrete Probability Distributions**.
**b.** In the dialog box select **Binomial**, the number of trials is *6,* the probability of a success is *.05*. If you wish to see a graph, click on **display graph**.

2.   The Excel commands necessary to determine the binomial probability distribution on page 193 are:

   a. On a blank Excel worksheet write the word *Success* in cell A1 and the word *Probability* in B1. In cells A2 through A14 write the integers 0 to 12. Enter *B2* as the active cell.

   b. From the toolbar select **Insert** and **Function Wizard**.

   c. In the first dialog box select **Statistical** in the function category and **BINOMDIST** in the function name category, then click **OK.**

   d. In the second dialog box enter the four items necessary to compute a binomial probability.

   1.   Enter *0* for the number of successes.

   2.   Enter *40* for the number of trials.

   3.   Enter *.09* for the probability of a success.

   4.   Enter the word *false* or the number *0* for the individual probabilities and click on **OK.**

   5.   Excel will compute the probability of 0 successes in 40 trials, with a .09 probability of success. The result, .02299618, is stored in cell B2.

   e. To find the complete probability distribution, go to the formula bar and replace the *0* to the right of the open parentheses with *A2:A14.*

   f. Move the mouse to the lower right corner of cell B2 and highlight the B column to cell B14. The probability of a success for the various values of the random variable will appear.

3.   The Excel commands necessary to determine the hypergeometric distribution on page 200 are:

   a. On a blank Excel worksheet write the word *Success* in cell D5 and the word *Probability* in E5. In cells D6 to D11 write the integers 0 to 5. Enter *E6* as the active cell.

   b. From the toolbar choose **Insert** and **Function.**

   c. In the first dialog box select **Statistical** and **HYPGEOMDIST**, and then click **OK.**

   d. In the second dialog box enter the four items necessary to compute a hypergeometric probability.

   1.   Enter *0* for the number of successes.

   2.   Enter *5* for the number of trials.

   3.   Enter *40* for the number of successes in the population.

   4.   Enter *50* for the size of the population and click **OK.**

   5.   Excel will compute the probability of 0 successes in 5 trials (.000118937) and store that result in cell B2.

   e. To find the complete probability distribution, go to the formula bar and replace the *0* to the right of the open parentheses with *D6:D11.*

   f. Move the mouse to the lower right corner of cell E6 and highlight the B column to cell E11. The probability of a success for the various outcomes will appear.

4.   The MINITAB commands to generate the Poisson distribution on page 202 are:

   a. Label column C1 as *Successes* and C2 as *Probability.* Enter the integers 0 though 5 in the first column.

   b. Select **Calc,** then **Probability Distributions,** and **Poisson.**

   c. In the dialog box click on **Probability,** set the mean equal to *.3,* and select *C1* as the Input column. Designate *C2* as Optional storage, and then click **OK.**

# Chapter 6 Answers to Self-Review

**6–1  a.**

| Number of Spots | Probability |
|---|---|
| 1 | $\frac{1}{6}$ |
| 2 | $\frac{1}{6}$ |
| 3 | $\frac{1}{6}$ |
| 4 | $\frac{1}{6}$ |
| 5 | $\frac{1}{6}$ |
| 6 | $\frac{1}{6}$ |
| Total | $\frac{6}{6} = 1.00$ |

**b.**

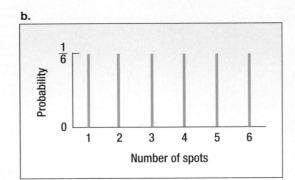

**c.** $\frac{6}{6}$, or 1.

**6–2  a.** It is discrete, because the values .80, .90, and 1.20 are clearly separated from each other. Also the sum of the probabilities is 1.00, and the outcomes are mutually exclusive.

**b.**

| x | P(x) | xP(x) |
|---|---|---|
| $ .80 | .30 | 0.24 |
| .90 | .50 | 0.45 |
| 1.20 | .20 | 0.24 |
| | | 0.93 |

The mean is 93 cents.

**c.**

| x | P(x) | (x − μ) | (x − μ)² P(x) |
|---|---|---|---|
| $0.80 | .30 | −0.13 | .00507 |
| 0.90 | .50 | −0.03 | .00045 |
| 1.20 | .20 | 0.27 | .01458 |
| | | | .02010 |

The variance is .02010, and the standard deviation is .14 cents.

**6–3  a.** It is reasonable because: each employee either uses direct deposit or does not; employees are independent; the probability of using direct deposit is .80 for all; and we count the number using the service out of 7.

**b.** $P(7) = {}_7C_7\,(.80)^7\,(.20)^0 = .2097$

**c.** $P(4) = {}_7C_4\,(.80)^4\,(.20)^3 = .1147$

**d.** Answers are in agreement.

**6–4** $n = 4$, $\pi = .60$

**a.** $P(x = 2) = .346$

**b.** $P(x \le 2) = .526$

**c.** $P(x > 2) = 1 - .526 = .474$

**6–5** $P(3) = \dfrac{{}_8C_3\,{}_4C_2}{{}_{12}C_5} = \dfrac{\left(\dfrac{8!}{3!5!}\right)\left(\dfrac{4!}{2!2!}\right)}{\dfrac{12!}{5!7!}}$

$= \dfrac{(56)(6)}{792} = .424$

**6–6** $\mu = 4{,}000(.0002) = 0.8$

$P(1) = \dfrac{0.8^1 e^{-0.8}}{1!} = .3595$

# 7

# Continuous Probability Distributions

Most retail stores offer their own credit cards. At the time of the credit application the customer is given a 10% discount on his or her purchase. The time it takes to fill out the credit application form follows a uniform distribution with the times ranging from 4 to 10 minutes. What is the standard deviation for the process time? (See Goal 2 and Exercise 35.)

# Introduction

Chapter 6 began our study of probability distributions. We considered three *discrete* probability distributions: binomial, hypergeometric, and Poisson. These distributions are based on discrete random variables, which can assume only clearly separated values. For example, we select for study 10 small businesses which began operations during the year 2000. The number still operating in 2004 can be 0, 1, 2, . . . , 10. There cannot be 3.7, 12, or −7 still operating in 2004. In this example, only certain outcomes are possible and these outcomes are represented by clearly separated values. In addition, the result is usually found by counting the number of successes. We count the number of the businesses in the study that are still in operation in 2004.

In this chapter, we continue our study of probability distributions by examining *continuous* probability distributions. A continuous probability distribution usually results from measuring something, such as the distance from the dormitory to the classroom, the weight of an individual, or the amount of bonus earned by CEOs. Suppose we select five students and find the distance, in miles, they travel to attend class as 12.2, 8.9, 6.7, 3.6, and 14.6. When examining a continuous distribution we are usually interested in information such as the percent of students who travel less than 10 miles or the percent who travel more than 8 miles. In other words, for a continuous distribution we may wish to know the percent of observations that occur within a certain range. It is important to realize that a continuous random variable has an infinite number of values within a particular range. So you think of the probability a variable will have a value within a specified range, rather than the probability for a specific value.

We consider two families of continuous probability distributions, the **uniform probability distribution** and the **normal probability distribution**. These distributions describe the likelihood that a continuous random variable that has an infinite number of possible values will fall within a specified range. For example, suppose the time to access the McGraw-Hill web page (www.mhhe.com) is uniformly distributed with a minimum time of 20 milliseconds and a maximum time of 60 milliseconds. Then we can determine the probability the page can be accessed in 30 milliseconds or less. The access time is measured on a continuous scale.

The second continuous distribution discussed in this chapter is the normal probability distribution. The normal distribution is described by its mean and standard deviation. For example, assume the life of an Energizer C-size battery follows a normal distribution with a mean of 45 hours and a standard deviation of 10 hours when used in a particular toy. We can determine the likelihood the battery will last more than 50 hours, between 35 and 62 hours, or less than 39 hours. The life of the battery is measured on a continuous scale.

# The Family of Uniform Distributions

The uniform probability distribution is perhaps the simplest distribution for a continuous random variable. This distribution is rectangular in shape and is defined by minimum and maximum values. Here are some examples that follow a uniform distribution.

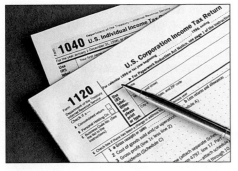

- The time to fly via a commercial airliner from Orlando, Florida, to Atlanta, Georgia, ranges from 60 minutes to 120 minutes. The random variable is the flight time within this interval. Note the variable of interest, flight time in minutes, is continuous in the interval from 60 minutes to 120 minutes.
- Volunteers at the Grand Strand Public Library prepare federal income tax forms. The time to prepare form 1040-EZ follows a uniform distribution over the interval between 10 minutes and 30 minutes. The random variable is the number of minutes to complete the form, and it can assume any value between 10 and 30.

A uniform distribution is shown in Chart 7–1. The distribution's shape is rectangular and has a minimum value of *a* and a maximum of *b*. Also notice in Chart 7–1 the height of the distribution is constant or uniform for all values between *a* and *b*. This implies that all the values in the range are equally likely.

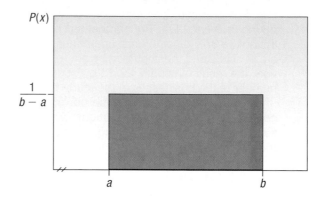

**CHART 7–1** A Continuous Uniform Distribution

The mean of a uniform distribution is located in the middle of the interval between the minimum and maximum values. It is computed as:

| | | |
|---|---|---|
| **MEAN OF THE UNIFORM DISTRIBUTION** | $\mu = \dfrac{a + b}{2}$ | **[7–1]** |

The standard deviation describes the dispersion of a distribution. In the uniform distribution, the standard deviation is also related to the interval between the maximum and minimum values.

| | | |
|---|---|---|
| **STANDARD DEVIATION OF THE UNIFORM DISTRIBUTION** | $\sigma = \sqrt{\dfrac{(b - a)^2}{12}}$ | **[7–2]** |

The height of the distribution, $P(x)$, is equal for all values of the random variable, *x*. The height of the uniform probability distribution can be computed as:

| | | | |
|---|---|---|---|
| **UNIFORM DISTRIBUTION** | $P(x) = \dfrac{1}{b - a}$ | if $a \le x \le b$ and 0 elsewhere | **[7–3]** |

As shown in Chapter 6, probability distributions are useful for making probability statements concerning the values of a random variable. For distributions describing a continuous random variable, areas within the distribution represent probabilities. In the uniform distribution, its rectangular shape allows us to apply the area formula for a rectangle. Recall we find the area of a rectangle by multiplying its length by its height. For the uniform distribution the height of the rectangle is $P(x)$, which is $1/(b - a)$. The length or base of the distribution is $b - a$. Notice that if we multiply the height of the distribution by its entire range to find the area, the result is always 1.00. To put it another way, the total area within a continuous probability distribution is equal to 1.00. In general

$$\text{Area} = (\text{height})(\text{base}) = \frac{1}{(b - a)} (b - a) = 1.00$$

So if a uniform distribution ranges from 10 to 15 the height is 0.20, found by 1/(15 − 10). The base is 5, found by 15 − 10. The total area is:

$$\text{Area} = (\text{height})(\text{base}) = \frac{1}{(15 - 10)}(15 - 10) = 1.00$$

An example will illustrate the features of a uniform distribution and how we calculate probabilities using it.

**EXAMPLE**

Southwest Arizona State University provides bus service to students while they are on campus. A bus arrives at the North Main Street and College Drive stop every 30 minutes between 6 A.M. and 11 P.M. during weekdays. Students arrive at the bus stop at random times. The time that a student waits is uniformly distributed from 0 to 30 minutes.

1. Draw a graph of this distribution.
2. Show that the area of this uniform distribution is 1.00.
3. How long will a student "typically" have to wait for a bus? In other words what is the mean waiting time? What is the standard deviation of the waiting times?
4. What is the probability a student will wait more than 25 minutes?
5. What is the probability a student will wait between 10 and 20 minutes?

**SOLUTION**

In this case the random variable is the length of time a student must wait. Time is measured on a continuous scale, and the wait times may range from 0 minutes up to 30 minutes.

1. The graph of the uniform distribution is shown in Chart 7–2. The horizontal line is drawn at a height of .0333, found by 1/(30 − 0). The range of this distribution is 30 minutes.

**CHART 7–2** Uniform Probability Distribution of Student Waiting Times

2. The times students must wait for the bus is uniform over the interval from 0 minutes to 30 minutes, so in this case *a* is 0 and *b* is 30.

$$\text{Area} = (\text{height})(\text{base}) = \frac{1}{(30 - 0)}(30 - 0) = 1.00$$

3. To find the mean, we use formula (7–1).

$$\mu = \frac{a + b}{2} = \frac{0 + 30}{2} = 15$$

The mean of the distribution is 15 minutes, so the typical wait time for bus service is 15 minutes.

To find the standard deviation of the wait times, we use formula (7–2).

$$\sigma = \sqrt{\frac{(b-a)^2}{12}} = \sqrt{\frac{(30-0)^2}{12}} = 8.66$$

The standard deviation of the distribution is 8.66 minutes. This measures the variation in the student wait times.

4.  The area within the distribution for the interval, 25 to 30, represents this particular probability. From the area formula:

$$P(25 < \text{wait time} < 30) = (\text{height})(\text{base}) = \frac{1}{(30-0)}(5) = .1667$$

So the probability a student waits between 25 and 30 minutes is .1667. This conclusion is illustrated by the following graph.

5.  The area within the distribution for the interval, 10 to 20, represents the probability.

$$P(10 < \text{wait time} < 20) = (\text{height})(\text{base}) = \frac{1}{(30-0)}(10) = .3333$$

We can illustrate this probability as follows.

**Self Review 7–1**  Australian sheep dogs have a relatively short life. The length of their life follows a uniform distribution between 8 and 14 years.
(a)  Draw this uniform distribution. What are the height and base values?
(b)  Show the total area under the curve is 1.00.
(c)  Calculate the mean and the standard deviation of this distribution.
(d)  What is the probability a particular dog lives between 10 and 14 years?
(e)  What is the probability a dog will live less than 9 years?

# Exercises

1.  A uniform distribution is defined over the interval from 6 to 10.
    **a.** What are the values for a and b?
    **b.** What is the mean of this uniform distribution?

    **c.** What is the standard deviation?
    **d.** Show that the total area is 1.00.
    **e.** Find the probability of a value more than 7.
    **f.** Find the probability of a value between 7 and 9.
2. A uniform distribution is defined over the interval from 2 to 5.
    **a.** What are the values for *a* and *b*?
    **b.** What is the mean of this uniform distribution?
    **c.** What is the standard deviation?
    **d.** Show that the total area is 1.00.
    **e.** Find the probability of a value more than 2.6.
    **f.** Find the probability of a value between 2.9 and 3.7.
3. America West Airlines reports the flight time from Los Angeles International Airport to Las Vegas is 1 hour and 5 minutes, or 65 minutes. Suppose the actual flying time is uniformly distributed between 60 and 70 minutes.
    **a.** Show a graph of the continuous probability distribution.
    **b.** What is the mean flight time? What is the variance of the flight times?
    **c.** What is the probability the flight time is less than 68 minutes?
    **d.** What is the probability the flight takes more than 64 minutes?
4. According to the Insurance Institute of America, a family of four spends between $400 and $3,800 per year on all types of insurance. Suppose the money spent is uniformly distributed between these amounts.
    **a.** What is the mean amount spent on insurance?
    **b.** What is the standard deviation of the amount spent?
    **c.** If we select a family at random, what is the probability they spend less than $2,000 per year on insurance per year?
    **d.** What is the probability a family spends more than $3,000 per year?

# The Family of Normal Probability Distributions

Next we consider the normal probability distribution. Unlike the uniform distribution [see formula (7–3)] the normal probability distribution has a very complex formula.

| | | |
|---|---|---|
| **NORMAL PROBABILITY DISTRIBUTION** | $$P(x) = \dfrac{1}{\sigma\sqrt{2\pi}}\, e^{-\left[\frac{(X-\mu)^2}{2\sigma^2}\right]}$$ | **[7–4]** |

However, do not be bothered by how complex this formula looks. You are already familiar with many of the values. The symbols $\mu$ and $\sigma$ refer to the mean and the standard deviation, as usual. The value of $\pi$ is the mathematical constant of 22/7, or 3.1416, from your high school algebra. The letter *e* is also a mathematical constant. It is the base of the natural log system and is equal to 2.718. *X* is the value of a continuous random variable. So a normal distribution is based on—that is, it is defined by—its mean and standard deviation.

    You will not need to make any calculations from formula (7–4). Instead you will be using a table, which is given as Appendix D, to look up the various probabilities.

    The normal probability distribution has the following major characteristics.

1. It is **bell-shaped** and has a single peak at the center of the distribution. The arithmetic mean, median, and mode are equal and located in the center of the distribution. Thus half the area under the normal curve is to the right of this center point and the other half to the left of it.
2. It is symmetrical about the mean. If we cut the normal curve vertically at the center value, the two halves will be mirror images.
3. It falls off smoothly in either direction from the central value. That is, the distribution is asymptotic: The curve gets closer and closer to the *X*-axis but never

actually touches it. To put it another way, the tails of the curve extend indefinitely in both directions.

4.  The location of a normal distribution is determined by the mean, $\mu$. The dispersion or spread of the distribution is determined by the standard deviation, $\sigma$.

These characteristics are shown graphically in Chart 7–3.

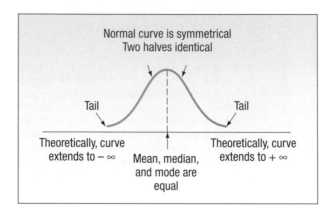

**CHART 7–3**  Characteristics of a Normal Distribution

There is not just one normal probability distribution, but rather a "family" of them. For example, in Chart 7–4 the probability distributions of length of employee service in three different plants can be compared. In the Camden plant, the mean is 20 years and the standard deviation is 3.1 years. There is another normal probability distribution for the length of service in the Dunkirk plant, where $\mu = 20$ years and $\sigma = 3.9$ years. In the Elmira plant, $\mu = 20$ years and $\sigma = 5.0$. Note that the means are the same but the standard deviations are different.

**Equal means, unequal standard deviations**

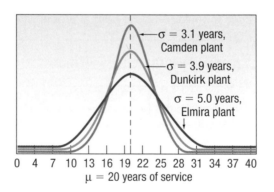

**CHART 7–4**  Normal Probability Distributions with Equal Means but Different Standard Deviations

Chart 7–5 shows the distribution of box weights of three different cereals. The weights follow a normal distribution with different means but identical standard deviations.

Finally, Chart 7–6 shows three normal distributions having different means and standard deviations. They show the distribution of tensile strengths, measured in pounds per square inch (psi), for three types of cables.

In Chapter 6, recall that discrete probability distributions show the specific likelihood a discrete value will occur. For example, on page 189, the binomial distribution

Unequal means, equal
standard deviations

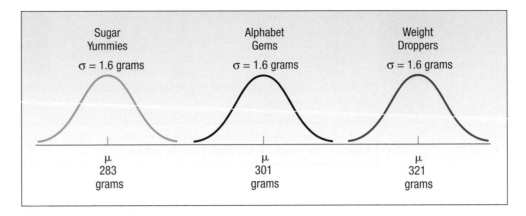

**CHART 7–5** Normal Probability Distributions Having Different Means but Equal Standard
Deviations

Unequal means, unequal
standard deviations

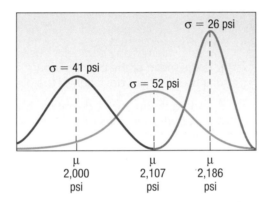

**CHART 7–6** Normal Probability Distributions with Different Means and Standard Deviations

is used to calculate the probability that none of the five flights arriving at the Bradford
Pennsylvania Regional Airport would be late.

With a continuous probability distribution, areas below the curve define probabilities. The total area under the normal curve is 1.0. This accounts for all possible outcomes. Since a normal probability distribution is symmetric, the area under the curve to the left of the mean is 0.5, and the area under the curve to the right of the mean is 0.5. Apply this to the distribution of Sugar Yummies in Chart 7–5. It is normally distributed with a mean of 283 grams. Therefore, the probability of filling a box with more than 283 grams is 0.5 and the probability of filling a box with less than 283 grams is 0.5. We can also determine the probability that a box weighs between 280 and 286 grams. However, to determine this probability we need to know about the standard normal probability distribution.

# The Standard Normal Distribution

The number of normal distributions is unlimited, each having a different mean ($\mu$), standard deviation ($\sigma$), or both. While it is possible to provide probability tables for discrete distributions such as the binomial and the Poisson, providing tables for the infinite number of normal distributions is impossible. Fortunately, one member of the family can be used to determine the probabilities for all normal distributions. It is called the **standard normal distribution,** and it is unique because it has a mean of 0 and a standard deviation of 1.

Any *normal distribution* can be converted into a *standard normal distribution* by subtracting the mean from each observation and dividing this difference by the standard deviation. The results are called **z values.** They are also referred to as **z scores,** the **z statistics,** the **standard normal deviates,** the **standard normal values,** or just the **normal deviate.**

> **z VALUE**  The signed distance between a selected value, designated X, and the mean, $\mu$, divided by the standard deviation, $\sigma$.

So, a z value is the distance from the mean, measured in units of the standard deviation. In terms of a formula:

| STANDARD NORMAL VALUE | $z = \dfrac{X - \mu}{\sigma}$ | [7–5] |
|---|---|---|

where:

X is the value of any particular observation or measurement.
$\mu$ is the mean of the distribution.
$\sigma$ is the standard deviation of the distribution.

As noted in the above definition, a z value expresses the distance or difference between a particular value of X and the arithmetic mean in units of the standard deviation. Once the normally distributed observations are standardized, the z values are normally distributed with a mean of 0 and a standard deviation of 1. The table in Appendix D (also on the inside back cover) lists the probabilities for the standard normal probability distribution.

To explain, suppose we wish to compute the probability that boxes of Sugar Yummies weigh between 283 and 285.4 grams. From Chart 7–5, we know that the box weight of Sugar Yummies follows the normal distribution with a mean of 283 grams and a standard deviation of 1.6 grams. We want to know the probability or area under the curve between the mean, 283 grams, and 285.4 grams. We can also express this problem using probability notation, similar to the style used in the previous chapter: $P(283 < \text{weight} < 285.4)$. To find the probability, it is necessary to convert both 283 grams and 285.4 grams to z values using formula (7–5). The z value corresponding to 283 is 0, found by $(283 - 283)/1.6$. The z value corresponding to 285.4 is 1.50 found by $(285.4 - 283)/1.6$. Next we go to the table in Appendix D. A portion of the table is repeated as Table 7–1. Go down the column of the table headed by the letter z to 1.5. Then move horizontally to the right and read the probability under the column headed

**TABLE 7–1**  Areas under the Normal Curve

| z | 0.00 | 0.01 | 0.02 | 0.03 | 0.04 | 0.05 | ⋯ |
|---|---|---|---|---|---|---|---|
| 1.3 | 0.4032 | 0.4049 | 0.4066 | 0.4082 | 0.4099 | 0.4115 | |
| 1.4 | 0.4192 | 0.4207 | 0.4222 | 0.4236 | 0.4251 | 0.4265 | |
| 1.5 | 0.4332 | 0.4345 | 0.4357 | 0.4370 | 0.4382 | 0.4394 | |
| 1.6 | 0.4452 | 0.4463 | 0.4474 | 0.4484 | 0.4495 | 0.4505 | |
| 1.7 | 0.4554 | 0.4564 | 0.4573 | 0.4582 | 0.4591 | 0.4599 | |
| 1.8 | 0.4641 | 0.4649 | 0.4656 | 0.4664 | 0.4671 | 0.4678 | |
| 1.9 | 0.4713 | 0.4719 | 0.4726 | 0.4732 | 0.4738 | 0.4744 | |

0.00. It is 0.4332. This means the area under the curve between 0.00 and 1.50 is 0.4332. This is the probability that a randomly selected box of Sugar Yummies will weigh between 283 and 285.4 grams. This is illustrated in the following graph.

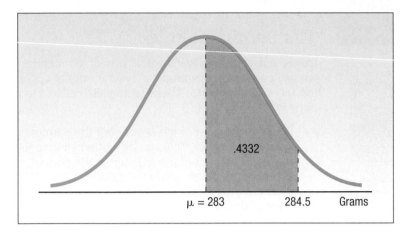

## Applications of the Standard Normal Distribution

What is the area under the curve between the mean and *X* for the following *z* values? Check your answers against those given. Not all the values are available in Table 7–5. You will need to use Appendix D or the table located on the inside back cover of the text.

| Computed *z* Value | Area under Curve |
|---|---|
| 2.84 | .4977 |
| 1.00 | .3413 |
| 0.49 | .1879 |

Now we will compute the *z* value given the population mean, μ, the population standard deviation, σ, and a selected *X*.

**EXAMPLE**

The weekly incomes of shift foremen in the glass industry are normally distributed with a mean of $1,000 and a standard deviation of $100. What is the *z* value for the income *X* of a foreman who earns $1,100 per week? For a foreman who earns $900 per week?

**SOLUTION**

Using formula (7–5), the *z* values for the two *X* values ($1,100 and $900) are:

For *X* = $1,100:

$$z = \frac{X - \mu}{\sigma}$$

$$= \frac{\$1,100 - \$1,000}{\$100}$$

$$= 1.00$$

For *X* = $900:

$$z = \frac{X - \mu}{\sigma}$$

$$= \frac{\$900 - \$1,000}{\$100}$$

$$= -1.00$$

The *z* of 1.00 indicates that a weekly income of $1,100 is one standard deviation above the mean, and a *z* of −1.00 shows that a $900 income is one standard deviation below the mean. Note that both incomes ($1,100 and $900) are the same distance ($100) from the mean.

Using the information in the preceding example ($\mu$ = $1,000, $\sigma$ = $100), convert:
(a)  The weekly income of $1,225 to a z value.
(b)  The weekly income of $775 to a z value.

**Statistics in Action**

An individual's skills depend on a combination of many hereditary and environmental factors, each having about the same amount of weight or influence on the skills. Thus, much like a binomial distribution with a large number of trials, many skills and attributes follow the normal distribution. For example, scores on the Scholastic Aptitude Test (SAT) are normally distributed with a mean of 1000 and a standard deviation of 140.

# The Empirical Rule

Before examining further applications of the standard normal probability distribution, we will consider three areas under the normal curve that will be used extensively in the following chapters. These facts were called the Empirical Rule in Chapter 3, see page 80.

1.  About 68 percent of the area under the normal curve is within one standard deviation of the mean. This can be written as $\mu \pm 1\sigma$.
2.  About 95 percent of the area under the normal curve is within two standard deviations of the mean, written $\mu \pm 2\sigma$.
3.  Practically all of the area under the normal curve is within three standard deviations of the mean, written $\mu \pm 3\sigma$.

This information is summarized in the following graph.

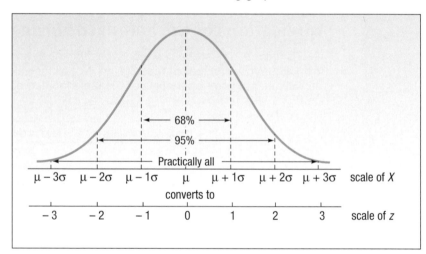

Transforming measurements to standard normal deviates changes the scale. The conversions are also shown in the graph. For example, $\mu + 1\sigma$ is converted to a z value of 1.00. Likewise, $\mu - 2\sigma$ is transformed to a z value of $-2.00$. Note that the center of the z distribution is zero, indicating no deviation from the mean, $\mu$.

**EXAMPLE**

As part of their quality assurance program, the Autolite Battery Company conducts tests on battery life. For a particular D cell alkaline battery, the mean life is 19 hours. The useful life of the battery follows a normal distribution with a standard deviation of 1.2 hours. Answer the following questions.

1.  About 68 percent of the batteries failed between what two values?
2.  About 95 percent of the batteries failed between what two values?
3.  Virtually all of the batteries failed between what two values?

**SOLUTION**

We can use the results of the Empirical Rule to answer these questions.

1.  About 68 percent of the batteries will fail between 17.8 and 20.2 hours, found by 19.0 ± 1(1.2) hours.

2. About 95 percent of the batteries will fail between 16.6 and 21.4 hours, found by 19.0 ± 2(1.2) hours.
3. Virtually all failed between 15.4 and 22.6 hours, found by 19.0 ± 3(1.2) hours.

This information is summarized on the following chart.

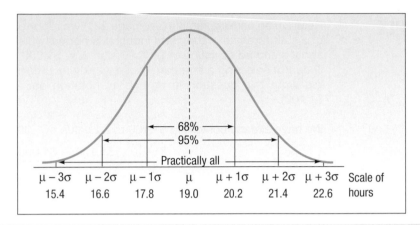

| μ − 3σ | μ − 2σ | μ − 1σ | μ | μ + 1σ | μ + 2σ | μ + 3σ | Scale of |
|--------|--------|--------|------|--------|--------|--------|----------|
| 15.4   | 16.6   | 17.8   | 19.0 | 20.2   | 21.4   | 22.6   | hours    |

**Self-Review 7–3**  The distribution of the annual incomes of a group of middle-management employees at Compton Plastics approximates a normal distribution with a mean of $47,200 and a standard deviation of $800.
(a) About 68 percent of the incomes lie between what two amounts?
(b) About 95 percent of the incomes lie between what two amounts?
(c) Virtually all of the incomes lie between what two amounts?
(d) What are the median and the modal incomes?
(e) Is the distribution of incomes symmetrical?

# Exercises

5. Explain what is meant by this statement: "There is not just one normal probability distribution but a 'family' of them."
6. List the major characteristics of a normal probability distribution.
7. The mean of a normal probability distribution is 500; the standard deviation is 10.
   a. About 68 percent of the observations lie between what two values?
   b. About 95 percent of the observations lie between what two values?
   c. Practically all of the observations lie between what two values?
8. The mean of a normal probability distribution is 60; the standard deviation is 5.
   a. About what percent of the observations lie between 55 and 65?
   b. About what percent of the observations lie between 50 and 70?
   c. About what percent of the observations lie between 45 and 75?
9. The Kamp family has twins, Rob and Rachel. Both Rob and Rachel graduated from college 2 years ago, and each is now earning $50,000 per year. Rachel works in the retail industry, where the mean salary for executives with less than 5 years' experience is $35,000 with a standard deviation of $8,000. Rob is an engineer. The mean salary for engineers with less than 5 years' experience is $60,000 with a standard deviation of $5,000. Compute the z values for both Rob and Rachel and comment on your findings.
10. A recent article in the *Cincinnati Enquirer* reported that the mean labor cost to repair a heat pump is $90 with a standard deviation of $22. Monte's Plumbing and Heating Service completed repairs on two heat pumps this morning. The labor cost for the first was $75 and it was $100 for the second. Compute z values for each and comment on your findings.

# Finding Areas under the Normal Curve

The next application of the standard normal distribution involves finding the area in a normal distribution between the mean and a selected value, which we identify as *X*. The following example will illustrate the details.

**EXAMPLE**

Recall in an earlier example (see page 221) we reported that the mean weekly income of a shift foreman in the glass industry is normally distributed with a mean of $1,000 and a standard deviation of $100. That is, $\mu = \$1,000$ and $\sigma = \$100$. What is the likelihood of selecting a foreman whose weekly income is between $1,000 and $1,100? We write this question in probability notation as: $P(\$1,000 <$ weekly income $< \$1,100)$.

**SOLUTION**

We have already converted $1,100 to a *z* value of 1.00 using formula (7–5). To repeat:

$$z = \frac{X - \mu}{\sigma} = \frac{\$1,100 - \$1,000}{\$100} = 1.00$$

The probability associated with a *z* of 1.00 is available in Appendix D. A portion of Appendix D follows. To locate the probability, go down the left column to 1.0, and then move horizontally to the column headed .00. The value is .3413.

| z | .00 | .01 | .02 |
|-----|-------|-------|-------|
| . | . | . | . |
| . | . | . | . |
| . | . | . | . |
| 0.7 | .2580 | .2611 | .2642 |
| 0.8 | .2881 | .2910 | .2939 |
| 0.9 | .3159 | .3186 | .3212 |
| 1.0 | .3413 | .3438 | .3461 |
| 1.1 | .3643 | .3665 | .3686 |
| . | . | . | . |
| . | . | . | . |
| . | . | . | . |

The area under the normal curve between $1,000 and $1,100 is .3413. We could also say 34.13 percent of the shift foremen in the glass industry earn between $1,000 and $1,100 weekly, or the likelihood of selecting a foreman and finding his or her income is between $1,000 and $1,100 is .3413.

This information is summarized in the following diagram.

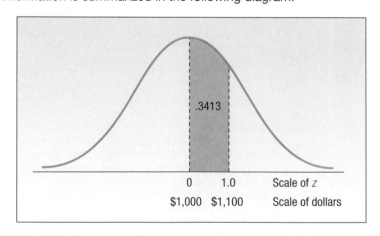

**Statistics in Action**

Many processes, such as filling soda bottles and canning fruit, are normally distributed. Manufacturers must guard against both over- and underfilling. If they put too much in the can or bottle, they are giving away their product. If they put too little in, the customer may feel cheated and the government may question the label description. "Control charts," with limits drawn three standard deviations above and below the mean, are routinely used to monitor this type of production process.

In the example just completed, we are interested in the probability between the mean and a given value. Let's change the question. Instead of wanting to know the probability of selecting at random a foreman who earned between $1,000 and $1,100, suppose we wanted the probability of selecting a foreman who earned less than $1,100. In probability notation we write this statement as $P$(weekly income < $1,100). The method of solution is the same. We find the probability of selecting a foreman who earns between $1,000, the mean, and $1,100. This probability is .3413. Next, recall that half the area, or probability, is above the mean and half is below. So the probability of selecting a foreman earning less than $1,000 is .5000. Finally, we add the two probabilities, so .3413 + .5000 = .8413. About 84 percent of the foremen in the glass industry earn less than $1,100 per month. See the following diagram.

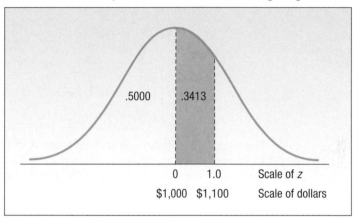

Excel will calculate this probability. The necessary commands are in the **Software Commands** section at the end of the chapter. The answer is .8413, the same as we calculated.

**EXAMPLE**

Refer to the information regarding the weekly income of shift foremen in the glass industry. The distribution of weekly incomes follows the normal distribution, with a mean of $1,000 and a standard deviation of $100. What is the probability of selecting a shift foreman in the glass industry whose income is:

1. Between $790 and $1,000?
2. Less than $790?

**SOLUTION**

We begin by finding the $z$ value corresponding to a weekly income of $790. From formula (7–5):

$$z = \frac{X - \mu}{s} = \frac{\$790 - \$1,000}{\$100} = -2.10$$

See Appendix D. Move down the left margin to the row 2.1 and across that row to the column headed 0.00. The value is .4821. So the area under the standard normal curve corresponding to a z value of 2.10 is .4821. However, because the normal distribution is symmetric, the area between 0 and a negative z value is the same as that between 0 and the corresponding positive z value. The likelihood of finding a foreman earning between $790 and $1,000 is .4821. In probability notation we write P($790 < weekly income < $1000) = .4821.

| z | 0.00 | 0.01 | 0.02 |
|---|------|------|------|
| . | . | . | . |
| . | . | . | . |
| . | . | . | . |
| 2.0 | .4772 | .4778 | .4783 |
| 2.1 | .4821 | .4826 | .4830 |
| 2.2 | .4861 | .4864 | .4868 |
| 2.3 | .4893 | .4896 | .4898 |
| . | . | . | . |
| . | . | . | . |
| . | . | . | . |

The mean divides the normal curve into two identical halves. The area under the half to the left of the mean is .5000, and the area to the right is also .5000. Because the area under the curve between $790 and $1,000 is .4821, the area below $790 is .0179, found by .5000 − .4821. In probability notation we write P(weekly income < $790) = .0179.

This means that 48.21 percent of the foremen have weekly incomes between $790 and $1,000. Further, we can anticipate that 1.79 percent earn less than $790 per week. This information is summarized in the following diagram.

---

**Self-Review 7–4**

The employees of Cartwright Manufacturing are awarded efficiency ratings. The distribution of the ratings follows a normal distribution. The mean is 400, the standard deviation 50.
(a) What is the area under the normal curve between 400 and 482? Write this area in probability notation.
(b) What is the area under the normal curve for ratings greater than 482? Write this area in probability notation.
(c) Show the facets of this problem in a chart.

## Exercises

**11.** A normal population has a mean of 20.0 and a standard deviation of 4.0.
    **a.** Compute the z value associated with 25.0.
    **b.** What proportion of the population is between 20.0 and 25.0?

   **c.** What proportion of the population is less than 18.0?

**12.** A normal population has a mean of 12.2 and a standard deviation of 2.5.

   **a.** Compute the $z$ value associated with 14.3.

   **b.** What proportion of the population is between 12.2 and 14.3?

   **c.** What proportion of the population is less than 10.0?

**13.** A recent study of the hourly wages of maintenance crew members for major airlines showed that the mean hourly salary was $20.50, with a standard deviation of $3.50. If we select a crew member at random, what is the probability the crew member earns:

   **a.** Between $20.50 and $24.00 per hour?

   **b.** More than $24.00 per hour?

   **c.** Less than $19.00 per hour?

**14.** The mean of a normal distribution is 400 pounds. The standard deviation is 10 pounds.

   **a.** What is the area between 415 pounds and the mean of 400 pounds?

   **b.** What is the area between the mean and 395 pounds?

   **c.** What is the probability of selecting a value at random and discovering that it has a value of less than 395 pounds?

Another application of the normal distribution involves combining two areas, or probabilities. One of the areas is to the right of the mean and the other to the left.

**EXAMPLE**

Recall the distribution of weekly incomes of shift foremen in the glass industry. The weekly incomes follow the normal distribution, with a mean of $1,000 and a standard deviation of $100. What is the area under this normal curve between $840 and $1,200?

**SOLUTION**

The problem can be divided into two parts. For the area between $840 and the mean of $1,000:

$$z = \frac{\$840 - \$1,000}{\$100} = \frac{-\$160}{\$100} = -1.60$$

For the area between the mean of $1,000 and $1,200:

$$z = \frac{\$1,200 - \$1,000}{\$100} = \frac{\$200}{\$100} = 2.00$$

The area under the curve for a $z$ of $-1.60$ is .4452 (from Appendix D). The area under the curve for a $z$ of 2.00 is .4772. Adding the two areas: .4452 + .4772 = .9224. Thus, the probability of selecting an income between $840 and $1,200 is .9224. In probability notation we write $P(\$840 < \text{weekly income} < \$1,200) = .4452 + .4772 = .9224$. To summarize, 92.24 percent of the foremen have weekly incomes between $840 and $1,200. This is shown in a diagram:

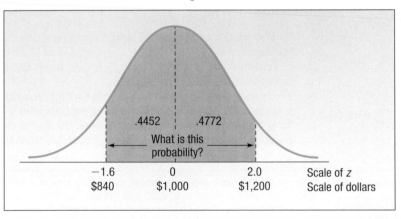

Another application of the normal distribution involves determining the area between values on the *same* side of the mean.

**EXAMPLE**

Returning to the weekly income distribution of shift foremen in the glass industry ($\mu$ = $1,000, $\sigma$ = $100), what is the area under the normal curve between $1,150 and $1,250?

**SOLUTION**

The situation is again separated into two parts, and formula (7–5) is used. First, we find the z value associated with a weekly salary of $1,250:

$$z = \frac{\$1,250 - \$1,000}{\$100} = 2.50$$

Next we find the z value for a weekly salary of $1,150:

$$z = \frac{\$1,150 - \$1,000}{\$100} = 1.50$$

From Appendix D the area associated with a z value of 2.50 is .4938. So the probability of a weekly salary between $1,000 and $1,250 is .4938. Similarly, the area associated with a z value of 1.50 is .4332, so the probability of a weekly salary between $1,000 and $1,150 is .4332. The probability of a weekly salary between $1,150 and $1,250 is found by subtracting the area associated with a z value of 1.50 (.4332) from that associated with a z of 2.50 (.4938). Thus, the probability of a weekly salary between $1,150 and $1,250 is .0606. In probability notation we write $P(\$1,150 <$ weekly income $< \$1,250) = .4938 - .4332 = .0606$.

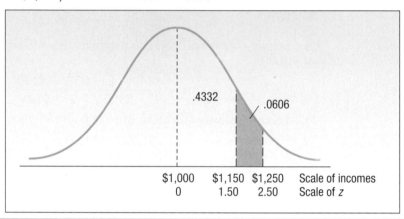

| | $1,000 | $1,150 | $1,250 | Scale of incomes |
| | 0 | 1.50 | 2.50 | Scale of z |

In brief, there are four situations for finding the area under the standard normal distribution.

1. To find the area between 0 and z (or −z), look up the probability directly in the table.
2. To find the area beyond z or (−z), locate the probability of z in the table and subtract that probability from .5000.
3. To find the area between two points on different sides of the mean, determine the z values and add the corresponding probabilities.
4. To find the area between two points on the same side of the mean, determine the z values and subtract the smaller probability from the larger.

---

**Self-Review 7–5**

Refer to the previous example, where the distribution of weekly incomes follows the normal distribution with a mean of $1,000 and the standard deviation is $100.
(a) What percent of the shift foremen earn a weekly income between $750 and $1,225? Draw a normal curve and shade the desired area on your diagram.
(b) What percent of the shift foremen earn a weekly income between $1,100 and $1,225? Draw a normal curve and shade the desired area on your diagram.

# Exercises

15. A normal distribution has a mean of 50 and a standard deviation of 4.
    a. Compute the probability of a value between 44.0 and 55.0.
    b. Compute the probability of a value greater than 55.0.
    c. Compute the probability of a value between 52.0 and 55.0.
16. A normal population has a mean of 80.0 and a standard deviation of 14.0.
    a. Compute the probability of a value between 75.0 and 90.0.
    b. Compute the probability of a value 75.0 or less.
    c. Compute the probability of a value between 55.0 and 70.0.
17. A cola-dispensing machine is set to dispense on average 7.00 ounces of cola per cup. The standard deviation is 0.10 ounces. The distribution amounts dispensed follows a normal distribution.
    a. What is the probability that the machine will dispense between 7.10 and 7.25 ounces of cola?
    b. What is the probability that the machine will dispense 7.25 ounces of cola or more?
    c. What is the probability that the machine will dispense between 6.80 and 7.25 ounces of cola?
18. The amounts of money requested on home loan applications at Down River Federal Savings follow the normal distribution, with a mean of $70,000 and a standard deviation of $20,000. A loan application is received this morning. What is the probability:
    a. The amount requested is $80,000 or more?
    b. The amount requested is between $65,000 and $80,000?
    c. The amount requested is $65,000 or more?
19. WNAE, an all-news AM station, finds that the distribution of the lengths of time listeners are tuned to the station follows the normal distribution. The mean of the distribution is 15.0 minutes and the standard deviation is 3.5 minutes. What is the probability that a particular listener will tune in:
    a. More than 20 minutes?
    b. For 20 minutes or less?
    c. Between 10 and 12 minutes?
20. The mean starting salary for college graduates in the spring of 2004 was $36,280. Assume that the distribution of starting salaries follows the normal distribution with a standard deviation of $3,300. What percent of the graduates have starting salaries:
    a. Between $35,000 and $40,000?
    b. More than $45,000?
    c. Between $40,000 and $45,000?

Previous examples require finding the percent of the observations located between two observations or the percent of the observations above, or below, a particular observation $X$. A further application of the normal distribution involves finding the value of the observation $X$ when the percent above or below the observation is given.

**EXAMPLE**

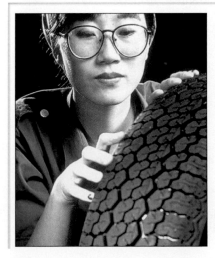

The Layton Tire and Rubber Company wishes to set a minimum mileage guarantee on its new MX100 tire. Tests reveal the mean mileage is 67,900 with a standard deviation of 2,050 miles and that the distribution of miles follows the normal distribution. They want to set the minimum guaranteed mileage so that no more than 4 percent of the tires will have to be replaced. What minimum guaranteed mileage should Layton announce?

**SOLUTION**

The facets of this case are shown in the following diagram, where $X$ represents the minimum guaranteed mileage.

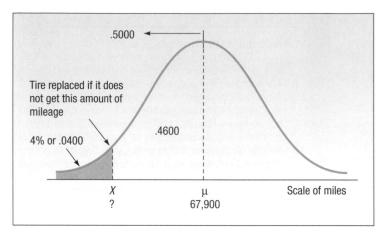

Inserting these values in formula (7–5) for z gives:

$$z = \frac{X - \mu}{\sigma} = \frac{X - 67{,}900}{2{,}050}$$

Notice that there are two unknowns, $z$ and $X$. To find $X$, we first find $z$, and then solve for $X$. Notice the area under the normal curve to the left of $\mu$ is .5000. The area between $\mu$ and $X$ is .4600, found by .5000 − .0400. Now refer to Appendix D. Search the body of the table for the area closest to .4600. The closest area is .4599. Move to the margins from this value and read the $z$ value of 1.75. Because the value is to the left of the mean, it is actually −1.75. These steps are illustrated in Table 7–2.

**TABLE 7–2** Selected Areas under the Normal Curve

| z | .03 | .04 | .05 | .06 |
|---|-----|-----|-----|-----|
| . | . | . | . | . |
| . | . | . | . | . |
| . | . | . | . | . |
| 1.5 | .4370 | .4382 | .4394 | .4406 |
| 1.6 | .4484 | .4495 | .4505 | .4515 |
| 1.7 | .4582 | .4591 | .4599 | .4608 |
| 1.8 | .4664 | .4671 | .4678 | .4686 |

Knowing that the distance between $\mu$ and $X$ is $-1.75\sigma$ or $z = -1.75$, we can now solve for $X$ (the minimum guaranteed mileage):

$$z = \frac{X - 67{,}900}{2{,}050}$$

$$-1.75 = \frac{X - 67{,}900}{2{,}050}$$

$$-1.75(2{,}050) = X - 67{,}900$$

$$X = 67{,}900 - 1.75(2{,}050) = 64{,}312$$

So Layton can advertise that it will replace for free any tire that wears out before it reaches 64,312 miles, and the company will know that only 4 percent of the tires will be replaced under this plan.

Excel will also find the mileage value. See the following output. The necessary commands are given in the **Software Commands** section at the end of the chapter.

**Self-Review 7–6**

An analysis of the final test scores for Introduction to Business reveals the scores follow the normal distribution. The mean of the distribution is 75 and the standard deviation is 8. The professor wants to award an A to students whose score is in the highest 10 percent. What is the dividing point for those students who earn an A and those earning a B?

# Exercises

21. A normal distribution has a mean of 50 and a standard deviation of 4. Determine the value below which 95 percent of the observations will occur.

22. A normal distribution has a mean of 80 and a standard deviation of 14. Determine the value above which 80 percent of the values will occur.

23. The amounts dispensed by a cola machine follow the normal distribution with a mean of 7 ounces and a standard deviation of 0.10 ounces per cup. How much cola is dispensed in the largest 1 percent of the cups?

24. Refer to Exercise 18, where the amount requested for home loans followed the normal distribution with a mean of $70,000 and a standard deviation of $20,000.
    a. How much is requested on the largest 3 percent of the loans?
    b. How much is requested on the smallest 10 percent of the loans?

25. Assume that the mean hourly cost to operate a commercial airplane follows the normal distribution with a mean $2,100 per hour and a standard deviation of $250. What is the operating cost for the lowest 3 percent of the airplanes?

26. The monthly sales of mufflers in the Richmond, Virginia, area follow the normal distribution with a mean of 1,200 and a standard deviation of 225. The manufacturer would like to establish inventory levels such that there is only a 5 percent chance of running out of stock. Where should the manufacturer set the inventory levels?

# The Normal Approximation to the Binomial

Chapter 6 describes the binomial probability distribution, which is a discrete distribution. The table of binomial probabilities in Appendix A goes successively from an *n* of 1 to an *n* of 15. If a problem involved taking a sample of 60, generating a binomial distribution for that large a number would be very time consuming. A more efficient approach is to apply the *normal approximation to the binomial*.

Using the normal distribution (a continuous distribution) as a substitute for a binomial distribution (a discrete distribution) for large values of $n$ seems reasonable because, as $n$ increases, a binomial distribution gets closer and closer to a normal distribution. Chart 7–7 depicts the change in the shape of a binomial distribution with $\pi = .50$ from an $n$ of 1, to an $n$ of 3, to an $n$ of 20. Notice how the case where $n = 20$ approximates the shape of the normal distribution. That is, compare the case where $n = 20$ to the normal curve in Chart 7–3 on page 218.

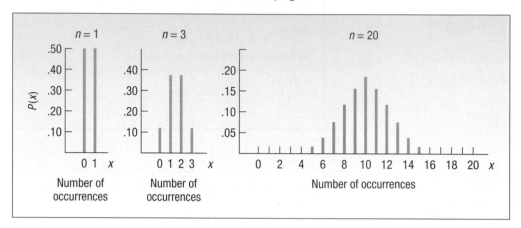

**CHART 7–7** Binomial Distributions for an $n$ of 1, 3, and 20, Where $\pi = .50$

When to use the normal approximation

When can we use the normal approximation to the binomial? The normal probability distribution is a good approximation to the binomial probability distribution when $n\pi$ and $n(1 - \pi)$ are both at least 5. However, before we apply the normal approximation, we must make sure that our distribution of interest is in fact a binomial distribution. Recall from Chapter 6 that four criteria must be met:

1. There are only two mutually exclusive outcomes to an experiment: a "success" and a "failure."
2. The distribution results from counting the number of successes in a fixed number of trials.
3. The probability of a success, $\pi$, remains the same from trial to trial.
4. Each trial is independent.

## Continuity Correction Factor

To show the application of the normal approximation to the binomial and the need for a correction factor, suppose the management of the Santoni Pizza Restaurant found

that 70 percent of their new customers return for another meal. For a week in which 80 new (first-time) customers dined at Santoni's, what is the probability that 60 or more will return for another meal?

Notice the binomial conditions are met: (1) There are only two possible outcomes—a customer either returns for another meal or does not return. (2) We can count the number of successes, meaning, for example, that 57 of the 80 customers return. (3) The trials are independent, meaning that if the 34th person returns for a second meal, that does not affect whether the 58th person returns. (4) The probability of a customer returning remains at .70 for all 80 customers.

Therefore, we could use the binomial formula (6–3) described on page 189.

$$P(x) = {}_nC_x\,(\pi)^x\,(1 - \pi)^{n - x}$$

To find the probability 60 or more customers return for another pizza, we need to first find the probability exactly 60 customers return. That is:

$$P(x = 60) = {}_{80}C_{60} \, (.70)^{60} \, (1 - .70)^{20} = .063$$

Next we find the probability that exactly 61 customers return. It is:

$$P(x = 61) = {}_{80}C_{61} \, (.70)^{61} \, (1 - .70)^{19} = .048$$

We continue this process until we have the probability all 80 customers return. Finally, we add the probabilities from 60 to 80. Solving the above problem in this manner is tedious. We can also use a computer software package such as MINITAB or Excel to find the various probabilities. Listed below are the binomial probabilities for $n = 80$, $\pi = .70$, and $x$, the number of customers returning, ranging from 43 to 68. The probability of any number of customers less than 43 or more than 68 returning is less than .001. We can assume these probabilities are 0.000.

| Number Returning | Probability | Number Returning | Probability |
|---|---|---|---|
| 43 | .001 | 56 | .097 |
| 44 | .002 | 57 | .095 |
| 45 | .003 | 58 | .088 |
| 46 | .006 | 59 | .077 |
| 47 | .009 | 60 | .063 |
| 48 | .015 | 61 | .048 |
| 49 | .023 | 62 | .034 |
| 50 | .033 | 63 | .023 |
| 51 | .045 | 64 | .014 |
| 52 | .059 | 65 | .008 |
| 53 | .072 | 66 | .004 |
| 54 | .084 | 67 | .002 |
| 55 | .093 | 68 | .001 |

We can find the probability of 60 or more returning by summing .063 + .048 + · · · + .001, which is .197. However, a look at the plot below shows the similarity of this distribution to a normal distribution. All we need do is "smooth out" the discrete probabilities into a continuous distribution. Furthermore, working with a normal distribution will involve far fewer calculations than working with the binomial.

The trick is to let the discrete probability for 56 customers be represented by an area under the continuous curve between 55.5 and 56.5. Then let the probability for 57 customers be represented by an area between 56.5 and 57.5 and so on. This is just the opposite of rounding off the numbers to a whole number.

Because we use the normal distribution to determine the binomial probability of 60 or more successes, we must subtract, in this case, .5 from 60. The value .5 is called the **continuity correction factor.** This small adjustment must be made because a continuous distribution (the normal distribution) is being used to approximate a discrete distribution (the binomial distribution). Subtracting, $60 - .5 = 59.5$.

> **CONTINUITY CORRECTION FACTOR** The value .5 subtracted or added, depending on the question, to a selected value when a discrete probability distribution is approximated by a continuous probability distribution.

# How to Apply the Correction Factor

Only four cases may arise. These cases are:

1. For the probability *at least X* occur, use the area *above* $(X - .5)$.
2. For the probability that *more than X* occur, use the area *above* $(X + .5)$.
3. For the probability that *X or fewer* occur, use the area *below* $(X + .5)$.
4. For the probability that *fewer than X* occur, use the area *below* $(X - .5)$.

To use the normal distribution to approximate the probability that 60 or more first-time Santoni customers out of 80 will return, follow the procedure shown below.

**Step 1.** Find the z corresponding to an X of 59.5 using formula (7–5), and formulas (6–4) and (6–5) for the mean and the variance of a binomial distribution:

$$\mu = n\pi = 80(.70) = 56$$
$$\sigma^2 = n\pi(1 - \pi) = 80(.70)(1 - .70) = 16.8$$
$$\sigma = \sqrt{16.8} = 4.10$$
$$z = \frac{X - \mu}{\sigma} = \frac{59.5 - 56}{4.10} = 0.85$$

**Step 2.** Determine the area under the normal curve between a $\mu$ of 56 and an X of 59.5. From step 1, we know that the z value corresponding to 59.5 is 0.85. So we go to Appendix D and read down the left margin to 0.8, and then we go horizontally to the area under the column headed by .05. That area is .3023.

**Step 3.** Calculate the area beyond 59.5 by subtracting .3023 from .5000 (.5000 − .3023 = .1977). Thus, .1977 is the probability that 60 or more first-time Santoni customers out of 80 will return for another meal. In probability notation $P(\text{customers} > 59.5) = .5000 - .3023 = .1977$. The facets of this problem are shown graphically:

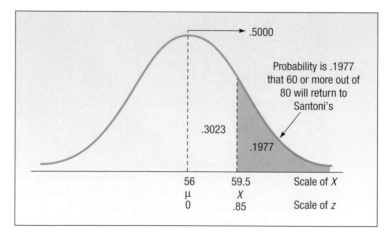

No doubt you will agree that using the normal approximation to the binomial is a more efficient method of estimating the probability of 60 or more first-time customers returning. The result compares favorably with that computed on page 233, using the binomial distribution. The probability using the binomial distribution is .197, whereas the probability using the normal approximation is .1977.

| | |
|---|---|
| **Self-Review 7–7**  | A study by Great Southern Home Insurance revealed that none of the stolen goods were recovered by the homeowners in 80 percent of reported thefts. <br> (a) During a period in which 200 thefts occurred, what is the probability that no stolen goods were recovered in 170 or more of the robberies? <br> (b) During a period in which 200 thefts occurred, what is the probability that no stolen goods were recovered in 150 or more robberies? |

# Exercises

27. Assume a binomial probability distribution with $n = 50$ and $\pi = .25$. Compute the following:
    a. The mean and standard deviation of the random variable.
    b. The probability that $X$ is 15 or more.
    c. The probability that $X$ is 10 or less.
28. Assume a binomial probability distribution with $n = 40$ and $\pi = .55$. Compute the following:
    a. The mean and standard deviation of the random variable.
    b. The probability that $X$ is 25 or greater.
    c. The probability that $X$ is 15 or less.
    d. The probability that $X$ is between 15 and 25 inclusive.
29. Dottie's Tax Service specializes in federal tax returns for professional clients, such as physicians, dentists, accountants, and lawyers. A recent audit by the IRS of the returns she prepared indicated that an error was made on 5 percent of the returns she prepared last year. Assuming this rate continues into this year and she prepares 60 returns, what is the probability that she makes errors on:
    a. More than six returns?
    b. At least six returns?
    c. Exactly six returns?
30. Shorty's Muffler advertises they can install a new muffler in 30 minutes or less. However, the work standards department at corporate headquarters recently conducted a study and found that 20 percent of the mufflers were not installed in 30 minutes or less. The Maumee branch installed 50 mufflers last month. If the corporate report is correct:
    a. How many of the installations at the Maumee branch would you expect to take more than 30 minutes?
    b. What is the likelihood that fewer than eight installations took more than 30 minutes?
    c. What is the likelihood that eight or fewer installations took more than 30 minutes?
    d. What is the likelihood that exactly 8 of the 50 installations took more than 30 minutes?
31. A study conducted by the nationally known Taurus Health Club revealed that 30 percent of its new members are significantly overweight. A membership drive in a metropolitan area resulted in 500 new members.
    a. It has been suggested that the normal approximation to the binomial be used to determine the probability that 175 or more of the new members are significantly overweight. Does this problem qualify as a binomial problem? Explain.
    b. What is the probability that 175 or more of the new members are significantly overweight?
    c. What is the probability that 140 or more new members are significantly overweight?
32. A recent issue of *Bride Magazine* suggested that couples planning their wedding should expect two-thirds of those who are sent an invitation to respond that they will attend. Rich and Stacy are planning to be married later this year. They plan to send 197 invitations.
    a. How many guests would you expect to accept the invitation?
    b. What is the standard deviation?
    c. What is the probability 140 or more will accept the invitation?
    d. What is the probability exactly 140 will accept the invitation?

# Chapter Outline

I. The uniform distribution is a continuous probability distribution with the following characteristics.
   A. It is rectangular in shape.
   B. The mean and the median are equal.
   C. It is completely described by its minimum value $a$ and its maximum value $b$.
   D. It is also described by the following equation for the region from $a$ to $b$:

$$P(x) = \frac{1}{b - a}$$        [7–3]

   E. The mean and standard deviation of a uniform distribution are computed as follows:

$$\mu = \frac{(a + b)}{2}$$        [7–1]

$$\sigma = \sqrt{\frac{(b - a)^2}{12}}$$        [7–2]

II. The normal distribution is a continuous distribution with the following characteristics.
   A. It is bell-shaped and has a single peak at the center of the distribution.
   B. The distribution is symmetric.
   C. It is asymptotic, meaning the curve approaches but never touches the $X$-axis.
   D. It is completely described by its mean and standard deviation.
   E. There is a family of normal distributions.
      1. Another normal distribution is created when either the mean or the standard deviation changes.
      2. A normal distribution is described by the following formula:

$$P(x) = \frac{1}{\sigma\sqrt{2\pi}}\, e^{-\left[\frac{(X - \mu)^2}{2\sigma^2}\right]}$$        [7–4]

III. The standard normal distribution is a particular normal distribution.
   A. It has a mean of 0 and a standard deviation of 1.
   B. Any normal distribution can be converted to the standard normal distribution by the following formula.

$$z = \frac{X - \mu}{\sigma}$$        [7–5]

   C. By standardizing a normal distribution, we can report the distance of a value from the mean in units of the standard deviation.
IV. The normal distribution can approximate a binomial distribution under certain conditions.
   A. $n\pi$ and $n(1 - \pi)$ must both be at least 5.
      1. $n$ is the number of observations.
      2. $\pi$ is the probability of a success.
   B. The four conditions for a binomial distribution are:
      1. There are only two possible outcomes.
      2. $\pi$ remains the same from trial to trial.
      3. The trials are independent.
      4. The distribution results from a count of the number of successes in a fixed number of trials.
   C. The mean and variance of a binomial distribution are computed as follows:

$$\mu = n\pi$$

$$\sigma^2 = n\pi(1 - \pi)$$

   D. The continuity correction factor of .5 is used to extend the continuous value of $X$ one-half unit in either direction. This correction compensates for approximating a discrete distribution by a continuous distribution.

# Chapter Exercises

**33.** The amount of cola in a 12-ounce can is uniformly distributed between 11.96 ounces and 12.05 ounces.
  **a.** What is the mean amount per can?
  **b.** What is the standard deviation amount per can?
  **c.** What is the probability of selecting a can of cola and finding it has less than 12 ounces?
  **d.** What is the probability of selecting a can of cola and finding it has more than 11.98 ounces?
  **e.** What is the probability of selecting a can of cola and finding it has more than 11.00 ounces?

**34.** A tube of Listerine Tartar Control toothpaste contains 4.2 ounces. As people use the toothpaste, the amount remaining in any tube is random. Assume the amount of toothpaste left in the tube follows a uniform distribution. From this information, we can determine the following information about the amount remaining in a toothpaste tube without invading anyone's privacy.
  **a.** How much toothpaste would you expect to be remaining in the tube?
  **b.** What is the standard deviation of the amount remaining in the tube?
  **c.** What is the likelihood there is less than 3.0 ounces remaining in the tube?
  **d.** What is the probability there is more than 1.5 ounces remaining in the tube?

**35.** Many retail stores offer their own credit cards. At the time of the credit application the customer is given a 10 percent discount on the purchase. The time required for the credit application process follows a uniform distribution with the times ranging from 4 minutes to 10 minutes.
  **a.** What is the mean time for the application process?
  **b.** What is the standard deviation of the process time?
  **c.** What is the likelihood a particular application will take less than 6 minutes?
  **d.** What is the likelihood an application will take more than 5 minutes?

**36.** The times patrons at the Grande Dunes Hotel in the Bahamas spend waiting for an elevator follows a uniform distribution between 0 and 3.5 minutes.
  **a.** Show that the area under the curve is 1.00.
  **b.** How long does the typical patron wait for elevator service?
  **c.** What is the standard deviation of the waiting time?
  **d.** What percent of the patrons wait for less than a minute?
  **e.** What percent of the patrons wait more than 2 minutes?

**37.** The net sales and the number of employees for aluminum fabricators with similar characteristics are organized into frequency distributions. Both are normally distributed. For the net sales, the mean is $180 million and the standard deviation is $25 million. For the number of employees, the mean is 1,500 and the standard deviation is 120. Clarion Fabricators had sales of $170 million and 1,850 employees.
  **a.** Convert Clarion's sales and number of employees to $z$ values.
  **b.** Locate the two $z$ values.
  **c.** Compare Clarion's sales and number of employees with those of the other fabricators.

**38.** The accounting department at Weston Materials, Inc., a national manufacturer of unattached garages, reports that it takes two construction workers a mean of 32 hours and a standard deviation of 2 hours to erect the Red Barn model. Assume the assembly times follow the normal distribution.
  **a.** Determine the $z$ values for 29 and 34 hours. What percent of the garages take between 32 hours and 34 hours to erect?
  **b.** What percent of the garages take between 29 hours and 34 hours to erect?
  **c.** What percent of the garages take 28.7 hours or less to erect?
  **d.** Of the garages, 5 percent take how many hours or more to erect?

**39.** A recent report in *USA Today* indicated a typical family of four spends $490 per month on food. Assume the distribution of food expenditures for a family of four follows the normal distribution, with a mean of $490 and a standard deviation of $90.
  **a.** What percent of the families spend more than $30 but less than $490 per month on food?
  **b.** What percent of the families spend less than $430 per month on food?
  **c.** What percent spend between $430 and $600 per month on food?
  **d.** What percent spend between $500 and $600 per month on food?

**40.** A study of long distance phone calls made from the corporate offices of the Pepsi Bottling Group, Inc., in Somers, New York, showed the calls follow the normal distribution. The mean length of time per call was 4.2 minutes and the standard deviation was 0.60 minutes.

**a.** What fraction of the calls last between 4.2 and 5 minutes?

**b.** What fraction of the calls last more than 5 minutes?

**c.** What fraction of the calls last between 5 and 6 minutes?

**d.** What fraction of the calls last between 4 and 6 minutes?

**e.** As part of her report to the president, the Director of Communications would like to report the length of the longest (in duration) 4 percent of the calls. What is this time?

**41.** Shaver Manufacturing, Inc. offers dental insurance to its employees. A recent study by the Human Resource Director shows the annual cost per employee per year followed the normal distribution, with a mean of $1,280 and a standard deviation of $420 per year.

**a.** What fraction of the employees cost more than $1,500 per year for dental expenses?

**b.** What fraction of the employees cost between $1,500 and $2,000 per year?

**c.** Estimate the percent that did not have any dental expense.

**d.** What was the cost for the 10 percent of employees who incurred the highest dental expense?

**42.** The annual commissions earned by sales representatives of Machine Products, Inc. a manufacturer of light machinery, follow the normal distribution. The mean yearly amount earned is $40,000 and the standard deviation is $5,000.

**a.** What percent of the sales representatives earn more than $42,000 per year?

**b.** What percent of the sales representatives earn between $32,000 and $42,000?

**c.** What percent of the sales representatives earn between $32,000 and $35,000?

**d.** The sales manager wants to award the sales representatives who earn the largest commissions a bonus of $1,000. He can award a bonus to 20 percent of the representatives. What is the cutoff point between those who earn a bonus and those who do not?

**43.** The weights of cans of Monarch pears follow the normal distribution with a mean of 1,000 grams and a standard deviation of 50 grams. Calculate the percentage of the cans that weigh:

**a.** Less than 860 grams.

**b.** Between 1,055 and 1,100 grams.

**c.** Between 860 and 1,055 grams.

**44.** The number of passengers on the *Carnival Sensation* during one-week cruises in the Caribbean follows the normal distribution. The mean number of passengers per cruise is 1,820 and the standard deviation is 120.

**a.** What percent of the cruises will have between 1,820 and 1,970 passengers?

**b.** What percent of the cruises will have 1,970 passengers or more?

**c.** What percent of the cruises will have 1,600 or fewer passengers?

**d.** How many passengers are on the cruises with the fewest 25 percent of passengers?

**45.** Management at Gordon Electronics is considering adopting a bonus system to increase production. One suggestion is to pay a bonus on the highest 5 percent of production based on past experience. Past records indicate weekly production follows the normal distribution. The mean of this distribution is 4,000 units per week and the standard deviation is 60 units per week. If the bonus is paid on the upper 5 percent of production, the bonus will be paid on how many units or more?

**46.** Fast Service Truck Lines uses the Ford Super Duty F-750 exclusively. Management made a study of the maintenance costs and determined the number of miles traveled during the year followed the normal distribution. The mean of the distribution was 60,000 miles and the standard deviation 2,000 miles.

**a.** What percent of the Ford Super Duty F-750s logged 65,200 miles or more?

**b.** What percent of the trucks logged more than 57,060 but less than 58,280 miles?

**c.** What percent of the Fords traveled 62,000 miles or less during the year?

**d.** Is it reasonable to conclude that any of the trucks were driven more than 70,000 miles? Explain.

**47.** Best Electronics, Inc. offers a "no hassle" returns policy. The number of items returned per day follows the normal distribution. The mean number of customer returns is 10.3 per day and the standard deviation is 2.25 per day.

**a.** In what percent of the days are there 8 or fewer customers returning items?

**b.** In what percent of the days are between 12 and 14 customers returning items?

**c.** Is there any chance of a day with no returns?

**48.** A recent report in *Business Week* indicated that 20 percent of all employees steal from their company each year. If a company employs 50 people, what is the probability that:

**a.** Fewer than 5 employees steal?

**b.** More than 5 employees steal?

    **c.** Exactly 5 employees steal?

    **d.** More than 5 but fewer than 15 employees steal?

**49.** The *Orange County Register,* as part of its Sunday health supplement, reported that 64 percent of American men over the age of 18 consider nutrition a top priority in their lives. Suppose we select a sample of 60 men. What is the likelihood that:

    **a.** 32 or more consider nutrition important?

    **b.** 44 or more consider nutrition important?

    **c.** More than 32 but fewer than 43 consider nutrition important?

    **d.** Exactly 44 consider diet important?

**50.** It is estimated that 10 percent of those taking the quantitative methods portion of the CPA examination fail that section. Sixty students are taking the exam this Saturday.

    **a.** How many would you expect to fail? What is the standard deviation?

    **b.** What is the probability that exactly two students will fail?

    **c.** What is the probability at least two students will fail?

**51.** The Georgetown, South Carolina, Traffic Division reported 40 percent of the high-speed chases involving automobiles result in a minor or major accident. During a month in which 50 high-speed chases occur, what is the probability that 25 or more will result in a minor or major accident?

**52.** Cruise ships of the Royal Viking line report that 80 percent of their rooms are occupied during September. For a cruise ship having 800 rooms, what is the probability that 665 or more are occupied in September?

**53.** The goal at U.S. airports handling international flights is to clear these flights within 45 minutes. Let's interpret this to mean that 95 percent of the flights are cleared in 45 minutes, so 5 percent of the flights take longer to clear. Let's also assume that the distribution is approximately normal.

    **a.** If the standard deviation of the time to clear an international flight is 5 minutes, what is the mean time to clear a flight?

    **b.** Suppose the standard deviation is 10 minutes, not the 5 minutes suggested in part a. What is the new mean?

    **c.** A customer has 30 minutes from the time her flight landed to catch her limousine. Assuming a standard deviation of 10 minutes, what is the likelihood that she will be cleared in time?

**54.** Jon Molnar will graduate from Carolina Forest High School this year. He took the American College Test (ACT) for college admission and received a score of 30. The high school principal informed him that only 2 percent of the students taking the exam receive a higher score. The mean score for all students taking the exam is 18.3. Jon's friends Karrie and George also took the test but were not given any information by the principal other than their scores. Karrie scored 25 and George 18. On the basis of this information, what were Karrie's and George's percentile ranks? Assume that the distribution of scores follows the normal distribution.

**55.** The weights of canned hams processed at the Henline Ham Company follow the normal distribution, with a mean of 9.20 pounds and a standard deviation of 0.25 pounds. The label weight is given as 9.00 pounds.

    **a.** What proportion of the hams actually weigh less than the amount claimed on the label?

    **b.** The owner, Glen Henline, is considering two proposals to reduce the proportion of hams below label weight. He can increase the mean weight to 9.25 and leave the standard deviation the same, or he can leave the mean weight at 9.20 and reduce the standard deviation from 0.25 pounds to 0.15. Which change would you recommend?

**56.** The *Cincinnati Enquirer,* as part of the Sunday business supplement, reported that the mean number of hours worked per week by those employed full time is 43.9. The article further indicated that about one-third of those employed full time work less than 40 hours per week.

    **a.** Given this information and assuming that number of hours worked follows the normal distribution, what is the standard deviation of the number of hours worked?

    **b.** The article also indicated that 20 percent of those working full time work more than 49 hours per week. Determine the standard deviation with this information. Are the two estimates of the standard deviation similar? What would you conclude?

**57.** Most four-year automobile leases allow up to 60,000 miles. If the lessee goes beyond this amount, a penalty of 20 cents per mile is added to the lease cost. Suppose the distribution of miles driven on four-year leases follows the normal distribution. The mean is 52,000 miles and the standard deviation is 5,000 miles.

    **a.** What percent of the leases will yield a penalty because of excess mileage?

    **b.** If the automobile company wanted to change the terms of the lease so that 25 percent of the leases went over the limit, where should the new upper limit be set?

    **c.** One definition of a low-mileage car is one that is 4 years old and has been driven less than 45,000 miles. What percent of the cars returned are considered low-mileage?

**58.** The price of shares of Bank of Florida at the end of trading each day for the last year followed the normal distribution. Assume there were 240 trading days in the year. The mean price was $42.00 per share and the standard deviation was $2.25 per share.

    **a.** What percent of the days was the price over $45.00? How many days would you estimate?

    **b.** What percent of the days was the price between $38.00 and $40.00?

    **c.** What was the stock's price on the *highest* 15 percent of days?

**59.** The annual sales of romance novels follow the normal distribution. However, the mean and the standard deviation are unknown. Forty percent of the time sales are more than 470,000, and 10 percent of the time sales are more than 500,000. What are the mean and the standard deviation?

**60.** In establishing warranties on HDTV sets, the manufacturer wants to set the limits so that few will need repair at manufacturer expense. On the other hand, the warranty period must be long enough to make the purchase attractive to the buyer. For a new HDTV the mean number of months until repairs are needed is 36.84 with a standard deviation of 3.34 months. Where should the warranty limits be set so that only 10 percent of the HDTVs need repairs at the manufacturer's expense?

**61.** DeKorte Tele-Marketing, Inc., is considering purchasing a machine that randomly selects and automatically dials telephone numbers. DeKorte Tele-Marketing makes most of its calls during the evening, so calls to business phones are wasted. The manufacturer of the machine claims that their programming reduces the calling to business phones to 15 percent of all calls. To test this claim the Director of Purchasing at DeKorte programmed the machine to select a sample of 150 phone numbers. What is the likelihood that more than 30 of the phone numbers selected are those of businesses, assuming the manufacturer's claim is correct?

# Dataset Exercises

**62.** Refer to the Real Estate dataset, which reports information on homes sold in the Denver, Colorado, area during the last year.

    **a.** The mean selling price (in $ thousands) of the homes was computed earlier to be $221.10, with a standard deviation of $47.11. Use the normal distribution to estimate the percent of homes selling for more than $280.0. Compare this to the actual results. Does the normal distribution yield a good approximation of the actual results?

    **b.** The mean distance from the center of the city is 14.629 miles with a standard deviation of 4.874 miles. Use the normal distribution to estimate the number of homes 18 or more miles but less than 22 miles from the center of the city. Compare this to the actual results. Does the normal distribution yield a good approximation of the actual results?

**63.** Refer to the Baseball 2002 dataset, which reports information on the 30 Major League Baseball teams for the 2002 season.

    **a.** The mean attendance per team for the season was 2,265 (in 000s) with a standard deviation of 753 (in 000s). Use the normal distribution to estimate the number of teams with attendance of more than 3.5 million. Compare that estimate with the actual number. Comment on the accuracy of your estimate.

    **b.** The mean team salary was $83.55 million with a standard deviation of $29.15 million. Use the normal distribution to estimate the number of teams with a team salary of more than $50 million. Compare that estimate with the actual number. Comment on the accuracy of the estimate.

**64.** Refer to the CIA data, which report demographic and economic information on 46 countries.

    **a.** The mean of the GDP/capita variable is 16.58 with a standard deviation of 9.27. Use the normal distribution to estimate the percentage of countries with exports above 24. Compare this estimate with the actual proportion. Does the normal distribution appear accurate in this case? Explain.

    **b.** The mean of the Exports is 116.3 with a standard deviation of 157.4. Use the normal distribution to estimate the percentage of countries with Exports above 170. Compare this estimate with the actual proportion. Does the normal distribution appear accurate in this case? Explain.

# Software Commands

1. The Excel commands necessary to produce the output on page 225 are:
   a. Select **Insert** and **Function,** then from the box select **Statistical** and **NORMDIST** and click *OK.*
   b. In the dialog box put *1100* in the box for *X, 1000* for the **Mean,** *100* for the **Standard_dev,** *True* in the **Cumulative** box, and click **OK.**
   c. The result will appear in the dialog box. If you click **OK,** the answer appears in your spreadsheet.
2. The Excel Commands necessary to produce the output on page 231 are:
   a. Select **Insert** and **Function,** then from the box select **Statistical** and **NORMINV** and click **OK.**
   b. In the dialog box, set the **Probability** to 0.04, the **Mean** to 67900, and the **Standard_dev** to 2050.
   c. The results will appear in the dialog box. Note that the answer is different from page 230 because of rounding error. If you click **OK,** the answer also appears in your spreadsheet.
   d. Try entering a **Probability** of 0.04, a **Mean** of zero, and a **Standard_dev** of one. The *z* value will be computed.

# Chapter 7 Answers to Self-Review

**7–1** **a.**

$P(x)$

.167

8          14

**b.** $P(x) = \text{(height)(base)}$

$$= \left(\frac{1}{14-8}\right)(14-8)$$

$$= \left(\frac{1}{6}\right)(6) = 1.00$$

**c.** $\mu = \dfrac{a+b}{2} = \dfrac{14+8}{2} = \dfrac{22}{2} = 11$

$$\sigma = \sqrt{\frac{(b-a)^2}{12}} = \sqrt{\frac{(14-8)^2}{12}} = \sqrt{\frac{36}{12}} = \sqrt{3}$$

$$= 1.73$$

**d.** $P(10 \le x \le 14) = \text{(height)(base)}$

$$= \left(\frac{1}{14-8}\right)(14-10)$$

$$= \frac{1}{6}(4)$$

$$= .667$$

**e.** $P(x \le 9) = \text{(height)(base)}$

$$= \left(\frac{1}{14-8}\right)(9-8)$$

$$= 0.167$$

**7–2** **a.** 2.25, found by:

$$z = \frac{\$1{,}225 - \$1{,}000}{\$100} = \frac{\$225}{\$100} = 2.25$$

**b.** −2.25, found by:

$$z = \frac{\$775 - \$1{,}000}{\$100} = \frac{-\$225}{\$100} = -2.25$$

**7–3** **a.** \$46,400 and \$48,000, found by \$47,200 ± 1(\$800).

**b.** \$45,600 and \$48,800, found by \$47,200 ± 2(\$800).

**c.** \$44,800 and \$49,600, found by \$47,200 ± 3(\$800).

**d.** \$47,200. The mean, median, and mode are equal for a normal distribution.

**e.** Yes, a normal distribution is symmetrical.

**7–4** **a.** Computing z:

$$z = \frac{482 - 400}{50} = +1.64$$

Referring to Appendix D, the area is .4495.
$P(400 < \text{rating} < 482) = .4495$

**b.** .0505, found by .5000 − .4495
$P(\text{rating} > 482) = .5000 - .4495 = .0505$

**c.**

.5000

.4495

.0505

0      1.64  Scale of z
400      482  Scale of days

**7–5** **a.** 98.16%, found by 0.4938 + 0.4878.

750      1,000      1,225 ← \$ scale
−2.50      0      2.25 ← z scale

**b.** 14.65%, found by 0.4878 − 0.3413.

1,000  1,100      1,225 ← \$ scale
0      1.00      2.25 ← z scale

**7–6** 85.24 (instructor would no doubt make it 85). The closest area to .4000 is .3997; z is 1.28. Then:

$$1.28 = \frac{X - 75}{8}$$

$$10.24 = X - 75$$

$$X = 85.24$$

**7–7** **a.** .0465, found by $\mu = n\pi = 200(.80) = 160$, and $\sigma^2 = n\pi(1 - \pi) = 200(.80)(1 - .80) = 32$. Then,

$$\sigma = \sqrt{32} = 5.66$$

$$z = \frac{169.5 - 160}{5.66} = 1.68$$

Area from Appendix D is .4535. Subtracting from .5000 gives .0465.

**b.** .9686, found by .4686 + .5000. First calculate z:

$$z = \frac{149.5 - 160}{5.66} = -1.86$$

Area from Appendix D is .4686.

# A Review of Chapters 5–7

This section is a review of the major concepts, terms, symbols, and equations introduced in Chapters 5, 6, and 7. These three chapters are concerned with methods of dealing with uncertainty. As an example of the uncertainty in business, consider the role of the quality assurance department in most mass-production firms. Usually, the department has neither the personnel nor the time to check, say, all 200 plug-in modules produced during a two-hour period. Standard operating procedure may call for selecting a sample of 5 modules and shipping all 200 modules if the 5 operate correctly. However, if 1 or more in the sample are defective, all 200 are checked. Assuming that all 5 function correctly, quality assurance personnel cannot be absolutely certain that their action (allowing shipment of the modules) will prove to be correct. It could be that the 5 selected at random are the only ones out of the 200 that function properly! Probability theory lets us measure the uncertainty involved, in this case, of shipping out defective modules. Also, probability as a measurement of uncertainty comes into play when Gallup, Harris, and other pollsters predict that Jim Barstow will win the vacant senatorial seat in Georgia.

Chapter 5 notes that a *probability* is a value between 0 and 1, inclusive, that expresses one's belief that a particular event will occur. A weather forecaster might state that the probability of rain tomorrow is .20. The project director of a firm bidding on a subway station in Bangkok might assess the firm's chance of being awarded the contract at .50. We looked at the ways probabilities can be combined using rules of addition and multiplication, some principles of counting, and the importance of Bayes' theorem.

Chapter 6 presents *discrete* probability distributions—the *binomial distribution,* the *hypergeometric distribution,* and the *Poisson distribution.* Other probability distributions will be discussed in forthcoming chapters (*t* distribution, chi-square distribution, etc.). Probability distributions are listings of all the possible outcomes of an experiment and the probability associated with each outcome. A probability distribution allows us to evaluate sample results.

Chapter 7 describes two continuous probability distributions, the *uniform probability distribution* and the *normal probability distribution.* The uniform distribution is used to describe phenomena that are equally likely over a range of values. It is rectangular in shape, its mean and median are equal, and it does not have a mode. The uniform distribution is completely described by its minimum and maximum values. Also, the distribution's minimum and maximum values are used to compute the probability for any event.

A normal probability distribution is used to describe phenomena that follow a normal bell-shaped distribution, such as the tensile strength of wires and the weights or volumes of cans and bottles. Actually, there is a family of normal distributions—each with its own mean and standard deviation. There is a normal distribution, for example, for a mean of $100 and a standard deviation of $5, another for a mean of $149 and a standard deviation of $5.26, and so on. It was noted that a normal probability distribution is symmetrical about its mean and that the tails of the normal curve extend in either direction infinitely.

Since there are an unlimited number of normal distributions, it is difficult to assign probabilities. Instead, any normal distribution can be changed to a *standard normal distribution* by computing *z scores.* The standard normal distribution has a mean of 0 and a standard deviation of 1. It is useful because the probability for any event from a normal distribution can be computed using standard normal probability tables.

## Glossary

### Chapter 5

**Bayes' theorem**   Developed by Reverend Bayes in the 1700s, it is designed to find the probability of one event, *A*, occurring, given that another event, *B*, has already occurred.

**Classical probability**   Probability based on the assumption that each of the outcomes is equally likely. According to this concept of probability, if there are *n* possible outcomes, the probability of a particular outcome is $1/n$. Thus, on the toss of a coin, the probability of a head is $1/n = 1/2$.

**Combination formula**   A formula to count the number of possible outcomes. If the order *a, b, c* is considered the same as *b, a, c,* or *c, b, a,* and so on, the number of arrangements is found by:

$$_nC_r = \frac{n!}{r!(n-r)!}$$

**Conditional probability**   The likelihood that an event will occur given that another event has already occurred.

**Empirical probability**   A concept of probability based on past experience. For example, the Metropolitan Life Insurance Company reported that during the year, 100.2 of every 100,000 persons in Wyoming died of accidental causes (motor vehicle accidents, falls, drowning, firearms, etc.). On the basis of this experience, Metropolitan can estimate the probability of accidental death for a particular person in Wyoming: 100.2/100,000 = .001002.

**Event**   A collection of one or more outcomes of an experiment. For example, an event may be three defective valves in an incoming shipment of valves for a 3.8 liter Ford engine.

**Experiment**   An activity that is either observed or measured. An experiment may be counting the number of correct responses to a question, for example.

**General rule of addition**   Used to find the probabilities of complex events made up of A or B.

$$P(A \text{ or } B) = P(A) + P(B) - P(A \text{ and } B)$$

**General rule of multiplication**   Used to find the probabilities of complex events made up of A and B. Example: It is known that there are 3 defective radios in a box containing 10 radios. What is the probability of selecting 2 defective radios on the first two selections from the box?

$$P(A \text{ and } B) = P(A)P(B \mid A) = \frac{3}{10} \times \frac{2}{9} = \frac{6}{90} = .067$$

Where $P(B \mid A)$ is the conditional probability and means "the probability of B occurring given that A has already occurred."

**Independent**   The occurrence of one event has no effect on the probability of the occurrence of another event.

**Multiplication formula**   One of the formulas used to count the number of possible outcomes of an experiment. It states that if there are m ways of doing one thing and n ways of doing another, there are $m \times n$ ways of doing both. Example: A sports shop offers two sport coats and three contrasting pants for $400. How many different outfits can there be? Answer: $m \times n = 2 \times 3 = 6$.

**Outcome**   A particular observation or measurement of an experiment.

**Permutation formula**   A formula to count the number of possible outcomes. If a, b, c is one arrangement, b, a, c another, c, a, b another; and so on, the total number of arrangements is determined by

$$_nP_r = \frac{n!}{(n-r)!}$$

**Probability**   A value between 0 and 1, inclusive, that reports the likelihood that a specific event will occur.

**Special rule of addition**   For this rule to apply, the events must be mutually exclusive. For two events, the probability of A or B occurring is found by:

$$P(A \text{ or } B) = P(A) + P(B)$$

Example:   The probability of a one-spot or a two-spot occurring on the toss of one die.

$$P(A \text{ or } B) = \frac{1}{6} + \frac{1}{6} = \frac{2}{6} = \frac{1}{3}$$

**Special rule of multiplication**   If two events are not related—that is, they are independent—this rule can be applied to determine the probability of their joint occurrence.

$$P(A \text{ and } B) = P(A)P(B)$$

Example:   The probability of two heads on two tosses of a coin is:

$$P(A \text{ and } B) = P(A)P(B) = \frac{1}{2} \times \frac{1}{2} = \frac{1}{4}$$

**Subjective probability**   The chance of an event happening based on whatever information is available—hunches, personal opinion, opinions of others, rumors, and so on.

## Chapter 6

**Binomial probability distribution**   A discrete random variable with the following characteristics:

1.   Each outcome can be classified into one of two mutually exclusive categories.
2.   The distribution is the result of counting the number of successes.
3.   Each trial is independent, meaning that the answer to trial 1 (correct or wrong) in no way affects the answer to trial 2.
4.   The probability of a success stays the same from trial to trial.

**Continuous random variable**   A random variable that may assume an infinite number of values within a given range.

**Discrete random variable**   A random variable that can assume only certain separate values.

**Hypergeometric probability distribution**   A probability distribution based on a discrete random variable. Its major characteristics are:

1.   There is a fixed number of trials.
2.   The probability of success is not the same from trial to trial.
3.   There are only two possible outcomes.

**Poisson distribution**   A distribution often used to approximate binomial probabilities when n is large and $\pi$ is small. What is considered "large" or "small" is not precisely defined, but a general rule is that n should be equal to or greater than 20 and $\pi$ equal to or less than .05.

**Probability distribution**   A listing of the possible outcomes of an experiment and the probability associated with each outcome.

**Random variable**   A quantity obtained from an experiment that may, by chance, result in different values. For example, a count of the number of accidents (the experiment) on I-75 during a week might be 10, or 11, or 12, or some other number.

## Chapter 7

**Continuity correction factor**   Used to improve the accuracy of the approximation of a discrete distribution by a continuous distribution.

**Normal probability distribution**   A continuous distribution that is bell-shaped, with the mean dividing the distribution into two equal parts. Further, the normal curve extends indefinitely in either direction; and, it never touches the X-axis.

**Uniform probability distribution** A continuous probability distribution that is rectangular in shape. It is completely described by using the minimum and maximum values of the distribution to compute the mean and standard deviation. Also, minimum and maximum values are used to compute the probability for any event.

**z value** The distance between a selected value and the population mean measured in units of the standard deviation.

## Exercises

### Part I—Multiple Choice

1. Based on your assessment of the stock market, you state that the chances that stock prices will start to go down within two months are 50-50. This concept of probability based on your beliefs is called
   a. Classical probability
   b. Empirical probability
   c. Subjective probability
   d. Independence

2. A study of absenteeism from the classroom is being conducted. In terms of statistics, the study is called:
   a. An experiment
   b. An event
   c. An outcome
   d. A joint probability

3. In a study of absenteeism, the results showed that 126 students were absent from Monday morning classes. This number (126) is called
   a. An experiment
   b. An event
   c. An outcome
   d. A joint probability

4. To apply this rule of addition, $P(A \text{ or } B \text{ or } C) = P(A) + P(B) + P(C)$, the events must be
   a. Joint events
   b. Conditional events
   c. Mutually exclusive events
   d. Independent events

5. Management claims that the probability of a defective relay is only 0.001. The rule used for finding the probability of the relay *not* being defective is the
   a. Addition rule
   b. Multiplication rule
   c. Complementary rule
   d. Special rule of probability

6. Management claims that the probability of a defective relay is only 0.001. The probability of the relay *not* being defective is
   a. 0.002
   b. 0.000001
   c. 0.999
   d. 1.0

7. For a probability distribution, the sum of the probabilities for all possible outcomes must equal
   a. 0.5
   b. 1.0
   c. 1.5
   d. 0.0

8. The binomial and Poisson probability distributions are
   a. Continuous
   b. Either discrete or continuous
   c. Discrete
   d. Normal

9. A normal probability distribution is
   a. Symmetric around the mean
   b. Bell shaped
   c. Asymptotic to the X-axis
   d. All of the above
10. A uniform probability distribution is
    a. Symmetric around the mean
    b. Bell shaped
    c. Asymptotic to the X-axis
    d. All of the above
11. For the uniform probability distribution and the normal probability distribution,
    a. The areas within the distributions are equal to 1.0.
    b. The modes are located in the center of the distribution.
    c. The ranges of a random variable are infinite.
    d. z scores can be used to convert each distribution to a standard normal distribution.
12. If we use z scores to convert any normal distribution, the new distribution is
    a. A binomial distribution with mean 0 and standard deviation $\sigma$
    b. A standard normal distribution with a mean of 0 and standard deviation of 1
    c. A standard normal distribution with a mean of $\mu$ and variance $\sigma^2$
    d. A Poisson distribution with mean 0

## Part II—Problems

13. A self-study course on management principles was offered to all employees of TMC Electronics. At the end of the time period, the employees were tested, with the following results:

| Course Grade | Number of Employees |
|---|---|
| A | 20 |
| B | 35 |
| C | 90 |
| D | 40 |
| F | 10 |
| Withdrew | 5 |

What is the probability that an employee selected at random:
a. Earned an A?
b. Earned a C or better?
c. Did not fail or withdraw?

14. It is claimed that Proactine, a new medicine for acne, is 80 percent effective—that is, of every 100 persons who apply it, 80 show significant improvement. It is applied to the affected area of a group of 15 people. What is the probability that:
a. All 15 will show significant improvement?
b. Fewer than 9 of 15 will show significant improvement?
c. That 12 or more people will show significant improvement?

15. First National Bank thoroughly investigates its applicants for small home-improvement loans. Their default record is very impressive: the probability that a homeowner will default is only .005. The bank has approved 400 small home-improvement loans. Assuming the Poisson probability distribution applies to this problem:
a. What is the probability that no homeowners out of the 400 will default?
b. How many of the 400 are expected not to default?
c. What is the probability that 3 or more homeowners will default on their small home-improvement loans?

16. A study of the attendance at the University of Alabama's basketball games revealed that the distribution of attendance is normally distributed with a mean of 10,000 and a standard deviation of 2,000.
a. What is the probability a particular game has an attendance of 13,500 or more?
b. What percent of the games have an attendance between 8,000 and 11,500?
c. Ten percent of the games have an attendance of how many or less?

**17.** The following table shows a breakdown of the One Hundred Eighth U.S. Congress by party affiliation.

| | Party | | |
| --- | --- | --- | --- |
| | Democrats | Republicans | Others |
| House | 205 | 229 | 1 |
| Senate | 48 | 51 | 1 |

  **a.** A member of Congress is selected at random. What is the probability of selecting a Republican?
  **b.** Given that the person selected is a member of the House of Representatives, what is the probability he or she is a Republican?
  **c.** What is the probability of selecting a member of the House of Representatives or a Democrat?
**18.** The Internal Revenue Service has set aside 200 tax returns where the amount of charitable contributions seemed excessive. A sample of six returns is selected from the group. If two or more of this sampled group have "excessive" amounts deducted for charitable contributions, the entire group will be audited. What is the probability the entire group will be audited, if the true proportion of "excessive" deductions is 20 percent? What if the true proportion is 30 percent?
**19.** The Daniel-James Insurance Company will insure an offshore Mobil Oil production platform against weather losses for one year. The president of Daniel-James estimates the following losses for that platform (in millions of dollars) with the accompanying probabilities:

| Amount of Loss ($ millions) | Probability of Loss |
| --- | --- |
| 0 | .98 |
| 40 | .016 |
| 300 | .004 |

  **a.** What is the expected amount Daniel-James will have to pay to Mobil in claims?
  **b.** What is the likelihood that Daniel-James will actually lose less than the expected amount?
  **c.** Given that Daniel-James suffers a loss, what is the likelihood that it is for $300 million?
  **d.** Daniel-James has set the annual premium at $2.0 million. Does that seem like a fair premium? Will it cover their risk?
**20.** The distribution of the number of school-age children per family in the Whitehall Estates area of Boise, Idaho, is:

| Number of children | 0 | 1 | 2 | 3 | 4 |
| --- | --- | --- | --- | --- | --- |
| Percent of families | 40 | 30 | 15 | 10 | 5 |

  **a.** Determine the mean and standard deviation of the number of school-age children per family in Whitehall Estates.
  **b.** A new school is planned in Whitehall Estates. An estimate of the number of school-age children is needed. There are 500 family units. How many children would you estimate?
  **c.** Some additional information is needed about only the families having children. Convert the preceding distribution to one for families with children. What is the mean number of children among families that have children?

# Cases

## A. Century National Bank
Refer to the Century National Bank data. Is it reasonable that the distribution of checking account balances approximates a normal distribution? Determine the mean and the standard deviation for the sample of 60 customers. Compare the actual distribution with the theoretical distribution. Cite some specific examples and comment on your findings.

Divide the account balances into three groups, of about 20 each, with the smallest third of the balances in the first group, the middle third in the second group, and those with the largest balances in the third group. Next, develop a table that shows the number in each of the categories of the account balances by branch. Does it appear that account balances are related to the branch? Cite some examples and comment on your findings.

## B. Elections Auditor

An item such as an increase in taxes, recall of elected officials, or an expansion of public services can be placed on the ballot if a required number of valid signatures are collected on the petition. Unfortunately, many people will sign the petition even though they are not registered to vote in that particular district, or they will sign the petition more than once.

Sara Ferguson, the elections auditor in Venango County, must certify the validity of these signatures after the petition is officially presented. Not surprisingly, her staff is overloaded, so she is considering using statistical methods to validate the pages of 200 signatures, instead of validating each individual signature. At a recent professional meeting, she found that in some communities in the state, election officials were checking only five signatures on each page, rejecting the entire page if two or more signatures were invalid. Some people are concerned that five may not be enough to make a good decision. They suggest that you should check 10 signatures and reject the page if three or more are invalid.

In order to investigate these methods, Sara asks her staff to pull the results from the last election and sample 30 pages. It happens that the staff selected 14 pages from the Avondale district, 9 pages from the Midway district, and 7 pages from the Kingston district. Each page had 200 signatures, and the data below show the number of invalid signatures on each.

Use the data to evaluate Sara's two proposals. Calculate the probability of rejecting a page under each of the approaches. Would you get about the same results by examining every single signature? Offer a plan of your own, and discuss how it might be better or worse than the two plans proposed by Sara.

| Avondale | Midway | Kingston |
|----------|--------|----------|
| 9        | 19     | 38       |
| 14       | 22     | 39       |
| 11       | 23     | 41       |
| 8        | 14     | 39       |
| 14       | 22     | 41       |
| 6        | 17     | 39       |
| 10       | 15     | 39       |
| 13       | 20     |          |
| 8        | 18     |          |
| 8        |        |          |
| 9        |        |          |
| 12       |        |          |
| 7        |        |          |
| 13       |        |          |

## C. Geoff "Applies" His Education

Geoff Brown is the manager for a small telemarketing firm and is evaluating the sales rate of experienced workers in order to set minimum standards for new hires. During the past few weeks, he has recorded the number of successful calls per hour for the staff. These data appear below along with some summary statistics he worked out with a statistical software package. Geoff has been a student at the local community college and has heard of many different kinds of probability distributions (binomial, normal, hypergeometric, Poisson, etc.). Could you give Geoff some advice on which distribution to use to fit these data as well as possible and how to decide when a probationary employee should be accepted as having reached full production status? This is important because it means a pay raise for the employee, and there have been some probationary employees in the past who have quit because of discouragement that they would never meet the standard.

Successful sales calls per hour during the week of August 14:

| 4 | 2 | 3 | 1 | 4 | 5 | 5 | 2 | 3 | 2 | 2 | 4 | 5 | 2 | 5 | 3 | 3 | 0 |
| 1 | 3 | 2 | 8 | 4 | 5 | 2 | 2 | 4 | 1 | 5 | 5 | 4 | 5 | 1 | 2 | 4 | |

Descriptive statistics:

| N | MEAN | MEDIAN | TRMEAN | STDEV | SEMEAN |
|-----|-------|--------|--------|-------|--------|
| 35  | 3.229 | 3.000  | 3.194  | 1.682 | 0.284  |
| MIN | MAX   | Q1     | Q3     |       |        |
| 0.0 | 8.000 | 2.000  | 5.000  |       |        |

Which distribution do you think Geoff should use for his analysis?

## D. CNP Bank Card

Before banks issue a credit card, they usually rate or score the customer in terms of his or her projected probability of being a profitable customer. A typical scoring table appears below.

| Age | Under 25 | 25–29 | 30–34 | 35+ |
|-----|----------|-------|-------|-----|
| | (12 pts.) | (5 pts.) | (0 pts.) | (18 pts.) |
| **Time at same address** | < 1 yr. | 1–2 yrs. | 3–4 yrs. | 5+ yrs. |
| | (9 pts.) | (0 pts.) | (13 pts.) | (20 pts.) |
| **Auto age** | None | 0–1 yr. | 2–4 yrs. | 5+ yrs. |
| | (18 pts.) | (12 pts.) | (13 pts.) | (3 pts.) |
| **Monthly car payment** | None | $1–$99 | $100–$299 | $300+ |
| | (15 pts.) | (6 pts.) | (4 pts.) | (0 pts.) |
| **Housing cost** | $1–$199 | $200–$399 | Owns | Lives with relatives |
| | (0 pts.) | (10 pts.) | (12 pts.) | (24 pts.) |
| **Checking/ savings accounts** | Both | Checking only | Savings only | Neither |
| | (15 pts.) | (3 pts.) | (2 pts.) | (0 pts.) |

The score is the sum of the points on the six items. For example, Sushi Brown is under 25 years old (12 pts.), has lived at the same address for 2 years (0 pts.), owns a 4-year-old car (13 pts.), with car payments of $75 (6 pts.), housing cost of $200 (10 pts.), and a checking account (3 pts.). She would score 44.

A second chart is then used to convert scores into the probability of being a profitable customer. A sample chart of this type appears below.

| Score | 30 | 40 | 50 | 60 | 70 | 80 | 90 |
|---|---|---|---|---|---|---|---|
| Probability | .70 | .78 | .85 | .90 | .94 | .95 | .96 |

Sushi's score of 44 would translate into a probability of being profitable of approximately .81. In other words 81 percent of customers like Sushi will make money for the bank card operations.

Here are the interview results for three potential customers.

| Name | David Born | Edward Brendan | Ann McLaughlin |
|---|---|---|---|
| Age | 42 | 23 | 33 |
| Time at same address | 9 | 2 | 5 |
| Auto age | 2 | 3 | 7 |
| Monthly car payment | $140 | $99 | $175 |
| Housing cost | $300 | $200 | Owns clear |
| Checking/savings accounts | Both | Checking only | Neither |

a. Score each of these customers and estimate their probability of being profitable.
b. What is the probability that all three are profitable?
c. What is the probability that none of them are profitable?
d. Find the entire probability distribution for the number of profitable customers among this group of three.

# 8

# Sampling Methods and the Central Limit Theorem

## GOALS

*When you have completed this chapter you will be able to:*

1 Explain why a sample is often the only feasible way to learn something about a population.

2 Describe methods to select a sample.

3 Define and construct a sampling distribution of the sample mean.

4 Explain the *central limit theorem.*

5 Use the central limit theorem to find probabilities of selecting possible sample means from a specified population.

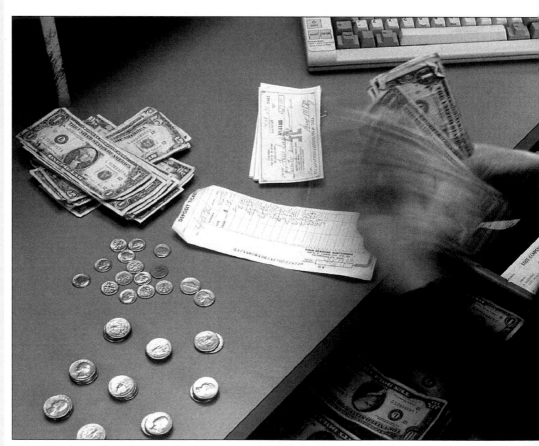

At the downtown office of First National Bank there are five tellers. How many different samples of two tellers are possible? (See Goal 3 and Exercise 28.)

**Statistics in Action**

With the significant role played by inferential statistics in all branches of science, the availability of large sources of random numbers has become a necessity. The first book of random numbers, containing 41,600 random digits generated by L. Tippett, was published in 1927. In 1938, R. A. Fisher and F. Yates published 15,000 random digits generated using two decks of cards. In 1955, RAND Corporation published a million random digits, generated by the random frequency pulses of an electronic roulette wheel. By 1970, applications of sampling required billions of random numbers. Methods have since been developed for generating, using a computer, digits that are "almost" random and hence are called *pseudo-random*. The question of whether a computer progam can be used to generate numbers that are truly random remains a debatable issue.

# Introduction

Chapters 1 through 4 emphasize techniques to describe data. To illustrate these techniques, we organize the prices for the 80 vehicles sold last month at Whitner Autoplex into a frequency distribution and compute various measures of location and dispersion. Such measures as the mean and the standard deviation describe the typical selling price and the spread in the selling prices. In these chapters the emphasis is on describing the condition of the data. That is, we describe something that has already happened.

Chapter 5 starts to lay the foundation for statistical inference with the study of probability. Recall that in statistical inference our goal is to determine something about a *population* based only on the *sample.* The population is the entire group of individuals or objects under consideration, and the sample is a part or subset of that population. Chapter 6 extends the probability concepts by describing three discrete probability distributions: the binomial, the hypergeometric, and the Poisson. Chapter 7 describes the uniform probability distribution and the normal probability distribution. Both of these are continuous distributions. Probability distributions encompass all possible outcomes of an experiment and the probability associated with each outcome. We use probability distributions to evaluate the likelihood something occurs in the future.

This chapter begins our study of sampling. A sample is a tool to infer something about a population. We begin this chapter by discussing methods of selecting a sample from a population. Next, we construct a distribution of the sample mean to understand how the sample means tend to cluster around the population mean. Finally, we show that for any population the shape of this sampling distribution tends to follow the normal probability distribution.

# Sampling Methods

In Chapter 1, we said the purpose of inferential statistics is to find something about a population based on a sample. A sample is a portion or part of the population of interest. In many cases, sampling is more feasible than studying the entire population. In this section, we show major reasons for sampling, and then several methods for selecting a sample.

## Reasons to Sample

When studying characteristics of a population, there are many practical reasons why we prefer to select portions or samples of a population to observe and measure. Some of the reasons for sampling are:

1. **To contact the whole population would be time consuming.** A candidate for a national office may wish to determine her chances for election. A sample poll using the regular staff and field interviews of a professional polling firm would take only 1 or 2 days. By using the same staff and interviewers and working 7 days a week, it would take nearly 200 years to contact all the voting population! Even if a large staff of interviewers could be assembled, the benefit of contacting all of the voters would probably not be worth the time.

2. **The cost of studying all the items in a population may be prohibitive.** Public opinion polls and consumer testing organizations, such as Gallup Polls and Roper ASW, usually contact fewer than 2,000 of the nearly 60 million families in the

United States. One consumer panel-type organization charges about $40,000 to mail samples and tabulate responses in order to test a product (such as breakfast cereal, cat food, or perfume). The same product test using all 60 million families would cost about $1 billion.

3. **The physical impossibility of checking all items in the population.** The populations of fish, birds, snakes, mosquitoes, and the like are large and are constantly moving, being born, and dying. Instead of even attempting to count all the ducks in Canada or all the fish in Lake Erie, we make estimates using various techniques—such as counting all the ducks on a pond picked at random, making creel checks, or setting nets at predetermined places in the lake.

4. **The destructive nature of some tests.** If the wine tasters at the Sutter Home Winery in California drank all the wine to evaluate the vintage, they would consume the entire crop, and none would be available for sale. In the area of industrial production, steel plates, wires, and similar products must have a certain minimum tensile strength. To ensure that the product meets the minimum standard, the Quality Assurance Department selects a sample from the current production. Each piece is stretched until it breaks, and the breaking point (usually measured in pounds per square inch) recorded. Obviously, if all the wire or all the plates were tested for tensile strength, none would be available for sale or use. For the same reason, only a sample of photographic film is selected and tested by Kodak to determine the quality of all the film produced, and only a few seeds are tested for germination by Burpee prior to the planting season.

5. **The sample results are adequate.** Even if funds were available, it is doubtful the additional accuracy of a 100 percent sample—that is, studying the entire population—is essential in most problems. For example, the federal government uses a sample of grocery stores scattered throughout the United States to determine the monthly index of food prices. The prices of bread, beans, milk, and other major food items are included in the index. It is unlikely that the inclusion of all grocery stores in the United States would significantly affect the index, since the prices of milk, bread, and other major foods usually do not vary by more than a few cents from one chain store to another.

When selecting a sample, researchers or analysts must be very careful that the sample is a fair representation of the population. In other words, the sample must be unbiased. In Chapter 1, an example of abusing statistics was the intentional selection of dentists to report that "2 out of 3 dentists surveyed indicated they would recommend Brand X toothpaste to their patients." Clearly, people can select a sample that supports their own biases. The ethical side of statistics always requires unbiased sampling and objective reporting of results. Next, several sampling methods show how to select a fair and unbiased sample from a population.

## Simple Random Sampling

The most widely used type of sampling is a **simple random sample.**

> **SIMPLE RANDOM SAMPLE** A sample selected so that each item or person in the population has the same chance of being included.

A table of random numbers is an efficient way to select members of the sample

To illustrate simple random sampling and selection, suppose a population consists of 845 employees of Nitra Industries. A sample of 52 employees is to be selected from that population. One way of ensuring that every employee in the population has the same chance of being chosen is to first write the name of each employee on a small slip of paper and deposit all of the slips in a box. After they have been thoroughly mixed, the first selection is made by drawing a slip out of the box without looking at it. This process is repeated until the sample size of 52 is chosen.

A more convenient method of selecting a random sample is to use the identification number of each employee and a **table of random numbers** such as the one in Appendix E. As the name implies, these numbers have been generated by a random process (in this case, by a computer). For each digit of a number, the probability of 0, 1, 2, . . . , 9 is the same. Thus, the probability that employee number 011 will be selected is the same as for employee 722 or employee 382. By using random numbers to select employees, bias is eliminated from the selection process.

A portion of a table of random numbers is shown in the following illustration. To select a sample of employees, you first choose a starting point in the table. Any starting point will do. Suppose the time is 3:04. You might look at the third column and then move down to the fourth set of numbers. The number is 03759. Since there are only 845 employees, we will use the first three digits of a five-digit random number. Thus, 037 is the number of the first employee to be a member of the sample. Another way of selecting the starting point is to close your eyes and point at a number in the table. To continue selecting employees, you could move in any direction. Suppose you move right. The first three digits of the number to the right of 03759 are 447—the number of the employee selected to be the second member of the sample. The next three-digit number to the right is 961. You skip 961 because there are only 845 employees. You continue to the right and select employee 784, then 189, and so on.

| 50525 | 57454 | 28455 | 68226 | 34656 | 38884 | 39018 |
| 72507 | 53380 | 53827 | 42486 | 54465 | 71819 | 91199 |
| 34986 | 74297 | 00144 | 38676 | 89967 | 98869 | 39744 |
| 68851 | 27305 | 03759 | 44723 | 96108 | 78489 | 18910 |
| 06738 | 62879 | 03910 | 17350 | 49169 | 03850 | 18910 |
| 11448 | 10734 | 05837 | 24397 | 10420 | 16712 | 94496 |
| | | Starting point | Second employee | | Third employee | Fourth employee |

---

**Self-Review 8–1**

The following class roster lists the students enrolling in an introductory course in business statistics. Three students are to be randomly selected and asked various questions regarding course content and method of instruction.
(a)   The numbers 00 through 45 are handwritten on slips of paper and placed in a bowl. The three numbers selected are 31, 7, and 25. Which students would be included in the sample?
(b)   Now use the table of random digits, Appendix E, to select your own sample.
(c)   What would you do if you encountered the number 59 in the table of random digits?

---

# Systematic Random Sampling

The simple random sampling procedure may be awkward in some research situations. For example, suppose the sales division of Computer Printers Unlimited needs to quickly estimate the mean dollar revenue per sale during the past month. They find that 2,000 sales invoices were recorded and stored in file drawers, and decide to select 100 invoices to estimate the mean dollar revenue. Simple random sampling requires the numbering of each invoice before using the random number table to select

```
                    CSPM 264 01 BUSINESS & ECONOMIC STAT
                       8:00 AM 9:40 AM MW ST 118 LIND D
```

| RANDOM NUMBER | NAME | CLASS RANK | RANDOM NUMBER | NAME | CLASS RANK |
|---|---|---|---|---|---|
| 00 | ANDERSON, RAYMOND | SO | 23 | MEDLEY, CHERYL ANN | SO |
| 01 | ANGER, CHERYL RENEE | SO | 24 | MITCHELL, GREG R | FR |
| 02 | BALL, CLAIRE JEANETTE | FR | 25 | MOLTER, KRISTI MARIE | SO |
| 03 | BERRY, CHRISTOPHER G | FR | 26 | MULCAHY, STEPHEN ROBERT | SO |
| 04 | BOBAK, JAMES PATRICK | SO | 27 | NICHOLAS, ROBERT CHARLES | JR |
| 05 | BRIGHT, M. STARR | JR | 28 | NICKENS, VIRGINIA | SO |
| 06 | CHONTOS, PAUL JOSEPH | SO | 29 | PENNYWITT, SEAN PATRICK | SO |
| 07 | DETLEY, BRIAN HANS | JR | 30 | POTEAU, KRIS E | JR |
| 08 | DUDAS, VIOLA | SO | 31 | PRICE, MARY LYNETTE | SO |
| 09 | DULBS, RICHARD ZALFA | JR | 32 | RISTAS, JAMES | SR |
| 10 | EDINGER, SUSAN KEE | SR | 33 | SAGER, ANNE MARIE | SO |
| 11 | FINK, FRANK JAMES | SR | 34 | SMILLIE, HEATHER MICHELLE | SO |
| 12 | FRANCIS, JAMES P | JR | 35 | SNYDER, LEISHA KAY | SR |
| 13 | GAGHEN, PAMELA LYNN | JR | 36 | STAHL, MARIA TASHERY | SO |
| 14 | GOULD, ROBYN KAY | SO | 37 | ST. JOHN, AMY J | SO |
| 15 | GROSENBACHER, SCOTT ALAN | SO | 38 | STURDEVANT, RICHARD K | SO |
| 16 | HEETFIELD, DIANE MARIE | SO | 39 | SWETYE, LYNN MICHELE | SO |
| 17 | KABAT, JAMES DAVID | JR | 40 | WALASINSKI, MICHAEL | SO |
| 18 | KEMP, LISA ADRIANE | FR | 41 | WALKER, DIANE ELAINE | SO |
| 19 | KILLION, MICHELLE A | SO | 42 | WARNOCK, JENNIFER MARY | SO |
| 20 | KOPERSKI, MARY ELLEN | SO | 43 | WILLIAMS, WENDY A | SO |
| 21 | KOPP, BRIDGETTE ANN | SO | 44 | YAP, HOCK BAN | SO |
| 22 | LEHMANN, KRISTINA MARIE | JR | 45 | YODER, ARLAN JAY | JR |

the 100 invoices. The numbering process would be a very time consuming task. Instead, **systematic random sampling** can be used.

> **SYSTEMATIC RANDOM SAMPLE** A random starting point is selected, and then every $k$th member of the population is selected.

First, $k$ is calculated as the population size divided by the sample size. For Computer Printers Unlimited, we would select every 20th (2,000/100) invoice from the file drawers; in so doing the numbering process is avoided. If $k$ is not a whole number, then round down.

Random sampling is used in the selection of the first invoice. For example, a number from a random number table between 1 and $k$, or 20, would be selected. Say, the random number was 18. Then, starting with the 18th invoice, every 20th invoice (18, 38, 58, etc.) would be selected as the sample.

Before using systematic random sampling, we should carefully observe the physical order of the population. When the physical order is related to the population characteristic, then systematic random sampling should not be used. For example, if the invoices in the example were filed in order of increasing sales, systematic random sampling would not guarantee a random sample. Other sampling methods should be used.

## Stratified Random Sampling

When a population can be clearly divided into groups based on some characteristic, then **stratified random sampling** can be used to guarantee that each group is represented in the sample. The groups are also called **strata.** For example, college students can be grouped as full time or part time, male or female, or traditional or nontraditional. Once the strata are defined, we can apply simple random sampling within each group or strata to collect the sample.

> **STRATIFIED RANDOM SAMPLE** A population is divided into subgroups, called strata, and a sample is randomly selected from each stratum.

For instance, we might study the advertising expenditures for the 352 largest companies in the United States. Suppose the objective of the study is to determine whether firms with high returns on equity (a measure of profitability) spent more of each sales dollar on advertising than firms with a low return or deficit. To make sure that the sample is a fair representation of the 352 companies, the companies are grouped on percent return on equity. Table 8–1 shows the strata and the relative frequencies. If simple random sampling was used, observe that firms in the 3rd and 4th strata have a high chance of selection (probability of 0.87) while firms in the other strata have a low chance of selection (probability of 0.13). We might not select any firms in stratum 1 or 5 *simply by chance.* However, stratified random sampling will guarantee that at least one firm in strata 1 and 5 are represented in the sample. Let's say that 50 firms are selected for intensive study. Then 1 (0.02 × 50) firm from stratum 1 would be randomly selected, 5 (0.10 × 50) firms from stratum 2 would be randomly selected, and so on. In this case, the number of firms sampled from each stratum is proportional to the stratum's relative frequency in the population. Stratified sampling has the advantage, in some cases, of more accurately reflecting the characteristics of the population than does simple random or systematic random sampling.

**TABLE 8–1** Number Selected for a Proportional Stratified Random Sample

| Stratum | Profitability (return on equity) | Number of Firms | Relative Frequency | Number Sampled |
|---|---|---|---|---|
| 1 | 30 percent and over | 8 | 0.02 | 1* |
| 2 | 20 up to 30 percent | 35 | 0.10 | 5* |
| 3 | 10 up to 20 percent | 189 | 0.54 | 27 |
| 4 | 0 up to 10 percent | 115 | 0.33 | 16 |
| 5 | Deficit | 5 | 0.01 | 1 |
| Total | | 352 | 1.00 | 50 |

*0.02 of 50 = 1, 0.10 of 50 = 5, etc.

## Cluster Sampling

Another common type of sampling is **cluster sampling.** It is often employed to reduce the cost of sampling a population scattered over a large geographic area.

> **CLUSTER SAMPLING** A population is divided into clusters using naturally occurring geographic or other boundaries. Then, clusters are randomly selected and a sample is collected by randomly selecting from each cluster.

Suppose you want to determine the views of residents in a particular state about state and federal environmental protection policies. Selecting a random sample of residents in the state and personally contacting each one would be time consuming and very expensive. Instead, you could employ cluster sampling by subdividing the state into small units—either counties or regions. These are often called *primary units.*

Suppose you divided the state into 12 primary units, then selected at random four regions—2, 7, 4, and 12—and concentrated your efforts in these primary units. You could take a random sample of the residents in each of these regions and interview them. (Note that this is a combination of cluster sampling and simple random sampling.)

**Statistics in Action**

Random and unbiased sampling methods are extremely important to making valid statistical inferences. In 1936, a straw vote to predict the outcome of the presidential race between Franklin Roosevelt and Alfred Landon was done. Ten million ballots in the form of returnable postcards were sent to addresses taken from telephone directories and automobile registrations. A high proportion of the ballots were returned, with 59 percent in favor of Landon and 41 percent favoring Roosevelt. On Election Day, Roosevelt won with 61 percent of the vote. Landon had 39 percent. In the mid-1930s people who had telephones and drove automobiles clearly did not represent American voters!

**Many other sampling methods**

The discussion of sampling methods in the preceding sections did not include all the sampling methods available to a researcher. Should you become involved in a major research project in marketing, finance, accounting, or other areas, you would need to consult books devoted solely to sample theory and sample design.

---

**Self-Review 8–2**

Refer to Self-Review 8–1 (page 253) and the class roster on page 254. Suppose a systematic random sample will select every ninth student enrolled in the class. Initially, the fourth student on the list was selected at random. That student is numbered 03. Remembering that the random numbers start with 00, which students will be chosen to be members of the sample?

---

# Exercises

1. The following is a list of Marco's Pizza stores in Lucas County. Also noted is whether the store is corporate-owned (C) or manager-owned (M). A sample of four locations is to be selected and inspected for customer convenience, safety, cleanliness, and other features.

| ID No. | Address | Type | ID No. | Address | Type |
|--------|---------|------|--------|---------|------|
| 00 | 2607 Starr Av | C | 12 | 2040 Ottawa River Rd | C |
| 01 | 309 W Alexis Rd | C | 13 | 2116 N Reynolds Rd | C |
| 02 | 2652 W Central Av | C | 14 | 3678 Rugby Dr | C |
| 03 | 630 Dixie Hwy | M | 15 | 1419 South Av | C |
| 04 | 3510 Dorr St | C | 16 | 1234 W Sylvania Av | C |
| 05 | 5055 Glendale Av | C | 17 | 4624 Woodville Rd | M |
| 06 | 3382 Lagrange St | M | 18 | 5155 S Main | M |
| 07 | 2525 W Laskey Rd | C | 19 | 106 E Airport Hwy | C |
| 08 | 303 Louisiana Av | C | 20 | 6725 W Central | M |
| 09 | 149 Main St | C | 21 | 4252 Monroe | C |
| 10 | 835 S McCord Rd | M | 22 | 2036 Woodville Rd | C |
| 11 | 3501 Monroe St | M | 23 | 1316 Michigan Av | M |

   a. The random numbers selected are 08, 18, 11, 54, 02, 41, and 54. Which stores are selected?
   b. Use the table of random numbers to select your own sample of locations.
   c. A sample is to consist of every seventh location. The number 03 is the starting point. Which locations will be included in the sample?
   d. Suppose a sample is to consist of three locations, of which two are corporate-owned and one is manager-owned. Select a sample accordingly.

2. The following is a list of hospitals in the Cincinnati (Ohio) and Northern Kentucky Region. Also included is whether the hospital is a general medical/surgical hospital (M/S) or a specialty hospital (S). We are interested in estimating the average number of full- and part-time nurses employed in the area hospitals.
   a. A sample of five hospitals is to be randomly selected. The random numbers are 09, 16, 00, 49, 54, 12, and 04. Which hospitals are included in the sample?
   b. Use a table of random numbers to develop your own sample of five hospitals.

| ID Number | Name | Address | Type | ID Number | Name | Address | Type |
|---|---|---|---|---|---|---|---|
| 00 | Bethesda North | 10500 Montgomery Cincinnati, Ohio 45242 | M/S | 15 | Providence Hospital | 2446 Kipling Avenue Cincinnati, Ohio 45239 | M/S |
| 01 | Ft. Hamilton-Hughes | 630 Eaton Avenue Hamilton, Ohio 45013 | M/S | 16 | St. Francis-St. George Hospital | 3131 Queen City Avenue Cincinnati, Ohio 45238 | M/S |
| 02 | Jewish Hospital-Kenwood | 4700 East Galbraith Rd. Cincinnati, Ohio 45236 | M/S | 17 | St. Elizabeth Medical Center, North Unit | 401 E. 20th Street Covington, Kentucky 41014 | M/S |
| 03 | Mercy Hospital-Fairfield | 3000 Mack Road Fairfield, Ohio 45014 | M/S | 18 | St. Elizabeth Medical Center, South Unit | One Medical Village Edgewood, Kentucky 41017 | M/S |
| 04 | Mercy Hospital-Hamilton | 100 Riverfront Plaza Hamilton, Ohio 45011 | M/S | 19 | St. Luke's Hospital West | 7380 Turfway Dr. Florence, Kentucky 41075 | M/S |
| 05 | Middletown Regional | 105 McKnight Drive Middletown, Ohio 45044 | M/S | 20 | St. Luke's Hospital East | 85 North Grand Avenue Ft. Thomas, Kentucky 41042 | M/S |
| 06 | Clermont Mercy Hospital | 3000 Hospital Dr. Batavia, Ohio 45103 | M/S | 21 | Care Unit Hospital Cinti. | 3156 Glenmore Avenue Cincinnati, Ohio 45211 | S |
| 07 | Mercy Hospital-Anderson | 7500 State Road Cincinnati, Ohio 45255 | M/S | 22 | Emerson Behavioral Science | 2446 Kipling Avenue Cincinnati, Ohio 45239 | S |
| 08 | Bethesda Oak Hospital | 619 Oak Street Cincinnati, Ohio 45206 | M/S | 23 | Pauline Warfield Lewis Center for Psychiatric Treat. | 1101 Summit Rd. Cincinnati, Ohio 45237 | S |
| 09 | Children's Hospital Medical Center | 3333 Burnet Avenue Cincinnati, Ohio 45229 | M/S | 24 | Children's Psychiatric No. Kentucky | 502 Farrell Drive Covington, Kentucky 41011 | S |
| 10 | Christ Hospital | 2139 Auburn Avenue Cincinnati, Ohio 45219 | M/S | 25 | Drake Center Rehab—Long Term | 151 W. Galbraith Road Cincinnati, Ohio 45216 | S |
| 11 | Deaconess Hospital | 311 Straight Street Cincinnati, Ohio 45219 | M/S | 26 | No. Kentucky Rehab Hospital—Short Term | 201 Medical Village Edgewood, Kentucky | S |
| 12 | Good Samaritan Hospital | 375 Dixmyth Avenue Cincinnati, Ohio 45220 | M/S | 27 | Shriners Burns Institute | 3229 Burnet Avenue Cincinnati, Ohio 45229 | S |
| 13 | Jewish Hospital | 3200 Burnet Avenue Cincinnati, Ohio 45229 | M/S | 28 | VA Medical Center | 3200 Vine Cincinnati, Ohio 45220 | S |
| 14 | University Hospital | 234 Goodman Street Cincinnati, Ohio 45267 | M/S | | | | |

    **c.** A sample is to consist of every fifth location. We select 02 as the starting point. Which hospitals will be included in the sample?

    **d.** A sample is to consist of four medical and surgical hospitals and one specialty hospital. Select an appropriate sample.

**3.** Listed below are the 35 members of the Metro Toledo Automobile Dealers Association. We would like to estimate the mean revenue from dealer service departments.

| ID Number | Dealer | ID Number | Dealer | ID Number | Dealer |
|---|---|---|---|---|---|
| 00 | Dave White Acura | 12 | Spurgeon Chevrolet Motor Sales, Inc. | 24 | Lexus of Toledo |
| 01 | Autofair Nissan | 13 | Dunn Chevrolet | 25 | Mathews Ford Oregon, Inc. |
| 02 | Autofair Toyota-Suzuki | 14 | Don Scott Chevrolet-Pontiac-Geo, Inc. | 26 | Northtowne Chevrolet-GEO |
| 03 | George Ball's Buick GMC Truck | 15 | Dave White Chevrolet Co. | 27 | Quality Ford Sales, Inc. |
| 04 | Yark Automotive Group | 16 | Dick Wilson Pontiac | 28 | Rouen Chrysler Jeep Eagle |
| 05 | Bob Schmidt Chevrolet | 17 | Doyle Pontiac Buick | 29 | Saturn of Toledo |
| 06 | Bowling Green Lincoln Mercury Jeep Eagle | 18 | Franklin Park Lincoln Mercury | 30 | Ed Schmidt Pontiac Jeep Eagle |
| 07 | Brondes Ford | 19 | Genoa Motors | 31 | Southside Lincoln Mercury |
| 08 | Brown Honda | 20 | Great Lakes Ford Nissan | 32 | Valiton Chrysler |
| 09 | Brown Mazda | 21 | Grogan Towne Chrysler | 33 | Vin Divers |
| 10 | Charlie's Dodge | 22 | Hatfield Motor Sales | 34 | Whitman Ford |
| 11 | Thayer Chevrolet Geo Toyota | 23 | Kistler Ford, Inc. | | |

**a.** We want to select a random sample of five dealers. The random numbers are: 05, 20, 59, 21, 31, 28, 49, 38, 66, 08, 29, and 02. Which dealers would be included in the sample?

**b.** Use the table of random numbers to select your own sample of five dealers.

**c.** A sample is to consist of every seventh dealer. The number 04 is selected as the starting point. Which dealers are included in the sample?

**4.** Listed below are the 27 Nationwide Insurance agents in the Toledo, Ohio, metropolitan area. We would like to estimate the mean number of years employed with Nationwide.

| ID Number | Agent | ID Number | Agent | ID Number | Agent |
|---|---|---|---|---|---|
| 00 | **Bly Scott** 3332 W Laskey Rd | 09 | **Harris Ev** 2026 Albon Rd | 18 | **Priest Harvey** 5113 N Summit St |
| 01 | **Coyle Mike** 5432 W Central Av | 10 | **Heini Bernie** 7110 W Central | 19 | **Riker Craig** 2621 N Reynolds Rd |
| 02 | **Denker Brett** 7445 Airport Hwy | 11 | **Hinckley Dave** | 20 | **Schwab Dave** 572 W Dussel Dr |
| 03 | **Denker Rollie** 7445 Airport Hwy | | 14 N Holland Sylvania Rd | 21 | **Seibert John** H 201 S Main |
| 04 | **Farley Ron** 1837 W Alexis Rd | 12 | **Joehlin Bob** 3358 Navarre Av | 22 | **Smithers Bob** 229 Superior St |
| 05 | **George Mark** 7247 W Central Av | 13 | **Keisser David** 3030 W Sylvania Av | 23 | **Smithers Jerry** 229 Superior St |
| 06 | **Gibellato Carlo** 6616 Monroe St | 14 | **Keisser Keith** 5902 Sylvania Av | 24 | **Wright Steve** 105 S Third St |
| | 3521 Navarre Av | 15 | **Lawrence Grant** 342 W Dussel Dr | 25 | **Wood Tom** 112 Louisiana Av |
| 07 | **Glemser Cathy** 5602 Woodville Rd | 16 | **Miller Ken** 2427 Woodville Rd | 26 | **Yoder Scott** 6 Willoughby Av |
| 08 | **Green Mike** 4149 Holland Sylvania Rd | 17 | **O'Donnell Jim** 7247 W Central Av | | |

**a.** We want to select a random sample of four agents. The random numbers are: 02, 59, 51, 25, 14, 29, 77, 69, and 18. Which dealers would be included in the sample?

**b.** Use the table of random numbers to select your own sample of four agents.

**c.** A sample is to consist of every seventh dealer. The number 04 is selected as the starting point. Which agents will be included in the sample?

# Sampling "Error"

The previous section discussed sampling methods that can be used to select a sample that is a fair or unbiased representation of the population. In each method, it is important to note that the selection of every possible sample of a specified size from a population has a known chance or probability. This is another way to describe an unbiased sampling method.

Samples are used to estimate population characteristics. For example, the mean of a sample is used to estimate the population mean. However, since the sample is a part or portion of the population, it is unlikely that the sample mean would be *exactly equal* to the population mean. Similarly, it is unlikely that the sample standard deviation would be *exactly equal* to the population standard deviation. We can therefore expect a difference between a *sample statistic* and its corresponding *population parameter*. This difference is called **sampling error.**

---

**SAMPLING ERROR** The difference between a sample statistic and its corresponding population parameter.

---

Consider the population of five employees at Kiser Industries. Last week the output for each employee was 97, 103, 96, 99, and 105 units. Suppose we select a sample of two employees and the output of these two employees was 97 and 105. The mean of this sample is 101, found by (97 + 105)/2. Another sample of two employees resulted in outputs of 103 and 96, so the mean of this sample is 99.5. However, the mean of *all* the outputs (the population mean) is 100, found by

$$\mu = \frac{\Sigma X}{N} = \frac{97 + 103 + 96 + 99 + 105}{5} = 100$$

The sampling error for the first sample is 1.0, found by $\bar{X} - \mu = 101 - 100$. The sampling error for the second sample is $-0.5$, found by $\bar{X} - \mu = 99.5 - 100$. Each of these differences, 1.0 and $-0.5$, is the sampling error made in estimating the population mean based on the sample mean. These sampling errors are due to chance.

In this example, each of the 10 possible samples of size 2 [see page 168 formula (5–10) for the combination rule] has an equal chance of selection. Each sample may have a different sample mean and a different sampling error. The value of the sampling error is based on the random selection of a sample. Therefore, sampling errors are random and occur by chance.

Now that we have discovered the possibility of a sampling error when sample results are used to estimate a population parameter, how can we make an accurate prediction about the possible success of a newly developed toothpaste or other product, based only on sample results? How can the quality-assurance department in a mass-production firm release a shipment of microchips based only on a sample of 10 chips? How can the CNN/*USA Today* or ABC News/*Washington Post* polling organizations make an accurate prediction about a presidential race based on a sample of 2,000 registered voters out of a voting population of nearly 90 million? To answer these questions, we first develop a *sampling distribution of the sample mean.*

# Sampling Distribution of the Sample Mean

Sample means vary from sample to sample.

The production output in the above example showed the means for samples of a specified size vary from sample to sample. The mean output of the first sample of two employees was 101, and the second sample mean was 99.5. A third sample would probably result in a different mean. The population mean was 100. If we organized the means of all possible samples of 2 employees into a probability distribution, we would obtain the **sampling distribution of the sample mean.**

> **SAMPLING DISTRIBUTION OF THE SAMPLE MEAN** A probability distribution of all possible sample means of a given sample size.

The following example illustrates the construction of a sampling distribution of the sample mean.

**EXAMPLE**

Tartus Industries has seven production employees (considered the population). The hourly earnings of each employee are given in Table 8–2.

**TABLE 8–2** Hourly Earnings of the Production Employees of Tartus Industries

| Employee | Hourly Earnings |
|----------|-----------------|
| Joe | $7 |
| Sam | 7 |
| Sue | 8 |
| Bob | 8 |
| Jan | 7 |
| Art | 8 |
| Ted | 9 |

1. What is the population mean?
2. What is the sampling distribution of the sample mean for samples of size 2?

3. What is the mean of the sampling distribution?
4. What observations can be made about the population and the sampling distribution?

**SOLUTION**

1. The population mean is $7.71, found by:

$$\mu = \frac{\$7 + \$7 + \$8 + \$8 + \$7 + \$8 + \$9}{7}$$

We identify the population mean with the Greek letter $\mu$. Our policy, stated in Chapters 1, 3, and 4, is to identify population parameters with Greek letters.

2. To arrive at the sampling distribution of the sample mean, all possible samples of 2 were selected without replacement from the population, and their means were computed. There are 21 possible samples, found by using formula (5–10) on page 168.

$$_NC_n = \frac{N!}{n!(N - n)!} = \frac{7!}{2!(7 - 2)!} = 21$$

where $N = 7$ is the number of items in the population and $n = 2$ is the number of items in the sample.

   The 21 sample means from all possible samples of 2 that can be drawn from the population are shown in Table 8–3. These 21 sample means are used to construct a probability distribution which is the sampling distribution of the sample mean and is summarized in Table 8–4.

**TABLE 8–3** Sample Means for All Possible Samples of 2 Employees

| Sample | Employees | Hourly Earnings | Sum | Mean | Sample | Employees | Hourly Earnings | Sum | Mean |
|--------|-----------|-----------------|-----|------|--------|-----------|-----------------|-----|------|
| 1 | Joe, Sam | $7, $7 | $14 | $7.00 | 12 | Sue, Bob | $8, $8 | $16 | $8.00 |
| 2 | Joe, Sue | 7, 8 | 15 | 7.50 | 13 | Sue, Jan | 8, 7 | 15 | 7.50 |
| 3 | Joe, Bob | 7, 8 | 15 | 7.50 | 14 | Sue, Art | 8, 8 | 16 | 8.00 |
| 4 | Joe, Jan | 7, 7 | 14 | 7.00 | 15 | Sue, Ted | 8, 9 | 17 | 8.50 |
| 5 | Joe, Art | 7, 8 | 15 | 7.50 | 16 | Bob, Jan | 8, 7 | 15 | 7.50 |
| 6 | Joe, Ted | 7, 9 | 16 | 8.00 | 17 | Bob, Art | 8, 8 | 16 | 8.00 |
| 7 | Sam, Sue | 7, 8 | 15 | 7.50 | 18 | Bob, Ted | 8, 9 | 17 | 8.50 |
| 8 | Sam, Bob | 7, 8 | 15 | 7.50 | 19 | Jan, Art | 7, 8 | 15 | 7.50 |
| 9 | Sam, Jan | 7, 7 | 14 | 7.00 | 20 | Jan, Ted | 7, 9 | 16 | 8.00 |
| 10 | Sam, Art | 7, 8 | 15 | 7.50 | 21 | Art, Ted | 8, 9 | 17 | 8.50 |
| 11 | Sam, Ted | 7, 9 | 16 | 8.00 | | | | | |

**TABLE 8–4** Sampling Distribution of the Sample Mean for $n = 2$

| Sample Mean | Number of Means | Probability |
|-------------|-----------------|-------------|
| $7.00 | 3 | .1429 |
| 7.50 | 9 | .4285 |
| 8.00 | 6 | .2857 |
| 8.50 | 3 | .1429 |
| | 21 | 1.0000 |

3. The mean of the sampling distribution of the sample mean is obtained by summing the various sample means and dividing the sum by the number of samples. The mean of all the sample means is usually written $\mu_{\bar{x}}$. The $\mu$ reminds us that it

is a population value because we have considered all possible samples. The subscript $\overline{X}$ indicates that it is the sampling distribution of the sample mean.

*Population mean is equal to the mean of the sample means*

$$\mu_{\overline{X}} = \frac{\text{Sum of all sample means}}{\text{Total number of samples}} = \frac{\$7.00 + \$7.50 + \cdots + \$8.50}{21}$$

$$= \frac{\$162}{21} = \$7.71$$

4. Refer to Chart 8–1, which shows both the population distribution and the distribution of the sample mean. These observations can be made:
   a. The mean of the distribution of the sample mean ($7.71) is equal to the mean of the population: $\mu = \mu_{\overline{X}}$.
   b. The spread in the distribution of the sample mean is less than the spread in the population values. The sample mean ranges from $7.00 to $8.50, while the population values vary from $7.00 up to $9.00. In fact, the standard deviation of the distribution of the sample mean is equal to the population standard deviation divided by the square root of the sample size. So the formula for the standard deviation of the distribution of the sample mean is $\sigma/\sqrt{n}$. Notice, as we increase the size of the sample, the spread of the distribution of the sample mean becomes smaller.
   c. The shape of the sampling distribution of the sample mean and the shape of the frequency distribution of the population values are different. The distribution of the sample mean tends to be more bell-shaped and to approximate the normal probability distribution.

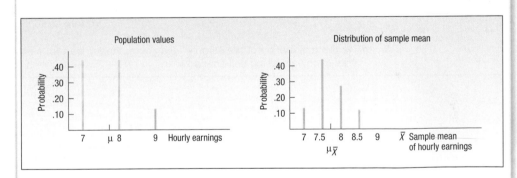

**CHART 8–1** Distributions of Population Values and Sample Mean

In summary, we took all possible random samples from a population and for each sample calculated a sample statistic (the mean amount earned). This example illustrates important relationships between the population distribution and the sampling distribution of the sample mean:

1. The mean of the sample means is exactly equal to the population mean.
2. The dispersion of the sampling distribution of sample means is narrower than the population distribution.
3. The sampling distribution of sample means tends to become bell-shaped and to approximate the normal probability distribution.

Given a bell-shaped or normal probability distribution, we will be able to apply concepts from Chapter 7 to determine the probability of selecting a sample with a specified sample mean. In the next section, we will show the importance of sample size as it relates to the sampling distribution of sample means.

**Self-Review 8–3**    The lengths of service of all the executives employed by Standard Chemicals are:

| Name | Years |
|------|-------|
| Mr. Snow | 20 |
| Ms. Tolson | 22 |
| Mr. Kraft | 26 |
| Ms. Irwin | 24 |
| Mr. Jones | 28 |

(a)    Using the combination formula, how many samples of size 2 are possible?
(b)    List all possible samples of 2 executives from the population and compute their means.
(c)    Organize the means into a sampling distribution.
(d)    Compare the population mean and the mean of the sample means.
(e)    Compare the dispersion in the population with that in the distribution of the sample mean.
(f)    A chart portraying the population values follows. Is the distribution of population values normally distributed (bell-shaped)?

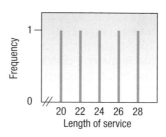

(g)    Is the distribution of the sample mean computed in part (c) starting to show some tendency toward being bell-shaped?

# Exercises

5.  A population consists of the following four values: 12, 12, 14, and 16.
    a. List all samples of size 2, and compute the mean of each sample.
    b. Compute the mean of the distribution of the sample mean and the population mean. Compare the two values.
    c. Compare the dispersion in the population with that of the sample mean.
6.  A population consists of the following five values: 2, 2, 4, 4, and 8.
    a. List all samples of size 2, and compute the mean of each sample.
    b. Compute the mean of the distribution of sample means and the population mean. Compare the two values.
    c. Compare the dispersion in the population with that of the sample means.
7.  A population consists of the following five values: 12, 12, 14, 15, and 20.
    a. List all samples of size 3, and compute the mean of each sample.
    b. Compute the mean of the distribution of sample means and the population mean. Compare the two values.
    c. Compare the dispersion in the population with that of the sample means.
8.  A population consists of the following five values: 0, 0, 1, 3, 6.
    a. List all samples of size 3, and compute the mean of each sample.
    b. Compute the mean of the distribution of sample means and the population mean. Compare the two values.
    c. Compare the dispersion in the population with that of the sample means.
9.  In the law firm Tybo and Associates, there are six partners. Listed below is the number of cases each associate actually tried in court last month.

| Associate | Number of Cases |
|-----------|-----------------|
| Ruud | 3 |
| Wu | 6 |
| Sass | 3 |
| Flores | 3 |
| Wilhelms | 0 |
| Schueller | 1 |

    **a.** How many different samples of 3 are possible?
    **b.** List all possible samples of size 3, and compute the mean number of cases in each sample.
    **c.** Compare the mean of the distribution of sample means to the population mean.
    **d.** On a chart similar to Chart 8–1, compare the dispersion in the population with that of the sample means.

**10.** There are five sales associates at Mid-Motors Ford. The five representatives and the number of cars they sold last week are:

| Sales Representative | Cars Sold |
|----------------------|-----------|
| Peter Hankish | 8 |
| Connie Stallter | 6 |
| Juan Lopez | 4 |
| Ted Barnes | 10 |
| Peggy Chu | 6 |

    **a.** How many different samples of size 2 are possible?
    **b.** List all possible samples of size 2, and compute the mean of each sample.
    **c.** Compare the mean of the sampling distribution of sample means with that of the population.
    **d.** On a chart similar to Chart 8–1, compare the dispersion in sample means with that of the population.

# The Central Limit Theorem

In this section, we examine the **central limit theorem.** Its application to the sampling distribution of the sample mean, introduced in the previous section, allows us to use the normal probability distribution to create confidence intervals for the population mean (described in Chapter 9) and perform tests of hypothesis (described in Chapter 10). The central limit theorem states that, for large random samples, the shape of the sampling distribution of the sample mean is close to a normal probability distribution. The approximation is more accurate for large samples than for small samples. This is one of the most useful conclusions in statistics. We can reason about the distribution of the sample mean with absolutely no information about the shape of the population distribution from which the sample is taken. In other words, the central limit theorem is true for all distributions.

A formal statement of the central limit theorem follows.

> **CENTRAL LIMIT THEOREM** If all samples of a particular size are selected from any population, the sampling distribution of the sample mean is approximately a normal distribution. This approximation improves with larger samples.

If the population follows a normal probability distribution, then for any sample size the sampling distribution of the sample mean will also be normal. If the population distribution is symmetrical (but not normal), you will see the normal shape of the distribution of the sample mean emerge with samples as small as 10. On the other hand, if you start with a distribution that is skewed or has thick tails, it may require samples of 30 or more to observe the normality feature. This concept is summarized in Chart 8–2. Observe the convergence to a normal distribution regardless of the shape of the population distribution. Most statisticians consider a sample of 30 or more to be large enough for the central limit theorem to be employed.

The idea that the distribution of the sample means from a population that is not normal will converge to normality is illustrated in Charts 8–3, 8–4, and 8–5. We will discuss this example in more detail shortly, but Chart 8–3 is a graph of a discrete probability distribution that is positively skewed. There are many possible samples of 5 that might be selected from this population. Suppose we randomly select 25 samples of size 5 each and compute the mean of each sample. These results are shown in Chart 8–4. Notice that the shape of the distribution of sample means has changed from the shape of the original population even though we selected only 25 of the many possible samples. To put it another way, we selected 25 random samples of 5 each from a population that is positively skewed and found the distribution of sample means has changed from the shape of the population. As we take larger samples, that is, $n = 20$ instead of $n = 5$, we will find the distribution of the sample mean will approach the normal distribution. Chart 8–5 shows the results of 25 random samples of 20 observations each from the same population. Observe the clear trend toward the normal probability distribution. This is the point of the central limit theorem. The following example will underscore this condition.

**EXAMPLE**

Ed Spence began his sprocket business 20 years ago. The business has grown over the years and now employs 40 people. Spence Sprockets, Inc. faces some major decisions regarding health care for these employees. Before making a final decision on what health care plan to purchase, Ed decides to form a committee of five representative employees. The committee will be asked to study the health care issue carefully and make a recommendation as to what plan best fits the employees' needs. Ed feels the views of newer employees toward health care may differ from those of more experienced employees. If Ed randomly selects this committee, what can he expect in terms of the mean years with Spence Sprockets for those on the committee? How does the shape of the distribution of years of experience of all employees (the population) compare with the shape of the sampling distribution of the mean? The lengths of service (rounded to the nearest year) of the 40 employees currently on the Spence Sprockets, Inc. payroll are as follows.

| 11 | 4 | 18 | 2 | 1 | 2 | 0 | 2 | 2 | 4 |
|----|---|----|---|---|---|---|----|---|----|
| 3 | 4 | 1 | 2 | 2 | 3 | 3 | 19 | 8 | 3 |
| 7 | 1 | 0 | 2 | 7 | 0 | 4 | 5 | 1 | 14 |
| 16 | 8 | 9 | 1 | 1 | 2 | 5 | 10 | 2 | 3 |

**SOLUTION**

Chart 8–3 shows the distribution of the years of experience for the population of 40 current employees. This distribution of lengths of service is positively skewed because there are a few employees who have worked at Spence Sprockets for a longer period of time. Specifically, six employees have been with the company 10 years or more. However, because the business has grown, the number of employees has increased in the last few years. Of the 40 employees, 18 have been with the company two years or less.

Let's consider the first of Ed Spence's problems. He would like to form a committee of five employees to look into the health care question and suggest what type of health care coverage would be most appropriate for the majority of workers. How

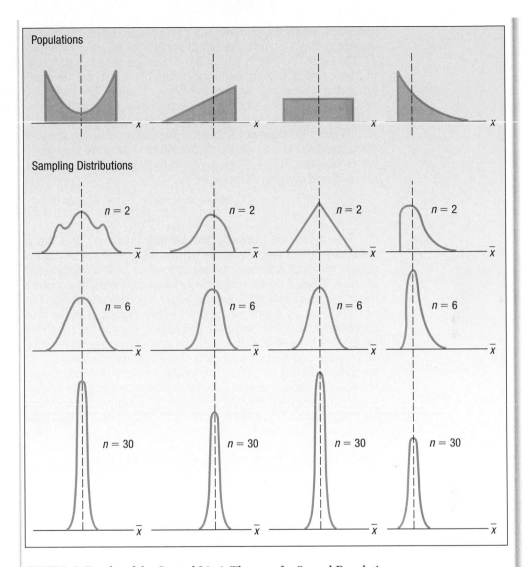

**CHART 8–2** Results of the Central Limit Theorem for Several Populations

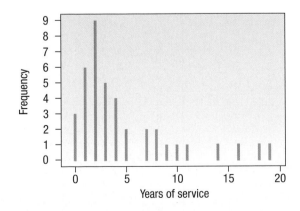

**CHART 8–3** Length of Service for Spence Sprockets, Inc. Employees

should he select the committee? If he selects the committee randomly, what might he expect in terms of mean length of service for those on the committee?

To begin, Ed writes the length of service for each of the 40 employees on pieces of paper and puts them into an old baseball hat. Next, he shuffles the pieces of paper around and randomly selects five slips of paper. The lengths of service for these five employees are 1, 9, 0, 19, and 14 years. Thus, the mean length of service for these five sampled employees is 8.60 years. How does that compare with the population mean? At this point Ed does not know the population mean, but the number of employees in the population is only 40, so he decides to calculate the mean length of service for *all* his employees. It is 4.8 years, found by adding the lengths of service for *all* the employees and dividing the total by 40.

$$\mu = \frac{11 + 4 + 18 + \cdots + 2 + 3}{40} = 4.80$$

The difference between the sample mean ($\overline{X}$) and the population mean ($\mu$) is called **sampling error.** In other words, the difference of 3.80 years between the population mean of 4.80 and the sample mean of 8.60 is the sampling error. It is due to chance. Thus, if Ed selected these five employees to constitute the committee, their mean length of service would be larger than the population mean.

What would happen if Ed put the five pieces of paper back into the baseball hat and selected another sample? Would you expect the mean of this second sample to be exactly the same as the previous one? Suppose he selects another sample of five employees and finds the lengths of service in this sample to be 7, 4, 4, 1, and 3. This sample mean is 3.80 years. The result of selecting 25 samples of five employees each is shown in Table 8–5 and Chart 8–4. There are actually 658,008 possible samples of 5 from the population of 40 employees, found by the combination formula (5–10) for 40 things taken 5 at a time. Notice the difference in the shape of the population and

**TABLE 8–5** Twenty-Five Random Samples of Five Employees

| Sample I.D. | Sample Data | | | | | Sample Mean |
|---|---|---|---|---|---|---|
| A | 1 | 9 | 0 | 19 | 14 | 8.6 |
| B | 7 | 4 | 4 | 1 | 3 | 3.8 |
| C | 8 | 19 | 8 | 2 | 1 | 7.6 |
| D | 4 | 18 | 2 | 0 | 11 | 7.0 |
| F | 4 | 2 | 4 | 7 | 18 | 7.0 |
| G | 1 | 2 | 0 | 3 | 2 | 1.6 |
| F | 2 | 3 | 2 | 0 | 2 | 1.8 |
| H | 11 | 2 | 9 | 2 | 4 | 5.6 |
| I | 9 | 0 | 4 | 2 | 7 | 4.4 |
| J | 1 | 1 | 1 | 11 | 1 | 3.0 |
| K | 2 | 0 | 0 | 10 | 2 | 2.8 |
| L | 0 | 2 | 3 | 2 | 16 | 4.6 |
| M | 2 | 3 | 1 | 1 | 1 | 1.6 |
| N | 3 | 7 | 3 | 4 | 3 | 4.0 |
| 0 | 1 | 2 | 3 | 1 | 4 | 2.2 |
| P | 19 | 0 | 1 | 3 | 8 | 6.2 |
| Q | 5 | 1 | 7 | 14 | 9 | 7.2 |
| R | 5 | 4 | 2 | 3 | 4 | 3.6 |
| S | 14 | 5 | 2 | 2 | 5 | 5.6 |
| T | 2 | 1 | 1 | 4 | 7 | 3.0 |
| U | 3 | 7 | 1 | 2 | 1 | 2.8 |
| V | 0 | 1 | 5 | 1 | 2 | 1.8 |
| W | 0 | 3 | 19 | 4 | 2 | 5.6 |
| X | 4 | 2 | 3 | 4 | 0 | 2.6 |
| Y | 1 | 1 | 2 | 3 | 2 | 1.8 |

the distribution of these sample means. The population of the lengths of service for employees (Chart 8–3) is positively skewed, but the distribution of these 25 sample means does not reflect the same positive skew. There is also a difference in the range of the sample means versus the range of the population. The population ranged from 0 to 19 years, whereas the sample means range from 1.6 to 8.6 years.

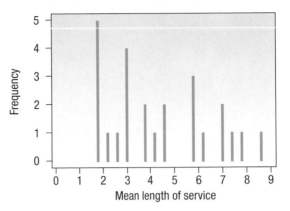

**CHART 8–4** Histogram of Mean Lengths of Service for 25 Samples of Five Employees

Table 8–6 reports the result of selecting 25 samples of 20 employees each and computing their sample means. These sample means are shown graphically in Chart 8–5. Compare the shape of this distribution to the population (Chart 8–3) and to the distribution of sample means where the sample is $n = 5$ (Chart 8–4). You should observe two important features:

**TABLE 8–6** Random Samples and Sample Means of 25 Samples of 20 Spence Sprocket, Inc. Employees

| Sample Number | Sample Data (Length of Service) | | | | | | | | | | | | | | | | | | | | Sample Mean |
|---|---|---|---|---|---|---|---|---|---|---|---|---|---|---|---|---|---|---|---|---|---|
| A | 3 | 8 | 3 | 0 | 2 | 1 | 2 | 3 | 11 | 5 | 1 | 3 | 4 | 2 | 7 | 1 | 1 | 2 | 4 | 16 | 3.95 |
| B | 2 | 3 | 8 | 2 | 1 | 5 | 2 | 0 | 3 | 1 | 0 | 7 | 1 | 4 | 3 | 11 | 4 | 4 | 3 | 1 | 3.25 |
| C | 14 | 5 | 0 | 3 | 2 | 14 | 11 | 9 | 2 | 2 | 1 | 2 | 19 | 1 | 0 | 1 | 4 | 2 | 19 | 8 | 5.95 |
| D | 9 | 2 | 1 | 1 | 4 | 10 | 0 | 8 | 4 | 3 | 2 | 1 | 0 | 8 | 1 | 14 | 5 | 10 | 1 | 3 | 4.35 |
| E | 18 | 1 | 2 | 2 | 4 | 3 | 2 | 8 | 2 | 1 | 0 | 19 | 4 | 19 | 0 | 1 | 4 | 0 | 3 | 14 | 5.35 |
| F | 10 | 4 | 4 | 18 | 3 | 3 | 1 | 0 | 0 | 2 | 2 | 4 | 7 | 10 | 2 | 0 | 3 | 4 | 2 | 1 | 4.00 |
| G | 5 | 7 | 11 | 8 | 11 | 18 | 1 | 1 | 16 | 2 | 2 | 16 | 2 | 3 | 2 | 16 | 2 | 2 | 2 | 4 | 6.55 |
| H | 3 | 0 | 2 | 0 | 5 | 4 | 5 | 3 | 8 | 3 | 2 | 5 | 1 | 1 | 2 | 9 | 8 | 3 | 16 | 5 | 4.25 |
| I | 0 | 0 | 18 | 2 | 1 | 7 | 4 | 1 | 3 | 0 | 3 | 2 | 11 | 7 | 2 | 8 | 5 | 1 | 2 | 3 | 4.00 |
| J | 2 | 7 | 2 | 4 | 1 | 3 | 3 | 2 | 5 | 10 | 0 | 1 | 1 | 2 | 9 | 3 | 2 | 19 | 3 | 2 | 4.05 |
| K | 7 | 4 | 5 | 3 | 3 | 0 | 18 | 2 | 0 | 4 | 2 | 7 | 2 | 7 | 4 | 2 | 10 | 1 | 1 | 2 | 4.20 |
| L | 0 | 3 | 10 | 5 | 9 | 2 | 1 | 4 | 1 | 2 | 1 | 8 | 18 | 1 | 4 | 3 | 3 | 2 | 0 | 4 | 4.05 |
| M | 4 | 1 | 2 | 1 | 7 | 3 | 9 | 14 | 8 | 19 | 4 | 4 | 1 | 2 | 0 | 3 | 1 | 2 | 1 | 2 | 4.40 |
| N | 3 | 16 | 1 | 2 | 4 | 4 | 4 | 2 | 1 | 5 | 2 | 3 | 5 | 3 | 4 | 7 | 16 | 1 | 11 | 1 | 4.75 |
| O | 2 | 19 | 2 | 0 | 2 | 2 | 16 | 2 | 3 | 11 | 9 | 2 | 8 | 0 | 8 | 2 | 7 | 3 | 2 | 2 | 5.10 |
| P | 2 | 18 | 16 | 5 | 2 | 2 | 19 | 0 | 1 | 2 | 11 | 4 | 2 | 2 | 1 | 4 | 2 | 0 | 4 | 3 | 5.00 |
| Q | 3 | 2 | 3 | 11 | 10 | 1 | 1 | 5 | 19 | 16 | 7 | 10 | 3 | 1 | 1 | 1 | 2 | 2 | 3 | 1 | 5.10 |
| R | 2 | 3 | 1 | 2 | 7 | 4 | 3 | 19 | 9 | 2 | 2 | 1 | 1 | 2 | 2 | 2 | 1 | 8 | 0 | 2 | 3.65 |
| S | 2 | 14 | 19 | 1 | 19 | 2 | 8 | 4 | 2 | 2 | 14 | 2 | 8 | 16 | 4 | 7 | 2 | 9 | 0 | 7 | 7.10 |
| T | 0 | 1 | 3 | 3 | 2 | 2 | 3 | 1 | 1 | 0 | 3 | 2 | 3 | 5 | 2 | 10 | 14 | 4 | 2 | 0 | 3.05 |
| U | 1 | 0 | 1 | 2 | 16 | 1 | 1 | 2 | 5 | 1 | 4 | 1 | 2 | 2 | 2 | 2 | 2 | 8 | 9 | 3 | 3.25 |
| V | 1 | 9 | 4 | 4 | 2 | 8 | 7 | 1 | 14 | 18 | 1 | 5 | 10 | 11 | 19 | 0 | 3 | 7 | 2 | 11 | 6.85 |
| W | 8 | 1 | 9 | 19 | 3 | 19 | 0 | 5 | 2 | 1 | 5 | 3 | 3 | 4 | 1 | 5 | 3 | 1 | 8 | 7 | 5.35 |
| X | 4 | 2 | 0 | 3 | 1 | 16 | 1 | 11 | 3 | 3 | 2 | 18 | 2 | 0 | 1 | 5 | 0 | 7 | 2 | 5 | 4.30 |
| Y | 1 | 2 | 1 | 2 | 0 | 2 | 7 | 2 | 4 | 8 | 19 | 2 | 5 | 3 | 3 | 0 | 19 | 2 | 1 | 18 | 5.05 |

1. The shape of the distribution of the sample mean is different from that of the population. In Chart 8–3 the distribution of all employees is positively skewed. However, as we select random samples from this population, the shape of the distribution of the sample mean changes. As we increase the size of the sample, the distribution of the sample mean approaches the normal probability distribution. This illustrates the central limit theorem.

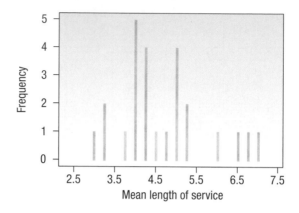

**CHART 8–5** Histogram of Mean Lengths of Service for 25 Samples of 20 Employees

2. There is less dispersion in the sampling distribution of sample means than in the population distribution. In the population the lengths of service ranged from 0 to 19 years. When we selected samples of 5, the sample means ranged from 1.6 to 8.6 years, and when we selected samples of 20, the means ranged from 3.05 to 7.10 years.

We can also compare the mean of the sample means to the population mean. The mean of the 25 samples reported in Table 8–6 is 4.676 years.

$$\mu_{\bar{X}} = \frac{3.95 + 3.25 + \cdots + 4.30 + 5.05}{25} = 4.676$$

We use the symbol $\mu_{\bar{X}}$ to identify the mean of the distribution of the sample mean. The subscript reminds us that the distribution is of the sample mean. It is read "mu sub X bar." We observe that the mean of the sample means, 4.676 years, is very close to the population mean of 4.80.

What should we conclude from this example? The central limit theorem indicates that, regardless of the shape of the population distribution, the sampling distribution of the sample mean will move toward the normal probability distribution. The larger the number of observations in each sample, the stronger the convergence. The Spence Sprockets, Inc., example shows how the central limit theorem works. We began with a positively skewed population (Chart 8–3). Next, we selected 25 random samples of 5 observations, computed the mean of each sample, and finally organized these 25 sample means into a graph (Chart 8–4). We observe a change in the shape of the sampling distribution of sample mean from that of the population. The movement is from a positively skewed distribution to a distribution that has the shape of the normal probability distribution.

To further illustrate the effects of the central limit theorem, we increased the number of observations in each sample from 5 to 20. We selected 25 samples of 20 observations each and calculated the mean of each sample. Finally, we organized these sample means into a graph (Chart 8–5). The shape of the histogram in Chart 8–5 is clearly moving toward the normal probability distribution.

If you go back to Chapter 6 where several binomial distributions with a "success" proportion of .10 are shown in Chart 6–4, you can see yet another demonstration of the Central Limit Theorem. Observe as *n* increases from 7 through 12 and 20 up to 40 that the profile of the probability distributions moves closer and closer to a normal probability distribution. Chart 8–5 on page 268 also shows the convergence to normality as *n* increases. This again reinforces the fact that as more observations are sampled from any population distribution, the shape of the sampling distribution of the sample mean will get closer and closer to a normal distribution.

The central limit theorem itself (reread the definition on page 263) does not say anything about the dispersion of the sampling distribution of sample mean or about the comparison of the mean of the sampling distribution of sample mean to the mean of the population. However, in our Example we did observe that there was less dispersion in the distribution of the sample mean than in the population distribution by noting the difference in the range in the population and the range of the sample means. We observe that the mean of the sample means is close to the mean of the population. It can be demonstrated that the mean of the sampling distribution is the population mean, i.e., $\mu_{\bar{x}} = \mu$, and if the standard deviation in the population is $\sigma$, the standard deviation of the sample means is $\sigma/\sqrt{n}$, where *n* is the number of observations in each sample. We refer to $\sigma/\sqrt{n}$ as the **standard error of the mean**. Its longer name is actually the *standard deviation of the sampling distribution of the sample mean.*

| STANDARD ERROR OF THE MEAN | $\sigma_{\bar{x}} = \dfrac{\sigma}{\sqrt{n}}$ | [8–1] |
|---|---|---|

In this section we also came to other important conclusions.

1. The mean of the distribution of sample means will be *exactly* equal to the population mean if we are able to select all possible samples of the same size from a given population. That is:

$$\mu = \mu_{\bar{x}}$$

   Even if we do not select all samples, we can expect the mean of the distribution of sample means to be close to the population mean.

2. There will be less dispersion in the sampling distribution of the sample mean than in the population. If the standard deviation of the population is $\sigma$, the standard deviation of the distribution of sample means is $\sigma/\sqrt{n}$. Note that when we increase the size of the sample the standard error of the mean decreases.

---

**Self-Review 8–4**

Refer to the Spence Sprockets, Inc. data on page 264. Select 10 random samples of 5 employees each. Use the methods described earlier in the chapter and the Table of Random Numbers (Appendix E) to find the employees to include in the sample. Compute the mean of each sample and plot the sample means on a chart similar to Chart 8–3. What is the mean of your ten sample means?

## Exercises

**11.** Appendix E is a table of random numbers. Hence, each digit from 0 to 9 has the same likelihood of occurrence.
   **a.** Draw a graph showing the population distribution. What is the population mean? Is this an example of the uniform distribution?
   **b.** Following are the first 10 rows of five digits from Appendix E. Assume that these are 10 random samples of five values each. Determine the mean of each sample and plot the means on a chart similar to Chart 8–3. Compare the mean of the sampling distribution of the sample means with the population mean.

| 0 | 2 | 7 | 1 | 1 |
|---|---|---|---|---|
| 9 | 4 | 8 | 7 | 3 |
| 5 | 4 | 9 | 2 | 1 |
| 7 | 7 | 6 | 4 | 0 |
| 6 | 1 | 5 | 4 | 5 |
| 1 | 7 | 1 | 4 | 7 |
| 1 | 3 | 7 | 4 | 8 |
| 8 | 7 | 4 | 5 | 5 |
| 0 | 8 | 9 | 9 | 9 |
| 7 | 8 | 8 | 0 | 4 |

12. The Scrapper Elevator Company has 20 sales representatives who sell their product throughout the United States and Canada. The number of units sold by each representative is listed below. Assume these sales figures to be the population values.

| 2 | 3 | 2 | 3 | 3 | 4 | 2 | 4 | 3 | 2 | 2 | 7 | 3 | 4 | 5 | 3 | 3 | 3 | 3 | 5 |
|---|---|---|---|---|---|---|---|---|---|---|---|---|---|---|---|---|---|---|---|

   a. Draw a graph showing the population distribution.
   b. Compute the mean of the population.
   c. Select five random samples of 5 each. Compute the mean of each sample. Use the methods described in this chapter and Appendix E to determine the items to be included in the sample.
   d. Compare the mean of the sampling distribution of the sample means to the population mean. Would you expect the two values to be about the same?
   e. Draw a histogram of the sample means. Do you notice a difference in the shape of the distribution of sample means compared to the shape of the population distribution?
13. Consider all of the coins (pennies, nickels, quarters, etc.) in your pocket or purse as a population. Make a frequency table beginning with the current year and counting backward to record the ages (in years) of the coins. For example, if the current year is 2004, then a coin with 2002 stamped on it is 2 years old.
   a. Draw a histogram or other graph showing the population distribution.
   b. Randomly select five coins and record the mean age of the sampled coins. Repeat this sampling process 20 times. Now draw a histogram or other graph showing the distribution of the sample means.
   c. Compare the shapes of the two histograms.
14. Consider the digits in the phone numbers on a randomly selected page of your local phone book a population. Make a frequency table of the final digit of 30 randomly selected phone numbers. For example, if a phone number is 555-9704, record a 4.
   a. Draw a histogram or other graph of this population distribution. Using the uniform distribution, compute the population mean and the population standard deviation.
   b. Also record the sample mean of the final four digits (9704 would lead to a mean of 5). Now draw a histogram or other graph showing the distribution of the sample means.
   c. Compare the shapes of the two histograms.

# Using the Sampling Distribution of the Sample Mean

The previous discussion is important because most business decisions are made on the basis of sampling results. Here are some examples.

1. The Arm and Hammer Company wants to ensure that their laundry detergent actually contains 100 fluid ounces, as indicated on the label. Historical summaries from the filling process indicate the mean amount per container is 100 fluid

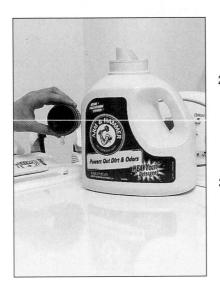

ounces and the standard deviation is 2 fluid ounces. The quality technician in her 10 A.M. check of 40 containers finds the mean amount per container is 99.8 fluid ounces. Should the technician shut down the filling operation or is the sampling error reasonable?

2. The A. C. Nielsen Company provides information to companies advertising on television. Prior research indicates that adult Americans watch an average of 6.0 hours per day of television. The standard deviation is 1.5 hours. For a sample of 50 adults in the Greater Boston area, would it be reasonable that we could randomly select a sample and find that they watch an average of 6.5 hours of television per day?

3. The Haughton Elevator Company wishes to develop specifications for the number of people who can ride in a new oversized elevator. Suppose the mean weight for an adult is 160 pounds and the standard deviation is 15 pounds. However, the distribution of weights does not follow the normal probability distribution. It is positively skewed. What is the likelihood that for a sample of 30 adults their mean weight is 170 pounds or more?

In each of these situations we have a population about which we have some information. We take a sample from that population and wish to conclude whether the sampling error, that is, the difference between the population parameter and the sample statistic, is due to chance.

Using ideas discussed in the previous section, we can compute the probability that a sample mean will fall within a certain range. We know that the sampling distribution of the sample mean will follow the normal probability distribution under two conditions:

1. When the samples are taken from populations known to follow the normal distribution. In this case the size of the sample is not a factor.

2. When the shape of the population distribution is not known or the shape is known to be nonnormal, but our sample contains at least 30 observations.

We can use formula (7–5), from the previous chapter, to convert any normal distribution to the standard normal distribution. We also refer to this as a *z* value. Then we can use the standard normal table, Appendix D, to find the probability of selecting an observation that would fall within a specific range. The formula for finding a *z* value is:

$$z = \frac{X - \mu}{\sigma}$$

In this formula $X$ is the value of the random variable, $\mu$ is the population mean, and $\sigma$ the population standard deviation.

However, most business decisions refer to a sample—not just one observation. So we are interested in the distribution of $\overline{X}$, the sample mean, instead of $X$, the value of one observation. That is the first change we make in formula (7–5). The second is that we use the standard error of the mean of $n$ observations instead of the population standard deviation. That is, we use $\sigma/\sqrt{n}$ in the denominator rather than $\sigma$. Therefore, to find the likelihood of a sample mean with a specified range, we first use the following formula to find the corresponding *z* value. Then we use Appendix D to locate the probability.

| FINDING THE *z* VALUE OF $\overline{X}$ WHEN THE POPULATION STANDARD DEVIATION IS KNOWN | $z = \dfrac{\overline{X} - \mu}{\sigma/\sqrt{n}}$ | [8–2] |
|---|---|---|

The following example will show the application.

**EXAMPLE**

The Quality Assurance Department for Cola, Inc., maintains records regarding the amount of cola in their "Jumbo" bottle. The actual amount of cola in each bottle is critical, but varies a small amount from one bottle to the next. Cola, Inc., does not wish to underfill the bottles, because they will have a problem with truth in labeling. On the other hand, they cannot overfill each bottle, because they would be giving cola away, hence reducing their profits. Their records indicate that the amount of cola follows the normal probability distribution. The mean amount per bottle is 31.2 ounces and the population standard deviation is 0.4 ounces. At 8 A.M. today the quality technician randomly selected 16 bottles from the filling line. The mean amount of cola contained in the bottles is 31.38 ounces. Is this an unlikely result? Is it likely the process is putting too much soda in the bottles? To put it another way, is the sampling error of 0.18 ounces unusual?

**SOLUTION**

We can use the results of the previous section to find the likelihood that we could select a sample of 16 ($n$) bottles from a normal population with a mean of 31.2 ($\mu$) ounces and a population standard deviation of 0.4 ($\sigma$) ounces and find the sample mean to be 31.38 ($\overline{X}$). We use formula (8–2) to find the value of $z$.

$$z = \frac{\overline{X} - \mu}{\sigma/\sqrt{n}} = \frac{31.38 - 31.20}{0.4/\sqrt{16}} = 1.80$$

The numerator of this equation, $\overline{X} - \mu = 31.38 - 31.20 = .18$, is the sampling error. The denominator, $\sigma/\sqrt{n} = 0.40/\sqrt{16} = 0.1$, is the standard error of the sampling distribution of the sample mean. So the $z$ values express the sampling error in standard units, in other words, the standard error.

Next, we compute the likelihood of a $z$ value greater than 1.80. In Appendix D locate the probability corresponding to a $z$ value of 1.80. It is .4641. The likelihood of a $z$ value greater than 1.80 is .0359, found by .5000 − .4641.

What do we conclude? It is unlikely, less than a 4 percent chance, we could select a sample of 16 observations from a normal population with a mean of 31.2 ounces and a population standard deviation of 0.4 ounces and find the sample mean equal to or greater than 31.38 ounces. We conclude the process is putting too much cola in the bottles. The quality technician should see the production supervisor about reducing the amount of soda in each bottle. This information is summarized in Chart 8–6.

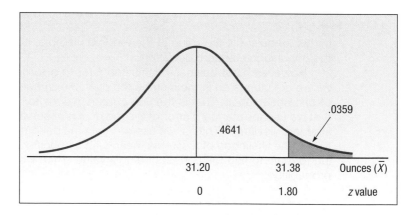

**CHART 8–6** Sampling Distribution of the Mean Amount of Cola in a Jumbo Bottle

Refer to the Cola, Inc., information. Suppose the quality technician selected a sample of 16 Jumbo bottles that averaged 31.08 ounces. What can you conclude about the filling process?

There are many sampling situations in business when we wish to make an inference about the population, but we do not have much knowledge about the population. Here the power of the central limit theorem helps. We know that, for any shape of the population distribution, if we select a sample sufficiently large, the sampling distribution of the sample mean will follow the normal distribution. Statistical theory has shown that samples of at least 30 are sufficiently large to allow us to assume that the sampling distribution follows the normal distribution.

Often we do not know the value of the population standard deviation, $\sigma$. Again, since the sample is at least 30, we estimate the population standard deviation with the sample standard deviation. The actual distribution of the statistic is Student's $t$ distribution which will be discussed in the next chapter. When we use $s$ to replace $\sigma$, the new formula for finding the value of $z$ is:

| FINDING THE $z$ VALUE OF $\overline{X}$ WHEN THE POPULATION STANDARD DEVIATION IS UNKNOWN | $z = \dfrac{\overline{X} - \mu}{s/\sqrt{n}}$ | [8–3] |
|---|---|---|

**EXAMPLE**

The Metropolitan New York Gas Station Dealers' Association estimates that the mean number of gallons of gasoline sold per day at a gas station is 20,000. The shape of this distribution is unknown. A sample of 70 dealers yesterday revealed the mean number of gallons sold was 19,480. The standard deviation of the sample of 70 dealers was 4,250 gallons. Is the assertion that the population mean is 20,000 gallons reasonable? What is the likelihood of finding a sample with the given statistics from the proposed population? What assumptions do you need to make?

**SOLUTION**

We are unsure of the shape of the population of gallons sold. However, the sample is sufficiently large to allow us to assume that the sampling distribution of the sample mean follows the normal distribution. The central limit theorem provides the necessary statistical theory. Again, because of the size of the sample, we can substitute the sample standard deviation for the population standard deviation. Formula (8–3) is appropriate for finding the $z$ value.

$$z = \frac{\overline{X} - \mu}{s/\sqrt{n}} = \frac{19,480 - 20,000}{4,250/\sqrt{70}} = -1.02$$

Referring to Appendix D, the likelihood of finding a $z$ value between 0 and $-1.02$ is .3461. The probability of finding a sample mean of 19,480 gallons or less from the specified population is .1539, found by .5000 − .3461. To put it another way, there is about a 15 percent chance we could select a sample of 70 gas stations and find the mean of this sample is 19,480 gallons or less, when the population mean is 20,000. It is reasonable to conclude that the population mean is 20,000 gallons. This information is summarized in Chart 8–7.

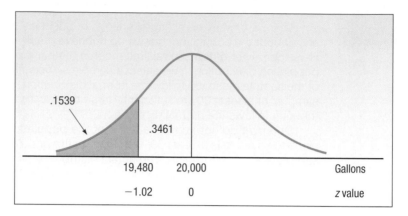

**CHART 8–7** Sampling Distribution for the Sample Mean of the Number of Gallons Sold per Day

---

**Self-Review 8–6**   The mean hourly wage for plumbers in the Atlanta, Georgia, region is $28.00. What is the likelihood that we could select a sample of 50 plumbers with a mean wage of $28.50 or more? The standard deviation of the sample is $2.00 per hour.

# Exercises

15. A normal population has a mean of 60 and a standard deviation of 12. You select a random sample of 9. Compute the probability the sample mean is:
    a. Greater than 63.
    b. Less than 56.
    c. Between 56 and 63.

16. A population of unknown shape has a mean of 75. You select a sample of 40. The standard deviation of the sample is 5. Compute the probability the sample mean is:
    a. Less than 74.
    b. Between 74 and 76.
    c. Between 76 and 77.
    d. Greater than 77.

17. The mean rent for a one-bedroom apartment in Southern California is $2,200 per month. The distribution of the monthly costs does not follow the normal distribution. In fact, it is positively skewed. What is the probability of selecting a sample of 50 one-bedroom apartments and finding the mean to be at least $1,950 per month? The standard deviation of the sample is $250.

18. According to an IRS study, it takes an average of 330 minutes for taxpayers to prepare, copy, and electronically file a 1040 tax form. A consumer watchdog agency selects a random sample of 40 taxpayers and finds the standard deviation of the time to prepare, copy, and electronically file form 1040 is 80 minutes.
    a. What assumption or assumptions do you need to make about the shape of the population?
    b. What is the standard error of the mean in this example?
    c. What is the likelihood the sample mean is greater than 320 minutes?
    d. What is the likelihood the sample mean is between 320 and 350 minutes?
    e. What is the likelihood the sample mean is greater than 350 minutes?

# Chapter Outline

I. There are many reasons for sampling a population.
    A. The results of a sample may adequately estimate the value of the population parameter, thus saving time and money.
    B. It may be too time consuming to contact all members of the population.
    C. It may be impossible to check or locate all the members of the population.
    D. The cost of studying all the items in the population may be prohibitive.
    E. Often testing destroys the sampled item and it cannot be returned to the population.

II. In an unbiased sample all members of the population have a chance of being selected for the sample. There are several probability sampling methods.
    A. In a simple random sample all members of the population have the same chance of being selected for the sample.
    B. In a systematic sample a random starting point is selected, and then every $k$th item thereafter is selected for the sample.
    C. In a stratified sample the population is divided into several groups, called strata, and then a random sample is selected from each stratum.
    D. In cluster sampling the population is divided into primary units, then samples are drawn from the primary units.

III. The sampling error is the difference between a population parameter and a sample statistic.

IV. The sampling distribution of the sample mean is a probability distribution of all possible sample means of the same sample size.
    A. For a given sample size, the mean of all possible sample means selected from a population is equal to the population mean.
    B. There is less variation in the distribution of the sample mean than in the population distribution.
        1. The standard error of the mean measures the variation in the sampling distribution of the sample mean.
            a. If we know the population standard deviation, the standard error is

$$\sigma_{\bar{X}} = \frac{\sigma}{\sqrt{n}} \qquad\qquad [8\text{--}1]$$

            b. If we do not know the population standard deviation, the standard error is estimated by

$$s_{\bar{X}} = \frac{s}{\sqrt{n}}$$

    C. If the population follows a normal distribution, the sampling distribution of the sample mean will also follow the normal distribution for samples of any size. Assume the population standard deviation is known. To determine the probability that a sample mean falls in a particular region, use the following formula.

$$z = \frac{\bar{X} - \mu}{\sigma/\sqrt{n}} \qquad\qquad [8\text{--}2]$$

    D. If the population is not normally distributed but the sample is of at least 30 observations, the sampling distribution of the sample mean is approximately normal. Assume the population standard deviation is not known. To determine the probability that a sample mean falls in a particular region, use the normal distribution and the following standardizing formula:

$$z = \frac{\bar{X} - \mu}{s/\sqrt{n}} \qquad\qquad [8\text{--}3]$$

# Pronunciation Key

| SYMBOL | MEANING | PRONUNCIATION |
|---|---|---|
| $\mu_{\bar{X}}$ | Mean of the sampling distribution of the sample mean | *mu sub X bar* |
| $\sigma_{\bar{X}}$ | Population standard error of the sample mean | *sigma sub X bar* |
| $s_{\bar{X}}$ | Estimate of the standard error of the sample mean | *s sub X bar* |

# Chapter Exercises

**19.** The retail stores located in the North Towne Square Mall are:

| | | | | | |
|---|---|---|---|---|---|
| 00 | Elder-Beerman | 09 | Lion Store | 18 | County Seat |
| 01 | Montgomery Ward | 10 | Bootleggers | 19 | Kid Mart |
| 02 | Deb Shop | 11 | Formal Man | 20 | Lerner |
| 03 | Frederick's of Hollywood | 12 | Leather Ltd. | 21 | Coach House Gifts |
| 04 | Petries | 13 | B Dalton Bookseller | 22 | Spence Gifts |
| 05 | Easy Dreams | 14 | Pat's Hallmark | 23 | CPI Photo Finish |
| 06 | Summit Stationers | 15 | Things Remembered | 24 | Regis Hairstylists |
| 07 | E. B. Brown Opticians | 16 | Pearle Vision Express | | |
| 08 | Kay-Bee Toy & Hobby | 17 | Dollar Tree | | |

    **a.** If the following random numbers are selected, which retail stores should be contacted for a survey? 11, 65, 86, 62, 06, 10, 12, 77, and 04

    **b.** Select a random sample of four retail stores. Use Appendix E.

    **c.** A systematic sampling procedure is to be used. The first store is to be contacted and then every third store. Which stores will be contacted?

**20.** Medical Mutual Insurance is investigating the cost of a routine office visit to family-practice physicians in the Rochester, New York, area. The following is a list of family-practice physicians in the region. Physicians are to be randomly selected and contacted regarding their charges. The 39 physicians have been coded from 00 to 38. Also noted is whether they are in practice by themselves (S), have a partner (P), or are in a group practice (G).

| Number | Physician | Type of Practice | Number | Physician | Type of Practice |
|---|---|---|---|---|---|
| 00 | R. E. Scherbarth, M.D. | S | 20 | Gregory Yost, M.D. | P |
| 01 | Crystal R. Goveia, M.D. | P | 21 | J. Christian Zona, M.D. | P |
| 02 | Mark D. Hillard, M.D. | P | 22 | Larry Johnson, M.D. | P |
| 03 | Jeanine S. Huttner, M.D. | P | 23 | Sanford Kimmel, M.D. | P |
| 04 | Francis Aona, M.D. | P | 24 | Harry Mayhew, M.D. | S |
| 05 | Janet Arrowsmith, M.D. | P | 25 | Leroy Rodgers, M.D. | S |
| 06 | David DeFrance, M.D. | S | 26 | Thomas Tafelski, M.D. | S |
| 07 | Judith Furlong, M.D. | S | 27 | Mark Zilkoski, M.D. | G |
| 08 | Leslie Jackson, M.D. | G | 28 | Ken Bertka, M.D. | G |
| 09 | Paul Langenkamp, M.D. | S | 29 | Mark DeMichiei, M.D. | G |
| 10 | Philip Lepkowski, M.D. | S | 30 | John Eggert, M.D. | P |
| 11 | Wendy Martin, M.D. | S | 31 | Jeanne Fiorito, M.D. | P |
| 12 | Denny Mauricio, M.D. | P | 32 | Michael Fitzpatrick, M.D. | P |
| 13 | Hasmukh Parmar, M.D. | P | 33 | Charles Holt, D.O. | P |
| 14 | Ricardo Pena, M.D. | P | 34 | Richard Koby, M.D. | P |
| 15 | David Reames, M.D. | P | 35 | John Meier, M.D. | P |
| 16 | Ronald Reynolds, M.D. | G | 36 | Douglas Smucker, M.D. | S |
| 17 | Mark Steinmetz, M.D. | G | 37 | David Weldy, M.D. | P |
| 18 | Geza Torok, M.D. | S | 38 | Cheryl Zaborowski, M.D. | P |
| 19 | Mark Young, M.D. | P | | | |

    **a.** The random numbers obtained from Appendix E are: 31, 94, 43, 36, 03, 24, 17, and 09. Which physicians should be contacted?

    **b.** Select a random sample of four physicians using the random numbers of Appendix E.

    **c.** A sample is to consist of every fifth physician. The number 04 is selected as the starting point. Which physicians will be contacted?

    **d.** A sample is to consist of two physicians in solo practice (S), two in partnership (P), and one in group practice (G). Select a sample accordingly. Explain your procedure.

**21.** What is sampling error? Could the value of the sampling error be zero? If it were zero, what would this mean?

**22.** List the reasons for sampling. Give an example of each reason for sampling.

**23.** The commercial banks in Region III are to be surveyed. Some of them are very large, with assets of more than $500 million; others are medium-sized, with assets between $100 million and $500 million; and the remaining banks have assets of less than $100 million. Explain how you would select a sample of these banks.

**24.** Urban Plastic Products, Inc. is concerned about the inside diameter of the plastic PVC pipe it produces. A machine extrudes the pipe, which is then cut into 10-foot lengths. About 720 pipes are produced per machine during a two-hour period. How would you go about taking a sample from the two-hour production period?

**25.** A study of motel facilities in Rock Hill, South Carolina, showed there were 25 facilities. The city's convention and visitors bureau is studying the number of rooms at each location. The results are as follows:

| 90 72 75 60 75 72 84 72 88 74 105 115 68 74 80 64 104 82 48 58 60 80 48 58 100 |
|---|

  **a.** Using a table of random numbers (Appendix E), select a random sample of five motels from this population.
  **b.** Obtain a systematic sample by selecting a random starting point among the first five motels and then select every fifth motel.
  **c.** Suppose the last five motels are "cut-rate" motels. Describe how you would select a random sample of three regular motels and two cut-rate motels.

**26.** As a part of their customer-service program, United Airlines randomly selected 10 passengers from today's 9 A.M. Chicago–Tampa flight. Each sampled passenger is to be interviewed in depth regarding airport facilities, service, food, and so on. To identify the sample, each passenger was given a number on boarding the aircraft. The numbers started with 001 and ended with 250.
  **a.** Select 10 usable numbers at random using Appendix E.
  **b.** The sample of 10 could have been chosen using a systematic sample. Choose the first number using Appendix E, and then list the numbers to be interviewed.
  **c.** Evaluate the two methods by giving the advantages and possible disadvantages.
  **d.** In what other way could a random sample be selected from the 250 passengers?

**27.** Suppose your statistics instructor gave six examinations during the semester. You received the following grades (percent correct): 79, 64, 84, 82, 92, and 77. Instead of averaging the six scores, the instructor indicated he would randomly select two grades and report that grade to the student records office.
  **a.** How many different samples of two test grades are possible?
  **b.** List all possible samples of size two and compute the mean of each.
  **c.** Compute the mean of the sample means and compare it to the population mean.
  **d.** If you were a student, would you like this arrangement? Would the result be different from dropping the lowest score? Write a brief report.

**28.** At the downtown office of First National Bank there are five tellers. Last week the tellers made the following number of errors each: 2, 3, 5, 3, and 5.
  **a.** How many different samples of 2 tellers are possible?
  **b.** List all possible samples of size 2 and compute the mean of each.
  **c.** Compute the mean of the sample means and compare it to the population mean.

**29.** The quality control department employs five technicians during the day shift. Listed below is the number of times each technician instructed the production foreman to shut down the manufacturing process last week.

| Technician | Shutdowns |
|---|---|
| Taylor | 4 |
| Hurley | 3 |
| Gupta | 5 |
| Rousche | 3 |
| Huang | 2 |

  **a.** How many different samples of two technicians are possible from this population?
  **b.** List all possible samples of two observations each and compute the mean of each sample.

    **c.** Compare the mean of the sample means with the population mean.

    **d.** Compare the shape of the population distribution with the shape of the distribution of the sample means.

**30.** The Appliance Center has six sales representatives at their North Jacksonville outlet. Listed below is the number of refrigerators sold by each last month.

| Sales Representative | Number Sold |
|---|---|
| Zina Craft | 54 |
| Woon Junge | 50 |
| Ernie DeBrul | 52 |
| Jan Niles | 48 |
| Molly Camp | 50 |
| Rachel Myak | 52 |

    **a.** How many samples of size two are possible?

    **b.** Select all possible samples of size two and compute the mean number sold.

    **c.** Organize the sample means into a frequency distribution.

    **d.** What is the mean of the population? What is the mean of the sample means?

    **e.** What is the shape of the population distribution?

    **f.** What is the shape of the distribution of the sample mean?

**31.** The Sony Corporation produces a Walkman that requires two AA batteries. The mean life of these batteries in this product is 35.0 hours. The distribution of the battery lives closely follows the normal probability distribution with a standard deviation of 5.5 hours. As a part of their testing program Sony tests samples of 25 batteries.

    **a.** What can you say about the shape of the distribution of sample mean?

    **b.** What is the standard error of the distribution of the sample mean?

    **c.** What proportion of the samples will have a mean useful life of more than 36 hours?

    **d.** What proportion of the sample will have a mean useful life greater than 34.5 hours?

    **e.** What proportion of the sample will have a mean useful life between 34.5 and 36.0 hours?

**32.** CRA CDs, Inc. wants the mean lengths of the "cuts" on a CD to be 135 seconds (2 minutes and 15 seconds). This will allow the disk jockeys to have plenty of time for commercials within each 10-minute segment. Assume the distribution of the length of the cuts follows the normal distribution with a standard deviation of 8 seconds. Suppose we select a sample of 16 cuts from various CDs sold by CRA CDs, Inc.

    **a.** What can we say about the shape of the distribution of the sample mean?

    **b.** What is the standard error of the mean?

    **c.** What percent of the sample means will be greater than 140 seconds?

    **d.** What percent of the sample means will be greater than 128 seconds?

    **e.** What percent of the sample means will be greater than 128 but less than 140 seconds?

**33.** Recent studies indicate that the typical 50-year-old woman spends $350 per year for personal-care products. The distribution of the amounts spent is positively skewed. We select a random sample of 40 women. The mean amount spent for those sampled is $335, and the standard deviation of the sample is $45. What is the likelihood of finding a sample mean this large or larger from the specified population?

**34.** Information from the American Institute of Insurance indicates the mean amount of life insurance per household in the United States is $110,000. This distribution is positively skewed. The standard deviation of the population is not known.

    **a.** A random sample of 50 households revealed a mean of $112,000 and a standard deviation of $40,000. What is the standard error of the mean?

    **b.** Suppose that you selected 50 samples of households. What is the expected shape of the distribution of the sample mean?

    **c.** What is the likelihood of selecting a sample with a mean of at least $112,000?

    **d.** What is the likelihood of selecting a sample with a mean of more than $100,000?

    **e.** Find the likelihood of selecting a sample with a mean of more than $100,000 but less than $112,000.

**35.** The mean age at which men in the United States marry for the first time is 24.8 years. The shape and the standard deviation of the population are both unknown. For a random sample of 60 men, what is the likelihood that the age at which they were married for the first time is less than 25.1 years? Assume that the standard deviation of the sample is 2.5 years.

**36.** A recent study by the Greater Los Angeles Taxi Drivers Association showed that the mean fare charged for service from Hermosa Beach to the Los Angeles International Airport is $18.00 and the standard deviation is $3.50. We select a sample of 15 fares.
  **a.** What is the likelihood that the sample mean is between $17.00 and $20.00?
  **b.** What must you assume to make the above calculation?

**37.** The Crossett Trucking Company claims that the mean weight of their delivery trucks when they are fully loaded is 6,000 pounds and the standard deviation is 150 pounds. Assume that the population follows the normal distribution. Forty trucks are randomly selected and weighed. Within what limits will 95 percent of the sample means occur?

**38.** The mean amount purchased by each customer at Churchill's Grocery Store is $23.50. The population is positively skewed and the standard deviation is not known. For a sample of 50 customers, answer the following questions.
  **a.** If the standard deviation of the sample is $5.00, what is the likelihood the sample mean is at least $25.00?
  **b.** Again, assume the sample standard deviation is $5.00. What is the likelihood the sample mean is greater than $22.50 but less than $25.00?
  **c.** Again, assume the sample standard deviation is $5.00. Within what limits will 90 percent of the sample means occur?

**39.** The mean SAT score for Division I student-athletes is 947 with a standard deviation of 205. If you select a random sample of 60 of these students, what is the probability the mean is below 900?

**40.** Suppose we roll a fair die two times.
  **a.** How many different samples are there?
  **b.** List each of the possible samples and compute the mean.
  **c.** On a chart similar to Chart 8–1, compare the distribution of sample means with the distribution of the population.
  **d.** Compute the mean and the standard deviation of each distribution and compare them.

**41.** The following table lists the most recent data available on per capita personal income (in dollars) for each of the 50 states.

| Number | State | Income | Number | State | Income | Number | State | Income |
|---|---|---|---|---|---|---|---|---|
| | **New England** | | | **Plains** | | | **Southwest** | |
| 01 | Connecticut | $39,300 | 17 | Iowa | 25,615 | 36 | Arizona | 25,189 |
| 02 | Maine | 24,603 | 18 | Kansas | 26,824 | 37 | New Mexico | 21,853 |
| 03 | Massachusetts | 35,551 | 19 | Minnesota | 30,793 | 38 | Oklahoma | 22,953 |
| 04 | New Hampshire | 31,114 | 20 | Missouri | 26,376 | 39 | Texas | 26,858 |
| 05 | Rhode Island | 29,377 | 21 | Nebraska | 27,049 | | **Rocky Mountain** | |
| 06 | Vermont | 25,889 | 22 | North Dakota | 23,313 | 40 | Colorado | 31,546 |
| | **Mideast** | | 23 | South Dakota | 25,045 | 41 | Idaho | 22,835 |
| 07 | Delaware | 30,778 | | **Southeast** | | 42 | Montana | 22,019 |
| 08 | Maryland | 32,465 | 24 | Alabama | 22,987 | 43 | Utah | 23,288 |
| 09 | New Jersey | 35,551 | 25 | Arkansas | 22,244 | 44 | Wyoming | 26,396 |
| 10 | New York | 33,890 | 26 | Florida | 27,780 | | **Far West** | |
| 11 | Pennsylvania | 28,605 | 27 | Georgia | 27,340 | 45 | Alaska | 28,577 |
| | **Great Lakes** | | 28 | Kentucky | 23,237 | 46 | California | 29,910 |
| 12 | Illinois | 31,145 | 29 | Louisiana | 22,847 | 47 | Hawaii | 27,544 |
| 13 | Indiana | 26,143 | 30 | Mississippi | 20,688 | 48 | Nevada | 31,022 |
| 14 | Michigan | 28,113 | 31 | North Carolina | 26,003 | 49 | Oregon | 27,023 |
| 15 | Ohio | 27,152 | 32 | South Carolina | 23,545 | 50 | Washington | 30,392 |
| 16 | Wisconsin | 27,390 | 33 | Tennessee | 25,574 | | | |
| | | | 34 | Virginia | 29,789 | | | |
| | | | 35 | West Virginia | 20,921 | | | |

  **a.** You wish to select a sample of eight from this list. The selected random numbers are 45, 15, 81, 09, 39, 43, 90, 26, 06, 45, 01, and 42. Which states are included in the sample?
  **b.** You wish to use a systematic sample of every sixth item and the digit 02 is chosen as the starting point. Which states are included?
  **c.** A sample of one state from each region is to be selected. Describe how you would perform the sampling process in detail. That is, show the random numbers you selected and the corresponding states that are included in your sample.

# exercises.com

**42.** You need to find the "typical" or mean annual dividend per share for large banks. You decide to sample six banks listed on the New York Stock Exchange. These banks and their trading symbol follow.

| Bank | Symbol | Bank | Symbol |
|------|--------|------|--------|
| AmSouth Bancorporation | ASO | National City Corp. | NCC |
| Bank of America Corp. | BAC | Northern Trust Corp. | NTRS |
| Bank of New York | BK | PNC Financial Services Group | PNC |
| Bank One Corp. | ONE | Regions Financial Corp. | RGBK |
| BB&T Corporation | BBT | SouthTrust Corp. | SOTR |
| Charter One Financial | CF | SunTrust Banks | STI |
| Comerica, Inc. | CMA | Synovus Financial | SNV |
| Fifth Third Bancorp | FITB | Union Planters | UPC |
| FleetBoston Financial Corp. | FBF | U.S. Bancorp | USB |
| Golden West Financial | GDW | Wachovia Corp. | WB |
| Huntington Bancshares | HBAN | Washington Mutual, Inc. | WM |
| KeyCorp | KEY | Wells Fargo & Co. (New) | WFC |
| Mellon Financial Corp. | MEL | Zions Bancorp | ZION |

**a.** After numbering the banks from 01 to 26, which banks would be included in a sample if the random numbers were 14, 08, 24, 25, 05, 44, 02, and 22? Go to the following website: http://www.quicken.com. Enter the trading symbol for each of the sampled banks and record the Annual Dividend per share (Annual div/shr). Determine the mean annual dividend per share for the sample of banks.

**b.** Which banks are selected if you use a systematic sample of every fourth bank starting with the random number 03?

**43.** There are several websites that will report the 30 stocks that make up the Dow Jones Industrial Average (DJIA). One site is www.dbc.com/dbcfiles/dowt.html. Compute the mean of the 30 stocks.

**a.** Use a random number table, such as Appendix E, to select a random sample of five companies that make up the DJIA. Compute the sample mean. Compare the sample mean to the population mean. What did you find? What did you expect to find?

**b.** You should not expect to find that the mean of these 30 stocks is the same as the current DJIA. Go to the Dow Jones website at http://averages.dowjones.com/j-p/index.jsp and read the reasons.

# Dataset Exercises

**44.** Refer to the Real Estate data, which reports information on the homes sold in the Denver, Colorado, area last year.

**a.** Compute the mean and the standard deviation of the distribution of the selling prices for the homes. Assume this to be the population. Develop a histogram of the data. Would it seem reasonable from this histogram to conclude that the population of selling prices follows the normal distribution?

**b.** Let's assume a normal population. Select a sample of 10 homes. Compute the mean and the standard deviation of the sample. Determine the likelihood of finding a sample mean this large or larger from the population.

**45.** Refer to the CIA data, which reports demographic and economic information on 46 countries. Select a random sample of 10 countries. For this sample calculate the mean GDP/capita. Repeat this sampling and calculation process five more times. Then find the mean and standard deviation of your six sample means.

**a.** How do this mean and standard deviation compare with the mean and standard deviation of the original "population" of 46 countries?

**b.** Make a histogram of the six means and discuss whether the distribution is normal.

**c.** Suppose the population distribution is normal. For the first sample mean you computed, determine the likelihood of finding a sample mean this large or larger from the population.

# Chapter 8 Answers to Self-Review

**8–1** **a.** Students selected are Price, Detley, and Molter.
**b.** Answers will vary.
**c.** Skip it and move to the next random number.

**8–2** The students selected are Berry, Francis, Kopp, Poteau, and Sweiye.

**8–3** **a.** 10, found by:

$$_5C_2 = \frac{5!}{2!(5-2)!}$$

**b.**

| | Service | Sample Mean |
|---|---|---|
| Snow, Tolson | 20, 22 | 21 |
| Snow, Kraft | 20, 26 | 23 |
| Snow, Irwin | 20, 24 | 22 |
| Snow, Jones | 20, 28 | 24 |
| Tolson, Kraft | 22, 26 | 24 |
| Tolson, Irwin | 22, 24 | 23 |
| Tolson, Jones | 22, 28 | 25 |
| Kraft, Irwin | 26, 24 | 25 |
| Kraft, Jones | 26, 28 | 27 |
| Irwin, Jones | 24, 28 | 26 |

**c.**

| Mean | Number | Probability |
|---|---|---|
| 21 | 1 | .10 |
| 22 | 1 | .10 |
| 23 | 2 | .20 |
| 24 | 2 | .20 |
| 25 | 2 | .20 |
| 26 | 1 | .10 |
| 27 | 1 | .10 |
| | 10 | 1.00 |

**d.** Identical: population mean, $\mu$, is 24, and mean of sample means, $\mu_{\bar{x}}$, is also 24.
**e.** Sample means range from 21 to 27. Population values go from 20 to 28.
**f.** Nonnormal.
**g.** Yes.

**8–4** The answers will vary. Here is one solution.

| | Sample Number | | | | | | | | | |
|---|---|---|---|---|---|---|---|---|---|---|
| | 1 | 2 | 3 | 4 | 5 | 6 | 7 | 8 | 9 | 10 |
| | 8 | 2 | 2 | 19 | 3 | 4 | 0 | 4 | 1 | 2 |
| | 19 | 1 | 14 | 9 | 2 | 5 | 8 | 2 | 14 | 4 |
| | 8 | 3 | 4 | 2 | 4 | 4 | 1 | 14 | 4 | 1 |
| | 0 | 3 | 2 | 3 | 1 | 2 | 16 | 1 | 2 | 3 |
| | 2 | 1 | 7 | 2 | 19 | 18 | 18 | 16 | 3 | 7 |
| Total | 37 | 10 | 29 | 35 | 29 | 33 | 43 | 37 | 24 | 17 |
| $\bar{X}$ | 7.4 | 2 | 5.8 | 7.0 | 5.8 | 6.6 | 8.6 | 7.4 | 4.8 | 3.4 |

Mean of the 10 sample means is 5.88.

**8–5** $z = \dfrac{31.08 - 31.20}{0.4/\sqrt{16}} = -1.20$

The probability that $z$ is greater than $-1.20$ is $.5000 + .3849 = .8849$. There is less than a 12 percent chance of this event happening.

**8–6** $z = \dfrac{\$28.50 - \$28.00}{\$2.00/\sqrt{50}} = 1.77$

The probability that $z$ is greater than 1.77 is $.5000 - .4616 = .0384$.

# Estimation and Confidence Intervals

The American Restaurant Association collected information on the number of meals eaten outside the home per week by young married couples. A survey of 60 couples showed the sample mean number of meals eaten outside the home was 2.76 meals per week. Construct a 97 percent confidence interval for the population mean. (See Goal 3 and Exercise 36.)

# Introduction

The previous chapter began our discussion of statistical inference. It introduced the reasons and methods of sampling. The reasons for sampling were:

- To contact the entire population is too time consuming
- The cost of studying all the items in the population is often too expensive
- The sample results are usually adequate
- The destructive nature of certain tests
- The physical impossibility of checking all the items

There are several methods of sampling. Simple random sampling is the most widely used method. With this type of sampling, each member of the population has the same chance of being selected to be a part of the sample. Other methods of sampling include systematic sampling, stratified sampling, and cluster sampling.

Chapter 8 assumes information about the population, such as the mean, the standard deviation, or the shape of the population. In most business situations, such information is not available. In fact, the purpose of sampling may be to estimate some of these values. For example, you select a sample from a population and use the mean of the sample to estimate the mean of the population.

This chapter considers several important aspects of sampling. We begin by studying point estimates. A point estimate is a particular value used to estimate a population value. For example, suppose we select a sample of 50 junior executives and ask each the number of hours they worked last week. Compute the mean of this sample of 50 and use the value of the sample mean as a point estimate of the unknown population mean. However, a point estimate is a single value. A more informative approach is to present a range of values in which we expect the population parameter to occur. Such a range of values is called a confidence interval.

Frequently in business we need to determine the size of a sample. How many voters should a polling organization contact to forecast the election outcome? How many products do we need to examine to ensure our quality level? This chapter also develops a strategy for determining the appropriate size of the sample.

# Point Estimates and Confidence Intervals

## Known σ or a Large Sample

In the previous chapter, the data on the length of service of Spence Sprockets employees, presented in the example on page 264, is a population because we present the length of service for all 40 employees. In that case we can easily compute the population mean. We have all the data and the population is not too large. In most situations, however, the population is large or it is difficult to identify all members of the population, so we need to rely on sample information. In other words, we do not know the population parameter and we therefore want to estimate the value from a sample statistic. Consider the following business situations.

1. Tourism is a major source of income for many Caribbean countries, such as Barbados. Suppose the Bureau of Tourism for Barbados wants an estimate of the mean amount spent by tourists visiting the country. It would not be feasible to contact each tourist. Therefore, 500 tourists are randomly selected as they depart the country and asked in detail about their spending while visiting the island. The mean amount spent by the sample of 500 tourists is an estimate of the unknown population parameter. That is, we let $\bar{X}$, the sample mean, serve as an estimate of $\mu$, the population mean.

2. Centex Home Builders, Inc., builds quality homes in the southeastern region of the United States. One of the major concerns of new buyers is the date on which the home will be completed. In recent times Centex has been telling customers, "Your home will be completed 45 working days from the date we begin installing

**Statistics in Action**

On all new cars, a fuel economy estimate is prominently displayed on the window sticker as required by the Environmental Protection Agency (EPA). Often, fuel economy is a factor in a consumer's choice of a new car because of fuel costs or environmental concerns. For example, a 2003 Toyota Camry's (4 cylinder) fuel estimates are 32 miles per gallon on the highway and 23 mpg in the city. The EPA recognizes that actual fuel economy may differ from the estimates by noting, "No test can simulate all possible combinations of conditions and climate, driver behavior, and car care habits. Actual mileage depends on how, when, and where the vehicle is driven. EPA has found that the mpg obtained by most drivers will be within a few mpg of the estimates . . ." In fact, the window sticker also includes an interval estimate for fuel economy: 19 to 27 mpg in the city and 27 to 37 mpg on the highway. http://www. fueleconomy.gov/

drywall." The customer relations department at Centex wishes to compare this pledge with recent experience. A sample of 50 homes completed this year revealed the mean number of working days from the start of drywall to the completion of the home was 46.7 days. Is it reasonable to conclude that the population mean is still 45 days and that the difference between the sample mean (46.7 days) and the proposed population mean is sampling error?

3. Recent medical studies indicate that exercise is an important part of a person's overall health. The director of human resources at OCF, a large glass manufacturer, wants an estimate of the number of hours per week employees spend exercising. A sample of 70 employees reveals the mean number of hours of exercise last week is 3.3. The sample mean of 3.3 hours estimates the unknown population mean, the mean hours of exercise for all employees.

A point estimate is a single statistic used to estimate a population parameter. Suppose Best Buy, Inc. wants to estimate the mean age of buyers of high-definition televisions. They select a random sample of 50 recent purchasers, determine the age of each purchaser, and compute the mean age of the buyers in the sample. The mean of this sample is a point estimate of the mean of the population.

> **POINT ESTIMATE** The statistic, computed from sample information, which is used to estimate the population parameter.

The sample mean, $\overline{X}$, is a point estimate of the population mean, $\mu$; $p$, a sample proportion, is a point estimate of $\pi$, the population proportion; and $s$, the sample standard deviation, is a point estimate of $\sigma$, the population standard deviation.

A point estimate, however, tells only part of the story. While we expect the point estimate to be close to the population parameter, we would like to measure how close it really is. A confidence interval serves this purpose.

> **CONFIDENCE INTERVAL** A range of values constructed from sample data so that the population parameter is likely to occur within that range at a specified probability. The specified probability is called the *level of confidence.*

For example, we estimate the mean yearly income for construction workers in the New York–New Jersey area is $65,000. The range of this estimate might be from $61,000 to $69,000. We can describe how confident we are that the population parameter is in the interval by making a probability statement. We might say, for instance, that we are 90 percent sure that the mean yearly income of construction workers in the New York–New Jersey area is between $61,000 and $69,000.

The information developed about the shape of a sampling distribution of the sample mean, that is, the sampling distribution of $\overline{X}$, allows us to locate an interval that has a specified probability of containing the population mean, $\mu$. For reasonably large samples, the results of the central limit theorem allow us to state the following:

1. Ninety-five percent of the sample means selected from a population will be within 1.96 standard deviations of the population mean $\mu$.
2. Ninety-nine percent of the sample means will lie within 2.58 standard deviations of the population mean.

The standard deviation discussed here is the standard deviation of the sampling distribution of the sample mean. It is usually called the "standard error." Intervals computed in this fashion are called the **95 percent confidence interval** and the

**99 percent confidence interval.** How are the values of 1.96 and 2.58 obtained? The *95 percent* and *99 percent* refer to the percent of similarly constructed intervals that would include the parameter being estimated. The *95 percent,* for example, refers to the middle 95 percent of the observations. Therefore, the remaining 5 percent are equally divided between the two tails.

See the following diagram.

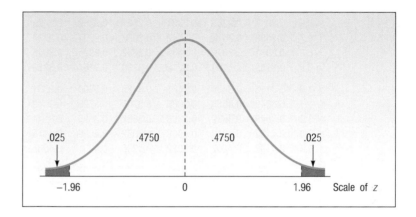

The central limit theorem, discussed in the previous chapter, states that the sampling distribution of the sample means is approximately normal when the sample contains at least 30 observations. Therefore, we can use Appendix D to find the appropriate *z* values. Locate .4750 in the body of the table. Read the corresponding row and column values. The value is 1.96. Thus, the probability of finding a *z* value between 0 and 1.96 is .4750. Likewise, the probability of being in the interval between −1.96 and 0 is also .4750. When we combine these two, the probability of being in the interval −1.96 to 1.96 is .9500. On the next page is a portion of Appendix D. The *z* value for the 90 percent level of confidence is determined in a similar manner. It is 1.65. For a 99 percent level of confidence the *z* value is 2.58.

How do you compute a 95 percent confidence interval? Assume your research involves the annual starting salary of accounting majors with a Bachelor's degree. You compute the sample mean to be $39,000 and the standard deviation (that is, the "standard error") of the sample mean to be $200. Assume your sample contains at least 30 observations. The 95 percent confidence interval is between $38,608 and $39,392, found by $39,000 ± 1.96($200). If 100 samples of the same size were selected from the population of interest and the corresponding 100 confidence intervals determined, you expect to find the population mean in 95 of the 100 confidence intervals.

In the above example, the standard error of the sampling distribution of the sample mean was $200. This is, of course, the standard error of the sample means, discussed in the previous chapter. See formula (8–1) for the case when the population standard deviation is available. In most applied situations, the population standard deviation is not available, so we estimate it as follows:

$$s_{\bar{x}} = \frac{s}{\sqrt{n}}$$

The size of the standard error is affected by two values. The first is the standard deviation. If the standard deviation is large, then the standard error will also be large. However, the standard error is also affected by the sample size. As the sample size is increased, the standard error decreases, indicating that there is less variability in the sampling distribution of the sample mean. This conclusion is logical, because an estimate made with a large sample should be more precise than one made from a small sample.

| z | 0.00 | 0.01 | 0.02 | 0.03 | 0.04 | 0.05 | 0.06 | 0.07 | 0.08 | 0.09 |
|---|------|------|------|------|------|------|------|------|------|------|
| 0.0 | 0.0000 | 0.0040 | 0.0080 | 0.0120 | 0.0160 | 0.0199 | 0.0239 | 0.0279 | 0.0319 | 0.0359 |
| 0.1 | 0.0398 | 0.0438 | 0.0478 | 0.0517 | 0.0557 | 0.0596 | 0.0636 | 0.0675 | 0.0714 | 0.0753 |
| 0.2 | 0.0793 | 0.0832 | 0.0871 | 0.0910 | 0.0948 | 0.0987 | 0.1026 | 0.1064 | 0.1103 | 0.1141 |
| 0.3 | 0.1179 | 0.1217 | 0.1255 | 0.1293 | 0.1331 | 0.1368 | 0.1406 | 0.1443 | 0.1480 | 0.1517 |
| 0.4 | 0.1554 | 0.1591 | 0.1628 | 0.1664 | 0.1700 | 0.1736 | 0.1772 | 0.1808 | 0.1844 | 0.1879 |
| 0.5 | 0.1915 | 0.1950 | 0.1985 | 0.2019 | 0.2054 | 0.2088 | 0.2123 | 0.2157 | 0.2190 | 0.2224 |
| 0.6 | 0.2257 | 0.2291 | 0.2324 | 0.2357 | 0.2389 | 0.2422 | 0.2454 | 0.2486 | 0.2517 | 0.2549 |
| 0.7 | 0.2580 | 0.2611 | 0.2642 | 0.2673 | 0.2704 | 0.2734 | 0.2764 | 0.2794 | 0.2823 | 0.2852 |
| 0.8 | 0.2881 | 0.2910 | 0.2939 | 0.2967 | 0.2995 | 0.3023 | 0.3051 | 0.3078 | 0.3106 | 0.3133 |
| 0.9 | 0.3159 | 0.3186 | 0.3212 | 0.3238 | 0.3264 | 0.3289 | 0.3315 | 0.3340 | 0.3365 | 0.3389 |
| 1.0 | 0.3413 | 0.3438 | 0.3461 | 0.3485 | 0.3508 | 0.3531 | 0.3554 | 0.3577 | 0.3599 | 0.3621 |
| 1.1 | 0.3643 | 0.3665 | 0.3686 | 0.3708 | 0.3729 | 0.3749 | 0.3770 | 0.3790 | 0.3810 | 0.3830 |
| 1.2 | 0.3849 | 0.3869 | 0.3888 | 0.3907 | 0.3925 | 0.3944 | 0.3962 | 0.3980 | 0.3997 | 0.4015 |
| 1.3 | 0.4032 | 0.4049 | 0.4066 | 0.4082 | 0.4099 | 0.4115 | 0.4131 | 0.4147 | 0.4162 | 0.4177 |
| 1.4 | 0.4192 | 0.4207 | 0.4222 | 0.4236 | 0.4251 | 0.4265 | 0.4279 | 0.4292 | 0.4306 | 0.4319 |
| 1.5 | 0.4332 | 0.4345 | 0.4357 | 0.4370 | 0.4382 | 0.4394 | 0.4406 | 0.4418 | 0.4429 | 0.4441 |
| 1.6 | 0.4452 | 0.4463 | 0.4474 | 0.4484 | 0.4495 | 0.4505 | 0.4515 | 0.4525 | 0.4535 | 0.4545 |
| 1.7 | 0.4554 | 0.4564 | 0.4573 | 0.4582 | 0.4591 | 0.4599 | 0.4608 | 0.4616 | 0.4625 | 0.4633 |
| 1.8 | 0.4641 | 0.4649 | 0.4656 | 0.4664 | 0.4671 | 0.4678 | 0.4686 | 0.4693 | 0.4699 | 0.4706 |
| 1.9 | 0.4713 | 0.4719 | 0.4726 | 0.4732 | 0.4738 | 0.4744 | 0.4750 | 0.4756 | 0.4761 | 0.4767 |
| 2.0 | 0.4772 | 0.4778 | 0.4783 | 0.4788 | 0.4793 | 0.4798 | 0.4803 | 0.4808 | 0.4812 | 0.4817 |
| 2.1 | 0.4821 | 0.4826 | 0.4830 | 0.4834 | 0.4838 | 0.4842 | 0.4846 | 0.4850 | 0.4854 | 0.4857 |
| 2.2 | 0.4861 | 0.4864 | 0.4868 | 0.4871 | 0.4875 | 0.4878 | 0.4881 | 0.4884 | 0.4887 | 0.4890 |
| 2.3 | 0.4893 | 0.4896 | 0.4898 | 0.4901 | 0.4904 | 0.4906 | 0.4909 | 0.4911 | 0.4913 | 0.4916 |
| 2.4 | 0.4918 | 0.4920 | 0.4922 | 0.4925 | 0.4927 | 0.4929 | 0.4931 | 0.4932 | 0.4934 | 0.4936 |

As we state in Chapter 8, when the sample size, $n$, is at least 30, it is generally agreed that the central limit theorem will ensure that the sample mean follows the normal distribution. This is an important consideration. If the sample mean is normally distributed, we can use the standard normal distribution, that is, $z$, in our calculations.

The 95 percent confidence interval is computed as follows, when the number of observations in the sample is at least 30.

$$\overline{X} \pm 1.96 \frac{s}{\sqrt{n}}$$

Similarly, the 99 percent confidence interval is computed as follows. Again we assume that the sample size is at least 30.

$$\overline{X} \pm 2.58 \frac{s}{\sqrt{n}}$$

As we discussed earlier, the values 1.96 and 2.58 are the $z$ values corresponding to the middle 95 percent and the middle 99 percent of the observations, respectively.

We can use other levels of confidence. For those cases the value of $z$ changes accordingly. In general, a confidence interval for the population mean is computed by:

| CONFIDENCE INTERVAL FOR THE POPULATION MEAN ($n \geq 30$) | $\overline{X} \pm z \dfrac{s}{\sqrt{n}}$ | [9–1] |
|---|---|---|

where $z$ depends on the level of confidence. Thus, for a 92 percent level of confidence, the value of $z$ in formula (9–1) is 1.75. The value of $z$ is from Appendix D. This table is based on half the normal distribution, so .9200/2 = .4600. The closest value in the body of the table is .4599 and the corresponding $z$ value is 1.75.

Frequently, we also use the 90 percent level of confidence. In this case, we want the area between 0 and $z$ to be .4500, found by .9000/2. To find the $z$ value for this level of confidence, move down the left column of Appendix D to 1.6 and then over to the columns headed 0.04 and 0.05. The area corresponding to a $z$ value of 1.64 is .4495, and for 1.65 it is .4505. To be conservative, we use 1.65. Try looking up the following levels of confidence and check your answers with the corresponding $z$ values given on the right.

| Confidence Level | Nearest Probability | $z$ Value |
|---|---|---|
| 80 percent | .3997 | 1.28 |
| 94 percent | .4699 | 1.88 |
| 96 percent | .4798 | 2.05 |

The following example shows the details for calculating a confidence interval and interpreting the result.

**EXAMPLE**

The American Management Association wishes to have information on the mean income of middle managers in the retail industry. A random sample of 256 managers reveals a sample mean of $45,420. The standard deviation of this sample is $2,050. The association would like answers to the following questions:

1. What is the population mean?
2. What is a reasonable range of values for the population mean?
3. What do these results mean?

**SOLUTION**

Generally, distributions of salary and income are positively skewed, because a few individuals earn considerably more than others, thus skewing the distribution in the positive direction. Fortunately, the central limit theorem stipulates that if we select a large sample, the distribution of the sample means will follow the normal distribution. In this instance, with a sample of 256 middle managers (remember, at least 30 is usually large enough), we can be assured that the sampling distribution will follow the normal distribution.

Another issue is that the population standard deviation is not known. Again, it is sound practice to use the sample standard deviation when we have a large sample. Now to answer the questions posed in the problem.

1. **What is the population mean?** In this case, we do not know. We do know the sample mean is $45,420. Hence, our best estimate of the unknown population value is the corresponding sample statistic. Thus the sample mean of $45,420 is a *point estimate* of the unknown population mean.
2. **What is a reasonable range of values for the population mean?** The Association decides to use the 95 percent level of confidence. To determine the corresponding confidence interval we use formula (9–1).

$$\bar{X} \pm z\frac{s}{\sqrt{n}} = \$45,420 \pm 1.96 \frac{\$2,050}{\sqrt{256}} = \$45,420 \pm \$251$$

The usual practice is to round these endpoints to $45,169 and $45,671. These endpoints are called the *confidence limits*. The degree of confidence or the *level of confidence* is 95 percent and the confidence interval is from $45,169 to $45,671.

3. **What do these results mean?** Suppose we select many samples of 256 managers, perhaps several hundred. For each sample, we compute the mean and the

288                    Chapter 9

standard deviation and then construct a 95 percent confidence interval, such as we did in the previous section. We could expect about 95 percent of these confidence intervals to contain the *population* mean. About 5 percent of the intervals would not contain the population mean annual income, which is $\mu$. However, a particular confidence interval either contains the population parameter or it does not. The following diagram shows the results of selecting samples from the population of middle managers in the retail industry, computing the mean and standard deviation of each, and then, using formula (9–1), determining a 95 percent confidence interval for the population mean. Note that not all intervals include the population mean. Both the endpoints of the fifth sample are less than the population mean. We attribute this to sampling error, and it is the risk we assume when we select the level of confidence.

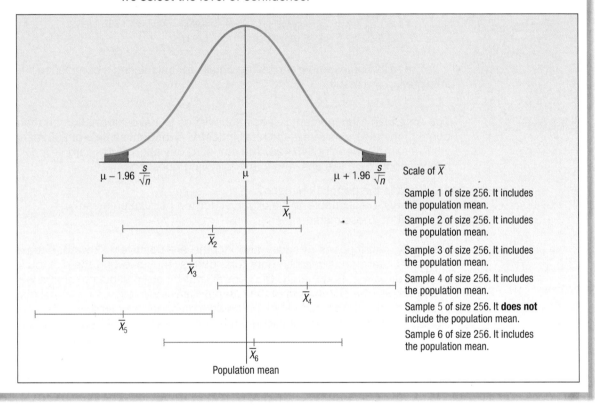

## A Computer Simulation

With the aid of a computer, we can randomly select samples from a population, quickly compute the confidence interval, and show how confidence intervals usually, but not always, include the population parameter. The following example will help to explain.

**EXAMPLE**

From many years in the automobile leasing business, Town Bank knows the mean distance driven on a four-year lease is 50,000 miles and the standard deviation is 5,000. Suppose, using the MINITAB statistical software system, we want to find what proportion of the 95 percent confidence intervals will include the population mean of 50. To make the calculations easier to understand, we'll conduct the study in thousands of miles, instead of miles. We select 60 random samples of size 30 from a population with a mean of 50 and a standard deviation of 5.

**SOLUTION**

The results of 60 random samples of 30 automobiles each are summarized in the table below. Of the 60 confidence intervals with a 95 percent confidence level, 2, or 3.33 percent, did not include the population mean of 50. The intervals (C3 and C59) that do *not* include the population mean are highlighted. 3.33 percent is close to the estimate that 5 percent of the intervals will not include the population mean, and the 58 of 60, or 96.67 percent, is close to 95 percent.

To explain the first calculation in more detail: MINITAB began by selecting a random sample of 30 observations from a population with a mean of 50 and a standard deviation of 5. The mean of these 30 observations is 50.053. The sampling error is 0.053, found by $\overline{X} - \mu = 50.053 - 50.000$. The endpoints of the confidence interval are 48.264 and 51.842. These endpoints are determined by using formula (9–1), but using $\sigma$ instead of $s$.

$$\overline{X} \pm 1.96 \frac{\sigma}{\sqrt{n}} = 50.053 \pm 1.96 \frac{5}{\sqrt{30}} = 50.053 \pm 1.789$$

```
One-Sample Z:

The assumed sigma = 5
```

| Variable | N | Mean | StDev | SE Mean | 95.0% CI |
|---|---|---|---|---|---|
| C1 | 30 | 50.053 | 5.002 | 0.913 | ( 48.264, 51.842) |
| C2 | 30 | 49.025 | 4.450 | 0.913 | ( 47.236, 50.815) |
| C3 | 30 | 52.023 | 5.918 | 0.913 | ( 50.234, 53.812) |
| C4 | 30 | 50.056 | 3.364 | 0.913 | ( 48.267, 51.845) |
| C5 | 30 | 49.737 | 4.784 | 0.913 | ( 47.948, 51.526) |
| C6 | 30 | 51.074 | 5.495 | 0.913 | ( 49.285, 52.863) |
| C7 | 30 | 50.040 | 5.930 | 0.913 | ( 48.251, 51.829) |
| C8 | 30 | 48.910 | 3.645 | 0.913 | ( 47.121, 50.699) |
| C9 | 30 | 51.033 | 4.918 | 0.913 | ( 49.244, 52.822) |
| C10 | 30 | 50.692 | 4.571 | 0.913 | ( 48.903, 52.482) |
| C11 | 30 | 49.853 | 4.525 | 0.913 | ( 48.064, 51.642) |
| C12 | 30 | 50.286 | 3.422 | 0.913 | ( 48.497, 52.076) |
| C13 | 30 | 50.257 | 4.317 | 0.913 | ( 48.468, 52.046) |
| C14 | 30 | 49.605 | 4.994 | 0.913 | ( 47.816, 51.394) |
| C15 | 30 | 51.474 | 5.497 | 0.913 | ( 49.685, 53.264) |
| C16 | 30 | 48.930 | 5.317 | 0.913 | ( 47.141, 50.719) |
| C17 | 30 | 49.870 | 4.847 | 0.913 | ( 48.081, 51.659) |
| C18 | 30 | 50.739 | 6.224 | 0.913 | ( 48.950, 52.528) |
| C19 | 30 | 50.979 | 5.520 | 0.913 | ( 49.190, 52.768) |
| C20 | 30 | 48.848 | 4.130 | 0.913 | ( 47.059, 50.638) |
| C21 | 30 | 49.481 | 4.056 | 0.913 | ( 47.692, 51.270) |
| C22 | 30 | 49.183 | 5.409 | 0.913 | ( 47.394, 50.973) |
| C23 | 30 | 50.084 | 4.522 | 0.913 | ( 48.294, 51.873) |
| C24 | 30 | 50.866 | 5.142 | 0.913 | ( 49.077, 52.655) |
| C25 | 30 | 48.768 | 5.582 | 0.913 | ( 46.979, 50.557) |
| C26 | 30 | 50.904 | 6.052 | 0.913 | ( 49.115, 52.694) |
| C27 | 30 | 49.481 | 5.535 | 0.913 | ( 47.691, 51.270) |
| C28 | 30 | 50.949 | 5.916 | 0.913 | ( 49.160, 52.739) |
| C29 | 30 | 49.106 | 4.641 | 0.913 | ( 47.317, 50.895) |
| C30 | 30 | 49.994 | 5.853 | 0.913 | ( 48.205, 51.784) |
| C31 | 30 | 49.601 | 5.064 | 0.913 | ( 47.811, 51.390) |
| C32 | 30 | 51.494 | 5.597 | 0.913 | ( 49.705, 53.284) |
| C33 | 30 | 50.460 | 4.393 | 0.913 | ( 48.671, 52.249) |
| C34 | 30 | 50.378 | 4.075 | 0.913 | ( 48.589, 52.167) |
| C35 | 30 | 49.808 | 4.155 | 0.913 | ( 48.019, 51.597) |
| C36 | 30 | 49.934 | 5.012 | 0.913 | ( 48.145, 51.723) |
| C37 | 30 | 50.017 | 4.082 | 0.913 | ( 48.228, 51.806) |
| C38 | 30 | 50.074 | 3.631 | 0.913 | ( 48.285, 51.863) |
| C39 | 30 | 48.656 | 4.833 | 0.913 | ( 46.867, 50.445) |
| C40 | 30 | 50.568 | 3.855 | 0.913 | ( 48.779, 52.357) |
| C41 | 30 | 50.916 | 3.775 | 0.913 | ( 49.127, 52.705) |
| C42 | 30 | 49.104 | 4.321 | 0.913 | ( 47.315, 50.893) |
| C43 | 30 | 50.308 | 5.467 | 0.913 | ( 48.519, 52.097) |

| Variable | N | Mean | StDev | SE Mean | 95.0% CI |
|----------|---|------|-------|---------|----------|
| C44 | 30 | 49.034 | 4.405 | 0.913 | ( 47.245, 50.823) |
| C45 | 30 | 50.399 | 4.729 | 0.913 | ( 48.610, 52.188) |
| C46 | 30 | 49.634 | 3.996 | 0.913 | ( 47.845, 51.424) |
| C47 | 30 | 50.479 | 4.881 | 0.913 | ( 48.689, 52.268) |
| C48 | 30 | 50.529 | 5.173 | 0.913 | ( 48.740, 52.318) |
| C49 | 30 | 51.577 | 5.822 | 0.913 | ( 49.787, 53.366) |
| C50 | 30 | 50.403 | 4.893 | 0.913 | ( 48.614, 52.192) |
| C51 | 30 | 49.717 | 5.218 | 0.913 | ( 47.927, 51.506) |
| C52 | 30 | 49.796 | 5.327 | 0.913 | ( 48.007, 51.585) |
| C53 | 30 | 50.549 | 4.680 | 0.913 | ( 48.760, 52.338) |
| C54 | 30 | 50.200 | 5.840 | 0.913 | ( 48.410, 51.989) |
| C55 | 30 | 49.138 | 5.074 | 0.913 | ( 47.349, 50.928) |
| C56 | 30 | 49.667 | 3.843 | 0.913 | ( 47.878, 51.456) |
| C57 | 30 | 49.603 | 5.614 | 0.913 | ( 47.814, 51.392) |
| C58 | 30 | 49.441 | 5.702 | 0.913 | ( 47.652, 51.230) |
| C59 | 30 | 47.873 | 4.685 | 0.913 | ( 46.084, 49.662) |
| C60 | 30 | 51.087 | 5.162 | 0.913 | ( 49.297, 52.876) |

**Self-Review 9–1**

The mean daily sales at the Bun-and-Run, a fast food outlet, is $20,000 for a sample of 40 days. The standard deviation of the sample is $3,000.
(a)  What is the estimated mean daily sales of the population? What is this estimate called?
(b)  What is the 99 percent confidence interval?
(c)  Interpret your findings.

# Exercises

1. A sample of 49 observations is taken from a normal population. The sample mean is 55, and the sample standard deviation is 10. Determine the 99 percent confidence interval for the population mean.
2. A sample of 81 observations is taken from a normal population. The sample mean is 40, and the sample standard deviation is 5. Determine the 95 percent confidence interval for the population mean.
3. A sample of 10 observations is selected from a normal population for which the population standard deviation is known to be 5. The sample mean is 20.
   a. Determine the standard error of the mean.
   b. Explain why we can use formula (9–1) to determine the 95 percent confidence interval even though the sample is less than 30.
   c. Determine the 95 percent confidence interval for the population mean.
4. Suppose you want an 85 percent confidence level. What value would you use to multiply the standard error of the mean?
5. A research firm conducted a survey to determine the mean amount steady smokers spend on cigarettes during a week. A sample of 49 steady smokers revealed that $\overline{X}$ = $20 and $s$ = $5.
   a. What is the point estimate of the population mean? Explain what it indicates.
   b. Using the 95 percent level of confidence, determine the confidence interval for $\mu$. Explain what it indicates.
6. Refer to the previous exercise. Suppose that 64 smokers (instead of 49) were sampled. Assume the sample mean and the sample standard deviation remained the same ($20 and $5, respectively).
   a. What is the 95 percent confidence interval estimate of $\mu$?
   b. Explain why this confidence interval is narrower than the one determined in the previous exercise.
7. Bob Nale is the owner of Nale's Texaco GasTown. Bob would like to estimate the mean number of gallons of gasoline sold to his customers. From his records, he selects a random sample of 60 sales and finds the mean number of gallons sold is 8.60 and the standard deviation is 2.30 gallons.

**a.** What is the point estimate of the population mean?
**b.** Develop a 99 percent confidence interval for the population mean.
**c.** Interpret the meaning of part b.
**8.** Dr. Patton is a Professor of English. Recently he counted the number of misspelled words in a group of student essays. For his class of 40 students, the mean number of misspelled words was 6.05 and the standard deviation 2.44 per essay. Construct a 95 percent confidence interval for the mean number of misspelled words in the population of student essays.

# Unknown Population Standard Deviation and a Small Sample

**Statistics in Action**

William Gosset was born in England in 1876 and died there in 1937. He worked for many years at Arthur Guinness & Sons Brewery. In fact, in his later years he was in charge of the Guinness Brewery in London. Guinness preferred their employees to use pen names when publishing papers, so in 1908, when Gosset wrote "The Probable Error of a Mean," he used the name "Student." In this paper he first described the properties of the *t* distribution.

In the previous section we used the standard normal distribution to express the level of confidence. We assumed either:

1. The population followed the normal distribution and the population standard deviation was known, or
2. The shape of the population was not known, but the number of observations in the sample was at least 30.

What do we do if the sample is less than 30 and we do not know the population standard deviation? This situation is not covered by the results of the central limit theorem but exists in many cases. Often we can reason that the population is normal or reasonably close to a normal distribution. Under these conditions, the correct statistical procedure is to replace the standard normal distribution with the *t* distribution. The *t* distribution is a continuous distribution with many similarities to the standard normal distribution. William Gosset, an English brewmaster, was the first to study the *t* distribution. He did his work in the early 1900s. The brewery that employed Gosset preferred its employees to use pen names when publishing papers. For this reason Gosset's work was published under the pen name "Student." Hence, you will frequently see this distribution referred to as Student's *t*.

Gosset was concerned with the behavior of the following term:

$$t = \frac{\overline{X} - \mu}{s/\sqrt{n}}$$

*s* is an estimate of $\sigma$. He was especially worried about the discrepancy between *s* and $\sigma$ when *s* was calculated from a very small sample. The *t* distribution and the standard normal distribution are shown graphically in Chart 9–1. Note particularly that the *t* distribution is flatter, more spread out, than the standard normal distribution. This is because the standard deviation of the *t* distribution is larger than the standard normal distribution.

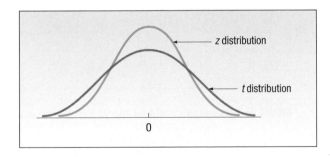

**CHART 9–1** The Standard Normal Distribution and Student's *t* Distribution

The following characteristics of the *t* distribution are based on the assumption that the population of interest is normal, or nearly normal.

1.   It is, like the *z* distribution, a continuous distribution.
2.   It is, like the *z* distribution, bell-shaped and symmetrical.
3.   There is not one *t* distribution, but rather a "family" of *t* distributions. All *t* distributions have a mean of 0, but their standard deviations differ according to the sample size, *n*. There is a *t* distribution for a sample size of 20, another for a sample size of 22, and so on. The standard deviation for a *t* distribution with 5 observations is larger than for a *t* distribution with 20 observations.
4.   The *t* distribution is more spread out and flatter at the center than the standard normal distribution (see Chart 9–1). As the sample size increases, however, the *t* distribution approaches the standard normal distribution, because the errors in using *s* to estimate σ decrease with larger samples.

Because Student's *t* distribution has a greater spread than the *z* distribution, the value of *t* for a given level of confidence is larger in magnitude than the corresponding *z* values. Chart 9–2 shows the values of *z* for a 95 percent level of confidence and of *t* for the same level of confidence when the sample size is *n* = 5. How we obtained the actual value of *t* will be explained shortly. For now, observe that for the same level of confidence the *t* distribution is flatter or more spread out than the standard normal distribution.

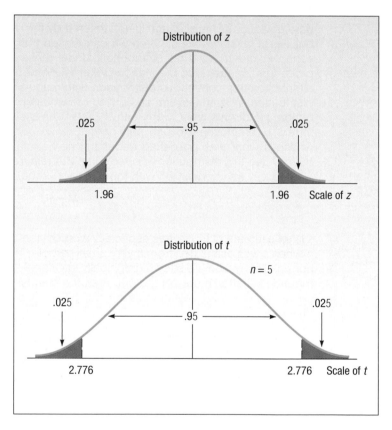

**CHART 9–2** Values of *z* and *t* for the 95 Percent Level of Confidence

To develop a confidence interval for the population mean using the *t* distribution, we adjust formula (9–1) as follows.

| CONFIDENCE INTERVAL FOR THE POPULATION MEAN, σ UNKNOWN | $\bar{X} \pm t \dfrac{s}{\sqrt{n}}$ | **[9–2]** |
|---|---|---|

To put it another way, to develop a confidence interval for the population mean with an unknown population standard deviation we:

1.  Assume the sample is from a normal population.
2.  Estimate the population standard deviation ($\sigma$) with the sample standard deviation ($s$).
3.  Use the $t$ distribution rather than the $z$ distribution.

We should be clear at this point. We usually employ the standard normal distribution when the sample size is at least 30. We should, strictly speaking, base the decision whether to use $z$ or $t$ on whether $\sigma$ is known or not. When $\sigma$ is known, we use $z$; when it is not, we use $t$. The rule of using $z$ when the sample is 30 or more is based on the fact that the $t$ distribution approaches the normal distribution as the sample size increases. When the sample reaches 30, there is little difference between the $z$ and $t$ values, so we may ignore the difference and use $z$. We will show this when we discuss the details of the $t$ distribution and how to find values in a $t$ distribution. Chart 9–3 summarizes the decision-making process.

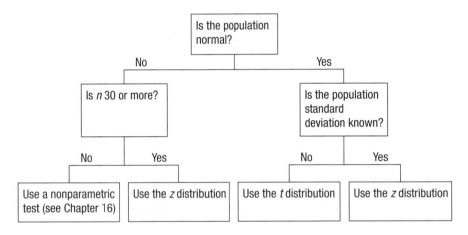

**CHART 9–3** Determining When to Use the $z$ Distribution or the $t$ Distribution

The following example will illustrate a confidence interval for a population mean when the population standard deviation is unknown and how to find the appropriate value of $t$ in a table.

**EXAMPLE**

A tire manufacturer wishes to investigate the tread life of its tires. A sample of 10 tires driven 50,000 miles revealed a sample mean of 0.32 inch of tread remaining with a standard deviation of 0.09 inch. Construct a 95 percent confidence interval for the population mean. Would it be reasonable for the manufacturer to conclude that after 50,000 miles the population mean amount of tread remaining is 0.30 inches?

**SOLUTION**

To begin, we assume the population distribution is normal. In this case, we don't have a lot of evidence, but the assumption is probably reasonable. We do not know the population standard deviation, but we know the sample standard deviation, which is .09 inches. To use the central limit theorem, we need a large sample, that is, a sample of 30 or more. In this instance there are only 10 observations in the sample. Hence, we cannot use the central limit theorem. That is, formula (9–1) is not applicable. We use formula (9–2):

$$\overline{X} \pm t \frac{s}{\sqrt{n}}$$

From the information given, $\bar{X} = 0.32$, $s = 0.09$, and $n = 10$. To find the value of $t$ we use Appendix F, a portion of which is reproduced below as Chart 9–4. Appendix F is also reproduced on the back inside cover of the text. The first step for locating $t$ is to move across the row identified for "Confidence Intervals" to the level of confidence requested. In this case we want the 95 percent level of confidence, so we move to the column headed "95%." The column on the left margin is identified as "*df.*" This refers to the number of degrees of freedom. The number of degrees of freedom is the number of observations in the sample minus the number of samples, written $n - 1$.[1] In this case it is $10 - 1 = 9$. For a 95 percent level of confidence and 9 degrees of freedom, we select the row with 9 degrees of freedom. The value of $t$ is 2.262.

| | 80% | 90% | 95% | 98% | 99% |
|---|---|---|---|---|---|
| | Confidence Intervals | | | | |

| df | Level of Significance for One-Tailed Test | | | | |
|---|---|---|---|---|---|
| | 0.100 | 0.050 | 0.025 | 0.010 | 0.005 |

| | Level of Significance for Two-Tailed Test | | | | |
|---|---|---|---|---|---|
| | 0.20 | 0.10 | 0.05 | 0.02 | 0.01 |
| 1 | 3.078 | 6.314 | 12.706 | 31.821 | 63.657 |
| 2 | 1.886 | 2.920 | 4.303 | 6.965 | 9.925 |
| 3 | 1.638 | 2.353 | 3.182 | 4.541 | 5.841 |
| 4 | 1.533 | 2.132 | 2.776 | 3.747 | 4.604 |
| 5 | 1.476 | 2.015 | 2.571 | 3.365 | 4.032 |
| 6 | 1.440 | 1.943 | 2.447 | 3.143 | 3.707 |
| 7 | 1.415 | 1.895 | 2.365 | 2.998 | 3.499 |
| 8 | 1.397 | 1.860 | 2.306 | 2.896 | 3.355 |
| 9 | 1.383 | 1.833 | 2.262 | 2.821 | 3.250 |
| 10 | 1.372 | 1.812 | 2.228 | 2.764 | 3.169 |

**CHART 9–4** A Portion of the $t$ Distribution

To determine the confidence interval we substitute the values in formula (9–2).

$$\bar{X} \pm t \frac{s}{\sqrt{n}} = 0.32 \pm 2.262 \frac{0.09}{\sqrt{10}} = 0.32 \pm .064$$

The endpoints of the confidence interval are 0.256 and 0.384. How do we interpret this result? It is reasonable to conclude that the population mean is in this interval. The manufacturer can be reasonably sure (95 percent confident) that the mean remaining tread depth is between 0.256 and 0.384 inches. Because the value of 0.30 is in this interval, it is possible that the mean of the population is 0.30.

---

[1] In brief summary, because sample statistics are being used, it is necessary to determine the number of values that are *free to vary.* To illustrate: assume that the mean of four numbers is known to be 5. The four numbers are 7, 4, 1, and 8. The deviations of these numbers from the mean must total 0. The deviations of +2, −1, −4, and +3 do total 0. If the deviations of +2, −1, and −4 are known, then the value of +3 is fixed (restricted) in order to satisfy the condition that the sum of the deviations must equal 0. Thus, 1 degree of freedom is lost in a sampling problem involving the standard deviation of the sample because one number (the arithmetic mean) is known.

Here is another example to clarify the use of confidence intervals. Suppose an article in your local newspaper reported that the mean time to sell a residential property in the area is 60 days. You select a random sample of 20 homes sold in the last year and find the mean selling time is 65 days. Based on the sample data, you develop a 95 percent confidence interval for the population mean. You find that the endpoints of the confidence interval are 62 days and 68 days. How do you interpret this result? You can be reasonably confident the population mean is within this range. The value proposed for the population mean, that is, 60 days, is not included in the interval. It is not likely that the population mean is 60 days. The evidence indicates the statement by the local newspaper may not be correct. To put it another way, it seems unreasonable to obtain the sample you did from a population that had a mean selling time of 60 days.

The following example will show additional details for determining and interpreting a confidence interval. We used MINITAB to perform the calculations.

**EXAMPLE**

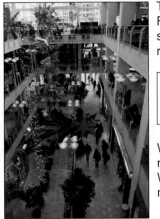

The manager of the Inlet Square Mall, near Ft. Myers, Florida, wants to estimate the mean amount spent per shopping visit by customers. A sample of 20 customers reveals the following amounts spent.

| $48.16 | $42.22 | $46.82 | $51.45 | $23.78 | $41.86 | $54.86 |
|--------|--------|--------|--------|--------|--------|--------|
| 37.92  | 52.64  | 48.59  | 50.82  | 46.94  | 61.83  | 61.69  |
| 49.17  | 61.46  | 51.35  | 52.68  | 58.84  | 43.88  |        |

What is the best estimate of the population mean? Determine a 95 percent confidence interval. Interpret the result. Would it be reasonable to conclude that the population mean is $50? What about $60?

**SOLUTION**

The mall manager assumes that the population of the amounts spent follows the normal distribution. This is a reasonable assumption in this case. Additionally, the confidence interval technique is quite powerful and tends to commit any errors on the conservative side if the population is not normal. We should not make the normality assumption when the population is severely skewed or when the distribution has "thick tails." In Chapter 16 we present methods for handling this problem if we cannot make the normality assumption. In this case, the normality assumption is reasonable.

The population standard deviation is not known and the size of the sample is less than 30. Hence, it is appropriate to use the *t* distribution and formula (9–2) to find the confidence interval. We use the MINITAB system to find the mean and standard deviation of this sample. The results are shown below.

The mall manager does not know the population mean. The sample mean is the best estimate of that value. From the above MINITAB output, the mean is $49.35, which is the best estimate, the *point estimate*, of the unknown population mean.

We use formula (9–2) to find the confidence interval. The value of $t$ is available from Appendix F. There are $n - 1 = 20 - 1 = 19$ degrees of freedom. We move across the row with 19 degrees of freedom to the column for the 95% confidence level. The value at this intersection is 2.093. We substitute these values into formula (9–2) to find the confidence interval.

$$\bar{X} \pm t \frac{s}{\sqrt{n}} = \$49.35 \pm 2.093 \frac{\$9.01}{\sqrt{20}} = \$49.35 \pm \$4.22$$

The endpoints of the confidence interval are $45.13 and $53.57. It is reasonable to conclude that the population mean is in that interval.

The manager of Inlet Square wondered whether the population mean could have been $50 or $60. The value of $50 is within the confidence interval. It is reasonable that the population mean could be $50. The value of $60 is not in the confidence interval. Hence, we conclude that the population mean is unlikely to be $60.

---

**Self-Review 9–2**

Dottie Kleman is the "Cookie Lady." She bakes and sells cookies at 50 different locations in the Philadelphia area. Ms. Kleman is concerned about absenteeism among her workers. The information below reports the number of days absent for a sample of 10 workers during the last two-week pay period.

| 4 | 1 | 2 | 2 | 1 | 2 | 2 | 1 | 0 | 3 |

(a) Determine the mean and the standard deviation of the sample.
(b) What is the population mean? What is the best estimate of that value?
(c) Develop a 95 percent confidence interval for the population mean.
(d) Explain why the $t$ distribution is used as a part of the confidence interval.
(e) Is it reasonable to conclude that the typical worker does not miss any days during a pay period?

## Exercises

9. Use Appendix F to locate the value of $t$ under the following conditions.
   a. The sample size is 12 and the level of confidence is 95 percent.
   b. The sample size is 20 and the level of confidence is 90 percent.
   c. The sample size is 8 and the level of confidence is 99 percent.
10. Use Appendix F to locate the value of $t$ under the following conditions.
   a. The sample size is 15 and the level of confidence is 95 percent.
   b. The sample size is 24 and the level of confidence is 98 percent.
   c. The sample size is 12 and the level of confidence is 90 percent.
11. The owner of Britten's Egg Farm wants to estimate the mean number of eggs laid per chicken. A sample of 20 chickens shows they laid an average of 20 eggs per month with a standard deviation of 2 eggs per month.
   a. What is the value of the population mean? What is the best estimate of this value?
   b. Explain why we need to use the $t$ distribution. What assumption do you need to make?
   c. For a 95 percent confidence interval, what is the value of $t$?
   d. Develop the 95 percent confidence interval for the population mean.
   e. Would it be reasonable to conclude that the population mean is 21 eggs? What about 25 eggs?

**12.** The American Sugar Producers Association wants to estimate the mean yearly sugar consumption. A sample of 16 people reveals the mean yearly consumption to be 60 pounds with a standard deviation of 20 pounds.
  **a.** What is the value of the population mean? What is the best estimate of this value?
  **b.** Explain why we need to use the *t* distribution. What assumption do you need to make?
  **c.** For a 90 percent confidence interval, what is the value of *t*?
  **d.** Develop the 90 percent confidence interval for the population mean.
  **e.** Would it be reasonable to conclude that the population mean is 63 pounds?
**13.** Merrill Lynch Securities and Health Care Retirement, Inc., are two large employers in downtown Toledo, Ohio. They are considering jointly offering child care for their employees. As a part of the feasibility study, they wish to estimate the mean weekly child-care cost of their employees. A sample of 10 employees who use child care reveals the following amounts spent last week.

| $107 | $92 | $97 | $95 | $105 | $101 | $91 | $99 | $95 | $104 |
|------|-----|-----|-----|------|------|-----|-----|-----|------|

Develop a 90 percent confidence interval for the population mean. Interpret the result.

**14.** The Greater Pittsburgh Area Chamber of Commerce wants to estimate the mean time workers who are employed in the downtown area spend getting to work. A sample of 15 workers reveals the following number of minutes traveled.

| 29 | 38 | 38 | 33 | 38 | 21 | 45 | 34 |
|----|----|----|----|----|----|----|----|
| 40 | 37 | 37 | 42 | 30 | 29 | 35 |    |

Develop a 98 percent confidence interval for the population mean. Interpret the result.

# A Confidence Interval for a Proportion

The material presented so far in this chapter uses the ratio scale of measurement. That is, we use such variables as incomes, weights, distances, and ages. We now want to consider situations such as the following:

- The career services director at Southern Technical Institute reports that 80 percent of its graduates enter the job market in a position related to their field of study.
- A company representative claims that 45 percent of Burger King sales are made at the drive-through window.
- A survey of homes in the Chicago area indicated that 85 percent of the new construction had central air conditioning.
- A recent survey of married men between the ages of 35 and 50 found that 63 percent felt that both partners should earn a living.

These examples illustrate the nominal scale of measurement. In the nominal scale an observation is classified into one of two or more mutually exclusive groups. For example, a graduate of Southern Tech either entered the job market in a position related to his or her field of study or not. A particular Burger King customer either made a purchase at the drive-through window or did not make a purchase at the drive-through window. There are only two possibilities, and the outcome must be classified into one of the two groups.

> **PROPORTION** The fraction, ratio, or percent indicating the part of the sample or the population having a particular trait of interest.

**Statistics In Action**

Many survey results reported in newspapers, in news magazines, and on TV use confidence intervals. For example, a recent survey of 800 TV viewers in Toledo, Ohio, found 44 percent watched the evening news on the local CBS affiliate. The article went on to indicate the margin of error was 3.4 percent. The margin of error is actually the amount that is added and subtracted from the point estimate to find the endpoints of a confidence interval. From formula (9–6) and the 95 percent level of confidence:

$$z\sqrt{\frac{p(1-p)}{n}}$$

$$= 1.96\sqrt{\frac{.44(1-44)}{800}}$$

$$= 0.034$$

As an example of a proportion, a recent survey indicated that 92 out of 100 surveyed favored the continued use of daylight savings time in the summer. The sample proportion is 92/100, or .92, or 92 percent. If we let $p$ represent the sample proportion, $X$ the number of "successes," and $n$ the number of items sampled, we can determine a sample proportion as follows.

| SAMPLE PROPORTION | $p = \dfrac{X}{n}$ | [9–3] |
|---|---|---|

The population proportion is identified by $\pi$. Therefore, $\pi$ refers to the percent of successes in the population. Recall from Chapter 6 that $\pi$ is the proportion of "successes" in a binomial distribution. This continues our practice of using Greek letters to identify population parameters and Roman letters to identify sample statistics.

To develop a confidence interval for a proportion, we need to meet the following assumptions.

1. The binomial conditions, discussed in Chapter 6, have been met. Briefly, these conditions are:
   a. The sample data is the result of counts.
   b. There are only two possible outcomes. (We usually label one of the outcomes a "success" and the other a "failure.")
   c. The probability of a success remains the same from one trial to the next.
   d. The trials are independent. This means the outcome on one trial does not affect the outcome on another.
2. The values $n\pi$ and $n(1-\pi)$ should both be greater than or equal to 5. This condition allows us to invoke the central limit theorem and employ the standard normal distribution, that is, $z$, to complete a confidence interval.

Developing a point estimate for a population proportion and a confidence interval for a population proportion is similar to doing so for a mean. To illustrate, John Gail is running for Congress from the third district of Nebraska. From a random sample of 100 voters in the district, 60 indicate they plan to vote for him in the upcoming election. The sample proportion is .60, but the population proportion is unknown. That is, we do not know what proportion of voters in the *population* will vote for Mr. Gail. The sample value, .60, is the best estimate we have of the unknown population parameter. So we let $p$, which is .60, be an estimate of $\pi$, which is not known.

To develop a confidence interval for a population proportion, we change formula (9–1) slightly:

| CONFIDENCE INTERVAL FOR A POPULATION PROPORTION | $p \pm z\sigma_p$ | [9–4] |
|---|---|---|

The term $\sigma_p$ is the "standard error" of the proportion. It measures the variability in the sampling distribution of the sample proportion.

| STANDARD ERROR OF THE SAMPLE PROPORTION | $\sigma_p = \sqrt{\dfrac{p(1-p)}{n}}$ | [9–5] |
|---|---|---|

We can then construct a confidence interval for a population proportion from the following formula.

| CONFIDENCE INTERVAL FOR A POPULATION PROPORTION | $p \pm z\sqrt{\dfrac{p(1-p)}{n}}$ | [9–6] |
|---|---|---|

**EXAMPLE**

The union representing the Bottle Blowers of America (BBA) is considering a proposal to merge with the Teamsters Union. According to BBA union bylaws, at least three-fourths of the union membership must approve any merger. A random sample of 2,000 current BBA members reveals 1,600 plan to vote for the merger proposal. What is the estimate of the population proportion? Develop a 95 percent confidence interval for the population proportion. Basing your decision on this sample information, can you conclude that the necessary proportion of BBA members favor the merger? Why?

**SOLUTION**

First, calculate the sample proportion from formula (9–3). It is .80, found by

$$p = \frac{X}{n} = \frac{1{,}600}{2{,}000} = .80$$

Thus, we estimate that 80 percent of the population favor the merger proposal. We determine the 95 percent confidence interval using formula (9–6). The z value corresponding to the 95 percent level of confidence is 1.96.

$$p \pm z \sqrt{\frac{p(1-p)}{n}} = .80 \pm 1.96 \sqrt{\frac{.80(1-.80)}{2{,}000}} = .80 \pm .018$$

The endpoints of the confidence interval are .782 and .818. The lower endpoint is greater than .75. Hence, we conclude that the merger proposal will likely pass because the interval estimate includes values greater than 75 percent of the union membership.

**Self-Review 9–3**

A market survey was conducted to estimate the proportion of homemakers who would recognize the brand name of a cleanser based on the shape and the color of the container. Of the 1,400 homemakers sampled, 420 were able to identify the brand by name.
(a) Estimate the value of the population proportion.
(b) Compute the standard error of the proportion.
(c) Develop a 99 percent confidence interval for the population proportion.
(d) Interpret your findings.

# Exercises

15. The owner of the West End Kwick Fill Gas Station wished to determine the proportion of customers who use a credit card or debit card to pay at the pump. He surveys 100 customers and finds that 80 paid at the pump.
    **a.** Estimate the value of the population proportion.
    **b.** Compute the standard error of the proportion.
    **c.** Develop a 95 percent confidence interval for the population proportion.
    **d.** Interpret your findings.
16. Ms. Maria Wilson is considering running for mayor of the town of Bear Gulch, Montana. Before completing the petitions, she decides to conduct a survey of voters in Bear Gulch. A sample of 400 voters reveals that 300 would support her in the November election.
    **a.** Estimate the value of the population proportion.
    **b.** Compute the standard error of the proportion.
    **c.** Develop a 99 percent confidence interval for the population proportion.
    **d.** Interpret your findings.
17. The Fox TV network is considering replacing one of its prime-time crime investigation shows with a new family-oriented comedy show. Before a final decision is made, network executives commission a sample of 400 viewers. After viewing the comedy, 250 indicated they would watch the new show and suggested it replace the crime investigation show.
    **a.** Estimate the value of the population proportion.
    **b.** Compute the standard error of the proportion.
    **c.** Develop a 99 percent confidence interval for the population proportion.
    **d.** Interpret your findings.

**18.** Schadek Silkscreen Printing, Inc. purchases plastic cups on which to print logos for sporting events, proms, birthdays, and other special occasions. Zack Schadek, the owner, received a large shipment this morning. To ensure the quality of the shipment, he selected a random sample of 300 cups. He found 15 to be defective.
  **a.** What is the estimated proportion defective in the population?
  **b.** Develop a 95 percent confidence interval for the proportion defective.
  **c.** Zack has an agreement with his supplier that he is to return lots that are 10 percent or more defective. Should he return this lot? Explain your decision.

# Finite-Population Correction Factor

The populations we have sampled so far have been very large or infinite. What if the sampled population is not very large? We need to make some adjustments in the way we compute the standard error of the sample means and the standard error of the sample proportions.

A population that has a fixed upper bound is *finite.* For example, there are 21,376 students enrolled at Eastern Illinois University, there are 40 employees at Spence Sprockets, DaimlerChrysler assembled 917 Jeep Wranglers at the Alexis Avenue plant yesterday, or there were 65 surgical patients at St. Rose Memorial Hospital in Sarasota yesterday. A finite population can be rather small; it could be all the students registered for this class. It can also be very large, such as all senior citizens living in Florida.

For a finite population, where the total number of objects is *N* and the size of the sample is *n,* the following adjustment is made to the standard errors of the sample means and proportions:

| | | |
|---|---|---|
| STANDARD ERROR OF THE SAMPLE MEAN, USING A FINITE POPULATION CORRECTION FACTOR | $\sigma_{\bar{x}} = \dfrac{\sigma}{\sqrt{n}} \sqrt{\dfrac{N - n}{N - 1}}$ | **[9–7]** |

| | | |
|---|---|---|
| STANDARD ERROR OF THE SAMPLE PROPORTION, USING A FINITE POPULATION CORRECTION FACTOR | $\sigma_p = \sqrt{\dfrac{p(1 - p)}{n}} \sqrt{\dfrac{N - n}{N - 1}}$ | **[9–8]** |

This adjustment is called the **finite-population correction factor.** Why is it necessary to apply a factor, and what is its effect? Logically, if the sample is a substantial percentage of the population, the estimate is more precise. Note the effect of the term $(N - n)/(N - 1)$. Suppose the population is 1,000 and the sample is 100. Then this ratio is $(1,000 - 100)/(1,000 - 1)$, or 900/999. Taking the square root gives the correction factor, .9492. Multiplying this correction factor by the standard error *reduces* the standard error by about 5 percent $(1 - .9492 = .0508)$. This reduction in the size of the standard error yields a smaller range of values in estimating the population mean or the population proportion. If the sample is 200, the correction factor is .8949, meaning that the standard error has been reduced by more than 10 percent. Table 9–1

**TABLE 9–1** Finite-Population Correction Factor for Selected Samples When the Population Is 1,000

| Sample Size | Fraction of Population | Correction Factor |
|---|---|---|
| 10 | .010 | .9955 |
| 25 | .025 | .9879 |
| 50 | .050 | .9752 |
| 100 | .100 | .9492 |
| 200 | .200 | .8949 |
| 500 | .500 | .7075 |

shows the effects of various sample sizes. Note that when the sample is less than about 5 percent of the population, the impact of the correction factor is quite small. The usual rule is if the ratio of $n/N$ is less than .05, the correction factor is ignored.

**EXAMPLE**

There are 250 families in Scandia, Pennsylvania. A poll of 40 families reveals the mean annual church contribution is $450 with a standard deviation of $75. Construct a 90 percent confidence interval for the mean annual contribution.

**SOLUTION**

First, note that the population is finite. That is, there is a limit to the number of people in Scandia. Second, note that the sample constitutes more than 5 percent of the population; that is, $n/N = 40/250 = .16$. Hence, we use the finite-population correction factor. The 90 percent confidence interval is constructed as follows, using formula (9–7).

$$\bar{X} \pm z\frac{s}{\sqrt{n}}\left(\sqrt{\frac{N-n}{N-1}}\right) = \$450 \pm 1.65\frac{\$75}{\sqrt{40}}\left(\sqrt{\frac{250-40}{250-1}}\right) = \$450 \pm \$19.57(\sqrt{.8434})$$

$$= \$450 \pm \$17.97$$

The endpoints of the confidence interval are $432.03 and $467.97. It is likely that the population mean falls within this interval.

---

**Self-Review 9–4**

The same study of church contributions in Scandia revealed that 15 of the 40 families sampled attend church regularly. Construct the 95 percent confidence interval for the proportion of families attending church regularly. Should the finite-population correction factor be used? Why or why not?

## Exercises

**19.** Thirty-six items are randomly selected from a population of 300 items. The sample mean is 35 and the sample standard deviation 5. Develop a 95 percent confidence interval for the population mean.

**20.** Forty-nine items are randomly selected from a population of 500 items. The sample mean is 40 and the sample standard deviation 9. Develop a 99 percent confidence interval for the population mean.

**21.** The attendance at the Savannah Colts minor league baseball game last night was 400. A random sample of 50 of those in attendance revealed that the mean number of soft drinks consumed per person was 1.86 with a standard deviation of 0.50. Develop a 99 percent confidence interval for the mean number of soft drinks consumed per person.

**22.** There are 300 welders employed at the Maine Shipyards Corporation. A sample of 30 welders revealed that 18 graduated from a registered welding course. Construct the 95 percent confidence interval for the proportion of all welders who graduated from a registered welding course.

## Choosing an Appropriate Sample Size

A concern that usually arises when designing a statistical study is "How many items should be in the sample?" If a sample is too large, money is wasted collecting the data. Similarly, if the sample is too small, the resulting conclusions will be uncertain. The necessary sample size depends on three factors:

1.  The level of confidence desired.
2.  The margin of error the researcher will tolerate.
3.  The variability in the population being studied.

The first factor is the *level of confidence*. Those conducting the study select the level of confidence. The 95 percent and the 99 percent levels of confidence are the most common, but any value between 0 and 100 percent is possible. The 95 percent level of confidence corresponds to a *z* value of 1.96, and a 99 percent level of confidence corresponds to a *z* value of 2.58. The higher the level of confidence selected, the larger the size of the corresponding sample.

The second factor is the *allowable error*. The maximum allowable error, designated as *E,* is the amount that is added and subtracted to the sample mean (or sample proportion) to determine the endpoints of the confidence interval. It is the amount of error those conducting the study are willing to tolerate. It is also one-half the width of the corresponding confidence interval. A small allowable error will require a large sample. A large allowable error will permit a smaller sample.

The third factor in determining the size of a sample is the *population standard deviation*. If the population is widely dispersed, a large sample is required. On the other hand, if the population is concentrated (homogeneous), the required sample size will be smaller. However, it may be necessary to use an estimate for the population standard deviation. Here are three suggestions for finding that estimate.

1. **Use a comparable study.** Use this approach when there is an estimate of the dispersion available from another study. Suppose we want to estimate the number of hours worked per week by refuse workers. Information from certain state or federal agencies who regularly sample the workforce might be useful to provide an estimate of the standard deviation. If a standard deviation observed in a previous study is thought to be reliable, it can be used in the current study to help provide an approximate sample size.

2. **Use a range-based approach.** To use this approach we need to know or have an estimate of the largest and smallest values in the population. Recall from Chapter 3, where we described the Empirical Rule, that virtually all the observations could be expected to be within plus or minus 3 standard deviations of the mean, assuming that the distribution was approximately normal. Thus, the distance between the largest and the smallest values is 6 standard deviations. We could estimate the standard deviation as one-sixth of the range. For example, the director of operations at University Bank wants an estimate of the number of checks written per month by college students. She believes that the distribution is approximately normal, the minimum number of checks written is 2 per month, and the most is 50 per month. The range of the number of checks written per month is 48, found by $50 - 2$. The estimate of the standard deviation then would be 8 checks per month, 48/6.

3. **Conduct a pilot study.** This is the most common method. Suppose we want an estimate of the number of hours per week worked by students enrolled in the College of Business at the University of Texas. To test the validity of our questionnaire, we use it on a small sample of students. From this small sample we compute the standard deviation of the number of hours worked and use this value to determine the appropriate sample size.

We can express the interaction among these three factors and the sample size in the following formula.

$$E = z \frac{s}{\sqrt{n}}$$

Solving this equation for *n* yields the following result.

| SAMPLE SIZE FOR ESTIMATING THE POPULATION MEAN | $n = \left( \dfrac{zs}{E} \right)^2$ | [9–9] |
|---|---|---|

where:

> $n$ is the size of the sample.
> $z$ is the standard normal value corresponding to the desired level of confidence.
> $s$ is an estimate of the population standard deviation.
> $E$ is the maximum allowable error.

The result of this calculation is not always a whole number. When the outcome is not a whole number, the usual practice is to round up *any* fractional result. For example, 201.22 would be rounded up to 202.

**EXAMPLE**

A student in public administration wants to determine the mean amount members of city councils in large cities earn per month as remuneration for being a council member. The error in estimating the mean is to be less than $100 with a 95 percent level of confidence. The student found a report by the Department of Labor that estimated the standard deviation to be $1,000. What is the required sample size?

**SOLUTION**

The maximum allowable error, $E$, is $100. The value of $z$ for a 95 percent level of confidence is 1.96, and the estimate of the standard deviation is $1,000. Substituting these values into formula (9–9) gives the required sample size as:

$$n = \left(\frac{zs}{E}\right)^2 = \left(\frac{(1.96)(\$1,000)}{\$100}\right)^2 = (19.6)^2 = 384.16$$

The computed value of 384.16 is rounded up to 385. A sample of 385 is required to meet the specifications. If the student wants to increase the level of confidence, for example to 99 percent, this will require a larger sample. The $z$ value corresponding to the 99 percent level of confidence is 2.58.

$$n = \left(\frac{zs}{E}\right)^2 = \left(\frac{(2.58)(\$1,000)}{\$100}\right)^2 = (25.8)^2 = 665.64$$

We recommend a sample of 666. Observe how much the change in the confidence level changed the size of the sample. An increase from the 95 percent to the 99 percent level of confidence resulted in an increase of 281 observations. This could greatly increase the cost of the study, both in terms of time and money. Hence, the level of confidence should be considered carefully.

The procedure just described can be adapted to determine the sample size for a proportion. Again, three items need to be specified:

1. The desired level of confidence.
2. The margin of error in the population proportion.
3. An estimate of the population proportion.

The formula to determine the sample size of a proportion is:

| SAMPLE SIZE FOR THE POPULATION PROPORTION | $n = p(1 - p)\left(\frac{z}{E}\right)^2$ | [9–10] |
|---|---|---|

If an estimate of $\pi$ is available from a pilot study or some other source, it can be used. Otherwise, .50 is used because the term $p(1 - p)$ can never be larger than when $p = .50$. For example, if $p = .30$, then $p(1 - p) = .3(1 - 3) = .21$, but when $p = .50$, $p(1 - p) = .5(1 - 5) = .25$

**EXAMPLE**

The study in the previous example also estimates the proportion of cities that have private refuse collectors. The student wants the estimate to be within .10 of the population proportion, the desired level of confidence is 90 percent, and no estimate is available for the population proportion. What is the required sample size?

**SOLUTION**

The estimate of the population proportion is to be within .10, so $E = .10$. The desired level of confidence is .90, which corresponds to a $z$ value of 1.65. Because no estimate of the population proportion is available, we use .50. The suggested number of observations is

$$n = (.5)(1 - .5)\left(\frac{1.65}{.10}\right)^2 = 68.0625$$

The student needs a random sample of 69 cities.

**Self-Review 9–5**

Will you assist the college registrar in determining how many transcripts to study? The registrar wants to estimate the arithmetic mean grade point average (GPA) of all graduating seniors during the past 10 years. GPAs range between 2.0 and 4.0. The mean GPA is to be estimated within plus or minus .05 of the population mean. The standard deviation is estimated to be 0.279. Use the 99 percent level of confidence.

## Exercises

**23.** A population is estimated to have a standard deviation of 10. We want to estimate the population mean within 2, with a 95 percent level of confidence. How large a sample is required?

**24.** We want to estimate the population mean within 5, with a 99 percent level of confidence. The population standard deviation is estimated to be 15. How large a sample is required?

**25.** The estimate of the population proportion is to be within plus or minus .05, with a 95 percent level of confidence. The best estimate of the population proportion is .15. How large a sample is required?

**26.** The estimate of the population proportion is to be within plus or minus .10, with a 99 percent level of confidence. The best estimate of the population proportion is .45. How large a sample is required?

**27.** A survey is being planned to determine the mean amount of time corporation executives watch television. A pilot survey indicated that the mean time per week is 12 hours, with a standard deviation of 3 hours. It is desired to estimate the mean viewing time within one-quarter hour. The 95 percent level of confidence is to be used. How many executives should be surveyed?

**28.** A processor of carrots cuts the green top off each carrot, washes the carrots, and inserts six to a package. Twenty packages are inserted in a box for shipment. To test the weight of the boxes, a few were checked. The mean weight was 20.4 pounds, the standard deviation 0.5 pounds. How many boxes must the processor sample to be 95 percent confident that the sample mean does not differ from the population mean by more than 0.2 pounds?

**29.** Suppose the President wants an estimate of the proportion of the population who support his current policy toward gun control. The President wants the estimate to be within .04 of the true proportion. Assume a 95 percent level of confidence. The President's political advisors estimated the proportion supporting the current policy to be .60.
   **a.** How large of a sample is required?
   **b.** How large of a sample would be necessary if no estimate were available for the proportion that support current policy?

**30.** Past surveys reveal that 30 percent of tourists going to Las Vegas to gamble during a weekend spend more than $1,000. Management wants to update this percentage.
   **a.** The new study is to use the 90 percent confidence level. The estimate is to be within 1 percent of the population proportion. What is the necessary sample size?
   **b.** Management said that the sample size determined above is too large. What can be done to reduce the sample? Based on your suggestion recalculate the sample size.

# Chapter Outline

**I.** A point estimate is a single value (statistic) used to estimate a population value (parameter).

**II.** A confidence interval is a range of values within which the population parameter is expected to occur.

 **A.** The factors that determine the width of a confidence interval for a mean are:

  **1.** The number of observations in the sample, $n$.

  **2.** The variability in the population, usually estimated by the sample standard deviation, $s$.

  **3.** The level of confidence.

   **a.** To determine the confidence limits when the population standard deviation is known or the sample is 30 or more, we use the $z$ distribution. The formula is

$$\overline{X} \pm z \frac{s}{\sqrt{n}} \qquad \textbf{[9–1]}$$

   **b.** To determine the confidence limits when the population standard deviation is unknown and the sample is less than 30, we use the $t$ distribution. The formula is

$$\overline{X} \pm t \frac{s}{\sqrt{n}} \qquad \textbf{[9–2]}$$

**III.** The major characteristics of the $t$ distribution are:

 **A.** It is a continuous distribution.

 **B.** It is mound-shaped and symmetrical.

 **C.** It is flatter, or more spread out, than the standard normal distribution.

 **D.** There is a family of $t$ distributions, depending on the number of degrees of freedom.

**IV.** A proportion is a ratio, fraction, or percent that indicates the part of the sample or population that has a particular characteristic.

 **A.** A sample proportion is found by $X$, the number of successes, divided by $n$, the number of observations.

 **B.** The standard error of the sample proportion reports the variability in the distribution of sample proportions. It is found by

$$\sigma_p = \sqrt{\frac{p(1 - p)}{n}} \qquad \textbf{[9–5]}$$

 **C.** We construct a confidence interval for a sample proportion from the following formula.

$$p \pm z \sqrt{\frac{p(1 - p)}{n}} \qquad \textbf{[9–6]}$$

**V.** We can determine an appropriate sample size for estimating both means and proportions.

 **A.** There are three factors that determine the sample size when we wish to estimate the mean.

  **1.** The desired level of confidence, which is usually expressed by $z$.

  **2.** The maximum allowable error, $E$.

  **3.** The variation in the population, expressed by $s$.

  **4.** The formula to determine the sample size for the mean is

$$n = \left(\frac{zs}{E}\right)^2 \qquad \textbf{[9–9]}$$

 **B.** There are three factors that determine the sample size when we wish to estimate a proportion.

  **1.** The desired level of confidence, which is usually expressed by $z$.

  **2.** The maximum allowable error, $E$.

  **3.** An estimate of the population proportion. If no estimate is available, use .50.

  **4.** The formula to determine the sample size for a proportion is

$$n = p(1 - p)\left(\frac{z}{E}\right)^2 \qquad \textbf{[9–10]}$$

**VI.** For a finite population, the standard error is adjusted by the factor $\sqrt{\dfrac{N - n}{N - 1}}$.

# Pronunciation Key

| SYMBOL | MEANING | PRONUNCIATION |
|---|---|---|
| $\sigma_{\bar{x}}$ | The standard error of the sample means | *sigma sub X bar* |
| $\sigma_p$ | Standard error of the sample proportion | *sigma sub p* |

# Chapter Exercises

31. A random sample of 85 group leaders, supervisors, and similar personnel at General Motors revealed that, on the average, they spent 6.5 years on the job before being promoted. The standard deviation of the sample was 1.7 years. Construct a 95 percent confidence interval.

32. A state meat inspector in Iowa has been given the assignment of estimating the mean net weight of packages of ground chuck labeled "3 pounds." Of course, he realizes that the weights cannot be precisely 3 pounds. A sample of 36 packages reveals the mean weight to be 3.01 pounds, with a standard deviation of 0.03 pounds.
    a. What is the estimated population mean?
    b. Determine a 95 percent confidence interval for the population mean.

33. A recent study of 50 self-service gasoline stations in the Greater Cincinnati–Northern Kentucky metropolitan area revealed that the mean price of unleaded gas was $1.519 per gallon. The sample standard deviation was $0.03 per gallon.
    a. Determine a 99 percent confidence interval for the population mean price.
    b. Would it be reasonable to conclude that the population mean was $1.50? Why or why not?

34. A recent survey of 50 executives who were laid off from their previous position revealed it took a mean of 26 weeks for them to find another position. The standard deviation of the sample was 6.2 weeks. Construct a 95 percent confidence interval for the population mean. Is it reasonable that the population mean is 28 weeks? Justify your answer.

35. The Badik Construction Company limits its business to constructing decks. The mean time to construct one of their standard decks is 8 hours for a two-person construction crew. The information is based on a sample of 40 decks recently constructed. The standard deviation of the sample was 3 hours.
    a. Determine a 90 percent confidence interval for the population mean.
    b. Would it be reasonable to conclude that the population mean is actually 9 hours? Justify your answer.

36. The American Restaurant Association collected information on the number of meals eaten outside the home per week by young married couples. A survey of 60 couples showed the sample mean number of meals eaten outside the home was 2.76 meals per week, with a standard deviation of 0.75 meals per week. Construct a 97 percent confidence interval for the population mean.

37. The National Collegiate Athletic Association (NCAA) reported that the mean number of hours spent per week on coaching and recruiting by college football assistant coaches during the season is 70. A random sample of 50 assistant coaches showed the sample mean to be 68.6 hours, with a standard deviation of 8.2 hours.
    a. Using the sample data, construct a 99 percent confidence interval for the population mean.
    b. Does the 99 percent confidence interval include the value suggested by the NCAA? Interpret this result.
    c. Suppose you decided to switch from a 99 to a 95 percent confidence interval. Without performing any calculations, will the interval increase, decrease, or stay the same? Which of the values in the formula will change?

38. The Human Relations Department of Electronics, Inc., would like to include a dental plan as part of the benefits package. The question is: How much does a typical employee and his or her family spend per year on dental expenses? A sample of 45 employees reveals the mean amount spent last year was $1,820, with a standard deviation of $660.
    a. Construct a 95 percent confidence interval for the population mean.
    b. The information from part (a) was given to the president of Electronics, Inc. He indicated he could afford $1,700 of dental expenses per employee. Is it possible that the population mean could be $1,700? Justify your answer.

**39.** A student conducted a study and reported that the 95 percent confidence interval for the mean ranged from 46 to 54. He was sure that the mean of the sample was 50, that the standard deviation of the sample was 16, and that the sample was at least 30, but could not remember the exact number. Can you help him out?

**40.** A recent study by the American Automobile Dealers Association revealed the mean amount of profit per car sold for a sample of 20 dealers was $290, with a standard deviation of $125. Develop a 95 percent confidence interval for the population mean.

**41.** A study of 25 graduates of four-year colleges by the American Banker's Association revealed the mean amount owed by a student in student loans was $14,381. The standard deviation of the sample was $1,892. Construct a 90 percent confidence interval for the population mean. Is it reasonable to conclude that the mean of the population is actually $15,000? Tell why or why not.

**42.** An important factor in selling a residential property is the number of people who look through the home. A sample of 15 homes recently sold in the Buffalo, New York, area revealed the mean number looking through each home was 24 and the standard deviation of the sample was 5 people. Develop a 98 percent confidence interval for the population mean.

**43.** The Warren County Telephone Company claims in its annual report that "the typical customer spends $60 per month on local and long distance service." A sample of 12 subscribers revealed the following amounts spent last month.

| $64 | $66 | $64 | $66 | $59 | $62 | $67 | $61 | $64 | $58 | $54 | $66 |
|-----|-----|-----|-----|-----|-----|-----|-----|-----|-----|-----|-----|

**a.** What is the point estimate of the population mean?
**b.** Develop a 90 percent confidence interval for the population mean.
**c.** Is the company's claim that the "typical customer" spends $60 per month reasonable? Justify your answer.

**44.** The manufacturer of a new line of ink jet printers would like to include as part of their advertising the number of pages a user can expect from a print cartridge. A sample of 10 cartridges revealed the following number of pages printed.

| 2,698 | 2,028 | 2,474 | 2,395 | 2,372 | 2,475 | 1,927 | 3,006 | 2,334 | 2,379 |
|-------|-------|-------|-------|-------|-------|-------|-------|-------|-------|

**a.** What is the point estimate of the population mean?
**b.** Develop a 95 percent confidence interval for the population mean.

**45.** Dr. Susan Benner is an industrial psychologist. She is currently studying stress among executives of Internet companies. She has developed a questionnaire that she believes measures stress. A score above 80 indicates stress at a dangerous level. A random sample of 15 executives revealed the following stress level scores.

| 94 | 78 | 83 | 90 | 78 | 99 | 97 | 90 | 97 | 90 | 93 | 94 | 100 | 75 | 84 |
|----|----|----|----|----|----|----|----|----|----|----|----|-----|----|----|

**a.** Find the mean stress level for this sample. What is the point estimate of the population mean?
**b.** Construct a 95 percent confidence level for the population mean.
**c.** Is it reasonable to conclude that Internet executives have a mean stress level in the dangerous level, according to Dr. Benner's test?

**46.** Furniture Land South surveyed 600 consumers and found that 414 were enthusiastic about a new home décor they plan to show in their store in High Point, North Carolina. Construct the 99 percent confidence interval for the population proportion.

**47.** There are 20,000 eligible voters in York County, South Carolina. A random sample of 500 York County voters revealed 350 plan to vote to return Louella Miller to the state senate. Construct a 99 percent confidence interval for the proportion of voters in the county who plan to vote for Ms. Miller. From this sample information, can you confirm she will be reelected?

**48.** In a poll to estimate presidential popularity, each person in a random sample of 1,000 voters was asked to agree with one of the following statements:
  **1.** The President is doing a good job.
  **2.** The President is doing a poor job.
  **3.** I have no opinion.

A total of 560 respondents selected the first statement, indicating they thought the President was doing a good job.

   **a.** Construct a 95 percent confidence interval for the proportion of respondents who feel the President is doing a good job.

   **b.** Based on your interval in part (a), is it reasonable to conclude that a majority (more than half) of the population believes the President is doing a good job?

**49.** Police Chief Aaron Ard of River City reports 500 traffic citations were issued last month. A sample of 35 of these citations showed the mean amount of the fine was $54, with a standard deviation of $4.50. Construct a 95 percent confidence interval for the mean amount of a citation in River City.

**50.** The First National Bank of Wilson has 650 checking account customers. A recent sample of 50 of these customers showed 26 to have a Visa card with the bank. Construct the 99 percent confidence interval for the proportion of checking account customers who have a Visa card with the bank.

**51.** It is estimated that 60 percent of U.S. households subscribe to cable TV. You would like to verify this statement for your class in mass communications. If you want your estimate to be within 5 percentage points, with a 95 percent level of confidence, how large of a sample is required?

**52.** You need to estimate the mean number of travel days per year for outside salespeople. The mean of a small pilot study was 150 days, with a standard deviation of 14 days. If you must estimate the population mean within 2 days, how many outside salespeople should you sample? Use the 90 percent confidence level.

**53.** You are to conduct a sample survey to determine the mean family income in a rural area of central Florida. The question is, how many families should be sampled? In a pilot sample of 10 families, the standard deviation of the sample was $500. The sponsor of the survey wants you to use the 95 percent confidence level. The estimate is to be within $100. How many families should be interviewed?

**54.** You plan to conduct a survey to find what proportion of the workforce has two or more jobs. You decide on the 95 percent confidence level and state that the estimated proportion must be within 2 percent of the population proportion. A pilot survey reveals that 5 of the 50 sampled hold two or more jobs. How many in the workforce should be interviewed to meet your requirements?

**55.** The proportion of public accountants who have changed companies within the last three years is to be estimated within 3 percent. The 95 percent level of confidence is to be used. A study conducted several years ago revealed that the percent of public accountants changing companies within three years was 21.

   **a.** To update this study, the files of how many public accountants should be studied?

   **b.** How many public accountants should be contacted if no previous estimates of the population proportion are available?

**56.** The Huntington National Bank, like most other large banks, found that using automatic teller machines (ATMs) reduces the cost of routine bank transactions. Huntington installed an ATM in the corporate offices of the Fun Toy Company. The ATM is for the exclusive use of Fun's 605 employees. After several months of operation, a sample of 100 employees revealed the following use of the ATM machine by Fun employees in a month.

| Number of Times ATM Used | Frequency |
| --- | --- |
| 0 | 25 |
| 1 | 30 |
| 2 | 20 |
| 3 | 10 |
| 4 | 10 |
| 5 | 5 |

   **a.** What is the estimate of the proportion of employees who do not use the ATM in a month?

   **b.** Develop a 95 percent confidence interval for this estimate. Can Huntington be sure that at least 40 percent of the employees of Fun Toy Company will use the ATM?

   **c.** How many transactions does the average Fun employee make per month?

   **d.** Develop a 95 percent confidence interval for the mean number of transactions per month.

   **e.** Is it possible that the population mean is 0? Explain.

**57.** In a recent Zogby poll of 1,000 adults nationwide, 613 said they believe other forms of life exist elsewhere in the universe. Construct the 99 percent confidence interval for the population proportion of those believing life exists elsewhere in the universe. Does your result imply that a majority of Americans believe life exists outside of Earth?

**58.** As part of an annual review of its accounts, a discount brokerage selects a random sample of 36 customers. Their accounts are reviewed for total account valuation, which showed a mean of $32,000, with a sample standard deviation of $8,200. What is a 90 percent confidence interval for the mean account valuation of the population of customers?

**59.** A sample of 352 subscribers to *Wired* magazine shows the mean time spent using the Internet is 13.4 hours per week, with a sample standard deviation of 6.8 hours. Find the 95 percent confidence interval for the mean time *Wired* subscribers spend on the Internet.

**60.** The Tennessee Tourism Institute (TTI) plans to sample information center visitors entering the state to learn the fraction of visitors who plan to camp in the state. Current estimates are that 35 percent of visitors are campers. How large a sample would you take to estimate at a 95 percent confidence level the population proportion with an allowable error of 2 percent?

# exercises.com

**61.** Hoover is an excellent source of business information. It includes daily summaries as well as information about various industries and specific companies. Go to the site at www.hoovers.com. Click on **Companies and Industries.** Then, click on **Industries** in the next menu, then go to **Sector** and select an **Industry Sector,** such as chemicals or retail. Then, select an industry within the sector. For example, **Chemicals—Diversified** is an industry within the **Chemicals** sector. This should give you a list of companies. Use a table of random numbers, such as Appendix E, to randomly select 5 to 10 companies in the list. Click on **Capsule,** and then the **Financials** tab to get information about the selected companies. One suggestion is to find the earnings per share. Compute the mean of each sample, and then develop a confidence interval for the mean earnings per share. Because the sample is a large part of the population, you will want to include the correction factor. Interpret the result.

**62.** The online edition of the *Information Please Almanac* is a valuable source of business information. Go to the Website at www.infoplease.com. Click on **Business.** Then in the **Almanac Section,** click on **Taxes,** then click on **State Taxes on Individuals.** The result is a listing of the 50 states and the District of Columbia. Use a table of random numbers to randomly select 5 to 10 states. Compute the mean state tax rate on individuals. Develop a confidence interval for the mean amount. Because the sample is a large part of the population, you will want to include the finite population correction factor. Interpret your result. You might, as an additional exercise, download all the information and use Excel or MINITAB to compute the population mean. Compare that value with the results of your confidence interval.

# Dataset Exercises

**63.** Refer to the Real Estate data, which reports information on the homes sold in Denver, Colorado, last year.
   **a.** Develop a 95 percent confidence interval for the mean selling price of the homes.
   **b.** Develop a 95 percent confidence interval for the mean distance the home is from the center of the city.
   **c.** Develop a 95 percent confidence interval for the proportion of homes with an attached garage.

**64.** Refer to the Baseball 2002 data, which reports information on the 30 Major League Baseball teams for the 2002 season.
   **a.** Develop a 95 percent confidence interval for the mean number of home runs per team.
   **b.** Develop a 95 percent confidence interval for the mean number of errors committed by each team.
   **c.** Develop a 95 percent confidence interval for the mean number of stolen bases for each team.

**65.** Refer to the Wage data, which reports information on annual wages for a sample of 100 workers. Also included are variables relating to industry, years of education, and gender for each worker.
   **a.** Develop a 95 percent confidence interval for the mean wage of the workers. Is it reasonable to conclude that the population mean is $35,000?

    **b.** Develop a 95 percent confidence interval for the mean years of education. Is it reasonable that the population mean is 13 years?

    **c.** Develop a 95 percent confidence interval for the mean age of the workers. Could the mean age be 40 years?

**66.** Refer to the CIA data, which reports demographic and economic information on 46 countries.

    **a.** Develop a 90 percent confidence interval for the mean percent of the population over 65 years.

    **b.** Develop a 90 percent confidence interval for the mean Gross Domestic Product (GDP) per capita.

    **c.** Develop a 90 percent confidence interval for the mean imports.

# Software Commands

**1.** The MINITAB commands for the 60 columns of 30 random numbers used in the Example/Solution on page 289 are:

    **a.** Select **Calc, Random Data,** and then click on **Normal.**

    **b.** From the dialog box click on **Generate** and type *30* for the number of rows of data, **Store** in *C1-C60,* the **Mean** is *50,* the **Standard Deviation** is *5.0,* and finally click **OK.**

**2.** The MINITAB commands for the 60 confidence intervals on page 289 follow.

    **a.** Select **Stat, Basic Statistics,** and then click on **1-Sample-z.**

    **b.** In the dialog box indicate that the **Variables** are *C1-C60* and that **Sigma** is *5.0.* Next click on **Options** in the lower right corner, in the next dialog box indicate that the **Confidence level** is *95.0,* and then click **OK.** Click **OK** in the main dialog box.

**3.** The MINITAB commands for the descriptive statistics on page 295 are the same as those used on page 78 in Chapter 3. Enter the data in the first column and label this column *Amount*. On the Toolbar select **Stat, Basic Statistics,** and **Display Basic Statistics.** In the dialog box select *Amount* as the **Variable** and click **OK.**

**4.** The MINITAB commands for the confidence interval for the amount spent at the Inlet Square Mall on page 95 are:

    **a.** Enter the 20 amounts spent in column c1 and name the variable *Amounts*, or locate the data on the student data disk. It is named "Shopping" and is found in the folder for Chapter 8.

    **b.** On the Toolbar select **Stat, Basic Statistics,** and click on **1-Sample t.**

    **c.** Select *Amount* as the **Variable** and click **OK.**

# Chapter 9 Answers to Self-Review

**9–1** **a.** $20,000. This is called the point estimate.

**b.** $20,000 \pm 2.58 \dfrac{\$3000}{\sqrt{40}} = \$20,000 \pm 1224$

**c.** The endpoints of the confidence interval are $18,776 and $21,224. About 99 percent of the intervals similarly constructed would include the population mean.

**9–2** **a.** $\bar{X} = \dfrac{18}{10} = 1.8 \qquad s = \sqrt{\dfrac{11.6}{10-1}} = 1.1353$

**b.** The population mean is not known. The best estimate is the sample mean, 1.8 days.

**c.** $1.80 \pm 2.262 \dfrac{1.1353}{\sqrt{10}} = 1.80 \pm 0.81$

**d.** $t$ is used because the population standard deviation is unknown and the sample contains less than 30 observations.

**e.** The value of 0 is not in the interval. It is unreasonable to conclude that the mean number of days of work missed is 0 per employee.

**9–3** **a.** $p = \dfrac{420}{1400} = .30$

**b.** $\sigma_p = \sqrt{\dfrac{.30(1-.30)}{1400}} = .0122$

**c.** $.30 \pm 2.58(.0122) = .30 \pm .03$

**d.** The interval is between .27 and .33. About 99 percent of the similarly constructed intervals would include the population mean.

**9–4** $.375 \pm 1.96 \sqrt{\dfrac{.375(1-.375)}{40}} \sqrt{\dfrac{250-40}{250-1}} =$

$.375 \pm 1.96(.0765)(.9184) = .375 \pm .138$

The correction factor should be applied because $40/250 > .05$.

**9–5** $n = \left(\dfrac{2.58(.279)}{.05}\right)^2 = 207.26$. The sample should be rounded to 208.

# A Review of Chapters 8 and 9

Chapter 8 began by describing the reasons sampling is necessary. We sample because it is often impossible to study every item, or individual, in some populations. It would be too expensive and time consuming, for example, to contact and record the annual incomes of all U.S. bank officers. Also, sampling often destroys the product. A drug manufacturer cannot test the properties of each tablet manufactured, because there would be none left to sell. To estimate a population parameter, therefore, we sample the population. A sample is a part of the population. Care must be taken to ensure that every member of our population has a chance of being selected; otherwise, the conclusions might be biased. A number of probability-type sampling methods can be used, including *simple random, systematic, stratified,* and *cluster sampling.*

Regardless of the sampling method selected, a sample statistic is seldom equal to the corresponding population parameter. For example, the mean of a sample is seldom exactly the same as the mean of the population. The difference between this sample statistic and the population parameter is the *sampling error.*

In Chapter 8 we demonstrated that if we selected all possible samples of a specified size from a population and calculated the mean of these samples, it would be exactly equal to the population mean. We also showed that the dispersion in the distribution of the sample means was equal to the population standard deviation divided by the square root of the sample size. Hence, we concluded that there was less dispersion in the distribution of the sample means than in the population. In addition, as we increased the number of observations in each sample, we decreased the variation in the sampling distribution.

The central limit theorem is the foundation of statistical inference. It states that if the population from which we select the samples follows the normal probability distribution, the distribution of the sample means will also follow the normal distribution. If the population is not normal, it will approach the normal probability distribution as we increase the size of the sample. From a practical standpoint, when the sample contains at least 30 observations, we conclude that the distribution of the sample means will follow the normal distribution.

Our focus in Chapter 9 was point estimates and interval estimates. A point estimate is a single value used to estimate a population parameter. An interval estimate is a range of values within which we expect the population parameter to occur. For example, based on a sample, we estimate that the mean annual income of all professional house painters in Atlanta, Georgia (the population), is $45,300. That estimate is called a *point estimate.* If we state that the population mean is probably in the interval between $45,200 and $45,400, that estimate is called an *interval estimate.* The two endpoints ($45,200 and $45,400) are the *confidence limits* for the population mean. We described the procedure for establishing a confidence interval for both large and small sample means as well as for sample proportions. In this chapter we also provided a method to determine the necessary sample size based on the dispersion in the population, the level of confidence desired, and the desired precision of the estimate.

# Glossary

**Bias**   A possible consequence if certain members of the population are denied the chance to be selected for the sample. As a result, the sample may not be representative of the population.

**Central limit theorem**   If the size of the sample is sufficiently large, the sampling distribution of the sample mean will approach a normal distribution regardless of the shape of the population.

**Cluster sampling**   A method often used to lower the cost of sampling if the population is dispersed over a wide geographic area. The area is divided into smaller units (counties, precincts, blocks, etc.) called primary units. Then a few primary units are chosen, and a random sample is selected from each unit.

**Interval estimate**   The interval within which a population parameter probably lies, based on sample information. Example: According to sample data, the population mean is in the interval between 1.9 and 2.0 pounds.

**Point estimate**   A single value computed from a sample and used to estimate a population parameter. Example: If

the sample mean is 1,020 psi, it is the best estimate of the mean tensile strength of the population.

**Probability sample**   A sample of items or individuals chosen so that each member of the population has a chance of being included in the sample.

**Sampling distribution of the sample mean**   A probability distribution consisting of all possible means of samples of a given size selected from the population.

**Sampling error**   The difference between a sample statistic and the corresponding population parameter. Example: The sample mean income is $22,100; the population mean is $22,000. The sampling error is $22,100 − $22,000 = $100. This error can be attributed to sampling, that is, chance.

**Simple random sampling**   A sampling scheme such that each member of the population has the *same* chance of being selected as part of the sample.

**Stratified random sampling**   A population is first divided into subgroups called strata. A sample is then chosen from each stratum. If, for example, the population of interest consisted of all undergraduate students, the sample design might call for sampling 62 freshmen, 51 sophomores, 40 juniors, and 39 seniors.

**Systematic random sampling** Assuming the population is arranged in some way, such as alphabetically, by height, or in a file drawer. A random starting point is selected, then every *k*th item becomes a member of the sample. If a sample design called for interviewing every ninth household on Main Street starting with 932 Main, the sample would consist of households at 932 Main, 941 Main, 950 Main, and so on.

## Exercises

### Part I—Multiple Choice

1. Each new employee is given an identification number. The personnel files are arranged sequentially starting with employee number 0001. To sample the employees, the number 0153 was first selected. Then numbers 0253, 0353, 0453, and so on became members of the sample. This type of sampling is called:
   a. Simple random sampling.
   b. Systematic sampling.
   c. Stratified random sampling.
   d. Cluster sampling.

2. You divide a precinct into blocks. Then you select 12 blocks at random and concentrate your sampling efforts in those 12 blocks. This type of sampling is called:
   a. Simple random sampling.
   b. Systematic sampling.
   c. Stratified random sampling.
   d. Cluster sampling.

3. The sampling error is:
   a. Equal to the population mean.
   b. A population parameter.
   c. Always positive.
   d. The difference between the sample statistic and the population parameter.

4. Which of the following are correct statements about confidence intervals?
   a. They cannot contain negative numbers.
   b. They are always based on the *z* distribution.
   c. They must always include the population parameter.
   d. None of the above are always correct.

5. The endpoints of a confidence interval are called:
   a. Confidence levels.
   b. The test statistics.
   c. The degrees of confidence.
   d. The confidence limits.

6. We compute the mean and the standard deviation of a sample of 50 observations from a population that is positively skewed. We wish to develop a confidence interval for the mean. Which of the following statements is correct?
   a. We cannot develop a confidence interval because the population is not normal.
   b. We cannot use the *z* distribution because we do not know the population standard deviation.
   c. We can use the *z* distribution because the central limit theorem shows that the distribution of the sample means will approximate the normal distribution.
   d. None of the above statements are correct.

7. Which of the following is *not* a correct statement about the *t* distribution?
   a. It is positively skewed.
   b. It is a continuous distribution.
   c. It has a mean of 0.
   d. There is a family of *t* distributions.

8. As the number of degrees of freedom increases in the *t* distribution:
   a. It approaches the standard normal distribution.
   b. The level of confidence increases.
   c. It becomes a continuous distribution.
   d. It becomes flatter.

9. The degrees of freedom are:
   a. The total number of observations.
   b. The number of observations minus the number of samples.
   c. The number of samples.
   d. The number of samples minus one.

**10.** We select a sample of 15 observations from a normal population and wish to develop a 98 percent confidence interval for the mean. The appropriate value of *t* is:
   **a.** 2.947
   **b.** 2.977
   **c.** 2.624
   **d.** None of the above.

## Part II—Problems

**11.** A recent study indicated that women took an average of 8.6 weeks of unpaid leave from their jobs after the birth of a child. Assume that this distribution follows the normal probability distribution with a standard deviation of 2.0 weeks. We select a sample of 35 women who recently returned to work after the birth of a child. What is the likelihood that the mean of this sample is at least 8.8 weeks?

**12.** The manager of the Tee Shirt Emporium reports that the mean number of shirts sold per week is 1,210, with a standard deviation of 325. The distribution of sales follows the normal distribution. What is the likelihood of selecting a sample of 25 weeks and finding the sample mean to be 1,100 or less?

**13.** The owner of the Gulf Stream Café wished to estimate the mean number of lunch customers per day. A sample of 40 days revealed a mean of 160 per day, with a standard deviation of 20 per day. Develop a 92 percent confidence interval for the mean number of customers per day.

**14.** The manager of the local Hamburger Express wishes to estimate the mean time customers spend in the drive-through window. A sample of 80 customers experienced a mean waiting time of 2.65 minutes, with a standard deviation of 0.45 minutes. Develop an 85 percent confidence interval for the mean waiting time.

**15.** The office manager for a large company is studying the usage of its copy machines. A random sample of six copy machines revealed the following number of copies (reported in 000s) made yesterday.

| 826 | 931 | 1,126 | 918 | 1,011 | 1,101 |

Develop a 95 percent confidence interval for the mean number of copies per machine.

**16.** John Kleman is the host of KXYZ Radio 55 AM drive-time news in Chicago. During his morning program, John asks listeners to call in and discuss current local and national news. This morning, John was concerned with the number of hours children under 12 years of age watch TV per day. The last 5 callers reported that their children watched the following number of hours of TV last night.

| 3.0 | 3.5 | 4.0 | 4.5 | 3.0 |

Would it be reasonable to develop a confidence interval from these data to show the mean number of hours of TV watched? If yes, construct an appropriate confidence interval and interpret the result. If no, why would a confidence interval not be appropriate?

**17.** Historically, Widgets Manufacturing, Inc. produces 250 widgets per day. Recently the new owner bought a new machine to produce more widgets per day. A sample of 16 days production revealed a mean of 240 units with a standard deviation of 35. Construct a confidence interval for the mean number of widgets produced per day. Does it seem reasonable to conclude that the mean daily widget production has increased? Justify your conclusion.

**18.** The manufacturer of a power chip used in expensive stereo equipment wishes to estimate the useful life of the chip (in thousands of hours). The estimate is to be within 0.10 (100) hours. Assume a 95 percent level of confidence and that the standard deviation of the useful life of the chip is 0.90 (900 hours). Determine the required sample size.

**19.** The manager of a home improvement store wishes to estimate the mean amount of money spent in the store. The estimate is to be within $4.00 with a 95 percent level of confidence. The manager does not know the standard deviation of the amounts spent. However, he does estimate that the range is from $5.00 up to $155.00. How large of a sample is needed?

**20.** In a sample of 200 residents of Georgetown County, 120 reported they believed the county real estate taxes were too high. Develop a 95 percent confidence interval for the proportion of residents who believe the tax rate is too high. Would it be reasonable to conclude that the majority of the taxpayers feel that the taxes are too high?

21. In recent times, the percent of buyers purchasing a new vehicle via the Internet has been large enough that local automobile dealers are concerned about its impact on their business. The information needed is an estimate of the proportion of purchases via the Internet. How large of a sample of purchasers is necessary for the estimate to be within 2 percentage points with a 98 percent level of confidence? Current thinking is that about 8 percent of the vehicles are purchased via the Internet.

22. Historically, the proportion of adults over the age of 24 who smoke has been .30. In recent years, much information has been published and aired on radio and TV that smoking is not good for one's health. A sample of 500 adults revealed only 25 percent of those sampled smoked. Develop a 98 percent confidence interval for the proportion of adults who currently smoke. Would you agree that the proportion is less than 30 percent?

23. The auditor of the State of Ohio needs an estimate of the proportion of residents who regularly play the state lottery. Historically, about 40 percent regularly play, but the auditor would like some current information. How large a sample is necessary for the estimate to be within 3 percentage points, with a 98 percent level of confidence?

# Case

## Century National Bank

Refer to the description of the Century National Bank at the end of the Review of Chapters 1–4 on page 137. When Mr. Selig took over as president of Century several years ago, the use of debit cards was just beginning. He would like an update on the use of these cards. Develop a 95 percent confidence interval for the proportion of customers using these cards. On the basis of the confidence interval, is it reasonable to conclude that more than half of the customers use a debit card? Interpret the results.

# 10

# One-Sample Tests of Hypothesis

Many grocery stores and large retailers such as Wal-Mart and K-Mart have installed self-checkout systems so shoppers can scan their own items and cash out themselves. A sample of customers using the service was taken for 15 days at the Wal-Mart on Highway 544 in Surfside Beach, South Carolina, to see how often it is used. Using the .05 significance level, is it reasonable to conclude that the mean number of customers using the system is more than 100 per day? (See Goal 4 and Exercise 51.)

# Introduction

Chapter 8 began our study of statistical inference. We described how we could select a random sample and from this sample estimate the value of a population parameter. For example, we selected a sample of 5 employees at Spence Sprockets, found the number of years of service for each sampled employee, computed the mean years of service, and used the sample mean to estimate the mean years of service for all employees. In other words, we estimated a population parameter from a sample statistic.

Chapter 9 continued the study of statistical inference by developing a confidence interval. A confidence interval is a range of values within which we expect the population parameter to occur. In this chapter, rather than develop a range of values within which we expect the population parameter to occur, we develop a procedure to test the validity of a statement about a population parameter. Some examples of statements we might want to test are:

- The mean speed of automobiles passing milepost 150 on the West Virginia Turnpike is 68 miles per hour.

- The mean number of miles driven by those leasing a Chevy Trail Blazer for three years is 32,000 miles.
- The mean time an American family lives in a particular single-family dwelling is 11.8 years.
- The mean starting salary for graduates of four-year business schools is $3,200 per month.
- Thirty-five percent of retirees in the upper Midwest sell their home and move to a warm climate within 1 year of their retirement.
- Eighty percent of those who play the state lotteries regularly never win more than $100 in any one play.

This chapter and several of the following chapters are concerned with statistical hypothesis testing. We begin by defining what we mean by a statistical hypothesis and statistical hypothesis testing. Next, we outline the steps in statistical hypothesis testing. Then we conduct tests of hypothesis for means and proportions. In the last section of the chapter, we describe possible errors due to sampling in hypothesis testing.

# What Is a Hypothesis?

A hypothesis is a statement about a population parameter.

A hypothesis is a statement about a population. Data are then used to check the reasonableness of the statement. To begin we need to define the word *hypothesis.* In the United States legal system, a person is innocent until proven guilty. A jury hypothesizes that a person charged with a crime is innocent and subjects this hypothesis to verification by reviewing the evidence and hearing testimony before reaching a verdict. In a similar sense, a patient goes to a physician and reports various symptoms. On the basis of the symptoms, the physician will order certain diagnostic tests, then, according to the symptoms and the test results, determine the treatment to be followed.

In statistical analysis we make a claim, that is, state a hypothesis, collect data, then use the data to test the assertion. We define a statistical hypothesis as follows.

> **HYPOTHESIS** A statement about a population parameter developed for the purpose of testing.

In most cases the population is so large that it is not feasible to study all the items, objects, or persons in the population. For example, it would not be possible to contact every systems analyst in the United States to find his or her monthly income. Likewise, the quality assurance department at Cooper Tire cannot check each tire produced to determine whether it will last more than 60,000 miles.

As noted in Chapter 8, an alternative to measuring or interviewing the entire population is to take a sample from the population. We can, therefore, test a statement to determine whether the sample does or does not support the statement concerning the population.

# What Is Hypothesis Testing?

The terms *hypothesis testing* and *testing a hypothesis* are used interchangeably. Hypothesis testing starts with a statement, or assumption, about a population parameter— such as the population mean. As noted, this statement is referred to as a *hypothesis.* A hypothesis might be that the mean monthly commission of salespeople in retail electronics stores, such as Circuit City, is $2,000. We cannot contact all these salespeople to ascertain that the mean is in fact $2,000. The cost of locating and interviewing every electronics salesperson in the United States would be exorbitant. To test the validity of the assumption ($\mu$ = $2,000), we must select a sample from the population of all electronics salespeople, calculate sample statistics, and based on certain decision rules accept or reject the hypothesis. A sample mean of $1,000 for the electronics salespeople would certainly cause rejection of the hypothesis. However, suppose the sample mean is $1,995. Is that close enough to $2,000 for us to accept the assumption that the population mean is $2,000? Can we attribute the difference of $5 between the two means to sampling error, or is that difference statistically significant?

> **HYPOTHESIS TESTING**  A procedure based on sample evidence and probability theory to determine whether the hypothesis is a reasonable statement.

# Five-Step Procedure for Testing a Hypothesis

There is a five-step procedure that systematizes hypothesis testing; when we get to step 5, we are ready to reject or not reject the hypothesis. However, hypothesis testing as used by statisticians does not provide proof that something is true, in the manner in which a mathematician "proves" a statement. It does provide a kind of "proof beyond a reasonable doubt," in the manner of the court system. Hence, there are specific rules of evidence, or procedures, that are followed. The steps are shown in the diagram at the bottom of this page. We will discuss in detail each of the steps.

# Step 1: State the Null Hypothesis ($H_0$) and the Alternate Hypothesis ($H_1$)

The first step is to state the hypothesis being tested. It is called the **null hypothesis,** designated $H_0$, and read "*H sub zero.*" The capital letter *H* stands for hypothesis, and the subscript zero implies "no difference." There is usually a "not" or a "no" term in the null hypothesis, meaning that there is "no change." For example, the null hypothesis is that the mean number of miles driven on the steel-belted tire is not different from 60,000. The null hypothesis would be written $H_0$: $\mu = 60,000$. Generally speaking, the null hypothesis is developed for the purpose of testing. We either reject or fail to reject the null hypothesis. The null hypothesis is a statement that is not rejected unless our sample data provide convincing evidence that it is false.

We should emphasize that if the null hypothesis is not rejected on the basis of the sample data, we cannot say that the null hypothesis is true. To put it another way, failing to reject the null hypothesis does not prove that $H_0$ is true, it means we have *failed to disprove $H_0$.* To prove without any doubt the null hypothesis is true, the population parameter would have to be known. To actually determine it, we would have to test, survey, or count every item in the population. This is usually not feasible. The alternative is to take a sample from the population.

It should also be noted that we often begin the null hypothesis by stating, "There is no *significant* difference between . . . ," or "The mean impact strength of the glass is not *significantly* different from. . . . " When we select a sample from a population, the sample statistic is usually numerically different from the hypothesized population parameter. As an illustration, suppose the hypothesized impact strength of a glass plate is 70 psi, and the mean impact strength of a sample of 12 glass plates is 69.5 psi. We must make a decision about the difference of 0.5 psi. Is it a true difference, that is, a significant difference, or is the difference between the sample statistic (69.5) and the hypothesized population parameter (70.0) due to chance (sampling)? As noted, to answer this question we conduct a test of significance, commonly referred to as a test of hypothesis. To define what is meant by a null hypothesis:

> **NULL HYPOTHESIS** A statement about the value of a population parameter.

The **alternate hypothesis** describes what you will conclude if you reject the null hypothesis. It is written $H_1$ and is read "*H sub one.*" It is also referred to as the research hypothesis. The alternate hypothesis is accepted if the sample data provide us with enough statistical evidence that the null hypothesis is false.

> **ALTERNATE HYPOTHESIS** A statement that is accepted if the sample data provide sufficient evidence that the null hypothesis is false.

The following example will help clarify what is meant by the null hypothesis and the alternate hypothesis. A recent article indicated the mean age of U.S. commercial aircraft is 15 years. To conduct a statistical test regarding this statement, the first step is to determine the null and the alternate hypotheses. The null hypothesis represents the current or reported condition. It is written $H_0$: $\mu = 15$. The alternate hypothesis is that the statement is not true, that is, $H_1$: $\mu \neq 15$. It is important to remember that no matter how the problem is stated, *the null hypothesis will always contain the equal sign.* The equal sign ($=$) will never appear in the alternate hypothesis. Why? Because the null hypothesis is the statement being tested, and we need a specific value to include in our calculations. We turn to the alternate hypothesis only if the data suggests the null hypothesis is untrue.

# Step 2: Select a Level of Significance

Select a level of
significance or risk.

After setting up the null hypothesis and alternate hypothesis, the next step is to state the level of significance.

> **LEVEL OF SIGNIFICANCE** The probability of rejecting the null hypothesis when it is true.

The level of significance is designated $\alpha$, the Greek letter alpha. It is also sometimes called the level of risk. This may be a more appropriate term because it is the risk you take of rejecting the null hypothesis when it is really true.

There is no one level of significance that is applied to all tests. A decision is made to use the .05 level (often stated as the 5 percent level), the .01 level, the .10 level, or any other level between 0 and 1. Traditionally, the .05 level is selected for consumer research projects, .01 for quality assurance, and .10 for political polling. You, the researcher, must decide on the level of significance *before* formulating a decision rule and collecting sample data.

To illustrate how it is possible to reject a true hypothesis, suppose a firm manufacturing personal computers uses a large number of printed circuit boards. Suppliers

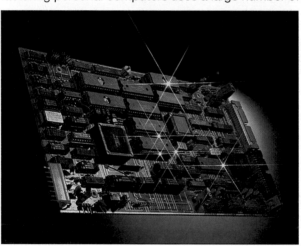

bid on the boards, and the one with the lowest bid is awarded a sizable contract. Suppose the contract specifies that the computer manufacturer's quality-assurance department will sample all incoming shipments of circuit boards. If more than 6 percent of the boards sampled are substandard, the shipment will be rejected. The null hypothesis is that the incoming shipment of boards contains 6 percent or less substandard boards. The alternate hypothesis is that more than 6 percent of the boards are defective.

A sample of 50 circuit boards received July 21 from Allied Electronics revealed that 4 boards, or 8 percent, were substandard. The shipment was rejected because it exceeded the maximum of 6 percent substandard printed circuit boards. If the shipment was actually substandard, then the decision to return the boards to the supplier was correct. However, suppose the 4 substandard printed circuit boards selected in the sample of 50 were the only substandard boards in the shipment of 4,000 boards. Then only $\frac{1}{10}$ of 1 percent were defective (4/4,000 = .001). In that case, less than 6 percent of the entire shipment was substandard and rejecting the shipment was an error. In terms of hypothesis testing, we rejected the null hypothesis that the shipment was not substandard when we should have accepted the null hypothesis. By rejecting a true null hypothesis, we committed a Type I error. The probability of committing a Type I error is $\alpha$.

> **TYPE I ERROR** Rejecting the null hypothesis, $H_0$, when it is true.

The probability of committing another type of error, called a Type II error, is designated by the Greek letter beta ($\beta$).

> **TYPE II ERROR** Accepting the null hypothesis when it is false.

The firm manufacturing personal computers would commit a Type II error if, unknown to the manufacturer, an incoming shipment of printed circuit boards from Allied Electronics contained 15 percent substandard boards, yet the shipment was accepted. How could this happen? Suppose 2 of the 50 boards in the sample (4 percent) tested were substandard, and 48 of the 50 were good boards. According to the stated procedure, because the sample contained less than 6 percent substandard boards, the shipment was accepted. It could be that *by chance* the 48 good boards selected in the sample were the only acceptable ones in the entire shipment consisting of thousands of boards!

In retrospect, the researcher cannot study every item or individual in the population. Thus, there is a possibility of two types of error—a Type I error, wherein the null hypothesis is rejected when it should have been accepted, and a Type II error, wherein the null hypothesis is not rejected when it should have been rejected.

We often refer to the probability of these two possible errors as *alpha,* $\alpha$, and *beta,* $\beta$. Alpha ($\alpha$) is the probability of making a Type I error, and beta ($\beta$) is the probability of making a Type II error.

The following table summarizes the decisions the researcher could make and the possible consequences.

| Null Hypothesis | Researcher | |
|---|---|---|
| | **Accepts** $H_0$ | **Rejects** $H_0$ |
| $H_0$ is true | Correct decision | Type I error |
| $H_0$ is false | Type II error | Correct decision |

# Step 3: Select the Test Statistic

There are many test statistics. In this chapter we use both *z* and *t* as the test statistic. In other chapters we will use such test statistics as *F* and $\chi^2$, called chi-square.

> **TEST STATISTIC** A value, determined from sample information, used to determine whether to reject the null hypothesis.

In hypothesis testing for the mean ($\mu$) when $\sigma$ is known or the sample size is large, the test statistic *z* is computed by:

| *z* DISTRIBUTION AS A TEST STATISTIC | $z = \dfrac{\overline{X} - \mu}{\sigma/\sqrt{n}}$ | [10–1] |
|---|---|---|

The *z* value is based on the sampling distribution of $\overline{X}$, which follows the normal distribution when the sample is reasonably large with a mean ($\mu_{\bar{x}}$) equal to $\mu$, and a standard deviation $\sigma_{\bar{x}}$, which is equal to $\sigma/\sqrt{n}$. We can thus determine whether the difference between $\overline{X}$ and $\mu$ is statistically significant by finding the number of standard deviations $\overline{X}$ is from $\mu$, using formula (10–1).

# Step 4: Formulate the Decision Rule

The decision rule states the conditions when $H_0$ is rejected.

A decision rule is a statement of the specific conditions under which the null hypothesis is rejected and the conditions under which it is not rejected. The region or area of

**Statistics in Action**

During World War II, allied military planners needed estimates of the number of German tanks. The information provided by traditional spying methods was not reliable, but statistical methods proved to be valuable. For example, espionage and reconnaissance led analysts to estimate that 1,550 tanks were produced during June of 1941. However, using the serial numbers of captured tanks and statistical analysis, military planners estimated 244. The actual number produced, as determined from German production records, was 271. The estimate using statistical analysis turned out to be much more accurate. A similar type of analysis was used to estimate the number of Iraqi tanks destroyed during Desert Storm.

rejection defines the location of all those values that are so large or so small that the probability of their occurrence under a true null hypothesis is rather remote.

Chart 10–1 portrays the rejection region for a test of significance that will be conducted later in the chapter.

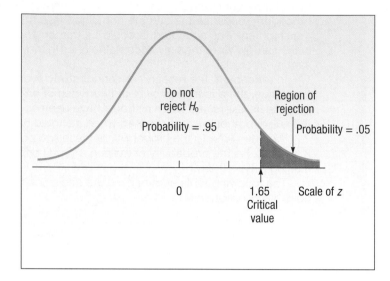

**CHART 10–1** Sampling Distribution of the Statistic $z$, a Right-Tailed Test, .05 Level of Significance

Note in the chart that:

1. The area where the null hypothesis is not rejected is to the left of 1.65. We will explain how to get the 1.65 value shortly.
2. The area of rejection is to the right of 1.65.
3. A one-tailed test is being applied. (This will also be explained later.)
4. The .05 level of significance was chosen.
5. The sampling distribution of the statistic $z$ is normally distributed.
6. The value 1.65 separates the regions where the null hypothesis is rejected and where it is not rejected.
7. The value 1.65 is the **critical value.**

> **CRITICAL VALUE** The dividing point between the region where the null hypothesis is rejected and the region where it is not rejected.

## Step 5: Make a Decision

The fifth and final step in hypothesis testing is computing the test statistic, comparing it to the critical value, and making a decision to reject or not to reject the null hypothesis. Referring to Chart 10–1, if, based on sample information, $z$ is computed to be 2.34, the null hypothesis is rejected at the .05 level of significance. The decision to reject $H_0$ was made because 2.34 lies in the region of rejection, that is, beyond 1.65. We would reject the null hypothesis, reasoning that it is highly improbable that a computed $z$ value this large is due to sampling variation (chance).

Had the computed value been 1.65 or less, say 0.71, the null hypothesis would not be rejected. It would be reasoned that such a small computed value could be attributed to chance, that is, sampling variation.

As noted, only one of two decisions is possible in hypothesis testing—either accept or reject the null hypothesis. Instead of "accepting" the null hypothesis, $H_0$, some researchers prefer to phrase the decision as: "Do not reject $H_0$," "We fail to reject $H_0$," or "The sample results do not allow us to reject $H_0$."

It should be reemphasized that there is always a possibility that the null hypothesis is rejected when it should not be rejected (a Type I error). Also, there is a definable chance that the null hypothesis is accepted when it should be rejected (a Type II error).

Before actually conducting a test of hypothesis, we will differentiate between a one-tailed test of significance and a two-tailed test.

---

**SUMMARY OF THE STEPS IN HYPOTHESIS TESTING**
1. Establish the null hypothesis ($H_0$) and the alternate hypothesis ($H_1$).
2. Select the level of significance, that is $\alpha$.
3. Select an appropriate test statistic.
4. Formulate a decision rule based on steps 1, 2, and 3 above.
5. Make a decision regarding the null hypothesis based on the sample information. Interpret the results of the test.

---

# One-Tailed and Two-Tailed Tests of Significance

Refer to Chart 10–1. It depicts a one-tailed test. The region of rejection is only in the right (upper) tail of the curve. To illustrate, suppose that the packaging department at General Foods Corporation is concerned that some boxes of Grape Nuts are significantly overweight. The cereal is packaged in 453-gram boxes, so the null hypothesis is $H_0$: $\mu \leq 453$. This is read, "the population mean ($\mu$) is equal to or less than 453." The alternate hypothesis is, therefore, $H_1$: $\mu > 453$. This is read, "$\mu$ is greater than 453." Note that the inequality sign in the alternate hypothesis ($>$) points to the region of rejection in the upper tail. (See Chart 10–1.) Also note that the null hypothesis includes the equal sign. That is, $H_0$: $\mu \leq 453$. The equality condition always appears in $H_0$, never in $H_1$.

Chart 10–2 portrays a situation where the rejection region is in the left (lower) tail of the normal distribution. As an illustration, consider the problem of automobile manufacturers, large automobile leasing companies, and other organizations that purchase large quantities of tires. They want the tires to average, say, 60,000 miles of wear under normal usage. They will, therefore, reject a shipment of tires if tests reveal that the life of the tires is significantly below 60,000 miles on the average. They gladly accept a

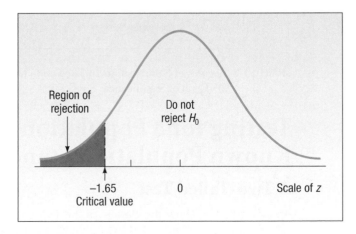

**CHART 10–2** Sampling Distribution for the Statistic $z$, Left-Tailed Test, .05 Level of Significance

shipment if the mean life is greater than 60,000 miles! They are not concerned with this possibility, however. They are concerned only if they have sample evidence to conclude that the tires will average less than 60,000 miles of useful life. Thus, the test is set up to satisfy the concern of the automobile manufacturers that *the mean life of the tires is less than 60,000 miles.* The null and alternate hypotheses in this case are written $H_0$: $\mu \geq 60,000$ and $H_1$: $\mu < 60,000$.

Test is one-tailed if $H_1$ states $\mu >$ or $\mu <$.

If $H_1$ states a direction, test is one-tailed.

One way to determine the location of the rejection region is to look at the direction in which the inequality sign in the alternate hypothesis is pointing (either < or >). In this problem it is pointing to the left, and the rejection region is therefore in the left tail.

In summary, a test is *one-tailed* when the alternate hypothesis, $H_1$, states a direction, such as:

$H_0$:   The mean income of women stockbrokers is *less than or equal to* $65,000 per year.
$H_1$:   The mean income of women stockbrokers is *greater* than $65,000 per year.

If no direction is specified in the alternate hypothesis, we use a *two-tailed* test. Changing the previous problem to illustrate, we can say:

$H_0$:   The mean income of women stockbrokers is $65,000 per year.
$H_1$:   The mean income of women stockbrokers is *not equal to* $65,000 per year.

If the null hypothesis is rejected and $H_1$ accepted in the two-tailed case, the mean income could be significantly greater than $65,000 per year, or it could be significantly less than $65,000 per year. To accommodate these two possibilities, the 5 percent area of rejection is divided equally into the two tails of the sampling distribution (2.5 percent each). Chart 10–3 shows the two areas and the critical values. Note that the total area in the normal distribution is 1.0000, found by .9500 + .0250 + .0250.

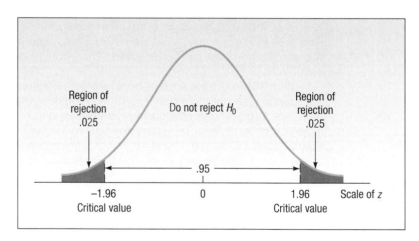

**CHART 10–3**  Regions of Nonrejection and Rejection for a Two-Tailed Test, .05 Level of Significance

# Testing for a Population Mean with a Known Population Standard Deviation

## A Two-Tailed Test

An example will show the details of the five-step hypothesis testing procedure. We also wish to use a two-tailed test. That is, we are *not* concerned whether the sample results are larger or smaller than the proposed population mean. Rather, we are interested in whether it is *different from* the proposed value for the population mean. We begin, as we did in the previous chapter, with a situation in which we have historical information about the population and in fact know its standard deviation.

**EXAMPLE**

The Jamestown Steel Company manufactures and assembles desks and other office equipment at several plants in western New York State. The weekly production of the Model A325 desk at the Fredonia Plant is normally distributed, with a mean of 200 and a standard deviation of 16. Recently, because of market expansion, new production methods have been introduced and new employees hired. The vice president of manufacturing would like to investigate whether there has been a change in the weekly production of the Model A325 desk. To put it another way, is the mean number of desks produced at the Fredonia Plant different from 200 at the .01 significance level?

**SOLUTION**

We use the statistical hypothesis testing procedure to investigate whether the production rate has changed from 200 per week.

**Step 1: State the null hypothesis and the alternate hypothesis.** The null hypothesis is "The population mean is 200." The alternate hypothesis is "The mean is different from 200" or "The mean is not 200." These two hypotheses are written:

$$H_0: \mu = 200$$
$$H_1: \mu \neq 200$$

This is a *two-tailed test* because the alternate hypothesis does not state a direction. In other words, it does not state whether the mean production is greater than 200 or less than 200. The vice president wants only to find out whether the production rate is different from 200.

**Step 2: Select the level of significance.** As noted, the .01 level of significance is used. This is $\alpha$, the probability of committing a Type I error, and it is the probability of rejecting a true null hypothesis.

**Step 3: Select the test statistic.** The large sample test statistic for a mean is $z$. It was discussed at length in Chapter 7. Transforming the production data to standard units ($z$ values) permits their use not only in this problem but also in other hypothesis-testing problems. Formula (10–1) for $z$ is repeated below with the various letters identified.

Formula for the test statistic

**[10–1]**

| Sample mean | | Population mean |
|---|---|---|
| | $z = \dfrac{\bar{X} - \mu}{\sigma/\sqrt{n}}$ | |
| Standard deviation of population | | Number in sample |

**Step 4: Formulate the decision rule.** The decision rule is formulated by finding the critical values of $z$ from Appendix D. Since this is a two-tailed test, half of .01, or .005, is placed in each tail. The area where $H_0$ is not rejected, located between the two tails, is therefore .99. Appendix D is based on half of the area under the curve, or .5000. Then, .5000 − .0050 is .4950, so .4950 is the area between 0 and the critical value. Locate .4950 in the body of the table. The value nearest to .4950 is .4951. Then read the critical value in the row and column corresponding to .4951. It is

2.58. For your convenience, Appendix D, Areas under the Normal Curve, is repeated in the inside back cover.

All the facets of this problem are shown in the diagram in Chart 10–4.

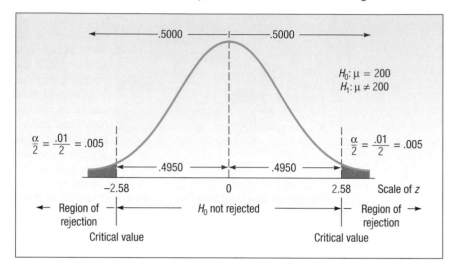

**CHART 10–4** Decision Rule for the .01 Significance Level

The decision rule is, therefore: Reject the null hypothesis and accept the alternate hypothesis (which states that the population mean is not 200) if the computed value of $z$ is not between $-2.58$ and $+2.58$. Do not reject the null hypothesis if $z$ falls between $-2.58$ and $+2.58$.

**Step 5: Make a decision and interpret the result.** Take a sample from the population (weekly production), compute $z$, apply the decision rule, and arrive at a decision to reject $H_0$ or not to reject $H_0$. The mean number of desks produced last year (50 weeks, because the plant was shut down 2 weeks for vacation) is 203.5. The standard deviation of the population is 16 desks per week. Computing the $z$ value from formula (10–1):

$$z = \frac{\overline{X} - \mu}{\sigma/\sqrt{n}} = \frac{203.5 - 200}{16/\sqrt{50}} = 1.55$$

Because 1.55 does not fall in the rejection region, $H_0$ is not rejected. We conclude that the population mean is *not* different from 200. So we would report to the vice president of manufacturing that the sample evidence does not show that the production rate at the Fredonia Plant has changed from 200 per week. The difference of 3.5 units between the historical weekly production rate and that last year can reasonably be attributed to sampling error. This information is summarized in the following chart.

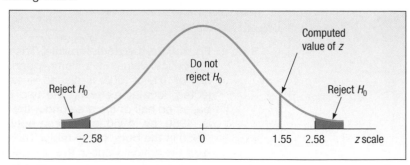

Did we prove that the assembly rate is still 200 per week? Not really. What we did, technically, was *fail to disprove the null hypothesis.* Failing to disprove the hypothesis that the population mean is 200 is not the same thing as proving it to be true. As we suggested in the chapter introduction, the conclusion is analogous to the American judicial system. To explain, suppose a person is accused of a crime but is acquitted by a jury. If a person is acquitted of a crime, the conclusion is that there was not enough evidence to prove the person guilty. The trial did not prove that the individual was innocent, only that there was not enough evidence to prove the defendant guilty. That is what we do in statistical hypothesis testing when we do not reject the null hypothesis. The correct interpretation is that we have failed to disprove the null hypothesis.

We selected the significance level, .01 in this case, before setting up the decision rule and sampling the population. This is the appropriate strategy. The significance level should be set by the investigator, but it should be determined *before* gathering the sample evidence and not changed based on the sample evidence.

How does the hypothesis testing procedure just described compare with that of confidence intervals discussed in the previous chapter? When we conducted the test of hypothesis regarding the production of desks we changed the units from desks per week to a $z$ value. Then we compared the computed value of the test statistic (1.55) to that of the critical values ($-2.58$ and 2.58). Because the computed value was in the region where the null hypothesis was not rejected, we concluded that the population mean could be 200. To use the confidence interval approach, on the other hand, we would develop a confidence interval, based on formula (9–1). See page 286. The interval would be from 197.66 to 209.34, found by $203.5 \pm 2.58(16/\sqrt{50})$. Note that the proposed population value, 200, is within this interval. Hence, we would conclude that the population mean could reasonably be 200.

In general, $H_0$ is rejected if the confidence interval does not include the hypothesized value. If the confidence interval includes the hypothesized value, then $H_0$ is not rejected. So the "do not reject region" for a test of hypothesis is equivalent to the proposed population value occurring in the confidence interval. The primary difference between a confidence interval and the "do not reject" region for a hypothesis test is whether the interval is centered around the sample statistic, such as $\bar{X}$, as in the confidence interval, or around 0, as in the test of hypothesis.

---

**SELF-REVIEW 10–1**

The mean annual turnover rate of the 200-count bottle of Bayer Aspirin is 6.0 with a standard deviation of 0.50. (This indicates that the stock of Bayer turns over on the pharmacy shelves an average of 6 times per year.) It is suspected that the mean turnover has changed and is not 6.0. Use the .05 significance level.
(a)   State the null hypothesis and the alternate hypothesis.
(b)   What is the probability of a Type I error?
(c)   Give the formula for the test statistic.
(d)   State the decision rule.
(e)   A random sample of 64 bottles of the 200-count size Bayer Aspirin showed a mean turnover rate of 5.84. Shall we reject the hypothesis that the population mean is 6.0? Interpret the result.

---

# A One-Tailed Test

In the previous example, we emphasized that we were concerned only with reporting to the vice president whether there had been a change in the mean number of desks assembled at the Fredonia Plant. We were not concerned with whether the change was an increase or a decrease in the production.

To illustrate a one-tailed test, let's change the problem. Suppose the vice president wants to know whether there has been an *increase* in the number of units assembled. To put it another way, can we conclude, because of the improved production methods, that the mean number of desks assembled in the last 50 weeks was more than 200? Look at the difference in the way the problem is formulated. In the first case we wanted to know whether there was a *difference* in the mean number assembled, but now we want to know whether there has been an *increase.* Because we are investigating different questions, we will set our hypotheses differently. The biggest difference occurs in the alternate hypothesis. Before, we stated the alternate hypothesis as "different from"; now we want to state it as "greater than." In symbols:

A two-tailed test:      A one-tailed test:

$H_0$: $\mu = 200$        $H_0$: $\mu \leq 200$

$H_1$: $\mu \neq 200$        $H_1$: $\mu > 200$

The critical values for a one-tailed test are different from a two-tailed test at the same significance level. In the previous example, we split the significance level in half and put half in the lower tail and half in the upper tail. In a one-tailed test we put all the rejection region in one tail. See Chart 10–5.

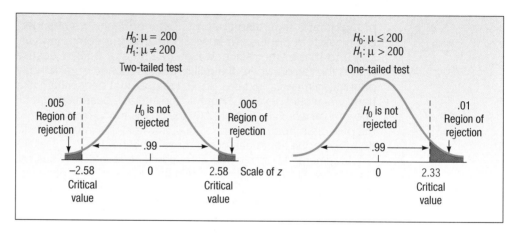

**CHART 10-5** Rejection Regions for Two-Tailed and One-Tailed Tests, $\alpha = .01$

For the one-tailed test, the critical value is 2.33, found by: (1) subtracting .01 from .5000 and (2) finding the *z* value corresponding to .4900.

# *p*-Value in Hypothesis Testing

In testing a hypothesis, we compare the test statistic to a critical value. A decision is made to either reject the null hypothesis or not to reject it. So, for example, if the critical value is 1.96 and the computed value of the test statistic is 2.19, the decision is to reject the null hypothesis.

In recent years, spurred by the availability of computer software, additional information is often reported on the strength of the rejection or acceptance. That is, how confident are we in rejecting the null hypothesis? This approach reports the probability (assuming that the null hypothesis is true) of getting a value of the test statistic at least as extreme as the value actually obtained. This process compares the probability, called the **p-value,** with the significance level. If the *p*-value is smaller than the significance level, $H_0$ is rejected. If it is larger than the significance level, $H_0$ is not rejected.

> **p-VALUE** The probability of observing a sample value as extreme as, or more extreme than, the value observed, given that the null hypothesis is true.

Determining the *p*-value not only results in a decision regarding $H_0$, but it gives us additional insight into the strength of the decision. A very small *p*-value, such as

.0001, indicates that there is little likelihood the $H_0$ is true. On the other hand, a $p$-value of .2033 means that $H_0$ is not rejected, and there is little likelihood that it is false.

How do we compute the $p$-value? To illustrate we will use the example in which we tested the null hypothesis that the mean number of desks produced per week at Fredonia was 200. We did not reject the null hypothesis, because the $z$ value of 1.55 fell in the region between $-2.58$ and 2.58. We agreed not to reject the null hypothesis if the computed value of $z$ fell in this region. The probability of finding a $z$ value of 1.55 or more is .0606, found by $.5000 - .4394$. To put it another way, the probability of obtaining an $\bar{X}$ greater than 203.5 if $\mu = 200$ is .0606. To compute the $p$-value, we need to be concerned with the region less than $-1.55$ as well as the values greater than 1.55 (because the rejection region is in both tails). The two-tailed $p$-value is .1212, found by 2(.0606). The $p$-value of .1212 is greater than the significance level of .01 decided upon initially, so $H_0$ is not rejected. The details are shown in the following graph. In general, the area is doubled in a two-sided test. Then the $p$-value can easily be compared with the significance level. The same decision rule is used as in the one-sided test.

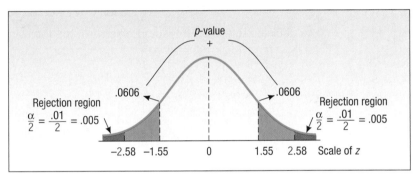

A $p$-value is a way to express the likelihood that $H_0$ is false. But how do we interpret a $p$-value? We have already said that if the $p$-value is less than the significance level, then we reject $H_0$; if it is greater than the significance level, then we do not reject $H_0$. Also, if the $p$-value is very large, then it is likely that $H_0$ is true. If the $p$-value is small, then it is likely that $H_0$ is not true. The following box will help to interpret $p$-values.

---

**INTERPRETING THE WEIGHT OF EVIDENCE AGAINST $H_0$** If the $p$-value is less than

(a) .10, we have *some* evidence that $H_0$ is not true.
(b) .05, we have *strong evidence* that $H_0$ is not true.
(c) .01, we have *very strong evidence* that $H_0$ is not true.
(d) .001, we have *extremely strong evidence* that $H_0$ is not true.

---

# Testing for a Population Mean: Large Sample, Population Standard Deviation Unknown

In the preceding example, we knew $\sigma$, the population standard deviation. In most cases, however, the population standard deviation is unknown. Thus, $\sigma$ must be based on prior studies or estimated by the sample standard deviation, $s$. The population standard deviation in the following example is not known, so the sample standard deviation is used to estimate $\sigma$. As long as the sample size, $n$, is at least 30, $s$ can be substituted for $\sigma$, as illustrated in the following formula:

| | | |
|---|---|---|
| $z$ STATISTIC, $\sigma$ UNKNOWN | $z = \dfrac{\bar{X} - \mu}{s/\sqrt{n}}$ | **[10–2]** |

**EXAMPLE**

The Thompson's Discount Appliance Store issues its own credit card. The credit manager wants to find whether the mean monthly unpaid balance is more than $400. The level of significance is set at .05. A random check of 172 unpaid balances revealed the sample mean is $407 and the standard deviation of the sample is $38. Should the credit manager conclude the population mean is greater than $400, or is it reasonable that the difference of $7 ($407 − $400 = $7) is due to chance?

**SOLUTION**

The null and alternate hypotheses are:

$H_0$: $\mu \leq \$400$
$H_1$: $\mu > \$400$

Because the alternate hypothesis states a direction, a one-tailed test is applied. The critical value of $z$ is 1.65. The computed value of $z$ is 2.42, found by using formula (10–2):

$$z = \frac{\bar{X} - \mu}{s/\sqrt{n}} = \frac{\$407 - \$400}{\$38/\sqrt{172}} = \frac{\$7}{\$2.8975} = 2.42$$

The decision rule is portrayed graphically in the following chart.

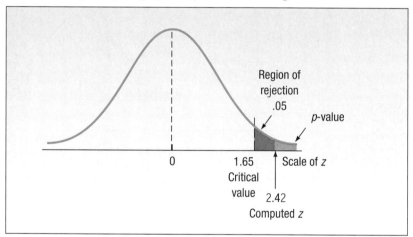

Because the computed value of the test statistic (2.42) is larger than the critical value (1.65), the null hypothesis is rejected. The credit manager can conclude the mean unpaid balance is greater than $400.

The $p$-value provides additional insight into the decision. Recall the $p$-value is the probability of finding a test statistic as large as or larger than that obtained, when the null hypothesis is true. So we find the probability of a $z$ value greater than 2.42. From Appendix D the probability of a $z$ value between 0 and 2.42 is .4922. We want to determine the likelihood of a value *greater than* 2.42, so .5000 − .4922 = .0078. We conclude that the likelihood of finding a $z$ value of 2.42 or larger when the null hypothesis is true is 0.78 percent. It is unlikely, therefore, that the null hypothesis is true.

---

**SELF-REVIEW 10–2**

Refer to Self-Review 10–1.

(a) Suppose the hypothesis-testing problem was changed to a one-tailed test. How would the null hypothesis be written symbolically if it read, "The population mean is equal to or greater than 6.0"?

(b) How would the alternate hypothesis be written symbolically if it read, "The population mean is less than 6.0"?

(c) Show the decision rule graphically. Show the rejection region and indicate the critical value.

(d) Calculate the $p$-value. Recall from Self-Review 10–1 on page 327 that $z = -2.56$.

# Exercises

For Exercises 1–4 answer the questions: (a) Is this a one- or two-tailed test? (b) What is the decision rule? (c) What is the value of the test statistic? (d) What is your decision regarding $H_0$? (e) What is the $p$-value? Interpret it.

1.  The following information is available.

    $H_0$: $\mu = 50$
    $H_1$: $\mu \neq 50$

    The sample mean is 49, and the sample size is 36. The population standard deviation is 5. Use the .05 significance level.

2.  The following information is available.

    $H_0$: $\mu \leq 10$
    $H_1$: $\mu > 10$

    The sample mean is 12 for a sample of 36. The population standard deviation is 3. Use the .02 significance level.

3.  A sample of 36 observations is selected from a normal population. The sample mean is 21, and the sample standard deviation is 5. Conduct the following test of hypothesis using the .05 significance level.

    $H_0$: $\mu \leq 20$
    $H_1$: $\mu > 20$

4.  A sample of 64 observations is selected from a normal population. The sample mean is 215, and the sample standard deviation is 15. Conduct the following test of hypothesis using the .03 significance level.

    $H_0$: $\mu \geq 220$
    $H_1$: $\mu < 220$

    For Exercises 5–8: (a) State the null hypothesis and the alternate hypothesis. (b) State the decision rule. (c) Compute the value of the test statistic. (d) What is your decision regarding $H_0$? (e) What is the $p$-value? Interpret it.

5.  The manufacturer of the X-15 steel-belted radial truck tire claims that the mean mileage the tire can be driven before the tread wears out is 60,000 miles. The standard deviation of the mileage is 5,000 miles. The Crosset Truck Company bought 48 tires and found that the mean mileage for their trucks is 59,500 miles. Is Crosset's experience different from that claimed by the manufacturer at the .05 significance level?

6.  The MacBurger restaurant chain claims that the waiting time of customers for service is normally distributed, with a mean of 3 minutes and a standard deviation of 1 minute. The quality-assurance department found in a sample of 50 customers at the Warren Road MacBurger that the mean waiting time was 2.75 minutes. At the .05 significance level, can we conclude that the mean waiting time is less than 3 minutes?

7.  A recent national survey found that high school students watched an average (mean) of 6.8 DVDs per month. A random sample of 36 college students revealed that the mean number of DVDs watched last month was 6.2, with a standard deviation of 0.5. At the .05 significance level, can we conclude that college students watch fewer DVDs a month than high school students?

8.  At the time she was hired as a server at the Grumney Family Restaurant, Beth Brigden was told, "You can average more than $20 a day in tips." Over the first 35 days she was employed at the restaurant, the mean daily amount of her tips was $24.85, with a standard deviation of $3.24. At the .01 significance level, can Ms. Brigden conclude that she is earning an average of more than $20 in tips?

# Tests Concerning Proportions

In the previous chapter we discussed confidence intervals for proportions. We can also conduct a test of hypothesis for a proportion. Recall that a proportion is the ratio of the number of successes to the number of observations. We let $X$ refer to the number of successes and $n$ the number of observations, so the proportion of successes in a fixed number of trials is $X/n$. Thus, the formula for computing a sample proportion, $p$, is $p = X/n$. Consider the following potential hypothesis-testing situations.

- Historically, General Motors reports that 70 percent of leased vehicles are returned with less than 36,000 miles. A recent sample of 200 vehicles returned at the end of their lease showed 158 had less than 36,000 miles. Has the proportion increased?
- The American Association of Retired Persons (AARP) reports that 60 percent of retired persons under the age of 65 would return to work on a full-time basis if a suitable job were available. A sample of 500 retirees under 65 revealed 315 would return to work. Can we conclude that more than 60 percent would return to work?
- Able Moving and Storage, Inc., advises its clients for long distance residential moves that their household goods will be delivered in 3 to 5 days from the time they are picked up. Able's records show that they are successful 90 percent of the time with this claim. A recent audit revealed they were successful 190 times out of 200. Can they conclude that their success rate has increased?

Some assumptions must be made and conditions met before testing a population proportion. To test a hypothesis about a population proportion, a random sample is chosen from the population. It is assumed that the binomial assumptions discussed in Chapter 6 are met: (1) the sample data collected are the result of counts; (2) the outcome of an experiment is classified into one of two mutually exclusive categories—a "success" or a "failure"; (3) the probability of a success is the same for each trial; and (4) the trials are independent, meaning the outcome of one trial does not affect the outcome of any other trial. The test we will conduct shortly is appropriate when both $n\pi$ and $n(1 - \pi)$ are at least 5. $n$ is the sample size, and $p$ is the population proportion. It takes advantage of the fact that a binomial distribution can be approximated by the normal distribution.

*$n\pi$ and $n(1 - \pi)$ must be at least 5.*

**EXAMPLE**

Suppose prior elections in a state indicated it is necessary for a candidate for governor to receive at least 80 percent of the vote in the northern section of the state to be elected. The incumbent governor is interested in assessing his chances of returning to office and plans to conduct a survey of 2,000 registered voters in the northern section of the state.

Using the hypothesis-testing procedure, assess the governor's chances of reelection.

**SOLUTION**

The following test of hypothesis can be conducted because both $n\pi$ and $n(1 - \pi)$ exceed 5. In this case, $n = 2,000$ and $\pi = .80$ ($\pi$ is the proportion of the vote in the northern part of the state, or 80 percent, needed to be elected). Thus, $n\pi = 2,000(.80) = 1,600$ and $n(1 - \pi) = 2,000(1 - .80) = 400$. Both 1,600 and 400 are greater than 5.

Step 1: **State the null hypothesis and the alternate hypothesis.** The null hypothesis, $H_0$, is that the population proportion $\pi$ is .80 or larger. The alternate hypothesis, $H_1$, is that the proportion is less than .80. From a practical standpoint, the incumbent governor is concerned only when the proportion is less than .80. If it is equal to or greater than .80, he will have no problem; that is, the sample data would indicate he will probably be reelected. These hypotheses are written symbolically as:

$$H_0: \pi \geq .80$$
$$H_1: \pi < .80$$

$H_1$ states a direction. Thus, as noted previously, the test is one-tailed with the inequality sign pointing to the tail of the distribution containing the region of rejection.

**Step 2:** **Select the level of significance.** The level of significance is .05. This is the likelihood that a true hypothesis will be rejected.

**Step 3:** **Select the test statistic.** $z$ is the appropriate statistic, found by:

| TEST OF HYPOTHESIS, ONE PROPORTION | $z = \dfrac{p - \pi}{\sigma_p}$ | **[10–3]** |

where:

$\pi$ is the population proportion.

$p$ is the sample proportion.

$n$ is the sample size.

$\sigma_p$ is the standard error of the proportion. It is computed by $\sqrt{\pi(1 - \pi)/n}$, so the formula for $z$ becomes:

| TEST OF HYPOTHESIS, ONE PROPORTION | $z = \dfrac{p - \pi}{\sqrt{\dfrac{\pi(1 - \pi)}{n}}}$ | **[10–4]** |

Finding the critical value

**Step 4:** **Formulate the decision rule.** The critical value or values of $z$ form the dividing point or points between the regions where $H_0$ is rejected and where it is not rejected. Since the alternate hypothesis states a direction, this is a one-tailed test. The sign of the inequality points to the left, so only the left side of the curve is used. (See Chart 10–6.) The significance level was given as .05 in step 2. This probability is in the left tail and determines the region of rejection. The area between zero and the critical value is .4500, found by .5000 − .0500. Referring to Appendix D and searching for .4500, we find the critical value of $z$ is 1.65. The decision rule is, therefore: Reject the null hypothesis and accept the alternate hypothesis if the computed value of $z$ falls to the left of −1.65; otherwise do not reject $H_0$.

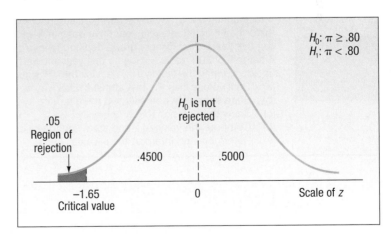

**CHART 10–6** Rejection Region for the .05 Level of Significance, One-Tailed Test

Select a sample and make a decision regarding $H_0$.

**Step 5:** **Make a decision and interpret the result.** Select a sample and make a decision about $H_0$. A sample survey of 2,000 potential voters in the northern part of the state revealed that 1,550 planned to vote for the incumbent governor. Is the sample proportion of .775 (found by 1,550/2,000) close enough to .80 to conclude that the difference is due to sampling error? In this case:

p is .775, the proportion in the sample who plan to vote for the governor.

n is 2,000, the number of voters surveyed.

$\pi$ is .80, the hypothesized population proportion.

z is a normally distributed test statistic when the hypothesis is true and the other assumptions are true.

Using formula (10–4) and computing z gives

$$z = \frac{p - \pi}{\sqrt{\dfrac{\pi(1 - \pi)}{n}}} = \frac{\dfrac{1{,}550}{2{,}000} - .80}{\sqrt{\dfrac{.80(1 - .80)}{2{,}000}}} = \frac{.775 - .80}{\sqrt{.00008}} = -2.80$$

The computed value of z (−2.80) is in the rejection region, so the null hypothesis is rejected at the .05 level. The difference of 2.5 percentage points between the sample percent (77.5 percent) and the hypothesized population percent in the northern part of the state necessary to carry the state (80 percent) is statistically significant. It is probably not due to sampling variation. To put it another way, the evidence at this point does not support the claim that the incumbent governor will return to the governor's mansion for another four years.

The p-value is the probability of finding a z value less than −2.80. From Appendix D, the probability of a z value between zero and −2.80 is .4974. So the p-value is .0026, found by .5000 − .4974. The governor cannot be confident of reelection because the p-value is less than the significance level.

---

**SELF-REVIEW 10–3**

A recent insurance industry report indicated that 40 percent of those persons involved in minor traffic accidents this year have been involved in a least one other traffic accident in the last five years. An advisory group decided to investigate this claim, believing it was too large. A sample of 200 traffic accidents this year showed 74 persons were also involved in another accident within the last five years. Use the .01 significance level.
(a) Can we use z as the test statistic? Tell why or why not.
(b) State the null hypothesis and the alternate hypothesis.
(c) Show the decision rule graphically.
(d) Compute the value of z and state your decision regarding the null hypothesis.
(e) Determine and interpret the p-value.

---

# Exercises

9. The following hypotheses are given.

$H_0$: $\pi \le .70$
$H_1$: $\pi > .70$

A sample of 100 observations revealed that $p = .75$. At the .05 significance level, can the null hypothesis be rejected?
a. State the decision rule.
b. Compute the value of the test statistic.
c. What is your decision regarding the null hypothesis?

10. The following hypotheses are given.

$$H_0: \pi = .40$$
$$H_1: \pi \neq .40$$

A sample of 120 observations revealed that $p = .30$. At the .05 significance level, can the null hypothesis be rejected?
   **a.** State the decision rule.
   **b.** Compute the value of the test statistic.
   **c.** What is your decision regarding the null hypothesis?

*Note:* It is recommended that you use the five-step hypothesis-testing procedure in solving the following problems.

11. The National Safety Council reported that 52 percent of American turnpike drivers are men. A sample of 300 cars traveling southbound on the New Jersey Turnpike yesterday revealed that 170 were driven by men. At the .01 significance level, can we conclude that a larger proportion of men were driving on the New Jersey Turnpike than the national statistics indicate?

12. A recent article in *USA Today* reported that a job awaits only one in three new college graduates. The major reasons given were an overabundance of college graduates and a weak economy. A survey of 200 recent graduates from your school revealed that 80 students had jobs. At the .02 significance level, can we conclude that a larger proportion of students at your school have jobs?

13. Chicken Delight claims that 90 percent of its orders are delivered within 10 minutes of the time the order is placed. A sample of 100 orders revealed that 82 were delivered within the promised time. At the .10 significance level, can we conclude that less than 90 percent of the orders are delivered in less than 10 minutes?

14. Research at the University of Toledo indicates that 50 percent of the students change their major area of study after their first year in a program. A random sample of 100 students in the College of Business revealed that 48 had changed their major area of study after their first year of the program. Has there been a significant decrease in the proportion of students who change their major after the first year in this program? Test at the .05 level of significance.

# Testing for a Population Mean: Small Sample, Population Standard Deviation Unknown

We are able to use the standard normal distribution, that is $z$, under two conditions:

1. The population is known to follow a normal distribution and the population standard deviation is known, or
2. The shape of the population is not known, but the number of observations in the sample is at least 30.

What do we do when the sample is less than 30 and the population standard deviation is not known? We encountered this same situation when constructing confidence intervals in the previous chapter. See pages 291–293 in Chapter 9. We summarized this problem in Chart 9–3 on page 293. Under these conditions the correct statistical procedure is to replace the standard normal distribution with the $t$ distribution. To review, the major characteristics of the $t$ distribution are:

1. It is a continuous distribution.
2. It is bell-shaped and symmetrical.
3. There is a family of $t$ distributions. Each time the degrees of freedom change, a new distribution is created.
4. As the number of degrees of freedom increases the shape of the $t$ distribution approaches that of the standard normal distribution.

5. The *t* distribution is flatter, or more spread out, than the standard normal distribution.

To conduct a test of hypothesis using the *t* distribution, we adjust formula (10–2) as follows.

| TEST OF MEAN, SMALL SAMPLE | $t = \dfrac{\overline{X} - \mu}{s/\sqrt{n}}$ | [10–5] |
|---|---|---|

with $n - 1$ degrees of freedom, where:

$\overline{X}$ is the mean of the sample.
$\mu$ is the hypothesized population mean.
$s$ is the standard deviation of the sample.
$n$ is the number of observations in the sample.

The following example shows the details

**EXAMPLE**

The McFarland Insurance Company Claims Department reports the mean cost to process a claim is $60. An industry comparison showed this amount to be larger than most other insurance companies, so they instituted cost-cutting measures. To evaluate the effect of the cost-cutting measures, the Supervisor of the Claims Department selected a random sample of 26 claims processed last month. The sample information is reported below.

| $45 | $49 | $62 | $40 | $43 | $61 |
|---|---|---|---|---|---|
| 48 | 53 | 67 | 63 | 78 | 64 |
| 48 | 54 | 51 | 56 | 63 | 69 |
| 58 | 51 | 58 | 59 | 56 | 57 |
| 38 | 76 | | | | |

At the .01 significance level is it reasonable to conclude that mean cost to process a claim is now less than $60?

**SOLUTION**

We will use the five-step hypothesis testing procedure.

**Step 1: State the null hypothesis and the alternate hypothesis.** The null hypothesis is that the population mean is at least $60. The alternate hypothesis is that the population mean is less than $60. We can express the null and alternate hypotheses as follows:

$H_0$: $\mu \geq \$60$
$H_1$: $\mu < \$60$

The test is *one*-tailed because we want to determine whether there has been a *reduction* in the cost. The inequality in the alternate hypothesis points to the region of rejection in the left tail of the distribution.

**Step 2: Select the level of significance.** We decided on the .01 significance level.

**Step 3: Select the test statistic.** The test statistic in this situation is the *t* distribution. Why? First it is reasonable to conclude that the distribution of the cost per claim follows the normal distribution. We can confirm this from the histogram on the right-hand side of the following MINITAB output. Observe the normal distribution superimposed on the frequency distribution.

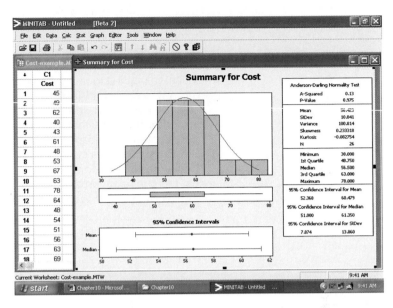

We do not know the standard deviation of the population. So we substitute the sample standard deviation. When the sample is large we can make the substitution and still use the standard normal distribution. We usually define large as 30 or more observations. In this case there are only 26 observations. Consequently we cannot use the standard normal distribution. Instead, we use *t*. The value of the test statistic is computed by formula (10–5):

$$t = \frac{\overline{X} - \mu}{s/\sqrt{n}}$$

**Step 4: Formulate the decision rule.** The critical values of *t* are given in Appendix F, a portion of which is shown in Table 10–1. Appendix F is also repeated in the back inside cover of the text. The far left column of the table

**TABLE 10–1** A Portion of the *t* Distribution Table

| Confidence Intervals | | | | | |
|---|---|---|---|---|---|
| **80%** | **90%** | **95%** | **98%** | **99%** | **99.9%** |
| Level of Significance for One-Tailed Test | | | | | |
| **0.100** | **0.050** | **0.025** | **0.010** | **0.005** | **0.0005** |
| Level of Significance for Two-Tailed Test | | | | | |
| **0.20** | **0.10** | **0.05** | **0.02** | **0.01** | **0.001** |
| ⋮ | ⋮ | ⋮ | ⋮ | ⋮ | ⋮ |
| 1.323 | 1.721 | 2.080 | 2.518 | 2.831 | 3.819 |
| 1.321 | 1.717 | 2.074 | 2.508 | 2.819 | 3.792 |
| 1.319 | 1.714 | 2.069 | 2.500 | 2.807 | 3.768 |
| 1.318 | 1.711 | 2.064 | 2.492 | 2.797 | 3.745 |
| 1.316 | 1.708 | 2.060 | 2.485 | 2.787 | 3.725 |
| 1.315 | 1.706 | 2.056 | 2.479 | 2.779 | 3.707 |
| 1.314 | 1.703 | 2.052 | 2.473 | 2.771 | 3.690 |
| 1.313 | 1.701 | 2.048 | 2.467 | 2.763 | 3.674 |
| 1.311 | 1.699 | 2.045 | 2.462 | 2.756 | 3.659 |
| 1.310 | 1.697 | 2.042 | 2.457 | 2.750 | 3.646 |

The *df* column values, left of the table, are: 21, 22, 23, 24, 25, 26, 27, 28, 29, 30.

is labeled "df" for degrees of freedom. The number of degrees of freedom is the total number of observations in the sample minus the number of samples, written $n - 1$. In this case the number of observations in the sample is 26, so there are $26 - 1 = 25$ degrees of freedom. To find the critical value, first locate the row with the appropriate degrees of freedom. This row is shaded in Table 10–1. Next, determine whether the test is one-tailed or two-tailed. In this case, we have a one-tailed test, so find the portion of the table that is labeled "one-tailed." Locate the column with the selected significance level. In this example, the significance level is .01. Move down the column labeled "0.01" until it intersects the row with 25 degrees of freedom. The value is 2.485. Because this is a one-sided test and the rejection region is in the left tail, the critical value is negative. The decision rule is to reject $H_0$ if the value of $t$ is less than $-2.485$.

**CHART 10-7** Rejection Region, $t$ Distribution, .01 Significance Level

**Step 5: Make a decision and interpret the result.** From the MINITAB output on page 337, next to the histogram, the mean cost per claim for the sample of 26 observations is $56.42. The standard deviation of this sample is $10.04. We insert these values in formula (10–5) and compute the value of $t$:

$$t = \frac{\bar{X} - \mu}{s/\sqrt{n}} = \frac{\$56.42 - \$60}{\$10.04/\sqrt{26}} = -1.818$$

Because $-1.818$ lies in the region to the right of the critical value of $-2.485$, the null hypothesis is not rejected at the .01 significance level. We have not demonstrated that the cost-cutting measures reduced the mean cost per claim to less than $60. To put it another way, the difference of $3.58 ($56.42 − $60) between the sample mean and the population mean could be due to sampling error. The computed value of $t$ is shown in Chart 10–7. It is in the region where the null hypothesis is *not* rejected.

In the previous example the mean and the standard deviation were included in the problem. The following example requires this information to be computed from the sample data.

**EXAMPLE**

The mean length of a small counterbalance bar is 43 millimeters. The production supervisor is concerned that the adjustments of the machine producing the bars have changed. He asks the Engineering Department to investigate. Engineering selects a random sample of 12 bars and measures each. The results are reported below in millimeters.

| 42 | 39 | 42 | 45 | 43 | 40 | 39 | 41 | 40 | 42 | 43 | 42 |
|----|----|----|----|----|----|----|----|----|----|----|----|

Is it reasonable to conclude that there has been a change in the mean length of the bars? Use the .02 significance level.

**SOLUTION**

We begin by stating the null hypothesis and the alternate hypothesis.

$H_0$: $\mu = 43$
$H_1$: $\mu \neq 43$

The alternate hypothesis does not state a direction, so this is a two-tailed test. There are 11 degrees of freedom, found by $n - 1 = 12 - 1 = 11$. The $t$ value is 2.718, found by referring to Appendix F for a two-tailed test, using the .02 significance level, with 11 degrees of freedom. The decision rule is: Reject the null hypothesis if the computed $t$ is to the left of $-2.718$ or to the right of 2.718. This information is summarized in Chart 10–8.

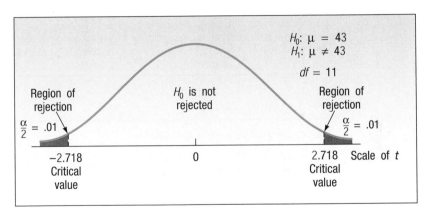

**CHART 10–8** Regions of Rejection, Two-Tailed Test, Student's $t$ Distribution, $\alpha = .02$

We calculate the standard deviation of the sample using formula (3–11). The mean, $\overline{X}$, is 41.5 millimeters, and the standard deviation, $s$, is 1.784 millimeters. The details are shown in Table 10–2.

Now we are ready to compute the value of $t$, using formula (10–5).

$$t = \frac{\overline{X} - \mu}{s/\sqrt{n}} = \frac{41.5 - 43.0}{1.784/\sqrt{12}} = -2.91$$

The null hypothesis that the population mean is 43 millimeters is rejected because the computed $t$ of $-2.91$ lies in the area to the left of $-2.718$. We accept the alternate hypothesis and conclude that the population mean is not 43 millimeters. The machine is out of control and needs adjustment.

**TABLE 10–2** Calculations of the Sample Standard Deviation

| X (mm) | X − X̄ | (X − X̄)² |
|---|---|---|
| 42 | 0.5 | 0.25 |
| 39 | −2.5 | 6.25 |
| 42 | 0.5 | 0.25 |
| 45 | 3.5 | 12.25 |
| 43 | 1.5 | 2.25 |
| 40 | −1.5 | 2.25 |
| 39 | −2.5 | 6.25 |
| 41 | −0.5 | 0.25 |
| 40 | −1.5 | 2.25 |
| 42 | 0.5 | 0.25 |
| 43 | 1.5 | 2.25 |
| 42 | 0.5 | 0.25 |
| 498 | 0 | 35.00 |

$$\bar{X} = \frac{498}{12} = 41.5 \text{ mm}$$

$$s = \sqrt{\frac{\Sigma(X - \bar{X})^2}{n - 1}} = \sqrt{\frac{35}{12 - 1}} = 1.784$$

---

**SELF-REVIEW 10–4**

The mean life of a battery used in a digital clock is 305 days. The lives of the batteries follow the normal distribution. The battery was recently modified to last longer. A sample of 20 of the modified batteries had a mean life of 311 days with a standard deviation of 12 days. Did the modification increase the mean life of the battery?
(a) State the null hypothesis and the alternate hypothesis.
(b) Show the decision rule graphically. Use the .05 significance level.
(c) Compute the value of t. What is your decision regarding the null hypothesis? Briefly summarize your results.

## Exercises

15. Given the following hypothesis:

    $H_0$: $\mu \le 10$
    $H_1$: $\mu > 10$

    For a random sample of 10 observations, the sample mean was 12 and the sample standard deviation 3. Using the .05 significance level:
    **a.** State the decision rule.
    **b.** Compute the value of the test statistic.
    **c.** What is your decision regarding the null hypothesis?
16. Given the following hypothesis:

    $H_0$: $\mu = 400$
    $H_1$: $\mu \ne 400$

    For a random sample of 12 observations, the sample mean was 407 and the sample standard deviation 6. Using the .01 significance level:
    **a.** State the decision rule.
    **b.** Compute the value of the test statistic.
    **c.** What is your decision regarding the null hypothesis?
17. The Rocky Mountain district sales manager of Rath Publishing, Inc., a college textbook publishing company, claims that the sales representatives make an average of 40 sales calls per week on professors. Several reps say that this estimate is too low. To investigate, a random sample of 28 sales representatives reveals that the mean number of calls made last week was 42. The standard deviation of the sample is 2.1 calls. Using the .05 significance level, can we conclude that the mean number of calls per salesperson per week is more than 40?
18. The management of White Industries is considering a new method of assembling its golf cart. The present method requires 42.3 minutes, on the average, to assemble a cart. The mean assembly time for a random sample of 24 carts, using the new method, was 40.6

minutes, and the standard deviation of the sample was 2.7 minutes. Using the .10 level of significance, can we conclude that the assembly time using the new method is faster?

**19.** A spark plug manufacturer claimed that its plugs have a mean life in excess of 22,100 miles. Assume the life of the spark plugs follows the normal distribution. A fleet owner purchased a large number of sets. A sample of 18 sets revealed that the mean life was 23,400 miles and the standard deviation was 1,500 miles. Is there enough evidence to substantiate the manufacturer's claim at the .05 significance level?

**20.** Most air travelers now use e-tickets. Electronic ticketing allows passengers to not worry about a paper ticket, and it costs the airline companies less to handle than a paper ticketing. However, in recent times the airlines have received complaints from passengers regarding their e-tickets, particularly when connecting flights and a change of airlines were involved. To investigate the problem an independent watchdog agency contacted a random sample of 20 airports and collected information on the number of complaints the airport had with e-tickets for the month of March. The information is reported below.

| 14 | 14 | 16 | 12 | 12 | 14 | 13 | 16 | 15 | 14 |
| 12 | 15 | 15 | 14 | 13 | 13 | 12 | 13 | 10 | 13 |

At the .05 significance level can the watchdog agency conclude the mean number of complaints per airport is less than 15 per month?

**a.** What assumption is necessary before conducting a test of hypothesis?

**b.** Plot the number of complaints per airport in a frequency distribution or a dot plot. Is it reasonable to conclude that the population follows a normal distribution?

**c.** Conduct a test of hypothesis and interpret the results.

## A Software Solution

The MINITAB statistical software system, used in earlier chapters, provides an efficient way of conducting a one-sample test of hypothesis for a population mean. The steps to generate the following output are shown in the Software Commands section at the end of the chapter.

An additional feature of most statistical software packages is to report the *p*-value, which gives additional information on the null hypothesis. The *p*-value is the probability of a *t* value as extreme as that computed, given that the null hypothesis is true. In this case, the *p*-value of .014 is the likelihood of a *t* value of $-2.91$ or less plus the likelihood of a *t* value of 2.91 or larger, given a population mean of 43. Thus, comparing the *p*-value to the significance level tells us whether the null hypothesis was close to being rejected, barely rejected, and so on.

To explain further, refer to the following diagram, in which the $p$-value of .014 is shown in purple and the significance level is the yellow area plus the purple area. Because the $p$-value of .014 is less than the significance level of .02, the null hypothesis is rejected. Had the $p$-value been larger than the significance level—say, .06, .19, or .57—the null hypothesis would not be rejected. If the significance level had initially been selected as .01, the null hypothesis would not be rejected.

In the preceding example the alternate hypothesis was two-sided, so there were rejection areas in both the upper and the lower tails. To determine the $p$-value, it was necessary to determine the area to the left of $-2.91$ for a $t$ distribution with 11 degrees of freedom and add to it the value of the area to the right of 2.91, also with 11 degrees of freedom.

What if we were conducting a one-sided test, so that the entire rejection region would be in either the upper or the lower tail? In that case, we would report the area from only the one tail. In the counterbalance example, if $H_1$ were stated as $\mu < 43$, the inequality would point to the left. Thus, we would have reported the $p$-value as the area to the left of $-2.91$. This value is .007, found by .014/2. Thus, the $p$-value for a one-tailed test would be .007.

How can we estimate a $p$-value without a computer? To illustrate, recall that, in the example regarding the length of a counterbalance, we rejected the null hypothesis that $\mu = 43$ and accepted the alternate hypothesis that $\mu \neq 43$. The significance level was .02, so logically the $p$-value is less than .02. To estimate the $p$-value more accurately, go to Appendix F and find the row with 11 degrees of freedom. The computed $t$ value of 2.91 is between 2.718 and 3.106. (A portion of Appendix F is reproduced as Table 10–3.) The two-tailed significance level corresponding to 2.718 is .02, and for 3.106 it is .01. Therefore, the $p$-value is between .01 and .02. The usual practice is to report that the $p$-value is *less* than the larger of the two significance levels. So we would report, "the $p$-value is less than .02."

**TABLE 10–3** A Portion of Student's $t$ Distribution

| | Confidence Intervals | | | | | |
|---|---|---|---|---|---|---|
| | 80% | 90% | 95% | 98% | 99% | 99.9% |
| | Level of Significance for One-Tailed Test | | | | | |
| *df* | 0.100 | 0.050 | .0025 | 0.010 | 0.005 | 0.0005 |
| | Level of Significance for Two-Tailed Test | | | | | |
| | 0.20 | 0.10 | 0.05 | 0.02 | 0.01 | 0.001 |
| ⋮ | ⋮ | ⋮ | ⋮ | ⋮ | ⋮ | ⋮ |
| 9 | 1.383 | 1.833 | 2.262 | 2.821 | 3.250 | 4.781 |
| 10 | 1.372 | 1.812 | 2.228 | 2.764 | 3.169 | 4.587 |
| 11 | 1.363 | 1.796 | 2.201 | 2.718 | 3.106 | 4.437 |
| 12 | 1.356 | 1.782 | 2.179 | 2.681 | 3.055 | 4.318 |
| 13 | 1.350 | 1.771 | 2.160 | 2.650 | 3.012 | 4.221 |
| 14 | 1.345 | 1.761 | 2.145 | 2.624 | 2.977 | 4.140 |
| 15 | 1.341 | 1.753 | 2.131 | 2.602 | 2.947 | 4.073 |

**SELF-REVIEW 10–5**    A machine is set to fill a small bottle with 9.0 grams of medicine. A sample of eight bottles revealed the following amounts (grams) in each bottle.

| 9.2 | 8.7 | 8.9 | 8.6 | 8.8 | 8.5 | 8.7 | 9.0 |

At the .01 significance level, can we conclude that the mean weight is less than 9.0 grams?
(a)  State the null hypothesis and the alternate hypothesis.
(b)  How many degrees of freedom are there?
(c)  Give the decision rule.
(d)  Compute the value of $t$. What is your decision regarding the null hypothesis?
(e)  Estimate the $p$-value.

# Exercises

**21.** Given the following hypothesis:

$H_0$: $\mu \geq 20$
$H_1$: $\mu < 20$

A random sample of five resulted in the following values: 18, 15, 12, 19, and 21. Using the .01 significance level, can we conclude the population mean is less than 20?
**a.** State the decision rule.
**b.** Compute the value of the test statistic.
**c.** What is your decision regarding the null hypothesis?
**d.** Estimate the $p$-value.

**22.** Given the following hypothesis:

$H_0$: $\mu = 100$
$H_1$: $\mu \neq 100$

A random sample of six resulted in the following values: 118, 105, 112, 119, 105, and 111. Using the .05 significance level, can we conclude the mean is different from 100?
**a.** State the decision rule.
**b.** Compute the value of the test statistic.
**c.** What is your decision regarding the null hypothesis?
**d.** Estimate the $p$-value.

**23.** Experience raising New Jersey Red chickens revealed the mean weight of the chickens at five months is 4.35 pounds. The weights follow the normal distribution. In an effort to increase their weight, a special additive is added to the chicken feed. The subsequent weights of a sample of five-month-old chickens were (in pounds):

| 4.41 | 4.37 | 4.33 | 4.35 | 4.30 | 4.39 | 4.36 | 4.38 | 4.40 | 4.39 |

At the .01 level, has the special additive increased the mean weight of the chickens? Estimate the $p$-value.

**24.** The liquid chlorine added to swimming pools to combat algae has a relatively short shelf life before it loses its effectiveness. Records indicate that the mean shelf life of a 5-gallon jug of chlorine is 2,160 hours (90 days). As an experiment, Holdlonger was added to the chlorine to find whether it would increase the shelf life. A sample of nine jugs of chlorine had these shelf lives (in hours):

| 2,159 | 2,170 | 2,180 | 2,179 | 2,160 | 2,167 | 2,171 | 2,181 | 2,185 |

At the .025 level, has Holdlonger increased the shelf life of the chlorine? Estimate the $p$-value.

**25.** Wyoming fisheries contend that the mean number of cutthroat trout caught during a full day of fly-fishing on the Snake, Buffalo, and other rivers and streams in the Jackson Hole area is 4.0. To make their yearly update, the fishery personnel asked a sample of fly-fishermen to keep a count of the number caught during the day. The numbers were: 4, 4, 3, 2, 6, 8, 7, 1, 9, 3, 1, and 6. At the .05 level, can we conclude that the mean number caught is greater than 4.0? Estimate the $p$-value.

**26.** Hugger Polls contends that an agent conducts a mean of 53 in-depth home surveys every week. A streamlined survey form has been introduced, and Hugger wants to evaluate its effectiveness. The number of in-depth surveys conducted during a week by a random sample of agents are:

| 53 | 57 | 50 | 55 | 58 | 54 | 60 | 52 | 59 | 62 | 60 | 60 | 51 | 59 | 56 |
|----|----|----|----|----|----|----|----|----|----|----|----|----|----|----|

At the .05 level of significance, can we conclude that the mean number of interviews conducted by the agents is more than 53 per week? Estimate the $p$-value.

# Type II Error

Recall that the level of significance, identified by the symbol $\alpha$, is the probability that the null hypothesis is rejected when it is true. This is called a Type I error. The most common levels of significance are .05 and .01 and are set by the researcher at the outset of the test.

In a hypothesis-testing situation there is also the possibility that a null hypothesis is not rejected when it is actually false. That is, we accept a false null hypothesis. This is called a Type II error. The probability of a Type II error is identified by the Greek letter beta ($\beta$). The following examples illustrate the details of determining the value of $\beta$.

**EXAMPLE**

A manufacturer purchases steel bars to make cotter pins. Past experience indicates that the mean tensile strength of all incoming shipments is 10,000 psi and that the standard deviation, $\sigma$, is 400 psi.

In order to make a decision about incoming shipments of steel bars, the manufacturer set up this rule for the quality-control inspector to follow: "Take a sample of 100 steel bars. At the .05 significance level if the sample mean ($\overline{X}$) strength falls between 9,922 psi and 10,078 psi, accept the lot. Otherwise the lot is to be rejected." Refer to Chart 10–9, Region A. It shows the region where each lot is rejected and where it is not rejected. The mean of this distribution is designated $\mu_0$. The tails of the curve represent the probability of making a Type I error, that is, rejecting the incoming lot of steel bars when in fact it is a good lot, with a mean of 10,000 psi.

Suppose the unknown population mean of an incoming lot, designated $\mu_1$, is really 9,900 psi. What is the probability that the quality-control inspector will fail to reject the shipment (a Type II error)?

**SOLUTION**

The probability of committing a Type II error, as represented by the purple area in Chart 10–9, Region B, can be computed by determining the area under the normal curve that lies above 9,922 pounds. The calculation of the areas under the normal curve was discussed in Chapter 7. Reviewing briefly, it is necessary first to determine the probability of the sample mean falling between 9,900 and 9,922. Then this probability is subtracted from .5000 (which represents all the area beyond the mean of 9,900) to arrive at the probability of making a Type II error in this case.

The number of standard units ($z$ value) between the mean of the incoming lot (9,900), designated by $\mu_1$, and $\overline{X}_c$, representing the critical value for 9,922, is computed by:

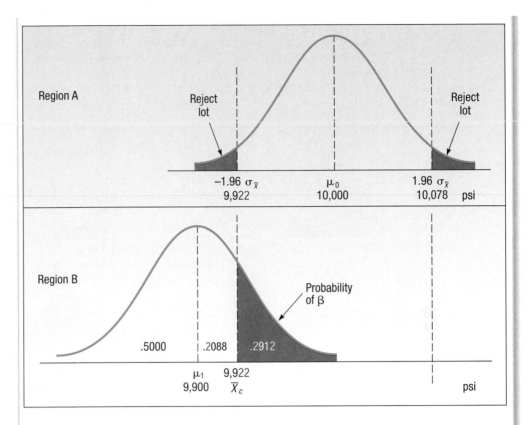

**CHART 10–9** Charts Showing Type I and Type II Errors

| TYPE II ERROR | $z = \dfrac{\bar{X}_c - \mu_1}{\sigma/\sqrt{n}}$ | **[10–6]** |
|---|---|---|

With $n = 100$ and $\sigma = 400$, the value of $z$ is 0.55:

$$z = \frac{\bar{X}_c - \mu_1}{\sigma/\sqrt{n}} = \frac{9{,}922 - 9{,}900}{400/\sqrt{100}} = \frac{22}{40} = 0.55$$

The area under the curve between 9,900 and 9,922 (a $z$ value of 0.55) is .2088. The area under the curve beyond 9,922 pounds is .5000 − .2088, or .2912; this is the probability of making a Type II error—that is, accepting an incoming lot of steel bars when the population mean is 9,900 psi.

Another illustration in Chart 10–10, Region C, depicts the probability of accepting a lot when the population mean is 10,120. To find the probability:

$$z = \frac{\bar{X}_c - \mu_1}{\sigma/\sqrt{n}} = \frac{10{,}078 - 10{,}120}{400/\sqrt{100}} = -1.05$$

The probability that $z$ is less than −1.05 is .1469, found by .5000 − .3531. Therefore, β, or the probability of a Type II error, is .1469.

Using the methods illustrated by Charts 10–9B and 10–10C, the probability of accepting a hypothesis as true when it is actually false can be determined for any value of $\mu_1$.

Type II error probabilities are shown in the center column of Table 10–4 for selected values of $\mu$, given in the left column. The right column gives the probability of not making a Type II error, which is also known as the power of a test.

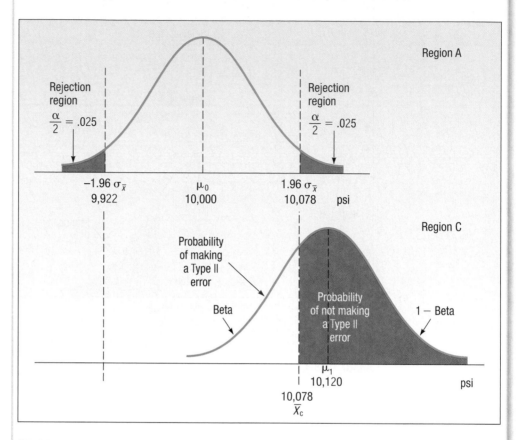

**CHART 10–10** Type I and Type II Errors (Another Example)

**TABLE 10–4** Probabilities of a Type II Error for $\mu_0 = 10,000$ Pounds and Selected Alternative Means, .05 Level of Significance

| Selected Alternative Mean (pounds) | Probability of Type II Error ($\beta$) | Probability of Not Making a Type II Error ($1 - \beta$) |
|---|---|---|
| 9,820 | .0054 | .9946 |
| 9,880 | .1469 | .8531 |
| 9,900 | .2912 | .7088 |
| 9,940 | .6736 | .3264 |
| 9,980 | .9265 | .0735 |
| 10,000 | — * | — |
| 10,020 | .9265 | .0735 |
| 10,060 | .6736 | .3264 |
| 10,100 | .2912 | .7088 |
| 10,120 | .1469 | .8531 |
| 10,180 | .0054 | .9946 |

*It is not possible to make a Type II error when $\mu = \mu_0$.

**SELF-REVIEW 10–6** Suppose the true mean of an incoming lot of steel bars is 10,180 psi. What is the probability that the quality control inspector will accept the bars as having a mean of 10,000 psi? (It sounds implausible that steel bars will be rejected if the tensile strength is higher than specified. However, it may be that the cotter pin has a dual function in an outboard motor. It may be designed not to shear off if the motor hits a small object, but to shear off if it hits a rock. Therefore, the steel should not be *too* strong.)

The light area in Chart 10–10, Region C, represents the probability of falsely accepting the hypothesis that the mean tensile strength of the incoming steel is 10,000 psi. What is the probability of committing a Type II error?

# Exercises

**27.** Refer to Table 10–4 and the example just completed. With $n = 100$, $\sigma = 400$, $\bar{X}_c = 9,922$, and $\mu_1 = 9,880$, verify that the probability of a Type II error is .1469.

**28.** Refer to Table 10–4 and the example just completed. With $n = 100$, $\sigma = 400$, $\bar{X}_c = 9,922$, and $\mu_1 = 9,940$, verify that the probability of a Type II error is .6736.

# Chapter Outline

**I.** The objective of hypothesis testing is to check the validity of a statement about a population parameter.

**II.** The steps in conducting a test of hypothesis are:

  **A.** State the null hypothesis ($H_0$) and the alternate hypothesis ($H_1$).

  **B.** Select the level of significance.

    **1.** The level of significance is the likelihood of rejecting a true null hypothesis.

    **2.** The most frequently used significance levels are .01, .05, and .10, but any value between 0 and 1.00 is possible.

  **C.** Select the test statistic.

    **1.** A test statistic is a value calculated from sample information used to determine whether to reject the null hypothesis.

    **2.** Two test statistics were considered in this chapter.

      **a.** The standard normal distribution is used when the population follows the normal distribution and the population standard deviation is known.

      **b.** The standard normal distribution is used when the population follows the normal distribution, the population standard deviation is unknown, but the sample contains at least 30 observations.

      **c.** The *t* distribution is used when the population follows the normal distribution, the population standard deviation is unknown, and the sample contains fewer than 30 observations.

  **D.** State the decision rule.

    **1.** The decision rule indicates the condition or conditions when the null hypothesis is rejected.

    **2.** In a two-tailed test, the rejection region is evenly split between the upper and lower tails.

    **3.** In a one-sample test, all of the rejection region is in either the upper or the lower tail.

  **E.** Select a sample, compute the value of the test statistic, make a decision regarding the null hypothesis, and interpret the results.

**III.** A *p*-value is the probability that the value of the test statistic is as extreme as the value computed, when the null hypothesis is true.

**IV.** Testing a hypothesis about a population mean.

  **A.** If the population standard deviation, $\sigma$, is known, the test statistic is the standard normal distribution and is determined from:

$$z = \frac{\bar{X} - \mu}{\sigma/\sqrt{n}}$$

[10–1]

**B.** If the population standard deviation is not known, but there are at least 30 observations in the sample, $s$ is substituted for $\sigma$. The test statistic is the standard normal distribution, and its value is determined from:

$$z = \frac{\bar{X} - \mu}{s/\sqrt{n}}$$ [10–2]

**C.** If the population standard deviation is not known, but there are fewer than 30 observations in the sample, $s$ is substituted for $\sigma$. The test statistic is the $t$ distribution, and its value is determined from:

$$t = \frac{\bar{X} - \mu}{s/\sqrt{n}}$$ [10–5]

The major characteristics of the $t$ distribution are:
1. It is a continuous distribution.
2. It is mound-shaped and symmetrical.
3. It is flatter, or more spread out, than the standard normal distribution.
4. There is a family of $t$ distributions, depending on the number of degrees of freedom.

**V.** Testing about a population proportion.
   **A.** Both $n\pi$ and $n(1 - \pi)$ must be at least 5.
   **B.** The test statistic is

$$z = \frac{p - \pi}{\sqrt{\dfrac{\pi(1 - \pi)}{n}}}$$ [10-4]

**VI.** There are two types of errors that can occur in a test of hypothesis.
   **A.** A Type I error occurs when a true null hypothesis is rejected.
      1. The probability of making a Type I error is equal to the level of significance.
      2. This probability is designated by the Greek letter $\alpha$.
   **B.** A Type II error occurs when a false null hypothesis is not rejected.
      1. The probability of making a Type II error is designated by the Greek letter $\beta$.
      2. The likelihood of a Type II error is found by

$$z = \frac{\bar{X}_c - \mu_1}{\sigma/\sqrt{n}}$$ [10-6]

   **C.** A power curve shows the chance of rejecting the null hypothesis for each value of a parameter.

# Pronunciation Key

| SYMBOL | MEANING | PRONUNCIATION |
|---|---|---|
| $H_0$ | Null hypothesis | *H sub zero* |
| $H_1$ | Alternate hypothesis | *H sub one* |
| $\alpha/2$ | Two-tailed significance level | *Alpha over 2* |
| $\bar{X}_c$ | Limit of the sample mean | *X bar sub c* |
| $\mu_0$ | Assumed population mean | *mu sub zero* |

# Chapter Exercises

**29.** A new weight-watching company, Weight Reducers International, advertises that those who join will lose, on the average, 10 pounds the first two weeks. A random sample of 50 people who joined the new weight reduction program revealed the mean loss to be 9 pounds with a standard deviation of 2.8 pounds. At the .05 level of significance, can we conclude that those joining Weight Reducers on average will lose less than 10 pounds? Determine the *p*-value.

**30.** Dole Pineapple, Inc. is concerned that the 16-ounce can of sliced pineapple is being overfilled. The quality-control department took a random sample of 50 cans and found that the arithmetic mean weight was 16.05 ounces, with a sample standard deviation of 0.03 ounces. At the 5 percent level of significance, can we conclude that the mean weight is greater than 16 ounces? Determine the *p*-value.

**31.** According to a recent survey, Americans get a mean of 7 hours of sleep per night. A random sample of 50 students at West Virginia University revealed the mean number of hours slept last night was 6 hours and 48 minutes (6.8 hours). The standard deviation of the sample was 0.9 hours. Is it reasonable to conclude that students at West Virginia sleep less than the typical American? Compute the *p*-value.

**32.** A statewide real estate sales agency, Farm Associates, specializes in selling farm property in the state of Nebraska. Their records indicate that the mean selling time of farm property is 90 days. Because of recent drought conditions, they believe that the mean selling time is now greater than 90 days. A statewide survey of 100 farms sold recently revealed that the mean selling time was 94 days, with a standard deviation of 22 days. At the .10 significance level, has there been an increase in selling time?

**33.** According to the local union president, the mean gross income of plumbers in the Salt Lake City area is normally distributed, with a mean of $45,000 and a standard deviation of $3,000. A recent investigative reporter for KYAK TV found, for a sample of 120 plumbers, the mean gross income was $45,500. At the .10 significance level, is it reasonable to conclude that the mean income is not equal to $45,000? Determine the *p*-value.

**34.** A recent article in *Vitality* magazine reported that the mean amount of leisure time per week for American men is 40.0 hours. You believe this figure is too large and decide to conduct your own test. In a random sample of 60 men, you find that the mean is 37.8 hours of leisure per week and that the standard deviation of the sample is 12.2 hours. Can you conclude that the information in the article is untrue? Use the .05 significance level. Determine the *p*-value and explain its meaning.

**35.** NBC TV news, in a segment on the price of gasoline, reported last evening that the mean price nationwide is $1.50 per gallon for self-serve regular unleaded. A random sample of 35 stations in the Milwaukee, Wisconsin, area revealed that the mean price was $1.52 per gallon and that the standard deviation was $0.05 per gallon. At the .05 significance level, can we conclude that the price of gasoline is higher in the Milwaukee area? Determine the *p*-value.

**36.** The Rutter Nursery Company packages their pine bark mulch in 50-pound bags. From a long history, the production department reports that the distribution of the bag weights follows the normal distribution and the standard deviation of this process is 3 pounds per bag. At the end of each day, Jeff Rutter, the production manager, weighs 10 bags and computes the mean weight of the sample. Below are the weights of 10 bags from today's production.

| 45.6 | 47.7 | 47.6 | 46.3 | 46.2 | 47.4 | 49.2 | 55.8 | 47.5 | 48.5 |
| --- | --- | --- | --- | --- | --- | --- | --- | --- | --- |

**a.** Can Mr. Rutter conclude that the mean weight of the bags is less than 50 pounds? Use the .01 significance level.
**b.** In a brief report, tell why Mr. Rutter can use the *z* distribution as the test statistic.
**c.** Compute the *p*-value.

**37.** Tina Dennis is the comptroller for Meek Industries. She believes that the current cash-flow problem at Meek is due to the slow collection of accounts receivable. She believes that more than 60 percent of the accounts are in arrears more than three months. A random sample of 200 accounts showed that 140 were more than three months old. At the .01 significance level, can she conclude that more than 60 percent of the accounts are in arrears for more than three months?

**38.** The policy of the Suburban Transit Authority is to add a bus route if more than 55 percent of the potential commuters indicate they would use the particular route. A sample of 70 commuters revealed that 42 would use a proposed route from Bowman Park to the downtown area. Does the Bowman-to-downtown route meet the STA criterion? Use the .05 significance level.

**39.** Past experience at the Crowder Travel Agency indicated that 44 percent of those persons who wanted the agency to plan a vacation for them wanted to go to Europe. During the most recent busy season, a sampling of 1,000 plans was selected at random from the files. It was found that 480 persons wanted to go to Europe on vacation. Has there been a significant shift upward in the percentage of persons who want to go to Europe? Test at the .05 significance level.

**40.** From past experience a television manufacturer found that 10 percent or less of its sets needed any type of repair in the first two years of operation. In a sample of 50 sets manufactured two years ago, 9 needed repair. At the .05 significance level, has the percent of sets needing repair increased? Determine the *p*-value.

41. An urban planner claims that, nationally, 20 percent of all families renting condominiums move during a given year. A random sample of 200 families renting condominiums in Dallas Metroplex revealed that 56 had moved during the past year. At the .01 significance level, does this evidence suggest that a larger proportion of condominium owners moved in the Dallas area? Determine the *p*-value.

42. The manufacturer of the Ososki motorcycle advertises that the cycle will average 87 miles per gallon of gasoline. A sample of eight bikes revealed the following mileage.

| 88 | 82 | 81 | 87 | 80 | 78 | 79 | 89 |
|----|----|----|----|----|----|----|----|

At the .05 level, is the mean mileage less than the advertised 87 miles per gallon?

43. The Myers Summer Casual Furniture Store tells customers that a special order will take six weeks (42 days). During recent months the owner has received several complaints that the special orders are taking longer than 42 days. A sample of 12 special orders delivered in the last month showed that the mean waiting time was 51 days, with a standard deviation of 8 days. At the .05 significance level, are customers waiting an average of more than 42 days? Estimate the *p*-value.

44. A recent article in the *Wall Street Journal* reported that the 30-year mortgage rate is now less than 6 percent. A sample of eight small banks in the Midwest revealed the following 30-year rates (in percent):

| 4.8 | 5.3 | 6.5 | 4.8 | 6.1 | 5.8 | 6.2 | 5.6 |
|-----|-----|-----|-----|-----|-----|-----|-----|

At the .01 significance level, can we conclude that the 30-year mortgage rate for small banks is less than 6 percent? Estimate the *p*-value.

45. According to the Coffee Research Organization (http://www.coffeeresearch.org) the typical American coffee drinker consumes an average of 3.1 cups per day. A sample of 12 senior citizens revealed they consumed the following amounts, reported in cups, of coffee yesterday.

| 3.1 | 3.3 | 3.5 | 2.6 | 2.6 | 4.3 | 4.4 | 3.8 | 3.1 | 4.1 | 3.1 | 3.2 |
|-----|-----|-----|-----|-----|-----|-----|-----|-----|-----|-----|-----|

At the .05 significance level does this sample data suggest there is a difference between the national average and the sample mean from senior citizens?

46. The postanesthesia care area (recovery room) at St. Luke's Hospital in Maumee, Ohio, was recently enlarged. The hope was that with the enlargement the mean number of patients per day would be more than 25. A random sample of 15 days revealed the following numbers of patients.

| 25 | 27 | 25 | 26 | 25 | 28 | 28 | 27 | 24 | 26 | 25 | 29 | 25 | 27 | 24 |
|----|----|----|----|----|----|----|----|----|----|----|----|----|----|----|

At the .01 significance level, can we conclude that the mean number of patients per day is more than 25? Estimate the *p*-value and interpret it.

47. *egolf.com* receives an average of 6.5 returns per day from online shoppers. For a sample of 12 days, they received the following number of returns.

| 0 | 4 | 3 | 4 | 9 | 4 | 5 | 9 | 1 | 6 | 7 | 10 |
|---|---|---|---|---|---|---|---|---|---|---|----|

At the .01 significance level, can we conclude the mean number of returns is less than 6.5?

48. During recent seasons, Major League Baseball has been criticized for the length of the games. A report indicated that the average game lasts 3 hours and 30 minutes. A sample of 17 games revealed the following times to completion. (Note that the minutes have been changed to fractions of hours, so that a game that lasted 2 hours and 24 minutes is reported at 2.40 hours.)

| 2.98 | 2.40 | 2.70 | 2.25 | 3.23 | 3.17 | 2.93 | 3.18 | 2.80 |
|------|------|------|------|------|------|------|------|------|
| 2.38 | 3.75 | 3.20 | 3.27 | 2.52 | 2.58 | 4.45 | 2.45 |      |

Can we conclude that the mean time for a game is less than 3.50 hours? Use the .05 significance level.

**49.** The Watch Corporation of Switzerland claims that their watches on average will neither gain nor lose time during a week. A sample of 18 watches provided the following gains (+) or losses (−) in seconds per week.

| | | | | | | | | |
|---|---|---|---|---|---|---|---|---|
| −0.38 | −0.20 | −0.38 | −0.32 | +0.32 | −0.23 | +0.30 | +0.25 | −0.10 |
| −0.37 | −0.61 | −0.48 | −0.47 | −0.64 | −0.04 | −0.20 | −0.68 | +0.05 |

Is it reasonable to conclude that the mean gain or loss in time for the watches is 0? Use the .05 significance level. Estimate the *p*-value.

**50.** Listed below is the rate of return for one year (reported in percent) for a sample of 12 mutual funds that are classified as taxable money market funds.

| | | | | | | | | | | | |
|---|---|---|---|---|---|---|---|---|---|---|---|
| 4.63 | 4.15 | 4.76 | 4.70 | 4.65 | 4.52 | 4.70 | 5.06 | 4.42 | 4.51 | 4.24 | 4.52 |

Using the .05 significance level is it reasonable to conclude that the mean rate of return is more than 4.50 percent?

**51.** Many grocery stores and large retailers such as Wal-Mart and K-Mart have installed self-checkout systems so shoppers can scan their own items and cash out themselves. How do customers like this service and how often do they use it? Listed below is the number of customers using the service for a sample of 15 days at the Wal-Mart on Highway 544 in Surfside, South Carolina.

| | | | | | | | | | |
|---|---|---|---|---|---|---|---|---|---|
| 120 | 108 | 120 | 114 | 118 | 91 | 118 | 92 | 104 | 104 |
| 112 | 97 | 118 | 108 | 117 | | | | | |

Is it reasonable to conclude that the mean number of customers using the self-checkout system is more than 100 per day? Use the .05 significance level.

**52.** In the year 2003 the mean fare to fly from Charlotte, North Carolina, to Seattle, Washington, on a discount ticket was $267. A random sample of round-trip discount fares on this route last month gives:

| | | | | | | | | | | | | |
|---|---|---|---|---|---|---|---|---|---|---|---|---|
| $321 | $286 | $290 | $330 | $310 | $250 | $270 | $280 | $299 | $265 | $291 | $275 | $281 |

At the .01 significance level can we conclude that the mean fare has increased? What is the *p*-value?

**53.** The President's call for designing and building a missile defense system that ignores restrictions of the Anti-Ballistic Missile Defense System treaty (ABM) is supported by 483 of the respondents in a nationwide poll of 1,002 adults. Is it reasonable to conclude that the nation is evenly divided on the issue? Use the .05 significance level.

**54.** One of the major U.S. automakers wishes to review its warranty. The warranty covers the engine, transmission, and drive train of all new cars for up to two years or 24,000 miles, whichever comes first. The manufacturer's quality-assurance department believes that the mean number of miles driven by owners is more than 24,000. A sample of 35 cars revealed that the mean number of miles was 24,421, with a standard deviation of 1,944 miles.

**a.** Conduct the following hypothesis test. Use the .05 significance level.

$H_0$: $\mu \leq 24{,}000$
$H_1$: $\mu > 24{,}000$

**b.** What is the largest value for the sample mean for which $H_0$ is not rejected?

**c.** Suppose the population mean shifts to 25,000 miles. What is the probability this change will not be detected?

**55.** A cola-dispensing machine is set to dispense 9.00 ounces of cola per cup, with a standard deviation of 1.00 ounces. The manufacturer of the machine would like to set the control limit in such a way that for samples of 36, 5 percent of the sample means will be greater than the upper control limit, and 5 percent of the sample means will be less than the lower control limit.

**a.** At what value should the control limit be set?

**b.** What is the probability that if the population mean shifts to 8.9, this change will not be detected?

**c.** What is the probability that if the population mean shifts to 9.3, this change will not be detected?

**56.** The owners of the Franklin Park Mall wished to study customer shopping habits. From earlier studies the owners are under the impression that a typical shopper spends 0.75 hours at the mall, with a standard deviation of 0.10 hours. Recently the mall owners added some specialty restaurants designed to keep shoppers in the mall longer. The consulting firm, Brunner and Swanson Marketing Enterprises, has been hired to evaluate the effects of the restaurants. A sample of 45 shoppers by Brunner and Swanson revealed that the mean time spent in the mall had increased to 0.80 hours.

**a.** Develop a test of hypothesis to determine if the mean time spent in the mall is more than 0.75 hours. Use the .05 significance level.

**b.** Suppose the mean shopping time actually increased from 0.75 hours to 0.77 hours. What is the probability this increase would not be detected?

**c.** When Brunner and Swanson reported the information in part (b) to the mall owners, the owners were upset with the statement that a survey could not detect a change from 0.75 to 0.77 hours of shopping time. How could this probability be reduced?

**57.** The following null and alternate hypotheses are given.

$$H_0: \mu \leq 50$$
$$H_1: \mu > 50$$

Suppose the population standard deviation is 10. The probability of a Type I error is set at .01 and the probability of a Type II error at .30. Assume that the population mean shifts from 50 to 55. How large a sample is necessary to meet these requirements?

**58.** An insurance company, based on past experience, estimates the mean damage for a natural disaster in its area is $5,000. After introducing several plans to prevent loss, they randomly sample 200 policyholders and find the mean amount per claim was $4,800 with a standard deviation of $1,300. Does it appear the prevention plans were effective in reducing the mean amount of a claim? Use the .05 significance level.

**59.** A national grocer's magazine reports the typical shopper spends eight minutes in line waiting to check out. A sample of 24 shoppers at the local Farmer Jack's showed a mean of 7.5 minutes with a standard deviation of 3.2 minutes. Is the waiting time at the local Farmer Jack's less than that reported in the national magazine? Use the .05 significance level.

# exercises.com

**60.** The *USA Today* (http://www.usatoday.com/sports/baseball/front.htm) and Major League Baseball (http://www.majorleaguebaseball.com) websites regularly report information on individual player salaries. Go to one of these sites and find the individual salaries for your favorite team. Compute the mean and the standard deviation. Is it reasonable to conclude that the mean salary on your favorite team is *different from* $1.80 million? If you are more of a football, basketball, or hockey enthusiast, information is also available on their teams' salaries.

**61.** The Gallup Organization in Princeton, New Jersey, is one of the best-known polling organizations in the United States. They often combine with *USA Today* or CNN to conduct polls of current interest. They also maintain a website at: http://www.gallup.com/. Consult this website to find the most recent polling results on Presidential approval ratings. You may need to click on Fast Facts. Test whether the majority (more than 50 percent) approve of the President's performance. If the article does not report the number of respondents included in the survey, assume that it is 1,000, a number that is typically used.

# Dataset Exercises

**62.** Refer to the Real Estate data, which reports information on the homes sold in Denver, Colorado, last year.

**a.** A recent article in the *Denver Post* indicated that the mean selling price of the homes in the area is more than $220,000. Can we conclude that the mean selling price in the Denver area is more than $220,000? Use the .01 significance level. What is the *p*-value?

**b.** The same article reported the mean size was more than 2,100 square feet. Can we conclude that the mean size of homes sold in the Denver area is more than 2,100 square feet? Use the .01 significance level. What is the *p*-value?

**c.** Determine the proportion of homes that have an attached garage. At the .05 significance level can we conclude that more than 60 percent of the homes sold in the Denver area had an attached garage? What is the *p*-value?

**d.** Determine the proportion of homes that have a pool. At the .05 significance level, can we conclude that less than 40 percent of the homes sold in the Denver area had a pool? What is the *p*-value?

**63.** Refer to the Baseball 2002 data, which reports information on the 30 Major League Baseball teams for the 2002 season.

**a.** Conduct a test of hypothesis to determine whether the mean salary of the teams was different from $80.0 million. Use the .05 significance level.

**b.** Conduct a test of hypothesis to determine whether the mean attendance was more than 2,000,000 per team.

**64.** Refer to the Wage data, which reports information on the annual wages for a sample of 100 workers. Also included are variables relating to the industry, years of education, and gender for each worker.

**a.** Conduct a test of hypothesis to determine if the mean annual wage is greater than $30,000. Use the .05 significance level. Determine the *p*-value and interpret the result.

**b.** Conduct a test of hypothesis to determine if the mean years of experience is different from 20. Use the .05 significance level. Determine the *p*-value and interpret the result.

**c.** Conduct a test of hypothesis to determine if the mean age is less than 40. Use the .05 significance level. Determine the *p*-value and interpret the result.

**d.** Conduct a test of hypothesis to determine if the proportion of union workers is greater than 15 percent. Use the .05 significance level and report the *p*-value.

**65.** Refer to the CIA data, which reports demographic and economic information on 46 different countries.

**a.** Conduct a test of hypothesis to determine if the mean number of cell phones is greater than 4.0. Use the .05 significance level. What is the *p*-value?

**b.** Conduct a test of hypothesis to determine if the mean size of the labor force is less than 50. Use the .05 significance level. What is the *p*-value?

# Software Commands

**1.** The MINITAB commands for the histogram and the descriptive statistics on page 337 are:

**a.** Enter the 26 sample observations in column C1 and name the variable **Cost**.

**b.** From the menu bar select **Stat**, **Basic Statistics**, and **Graphical Summary.** In the dialog box select **Cost** as the variable and click **OK**.

**2.** The MINITAB commands for the one-sample *t* test on page 341 are:

**a.** Enter the sample data into column C1 and name the variable **Length.**

**b.** From the menu bar select **Stat, Basic Statistics,** and **1-Sample t** and then hit **Enter.**

**c.** Select **Length** as the variable, select **Test mean,** insert the number **43** and click **OK**.

# Chapter 10  Answers to Self-Review

**10–1 a.** $H_0$: $\mu = 6.0$; $H_1$: $\mu \neq 6.0$
**b.** .05.
**c.** $z = \dfrac{\bar{X} - \mu}{\sigma/\sqrt{n}}$
**d.** Do not reject the null hypothesis if the computed $z$ value falls between $-1.96$ and $+1.96$.
**e.** Yes. Computed $z = -2.56$, found by:

$$z = \frac{5.84 - 6.0}{0.5/\sqrt{64}} = \frac{-0.16}{.0625} = -2.56$$

Reject $H_0$ at the .05 level. Accept $H_1$. The mean turnover rate is not equal to 6.0.

**10–2 a.** $H_0$: $\mu \geq 6.0$
**b.** $H_1$: $\mu < 6.0$
**c.** Note that the inequality sign ($<$) in the alternate hypothesis points in the direction of the region of rejection. To determine the critical value: $.5000 - .05 = .4500$. $z$ from Appendix D is about $-1.65$.

**d.** $p$-value $= .5000 - .4948 = .0052$
**10–3 a.** Yes, because both $n\pi$ and $n(1 - \pi)$ exceed 5: $n\pi = 200(.40) = 80$, and $n(1 - \pi) = 200(.60) = 120$.
**b.** $H_0$: $\pi \geq .40$
    $H_1$: $\pi < .40$
**c.**

**d.** $z = -0.87$, found by:

$$z = \frac{.37 - .40}{\sqrt{\dfrac{.40(1 - .40)}{200}}} = \frac{-.03}{\sqrt{.0012}} = -0.87$$

Do not reject $H_0$.
**e.** The $p$-value is .1922, found by $.5000 - .3078$.

**10–4 a.** $H_0$: $\mu \leq 305$, $H_1$: $\mu > 305$.
**b.** $df = n - 1 = 20 - 1 = 19$

**c.** $t = \dfrac{\bar{X} - \mu}{s/\sqrt{n}} = \dfrac{311 - 305}{12/\sqrt{20}} = 2.236$
Reject $H_0$ because $2.236 > 1.729$. The modification increased the mean battery life to more than 305 days.
**10–5 a.** $H_0$: $\mu \geq 9.0$, $H_1$: $\mu < 9.0$.
**b.** 7, found by $n - 1 = 8 - 1 = 7$.
**c.** Reject $H_0$ if $t < -2.998$.

**d.** $t = -2.494$, found by:

$$s = \sqrt{\frac{0.36}{8 - 1}} = 0.2268$$

$$\bar{X} = \frac{70.4}{8} = 8.8$$

Then

$$t = \frac{8.8 - 9.0}{0.2268/\sqrt{8}} = -2.494$$

Since $-2.494$ lies to the right of $-2.998$, $H_0$ is not rejected. We have not shown that the mean is less than 9.0.
**e.** The $p$-value is between .025 and .010.
**10–6** .0054, found by determining the area under the curve between 10,078 and 10,180 (Chart 10–10B).

$$z = \frac{\bar{X}_C - \mu_1}{\sigma/\sqrt{n}}$$

$$= \frac{10,078 - 10,180}{400/\sqrt{100}} = -2.55$$

The area under the curve for a $z$ of $-2.55$ is .4946 (Appendix D), and $.5000 - .4946 = .0054$.

# Two-Sample Tests of Hypothesis

## GOALS

*When you have completed this chapter, you will be able to:*

**1** Conduct a test of a hypothesis about the difference between two independent population means.

**2** Conduct a test of a hypothesis about the difference between two population proportions.

**3** Conduct a test of a hypothesis about the mean difference between paired or dependent observations.

**4** Understand the difference between dependent and independent samples.

Data was collected on annual rates of return for five stocks listed on the New York Stock Exchange and five stocks listed on NASDAQ. At the .10 significance level, can we conclude that the annual rates of return are higher on the big board? (See Goal 1 and Exercise 46.)

# Introduction

Chapter 10 began our study of hypothesis testing. We described the nature of hypothesis testing and conducted tests of a hypothesis in which we compared the results of a single sample to a population value. That is, we selected a single random sample from a population and conducted a test of whether the proposed population value was reasonable. Recall, in Chapter 10 we selected a sample of the number of desks assembled per week at the Jamestown Steel Company to determine whether there was a change in the production rate. Similarly, we sampled voters in one area of a particular state to determine whether the population proportion that would support the governor for reelection was less than .80. In both of these cases, we compared the results of a *single* sample statistic to a population parameter.

In this chapter we expand the idea of hypothesis testing to two samples. That is, we select random samples from two different populations to determine whether the population means are equal. Some questions we might want to test are:

1. Is there a difference in the mean value of residential real estate sold by male agents and female agents in south Florida?
2. Is there a difference in the mean number of defects produced on the day and the afternoon shifts at Kimble Products?
3. Is there a difference in the mean number of days absent between young workers (under 21 years of age) and older workers (more than 60 years of age) in the fast-food industry?

4. Is there is a difference in the proportion of Ohio State University graduates and University of Cincinnati graduates who pass the state Certified Public Accounting Examination on their first attempt?
5. Is there an increase in the production rate if music is piped into the production area?

We begin this chapter with the case in which we select random samples from two populations and wish to investigate whether these populations have the same mean.

# Two-Sample Tests of Hypothesis: Independent Samples

A city planner in Florida wishes to know whether there is a difference in the mean hourly wage rate of plumbers and electricians in central Florida. A financial accountant wishes to know whether the mean rate of return for high yield mutual funds is different from the mean rate of return on global mutual funds. In each of these cases there are two independent populations. In the first case, the plumbers represent one population and the electricians the other. In the second case, high yield mutual funds are one population and global mutual funds the other.

In each of these cases, to investigate the question, we would select a random sample from each population and compute the mean of the two samples. If the two population means are the same, that is, the mean hourly rate is the same for the plumbers and the electricians, we would expect the *difference* between the two sample means to be zero. But what if our sample results yield a difference other than zero? Is that difference due to chance or is it because there is a real difference in the hourly earnings? A two-sample test of means will help to answer this question.

We do need to return to the results of Chapter 8. Recall that we showed that a distribution of sample means would tend to approximate the normal distribution when the sample size is at least 30. We need to again assume that a distribution of sample means will follow the normal distribution. It can be shown mathematically that the distribution of the differences between sample means for two normal distributions is also normal.

We can illustrate this theory in terms of the city planner in Tampa, Florida. To begin, let's assume some information that is not usually available. Suppose that the population of plumbers has a mean of $30.00 per hour and a standard deviation of $5.00 per hour. The population of electricians has a mean of $29.00 and a standard deviation of $4.50. Now, from this information it is clear that the two population means are not the same. The plumbers actually earn $1.00 per hour more than the electricians. But we cannot expect to uncover this difference each time we sample the two populations.

Suppose we select a random sample of 40 plumbers and a random sample of 35 electricians and compute the mean of each sample. Then, we determine the difference between the sample means. It is this difference between the sample means that holds our interest. If the populations have the same mean, then we would expect the difference between the two sample means to be zero. If there is a difference between the population means, then we expect to find a difference between the sample means.

To understand the theory, we need to take several pairs of samples, compute the mean of each, determine the difference between the sample means, and study the distribution of the differences in the sample means. Because of our study of the distribution of sample means in Chapter 8, we know that the distribution of the sample means follows the normal distribution (assume at least $n = 30$). If the two distributions of sample means follow the normal distribution, then we can reason that the distribution of their differences will also follow the normal distribution. This is the first hurdle.

The second hurdle refers to the mean of this distribution of differences. If we find the mean of this distribution is zero, that implies that there is no difference in the two populations. On the other hand, if the mean of the distribution of differences is equal to some value other than zero, either positive or negative, then we conclude that the two populations do not have the same mean.

To report some concrete results, let's return to the city planner in Tampa, Florida. Table 11–1 shows the result of selecting 20 different samples of 40 plumbers and 35 electricians, computing the mean of each sample, and finding the difference between the two sample means. In the first case the sample of 40 plumbers has a mean of $29.80, and for the 35 electricians the mean is $28.76. The difference between the sample means is $1.04. This process was repeated 19 more times. Observe that in 17 of the 20 cases the mean of the plumbers is larger than the mean of the electricians.

Our final hurdle is that we need to know something about the *variability* of the distribution of differences. To put it another way, what is the standard deviation of this distribution of differences? Statistical theory shows that when we have independent populations, such as the case here, the distribution of the differences has a variance (standard deviation squared) equal to the sum of the two individual variances. This means that we can add the variances of the two sampling distributions.

| VARIANCE OF THE DISTRIBUTION OF DIFFERENCES IN MEANS | $s^2_{\bar{X}_1 - \bar{X}_2} = \dfrac{s^2_1}{n_1} + \dfrac{s^2_2}{n_2}$ | **[11–1]** |
|---|---|---|

The term $s^2_{\bar{X}_1 - \bar{X}_2}$ looks complex but need not be difficult to interpret. The $s^2$ portion reminds us that it is a sample variance, and the subscript $\bar{X}_1 - \bar{X}_2$ that it is a distribution of differences in the sample means.

**TABLE 11–1** The Means of Random Samples of Plumbers and Electricians

| Sample | Plumbers | Electricians | Difference |
|--------|----------|--------------|------------|
| 1 | $29.80 | $28.76 | $1.04 |
| 2 | 30.32 | 29.40 | 0.92 |
| 3 | 30.57 | 29.94 | 0.63 |
| 4 | 30.04 | 28.93 | 1.11 |
| 5 | 30.09 | 29.78 | 0.31 |
| 6 | 30.02 | 28.66 | 1.36 |
| 7 | 29.60 | 29.13 | 0.47 |
| 8 | 29.63 | 29.42 | 0.21 |
| 9 | 30.17 | 29.29 | 0.88 |
| 10 | 30.81 | 29.75 | 1.06 |
| 11 | 30.09 | 28.05 | 2.04 |
| 12 | 29.35 | 29.07 | 0.28 |
| 13 | 29.42 | 28.79 | 0.63 |
| 14 | 29.78 | 29.54 | 0.24 |
| 15 | 29.60 | 29.60 | 0.00 |
| 16 | 30.60 | 30.19 | 0.41 |
| 17 | 30.79 | 28.65 | 2.14 |
| 18 | 29.14 | 29.95 | −0.81 |
| 19 | 29.91 | 28.75 | 1.16 |
| 20 | 28.74 | 29.21 | −0.47 |

We can put this equation in a more usable form by taking the square root, so that we have the standard deviation of the distribution of the differences. Finally, we standardize the distribution of the differences. The result is the following equation.

| | | |
|---|---|---|
| **TEST STATISTIC FOR THE DIFFERENCE BETWEEN TWO MEANS** | $$z = \dfrac{\bar{X}_1 - \bar{X}_2}{\sqrt{\dfrac{s_1^2}{n_1} + \dfrac{s_2^2}{n_2}}}$$ | **[11–2]** |

Before we present an example, let's review the assumptions necessary for using formula (11–2).

Assumptions for large sample test

1. The two samples must be unrelated, that is, independent.
2. The samples must be large enough that the distribution of the sample means follows the normal distribution. The usual practice is to require that both samples have at least 30 observations.

The following example shows the details of the two-sample test of hypothesis for two population means.

**EXAMPLE**

Customers at FoodTown Super Markets have a choice when paying for their groceries. They may check out and pay using the standard cashier assisted checkout, or they may use the new U-Scan procedure. In the standard procedure a FoodTown employee scans each item, puts it on a short conveyor where another employee puts it in a bag and then into the grocery cart. In the U-Scan procedure the customer scans each item, bags it, and places the bags in the cart themselves. The U-Scan procedure is designed to reduce the time a customer spends in the checkout line.

The U-Scan facility was recently installed at the Byrne Road FoodTown location. The store manager would like to know if the mean checkout time using the standard checkout method is longer than using the U-Scan. She gathered the following sample information. The time is measured from when the customer enters the line until their bags are in the cart. Hence the time includes both waiting in line and checking out. What is the *p*-value?

| Customer Type | Sample Mean | Sample Standard Deviation | Sample Size |
|---|---|---|---|
| Standard | 5.50 minutes | 0.40 minutes | 50 |
| U-Scan | 5.30 minutes | 0.30 minutes | 100 |

**Statistics in Action**

Do you live to work or work to live? A recent poll of 802 working Americans revealed that, among those who considered their work as a career, the mean number of hours worked per day was 8.7. Among those who considered their work a job, the mean number of hours worked per day was 7.6.

We use the five-step hypothesis testing procedure to investigate the question.

**Step 1:** **State the null hypothesis and the alternate hypothesis.** The null hypothesis is that there is no difference in the mean checkout times for the two groups. In other words, the difference of 0.20 minutes between the mean checkout time for the standard method and the mean checkout time for U-Scan is due to chance. The alternate hypothesis is that the mean checkout time is longer for those using the standard method. We will let $\mu_s$ refer to the mean checkout time for the population of standard customers and $\mu_u$ the mean checkout time for the U-Scan customers. The null and alternative hypotheses are:

$$H_0: \mu_s \leq \mu_u$$
$$H_1: \mu_s > \mu_u$$

**Step 2:** **Select the level of significance.** The significance level is the probability that we reject the null hypothesis when it is actually true. This likelihood is determined prior to selecting the sample or performing any calculations. The .05 and .01 significance levels are the most common, but other values, such as .02 and .10, are also used. In theory, we may select any value between 0 and 1 for the significance level. In this case we selected the .01 significance level.

**Step 3:** **Determine the test statistic.** In Chapter 10 we used the standard normal distribution (that is *z*) and *t* as test statistics. In this case, because the samples are large, we use the *z* distribution as the test statistic.

**Step 4:** **Formulate a decision rule.** The decision rule is based on the null and the alternate hypotheses (i.e., one-tailed or two-tailed test), the level of significance, and the test statistic used. We selected the .01 significance level, the *z* distribution as the test statistic, and we wish to determine whether the mean checkout time is longer using the standard method. We set the alternate hypothesis to indicate that the mean checkout time is longer for those using the standard method than the U-Scan method. Hence, the rejection region is in the upper tail of the standard normal distribution. To find the critical value, place .01 of the total area in the upper tail. This means that .4900 (.5000 − .0100) of the area is located between the *z* value of 0 and the critical value. Next, we search the body of Appendix D for a value located near .4900. It is 2.33, so our decision rule is to reject $H_0$ if the value computed from the test statistic exceeds 2.33. Chart 11–1 depicts the decision rule.

**Step 5:** **Make the decision regarding $H_0$ and interpret the result.** We use formula (11–2) to compute the value of the test statistic.

$$z = \frac{\bar{X}_s - \bar{X}_u}{\sqrt{\dfrac{s_s^2}{n_s} + \dfrac{s_u^2}{n_u}}} = \frac{5.5 - 5.3}{\sqrt{\dfrac{0.40^2}{50} + \dfrac{0.30^2}{100}}} = \frac{0.2}{0.064} = 3.13$$

**CHART 11–1** Decision Rule for One-Tailed Test at .01 Significance Level

The computed value of 3.13 is larger than the critical value of 2.33. Our decision is to reject the null hypothesis and accept the alternate hypothesis. The difference of .20 minutes between the mean checkout time using the standard method is too large to have occurred by chance. To put it another way, we conclude the U-Scan method is faster.

What is the *p*-value for the test statistic? Recall that the *p*-value is the probability of finding a value of the test statistic this extreme when the null hypothesis is true. To calculate the *p*-value we need the probability of a *z* value larger than 3.13. From Appendix D we cannot find the probability associated with 3.13. The largest value available is 3.09. The area corresponding to 3.09 is .4990. In this case we can report that the *p*-value is less than .0010, found by .5000 − .4990. We conclude that there is very little likelihood that the null hypothesis is true!

In summary, the criteria for using the large sample test of means are:

1. *The samples are from independent populations*. This means, for example, that the sample checkout time for the U-Scan customers is unrelated to the checkout time for the other customers. If Mr. Smith is a FoodTown customer and his response time is sampled, that does not affect the checkout time for any other customers.
2. *Both sample sizes are at least 30*. In the FoodTown example, one sample was 50 and the other 100. Because both samples are considered large, we can substitute the sample standard deviations for the population standard deviations and use formula (11–2) to find the value of the test statistic.

---

**Self-Review 11–1**

Tom Sevits is the owner of the Appliance Patch. Recently Tom observed a difference in the dollar value of sales between the men and women he employs as sales associates. A sample of 40 days revealed the men sold a mean of $1,400 worth of appliances per day with a standard deviation of $200. For a sample of 50 days, the women sold a mean of $1,500 worth of appliances per day with a standard deviation of $250. At the .05 significance level can Mr. Sevits conclude that the mean amount sold per day is larger for the women?
(a) State the null hypothesis and the alternate hypothesis.
(b) What is the decision rule?
(c) What is the value of the test statistic?
(d) What is your decision regarding the null hypothesis?
(e) What is the *p*-value?
(f) Interpret the result.

# Exercises

1. A sample of 40 observations is selected from one population. The sample mean is 102 and the sample standard deviation is 5. A sample of 50 observations is selected from a second population. The sample mean is 99 and the sample standard deviation is 6. Conduct the following test of hypothesis using the .04 significance level.

$H_0$: $\mu_1 = \mu_2$
$H_1$: $\mu_1 \neq \mu_2$

a. Is this a one-tailed or a two-tailed test?
b. State the decision rule.
c. Compute the value of the test statistic.
d. What is your decision regarding $H_0$?
e. What is the $p$-value?

2. A sample of 65 observations is selected from one population. The sample mean is 2.67 and the sample standard deviation is 0.75. A sample of 50 observations is selected from a second population. The sample mean is 2.59 and the sample standard deviation is 0.66. Conduct the following test of hypothesis using the .08 significance level.

$H_0$: $\mu_1 \leq \mu_2$
$H_1$: $\mu_1 > \mu_2$

a. Is this a one-tailed or a two-tailed test?
b. State the decision rule.
c. Compute the value of the test statistic.
d. What is your decision regarding $H_0$?
e. What is the $p$-value?

*Note:* Use the five-step hypothesis testing procedure to solve the following exercises.

3. The Gibbs Baby Food Company wishes to compare the weight gain of infants using their brand versus their competitor's. A sample of 40 babies using the Gibbs products revealed a mean weight gain of 7.6 pounds in the first three months after birth. The standard deviation of the sample was 2.3 pounds. A sample of 55 babies using the competitor's brand revealed a mean increase in weight of 8.1 pounds, with a standard deviation of 2.9 pounds. At the .05 significance level, can we conclude that babies using the Gibbs brand gained less weight? Compute the $p$-value and interpret it.

4. As part of a study of corporate employees, the Director of Human Resources for PNC, Inc. wants to compare the distance traveled to work by employees at their office in downtown Cincinnati with the distance for those in downtown Pittsburgh. A sample of 35 Cincinnati employees showed they travel a mean of 370 miles per month, with a standard deviation of 30 miles per month. A sample of 40 Pittsburgh employees showed they travel a mean of 380 miles per month, with a standard deviation of 26 miles per month. At the .05 significance level, is there a difference in the mean number of miles traveled per month between Cincinnati and Pittsburgh employees? Use the five-step hypothesis-testing procedure.

5. A financial analyst wants to compare the turnover rates, in percent, for shares of oil-related stocks versus other stocks, such as GE and IBM. She selected 32 oil-related stocks and 49 other stocks. The mean turnover rate of oil-related stocks is 31.4 percent and the standard deviation 5.1 percent. For the other stocks, the mean rate was computed to be 34.9 percent and the standard deviation 6.7 percent. Is there a significant difference in the turnover rates of the two types of stock? Use the .01 significance level.

6. Mary Jo Fitzpatrick is the Vice President for Nursing Services at St. Luke's Memorial Hospital. Recently she noticed in the job postings for nurses that those that are unionized seem to offer higher wages. She decided to investigate and gathered the following sample information.

| Group | Mean Wage | Sample Standard Deviation | Sample Size |
|---|---|---|---|
| Union | $20.75 | $2.25 | 40 |
| Nonunion | $19.80 | $1.90 | 45 |

Would it be reasonable for her to conclude that union nurses earn more? Use the .02 significance level. What is the $p$-value?

# Two-Sample Tests about Proportions

In the previous section, we considered a test involving population means. However, we are often interested also in whether two sample proportions came from populations that are equal. Here are several examples.

- The Vice President of Human Resources wishes to know whether there is a difference in the proportion of hourly employees who miss more than 5 days of work per year at the Atlanta and the Houston plants.
- General Motors is considering a new design for the Pontiac Grand Am. The design is shown to a group of potential buyers under 30 years of age and another group over 60 years of age. Pontiac wishes to know whether there is a difference in the proportion of the two groups who like the new design.
- A consultant to the airline industry is investigating the fear of flying among adults. Specifically, they wish to know whether there is a difference in the proportion of men versus women who are fearful of flying.

In the above cases each sampled item or individual can be classified as a "success" or a "failure." That is, in the Pontiac Grand Am example each potential buyer is classified as "liking the new design" or "not liking the new design." We then compare the proportion in the under 30 group with the proportion in the over 60 group who indicated they liked the new design. Can we conclude that the differences are due to chance? In this study there is no measurement obtained, only classifying the individuals or objects. Then we assume the nominal scale of measurement.

To conduct the test, we assume each sample is large enough that the normal distribution will serve as a good approximation of the binomial distribution. The test statistic follows the standard normal distribution. We compute the value of $z$ from the following formula:

| | | |
|---|---|---|
| **TWO-SAMPLE TEST OF PROPORTIONS** | $$z = \frac{p_1 - p_2}{\sqrt{\dfrac{p_c(1 - p_c)}{n_1} + \dfrac{p_c(1 - p_c)}{n_2}}}$$ | **[11–3]** |

Formula (11–3) is formula (11–2) with the respective sample proportions replacing the sample means and $p_c(1 - p_c)$ replacing the two sample standard deviations. In addition:

$n_1$ is the number of observations in the first sample.
$n_2$ is the number of observations in the second sample.
$p_1$ is the proportion in the first sample possessing the trait.
$p_2$ is the proportion in the second sample possessing the trait.
$p_c$ is the pooled proportion possessing the trait in the combined samples. It is called the pooled estimate of the population proportion and is computed from the following formula.

| | | |
|---|---|---|
| **POOLED PROPORTION** | $$p_c = \frac{X_1 + X_2}{n_1 + n_2}$$ | **[11–4]** |

where:

$X_1$ is the number possessing the trait in the first sample.
$X_2$ is the number possessing the trait in the second sample.

The following example will illustrate the two-sample test of proportions.

**EXAMPLE**

The Manelli Perfume Company recently developed a new fragrance that they plan to market under the name "Heavenly." A number of market studies indicate that Heavenly has very good market potential. The Sales Department at Manelli is particularly interested in whether there is a difference in the proportions of younger and older women who would purchase Heavenly if it were marketed. There are two independent populations, a population consisting of the younger women and a population consisting of the older women. Each sampled woman will be asked to smell Heavenly and indicate whether she likes the fragrance well enough to purchase a bottle.

**SOLUTION**

We will use the usual five-step hypothesis-testing procedure.

**Step 1:** **State $H_0$ and $H_1$.** In this case the null hypothesis is: "There is no difference in the proportion of young women and older women who prefer Heavenly." We designate $\pi_1$ as the proportion of young women who would purchase Heavenly and $\pi_2$ as the proportion of older women who would purchase. The alternate hypothesis is that the two proportions are not equal.

$$H_0: \pi_1 = \pi_2$$
$$H_1: \pi_1 \neq \pi_2$$

**Step 2:** **Select the level of significance.** We choose the .05 significance level in this example.

**Step 3:** **Determine the test statistic.** If each sample is large enough, the test statistic follows the standard normal distribution. The value of the test statistic can be computed from formula (11–3).

**Step 4:** **Formulate the decision rule.** Recall that the alternate hypothesis from step 1 does not state a direction, so this is a two-tailed test. To determine the critical value, we divide the significance level in half and place this amount in each tail of the $z$ distribution. Next, we subtract this amount from the total area to the right of zero. That is .5000 − .0250 = .4750. Finally, we search the body of the $z$ table (Appendix D) for the closest value. It is 1.96. The critical values are −1.96 and +1.96. As before, if the computed $z$ value falls in the region between +1.96 and −1.96, the null hypothesis is not rejected. If that does occur, it is assumed that any difference between the two sample proportions is due to chance variation. This information is summarized in Chart 11–2.

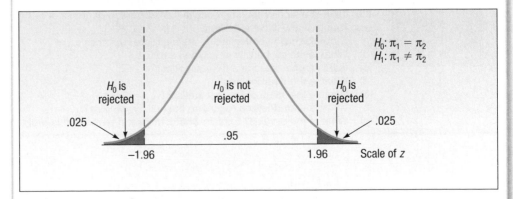

**CHART 11–2 Decision Rules for Heavenly Fragrance Test, .05 Significance Level**

**Step 5:** **Select a sample and make a decision.** A random sample of 100 young women revealed 20 liked the Heavenly fragrance well enough to purchase it. Similarly, a sample of 200 older women revealed 100 liked the fragrance well enough to make a purchase. We let $p_1$ refer to the young women and $p_2$ to the older women.

$$p_1 = \frac{X_1}{n_1} = \frac{20}{100} = .20 \qquad p_2 = \frac{X_2}{n_2} = \frac{100}{200} = .50$$

The research question is whether the difference of .30 in the two sample proportions is due to chance or whether there is a difference in the proportion of younger and older women who like the Heavenly fragrance.

Next, we combine or pool the sample proportions. We use formula (11–4).

$$p_c = \frac{X_1 + X_2}{n_1 + n_2} = \frac{20 + 100}{100 + 200} = .40$$

Note that the pooled proportion is closer to .50 than to .20 because more older women than younger women were sampled.

We use formula (11–3) to find the value of the test statistic.

$$z = \frac{p_1 - p_2}{\sqrt{\dfrac{p_c(1 - p_c)}{n_1} + \dfrac{p_c(1 - p_c)}{n_2}}} = \frac{.20 - .50}{\sqrt{\dfrac{.40(1 - .40)}{100} + \dfrac{.40(1 - .40)}{200}}} = -5.00$$

The computed value of $-5.00$ is in the area of rejection; that is, it is to the left of $-1.96$. Therefore, the null hypothesis is rejected at the .05 significance level. To put it another way, we reject the null hypothesis that the proportion of young women who would purchase Heavenly is equal to the proportion of older women who would purchase Heavenly. It is unlikely that the difference between the two sample proportions is due to chance. To find the $p$-value we go to Appendix D and look for the likelihood of finding a $z$ value less than $-5.00$ or greater than 5.00. The largest value of $z$ reported is 3.09, with a corresponding probability of .4990. So the probability of finding a $z$ value greater than 5.00 or less than $-5.00$ is virtually zero. So we report zero as the $p$-value. There is very little likelihood the null hypothesis is true. We conclude that there is a difference in the proportion of younger and older women who would purchase Heavenly.

---

**Self-Review 11–2**

Of 150 adults who tried a new peach-flavored peppermint patty, 87 rated it excellent. Of 200 children sampled, 123 rated it excellent. Using the .10 level of significance, can we conclude that there is a significant difference in the proportion of adults and the proportion of children who rate the new flavor excellent?
(a)   State the null hypothesis and the alternate hypothesis.
(b)   What is the probability of a Type I error?
(c)   Is this a one-tailed or a two-tailed test?
(d)   What is the decision rule?
(e)   What is the value of the test statistic?
(f)   What is your decision regarding the null hypothesis?
(g)   What is the $p$-value? Explain what it means in terms of this problem.

# Exercises

**7.** The null and alternate hypotheses are:

$$H_0: \pi_1 \leq \pi_2$$
$$H_1: \pi_1 > \pi_2$$

A sample of 100 observations from the first population indicated that $X_1$ is 70. A sample of 150 observations from the second population revealed $X_2$ to be 90. Use the .05 significance level to test the hypothesis.

a. State the decision rule.
b. Compute the pooled proportion.
c. Compute the value of the test statistic.
d. What is your decision regarding the null hypothesis?

8. The null and alternate hypotheses are:

$H_0$: $\pi_1 = \pi_2$
$H_1$: $\pi_1 \neq \pi_2$

A sample of 200 observations from the first population indicated that $X_1$ is 170. A sample of 150 observations from the second population revealed $X_2$ to be 110. Use the .05 significance level to test the hypothesis.

a. State the decision rule.
b. Compute the pooled proportion.
c. Compute the value of the test statistic.
d. What is your decision regarding the null hypothesis?

*Note:* Use the five-step hypothesis-testing procedure in solving the following exercises.

9. The Damon family owns a large grape vineyard in western New York along Lake Erie. The grapevines must be sprayed at the beginning of the growing season to protect against various insects and diseases. Two new insecticides have just been marketed: Pernod 5 and Action. To test their effectiveness, three long rows were selected and sprayed with Pernod 5, and three others were sprayed with Action. When the grapes ripened, 400 of the vines treated with Pernod 5 were checked for infestation. Likewise, a sample of 400 vines sprayed with Action were checked. The results are:

| Insecticide | Number of Vines Checked (sample size) | Number of Infested Vines |
|---|---|---|
| Pernod 5 | 400 | 24 |
| Action | 400 | 40 |

At the .05 significance level, can we conclude that there is a difference in the proportion of vines infested using Pernod 5 as opposed to Action?

10. The Roper Organization conducted identical surveys in 1990 and 2000. One question asked women was "Are most men basically kind, gentle, and thoughtful?" The 1990 survey revealed that, of the 3,000 women surveyed, 2,010 said that they were. In 2000, 1,530 of the 3,000 women surveyed thought that men were kind, gentle, and thoughtful. At the .05 level, can we conclude that women think men are less kind, gentle, and thoughtful in 2000 compared with 1990?

11. A nationwide sample of influential Republicans and Democrats was asked as a part of a comprehensive survey whether they favored lowering environmental standards so that high-sulfur coal could be burned in coal-fired power plants. The results were:

| | Republicans | Democrats |
|---|---|---|
| Number sampled | 1,000 | 800 |
| Number in favor | 200 | 168 |

At the .02 level of significance, can we conclude that there is a larger proportion of Democrats in favor of lowering the standards?

12. The research department at the home office of New Hampshire Insurance conducts ongoing research on the causes of automobile accidents, the characteristics of the drivers, and so on. A random sample of 400 policies written on single persons revealed 120 had at least one accident in the previous three-year period. Similarly, a sample of 600 policies written on married persons revealed that 150 had been in at least one accident. At the .05 significance level, is there a significant difference in the proportions of single and married persons having an accident during a three-year period?

# Comparing Population Means with Small Samples

In an earlier section we assumed that the two population standard deviations were un-known but that we selected random samples containing 30 or more observations each. In this section we consider the case in which the population standard deviations are unknown and the number of observations in at least one of the samples is less than 30. We often refer to this as a "small sample test of means." The requirements for the small sample test are more stringent. The three required assumptions are:

**Assumptions for small sample test of means**

1. The sampled populations follow the normal distribution.
2. The two samples are from independent populations.
3. The standard deviations of the two populations are equal.

In this case, the $t$ distribution is used to compare two population means. The formula for computing the test statistic $t$ is similar to (11–2), but an additional calculation is necessary. The third assumption above indicates that the population standard deviations must be equal. The two sample standard deviations are pooled to form a single estimate of the unknown population standard deviation. In essence, we compute a weighted mean of the two sample standard deviations and use this as an estimate of the population standard deviation. The weights are the degrees of freedom that each sample provides. Why do we need to pool the standard deviations? In most cases when the samples each have fewer than 30 observations, the population standard deviations are not known. Thus, we calculate $s$, the sample standard deviation, and sub-stitute it for $\sigma$, the population standard deviation. Because we assume that the two populations have equal standard deviations, the best estimate we can make of that value is to combine or pool all the information we have about the value of the popula-tion standard deviation.

The following formula is used to pool the sample standard deviations. Notice that two factors are involved: the number of observations in each sample and the sample standard deviations themselves.

| POOLED VARIANCE | $s_p^2 = \dfrac{(n_1 - 1)s_1^2 + (n_2 - 1)s_2^2}{n_1 + n_2 - 2}$ | [11–5] |
|---|---|---|

where:

$s_1^2$ is the variance (standard deviation squared) of the first sample.
$s_2^2$ is the variance of the second sample.

The value of $t$ is computed from the following equation.

| TWO-SAMPLE TEST OF MEANS—SMALL SAMPLES | $t = \dfrac{\bar{X}_1 - \bar{X}_2}{\sqrt{s_p^2\left(\dfrac{1}{n_1} + \dfrac{1}{n_2}\right)}}$ | [11–6] |
|---|---|---|

where:

$\bar{X}_1$ is the mean of the first sample.
$\bar{X}_2$ is the mean of the second sample.
$n_1$ is the number of observations in the first sample.
$n_2$ is the number of observations in the second sample.
$s_p^2$ is the pooled estimate of the population variance.

The number of degrees of freedom in the test is the total number of items sam-pled minus the total number of samples. Because there are two samples, there are $n_1 + n_2 - 2$ degrees of freedom.

**EXAMPLE**

Owens Lawn Care, Inc. manufactures and assembles lawnmowers that are shipped to dealers throughout the United States and Canada. Two different procedures have been proposed for mounting the engine on the frame of the lawnmower. The question is: Is there a difference in the mean time to mount the engines on the frames of the lawnmowers? The first procedure was developed by longtime Owens employee Herb Welles (designated as procedure 1), and the other procedure was developed by Owens Vice-President of Engineering William Atkins (designated as procedure 2). To evaluate the two methods, it was decided to conduct a time and motion study. A sample of five employees was timed using the Welles method and six using the Atkins method. The results, in minutes, are shown below. Is there a difference in the mean mounting times? Use the .10 significance level.

| Welles (minutes) | Atkins (minutes) |
|:---:|:---:|
| 2 | 3 |
| 4 | 7 |
| 9 | 5 |
| 3 | 8 |
| 2 | 4 |
|   | 3 |

**SOLUTION**

Following the five steps to test a hypothesis, the null hypothesis states that there is no difference in mean mounting times between the two procedures. The alternate hypothesis indicates that there is a difference.

$H_0$: $\mu_1 = \mu_2$
$H_1$: $\mu_1 \neq \mu_2$

The required assumptions are:

1. The observations in the Welles sample are *independent* of the observations in the Atkins sample.
2. The two populations follow the normal distribution.
3. The two populations have equal standard deviations.

Is there a difference between the mean assembly times using the Welles and the Atkins methods? The degrees of freedom are equal to the total number of items sampled minus the number of samples. In this case that is $n_1 + n_2 - 2$. Five assemblers used the Welles method and six the Atkins method. Thus, there are 9 degrees of freedom, found by $5 + 6 - 2$. The critical values of $t$, from Appendix F for $df = 9$, a two-tailed test, and the .10 significance level, are $-1.833$ and $1.833$. The decision rule is portrayed graphically in Chart 11–3. We do not reject the null hypothesis if the computed value of $t$ falls between $-1.833$ and $1.833$.

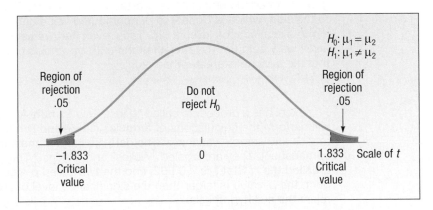

**CHART 11–3** Regions of Rejection, Two-Tailed Test, $df = 9$, and .10 Significance Level

We use three steps to compute the value of $t$.

**Step 1: Calculate the Sample Standard Deviations.** See the details below.

| Welles Method | | Atkins Method | |
|---|---|---|---|
| $X_1$ | $(X_1 - \bar{X}_1)^2$ | $X_2$ | $(X_2 - \bar{X}_2)^2$ |
| 2 | $(2 - 4)^2 = 4$ | 3 | $(3 - 5)^2 = 4$ |
| 4 | $(4 - 4)^2 = 0$ | 7 | $(7 - 5)^2 = 4$ |
| 9 | $(9 - 4)^2 = 25$ | 5 | $(5 - 5)^2 = 0$ |
| 3 | $(3 - 4)^2 = 1$ | 8 | $(8 - 5)^2 = 9$ |
| 2 | $(2 - 4)^2 = 4$ | 4 | $(4 - 5)^2 = 1$ |
| 20 | 34 | 3 | $(3 - 5)^2 = 4$ |
| | | 30 | 22 |

$$\bar{X}_1 = \frac{\Sigma X_1}{n_1} = \frac{20}{5} = 4 \qquad \bar{X}_2 = \frac{\Sigma X_2}{n_2} = \frac{30}{6} = 5$$

$$s_1 = \sqrt{\frac{\Sigma(X_1 - \bar{X}_1)^2}{n_1 - 1}} = \sqrt{\frac{34}{5 - 1}} = 2.9155 \qquad s_2 = \sqrt{\frac{\Sigma(X_2 - \bar{X}_2)^2}{n_2 - 1}} = \sqrt{\frac{22}{6 - 1}} = 2.0976$$

**Step 2: Pool the Sample Variances.** We use formula (11–5) to pool the sample variances (standard deviations squared).

$$s_p^2 = \frac{(n_1 - 1)s_1^2 + (n_2 - 1)s_2^2}{n_1 + n_2 - 2} = \frac{(5 - 1)(2.9155)^2 + (6 - 1)(2.0976)^2}{5 + 6 - 2} = 6.2222$$

**Step 3: Determine the value of $t$.** The mean mounting time for the Welles method is 4.00 minutes, found by $\bar{X}_1 = 20/5$. The mean mounting time for the Atkins method is 5.00 minutes, found by $\bar{X}_2 = 30/6$. We use formula (11–6) to calculate the value of $t$.

$$t = \frac{\bar{X}_1 - \bar{X}_2}{\sqrt{s_p^2 \left( \frac{1}{n_1} + \frac{1}{n_2} \right)}} = \frac{4.00 - 5.00}{\sqrt{6.2222 \left( \frac{1}{5} + \frac{1}{6} \right)}} = -0.662$$

The decision is not to reject the null hypothesis, because $-0.662$ falls in the region between $-1.833$ and $1.833$. We conclude that there is no difference in the mean times to mount the engine on the frame using the two methods.

We can also estimate the $p$-value using Appendix F. Locate the row with 9 degrees of freedom, and use the two-tailed test column. Find the $t$ value, without regard to the sign, which is closest to our computed value of 0.662. It is 1.383, corresponding to a significance level of .20. Thus, even had we used the 20 percent significance level, we would not have rejected the null hypothesis of equal means. We can report that the $p$-value is greater than .20.

Excel has a procedure called "t-Test: Two Sample Assuming Equal Variances" that will perform the calculations of formulas (11–5) and (11–6) as well as find the sample means and sample variances. The data are input in the first two columns of the Excel spreadsheet. They are labeled "Welles" and "Atkins." The output follows. The value of $t$, called the "$t$ Stat," is $-0.662$, and the two-tailed $p$-value is .525. As we would expect, the $p$-value is larger than the significance level of .10. The conclusion is not to reject the null hypothesis.

**Self-Review 11–3** The production manager at Bellevue Steel, a manufacturer of wheelchairs, wants to compare the number of defective wheelchairs produced on the day shift with the number on the afternoon shift. A sample of the production from 6 day shifts and 8 afternoon shifts revealed the following number of defects.

| Day | 5 | 8 | 7 | 6 | 9 | 7 | | |
|---|---|---|---|---|---|---|---|---|
| Afternoon | 8 | 10 | 7 | 11 | 9 | 12 | 14 | 9 |

At the .05 significance level, is there a difference in the mean number of defects per shift?
(a) State the null hypothesis and the alternate hypothesis.
(b) What is the decision rule?
(c) What is the value of the test statistic?
(d) What is your decision regarding the null hypothesis?
(e) What is the $p$-value?
(f) Interpret the result.
(g) What are the assumptions necessary for this test?

# Exercises

For Exercises 13 and 14: (a) state the decision rule, (b) compute the pooled estimate of the population variance, (c) compute the test statistic, (d) state your decision about the null hypothesis, and (e) estimate the $p$-value.

**13.** The null and alternate hypotheses are:

$H_0$: $\mu_1 = \mu_2$
$H_1$: $\mu_1 \neq \mu_2$

A random sample of 10 observations from one population revealed a sample mean of 23 and a sample deviation of 4. A random sample of 8 observations from another population revealed a sample mean of 26 and a sample standard deviation of 5. At the .05 significance level, is there a difference between the population means?

**14.** The null and alternate hypotheses are:

$$H_0: \mu_1 = \mu_2$$
$$H_1: \mu_1 \neq \mu_2$$

A random sample of 15 observations from the first population revealed a sample mean of 350 and a sample standard deviation of 12. A random sample of 17 observations from the second population revealed a sample mean of 342 and a sample standard deviation of 15. At the .10 significance level, is there a difference in the population means?

*Note:* Use the five-step hypothesis testing procedure for the following exercises.

**15.** A sample of scores on an examination given in Statistics 201 are:

| Men   | 72 | 69 | 98 | 66 | 85 | 76 | 79 | 80 | 77 |
|-------|----|----|----|----|----|----|----|----|----|
| Women | 81 | 67 | 90 | 78 | 81 | 80 | 76 |    |    |

At the .01 significance level, is the mean grade of the women higher than that of the men?

**16.** A recent study compared the time spent together by single- and dual-earner couples. According to the records kept by the wives during the study, the mean amount of time spent together watching television among the single-earner couples was 61 minutes per day, with a standard deviation of 15.5 minutes. For the dual-earner couples, the mean number of minutes spent watching television was 48.4 minutes, with a standard deviation of 18.1 minutes. At the .01 significance level, can we conclude that the single-earner couples on average spend more time watching television together? There were 15 single-earner and 12 dual-earner couples studied.

**17.** Ms. Lisa Monnin is the budget director for Nexus Media, Inc. She would like to compare the daily travel expenses for the sales staff and the audit staff. She collected the following sample information.

| Sales ($) | 131 | 135 | 146 | 165 | 136 | 142 |     |
|-----------|-----|-----|-----|-----|-----|-----|-----|
| Audit ($) | 130 | 102 | 129 | 143 | 149 | 120 | 139 |

At the .10 significance level, can she conclude that the mean daily expenses are greater for the sales staff than the audit staff? What is the *p*-value?

**18.** The Tampa Bay (Florida) Area Chamber of Commerce wanted to know whether the mean weekly salary of nurses was larger than that of school teachers. To investigate, they collected the following information on the amounts earned last week by a sample of school teachers and nurses.

| School teachers ($) | 845 | 826 | 827 | 875 | 784 | 809 | 802 | 820 | 829 | 830 | 842 | 832 |
|---------------------|-----|-----|-----|-----|-----|-----|-----|-----|-----|-----|-----|-----|
| Nurses ($)          | 841 | 890 | 821 | 771 | 850 | 859 | 825 | 829 |     |     |     |     |

Is it reasonable to conclude that the mean weekly salary of nurses is higher? Use the .01 significance level. What is the *p*-value?

# Two-Sample Tests of Hypothesis: Dependent Samples

On page 367, we tested the difference between the means from two independent samples. We compared the mean time required to mount an engine using the Welles method to the time to mount the engine using the Atkins method. The samples were *independent,* meaning that the sample of assembly times using the Welles method was in no way related to the sample of assembly times using the Atkins method.

There are situations, however, in which the samples are not independent. To put it another way, the samples are **dependent** or related. As an example, Nickel Savings and Loan employs two firms, Schadek Appraisals and Bowyer Real Estate, to appraise the value of the real estate properties on which they make loans. It is important that these two firms be similar in their appraisal values. To review the consistency of the two appraisal firms, Nickel Savings randomly selects 10 homes and has both

Schadek Appraisals and Bowyer Real Estate appraise the value of the selected homes. For each home, there will be a pair of appraisal values. That is, for each home there will be an appraised value from both Schadek Appraisals and Bowyer Real Estate. The appraised values depend on, or are related to, the home selected. This is also referred to as a **paired sample.**

For hypothesis testing, we are interested in the distribution of the *differences* in the appraised value of each home. Hence, there is only one sample. To put it more formally, we are investigating whether the mean of the distribution of differences in the appraised values is 0. The sample is made up of the *differences* between the appraised values determined by Schadek Appraisals and the values from Bowyer Real Estate. If the two appraisal firms are reporting similar estimates, then sometimes Schadek Appraisals will be the higher value and sometimes Bowyer Real Estate will have the higher value. However, the mean of the distribution of differences will be 0. On the other hand, if one of the firms consistently reports the larger appraisal values, then the mean of the distribution of the differences will not be 0.

We will use the symbol $\mu_d$ to indicate the population mean of the distribution of differences. We assume the distribution of the population of differences follows the normal distribution. The test statistic follows the *t* distribution and we calculate its value from the following formula:

| PAIRED *t* TEST | $t = \dfrac{\bar{d}}{s_d/\sqrt{n}}$ | [11–7] |
|---|---|---|

There are $n - 1$ degrees of freedom and

$\bar{d}$ is the mean of the difference between the paired or related observations.
$s_d$ is the standard deviation of the differences between the paired or related observations.
$n$ is the number of paired observations.

The standard deviation of the differences is computed by the familiar formula for the standard deviation, except $d$ is substituted for $X$. The formula is:

$$s_d = \sqrt{\frac{\Sigma(d - \bar{d})^2}{n - 1}}$$

The following example illustrates this test.

**EXAMPLE**

Recall that Nickel Savings and Loan wishes to compare the two companies they use to appraise the value of residential homes. Nickel Savings selected a sample of 10 residential properties and scheduled both firms for an appraisal. The results, reported in $000, are:

| Home | Schadek | Bowyer |
|---|---|---|
| 1 | 135 | 128 |
| 2 | 110 | 105 |
| 3 | 131 | 119 |
| 4 | 142 | 140 |
| 5 | 105 | 98 |
| 6 | 130 | 123 |
| 7 | 131 | 127 |
| 8 | 110 | 115 |
| 9 | 125 | 122 |
| 10 | 149 | 145 |

At the .05 significance level, can we conclude there is a difference in the mean appraised values of the homes?

**SOLUTION**   The first step is to state the null and the alternate hypotheses. In this case a two-tailed alternative is appropriate because we are interested in determining whether there is a *difference* in the appraised values. We are not interested in showing whether one particular firm appraises property at a higher value than the other. The question is whether the sample differences in the appraised values could have come from a population with a mean of 0. If the population mean of the differences is 0, then we conclude that there is no difference in the appraised values. The null and alternate hypotheses are:

$H_0$: $\mu_d = 0$
$H_1$: $\mu_d \neq 0$

There are 10 homes appraised by both firms, so $n = 10$, and $df = n - 1 = 10 - 1 = 9$. We have a two-tailed test, and the significance level is .05. To determine the critical value, go to Appendix F, move across the row with 9 degrees of freedom to the column for a two-tailed test and the .05 significance level. The value at the intersection is 2.262. This value appears in the box in Table 11–2. The decision rule is to reject the null hypothesis if the computed value of $t$ is less than $-2.262$ or greater than 2.262. Here are the computational details.

| Home | Schadek | Bowyer | Difference, $d$ | $(d - \bar{d})$ | $(d - \bar{d})^2$ |
|------|---------|--------|-----------------|-----------------|-------------------|
| 1 | 135 | 128 | 7 | 2.4 | 5.76 |
| 2 | 110 | 105 | 5 | 0.4 | 0.16 |
| 3 | 131 | 119 | 12 | 7.4 | 54.76 |
| 4 | 142 | 140 | 2 | −2.6 | 6.76 |
| 5 | 105 | 98 | 7 | 2.4 | 5.76 |
| 6 | 130 | 123 | 7 | 2.4 | 5.76 |
| 7 | 131 | 127 | 4 | −0.6 | 0.36 |
| 8 | 110 | 115 | −5 | −9.6 | 92.16 |
| 9 | 125 | 122 | 3 | −1.6 | 2.56 |
| 10 | 149 | 145 | 4 | −0.6 | 0.36 |
| | | | 46 | 0 | 174.40 |

$$\bar{d} = \frac{\Sigma d}{n} = \frac{46}{10} = 4.60$$

$$s_d = \sqrt{\frac{\Sigma(d - \bar{d})^2}{n - 1}} = \sqrt{\frac{174.4}{10 - 1}} = 4.402$$

Using formula (11–7), the value of the test statistic is 3.305, found by

$$t = \frac{\bar{d}}{s_d/\sqrt{n}} = \frac{4.6}{4.402/\sqrt{10}} = 3.305$$

Because the computed $t$ falls in the rejection region, the null hypothesis is rejected. The population distribution of differences does not have a mean of 0. We conclude that there is a difference in the mean appraised values of the homes. The largest difference of $12,000 is for Home 3. Perhaps that would be an appropriate place to begin a more detailed review.

To find the $p$-value, we use Appendix F and the section for a two-tailed test. Move along the row with 9 degrees of freedom and find the values of $t$ that are closest to our calculated value. For a .01 significance level, the value of $t$ is 3.250. The computed value is larger than this value, but smaller than the value of 4.781 corresponding to the

.001 significance level. Hence, the *p*-value is less than .01. This information is highlighted in Table 11–2.

**TABLE 11–2** A Portion of the *t* Distribution from Appendix F

| | | | Confidence Intervals | | | |
|---|---|---|---|---|---|---|
| | **80%** | **90%** | **95%** | **98%** | **99%** | **99.9%** |
| | Level of Significance for One-Tailed Test | | | | | |
| **df** | **0.100** | **0.050** | **0.025** | **0.010** | **0.005** | **0.0005** |
| | Level of Significance for Two-Tailed Test | | | | | |
| | **0.20** | **0.10** | **0.05** | **0.02** | **0.01** | **0.001** |
| 1 | 3.078 | 6.314 | 12.706 | 31.821 | 63.657 | 636.619 |
| 2 | 1.886 | 2.920 | 4.303 | 6.965 | 9.925 | 31.599 |
| 3 | 1.638 | 2.353 | 3.182 | 4.541 | 5.841 | 12.924 |
| 4 | 1.533 | 2.132 | 2.776 | 3.747 | 4.604 | 8.610 |
| 5 | 1.476 | 2.015 | 2.571 | 3.365 | 4.032 | 6.869 |
| 6 | 1.440 | 1.943 | 2.447 | 3.143 | 3.707 | 5.959 |
| 7 | 1.415 | 1.895 | 2.365 | 2.998 | 3.499 | 5.408 |
| 8 | 1.397 | 1.860 | 2.306 | 2.896 | 3.355 | 5.041 |
| 9 | 1.383 | 1.833 | 2.262 | 2.821 | 3.250 | 4.781 |
| 10 | 1.372 | 1.812 | 2.228 | 2.764 | 3.169 | 4.587 |

Excel has a procedure called "t-Test: Paired Two-Sample for Means" that will perform the calculations of formula (11–7). The output from this procedure is given below.

The computed value of *t* is 3.3045, and the two-tailed *p*-value is .00916. Because the *p*-value is less than .05, we reject the hypothesis that the mean of the distribution of the differences between the appraised values is zero. In fact, this *p*-value is less than 1.0 percent. There is a small likelihood that the null hypothesis is true.

EXCEL

| | A | B | C | D | E | F | G | H | I | J |
|---|---|---|---|---|---|---|---|---|---|---|
| 1 | Home | Schadek | Bowyer | | | | | | | |
| 2 | 1 | 135 | 128 | | **t-Test: Paired Two Sample for Means** | | | | | |
| 3 | 2 | 110 | 105 | | | | | | | |
| 4 | 3 | 131 | 119 | | | Schade | Bowyer | | | |
| 5 | 4 | 142 | 140 | | Mean | 126.8 | 122.2 | | | |
| 6 | 5 | 105 | 98 | | Variance | 208.8 | 204.1777778 | | | |
| 7 | 6 | 130 | 123 | | Observations | 10 | 10 | | | |
| 8 | 7 | 131 | 127 | | Pearson Correlation | 0.953 | | | | |
| 9 | 8 | 110 | 115 | | Hypothesized Mean Difference | 0 | | | | |
| 10 | 9 | 125 | 122 | | df | 9 | | | | |
| 11 | 10 | 149 | 145 | | t Stat | 3.305 | | | | |
| 12 | | | | | P(T<=t) one-tail | 0.005 | | | | |
| 13 | | | | | t Critical one-tail | 1.833 | | | | |
| 14 | | | | | P(T<=t) two-tail | 0.009 | | | | |
| 15 | | | | | t Critical two-tail | 2.262 | | | | |

# Comparing Dependent and Independent Samples

Beginning students are often confused by the difference between tests for independent samples [formula (11–6)] and tests for dependent samples [formula (11–7)]. How do we tell the difference between dependent and independent samples? There are two types of dependent samples: (1) those characterized by a measurement, an intervention of some type, and then another measurement; and (2) a matching or pairing of the observations. To explain further:

1.  The first type of dependent sample is characterized by a measurement followed by an intervention of some kind and then another measurement. This could be called a "before" and "after" study. Two examples will help to clarify. Suppose we want to show that, by placing speakers in the production area and playing soothing music, we are able to increase production. We begin by selecting a sample of workers and measuring their output under the current conditions. The speakers are then installed in the production area, and we again measure the output of the same workers. There are two measurements, before placing the speakers in the production area and after. The intervention is placing speakers in the production area.

    A second example involves an educational firm that offers courses designed to increase test scores and reading ability. Suppose the firm wants to offer a course that will help high school juniors increase their SAT scores. To begin, each student takes the SAT in the junior year in high school. During the summer between the junior and senior year, they participate in the course that gives them tips on taking tests. Finally, during the fall of their senior year in high school, they retake the SAT. Again, the procedure is characterized by a measurement (taking the SAT as a junior), an intervention (the summer workshops), and another measurement (taking the SAT during their senior year).

2.  The second type of dependent sample is characterized by matching or pairing observations. Nickel Savings in the previous example is a dependent sample of this type. They selected a property for appraisal and then had two appraisals on the same property. As a second example, suppose an industrial psychologist wishes to study the intellectual similarities of newly married couples. She selects a sample of newlyweds. Next, she administers a standard intelligence test to both the man and woman to determine the difference in the scores. Notice the matching that occurred: comparing the scores that are paired or matched by marriage.

Why do we prefer dependent samples to independent samples? By using dependent samples, we are able to reduce the variation in the sampling distribution. To illustrate, we will use the Nickel Savings and Loan example just completed. Suppose we assume that we have two independent samples of real estate property for appraisal and conduct the following test of hypothesis, using formula (11–6). The null and alternate hypotheses are:

$$H_0: \mu_1 = \mu_2$$
$$H_1: \mu_1 \neq \mu_2$$

There are now two independent samples of 10 each. So the number of degrees of freedom is $10 + 10 - 2 = 18$. From Appendix D, for the .05 significance level, $H_0$ is rejected if $t$ is less than $-2.101$ or greater than $2.101$.

We use the same Excel commands as on page 66 in Chapter 3 to find the mean and the standard deviation of the two independent samples. We use the Excel commands on page 384 of this chapter to find the pooled variance and the value of the "$t$-Stat." These values are highlighted in yellow.

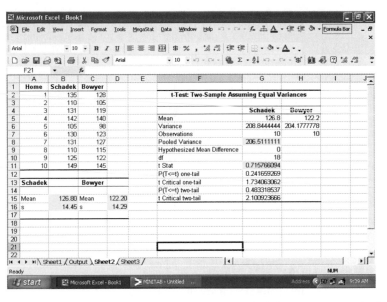

The mean of the appraised value of the 10 properties by Schadek is $126,800, and the standard deviation is $14,500. For Bowyer Real Estate the mean appraised value is $122,200, and the standard deviation is $14,300. To make the calculations easier, we use $000 instead of $. The value of the pooled estimate of the variance from formula (11–5) is

$$s_p^2 = \frac{(n_1 - 1)s_1^2 + (n_2 - 1)s_2^2}{n_1 + n_2 - 2} = \frac{(10 - 1)(14.45^2) + (10 - 1)(14.29)^2}{10 + 10 - 2} = 206.50$$

From formula (11–6), $t$ is 0.716.

$$t = \frac{\bar{X}_1 - \bar{X}_2}{\sqrt{s_p^2 \left(\frac{1}{n_1} + \frac{1}{n_2}\right)}} = \frac{126.8 - 122.2}{\sqrt{206.50 \left(\frac{1}{10} + \frac{1}{10}\right)}} = \frac{4.6}{6.4265} = 0.716$$

The computed $t$ (0.716) is less than 2.101, so the null hypothesis is not rejected. We cannot show that there is a difference in the mean appraisal value. That is not the same conclusion that we got before! Why does this happen? The numerator is the same in the paired observations test (4.6). However, the denominator is smaller. In the paired test the denominator is 1.3920 (see the calculations on page 372). In the case of the independent samples, the denominator is 6.4403. There is more variation or uncertainty. This accounts for the difference in the $t$ values and the difference in the statistical decisions. The denominator measures the standard error of the statistic. When the samples are *not* paired, two kinds of variation are present: differences between the two appraisal firms and the difference in the value of the real estate. Properties numbered 4 and 10 have relatively high values, whereas number 5 is relatively low. These data show how different the values of the property are, but we are really interested in the difference between the two appraisal firms.

The trick is to pair the values to reduce the variation among the properties. The paired test uses only the difference between the two appraisal firms for the same property. Thus, the paired or dependent statistic focuses on the variation between Schadek Appraisals and Bowyer Real Estate. Thus, its standard error is always smaller. That, in turn, leads to a larger test statistic and a greater chance of rejecting the null hypothesis. So whenever possible you should pair the data.

There is a bit of bad news here. In the paired observations test, the degrees of freedom are half of what they are if the samples are not paired. For the real estate example, the degrees of freedom drop from 18 to 9 when the observations are paired. However, in most cases, this is a small price to pay for a better test.

**Self-Review 11–4**

Advertisements by Sylph Fitness Center claim that completing their course will result in losing weight. A random sample of eight recent participants showed the following weights before and after completing the course. At the .01 significance level, can we conclude the students lost weight?

| Name | Before | After |
|------|--------|-------|
| Hunter | 155 | 154 |
| Cashman | 228 | 207 |
| Mervine | 141 | 147 |
| Massa | 162 | 157 |
| Creola | 211 | 196 |
| Peterson | 164 | 150 |
| Redding | 184 | 170 |
| Poust | 172 | 165 |

(a) State the null hypothesis and the alternate hypothesis.
(b) What is the critical value of $t$?
(c) What is the computed value of $t$?
(d) Interpret the result. What is the $p$-value?
(e) What assumption needs to be made about the distribution of the differences?

## Exercises

**19.** The null and alternate hypotheses are:

$H_0$: $\mu_d \leq 0$
$H_1$: $\mu_d > 0$

The following sample information shows the number of defective units produced on the day shift and the afternoon shift for a sample of four days last month.

| | Day | | | |
|---|---|---|---|---|
| | 1 | 2 | 3 | 4 |
| Day shift | 10 | 12 | 15 | 19 |
| Afternoon shift | 8 | 9 | 12 | 15 |

At the .05 significance level, can we conclude there are more defects produced on the afternoon shift?

**20.** The null and alternate hypotheses are:

$H_0$: $\mu_d = 0$
$H_1$: $\mu_d \neq 0$

The following paired observations show the number of traffic citations given for speeding by Officer Dhondt and Officer Meredith of the South Carolina Highway Patrol for the last five months.

| | Day | | | | |
|---|---|---|---|---|---|
| | May | June | July | August | September |
| Officer Dhondt | 30 | 22 | 25 | 19 | 26 |
| Officer Meredith | 26 | 19 | 20 | 15 | 19 |

At the .05 significance level, is there a difference in the mean number of citations given by the two officers?

*Note:* Use the five-step hypothesis testing procedure to solve the following exercises.

21. The management of Discount Furniture, a chain of discount furniture stores in the Northeast, designed an incentive plan for salespeople. To evaluate this innovative plan, 12 salespeople were selected at random, and their weekly incomes before and after the plan were recorded.

| Salesperson | Before | After |
|-------------|--------|-------|
| Sid Mahone | $320 | $340 |
| Carol Quick | 290 | 285 |
| Tom Jackson | 421 | 475 |
| Andy Jones | 510 | 510 |
| Jean Sloan | 210 | 210 |
| Jack Walker | 402 | 500 |
| Peg Mancuso | 625 | 631 |
| Anita Loma | 560 | 560 |
| John Cuso | 360 | 365 |
| Carl Utz | 431 | 431 |
| A. S. Kushner | 506 | 525 |
| Fern Lawton | 505 | 619 |

Was there a significant increase in the typical salesperson's weekly income due to the innovative incentive plan? Use the .05 significance level. Estimate the *p*-value, and interpret it.

22. The federal government recently granted funds for a special program designed to reduce crime in high-crime areas. A study of the results of the program in eight high-crime areas of Miami, Florida, yielded the following results.

| | A | B | C | D | E | F | G | H |
|--------|----|----|----|----|----|----|----|----|
| Before | 14 | 7 | 4 | 5 | 17 | 12 | 8 | 9 |
| After | 2 | 7 | 3 | 6 | 8 | 13 | 3 | 5 |

*Number of Crimes by Area*

Has there been a decrease in the number of crimes since the inauguration of the program? Use the .01 significance level. Estimate the *p*-value.

# Chapter Outline

I. In comparing two population means we wish to know whether they could be equal.
   A. We are investigating whether the distribution of the difference between the means could have a mean of 0.
   B. The test statistic is the standard normal (*z*) if the samples both contain at least 30 observations and the population standard deviations are unknown.
      1. No assumption about the shape of either population is required.
      2. The samples are from independent populations.
      3. The formula to compute the value of *z* is

$$z = \frac{\bar{X}_1 - \bar{X}_2}{\sqrt{\dfrac{s_1^2}{n_1} + \dfrac{s_2^2}{n_2}}}$$

[11–2]

II. We can also test whether two samples came from populations with an equal proportion of successes.
   A. The two sample proportions are pooled using the following formula:

$$p_c = \frac{X_1 + X_2}{n_1 + n_2}$$

[11–4]

**B.** We compute the value of the test statistic from the following formula:

$$z = \frac{p_1 - p_2}{\sqrt{\dfrac{p_c(1 - p_c)}{n_1} + \dfrac{p_c(1 - p_c)}{n_2}}}$$    [11–3]

**III.** The test statistic to compare two means is the $t$ distribution if one or both of the samples contain fewer than 30 observations.
   **A.** Both populations must follow the normal distribution.
   **B.** The populations must have equal standard deviations.
   **C.** The samples are independent.
   **D.** Finding the value of $t$ requires two steps.
      **1.** The first step is to pool the standard deviations according to the following formula:

$$s_p^2 = \frac{(n_1 - 1)s_1^2 + (n_2 - 1)s_2^2}{n_1 + n_2 - 2}$$    [11–5]

   **2.** The value of $t$ is computed from the following formula:

$$t = \frac{\bar{X}_1 - \bar{X}_2}{\sqrt{s_p^2\left(\dfrac{1}{n_1} + \dfrac{1}{n_2}\right)}}$$    [11–6]

**IV.** For dependent samples, we assume the distribution of the paired differences between the populations has a mean of 0.
   **A.** We first compute the mean and the standard deviation of the sample differences.
   **B.** The value of the test statistic is computed from the following formula:

$$t = \frac{\bar{d}}{s_d/\sqrt{n}}$$    [11–7]

# Pronunciation Key

| SYMBOL | MEANING | PRONUNCIATION |
|--------|---------|---------------|
| $p_c$ | Pooled proportion | p sub c |
| $s_p^2$ | Pooled sample variance | s sub p squared |
| $\bar{X}_1$ | Mean of the first sample | X bar sub 1 |
| $\bar{X}_2$ | Mean of the second sample | X bar sub 2 |
| $\bar{d}$ | Mean of the difference between dependent observations | d bar |
| $s_d$ | Standard deviation of the difference between dependent observations | s sub d |

# Chapter Exercises

**23.** A recent study focused on the number of times men and women who live alone buy take-out dinner in a month. The information is summarized below.

| Statistic | Men | Women |
|-----------|-----|-------|
| Mean | 24.51 | 22.69 |
| Standard deviation | 4.48 | 3.86 |
| Sample size | 35 | 40 |

At the .01 significance level, is there a difference in the mean number of times men and women order takeout dinners in a month? What is the $p$-value?

**24.** Clark Heter is an industrial engineer at Lyons Products. He would like to determine whether there are more units produced on the afternoon shift than on the day shift. A sample of 54 day-shift workers showed that the mean number of units produced was 345, with a standard deviation of 21. A sample of 60 afternoon-shift workers showed that the mean number of units produced was 351, with a standard deviation of 28 units. At the .05 significance level, is the number of units produced on the afternoon shift larger?

25. Fry Brothers Heating and Air Conditioning, Inc. employs Larry Clark and George Murnen to make service calls to repair furnaces and air conditioning units in homes. Tom Fry, the owner, would like to know whether there is a difference in the mean number of service calls they make per day. A random sample of 40 days last year showed that Larry Clark made an average of 4.77 calls per day, with a standard deviation of 1.05 calls per day. For a sample of 50 days George Murnen made an average of 5.02 calls per day, with a standard deviation of 1.23 calls per day. At the .05 significance level, is there a difference in the mean number of calls per day between the two employees? What is the p-value?

26. A coffee manufacturer is interested in whether the mean daily consumption of regular-coffee drinkers is less than that of decaffeinated-coffee drinkers. A random sample of 50 regular-coffee drinkers showed a mean of 4.35 cups per day, with a standard deviation of 1.20 cups per day. A sample of 40 decaffeinated-coffee drinkers showed a mean of 5.84 cups per day, with a standard deviation of 1.36 cups per day. Use the .01 significance level. Compute the p-value.

27. A cell phone company offers two plans to it subscribers. At the time new subscribers sign up, they are asked to provide some demographic information. The mean yearly income for a sample of 40 subscribers to Plan A is $57,000 with a standard deviation of $9,200. This distribution is positively skewed; the actual coefficient of skewness is 2.11. For a sample of 30 subscribers to Plan B the mean income is $61,000 with a standard deviation of $7,100. The distribution of Plan B subscribers is also positively skewed, but not as severely. The coefficient of skewness is 1.54. At the .05 significance level, is it reasonable to conclude the mean income of those selecting Plan B is larger? What is the p-value? Do the coefficients of skewness affect the results of the hypothesis test? Why?

28. A computer manufacturer offers a help line that purchasers can call for help 24 hours a day 7 days a week. Clearing these calls for help in a timely fashion is important to the company's image. After telling the caller that resolution of the problem is important the caller is asked whether the issue is "software" or "hardware" related. The mean time it takes a technician to resolve a software issue is 18 minutes with a standard deviation of 4.2 minutes. This information was obtained from a sample of 35 monitored calls. For a study of 45 hardware issues, the mean time for the technician to resolve the problem was 15.5 minutes with a standard deviation of 3.9 minutes. This information was also obtained from monitored calls. At the .05 significance level is it reasonable to conclude that it takes longer to resolve software issues? What is the p-value?

29. The manufacturer of Advil, a common headache remedy, recently developed a new formulation of the drug that is claimed to be more effective. To evaluate the new drug, a sample of 200 current users is asked to try it. After a one-month trial, 180 indicated the new drug was more effective in relieving a headache. At the same time a sample of 300 current Advil users is given the current drug but told it is the new formulation. From this group, 261 said it was an improvement. At the .05 significance level can we conclude that the new drug is more effective?

30. Each month the National Association of Purchasing Managers publishes the NAPM index. One of the questions asked on the survey to purchasing agents is: Do you think the economy is expanding? Last month, of the 300 responses 160 answered yes to the question. This month, 170 of the 290 responses indicated they felt the economy was expanding. At the .05 significance level, can we conclude that a larger proportion of the agents believe the economy is expanding this month?

31. As part of a recent survey among dual-wage-earner couples, an industrial psychologist found that 990 men out of the 1,500 surveyed believed the division of household duties was fair. A sample of 1,600 women found 970 believed the division of household duties was fair. At the .01 significance level, is it reasonable to conclude that the proportion of men who believe the division of household duties is fair is larger? What is the p-value?

32. There are two major Internet providers in the Colorado Springs, Colorado, area, one called HTC and the other Mountain Communications. We want to investigate whether there is a difference in the proportion of times a customer is able to access the Internet. During a one-week period, 500 calls were placed at random times throughout the day and night to HTC. A connection was made to the Internet on 450 occasions. A similar one-week study with Mountain Communications showed the Internet to be available on 352 of 400 trials. At the .01 significance level, is there a difference in the percent of time that access to the Internet is successful?

33. The owner of Bun 'N' Run Hamburger wishes to compare the sales per day at two locations. The mean number sold for 10 randomly selected days at the Northside site was 83.55, and the standard deviation was 10.50. For a random sample of 12 days at the Southside location, the mean number sold was 78.80 and the standard deviation was 14.25. At the .05 significance level, is there a difference in the mean number of hamburgers sold at the two locations? What is the p-value?

34. The Engineering Department at Sims Software, Inc., recently developed two chemical solutions designed to increase the usable life of computer disks. A sample of disks treated with the first solution lasted 86, 78, 66, 83, 84, 81, 84, 109, 65, and 102 hours. Those treated with the second solution lasted 91, 71, 75, 76, 87, 79, 73, 76, 79, 78, 87, 90, 76, and 72 hours. At the .10 significance level, can we conclude that there is a difference in the length of time the two types of treatment lasted?

35. The Willow Run Outlet Mall has two Haggar Outlet Stores, one located on Peach Street and the other on Plum Street. The two stores are laid out differently, but both store managers claim their layout maximizes the amounts customers will purchase on impulse. A sample of 10 customers at the Peach Street store revealed they spent the following amounts more than planned: $17.58, $19.73, $12.61, $17.79, $16.22, $15.82, $15.40, $15.86, $11.82, and $15.85. A sample of 14 customers at the Plum Street store revealed they spent the following amounts more than they planned: $18.19, $20.22, $17.38, $17.96, $23.92, $15.87, $16.47, $15.96, $16.79, $16.74, $21.40, $20.57, $19.79, and $14.83. At the .01 significance level, is there a difference in the mean amounts purchased on impulse at the two stores?

36. The Grand Strand Family Medical Center is specifically set up to treat minor medical emergencies for visitors to the Myrtle Beach area. There are two facilities, one in the Little River Area and the other in Murrells Inlet. The Quality Assurance Department wishes to compare the mean waiting time for patients at the two locations. Samples of the waiting times, reported in minutes, follow:

| Location | Waiting Time |
|---|---|
| Little River | 31.73  28.77  29.53  22.08  29.47  18.60  32.94  25.18  29.82  26.49 |
| Murrells Inlet | 22.93  23.92  26.92  27.20  26.44  25.62  30.61  29.44  23.09  23.10  26.69  22.31 |

At the .05 significance level, is there a difference in the mean waiting time?

37. The Commercial Bank and Trust Company is studying the use of its automatic teller machines (ATMs). Of particular interest is whether young adults (under 25 years) use the machines more than senior citizens. To investigate further, samples of customers under 25 years of age and customers over 60 years of age were selected. The number of ATM transactions last month was determined for each selected individual, and the results are shown below. At the .01 significance level, can bank management conclude that younger customers use the ATMs more?

| Under 25 | 10 | 10 | 11 | 15 | 7 | 11 | 10 | 9 | | |
|---|---|---|---|---|---|---|---|---|---|---|
| Over 60 | 4 | 8 | 7 | 7 | 4 | 5 | 1 | 7 | 4 | 10 | 5 |

38. Two boats, the *Prada* (Italy) and the *Oracle* (U.S.A.), are competing for a spot in the upcoming *America's Cup* race. They race over a part of the course several times. Below are the sample times in minutes. At the .05 significance level, can we conclude that there is a difference in their mean times?

| Boat | Times (minutes) |
|---|---|
| *Prada* (Italy) | 12.9  12.5  11.0  13.3  11.2  11.4  11.6  12.3  14.2  11.3 |
| *Oracle* (U.S.A.) | 14.1  14.1  14.2  17.4  15.8  16.7  16.1  13.3  13.4  13.6  10.8  19.0 |

39. The manufacturer of an MP3 player wanted to know whether a 10 percent reduction in price is enough to increase the sales of their product. To investigate, the owner randomly selected eight outlets and sold the MP3 player at the reduced price. At seven randomly selected outlets, the MP3 player was sold at the regular price. Reported below is the number of units sold last month at the sampled outlets. At the .01 significance level, can the manufacturer conclude that the price reduction resulted in an increase in sales?

| Regular price | 138 | 121 | 88 | 115 | 141 | 125 | 96 | |
|---|---|---|---|---|---|---|---|---|
| Reduced price | 128 | 134 | 152 | 135 | 114 | 106 | 112 | 120 |

40. A number of minor automobile accidents occur at various high-risk intersections in Teton County despite traffic lights. The Traffic Department claims that a modification in the type of light will reduce these accidents. The county commissioners have agreed to a proposed experiment. Eight intersections were chosen at random, and the lights at those intersections were modified. The numbers of minor accidents during a six-month period before and after the modifications were:

| | Number of Accidents | | | | | | | |
|---|---|---|---|---|---|---|---|---|
| | A | B | C | D | E | F | G | H |
| Before modification | 5 | 7 | 6 | 4 | 8 | 9 | 8 | 10 |
| After modification | 3 | 7 | 7 | 0 | 4 | 6 | 8 | 2 |

At the .01 significance level is it reasonable to conclude that the modification reduced the number of traffic accidents?

41. Lester Hollar is Vice President for Human Resources for a large manufacturing company. In recent years he has noticed an increase in absenteeism that he thinks is related to the general health of the employees. Four years ago, in an attempt to improve the situation, he began a fitness program in which employees exercise during their lunch hour. To evaluate the program, he selected a random sample of eight participants and found the number of days each was absent in the six months before the exercise program began and in the last six months. Below are the results. At the .05 significance level, can he conclude that the number of absences has declined? Estimate the p-value.

| Employee | Before | After |
|---|---|---|
| 1 | 6 | 5 |
| 2 | 6 | 2 |
| 3 | 7 | 1 |
| 4 | 7 | 3 |
| 5 | 4 | 3 |
| 6 | 3 | 6 |
| 7 | 5 | 3 |
| 8 | 6 | 7 |

42. The president of the American Insurance Institute wants to compare the yearly costs of auto insurance offered by two leading companies. He selects a sample of 15 families, some with only a single insured driver, others with several teenage drivers, and pays each family a stipend to contact the two companies and ask for a price quote. To make the data comparable, certain features, such as the amount deductible and limits of liability, are standardized. The sample information is reported below. At the .10 significance level, can we conclude that there is a difference in the amounts quoted?

| Family | Progressive Car Insurance | GEICO Mutual Insurance |
|---|---|---|
| Becker | $2,090 | $1,610 |
| Berry | 1,683 | 1,247 |
| Cobb | 1,402 | 2,327 |
| Debuck | 1,830 | 1,367 |
| DuBrul | 930 | 1,461 |
| Eckroate | 697 | 1,789 |
| German | 1,741 | 1,621 |
| Glasson | 1,129 | 1,914 |
| King | 1,018 | 1,956 |
| Kucic | 1,881 | 1,772 |
| Meredith | 1,571 | 1,375 |
| Obeid | 874 | 1,527 |
| Price | 1,579 | 1,767 |
| Phillips | 1,577 | 1,636 |
| Tresize | 860 | 1,188 |

43. Fairfield Homes is developing two parcels near Pigeon Fork, Tennessee. In order to test different advertising approaches, they use different media to reach potential buyers. The mean annual family income for 75 people making inquiries at the first development is $150,000, with a standard deviation of $40,000. A corresponding sample of 120 people at the second development had a mean of $180,000, with a standard deviation of $30,000. At the .05 significance level, can Fairfield conclude that the population means are different?

44. The following data resulted from a taste test of two different chocolate bars. The first number is a rating of the taste, which could range from 0 to 5, with a 5 indicating the person liked the taste. The second number indicates whether a "secret ingredient" was present. If the ingredient was present a code of "1" was used and a "0" otherwise. At the .05 significance level, does this data show a difference in the taste ratings?

| Rating | "With/Without" | Rating | "With/Without" |
|--------|----------------|--------|----------------|
| 3 | 1 | 1 | 1 |
| 1 | 1 | 4 | 0 |
| 0 | 0 | 4 | 0 |
| 2 | 1 | 2 | 1 |
| 3 | 1 | 3 | 0 |
| 1 | 1 | 4 | 0 |

45. An investigation of the effectiveness of an antibacterial soap in reducing operating room contamination resulted in the accompanying table. The new soap was tested in a sample of eight operating rooms in the greater Seattle area during the last year.

| | Operating Room | | | | | | | |
|--------|-----|-----|-----|------|------|-----|-----|------|
| | A | B | C | D | E | F | G | H |
| Before | 6.6 | 6.5 | 9.0 | 10.3 | 11.2 | 8.1 | 6.3 | 11.6 |
| After | 6.8 | 2.4 | 7.4 | 8.5 | 8.1 | 6.1 | 3.4 | 2.0 |

At the 0.05 significance level, can we conclude the contamination measurements are lower after use of the new soap?

46. The following data on annual rates of return were collected from five stocks listed on the New York Stock Exchange ("the big board") and five stocks listed on NASDAQ. At the .10 significance level, can we conclude that the annual rates of return are higher on the big board?

| NYSE | NASDAQ |
|-------|--------|
| 17.16 | 15.80 |
| 17.08 | 16.28 |
| 15.51 | 16.21 |
| 8.43 | 17.97 |
| 25.15 | 7.77 |

47. The city of Laguna Beach operates two public parking lots. The one on Ocean Drive can accommodate up to 125 cars and the one on Rio Rancho can accommodate up to 130 cars. City planners are considering both increasing the size of the lots and changing the fee structure. To begin, the Planning Office would like some information on the number of cars in the lots at various times of the day. A junior planner officer is assigned the task of visiting the two lots at random times of the day and evening and counting the number of cars in the lots. The study lasted over a period of one month. Below is the number of cars in the lots for 25 visits of the Ocean Drive lot and 28 visits of the Rio Rancho lot.

**Ocean**

| | | | | | | | | | | | | |
|----|-----|----|-----|-----|----|----|----|-----|-----|-----|----|----|
| 89 | 115 | 93 | 79 | 113 | 77 | 51 | 75 | 118 | 105 | 106 | 91 | 54 |
| 63 | 121 | 53 | 81 | 115 | 67 | 53 | 69 | 95 | 121 | 88 | 64 | |

**Rio Rancho**

| | | | | | | | | | | | | |
|-----|-----|----|-----|-----|-----|-----|----|----|----|-----|----|-----|
| 128 | 110 | 81 | 126 | 82 | 114 | 93 | 40 | 94 | 45 | 84 | 71 | 74 |
| 92 | 66 | 69 | 100 | 114 | 113 | 107 | 62 | 77 | 80 | 107 | 90 | 129 |
| 105 | 124 | | | | | | | | | | | |

Is it reasonable to conclude that there is a difference in the mean number of cars in the two lots? Use the .05 significance level.

48. The amount of money out of income spent on housing is an important component of the cost of living. The total costs of housing for homeowners might include mortgage payments, property taxes, and utility costs (water, heat, electricity). An economist selected a sample of 20 homeowners in New England and then calculated these total housing costs

as a percent of monthly income, five years ago and now. The information is reported below. Is it reasonable to conclude the percent is less now than five years ago?

| Homeowner | Five Years Ago | Now | Homeowner | Five Years Ago | Now |
|-----------|----------------|-----|-----------|----------------|-----|
| 1 | 17 | 10 | 11 | 35 | 32 |
| 2 | 20 | 39 | 12 | 16 | 32 |
| 3 | 29 | 37 | 13 | 23 | 21 |
| 4 | 43 | 27 | 14 | 33 | 12 |
| 5 | 36 | 12 | 15 | 44 | 40 |
| 6 | 43 | 41 | 16 | 44 | 42 |
| 7 | 45 | 24 | 17 | 28 | 22 |
| 8 | 19 | 26 | 18 | 29 | 19 |
| 9 | 49 | 28 | 19 | 39 | 35 |
| 10 | 49 | 26 | 20 | 22 | 12 |

# exercises.com

**49.** Listed below are several prominent companies and their stock prices in February 2003. Go to the Web and look up today's price. There are many sources to find stock prices, such as Yahoo and CNNFI. The Yahoo address is http://www.quote.yahoo.com. Enter the symbol identification to find the current price. At the .05 significance level, can we conclude that the prices have changed?

| Company | Symbol | Price |
|---------|--------|-------|
| Coca-Cola | KO | $41.10 |
| Walt Disney | DIS | 17.30 |
| Eastman Kodak | EK | 30.95 |
| Ford Motor Company | F | 8.93 |
| General Motors | GM | 34.46 |
| Goodyear Tire | GT | 4.25 |
| IBM | IBM | 79.33 |
| McDonald's | MCD | 13.45 |
| McGraw-Hill Publishing | MHP | 56.59 |
| Oracle | ORCL | 12.42 |
| Johnson and Johnson | JNJ | 53.06 |
| General Electric | GE | 22.91 |
| Home Depot | HD | 21.90 |

**50.** The *USA Today* (http://www.usatoday.com/sports/baseball/front.htm) and Major League Baseball's (http://www.majorleaguebaseball.com) websites regularly report information on individual player salaries. Go to one of these sites and find the individual salaries for your favorite team. Compute the mean and the standard deviation. Is it reasonable to conclude that your favorite (or local) team has a mean player salary different from $1,500,000?

# Dataset Exercises

**51.** Refer to the Real Estate data, which reports information on the homes sold in Denver, Colorado, last year.
  **a.** At the .05 significance level, can we conclude that there is a difference in the mean selling price of homes with a pool and homes without a pool?
  **b.** At the .05 significance level, can we conclude that there is a difference in the mean selling price of homes with an attached garage and homes without a garage?
  **c.** At the .05 significance level, can we conclude that there is a difference in the mean selling price of homes in Township 1 and Township 2?
  **d.** Find the median selling price of the homes. Divide the homes into two groups, those that sold for more than (or equal to) the median price and those that sold for less. Is there a difference in the proportion of homes with a pool for those that sold at or above the median price versus those that sold for less than the median price? Use the .05 significance level.

52. Refer to the Baseball 2002 data, which reports information on the 30 Major League Baseball teams for the 2002 season.
    a. At the .05 significance level, can we conclude that there is a difference in the mean salary of teams in the American League versus teams in the National League?
    b. At the .05 significance level, can we conclude that there is a difference in the mean home attendance of teams in the American League versus teams in the National League?
    c. At the .05 significance level, can we conclude that there is a difference in the mean number of wins for teams that have artificial turf home fields versus teams that have grass home fields?
    d. At the .05 significance level, can we conclude that there is a difference in the mean number of home runs for teams that have artificial turf home fields versus teams that have grass home fields?
53. Refer to the Wage data, which reports information on annual wages for a sample of 100 workers. Also included are variables relating to industry, years of education, and gender for each worker.
    a. Conduct a test of hypothesis to determine if there is a difference in the mean annual wages of southern residents versus nonsouthern residents.
    b. Conduct a test of hypothesis to determine if there is a difference in the mean annual wages of white and nonwhite wage earners.
    c. Conduct a test of hypothesis to determine if there is a difference in the mean annual wages of Hispanic and non-Hispanic wage earners.
    d. Conduct a test of hypothesis to determine if there is a difference in the mean annual wages of female and male wage earners.
    e. Conduct a test of hypothesis to determine if there is a difference in the mean annual wages of married and nonmarried wage earners.
54. Refer to the CIA data, which reports demographic and economic information on 46 countries. Conduct a test of hypothesis to determine whether the mean percent of the population over 65 years of age in G20 countries is different from those that are not G20 members.

# Software Commands

1. The Excel commands for the two-sample *t*-test on page 369 are:
   a. Enter the data into columns A and B (or any other columns) in the spreadsheet. Use the first row of each column to enter the variable name.
   b. From the menu bar select **Tools** and **Data Analysis.** Select **t-Test: Two-Sample Assuming Equal Variances,** then click **OK.**
   c. In the dialog box indicate that the range of **Variable 1** is from *A1* to *A6* and **Variable 2** from *B1* to *B7*, the **Hypothesized Mean Difference** is 0, the **Labels** are in the first row, **Alpha** is *0.05*, and the **Output Range** is *D2*. Click **OK.**

2. The Excel commands for the paired *t*-test on page 373 are:
   a. Enter the data into columns B and C (or any other two columns) in the spreadsheet, with the variable names in the first row.
   b. From the menu bar select **Tools** and **Data Analysis.** Select **t-Test: Paired Two Sample for Means,** then click **OK.**
   c. In the dialog box indicate that the range of **Variable 1** is from *B1* to *B11* and **Variable 2** from *C1* to *C11*, the **Hypothesized Mean Difference** is *0*, the **Labels** are in the first row, **Alpha** is *.05*, and the **Output Range** is *D2*. Click **OK.**

# Chapter 11  Answers to Self-Review

**11–1  a.** $H_0$: $\mu_W \leq \mu_M$
  $H_1$: $\mu_W > \mu_M$
  The subscript $W$ refers to the women and $M$ to the men.
  **b.** Reject $H_0$ if $z > 1.65$
  **c.** $z = \dfrac{\$1{,}500 - \$1{,}400}{\sqrt{\dfrac{(\$250)^2}{50} + \dfrac{(\$200)^2}{40}}} = 2.11$
  **d.** Reject the null hypothesis
  **e.** $p$-value $= .5000 - .4826 = .0174$
  **f.** The mean amount sold per day is larger for women.

**11–2  a.** $H_0$: $\pi_1 = \pi_2$
  $H_1$: $\pi_1 \neq \pi_2$
  **b.** .10
  **c.** Two-tailed
  **d.** Reject $H_0$ if $z$ is less than $-1.65$ or greater than 1.65.
  **e.** $p_c = \dfrac{87 + 123}{150 + 200} = \dfrac{210}{350} = .60$
  $p_1 = \dfrac{87}{150} = .58 \qquad p_2 = \dfrac{123}{200} = .615$
  $z = \dfrac{.58 - .615}{\sqrt{\dfrac{.60(.40)}{150} + \dfrac{.60(.40)}{200}}} = -0.66$
  **f.** Do not reject $H_0$.
  **g.** $p$-value $= 2(.5000 - .2454) = .5092$
  There is no difference in the proportion of adults and children that liked the proposed flavor.

**11–3  a.** $H_0$: $\mu_d = \mu_a$
  $H_1$: $\mu_d \neq \mu_a$
  **b.** $df = 6 + 8 - 2 = 12$
  Reject $H_0$ if $t$ is less than $-2.179$ or $t$ is greater than 2.179.
  **c.** $\bar{X}_1 = \dfrac{42}{6} = 7.00 \quad s_1 = \sqrt{\dfrac{10}{6 - 1}} = 1.4142$
  $\bar{X}_2 = \dfrac{80}{8} = 10.00 \quad s_2 = \sqrt{\dfrac{36}{8 - 1}} = 2.2678$
  $s_p^2 = \dfrac{(6 - 1)(1.4142)^2 + (8 - 1)(2.2678)^2}{6 + 8 - 2}$
  $= 3.8333$
  $t = \dfrac{7.00 - 10.00}{\sqrt{3.8333\left(\dfrac{1}{6} + \dfrac{1}{8}\right)}} = -2.837$

  **d.** Reject $H_0$ because $-2.837$ is less than the critical value.
  **e.** The $p$-value is less than .02.
  **f.** The mean number of defects is not the same on the two shifts.
  **g.** Independent populations, populations follow the normal distribution, populations have equal standard deviations.

**11–4  a.** $H_0$: $\mu_d \leq 0$, $H_1$: $\mu_d > 0$.
  **b.** Reject $H_0$ if $t > 2.998$.
  **c.**

| Name | Before | After | $d$ | $(d - \bar{d})$ | $(d - \bar{d})^2$ |
|---|---|---|---|---|---|
| Hunter | 155 | 154 | 1 | $-7.875$ | 62.0156 |
| Cashman | 228 | 207 | 21 | 12.125 | 147.0156 |
| Mervine | 141 | 147 | $-6$ | $-14.875$ | 221.2656 |
| Massa | 162 | 157 | 5 | $-3.875$ | 15.0156 |
| Creola | 211 | 196 | 15 | 6.125 | 37.5156 |
| Peterson | 164 | 150 | 14 | 5.125 | 26.2656 |
| Redding | 184 | 170 | 14 | 5.125 | 26.2656 |
| Poust | 172 | 165 | 7 | $-1.875$ | 3.5156 |
|  |  |  | 71 |  | 538.8750 |

  $\bar{d} = \dfrac{71}{8} = 8.875$

  $s_d = \sqrt{\dfrac{538.875}{8 - 1}} = 8.774$

  $t = \dfrac{8.875}{8.774/\sqrt{8}} = 2.861$

  **d.** Do not reject $H_0$. We cannot conclude that the students lost weight. The $p$-value is less than .025 but larger than .01.
  **e.** The distribution of the differences must follow a normal distribution.

# 12

# Analysis of Variance

## GOALS

*When you have completed this chapter, you will be able to:*

1 List the characteristics of the *F* distribution.

2 Conduct a test of hypothesis to determine whether the variances of two populations are equal.

3 Discuss the general idea of analysis of variance.

4 Organize data into a one-way and a two-way ANOVA table.

5 Conduct a test of hypothesis among three or more treatment means.

6 Develop confidence intervals for the difference in treatment means.

7 Define and understand the terms *treatments* and *blocks.*

8 Conduct a test of hypothesis to determine whether there is a difference among block means.

Three assembly lines are used to produce a certain component for an airliner. To examine the production rate, a random sample of six hourly periods is chosen for each assembly line and the number of components produced during these periods for each line is recorded. Develop a 99 percent confidence interval for the difference in the means between lines B and C. (See Goal 6 and Exercise 32.)

# Introduction

In this chapter we continue our discussion of hypothesis testing. Recall that in Chapters 10 and 11 we examined the general theory of hypothesis testing. We described the case where a large sample was selected from the population. We used the $z$ distribution (the standard normal distribution) to determine whether it was reasonable to conclude that the population mean was equal to a specified value. We tested whether two population means are the same. We also conducted both one- and two-sample tests for population proportions, again using the standard normal distribution as the distribution of the test statistic. We described methods for conducting tests of means where the populations were assumed normal but the samples were small (contained fewer than 30 observations). In that case the $t$ distribution was used as the distribution of the test statistic. In this chapter we expand further our idea of hypothesis tests. We describe a test for variances and then a test that simultaneously compares several means to determine if they came from equal populations.

# The $F$ Distribution

The probability distribution used in this chapter is the $F$ distribution. It was named to honor Sir Ronald Fisher, one of the founders of modern-day statistics. This probability distribution is used as the distribution of the test statistic for several situations. It is used to test whether two samples are from populations having equal variances, and it is also applied when we want to compare several population means simultaneously. The simultaneous comparison of several population means is called **analysis of variance (ANOVA).** In both of these situations, the populations must follow a normal distribution, and the data must be at least interval-scale.

What are the characteristics of the $F$ distribution?

Characteristics of the $F$ distribution

1. **There is a "family" of $F$ distributions.** A particular member of the family is determined by two parameters: the degrees of freedom in the numerator and the degrees of freedom in the denominator. The shape of the distribution is illustrated by the following graph. There is one $F$ distribution for the combination of 29 degrees of freedom in the numerator and 28 degrees of freedom in the denominator. There is another $F$ distribution for 19 degrees in the numerator and 6 degrees of freedom in the denominator. Note that the shape of the curves change as the degrees of freedom change.

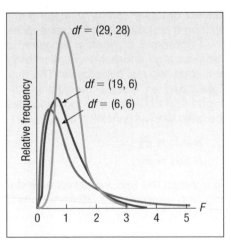

2. **The $F$ distribution is continuous.** This means that it can assume an infinite number of values between zero and positive infinity.

3. **The F distribution cannot be negative.** The smallest value $F$ can assume is 0.
4. **It is positively skewed.** The long tail of the distribution is to the right-hand side. As the number of degrees of freedom increases in both the numerator and denominator the distribution approaches a normal distribution.
5. **It is asymptotic.** As the values of $X$ increase, the $F$ curve approaches the $X$-axis but never touches it. This is similar to the behavior of the normal distribution, described in Chapter 7.

# Comparing Two Population Variances

The $F$ distribution is used to test the hypothesis that the variance of one normal population equals the variance of another normal population. The following examples will show the use of the test:

- Two Barth shearing machines are set to produce steel bars of the same length. The bars, therefore, should have the same mean length. We want to ensure that in addition to having the same mean length they also have similar variation.

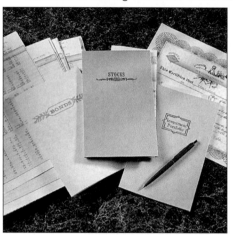

- The mean rate of return on two types of common stock may be the same, but there may be more variation in the rate of return in one than the other. A sample of 10 Internet stocks and 10 utility stocks shows the same mean rate of return, but there is likely more variation in the Internet stocks.
- A study by the marketing department for a large newspaper found that men and women spent about the same amount of time per day reading the paper. However, the same report indicated there was nearly twice as much variation in time spent per day among the men than the women.

The $F$ distribution is also used to test assumptions for some statistical tests. Recall that in the previous chapter when small samples were assumed, we used the $t$ test to investigate whether the means of two independent populations differed. To employ that test, we assume that the variances of two normal populations are the same. See this list of assumptions on page 366. The $F$ distribution provides a means for conducting a test regarding the variances of two normal populations.

Regardless of whether we want to determine whether one population has more variation than another population or validate an assumption for a statistical test, we first state the null hypothesis. The null hypothesis is that the variance of one normal population, $\sigma_1^2$, equals the variance of the other normal population, $\sigma_2^2$. The alternate hypothesis could be that the variances differ. In this instance the null hypothesis and the alternate hypothesis are:

$H_0: \sigma_1^2 = \sigma_2^2$
$H_1: \sigma_1^2 \neq \sigma_2^2$

To conduct the test, we select a random sample of $n_1$ observations from one population, and a sample of $n_2$ observations from the second population. The test statistic is defined as follows.

| TEST STATISTIC FOR COMPARING TWO VARIANCES | $F = \dfrac{s_1^2}{s_2^2}$ | [12–1] |
|---|---|---|

The terms $s_1^2$ and $s_2^2$ are the respective sample variances. If the null hypothesis is true, the test statistic follows the $F$ distribution with $n_1 - 1$ and $n_2 - 1$ degrees of freedom. In order to reduce the size of the table of critical values, the *larger* sample variance is placed in the numerator; hence, the tabled $F$ ratio is always larger than 1.00. Thus, the right-tail critical value is the only one required. The critical value of $F$ for a two-tailed test is found by dividing the significance level in half ($\alpha/2$) and then referring to the appropriate degrees of freedom in Appendix G. An example will illustrate.

**EXAMPLE**

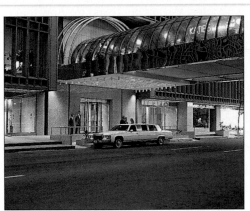

Lammers Limos offers limousine service from the city hall in Toledo, Ohio, to Metro Airport in Detroit. Sean Lammers, president of the company, is considering two routes. One is via U.S. 25 and the other via I-75. He wants to study the time it takes to drive to the airport using each route and then compare the results. He collected the following sample data, which is reported in minutes. Using the .10 significance level, is there a difference in the variation in the driving times for the two routes?

| U.S. Route 25 | Interstate 75 |
|---|---|
| 52 | 59 |
| 67 | 60 |
| 56 | 61 |
| 45 | 51 |
| 70 | 56 |
| 54 | 63 |
| 64 | 57 |
|  | 65 |

**SOLUTION**

The mean driving times along the two routes are nearly the same. The mean time is 58.29 minutes for the U.S. 25 route and 59.0 minutes along the I-75 route. However, in evaluating travel times, Mr. Lammers is also concerned about the variation in the travel times. The first step is to compute the two sample variances. We'll use formula (3–11) to compute the sample standard deviations. To obtain the sample variances, we square the standard deviations.

## U.S. Route 25

$$\bar{X} = \frac{\Sigma X}{n} = \frac{408}{7} = 58.29 \qquad s = \sqrt{\frac{\Sigma(X - \bar{X})^2}{n - 1}} = \sqrt{\frac{485.43}{7 - 1}} = 8.9947$$

## Interstate 75

$$\bar{X} = \frac{\Sigma X}{n} = \frac{472}{8} = 59.00 \qquad s = \sqrt{\frac{\Sigma(X - \bar{X})^2}{n - 1}} = \sqrt{\frac{134}{8 - 1}} = 4.3753$$

There is more variation, as measured by the standard deviation, in the U.S. 25 route than in the I-75 route. This is somewhat consistent with his knowledge of the two routes; the U.S. 25 route contains more stoplights, whereas I-75 is a limited-access interstate highway. However, the I-75 route is several miles longer. It is important that the service offered be both timely and consistent, so he decides to conduct a statistical test to determine whether there really is a difference in the variation of the two routes.

The usual five-step hypothesis-testing procedure will be employed.

**Step 1:** We begin by stating the null hypothesis and the alternate hypothesis. The test is two-tailed because we are looking for a difference in the variation of the two routes. We are *not* trying to show that one route has more variation than the other.

$$H_0: \sigma_1^2 = \sigma_2^2$$
$$H_1: \sigma_1^2 \neq \sigma_2^2$$

**Step 2:** We selected the .10 significance level.

**Step 3:** The appropriate test statistic follows the $F$ distribution.

**Step 4:** The critical value is obtained from Appendix G, a portion of which is reproduced as Table 12–1. Because we are conducting a two-tailed test, the tabled significance level is .05, found by $\alpha/2 = .10/2 = .05$. There are $n_1 - 1 = 7 - 1 = 6$ degrees of freedom in the numerator, and $n_2 - 1 = 8 - 1 = 7$ degrees of freedom in the denominator. To find the critical value, move horizontally across the top portion of the $F$ table (Table 12–1 or Appendix G) for the .05 significance level to 6 degrees of freedom in the numerator. Then move down that column to the critical value opposite 7 degrees of freedom in the denominator. The critical value is 3.87. Thus, the decision rule is: Reject the null hypothesis if the ratio of the sample variances exceeds 3.87.

**TABLE 12–1** Critical Values of the $F$ Distribution, $\alpha = .05$

| Degrees of Freedom for Denominator | Degrees of Freedom for Numerator | | | |
|---|---|---|---|---|
| | 5 | 6 | 7 | 8 |
| 1 | 230 | 234 | 237 | 239 |
| 2 | 19.3 | 19.3 | 19.4 | 19.4 |
| 3 | 9.01 | 8.94 | 8.89 | 8.85 |
| 4 | 6.26 | 6.16 | 6.09 | 6.04 |
| 5 | 5.05 | 4.95 | 4.88 | 4.82 |
| 6 | 4.39 | 4.28 | 4.21 | 4.15 |
| 7 | 3.97 | 3.87 | 3.79 | 3.73 |
| 8 | 3.69 | 3.58 | 3.50 | 3.44 |
| 9 | 3.48 | 3.37 | 3.29 | 3.23 |
| 10 | 3.33 | 3.22 | 3.14 | 3.07 |

**Step 5:** The final step is to take the ratio of the two sample variances, determine the value of the test statistic, and make a decision regarding the null hypothesis. Note that formula (12–1) refers to the sample *variances* but we calculated the sample *standard deviations*. We need to square the standard deviations to determine the variances.

$$F = \frac{s_1^2}{s_2^2} = \frac{(8.9947)^2}{(4.3753)^2} = 4.23$$

The decision is to reject the null hypothesis, because the computed $F$ value (4.23) is larger than the critical value (3.87). We conclude that there is a difference in the variation of the travel times along the two routes.

As noted, the usual practice is to determine the $F$ ratio by putting the larger of the two sample variances in the numerator. This will force the $F$ ratio to be at least 1.00. This allows us to always use the right tail of the $F$ distribution, thus avoiding the need for more extensive $F$ tables.

A logical question arises regarding one-tailed tests. For example, suppose in the previous example we suspected that the variance of the times using the U.S. 25 route is *larger* than the variance of the times along the I-75 route. We would state the null and the alternate hypothesis as

$$H_0: \sigma_1^2 \leq \sigma_2^2$$
$$H_1: \sigma_1^2 > \sigma_2^2$$

The test statistic is computed as $s_1^2/s_2^2$. Notice that we labeled the population with the suspected largest variance as population 1. So $s_1^2$ appears in the numerator. The $F$ ratio will be larger than 1.00, so we can use the upper tail of the $F$ distribution. Under these conditions, it is not necessary to divide the significance level in half. Because Appendix G gives us only the .05 and .01 significance levels, we are restricted to these levels for one-tailed tests and .10 and .02 for two-tailed tests unless we consult a more complete table or use statistical software to compute the $F$ statistic.

The Excel software system has a procedure to perform a test of variances. Below is the output. The computed value of $F$ is the same as determined by using formula (12–1).

---

**Self-Review 12–1**

Steele Electric Products, Inc. assembles electrical components for cell phones. For the last 10 days Mark Nagy has averaged 9 rejects, with a standard deviation of 2 rejects per day. Debbie Richmond averaged 8.5 rejects, with a standard deviation of 1.5 rejects, over the same period. At the .05 significance level, can we conclude that there is more variation in the number of rejects per day attributed to Mark?

# Exercises

1. What is the critical $F$ value for a sample of six observations in the numerator and four in the denominator? Use a two-tailed test and the .10 significance level.

**2.** What is the critical $F$ value for a sample of four observations in the numerator and seven in the denominator? Use a one-tailed test and the .01 significance level.

**3.** The following hypotheses are given.

$H_0$: $\sigma_1^2 = \sigma_2^2$

$H_1$: $\sigma_1^2 \neq \sigma_2^2$

A random sample of eight observations from the first population resulted in a standard deviation of 10. A random sample of six observations from the second population resulted in a standard deviation of 7. At the .02 significance level, is there a difference in the variation of the two populations?

**4.** The following hypotheses are given.

$H_0$: $\sigma_1^2 \leq \sigma_2^2$

$H_1$: $\sigma_1^2 > \sigma_2^2$

A random sample of five observations from the first population resulted in a standard deviation of 12. A random sample of seven observations from the second population showed a standard deviation of 7. At the .01 significance level, is there more variation in the first population?

**5.** Arbitron Media Research, Inc. conducted a study of the radio listening habits of men and women. One facet of the study involved the mean listening time. It was discovered that the mean listening time for men was 35 minutes per day. The standard deviation of the sample of the 10 men studied was 10 minutes per day. The mean listening time for the 12 women studied was also 35 minutes, but the standard deviation of the sample was 12 minutes. At the .10 significance level, can we conclude that there is a difference in the variation in the listening times for men and women?

**6.** A stockbroker at Critical Securities reported that the mean rate of return on a sample of 10 oil stocks was 12.6 percent with a standard deviation of 3.9 percent. The mean rate of return on a sample of 8 utility stocks was 10.9 percent with a standard deviation of 3.5 percent. At the .05 significance level, can we conclude that there is more variation in the oil stocks?

# ANOVA Assumptions

Another use of the $F$ distribution is the analysis of variance (ANOVA) technique in which we compare three or more population means to determine whether they could be equal. To use ANOVA, we assume the following:

1. The populations follow the normal distribution.
2. The populations have equal standard deviations ($\sigma$).
3. The populations are independent.

When these conditions are met, $F$ is used as the distribution of the test statistic.

Why do we need to study ANOVA? Why can't we just use the test of differences in population means discussed in the previous chapter? We could compare the treatment means two at a time. The major reason is the unsatisfactory buildup of Type I error. To explain further, suppose we have four different methods (A, B, C, and D) of training new recruits to be firefighters. We randomly assign each of the 40 recruits in this year's class to one of the four methods. At the end of the training program, we administer to the four groups a common test to measure understanding of firefighting techniques. The question is: Is there a difference in the mean test scores among the four groups? An answer to this question will allow us to compare the four training methods.

Using the $t$ distribution to compare the four population means, we would have to conduct six different $t$ tests. That is, we would need to compare the mean scores for the four methods as follows: A versus B, A versus C, A versus D, B versus C, B versus D, and C versus D. If we set the significance level at .05, the probability of a correct statistical decision is .95, found by $1 - .05$. Because we conduct six separate

*Using the $t$ distribution leads to a buildup of Type I error.*

(independent) tests the probability that we do *not* make an incorrect decision due to sampling in any of the six independent tests is:

$$P(\textit{All correct}) = (.95)(.95)(.95)(.95)(.95)(.95) = .735$$

To find the probability of at least one error due to sampling, we subtract this result from 1. Thus, the probability of at least one incorrect decision due to sampling is $1 - .735 = .265$. To summarize, if we conduct six independent tests using the $t$ distribution, the likelihood of rejecting a true null hypothesis because of sampling error is increased from .05 to an unsatisfactory level of .265. It is obvious that we need a better method than conducting six $t$ tests. ANOVA will allow us to compare the treatment means simultaneously and avoid the buildup of the Type I error.

ANOVA was developed for applications in agriculture, and many of the terms related to that context remain. In particular the term *treatment* is used to identify the different populations being examined. The following illustration will clarify the term *treatment* and demonstrate an application of ANOVA.

**EXAMPLE**

Joyce Kuhlman manages a regional financial center. She wishes to compare the productivity, as measured by the number of customers served, among three employees. Four days are randomly selected and the number of customers served by each employee is recorded. The results are:

| Wolfe | White | Korosa |
|-------|-------|--------|
| 55 | 66 | 47 |
| 54 | 76 | 51 |
| 59 | 67 | 46 |
| 56 | 71 | 48 |

**SOLUTION**

Is there a difference in the mean number of customers served? Chart 12–1 illustrates how the populations would appear if there was a difference in the treatment means. Note that the populations follow the normal distribution and the variation in each population is the same. However, the means are *not* the same.

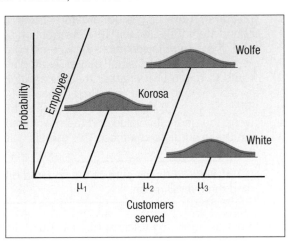

**CHART 12–1** Case Where Treatment Means Are Different

Suppose the populations are the same. That is, there is no difference in the (treatment) means. This is shown in Chart 12–2. This would indicate that the population means are the same. Note again that the populations follow the normal distribution and the variation in each of the populations is the same.

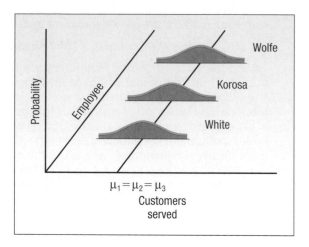

**CHART 12–2** Case Where Treatment Means Are the Same

# The ANOVA Test

How does the ANOVA test work? Recall that we want to determine whether the various sample means came from a single population or populations with different means. We actually compare these sample means through their variances. To explain, recall that on page 392 we listed the assumptions required for ANOVA. One of those assumptions was that the standard deviations of the various normal populations had to be the same. We take advantage of this requirement in the ANOVA test. The underlying strategy is to estimate the population variance (standard deviation squared) two ways and then find the ratio of these two estimates. If this ratio is about 1, then logically the two estimates are the same, and we conclude that the population means are the same. If the ratio is quite different from 1, then we conclude that the population means are not the same. The $F$ distribution serves as a referee by indicating when the ratio of the sample variances is too much greater than 1 to have occurred by chance.

Refer to the financial center example in the previous section. The manager wants to determine whether there is a difference in the mean number of customers served. To begin, find the overall mean of the 12 observations. It is 58, found by $(55 + 54 + \cdots + 48)/12$. Next, for each of the 12 observations find the difference between the particular value and the overall mean. Each of these differences is squared and these squares summed. This term is called the **total variation.**

> **TOTAL VARIATION** The sum of the squared differences between each observation and the overall mean.

In our example the total variation is 1,082, found by $(55 - 58)^2 + (54 - 58)^2 + \cdots + (48 - 58)^2$.

Next, break this total variation into two components: that which is due to the **treatments** and that which is **random.** To find these two components, determine the mean of each of the treatments. The first source of variation is due to the treatments.

> **TREATMENT VARIATION** The sum of the squared differences between each treatment mean and the grand or overall mean.

In the example the variation due to the treatments is the sum of the squared differences between the mean of each employee and the overall mean. This term is 992. To calculate it we first find the mean of each of the three treatments. The mean for Wolfe is 56, found by (55 + 54 + 59 + 56)/4. The other means are 70 and 48, respectively. The sum of the squares due to the treatments is:

$$(56 - 58)^2 + (56 - 58)^2 + \cdots + (48 - 58)^2 = 4(56 - 58)^2 + 4(70 - 58)^2 + 4(48 - 58)^2$$
$$= 992$$

If there is considerable variation among the treatment means, it is logical that this term will be large. If the treatment means are similar, this term will be a small value. The smallest possible value would be zero. This would occur when all the treatment means are the same.

The other source of variation is referred to as the **random** component, or the error component.

---

**RANDOM VARIATION** The sum of the squared differences between each observation and its treatment mean.

---

In the example this term is the sum of the squared differences between each value and the mean for that particular employee. The error variation is 90.

$$(55 - 56)^2 + (54 - 56)^2 + \cdots + (48 - 48)^2 = 90$$

We determine the test statistic, which is the ratio of the two estimates of the population variance, from the following equation.

$$F = \frac{\text{Estimate of the population variance}}{\text{based on the differences among the sample means}} \Big/ \frac{\text{Estimate of the population variance}}{\text{based on the variation within the sample}}$$

Our first estimate of the population variance is based on the treatments, that is, the difference *between* the means. It is 992/2. Why did we divide by 2? Recall from Chapter 3, to find a sample variance [see formula (3–11)], we divide by the number of observations minus one. In this case there are three treatments, so we divide by 2. Our first estimate of the population variance is 992/2.

The variance estimate *within* the treatments is the random variation divided by the total number of observations less the number of treatments. That is 90/(12 − 3). Hence, our second estimate of the population variance is 90/9. This is actually a generalization of formula (11–5), where we pooled the sample variances from two populations.

The last step is to take the ratio of these two estimates.

$$F = \frac{992/2}{90/9} = 49.6$$

Because this ratio is quite different from 1, we can conclude that the treatment means are not the same. There is a difference in the mean number of customers served by the three employees.

Here's another example, which deals with samples of different sizes.

**EXAMPLE**

Professor James Brunner had students in his marketing class rate his performance as Excellent, Good, Fair, or Poor. A graduate student collected the ratings and assured the students that Professor Brunner would not receive them until after course grades had been sent to the records office. The rating (i.e., the treatment) a student gave the professor was matched with his or her course grade, which could range from 0 to 100. The sample information is reported below. Is there a difference in the mean score of the students in each of the four rating categories? Use the .01 significance level.

| Course Grades | | | |
|---|---|---|---|
| **Excellent** | **Good** | **Fair** | **Poor** |
| 94 | 75 | 70 | 68 |
| 90 | 68 | 73 | 70 |
| 85 | 77 | 76 | 72 |
| 80 | 83 | 78 | 65 |
|  | 88 | 80 | 74 |
|  |  | 68 | 65 |
|  |  | 65 |  |

**SOLUTION**

We will follow the usual five-step hypothesis-testing procedure.

> **Step 1: State the null hypothesis and the alternate hypothesis.** The null hypothesis is that the mean scores are the same for the four ratings.
>
> $$H_0: \mu_1 = \mu_2 = \mu_3 = \mu_4$$
>
> The alternate hypothesis is that the mean scores are not all the same for the four ratings.
>
> $H_1$: The mean scores are not all equal.
>
> We can also think of the alternate hypothesis as "at least two mean scores are not equal."
>
> If the null hypothesis is not rejected, we conclude that there is no difference in the mean course grades based on the instructor ratings. If $H_0$ is rejected, we conclude that there is a difference in at least one pair of mean ratings, but at this point we do not know which pair or how many pairs differ.
>
> **Step 2: Select the level of significance.** We selected the .01 significance level.
>
> **Step 3: Determine the test statistic.** The test statistic follows the $F$ distribution.
>
> **Step 4: Formulate the decision rule.** To determine the decision rule, we need the critical value. The critical value for the $F$ statistic is found in Appendix G. The critical values for the .05 significance level are found on the first page and the .01 significance level on the second page. To use this table we need to know the degrees of freedom in the numerator and the denominator. The degrees of freedom in the numerator equals the number of treatments, designated as $k$, minus 1. The degrees of freedom in the denominator is the total number of observations, $n$, minus the number of treatments. For this problem there are four treatments and a total of 22 observations.
>
> > Degrees of freedom in the numerator $= k - 1 = 4 - 1 = 3$
> > Degrees of freedom in the denominator $= n - k = 22 - 4 = 18$
>
> Refer to Appendix G and the .01 significance level. Move horizontally across the top of the page to 3 degrees of freedom in the numerator.

Then move down that column to the row with 18 degrees of freedom. The value at this intersection is 5.09. So the decision rule is to reject $H_0$ if the computed value of $F$ exceeds 5.09.

**Step 5: Select the sample, perform the calculations, and make a decision.** It is convenient to summarize the calculations of the $F$ statistic in an **ANOVA table.** The format for an ANOVA table is as follows. Statistical software packages also use this format.

| ANOVA Table | | | | |
|---|---|---|---|---|
| **Source of Variation** | **Sum of Squares** | **Degrees of Freedom** | **Mean Square** | **F** |
| Treatments | SST | $k - 1$ | SST/$(k - 1)$ = MST | MST/MSE |
| Error | SSE | $n - k$ | SSE/$(n - k)$ = MSE | |
| Total | SS total | $n - 1$ | | |

There are three values, or sum of squares, used to compute the test statistic $F$. You can determine these values by obtaining SS total and SSE, then finding SST by subtraction. The SS total term is the total variation, SST is the variation due to the treatments, and SSE is the variation within the treatments.

We usually start the process by finding SS total. This is the sum of the squared differences between each observation and the overall mean. The formula for finding SS total is:

$$SS\ total = \Sigma(X - \bar{X}_G)^2 \qquad \textbf{[12–2]}$$

where:

$X$ is each sample observation.
$\bar{X}_G$ is the overall or grand mean.

Next determine SSE or the sum of the squared errors. This is the sum of the squared differences between each observation and its respective treatment mean. The formula for finding SSE is:

$$SSE = \Sigma(X - \bar{X}_c)^2 \qquad \textbf{[12–3]}$$

where:

$\bar{X}_c$ is the sample mean for treatment $c$.

The detailed calculations of SS total and SSE for this example follow. To determine the values of SS total and SSE we start by calculating the overall or grand mean. There are 22 observations and the total is 1,664, so the grand mean is 75.64.

| | **Excellent** | **Good** | **Fair** | **Poor** | **Total** |
|---|---|---|---|---|---|
| | 94 | 75 | 70 | 68 | |
| | 90 | 68 | 73 | 70 | |
| | 85 | 77 | 76 | 72 | |
| | 80 | 83 | 78 | 65 | |
| | | 88 | 80 | 74 | |
| | | | 68 | 65 | |
| | | | 65 | | |
| Column total | 349 | 391 | 510 | 414 | 1664 |
| $n$ | 4 | 5 | 7 | 6 | 22 |
| Mean | 87.25 | 78.20 | 72.86 | 69.00 | 75.64 |

Next we find the deviation of each observation from the grand mean, square those deviations, and sum this result for all 22 observations. For example, the first student had a score of 94 and the overall or grand mean is 75.64. So $(X - \bar{X}_G) = 94 - 75.64 = 18.36$. The calculations for all students follow.

| Excellent | Good | Fair | Poor |
|-----------|-------|-------|--------|
| 18.36 | −0.64 | −5.64 | −7.64 |
| 14.36 | −7.64 | −2.64 | −5.64 |
| 9.36 | 1.36 | 0.36 | −3.64 |
| 4.36 | 7.36 | 2.36 | −10.64 |
| | 12.36 | 4.36 | −1.64 |
| | | −7.64 | −10.64 |
| | | −10.64 | |

Then square each of these differences and sum all the values. Thus for the first student:

$$(X - \bar{X}_G)^2 = (94 - 75.64) = (18.36)^2 = 337.09.$$

Finally sum all the squared differences as formula (12–2) directs. Our SS total value is 1,485.09.

| | Excellent | Good | Fair | Poor | Total |
|---|-----------|-------|-------|--------|-------|
| | 337.09 | 0.41 | 31.81 | 58.37 | |
| | 206.21 | 58.37 | 6.97 | 31.81 | |
| | 87.61 | 1.85 | 0.13 | 13.25 | |
| | 19.0 | 54.17 | 5.57 | 113.21 | |
| | | 152.77 | 19.01 | 2.69 | |
| | | | 58.37 | 113.21 | |
| | | | 113.21 | | |
| Total | 649.91 | 267.57 | 235.07 | 332.54 | 1,485.09 |

To compute the term SSE find the deviation between each observation and its treatment mean. In the example the mean of the first treatment (that is the students who rated Professor Brunner "Excellent") is 87.25. The first student earned a score of 94, so $(X - \bar{X}_c) = (94 - 87.25) = 6.75$. For the first student in the "Good" group $(X - \bar{X}_c) = (75 - 78.20) = -3.20$. The details of each of these calculations follow.

| Excellent | Good | Fair | Poor |
|-----------|-------|-------|------|
| 6.75 | −3.2 | −2.86 | −1 |
| 2.75 | −10.2 | 0.14 | 1 |
| −2.25 | −1.2 | 3.14 | 3 |
| −7.25 | 4.8 | 5.14 | −4 |
| | 9.8 | 7.14 | 5 |
| | | −4.86 | −4 |
| | | −7.86 | |

Each of these values is squared and then summed for all 22 observations. The values are shown in the following table.

| | Excellent | Good | Fair | Poor | Total |
|---|---|---|---|---|---|
| | 45.5625 | 10.24 | 8.18 | 1 | |
| | 7.5625 | 104.04 | 0.02 | 1 | |
| | 5.0625 | 1.44 | 9.86 | 9 | |
| | 52.5625 | 23.04 | 26.42 | 16 | |
| | | 96.04 | 50.98 | 25 | |
| | | | 23.62 | 16 | |
| | | | 61.78 | | |
| Total | 110.7500 | 234.80 | 180.86 | 68 | 594.41 |

So the SSE value is 594.41. That is $\Sigma(X - \bar{X}_c)^2 = 594.41$.

Finally we determine SST, the sum of the squares due to the treatments, by subtraction.

$$SST = SS\ total - SSE \qquad\qquad [12\text{–}4]$$

For this example:

$$SST = SS\ total - SSE = 1{,}485.09 - 594.41 = 890.68.$$

To find the computed value of $F$, work your way across the ANOVA table. The degrees of freedom for the numerator and the denominator are the same as in step 4 above when we were finding the critical value of $F$. The term **mean square** is another expression for an estimate of the variance. The mean square for treatments is SST divided by its degrees of freedom. The result is the **mean square for treatments** and is written MST. Compute the **mean square error** in a similar fashion. To be precise, divide SSE by its degrees of freedom. To complete the process and find $F$, divide MST by MSE.

Insert the particular values of $F$ into an ANOVA table and compute the value of $F$ as follows.

| Source of Variation | Sum of Squares | Degrees of Freedom | Mean Square | F |
|---|---|---|---|---|
| Treatments | 890.68 | 3 | 296.89 | 8.99 |
| Error | 594.41 | 18 | 33.02 | |
| Total | 1,485.09 | 21 | | |

The computed value of $F$ is 8.99, which is greater than the critical value of 5.09, so the null hypothesis is rejected. We conclude the population means are not all equal. The mean scores are not the same in each of the four ratings groups. It is likely that the grades students earned in the course are related to the opinion they have of the overall competency and classroom performance of the instructor. At this point we can only conclude there is a difference in the treatment means. We cannot determine which treatment groups differ or how many treatment groups differ.

As noted in the previous example, the calculations are tedious if the number of observations in each treatment is large. There are many software packages that will output the results. Following is the Excel output in the form of an ANOVA table for the previous example involving student ratings in a marketing class. There are some slight differences between the software output and the previous calculations. These differences are due to rounding.

**Statistics in Action**

Have you ever waited in line for a telephone and it seemed like the person using the phone talked on and on? There is evidence that people actually talk longer on public telephones when someone is waiting. In a recent survey, researchers measured the length of time that 56 shoppers in a mall spent on the phone (1) when they were alone, (2) when a person was using the adjacent phone, and (3) when a person was using an adjacent phone and someone was waiting to use the phone. The study, using the one-way ANOVA technique, showed that the mean time using the telephone was significantly less when the person was alone.

Notice Excel uses the term "Between Groups" for "Treatments" and "Within Groups" for "Error." However, they have the same meanings. The *p*-value is .0007. This is the probability of finding a value of the test statistic this large or larger when the null hypothesis is true. To put it another way, it is the likelihood of calculating an *F* value larger than 8.99 with 3 degrees of freedom in the numerator and 18 degrees of freedom in the denominator. So when we reject the null hypothesis in this instance there is a very small likelihood of committing a Type I error!

Following is the MINITAB output from the student ratings example, which is similar to the Excel output. The output is also in the form of an ANOVA table. In addition, MINITAB provides information about the differences between means. This is discussed in the next section.

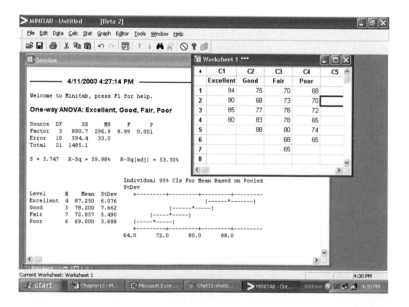

The MINITAB system uses the term *factor* instead of *treatment,* with the same intended meaning.

**Self-Review 12–2**

Citrus Clean is a new all-purpose cleaner being test marketed by placing displays in three different locations within various supermarkets. The number of 12-ounce bottles sold from each location within the supermarket is reported below.

| | | | | |
|---|---|---|---|---|
| Near bread | 18 | 14 | 19 | 17 |
| Near beer | 12 | 18 | 10 | 16 |
| Other cleaners | 26 | 28 | 30 | 32 |

At the .05 significance level, is there a difference in the mean number of bottles sold at the three locations?
(a) State the null hypothesis and the alternate hypothesis.
(b) What is the decision rule?
(c) Compute the values of SS total, SST, and SSE.
(d) Develop an ANOVA table.
(e) What is your decision regarding the null hypothesis?

# Exercises

7. The following is sample information. Test the hypothesis that the treatment means are equal. Use the .05 significance level.

| Treatment 1 | Treatment 2 | Treatment 3 |
|---|---|---|
| 8 | 3 | 3 |
| 6 | 2 | 4 |
| 10 | 4 | 5 |
| 9 | 3 | 4 |

a. State the null hypothesis and the alternate hypotheses.
b. What is the decision rule?
c. Compute SST, SSE, and SS total.
d. Complete an ANOVA table.
e. State your decision regarding the null hypothesis.

8. The following is sample information. Test the hypothesis at the .05 significance level that the treatment means are equal.

| Treatment 1 | Treatment 2 | Treatment 3 |
|---|---|---|
| 9 | 13 | 10 |
| 7 | 20 | 9 |
| 11 | 14 | 15 |
| 9 | 13 | 14 |
| 12 | | 15 |
| 10 | | |

a. State the null hypothesis and the alternate hypotheses.
b. What is the decision rule?
c. Compute SST, SSE, and SS total.
d. Complete an ANOVA table.
e. State your decision regarding the null hypothesis.

9. A real estate developer is considering investing in a shopping mall on the outskirts of Atlanta, Georgia. Three parcels of land are being evaluated. Of particular importance is the income in the area surrounding the proposed mall. A random sample of four families is selected near each proposed mall. Following are the sample results. At the .05 significance

level, can the developer conclude there is a difference in the mean income? Use the usual five-step hypothesis testing procedure.

| Southwyck Area ($000) | Franklin Park ($000) | Old Orchard ($000) |
|---|---|---|
| 64 | 74 | 75 |
| 68 | 71 | 80 |
| 70 | 69 | 76 |
| 60 | 70 | 78 |

10. The manager of a computer software company wishes to study the number of hours senior executives spend at their desktop computers by type of industry. The manager selected a sample of five executives from each of three industries. At the .05 significance level, can she conclude there is a difference in the mean number of hours spent per week by industry?

| Banking | Retail | Insurance |
|---|---|---|
| 12 | 8 | 10 |
| 10 | 8 | 8 |
| 10 | 6 | 6 |
| 12 | 8 | 8 |
| 10 | 10 | 10 |

# Inferences about Pairs of Treatment Means

Suppose we carry out the ANOVA procedure and make the decision to reject the null hypothesis. This allows us to conclude that all the treatment means are not the same. Sometimes we may be satisfied with this conclusion, but in other instances we may want to know which treatment means differ. This section provides the details for such a test.

Recall that in the example regarding student opinions and grades there was a difference in the treatment means. That is, the null hypothesis was rejected and the alternate hypothesis accepted. If the student opinions do differ, the question is: Between which groups do the treatment means differ?

Several procedures are available to answer this question. The simplest is through the use of confidence intervals, that is, formula (9–2). From the computer output of the previous example (see page 400), note that the sample mean score for those students rating the instruction Excellent is 87.250, and for those rating the instruction Poor it is 69.000. Thus, those students who rated the instruction Excellent seemingly earned higher grades than those who rated the instruction Poor. Is there enough disparity to justify the conclusion that there is a significant difference in the mean scores of the two groups?

The $t$ distribution, described in Chapters 10 and 11, is used as the basis for this test. Recall that one of the assumptions of ANOVA is that the population variances are the same for all treatments. This common population value is the **mean square error,** or MSE, and is determined by SSE/$(n - k)$. A confidence interval for the difference between two populations is found by:

| CONFIDENCE INTERVAL FOR THE DIFFERENCE IN TREATMENT MEANS | $(\bar{X}_1 - \bar{X}_2) \pm t\sqrt{MSE\left(\dfrac{1}{n_1} + \dfrac{1}{n_2}\right)}$ | [12–5] |
|---|---|---|

where:

$\bar{X}_1$ is the mean of the first sample.

$\bar{X}_2$ is the mean of the second sample.

$t$ is obtained from Appendix F. The degrees of freedom is equal to $n - k$.

MSE is the mean square error term obtained from the ANOVA table [SSE/$(n - k)$].

$n_1$ is the number of observations in the first sample.

$n_2$ is the number of observations in the second sample.

How do we decide whether there is a difference in the treatment means? If the confidence interval includes zero, there is *not* a difference between the treatment means. For example, if the left endpoint of the confidence interval has a negative sign and the right endpoint has a positive sign, the interval includes zero and the two means do not differ. So if we develop a confidence interval from formula (12–5) and find the difference in the sample means was 5.00, that is, if $\bar{X}_1 - \bar{X}_2 = 5$ and $t\sqrt{\text{MSE}\left(\dfrac{1}{n_1} + \dfrac{1}{n_2}\right)} = 12$, the confidence interval would range from $-7.00$ up to 17.00. To put it in symbols:

$$(\bar{X}_1 - \bar{X}_2) \pm t\sqrt{\text{MSE}\left(\frac{1}{n_1} + \frac{1}{n_2}\right)} = 5.00 \pm 12.00 = -7.00 \text{ up to } 17.00$$

Note that zero is included in this interval. Therefore, we conclude that there is no significant difference in the selected treatment means.

On the other hand, if the endpoints of the confidence interval have the same sign, this indicates that the treatment means differ. For example, if $\bar{X}_1 - \bar{X}_2 = -0.35$ and $t\sqrt{\text{MSE}\left(\dfrac{1}{n_1} + \dfrac{1}{n_2}\right)} = 0.25$, the confidence interval would range from $-0.60$ up to $-0.10$. Because $-0.60$ and $-0.10$ have the same sign, both negative, zero is not in the interval and we conclude that these treatment means differ.

Using the previous student opinion example let us compute the confidence interval for the difference between the mean scores of all students who provide "Excellent" and "Poor" ratings. Assume the populations are labeled 1 and 4. With a 95 percent level of confidence, the endpoints of the confidence interval are 10.46 and 26.04.

$$(\bar{X}_1 - \bar{X}_4) \pm t\sqrt{\text{MSE}\left(\frac{1}{n_1} + \frac{1}{n_4}\right)} = (87.25 - 69.00) \pm 2.101\sqrt{33.0\left(\frac{1}{4} + \frac{1}{6}\right)}$$

$$= 18.25 \pm 7.79$$

where:

$\bar{X}_1$ is 87.25.

$\bar{X}_4$ is 69.00.

$t$ is 2.101: from Appendix F with $(n - k) = 22 - 4 = 18$ degrees of freedom.

MSE is 33.0: from the ANOVA table with SSE/$(n - k)$ = 594.4/18.

$n_1$ is 4.

$n_4$ is 6.

The 95 percent confidence interval ranges from 10.46 up to 26.04. Both endpoints are positive; hence, we can conclude these treatment means differ significantly. That is, students who rated the instructor Excellent have significantly higher grades than those who rated the instructor as Poor.

Approximate results can also be obtained directly from the MINITAB output. On the next page is the lower portion of the output from page 400. On the left side is the number of observations, the mean, and the standard deviation for each treatment. Seven students, for example, rated the instructor as Fair. The mean course grade they earned is 72.857. The standard deviation of their scores is 5.490.

```
                                    Individual 95% CIs For Mean
                                    Based on Pooled StDev
Level     N     Mean    StDev    ----------+---------+---------+------
Excellen  4    87.250   6.076                           (------*------)
Good      5    78.200   7.662              (------*-----)
Fair      7    72.857   5.490       (-----*-----)
Poor      6    69.000   3.688    (-----*-----)
                                    ----------+---------+---------+------
Pooled StDev = 5.747                    72.0      80.0      88.0
```

On the right side of the printout is a confidence interval for each treatment mean. The asterisk (*) indicates the location of the treatment mean and the open parenthesis and close parenthesis, the endpoints of the confidence interval. In those instances where the intervals overlap, the treatment means may not differ. If there is no common area in the confidence intervals, that pair of means differ.

The endpoints of a 95 percent confidence interval for the scores of students rating the instructor Fair are about 69 and 77. For students rating the instructor Poor, the endpoints of the confidence interval are about 64 and 74. There is common area in this confidence interval, so we conclude that this pair of means does not differ. In other words, there is no significant difference between the scores of students rating the instructor Fair and those rating him Poor.

There are two pairs of means that differ. The scores of students who rated the instructor Excellent differ from the scores of the students who rated the instructor Fair and those who rated the instructor Poor. There is no common area between the two pairs of confidence intervals.

We should emphasize that this investigation is a step-by-step process. The initial step is to conduct the ANOVA test. Only if the null hypothesis that the treatment means are equal is rejected should any analysis of the individual treatment means be attempted.

**Self-Review 12–3**

The following data are the semester tuition charges ($000) for a sample of private colleges in various regions of the United States. At the .05 significance level, can we conclude there is a difference in the mean tuition rates for the various regions?

| Northeast ($000) | Southeast ($000) | West ($000) |
|---|---|---|
| 10 | 8 | 7 |
| 11 | 9 | 8 |
| 12 | 10 | 6 |
| 10 | 8 | 7 |
| 12 |  | 6 |

(a) State the null and the alternate hypotheses.
(b) What is the decision rule?
(c) Develop an ANOVA table. What is the value of the test statistic?
(d) What is your decision regarding the null hypothesis?
(e) Could there be a significant difference between the mean tuition in the Northeast and that of the West? If so, develop a 95 percent confidence interval for that difference.

# Exercises

**11.** Given the following sample information, test the hypothesis that the treatment means are equal at the .05 significance level.

| Treatment 1 | Treatment 2 | Treatment 3 |
|:-----------:|:-----------:|:-----------:|
| 8  | 3 | 3 |
| 11 | 2 | 4 |
| 10 | 1 | 5 |
|    | 3 | 4 |
|    | 2 |   |

    **a.** State the null hypothesis and the alternate hypothesis.
    **b.** What is the decision rule?
    **c.** Compute SST, SSE, and SS total.
    **d.** Complete an ANOVA table.
    **e.** State your decision regarding the null hypothesis.
    **f.** If $H_0$ is rejected, can we conclude that treatment 1 and treatment 2 differ? Use the 95 percent level of confidence.

**12.** Given the following sample information, test the hypothesis that the treatment means are equal at the .05 significance level.

| Treatment 1 | Treatment 2 | Treatment 3 |
|:-----------:|:-----------:|:-----------:|
| 3 | 9 | 6 |
| 2 | 6 | 3 |
| 5 | 5 | 5 |
| 1 | 6 | 5 |
| 3 | 8 | 5 |
| 1 | 5 | 4 |
|   | 4 | 1 |
|   | 7 | 5 |
|   | 6 |   |
|   | 4 |   |

    **a.** State the null hypothesis and the alternate hypothesis.
    **b.** What is the decision rule?
    **c.** Compute SST, SSE, and SS total.
    **d.** Complete an ANOVA table.
    **e.** State your decision regarding the null hypothesis.
    **f.** If $H_0$ is rejected, can we conclude that treatment 2 and treatment 3 differ? Use the 95 percent level of confidence.

**13.** A senior accounting major at Midsouth State University has job offers from four CPA firms. To explore the offers further, she asked a sample of recent trainees how many months each worked for the firm before receiving a raise in salary. The sample information is submitted to MINITAB with the following results:

```
Analysis of Variance
Source    DF        SS        MS        F         P
Factor     3     32.33     10.78     2.36     0.133
Error     10     45.67      4.57
Total     13     78.00
```

At the .05 level of significance, is there a difference in the mean number of months before a raise was granted among the four CPA firms?

**14.** A stock analyst wants to determine whether there is a difference in the mean rate of return for three types of stock: utility, retail, and banking stocks. The following output is obtained:

```
Analysis of Variance
Source      DF        SS        MS         F         P
Factor       2      86.49     43.25     13.09     0.001
Error       13      42.95      3.30
Total       15     129.44
                                    Individual 95% CIs For Mean
                                    Based on Pooled StDev
Level        N      Mean      StDev  ---------+---------+---------+------
Utility      5     17.400     1.916                      (------*------)
Retail       5     11.620     0.356  (------*------)
Banking      6     15.400     2.356              (------*------)
                                           ---------+---------+---------+------
Pooled StDev = 1.818                        12.0      15.0      18.0
```

a. Using the .05 level of significance, is there a difference in the mean rate of return among the three types of stock?

b. Suppose the null hypothesis is rejected. Can the analyst conclude there is a difference between the mean rates of return for the utility and the retail stocks? Explain.

# Two-Way Analysis of Variance

In the student ratings example, we divided the total variation into two categories: the variation between the treatments and the variation within the treatments. We also called the variation within the treatments the error or the random variation. To put it another way, we considered only two sources of variation, that due to the treatments and the random differences. In the student ratings example there may be other causes of variation in the student grades in addition to the instructor rating. These factors might include the number of hours per week the student studied, the mathematics ability of the student, or the gender of the student.

The benefit of considering other factors is that we can reduce the error variance. That is, if we can reduce the denominator of the $F$ statistic (reducing the error variance or, more directly, the SSE term) the value of $F$ will be larger, causing us to reject the hypothesis of equal treatment means. In other words, if we can explain more of the variation, then there is less "error." An example will clarify the reduction in the error variance.

**EXAMPLE**

WARTA, the Warren Area Regional Transit Authority, is expanding bus service from the suburb of Starbrick into the central business district of Warren. There are four routes being considered from Starbrick to downtown Warren: (1) via U.S. 6, (2) via the west end, (3) via the Hickory Street Bridge, and (4) via Route 59. WARTA conducted several tests to determine whether there was a difference in the mean travel times along the four routes. Because there will be many different drivers, the test was set up so each driver drove along each of the four routes. Below is the travel time, in minutes, for each driver-route combination.

| | Travel Time from Starbrick to Warren (minutes) | | | |
|---|---|---|---|---|
| Driver | U.S. 6 | West End | Hickory St. | Rte. 59 |
| Deans | 18 | 20 | 20 | 22 |
| Snaverly | 21 | 22 | 24 | 24 |
| Ormson | 20 | 23 | 25 | 23 |
| Zollaco | 25 | 21 | 28 | 25 |
| Filbeck | 26 | 24 | 28 | 25 |

At the .05 significance level, is there a difference in the mean travel time along the four routes? If we remove the effect of the drivers, is there a difference in the mean travel time?

SOLUTION

To begin, we conduct a test of hypothesis using a one-way ANOVA. That is, we consider only the four routes. Under this condition the variation in travel times is either due to the treatments or it is random. The null hypothesis and the alternate hypothesis for comparing the mean travel time along the four routes are:

$H_0$: $\mu_1 = \mu_2 = \mu_3 = \mu_4$
$H_1$: Not all treatment means are the same.

There are four routes, so for the numerator the degrees of freedom is $k - 1 = 4 - 1 = 3$. There are 20 observations, so the degrees of freedom in the denominator is $n - k = 20 - 4 = 16$. From Appendix G, with the .05 significance level, the critical value of $F$ is 3.24. The decision rule is to reject the null hypothesis if the computed value of $F$ is greater than 3.24.

We use Excel to perform the calculations. The computed value of $F$ is 1.618, so our decision is to not reject the null hypothesis. We conclude there is no difference in the mean travel time along the four routes. There is no reason to select one of the routes as faster than the other.

EXCEL

Microsoft Excel - Book2

Travel Time From Starbrick to Warren (minutes)

Anova: Single Factor

| Driver | U.S. 6 | West End | Hickory St | Rte. 59 |
|---|---|---|---|---|
| Deans | 18 | 20 | 20 | 22 |
| Snaverly | 21 | 22 | 24 | 24 |
| Ormson | 20 | 23 | 25 | 23 |
| Zollaco | 25 | 21 | 28 | 25 |
| Filbeck | 26 | 24 | 28 | 25 |

SUMMARY

| Groups | Count | Sum | Average | Variance |
|---|---|---|---|---|
| U.S. 6 | 5 | 110 | 22 | 11.5 |
| West End | 5 | 110 | 22 | 2.5 |
| Hickory St | 5 | 125 | 25 | 11 |
| Rte. 59 | 5 | 119 | 23.8 | 1.7 |

ANOVA

| Source of Variation | SS | df | MS | F |
|---|---|---|---|---|
| Between Groups | 32.4 | 3 | 10.8 | 1.6180 |
| Within Groups | 106.8 | 16 | 6.675 | |
| | | | | |
| Total | 139.2 | 19 | | |

From the above Excel output the mean travel times along the routes were: 22 minutes along U.S. 6, 22 minutes along the West End route, 25 minutes using Hickory Street, and 23.8 minutes using Route 59. From the ANOVA table we note: SST is 32.4, SSE is 106.8, and SS total is 139.2. We conclude these differences could reasonably be attributed to chance.

In the above example we considered the variation due to the treatments (routes) and took all the remaining variation to be random. However, we did not set up the trials so that each of the five drivers drove along each of the four routes. If we could consider the effect of the several drivers, this would allow us to reduce the SSE term, which would lead to a larger value of $F$. The second treatment variable, the drivers in this case, is referred to as a **blocking variable.**

**BLOCKING VARIABLE**  A second treatment variable that when included in the ANOVA analysis will have the effect of reducing the SSE term.

In this case we let the drivers be the blocking variable, and removing the effect of the drivers from the SSE term will change the $F$ ratio for the treatment variable. First, we need to determine the sum of squares due to the blocks.

In a two-way ANOVA, the sum of squares due to blocks is found by the following formula.

$$SSB = k\Sigma(\overline{X}_b - \overline{X}_G)^2 \qquad \textbf{[12–6]}$$

where

    $k$ is the number of treatments.
    $b$ is the number of blocks.
    $\overline{X}_b$ is the sample mean of block $b$.
    $\overline{X}_G$ is the overall or grand mean.

From the calculations below, the means for the respective drivers are 20 minutes, 22.75 minutes, 22.75 minutes, 24.75 minutes, and 25.75 minutes. The overall mean is 23.2 minutes, found by adding the travel time for all 20 drives (464 minutes) and dividing by 20.

| Driver | U.S. 6 | West End | Hickory St | Rte. 59 | Driver Sums | Driver Means |
|--------|--------|----------|------------|---------|-------------|--------------|
| Deans | 18 | 20 | 20 | 22 | 80 | 20 |
| Snaverly | 21 | 22 | 24 | 24 | 91 | 22.75 |
| Ormson | 20 | 23 | 25 | 23 | 91 | 22.75 |
| Zollaco | 25 | 21 | 28 | 25 | 99 | 24.75 |
| Filbeck | 26 | 24 | 28 | 25 | 103 | 25.75 |

Substituting this information into formula (12–6) we determine SSB, the sum of squares due to the drivers (the blocking variable) is 78.2.

$SSB = k\Sigma(\overline{X}_b - \overline{X}_G)^2$

    $= 4(20.0 - 23.2)^2 + 4(22.75 - 23.2)^2 + 4(22.75 - 23.2)^2 + 4(24.75 - 23.2)^2 +$
        $4(25.75 - 23.2)^2$

    $= 78.2$

The same format is used in the two-way ANOVA table as in the one-way case, except there is an additional row for the blocking variable. SS total and SST are calculated as before, and SSB is found from formula (12–6). The SSE term is found by subtraction.

| SUM OF SQUARES ERROR, TWO-WAY | SSE = SS total − SST − SSB | **[12–7]** |
|---|---|---|

The values for the various components of the ANOVA table are computed as follows.

| Source of Variation | Sum of Squares | Degrees of Freedom | Mean Square | F |
|---------------------|----------------|---------------------|-------------|---|
| Treatments | SST | $k - 1$ | $SST/(k - 1) = MST$ | MST/MSE |
| Blocks | SSB | $b - 1$ | $SSB/(b - 1) = MSB$ | MSB/MSE |
| Error | SSE | $(k - 1)(b - 1)$ | $SSE/(k - 1)(b - 1) = MSE$ | |
| Total | SS total | $n - 1$ | | |

SSE is found by formula (12–7).

    SSE = SS total − SST − SSB = 139.2 − 32.4 − 78.2 = 28.6

| Source of Variation | (1) Sum of Squares | (2) Degrees of Freedom | (3) Mean Square (1)/(2) |
|---|---|---|---|
| Treatments | 32.4 | 3 | 10.80 |
| Blocks | 78.2 | 4 | 19.550 |
| Error | 28.6 | 12 | 2.383 |
| Total | 139.2 | | |

There is disagreement at this point. If the purpose of the blocking variable (the drivers in this example) was only to reduce the error variation, we should not conduct a test of hypothesis for the difference in block means. That is, if our goal was to reduce the MSE term, then we should not test a hypothesis regarding the blocking variable. On the other hand, we may wish to give the blocks the same status as the treatments and conduct a test of hypothesis. In the latter case, when the blocks are important enough to be considered as a second factor, we refer to this as a **two-factor experiment.** In many cases the decision is not clear. In our example we are concerned about the difference in the travel time for the different drivers, so we will conduct the test of hypothesis. The two sets of hypotheses are:

1.  $H_0$: The treatment means are the same ($\mu_1 = \mu_2 = \mu_3 = \mu_4$).
    $H_1$: The treatment means are not the same.
2.  $H_0$: The block means are the same ($\mu_1 = \mu_2 = \mu_3 = \mu_4 = \mu_5$).
    $H_1$: The block means are not the same.

First, we will test the hypothesis concerning the treatment means. There are $k - 1 = 4 - 1 = 3$ degrees of freedom in the numerator and $(b - 1)(k - 1) = (5 - 1)(4 - 1) = 12$ degrees of freedom in the denominator. Using the .05 significance level, the critical value of $F$ is 3.49. The null hypothesis that the mean times for the four routes are the same is rejected if the $F$ ratio exceeds 3.49.

$$F = \frac{\text{MST}}{\text{MSE}} = \frac{10.80}{2.383} = 4.53$$

The null hypothesis is rejected and the alternate accepted. We conclude that the mean travel time is not the same for all routes. WARTA will want to conduct some tests to determine which treatment means differ.

Next, we test to find whether the travel time is the same for the various drivers. The degrees of freedom in the numerator for blocks is $b - 1 = 5 - 1 = 4$. The degrees of freedom for the denominator are the same as before: $(b - 1)(k - 1) = (5 - 1)(4 - 1) = 12$. The null hypothesis that the block means are the same is rejected if the $F$ ratio exceeds 3.26.

$$F = \frac{\text{MSB}}{\text{MSE}} = \frac{19.550}{2.383} = 8.20$$

The null hypothesis is rejected, and the alternate is accepted. The mean time is not the same for the various drivers. Thus, WARTA management can conclude, based on the sample results, that there is a difference in the routes and in the drivers.

The Excel spreadsheet has a two-factor ANOVA procedure. The output for the WARTA example just completed is repeated on the next page. The results are the same as reported earlier. In addition the Excel output reports the $p$-values. The $p$-value for the null hypothesis regarding the drivers is .002 and .024 for the routes. These $p$-values confirm that the null hypotheses for treatments and blocks should both be rejected using the .05 significance level because the $p$-value is less than the significance level.

**Self-Review 12–4**　Rudduck Shampoo sells three shampoos, one each for dry, normal, and oily hair. Sales, in millions of dollars, for the past five months are given in the following table. Using the .05 significance level, test whether the mean sales differ for the three types of shampoo or by month.

| Sales ($ million) | | | |
|---|---|---|---|
| Month | Dry | Normal | Oily |
| June | 7 | 9 | 12 |
| July | 11 | 12 | 14 |
| August | 13 | 11 | 8 |
| September | 8 | 9 | 7 |
| October | 9 | 10 | 13 |

# Exercises

For exercises 15 and 16, conduct a test of hypothesis to determine whether the block or the treatment means differ. Using the .05 significance level: (a) state the null and alternate hypotheses for treatments; (b) state the decision rule for treatments; and (c) state the null and alternate hypotheses for blocks. Also, state the decision rule for blocks, then: (d) compute SST, SSB, SS total, and SSE; (e) complete an ANOVA table; and (f) give your decision regarding the two sets of hypotheses.

**15.** The following data are given for a two-factor ANOVA.

| | Treatment | |
|---|---|---|
| Block | 1 | 2 |
| A | 46 | 31 |
| B | 37 | 26 |
| C | 44 | 35 |

16. The following data are given for a two-factor ANOVA.

| Block | Treatment 1 | 2 | 3 |
|-------|-----|-----|-----|
| A | 12 | 14 | 8 |
| B | 9 | 11 | 9 |
| C | 7 | 8 | 8 |

17. The Chapin Manufacturing Company operates 24 hours a day, five days a week. The workers rotate shifts each week. Management is interested in whether there is a difference in the number of units produced when the employees work on various shifts. A sample of five workers is selected and their output recorded on each shift. At the .05 significance level, can we conclude there is a difference in the mean production rate by shift or by employee?

| Employee | Units Produced Day | Afternoon | Night |
|----------|-----|-----------|-------|
| Skaff | 31 | 25 | 35 |
| Lum | 33 | 26 | 33 |
| Clark | 28 | 24 | 30 |
| Treece | 30 | 29 | 28 |
| Morgan | 28 | 26 | 27 |

18. There are three hospitals in the Tulsa, Oklahoma, area. The following data show the number of outpatient surgeries performed at each hospital last week. At the .05 significance level, can we conclude there is a difference in the mean number of surgeries performed by hospital or by day of the week?

| Day | Number of Surgeries Performed St. Luke's | St. Vincent | Mercy |
|-----|---------|-------------|-------|
| Monday | 14 | 18 | 24 |
| Tuesday | 20 | 24 | 14 |
| Wednesday | 16 | 22 | 14 |
| Thursday | 18 | 20 | 22 |
| Friday | 20 | 28 | 24 |

# Chapter Outline

I. The characteristics of the $F$ distribution are:
   A. It is continuous.
   B. Its values cannot be negative.
   C. It is positively skewed.
   D. There is a family of $F$ distributions. Each time the degrees of freedom in either the numerator or the denominator changes, a new distribution is created.
II. The $F$ distribution is used to test whether two population variances are the same.
   A. The sampled populations must follow the normal distribution.
   B. The larger of the two sample variances is placed in the numerator, forcing the ratio to be at least 1.00.
   C. The value of $F$ is computed using the following equation:

$$F = \frac{s_1^2}{s_2^2}$$

[12–1]

**III.** A one-way ANOVA is used to compare several treatment means.
 **A.** A treatment is a source of variation.
 **B.** The assumptions underlying ANOVA are:
  **1.** The samples are from populations which follow the normal distribution.
  **2.** The populations have equal standard deviations.
  **3.** The samples are independent.
 **C.** The information for finding the value of $F$ is summarized in an ANOVA table.
  **1.** The formula for SS total, the sum of squares total, is:

$$\text{SS total} = \Sigma(X - \bar{X}_G)^2 \qquad \text{[12–2]}$$

  **2.** The SSE, the sum of squares error, is found by subtraction.

$$\text{SSE} = \Sigma(X - \bar{X}_c)^2 \qquad \text{[12–3]}$$

  **3.** The formula for the SST, the sum of squares treatment, is:

$$\text{SST} = \text{SS total} - \text{SSE} \qquad \text{[12–4]}$$

  **4.** This information is summarized in the following table and the value of $F$ determined.

| Source of Variation | Sum of Squares | Degrees of Freedom | Mean Square | F |
|---|---|---|---|---|
| Treatments | SST | $k - 1$ | $\text{SST}/(k - 1) = \text{MST}$ | MST/MSE |
| Error | SSE | $n - k$ | $\text{SSE}/(n - k) = \text{MSE}$ | |
| Total | SS total | $n - 1$ | | |

**IV.** If a null hypothesis of equal treatment means is rejected, we can identify the pairs of means that differ from the following confidence interval.

$$(\bar{X}_1 - \bar{X}_2) \pm t\sqrt{\text{MSE}\left(\frac{1}{n_1} + \frac{1}{n_2}\right)} \qquad \text{[12–5]}$$

**V.** In a two-way ANOVA we consider a second treatment variable.
 **A.** The second treatment variable is called the blocking variable.
 **B.** It is determined using the following equation:

$$\text{SSB} = k\Sigma(\bar{X}_b - \bar{X}_G)^2 411 \qquad \text{[12–6]}$$

 **C.** The SSE term, or sum of squares error, is found from the following equation.

$$\text{SSE} = \text{SS total} - \text{SST} - \text{SSB} \qquad \text{[12–7]}$$

 **D.** The $F$ statistics for the treatment variable and the blocking variable are determined in the following table.

| Source of Variation | Sum of Squares | Degrees of Freedom | Mean Square | F |
|---|---|---|---|---|
| Treatments | SST | $k - 1$ | $\text{SST}/(k - 1) = \text{MST}$ | MST/MSE |
| Blocks | SSB | $b - 1$ | $\text{SSB}/(b - 1) = \text{MSB}$ | MSB/MSE |
| Error | SSE | $(k - 1)(b - 1)$ | $\text{SSE}/(k - 1)(b - 1) = \text{MSE}$ | |
| Total | SS total | $n - 1$ | | |

# Pronunciation Key

| SYMBOL | MEANING | PRONUNCIATION |
|---|---|---|
| SS total | Sum of squares total | S S total |
| SST | Sum of squares treatment | S S T |
| SSE | Sum of squares error | S S E |
| MSE | Mean square error | M S E |
| SSB | Block sum of squares | S S B |

# Chapter Exercises

**19.** A real estate agent in the coastal area of Georgia wants to compare the variation in the selling price of homes on the oceanfront with those one to three blocks from the ocean. A sample of 21 oceanfront homes sold within the last year revealed the standard deviation of the selling prices was $45,600. A sample of 18 homes, also sold within the last year, that were one to three blocks from the ocean revealed that the standard deviation was $21,330. At the .01 significance level, can we conclude that there is more variation in the selling prices of the oceanfront homes?

**20.** A computer manufacturer is about to unveil a new, faster personal computer. The new machine clearly is faster, but initial tests indicate there is more variation in the processing time. The processing time depends on the particular program being run, the amount of input data, and the amount of output. A sample of 16 computer runs, covering a range of production jobs, showed that the standard deviation of the processing time was 22 (hundredths of a second) for the new machine and 12 (hundredths of a second) for the current machine. At the .05 significance level can we conclude that there is more variation in the processing time of the new machine?

**21.** There are two Chevrolet dealers in Jamestown, New York. The mean monthly sales at Sharkey Chevy and Dave White Chevrolet are about the same. However, Tom Sharkey, the owner of Sharkey Chevy, believes his sales are more consistent. Below is the number of new cars sold at Sharkey in the last seven months and for the last eight months at Dave White. Do you agree with Mr. Sharkey? Use the .01 significance level.

| Sharkey    | 98 | 78 | 54 | 57 | 68 | 64 | 70 |     |
|------------|----|----|----|----|----|----|----|-----|
| Dave White | 75 | 81 | 81 | 30 | 82 | 46 | 58 | 101 |

**22.** Random samples of five were selected from each of three populations. The sum of squares total was 100. The sum of squares due to the treatments was 40.
   **a.** Set up the null hypothesis and the alternate hypothesis.
   **b.** What is the decision rule? Use the .05 significance level.
   **c.** Complete the ANOVA table. What is the value of $F$?
   **d.** What is your decision regarding the null hypothesis?

**23.** In an ANOVA table MSE was equal to 10. Random samples of six were selected from each of four populations, where the sum of squares total was 250.
   **a.** Set up the null hypothesis and the alternate hypothesis.
   **b.** What is the decision rule? Use the .05 significance level.
   **c.** Complete the ANOVA table. What is the value of $F$?
   **d.** What is your decision regarding the null hypothesis?

**24.** The following is a partial ANOVA table.

| Source    | Sum of Squares | df | Mean Square | F |
|-----------|----------------|----|-------------|---|
| Treatment |                | 2  |             |   |
| Error     |                |    | 20          |   |
| Total     | 500            | 11 |             |   |

Complete the table and answer the following questions. Use the .05 significance level.
   **a.** How many treatments are there?
   **b.** What is the total sample size?
   **c.** What is the critical value of $F$?
   **d.** Write out the null and alternate hypotheses.
   **e.** What is your conclusion regarding the null hypothesis?

**25.** A consumer organization wants to know whether there is a difference in the price of a particular toy at three different types of stores. The price of the toy was checked in a sample of five discount stores, five variety stores, and five department stores. The results are shown below. Use the .05 significance level.

| Discount | Variety | Department |
|----------|---------|------------|
| $12 | $15 | $19 |
| 13 | 17 | 17 |
| 14 | 14 | 16 |
| 12 | 18 | 20 |
| 15 | 17 | 19 |

**26.** A physician who specializes in weight control has three different diets she recommends. As an experiment, she randomly selected 15 patients and then assigned 5 to each diet. After three weeks the following weight losses, in pounds, were noted. At the .05 significance level, can she conclude that there is a difference in the mean amount of weight loss among the three diets?

| Plan A | Plan B | Plan C |
|--------|--------|--------|
| 5 | 6 | 7 |
| 7 | 7 | 8 |
| 4 | 7 | 9 |
| 5 | 5 | 8 |
| 4 | 6 | 9 |

**27.** The City of Maumee comprises four districts. Chief of police Andy North wants to determine whether there is a difference in the mean number of crimes committed among the four districts. He recorded the number of crimes reported in each district for a sample of six days. At the .05 significance level, can the chief of police conclude there is a difference in the mean number of crimes?

| Number of Crimes | | | |
|------------------|-----------|----------|------------|
| Rec Center | Key Street | Monclova | Whitehouse |
| 13 | 21 | 12 | 16 |
| 15 | 13 | 14 | 17 |
| 14 | 18 | 15 | 18 |
| 15 | 19 | 13 | 15 |
| 14 | 18 | 12 | 20 |
| 15 | 19 | 15 | 18 |

**28.** The personnel director of Cander Machine Products is investigating "perfectionism" on the job. A test designed to measure perfectionism was administered to a random sample of 18 employees. The scores ranged from 20 to about 40. One of the facets of the study involved the early background of each employee. Did the employee come from a rural background, a small city, or a large city? The scores are:

| Rural Area | Small Urban Area | Large Urban Area |
|------------|------------------|------------------|
| 35 | 28 | 24 |
| 30 | 24 | 28 |
| 36 | 25 | 26 |
| 38 | 30 | 30 |
| 29 | 32 | 34 |
| 34 | 28 | |
| 31 | | |

**a.** At the .05 level, can it be concluded that there is a difference in the three mean scores?
**b.** If the null hypothesis is rejected, can you state that the mean score of those with a rural background is different from the score of those with a large-city background?

**29.** When only two treatments are involved, ANOVA and the Student $t$ test (Chapter 10) result in the same conclusions. Also, $t^2 = F$. As an example, suppose that 14 randomly selected students were divided into two groups, one consisting of 6 students and the other of 8. One group was taught using a combination of lecture and programmed instruction, the other using a combination of lecture and television. At the end of the course, each group was given a 50-item test. The following is a list of the number correct for each of the two groups.

| Lecture and Programmed Instruction | Lecture and Television |
|:---:|:---:|
| 19 | 32 |
| 17 | 28 |
| 23 | 31 |
| 22 | 26 |
| 17 | 23 |
| 16 | 24 |
| | 27 |
| | 25 |

**a.** Using analysis of variance techniques, test $H_0$ that the two mean test scores are equal; $\alpha = .05$.
**b.** Using the $t$ test from Chapter 10, compute $t$.
**c.** Interpret the results.

**30.** There are four auto body shops in a community and all claim to promptly serve customers. To check if there is any difference in service, customers are randomly selected from each repair shop and their waiting times in days are recorded. The output from a statistical software package is:

| Summary | | | | |
|---|:---:|:---:|:---:|:---:|
| **Groups** | **Count** | **Sum** | **Average** | **Variance** |
| Body Shop A | 3 | 15.4 | 5.133333 | 0.323333 |
| Body Shop B | 4 | 32 | 8 | 1.433333 |
| Body Shop C | 5 | 25.2 | 5.04 | 0.748 |
| Body Shop D | 4 | 25.9 | 6.475 | 0.595833 |

| ANOVA | | | | | |
|---|:---:|:---:|:---:|:---:|:---:|
| **Source of Variation** | **SS** | **df** | **MS** | **F** | **p-value** |
| Between Groups | 23.37321 | 3 | 7.791069 | 9.612506 | 0.001632 |
| Within Groups | 9.726167 | 12 | 0.810514 | | |
| Total | 33.09938 | 15 | | | |

Is there evidence to suggest a difference in the mean waiting times at the four body shops? Use the .05 significance level.

**31.** The fuel efficiencies for a sample of 27 compact, midsize, and large cars are entered into a statistical software package. Analysis of variance is used to investigate if there is a difference in the mean mileage of the three cars. What do you conclude? Use the .01 significance level.

| Summary | | | | |
|---|:---:|:---:|:---:|:---:|
| **Groups** | **Count** | **Sum** | **Average** | **Variance** |
| Compact | 12 | 268.3 | 22.35833 | 9.388106 |
| Midsize | 9 | 172.4 | 19.15556 | 7.315278 |
| Large | 6 | 100.5 | 16.75 | 7.303 |

Additional results are shown on the next page.

| ANOVA | | | | | |
|---|---|---|---|---|---|
| Source of Variation | SS | df | MS | F | p-value |
| Between Groups | 136.4803 | 2 | 68.24014 | 8.258752 | 0.001866 |
| Within Groups | 198.3064 | 24 | 8.262766 | | |
| Total | 334.7867 | 26 | | | |

**32.** Three assembly lines are used to produce a certain component for an airliner. To examine the production rate, a random sample of six hourly periods is chosen for each assembly line and the number of components produced during these periods for each line is recorded. The output from a statistical software package is:

| Summary | | | | |
|---|---|---|---|---|
| Groups | Count | Sum | Average | Variance |
| Line A | 6 | 250 | 41.66667 | 0.266667 |
| Line B | 6 | 260 | 43.33333 | 0.666667 |
| Line C | 6 | 249 | 41.5 | 0.7 |

| ANOVA | | | | | |
|---|---|---|---|---|---|
| Source of Variation | SS | df | MS | F | p-value |
| Between Groups | 12.33333 | 2 | 6.166667 | 11.32653 | 0.001005 |
| Within Groups | 8.166667 | 15 | 0.544444 | | |
| Total | 20.5 | 17 | | | |

**a.** Use a .01 level of significance to test if there is a difference in the mean production of the three assembly lines.

**b.** Develop a 99 percent confidence interval for the difference in the means between Line B and Line C.

**33.** A grocery store wants to monitor the amount of withdrawals that its customers make from automatic teller machines (ATMs) located within their stores. They sample 10 withdrawals from each location and the output from a statistical software package is:

| Summary | | | | |
|---|---|---|---|---|
| Groups | Count | Sum | Average | Variance |
| Location X | 10 | 825 | 82.5 | 1,808.056 |
| Location Y | 10 | 540 | 54 | 921.1111 |
| Location Z | 10 | 382 | 38.2 | 1,703.733 |

| ANOVA | | | | | |
|---|---|---|---|---|---|
| Source of Variation | SS | df | MS | F | p-value |
| Between Groups | 1,0081.27 | 2 | 5,040.633 | 3.411288 | 0.047766 |
| Within Groups | 3,9896.1 | 27 | 1,477.633 | | |
| Total | 4,9977.37 | 29 | | | |

**a.** Use a .01 level of significance to test if there is a difference in the mean amount of money withdrawn.

**b.** Develop a 90 percent confidence interval for the difference in the means between Location X and Location Z.

**34.** One reads that a business school graduate with an undergraduate degree earns more than a high school graduate with no additional education, and a person with a master's degree or a doctorate earns even more. To investigate we select a sample of 25 mid-level managers of companies with less than 200 employees. Their incomes, classified by highest level of education, follow.

| Income ($ thousands) | | |
|---|---|---|
| High School or Less | Undergraduate Degree | Master's Degree or More |
| 45 | 49 | 51 |
| 47 | 57 | 73 |
| 53 | 85 | 82 |
| 62 | 73 | 59 |
| 39 | 81 | 94 |
| 43 | 84 | 89 |
| 54 | 89 | 89 |
| | 92 | 95 |
| | 62 | 73 |

Test at the .05 level of significance that there is no difference in the arithmetic mean salaries of the three groups. If the null hypothesis is rejected, conduct further tests to determine which groups differ.

**35.** Shank's, Inc., a nationwide advertising firm, wants to know whether the size of an advertisement and the color of the advertisement make a difference in the response of magazine readers. A random sample of readers is shown ads of four different colors and three different sizes. Each reader is asked to give the particular combination of size and color a rating between 1 and 10. Assume that the ratings follow the normal distribution. The rating for each combination is shown in the following table (for example, the rating for a small red ad is 2).

| Size of Ad | Color of Ad | | | |
|---|---|---|---|---|
| | Red | Blue | Orange | Green |
| Small | 2 | 3 | 3 | 8 |
| Medium | 3 | 5 | 6 | 7 |
| Large | 6 | 7 | 8 | 8 |

Is there a difference in the effectiveness of an advertisement by color and by size? Use the .05 level of significance.

**36.** There are four McBurger restaurants in the Columbus, Georgia, area. The numbers of burgers sold at the respective restaurants for each of the last six weeks are shown below. At the .05 significance level, is there a difference in the mean number sold among the four restaurants, when the factor of week is considered?

| Week | Restaurant | | | |
|---|---|---|---|---|
| | Metro | Interstate | University | River |
| 1 | 124 | 160 | 320 | 190 |
| 2 | 234 | 220 | 340 | 230 |
| 3 | 430 | 290 | 290 | 240 |
| 4 | 105 | 245 | 310 | 170 |
| 5 | 240 | 205 | 280 | 180 |
| 6 | 310 | 260 | 270 | 205 |

**a.** Is there a difference in the treatment means?
**b.** Is there a difference in the block means?

**37.** The city of Tucson, Arizona, employs people to assess the value of homes for the purpose of establishing real estate tax. The city manager routinely sends each assessor to five homes and then compares the results. The information is given below, in thousands of dollars. Can we conclude that there is a difference in the assessors, at $\alpha = .05$?

| Home | Assessor | | | |
|------|----------|--------|--------|---------|
|      | Zawodny | Norman | Cingle | Holiday |
| A | $53.0 | $55.0 | $49.0 | $45.0 |
| B | 50.0 | 51.0 | 52.0 | 53.0 |
| C | 48.0 | 52.0 | 47.0 | 53.0 |
| D | 70.0 | 68.0 | 65.0 | 64.0 |
| E | 84.0 | 89.0 | 92.0 | 86.0 |

**a.** Is there a difference in the treatment means?
**b.** Is there a difference in the block means?

**38.** Martin Motors has in stock three cars of the same make and model. The president would like to compare the gas consumption of the three cars (labeled car A, car B, and car C) using four different types of gasoline. For each trial, a gallon of gasoline was added to an empty tank, and the car was driven until it ran out of gas. The following table shows the number of miles driven in each trial.

| Types of Gasoline | Distance (miles) | | |
|-------------------|-------|-------|-------|
|                   | Car A | Car B | Car C |
| Regular | 22.4 | 20.8 | 21.5 |
| Super regular | 17.0 | 19.4 | 20.7 |
| Unleaded | 19.2 | 20.2 | 21.2 |
| Premium unleaded | 20.3 | 18.6 | 20.4 |

Using the .05 level of significance:
**a.** Is there a difference among types of gasoline?
**b.** Is there a difference in the cars?

**39.** A research firm wants to compare the miles per gallon of unleaded regular, mid-grade, and super premium gasolines. Because of differences in the performance of different automobiles, seven different automobiles were selected and treated as blocks. Therefore, each brand of gasoline was tested with each type of automobile. The results of the trials, in miles per gallon, are shown in the following table. At the .05 significance level, is there a difference in the gasolines or automobiles?

| Automobile | Regular | Mid-grade | Super Premium |
|------------|---------|-----------|---------------|
| 1 | 21 | 23 | 26 |
| 2 | 23 | 22 | 25 |
| 3 | 24 | 25 | 27 |
| 4 | 24 | 24 | 26 |
| 5 | 26 | 26 | 30 |
| 6 | 26 | 24 | 27 |
| 7 | 28 | 27 | 32 |

**40.** Three supermarket chains in the Denver area each claim to have the lowest overall prices. As part of an investigative study on supermarket advertising, the *Denver Daily News* conducted a study. First, a random sample of nine grocery items was selected. Next, the price of each selected item was checked at each of the three chains on the same day. At the .05 significance level, is there a difference in the mean prices at the supermarkets or for the items?

| Item | Super$ | Ralph's | Lowblaws |
|------|--------|---------|----------|
| 1 | $1.12 | $1.02 | $1.07 |
| 2 | 1.14 | 1.10 | 1.21 |
| 3 | 1.72 | 1.97 | 2.08 |
| 4 | 2.22 | 2.09 | 2.32 |
| 5 | 2.40 | 2.10 | 2.30 |
| 6 | 4.04 | 4.32 | 4.15 |
| 7 | 5.05 | 4.95 | 5.05 |
| 8 | 4.68 | 4.13 | 4.67 |
| 9 | 5.52 | 5.46 | 5.86 |

**41.** Listed below are the weights (in grams) of a sample of M&M's Plain candies, classified according to color. Use a statistical software system to determine whether there is a difference in the mean weights of candies of different colors. Use the .05 significance level.

| Red | Orange | Yellow | Brown | Tan | Green |
|-----|--------|--------|-------|-----|-------|
| 0.946 | 0.902 | 0.929 | 0.896 | 0.845 | 0.935 |
| 1.107 | 0.943 | 0.960 | 0.888 | 0.909 | 0.903 |
| 0.913 | 0.916 | 0.938 | 0.906 | 0.873 | 0.865 |
| 0.904 | 0.910 | 0.933 | 0.941 | 0.902 | 0.822 |
| 0.926 | 0.903 | 0.932 | 0.838 | 0.956 | 0.871 |
| 0.926 | 0.901 | 0.899 | 0.892 | 0.959 | 0.905 |
| 1.006 | 0.919 | 0.907 | 0.905 | 0.916 | 0.905 |
| 0.914 | 0.901 | 0.906 | 0.824 | 0.822 | 0.852 |
| 0.922 | 0.930 | 0.930 | 0.908 | | 0.965 |
| 1.052 | 0.883 | 0.952 | 0.833 | | 0.898 |
| 0.903 | | 0.939 | | | |
| 0.895 | | 0.940 | | | |
| | | 0.882 | | | |
| | | 0.906 | | | |

**42.** There are four radio stations in Midland. The stations have different formats (hard rock, classical, country/western, and easy listening), but each is concerned with the number of minutes of music played per hour. From a sample of 10 hours from each station, the following sample means were offered.

$$\bar{X}_1 = 51.32 \qquad \bar{X}_2 = 44.64 \qquad \bar{X}_3 = 47.2 \qquad \bar{X}_4 = 50.85$$

$$\text{SS total} = 650.75$$

**a.** Determine SST.
**b.** Determine SSE.
**c.** Complete an ANOVA table.
**d.** At the .05 significance level, is there a difference in the treatment means?
**e.** Is there a difference in the mean amount of music time between station 1 and station 4? Use the .05 significance level.

# exercises.com

**43.** Many real estate companies and rental agencies now publish their listings on the Web. One example is the Dunes Realty Company, located in Garden City Beach, South Carolina. Go to their website, http://www.dunes.com, select **Beach House Search,** then indicate 5 bedroom, accommodations for 14 people, second row (this means it is across the street from the beach), no pool or floating dock, select a period in July and August, indicate that you are willing to spend $8,000 per week, and then click on **Search the Beach Houses.** The output should include details on the beach houses that met your criteria. At the .05 significance level, is there a difference in the mean rental prices for the different number of bedrooms? (You may want to combine some of the larger homes, such as 8 or more bedrooms.) Which pairs of means differ?
**44.** The percentages of quarterly changes in the gross domestic product for 20 countries are available at the following site: http://www.oecd.org, select **Statistics, National Accounts,** and select **Quarterly Growth Rates in GDP.** Copy the data for Germany, Japan, and the United States into three columns in MINITAB or Excel. Perform an ANOVA to see whether there is a difference in the means. What can you conclude?

# Dataset Exercises

**45.** Refer to the Real Estate data, which reports information on the homes sold in the Denver, Colorado, area last year.
**a.** At the .02 significance level, is there a difference in the variability of the selling prices of the homes that have a pool versus those that do not have a pool?

**b.** At the .02 significance level, is there a difference in the variability of the selling prices of the homes with an attached garage versus those that do not have an attached garage?

**c.** At the .05 significance level, is there a difference in the mean selling price of the homes among the five townships?

**46.** Refer to the Baseball 2002 data, which reports information on the 30 Major League Baseball teams for the 2002 season.

**a.** At the .10 significance level, is there a difference in the variation of the number of stolen bases among the teams that play their home games on natural grass versus on artificial turf?

**b.** Create a variable that classifies a team's total attendance into three groups: less than 2.0 (million), 2.0 up to 3.0, and 3.0 or more. At the .05 significance level, is there a difference in the mean number of games won among the three groups? Use the .01 significance level.

**c.** Using the same attendance variable developed in part (b), is there a difference in the mean team batting average? Use the .01 significance level.

**d.** Using the same attendance variable developed in part (b), is there a difference in the mean salary of the three groups? Use the .01 significance level.

**47.** Refer to the Wage data, which reports information on annual wages for a sample of 100 workers. Also included are variables relating to industry, years of education, and gender for each worker.

**a.** Conduct a test of hypothesis to determine if there is a difference in the mean annual wages for workers in the three industries. If there is a difference in the means, which pair or pairs of means differ? Use the .05 significance level.

**b.** Conduct a test of hypothesis to determine if there is a difference in the mean annual wages for workers in the six different occupations. If there is a difference in the means, which pair or pairs of means differ? Use the .05 significance level.

# Software Commands

**1.** The Excel commands for the test of variances on page 391 are:

**a.** Enter the data for U.S. 25 in column A and for I-75 in column B. Label the two columns.

**b.** Click on **Tools**, **Data Analysis**, select **F-Test: Two-Sample for Variances,** and click **OK.**

**c.** The range of the first variable is *A1:A8* and *B1:B9* for the second, click on **Labels,** select *D1* for the output range, and click **OK.**

**2.** The Excel commands for the one-way ANOVA on page 400 are:

**a.** Key in data into four columns labeled: Excellent, Good, Fair, and Poor.

**b.** Click on **Tools** on the Excel Toolbar and select **Data Analysis.** In the dialog box select **ANOVA, Single Factor ANOVA,** and click **OK.**

**c.** In the subsequent dialog box make the input range *A1:D8,* click on **Grouped by Columns,** click on **Labels in First Row,** the **Alpha** text box is .05, and finally select **Output range** as *G1* and click **OK.**

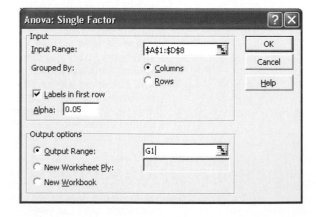

**3.** The MINITAB commands for the one-way ANOVA on page 400 are:

   **a.** Input the data into four columns and identify the columns as *Excellent, Good, Fair,* and *Poor.*

   **b.** Select **Stat**, **ANOVA**, and **Oneway (Unstacked)** and click **OK.**

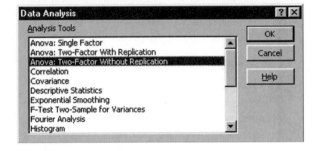

**4.** The Excel commands for the two-way ANOVA on page 410 are:

   **a.** In the first row of the first column write the word *Drivers,* then list the five drivers in the first column. In the first row of the next four columns enter the name of the routes. Enter the data under each route name.

   **b.** Select **Tools**, **Data Analysis**, and **ANOVA: Two-Factor Without Replication,** and then click **OK**.

   **c.** In the dialog box the **Input Range** is *AI:E6*, click on **Labels**, select *A10* for **Output Range**, and then click **OK**.

# Chapter 12  Answers to Self-Review

**12–1** Let Mark's assemblies be population 1, then
$H_0$: $\sigma_1^2 \le \sigma_2^2$; $H_1$: $\sigma_1^2 > \sigma_2^2$; $df_1 = 10 - 1 = 9$; and
$df_2$ also equals 9. $H_0$ is rejected if $F > 3.18$.

$$F = \frac{(2.0)^2}{(1.5)^2} = 1.78$$

$H_0$ is not rejected. The variation is the same for both employees.

**12–2** **a.** $H_0$: $\mu_1 = \mu_2 = \mu_3$
   $H_1$: At least one treatment mean is different.
   **b.** Reject $H_0$ if $F > 4.26$
   **c.**   $\bar{X} = \dfrac{240}{12} = 20$
   SS total $= (18 - 20)^2 + \cdots + (32 - 20)^2$
       $= 578$
       SSE $= (18 - 17)^2 + (14 - 17)^2 + \cdots +$
           $(32 - 29)^2$
           $= 74$
   SST $= 578 - 74 = 504$
   **d.**

| Source | Sum of Squares | Degrees of Freedom | Mean Square | F |
|---|---|---|---|---|
| Treatment | 504 | 2 | 252 | 30.65 |
| Error | 74 | 9 | 8.22 | |

   **e.** $H_0$ is rejected. There is a difference in the mean number of bottles sold at the various locations.

**12–3** **a.** $H_0$: $\mu_1 = \mu_2 = \mu_3$
   $H_1$: Not all means are equal.
   **b.** $H_0$ is rejected if $F > 3.98$.
   **c.** $\bar{X}_G = 8.86$, $\bar{X}_1 = 11$, $\bar{X}_2 = 8.75$, $\bar{X}_3 = 6.8$
   SS total $= 53.71$
       SST $= 44.16$
       SSE $= 9.55$

| Source | Sum of Squares | df | Mean Square | F |
|---|---|---|---|---|
| Treatment | 44.16 | 2 | 22.08 | 25.43 |
| Error | 9.55 | 11 | 0.8682 | |
| Total | 53.71 | 13 | | |

   **d.** $H_0$ is rejected. The treatment means differ.
   **e.** $(11.0 - 6.8) \pm 2.201 \sqrt{0.8682(\frac{1}{5} + \frac{1}{5})} =$
       $4.2 \pm 1.30 = 2.90$ and $5.50$

These treatment means differ because both endpoints of the confidence interval are of the same sign—positive in this problem.

**12–4** For types:

$H_0$: $\mu_1 = \mu_2 = \mu_3$
$H_1$: The treatment means are not equal.

Reject $H_0$ if $F > 4.46$.
For months:

$H_0$: $\mu_1 = \mu_2 = \mu_3 = \mu_4 = \mu_5$
$H_1$: The block means are not equal.

Reject $H_0$ if $F > 3.84$.
The analysis of variance table is as follows:

| Source: | df | SS | MS | F |
|---|---|---|---|---|
| Types | 2 | 3.60 | 1.80 | 0.39 |
| Months | 4 | 31.73 | 7.93 | 1.71 |
| Error | 8 | 37.07 | 4.63 | |
| Total | 14 | 72.40 | | |

The null hypotheses cannot be rejected for either types or months. There is no difference in the mean sales among types or months.

# A Review of Chapters 10–12

This section is a review of the major concepts and terms introduced in Chapters 10, 11, and 12. Chapter 10 began our study of hypothesis testing. A hypothesis is a statement about the value of a population parameter. In statistical hypothesis testing, we begin by making a statement about the value of the population parameter in the null hypothesis. We establish the null hypothesis for the purpose of testing. When we complete the testing, our decision is either to reject or to fail to reject the null hypothesis. If we reject the null hypothesis, we conclude that the alternate hypothesis is true. The alternate hypothesis is "accepted" only if we show that the null hypothesis is false. We also refer to the alternate hypothesis as the research hypothesis. Most of the time we want to prove the alternate hypothesis.

In Chapter 10 we selected random samples from a single population and tested whether it was reasonable that the population parameter under study equals a particular value. For example, we wish to investigate whether the mean tenure time of those holding the position of CEO in large firms is 12 years. We select a sample of CEOs, compute the sample mean, and compare the mean of the sample to the population. The single population under consideration is the CEOs of large firms. We described methods for conducting the test when the population standard deviation was available, when the sample was large (usually 30 or more), and when the sample was small. Also, in Chapter 10 we conducted tests of hypothesis about a population proportion. A proportion is the fraction of individuals or objects possessing a certain characteristic. For example, industry records indicate that 70 percent of gasoline sales for automobiles are for the regular grade of gasoline. A sample of the 100 sales from last month at the Pantry in Conway revealed 76 were for the regular grade. Can the owners conclude that more than 70 percent of their customers purchase the regular grade?

In Chapter 11 we extended the idea of hypothesis testing to comparing whether two independent random samples came from populations having the same or equal population means. For example, St. Mathews Hospital operates an urgent care facility on both the north and south sides of Knoxville, Tennessee. The research question is: Is the mean waiting time for patients visiting the two facilities the same? To investigate, we select a random sample from each of the facilities and compute the sample means. We test the null hypothesis that the mean waiting time is the same at the two facilities. The alternate hypothesis is that the mean waiting time is not the same for the two facilities. If both samples are at least 30, then we use the $z$ distribution as the distribution of the test statistic. If one of the samples is less than 30, the test statistic follows the $t$.

Our discussion in Chapter 11 also concerned dependent samples. For *dependent* samples, we applied the *paired difference test.* The test statistic is the $t$ distribution. One typical paired sample problem calls for recording an individual's blood pressure before administering medication and then again afterward in order to evaluate the effectiveness of the medication. We also considered the case of testing two population proportions. For example, the production manager wished to compare the proportion of defects on the day shift with that of the second shift.

Chapter 11 dealt with the difference between two population means. Chapter 12 presented tests for variances and a procedure called the *analysis of variance,* or *ANOVA,* used to simultaneously determine whether several independent normal populations have the same mean. This is accomplished by comparing the variances of the random samples selected from these populations. We apply the usual hypothesis-testing procedure, but we use the $F$ distribution as the test statistic. Often the calculations are tedious, so a software package is recommended.

As an example of the analysis of variance, a test could be conducted to resolve whether there is any difference in effectiveness among five fertilizers on the weight of popcorn ears. This type of analysis is referred to as *one-factor ANOVA* because we are able to draw conclusions about only one factor, called a *treatment.* If we want to draw conclusions about the simultaneous effects of more than one factor or variable, the *two-factor ANOVA* technique is applied. Both the one-factor and two-factor tests use the $F$ *distribution* as the distribution of the test statistic. The $F$ distribution is also the distribution of the test statistic used to find whether one normal population has more variation than another.

## Glossary

### Chapter 10
**Alpha**  The probability of a Type I error or the level of significance. Its symbol is the Greek letter $\alpha$.
**Alternate hypothesis**  The conclusion we accept when we demonstrate that the null hypothesis is false. It is also called the research hypothesis.

**Critical value**  A value that is the dividing point between the region where the null hypothesis is not rejected and the region where it is rejected.
**Degrees of freedom**  The number of items in a sample that are free to vary. Suppose there are two items in a sample, and we know the mean. We are free to specify

only one of the two values, because the other value is automatically determined (since the two values total twice the mean). Example: If the mean is $6, we are free to choose only one value. Choosing $4 makes the other value $8 because $4 + $8 = 2($6). So there is 1 degree of freedom in this illustration. We can determine the degrees of freedom by $n - 1 = 2 - 1 = 1$. If $n$ is 4, then there are 3 degrees of freedom, found by $n - 1 = 4 - 1 = 3$.

**Hypothesis**   A statement or claim about the value of a population parameter. Examples: 40.7 percent of all persons 65 years old or older live alone. The mean number of people in a car is 1.33.

**Hypothesis testing**   A statistical procedure, based on sample evidence and probability theory, used to determine whether the statement about the population parameter is a reasonable statement.

**One-tailed test**   Used when the alternate hypothesis states a direction such as $H_1$: $\mu > 40$, read "the population mean is greater than 40." Here the rejection region is only in one tail (the right tail).

**Proportion**   A fraction or percentage of a sample or a population having a particular trait. If 5 out of 50 in a sample liked a new cereal, the proportion is 5/50, or .10.

**p-value**   The probability of computing a value of the test statistic at least as extreme as the one found in the sample data when the null hypothesis is true.

**Two-tailed test**   Used when the alternate hypothesis does not state a direction, such as $H_1$: $\mu \neq 75$, read "the population mean is not equal to 75." There is a region of rejection in each tail.

**Type I error**   Occurs when a true $H_0$ is rejected.

**Type II error**   Occurs when a false $H_0$ is accepted.

## Chapter 11

**Dependent samples**   Dependent samples are characterized by a measurement, then some type of intervention, followed by another measurement. Paired samples are also dependent because the same individual or item is a member of both samples. Example: Ten participants in a marathon were weighed prior to and after competing in the race. We wish to study the mean amount of weight loss.

**Independent samples**   The samples chosen at random are not related to each other. We wish to study the mean age of the inmates at the Auburn and Allegheny prisons. We select a random sample of 28 inmates from the Auburn

prison and a sample of 19 inmates at Allegheny prison. A person cannot be an inmate in both prisons. The samples are independent, that is, unrelated.

**Pooled estimate of the population variance**   A weighted average of $s_1^2$ and $s_2^2$ used to estimate the common variance, $\sigma^2$, when using small samples to test the difference between two population means.

**t distribution**   Investigated and reported by William S. Gossett in 1908 and published under the pseudonym *Student*. It is similar to the standard normal distribution presented in Chapter 7. The major characteristics of $t$ are:

1. It is a continuous distribution.
2. It can assume values between minus infinity and plus infinity.
3. It is symmetrical about its mean of zero. However, it is more spread out and flatter at the apex than the standard normal distribution.
4. It approaches the standard normal distribution as $n$ gets larger.
5. There is a family of $t$ distributions. One $t$ distribution exists for a sample of 15 observations, another for 25, and so on.

## Chapter 12

**Analysis of variance (ANOVA)**   A technique used to test simultaneously whether the means of several populations are equal. It uses the $F$ distribution as the distribution of the test statistic.

**Block**   A second source of variation, in addition to treatments.

**F distribution**   It is used as the test statistic for ANOVA problems, as well as others. The major characteristics of the $F$ distribution are:

1. It is never negative.
2. It is a continuous distribution approaching the $X$-axis but never touching it.
3. It is positively skewed.
4. It is based on two sets of degrees of freedom.
5. Like the $t$ distribution, there is a "family" of $F$ distributions. There is one distribution for 17 degrees of freedom in the numerator and 9 degrees of freedom in the denominator, there is another $F$ distribution for 7 degrees of freedom in the numerator and 12 degrees of freedom in the denominator, and so on.

## Exercises

### Part I—Multiple Choice

1. In a one-tailed test using the $z$ distribution as the test statistic and the .01 significance level, the critical value is either
   a. $-1.96$ or $+1.96$.
   b. $-1.65$ or $+1.65$.
   c. $-2.58$ or $+2.58$.
   d. 0 or 1.
   e. None of these is correct.

2. A Type II error is committed if we:
   a. Reject a true null hypothesis.
   b. Accept a true alternate hypothesis.
   c. Reject a true alternate hypothesis.
   d. Accept both the null and alternate hypotheses at the same time.
   e. None of these is correct.
3. The hypotheses are $H_0$: $\mu = 240$ pounds of pressure and $H_1$: $\mu \neq 240$ pounds of pressure.
   a. A one-tailed test is being applied.
   b. A two-tailed test is being applied.
   c. A three-tailed test is being applied.
   d. The wrong test is being applied.
   e. None of these is correct.
4. The .01 significance level is used in an experiment, and a one-tailed test with the rejection region in the lower tail is applied. Computed $z$ is $-1.8$. This indicates:
   a. $H_0$ should not be rejected.
   b. We should reject $H_0$ and accept $H_1$.
   c. We should take a larger sample.
   d. We should have used the .05 level of significance.
   e. None of these is correct.
5. The test statistic for testing a hypothesis for small sample means when the population standard deviation is not known is:
   a. $z$.    b. $t$.    c. $F$.    d. $\chi^2$.
6. We want to test a hypothesis for the difference between two population means. The null and alternate hypotheses are stated as

   $H_0$: $\mu_1 = \mu_2$
   $H_1$: $\mu_1 \neq \mu_2$

   a. A left-tailed test should be applied.
   b. A two-tailed test should be applied.
   c. A right-tailed test should be applied.
   d. We cannot determine whether a left-, right-, or two-tailed test should be applied based on the information given.
   e. None of these is correct.
7. The $F$ distribution:
   a. Cannot be negative.
   b. Cannot be positive.
   c. Is the same as the $t$ distribution.
   d. Is the same as the $z$ distribution.
   e. None of these is correct.
8. As the sample size increases, the $t$ distribution approaches:
   a. ANOVA.
   b. The standard normal or $z$ distribution.
   c. The Poisson distribution.
   d. Zero.
   e. None of these is correct.
9. To conduct a paired difference test, the samples must be:
   a. Infinitely large.
   b. Equal to ANOVA.
   c. Independent.
   d. Dependent.
   e. None of these is correct.
10. An ANOVA test was conducted with respect to the population mean. The null hypothesis was rejected. This indicates
   a. There were too many degrees of freedom.
   b. There is no difference between the population means.
   c. There is a difference between at least two population means.
   d. A larger sample should be selected.
   e. None of these is correct.

## Part II—Problems

For each of the following problems, state: (a) the null and the alternate hypothesis, (b) the decision rule, and (c) the decision regarding the null hypothesis, (d) then interpret the result.

11. A machine is set to produce tennis balls so the mean bounce is 36 inches when the ball is dropped from a platform of a certain height. The supervisor suspects that the mean bounce has changed and is less than 36 inches. As an experiment 42 balls were dropped from the platform and the mean height of the bounce was 35.5 inches, with a standard deviation of 0.9 inches. At the .05 significance level, can the supervisor conclude that the mean bounce height is less than 36 inches?

12. Research by the Illinois Banking Company revealed that only 8 percent of their customers wait more than five minutes to do their banking when not using the drive-through facility. Management considers this reasonable and will not add more tellers unless the proportion becomes larger than 8 percent. The branch manager at the Litchfield Branch believes that the wait is longer than the standard at her branch and requested additional part-time tellers. To support her request she found that in a sample of 100 customers, 10 waited more than five minutes. At the .01 significance level, is it reasonable to conclude that more than 8 percent of the customers wait more than five minutes?

13. It was hypothesized that road construction workers do not engage in productive work 20 minutes on the average out of every hour. Some claimed the nonproductive time is greater than 20 minutes. An actual study was conducted at a construction site, using a stopwatch and other ways of checking the work habits. A random check of workers revealed the following unproductive times, in minutes, during a one-hour period (exclusive of regularly scheduled breaks):

| 10 | 25 | 17 | 20 | 28 | 30 | 18 | 23 | 18 |
|----|----|----|----|----|----|----|----|----|

Using the .05 significance level, is it reasonable to conclude the mean unproductive time is greater than 20 minutes?

14. A test is to be conducted involving the mean holding power of two glues designed for plastic. First, a small plastic hook was coated at one end with Epox glue and fastened to a sheet of plastic. After it dried, weight was added to the hook until it separated from the sheet of plastic. The weight was then recorded. This was repeated until 12 hooks were tested. The same procedure was followed for Holdtite glue, but only 10 hooks were used. The sample results, in pounds, were:

|                          | Epox | Holdtite |
|--------------------------|------|----------|
| Sample mean              | 250  | 252      |
| Sample standard deviation | 5    | 8        |
| Sample size              | 12   | 10       |

At the .01 significance level, is there a difference between the mean holding power of Epox and that of Holdtite?

15. Pittsburgh Paints wishes to test an additive formulated to increase the life of paints used in the Southwest. The top half of a piece of wood was painted using the regular paint. The bottom half was painted with the paint including the additive. The same procedure was followed for a total of 10 pieces. Then each piece was subjected to high-pressure water and brilliant light. The data, the number of hours each piece lasted before it faded beyond a certain point, follow:

| | Number of Hours by Sample | | | | | | | | | |
|-----------------|-----|-----|-----|-----|-----|-----|-----|-----|-----|-----|
| | A | B | C | D | E | F | G | H | I | J |
| Without additive | 325 | 313 | 320 | 340 | 318 | 312 | 319 | 330 | 333 | 319 |
| With additive | 323 | 313 | 326 | 343 | 310 | 320 | 313 | 340 | 330 | 315 |

Using the .05 significance level, determine whether the additive is effective in prolonging the life of the paint.

16. The Buffalo, New York, cola distributor is featuring a super-special sale on 12-packs. She wonders where in the grocery store to place the cola for maximum attention. Should it be near the front door of the grocery stores, in the cola section, at the checkout registers, or near the milk and other dairy products? Four stores with similar total sales cooperated in an

experiment. In one store the 12-packs were stacked near the front door, in another they were placed near the checkout registers, and so on. Sales were checked at specified times in each store for exactly four minutes. The results were:

| Cola at the Door | In Soft Drink Section | Near Registers | Dairy Section |
|---|---|---|---|
| $6 | $ 5 | $ 7 | $10 |
| 8 | 10 | 10 | 9 |
| 3 | 12 | 9 | 6 |
| 7 | 4 | 4 | 11 |
|  | 9 | 5 |  |
|  |  | 7 |  |

The Buffalo distributor wants to find out whether there is a difference in the mean sales for cola stacked at the four locations in the store. Use the .05 significance level.

# Cases

## A. Century National Bank

Refer to the description of Century National Bank at the end of the Review of Chapters 1–4 on page 137.

With many other options available, customers no longer let their money sit in a checking account. For many years the mean checking balance has been $1,600. Does the sample data indicate that the mean account balance has declined from this value?

Recent years have also seen an increase in the use of ATM machines. When Mr. Selig took over the bank, the mean number of transactions per month per customer was 8; now he believes it has increased to more than 10. In fact, the advertising agency that prepares TV commercials for Century would like to use this on the new commercial being designed. Is there sufficient evidence to conclude that the mean number of transactions per customer is more than 10 per month? Could the advertising agency say the mean is more than 9 per month?

The bank has branch offices in four different cities: Cincinnati, Ohio; Atlanta, Georgia; Louisville, Kentucky; and Erie, Pennsylvania. Mr. Selig would like to know whether there is a difference in the mean checking account balances among the four branches. If there are differences, between which branches do these differences occur?

Mr. Selig is also interested in the ATMs. Is there a difference in the ATM use among the branches? Also, do customers who have debit cards tend to use the ATMs differently from those who do not have debit cards? Is there a difference in ATM use by those with checking accounts that pay interest versus those that do not? Prepare a report for Mr. Selig answering these questions.

## B. Bell Grove Medical Center

Ms. Gene Dempsey manages the emergency care center at the Bell Grove Medical Center. One of her responsibilities is to have enough nurses so that incoming patients needing service can be handled promptly. It is stressful for patients to wait a long time for emergency care even when their care needs are not life threatening. Ms. Dempsey

gathered the following information regarding the number of patients over the last several weeks. The center is not open on weekends. Does it appear that there are any differences in the number of patients served by the day of the week? If there are differences, which days seem to be the busiest?

| Date | Day | Patients |
|---|---|---|
| 9-29-00 | Monday | 38 |
| 9-30-00 | Tuesday | 28 |
| 10-1-00 | Wednesday | 28 |
| 10-2-00 | Thursday | 30 |
| 10-3-00 | Friday | 35 |
| 10-6-00 | Monday | 35 |
| 10-7-00 | Tuesday | 25 |
| 10-8-00 | Wednesday | 22 |
| 10-9-00 | Thursday | 21 |
| 10-10-00 | Friday | 32 |
| 10-13-00 | Monday | 37 |
| 10-14-00 | Tuesday | 29 |
| 10-15-00 | Wednesday | 27 |
| 10-16-00 | Thursday | 28 |
| 10-17-00 | Friday | 35 |
| 10-20-00 | Monday | 37 |
| 10-21-00 | Tuesday | 26 |
| 10-22-00 | Wednesday | 28 |
| 10-23-00 | Thursday | 23 |
| 10-24-00 | Friday | 33 |

# 13

# Linear Regression and Correlation

## GOALS

*When you have completed this chapter, you will be able to:*

1 Draw a scatter diagram.

2 Understand and interpret the terms *dependent* and *independent variable.*

3 Calculate and interpret the coefficient of correlation, the coefficient of determination, and the standard error of estimate.

4 Conduct a test of hypothesis to determine whether the coefficient of correlation in the population is zero.

5 Calculate the least squares regression line.

6 Construct and interpret confidence and prediction intervals for the dependent variable.

7 Set up and interpret an ANOVA table.

An appliance store with outlets in New England plans to air a commercial for a digital camera on selected local TV stations prior to a weekend sale. The general sales manager plans to record sales information for Saturday–Sunday at the various outlets and compare them with the number of times the ad appeared on the local TV station. He hopes to find out whether there is a relationship between the number of times the ad aired and digital camera sales. Determine the coefficient of determination. (See Goal 3 and Exercise 3.)

# Introduction

Chapters 2 through 4 dealt with *descriptive statistics.* We organized raw data into a frequency distribution, and computed several measures of location and measures of

dispersion to describe the major characteristics of the data. Chapter 5 started the study of *statistical inference.* The main emphasis was on inferring something about a population parameter, such as the population mean, on the basis of a sample. We tested for the reasonableness of a population mean or a population proportion, the difference between two population means, or whether several population means were equal. All of these tests involved just *one* interval- or ratio-level variable, such as the weight of a plastic soft drink bottle, the income of bank presidents, or the number of patients admitted to a particular hospital.

We shift the emphasis in this chapter to the study of two variables. Recall in Chapter 4 we introduced the idea of showing the relationship between two variables with a scatter diagram. We plotted the price of vehicles sold at Whitner Autoplex on the vertical axis and the age of the buyer on the horizontal axis. See the statistical software output on page 119. In that case we observed that as the age of the buyer increased, the amount spent for the vehicle also increased. In this chapter we carry this idea further. That is, we develop numerical measures to express the relationship between two variables. Is the relationship strong or weak, is it direct or inverse? In addition we develop an equation to express the relationship between variables. This will allow us to estimate one variable on the basis of another. Here are some examples.

- Is there a relationship between the amount Healthtex spends per month on advertising and the sales in the month?
- Can we base an estimate of the cost to heat a home in January on the number of square feet in the home?
- Is there a relationship between the miles per gallon achieved by large pickup trucks and the size of the engine?
- Is there a relationship between the number of hours that students studied for an exam and the score earned?

Note in each of these cases there are two variables observed for each sampled observation. For the last example, we find, for each student selected for the sample, the hours studied and the score earned.

We begin this chapter by examining the meaning and purpose of **correlation analysis.** We continue our study by developing a mathematical equation that will allow us to estimate the value of one variable based on the value of another. This is called **regression analysis.** We will (1) determine the equation of the line that best fits the data, (2) use the equation to estimate the value of one variable based on another, (3) measure the error in our estimate, and (4) establish confidence and prediction intervals for our estimate.

# What Is Correlation Analysis?

Correlation analysis is the study of the relationship between variables. To explain, suppose the sales manager of Copier Sales of America, which has a large sales force throughout the United States and Canada, wants to determine whether there is a relationship between the number of sales calls made in a month and the number of copiers sold that month. The manager selects a random sample of 10 representatives and determines the number of sales calls each representative made last month and the number of copiers sold. The sample information is shown in Table 13–1.

TABLE 13–1  Sales Calls and Copiers Sold for 10 Salespeople

| Sales Representative | Number of Sales Calls | Number of Copiers Sold |
|---|---|---|
| Tom Keller | 20 | 30 |
| Jeff Hall | 40 | 60 |
| Brian Virost | 20 | 40 |
| Greg Fish | 30 | 60 |
| Susan Welch | 10 | 30 |
| Carlos Ramirez | 10 | 40 |
| Rich Niles | 20 | 40 |
| Mike Kiel | 20 | 50 |
| Mark Reynolds | 20 | 30 |
| Soni Jones | 30 | 70 |

By reviewing the data we observe that there does seem to be some relationship between the number of sales calls and the number of units sold. That is, the sales-people who made the most sales calls sold the most units. However, the relationship is not "perfect" or exact. For example, Soni Jones made fewer sales calls than Jeff Hall, but she sold more units.

Instead of talking in generalities as we did in Chapter 4 and have so far in this chapter, we will develop some statistical measures to portray more precisely the relationship between the two variables, sales calls and copiers sold. This group of statistical techniques is called **correlation analysis.**

> **CORRELATION ANALYSIS**  A group of techniques to measure the association between two variables.

The basic idea of correlation analysis is to report the association between two variables. The usual first step is to plot the data in a **scatter diagram.** An example will show how a scatter diagram is used.

**Statistics in Action**

The space shuttle Challenger exploded on January 28, 1986. An investigation of the cause examined four contractors: Rockwell International for the shuttle and engines, Lockheed for ground support, Martin Marietta for the external fuel tanks, and Morton Thiokol for the solid fuel booster rockets. After several months, the investigation blamed the explosion on defective O-rings produced by Morton Thiokol. A study of the contractor's stock prices showed an interesting happenstance. On the day of the crash, Morton Thiokol stock was down 11.86% and the stock of the other three lost only 2 to 3%. Can we conclude that financial markets predicted the outcome of the investigation?

**EXAMPLE**

Copier Sales of America sells copiers to businesses of all sizes throughout the United States and Canada. Ms. Marcy Bancer was recently promoted to the position of national sales manager. At the upcoming sales meeting, the sales representatives from all over the country will be in attendance. She would like to impress upon them the importance of making that extra sales call each day. She decides to gather some information on the relationship between the number of sales calls and the number of copiers sold. She selected a random sample of 10 sales representatives and determined the number of sales calls they made last month and the number of copiers they sold. The sample information is reported in Table 13–1. What observations can you make about the relationship between the number of sales calls and the number of copiers sold? Develop a scatter diagram to display the information.

**SOLUTION**

Based on the information in Table 13–1, Ms. Bancer suspects there is a relationship between the number of sales calls made in a month and the number of copiers sold. Soni Jones sold the most copiers last month, and she was one of three representatives making 30 or more sales calls. On the other hand, Susan Welch and Carlos

Ramirez made only 10 sales calls last month. Ms. Welch had the lowest number of copiers sold among the sampled representatives.

The implication is that the number of copiers sold is related to the number of sales calls made. As the number of sales calls increases, it appears the number of copiers sold also increases. We refer to number of sales calls as the **independent variable** and number of copiers sold as the **dependent variable.**

> **DEPENDENT VARIABLE** The variable that is being predicted or estimated.

> **INDEPENDENT VARIABLE** A variable that provides the basis for estimation. It is the predictor variable.

It is common practice to scale the dependent variable (copiers sold) on the vertical or $Y$-axis and the independent variable (number of sales calls) on the horizontal or $X$-axis. To develop the scatter diagram of the Copier Sales of America sales information, we begin with the first sales representative, Tom Keller. Tom made 20 sales calls last month and sold 30 copiers, so $X = 20$ and $Y = 30$. To plot this point, move along the horizontal axis to $X = 20$, then go vertically to $Y = 30$ and place a dot at the intersection. This process is continued until all the paired data are plotted, as shown in Chart 13–1.

**CHART 13–1** Scatter Diagram Showing Sales Calls and Copiers Sold

The scatter diagram shows graphically that the sales representatives who make more calls tend to sell more copiers. It is reasonable for Ms. Bancer, the national sales manager at Copier Sales of America, to tell her salespeople that the more sales calls they make the more copiers they can expect to sell. Note that while there appears to be a positive relationship between the two variables, all the points do not fall on a line. In the following section you will measure the strength and direction of this relationship between two variables by determining the coefficient of correlation.

# The Coefficient of Correlation

Interval- or ratio-level data are required

Originated by Karl Pearson about 1900, the **coefficient of correlation** describes the strength of the relationship between two sets of interval-scaled or ratio-scaled variables. Designated $r$, it is often referred to as *Pearson's r* and as the *Pearson product-moment correlation coefficient.* It can assume any value from $-1.00$ to $+1.00$ inclusive. A correlation coefficient of $-1.00$ or $+1.00$ indicates *perfect correlation.* For example, a correlation coefficient for the preceding example computed to be $+1.00$

would indicate that the number of sales calls and the number of copiers sold are perfectly related in a positive linear sense. A computed value of −1.00 reveals that sales calls and the number of copiers sold are perfectly related in an inverse linear sense. How the scatter diagram would appear if the relationship between the two sets of data were linear and perfect is shown in Chart 13–2.

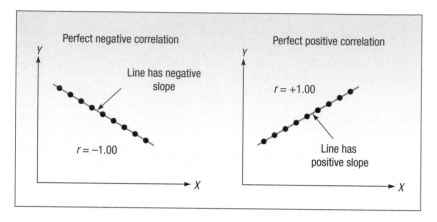

**CHART 13–2**  Scatter Diagrams Showing Perfect Negative Correlation and
              Perfect Positive Correlation

If there is absolutely no relationship between the two sets of variables, Pearson's *r* is zero. A coefficient of correlation *r* close to 0 (say, .08) shows that the linear relationship is quite weak. The same conclusion is drawn if $r = -.08$. Coefficients of −.91 and +.91 have equal strength; both indicate very strong correlation between the two variables. Thus, *the strength of the correlation does not depend on the direction (either − or +).*

Scatter diagrams for $r = 0$, a weak *r* (say, −.23), and a strong *r* (say, +.87) are shown in Chart 13–3. Note that if the correlation is weak, there is considerable scatter about a line drawn through the center of the data. For the scatter diagram representing a strong relationship, there is very little scatter about the line. This indicates, in the example shown on the chart, that hours studied is a good predictor of exam score.

**CHART 13–3**  Scatter Diagrams Depicting Zero, Weak, and Strong Correlation

The following drawing summarizes the strength and direction of the coefficient of correlation.

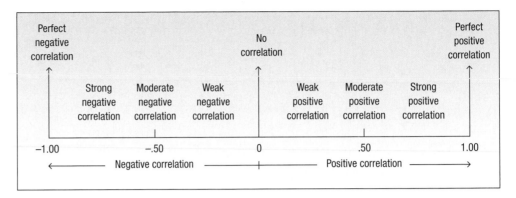

---

**COEFFICIENT OF CORRELATION** A measure of the strength of the linear relationship between two variables.

---

How is the value of the coefficient of correlation determined? We will use the Copier Sales of America data, which are reported in Table 13–2, as an example. We begin with a scatter diagram, similar to Chart 13–2. Draw a vertical line through the data values at the mean of the $X$-values and a horizontal line at the mean of the $Y$-values. In Chart 13–4 we've added a vertical line at 22.0 calls ($\bar{X} = \Sigma X/n = 220/10 = 22$) and a horizontal line at 45.0 copiers ($\bar{Y} = \Sigma Y/n = 450/10 = 45.0$). These lines pass through the "center" of the data and divide the scatter diagram into four quadrants. Think of moving the origin from (0, 0) to (22, 45).

**TABLE 13–2** Sales Calls and Copiers Sold for 10 Salespeople

| Sales Representative | Sales Calls ($X$) | Copiers Sold ($Y$) |
|---|---|---|
| Tom Keller | 20 | 30 |
| Jeff Hall | 40 | 60 |
| Brian Virost | 20 | 40 |
| Greg Fish | 30 | 60 |
| Susan Welch | 10 | 30 |
| Carlos Ramirez | 10 | 40 |
| Rich Niles | 20 | 40 |
| Mike Kiel | 20 | 50 |
| Mark Reynolds | 20 | 30 |
| Soni Jones | 30 | 70 |
| Total | 220 | 450 |

Two variables are positively related, when the number of copiers sold is above the mean and the number of sales calls is also above the mean. These points appear in the upper-right quadrant of Chart 13–4. Similarly, when the number of copiers sold is less than the mean, so is the number of sales calls. These points fall in the lower-left quadrant of Chart 13–4. For example, the last person on the list in Table 13–2, Soni Jones, made 30 sales calls and sold 70 copiers. These values are above their respective means, so this point is located in the upper-right quadrant. She made 8 ($X - \bar{X} = 30 - 22$) more sales calls than the mean and sold 25 ($Y - \bar{Y} = 70 - 45$)

**CHART 13–4** Computation of the Coefficient of Correlation

more copiers than the mean. Tom Keller, the first name on the list in Table 13–2, made 20 sales calls and sold 30 copiers. Both of these values are less than their respective mean; hence this point is in the lower-left quadrant. Tom made 2 less sales calls and sold 15 less copiers than the respective means. The deviations from the mean number of sales calls and for the mean number of copiers sold are summarized in Table 13–3 for the 10 sales representatives. The sum of the products of the deviations from the respective means is 900. That is, the term $\Sigma(X - \bar{X})(Y - \bar{Y}) = 900$.

**TABLE 13–3** Deviations from the Mean and Their Products

| Sales Representative | Calls Y | Sales X | $X - \bar{X}$ | $Y - \bar{Y}$ | $(X - \bar{X})(Y - \bar{Y})$ |
|---|---|---|---|---|---|
| Tom Keller | 20 | 30 | −2 | −15 | 30 |
| Jeff Hall | 40 | 60 | 18 | 15 | 270 |
| Brian Virost | 20 | 40 | −2 | −5 | 10 |
| Greg Fish | 30 | 60 | 8 | 15 | 120 |
| Susan Welch | 10 | 30 | −12 | −15 | 180 |
| Carlos Ramirez | 10 | 40 | −12 | −5 | 60 |
| Rich Niles | 20 | 40 | −2 | −5 | 10 |
| Mike Kiel | 20 | 50 | −2 | 5 | −10 |
| Mark Reynolds | 20 | 30 | −2 | −15 | 30 |
| Soni Jones | 30 | 70 | 8 | 25 | 200 |
| | | | | | 900 |

In both the upper-right and the lower-left quadrants, the product of $(X - \bar{X})(Y - \bar{Y})$ is positive because both of the factors have the same sign. In our example this happens for all sales representatives except Mike Kiel. We can therefore expect the coefficient of correlation to have a positive value.

If the two variables are inversely related, one variable will be above the mean and the other below the mean. Most of the points in this case occur in the upper-left and lower-right quadrants. Now $(X - \bar{X})$ and $(Y - \bar{Y})$ will have opposite signs, so their product is negative. The resulting correlation coefficient is negative.

What happens if there is no linear relationship between the two variables? The points in the scatter diagram will appear in all four quadrants. The negative products of $(X - \bar{X})(Y - \bar{Y})$ offset the positive products, so the sum is near zero. This leads to a correlation coefficient near zero.

Pearson also wanted the correlation coefficient to be unaffected by the units of the two variables. For example, if we had used hundreds of copiers sold instead of the number sold, the coefficient of correlation would be the same. The coefficient of correlation is independent of the scale used if we divide the term $\Sigma(X - \bar{X})(Y - \bar{Y})$ by the sample standard deviations. It is also made independent of the sample size and bounded by the values +1.00 and −1.00 if we divide by $(n - 1)$.

This reasoning leads to the following formula:

| CORRELATION COEFFICIENT | $r = \dfrac{\Sigma(X - \bar{X})(Y - \bar{Y})}{(n - 1) s_x s_y}$ | **[13–1]** |

To compute the coefficient of correlation, we use the standard deviations of the sample of 10 sales calls and 10 copiers sold. We could use formula (3–12) to calculate the sample standard deviations or we could use a software package. For the specific Excel and MINITAB commands see the Software Command section at the end of Chapter 3. The following is the Excel output. The standard deviation of the number of sales calls is 9.189 and of the number of copiers sold 14.337.

We now insert these values into formula (13–1) to determine the coefficient of correlation:

$$r = \frac{\Sigma(X - \bar{X})(Y - \bar{Y})}{(n - 1) s_x s_y} = \frac{900}{(10 - 1)(9.189)(14.337)} = 0.759$$

How do we interpret a correlation of 0.759? First, it is positive, so we see there is a direct relationship between the number of sales calls and the number of copiers sold. This confirms our reasoning based on the scatter diagram, Chart 13–4. The value of 0.759 is fairly close to 1.00, so we conclude that the association is strong. To put it another way, an increase in calls will likely lead to more sales.

# The Coefficient of Determination

In the previous example regarding the relationship between the number of sales calls and the units sold, the coefficient of correlation, 0.759, was interpreted as being "strong." Terms such as *weak, moderate,* and *strong,* however, do not have precise meaning. A measure that has a more easily interpreted meaning is the **coefficient of determination.** It is computed by squaring the coefficient of correlation. In the example, the coefficient of determination, $r^2$, is 0.576, found by $(0.759)^2$. This is a proportion or a percent; we can say that 57.6 percent of the variation in the number of copiers sold is explained, or accounted for, by the variation in the number of sales calls.

> **COEFFICIENT OF DETERMINATION** The proportion of the total variation in the dependent variable $Y$ that is explained, or accounted for, by the variation in the independent variable $X$.

Further discussion of the coefficient of determination is found later in the chapter.

## Correlation and Cause

If there is a strong relationship (say, .91) between two variables, we are tempted to assume that an increase or decrease in one variable *causes* a change in the other variable. For example, it can be shown that the consumption of Georgia peanuts and the consumption of aspirin have a strong correlation. However, this does not indicate that an increase in the consumption of peanuts *caused* the consumption of aspirin to increase. Likewise, the incomes of professors and the number of inmates in mental institutions have increased proportionately. Further, as the population of donkeys has decreased, there has been an increase in the number of doctoral degrees granted. Relationships such as these are called **spurious correlations.** What we can conclude when we find two variables with a strong correlation is that there is a relationship or association between the two variables, not that a change in one causes a change in the other.

**Self-Review 13–1**

Haverty's Furniture is a family business that has been selling to retail customers in the Chicago area for many years. They advertise extensively on radio, TV, and the Internet, emphasizing their low prices and easy credit terms. The owner would like to review the relationship between sales and the amount spent on advertising. Below is information on sales and advertising expense for the last four months.

| Month | Advertising Expense ($ million) | Sales Revenue ($ million) |
|---|---|---|
| July | 2 | 7 |
| August | 1 | 3 |
| September | 3 | 8 |
| October | 4 | 10 |

(a) The owner wants to forecast sales on the basis of advertising expense. Which variable is the dependent variable? Which variable is the independent variable?
(b) Draw a scatter diagram.
(c) Determine the coefficient of correlation.
(d) Interpret the strength of the correlation coefficient.
(e) Determine the coefficient of determination. Interpret.

## Exercises

**1.** The following sample observations were randomly selected.

| $X$: | 4 | 5 | 3 | 6 | 10 |
|---|---|---|---|---|---|
| $Y$: | 4 | 6 | 5 | 7 | 7 |

Determine the coefficient of correlation and the coefficient of determination. Interpret.

**2.** The following sample observations were randomly selected.

| $X$: | 5 | 3 | 6 | 3 | 4 | 4 | 6 | 8 |
|---|---|---|---|---|---|---|---|---|
| $Y$: | 13 | 15 | 7 | 12 | 13 | 11 | 9 | 5 |

Determine the coefficient of correlation and the coefficient of determination. Interpret the association between $X$ and $Y$.

3. Bi-lo Appliance Stores has outlets in several large metropolitan areas in New England. The general sales manager plans to air a commercial for a digital camera on selected local TV stations prior to a sale starting on Saturday and ending Sunday. She plans to get the information for Saturday–Sunday digital camera sales at the various outlets and pair them with the number of times the advertisement was shown on the local TV stations. The purpose is to find whether there is any relationship between the number of times the advertisement was aired and digital camera sales. The pairings are:

| Location of TV Station | Number of Airings | Saturday–Sunday Sales ($ thousands) |
|---|---|---|
| Providence | 4 | 15 |
| Springfield | 2 | 8 |
| New Haven | 5 | 21 |
| Boston | 6 | 24 |
| Hartford | 3 | 17 |

a. What is the dependent variable?
b. Draw a scatter diagram.
c. Determine the coefficient of correlation.
d. Determine the coefficient of determination.
e. Interpret these statistical measures.

4. The production department of NDB Electronics wants to explore the relationship between the number of employees who assemble a subassembly and the number produced. As an experiment, two employees were assigned to assemble the subassemblies. They produced 15 during a one-hour period. Then four employees assembled them. They produced 25 during a one-hour period. The complete set of paired observations follows.

| Number of Assemblers | One-Hour Production (units) |
|---|---|
| 2 | 15 |
| 4 | 25 |
| 1 | 10 |
| 5 | 40 |
| 3 | 30 |

The dependent variable is production; that is, it is assumed that the level of production depends upon the number of employees.

a. Draw a scatter diagram.
b. Based on the scatter diagram, does there appear to be any relationship between the number of assemblers and production? Explain.
c. Compute the coefficient of correlation.
d. Evaluate the strength of the relationship by computing the coefficient of determination.

5. The city council of Pine Bluffs is considering increasing the number of police in an effort to reduce crime. Before making a final decision, the council asks the Chief of Police to survey other cities of similar size to determine the relationship between the number of police and the number of crimes reported. The Chief gathered the following sample information.

| City | Police | Number of Crimes | City | Police | Number of Crimes |
|---|---|---|---|---|---|
| Oxford | 15 | 17 | Holgate | 17 | 7 |
| Starksville | 17 | 13 | Carey | 12 | 21 |
| Danville | 25 | 5 | Whistler | 11 | 19 |
| Athens | 27 | 7 | Woodville | 22 | 6 |

a. If we want to estimate crimes on the basis of the number of police, which variable is the dependent variable and which is the independent variable?
b. Draw a scatter diagram.

    **c.** Determine the coefficient of correlation.
    **d.** Determine the coefficient of determination.
    **e.** Interpret these statistical measures. Does it surprise you that the relationship is inverse?
**6.** The owner of Maumee Ford-Mercury wants to study the relationship between the age of a car and its selling price. Listed below is a random sample of 12 used cars sold at the dealership during the last year.

| Car | Age (years) | Selling Price ($000) | Car | Age (years) | Selling Price ($000) |
|-----|-------------|----------------------|-----|-------------|----------------------|
| 1 | 9 | 8.1 | 7 | 8 | 7.6 |
| 2 | 7 | 6.0 | 8 | 11 | 8.0 |
| 3 | 11 | 3.6 | 9 | 10 | 8.0 |
| 4 | 12 | 4.0 | 10 | 12 | 6.0 |
| 5 | 8 | 5.0 | 11 | 6 | 8.6 |
| 6 | 7 | 10.0 | 12 | 6 | 8.0 |

    **a.** If we want to estimate selling price on the basis of the age of the car, which variable is the dependent variable and which is the independent variable?
    **b.** Draw a scatter diagram.
    **c.** Determine the coefficient of correlation.
    **d.** Determine the coefficient of determination.
    **e.** Interpret these statistical measures. Does it surprise you that the relationship is inverse?

# Testing the Significance of the Correlation Coefficient

Recall the sales manager of Copier Sales of America found the correlation between the number of sales calls and the number of copiers sold was 0.759. This indicated a strong association between the two variables. However, only 10 salespeople were sampled. Could it be that the correlation in the population is actually 0? This would mean the correlation of 0.759 was due to chance. The population in this example is all the salespeople employed by the firm.

Could the correlation in the population be zero?

    Resolving this dilemma requires a test to answer the obvious question: Could there be zero correlation in the population from which the sample was selected? To put it another way, did the computed $r$ come from a population of paired observations with zero correlation? To continue our convention of allowing Greek letters to represent a population parameter, we will let $\rho$ represent the correlation in the population. It is pronounced "rho."

    We will continue with the illustration involving sales calls and copiers sold. We employ the same hypothesis testing steps described in Chapter 10. The null hypothesis and the alternate hypothesis are:

$H_0$: $\rho = 0$     (The correlation in the population is zero.)
$H_1$: $\rho \neq 0$     (The correlation in the population is different from zero.)

From the way $H_1$ is stated, we know that the test is two-tailed.
    The formula for $t$ is:

| | | |
|---|---|---|
| ***t* TEST FOR THE COEFFICIENT OF CORRELATION** | $$t = \frac{r\sqrt{n-2}}{\sqrt{1-r^2}} \quad \text{with } n-2 \text{ degrees of freedom}$$ | **[13–2]** |

Using the .05 level of significance, the decision rule states that if the computed $t$ falls in the area between plus 2.306 and minus 2.306, the null hypothesis is not rejected. To locate the critical value of 2.306, refer to Appendix F for $df = n - 2 = 10 - 2 = 8$. See Chart 13–5.

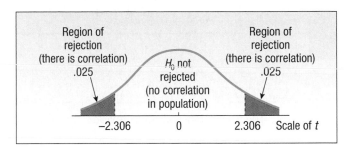

**CHART 13–5** Decision Rule for Test of Hypothesis at .05 Significance Level and 8 $df$

Applying formula (13–2) to the example regarding the number of sales calls and units sold:

$$t = \frac{r\sqrt{n-2}}{\sqrt{1-r^2}} = \frac{.759\sqrt{10-2}}{\sqrt{1-.759^2}} = 3.297$$

The computed $t$ is in the rejection region. Thus, $H_0$ is rejected at the .05 significance level. This means the correlation in the population is not zero. From a practical standpoint, it indicates to the sales manager that there is correlation with respect to the number of sales calls made and the number of copiers sold in the population of salespeople.

We can also interpret the test of hypothesis in terms of $p$-values. A $p$-value is the likelihood of finding a value of the test statistic more extreme than the one computed, when $H_0$ is true. To determine the $p$-value, go to the $t$ distribution in Appendix F and find the row for 8 degrees of freedom. The value of the test statistic is 3.297, so in the row for 8 degrees of freedom and a two-tailed test, find the value closest to 3.297. For a two-tailed test at the .02 significance level, the critical value is 2.896, and the critical value at the .01 significance level is 3.355. Because 3.297 is between 2.896 and 3.355 we conclude that the $p$-value is between .01 and .02.

Both MINITAB and Excel will report the correlation between two variables. In addition to the correlation, MINITAB reports the $p$-value for the test of hypothesis that the correlation in the population between the two variables is 0. The MINITAB output showing the results is below. They are the same as those calculated earlier.

**Self-Review 13–2**   A sample of 25 mayoral campaigns in cities with populations larger than 50,000 showed that the correlation between the percent of the vote received and the amount spent on the campaign by the candidate was .43. At the .05 significance level, is there a positive association between the variables?

# Exercises

**7.** The following hypotheses are given.

$H_0$: $\rho \leq 0$
$H_1$: $\rho > 0$

A random sample of 12 paired observations indicated a correlation of .32. Can we conclude that the correlation in the population is greater than zero? Use the .05 significance level.

**8.** The following hypotheses are given.

$H_0$: $\rho \geq 0$
$H_1$: $\rho < 0$

A random sample of 15 paired observations have a correlation of $-.46$. Can we conclude that the correlation in the population is less than zero? Use the .05 significance level.

**9.** The Pennsylvania Refining Company is studying the relationship between the pump price of gasoline and the number of gallons sold. For a sample of 20 stations last Tuesday, the correlation was .78. At the .01 significance level, is the correlation in the population greater than zero?

**10.** A study of 20 worldwide financial institutions showed the correlation between their assets and pretax profit to be .86. At the .05 significance level, can we conclude that there is positive correlation in the population?

# Regression Analysis

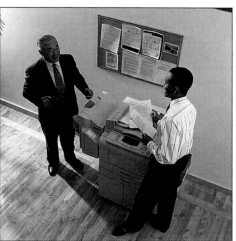

In the previous section we developed measures to express the strength and the direction of the relationship between two variables. In this section we wish to develop an equation to express the *linear* (straight line) relationship between two variables. In addition we want to be able to estimate the value of the dependent variable $Y$ based on a selected value of the independent variable $X$. The technique used to develop the equation and provide the estimates is called **regression analysis.**

In Table 13–1 we reported the number of sales calls and the number of units sold for a sample of 10 sales representatives employed by Copier Sales of America. Chart 13–1 portrayed this information in a scatter diagram. Now we want to develop a linear equation that expresses the relationship between the number of sales calls and the number of units sold. The equation for the line used to estimate $Y$ on the basis of $X$ is referred to as the **regression equation.**

**REGRESSION EQUATION**   An equation that expresses the linear relationship between two variables.

# Least Squares Principle

The scatter diagram in Chart 13–1 is reproduced in Chart 13–6, with a line drawn with a ruler through the dots to illustrate that a straight line would probably fit the data. However, the line drawn using a straight edge has one disadvantage: Its position is based in part on the judgment of the person drawing the line. The hand-drawn lines in Chart 13–7 represent the judgments of four people. All the lines except line *A* seem to be reasonable. However, each would result in a different estimate of units sold for a particular number of sales calls.

**CHART 13–6** Sales Calls and Copiers Sold for 10 Sales Representatives

**CHART 13–7** Four Lines Superimposed on the Scatter Diagram

Least squares line gives "best" fit; subjective method is unreliable.

Judgment is eliminated by determining the regression line using a mathematical method called the **least squares principle.** This method gives what is commonly referred to as the "best-fitting" line.

> **LEAST SQUARES PRINCIPLE** Determining a regression equation by minimizing the sum of the squares of the vertical distances between the actual *Y* values and the predicted values of *Y*.

To illustrate this concept, the same data are plotted in the three charts that follow. The regression line in Chart 13–8 was determined using the least squares method. It is the best-fitting line because the sum of the squares of the vertical deviations about it is at a minimum. The first plot ($X = 3$, $Y = 8$) deviates by 2 from the line, found by $10 - 8$. The deviation squared is 4. The squared deviation for the plot $X = 4$, $Y = 18$ is 16. The squared deviation for the plot $X = 5$, $Y = 16$ is 4. The sum of the squared deviations is 24, found by $4 + 16 + 4$.

Assume that the lines in Charts 13–9 and 13–10 were drawn with a straight edge. The sum of the squared vertical deviations in Chart 13–9 is 44. For Chart 13–10 it is 132. Both sums are greater than the sum for the line in Chart 13–8, found by using the least squares method.

The equation of a straight line has the form

| GENERAL FORM OF LINEAR REGRESSION EQUATION | $Y' = a + bX$ | **[13–3]** |
|---|---|---|

where:

$Y'$ read *Y* prime, is the predicted value of the *Y* variable for a selected *X* value.

$a$ is the *Y*-intercept. It is the estimated value of *Y* when $X = 0$. Another way to put it is: $a$ is the estimated value of *Y* where the regression line crosses the *Y*-axis when *X* is zero.

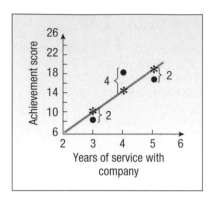

**CHART 13–8** The Least Squares Line

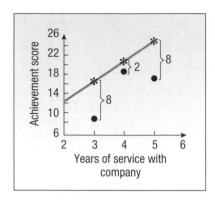

**CHART 13–9** Line Drawn with a Straight Edge

**CHART 13–10** Line Drawn with a Straight Edge

*b* is the slope of the line, or the average change in *Y′* for each change of one unit (either increase or decrease) in the independent variable *X*.

*X* is any value of the independent variable that is selected.

The formulas for *a* and *b* are:

---

**SLOPE OF THE REGRESSION LINE**        $b = r\dfrac{s_y}{s_x}$        **[13-4]**

---

where:

*r* is the correlation coefficient.

$s_y$ is the standard deviation of *Y* (the dependent variable).

$s_x$ is the standard deviation of *X* (the independent variable).

---

**Y-INTERCEPT**        $a = \bar{Y} - b\bar{X}$        **[13-5]**

---

where

$\bar{Y}$ is the mean of *Y* (the dependent variable).

$\bar{X}$ is the mean of *X* (the independent variable).

**EXAMPLE**

Recall the example involving Copier Sales of America. The sales manager gathered information on the number of sales calls made and the number of copiers sold for a random sample of 10 sales representatives. As a part of her presentation at the upcoming sales meeting, Ms. Bancer, the sales manager, would like to offer specific information about the relationship between the number of sales calls and the number of copiers sold. Use the least squares method to determine a linear equation to express the relationship between the two variables. What is the expected number of copiers sold by a representative who made 20 calls?

**SOLUTION**

The calculations necessary to determine the regression equation are:

$$b = r\left(\frac{s_y}{s_x}\right) = .759\left(\frac{14.337}{9.189}\right) = 1.1842$$

$$a = \bar{Y} - b\bar{X} = 45 - (1.1842)22 = 18.9476$$

Thus, the regression equation is $Y' = 18.9476 + 1.1842X$. So if a salesperson makes 20 calls, he or she can expect to sell 42.6316 copiers, found by $Y' = 18.9476 + 1.1842X = 18.9476 + 1.1842(20)$. The $b$ value of 1.1842 means that for each additional sales call made the sales representative can expect to increase the number of copiers sold by about 1.2. To put it another way, five additional sales calls in a month will result in about six more copiers being sold, found by $1.1842(5) = 5.921$.

The $a$ value of 18.9476 is the point where the equation crosses the $Y$-axis. A literal translation is that if no sales calls are made, that is, $X = 0$, 18.9476 copiers will be sold. Note that $X = 0$ is outside the range of values included in the sample and, therefore, should not be used to estimate the number of copiers sold. The sales calls ranged from 10 to 40, so estimates should be made within that range.

# Drawing the Line of Regression

The least squares equation, $Y' = 18.9476 + 1.1842X$, can be drawn on the scatter diagram. The first sales representative in the sample is Tom Keller. He made 20 calls. His estimated number of copiers sold is $Y' = 18.9476 + 1.1842(20) = 42.6316$. The plot $X = 20$ and $Y = 42.6316$ is located by moving to 20 on the $X$-axis and then going vertically to 42.6316. The other points on the regression equation can be determined by substituting the particular value of $X$ into the regression equation.

| Sales Representative | Sales Calls (X) | Estimated Sales (Y') | Sales Representative | Sales Calls (X) | Estimated Sales (Y') |
|---|---|---|---|---|---|
| Tom Keller | 20 | 42.6316 | Carlos Ramirez | 10 | 30.7896 |
| Jeff Hall | 40 | 66.3156 | Rich Niles | 20 | 42.6316 |
| Brian Virost | 20 | 42.6316 | Mike Kiel | 20 | 42.6316 |
| Greg Fish | 30 | 54.4736 | Mark Reynolds | 20 | 42.6316 |
| Susan Welch | 10 | 30.7896 | Soni Jones | 30 | 54.4736 |

All the other points are connected to give the line. See Chart 13–11.

**CHART 13–11** The Line of Regression Drawn on the Scatter Diagram

This line has some interesting features. As we have discussed, there is no other line through the data for which the sum of the squared deviations is smaller. In addition, this line will pass through the points represented by the mean of the $X$ values and the mean of the $Y$ values, that is, $\bar{X}$ and $\bar{Y}$. In this example $\bar{X} = 22.0$ and $\bar{Y} = 45.0$.

**Self-Review 13–3**

Refer to Self-Review 13–1, where the owner of Haverty's Furniture Company was studying the relationship between sales and the amount spent on advertising. The sales information for the last four months is repeated below.

| Month | Advertising Expense ($ million) | Sales Revenue ($ million) |
|---|---|---|
| July | 2 | 7 |
| August | 1 | 3 |
| September | 3 | 8 |
| October | 4 | 10 |

(a) Determine the regression equation.
(b) Interpret the values of *a* and *b*.
(c) Estimate sales when $3 million is spent on advertising.

# Exercises

11. The following sample observations were randomly selected.

| X: | 4 | 5 | 3 | 6 | 10 |
|---|---|---|---|---|---|
| Y: | 4 | 6 | 5 | 7 | 7 |

   **a.** Determine the regression equation.
   **b.** Determine the value of $Y'$ when $X$ is 7.

12. The following sample observations were randomly selected.

| X: | 5 | 3 | 6 | 3 | 4 | 4 | 6 | 8 |
|---|---|---|---|---|---|---|---|---|
| Y: | 13 | 15 | 7 | 12 | 13 | 11 | 9 | 5 |

   **a.** Determine the regression equation.
   **b.** Determine the value of $Y'$ when $X$ is 7.

13. The Bradford Electric Illuminating Company is studying the relationship between kilowatt-hours (thousands) used and the number of rooms in a private single-family residence. A random sample of 10 homes yielded the following.

| Number of Rooms | Kilowatt-Hours (thousands) | Number of Rooms | Kilowatt-Hours (thousands) |
|---|---|---|---|
| 12 | 9 | 8 | 6 |
| 9 | 7 | 10 | 8 |
| 14 | 10 | 10 | 10 |
| 6 | 5 | 5 | 4 |
| 10 | 8 | 7 | 7 |

   **a.** Determine the regression equation.
   **b.** Determine the number of kilowatt-hours, in thousands, for a six-room house.

14. Mr. James McWhinney, president of Daniel-James Financial Services, believes there is a relationship between the number of client contacts and the dollar amount of sales. To document this assertion, Mr. McWhinney gathered the following sample information. The X column indicates the number of client contacts last month, and the Y column shows the value of sales ($ thousands) last month for each client sampled.

| Number of Contacts, X | Sales ($ thousands), Y | Number of Contacts, X | Sales ($ thousands), Y |
|---|---|---|---|
| 14 | 24 | 23 | 30 |
| 12 | 14 | 48 | 90 |
| 20 | 28 | 50 | 85 |
| 16 | 30 | 55 | 120 |
| 46 | 80 | 50 | 110 |

   a. Determine the regression equation.
   b. Determine the estimated sales if 40 contacts are made.
15. A recent article in *Business Week* listed the "Best Small Companies." We are interested in the current results of the companies' sales and earnings. A random sample of 12 companies was selected and the sales and earnings, in millions of dollars, are reported below.

| Company | Sales ($ millions) | Earnings ($ millions) | Company | Sales ($ millions) | Earnings ($ millions) |
|---|---|---|---|---|---|
| Papa John's International | $89.2 | $4.9 | Checkmate Electronics | $17.5 | $ 2.6 |
| Applied Innovation | 18.6 | 4.4 | Royal Grip | 11.9 | 1.7 |
| Integracare | 18.2 | 1.3 | M-Wave | 19.6 | 3.5 |
| Wall Data | 71.7 | 8.0 | Serving-N-Slide | 51.2 | 8.2 |
| Davidson Associates | 58.6 | 6.6 | Daig | 28.6 | 6.0 |
| Chico's Fas | 46.8 | 4.1 | Cobra Golf | 69.2 | 12.8 |

   Let sales be the independent variable and earnings be the dependent variable.
   a. Draw a scatter diagram.
   b. Compute the coefficient of correlation.
   c. Compute the coefficient of determination.
   d. Interpret your findings in parts b and c.
   e. Determine the regression equation.
   f. For a small company with $50.0 million in sales, estimate the earnings.
16. We are studying mutual bond funds for the purpose of investing in several funds. For this particular study, we want to focus on the assets of a fund and its five-year performance. The question is: Can the five-year rate of return be estimated based on the assets of the fund? Nine mutual funds were selected at random, and their assets and rates of return are shown below.

| Fund | Assets ($ millions) | Return (%) | Fund | Assets ($ millions) | Return (%) |
|---|---|---|---|---|---|
| AARP High Quality Bond | $622.2 | 10.8 | MFS Bond A | $494.5 | 11.6 |
| Babson Bond L | 160.4 | 11.3 | Nichols Income | 158.3 | 9.5 |
| Compass Capital Fixed Income | 275.7 | 11.4 | T. Rowe Price Short-term | 681.0 | 8.2 |
| Galaxy Bond Retail | 433.2 | 9.1 | Thompson Income B | 241.3 | 6.8 |
| Keystone Custodian B-1 | 437.9 | 9.2 | | | |

   a. Draw a scatter diagram.
   b. Compute the coefficient of correlation.
   c. Compute the coefficient of determination.
   d. Write a brief report of your findings for parts b and c.
   e. Determine the regression equation. Use assets as the independent variable.
   f. For a fund with $400.0 million in sales, determine the five-year rate of return (in percent).
17. Refer to Exercise 5.
   a. Determine the regression equation.
   b. Estimate the number of crimes for a city with 20 police.
   c. Interpret the regression equation.

**18.** Refer to Exercise 6.
  **a.** Determine the regression equation.
  **b.** Estimate the selling price of a 10-year-old car.
  **c.** Interpret the regression equation.

# The Standard Error of Estimate

Note in the preceding scatter diagram (Chart 13–11) that all of the points do not lie exactly on the regression line. If they all were on the line, there would be no error in estimating the number of units sold. To put it another way, if all the points were on the regression line, units sold could be predicted with 100 percent accuracy. Thus, there would be no error in predicting the $Y$ variable based on an $X$ variable. This is true in the following hypothetical case (see Chart 13–12). Theoretically, if $X = 4$, then an exact $Y$ of 100 could be predicted with 100 percent confidence. Or if $X = 12$, then $Y = 300$. Because there is no difference between the observed values and the predicted values, there is no error in this estimate.

**CHART 13–12** Example of Perfect Prediction: Horsepower and Cost of Electricity

Perfect prediction unrealistic in business

Perfect prediction in economics and business is practically impossible. For example, the revenue for the year from gasoline sales ($Y$) based on the number of automobile registrations ($X$) as of a certain date could no doubt be approximated fairly closely, but the prediction would not be exact to the nearest dollar, or probably even to the nearest thousand dollars. Even predictions of tensile strength of steel wires based on the outside diameters of the wires are not always exact due to slight differences in the composition of the steel.

What is needed, then, is a measure that describes how precise the prediction of $Y$ is based on $X$ or, conversely, how inaccurate the estimate might be. This measure is called the **standard error of estimate.** The standard error of estimate, symbolized by $s_{y \cdot x}$, is the same concept as the standard deviation discussed in Chapter 3. The standard deviation measures the dispersion around the mean. The standard error of estimate measures the dispersion about the regression line.

> **STANDARD ERROR OF ESTIMATE** A measure of the scatter, or dispersion, of the observed values around the line of regression.

The standard error of estimate is found by the following equation. Note that the equation is quite similar to the one for the standard deviation of a sample.

| STANDARD ERROR OF ESTIMATE | $s_{y \cdot x} = \sqrt{\dfrac{\Sigma(Y - Y')^2}{n - 2}}$ | [13–6] |
|---|---|---|

The standard deviation is based on the squared deviations from the mean, whereas the standard error of estimate is based on squared deviations between each $Y$ and its predicted value, $Y'$. Remember that the regression line represents all the values of $Y'$. If $s_{y \cdot x}$ is small, this means that the data are relatively close to the regression line and the regression equation can be used to predict $Y$ with little error. If $s_{y \cdot x}$ is large, this means that the data are widely scattered around the regression line and the regression equation will not provide a precise estimate $Y$.

**EXAMPLE**

Recall the example involving Copier Sales of America. The sales manager determined the least squares regression equation to be $Y' = 18.9476 + 1.1842X$, where $Y$ refers to the number of copiers sold and $X$ the number of sales calls made. Determine the standard error of estimate as a measure of how well the values fit the regression line.

**SOLUTION**

To find the standard error, we begin by finding the difference between the value, $Y$, and the value estimated from the regression equation, $Y'$. Next we square this difference, that is, $(Y - Y')^2$. We do this for each of the $n$ observations and sum the results. That is, we compute $\Sigma(Y - Y')^2$, which is the numerator of formula (13–6). Finally, we divide by the number of observations minus 2. Why minus 2? We lose a degree of freedom each for estimating the intercept value, $a$, and the slope value, $b$. The details of the calculations are summarized in Table 13–4.

**TABLE 13–4** Computations Needed for the Standard Error of Estimate

| Sales Representative | Actual Sales ($Y$) | Estimated Sales ($Y'$) | Deviation ($Y - Y'$) | Deviation Squared ($Y - Y'$)² |
|---|---|---|---|---|
| Tom Keller | 30 | 42.6316 | −12.6316 | 159.557 |
| Jeff Hall | 60 | 66.3156 | −6.3156 | 39.887 |
| Brian Virost | 40 | 42.6316 | −2.6316 | 6.925 |
| Greg Fish | 60 | 54.4736 | 5.5264 | 30.541 |
| Susan Welch | 30 | 30.7896 | −0.7896 | 0.623 |
| Carlos Ramirez | 40 | 30.7896 | 9.2104 | 84.831 |
| Rich Niles | 40 | 42.6316 | −2.6316 | 6.925 |
| Mike Kiel | 50 | 42.6316 | 7.3684 | 54.293 |
| Mark Reynolds | 30 | 42.6316 | −12.6316 | 159.557 |
| Soni Jones | 70 | 54.4736 | 15.5264 | 241.069 |
|  |  |  | 0.0000 | 784.211 |

The standard error of estimate is 9.901, found by using formula (13–6).

$$s_{y \cdot x} = \sqrt{\frac{\Sigma(Y - Y')^2}{n - 2}} = \sqrt{\frac{784.211}{10 - 2}} = 9.901$$

The deviations $(Y - Y')$ are the vertical deviations from the regression line. To illustrate, the 10 deviations from Table 13–4 are shown in Chart 13–13. Note in Table 13–4 that the sum of the signed deviations is zero. This indicates that the positive deviations (above the regression line) are offset by the negative deviations (below the regression line).

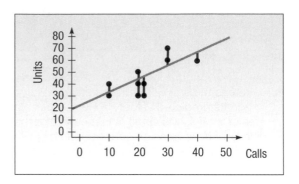

**CHART 13–13** Sales Calls and Copiers Sold for 10 Salespeople

Software eases computation when you are finding the least squares regression line, calculating fitted values, or finding the standard error. The Excel output from the Copier Sales of America example is included below. The slope and intercept are in the column "Coefficients" (cells G17 and G18). The fitted values for each sales representative are the column "Predicted Sales" (cells D2:D11). The "Residuals" or differences between the actual and the estimated values are in the next column (cells E2:E11). The standard error of estimate is in cell G7. All of these values are highlighted below.

| Microsoft Excel - Copier | | | | | | | |
|---|---|---|---|---|---|---|---|
| | A | B | C | D | E | F | G | H |
| 1 | Sales Representative | Calls | Sales | Predicted Sales | Residuals | | SUMMARY OUTPUT | |
| 2 | Tom Keller | 20 | 30 | 42.63158 | -12.631579 | | | |
| 3 | Jeff Hall | 40 | 60 | 66.31579 | -6.315789 | Regression Statistics | | |
| 4 | Brian Virost | 20 | 40 | 42.63158 | -2.631579 | Multiple R | 0.7590 | |
| 5 | Greg Fish | 30 | 60 | 54.47368 | 5.526316 | R Square | 0.5761 | |
| 6 | Susan Welch | 10 | 30 | 30.78947 | -0.789474 | Adjusted R Square | 0.5231 | |
| 7 | Carlos Ramirez | 10 | 40 | 30.78947 | 9.210526 | Standard Error | 9.9008 | |
| 8 | Rich Niles | 20 | 40 | 42.63158 | -2.631579 | Observations | 10.0000 | |
| 9 | Mike Keil | 20 | 50 | 42.63158 | 7.368421 | | | |
| 10 | Mark Reynolds | 20 | 30 | 42.63158 | -12.631579 | ANOVA | | |
| 11 | Soni Jones | 30 | 70 | 54.47368 | 15.526316 | | df | SS |
| 12 | | | | | | Regression | 1 | 1065.7 |
| 13 | | | | | | Residual | 8 | 784.21 |
| 14 | | | | | | Total | 9 | |
| 15 | | | | | | | | |
| 16 | | | | | | | Coefficients | Standard |
| 17 | | | | | | Intercept | 18.9474 | 8.4988 |
| 18 | | | | | | Calls | 1.1842 | 0.3591 |
| 19 | | | | | | | | |
| 20 | | | | | | | | |
| 21 | | | | | | | | |
| 22 | | | | | | | | |

Thus far we have presented linear regression only as a descriptive tool. In other words it is a simple summary ($Y' = a + bX$) of the relationship between the dependent $Y$ variable and the independent $X$ variable. When our data are a sample taken from a population, we are doing inferential statistics. Then we need to recall the distinction between population parameters and sample statistics. In this case, we "model" the linear relationship in the population by the equation:

$$Y = \alpha + \beta X$$

where:

$Y$ is any value of the dependent variable.
$\alpha$ is the $Y$-intercept (the value of $Y$ when $X = 0$) in the population.

**Statistics in Action**

Studies indicate that for both men and women, those who are considered good looking earn higher wages than those who are not. In addition, for men there is a correlation between height and salary. For each additional inch of height, a man can expect to earn an additional $250 per year. So a man 6'6" tall receives a $3,000 "stature" bonus over his 5'6" counterpart. Being overweight or underweight is also related to earnings, particularly among women. A study of young women showed the heaviest 10 percent earned about 6 percent less than their lighter counterparts.

$\beta$ is the slope (the amount by which $Y$ changes when $X$ increases by one unit) of the population line.

$X$ is any value of the independent variable.

Now $\alpha$ and $\beta$ are population parameters and $a$ and $b$, respectively, are estimates of those parameters. They are computed from a particular sample taken from the population. Fortunately, the formulas given earlier in the chapter for $a$ and $b$ do not change when we move from using regression as a descriptive tool to regression in statistical inference.

It should be noted that the linear regression equation for the sample of salespeople is only an estimate of the relationship between the two variables for the population. Thus, the values of $a$ and $b$ in the regression equation are usually referred to as the **estimated regression coefficients,** or simply the **regression coefficients.**

# Assumptions Underlying Linear Regression

To properly apply linear regression, several assumptions are necessary. Chart 13–14 illustrates these assumptions.

1. For each value of $X$, there is a group of $Y$ values. These $Y$ values follow the normal distribution.
2. The means of these normal distributions lie on the regression line.
3. The standard deviations of these normal distributions are all the same. The best estimate we have of this common standard deviation is the standard error of estimate ($s_{y \cdot x}$).
4. The $Y$ values are statistically independent. This means that in selecting a sample a particular $X$ does not depend on any other value of $X$. This assumption is particularly important when data are collected over a period of time. In such situations, the errors for a particular time period are often correlated with those of other time periods.

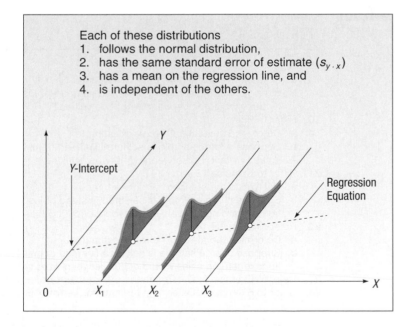

**CHART 13–14** Regression Assumptions Shown Graphically

Recall from Chapter 7 that if the values follow a normal distribution, then the mean plus or minus one standard deviation will encompass 68 percent of the observations, the mean plus or minus two standard deviations will encompass 95 percent of the observations, and the mean plus or minus three standard deviations will encompass virtually all of the observations. The same relationship exists between the predicted values $Y'$ and the standard error of estimate ($s_{y \cdot x}$).

1.  $Y' \pm s_{y \cdot x}$ will include the middle 68 percent of the observations.
2.  $Y' \pm 2s_{y \cdot x}$ will include the middle 95 percent of the observations.
3.  $Y' \pm 3s_{y \cdot x}$ will include virtually all the observations.

We can now relate these assumptions to Copier Sales of America, where we studied the relationship between the number of sales calls and the number of copiers sold. Assume that we took a much larger sample than $n = 10$, but that the standard error of estimate was still 9.901. If we drew a parallel line 9.901 units above the regression line and another 9.901 units below the regression line, about 68 percent of the points would fall between the two lines. Similarly, a line 19.802 [$2s_{y \cdot x} = 2(9.901)$] units above the regression line and another 19.802 units below the regression line should include about 95 percent of the data values.

As a rough check, refer to the second column from the right in Table 13–4 on page 447, i.e., the column headed "Deviation." Three of the 10 deviations exceed one standard error of estimate. That is, the deviation of $-12.6316$ for Tom Keller, $-12.6316$ for Mark Reynolds, and $+15.5264$ for Soni Jones all exceed the value of 9.901, which is one standard error from the regression line. All of the values are within 19.802 units of the regression line. To put it another way, 7 of the 10 deviations in the sample are within one standard error of the regression line and all are within two—a good result for a relatively small sample.

---

**Self-Review 13–4**

Refer to Self-Reviews 13–1 and 13–3, where the owner of Haverty's Furniture was studying the relationship between sales and the amount spent on advertising. Determine the standard error of estimate.

---

## Exercises

**19.** Refer to Exercise 11.
   **a.** Determine the standard error of estimate.
   **b.** Suppose a large sample is selected (instead of just five). About 68 percent of the predictions would be between what two values?
**20.** Refer to Exercise 12.
   **a.** Determine the standard error of estimate.
   **b.** Suppose a large sample is selected (instead of just eight). About 95 percent of the predictions would be between what two values?
**21.** Refer to Exercise 13.
   **a.** Determine the standard error of estimate.
   **b.** Suppose a large sample is selected (instead of just 10). About 95 percent of the predictions regarding kilowatt-hours would occur between what two values?
**22.** Refer to Exercise 14.
   **a.** Determine the standard error of estimate.
   **b.** Suppose a large sample is selected (instead of just 10). About 95 percent of the predictions regarding sales would occur between what two values?
**23.** Refer to Exercise 5. Determine the standard error of estimate.
**24.** Refer to Exercise 6. Determine the standard error of estimate.

# Confidence and Prediction Intervals

The standard error of estimate is also used to establish confidence intervals when the sample size is large and the scatter around the regression line approximates the normal distribution. In our example involving the number of sales calls and the number of copiers sold, the sample size is small; hence, we need a correction factor to account for the size of the sample. In addition, when we move away from the mean of the independent variable, our estimates are subject to more variation, and we also need to adjust for this.

We are interested in providing interval estimates of two types. The first, which is called a **confidence interval,** reports the *mean* value of Y for a given X. The second type of estimate is called a **prediction interval,** and it reports the *range of values* of Y for a *particular* value of X. To explain further, suppose we estimate the salary of executives in the retail industry based on their years of experience. If we want an interval estimate of the mean salary of *all* retail executives with 20 years of experience, we calculate a confidence interval. If we want an estimate of the salary of Curtis Bender, a particular retail executive with 20 years of experience, we calculate a prediction interval.

To determine the confidence interval for the mean value of Y for a given X, the formula is:

| | | |
|---|---|---|
| CONFIDENCE INTERVAL FOR THE MEAN OF Y, GIVEN X. | $$Y' \pm t(s_{y \cdot x}) \sqrt{\frac{1}{n} + \frac{(X - \bar{X})^2}{\Sigma(X - \bar{X})^2}}$$ | **[13–7]** |

where:

$Y'$ is the predicted value for any selected X value.
$X$ is any selected value of X.
$\bar{X}$ is the mean of the Xs, found by $\Sigma X/n$.
$n$ is the number of observations.
$s_{y \cdot x}$ is the standard error of estimate.
$t$ is the value of t from Appendix F with $n - 2$ degrees of freedom.

We first described the t distribution in Chapter 9. In review the concept of t was developed by William Gossett in the early 1900s. He noticed that $\bar{X} \pm z(s)$ was not precisely correct for small samples. He observed, for example, for degrees of freedom of 120, that 95 percent of the items fell within $\bar{X} \pm 1.98s$ instead of $\bar{X} \pm 1.96s$. This difference is not too critical, but note what happens as the sample size becomes smaller:

| df | t |
|---|---|
| 120 | 1.980 |
| 60 | 2.000 |
| 21 | 2.080 |
| 10 | 2.228 |
| 3 | 3.182 |

This is logical. The smaller the sample size, the larger the possible error. The increase in the t value compensates for this possibility.

**EXAMPLE**

We return to the Copier Sales of America illustration. Determine a 95 percent confidence interval for all sales representatives who make 25 calls and for Sheila Baker, a West Coast sales representative who made 25 calls.

**SOLUTION**

We use formula (13–7) to determine a confidence interval. Table 13–5 includes the necessary totals and a repeat of the information of Table 13–2 on page 433.

**TABLE 13–5** Calculations Needed for Determining the Confidence Interval and Prediction Interval

| Sales Representative | Sales Calls ($X$) | Copier Sales ($Y$) | $(X - \bar{X})$ | $(X - \bar{X})^2$ |
|---|---|---|---|---|
| Tom Keller | 20 | 30 | −2 | 4 |
| Jeff Hall | 40 | 60 | 18 | 324 |
| Brian Virost | 20 | 40 | −2 | 4 |
| Greg Fish | 30 | 60 | 8 | 64 |
| Susan Welch | 10 | 30 | −12 | 144 |
| Carlos Ramirez | 10 | 40 | −12 | 144 |
| Rich Niles | 20 | 40 | −2 | 4 |
| Mike Kiel | 20 | 50 | −2 | 4 |
| Mark Reynolds | 20 | 30 | −2 | 4 |
| Soni Jones | 30 | 70 | 8 | 64 |
| | | | 0 | 760 |

The first step is to determine the number of copiers we expect a sales representative to sell if he or she makes 25 calls. It is 48.5526, found by $Y' = 18.9476 + 1.1842X = 18.9476 + 1.1842(25)$.

To find the $t$ value, we need to first know the number of degrees of freedom. In this case the degrees of freedom is $n - 2 = 10 - 2 = 8$. We set the confidence level at 95 percent. To find the value of $t$, move down the left-hand column to 8 degrees of freedom, then move across to the column with the 95 percent level of confidence. The value of $t$ is 2.306.

In the previous section we calculated the standard error of estimate to be 9.901. We let $X = 25$, $\bar{X} = \Sigma X/n = 220/10 = 22$, and from Table 13–5 $\Sigma (X - \bar{X})^2 = 760$. Inserting these values in formula (13–7), we can determine the confidence interval.

$$\text{Confidence Interval} = Y' \pm ts_{y \cdot x} \sqrt{\frac{1}{n} + \frac{(X - \bar{X})^2}{\Sigma (X - \bar{X})^2}}$$

$$= 48.5526 \pm 2.306(9.901) \sqrt{\frac{1}{10} + \frac{(25 - 22)^2}{760}}$$

$$= 48.5526 \pm 7.6356$$

Thus, the 95 percent confidence interval for all sales representatives who make 25 calls is from 40.9170 up to 56.1882. To interpret, let's round the values. If a sales representative makes 25 calls, he or she can expect to sell 48.6 copiers. It is likely those sales will range from 40.9 to 56.2 copiers.

To determine the prediction interval for a particular value of $Y$ for a given $X$, formula (13–7) is modified slightly: A 1 is added under the radical. The formula becomes:

| PREDICTION INTERVAL FOR $Y$, GIVEN $X$ | $Y' \pm ts_{y \cdot x} \sqrt{1 + \dfrac{1}{n} + \dfrac{(X - \bar{X})^2}{\Sigma (X - \bar{X})^2}}$ | **[13–8]** |
|---|---|---|

Suppose we want to estimate the number of copiers sold by Sheila Baker, who made 25 sales calls. The 95 percent prediction interval is determined as follows:

$$\text{Prediction Interval} = Y' \pm t s_{y \cdot x} \sqrt{1 + \frac{1}{n} + \frac{(X - \bar{X})^2}{\Sigma(X - \bar{X})^2}}$$

$$= 48.5526 \pm 2.306(9.901)\sqrt{1 + \frac{1}{10} + \frac{(25 - 22)^2}{760}}$$

$$= 48.5526 \pm 24.0746$$

Thus, the interval is from 24.478 up to 72.627 copiers. We conclude that the number of copiers sold will be between about 24 and 73 for a particular sales representative. This interval is quite large. It is much larger than the confidence interval for all sales representatives who made 25 calls. It is logical, however, that there should be more variation in the sales estimate for an individual than for a group.

The following MINITAB graph shows the relationship between the regression line (in the center), the confidence interval (shown in crimson), and the prediction interval (shown in green). The bands for the prediction interval are always further from the regression line than for the confidence interval. Also, as the values of X move away from the mean number of calls (22) in either the positive or the negative direction the confidence interval and prediction interval bands widen. This is caused by the numerator of the right-hand term under the radical in formulas (13–7) and (13–8). That is, as the term $(X - \bar{X})^2$ increases, the widths of the confidence interval and the prediction interval also increase. To put it another way, there is less precision in our estimates as we move away, in either direction, from the mean of the independent variable.

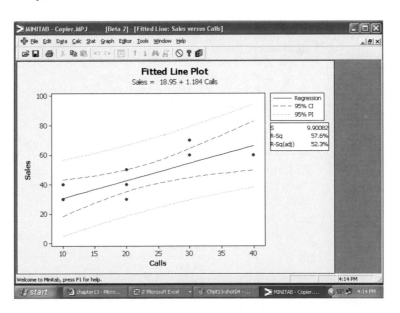

Confidence and Prediction Intervals for Copier Sales of America Data

We wish to emphasize again the distinction between a confidence interval and a prediction interval. A confidence interval refers to all cases with a given value of X and is computed by formula (13–7). A prediction interval refers to a particular case for a given value of X and is computed using formula (13–8). The prediction interval will always be wider because of the extra 1 under the radical in the second equation.

---

**Self-Review 13–5**

Refer to the sample data in Self-Reviews 13–1, 13–3, and 13–4, where the owner of Haverty's Furniture was studying the relationship between sales and the amount spent on advertising. The sales information for the last four months is repeated below.

| Month | Advertising Expense ($ million) | Sales Revenue ($ million) |
|---|---|---|
| July | 2 | 7 |
| August | 1 | 3 |
| September | 3 | 8 |
| October | 4 | 10 |

The regression equation was computed to be $Y' = 1.5 + 2.2X$, and the standard error is 0.9487. Both variables are reported in millions of dollars. Determine the 90 percent confidence interval for the typical month in which $3 million was spent on advertising.

---

# Exercises

25. Refer to Exercise 11.
    a. Determine the .95 confidence interval for the mean predicted when $X = 7$.
    b. Determine the .95 prediction interval for an individual predicted when $X = 7$.
26. Refer to Exercise 12.
    a. Determine the .95 confidence interval for the mean predicted when $X = 7$.
    b. Determine the .95 prediction interval for an individual predicted when $X = 7$.
27. Refer to Exercise 13.
    a. Determine the .95 confidence interval, in thousands of kilowatt-hours, for the mean of all six-room homes.
    b. Determine the .95 prediction interval, in thousands of kilowatt-hours, for a particular six-room home.
28. Refer to Exercise 14.
    a. Determine the .95 confidence interval, in thousands of dollars, for the mean of all sales personnel who make 40 contacts.
    b. Determine the .95 prediction interval, in thousands of dollars, for a particular salesperson who makes 40 contacts.

# More on the Coefficient of Determination

To further examine the basic concept of the coefficient of determination, suppose there is interest in the relationship between years on the job, $X$, and weekly production, $Y$. Sample data revealed:

| Employee | Years on Job, $X$ | Weekly Production, $Y$ |
|---|---|---|
| Gordon | 14 | 6 |
| James | 7 | 5 |
| Ford | 3 | 3 |
| Salter | 15 | 9 |
| Artes | 11 | 7 |

The sample data were plotted in a scatter diagram. Since the relationship between $X$ and $Y$ appears to be linear, a line was drawn through the plots (see Chart 13–15). The equation is $Y' = 2 + 0.4X$.

Note in Chart 13–15 that if we were to use that line to predict weekly production for an employee, in no case would our prediction be exact. That is, there would be some error in each of our predictions. As an example, for Gordon, who has been with the company 14 years, we would predict weekly production to be 7.6 units; however, he produces only 6 units.

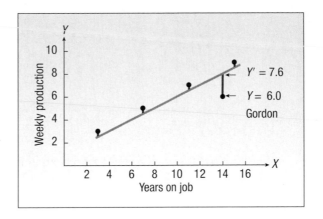

**CHART 13–15** Observed Data and the Least Squares Line

To measure the overall error in our prediction, every deviation from the line is squared and the squares summed. The predicted point on the line is designated $Y'$, read $Y$ prime, and the observed point is designated $Y$. For Gordon, $(Y - Y')^2 = (6 - 7.6)^2 = (-1.6)^2 = 2.56$. Logically, this variation cannot be explained by the independent variable, so it is referred to as the *unexplained variation*. Specifically, we cannot explain why Gordon's production of 6 units is 1.6 units below his predicted production of 7.6 units, based on the number of years he has been on the job.

The sum of the squared deviations, $\Sigma(Y - Y')^2$, is 4.00. (See Table 13–6.) The term $\Sigma(Y - Y')^2 = 4.00$ is the variation in $Y$ (production) that cannot be predicted from $X$. It is the "unexplained" variation in $Y$.

*Unexplained variation* (margin note)

**TABLE 13–6** Computations Needed for the Unexplained Variation

|        | $X$ | $Y$ | $Y'$ | $Y - Y'$ | $(Y - Y')^2$ |
|--------|-----|-----|------|----------|--------------|
| Gordon | 14  | 6   | 7.6  | −1.6     | 2.56         |
| James  | 7   | 5   | 4.8  | 0.2      | 0.04         |
| Ford   | 3   | 3   | 3.2  | −0.2     | 0.04         |
| Salter | 15  | 9   | 8.0  | 1.0      | 1.00         |
| Artes  | 11  | 7   | 6.4  | 0.6      | 0.36         |
| Total  | 50  | 30  |      | 0.0*     | 4.00         |

*Must be 0.

Now suppose *only* the $Y$ values (weekly production, in this problem) are known and we want to predict production for every employee. The actual production figures for the employees are 6, 5, 3, 9, and 7 (from Table 13–6). To make these predictions, we could assign the mean weekly production (6 units, found by $\Sigma Y/n = 30/5 = 6$) to each employee. This would keep the sum of the squared prediction errors at a minimum. (Recall from Chapter 3 that the sum of the squared deviations from the arithmetic mean for a set of numbers is smaller than the sum of the squared deviations from any other value, such as the median.) Table 13–7 shows the necessary calculations. The sum of the squared deviations is 20, as shown in Table 13–7. The value 20 is referred to as the *total variation in Y*.

*Total variation in Y* (margin note)

**TABLE 13–7** Calculations Needed for the Total Variation in Y

| Name | Weekly Production, $Y$ | Mean Weekly Production, $\bar{Y}$ | $Y - \bar{Y}$ | $(Y - \bar{Y})^2$ |
|------|------|------|------|------|
| Gordon | 6 | 6 | 0 | 0 |
| James | 5 | 6 | −1 | 1 |
| Ford | 3 | 6 | −3 | 9 |
| Salter | 9 | 6 | 3 | 9 |
| Artes | 7 | 6 | 1 | 1 |
| Total | | | 0* | 20 |

*Must be 0.

What we did to arrive at the total variation in $Y$ is shown diagrammatically in Chart 13–16.

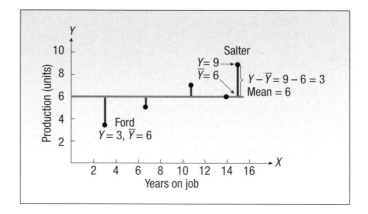

**CHART 13–16** Plots Showing Deviations from the Mean of Y

Logically, the total variation in $Y$ can be subdivided into unexplained variation and explained variation. To arrive at the explained variation, since we know the total variation and unexplained variation, we simply subtract: Explained variation = Total variation − Unexplained variation. Dividing the explained variation by the total variation gives the coefficient of determination, $r^2$, which is a proportion. In terms of a formula:

**COEFFICIENT OF DETERMINATION**

$$r^2 = \frac{\text{Total variation} - \text{Unexplained variation}}{\text{Total variation}}$$

$$= \frac{\Sigma(Y - \bar{Y})^2 - \Sigma(Y - Y')^2}{\Sigma(Y - \bar{Y})^2}$$

[13–9]

In this problem:

$$r^2 = \frac{20 - 4}{20} = \frac{16}{20}$$

Table 13–7
Table 13–6
Explained variation
Total variation

$$= .80$$

As mentioned, .80 is a proportion. We say that 80 percent of the variation in weekly production, $Y$, is determined, or accounted for, by its linear relationship with $X$ (years on the job).

As a check, formula (13–1) for the coefficient of correlation could be used. Squaring $r$ gives the coefficient of determination. Exercise 29 offers a check on the preceding problem.

## Exercises

**29.** Using the preceding problem, involving years on the job and weekly production, verify that the coefficient of determination is in fact .80.

**30.** The number of shares of Icom, Inc., turned over during a month, and the price at the end of the month, are listed in the following table. Also given are the $Y'$ values.

| Turnover (thousands of shares), $X$ | Actual Price, $Y$ | Estimated Price, $Y'$ |
|:---:|:---:|:---:|
| 4 | $2 | $2.7 |
| 1 | 1 | 0.6 |
| 5 | 4 | 3.4 |
| 3 | 2 | 2.0 |
| 2 | 1 | 1.3 |

    **a.** Draw a scatter diagram. Plot a line through the dots.
    **b.** Compute the coefficient of determination using formula (13–10).
    **c.** Interpret the coefficient of determination.

# The Relationships among the Coefficient of Correlation, the Coefficient of Determination, and the Standard Error of Estimate

In an earlier section, we discussed the standard error of estimate, which measures how close the actual values are to the regression line. When the standard error is small, it indicates that the two variables are closely related. In the calculation of the standard error, the key term is $\Sigma(Y - Y')^2$. If the value of this term is small, then the standard error will also be small.

The correlation coefficient measures the strength of the linear association between two variables. When the points on the scatter diagram appear close to the line, we note that the correlation coefficient tends to be large. Thus, the standard error of estimate and the coefficient of correlation relate the same information but use a different scale to report the strength of the association. However, both measures involve the term $\Sigma(Y - Y')^2$.

We also noted that the square of the correlation coefficient is the coefficient of determination. The coefficient of determination measures the percent of the variation in $Y$ that is explained by the variation in $X$.

A convenient vehicle for showing the relationship among these three measures is an ANOVA table. This table is similar to the analysis of variance table developed in Chapter 12. In that chapter, the total variation was divided into two components: that due to the *treatments* and that due to *random error*. The concept is similar in regression analysis. The total variation, $\Sigma(Y - \bar{Y})^2$, is divided into two components: (1) that explained by the *regression* (explained by the independent variable) and (2) the *error,* or unexplained variation. These two categories are identified in the first column of the ANOVA table that follows. The column headed "df" refers to the degrees of freedom associated with each category. The total number of degrees of freedom is $n - 1$. The number of degrees of freedom in the regression is 1, since there is only one independent variable. The number of degrees of freedom associated with the error term is $n - 2$. The term "SS" located in the middle of the ANOVA table refers to the sum of squares—the variation. The terms are computed as follows:

$$\text{Regression} = \text{SSR} = \Sigma(Y' - \bar{Y})^2$$

$$\text{Error variation} = \text{SSE} = \Sigma(Y - Y')^2$$

$$\text{Total variation} = \text{SS total} = \Sigma(Y - \bar{Y})^2$$

The format for the ANOVA table is:

| Source | df | SS | MS |
|--------|-----|--------|------------|
| Regression | 1 | SSR | SSR/1 |
| Error | $n - 2$ | SSE | SSE/($n - 2$) |
| Total | $n - 1$ | SS total* | |

*SS total = SSR + SSE.

The coefficient of determination, $r^2$, can be obtained directly from the ANOVA table by:

| COEFFICIENT OF DETERMINATION | $r^2 = \dfrac{\text{SSR}}{\text{SS total}} = 1 - \dfrac{\text{SSE}}{\text{SS total}}$ | [13–10] |
|---|---|---|

The term "SSR/SS total" is the proportion of the variation in $Y$ *explained* by the independent variable, $X$. Note the effect of the SSE term on $r^2$. As SSE decreases, $r^2$ will increase. Conversely, as the standard error decreases, the $r^2$ term increases.

The standard error of estimate can also be obtained from the ANOVA table using the following equation:

| STANDARD ERROR OF ESTIMATE | $s_{y \cdot x} = \sqrt{\dfrac{\text{SSE}}{n - 2}}$ | [13–11] |
|---|---|---|

The Copier Sales of America example is used to illustrate the computations of the coefficient of determination and the standard error of estimate from an ANOVA table.

**EXAMPLE**

In the Copier Sales of America example we studied the relationship between the number of sales calls made and the number of copiers sold. Use a computer software package to determine the least squares regression equation and the ANOVA table. Identify the regression equation, the standard error of estimate, and the coefficient of determination on the computer output. From the ANOVA table on the computer output, determine the coefficient of determination and the standard error of estimate using formulas (13–10) and (13–11).

**SOLUTION**

The output from Excel follows.

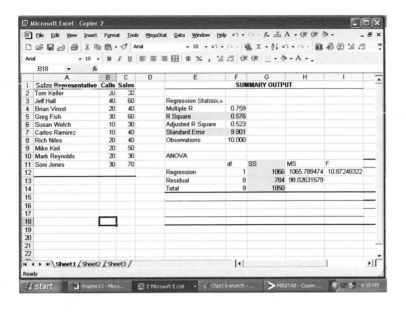

From formula (13–10) the coefficient of determination is .576, found by

$$r^2 = \frac{SSR}{SS\ total} = \frac{1,066}{1,850} = .576$$

This is the same value we computed earlier in the chapter, when we found the coefficient of determination by squaring the coefficient of correlation. Again, the interpretation is that the independent variable, *Calls,* explains 57.6 percent of the variation in the number of copiers sold. If we needed the coefficient of correlation, we could find it by taking the square root of the coefficient of determination:

$$r = \sqrt{r^2} = \sqrt{.576} = .759$$

A problem does remain, and that involves the sign for the coefficient of correlation. Recall that the square root of a value could have either a positive or a negative sign. The sign of the coefficient of correlation will always be the same as that of the slope. That is, *b* and *r* will always have the same sign. In this case the sign is positive, so the coefficient of correlation is .759.

To find the standard error of estimate, we use formula (13–11):

$$s_{y \cdot x} = \sqrt{\frac{SSE}{n - 2}} = \sqrt{\frac{784.2}{10 - 2}} = 9.901$$

Again, this is the same value calculated earlier in the chapter. These values are identified on the Excel computer output.

# Transforming Data

The coefficient of correlation describes the strength of the *linear* relationship between two variables. It could be that two variables are closely related, but this relationship is not linear. Be cautious when you are interpreting the coefficient of correlation. A value of *r* may indicate there is no linear relationship, but it could be there is a relationship of some other nonlinear or curvilinear form. To explain, below is a listing of 13 professional golfers, the amount they earned during the 2002 season, and their mean score per round. (In golf, the objective is to play 18 holes in the least number of strokes. So, the lower mean scores are related to the higher earnings.)

| Player | Earnings ($000) | Mean score |
|---|---|---|
| Tiger Woods | 6,912.6 | 68.56 |
| Phil Michelson | 4,312.0 | 69.58 |
| Fred Funk | 2,383.1 | 69.99 |
| Peter Lonard | 1,413.1 | 70.00 |
| Tim Herron | 954.9 | 70.68 |
| Paul Azinger | 769.9 | 71.54 |
| John Daly | 593.0 | 71.86 |
| Bob May | 407.8 | 71.16 |
| Hal Sutton | 320.0 | 71.95 |
| Jason Hill | 150.9 | 72.68 |
| Bradley Hughes | 85.4 | 71.50 |
| Gary Nicklaus | 42.0 | 72.81 |
| Jack Nicklaus | 8.9 | 74.83 |

For the above golf data the correlation between the variables, earnings and score, shows a fairly strong negative relationship. The correlation is −0.782, but when we use a scatter diagram to plot the data the relationship appears to be nonlinear. That is, the relationship does not follow a straight line.

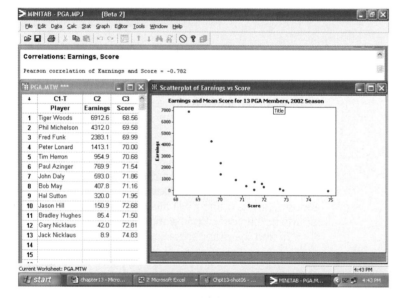

What can we do to explore other (nonlinear) relationships? One possibility is to transform one of the variables. For example, instead of using $X$ as the independent variable we might use its square as the independent variable. Another possibility is to transform the dependent variable.

In the golf-earnings example, changing the scale of the dependent variable is effective. We use MINITAB to determine the log of each golfer's earnings and then find the correlation between the log of earnings and score. The coefficient of correlation increases to −0.943, which means 88.9 percent of the variation in the log of earnings, is accounted for by the independent variable score. Clearly as the mean score increases for a golfer, he can expect his earnings to decrease.

There is no commonly accepted procedure to determine which variable to transform or what transformation to use. So experience and trial and error are your guides. The most common types of transformations are:

- Take the log of one of the variables.
- Square one of the variables.

- Take the square root of one of the variables.
- Take the reciprocal of one of the variables.

# Exercises

**31.** Given the following ANOVA table:

| SOURCE | DF | SS | MS | F |
|---|---|---|---|---|
| Regression | 1 | 1000.0 | 1000.00 | 26.00 |
| Error | 13 | 500.0 | 38.46 | |
| Total | 14 | 1500.0 | | |

 **a.** Determine the coefficient of determination.
 **b.** Assuming a direct relationship between the variables, what is the coefficient of correlation?
 **c.** Determine the standard error of estimate.
**32.** On the first statistics exam the coefficient of determination between the hours studied and the grade earned was 80 percent. The standard error of estimate was 10. There were 20 students in the class. Develop an ANOVA table.
**33.** Given the following sample observations, develop a scatter diagram. Compute the coefficient of correlation. Does the relationship between the variables appear to be linear? Try squaring the $X$-variable and then determine the correlation coefficient.

| $X$ | −8 | −16 | 12 | 2 | 18 |
|---|---|---|---|---|---|
| $Y$ | 58 | 247 | 153 | 3 | 341 |

**34.** According to basic economics as the demand for a product increases the price will decrease. Listed below is the number of units demanded and the price.

| Demand | Price |
|---|---|
| 2 | $120.0 |
| 5 | 90.0 |
| 8 | 80.0 |
| 12 | 70.0 |
| 16 | 50.0 |
| 21 | 45.0 |
| 27 | 31.0 |
| 35 | 30.0 |
| 45 | 25.0 |
| 60 | 21.0 |

**a.** Determine the correlation between price and demand. Plot the data in a scatter diagram. Does the relationship seem to be linear?

**b.** Transform the price to a log to the base 10. Plot the log of the price and the demand. Determine the correlation coefficient. Does this seem to improve the relationship between the variables?

# Chapter Outline

**I.** A scatter diagram is a graphic tool to portray the relationship between two variables.
   **A.** The dependent variable is scaled on the Y-axis and is the variable being estimated.
   **B.** The independent variable is scaled on the X-axis and is the variable used as the estimator.
**II.** The coefficient of correlation measures the strength of the linear association between two variables.
   **A.** Both variables must be at least the interval scale of measurement.
   **B.** The coefficient of correlation can range from −1.00 up to 1.00.
   **C.** If the correlation between two variables is 0, there is no association between them.
   **D.** A value of 1.00 indicates perfect positive correlation, and −1.00 perfect negative correlation.
   **E.** A positive sign means there is a direct relationship between the variables, and a negative sign means there is an inverse relationship.
   **F.** It is designated by the letter r and found by the following equation:

$$r = \frac{\Sigma(X - \bar{X})(Y - \bar{Y})}{(n - 1) s_x s_y}$$                    **[13–1]**

   **G.** The following equation is used to determine whether the correlation in the population is different from 0.

$$t = \frac{r\sqrt{n - 2}}{\sqrt{1 - r^2}}$$                    **[13–2]**

**III.** The coefficient of determination is the fraction of the variation in one variable that is explained by the variation in the other variable.
   **A.** It ranges from 0 to 1.0.
   **B.** It is the square of the coefficient of correlation.
**IV.** In regression analysis we estimate one variable based on another variable.
   **A.** The variable being estimated is the dependent variable.
   **B.** The variable used to make the estimate is the independent variable.
      **1.** The relationship between the variables must be linear.
      **2.** Both the independent and the dependent variables must be interval or ratio scale.
      **3.** The least squares criterion is used to determine the regression equation.
**V.** The least squares regression line is of the form $Y' = a + bX$.
   **A.** $Y'$ is the estimated value of Y for a selected value of X.
   **B.** a is the constant or intercept.
      **1.** It is the value of $Y'$ when $X = 0$.
      **2.** a is computed using the following equation.

$$a = \bar{Y} - b\bar{X}$$                    **[13–5]**

   **C.** b is the slope of the fitted line.
      **1.** It shows the amount of change in $Y'$ for a change of one unit in X.
      **2.** A positive value for b indicates a direct relationship between the two variables, and a negative value an inverse relationship.
      **3.** The sign of b and the sign of r, the coefficient of correlation, are always the same.
      **4.** b is computed using the following equation.

$$b = \frac{rs_y}{s_x}$$                    **[13–4]**

   **D.** X is the value of the independent variable.
**VI.** The standard error of estimate measures the variation around the regression line.
   **A.** It is in the same units as the dependent variable.
   **B.** It is based on squared deviations from the regression line.

**C.** Small values indicate that the points cluster closely about the regression line.

**D.** It is computed using the following formula.

$$s_{y \cdot x} = \sqrt{\frac{\Sigma(Y - Y')^2}{n - 2}}$$   **[13–6]**

**VII.** Inference about linear regression is based on the following assumptions.

**A.** For a given value of $X$, the values of $Y$ are normally distributed about the line of regression.

**B.** The standard deviation of each of the normal distributions is the same for all values of $X$ and is estimated by the standard error of estimate.

**C.** The deviations from the regression line are independent, with no pattern to the size or direction.

**VIII.** There are two types of interval estimates.

**A.** In a confidence interval the mean value of $Y$ is estimated for a given value of $X$.

**1.** It is computed from the following formula.

$$Y' \pm ts_{y \cdot x} \sqrt{\frac{1}{n} + \frac{(X - \bar{X})^2}{\Sigma(X - \bar{X})^2}}$$   **[13–7]**

**2.** The width of the interval is affected by the level of confidence, the size of the standard error of estimate, and the size of the sample, as well as the value of the independent variable.

**B.** In a prediction interval the individual value of $Y$ is estimated for a given value of $X$.

**1.** It is computed from the following formula.

$$Y' \pm ts_{y \cdot x} \sqrt{1 + \frac{1}{n} + \frac{(X - \bar{X})^2}{\Sigma(X - \bar{X})^2}}$$   **[13–8]**

**2.** The difference between formulas (13–7) and (13–8) is the 1 under the radical.

**a.** The prediction interval will be wider than the confidence interval.

**b.** The prediction interval is also based on the level of confidence, the size of the standard error of estimate, the size of the sample, and the value of the independent variable.

# Pronunciation Key

| SYMBOL | MEANING | PRONUNCIATION |
|---|---|---|
| $\Sigma XY$ | Sum of the products of $X$ and $Y$ | Sum X Y |
| $\rho$ | Coefficient of correlation in the population | Rho |
| $Y'$ | Estimated value of $Y$ | Y prime |
| $s_{y \cdot x}$ | Standard error of estimate | s sub y dot x |
| $r^2$ | Coefficient of determination | r square |

# Chapter Exercises

**35.** A regional commuter airline selected a random sample of 25 flights and found that the correlation between the number of passengers and the total weight, in pounds, of luggage stored in the luggage compartment is 0.94. Using the .05 significance level, can we conclude that there is a positive association between the two variables?

**36.** A sociologist claims that the success of students in college (measured by their GPA) is related to their family's income. For a sample of 20 students, the coefficient of correlation is 0.40. Using the 0.01 significance level, can we conclude that there is a positive correlation between the variables?

**37.** An Environmental Protection Agency study of 12 automobiles revealed a correlation of 0.47 between the engine size and emissions. At the .01 significance level, can we conclude that there is a positive association between these variables? What is the *p*-value? Interpret.

**38.** A study of college soccer games revealed the correlation between the number of shots attempted and the number of goals scored to be 0.21 for a sample of 20 games. Is it reasonable to conclude that there is a positive correlation between the two variables? Use the .05 significance level. Determine the *p*-value.

39. A sample of 30 used cars sold by Northcut Motors in 2003 revealed the correlation between the selling price and the number of miles driven was −.45. At the .05 significance level, can we conclude that there is a negative association in the population between the two variables?

40. For a sample of 32 large U.S. cities, the correlation between the mean number of square feet per office worker and the mean monthly rental rate in the central business district is −.363. At the .05 significance level, can we conclude that there is a negative association in the population between the two variables?

41. What is the relationship between the amount spent per week on food and the size of the family? Do larger families spend more on food? A sample of 10 families in the Chicago area revealed the following figures for family size and the amount spent on food per week.

| Family Size | Amount Spent on Food | Family Size | Amount Spent on Food |
|---|---|---|---|
| 3 | $ 99 | 3 | $111 |
| 6 | 104 | 4 | 74 |
| 5 | 151 | 4 | 91 |
| 6 | 129 | 5 | 119 |
| 6 | 142 | 3 | 91 |

a. Compute the coefficient of correlation.
b. Determine the coefficient of determination.
c. Can we conclude that there is a positive association between the amount spent on food and the family size? Use the .05 significance level.

42. A sample of 12 homes sold last week in St. Paul, Minnesota, is selected. Can we conclude that as the size of the home (reported below in thousands of square feet) increases, the selling price (reported in $ thousands) also increases?

| Home Size (thousands of square feet) | Selling Price ($ thousands) | Home Size (thousands of square feet) | Selling Price ($ thousands) |
|---|---|---|---|
| 1.4 | 100 | 1.3 | 110 |
| 1.3 | 110 | 0.8 | 85 |
| 1.2 | 105 | 1.2 | 105 |
| 1.1 | 120 | 0.9 | 75 |
| 1.4 | 80 | 1.1 | 70 |
| 1.0 | 105 | 1.1 | 95 |

a. Compute the coefficient of correlation.
b. Determine the coefficient of determination.
c. Can we conclude that there is a positive association between the size of the home and the selling price? Use the .05 significance level.

43. The manufacturer of Cardio Glide exercise equipment wants to study the relationship between the number of months since the glide was purchased and the length of time the equipment was used last week.

| Person | Months Owned | Hours Exercised | Person | Months Owned | Hours Exercised |
|---|---|---|---|---|---|
| Rupple | 12 | 4 | Massa | 2 | 8 |
| Hall | 2 | 10 | Sass | 8 | 3 |
| Bennett | 6 | 8 | Karl | 4 | 8 |
| Longnecker | 9 | 5 | Malrooney | 10 | 2 |
| Phillips | 7 | 5 | Veights | 5 | 5 |

**a.** Plot the information on a scatter diagram. Let hours of exercise be the dependent variable. Comment on the graph.

**b.** Determine the coefficient of correlation. Interpret.

**c.** At the .01 significance level, can we conclude that there is a negative association between the variables?

**44.** The following regression equation was computed from a sample of 20 observations:

$$Y' = 15 - 5X$$

SSE was found to be 100 and SS total 400.

**a.** Determine the standard error of estimate.

**b.** Determine the coefficient of determination.

**c.** Determine the coefficient of correlation. (Caution: Watch the sign!)

**45.** An ANOVA table is:

| SOURCE | DF | SS | MS | F |
|--------|----|----|----|----|
| Regression | 1 | 50 | | |
| Error | | | | |
| Total | 24 | 500 | | |

**a.** Complete the ANOVA table.

**b.** How large was the sample?

**c.** Determine the standard error of estimate.

**d.** Determine the coefficient of determination.

**46.** Following is a regression equation.

$$Y' = 17.08 + 0.16X$$

This information is also available: $s_{y \cdot x} = 4.05$, $\Sigma(X - \bar{X})^2 = 1030$, and $n = 5$.

**a.** Estimate the value of $Y'$ when $X = 50$.

**b.** Develop a 95 percent prediction interval for an individual value of $Y$ for $X = 50$.

**47.** The National Highway Association is studying the relationship between the number of bidders on a highway project and the winning (lowest) bid for the project. Of particular interest is whether the number of bidders increases or decreases the amount of the winning bid.

| Project | Number of Bidders, X | Winning Bid ($ millions), Y | Project | Number of Bidders, X | Winning Bid ($ millions), Y |
|---------|---------------------|----------------------------|---------|---------------------|----------------------------|
| 1 | 9 | 5.1 | 9 | 6 | 10.3 |
| 2 | 9 | 8.0 | 10 | 6 | 8.0 |
| 3 | 3 | 9.7 | 11 | 4 | 8.8 |
| 4 | 10 | 7.8 | 12 | 7 | 9.4 |
| 5 | 5 | 7.7 | 13 | 7 | 8.6 |
| 6 | 10 | 5.5 | 14 | 7 | 8.1 |
| 7 | 7 | 8.3 | 15 | 6 | 7.8 |
| 8 | 11 | 5.5 | | | |

**a.** Determine the regression equation. Interpret the equation. Do more bidders tend to increase or decrease the amount of the winning bid?

**b.** Estimate the amount of the winning bid if there were seven bidders.

**c.** A new entrance is to be constructed on the Ohio Turnpike. There are seven bidders on the project. Develop a 95 percent prediction interval for the winning bid.

**d.** Determine the coefficient of determination. Interpret its value.

**48.** Mr. William Profit is studying companies going public for the first time. He is particularly interested in the relationship between the size of the offering and the price per share. A sample of 15 companies that recently went public revealed the following information.

| Company | Size ($ millions), X | Price per Share, Y | Company | Size ($ millions), X | Price per Share, Y |
|---|---|---|---|---|---|
| 1 | 9.0 | 10.8 | 9 | 160.7 | 11.3 |
| 2 | 94.4 | 11.3 | 10 | 96.5 | 10.6 |
| 3 | 27.3 | 11.2 | 11 | 83.0 | 10.5 |
| 4 | 179.2 | 11.1 | 12 | 23.5 | 10.3 |
| 5 | 71.9 | 11.1 | 13 | 58.7 | 10.7 |
| 6 | 97.9 | 11.2 | 14 | 93.8 | 11.0 |
| 7 | 93.5 | 11.0 | 15 | 34.4 | 10.8 |
| 8 | 70.0 | 10.7 | | | |

  **a.** Determine the regression equation.
  **b.** Determine the coefficient of determination. Do you think Mr. Profit should be satisfied with using the size of the offering as the independent variable?

**49.** The Bardi Trucking Co., located in Cleveland, Ohio, makes deliveries in the Great Lakes region, the Southeast, and the Northeast. Jim Bardi, the president, is studying the relationship between the distance a shipment must travel and the length of time, in days, it takes the shipment to arrive at its destination. To investigate, Mr. Bardi selected a random sample of 20 shipments made last month. Shipping distance is the independent variable, and shipping time is the dependent variable. The results are as follows:

| Shipment | Distance (miles) | Shipping Time (days) | Shipment | Distance (miles) | Shipping Time (days) |
|---|---|---|---|---|---|
| 1 | 656 | 5 | 11 | 862 | 7 |
| 2 | 853 | 14 | 12 | 679 | 5 |
| 3 | 646 | 6 | 13 | 835 | 13 |
| 4 | 783 | 11 | 14 | 607 | 3 |
| 5 | 610 | 8 | 15 | 665 | 8 |
| 6 | 841 | 10 | 16 | 647 | 7 |
| 7 | 785 | 9 | 17 | 685 | 10 |
| 8 | 639 | 9 | 18 | 720 | 8 |
| 9 | 762 | 10 | 19 | 652 | 6 |
| 10 | 762 | 9 | 20 | 828 | 10 |

  **a.** Draw a scatter diagram. Based on these data, does it appear that there is a relationship between how many miles a shipment has to go and the time it takes to arrive at its destination?
  **b.** Determine the coefficient of correlation. Can we conclude that there is a positive correlation between distance and time? Use the .05 significance level.
  **c.** Determine and interpret the coefficient of determination.
  **d.** Determine the standard error of estimate.

**50.** Super Markets, Inc. is considering expanding into the Scottsdale, Arizona, area. Ms. Luann Miller, Director of Planning, must present an analysis of the proposed expansion to the operating committee of the board of directors. As a part of her proposal, she needs to include information on the amount people in the region spend per month for grocery items. She would also like to include information on the relationship between the amount spent for grocery items and income. She gathered the following sample information.

| Household | Monthly Amount | Monthly Income | Household | Monthly Amount | Monthly Income |
|---|---|---|---|---|---|
| 1 | $555 | $4,388 | 21 | $ 913 | $6,688 |
| 2 | 489 | 4,558 | 22 | 918 | 6,752 |
| 3 | 458 | 4,793 | 23 | 710 | 6,837 |
| 4 | 613 | 4,856 | 24 | 1,083 | 7,242 |
| 5 | 647 | 4,856 | 25 | 937 | 7,263 |
| 6 | 661 | 4,899 | 26 | 839 | 7,540 |
| 7 | 662 | 4,899 | 27 | 1,030 | 8,009 |
| 8 | 675 | 5,091 | 28 | 1,065 | 8,094 |
| 9 | 549 | 5,133 | 29 | 1,069 | 8,264 |
| 10 | 606 | 5,304 | 30 | 1,064 | 8,392 |
| 11 | 668 | 5,304 | 31 | 1,015 | 8,414 |
| 12 | 740 | 5,304 | 32 | 1,148 | 8,882 |
| 13 | 592 | 5,346 | 33 | 1,125 | 8,925 |
| 14 | 720 | 5,495 | 34 | 1,090 | 8,989 |
| 15 | 680 | 5,581 | 35 | 1,208 | 9,053 |
| 16 | 540 | 5,730 | 36 | 1,217 | 9,138 |
| 17 | 693 | 5,943 | 37 | 1,140 | 9,329 |
| 18 | 541 | 5,943 | 38 | 1,265 | 9,649 |
| 19 | 673 | 6,156 | 39 | 1,206 | 9,862 |
| 20 | 676 | 6,603 | 40 | 1,145 | 9,883 |

a. Let the amount spent be the dependent variable and monthly income the independent variable. Create a scatter diagram, using a software package.

b. Determine the regression equation. Interpret the slope value.

c. Determine the coefficient of correlation. Can you conclude that it is greater than 0?

**51.** Below is information on the price per share and the dividend for a sample of 30 companies.

| Company | Price per Share | Dividend | Company | Price per Share | Dividend |
|---|---|---|---|---|---|
| 1 | $20.00 | $ 3.14 | 16 | $57.06 | $ 9.53 |
| 2 | 22.01 | 3.36 | 17 | 57.40 | 12.60 |
| 3 | 31.39 | 0.46 | 18 | 58.30 | 10.43 |
| 4 | 33.57 | 7.99 | 19 | 59.51 | 7.97 |
| 5 | 35.86 | 0.77 | 20 | 60.60 | 9.19 |
| 6 | 36.12 | 8.46 | 21 | 64.01 | 16.50 |
| 7 | 36.16 | 7.62 | 22 | 64.66 | 16.10 |
| 8 | 37.99 | 8.03 | 23 | 64.74 | 13.76 |
| 9 | 38.85 | 6.33 | 24 | 64.95 | 10.54 |
| 10 | 39.65 | 7.96 | 25 | 66.43 | 21.15 |
| 11 | 43.44 | 8.95 | 26 | 68.18 | 14.30 |
| 12 | 49.08 | 9.61 | 27 | 69.56 | 24.42 |
| 13 | 53.73 | 11.11 | 28 | 74.90 | 11.54 |
| 14 | 54.41 | 13.28 | 29 | 77.91 | 17.65 |
| 15 | 55.10 | 10.22 | 30 | 80.00 | 17.36 |

a. Calculate the regression equation using selling price based on the annual dividend. Interpret the slope value.

b. Determine the coefficient of determination. Interpret its value.

c. Determine the coefficient of correlation. Can you conclude that it is greater than 0 using the .05 significance level?

**52.** A highway employee performed a regression analysis of the relationship between the number of construction work-zone fatalities and the number of unemployed people in a state. The regression equation is Fatalities $= 12.7 + 0.000114$ (Unemp). Some additional output is:

```
Predictor              Coef        SE Coef         T        P
Constant             12.726          8.115      1.57    0.134
Unemp            0.00011386     0.00002896      3.93    0.001

Analysis of Variance
Source              DF        SS         MS        F        P
Regression           1     10354      10354    15.46    0.001
Residual Error      18     12054        670
Total               19     22408
```

a. How many states were in the sample?
b. Determine the standard error of estimate.
c. Determine the coefficient of determination.
d. Determine the coefficient of correlation.
e. At the .05 significance level does the evidence suggest there is a positive association between fatalities and the number unemployed?

53. Regression analysis relating the current market value in dollars to the size in square feet of homes in Greene County has been developed. The computer output follows. The regression equation is: Value = −37,186 + 65.0 Size.

```
Predictor        Coef     SE Coef         T          P
Constant       -37186        4629     -8.03      0.000
Size           64.993       3.047     21.33      0.000

Analysis of Variance
Source              DF              SS                MS          F         P
Regression           1     13548662082       13548662082     454.98     0.000
Residual Error      33       982687392          29778406
Total               34     14531349474
```

a. How many homes were in the sample?
b. Compute the standard error of estimate.
c. Compute the coefficient of determination.
d. Compute the coefficient of correlation.
e. At the .05 significance level does the evidence suggest a positive association between the market value of homes and the size of the home in square feet?

54. The following table shows the mean annual percent return on capital (profitability) and the mean annual percentage sales growth for eight aerospace and defense companies.

| Company | Profitability | Growth |
|---|---|---|
| Alliant Techsystems | 23.1 | 8.0 |
| Boeing | 13.2 | 15.6 |
| General Dynamics | 24.2 | 31.2 |
| Honeywell | 11.1 | 2.5 |
| L-3 Communications | 10.1 | 35.4 |
| Northrop Grunmman | 10.8 | 6.0 |
| Rockwell Collins | 27.3 | 8.7 |
| United Technologies | 20.1 | 3.2 |

a. Compute the coefficient of correlation. Conduct a test of hypothesis to determine if it is reasonable to conclude that the population correlation is greater than zero. Use the .05 significance level.
b. Develop the regression equation for profitability based on growth. Comment on the slope value.
c. Use a software package to determine the residual for each observation. Which company has the largest residual?

55. The following data shows the retail price for 12 randomly selected laptop computers along with their corresponding processor speeds.

| Computers | Speed | Price |
|-----------|-------|-------|
| 1 | 2.0 | $2,689 |
| 2 | 1.6 | 1,229 |
| 3 | 1.6 | 1,419 |
| 4 | 1.8 | 2,589 |
| 5 | 2.0 | 2,849 |
| 6 | 1.2 | 1,349 |
| 7 | 2.0 | 2,929 |
| 8 | 1.6 | 1,849 |
| 9 | 2.0 | 2,819 |
| 10 | 1.6 | 2,669 |
| 11 | 1.0 | 1,249 |
| 12 | 1.4 | 1,159 |

   **a.** Develop a linear equation that can be used to describe how the price depends on the processor speed.

   **b.** Based on your regression equation, is there one machine that seems particularly over- or underpriced?

   **c.** Compute the correlation coefficient between the two variables. At the .05 significance level conduct a test of hypothesis to determine if the population correlation could be greater than zero.

**56.** A consumer buying cooperative tested the effective heating area of 20 different electric space heaters with different wattages. Here are the results.

| Heater | Wattage | Area |
|--------|---------|------|
| 1 | 1,500 | 205 |
| 2 | 750 | 70 |
| 3 | 1,500 | 199 |
| 4 | 1,250 | 151 |
| 5 | 1,250 | 181 |
| 6 | 1,250 | 217 |
| 7 | 1,000 | 94 |
| 8 | 2,000 | 298 |
| 9 | 1,000 | 135 |
| 10 | 1,500 | 211 |
| 11 | 1,250 | 116 |
| 12 | 500 | 72 |
| 13 | 500 | 82 |
| 14 | 1,500 | 206 |
| 15 | 2,000 | 245 |
| 16 | 1,500 | 219 |
| 17 | 750 | 63 |
| 18 | 1,500 | 200 |
| 19 | 1,250 | 151 |
| 20 | 500 | 44 |

   **a.** Compute the correlation between the wattage and heating area. Is there a direct or an indirect relationship?

   **b.** Conduct a test of hypothesis to determine if it is reasonable that the coefficient is greater than zero. Use the .05 significance level.

   **c.** Develop the regression equation for effective heating based on wattage.

   **d.** Which heater looks like the "best buy" based on the size of the residual?

**57.** A dog trainer is exploring the relationship between the size of the dog (weight) and its daily food consumption (measured in standard cups). Below is the result of a sample of 18 observations.

| Dog | Weight | Consumption |
|-----|--------|-------------|
| 1 | 41 | 3 |
| 2 | 148 | 8 |
| 3 | 79 | 5 |
| 4 | 41 | 4 |
| 5 | 85 | 5 |
| 6 | 111 | 6 |
| 7 | 37 | 3 |
| 8 | 111 | 6 |
| 9 | 41 | 3 |
| 10 | 91 | 5 |
| 11 | 109 | 6 |
| 12 | 207 | 10 |
| 13 | 49 | 3 |
| 14 | 113 | 6 |
| 15 | 84 | 5 |
| 16 | 95 | 5 |
| 17 | 57 | 4 |
| 18 | 168 | 9 |

   **a.** Compute the correlation coefficient. Is it reasonable to conclude that the correlation in the population is greater than zero? Use the .05 significance level.

   **b.** Develop the regression equation for cups based on the dog's weight. How much does each additional cup change the estimated weight of the dog?

   **c.** Is one of the dogs a big undereater or overeater?

# exercises.com

**58.** Suppose you want to study the association between the literacy rate in a country, the population, and the country's gross domestic product (GDP). Go to the website of *Information Please Almanac* (http://www.infoplease.com). Select the category **World,** and then select **Countries.** A list of 195 countries starting with Afghanistan and ending with Zimbabwe will appear. Randomly select a sample of about 20 countries. It may be convenient to use a systematic sample. In other words, randomly select 1 of the first 10 countries and then select every tenth country thereafter. Click on each country name and scan the information to find the literacy rate, the population, and the GDP. Compute the correlation among the variables. In other words, find the correlation between: literacy and population, literacy and GDP, and population and GDP. *Warning:* Be careful of the units. Sometimes population is reported in millions, other times in thousands. At the .05 significance level, can we conclude that the correlation is different from zero for each pair of variables?

**59.** Many real estate companies and rental agencies now publish their listings on the Web. One example is the Dunes Realty Company, located in Garden City and Surfside Beaches in South Carolina. Go to the Web site http://www.dunes.com and select **Cottages Search.** Then indicate 5 bedroom, accommodations for 14 people, second row (this means it is across the street from the beach), and no pool or floating dock; select a period in July or August; indicate that you are willing to spend $5,000 per week; and then click on **Search the Cottages.** The output should include details on the cottages that met your criteria.

   **a.** Determine the correlation between the number of baths in each cottage and the weekly rental price. Can you conclude that the correlation is greater than zero at the .05 significance level? Determine the coefficient of determination.

   **b.** Determine the regression equation using the number of bathrooms as the independent variable and the price per week as the dependent variable. Interpret the regression equation.

   **c.** Calculate the correlation between the number of people the cottage will accommodate and the weekly rental price. At the .05 significance level can you conclude that it is different from zero?

# Dataset Exercises

**60.** Refer to the Real Estate data, which reports information on homes sold in Denver, Colorado, last year.

   **a.** Let selling price be the dependent variable and size of the home the independent variable. Determine the regression equation. Estimate the selling price for a home with an area of 2,200 square feet. Determine the 95 percent confidence interval and the 95 percent prediction interval for the selling price of a home with 2,200 square feet.

   **b.** Let selling price be the dependent variable and distance from the center of the city the independent variable. Determine the regression equation. Estimate the selling price of a home 20 miles from the center of the city. Determine the 95 percent confidence interval and the 95 percent prediction interval for homes 20 miles from the center of the city.

   **c.** Can you conclude that the independent variables "distance from the center of the city" and "selling price" are negatively correlated and that the area of the home and the selling price are positively correlated? Use the .05 significance level. Report the *p*-value of the test.

**61.** Refer to the Baseball 2002 data, which reports information on the 2002 Major League Baseball season.

   **a.** Let the games won be the dependent variable and total team salary, in millions of dollars, be the independent variable. Can you conclude that there is a positive association between the two variables? Determine the regression equation. Interpret the slope, that is the value of *b*. How many additional wins will an additional $5 million in salary bring?

   **b.** Determine the correlation between games won and ERA and between games won and team batting average. Which has the stronger correlation? Can we conclude that there is a positive correlation between wins and team batting and a negative correlation between wins and ERA? Use the .05 significance level.

   **c.** Assume the number of games won is the dependent variable and attendance the independent variable. Can we conclude that the correlation between these two variables is greater than 0? Use the .05 significance level.

**62.** Refer to the Wage data, which reports information on annual wages for a sample of 100 workers. Also included are variables relating to industry, years of education, and gender for each worker.

   **a.** Determine the correlation between the annual wage and the years of education. At the .05 significance level can we conclude there is a positive correlation between the two variables?

   **b.** Determine the correlation between the annual wage and the years of work experience. At the .05 significance level can we conclude there is a positive correlation between the two variables?

**63.** Refer to the CIA data, which reports demographic and economic information on 46 countries.

   **a.** You wish to use the Labor force variable as the independent variable to predict the unemployment rate. Interpret the slope value. Use the appropriate linear regression equation to predict unemployment in the United Arab Emirates.

   **b.** Find the correlation coefficient between the levels of exports and imports. Use the .05 significance level to test whether there is a positive correlation between these two variables.

   **c.** Does there appear to be a relationship between the percentage of the population over 65 and the literacy percentage? Support your answer with statistical evidence. Conduct an appropriate test of hypothesis and interpret the result.

# Software Commands

1. The MINITAB commands for the output showing the coefficient of correlation on page 439 are:
   a. Enter the sales representative's name in C1, the number of calls in C2, and the sales in C3.
   b. Select **Stat, Basic Statistics,** and **Correlation.**
   c. Select *Calls* and *Sales* as the variables, click on **Display p-values,** and then click **OK.**

2. The computer commands for the Excel output on page 448 are:
   a. Enter the variable names in row 1 of columns A, B, and C. Enter the data in rows 2 through 11 in the same columns.
   b. Select **Tools, Data Analysis,** and then select **Regression.**
   c. For our spreadsheet we have *Calls* in column B and *Sales* in column C. The **Input Y-Range** is *C1:C11* and the **Input X-Range** is *B1:B11,* click on **Labels,** select *D1* as the **Output Range,** and click **OK.**

3. The MINITAB commands to the confidence intervals and prediction intervals on page 453 are:
   a. Select **Stat, Regression,** and **Fitted line plot.**
   b. In the next dialog box the **Response (Y)** is Sales and **Predictor (X)** is Calls. Select **Linear** for the type of regression model and then click on **Options.**
   c. In the **Options** dialog box click on **Display confidence and prediction bands,** use the **95.0 for confidence level,** and then in the **Title** box type an appropriate heading, then click **OK** and then **OK** again.

# Chapter 13 Answers to Self-Review

**13–1 a.** Advertising expense is the independent variable and sales revenue is the dependent variable.

**b.**

**c.**

| X | Y | $(X - \bar{X})$ | $(X - \bar{X})^2$ | $(Y - \bar{Y})$ | $(Y - \bar{Y})^2$ | $(X - \bar{X})(Y - \bar{Y})$ |
|---|---|---|---|---|---|---|
| 2 | 7 | −0.5 | .25 | 0 | 0 | 0 |
| 1 | 3 | −1.5 | 2.25 | −4 | 16 | 6 |
| 3 | 8 | 0.5 | .25 | 1 | 1 | 0.5 |
| 4 | 10 | 1.5 | 2.25 | 3 | 9 | 4.5 |
| 10 | 28 | | 5.00 | | 26 | 11 |

$$\bar{X} = \frac{10}{4} = 2.5 \qquad \bar{Y} = \frac{28}{4} = 7$$

$$s_x = \sqrt{\frac{5}{3}} = 1.2909944$$

$$s_y = \sqrt{\frac{26}{3}} = 2.9439203$$

$$r = \frac{\Sigma(X - \bar{X})(Y - \bar{Y})}{(n - 1)\, s_x s_y} = \frac{11}{(4 - 1)(1.2909944)(2.9439203)}$$

$$= 0.9648$$

**d.** There is a strong correlation between the advertising expense and sales.

**e.** $r^2 = .93$, 93% of the variation in sales is "explained" by variation in advertising.

**13–2** $H_0: \rho \le 0,\ H_1: \rho > 0.$ $H_0$ is rejected if $t > 1.714$.

$$t = \frac{.43\sqrt{25 - 2}}{\sqrt{1 - (.43)^2}} = 2.284$$

$H_0$ is rejected. There is a positive correlation between the percent of the vote received and the amount spent on the campaign.

**13–3 a.** See the calculations in Self-Review 13–1, part (c).

$$b = \frac{rs_y}{s_x} = \frac{(0.9648)(2.9439)}{1.2910} = 2.2$$

$$a = \frac{28}{4} - 2.2\left(\frac{10}{4}\right) = 7 - 5.5 = 1.5$$

**b.** The slope is 2.2. This indicates that an increase of $1 million in advertising will result in an increase of $2.2 million in sales. The intercept is 1.5. If there was no expenditure for advertising, sales would be $1.5 million.

**c.** $Y' = 1.5 + 2.2(3) = 8.1$

**13–4** 0.9487, found by:

| Y | Y′ | $(Y - Y')$ | $(Y - Y')^2$ |
|---|---|---|---|
| 7 | 5.9 | 1.1 | 1.21 |
| 3 | 3.7 | −0.7 | .49 |
| 8 | 8.1 | −0.1 | .01 |
| 10 | 10.3 | −0.3 | .09 |
| | | | 1.80 |

$$s_{y \cdot x} = \sqrt{\frac{\Sigma(Y - Y')^2}{n - 2}}$$

$$= \sqrt{\frac{1.80}{4 - 2}} = .9487$$

**13–5** 6.58 and 9.62, since $Y'$ for an $X$ of 3 is 8.1, found by $Y' = 1.5 + 2.2(3) = 8.1$, then $\bar{X} = 2.5$ and $\Sigma(X - \bar{X})^2 = 5$.

$t$ from Appendix F for $4 - 2 = 2$ degrees of freedom at the .10 level is 2.920.

$$Y' \pm t(s_{y \cdot x}) \sqrt{\frac{1}{n} + \frac{(X - \bar{X})^2}{\Sigma(X - \bar{X})^2}}$$

$$= 8.1 \pm 2.920(0.9487) \sqrt{\frac{1}{4} + \frac{(3 - 2.5)^2}{5}}$$

$$= 8.1 \pm 2.920(0.9487)(0.5477)$$

$$= 6.58 \text{ and } 9.62 \text{ (in \$ millions)}$$

# 14

# Multiple Regression and Correlation Analysis

## GOALS

*When you have completed this chapter, you will be able to:*

1 Describe the relationship between several independent variables and a dependent variable using a multiple regression equation.

2 Compute and interpret the multiple standard error of estimate and the coefficient of determination.

3 Interpret a correlation matrix.

4 Set up and interpret an ANOVA table.

5 Conduct a test of hypothesis to determine whether regression coefficients differ from zero.

6 Conduct a test of hypothesis on each of the regression coefficients.

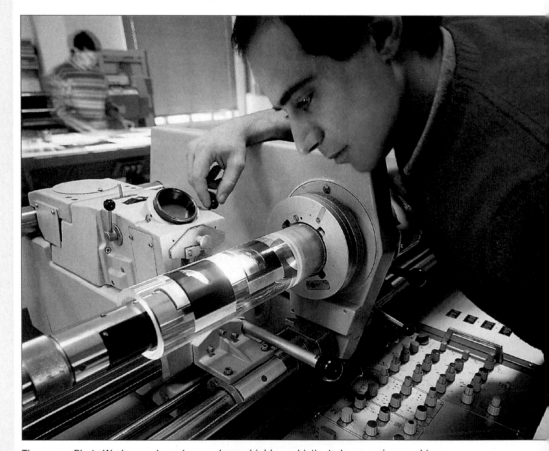

Thompson Photo Works purchased several new, highly sophisticated processing machines. The production department needed some guidance with respect to qualifications needed by an operator. In order to explore the factors needed to estimate performance on the new processing machines four variables were listed: length of time an employee was in the industry, mechanical aptitude test score, age, and prior on-the-job rating. How many dependent variables are there? (See Goal 1 and Exercise 2.)

# Introduction

In Chapter 13 we described the relationship between a pair of interval- or ratio-scaled measurements. We began the chapter by studying the coefficient of correlation, which measures strength of the relationship. A coefficient near plus or minus 1.00 ($-.88$ or .78, for example) indicates a very strong linear relationship, whereas a value near 0 ($-.12$ or .18, for example) means that the relationship is weak. Next we developed a procedure to determine a linear equation to express the relationship between the two variables. We referred to this as a *line of regression.* This line describes the relationship between the variables. It also describes the overall pattern of a dependent variable ($Y$) to a single independent or explanatory variable ($X$).

In multiple linear correlation and regression we use additional independent variables (denoted $X_1$, $X_2$, . . . , and so on) that help us better explain or predict the dependent variable ($Y$). Almost all of the ideas we saw in simple linear correlation and regression extend to this more general situation. However, the additional independent variables do lead to some new considerations. Multiple regression analysis can be used either as a descriptive or as an inferential technique.

# Multiple Regression Analysis

The general descriptive form of a multiple linear equation is shown in formula (14–1). We use $k$ to represent the number of independent variables. So $k$ can be any positive integer.

| GENERAL MULTIPLE REGRESSION EQUATION | $Y' = a + b_1X_1 + b_2X_2 + b_3X_3 + \cdots + b_kX_k$ | [14-1] |

where:

$a$ is the intercept, the value of $Y$ when all the $X$'s are zero.

$b_j$ is the amount by which $Y$ changes when that particular $X_j$ increases by one unit with all other values held the same. The subscript $j$ can assume values between 1 and $k$, which is the number of independent variables.

When there are only two independent variables, this equation can be portrayed graphically as a plane. Chart 14–1 is a graph of the relationship $Y' = a + b_1X_1 + b_2X_2$ used to summarize or "fit" 10 observations.

**CHART 14–1** Regression Plane with Ten Sample Points

To illustrate the interpretation of the intercept and the two regression coefficients, suppose a vehicle's mileage per gallon of gasoline is directly related to the octane rating of the gasoline being used $(X_1)$ and inversely related to the weight of the automobile $(X_2)$. Assume that the regression equation, calculated using statistical software, is:

$$Y' = 6.3 + 0.2X_1 - 0.001X_2$$

The intercept value of 6.3 indicates the regression equation intersects the $Y$-axis at 6.3 when both $X_1$ and $X_2$ are zero. Of course, this does not make any physical sense to own an automobile that has no (zero) weight and to use gasoline with no octane. It is important to keep in mind that a regression equation is not generally used outside the range of the sample values.

The $b_1$ of 0.2 indicates that for each increase of 1 in the octane rating of the gasoline, the automobile would travel 2/10 of a mile more per gallon, *regardless of the weight of the vehicle.* That is, the vehicle's weight is held constant. The $b_2$ value of $-0.001$ reveals that for each increase of one pound in the vehicle's weight, the number of miles traveled per gallon decreases by 0.001, *regardless of the octane of the gasoline being used.*

As an example, an automobile with 92-octane gasoline in the tank and weighing 2,000 pounds would travel an average 22.7 miles per gallon, found by:

$$Y' = a + b_1X_1 + b_2X_2 = 6.3 + 0.2(92) - 0.001(2,000) = 22.7$$

The value of 22.7 is in miles per gallon.

The values for the coefficients in the multiple linear equation are found by using the method of least squares. Recall from the previous chapter that the least squares method makes the sum of the squared differences between the fitted and actual values of $Y$ as small as possible. Because the calculations are very tedious, they are virtually always performed by a statistical software package, such as Excel or MINITAB. Fortunately, the information reported is fairly standard.

# Inferences in Multiple Linear Regression

Thus far, multiple regression analysis has been viewed only as a way to describe the relationship between a dependent variable and several independent variables. However, the least squares method also has the ability to draw inferences or generalizations about the relationship for an entire population. Recall that when you create confidence intervals or perform hypothesis tests as a part of inferential statistics, you view the data as a random sample taken from some population.

In the multiple regression setting, we assume there is an unknown population regression equation that relates the dependent variable to the $k$ independent variables. This is sometimes called a **model** of the relationship. In symbols we write:

$$Y' = \alpha + \beta_1X_1 + \beta_2X_2 + \cdots + \beta_kX_k$$

This equation is analogous to formula (14–1) except the coefficients are now reported as Greek letters. We use the Greek letters to denote *population parameters*. Then under a certain set of assumptions, which will be discussed shortly, the computed values of $a$ and $b_j$ are sample statistics. These sample statistics are point estimates of the corresponding population parameters $\alpha$ and $\beta_j$. These point estimates have normally distributed sampling distributions. These sampling distributions are each centered at their respective parameter values. To put it another way, the means of the sampling distributions are equal to the parameter values to be estimated. Thus, by using the properties of the sampling distributions of these statistics, inferences about the population parameters can be made.

We begin the discussion of multiple regression by describing a situation involving three independent variables.

**EXAMPLE**

Salsberry Realty sells homes along the east coast of the United States. One of the questions most frequently asked by prospective buyers is: If we purchase this home, how much can we expect to pay to heat it during the winter? The research department at Salsberry has been asked to develop some guidelines regarding heating costs for single-family homes. Three variables are thought to relate to the heating costs: (1) the mean daily outside temperature, (2) the number of inches of insulation in the attic, and (3) the age of the furnace. To investigate, Salsberry's research department selected a random sample of 20 recently sold homes. They determined the cost to heat the home last January, as well as the January outside temperature in the region, the number of inches of insulation in the attic, and the age of the furnace. The sample information is reported in Table 14–1.

**TABLE 14–1** Factors in January Heating Cost for a Sample of 20 Homes

| Home | Heating Cost ($) | Mean Outside Temperature (°F) | Attic Insulation (inches) | Age of Furnace (years) |
|------|------------------|-------------------------------|---------------------------|------------------------|
| 1 | $250 | 35 | 3 | 6 |
| 2 | 360 | 29 | 4 | 10 |
| 3 | 165 | 36 | 7 | 3 |
| 4 | 43 | 60 | 6 | 9 |
| 5 | 92 | 65 | 5 | 6 |
| 6 | 200 | 30 | 5 | 5 |
| 7 | 355 | 10 | 6 | 7 |
| 8 | 290 | 7 | 10 | 10 |
| 9 | 230 | 21 | 9 | 11 |
| 10 | 120 | 55 | 2 | 5 |
| 11 | 73 | 54 | 12 | 4 |
| 12 | 205 | 48 | 5 | 1 |
| 13 | 400 | 20 | 5 | 15 |
| 14 | 320 | 39 | 4 | 7 |
| 15 | 72 | 60 | 8 | 6 |
| 16 | 272 | 20 | 5 | 8 |
| 17 | 94 | 58 | 7 | 3 |
| 18 | 190 | 40 | 8 | 11 |
| 19 | 235 | 27 | 9 | 8 |
| 20 | 139 | 30 | 7 | 5 |

Determine the multiple regression equation. Which variables are the independent variables? Which variable is the dependent variable? Discuss the regression coefficients. What does it indicate if some coefficients are positive and some coefficients are negative? What is the intercept value? What is the estimated heating cost for a home if the mean outside temperature is 30 degrees, there are 5 inches of insulation in the attic, and the furnace is 10 years old?

SOLUTION

The MINITAB and Excel statistical software systems generate the outputs shown below.

MINITAB

**Regression Analysis: Cost versus Temp, Insul, Age**

The regression equation is
Cost = 427 - 4.58 Temp - 14.8 Insul + 6.10 Age

| Predictor | Coef | SE Coef | T | P |
|---|---|---|---|---|
| Constant | 427.19 | 59.60 | 7.17 | 0.000 |
| Temp | -4.5827 | 0.7723 | -5.93 | 0.000 |
| Insul | -14.831 | 4.754 | -3.12 | 0.007 |
| Age | 6.101 | 4.012 | 1.52 | 0.148 |

S = 51.0486   R-Sq = 80.4%   R-Sq(adj) = 76.7%

Analysis of Variance

| Source | DF | SS | MS | F | P |
|---|---|---|---|---|---|
| Regression | 3 | 171220 | 57073 | 21.90 | 0.000 |
| Residual Error | 16 | 41695 | 2606 | | |
| Total | 19 | 212916 | | | |

EXCEL

**SUMMARY OUTPUT**

**Regression Statistics**

| Multiple R | 0.897 |
|---|---|
| R Square | 0.804 |
| Adjusted R Square | 0.767 |
| Standard Error | 51.049 |
| Observations | 20.000 |

ANOVA

| | df | SS | MS |
|---|---|---|---|
| Regression | 3 | 171220.473 | 57073.49 |
| Residual | 16 | 41695.277 | 2605.95 |
| Total | 19 | 212915.750 | |

| | Coefficients | Standard Error | t Stat |
|---|---|---|---|
| Intercept | 427.194 | 59.6014 | 7.17 |
| Temp | -4.583 | 0.7723 | -5.93 |
| Insul | -14.831 | 4.7544 | -3.12 |
| Age | 6.101 | 4.0121 | 1.52 |

The dependent variable is the January heating cost. There are three independent variables, the mean outside temperature, the number of inches of insulation in the attic, and the age of the furnace.

The general form of a multiple regression equation with three independent variables is:

$$Y' = a + b_1X_1 + b_2X_2 + b_3X_3$$

In this case the estimated multiple regression equation is $Y' = 427 - 4.58X_1 - 14.8X_2 + 6.10X_3$. The intercept value is 427. This is the point where the regression equation crosses the Y-axis. The regression coefficients for the mean outside temperature and the amount of attic insulation are both negative. This is not surprising. As the outside temperature increases, the cost to heat the home will go down. Hence, we would expect an inverse relationship. For each degree the mean temperature increases, we expect the heating cost to decrease $4.58 per month. So if the mean temperature in Boston is 25 degrees and it is 35 degrees in Philadelphia, all other things being the same, we expect the heating cost would be $45.80 less in Philadelphia.

The variable "attic insulation" also shows an inverse relationship: the more insulation in the attic, the less the cost to heat the home. So the negative sign for this coefficient is logical. For each additional inch of insulation, we expect the cost to heat the home to decline $14.80 per month, regardless of the outside temperature or the age of the furnace.

The age of the furnace variable shows a direct relationship. With an older furnace, the cost to heat the home increases. Specifically, for each additional year older the furnace is, we expect the cost to increase $6.10 per month.

The estimated heating cost for the month is $276.60 if the mean outside temperature for the month is 30 degrees, there are 5 inches of insulation in the attic, and the furnace is 10 years old.

$$Y' = a + b_1X_1 + b_2X_2 + b_3X_3 = 427 - 4.58(30) - 14.8(5) + 6.10(10) = 276.60$$

---

**Self-Review 14–1**

The quality control engineer at Palmer Industries is interested in estimating the tensile strength of steel wire based on its outside diameter and the amount of molybdenum in the steel. As an experiment, she selected 25 pieces of wire, measured the outside diameters, and determined the molybdenum content. Then she measured the tensile strength of each piece. The results of the first four were:

| Piece | Tensile Strength (psi), $Y$ | Outside Diameter (mm), $X_1$ | Amount of Molybdenum (units), $X_2$ |
|---|---|---|---|
| A | 11 | .3 | 6 |
| B | 9 | .2 | 5 |
| C | 16 | .4 | 8 |
| D | 12 | .3 | 7 |

Using a statistical software package, the QC engineer determined the multiple regression equation to be $Y' = -0.5 + 20X_1 + 1X_2$.
(a) From the equation, what is the estimated tensile strength of a steel wire having an outside diameter of .35 mm and 6.4 units of molybdenum?
(b) Interpret the value of $b_1$ in the equation.

# Exercises

1. The director of marketing at Reeves Wholesale Products is studying monthly sales. Three independent variables were selected as estimators of sales: regional population, per-capita income, and regional unemployment rate. The regression equation was computed to be (in dollars):

$$Y' = 64,100 + 0.394X_1 + 9.6X_2 - 11,600X_3$$

   a. What is the full name of the equation?
   b. Interpret the number 64,100.
   c. What are the estimated monthly sales for a particular region with a population of 796,000, per-capita income of $6,940, and an unemployment rate of 6.0 percent?

2.  Thompson Photo Works purchased several new, highly sophisticated processing machines. The production department needed some guidance with respect to qualifications needed by an operator. Is age a factor? Is the length of service as an operator important? In order to explore further the factors needed to estimate performance on the new processing machines, four variables were listed:

    $X_1$ = Length of time an employee was in the industry.      $X_3$ = Prior on-the-job rating.
    $X_2$ = Mechanical aptitude test score.                      $X_4$ = Age.

    Performance on the new machine is designated $Y$.
       Thirty employees were selected at random. Data were collected for each, and their performances on the new machines were recorded. A few results are:

| Name | Performance on New Machine, $Y$ | Length of Time in Industry, $X_1$ | Mechanical Aptitude Score, $X_2$ | Prior On-the-Job Performance, $X_3$ | Age, $X_4$ |
|------|------|------|------|------|------|
| Andy Kosin | 112 | 12 | 312 | 121 | 52 |
| Sue Annis | 113 | 2 | 380 | 123 | 27 |

    The equation is:

    $$Y' = 11.6 + 0.4X_1 + 0.286X_2 + 0.112X_3 + 0.002X_4$$

    a.  What is the full designation of the equation?
    b.  How many dependent variables are there? Independent variables?
    c.  What is the number 0.286 called?
    d.  As age increases by one year, how much does estimated performance on the new machine increase?
    e.  Carl Knox applied for a job at Photo Works. He has been in the business for six years, and scored 280 on the mechanical aptitude test. Carl's prior on-the-job performance rating is 97, and he is 35 years old. Estimate Carl's performance on the new machine.

3.  A sample of General Mills employees was studied to determine their degree of satisfaction with their present life. A special index, called the index of satisfaction, was used to measure satisfaction. Six factors were studied, namely, age at the time of first marriage ($X_1$), annual income ($X_2$), number of children living ($X_3$), value of all assets ($X_4$), status of health in the form of an index ($X_5$), and the average number of social activities per week—such as bowling and dancing ($X_6$). Suppose the multiple regression equation is:

    $$Y' = 16.24 + 0.017X_1 + 0.0028X_2 + 42X_3 + 0.0012X_4 + 0.19X_5 + 26.8X_6$$

    a.  What is the estimated index of satisfaction for a person who first married at 18, has an annual income of $26,500, has three children living, has assets of $156,000, has an index of health status of 141, and has 2.5 social activities a week on the average?
    b.  Which would add more to satisfaction, an additional income of $10,000 a year or two more social activities a week?

4.  Cellulon, a manufacturer of a home insulation, wants to develop guidelines for builders and consumers regarding the effects (1) of the thickness of the insulation in the attic of a home and (2) of the outdoor temperature on natural gas consumption. In the laboratory they varied the insulation thickness and temperature. A few of the findings are:

| Monthly Natural Gas Consumption (cubic feet), $Y$ | Thickness of Insulation (inches), $X_1$ | Outdoor Temperature (°F), $X_2$ |
|------|------|------|
| 30.3 | 6 | 40 |
| 26.9 | 12 | 40 |
| 22.1 | 8 | 49 |

    On the basis of the sample results, the regression equation is:

    $$Y' = 62.65 - 1.86X_1 - 0.52X_2$$

**a.** How much natural gas can homeowners expect to use per month if they install 6 inches of insulation and the outdoor temperature is 40 degrees F?
**b.** What effect would installing 7 inches of insulation instead of 6 have on the monthly natural gas consumption (assuming the outdoor temperature remains at 40 degrees F)?
**c.** Why are the regression coefficients $b_1$ and $b_2$ negative? Is this logical?

# Multiple Standard Error of Estimate

In the Salsberry Realty example we estimated the cost to heat a home during the month of January when the mean outside temperature was 30 degrees, there were 5 inches of attic insulation, and the furnace was 10 years old to be $276.60. We would expect to find some random error in this estimate. Sometimes a home with these statistics would cost more than $276.60 to heat and other times less. The error in this estimate is measured by the **multiple standard error of estimate.** The standard error, as it is usually called, is denoted $s_{y \cdot 123}$. The subscripts indicate that three independent variables are being used to estimate the value of Y.

Recall from Chapter 13 the standard error of estimate described the variation around the regression line. A small standard error indicates the points are close to the regression line, whereas a large value indicates the points are scattered about the regression line. The same concept is true in multiple regression. If we have two independent variables, then we can think of the variation around a regression plane. See Chart 14–1 on page 475. If there are more than two independent variables, we do not have a geometric interpretation of the equation, but the standard error is still a measure of the "error" or variability in the prediction.

The formula to compute the standard error is similar to that used in the previous chapter. See formula (13–6) on page 447. The numerator is the sum of the squared differences between the estimated and the actual values of the dependent variable. In the denominator, we adjust for the fact that we are considering several, that is, *k,* independent variables.

| | | |
|---|---|---|
| **MULTIPLE STANDARD ERROR OF ESTIMATE** | $s_{y \cdot 12 \cdots k} = \sqrt{\dfrac{\Sigma(Y - Y')^2}{n - (k + 1)}}$ | **[14–2]** |

where:

Y is the observation.
Y' is the value estimated from the regression equation.
n is the number of observations in the sample.
k is the number of independent variables.

In the Salsberry Realty example, $k = 3$.

Again, we use the Salsberry Realty problem to illustrate. The first home had a mean outside temperature of 35 degrees, 3 inches of attic insulation, and a 6-year-old furnace. Substituting these values into the regression equation, the estimated heating cost is $258.90, determined by $427 - 4.58(35) - 14.80(3) + 6.10(6)$. The Y' values for the other homes are found similarly and are reported in Table 14–2.

The actual heating cost for the first home is $250, in contrast to the estimated cost of $258.90. That is, the error in the prediction is $-\$8.90$, found by ($250 - \$258.90$). This difference between the actual heating cost and the estimated heating cost is called the **residual.** To find the multiple standard error of estimate, we determine the residual for each of the sampled homes, square the residual, and then total the squared residuals. The total is reported in the lower right corner of Table 14–2.

In this example $n = 20$ and $k = 3$ (three independent variables), so the multiple standard error of estimate is:

$$s_{y \cdot 123} = \sqrt{\frac{\Sigma(Y - Y')^2}{n - (k + 1)}} = \sqrt{\frac{41,695.58}{20 - (3 + 1)}} = 51.05$$

**TABLE 14–2** Calculations Needed for the Multiple Standard Error of Estimate

| Home | Temperature (°F) | Insulation (inches) | Age (years) | Cost, Y | Y' | (Y − Y') | (Y − Y')² |
|---|---|---|---|---|---|---|---|
| 1 | 35 | 3 | 6 | $250 | 258.90 | −8.90 | 79.21 |
| 2 | 29 | 4 | 10 | 360 | 295.98 | 64.02 | 4,098.56 |
| 3 | 36 | 7 | 3 | 165 | 176.82 | −11.82 | 139.71 |
| 4 | 60 | 6 | 9 | 43 | 118.30 | −75.30 | 5,670.09 |
| 5 | 65 | 5 | 6 | 92 | 91.90 | 0.10 | 0.01 |
| 6 | 30 | 5 | 5 | 200 | 246.10 | −46.10 | 2,125.21 |
| 7 | 10 | 6 | 7 | 355 | 335.10 | 19.90 | 396.01 |
| 8 | 7 | 10 | 10 | 290 | 307.94 | −17.94 | 321.84 |
| 9 | 21 | 9 | 11 | 230 | 264.72 | −34.72 | 1,205.48 |
| 10 | 55 | 2 | 5 | 120 | 176.00 | −56.00 | 3,136.00 |
| 11 | 54 | 12 | 4 | 73 | 26.48 | 46.52 | 2,164.11 |
| 12 | 48 | 5 | 1 | 205 | 139.26 | 65.74 | 4,321.75 |
| 13 | 20 | 5 | 15 | 400 | 352.90 | 47.10 | 2,218.41 |
| 14 | 39 | 4 | 7 | 320 | 231.88 | 88.12 | 7,765.13 |
| 15 | 60 | 8 | 6 | 72 | 70.40 | 1.60 | 2.56 |
| 16 | 20 | 5 | 8 | 272 | 310.20 | −38.20 | 1,459.24 |
| 17 | 58 | 7 | 3 | 94 | 76.06 | 17.94 | 321.84 |
| 18 | 40 | 8 | 11 | 190 | 192.50 | −2.50 | 6.25 |
| 19 | 27 | 9 | 8 | 235 | 218.94 | 16.06 | 257.92 |
| 20 | 30 | 7 | 5 | 139 | 216.50 | −77.50 | 6,006.25 |
| Total | | | | | | | 41,695.58 |

How do we interpret the 51.05? It is the typical "error" we make when we use this equation to predict the cost. First, the units are the same as the dependent variable, so the standard error is in dollars. Second, if the errors are normally distributed, about 68 percent of the residuals should be less than ±51.05 and about 95 percent should be less than ±2(51.05) or ±102.10. Refer to the second column from the right in Table 14–2, the column headed (Y − Y'). Of the 20 residuals reported in this column, 14 are less than ±51.05 and all are less than ±102.10, which is quite close to the guidelines of 68 percent and 95 percent.

In Chapter 13 we used the standard error of estimate to construct confidence intervals and prediction intervals. We will not detail these procedures for multiple regression, but they are available on statistical software systems, such as MINITAB.

# Assumptions about Multiple Regression and Correlation

Before continuing our discussion, we list the assumptions underlying both multiple regression and multiple correlation. As noted in several previous chapters, we identify the assumptions because if they are not fully met, the results might be biased. For instance, in selecting a sample, we assume that all the items in the population have a chance of being selected. If our research involves surveying all those who ski, but we ignore those over 40 because we believe they are "too old," we would be biasing the responses toward the younger skiers. It should be mentioned, however, that in practice strict adherence to the following assumptions is not always possible in multiple regression and correlation problems involving the ever-changing business climate. But the statistical techniques discussed in this chapter appear to work well even when one or more of the assumptions are violated. Even if the values in the multiple regression equation are "off" slightly, our estimates based on the equation will be closer than any that could otherwise be made.

Each of the following assumptions will be discussed in more detail as we progress through the chapter.

1. The independent variables and the dependent variable have a linear relationship.
2. The dependent variable is continuous and at least interval scale.
3. The variation in the difference between the actual and the predicted values is the same for all fitted values of $Y$. That is, $(Y - Y')$ must be approximately the same for all values of $Y'$. When this is the case, differences exhibit **homoscedasticity.**
4. The residuals, computed by $Y - Y'$, are normally distributed with a mean of 0.
5. Successive observations of the dependent variable are uncorrelated. Violation of this assumption is called **autocorrelation.** Autocorrelation often happens when data are collected successively over periods of time.

**Homoscedasticity**

**Autocorrelation**

Statistical tests are available to detect homoscedasticity and autocorrelation. For those interested, these tests are covered in more advanced textbooks such as *Applied Linear Regression Models* by Kutner, Nachtscheim, and Neter (4th ed., 2004, published by McGraw-Hill/Irwin).

# The ANOVA Table

As mentioned previously, the multiple regression calculations are lengthy. Fortunately, many software systems are available to perform the calculations. Most of the systems report the results in a fairly standard format. The output from the MINITAB system shown on page 478 is typical. It includes the regression equation, the standard error of estimate, the coefficient of determination, as well as an analysis of variance table. We have already described the meaning of the regression coefficients in the equation $Y' = 427 - 4.58X_1 - 14.8X_2 + 6.10X_3$. We will discuss the "Coef," "StDev," and "T" (i.e., $t$ ratio) columns later in the chapter. A portion of the output from MINITAB is repeated here.

First, let's focus on the analysis of variance table. It is similar to the ANOVA table described in Chapter 12. In that chapter the variation was divided into two components: variance due to the *treatments* and variance due to random *error*. Here the total variance is also divided into two components: variance explained by the **regression,** that is, the independent variables, and the **error variance,** or unexplained variation. These two categories are identified in the "Source" column of the analysis of variance table. In the example there are 20 observations, so $n = 20$. The *total* number of degrees of freedom is $n - 1$, or $20 - 1 = 19$. The number of degrees of freedom in the "Regression" row is the number of independent variables. We let $k$ represent the number of independent variables, so $k = 3$. The number of degrees of freedom in the "Error" row is $n - (k + 1) = 20 - (3 + 1) = 16$ degrees of freedom.

The heading "SS" in the middle of the ANOVA table refers to the sum of squares, or the variation.

Total variation = SS total = $\Sigma(Y - \bar{Y})^2 = 212,916$
Error variation = SSE = $\Sigma(Y - Y')^2 = 41,695$
Regression variation = SSR = $\Sigma(Y' - \bar{Y})^2$ = SS total − SSE
$$= 212,916 - 41,695 = 171,220$$

The column headed "MS" (mean square) is determined by dividing the SS term by the *df* term. Thus, MSR, the mean square regression, is equal to SSR/$k$, and MSE equals SSE/$[n - (k + 1)]$. The general format of the ANOVA table is:

| Source | *df* | SS | MS | *F* |
|---|---|---|---|---|
| Regression | $k$ | SSR | MSR = SSR/$k$ | MSR/MSE |
| Error | $n - (k + 1)$ | SSE | MSE = SSE/$[n - (k + 1)]$ | |
| Total | $n - 1$ | SS total | | |

The **coefficient of multiple determination,** written as $R^2$, is the percent of the total variation explained by the regression. It is the sum of squares due to the regression, divided by the sum of squares total.

| COEFFICIENT OF MULTIPLE DETERMINATION | $R^2 = \dfrac{\text{SSR}}{\text{SS total}}$ | [14–3] |
|---|---|---|

$$R^2 = \frac{\text{SSR}}{\text{SS total}} = \frac{171,220}{212,916} = .804$$

The multiple standard error of estimate may also be found directly from the ANOVA table.

$$s_{y \cdot 123} = \sqrt{\frac{\text{SSE}}{n - (k + 1)}} = \sqrt{\frac{41,695}{[(20 - (3 + 1)]}} = 51.05$$

These values, $R^2 = .804$ and $s_{y \cdot 123} = 51.05$, are included in the MINITAB output.

---

**Self-Review 14–2**

Refer to the following ANOVA table.

```
SOURCE         DF     SS     MS       F
Regression      4     10    2.50    10.0
Error          20      5    0.25
Total          24     15
```

(a)  How large was the sample?
(b)  How many independent variables are there?
(c)  Compute the coefficient of multiple determination.
(d)  Compute the multiple standard error of estimate.

# Exercises

**5.** Refer to the following ANOVA table.

```
SOURCE        DF      SS      MS         F
Regression     3      21     7.0      2.33
Error         15      45     3.0
Total         18      66
```

    **a.** How large was the sample?
    **b.** How many independent variables are there?
    **c.** Compute the coefficient of multiple determination.
    **d.** Compute the multiple standard error of estimate.

**6.** Refer to the following ANOVA table.

```
SOURCE        DF      SS      MS         F
Regression     5      60      12     1.714
Error         20     140       7
Total         25     200
```

    **a.** How large was the sample?
    **b.** How many independent variables are there?
    **c.** Compute the coefficient of multiple determination.
    **d.** Compute the multiple standard error of estimate.

# Evaluating the Regression Equation

Earlier in the chapter we described an example in which Salsberry Realty developed, using multiple regression techniques, an equation to express the cost to heat a home during the month of January based on the mean outside temperature, the number of inches of attic insulation, and the age of the furnace. The equation seemed reasonable, but we may wish to verify that the multiple coefficient of determination is significantly larger than zero, evaluate the regression coefficients to see which are not equal to zero, and verify that the regression assumptions are met.

## Using a Scatter Diagram

There are three independent variables, designated $X_1$, $X_2$, and $X_3$. The dependent variable, the heating cost, is designated $Y$. In order to visualize the relationships between the dependent variable and each of the independent variables, we can draw the following scatter diagrams.

Of the three independent variables, the strongest association is between heating cost and the mean outside temperature. The relationships between cost and temperature and cost and insulation both are inverse. That is, as the independent variable increases, the dependent variable decreases. The relationship between the heating cost and the age of the furnace is direct. As the furnace gets older, it costs more to heat the home.

## Correlation Matrix

A correlation matrix is also useful in analyzing the factors involved in the cost to heat a home.

> **CORRELATION MATRIX** A matrix showing the coefficients of correlation between all pairs of variables.

The correlation matrix of the Salsberry Realty example follows. The matrix, which appears on the right-hand side of the output, was developed using the Excel software.

Cost is the dependent variable, *Y*. We are particularly interested in independent variables that have a strong correlation with the dependent variable. We may wish to develop a simpler multiple regression equation using fewer independent variables and the correlation matrix helps us identify which variables may be relatively more important. As indicated in the output, temperature has the strongest correlation with cost, −0.81151. The negative sign indicates the inverse relationship we were expecting. Age has a stronger correlation with cost than insulation and, again as we expected, the correlation between cost and the age of the furnace is direct. It is 0.53673.

A second use of the correlation matrix is to check for **multicollinearity.**

> **MULTICOLLINEARITY** Correlation among the independent variables.

Multicollinearity can distort the standard error of estimate and may, therefore, lead to incorrect conclusions as to which independent variables are statistically significant. In this case, the correlation between the age of the furnace and the temperature is the strongest, but it is not large enough to cause a problem. A common rule of thumb is that correlations among the independent variables between $-.70$ and $.70$ do not cause difficulties. The usual remedy for multicollinearity is to drop one of the independent variables that are strongly correlated and recompute the regression equation.

## Global Test: Testing the Multiple Regression Model

The ability of the independent variables $X_1$, $X_2$, . . . , $X_k$ to explain the behavior of the dependent variable $Y$ can be tested. To put this in question form: Can the dependent variable be estimated without relying on the independent variables? The test used is referred to as the **global test.** Basically, it investigates whether it is possible all the independent variables have zero net regression coefficients. To put it another way, could the amount of explained variation, $R^2$, occur by chance?

To relate this question to the heating cost example, we will test whether the independent variables (amount of insulation in the attic, mean daily outside temperature, and age of furnace) are capable of effectively estimating home heating costs.

Recall that in testing a hypothesis, we first state the null hypothesis and the alternate hypothesis. In the heating cost example, there are three independent variables. Recall that $b_1$, $b_2$, and $b_3$ are sample net regression coefficients. The corresponding coefficients in the population are given the symbols $\beta_1$, $\beta_2$, and $\beta_3$. We now test whether the net regression coefficients in the population are all zero. The null hypothesis is:

$H_0$: $\beta_1 = \beta_2 = \beta_3 = 0$

The alternate hypothesis is:

$H_1$: Not all the $\beta$s are 0.

If the null hypothesis is true, it implies the regression coefficients are all zero and, logically, are of no use in estimating the dependent variable (heating cost). Should that be the case, we would have to search for some other independent variables—or take a different approach—to predict home heating costs.

To test the null hypothesis that the multiple regression coefficients are all zero, we employ the $F$ distribution introduced in Chapter 12. We will use the .05 level of significance. Recall these characteristics of the $F$ distribution:

Characteristics of the
$F$ distribution

1.  It is positively skewed, with the critical value located in the right tail. The critical value is the point that separates the region where $H_0$ is not rejected from the region of rejection.
2.  It is constructed by knowing the number of degrees of freedom in the numerator and the number of degrees of freedom in the denominator.

The degrees of freedom for the numerator and the denominator may be found in the software summary in the analysis of variance table. That portion of the table is included below. The top number in the column marked "DF" is 3, indicating that there are 3 degrees of freedom in the numerator. The middle number in the "DF" column (16) indicates that there are 16 degrees of freedom in the denominator. The number 16 is found by $n - (k + 1) = 20 - (3 + 1) = 16$. The number 3 corresponds to the number of independent variables.

The value of $F$ is found from the following equation.

| GLOBAL TEST | $$F = \frac{SSR/k}{SSE/[n - (k + 1)]}$$ | [14–4] |
|---|---|---|

SSR is the sum of the squares "explained by" the regression, SSE the sum of squares error, $n$ the number of observations, and $k$ the number of independent variables. Inserting these values in formula (14–4) gives:

$$F = \frac{SSR/k}{SSE/[n - (k + 1)]} = \frac{171{,}220/3}{41{,}695/[20 - (3 + 1)]} = 21.90$$

The critical value of $F$ is found in Appendix G. Using the table for the .05 significance level, move horizontally to 3 degrees of freedom in the numerator, then down to 16 degrees of freedom in the denominator, and read the critical value. It is 3.24. The region where $H_0$ is not rejected and the region where $H_0$ is rejected are shown in the following diagram.

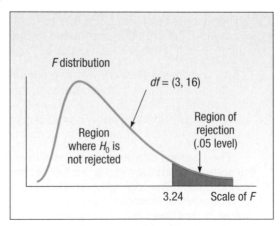

Continuing with the global test, the decision rule is: Do not reject the null hypothesis that all the regression coefficients are 0 if the computed value of $F$ is less than or equal to 3.24. If the computed $F$ is greater than 3.24, reject $H_0$ and accept the alternate hypothesis, $H_1$.

The computed value of $F$ is 21.90, which is in the rejection region. The null hypothesis that all the multiple regression coefficients are zero is therefore rejected. The $p$-value is 0.000 from the above analysis of variance table, so it is quite unlikely that $H_0$ is true. The null hypothesis is rejected, indicating that not all the regression coefficients are zero. From a practical standpoint, this means that some of the independent variables (amount of insulation, etc.) do have the ability to explain the variation in the dependent variable (heating cost). We expected this decision. Logically, the outside temperature, the amount of insulation, and age of the furnace have a great bearing on heating costs. The global test assures us that they do.

## Evaluating Individual Regression Coefficients

So far we have shown that some, but not necessarily all, of the regression coefficients are not equal to zero and thus useful for predictions. The next step is to test the variables *individually* to determine which regression coefficients may be 0 and which are not.

Why is it important to find whether it is possible that any of the βs equal 0? If a β could equal 0, it implies that this particular independent variable is of no value in explaining any variation in the dependent value. If there are coefficients for which $H_0$ cannot be rejected, we may want to eliminate them from the regression equation.

We will now conduct three separate tests of hypothesis—for temperature, for insulation, and for the age of the furnace.

| For temperature: | For insulation: | For furnace age: |
|---|---|---|
| $H_0: \beta_1 = 0$ | $H_0: \beta_2 = 0$ | $H_0: \beta_3 = 0$ |
| $H_1: \beta_1 \neq 0$ | $H_1: \beta_2 \neq 0$ | $H_1: \beta_3 \neq 0$ |

We will test the hypotheses at the .05 level. The way the alternate hypothesis is stated indicates that the test is two-tailed.

The test statistic follows the Student $t$ distribution with $n - (k + 1)$ degrees of freedom. The number of sample observations is $n$. There are 20 homes in the study, so $n = 20$. The number of independent variables is $k$, which is 3. Thus, there are $n - (k + 1) = 20 - (3 + 1) = 16$ degrees of freedom.

The critical value for $t$ is in Appendix F. For a two-tailed test with 16 degrees of freedom using the .05 significance level, $H_0$ is rejected if $t$ is less than $-2.120$ or greater than 2.120. The MINITAB software produced the following output.

The column headed "Coef" shows the regression coefficients for the multiple regression equation:

$$Y' = 427.19 - 4.5827X_1 - 14.831X_2 + 6.101X_3$$

Interpreting the term $-4.5827X_1$ in the equation: For each degree the temperature increases, it is expected that the heating cost will decrease about $4.58, holding the two other variables constant.

The column on the MINITAB output labeled "SE Coef" indicates the standard error of the sample regression coefficient. Recall that Salsberry Realty selected a sample of 20 homes along the east coast of the United States. If they were to select a second sample at random and compute the regression coefficients of that sample, the values would not be exactly the same. If they repeated the sampling process many times, however, we could design a sampling distribution of these regression coefficients. The column labeled "SE Coef" estimates the variability of these regression coefficients. The sampling distribution of Coef/SE Coef follows the $t$ distribution with $n - (k + 1)$ degrees of freedom. Hence, we are able to test the independent variables individually to determine whether the net regression coefficients differ from zero. The computed $t$ ratio is $-5.93$ for temperature and $-3.12$ for insulation. Both of these $t$ values are in the rejection region to the left of $-2.120$. Thus, we conclude that the regression coefficients for the temperature and insulation variables are *not* zero. The computed $t$ for age of the furnace is 1.52, so we conclude that $b_3$ could equal 0. The independent variable "age of the furnace" is not a significant predictor of heating cost. It can be dropped from the analysis. We can test individual regression coefficients using the $t$ distribution. The formula is:

| TESTING INDIVIDUAL REGRESSION COEFFICIENTS | $t = \dfrac{b_i - 0}{s_{b_i}}$ | [14–5] |
|---|---|---|

The $b_i$ refers to any one of the net regression coefficients and $s_{b_i}$ refers to standard deviation of that distribution of the net regression coefficient. We include 0 in the equation because the null hypothesis is $\beta_i = 0$.

To illustrate this formula, refer to the test of the regression coefficient for the independent variable Temperature. We let $b_1$ refer to the net regression coefficient. From the computer output on page 489 it is $-4.5827$. $s_{b_i}$ is the standard deviation of the sampling distribution of the net regression coefficient for the independent variable Temperature. Again, from the computer output on page 489, it is 0.7723. Inserting these values in formula (14–5):

$$t = \frac{b_1 - 0}{s_{b_1}} = \frac{-4.5827 - 0}{0.7723} = -5.93$$

This is the value found in the "T" column of the output.

In Self-Review 14–3, we run the multiple regression example again using MINITAB, but only two variables—"temperature" and "insulation"—are included. These two variables explained 77.6 percent of the variation in heating cost. Using all three variables—temperature, insulation, and furnace age—a total of 80.4 percent of the variation is explained. The additional variable increased $R^2$ by only 2.8 percent—a rather small increase for the addition of an independent variable.

At this point we should also develop a strategy for deleting independent variables. In the Salsberry Realty case there were three independent variables and one (age) had a regression coefficient that did not differ from 0. It is clear that we should drop that variable. So we delete that variable and rerun the regression equation. However, in some instances it may not be as clear-cut which variable to delete.

To explain, suppose we developed a multiple regression equation based on five independent variables. We conducted the global test and found that some of the regression coefficients were different from zero. Next, we tested the regression coefficients individually and found that three were significant and two were not. The preferred procedure is to drop the single independent variable with the *smallest absolute* t *value* or *largest* p-*value* and rerun the regression equation with the four remaining variables. Then, on the new regression equation with four independent variables, conduct the individual tests. If there are still regression coefficients that are not significant, again drop the variable with the smallest absolute *t* value. To describe the process in another way, we should delete only one variable at a time. Each time we delete a variable, we need to rerun the regression equation and check the remaining variables.

This process of selecting variables to include in a regression model can be automated, using Excel, MINITAB, Megastat, or other statistical software. Most of the software systems include methods to sequentially remove and/or add independent variables and at the same time provide estimates of the percentage of variation explained (the *R*-square term). Two of the common methods are **stepwise regression** and **best subset regression.** It may take a long time, but in the extreme you could compute every regression between the dependent variable and any possible subset of the independent variables.

Unfortunately, on occasion, the software may work "too hard" to find an equation that fits all the quirks of your particular data set. The resultant equation may not represent the relationship in the population. You will need to use your judgment to choose among the equations presented. Consider whether the results are logical. They should have a simple interpretation and be consistent with your knowledge of the application under study.

---

**Self-Review 14–3**

The multiple regression and correlation data for the preceding heating cost example were rerun using only the first two significant independent variables—temperature and insulation. (See the following MINITAB output.)

(a) What is the new multiple regression equation? (Temperature is $X_1$ and insulation $X_2$.)
(b) What is the coefficient of multiple determination? Interpret.
(c) How can you tell that these two independent variables are of value in predicting heating costs?
(d) What is the p-value of insulation? Interpret.

# Qualitative Independent Variables

The three variables used in the Salsberry Realty example were all quantitative; that is, numerical in nature. Frequently we wish to use nominal-scale variables—such as gender, whether the home has a swimming pool, or whether the sports team was the home or the visiting team—in our analysis. These are called *qualitative variables* because they describe a particular quality, such as male or female. To use a qualitative variable in regression analysis, we use a scheme of **dummy variables** in which one of the two possible conditions is coded 0 and the other 1.

> **DUMMY VARIABLE** A variable in which there are only two possible outcomes. For analysis, one of the outcomes is coded a 1 and the other a 0.

For example, we might be interested in estimating an executive's salary on the basis of years of job experience and whether he or she graduated from college. "Graduation from college" can take on only one of two conditions: yes or no. Thus, it is considered a qualitative variable.

Suppose in the Salsberry Realty example that the independent variable "garage" is added. For those homes without an attached garage, 0 is used; for homes with an attached garage, a 1 is used. We will refer to the "garage" variable as $X_4$. The data from Table 14–3 are entered into the MINITAB system.

**TABLE 14–3** Home Heating Costs, Temperature, Insulation, and Presence of a Garage for a Sample of 20 Homes

| Cost, $Y$ | Temperature, $X_1$ | Insulation, $X_2$ | Garage, $X_4$ |
|---|---|---|---|
| $250 | 35 | 3 | 0 |
| 360 | 29 | 4 | 1 |
| 165 | 36 | 7 | 0 |
| 43 | 60 | 6 | 0 |
| 92 | 65 | 5 | 0 |
| 200 | 30 | 5 | 0 |
| 355 | 10 | 6 | 1 |
| 290 | 7 | 10 | 1 |
| 230 | 21 | 9 | 0 |
| 120 | 55 | 2 | 0 |
| 73 | 54 | 12 | 0 |
| 205 | 48 | 5 | 1 |
| 400 | 20 | 5 | 1 |
| 320 | 39 | 4 | 1 |
| 72 | 60 | 8 | 0 |
| 272 | 20 | 5 | 1 |
| 94 | 58 | 7 | 0 |
| 190 | 40 | 8 | 1 |
| 235 | 27 | 9 | 0 |
| 139 | 30 | 7 | 0 |

The output from MINITAB is:

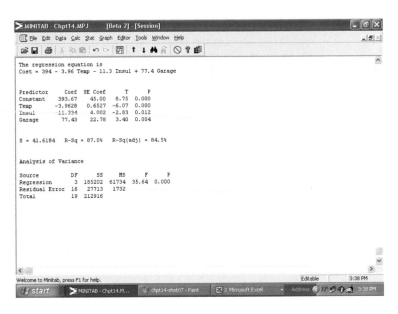

What is the effect of the variable "garage"? Should it be included in the analysis? To show the effect of the variable, suppose we have two houses exactly alike next to each other in Buffalo, New York; one has an attached garage, and the other does not. Both homes have 3 inches of insulation, and the mean January temperature in Buffalo is 20 degrees. For the house without an attached garage, a 0 is substituted for $X_4$ in the regression equation. The estimated heating cost is $280.90, found by:

$$Y' = 394 - 3.96X_1 - 11.3X_2 + 77.4X_4$$

$$= 394 - 3.96(20) - 11.3(3) + 77.4(0) = 280.90$$

For the house with an attached garage, a 1 is substituted for $X_4$ in the regression equation. The estimated heating cost is $358.30, found by:

$$Y' = 394 - 3.96X_1 - 11.3X_2 + 77.4X_4$$

$$= 394 - 3.96(20) - 11.3(3) + 77.4(1) = 358.30$$

The difference between the estimated heating costs is $77.40 ($358.30 − $280.90). Hence, we can expect the cost to heat a house with an attached garage to be $77.40 more than the cost for an equivalent house without a garage.

We have shown the difference between the two types of homes to be $77.40, but is the difference significant? We conduct the following test of hypothesis.

$$H_0: \beta_4 = 0$$

$$H_1: \beta_4 \neq 0$$

The information necessary to answer this question is on the MINITAB output above. The net regression coefficient for the independent variable Garage is 77.43, the standard deviation of the distribution of sampling distribution is 22.78. We identify this as the fourth independent variable, so we use a subscript of 4. Finally, we insert these values in formula (14–5).

$$t = \frac{b_4 - 0}{s_{b_4}} = \frac{77.43 - 0}{22.78} = 3.40$$

There are three independent variables in the analysis, so there are $n - (k + 1) = 20 - (3 + 1) = 16$ degrees of freedom. The critical value from Appendix F is 2.120. The decision rule, using a two-tailed test and the .05 significance level, is to reject $H_0$

if the computed $t$ is to the left of $-2.120$ or to the right of 2.120. Since the computed value of 3.40 is to the right of 2.120, the null hypothesis is rejected. It is concluded that the regression coefficient is not zero. The independent variable "garage" should be included in the analysis.

Is it possible to use a qualitative variable with more than two possible outcomes? Yes, but the coding scheme becomes more complex and will require a series of dummy variables. To explain, suppose a company is studying its sales as they relate to advertising expense by quarter for the last 5 years. Let sales be the dependent variable and advertising expense be the first independent variable, $X_1$. To include the qualitative information regarding the quarter, we use three additional independent variables. For the variable $X_2$, the five observations referring to the first quarter of each of the 5 years are coded 1 and the other quarters 0. Similarly, for $X_3$ the five observations referring to the second quarter are coded 1 and the other quarters 0. For $X_4$ the five observations referring to the third quarter are coded 1 and the other quarters 0. An observation that does not refer to any of the first three quarters must refer to the fourth quarter, so a distinct independent variable referring to this quarter is not necessary.

# Exercises

7.　Refer to the following information:

| Predictor | Coef | StDev | | |
|---|---|---|---|---|
| Constant | 20.00 | 10.00 | | |
| $X_1$ | −1.00 | 0.25 | | |
| $X_2$ | 12.00 | 8.00 | | |
| $X_3$ | −15.00 | 5.00 | | |
| | | | | |
| SOURCE | DF | SS | MS | F |
| Regression | 3 | 7,500.00 | | |
| Error | 18 | | | |
| Total | 21 | 10,000.0 | | |

　　a.　Complete the ANOVA table.
　　b.　Conduct a global test of hypothesis, using the .05 significance level. Can you conclude that any of the net regression coefficients are different from zero?
　　c.　Conduct a test of hypothesis on each of the regression coefficients. Could you delete any of the variables?

8.　Refer to the following information:

| Predictor | Coef | StDev | | |
|---|---|---|---|---|
| Constant | −150 | 90 | | |
| $X_1$ | 2000 | 500 | | |
| $X_2$ | −25 | 30 | | |
| $X_3$ | 5 | 5 | | |
| $X_4$ | −300 | 100 | | |
| $X_5$ | 0.60 | 0.15 | | |
| | | | | |
| SOURCE | DF | SS | MS | F |
| Regression | 5 | 1,500.0 | | |
| Error | 15 | | | |
| Total | 20 | 2,000.0 | | |

　　a.　Complete the ANOVA table.
　　b.　Conduct a global test of hypothesis, using the .05 significance level. Can you conclude that any of the net regression coefficients are different from zero?
　　c.　Conduct a test of hypothesis on each of the regression coefficients. Could you delete any of the variables?

# Analysis of Residuals

In an earlier section we describe the assumptions required for regression and correlation analysis. These assumptions are:

1. There is a linear relationship between the dependent variable and the independent variables.
2. The dependent variable is measured as an interval- or ratio-scale variable.
3. Successive observations of the dependent variable are not correlated.
4. The differences between the actual values and estimated values, that is, the residuals, are normally distributed.
5. The variation in the residuals is the same for all fitted values of $Y'$. That is, the distribution of $(Y - Y')$ is the same for all values of $Y'$.

The last two assumptions can be verified by plotting the residuals. That is, we want to confirm that the residuals follow a normal distribution and that residuals have the same variation whether the $Y'$ value is large or small. We present the necessary data in Table 14–4. The column headed "Actual Cost" is the original heating cost, first presented in Table 14–1. The next column, labeled "Estimated Cost," is the cost to heat the home as estimated from the regression equation. This is also referred to as the fitted value and is $Y'$. The value for the first home is found by substituting the actual values of the three variables into the regression equation. For example, from Table 14–3, the first home's mean outside temperature was 35 degrees, it had 3 inches of attic insulation, and did not have an attached garage. The actual heating cost was $250, and the estimated heating cost is $221.08, found by

$$Y' = 393.67 - 3.96(35) - 11.33(3) + 77.43(0) = 221.08$$

The residual is in the last column. It is 28.92, found by $250 - 221.08$. The residuals for the 19 other values are computed similarly.

**TABLE 14–4** Summary of Actual Costs, Estimated Costs, and Residuals for Salsberry Realty Problem

| Home | Actual Cost, $Y$ | Estimated Cost, $Y'$ | Residual $Y - Y'$ |
|---|---|---|---|
| 1 | 250 | 221.08 | 28.92 |
| 2 | 360 | 310.94 | 49.06 |
| 3 | 165 | 171.80 | −6.80 |
| 4 | 43 | 88.09 | −45.09 |
| 5 | 92 | 79.62 | 12.38 |
| 6 | 200 | 218.22 | −18.22 |
| 7 | 355 | 363.52 | −8.52 |
| 8 | 290 | 330.08 | −40.08 |
| 9 | 230 | 208.54 | 21.46 |
| 10 | 120 | 153.21 | −33.21 |
| 11 | 73 | 43.87 | 29.13 |
| 12 | 205 | 224.37 | −19.37 |
| 13 | 400 | 335.25 | 64.75 |
| 14 | 320 | 271.34 | 48.66 |
| 15 | 72 | 65.43 | 6.57 |
| 16 | 272 | 335.25 | −63.25 |
| 17 | 94 | 84.68 | 9.32 |
| 18 | 190 | 222.06 | −32.06 |
| 19 | 235 | 184.78 | 50.22 |
| 20 | 139 | 195.56 | −56.56 |

We can use the last column, the residuals, to verify the normality assumption. The following MINITAB output shows a stem-and-leaf display and a histogram of the residuals. Both charts indicate that the distribution of the residuals is somewhat normal, as required in the assumptions. To interpret the output, note that the residuals are tallied into classes with a class interval of 20: −70 up to −50, with a midpoint of −60; −50 up to −30, with a midpoint of −40; and so on. The details of the first three classes are:

| Class | Midpoint | Residuals | Count |
|---|---|---|---|
| −70 up to −50 | −60 | −63.25, −56.56 | 2 |
| −50 up to −30 | −40 | −45.09, −40.08, −33.21, −32.06 | 4 |
| −30 up to −10 | −20 | −19.37, −18.22 | 2 |

**Homoscedasticity**

The assumptions for regression analysis also require that the residuals remain constant for all values of $Y'$. Recall that this condition is called **homoscedasticity.** To check for homoscedasticity, the residuals are plotted against the fitted values of $Y$. That is, we develop a scatter plot with the values in the Estimated Cost column of Table 14–4 plotted on the horizontal axis and the residuals on the vertical axis. The first plot is 221.08 for $X$ and 28.92 for $Y$. Because the spread of the residuals is the same for any $Y'$, we conclude that the assumption has not been violated.

Following are two examples in which the homoscedasticity requirement is not met. Note in the first example, the plot of residuals is funnel-shaped. That is, as the fitted $Y$ values increase, so does the variation in the residuals. In the second example, there is a pattern to the residuals. The residuals seem to take the shape of a polynomial, or a second-degree equation.

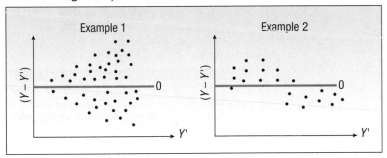

What problems are caused by residuals that fail to show homoscedasticity? The standard deviations of the regression coefficients will be understated (too small), causing potential independent variables to appear to be significant when they may not be. The remedy for this condition is to select other independent variables or to transform some of the variables. For a more detailed discussion of residual analysis, refer to an advanced text, such as *Applied Linear Regression Models* by Kutner, Nachtscheim, and Neter (4th ed., 2004, published by McGraw-Hill/Irwin).

In the following example we show how analysis of the residuals can lead to an improved regression model.

**EXAMPLE**

Paul Roseboro is an analyst for Bar Nun Trucking. He is studying the effect of tire pressure on fuel economy (Mpg) for a fleet of 24 sedans used by regional supervisors. He convinced management to have four different cars driven with a tire pressure of 30 pounds per square inch, four at 31, four at 32, and so forth. He obtained the following sample information.

| Pressure | Mileage |
|----------|---------|
| 30 | 29.8851 |
| 30 | 27.5577 |
| 30 | 27.0726 |
| 30 | 26.4422 |
| 31 | 31.7876 |
| 31 | 29.8017 |
| 31 | 30.2135 |
| 31 | 36.1228 |
| 32 | 35.6521 |
| 32 | 36.6301 |
| 32 | 37.7559 |
| 32 | 35.1194 |
| 33 | 37.0772 |
| 33 | 38.2858 |
| 33 | 36.1861 |
| 33 | 40.2397 |
| 34 | 33.0048 |
| 34 | 34.6957 |
| 34 | 35.4852 |
| 34 | 35.1910 |
| 35 | 34.3259 |
| 35 | 32.0578 |
| 35 | 29.4446 |
| 35 | 32.4416 |

Develop an appropriate regression model to relate tire pressure to fuel effectiveness. What appears to be the best level for tire pressure?

Paul used a statistical software package to develop a regression equation, with tire pressure as the independent variable and Mpg as the dependent variable. From this regression equation he obtained the residuals and the fitted values. Finally he plotted these values on a scatter diagram. Paul is looking at the following plot of the residuals versus the fitted values. What does it show? Are there any problems with the regression assumptions?

The residuals $(Y - Y')$ are on the vertical axis and fitted values of $Y'$ are on the horizontal axis. It appears that the errors or residuals are not random. Instead, there is a definite pattern to the residuals. They are consistently negative for high and low values of tire pressure and they are consistently positive in the middle of the range.

A data plot with the linear regression equation lends even more insight. Here we have the dependent variable Mpg on the vertical axis and tire pressure on the horizontal axis.

The regression equation is Mpg = 4.52403 + 0.889614 Pressure. Notice the value of $R^2$, namely 17 percent, is rather low. To put it another way, only 17 percent of the variation in mileage is accounted for by the differences in tire pressure. From the plot we can "see" that the relationship between the variables is not linear.

This pattern indicates the relationship may be curvilinear. So Paul decides to fit a quadratic or second-degree equation to the data. His new equation is of the general form:

$$Y' = a + b_1X_1 + b_2X_1^2$$

To create a second independent variable for this analysis, Paul squares each tire pressure. Generally, a variable and its square tend to behave independently of each other. Then he can use multiple regression to determine the second degree equation. In other words, he fits the tire pressure and the tire pressure squared with the Mpg. See the data on the left side of the MINITAB output below.

The new regression equation is:

$$\text{Mpg} = -1208 + 75.74 \text{ Pressure} - 1.152 \text{ Pressure**2}$$

The $R^2$ value has increased to 77.7 percent. That is, the independent variables tire pressure and tire pressure squared now account for nearly 78 percent of the variation in mileage. This is a substantial improvement.

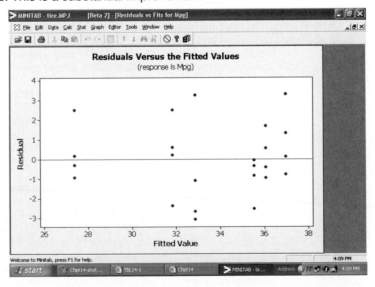

What about the problem with the residuals not being in a random pattern? Paul plots the residuals obtained from the quadratic equation against the variable tire pressure and there seems to be no pattern. The residuals look "more random" now.

What would be the optimum value for the tire pressure? If we look at the scatter plot with the fitted regression equation added, then we can see the mileage increased up to about 33 pounds and then began to decline.

This plot also suggests that the optimum tire pressure should be 33 pounds per square inch. In summary, by using a quadratic equation we were able to increase the explained variation from 17 percent to 78 percent, eliminate the problem with the residuals, and find the most favorable tire pressure of 33 pounds.

# Chapter Outline

I. Multiple regression and correlation analysis is based on these assumptions.
   A. There is a linear relationship between the independent variables and the dependent variable.
   B. The dependent variable is a continuous variable measured on either an interval or ratio scale.
   C. The residual variation is the same for all fitted values of $Y$.
   D. The residuals follow the normal distribution.
   E. Successive observations of the dependent variable are uncorrelated.

II. The general form of the multiple regression equation is:

$$Y' = a + b_1 X_1 + b_2 X_2 + \cdots + b_k X_k \qquad \text{[14–1]}$$

   where $Y'$ is the estimated value, $a$ is the $Y$-intercept, the $b_i$ refers to the sample regression coefficients, and the $X_i$ refers to the values of the various independent variables.
   A. There can be any number of independent variables.
   B. The least squares criterion is used to develop the equation.
   C. A statistical software package is needed to determine $a$ and the various $b$ values.

III. There are two measures of the effectiveness of the regression equation.
   A. The multiple standard error of estimate is similar to the standard deviation.
      1. It is measured in the same units as the dependent variable.
      2. It is difficult to determine what is a large value and what is a small value of the standard error.
   B. The coefficient of determination may range from 0 to 1 and show the fraction of the variation in $Y$ that is explained by the set of independent variables.

IV. An ANOVA table shows the variation in the dependent variable explained by the regression equation and the residual or error variation.

V. A correlation matrix shows all possible simple correlation coefficients between pairs of variables.

VI. A global test is used to investigate whether any of the independent variables have significant regression coefficients.
   A. The null hypothesis is: All the regression coefficients are zero.
   B. The alternate hypothesis is: At least one regression coefficient is not zero.
   C. The test statistic is the $F$ distribution with $k$ (the number of independent variables) degrees of freedom in the numerator and $n - (k + 1)$ degrees of freedom in the denominator, where $n$ is the sample size.
   D. The formula to calculate the value of the test statistic for the global test is:

$$F = \frac{\text{SSR}/k}{\text{SSE}/[n - (k + 1)]} \qquad \text{[14–4]}$$

VII. The test for individual variables determines which independent variables have nonzero regression coefficients.
   A. The variables that have zero regression coefficients are usually dropped from the analysis.

**B.** The test statistic is the $t$ distribution with $n - (k + 1)$ degrees of freedom.
**C.** The formula to calculate the value of the test statistic for the individual test is:

$$t = \frac{b_i - 0}{s_{b_i}}$$ [14–5]

**VIII.** Dummy variables are used to represent qualitative variables and can assume only one of two possible conditions.
**IX.** A residual is the difference between the actual value of $Y$ and the predicted value of $Y$.
    **A.** Residuals should be approximately normally distributed. Histograms and stem-and-leaf charts are useful in checking this requirement.
    **B.** A plot of the residuals and their corresponding $Y'$ values is useful for showing that there are no trends or patterns in the residuals.

# Pronunciation Key

| SYMBOL | MEANING | PRONUNCIATION |
|---|---|---|
| $b_1$ | Regression coefficient for the first independent variable | b sub 1 |
| $b_k$ | Regression coefficient for any independent variable | b sub k |
| $s_{y \cdot 12 \cdots k}$ | Multiple standard error of estimate | s sub y dot 1, 2 . . . k |

# Chapter Exercises

**9.** A multiple regression equation yields the following partial results.

| Source | Sum of Squares | df |
|---|---|---|
| Regression | 750 | 4 |
| Error | 500 | 35 |

    **a.** What is the total sample size?
    **b.** How many independent variables are being considered?
    **c.** Compute the coefficient of determination.
    **d.** Compute the standard error of estimate.
    **e.** Test the hypothesis that none of the regression coefficients is equal to zero. Let $\alpha = .05$.
**10.** In a multiple regression equation two independent variables are considered, and the sample size is 25. The regression coefficients and the standard errors are as follows.

$$b_1 = 2.676 \qquad s_{b_1} = 0.56$$
$$b_2 = -0.880 \qquad s_{b_2} = 0.71$$

Conduct a test of hypothesis to determine whether either independent variable has a coefficient equal to zero. Would you consider deleting either variable from the regression equation? Use the .05 significance level.
**11.** The following output was obtained.

```
Analysis of variance

SOURCE          DF          SS          MS
Regression       5         100          20
Error           20          40           2
Total           25         140

Predictor      Coef       StDev     t-ratio
Constant       3.00        1.50        2.00
    X₁         4.00        3.00        1.33
    X₂         3.00        0.20       15.00
    X₃         0.20        0.05        4.00
    X₄        -2.50        1.00       -2.50
    X₅         3.00        4.00        0.75
```

a. What is the sample size?
b. Compute the value of $R^2$.
c. Compute the multiple standard error of estimate.
d. Conduct a global test of hypothesis to determine whether any of the regression coefficients are significant. Use the .05 significance level.
e. Test the regression coefficients individually. Would you consider omitting any variable(s)? If so, which one(s)? Use the .05 significance level.

12. In a multiple regression equation $k = 5$ and $n = 20$, the MSE value is 5.10, and SS total is 519.68. At the .05 significance level, can we conclude that any of the regression coefficients are not equal to 0?

13. The district manager of Jasons, a large discount electronics chain, is investigating why certain stores in her region are performing better than others. She believes that three factors are related to total sales: the number of competitors in the region, the population in the surrounding area, and the amount spent on advertising. From her district, consisting of several hundred stores, she selects a random sample of 30 stores. For each store she gathered the following information.

$Y$ = total sales last year (in $ thousands).
$X_1$ = number of competitors in the region.
$X_2$ = population of the region (in millions).
$X_3$ = advertising expense (in $ thousands).

The sample data were run on MINITAB, with the following results.

```
Analysis of variance

SOURCE          DF          SS          MS
Regression       3     3050.00     1016.67
Error           26     2200.00       84.62
Total           29     5250.00

Predictor     Coef      StDev     t-ratio
Constant     14.00       7.00        2.00
   X₁        -1.00       0.70       -1.43
   X₂        30.00       5.20        5.77
   X₃         0.20       0.08        2.50
```

a. What are the estimated sales for the Bryne Store, which has four competitors, a regional population of 0.4 (400,000), and advertising expense of 30 ($30,000)?
b. Compute the $R^2$ value.
c. Compute the multiple standard error of estimate.
d. Conduct a global test of hypothesis to determine whether any of the regression coefficients are not equal to zero. Use the .05 level of significance.
e. Conduct tests of hypotheses to determine which of the independent variables have significant regression coefficients. Which variables would you consider eliminating? Use the .05 significance level.

14. Suppose that the sales manager of a large automotive parts distributor wants to estimate as early as April the total annual sales of a region. On the basis of regional sales, the total sales for the company can also be estimated. If, based on past experience, it is found that the April estimates of annual sales are reasonably accurate, then in future years the April forecast could be used to revise production schedules and maintain the correct inventory at the retail outlets.

Several factors appear to be related to sales, including the number of retail outlets in the region stocking the company's parts, the number of automobiles in the region registered as of April 1, and the total personal income for the first quarter of the year. Five independent variables were finally selected as being the most important (according to the sales manager). Then the data were gathered for a recent year. The total annual sales for that year for each region were also recorded. Note in the following table that for region 1 there were 1,739 retail outlets stocking the company's automotive parts, there were 9,270,000 registered automobiles in the region as of April 1, and sales for that year were $37,702,000.

| Annual Sales ($ millions), Y | Number of Retail Outlets, $X_1$ | Number of Automobiles Registered (millions), $X_2$ | Personal Income ($ billions), $X_3$ | Average Age of Automobiles (years), $X_4$ | Number of Supervisors, $X_5$ |
|---|---|---|---|---|---|
| 37.702 | 1,739 | 9.27 | 85.4 | 3.5 | 9.0 |
| 24.196 | 1,221 | 5.86 | 60.7 | 5.0 | 5.0 |
| 32.055 | 1,846 | 8.81 | 68.1 | 4.4 | 7.0 |
| 3.611 | 120 | 3.81 | 20.2 | 4.0 | 5.0 |
| 17.625 | 1,096 | 10.31 | 33.8 | 3.5 | 7.0 |
| 45.919 | 2,290 | 11.62 | 95.1 | 4.1 | 13.0 |
| 29.600 | 1,687 | 8.96 | 69.3 | 4.1 | 15.0 |
| 8.114 | 241 | 6.28 | 16.3 | 5.9 | 11.0 |
| 20.116 | 649 | 7.77 | 34.9 | 5.5 | 16.0 |
| 12.994 | 1,427 | 10.92 | 15.1 | 4.1 | 10.0 |

a. Consider the following correlation matrix. Which single variable has the strongest correlation with the dependent variable? The correlations between the independent variables "outlets" and "income" and between "cars" and "outlets" are fairly strong. Could this be a problem? What is this condition called?

|  | sales | outlets | cars | income | age |
|---|---|---|---|---|---|
| outlets | 0.899 | | | | |
| cars | 0.605 | 0.775 | | | |
| income | 0.964 | 0.825 | 0.409 | | |
| age | −0.323 | −0.489 | −0.447 | −0.349 | |
| bosses | 0.286 | 0.183 | 0.395 | 0.155 | 0.291 |

b. The following regression equation was obtained using the five independent variables. What percent of the variation is explained by the regression equation?

```
The regression equation is
sales = -19.7 - 0.00063 outlets + 1.74 cars + 0.410 income +
        2.04 age - 0.034 bosses

        Predictor         Coef        StDev     t-ratio
        Constant       -19.672        5.422       -3.63
        outlets      -0.000629     0.002638       -0.24
        cars            1.7399       0.5530        3.15
        income         0.40994      0.04385        9.35
        age             2.0357       0.8779        2.32
        bosses         -0.0344       0.1880       -0.18

Analysis of Variance
        SOURCE       DF          SS          MS
        Regression    5     1593.81      318.76
        Error         4        9.08        2.27
        Total         9     1602.89
```

c. Conduct a global test of hypothesis to determine whether any of the regression coefficients are not zero. Use the .05 significance level.
d. Conduct a test of hypothesis on each of the independent variables. Would you consider eliminating "outlets" and "bosses"? Use the .05 significance level.
e. The regression has been rerun below with "outlets" and "bosses" eliminated. Compute the coefficient of determination. How much has $R^2$ changed from the previous analysis?

```
The regression equation is
sales = -18.9 + 1.61 cars + 0.400 income + 1.96 age
            Predictor            Coef         StDev      t-ratio
            Constant          -18.924         3.636        -5.20
            Cars               1.6129        0.1979         8.15
            Income            0.40031       0.01569        25.52
            Age                1.9637        0.5846         3.36
Analysis of Variance
            SOURCE          DF            SS            MS
            Regression       3       1593.66        531.22
            Error            6          9.23          1.54
            Total            9       1602.89
```

**f.** Following is a histogram and a stem-and-leaf chart of the residuals. Does the normality assumption appear reasonable?

```
Histogram of residual N = 10        Stem-and-leaf of residual N = 10
                                     Leaf Unit = 0.10
Midpoint Count
    -1.5     1    *                  1  -1   7
    -1.0     1    *                  2  -1   2
    -0.5     2    **                 2  -0
    -0.0     2    **                 5  -0   440
     0.5     2    **                 5   0   24
     1.0     1    *                  3   0   68
     1.5     1    *                  1   1
                                     1   1   7
```

**g.** Following is a plot of the fitted values of $Y$ (i.e., $Y'$) and the residuals. Do you see any violations of the assumptions?

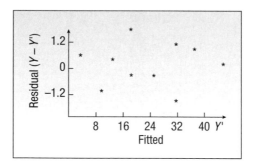

**15.** The administrator of a new paralegal program at Seagate Technical College wants to estimate the grade point average in the new program. He thought that high school GPA, the verbal score on the Scholastic Aptitude Test (SAT), and the mathematics score on the SAT would be good predictors of paralegal GPA. The data on nine students are:

| Student | High School GPA | SAT Verbal | SAT Math | Paralegal GPA |
|---------|-----------------|------------|----------|---------------|
| 1 | 3.25 | 480 | 410 | 3.21 |
| 2 | 1.80 | 290 | 270 | 1.68 |
| 3 | 2.89 | 420 | 410 | 3.58 |
| 4 | 3.81 | 500 | 600 | 3.92 |
| 5 | 3.13 | 500 | 490 | 3.00 |
| 6 | 2.81 | 430 | 460 | 2.82 |
| 7 | 2.20 | 320 | 490 | 1.65 |
| 8 | 2.14 | 530 | 480 | 2.30 |
| 9 | 2.63 | 469 | 440 | 2.33 |

**a.** Consider the following correlation matrix. Which variable has the strongest correlation with the dependent variable? Some of the correlations among the independent variables are strong. Does this appear to be a problem?

|      | legal | gpa   | verbal |
|------|-------|-------|--------|
| gpa    | 0.911 |       |        |
| verbal | 0.616 | 0.609 |        |
| math   | 0.487 | 0.636 | 0.599  |

**b.** Consider the following output. Compute the coefficient of multiple determination.

```
The regression equation is
legal = -0.411 + 1.20 gpa + 0.00163 verbal - 0.00194 math

Predictor              Coef            StDev          t-ratio
Constant            -0.4111           0.7823           -0.53
gpa                  1.2014           0.2955            4.07
verbal            0.001629          0.002147            0.76
math             -0.001939          0.002074           -0.94

Analysis of Variance
SOURCE           DF            SS            MS
Regression        3        4.3595        1.4532
Error             5        0.7036        0.1407
Total             8        5.0631
```

**c.** Conduct a global test of hypothesis from the preceding output. Does it appear that any of the regression coefficients are not equal to zero?

**d.** Conduct a test of hypothesis on each independent variable. Would you consider eliminating the variables "verbal" and "math"? Let $\alpha = .05$.

**e.** The analysis has been rerun without "verbal" and "math." See the following output. Compute the coefficient of determination. How much has $R^2$ changed from the previous analysis?

```
The regression equation is
legal = -0.454 + 1.16 gpa

Predictor              Coef          StDev        t-ratio
Constant            -0.4542         0.5542         -0.82
gpa                  1.1589         0.1977          5.86

Analysis of Variance
SOURCE           DF          SS            MS
Regression        1       4.2061        4.2061
Error             7       0.8570        0.1224
Total             8       5.0631
```

**f.** Following are a histogram and a stem-and-leaf diagram of the residuals. Does the normality assumption for the residuals seem reasonable?

```
Histogram of residual N = 9

Midpoint            Count
   -0.4              1    *
   -0.2              3    ***
    0.0              3    ***
    0.2              1    *
    0.4              0
    0.6              1    *

Stem-and-leaf of residual N = 9
Leaf unit = 0.10

  1    -0    4
  2    -0    2
 (3)   -0    110
  4     0    00
  2     0
  1     0
  1     0    6
```

**g.** Following is a plot of the residuals and the $Y'$ values. Do you see any violation of the assumptions?

The following problems require a software package.

**16.** Mike Wilde is president of the teachers' union for Otsego School District. In preparing for upcoming negotiations, he would like to investigate the salary structure of classroom teachers in the district. He believes there are three factors that affect a teacher's salary: years of experience, a rating of teaching effectiveness given by the principal, and whether the teacher has a master's degree. A random sample of 20 teachers resulted in the following data.

| Salary ($ thousands), $Y$ | Years of Experience, $X_1$ | Principal's Rating, $X_2$ | Master's Degree,* $X_3$ |
|---|---|---|---|
| 21.1 | 8 | 35 | 0 |
| 23.6 | 5 | 43 | 0 |
| 19.3 | 2 | 51 | 1 |
| 33.0 | 15 | 60 | 1 |
| 28.6 | 11 | 73 | 0 |
| 35.0 | 14 | 80 | 1 |
| 32.0 | 9 | 76 | 0 |
| 26.8 | 7 | 54 | 1 |
| 38.6 | 22 | 55 | 1 |
| 21.7 | 3 | 90 | 1 |
| 15.7 | 1 | 30 | 0 |
| 20.6 | 5 | 44 | 0 |
| 41.8 | 23 | 84 | 1 |
| 36.7 | 17 | 76 | 0 |
| 28.4 | 12 | 68 | 1 |
| 23.6 | 14 | 25 | 0 |
| 31.8 | 8 | 90 | 1 |
| 20.7 | 4 | 62 | 0 |
| 22.8 | 2 | 80 | 1 |
| 32.8 | 8 | 72 | 0 |

*1 = yes, 0 = no.

**a.** Develop a correlation matrix. Which independent variable has the strongest correlation with the dependent variable? Does it appear there will be any problems with multicollinearity?

**b.** Determine the regression equation. What salary would you estimate for a teacher with five years' experience, a rating by the principal of 60, and no master's degree?

**c.** Conduct a global test of hypothesis to determine whether any of the net regression coefficients differ from zero. Use the .05 significance level.

**d.** Conduct a test of hypothesis for the individual regression coefficients. Would you consider deleting any of the independent variables? Use the .05 significance level.

**e.** If your conclusion in part (d) was to delete one or more independent variables, run the analysis again without those variables.

**f.** Determine the residuals for the equation of part (e). Use a stem-and-leaf chart or a histogram to verify that the distribution of the residuals is approximately normal.

**g.** Plot the residuals computed in part (f) in a scatter diagram with the residuals on the $Y$-axis and the $Y'$ values on the $X$-axis. Does the plot reveal any violations of the assumptions of regression?

**17.** The district sales manager for a major automobile manufacturer is studying car sales. Specifically, he would like to determine what factors affect the number of cars sold at a dealership. To investigate, he randomly selects 12 dealers. From these dealers he obtains the number of cars sold last month, the minutes of radio advertising purchased last month, the number of full-time salespeople employed in the dealership, and whether the dealer is located in the city. The information is as follows:

| Cars Sold Last Month, Y | Advertising, $X_1$ | Sales Force, $X_2$ | City, $X_3$ | Cars Sold Last Month, Y | Advertising, $X_1$ | Sales Force, $X_2$ | City, $X_3$ |
|---|---|---|---|---|---|---|---|
| 127 | 18 | 10 | Yes | 161 | 25 | 14 | Yes |
| 138 | 15 | 15 | No | 180 | 26 | 17 | Yes |
| 159 | 22 | 14 | Yes | 102 | 15 | 7 | No |
| 144 | 23 | 12 | Yes | 163 | 24 | 16 | Yes |
| 139 | 17 | 12 | No | 106 | 18 | 10 | No |
| 128 | 16 | 12 | Yes | 149 | 25 | 11 | Yes |

**a.** Develop a correlation matrix. Which independent variable has the strongest correlation with the dependent variable? Does it appear there will be any problems with multi-collinearity?
**b.** Determine the regression equation. How many cars would you expect to be sold by a dealership employing 20 salespeople, purchasing 15 minutes of advertising, and located in a city?
**c.** Conduct a global test of hypothesis to determine whether any of the net regression coefficients differ from zero. Let $\alpha = .05$.
**d.** Conduct a test of hypothesis for the individual regression coefficients. Would you consider deleting any of the independent variables? Let $\alpha = .05$.
**e.** If your conclusion in part (d) was to delete one or more independent variables, run the analysis again without those variables.
**f.** Determine the residuals for the equation of part (e). Use a stem-and-leaf chart or a histogram to verify that the distribution of the residuals is approximately normal.
**g.** Plot the residuals computed in part (f) in a scatter diagram with the residuals on the $Y$-axis and the $Y'$ values on the $X$-axis. Does the plot reveal any violations of the assumptions of regression?

**18.** Fran's Convenience Marts are located throughout metropolitan Erie, Pennsylvania. Fran, the owner, would like to expand into other communities in northwestern Pennsylvania and southwestern New York, such as Jamestown, Corry, Meadville, and Warren. As part of her presentation to the local bank, she would like to better understand the factors that make a particular outlet profitable. She must do all the work herself, so she will not be able to study all her outlets. She selects a random sample of 15 marts and records the average daily sales (Y), the floor space (area), the number of parking spaces, and the median income of families in that ZIP code region for each. The sample information is reported below.

| Sampled Mart | Daily Sales | Store Area | Parking Spaces | Income ($ thousands) |
|---|---|---|---|---|
| 1 | $1,840 | 532 | 6 | 44 |
| 2 | 1,746 | 478 | 4 | 51 |
| 3 | 1,812 | 530 | 7 | 45 |
| 4 | 1,806 | 508 | 7 | 46 |
| 5 | 1,792 | 514 | 5 | 44 |
| 6 | 1,825 | 556 | 6 | 46 |
| 7 | 1,811 | 541 | 4 | 49 |
| 8 | 1,803 | 513 | 6 | 52 |
| 9 | 1,830 | 532 | 5 | 46 |
| 10 | 1,827 | 537 | 5 | 46 |
| 11 | 1,764 | 499 | 3 | 48 |
| 12 | 1,825 | 510 | 8 | 47 |
| 13 | 1,763 | 490 | 4 | 48 |
| 14 | 1,846 | 516 | 8 | 45 |
| 15 | 1,815 | 482 | 7 | 43 |

a. Determine the regression equation.
b. What is the value of $R^2$? Comment on the value.
c. Conduct a global hypothesis test to determine if any of the independent variables are different from zero.
d. Conduct individual hypothesis tests to determine if any of the independent variables can be dropped.
e. If variables are dropped, recompute the regression equation and $R^2$.

19. Steve Douglas has been hired as a management trainee by a large brokerage firm. As his first project, he is asked to study the gross profit of firms in the chemical industry. What factors affect profitability in that industry? Steve selects a random sample of 16 firms and obtains data on the number of employees, number of consecutive common stock dividends paid, the total value of inventory at the start of the current year, and the gross profit for each firm. His findings are:

| Company | Gross Profit ($ thousands), $Y$ | Number of Employees, $X_1$ | Consecutive Dividends, $X_2$ | Beginning Inventory ($ thousands), $X_3$ |
|---|---|---|---|---|
| 1 | 2,800 | 140 | 12 | 1,800 |
| 2 | 1,300 | 65 | 21 | 320 |
| 3 | 1,230 | 130 | 42 | 820 |
| 4 | 1,600 | 115 | 80 | 76 |
| 5 | 4,500 | 390 | 120 | 3,600 |
| 6 | 5,700 | 670 | 64 | 8,400 |
| 7 | 3,150 | 205 | 43 | 508 |
| 8 | 640 | 40 | 14 | 870 |
| 9 | 3,400 | 480 | 88 | 5,500 |
| 10 | 6,700 | 810 | 98 | 9,875 |
| 11 | 3,700 | 120 | 44 | 6,500 |
| 12 | 6,440 | 590 | 110 | 9,130 |
| 13 | 1,280 | 440 | 38 | 1,200 |
| 14 | 4,160 | 280 | 24 | 890 |
| 15 | 3,870 | 650 | 60 | 1,200 |
| 16 | 980 | 150 | 24 | 1,300 |

a. Determine the regression equation. The Master Chemical Company employs 220 people, has paid 64 consecutive common stock dividends, and has an inventory valued at $1,500,000 at the start of the year. What is the estimate of the gross profit?
b. Conduct a global test of hypothesis to determine whether any of the net regression coefficients differ from zero.
c. Conduct a test of hypothesis for the individual regression coefficients. Would you consider deleting any of the independent variables?
d. If your conclusion in part (c) was to delete one or more independent variables, run the analysis again, deleting those variables.
e. Determine the residuals for the equation of part (d). Use a stem-and-leaf chart or a histogram to verify that the distribution of the residuals is approximately normal.
f. Plot the residuals computed in part (e) in a scatter diagram with the residuals on the $Y$-axis and the $Y'$ values on the $X$-axis. Does the plot reveal any violations of the assumptions of regression?

20. The *Times-Observer* is a daily newspaper in Metro City. Like many city newspapers, the *Times-Observer* is suffering through difficult financial times. The circulation manager is studying other papers in similar cities in the United States and Canada. She is particularly interested in what variables relate to the number of subscriptions to the paper. She is able to obtain the following sample information on 25 newspapers in similar cities. The following notation is used:

  Sub = Number of subscriptions (in thousands).
  Popul = The metropolitan population (in thousands).
  Adv = The advertising budget of the paper (in $ hundreds).
  Income = The median family income in the metropolitan area (in $ thousands).

| Paper | Sub | Popul | Adv | Income | Paper | Sub | Popul | Adv | Income |
|---|---|---|---|---|---|---|---|---|---|
| 1 | 37.95 | 588.9 | 13.2 | 35.1 | 14 | 38.39 | 586.5 | 15.4 | 35.5 |
| 2 | 37.66 | 585.3 | 13.2 | 34.7 | 15 | 37.29 | 544.0 | 11.0 | 34.9 |
| 3 | 37.55 | 566.3 | 19.8 | 34.8 | 16 | 39.15 | 611.1 | 24.2 | 35.0 |
| 4 | 38.78 | 642.9 | 17.6 | 35.1 | 17 | 38.29 | 643.3 | 17.6 | 35.3 |
| 5 | 37.67 | 624.2 | 17.6 | 34.6 | 18 | 38.09 | 635.6 | 19.8 | 34.8 |
| 6 | 38.23 | 603.9 | 15.4 | 34.8 | 19 | 37.83 | 598.9 | 15.4 | 35.1 |
| 7 | 36.90 | 571.9 | 11.0 | 34.7 | 20 | 39.37 | 657.0 | 22.0 | 35.3 |
| 8 | 38.28 | 584.3 | 28.6 | 35.3 | 21 | 37.81 | 595.2 | 15.4 | 35.1 |
| 9 | 38.95 | 605.0 | 28.6 | 35.1 | 22 | 37.42 | 520.0 | 19.8 | 35.1 |
| 10 | 39.27 | 676.3 | 17.6 | 35.6 | 23 | 38.83 | 629.6 | 22.0 | 35.3 |
| 11 | 38.30 | 587.4 | 17.6 | 34.9 | 24 | 38.33 | 680.0 | 24.2 | 34.7 |
| 12 | 38.84 | 576.4 | 22.0 | 35.4 | 25 | 40.24 | 651.2 | 33.0 | 35.8 |
| 13 | 38.14 | 570.8 | 17.6 | 35.0 | | | | | |

a. Determine the regression equation.
b. Conduct a global test of hypothesis to determine whether any of the net regression coefficients are not equal to zero.
c. Conduct a test for the individual coefficients. Would you consider deleting any coefficients?
d. Determine the residuals and plot them against the fitted values. Do you see any problems?
e. Develop a histogram of the residuals. Do you see any problems with the normality assumption?

21. How important is GPA in determining the starting salary of recent business school graduates? Does graduating from a business school increase the starting salary? The Director of Undergraduate Studies at a major university wanted to study these questions. She gathered the following sample information on 15 graduates last spring to investigate these questions.

| Student | Salary | GPA | Business |
|---|---|---|---|
| 1 | $31.5 | 3.245 | 0 |
| 2 | 33.0 | 3.278 | 0 |
| 3 | 34.1 | 3.520 | 1 |
| 4 | 35.4 | 3.740 | 1 |
| 5 | 34.2 | 3.520 | 1 |
| 6 | 34.0 | 3.421 | 1 |
| 7 | 34.5 | 3.410 | 1 |
| 8 | 35.0 | 3.630 | 1 |
| 9 | 34.7 | 3.355 | 1 |
| 10 | 32.5 | 3.080 | 0 |
| 11 | 31.5 | 3.025 | 0 |
| 12 | 32.2 | 3.146 | 0 |
| 13 | 34.0 | 3.465 | 1 |
| 14 | 32.8 | 3.245 | 0 |
| 15 | 31.8 | 3.025 | 0 |

The salary is reported in $000, GPA on the traditional 4-point scale. A 1 indicates the student graduated from a school of business; a 0 indicates that the student graduated from one of the other schools.
a. Develop a correlation matrix. Do you see any problems with multicollinearity?
b. Determine the regression equation. Discuss the regression equation. How much does graduating from a college of business add to a starting salary? What starting salary would you estimate for a student with a GPA of 3.00 who graduated from a college of business?
c. What is the value of $R^2$? Can we conclude that this value is greater than 0?
d. Would you consider deleting either of the independent variables?

e. Plot the residuals in a histogram. Is there any problem with the normality assumption?

f. Plot the fitted values against the residuals. Does this plot indicate any problems with homoscedasticity?

22. A mortgage department of a large bank is studying its recent loans. Of particular interest is how such factors as the value of the home (in thousands of dollars), education level of the head of the household, age of the head of the household, current monthly mortgage payment (in dollars), and gender of the head of the household (male = 1, female = 0) relate to the family income. Are these variables effective predictors of the income of the household? A random sample of 25 recent loans is obtained.

| Income ($ thousands) | Value ($ thousands) | Years of Education | Age | Mortgage Payment | Gender |
|---|---|---|---|---|---|
| $40.3 | $190 | 14 | 53 | $230 | 1 |
| 39.6 | 121 | 15 | 49 | 370 | 1 |
| 40.8 | 161 | 14 | 44 | 397 | 1 |
| 40.3 | 161 | 14 | 39 | 181 | 1 |
| 40.0 | 179 | 14 | 53 | 378 | 0 |
| 38.1 | 99 | 14 | 46 | 304 | 0 |
| 40.4 | 114 | 15 | 42 | 285 | 1 |
| 40.7 | 202 | 14 | 49 | 551 | 0 |
| 40.8 | 184 | 13 | 37 | 370 | 0 |
| 37.1 | 90 | 14 | 43 | 135 | 0 |
| 39.9 | 181 | 14 | 48 | 332 | 1 |
| 40.4 | 143 | 15 | 54 | 217 | 1 |
| 38.0 | 132 | 14 | 44 | 490 | 0 |
| 39.0 | 127 | 14 | 37 | 220 | 0 |
| 39.5 | 153 | 14 | 50 | 270 | 1 |
| 40.6 | 145 | 14 | 50 | 279 | 1 |
| 40.3 | 174 | 15 | 52 | 329 | 1 |
| 40.1 | 177 | 15 | 47 | 274 | 0 |
| 41.7 | 188 | 15 | 49 | 433 | 1 |
| 40.1 | 153 | 15 | 53 | 333 | 1 |
| 40.6 | 150 | 16 | 58 | 148 | 0 |
| 40.4 | 173 | 13 | 42 | 390 | 1 |
| 40.9 | 163 | 14 | 46 | 142 | 1 |
| 40.1 | 150 | 15 | 50 | 343 | 0 |
| 38.5 | 139 | 14 | 45 | 373 | 0 |

a. Determine the regression equation.

b. What is the value of $R^2$? Comment on the value.

c. Conduct a global hypothesis test to determine whether any of the independent variables are different from zero.

d. Conduct individual hypothesis tests to determine whether any of the independent variables can be dropped.

e. If variables are dropped, recompute the regression equation and $R^2$.

23. Fred G. Hire is the manager of human resources at Crescent Tool and Die, Inc. As part of his yearly report to the CEO, he is required to present an analysis of the salaried employees. Because there are over 1,000 employees, he does not have the staff to gather information on each salaried employee, so he selects a random sample of 30. For each employee, he records monthly salary; service at Crescent, in months; gender (1 = male, 0 = female); and whether the employee has a technical or clerical job. Those working technical jobs are coded 1, and those who are clerical 0.

| Sampled Employee | Monthly Salary | Length of Service | Age | Gender | Job |
|---|---|---|---|---|---|
| 1 | $1,769 | 93 | 42 | 1 | 0 |
| 2 | 1,740 | 104 | 33 | 1 | 0 |
| 3 | 1,941 | 104 | 42 | 1 | 1 |
| 4 | 2,367 | 126 | 57 | 1 | 1 |
| 5 | 2,467 | 98 | 30 | 1 | 1 |
| 6 | 1,640 | 99 | 49 | 1 | 1 |
| 7 | 1,756 | 94 | 35 | 1 | 0 |
| 8 | 1,706 | 96 | 46 | 0 | 1 |
| 9 | 1,767 | 124 | 56 | 0 | 0 |
| 10 | 1,200 | 73 | 23 | 0 | 1 |
| 11 | 1,706 | 110 | 67 | 0 | 1 |
| 12 | 1,985 | 90 | 36 | 0 | 1 |
| 13 | 1,555 | 104 | 53 | 0 | 0 |
| 14 | 1,749 | 81 | 29 | 0 | 0 |
| 15 | 2,056 | 106 | 45 | 1 | 0 |
| 16 | 1,729 | 113 | 55 | 0 | 1 |
| 17 | 2,186 | 129 | 46 | 1 | 1 |
| 18 | 1,858 | 97 | 39 | 0 | 1 |
| 19 | 1,819 | 101 | 43 | 1 | 1 |
| 20 | 1,350 | 91 | 35 | 1 | 1 |
| 21 | 2,030 | 100 | 40 | 1 | 0 |
| 22 | 2,550 | 123 | 59 | 1 | 0 |
| 23 | 1,544 | 88 | 30 | 0 | 0 |
| 24 | 1,766 | 117 | 60 | 1 | 1 |
| 25 | 1,937 | 107 | 45 | 1 | 1 |
| 26 | 1,691 | 105 | 32 | 0 | 1 |
| 27 | 1,623 | 86 | 33 | 0 | 0 |
| 28 | 1,791 | 131 | 56 | 0 | 1 |
| 29 | 2,001 | 95 | 30 | 1 | 1 |
| 30 | 1,874 | 98 | 47 | 1 | 0 |

**a.** Determine the regression equation, using salary as the dependent variable and the other four variables as independent variables.
**b.** What is the value of $R^2$? Comment on this value.
**c.** Conduct a global test of hypothesis to determine whether any of the independent variables are different from 0.
**d.** Conduct an individual test to determine whether any of the independent variables can be dropped.
**e.** Rerun the regression equation, using only the independent variables that are significant. How much more does a man earn per month than a woman? Does it make a difference whether the employee has a technical or a clerical job?

**24.** Many regions along the coast in North and South Carolina and Georgia have experienced rapid population growth over the last 10 years. It is expected that the growth will continue over the next 10 years. This has resulted in many of the large grocery store chains building new stores in the region. The Kelley's Super Grocery Stores, Inc. chain is no exception. The director of planning for Kelley's Super Grocery Stores wants to study adding more stores in this region. He believes there are two main factors that indicate the amount families spend on groceries. The first is their income and the other is the number of people in the family. The director gathered the following sample information.

| Family | Food | Income | Size |
|--------|------|--------|------|
| 1 | $5.04 | $ 73.98 | 4 |
| 2 | 4.08 | 54.90 | 2 |
| 3 | 5.76 | 94.14 | 4 |
| 4 | 3.48 | 52.02 | 1 |
| 5 | 4.20 | 65.70 | 2 |
| 6 | 4.80 | 53.64 | 4 |
| 7 | 4.32 | 79.74 | 3 |
| 8 | 5.04 | 68.58 | 4 |
| 9 | 6.12 | 165.60 | 5 |
| 10 | 3.24 | 64.80 | 1 |
| 11 | 4.80 | 138.42 | 3 |
| 12 | 3.24 | 125.82 | 1 |
| 13 | 6.60 | 77.58 | 7 |
| 14 | 4.92 | 171.36 | 2 |
| 15 | 6.60 | 82.08 | 9 |
| 16 | 5.40 | 141.30 | 3 |
| 17 | 6.00 | 36.90 | 5 |
| 18 | 5.40 | 56.88 | 4 |
| 19 | 3.36 | 71.82 | 1 |
| 20 | 4.68 | 69.48 | 3 |
| 21 | 4.32 | 54.36 | 2 |
| 22 | 5.52 | 87.66 | 5 |
| 23 | 4.56 | 38.16 | 3 |
| 24 | 5.40 | 43.74 | 7 |
| 25 | 4.80 | 48.42 | 5 |

Food and income are reported in thousands of dollars per year, and the variable "Size" refers to the number of people in the household.

**a.** Develop a correlation matrix. Do you see any problems with multicollinearity?

**b.** Determine the regression equation. Discuss the regression equation. How much does an additional family member add to the amount spent on food?

**c.** What is the value of $R^2$? Can we conclude that this value is greater than 0?

**d.** Would you consider deleting either of the independent variables?

**e.** Plot the residuals in a histogram. Is there any problem with the normality assumption?

**f.** Plot the fitted values against the residuals. Does this plot indicate any problems with homoscedasticity?

**25.** An investment advisor is studying the relationship between a common stock's price to earnings ratio (P/E) and factors that she thinks would influence it. She has the following data on the earnings per share (EPS) and the dividend percentage (Yield) for a sample of 20 stocks.

| Stock | P/E | EPS | Yield |
|-------|-----|-----|-------|
| 1 | 20.79 | 2.46 | 1.42 |
| 2 | 3.03 | 2.69 | 4.05 |
| 3 | 44.46 | −0.28 | 4.16 |
| 4 | 41.72 | −0.45 | 1.27 |
| 5 | 18.96 | 1.60 | 3.39 |
| 6 | 18.42 | 2.32 | 3.86 |
| 7 | 34.82 | 0.81 | 4.56 |
| 8 | 30.43 | 2.13 | 1.62 |
| 9 | 29.97 | 2.22 | 5.10 |
| 10 | 10.86 | 1.44 | 1.17 |
| 11 | 1.35 | 2.93 | 2.59 |
| 12 | 25.43 | 2.07 | 1.04 |
| 13 | 22.14 | 2.19 | 3.52 |
| 14 | 24.21 | −0.83 | 1.56 |
| 15 | 30.91 | 2.29 | 2.23 |
| 16 | 35.79 | 1.64 | 3.36 |
| 17 | 18.99 | 3.07 | 1.98 |
| 18 | 30.21 | 1.71 | 3.07 |
| 19 | 32.88 | 0.35 | 2.21 |
| 20 | 15.19 | 5.02 | 3.50 |

a. Develop a multiple linear regression with P/E as the dependent variable.
b. Are either of the two independent variables an effective predictor of P/E?
c. Interpret the regression coefficients.
d. Do any of these stocks look particularly undervalued?
e. Plot the residuals and check the normality assumption. Plot the fitted values against the residuals.
f. Does there appear to be any problems with homoscedasticity?
g. Develop a correlation matrix. Do any of the correlations indicate multicollinearity?

26. Listed below is recent data from the United States Bureau of Labor Statistics on the percent changes in Output/Hour, Unit Labor Costs, and Real Hourly Compensation for nonfarm payrolls in the United States.

| Year | Quarter | Output/Hour | Labor Cost | Compensation |
|------|---------|-------------|------------|--------------|
| 1997 | 1 | 1.1 | 1.1 | −0.1 |
| 1997 | 2 | 4.5 | −2.6 | 0.9 |
| 1997 | 3 | 3.0 | 0.7 | 2.0 |
| 1997 | 4 | 0.5 | 5.6 | 0.8 |
| 1998 | 1 | 4.9 | 2.0 | 6.2 |
| 1998 | 2 | 0.6 | 5.1 | 4.6 |
| 1998 | 3 | 1.9 | 2.7 | 3.0 |
| 1998 | 4 | 4.3 | −0.4 | 2.0 |
| 1999 | 1 | 2.4 | 4.8 | 5.5 |
| 1999 | 2 | −0.8 | 1.3 | −2.2 |
| 1999 | 3 | 3.7 | 0.0 | 0.8 |
| 1999 | 4 | 6.3 | −0.5 | 2.5 |
| 2000 | 1 | 0.2 | 14.9 | 10.7 |
| 2000 | 2 | 6.0 | −3.6 | −0.7 |
| 2000 | 3 | 0.6 | 8.0 | 4.9 |
| 2000 | 4 | 1.7 | 1.4 | 0.2 |
| 2001 | 1 | −1.5 | 4.3 | −0.9 |
| 2001 | 2 | −0.1 | 0.3 | −2.9 |
| 2001 | 3 | 2.1 | −1.1 | 0.3 |
| 2001 | 4 | 7.3 | −5.4 | 1.8 |
| 2002 | 1 | 8.6 | −5.3 | 1.4 |
| 2002 | 2 | 1.7 | 2.2 | 0.5 |
| 2002 | 3 | 5.1 | −0.2 | 3.0 |

a. Develop a multiple regression equation with output and labor as independent variables and compensation as the dependent variable.
b. Conduct a global test. Can we conclude the value of $R^2$ is greater than zero?
c. Test each variable for significance. Should any be dropped?
d. Plot the residuals and verify the normality assumption.
e. Plot the fitted value against the residuals. Is there a problem with homoscedasticity?
f. Construct a correlation matrix. Is there a problem with multicollinearity?

# exercises.com

27. The National Institute of Standards and Technology provides several datasets to allow any user to test the accuracy of their statistical software. Go to the website: http://www.itl.nist. gov/div898/strd. Select the **Dataset Archives** section and, within that, the **Linear Regression** section. You will find the names of 11 small datasets stored in ASCII format on this page. Select one and run the data through your statistical software. Compare your results with the "official" results of the federal government.

28. As described in the examples in Chapters 12 and 13, many real estate companies and rental agencies now publish their listings on the Web. One example is the Dunes Realty Company, located in Garden City and Surfside Beaches in South Carolina. Go to the Web site http://www.dunes.com, select **Cottage Search,** then indicate 5 bedroom, accommodations for 14 people, oceanfront, and no pool or floating dock, select a period in July and August, indicate that you are willing to spend $5,000 per week, and then click on **Search**

**the Cottages.** The output should include details on the cottages that met your criteria. Develop a multiple linear regression equation using the rental price per week as the dependent variable and number of bedrooms, number of bathrooms, and how many people the cottage will accommodate as independent variables. Analyze the regression equations. Would you consider deleting any independent variables? What is the coefficient of determination? If you delete any of the variables, rerun the regression equation and discuss the new equation.

# Dataset Exercises

29. Refer to the Real Estate data which reports information on homes sold in the Denver, Colorado, area during the last year. Use the selling price of the home as the dependent variable and determine the regression equation with number of bedrooms, size of the house, whether there is a pool, whether there is an attached garage, distance from the center of the city, and number of bathrooms as independent variables.
    a. Write out the regression equation. Discuss each of the variables. For example, are you surprised that the regression coefficient for distance from the center of the city is negative? How much does a garage or a swimming pool add to the selling price of a home?
    b. Determine the value of $R^2$. Interpret.
    c. Develop a correlation matrix. Which independent variables have strong or weak correlations with the dependent variable? Do you see any problems with multicollinearity?
    d. Conduct the global test on the set of independent variables. Interpret.
    e. Conduct a test of hypothesis on each of the independent variables. Would you consider deleting any of the variables? If so, which ones?
    f. Rerun the analysis until only significant net regression coefficients remain in the analysis. Identify these variables.
    g. Develop a histogram or a stem-and-leaf display of the residuals from the final regression equation developed in part (f). Is it reasonable to conclude that the normality assumption has been met?
    h. Plot the residuals against the fitted values from the final regression equation developed in part (f) against the fitted values of $Y$. Plot the residuals on the vertical axis and the fitted values on the horizontal axis.

30. Refer to the Baseball 2002 data, which reports information on the 30 Major League Baseball teams for the 2002 season. Let the number of games won be the dependent variable and the following variables be independent variables: team batting average, number of stolen bases, number of errors committed, team ERA, number of home runs, and whether the team's home field is natural grass or artificial turf.
    a. Write out the regression equation. Discuss each of the variables. For example, are you surprised that the regression coefficient for ERA is negative? How many wins does playing on natural grass for a home field add to or subtract from the total wins for the season?
    b. Determine the value of $R^2$. Interpret.
    c. Develop a correlation matrix. Which independent variables have strong or weak correlations with the dependent variable? Do you see any problems with multicollinearity?
    d. Conduct a global test on the set of independent variables. Interpret.
    e. Conduct a test of hypothesis on each of the independent variables. Would you consider deleting any of the variables? If so, which ones?
    f. Rerun the analysis until only significant net regression coefficients remain in the analysis. Identify these variables.
    g. Develop a histogram or a stem-and-leaf display of the residuals from the final regression equation developed in part (f). Is it reasonable to conclude that the normality assumption has been met?
    h. Plot the residuals against the fitted values from the final regression equation developed in part (f) against the fitted values of $Y$. Plot the residuals on the vertical axis and the fitted values on the horizontal axis.

31. Refer to the Wage data, which reports information on annual wages for a sample of 100 workers. Also included are variables relating to industry, years of education, and gender for each worker. Determine the regression equation using annual wage as the dependent variable and years of education, gender, years of work experience, age in years, and whether or not the worker was a union member.
    a. Write out the regression equation. Discuss each variable.
    b. Determine and interpret the $R^2$ value.
    c. Develop a correlation matrix. Which independent variables have strong or weak correlations with the dependent variable? Do you see any problems with multicollinearity?

d. Conduct a global test of hypothesis on the set of independent variables. Interpret your findings. Is it reasonable to continue with the analysis or should you stop here?

e. Conduct a test of hypothesis on each of the independent variables. Would you consider deleting any of these variables? If so, which ones?

f. Rerun the analysis deleting any of the independent variables that are not significant. Delete the variables one at a time.

g. Develop a histogram or a stem-and-leaf chart of the residuals from the final regression equation. Is it reasonable to conclude that the normality assumption has been met?

h. Plot the residuals against the fitted values from the final regression equation. Plot the residuals on the vertical axis and the fitted values on the horizontal axis.

32. Refer to the CIA data, which reports demographic and economic information on 46 countries. Let unemployment be the dependent variable and percent of the population over 65, life expectancy, and literacy be the independent variables.

a. Determine the regression equation using a software package. Write out the regression equation.

b. What is the value of the coefficient of determination?

c. Check the independent variables for multicollinearity.

d. Conduct a global test on the set of independent variables.

e. Test each of the independent variables to determine if they differ from zero.

f. Would you delete any of the independent variables? If so, rerun the regression analysis and report the new equation.

g. Make a histogram of the residuals from your final regression equation. Is it reasonable to conclude that the residuals follow a normal distribution?

h. Plot the residuals versus the fitted values and check. Are there any problems?

# Software Commands

1. The MINITAB commands for the multiple regression output on page 478 are:
   a. Import the data from the CD. The file name is Tbl14–1.
   b. Select **Stat**, **Regression,** and then click on **Regression**.
   c. Select *Cost* as the **Response** variable, and *Temp, Insulation,* and *Age* as the **Predictors**, then click on **OK.**

2. The Excel commands to produce the multiple regression output on page 478 are:
   a. Import the data from the CD. The file name is Tbl14.
   b. Select **Tools**, then **Data Analysis**, highlight **Regression,** and click **OK**.
   c. Make the **Input Y Range** *A1:A21*, the **Input X Range** *B1:D21,* check the **Labels** box, the **Output Range** is *F1,* click **OK**.

3.  The Excel commands to develop the correlation matrix on page 486 are:
    a.  Import the data from the CD. The file name is Tbl14–1.
    b.  Select **Tools, Data Analysis,** then hit **Enter.** Select the command **Correlation** and then hit **OK.**
    c.  The **Input Range** is *A1:D21,* grouped by **Columns,** check the **Labels** box, select the **Output Range** as *G1,* and click **OK.**

4.  The MINITAB commands for the multiple regression output on page 496 are:
    a.  Import the data from the CD. The file name is Tbl14–1.
    b.  Select **Stat**, **Regression,** and then click on **Regression**.
    c.  Select *Cost* as the **Response** variable, and *Temp, Insulation,* and *Age* as the **Predictors**, then click on **OK.**
    d.  Click on **Storage,** then check **Residuals** and **Fits,** and click **OK** in both dialog boxes.

5.  The MINITAB commands for the fitted regression on page 499 are:
    a.  Import the data from the CD.
    b.  Select **Stat**, **Regression,** and then click on **Fitted Line Plot**.
    c.  Select Mpg as the **Response (Y)** and Pressure as the **Predictor (X),** and then select Quadratic as the **Type of Regression Model** and click on **OK.**

# Chapter 14  Answers to Self-Review

**14–1** **a.** 12.9 psi, found by $Y' = -0.5 + 20(.35) + 1(6.4)$.

    **b.** The $b_1$ of 20 indicates that the tensile strength of the wire will increase 20 psi for each increase of 1 mm in outside diameter, with the amount of molybdenum held constant. That is, tensile strength will increase 20 psi regardless of the amount of molybdenum in the wire.

**14–2** **a.** $n = 25$

    **b.** 4

    **c.** $R^2 = \dfrac{10}{15} = 0.6677$

    **d.** $s_{y \cdot 1234} = \sqrt{\dfrac{5}{20}} = 0.50$

**14–3** **a.** $Y' = 490 - 5.15X_1 - 14.7X_2$

    **b.** .776. A total of 77.6 percent of the variation in heating cost is explained by temperature and insulation.

    **c.** The results of the global test indicate that at least one of the regression coefficients is not zero. To arrive at that conclusion, we first stated the null hypothesis as $H_0$: $\beta_1 = \beta_2 = 0$. The critical value of $F$ is 3.59, and the computed value 29.4, found by $82,597/2,807$. Since 29.4 lies in the region of rejection beyond 3.59, we reject $H_0$.

    **d.** The $p$-value is .008. The probability of a $t$ value less than $-2.98$ or greater than 2.98, with 17 degrees of freedom, is .008.

# A Review of Chapters 13 and 14

Simple regression and correlation examine the relationship between two variables.

This section is a review of the major concepts and terms introduced in Chapters 13 and 14. Chapter 13 noted that the strength of the relationship between the independent variable and the dependent variable can be measured by the *coefficient of correlation.* Developed by Karl Pearson, Pearson's r can assume any value between $-1.00$ and $+1.00$ inclusive. Coefficients of $-1.00$ and $+1.00$ indicate perfect relationship, and 0 indicates no relationship. A value near 0, such as $-.14$ or $.14$, indicates a weak relationship. A value near $-1$ or $+1$, such as $-.90$ or $+.90$, indicates a strong relationship. Squaring r gives the *coefficient of determination,* also called $r^2$. It indicates the proportion of the total variation in the dependent variable explained by the independent variable.

Multiple regression and correlation is concerned with relationship between two or more independent variables and the dependent variable.

Likewise, the strength of the relationship between several independent variables and a dependent variable is measured by the *coefficient of multiple determination, $R^2$.* It measures the proportion of the variation in Y explained by two or more independent variables.

The linear relationship in the simple case involving one independent variable and one dependent variable is described by the equation $Y' = a + bX$. For three independent variables, $X_1$, $X_2$, and $X_3$, the same multiple regression equation is

$$Y' = a + b_1X_1 + b_2X_2 + b_3X_3$$

Computer invaluable in multiple regression and correlation.

Solving for $b_1, b_2, b_3, \ldots, b_k$ would involve tedious calculations. Fortunately, this type of problem can be quickly solved using one of the many statistical software packages and spreadsheet packages available for the computer. Various measures, such as the coefficient of determination, the multiple standard error of estimate, the results of the global test, and the test of the individual variables are reported in the output of most computer software programs.

## Glossary

### Chapter 13
**Coefficient of correlation**  A measure of the strength of association between two variables. It is computed by:

$$r = \frac{\Sigma(X - \bar{X})(Y - \bar{Y})}{(n - 1)\, s_x\, s_y} \qquad \textbf{[13–1]}$$

**Coefficient of determination**  The proportion of the total variation in the dependent variable that is explained by the independent variable. It can assume any value between 0 and $+1.00$ inclusive. A coefficient of .82 indicates that 82 percent of the variation in Y is accounted for by X. This coefficient is computed by squaring the coefficient of correlation, r.

**Correlation analysis**  A group of statistical techniques used to measure the strength of the relationship between two variables.

**Least squares method**  A technique used to arrive at the regression equation by minimizing the sum of the squares of the vertical distances between the actual Y values and the predicted Y values.

**Linear regression equation**  A mathematical equation that defines the relationship between two variables. It has the form $Y' = a + bX$. It is used to predict Y based on a selected X value. Y is the dependent variable and X the independent variable.

**Scatter diagram**  A chart that visually depicts the relationship between two variables.

**Standard error of estimate**  Measures the dispersion of the actual Y values about the regression line. It is reported in the same units as the dependent variable.

**Test of significance of r**  A formula to answer the question: Is the correlation in the population from which the sample was selected zero? The test statistic is t, and the number of degrees of freedom is $n - 2$.

$$t = \frac{r\sqrt{n - 2}}{\sqrt{1 - r^2}} \qquad \textbf{[13–2]}$$

### Chapter 14
**Autocorrelation**  Correlation of successive residuals. This condition frequently occurs when time is involved in the analysis.

**Correlation matrix**  A listing of all possible simple coefficients of correlation. A correlation matrix includes the correlations between each of the independent variables and the dependent variable, as well as those among all the independent variables.

**Homoscedasticity**  The standard error of estimate is the same for all fitted values of the dependent variable.

**Multicollinearity**  A condition that occurs in multiple regression analysis if the independent variables are themselves correlated.

**Multiple regression equation**  The relationship in the form of a mathematical equation between several independent variables and a dependent variable. The general form is $Y' = a + b_1X_1 + b_2X_2 + b_3X_3 + \cdots + b_kX_k$. It is used to estimate Y given selected X values and k independent variables.

**Qualitative variables**  A nominal-scale variable that can assume only one of two possible outcomes. For example, a person is considered either employed or unemployed.

**Residual**  The difference between the actual value of the dependent variable and the estimated value of the dependent variable, that is $Y - Y'$.

## Exercises

### Part I—Multiple Choice

1. The strength of the association between a set of independent variables $X$ and a dependent variable $Y$ is measured by the
   a. Coefficient of correlation.
   b. Coefficient of determination.
   c. Standard error of estimate.
   d. All of the above.

2. The percent of total variation of the dependent variable $Y$ explained by the independent variable $X$ is measured by
   a. Coefficient of correlation.
   b. Coefficient of determination.
   c. Standard error of estimate.
   d. Multicollinearity.

3. A coefficient of correlation was computed to be $-0.90$. This result means:
   a. The relationship between two variables is weak.
   b. The relationship between two variables is strong and positive.
   c. The relationship between two variables is strong and negative.
   d. The relationship between four variables is strong.

4. The coefficient of determination was computed to be .38 in a problem involving one independent variable and one dependent variable. This result means
   a. The relationship between the two variables is negative.
   b. The correlation coefficient is also .38.
   c. 38 percent of the total variation is explained by the independent variable.
   d. 38 percent of the total variation is explained by the dependent variable.

5. What is the relationship between the coefficient of correlation and the coefficient of determination?
   a. They are unrelated.
   b. The coefficient of determination is the coefficient of correlation squared.
   c. The coefficient of determination is the square root of the coefficient of correlation.
   d. They are equal.

6. Multicollinearity exists when
   a. Independent variables are correlated less than $-0.70$ or more than $0.70$.
   b. An independent variable is strongly associated with a dependent variable.
   c. There is only one independent variable.
   d. The relationship between the dependent and independent variables is nonlinear.

7. If "time" is used as the independent variable in a simple linear regression analysis, which of the following assumptions could be violated?
   a. There is a linear relationship between the independent and dependent variables.
   b. The residual variation is the same for all fitted values of $Y$.
   c. The residuals are normally distributed.
   d. Successive observations of the dependent variable are uncorrelated.

8. In multiple regression, when the global test of significance is rejected, we can conclude:
   a. All of the net sample regression coefficients are equal to zero.
   b. All of the net sample regression coefficients are not equal to zero.
   c. At least one net sample regression coefficient is not equal to zero.
   d. The regression equation intersects the $Y$-axis at zero.

9. A residual is defined as:
   a. $Y - Y'$.
   b. Error sum of squares.
   c. Regression sum of squares.
   d. Type I error.

10. What test statistic is used for a global test of significance?
    a. $z$ statistic.
    b. $t$ statistic.
    c. Chi-square statistic.
    d. $F$ statistic.

### Part II—Problems

11. The accounting department at Crate and Barrel wishes to estimate the profit for each of the chain's many stores on the basis of the number of employees in the store, overhead costs, average markup, and theft loss. A few statistics from the stores are:

| Store | Net Profit ($ thousands) | Number of Employees | Overhead Cost ($ thousands) | Average Markup (percent) | Theft Loss ($ thousands) |
|---|---|---|---|---|---|
| 1 | $846 | 143 | $79 | 69 | $52 |
| 2 | 513 | 110 | 64 | 50 | 45 |

**a.** The dependent variable is _____ .

**b.** The general equation for this problem is _____ .

**c.** The multiple regression equation was computed to be $Y' = 67 + 8X_1 - 10X_2 + 0.004X_3 - 3X_4$. What is predicted sales for a store with 112 employees, an overhead cost of $65,000, a markup rate of 50 percent, and a loss from theft of $50,000?

**d.** Suppose $R^2$ was computed to be .86. Explain.

**e.** Suppose that the multiple standard error of estimate was 3 (in $ thousands). Explain what this means in this problem.

**12.** Quick-print firms in a large downtown business area spend most of their advertising dollars on advertisements on bus benches. A research project involves predicting monthly sales based on the annual amount spent on placing ads on bus benches. A sample of quick-print firms revealed these advertising expenses and sales:

| Firm | Annual Bus Bench Advertising ($ thousands) | Monthly Sales ($ thousands) |
|---|---|---|
| A | 2 | 10 |
| B | 4 | 40 |
| C | 5 | 30 |
| D | 7 | 50 |
| E | 3 | 20 |

**a.** Draw a scatter diagram.

**b.** Determine the coefficient of correlation.

**c.** What is the coefficient of determination?

**d.** Compute the regression equation.

**e.** Estimate the monthly sales of a quick-print firm that spends $4,500 on bus bench advertisements.

**f.** Summarize your findings.

**13.** The following ANOVA output is given.

```
SOURCE          Sum of Squares      DF           MS
Regression              1050.8       4       262.70
Error                     83.8      20         4.19
Total                   1134.6      24

   Predictor        Coef      St.Dev.      t-ratio
   Constant        70.06         2.13        32.89
      X₁            0.42         0.17         2.47
      X₂            0.27         0.21         1.29
      X₃            0.75         0.30         2.50
      X₄            0.42         0.07         6.00
```

**a.** Compute the coefficient of determination.

**b.** Compute the multiple standard error of estimate.

**c.** Conduct a test of hypothesis to determine whether any of the net regression coefficients are different from zero.

**d.** Conduct a test of hypothesis on the individual regression coefficients. Can any of the variables be detected?

# Cases

## A. The Century National Bank

Refer to the Century National Bank data. Using checking account balance as the dependent variable and using the number of ATM transactions, the number of other services used, whether the individual has a debit card, and whether interest is paid on the particular account as independent variables, write a report indicating which of the variables seem related to the account balance and how well they explain the variation in account balances. Should all of the independent variables proposed be used in the analysis or can some be dropped?

## B. Terry and Associates: The Time to Deliver Medical Kits

Terry and Associates is a specialized medical testing center in Denver, Colorado. One of their major sources of revenue is a kit used to test for elevated amounts of lead in the blood. Workers in auto body shops, those in the lawn care industry, and commercial house painters are exposed to large amounts of lead and thus must be randomly tested. It is expensive to conduct the test, so the kits are delivered on demand to a variety of locations throughout the Denver area.

Kathleen Terry, the owner, is concerned about appropriate costing of each delivery. To investigate, Ms. Terry gathered information on a random sample of 50 recent deliveries. Factors thought to be related to the cost of delivering a kit are:

Prep    The time between when the customized order is phoned into the company and when it is ready for delivery.
Delivery  The actual travel time from Terry's plant to the customer.
Mileage  The distance in miles from Terry's plant to the customer.

| Sample Number | Cost | Prep | Delivery | Mileage |
|---|---|---|---|---|
| 1 | $32.60 | 10 | 51 | 20 |
| 2 | 23.37 | 11 | 33 | 12 |
| 3 | 31.49 | 6 | 47 | 19 |
| 4 | 19.31 | 9 | 18 | 8 |
| 5 | 28.35 | 8 | 88 | 17 |
| 6 | 22.63 | 9 | 20 | 11 |
| 7 | 22.63 | 9 | 39 | 11 |
| 8 | 21.53 | 10 | 23 | 10 |
| 9 | 21.16 | 13 | 20 | 8 |
| 10 | 21.53 | 10 | 32 | 10 |
| 11 | 28.17 | 5 | 35 | 16 |
| 12 | 20.42 | 7 | 23 | 9 |
| 13 | 21.53 | 9 | 21 | 10 |
| 14 | 27.55 | 7 | 37 | 16 |
| 15 | 23.37 | 9 | 25 | 12 |
| 18 | 15.99 | 8 | 13 | 4 |

| Sample Number | Cost | Prep | Delivery | Mileage |
|---|---|---|---|---|
| 19 | 17.96 | 12 | 12 | 4 |
| 20 | 25.22 | 6 | 41 | 14 |
| 21 | 24.29 | 3 | 28 | 13 |
| 22 | 22.76 | 4 | 26 | 10 |
| 23 | 28.17 | 9 | 54 | 16 |
| 24 | 19.68 | 7 | 18 | 8 |
| 25 | 25.15 | 6 | 50 | 13 |
| 26 | 20.36 | 9 | 19 | 7 |
| 27 | 21.16 | 3 | 19 | 8 |
| 28 | 25.95 | 10 | 45 | 14 |
| 29 | 18.76 | 12 | 12 | 5 |
| 30 | 18.76 | 8 | 16 | 5 |
| 31 | 24.29 | 7 | 35 | 13 |
| 32 | 19.56 | 2 | 12 | 6 |
| 33 | 22.63 | 8 | 30 | 11 |
| 34 | 21.16 | 5 | 13 | 8 |
| 35 | 21.16 | 11 | 20 | 8 |
| 36 | 19.68 | 5 | 19 | 8 |
| 37 | 18.76 | 5 | 14 | 7 |
| 38 | 17.96 | 5 | 11 | 4 |
| 39 | 23.37 | 10 | 25 | 12 |
| 40 | 25.22 | 6 | 32 | 14 |
| 41 | 27.06 | 8 | 44 | 16 |
| 42 | 21.96 | 9 | 28 | 9 |
| 43 | 22.63 | 8 | 31 | 11 |
| 44 | 19.68 | 7 | 19 | 8 |
| 45 | 22.76 | 8 | 28 | 10 |
| 46 | 21.96 | 13 | 18 | 9 |
| 47 | 25.95 | 10 | 32 | 14 |
| 48 | 26.14 | 8 | 44 | 15 |
| 49 | 24.29 | 8 | 34 | 13 |
| 50 | 24.35 | 3 | 33 | 12 |

1. Develop a multiple linear regression equation that describes the relationship between the cost of delivery and the other variables. Do these three variables explain a reasonable amount of the variation in the dependent variable? Estimate the delivery cost for a kit that takes 10 minutes for preparation, takes 30 minutes to deliver, and must cover a distance of 14 miles.

2. Test to determine that at least one net regression coefficient differs from zero. Also test to see whether any of the variables can be dropped from the analysis. If some of the variables can be dropped, rerun the regression equation until only significant variables are included. Write a brief report interpreting the final regression equation.

# 15

# Nonparametric Methods:

## Chi-Square Applications

## GOALS

*When you have completed this chapter, you will be able to:*

1 List the characteristics of the chi-square distribution.

2 Conduct a test of hypothesis comparing an observed set of frequencies to an expected distribution.

3 Conduct a test of hypothesis to determine whether two classification criteria are related.

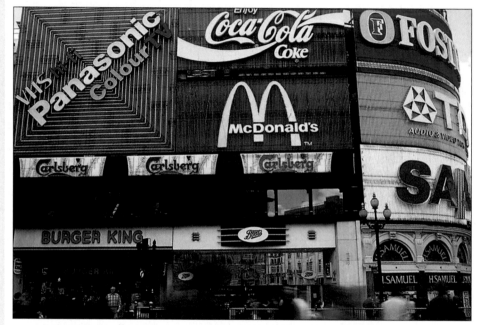

Refer to the Wage data, which reports information on annual wages for a sample of 100 workers. Also included are variables relating to industry, years of education, and gender for each worker. Develop a table showing the industry of employment by gender. At the .05 significance level is it reasonable to conclude that industry of employment and gender are related? (See Goal 3 and Exercise 33.)

# Introduction

Chapters 9 through 12 discuss data of interval or ratio scale, such as weights of steel ingots, incomes of minorities, and years of employment. We conduct hypothesis tests about a single population mean, two population means, and three or more population means. For these tests we assume the populations follow the normal distribution. However, there are tests available in which no assumption regarding the shape of the population is necessary. There are also tests exclusively for data of nominal scale of measurement. Recall from Chapter 1 that nominal data is the "lowest" or most primitive. For this type of measurement, data are classified into categories where there is no natural order. Examples include gender of Congressional representatives, state of birth of students, or brand of peanut butter purchased. In this chapter we introduce a new test statistic, the chi-square statistic. We can use it for data measured with a nominal scale.

# Goodness-of-Fit Test: Equal Expected Frequencies

The goodness-of-fit test is one of the most commonly used statistical tests. The first illustration of this test involves the case in which the expected cell frequencies are equal.

As the full name implies, the purpose of the goodness-of-fit test is to compare an observed distribution to an expected distribution. An example will describe the hypothesis-testing situation.

**EXAMPLE**

Ms. Jan Kilpatrick is the marketing manager for a manufacturer of sports cards. She plans to begin a series of cards with pictures and playing statistics of former Major League Baseball players. One of the problems is the selection of the former players. At the baseball card show at the Southwyck Mall last weekend, she set up a booth and offered cards of the following six Hall of Fame baseball players: Tom Seaver, Nolan Ryan, Ty Cobb, George Brett, Hank Aaron, and Johnny Bench. At the end of the day she sold a total of 120 cards. The number of cards sold for each old-time player is shown in Table 15–1. Can she conclude the sales are not the same for each player?

**TABLE 15–1**  Number of Cards Sold for Each Player

| Player | Cards Sold |
|--------|-----------|
| Tom Seaver | 13 |
| Nolan Ryan | 33 |
| Ty Cobb | 14 |
| George Brett | 7 |
| Hank Aaron | 36 |
| Johnny Bench | 17 |
| Total | 120 |

If there is no significant difference in the popularity of the players, we would expect that the observed frequencies ($f_o$) would be equal—or nearly equal. That is, we would expect to sell as many cards for Tom Seaver as for Nolan Ryan. Thus, any discrepancy in the observed and expected frequencies could be attributed to sampling (chance).

What about the level of measurement in this problem? Notice when a card is sold, the "measurement" of the card is based on the player's name. There is no natural order to the players. No one player is better than another. Therefore, a nominal scale is used to evaluate each observation.

Because there are 120 cards in the sample, we expect that 20 ($f_e$) cards, i.e., the expected frequency $f_e$, will fall in each of the six categories (Table 15–2). These categories are called **cells.** An examination of the set of observed frequencies in Table 15–1 indicates that the card for George Brett is sold rather infrequently, whereas the cards for Hank Aaron and Nolan Ryan are sold more often. Is the difference in sales due to chance, or can we conclude that there is a preference for the cards of certain players?

**TABLE 15–2** Observed and Expected Frequencies for the 120 Cards Sold

| Player | Cards Sold, $f_o$ | Expected Number Sold, $f_e$ |
|---|---|---|
| Tom Seaver | 13 | 20 |
| Nolan Ryan | 33 | 20 |
| Ty Cobb | 14 | 20 |
| George Brett | 7 | 20 |
| Hank Aaron | 36 | 20 |
| Johnny Bench | 17 | 20 |
| Total | 120 | 120 |

**SOLUTION**

We will use the same systematic five-step hypothesis-testing procedure followed in previous chapters.

**Step 1: State the null hypothesis and the alternate hypothesis.** The null hypothesis, $H_0$, is that there is no difference between the set of observed frequencies and the set of expected frequencies; that is, any difference between the two sets of frequencies can be attributed to sampling (chance). The alternate hypothesis, $H_1$, is that there is a difference between the observed and expected sets of frequencies. If $H_0$ is rejected and $H_1$ is accepted, it means that sales are not equally distributed among the six categories (cells).

**Step 2: Select the level of significance.** We selected the .05 level, which is the same as the Type I error probability. Thus, the probability is .05 that a true null hypothesis will be rejected.

**Step 3: Select the test statistic.** The test statistic follows the chi-square distribution, designated as $\chi^2$:

| CHI-SQUARE TEST STATISTIC | $\chi^2 = \Sigma \left[ \dfrac{(f_o - f_e)^2}{f_e} \right]$ | [15–1] |
|---|---|---|

with $k - 1$ degrees of freedom, where:

  $k$ is the number of categories.
  $f_o$ is an observed frequency in a particular category.
  $f_e$ is an expected frequency in a particular category.

We will examine the characteristics of the chi-square distribution in more detail shortly.

**Step 4: Formulate the decision rule.** Recall the decision rule in hypothesis testing requires finding a number that separates the region where we do not reject $H_0$ from the region of rejection. This number is called the *critical* *value.* As we will soon see, the chi-square distribution is really a family of distributions. Each distribution has a slightly different shape, depending on the number of degrees of freedom. The number of degrees of freedom in this type of problem is found by $k - 1$, where $k$ is the number of categories. In this particular problem there are six. Since there are six categories, there are $k - 1 = 6 - 1 = 5$ degrees of freedom. As noted, a category is called a *cell,* so there are six cells. The critical value for 5 degrees of freedom and the .05 level of significance is found in Appendix B. A portion of that table is shown in Table 15–3. The critical value is 11.070, found by locating 5 degrees of freedom in the left margin and then moving horizontally (to the right) and reading the critical value in the .05 column.

**TABLE 15–3** A Portion of the Chi-Square Table

| Degrees of Freedom df | Right-Tail Area | | | |
|---|---|---|---|---|
| | .10 | .05 | .02 | .01 |
| 1 | 2.706 | 3.841 | 5.412 | 6.635 |
| 2 | 4.605 | 5.991 | 7.824 | 9.210 |
| 3 | 6.251 | 7.815 | 9.837 | 11.345 |
| 4 | 7.779 | 9.488 | 11.668 | 13.277 |
| 5 | 9.236 | 11.070 | 13.388 | 15.086 |

The decision rule is to reject $H_0$ if the computed value of chi-square is greater than 11.070. If it is less than or equal to 11.070, do not reject $H_0$. Chart 15–1 shows the decision rule.

**CHART 15–1** Chi-Square Probability Distribution for 5 Degrees of Freedom, Showing the Region of Rejection, .05 Level of Significance

The decision rule indicates that if there are large differences between the observed and expected frequencies, resulting in a computed $\chi^2$ of more than 11.070, the null hypothesis should be rejected. However, if the differences between $f_o$ and $f_e$ are small, the computed $\chi^2$ value will be 11.070 or less, and the null hypothesis should not be rejected. The reasoning is that such small differences between the observed and expected frequencies are probably due to chance. Remember, the 120 observations are a sample of the population.

**Step 5:** **Compute the value of chi-square and make a decision.** Of the 120 cards sold in the sample, we counted the number of times Tom Seaver and Nolan Ryan, and each of the others were sold. The counts were reported in Table 15–1. The calculations for chi-square follow. (Note again that the expected frequencies are the same for each cell.)

Column 1:    Determine the differences between each $f_o$ and $f_e$. That is, $(f_o - f_e)$. The sum of these differences is zero.

Column 2:    Square the difference between each observed and expected frequency, that is, $(f_o - f_e)^2$.

Column 3:    Divide the result for each observation by the expected frequency. That is, $\dfrac{(f_o - f_e)^2}{f_e}$. Finally, sum these values.

The result is the value of $\chi^2$, which is 34.40.

| Baseball Player | $f_o$ | $f_e$ | (1) $(f_o - f_e)$ | (2) $(f_o - f_e)^2$ | (3) $\dfrac{(f_o - f_e)^2}{f_e}$ |
|---|---|---|---|---|---|
| Tom Seaver | 13 | 20 | −7 | 49 | 49/20 = 2.45 |
| Nolan Ryan | 33 | 20 | 13 | 169 | 169/20 = 8.45 |
| Ty Cobb | 14 | 20 | −6 | 36 | 36/20 = 1.80 |
| George Brett | 7 | 20 | −13 | 169 | 169/20 = 8.45 |
| Hank Aaron | 36 | 20 | 16 | 256 | 256/20 = 12.80 |
| Johnny Bench | 17 | 20 | −3 | 9 | 9/20 = 0.45 |
| | | | Must be → 0 | | $\chi^2$ → 34.40 |

The computed $\chi^2$ of 34.40 is in the rejection region beyond the critical value of 11.070. The decision, therefore, is to reject $H_0$ at the .05 level and to accept $H_1$. The difference between the observed and the expected frequencies is not due to chance. Rather, the differences between $f_o$ and $f_e$ are large enough to be considered significant. The chance these differences are due to sampling error is very small. So we conclude that it is unlikely that card sales are the same among the six players.

EXCEL

We can use software to compute the value of chi-square. The output of MegaStat follows. The steps are shown in the Software Commands section at the end of the chapter. The computed value of chi-square is 34.40, the same value obtained in our earlier calculations. Also note the p-value is much less than .05 (.00000198).

Microsoft Excel - Book1

File   Edit   View   Insert   Format   Tools   MegaStat   Data   Window   Help

A1

|   | A | B | C | D | E | F |
|---|---|---|---|---|---|---|
| 1 | | | | | | |
| 2 | Goodness of Fit Test | | | | | |
| 3 | | | | | | |
| 4 | | observed | expected | O - E | (O - E)²/ E | % of chisq |
| 5 | | 13 | 20.000 | -7.000 | 2.450 | 7.12 |
| 6 | | 33 | 20.000 | 13.000 | 8.450 | 24.56 |
| 7 | | 14 | 20.000 | -6.000 | 1.800 | 5.23 |
| 8 | | 7 | 20.000 | -13.000 | 8.450 | 24.56 |
| 9 | | 36 | 20.000 | 16.000 | 12.800 | 37.21 |
| 10 | | 17 | 20.000 | -3.000 | 0.450 | 1.31 |
| 11 | | 120 | 120.000 | 0.000 | 34.400 | 100.00 |
| 12 | | | | | | |
| 13 | | 34.40 | chi-square | | | |
| 14 | | 5 | df | | | |
| 15 | | 1.98E-06 | p-value | | | |

Output / Sheet1 / Sheet2 / Sheet3 /

Ready

The chi-square distribution, which is used as the test statistic in this chapter, has the following characteristics.

1. **Chi-square values are never negative.** This is because the difference between $f_o$ and $f_e$ is squared, that is, $(f_o - f_e)^2$.
2. **There is a family of chi-square distributions.** There is a chi-square distribution for 1 degree of freedom, another for 2 degrees of freedom, another for 3 degrees of freedom, and so on. In this type of problem the number of degrees of freedom is determined by $k - 1$, where $k$ is the number of categories. Therefore, the shape of the chi-square distribution does *not* depend on the size of the sample, but on the number of categories used. For example, if 200 employees of an airline were classified into one of three categories—flight personnel, ground support, and administrative personnel—there would be $k - 1 = 3 - 1 = 2$ degrees of freedom.
3. **The chi-square distribution is positively skewed.** However, as the number of degrees of freedom increases, the distribution begins to approximate the normal distribution. Chart 15–2 shows the distributions for selected degrees of freedom. Notice that for 10 degrees of freedom the curve is approaching a normal distribution.

Shape of $\chi^2$ distribution approaches normal distribution as *df* becomes larger

**CHART 15–2** Chi-Square Distributions for Selected Degrees of Freedom

---

**Self-Review 15–1**

The human resources director at Georgetown Paper, Inc. is concerned about absenteeism among hourly workers. She decides to sample the records to determine whether absenteeism is distributed evenly throughout the six-day workweek. The null hypothesis to be tested is: Absenteeism is distributed evenly throughout the week. The sample results are:

|  | Number Absent |  | Number Absent |
|---|---|---|---|
| Monday | 12 | Thursday | 10 |
| Tuesday | 9 | Friday | 9 |
| Wednesday | 11 | Saturday | 9 |

Use the .01 significance level and the five-step hypothesis testing procedure.
(a) What are the numbers 12, 9, 11, 10, 9, and 9 called?
(b) How many categories (cells) are there?
(c) What is the *expected* frequency for each day?

(d)   How many degrees of freedom are there?
(e)   What is the chi-square critical value at the 1 percent significance level?
(f)   Compute the $\chi^2$ test statistic.
(g)   What is the decision regarding the null hypothesis?
(h)   Specifically, what does this indicate to the human resources director?

# Exercises

**1.** In a particular chi-square goodness-of-fit test there are four categories and 200 observations. Use the .05 significance level.
   **a.** How many degrees of freedom are there?
   **b.** What is the critical value of chi-square?

**2.** In a particular chi-square goodness-of-fit test there are six categories and 500 observations. Use the .01 significance level.
   **a.** How many degrees of freedom are there?
   **b.** What is the critical value of chi-square?

**3.** The null hypothesis and the alternate are:

   $H_0$: The cell categories are equal.
   $H_1$: The cell categories are not equal.

| Category | $f_o$ |
|----------|-------|
| A | 10 |
| B | 20 |
| C | 30 |

   **a.** State the decision rule, using the .05 significance level.
   **b.** Compute the value of chi-square.
   **c.** What is your decision regarding $H_0$?

**4.** The null hypothesis and the alternate are:

   $H_0$: The cell categories are equal.
   $H_1$: The cell categories are not equal.

| Category | $f_o$ |
|----------|-------|
| A | 10 |
| B | 20 |
| C | 30 |
| D | 20 |

   **a.** State the decision rule, using the .05 significance level.
   **b.** Compute the value of chi-square.
   **c.** What is your decision regarding $H_0$?

**5.** A six-sided die is rolled 30 times and the numbers 1 through 6 appear as shown in the following frequency distribution. At the .10 significance level, can we conclude that the die is fair?

| Outcome | Frequency | Outcome | Frequency |
|---------|-----------|---------|-----------|
| 1 | 3 | 4 | 3 |
| 2 | 6 | 5 | 9 |
| 3 | 2 | 6 | 7 |

6. Classic Golf, Inc. manages five courses in the Jacksonville, Florida, area. The Director wishes to study the number of rounds of golf played per weekday at the five courses. He gathered the following sample information.

| Day | Rounds |
|-----|--------|
| Monday | 124 |
| Tuesday | 74 |
| Wednesday | 104 |
| Thursday | 98 |
| Friday | 120 |

At the .05 significance level, is there a difference in the number of rounds played by day of the week?

7. A group of department store buyers viewed a new line of dresses and gave their opinions of them. The results were:

| Opinion | Number of Buyers | Opinion | Number of Buyers |
|---------|------------------|---------|------------------|
| Outstanding | 47 | Good | 39 |
| Excellent | 45 | Fair | 35 |
| Very good | 40 | Undesirable | 34 |

Because the largest number (47) indicated the new line is outstanding, the head designer thinks that this is a mandate to go into mass production of the dresses. The head sweeper (who somehow became involved in this) believes that there is not a clear mandate and claims that the opinions are evenly distributed among the six categories. He further states that the slight differences among the various counts are probably due to chance. Test the null hypothesis that there is no significant difference among the opinions of the buyers. Test at the .01 level of risk. Follow a formal approach; that is, state the null hypothesis, the alternate hypothesis, and so on.

8. The safety director of Honda USA took samples at random from the file of minor work-related accidents and classified them according to the time the accident took place.

| Time | Number of Accidents | Time | Number of Accidents |
|------|---------------------|------|---------------------|
| 8 up to 9 A.M. | 6 | 1 up to 2 P.M. | 7 |
| 9 up to 10 A.M. | 6 | 2 up to 3 P.M. | 8 |
| 10 up to 11 A.M. | 20 | 3 up to 4 P.M. | 19 |
| 11 up to 12 P.M. | 8 | 4 up to 5 P.M. | 6 |

Using the goodness-of-fit test and the .01 level of significance, determine whether the accidents are evenly distributed throughout the day. Write a brief explanation of your conclusion.

# Goodness-of-Fit Test: Unequal Expected Frequencies

The expected frequencies ($f_e$) in the previous distribution involving baseball cards were all equal (20). According to the null hypothesis, it was expected that a picture of Tom Seaver would appear 20 times at random, a picture of Johnny Bench would appear 20 times out of 120 trials, and so on. The chi-square test can also be used if the expected frequencies are not equal.

Expected frequencies not equal in this problem

The following example illustrates the case of unequal frequencies and also gives a practical use of the chi-square goodness-of-fit test—namely, to find whether a local experience differs from the national experience.

**EXAMPLE**

The American Hospital Administrators Association (AHAA) reports the following information concerning the number of times senior citizens are admitted to a hospital during a one-year period. Forty percent are not admitted; 30 percent are admitted once; 20 percent are admitted twice, and the remaining 10 percent are admitted three or more times.

A survey of 150 residents of Bartow Estates, a community devoted to active seniors located in Central Florida, revealed 55 residents were not admitted during the last year, 50 were admitted to a hospital once, 32 were admitted twice, and the rest of those in the survey were admitted three or more times. Can we conclude the survey at Bartow Estates is consistent with the information suggested by the AHAA? Use the .05 significance level.

**SOLUTION**

We begin by organizing the above information into Table 15–4. Clearly, we cannot compare percentages given in the study by the Hospital Administrators to the frequencies reported for the Bartow Estates. However, these percentages can be converted to expected frequencies, $f_e$. According to the Hospital Administrators, 40 percent of the Bartow residents in the survey did not require hospitalization. Thus, if there is no difference between the national experience and those of Bartow Estates, then 40 percent of the 150 seniors surveyed (60 residents) would not have been hospitalized. Further, 30 percent of those surveyed were admitted once (45 residents), and so on. The observed frequencies for Bartow residents and the expected frequencies based on the percents in the national study are given in Table 15–4.

**Statistics in Action**

Many state governments operate lotteries to help fund education. In many lotteries, numbered balls are mixed and selected by a machine. In a "Select Three" game, numbered balls are selected randomly from three groups of balls numbered zero through nine. Randomness would predict that the frequency of each number is equal. How would you prove that the selection machine ensured randomness? A chi-square, goodness-of-fit test could be used to prove or disprove randomness.

**TABLE 15–4** Summary of Study by AHAA and a Survey of Bartow Estates Residents

| Number of Times Admitted | AHAA Percent of Total | Number of Bartow Residents ($f_o$) | Expected Number of Residents ($f_e$) |
|---|---|---|---|
| 0 | 40 | 55 | 60 |
| 1 | 30 | 50 | 45 |
| 2 | 20 | 32 | 30 |
| 3 or more | 10 | 13 | 15 |
| Total | 100 | 150 | 150 |

The null hypothesis and the alternate hypotheses are:

$H_0$: There is no difference between local and national experience for hospital admissions.

$H_1$: There is a difference between local and national experience for hospital admissions.

To find the decision rule we use Appendix B. There are four admitting categories, so the degrees of freedom are $df = 4 - 1 = 3$. The critical value is 7.815. Therefore, the decision rule is to reject the null hypothesis if $\chi^2 > 7.815$. The decision rule is portrayed in Chart 15–3.

Now to compute the chi-square test statistic:

| Number of Times Admitted | ($f_o$) | ($f_e$) | $f_o - f_e$ | $(f_o - f_e)^2/f_e$ |
|---|---|---|---|---|
| 0 | 55 | 60 | −5 | 0.4167 |
| 1 | 50 | 45 | 5 | 0.5556 |
| 2 | 32 | 30 | 2 | 0.1333 |
| 3 or more | 13 | 15 | −2 | 0.2667 |
| Total | 150 | 150 | 0 | 1.3723 |

**CHART 15–3** Decision Criteria for the Bartow Estates Research Study

The computed value of $\chi^2$ (1.3723) lies to the left of 7.815. Thus, we cannot reject the null hypothesis. We conclude that there is no evidence of a difference between the local and national experience for hospital admissions.

# Limitations of Chi-Square

Be careful in applying $\chi^2$ to some problems.

If there is an unusually small expected frequency in a cell, chi-square (if applied) might result in an erroneous conclusion. This can happen because $f_e$ appears in the denominator, and dividing by a very small number makes the quotient quite large! Two generally accepted rules regarding small cell frequencies are:

1. If there are only two cells, the *expected* frequency in each cell should be 5 or more. The computation of chi-square would be permissible in the following problem, involving a minimum $f_e$ of 6.

| Individual | $f_o$ | $f_e$ |
|---|---|---|
| Literate | 643 | 642 |
| Illiterate | 7 | 6 |

2. For more than two cells, chi-square should *not* be used if more than 20 percent of the $f_e$ cells have expected frequencies less than 5. According to this rule, it would not be appropriate to use the goodness-of-fit test on the following data. Three of the seven cells, or 43 percent, have expected frequencies ($f_e$) of less than 5.

| Level of Management | $f_o$ | $f_e$ |
|---|---|---|
| Foreman | 30 | 32 |
| Supervisor | 110 | 113 |
| Manager | 86 | 87 |
| Middle management | 23 | 24 |
| Assistant vice president | 5 | 2 |
| Vice president | 5 | 4 |
| Senior vice president | 4 | 1 |
| Total | 263 | 263 |

To show the reason for the 20 percent policy, we conducted the goodness-of-fit test on the above data on the levels of management. The MegaStat output follows.

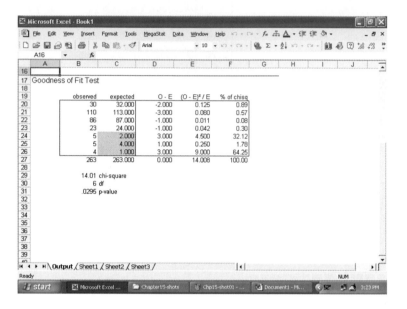

For this test at the .05 significance level, $H_0$ is rejected if the computed value of chi-square is greater than 12.592. The computed value is 14.01, so we reject the null hypothesis that the observed frequencies represent a random sample from the population of the expected values. Examine the MegaStat output. More than 98 percent of the computed chi-square value is accounted for by the three vice president categories ($[4.500 + .250 + 9.000]/14.008 = 0.9815$). Logically, too much weight is being given to these categories.

The dilemma can be resolved by combining categories if it is logical to do so. In the above example we combine the three vice-presidential categories, which satisfies the 20 percent rule.

| Level of Management | $f_o$ | $f_e$ |
|---|---|---|
| Foreman | 30 | 32 |
| Supervisor | 110 | 113 |
| Manager | 86 | 87 |
| Middle management | 23 | 24 |
| Vice president | 14 | 7 |
| Total | 263 | 263 |

The computed value of chi-square with the revised categories is 7.26. See the following output. This value is less than the critical value of 9.488 for the .05 significance level. The null hypothesis is, therefore, not rejected at the .05 significance level. This indicates there is no evidence of a significant difference between the observed distribution and the expected distribution.

**Self-Review 15–2** The American Accounting Association classifies accounts receivable as "current," "late," and "not collectible." Industry figures show that 60 percent of accounts receivable are current, 30 percent are late, and 10 percent are not collectible. Massa and Barr, attorneys in Greenville, Ohio, has 500 accounts receivable: 320 are current, 120 are late, and 60 are not collectible. Are these numbers in agreement with the industry distribution? Use the .05 significance level.

# Exercises

9. The following hypotheses are given:

   $H_0$: Forty percent of the observations are in category A, 40 percent are in B, and 20 percent are in C.
   $H_1$: The observations are not as described in $H_0$.

   We took a sample of 60, with the following results.

   | Category | $f_o$ |
   |----------|-------|
   | A | 30 |
   | B | 20 |
   | C | 10 |

   a. State the decision rule using the .01 significance level.
   b. Compute the value of chi-square.
   c. What is your decision regarding $H_0$?

10. The chief of security for the Mall of the Dakotas was directed to study the problem of missing goods. He selected a sample of 100 boxes that had been tampered with and ascertained that for 60 of the boxes, the missing pants, shoes, and so on were attributed to shoplifting. For 30 other boxes employees had stolen the goods, and for the remaining 10 boxes he blamed poor inventory control. In his report to the mall management, can he say that shoplifting is *twice* as likely to be the cause of the loss as compared with either employee theft or poor inventory control and that employee theft and poor inventory control are equally likely? Use the .02 significance level.

11. The bank credit card department of Carolina Bank knows from experience that 5 percent of the card holders have had some high school, 15 percent have completed high school, 25 percent have had some college, and 55 percent have completed college. Of the 500 card holders whose cards have been called in for failure to pay their charges this month, 50 had some high school, 100 had completed high school, 190 had some college, and 160 had completed college. Can we conclude that the distribution of card holders who do not pay their charges is different from all others? Use the .01 significance level.

12. For many years TV executives used the guideline that 30 percent of the audience were watching each of the prime-time networks and 10 percent were watching cable stations on a weekday night. A random sample of 500 viewers in the Tampa–St. Petersburg, Florida, area last Monday night showed that 165 homes were tuned in to the ABC affiliate, 140 to the CBS affiliate, 125 to the NBC affiliate, and the remainder were viewing a cable station. At the .05 significance level, can we conclude that the guideline is still reasonable?

# Contingency Table Analysis

In Chapter 4 we discuss bivariate data, where we study the relationship between two variables. We describe a contingency table which simultaneously summarizes two nominal-scale variables of interest. For example, a sample of students enrolled in the School of Business is classified by gender (male or female) and major (accounting, management, finance, marketing, or quantitative methods). This classification is based on the nominal scale, because there is no natural order to the classifications.

We discussed contingency tables earlier, in Chapter 5. On page 156, we illustrate the relationship between the loyalty to the company and the length of employment. Are older employees likely to be more loyal to the company?

We can use the chi-square statistic to formally test for a relationship between two nominal-scaled variables. To put it another way, Is one variable *independent* of the other? Here are some examples where we are interested in testing whether two variables are related.

- The Ford Motor Company operates an assembly plant in Dearborn, Michigan. The plant operates three shifts per day, 5 days a week. The quality control manager wishes to compare the quality level on the three shifts. Vehicles are classified by quality level (acceptable, unacceptable) and shift (day, afternoon, night). Is there a difference in the quality level on the three shifts? That is, is the quality of the product related to the shift when it was manufactured? Or, is the quality of the product independent of the shift on which it was manufactured?
- A sample of 100 drivers who were stopped for speeding violations was classified by gender and whether or not they were wearing a seat belt. For this sample, is wearing a seatbelt related to gender?
- Does a male released from federal prison make a different adjustment to civilian life if he returns to his hometown or if he goes elsewhere to live? The two variables are adjustment to civilian life and place of residence. Note that both variables are measured on the nominal scale.

**EXAMPLE**

The Federal Correction Agency is investigating the last question cited above: Does a male released from federal prison make a different adjustment to civilian life if he returns to his hometown or if he goes elsewhere to live? To put it another way, is there a relationship between adjustment to civilian life and place of residence after release from prison?

**SOLUTION**

As before, the first step in hypothesis testing is to state the null and alternate hypotheses.

$H_0$: There is no relationship between adjustment to civilian life and where the individual lives after being released from prison.

$H_1$: There is a relationship between adjustment to civilian life and where the individual lives after being released from prison.

The .01 level of significance will be used to test the hypothesis.

The agency's psychologists interviewed 200 randomly selected former prisoners. Using a series of questions, the psychologists classified the adjustment of each individual to civilian life as outstanding, good, fair, or unsatisfactory. The classifications for the 200 former prisoners were tallied as follows. Joseph Camden, for example, returned to his hometown and has shown outstanding adjustment to civilian life. His case is one of the 27 tallies in the upper left box.

| Residence after Release from Prison | Adjustment to Civilian Life | | | |
|---|---|---|---|---|
| | Outstanding | Good | Fair | Unsatisfactory |
| Hometown | /H/ /H/ /H/ /H/ /H/ // | /H/ /H/ /H/ /H/ /H/ /H/ /HI | /HI /HI /HI /HI /HI /HI /// | /HI /HI /HI /HI /HI |
| Not hometown | /HI /HI /// | /HI /HI /HI | /HI /HI /HI /HI /HI // | /HI /HI /HI /HI /HI |

**Contingency table consists of count data.**

The tallies in each box, or *cell,* were counted. The counts are given in the following **contingency table.** (See Table 15–5.) In this case, the Federal Correction Agency wondered whether adjustment to civilian life is *contingent on* where the prisoner goes after release from prison.

**TABLE 15–5** Adjustment to Civilian Life and Place of Residence

| Residence after Release from Prison | Adjustment to Civilian Life | | | | Total |
|---|---|---|---|---|---|
| | Outstanding | Good | Fair | Unsatisfactory | |
| Hometown | 27 | 35 | 33 | 25 | 120 |
| Not hometown | 13 | 15 | 27 | 25 | 80 |
| Total | 40 | 50 | 60 | 50 | 200 |

Once we know how many rows (2) and columns (4) there are in the contingency table, we can determine the critical value and the decision rule. For a chi-square test of significance where two traits are classified in a contingency table, the degrees of freedom are found by:

$$df = (\text{number of rows} - 1)(\text{number of columns} - 1) = (r - 1)(c - 1)$$

In this problem:

$$df = (r - 1)(c - 1) = (2 - 1)(4 - 1) = 3$$

To find the critical value for 3 degrees of freedom and the .01 level (selected earlier), refer to Appendix B. It is 11.345. The decision rule is to reject the null hypothesis if the computed value of $\chi^2$ is greater than 11.345. The decision rule is portrayed graphically in Chart 15–4.

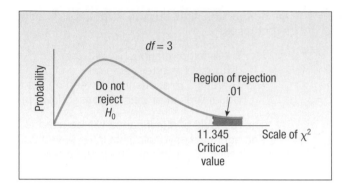

**CHART 15–4** Chi-Square Distribution for 3 Degrees of Freedom

Next we find the computed value of $\chi^2$. The observed frequencies, $f_o$, are shown in Table 15–5. How are the corresponding expected frequencies, $f_e$, determined? Note in the "Total" column of Table 15–5 that 120 of the 200 former prisoners (60 percent) returned to their hometowns. *If there were no relationship* between adjustment and residency after release from prison, we would expect 60 percent of the 40 ex-prisoners who made outstanding adjustment to civilian life to reside in their hometowns. Thus, the expected frequency $f_e$ for the upper left cell is $.60 \times 40 = 24$. Likewise, if there were no relationship between adjustment and present residence, we would expect 60 percent of the 50 ex-prisoners (30) who had "good" adjustment to civilian life to reside in their hometowns.

Further, notice that 80 of the 200 ex-prisoners studied (40 percent) did not return to their hometowns to live. Thus, of the 60 considered by the psychologists to have made "fair" adjustment to civilian life, $.40 \times 60$, or 24, would be expected not to return to their hometowns.

The expected frequency for any cell can be determined by

| EXPECTED FREQUENCY | $f_e = \dfrac{\text{(Row total)(Column total)}}{\text{Grand total}}$ | [15–2] |
|---|---|---|

From this formula, the expected frequency for the upper left cell in Table 15–5 is:

$$\text{Expected frequency} - \frac{\text{(Row total)(Column total)}}{\text{Grand total}} = \frac{(120)(40)}{200} = 24$$

The observed frequencies, $f_o$, and the expected frequencies, $f_e$, for all of the cells in the contingency table are listed in Table 15–6.

**TABLE 15–6** Observed and Expected Frequencies

| Residence after Release from Prison | Adjustment to Civilian Life | | | | | | | | Total | |
|---|---|---|---|---|---|---|---|---|---|---|
| | Outstanding | | Good | | Fair | | Unsatisfactory | | | |
| | $f_o$ | $f_e$ | $f_o$ | $f_e$ | $f_o$ | $f_e$ | $f_o$ | $f_e$ | $f_o$ | $f_e$ |
| Hometown | 27 | 24 | 35 | 30 | 33 | 36 | 25 | 30 | 120 | 120 |
| Not hometown | 13 | 16 | 15 | 20 | 27 | 24 | 25 | 20 | 80 | 80 |
| Total | 40 | 40 | 50 | 50 | 60 | 60 | 50 | 50 | 200 | 200 |

Must be equal

$\dfrac{(80)(50)}{200}$

Must be equal

Recall that the computed value of chi-square using formula (15–1) is found by:

$$\chi^2 = \Sigma\left[\frac{(f_o - f_e)^2}{f_e}\right]$$

Starting with the upper left cell:

$$\chi^2 = \frac{(27 - 24)^2}{24} + \frac{(35 - 30)^2}{30} + \frac{(33 - 36)^2}{36} + \frac{(25 - 30)^2}{30}$$

$$+ \frac{(13 - 16)^2}{16} + \frac{(15 - 20)^2}{20} + \frac{(27 - 24)^2}{24} + \frac{(25 - 20)^2}{20}$$

$$= 0.375 + 0.833 + 0.250 + 0.833 + 0.563 + 1.250 + 0.375 + 1.250$$

$$= 5.729$$

Because the computed value of chi-square (5.729) lies in the region to the left of 11.345, the null hypothesis is not rejected at the .01 significance level. We conclude there is no evidence of a relationship between adjustment to civilian life and where the prisoner resides after being released from prison. For the Federal Correction Agency's advisement program, adjustment to civilian life is not related to where the ex-prisoner lives.

The following output is from the MINITAB system.

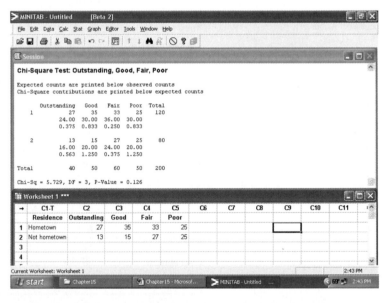

Observe that the value of chi-square is the same as that computed earlier. In addition, the p-value is reported, .126. So the probability of finding a value of the test statistic as large or larger is .126 when the null hypothesis is true. The p-value also results in the same decision, do not reject the null hypothesis.

**Self-Review 15–3**

A social scientist sampled 140 people and classified them according to income level and whether or not they played a state lottery in the last month. The sample information is reported below. Is it reasonable to conclude that playing the lottery is related to income level? Use the .05 significance level.

|              | Income |        |      |       |
|--------------|--------|--------|------|-------|
|              | Low    | Middle | High | Total |
| Played       | 46     | 28     | 21   | 95    |
| Did not play | 14     | 12     | 19   | 45    |
| Total        | 60     | 40     | 40   | 140   |

(a) What is this table called?
(b) State the null hypothesis and the alternate hypothesis.
(c) What is the decision rule?
(d) Determine the value of chi-square.
(e) Make a decision on the null hypothesis. Interpret the result.

# Exercises

**13.** The director of advertising for the *Carolina Sun Times,* the largest newspaper in the Carolinas, is studying the relationship between the type of community in which a subscriber resides and the section of the newspaper he or she reads first. For a sample of readers, she collected the following sample information.

|        | National News | Sports | Comics |
|--------|---------------|--------|--------|
| City   | 170           | 124    | 90     |
| Suburb | 120           | 112    | 100    |
| Rural  | 130           | 90     | 88     |

At the .05 significance level, can we conclude there is a relationship between the type of community where the person resides and the section of the paper read first?

**14.** Four brands of light bulbs are being considered for use in the final assembly area of the Saturn plant in Spring Hill, Tennessee. The director of purchasing asked for samples of 100 from each manufacturer. The numbers of acceptable and unacceptable bulbs from each manufacturer are shown below. At the .05 significance level, is there a difference in the quality of the bulbs?

|              | Manufacturer |     |     |     |
|--------------|-----|-----|-----|-----|
|              | A   | B   | C   | D   |
| Unacceptable | 12  | 8   | 5   | 11  |
| Acceptable   | 88  | 92  | 95  | 89  |
| Total        | 100 | 100 | 100 | 100 |

**15.** The Quality Control Department at Food Town, Inc., a grocery chain in upstate New York, conducts a monthly check on the comparison of scanned prices to posted prices. The chart below summarizes the results of a sample of 500 items last month. Company management would like to know whether there is any relationship between error rates on regular priced items and specially priced items. Use the .01 significance level.

|               | Regular Price | Advertised Special Price |
|---------------|---------------|--------------------------|
| Undercharge   | 20            | 10                       |
| Overcharge    | 15            | 30                       |
| Correct price | 200           | 225                      |

16. The use of cellular phones in automobiles has increased dramatically in the last few years. Of concern to traffic experts, as well as manufacturers of cellular phones, is the effect on accident rates. Is someone who is using a cellular phone more likely to be involved in a traffic accident? What is your conclusion from the following sample information? Use the .05 significance level.

| | Had Accident in the Last Year | Did Not Have an Accident in the Last Year |
|---|---|---|
| Cellular phone in use | 25 | 300 |
| Cellular phone not in use | 50 | 400 |

# Chapter Outline

  I. The characteristics of the chi-square distribution are:
  A. The value of chi-square is never negative.
  B. The chi-square distribution is positively skewed.
  C. There is a family of chi-square distributions.
  1. Each time the degrees of freedom change, a new distribution is formed.
  2. As the degrees of freedom increase, the distribution approaches a normal distribution.
  II. A goodness-of-fit test will show whether an observed set of frequencies could have come from a hypothesized population distribution.
  A. The degrees of freedom are $k - 1$, where $k$ is the number of categories.
  B. The formula for computing the value of chi-square is

$$\chi^2 = \Sigma \left[ \frac{(f_o - f_e)^2}{f_e} \right]$$  [15–1]

  III. A contingency table is used to test whether two traits or characteristics are related.
  A. Each observation is classified according to two traits.
  B. The expected frequency is determined as follows:

$$f_e = \frac{(\text{Row total})(\text{Column total})}{(\text{Grand total})}$$  [15–2]

  C. The degrees of freedom are found by:

$$df = (\text{Rows} - 1)(\text{Columns} - 1)$$

  D. The usual hypothesis testing procedure is used.

# Pronunciation Key

| SYMBOL | MEANING | PRONUNCIATION |
|---|---|---|
| $\chi^2$ | Probability distribution | *ki square* |
| $f_o$ | Observed frequency | *f sub oh* |
| $f_e$ | Expected frequency | *f sub e* |

# Chapter Exercises

17. Vehicles heading west on Front Street may turn right, left, or go straight ahead at Elm Street. The city traffic engineer believes that half of the vehicles will continue straight through the intersection. Of the remaining half, equal proportions will turn right and left. Two

hundred vehicles were observed, with the following results. Can we conclude that the traffic engineer is correct? Use the .10 significance level.

|  | Straight | Right Turn | Left Turn |
|---|---|---|---|
| Frequency | 112 | 48 | 40 |

18. The publisher of a sports magazine plans to offer new subscribers one of three gifts: a sweatshirt with the logo of their favorite team, a coffee cup with the logo of their favorite team, or a pair of earrings also with the logo of their favorite team. In a sample of 500 new subscribers, the number selecting each gift is reported below. At the .05 significance level, is there a preference for the gifts or should we conclude that the gifts are equally well liked?

| Gift | Frequency |
|---|---|
| Sweatshirt | 183 |
| Coffee cup | 175 |
| Earrings | 142 |

19. In a particular market there are three commercial television stations, each with its own evening news program from 6:00 to 6:30 P.M. According to a report in this morning's local newspaper, a random sample of 150 viewers last night revealed 53 watched the news on WNAE (channel 5), 64 watched on WRRN (channel 11), and 33 on WSPD (channel 13). At the .05 significance level, is there a difference in the proportion of viewers watching the three channels?

20. There are four entrances to the Government Center Building in downtown Philadelphia. The building maintenance supervisor would like to know if the entrances are equally utilized. To investigate, 400 people were observed entering the building. The number using each entrance is reported below. At the .01 significance level, is there a difference in the use of the four entrances?

| Entrance | Frequency |
|---|---|
| Main Street | 140 |
| Broad Street | 120 |
| Cherry Street | 90 |
| Walnut Street | 50 |
| Total | 400 |

21. The owner of a mail-order catalog would like to compare her sales with the geographic distribution of the population. According to the United States Bureau of the Census, 21 percent of the population lives in the Northeast, 24 percent in the Midwest, 35 percent in the South, and 20 percent in the West. Listed below is a breakdown of a sample of 400 orders randomly selected from those shipped last month. At the .01 significance level, does the distribution of the orders reflect the population?

| Region | Frequency |
|---|---|
| Northeast | 68 |
| Midwest | 104 |
| South | 155 |
| West | 73 |
| Total | 400 |

22. The Banner Mattress and Furniture Company wishes to study the number of credit applications received per day for the last 300 days. The information is reported on the next page.

| Number of Credit Applications | Frequency (Number of Days) |
|:---:|:---:|
| 0 | 50 |
| 1 | 77 |
| 2 | 81 |
| 3 | 48 |
| 4 | 31 |
| 5 or more | 13 |

To interpret, there were 50 days on which no credit applications were received, 77 days on which only one application was received, and so on. Would it be reasonable to conclude that the population distribution is Poisson with a mean of 2.0? Use the .05 significance level. *Hint:* To find the expected frequencies use the Poisson distribution with a mean of 2.0. Find the probability of exactly one success given a Poisson distribution with a mean of 2.0. Multiply this probability by 300 to find the expected frequency for the number of days in which there was exactly one application. Determine the expected frequency for the other days in a similar manner.

**23.** In the early 2000s the Deep Down Mining Company implemented new safety guidelines. Prior to these new guidelines, management expected there to be no accidents in 40 percent of the months, one accident in 30 percent of the months, two accidents in 20 percent of the months, and three accidents in 10 percent of the months. Over the last 10 years, or 120 months, there have been 46 months in which there were no accidents, 40 months in which there was one accident, 22 months in which there were two accidents, and 12 months in which there were 3 accidents. At the .05 significance level can the management at Deep Down conclude that there has been a change in the monthly accident distribution?

**24.** A recent study by a large retailer designed to determine whether there was a relationship between the importance a store manager placed on advertising and the size of the store revealed the following sample information:

|  | Important | Not Important |
|:---|:---:|:---:|
| Small | 40 | 52 |
| Medium | 106 | 47 |
| Large | 67 | 32 |

What is your conclusion? Use the .05 significance level.

**25.** Two hundred managers from various levels were randomly selected and interviewed regarding their concern about environmental issues. The response of each person was tallied into one of three categories: no concern, some concern, and great concern. The results were:

| Level of Management | No Concern | Some Concern | Great Concern |
|:---|:---:|:---:|:---:|
| Top management | 15 | 13 | 12 |
| Middle management | 20 | 19 | 21 |
| Supervisor | 7 | 7 | 6 |
| Group leader | 28 | 21 | 31 |

Use the .01 significance level to determine whether there is a relationship between management level and environmental concern.

**26.** A study regarding the relationship between age and the amount of pressure sales personnel feel in relation to their jobs revealed the following sample information. At the .01 significance level, is there a relationship between job pressure and age?

| Age (years) | Degree of Job Pressure | | |
| --- | --- | --- | --- |
| | Low | Medium | High |
| Less than 25 | 20 | 18 | 22 |
| 25 up to 40 | 50 | 46 | 44 |
| 40 up to 60 | 58 | 63 | 59 |
| 60 and older | 34 | 43 | 43 |

27. The claims department at the Wise Insurance Company believes that younger drivers have more accidents and, therefore, should be charged higher insurance rates. Investigating a sample of 1,200 Wise policyholders revealed the following breakdown on whether a claim had been filed in the last three years and the age of the policyholder. Is it reasonable to conclude that there is a relationship between the age of the policyholder and whether or not the person filed a claim? Use the .05 significance level.

| Age Group | No Claim | Claim |
| --- | --- | --- |
| 16 up to 25 | 170 | 74 |
| 25 up to 40 | 240 | 58 |
| 40 up to 55 | 400 | 44 |
| 55 or older | 190 | 24 |
| Total | 1,000 | 200 |

28. A sample of employees at a large chemical plant was asked to indicate a preference for one of three pension plans. The results are given in the following table. Does it seem that there is a relationship between the pension plan selected and the job classification of the employees? Use the .01 significance level.

| Job Class | Pension Plan | | |
| --- | --- | --- | --- |
| | Plan A | Plan B | Plan C |
| Supervisor | 10 | 13 | 29 |
| Clerical | 19 | 80 | 19 |
| Labor | 81 | 57 | 22 |

# exercises.com

29. Did you ever purchase a bag of M&M's candies and wonder about the distribution of colors? You can go to the website www.baking.m-ms.com and click the United States on the map, then click **About M&M's,** then **History, Products,** and **Peanut** and find the percentage breakdown according to the manufacturer, as well as a brief history of the product. Did you know in the beginning they were all brown? For M&M's peanuts 20 percent are blue, 20 percent brown, 20 percent yellow, 20 percent red, 10 percent green, and 10 percent orange. A 6 oz. bag purchased at the Book Store at Coastal Carolina University on March 7, 2003, had 13 blue, 17 brown, 20 yellow, 7 red, 9 orange, and 6 green. Is it reasonable to conclude that actual distribution agrees with the expected distribution? Use the .05 significance level. Conduct your own trial. Be sure to share with your instructor.

30. As described in earlier chapters, many real estate companies and rental agencies now publish their listings on the World Wide Web. One example is the Dunes Realty Company located in Garden City, South Carolina and Surfside Beach, South Carolina. Go to the website http://www.dunes.com and click on **Beach House Search,** then indicate at least 5 bedrooms, accommodations for at least 14 people, oceanfront, and no pool or floating dock; select a period in March; indicate that you are willing to spend up to $8,000 per week; and finally click on **Search the Cottages**. Sort the cottages offered into a contingency table by the number of bathrooms and whether the rental price is less than $2,000 for the week or $2,000 or more. You may need to combine some of the cells. Conduct a statistical test to determine if the number of bedrooms is related to the cost. Use the .05 significance level.

# Dataset Exercises

31. Refer to the Real Estate data, which reports information on homes sold in the Denver, Colorado, area last year.
    **a.** Develop a contingency table that shows whether a home has a pool and the township in which the house is located. Is there an association between the variables "pool" and "township"? Use the .05 significance level.
    **b.** Develop a contingency table that shows whether a home has an attached garage and the township in which the home is located. Is there an association between the variables "attached garage" and "township"? Use the .05 significance level.
32. Refer to the Baseball 2002 data, which reports information on the 30 Major League Baseball teams for the 2002 season. Set up a variable that divides the teams into two groups, those that had a winning season and those that did not. There are 162 games in the season, so define a winning season as having won 81 or more games. Next, divide the teams into two salary groups. Let the 15 teams with the largest salaries be in one group and the 15 teams with the smallest salaries in the other. At the .05 significance level is there a relationship between salaries and winning?
33. Refer to the Wage data, which reports information on annual wages for a sample of 100 workers. Also included are variables relating to industry, years of education, and gender for each worker. Develop a table showing the industry of employment by gender. At the .05 significance level is it reasonable to conclude that industry of employment and gender are related?
34. Refer to the CIA data, which reports demographic and economic information on 46 countries.
    **a.** Develop a contingency table that shows G-20 membership versus level of petroleum activity. Is there a significant association at the .05 level of significance between these variables?

**b.** Group the countries into "young" (percent of population over 65 is less than 10) and "old" (percent of population over 65 is more than 10). Then develop a contingency table between this "age" variable and the level of petroleum activity. At the .05 level of significance can we conclude these variables are related?

# Software Commands

1. The MegaStat commands to create the chi-square goodness-of-fit test on page 526 are:
   **a.** Enter the information from Table 15–1 into a worksheet as shown.
   **b.** Select **MegaStat, Chi-Square/Crosstabs,** and **Goodness-of-fit** and hit **Enter.**
   **c.** In the dialog box select *B2:B7* as the **Observed values,** *C2:C7* as the **Expected values,** and enter *0* as the **Number of parameters estimated from the data.** Click on **OK.**

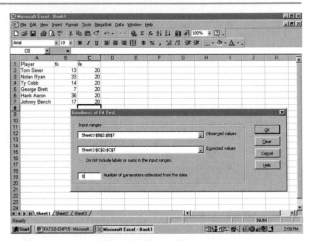

2. The MegaStat commands to create the chi-square goodness-of-fit tests on pages 532 and 533 are the same except for the number of items in the observed and expected frequency columns. Only one dialog box is shown.
   **a.** Enter the Levels of Management information shown on page 531.
   **b.** Select **MegaStat, Chi-Square/Crosstabs,** and **Goodness-of-fit** and hit **Enter.**
   **c.** In the dialog box select *B2:B8* as the **Observed values,** *C2:C8* as the **Expected values,** and enter *0* as the **Number of parameters estimated from the data.** Click on **OK.**

3. The MINITAB commands for the chi-square analysis on page 537 are:
   **a.** Enter the names of the variables in the first row and the data in the next two rows.
   **b.** Select **Stat, Table,** and then click on **Chi-square test** and hit **Enter.**
   **c.** In the dialog box select the columns labeled *Outstanding* to *Unsatisfactory* and click **OK.**

# Chapter 15 Answers to Self-Review

**15–1**
  **a.** Observed frequencies.
  **b.** Six (six days of the week).
  **c.** 10. Total observed frequencies ÷ 6 = 60/6 = 10.
  **d.** 5; $k - 1 = 6 - 1 = 5$.
  **e.** 15.086 (from the chi-square table in Appendix B).
  **f.**

$$\chi^2 = \Sigma \left[ \frac{(f_o - f_e)^2}{f_e} \right] = \frac{(12 - 10)^2}{10} + \cdots + \frac{(9 - 10)^2}{10} = 0.8$$

  **g.** No. We do not reject $H_0$.
  **h.** Absenteeism is distributed evenly throughout the week. The observed differences are due to sampling variation.

**15–2**   $H_0: P_C = .60$, $P_L = .30$, and $P_U = .10$.
$H_1$: Distribution is not as above.
Reject $H_0$ if $\chi^2 > 5.991$.

| Category | $f_o$ | $f_e$ | $\dfrac{(f_o - f_e)^2}{f_e}$ |
|---|---|---|---|
| Current | 320 | 300 | 1.33 |
| Late | 120 | 150 | 6.00 |
| Uncollectible | 60 | 50 | 2.00 |
| | 500 | 500 | 9.33 |

Reject $H_0$. The accounts receivable data does not reflect the national average.

**15–3**
  **a.** Contingency table
  **b.** $H_0$: There is no relationship between income and whether the person played the lottery.
$H_1$: There is a relationship between income and whether the person played the lottery.
  **c.** Reject $H_0$ if $\chi^2$ is greater than 5.991.
  **d.**

$$\chi^2 = \frac{(46 - 40.71)^2}{40.71} + \frac{(28 - 27.14)^2}{27.14} + \frac{(21 - 27.14)^2}{27.14}$$
$$+ \frac{(14 - 19.29)^2}{19.29} + \frac{(12 - 12.86)^2}{12.86} + \frac{(19 - 12.86)^2}{12.86}$$
$$= 6.544$$

  **e.** Reject $H_0$. There is a relationship between income level and playing the lottery.

# 16

## GOALS

*When you have completed this chapter, you will be able to:*

1 Conduct the sign test for dependent samples using the binomial and standard normal distributions as the test statistics.

2 Conduct a test of hypothesis for dependent samples using the Wilcoxon signed-rank test.

3 Conduct and interpret the Wilcoxon rank-sum test for independent samples.

4 Conduct and interpret the Kruskal-Wallis test for several independent samples.

5 Compute and interpret Spearman's coefficient of rank correlation.

6 Conduct a test of hypothesis to determine whether the correlation among the ranks in the population is different from zero.

# Nonparametric Methods

## Analysis of Ranked Data

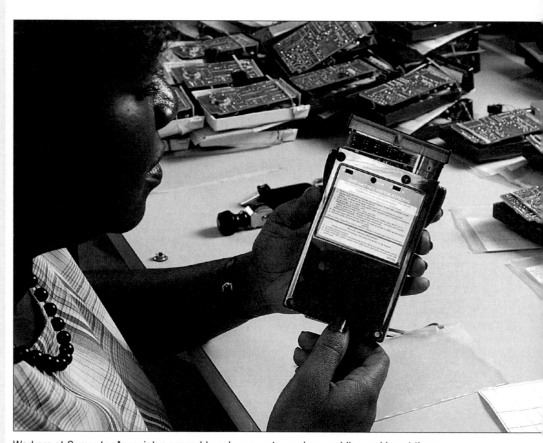

Workers at Computer Associates assemble only one or two subassemblies and insert them in "frames" at their individual stations. Executives at CA think employees might have higher morale if they were assigned to assemble all components and then test the completed computers. A sample of 25 employees was selected to experiment and try this new process. After a training program, each was asked his or her preference. Twenty stated that they preferred the new complete assembly system. At the .05 level, use the sign test to arrive at a decision regarding employee preference. (See Goal 1 and Exercise 8.)

# Introduction

Chapter 15 introduced tests of hypothesis for *nominal-scale* variables. Recall from Chapter 1 that nominal level of measurement implies that the data can only be classified into categories, and there is no particular order to the categories. The purpose of these tests is to determine whether an observed set of frequencies, $f_o$, is significantly different from a corresponding set of expected frequencies, $f_e$. Likewise, if you are interested in the relationship between two characteristics—such as the age of an individual and his or her music preference—you would tally the data into a contingency table and use the chi-square distribution as the test statistic. For both these types of problems, no assumptions need to be made about the shape of the population. We do not have to assume, for example, that the population of interest follows the normal distribution, as was done with tests of hypotheses in Chapters 10 through 12.

This chapter is a continuation of tests of hypotheses designed especially for nonparametric data. However, instead of being applicable to nominal-level data, these tests require that the responses be at least *ordinal* level. That is, the responses can be ranked from low to high. An example of ranking is the executive title. Executives are ranked assistant vice president, vice president, senior vice president, and president. A vice president is ranked higher than an assistant vice president, a senior vice president is ranked higher than a vice president, and so on.

In this chapter we consider five distribution-free tests and the Spearman coefficient of rank correlation. The tests are: the sign test, the median test, the Wilcoxon signed-rank test, the Wilcoxon rank-sum test, the Kruskal-Wallis analysis of variance by ranks.

# The Sign Test

The **sign test** is based on the sign of a difference between two related observations. We usually designate a plus sign for a positive difference and a minus sign for a negative difference. If, for example, sales increased from $34,698 in October to $51,276 in November, we record the $16,578 difference as a plus sign. If production dropped from 98,000 computers in the first quarter to 51,000 in the second quarter, a minus sign is recorded. For a sign test, we are not concerned with the magnitude of the difference, only the direction of the difference.

The sign test has many applications. One is for "before/after" experiments. To illustrate, suppose an evaluation is to be made on a new tune-up program for automobiles. We record the number of miles traveled per gallon of gasoline before the tune-up and again after the tune-up. If the tune-up is not effective, that is, had no effect on performance, then about half of the automobiles tested would show an increase in miles per gallon and the other half a decrease. A "+" sign is assigned to an increase, a "−" sign to a decrease.

A product-preference experiment illustrates another use of the sign test. Taster's Choice markets two kinds of coffee in a 4-ounce jar: decaffeinated and regular. Their

market research department wants to determine whether coffee drinkers prefer decaffeinated or regular coffee. Coffee drinkers are given two small, unmarked cups of coffee, and each is asked his or her preference. Preference for decaffeinated could be coded "+" and preference for regular "−." In a sense the data are ordinal level because the coffee drinkers give their preferred coffee the higher rank; they rank the other kind below it. Here again, if the population of consumers do not have a preference, we would expect half of the sample of coffee drinkers to prefer decaffeinated and the other half regular coffee.

We can best show the application of the sign test by an example. We will use a "before/after" experiment.

**EXAMPLE**

The director of information systems at Samuelson Chemicals recommended that an in-plant training program be instituted for managers. The objective is to improve the knowledge of database usage in accounting, procurement, production, and so on. Some managers thought it would be a worthwhile program; others resisted it, saying it would be of no value. Despite these objections, it was announced that the training sessions would commence the first of the month.

A sample of 15 managers was selected at random. A panel of database experts determined the general level of competence of each manager with respect to using the database. Their competence and understanding were rated as being either outstanding, excellent, good, fair, or poor. (See Table 16–1.) After the three-month training program, the same panel of information systems experts rated each manager again. The two ratings (before and after) are shown along with the sign of the difference. A "+" sign indicates improvement, and a "−" sign indicates that the manager's competence using databases had declined after the training program.

**TABLE 16–1** Competence before and after the Training Program

| | Name | Before | After | Sign of Difference |
|---|---|---|---|---|
| | T. J. Bowers | Good | Outstanding | + |
| | Sue Jenkins | Fair | Excellent | + |
| | James Brown | Excellent | Good | − |
| Dropped from analysis | Tad Jackson | Poor | Good | + |
| | ~~Andy Love~~ | ~~Excellent~~ | ~~Excellent~~ | ~~0~~ |
| | Sarah Truett | Good | Outstanding | + |
| | John Sinshi | Poor | Fair | + |
| | Jean Unger | Excellent | Outstanding | + |
| | Coy Farmer | Good | Poor | − |
| | Troy Archer | Poor | Good | + |
| | V. A. Jones | Good | Outstanding | + |
| | Coley Casper | Fair | Excellent | + |
| | Candy Fry | Good | Fair | − |
| | Arthur Seiple | Good | Outstanding | + |
| | Sandy Gumpp | Poor | Good | + |

We are interested in whether the in-plant training program was effective in increasing the competence of the managers using the company's database. That is, are the managers more competent after the training program than before?

**SOLUTION**

We will use the five-step hypothesis-testing procedure.

**Step 1: State the null hypothesis and the alternate hypothesis.**

$H_0$: $\pi \le .50$     There is no increase in competence as a result of the in-plant training program.

$H_1$: $\pi > .50$     The database competence of the managers has increased.

The symbol $\pi$ refers to the proportion in the population with a particular characteristic. If we *do not reject* the null hypothesis, it will indicate the training program has produced no change in the level of competence, or competence actually decreased. If we *reject* the null hypothesis, it will indicate that the competence of the managers has increased as a result of the training program.

The binomial distribution discussed in Chapter 6 is used as the test statistic. It is appropriate because the sign test meets all the binomial assumptions, namely:

1. There are only two outcomes: a "success" and a "failure." A manager either increased in database competence (a success) or did not.
2. For each trial the probability of success is assumed to be .50. Thus, the probability of a success is the same for all trials (managers in this case).
3. The total number of trials is fixed (15 in this experiment).
4. Each trial is independent. This means, for example, that Arthur Seiple's performance in the three-month course is unrelated to Sandy Gumpp's performance.

**Step 2:** **Select a level of significance.** We chose the .10 level.

**Step 3:** **Decide on the test statistic.** It is the *number of plus signs* resulting from the experiment.

**Step 4:** **Formulate a decision rule.** Fifteen managers were enrolled in the training course, but Andy Love showed no increase or decrease in competence. (See Table 16–1.) He was, therefore, eliminated from the study because he could not be assigned to either group, so $n = 14$. From the binomial probability distribution table in Appendix A, for an $n$ of 14 and a probability of .50, we copied the binomial probability distribution in Table 16–2. The number of successes is in column 1, the probability of success in column 2, and the cumulative probabilities in column 3. To arrive at the cumulative probabilities, we *add* the probabilities of success in column 2 from the bottom. For illustration, to get the cumulative probability of 11 or more successes, we add .000 + .001 + .006 + .022 = .029.

This is a one-tailed test because the alternate hypothesis gives a direction. The inequality (>) points to the right. Thus, the region of rejection is in the upper tail. If the inequality sign pointed toward the left tail (<), the region of rejection would be in the lower tail. If that were the case, we would add the probabilities in column 2 *down* to get the cumulative probabilities in column 3.

Recall that we selected the .10 level of significance. To arrive at the decision rule for this problem, we go to the cumulative probabilities in Table 16–2, column 3. We read up from the bottom until we come to the *cumulative probability nearest to but not exceeding the level of significance (.10).* That cumulative probability is .090. The number of successes (plus signs) corresponding to .090 in column 1 is 10. Therefore, the decision rule is: If the number of pluses in the sample is 10 or more, the null hypothesis is rejected and the alternate hypothesis accepted.

To repeat: We add the probabilities up from the bottom because the direction of the inequality (>) is toward the right, indicating that the region of rejection is in the upper tail. If the number of plus signs in the sample is 10 or more, we reject the null hypothesis; otherwise, we do not reject $H_0$. The region of rejection is portrayed in Chart 16–1.

What procedure is followed for a two-tailed test? We combine (add) the probabilities of success in the two tails until we come as close to the

**TABLE 16–2** Binomial Probability Distribution for $n = 14$, $\pi = .50$

| (1)<br>Number of<br>Successes | (2)<br>Probability of<br>Success | (3)<br>Cumulative<br>Probability | |
|---|---|---|---|
| 0 | .000 | 1.000 | |
| 1 | .001 | .999 | |
| 2 | .006 | .998 | |
| 3 | .022 | .992 | |
| 4 | .061 | .970 | |
| 5 | .122 | .909 | |
| 6 | .183 | .787 | |
| 7 | .209 | .604 | |
| 8 | .183 | .395 | |
| 9 | .122 | .212 | |
| 10 | .061 | .090 | ↑ |
| 11 | .022 | .029 | ← .000 + .001 + |
| 12 | .006 | .007 | .006 + .022 |
| 13 | .001 | .001 | Add up |
| 14 | .000 | .000 | |

**CHART 16–1** Region of Rejection, $n = 14$, $\pi = .50$

desired level of significance ($\alpha$) as possible without exceeding it. In this example $\alpha$ is .10. The probability of 3 or fewer successes is .029, found by .000 + .001 + .006 + .022. The probability of 11 or more successes is also .029. Adding the two probabilities gives .058. This is the closest we can come to .10 without exceeding it. Had we included the probabilities of 4 and 10 successes, the total would be .180, which exceeds .10. Hence, the decision rule for a two-tailed test would be to reject the null hypothesis if there are 3 or fewer plus signs, or 11 or more plus signs.

**Step 5: Make a decision regarding the null hypothesis.** Eleven out of the 14 managers in the training course increased their database competency. The number 11 is in the rejection region, which starts at 10, so $H_0$ is rejected. The three-month training course was effective. It increased the database competency of the managers.

It should be noted again that if the alternate hypothesis does not give a direction—for example, $H_0$: $\pi = .50$ and $H_1$: $\pi \neq 50$—the test of hypothesis is *two-tailed*. In such cases there will be two rejection regions—one in the lower tail and one in the upper tail. If $\alpha = .10$ and the test is two-tailed, the area in each tail is .05 ($\alpha/2 = .10/2 = .05$). Self-Review 16–1 illustrates this.

---

**Self-Review 16–1**

Recall the Taster's Choice example described on page 547, involving a consumer test to determine the preference for decaffeinated versus regular coffee. The null and alternate hypotheses are:

$$H_0: \pi = .50 \qquad n = 12 \qquad \alpha = .10$$
$$H_1: \pi \neq .50$$

(a) Is this a one-tailed or a two-tailed test of hypothesis?
(b) Show the decision rule in a chart.
(c) Letting consumer preference for decaffeinated coffee be a "+" and preference for regular coffee a "−," it was found that two customers preferred decaffeinated. What is your decision? Explain.

---

# Exercises

1. The following hypothesis-testing situation is given: $H_0$: $\pi \leq .50$ and $H_1$: $\pi > .50$. The significance level is .10, and the sample size is 12.
   **a.** What is the decision rule?
   **b.** There were nine successes. What is your decision regarding the null hypothesis? Explain.
2. The following hypothesis-testing situation is given: $H_0$: $\pi = .50$ and $H_1$: $\pi \neq .50$. The significance level is .05, and the sample size is 9.
   **a.** What is the decision rule?
   **b.** There were five successes. What is your decision regarding the null hypothesis?
3. Calorie Watchers has low-calorie breakfasts, lunches, and dinners. If you join the club, you receive two packaged meals a day. CW claims that you can eat anything you want for the third meal and still lose at least five pounds the first month. Members of the club are weighed before commencing the program and again at the end of the first month. The experiences of a random sample of 11 enrollees are:

| Name | Weight Change | Name | Weight Change |
|------|---------------|------|---------------|
| Foster | Lost | Hercher | Lost |
| Taoka | Lost | Camder | Lost |
| Lange | Gained | Hinckle | Lost |
| Rousos | Lost | Hinkley | Lost |
| Stephens | No change | Justin | Lost |
| Cantrell | Lost | | |

We are interested in whether there has been a weight loss as a result of the Calorie Watchers program.
   **a.** State $H_0$ and $H_1$.
   **b.** Using the .05 level of significance, what is the decision rule?
   **c.** What is your conclusion about the Calorie Watchers program?

**4.** Many new stockbrokers resist giving presentations to bankers and certain other groups. Sensing this lack of self-confidence, management arranged to have a confidence-building seminar for a sample of new stockbrokers and enlisted Career Boosters for a three-week course. Before the first session, Career Boosters measured the level of confidence of each participant. It was measured again after the three-week seminar. The before and after levels of self-confidence for the 14 in the course are shown below. Self-confidence was classified as being either negative, low, high, or very high.

| Stockbroker | Before Seminar | After Seminar | Stockbroker | Before Seminar | After Seminar |
|---|---|---|---|---|---|
| J. M. Martin | Negative | Low | F. M. Orphey | Low | Very high |
| T. D. Jagger | Negative | Negative | C. C. Ford | Low | High |
| A. D. Hammer | Low | High | A. R. Utz | Negative | Low |
| T. A. Jones, Jr. | Very high | Low | M. R. Murphy | Low | High |
| J. J. Cornwall | Low | High | P. A. Arms | Negative | Low |
| D. A. Skeen | Low | High | B. K. Pierre | Low | High |
| C. B. Simmer | Negative | High | N. S. Walker | Low | Very high |

The purpose of this study is to find whether Career Boosters was effective in raising the self-confidence of the new stockbrokers. That is, was the level of self-confidence higher after the seminar than before it? Use the .05 significance level.
**a.** State the null and alternate hypotheses.
**b.** Using the .05 level of significance, state the decision rule—either in words or in chart form.
**c.** Draw conclusions about the seminar offered by Career Boosters.

# Using the Normal Approximation to the Binomial

If the number of observations in the sample is larger than 10, the normal distribution can be used to approximate the binomial. Recall in Chapter 6, we computed the mean of the binomial distribution from $\mu = n\pi$ and the standard deviation from $\sigma = \sqrt{n\pi(1 - \pi)}$. In this case $\pi = .50$, so the equations reduce to $\mu = .50n$ and $\sigma = .50\sqrt{n}$, respectively.

The test statistic $z$ is

| | | |
|---|---|---|
| **SIGN TEST, LARGE SAMPLE** | $z = \dfrac{(X \pm .50) - \mu}{\sigma}$ | **[16–1]** |

If the number of pluses or minuses is *more than n/2,* we use the following form as the test statistic:

| | | |
|---|---|---|
| **SIGN TEST, LARGE SAMPLE, + SIGNS MORE THAN** *n/2* | $z = \dfrac{(X - .50) - \mu}{\sigma} = \dfrac{(X - .50) - .50n}{.50\sqrt{n}}$ | **[16–2]** |

If the number of pluses or minuses is *less than n/2,* the test statistic $z$ is

| | | |
|---|---|---|
| **SIGN TEST, LARGE SAMPLE, + SIGNS LESS THAN** *n/2* | $z = \dfrac{(X + .50) - \mu}{\sigma} = \dfrac{(X + .50) - .50n}{.50\sqrt{n}}$ | **[16–3]** |

In the preceding formulas, *X* is the number of plus (or minus) signs. The value $+.50$ or $-.50$ is the *continuity correction factor,* discussed in Chapter 7. Briefly, it is applied when a continuous distribution such as the normal distribution (which we are using) is used to approximate a discrete distribution (the binomial).

The following example illustrates the details of the large sample sign test.

**EXAMPLE**

The market research department of Cola, Inc., has been given the assignment of testing a new soft drink. Two versions of the drink are considered—a rather sweet drink and a somewhat bitter one. A preference test is to be conducted consisting of a sample of 64 consumers. Each consumer will taste both the sweet cola (labeled A) and the bitter one (labeled B) and indicate a preference. How will the test of hypothesis be conducted, and what cola, if any, is preferred?

**SOLUTION**

**Step 1: State the null and alternate hypotheses.**

$H_0$: $\pi = .50$    There is no preference.
$H_1$: $\pi \neq .50$    There is a preference.

**Step 2: Select a level of significance.** It is the .05 level.
**Step 3: Select the test statistic.** It is $z$, given in formula (16–1).

$$z = \frac{(X \pm .50) - \mu}{\sigma}$$

where $\mu = .50n$ and $\sigma = .50\sqrt{n}$.

**Step 4: Formulate the decision rule.** Referring to Appendix D, *Areas under the Normal Curve,* for a two-tailed test (because $H_1$ states that $\pi \neq .50$) and the .05 significance level, the critical values are $+1.96$ and $-1.96$. Recall from Chapter 10 that for a two-tailed test we split the rejection probability in half and place one half in each tail. That is, $\alpha/2 = .05/2 = .025$. Continuing, $.5000 - .0250 = .4750$. Searching for .4750 in the body of the table and reading the $z$ value in the left margin gives 1.96, the critical value. Therefore, do not reject $H_0$ if the computed $z$ value is between $+1.96$ and $-1.96$. Otherwise, reject $H_0$ and accept $H_1$.

**Step 5: Compute $z$, compare the computed value with the critical value, and make a decision regarding $H_0$.** Preference for cola A was given a "$+$" sign and preference for B a "$-$" sign. Out of the 64 in the sample, 42 preferred the sweet cola, A. Therefore, there are 42 pluses. Since 42 is *more than n/2 = 64/2 = 32,* we use formula (16–2) for $z$:

$$z = \frac{(X - .50) - .50n}{.50\sqrt{n}} = \frac{(42 - .50) - .50(64)}{.50\sqrt{64}} = 2.38$$

The computed $z$ of 2.38 is beyond the critical value of 1.96. Therefore, the null hypothesis of no difference is rejected at the .05 significance level. There is evidence of a difference in consumer preference. That is, we conclude consumers prefer one cola over another.

The p-value is the probability of finding a $z$ value larger than 2.38 or smaller than $-2.38$. From Appendix D, the probability of finding a $z$ value greater than 2.38 is $.5000 - .4913 = .0087$. Thus, the two-tailed p-value is .0174. So the probability of obtaining a sample statistic this extreme when the null hypothesis is true is less than 2 percent.

---

**Self-Review 16–2**

The Human Resources Department in a large automobile assembly plant began blood pressure screening and education for the 100 employees in the Paint Department the first of the year. As a follow-up in July the same 100 employees were again screened for blood pressure and 80 showed a reduction. Can we conclude the screening was effective in reducing blood pressure readings?

(a)  State the null hypothesis and the alternate hypothesis.
(b)  What is the decision rule for a significance level of .05?

(c)   Compute the value of the test statistic.
(d)   What is your decision regarding the null hypothesis?
(e)   Interpret your decision.

# Exercises

**5.** A sample of 45 overweight men participated in an exercise program. At the conclusion of the program 32 had lost weight. At the .05 significance level, can we conclude the program is effective?
   **a.** State the null hypothesis and the alternate hypothesis.
   **b.** State the decision rule.
   **c.** Compute the value of the test statistic.
   **d.** What is your decision regarding the null hypothesis?

**6.** A sample of 60 college students was given a special training program designed to improve their time management skills. One month after completing the course the students were contacted and asked whether the skills learned in the program were effective. A total of 42 responded yes. At the .05 significance level, can we conclude the program is effective?
   **a.** State the null hypothesis and the alternate hypothesis.
   **b.** State the decision rule.
   **c.** Compute the value of the test statistic.
   **d.** What is your decision regarding the null hypothesis?

**7.** Pierre's Restaurant announced that on Thursday night the menu would consist of unusual gourmet items, such as squid, rabbit, snails from Scotland, and dandelion greens. As part of a larger survey, a sample of 81 regular customers was asked whether they preferred the regular menu or the gourmet menu. Forty-three preferred the gourmet menu. Using the sign test and the .02 level, test whether the customers liked the gourmet menu better than the regular menu. Justify your conclusion.

**8.** Assembly workers at Computer Associates assemble just one or two subassemblies and insert them in a frame. The executives at CA think that the employees would have more pride in their work if they assembled all of the subassemblies and tested the complete computer. A sample of 25 employees was selected to experiment with the idea. After a training program, each was asked his or her preference. Twenty liked assembling the entire unit and testing it. At the .05 level, use the sign test to arrive at a decision regarding employee preference. Explain the steps you used to arrive at your decision.

## Testing a Hypothesis about a Median

Most of the tests of hypothesis we have conducted so far involved the population mean or a proportion. The sign test is one of the few tests that can be used to test the value of a median. Recall from Chapter 3 that the median is the value above which half of the observations lie and below which the other half lie. For hourly wages of $7, $9, $11, and $18, the median is $10. Half of the wages are above $10 an hour and the other half below $10.

To conduct a test of hypothesis, a value above the median is assigned a plus sign, and a value below the median is assigned a minus sign. If a value is the same as the median, it is dropped from further analysis. The procedure is identical to that followed in the small-sample and large-sample sign tests just discussed.

**EXAMPLE**

A study several years ago by the Consumer Research Department of Superior Grocers found the median weekly amount spent on grocery items by young married couples was $123. The CEO would like to repeat the research to determine whether the median amount spent has changed. Consumer Research's new sample information showed that, in a random sample of 102 young adult married couples, 60 spent more than $123 last week on grocery items, 40 spent less, and 2 spent exactly $123. At the

.10 significance level, is it reasonable to conclude that the median amount spent is not equal to $123?

**SOLUTION**

If the population median is $123, then we expect about half the sampled couples to have spent more than $123 last week and about half less than $123. After discarding the two customers who spent exactly $123, we would expect 50 to be above the median and 50 to be below the median. Is this difference attributable to chance, or is the median some value other than $123? The statistical test for the median will help answer that question.

The null and the alternate hypotheses are:

$H_0$: Median = $123
$H_1$: Median ≠ $123

This is a two-tailed test because the alternate hypothesis does not indicate a direction. That is, we are not interested in whether the median is less than or greater than $123, only that it is different from $123. The test statistic meets the binomial assumptions. That is:

1.  An observation is either larger or smaller than the proposed median, so there are only two possible outcomes.
2.  The probability of a success remains constant at .50. That is, $\pi = .50$.
3.  The couples selected as part of the sample represent independent trials.
4.  We count the number of successes in a fixed number of trials. In this case we consider 100 couples and count the number who spend more than $123 per week on grocery items.

The usable sample size is 100 and $\pi$ is .50, so $n\pi = 100(.50) = 50$ and $n(1 - \pi) = 100(1 - .50) = 50$, which are both larger than 5, so we use the normal distribution to approximate the binomial. That is, we actually use the standard normal distribution as the test statistic. The significance level is .10, so $\alpha/2 = .10/2 = .05$ of the area is in each tail of a normal distribution. From Appendix D, which shows the areas under a normal curve, the critical values are $-1.65$ and $1.65$. The decision rule is to reject $H_0$ if $z$ is less than $-1.65$ or greater than $1.65$.

We use formula (16–2) for $z$ because 60 is greater than $n/2$ ($100/2 = 50$).

$$z = \frac{(X - .50) - .50n}{.50\sqrt{n}} = \frac{(60 - .5) - .50(100)}{.50\sqrt{100}} = 1.90$$

The null hypothesis is rejected because the computed value of 1.90 is greater than the critical value of 1.65. The sample evidence indicates that the median amount spent per week on grocery items by young couples is *not* $123. The p-value for this test is .0574, found by 2(.5000 − .4713).

---

**Self-Review 16–3**

After receiving the results regarding the weekly amount spent on grocery items for young couples from the Consumer Research Department, the CEO of Superior Grocers wondered whether the same was true for senior citizen couples. In this case the CEO wants the Customer Research Department to investigate whether the median weekly amount spent per week by senior citizens is *greater than* $123. A sample of 64 senior citizen couples revealed 42 spent more than $123 per week on grocery items. Use the .05 significance level.

## Exercises

9. At www.payscale.com, the median salary for a chiropractor in Kansas is $82,400 per year. A group of recent graduates believe this amount is too low. In a random sample of 205

chiropractors who recently graduated, 170 began with a salary of more than $82,400 and five earned a salary of exactly $82,400.
  **a.** State the null and alternate hypotheses.
  **b.** State the decision rule. Use the .05 significance level.
  **c.** Do the necessary computations and interpret the results.
10. Central Airlines claims that the median price of a round-trip ticket to Jackson Hole, Wyoming, is $503. This claim is being challenged by the Association of Travel Agents, who believe the median price is less than $503. To resolve the issue, a random sample of 400 round-trip tickets was selected. Of these, 160 tickets were below $503. None of the tickets were exactly $503. Let $\alpha = .05$.
  **a.** State the null and alternate hypotheses.
  **b.** Reach a decision regarding the controversy.

# Wilcoxon Signed-Rank Test

The paired $t$ test, described in Chapter 11, had two requirements. First, the samples must be dependent. Recall that dependent samples are characterized by a measurement, some type of intervention, and then another measurement. For example, a large company began a "wellness" program at the start of the year. Twenty workers are enrolled in the weight reduction portion of the program. To begin, all participants were weighed. Next they dieted, did the exercise, and so forth in an attempt to lose weight. At the end of the program, which lasted six months, all participants were weighed again. The difference in their weight between the start and the end of the program is the variable of interest. Note that there is a measurement, an intervention, and then another measurement.

The second requirement for the paired $t$ test is that the distribution of the differences follow a normal distribution. In the company wellness example in the previous

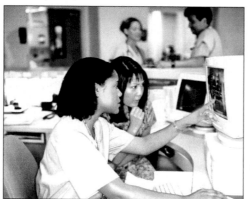

paragraph, this would require that the differences in the weights of the 20 participants follow the normal distribution. In that case this assumption is reasonable. However, there are instances when we want to study the differences between dependent observations where we cannot assume that the distribution of the differences approximates a normal distribution. Frequently we encounter a problem with the normality assumption when the level of measurement in the samples is ordinal, rather than interval or ratio. For example, suppose there are 10 surgical patients on 3 East today. The nursing supervisor asks Nurse Benner and Nurse Jurris to rate each of the 10 patients on a scale of 1 to 10, according to the difficulty of patient care. The distribution of the differences in the ratings probably would not approximate the normal distribution, and, therefore, the paired $t$ test would not be appropriate.

In 1945, Frank Wilcoxon developed a nonparametric test, based on the differences in dependent samples, where the normality assumption is not required. This test is called the **Wilcoxon signed-rank test.** The following example details its application.

**EXAMPLE**

Fricker's is a family restaurant chain located primarily in the southeastern part of the United States. They offer a full dinner menu, but their specialty is chicken. Recently, Bernie Frick, the owner and founder, developed a new spicy flavor for the batter in which the chicken is cooked. Before replacing the current flavor, he wants to conduct some tests to be sure that patrons will like the spicy flavor better.

To begin, Bernie selects a random sample of 15 customers. Each sampled customer is given a small piece of the current chicken and asked to rate its overall taste on a scale of 1 to 20. A value near 20 indicates the participant liked the flavor, whereas a score near 0 indicates they did not like the flavor. Next, the same 15 participants are given a sample of the new chicken with the spicier flavor and again asked to rate its taste on a scale of 1 to 20. The results are reported below. Is it reasonable to conclude that the spicy flavor is preferred? Use the .05 significance level.

| Participant | Spicy Flavor Score | Current Flavor Score | Participant | Spicy Flavor Score | Current Flavor Score |
|---|---|---|---|---|---|
| Arquette | 14 | 12 | Garcia | 19 | 10 |
| Jones | 8 | 16 | Sundar | 18 | 10 |
| Fish | 6 | 2 | Miller | 16 | 13 |
| Wagner | 18 | 4 | Peterson | 18 | 2 |
| Badenhop | 20 | 12 | Boggart | 4 | 13 |
| Hall | 16 | 16 | Hein | 7 | 14 |
| Fowler | 14 | 5 | Whitten | 16 | 4 |
| Virost | 6 | 16 | | | |

**SOLUTION**

The samples are dependent or related. That is, the participants are asked to rate both flavors of chicken. Thus, if we compute the difference between the rating for the spicy flavor and the current flavor, the resulting value shows the amount the participants favor one flavor over the other. If we choose to subtract the current flavor score from the spicy flavor score, a positive result is the "amount" the participant favors the spicy flavor. Negative difference scores indicate the participant favored the current flavor. Because of the somewhat subjective nature of the scores, we are not sure the distribution of the differences follows the normal distribution. We decide to use the nonparametric Wilcoxon signed-rank test.

As usual, we will use the five-step hypothesis-testing procedure. The null hypothesis is that there is no difference in the rating of the chicken flavors by the participants. That is, as many participants in the study rated the spicy flavor higher as rated the regular flavor higher. The alternate hypothesis is that the ratings are higher for the spicy flavor. More formally:

$H_0$: There is no difference in the ratings of the two flavors.
$H_1$: The spicy ratings are higher.

This is a one-tailed test. Why? Because Bernie Frick, the owner of Fricker's, will want to change his chicken flavor only if the sample participants show that the population of customers like the new flavor better. The significance level is .05, as stated in the problem above.

The steps to conduct the Wilcoxon signed-rank test are as follows.

1. Compute the difference between the spicy flavor score and the current flavor score for each participant. For example, Arquette's spicy flavor score was 14 and current flavor score was 12, so the amount of the difference is 2. For Jones, the difference is −8, found by 8 − 16, and for Fish it is 4, found by 6 − 2. The differences for all participants are shown in column 4 of Table 16–3.
2. Only the positive and negative differences are considered further. That is, if the difference in flavor scores is 0, that participant is dropped from further analysis and the number in the sample reduced. From Table 16–3, Hall, the sixth participant, scored both the spicy and the current flavor a 16. Hence, Hall is dropped from the study and the usable sample size reduced from 15 to 14.

3. Determine the absolute differences for the values computed in column 4. Recall that in an absolute difference we ignore the sign of the difference. The absolute differences are shown in column 5.
4. Next, rank the absolute differences from smallest to largest. Arquette, the first participant scored the spicy chicken a 14 and the current a 12. The difference of 2 in the two taste scores is the smallest absolute difference, so it is given a ranking of 1. The next largest difference is 3, given by Miller, so it is given a rank of 2. The other differences are ranked in a similar manner. There are three participants who rated the difference in the flavor as 8. That is, Jones, Badenhop, and Sundar each had a difference of 8 between their rating of the spicy flavor and the current flavor. To resolve this problem, we average the ranks involved and report the average rank for each. This situation involves the ranks 5, 6, and 7, so all three participants are assigned the rank of 6. The same situation occurs for those participants with a difference of 9. The ranks involved are 8, 9, and 10, so those participants are assigned a rank of 9.

**TABLE 16–3** Flavor Rating for Current and Spicy Flavors

| (1) Participant | (2) Spicy Score | (3) Current Score | (4) Difference in Score | (5) Absolute Difference | (6) Rank | (7) Signed Rank $R^+$ | $R^-$ |
|---|---|---|---|---|---|---|---|
| Arquette | 14 | 12 | 2 | 2 | 1 | 1 | |
| Jones | 8 | 16 | −8 | 8 | 6 | | 6 |
| Fish | 6 | 2 | 4 | 4 | 3 | 3 | |
| Wagner | 18 | 4 | 14 | 14 | 13 | 13 | |
| Badenhop | 20 | 12 | 8 | 8 | 6 | 6 | |
| Hall | 16 | 16 | * | * | * | * | |
| Fowler | 14 | 5 | 9 | 9 | 9 | 9 | |
| Virost | 6 | 16 | −10 | 10 | 11 | | 11 |
| Garcia | 19 | 10 | 9 | 9 | 9 | 9 | |
| Sunder | 18 | 10 | 8 | 8 | 6 | 6 | |
| Miller | 16 | 13 | 3 | 3 | 2 | 2 | |
| Peterson | 18 | 2 | 16 | 16 | 14 | 14 | |
| Boggart | 4 | 13 | −9 | 9 | 9 | | 9 |
| Hein | 7 | 14 | −7 | 7 | 4 | | 4 |
| Whitten | 16 | 4 | 12 | 12 | 12 | 12 | |
| Total | | | | | | 75 | 30 |

5. Each assigned rank in column 6 is then given the same sign as the original difference, and the results are reported in column 7. For example, the second participant has a difference score of −8 and a rank of 6. This value is located in the $R^-$ section of column 7.
6. The $R^+$ and $R^-$ columns are totaled. The sum of the positive ranks is 75 and the sum of the negative ranks is 30. The smaller of the two rank sums is used as the test statistic and referred to as $T$.

The critical values for the Wilcoxon signed-rank test are located in Appendix H. A portion of that table is shown on the following page. The $\alpha$ row is used for one-tailed tests and the $2\alpha$ row for two-tailed tests. In this case we want to show that customers like the spicy taste better, which is a one-tailed test, so we select the $\alpha$ row. We chose the .05 significance level, so move to the right to the column headed .05. Go down that column to the row where $n$ is 14. (Recall that one person in the study rated the chicken flavors the same and was dropped from the study, making the usable sample size 14.) The value at the intersection is 25, so the critical value is 25. The decision rule is to reject the null hypothesis if the *smaller* of the rank sums is 25 or less. The value obtained from Appendix H is the *largest value in the rejection region.* In this case the smaller rank sum is 30, so the decision is not to reject the null hypothesis. We cannot conclude there is a difference in the flavor ratings between the current and the spicy. Mr. Frick has not shown that customers prefer the new flavor.

| $n$ | $2\alpha$ .15<br>$\alpha$ .075 | .10<br>.050 | .05<br>.025 | .04<br>.020 | .03<br>.015 | .02<br>.010 | .01<br>.005 |
|-----|------|------|------|------|------|------|------|
| 4 | 0 | | | | | | |
| 5 | 1 | 0 | | | | | |
| 6 | 2 | 2 | 0 | 0 | | | |
| 7 | 4 | 3 | 2 | 1 | 0 | 0 | |
| 8 | 7 | 5 | 3 | 3 | 2 | 1 | 0 |
| 9 | 9 | 8 | 5 | 5 | 4 | 3 | 1 |
| 10 | 12 | 10 | 8 | 7 | 6 | 5 | 3 |
| 11 | 16 | 13 | 10 | 9 | 8 | 7 | 5 |
| 12 | 19 | 17 | 13 | 12 | 11 | 9 | 7 |
| 13 | 24 | 21 | 17 | 16 | 14 | 12 | 9 |
| 14 | 28 | 25 | 21 | 19 | 18 | 15 | 12 |
| 15 | 33 | 30 | 25 | 23 | 21 | 19 | 15 |

**Self-Review 16–4**

The assembly area of Gotrac Products was recently redesigned. Installing a new lighting system and purchasing new workbenches were two features of the redesign. The production supervisor would like to know if the changes resulted in an improvement in worker productivity. To investigate she selected a sample of 11 workers and determined the production rate before and after the changes. The sample information is reported below.

| Operator | Production Before | Production After | Operator | Production Before | Production After |
|----------|-------------------|------------------|----------|-------------------|------------------|
| S. M. | 17 | 18 | U. Z. | 10 | 22 |
| D. J. | 21 | 23 | Y. U. | 20 | 19 |
| M. D. | 25 | 22 | U. T. | 17 | 20 |
| B. B. | 15 | 25 | Y. H. | 24 | 30 |
| M. F. | 10 | 28 | Y. Y. | 23 | 26 |
| A. A. | 16 | 16 | | | |

(a) How many usable pairs are there? That is, what is $n$?
(b) Using the Wilcoxon signed-rank test, determine whether the new procedures actually increased production. Use the .05 level and a one-tailed test.

# Exercises

11. An industrial psychologist selected a random sample of seven young urban professional couples who own their homes. The size of their home (square feet) is compared with that of their parents. At the .05 significance level, can we conclude that the yuppies live in larger homes than their parents?

| Couple Name | Professional | Parent | Couple Name | Professional | Parent |
|-------------|--------------|--------|-------------|--------------|--------|
| Gordon | 1,725 | 1,175 | Kuhlman | 1,290 | 1,360 |
| Sharkey | 1,310 | 1,120 | Welch | 1,880 | 1,750 |
| Uselding | 1,670 | 1,420 | Anderson | 1,530 | 1,440 |
| Bell | 1,520 | 1,640 | | | |

12. Suppose Toyota Motor Corporation is studying the effect of regular versus high-octane gasoline on fuel economy of its new high-performance, 3.5-liter, V6 engine. Ten executives are selected and asked to maintain records on the number of miles traveled per gallon of gas. The results are:

| | Miles per Gallon | | | | Miles per Gallon | |
|---|---|---|---|---|---|---|
| Executive | Regular | High-Octane | Executive | Regular | High-Octane |
| Bowers | 25 | 28 | Rau | 38 | 40 |
| Demars | 33 | 31 | Greolke | 29 | 29 |
| Grasser | 31 | 35 | Burns | 42 | 37 |
| DeToto | 45 | 44 | Snow | 41 | 44 |
| Kleg | 42 | 47 | Lawless | 30 | 44 |

At the .05 significance level, is there a difference in the number of miles traveled per gallon between regular and high-octane gasoline?

13. A new assembly-line procedure to increase production has been suggested by Mr. Mump. To test whether the new procedure is superior to the old procedure, a sample group of 15 assembly line workers was selected at random. First their production under the old system was determined. Then the new Mump procedure was introduced. After an appropriate break-in period, their production was measured again. The results were:

| | Production | | | | Production | |
|---|---|---|---|---|---|---|
| Employee | Old System | Mump Method | Employee | Old System | Mump Method |
| A | 60 | 64 | I | 87 | 84 |
| B | 40 | 52 | J | 80 | 80 |
| C | 59 | 58 | K | 56 | 57 |
| D | 30 | 37 | L | 21 | 21 |
| E | 70 | 71 | M | 99 | 108 |
| F | 78 | 83 | N | 50 | 56 |
| G | 43 | 46 | O | 56 | 62 |
| H | 40 | 52 | | | |

At the .05 significance level can we conclude the production is greater using the Mump method?
   a. State the null and alternate hypotheses.
   b. State the decision rule.
   c. Arrive at a decision regarding the null hypothesis.

14. It has been suggested that daily production of a subassembly would be increased if better lighting were installed and background music and free coffee and doughnuts were provided during the day. Management agreed to try the scheme for a limited time. The number of subassemblies produced per week by a sample of employees follows.

| Employee | Past Production Record | Production after Installing, Lighting, Music, etc. | Employee | Past Production Record | Production after Installing, Lighting, Music, etc. |
|---|---|---|---|---|---|
| JD | 23 | 33 | WWJ | 21 | 25 |
| SB | 26 | 26 | OP | 25 | 22 |
| MD | 24 | 30 | CD | 21 | 23 |
| RCF | 17 | 25 | PA | 16 | 17 |
| MF | 20 | 19 | RRT | 20 | 15 |
| UHH | 24 | 22 | AT | 17 | 9 |
| IB | 30 | 29 | QQ | 23 | 30 |

Using the Wilcoxon signed-rank test, determine whether the suggested changes are worthwhile.
   a. State the null hypothesis.
   b. You decide on the alternate hypothesis.

**c.** You decide on the level of significance.
**d.** State the decision rule.
**e.** Compute $T$ and arrive at a decision.

# Wilcoxon Rank-Sum Test

One test specifically designed to determine whether two independent samples came from equivalent populations is the **Wilcoxon rank-sum test.** This test is an alternative to the two-sample $t$ test described in Chapter 11. Recall that the $t$ test requires that the two populations follow the normal distribution and have equal population variances. These conditions are not required for the Wilcoxon rank-sum test.

The Wilcoxon rank-sum test is based on the average of ranks. The data are ranked as if the observations were part of a single sample. If the null hypothesis is true, then the ranks will be about evenly distributed between the two samples, and the average of the ranks for the two samples will be about the same. That is, the low, medium, and high ranks should be about equally divided between the two samples. If the alternate hypothesis is true, one of the samples will have more of the lower ranks and, thus, a smaller rank average. The other sample will have more of the higher ranks and, therefore, a larger average. If each of the samples contains *at least eight observations,* the standard normal distribution is used as the test statistic. The formula is:

| | | |
|---|---|---|
| **WILCOXON RANK-SUM TEST** | $$z = \dfrac{W - \dfrac{n_1(n_1 + n_2 + 1)}{2}}{\sqrt{\dfrac{n_1 n_2 (n_1 + n_2 + 1)}{12}}}$$ | **[16–4]** |

*Test using independent samples*

where:

$n_1$ is the number of observations from the first population.
$n_2$ is the number of observations from the second population.
$W$ is the sum of the ranks from the first population.

**EXAMPLE**

Dan Thompson, the president of CEO Airlines, recently noted an increase in the number of no-shows for flights out of Atlanta. He is particularly interested in determining whether there are more no-shows for flights that originate from Atlanta compared with flights leaving Chicago. A sample of nine flights from Atlanta and eight from Chicago are reported in Table 16–4. At the .05 significance level, can we conclude that there are more no-shows for the flights originating in Atlanta?

**TABLE 16–4** Number of No-Shows for Scheduled Flights

| Atlanta | Chicago | Atlanta | Chicago |
|---------|---------|---------|---------|
| 11 | 13 | 20 | 9 |
| 15 | 14 | 24 | 17 |
| 10 | 10 | 22 | 21 |
| 18 | 8 | 25 | |
| 11 | 16 | | |

**SOLUTION**

If the populations of no-shows followed the normal distribution and had equal variances, the two-sample $t$ test, discussed in Chapter 11, would be appropriate. In this case Mr. Thompson believes these two conditions cannot be met. Therefore, a nonparametric test, the Wilcoxon rank-sum test, is appropriate.

If the number of no-shows is the same for Atlanta and Chicago, then we expect the means of the two ranks to be about the same. If the number of no-shows is not the same, we expect the two sums of ranks to be quite different.

Mr. Thompson believes there are more no-shows for Atlanta flights. Thus, a one-tailed test is appropriate, with the rejection region located in the upper tail. The null and alternate hypotheses are:

$H_0$: The population distribution of no-shows is the same or less for Atlanta and Chicago.

$H_1$: The population distribution of no-shows is larger for Atlanta than for Chicago.

The test statistic follows the standard normal distribution. At the .05 significance level, we find from Appendix D the critical value of $z$ is 1.65. The null hypothesis is rejected if the computed value of $z$ is greater than 1.65.

The alternate hypothesis is that there are more no-shows in Atlanta, which means that distribution is located to the right of the Chicago distribution. The value of $W$ is calculated for the Atlanta group and is found to be 96.5, which is the sum of the ranks for the no-shows for the Atlanta flights. The details of rank assignment are shown in Table 16–5. We rank the observations from *both* samples as if they were a single group. The Chicago flight with only 8 no-shows had the fewest, so it is assigned a rank of 1. The Chicago flight with 9 no-shows is ranked 2, and so on. The Atlanta flight with 25 no-shows is the highest, so it is assigned the largest rank, 17. There are also two instances of tied ranks. There are an Atlanta and a Chicago flight that each had 10 no-shows and two Atlanta flights with 11 no-shows. How do we handle these ties? The solution is to average the ranks involved and assign the average rank to both flights. In the case involving 10 no-shows the ranks involved are 3 and 4. The mean of these ranks is 3.5, so a rank of 3.5 is assigned to both the Atlanta and the Chicago flights with 10 no-shows.

**TABLE 16–5** Ranked Number of No-Shows for Scheduled Flights

| Atlanta | | Chicago | |
|---|---|---|---|
| No-Shows | Rank | No-Shows | Rank |
| 11 | 5.5 | 13 | 7 |
| 15 | 9 | 14 | 8 |
| 10 | 3.5 | 10 | 3.5 |
| 18 | 12 | 8 | 1 |
| 11 | 5.5 | 16 | 10 |
| 20 | 13 | 9 | 2 |
| 24 | 16 | 17 | 11 |
| 22 | 15 | 21 | 14 |
| 25 | 17 | | |
| | 96.5 | | 56.5 |

Note from Table 16–5 that there are nine flights originating in Atlanta and eight in Chicago, so $n_1 = 9$ and $n_2 = 8$. Computing $z$ from formula (16–4) gives:

$$z = \frac{W - \dfrac{n_1(n_1 + n_2 + 1)}{2}}{\sqrt{\dfrac{n_1 n_2 (n_1 + n_2 + 1)}{12}}} = \frac{96.5 - \dfrac{9(9 + 8 + 1)}{2}}{\sqrt{\dfrac{9(8)(9 + 8 + 1)}{12}}} = 1.49$$

Because the computed $z$ value (1.49) is less than 1.65, the null hypothesis is not rejected. The evidence does not show a difference in the typical number of no-shows.

That is, it appears that the number of no-shows is the same in Atlanta as in Chicago. The *p*-value is .0681, found by determining the area to the right of 1.49 (.5000 − .4319).

The MegaStat software can produce the same results. The MegaStat *p*-value is .0742, which is close to the value we calculated. The difference is due to rounding in the system and correcting for ties.

In using the Wilcoxon rank-sum test, you may number the two populations in either order. However, once you have made a choice, *W* must be the sum of the ranks identified as population 1. If, in the no-show example, the population of Chicago was identified as number 1, the direction of the alternate hypothesis would be changed, but the *absolute value of z* would remain the same.

$H_0$: The population distribution of no-shows is the same or larger for Chicago than for Atlanta.

$H_1$: The population distribution of no-shows is smaller for Chicago than for Atlanta.

The computed value of *z* is −1.49, found by:

$$z = \frac{W - \dfrac{n_1(n_1 + n_2 + 1)}{2}}{\sqrt{\dfrac{n_1 n_2(n_1 + n_2 + 1)}{12}}} = \frac{56.5 - \dfrac{8(8 + 9 + 1)}{2}}{\sqrt{\dfrac{8(9)(8 + 9 + 1)}{12}}} = -1.49$$

---

**Self-Review 16–5**

The research director for Top Flite wants to know whether there is a difference in the distribution of the distances traveled by two of the company's golf balls. Eight of their XL-550 brand and eight of their DL-300 brand balls were hit by an automatic driver. The distances (in yards) were as follows:

| | |
|---|---|
| XL-550: | 252, 263, 279, 273, 271, 265, 257, 280 |
| DL-300: | 262, 242, 256, 260, 258, 243, 239, 265 |

Assume the distributions of the distances traveled do not follow the normal distribution. At the .05 significance level, is there a difference between the two distributions?

# Exercises

15. The following observations were randomly selected from populations that were not necessarily normally distributed. Use the .05 significance level, a two-tailed test, and the Wilcoxon rank-sum test to determine whether there is a difference between the two populations.

| Population A: | 38, 45, 56, 57, 61, 69, 70, 79 |
|---|---|
| Population B: | 26, 31, 35, 42, 51, 52, 57, 62 |

16. The following observations were randomly selected from populations that are not necessarily normally distributed. Use the .05 significance level, a two-tailed test, and the Wilcoxon rank-sum test to determine whether there is a difference between the two populations.

| Population A: | 12, 14, 15, 19, 23, 29, 33, 40, 51 |
|---|---|
| Population B: | 13, 16, 19, 21, 22, 33, 35, 43 |

17. Tucson State University offers two MBA programs. In the first program the students meet two nights per week at the University's main campus in downtown Tucson. In the second program students only communicated on-line with the instructor. The director of the MBA experience at Tucson wishes to compare the number of hours studied last week by the two groups of students. A sample of 10 on-campus students and 12 on-line students revealed the following information.

| Campus | 28, 16, 42, 29, 31, 22, 50, 42, 23, 25 |
|---|---|
| Online | 26, 42, 65, 38, 29, 32, 59, 42, 27, 41, 46, 18 |

Do not assume the two distributions of study times, which are reported in hours, follow a normal distribution. At the .05 significance level, can we conclude the on-line students study more?

18. In recent times, with mortgage rates at low levels, financial institutions have had to provide more customer convenience. One of the innovations offered by Coastal National Bank and Trust is the on-line entry of mortgage applications. Listed below is the time, in minutes, to complete the application process for customers applying for a 15-year fixed-rate and a 30-year fixed-rate mortgage.

| 15 years, fixed rate | 41, 36, 42, 39, 36, 48, 49, 38 |
|---|---|
| 30 years, fixed rate | 21, 27, 36, 20, 19, 21, 39, 24, 22 |

At the .05 significance level, is it reasonable to conclude that it takes less time for those customers applying for the 30-year fixed-rate mortgage? Do not assume the distribution times follow a normal distribution for either group.

# Kruskal-Wallis Test: Analysis of Variance by Ranks

Kruskal-Wallis test less restrictive than ANOVA

The analysis of variance (ANOVA) procedure discussed in Chapter 12 was concerned with whether several population means are equal. The data were interval or ratio level. Also, it was assumed the populations follow the normal distribution and their standard deviations were equal. What if the data are ordinal scale and/or the populations do not follow a normal distribution? W. H. Kruskal and W. A. Wallis reported a nonparametric test in 1952 requiring only ordinal-level (ranked) data. No assumptions about the shape of the populations are required. The test is referred to as the **Kruskal-Wallis one-way analysis of variance by ranks.**

For the Kruskal-Wallis test to be applied, the samples selected from the populations must be *independent*. For example, if samples from three groups—executives, staff, and supervisors—are to be selected and interviewed, the responses of one group (say, the executives) must in no way influence the responses of the others.

To compute the Kruskal-Wallis test statistic, (1) all the samples are combined, (2) the combined values are ordered from low to high, and (3) the ordered values are *replaced by ranks, starting with 1 for the smallest value.* An example will clarify the procedure.

**EXAMPLE**

A management seminar consists of executives from manufacturing, finance, and engineering. Before scheduling the seminar sessions, the seminar leader is interested in whether the three groups are equally knowledgeable about management principles. Plans are to take samples of the executives in manufacturing, in finance, and in engineering and to administer a test to each executive. If there is no difference in the scores for the three distributions, the seminar leader will conduct just one session. However, if there is a difference in the scores, separate sessions will be given.

We will use the Kruskal-Wallis test instead of ANOVA because the seminar leader is unwilling to assume that (1) the populations of management scores follow the normal distribution or (2) the population standard deviations are the same.

**SOLUTION**

The usual first step in hypothesis testing is to state the null and the alternate hypotheses.

$H_0$: The population distributions of the management scores for the populations of executives in manufacturing, finance, and engineering are the same.

$H_1$: The population distributions are not all the same.

The seminar leader selected the .05 level of risk.

The test statistic used for the Kruskal-Wallis test is designated $H$. Its formula is:

| KRUSKAL-WALLIS TEST | $H = \dfrac{12}{n(n+1)}\left[\dfrac{(\Sigma R_1)^2}{n_1} + \dfrac{(\Sigma R_2)^2}{n_2} + \cdots + \dfrac{(\Sigma R_k)^2}{n_k}\right] - 3(n+1)$ | **[16–5]** |
|---|---|---|

with $k - 1$ degrees of freedom ($k$ is the number of populations), where:

$\Sigma R_1, \Sigma R_2, \ldots, \Sigma R_k$ are the sums of the ranks of samples 1, 2, ..., $k$, respectively.

$n_1, n_2, \ldots, n_k$ are the sizes of samples 1, 2, ..., $k$, respectively.

$n$ is the combined number of observations for all samples.

Chi-square used if every sample is at least 5

The distribution of the sample $H$ statistic is very close to the chi-square distribution with $k - 1$ degrees of freedom *if every sample includes at least 5 observations.* Therefore, we will use the chi-square to formulate the decision rule. In this example there are three populations—a population of executives in manufacturing, another for executives in finance, and a third population of engineering executives. Thus, there are $k - 1$, or $3 - 1 = 2$ degrees of freedom. Refer to the chi-square table of critical values in Appendix I. The critical value for 2 degrees of freedom and the .05 level of risk is 5.991. Do not reject $H_0$ if the computed value of the test statistic $H$ is less than or equal to 5.991. Reject $H_0$ if the computed value of $H$ is greater than 5.991, and accept $H_1$.

The next step is to select random samples from the three populations. A sample of seven manufacturing, eight finance, and six engineering executives was selected. Their scores on the test are recorded in Table 16–6.

**TABLE 16–6** Management Test Scores for Manufacturing, Finance, and Engineering
Executives

| Manufacturing Executives | Finance Executives | Engineering Executives |
|---|---|---|
| 56 | 103 | 42 |
| 39 | 87 | 38 ⟵ tie for next lowest |
| 48 | 51 | 89 |
| 38 ⟵ tie for next lowest | 95 | 75 |
| 73 | 68 | 35 ⟵ lowest |
| 50 | 42 | 61 |
| 62 | 107 ⟵ highest score | |
| | 89 | |

Considering the scores as a single population, the trade executive with a score of 35 is the lowest, so it is ranked 1. There are two scores of 38. To resolve this tie, each score is given a rank of 2.5, found by (2 + 3)/2. This process is continued for all scores. The highest score is 107, and that finance executive is given a rank of 21. The scores, the ranks, and the sum of the ranks for each of the three samples are given in Table 16–7.

**TABLE 16–7** Scores, Ranks, and Sums of Ranks for Management Test Scores

| Manufacturing Executives | | Finance Executives | | Engineering Executives | |
|---|---|---|---|---|---|
| Scores | Ranks ($R_1$) | Scores | Ranks ($R_2$) | Scores | Ranks ($R_3$) |
| 56 | 10.0 | 103 | 20.0 | 42 | 5.5 |
| 39 | 4.0 | 87 | 16.0 | 38 | 2.5 |
| 48 | 7.0 | 51 | 9.0 | 89 | 17.5 |
| 38 | 2.5 | 95 | 19.0 | 75 | 15.0 |
| 73 | 14.0 | 68 | 13.0 | 35 | 1.0 |
| 50 | 8.0 | 42 | 5.5 | 61 | 11.0 |
| 62 | 12.0 | 107 | 21.0 | | |
| | | 89 | 17.5 | | |
| | $\Sigma R_1 = 57.5$ | | $\Sigma R_2 = 121.0$ | | $\Sigma R_3 = 52.5$ |

Solving for $H$ gives

$$H = \frac{12}{n(n+1)}\left[\frac{(\Sigma R_1)^2}{n_1} + \frac{(\Sigma R_2)^2}{n_2} + \frac{(\Sigma R_3)^2}{n_3}\right] - 3(n+1)$$

$$= \frac{12}{21(21+1)}\left[\frac{57.5^2}{7} + \frac{121^2}{8} + \frac{52.5^2}{6}\right] - 3(21+1) = 5.736$$

Because the computed value of $H$ (5.736) is not beyond 5.991, the null hypothesis is not rejected. There is no evidence of a difference among the executives from manufacturing, finance, and engineering with respect to their typical knowledge of management principles. From a practical standpoint, the seminar leader should consider offering only one session including executives from all areas.

The Kruskal-Wallis procedure is available on the MINITAB system. Output for the example regarding the knowledge of management principles of executives from several industries follows. The computed value of $H$ is 5.74 and the $p$-value reported on the output is .057. This agrees with our earlier calculations.

Recall from Chapter 12 that for the analysis of variance technique to apply, we assume that: (1) the populations are normally distributed, (2) these populations have equal standard deviations, and (3) the samples are selected independently. If these assumptions are met, we use the $F$ distribution as the test statistic. If these assumptions cannot be met, we apply the distribution-free test by Kruskal-Wallis. To highlight the similarities between the two approaches, we will solve the example regarding executive knowledge of management principles using the ANOVA technique.

To begin, we state the null and the alternate hypotheses for the three groups.

$H_0$: $\mu_1 = \mu_2 = \mu_3$
$H_1$: The treatment means are not all the same.

For the .05 significance level, with $k - 1 = 3 - 1 = 2$ degrees of freedom in the numerator and $n - k = 21 - 3 = 18$ degrees of freedom in the denominator, the critical value of $F$ is 3.55. The decision rule is to reject the null hypothesis if the computed value of $F$ is greater than 3.55. The output from the Excel system follows.

From the previous output, the computed value of $F$ is 4.12 and the $p$-value is .0336. Our decision is to reject the null hypothesis and accept the alternate hypothesis. Using this test we conclude that the treatment means are not the same. That is, the knowledge of management principles is different among the three executive groups.

We have contradictory conclusions on the same data. How can this happen? If we compare the results using $p$-values, the answers are similar. For the Kruskal-Wallis test the $p$-value was .057, which is only slightly more than the significance level of .05, but our decision was not to reject $H_0$. The $p$-value using ANOVA is .034, which is not far beyond the critical value into the rejection region. So, to summarize, we just missed rejecting $H_0$ with the Kruskal-Wallis test, and we were just in the rejection region using ANOVA. The difference in the $p$-values is .023. Thus, the results are actually quite close in terms of the $p$-values.

---

**Self-Review 16–6**

The regional bank manager of Statewide Financial is interested in the turnover rate of personal checking accounts in four of the large branch banks. (Turnover rate is the speed at which the money in an account is deposited and withdrawn. An extremely active account may have a rate of 300; if only one or two checks were written, the rate could be about 30.) The turnover rates of the samples selected from the four branch banks are shown. Using the .01 level and the Kruskal-Wallis test, determine whether there is a difference in the turnover rates of the personal checking accounts among the four branches.

| Englewood Branch | West Side Branch | Great Northern Branch | Sylvania Branch |
|---|---|---|---|
| 208 | 91 | 302 | 99 |
| 307 | 62 | 103 | 116 |
| 199 | 86 | 319 | 189 |
| 142 | 91 | 340 | 103 |
| 91 | 80 | 180 | 100 |
| 296 | | | 131 |

---

# Exercises

19. Under what conditions should the Kruskal-Wallis test be used instead of analysis of variance?
20. Under what conditions should the Kruskal-Wallis test be used instead of the Wilcoxon rank-sum test?
21. The following sample data were obtained from three populations that did not follow a normal distribution.

| Sample 1 | Sample 2 | Sample 3 |
|---|---|---|
| 50 | 48 | 39 |
| 54 | 49 | 41 |
| 59 | 49 | 44 |
| 59 | 52 | 47 |
| 65 | 56 | 51 |
| | 57 | |

a. State the null hypothesis.
b. Using the .05 level of risk, state the decision rule.
c. Compute the value of the test statistic.
d. What is your decision on the null hypothesis?

**22.** The following sample data were obtained from three populations where the variances were not equal, and you wish to compare the populations.

| Sample 1 | Sample 2 | Sample 3 |
|----------|----------|----------|
| 21 | 15 | 38 |
| 29 | 17 | 40 |
| 35 | 22 | 44 |
| 45 | 27 | 51 |
| 56 | 31 | 53 |
| 71 |  |  |

    **a.** State the null hypothesis.
    **b.** Using the .01 level of risk, state the decision rule.
    **c.** Compute the value of the test statistic.
    **d.** What is your decision on the null hypothesis?

**23.** Davis Outboard Motors, Inc. recently developed an epoxy painting process for corrosion protection on exhaust components. Bill Davis, the owner, wishes to determine whether the lengths of life for the paint are equal for three different conditions: salt water, fresh water without weeds, and fresh water with a heavy concentration of weeds. Accelerated-life tests were conducted in the laboratory, and the number of hours the paint lasted before peeling was recorded.

| Salt Water | Fresh Water | Fresh Water with Weeds |
|------------|-------------|------------------------|
| 167.3 | 160.6 | 182.7 |
| 189.6 | 177.6 | 165.4 |
| 177.2 | 185.3 | 172.9 |
| 169.4 | 168.6 | 169.2 |
| 180.3 | 176.6 | 174.7 |

Use the Kruskal-Wallis test and the .01 level to determine whether the lasting quality of the paint is the same for the three water conditions.

**24.** The National Turkey Association wants to experiment with three different feed mixtures for very young turkeys. Since no experience exists regarding the three mixtures, no assumptions can be made about the distribution of weights. The Kruskal-Wallis test must be used to test whether the turkeys are equal in weight after eating the feed for a specified length of time. Five young turkeys were given feed A, six were given feed B, and five were given feed C. Test at the .05 level whether the mean weights of the turkeys who ate feed A, feed B, and feed C are equal.

| Weight (in pounds) | | |
|--------------------|--|--|
| Feed Mixture A | Feed Mixture B | Feed Mixture C |
| 11.2 | 12.6 | 11.3 |
| 12.1 | 10.8 | 11.9 |
| 10.9 | 11.3 | 12.4 |
| 11.3 | 11.0 | 10.6 |
| 12.0 | 12.0 | 12.0 |
|  | 10.7 |  |

# Rank-Order Correlation

In Chapter 13, we discussed $r$, the sample coefficient of correlation. Recall that it measures the association between two interval- or ratio-scaled variables. For example, the coefficient of correlation reports the association between the salary of executives and their years of experience, or the association between the number of miles a shipment had to travel and the number of days it took to arrive at its destination.

Charles Spearman, a British statistician, introduced a measure of correlation for ordinal-level data. This measure allows us to describe the relationship between sets of ranked data. For example, two staff members in the Office of Research at the University of the Valley are asked to rank 10 faculty research proposals for funding purposes. We want to study the association between the ratings of the two staff members. That is, do the two staff members rate the same proposals as the most worthy and the least worthy of funding? Spearman's coefficient of rank correlation, denoted $r_s$, provides a measure of the association.

The coefficient of rank correlation is computed by the following formula.

| SPEARMAN'S COEFFICIENT OF RANK CORRELATION | $r_s = 1 - \dfrac{6\Sigma d^2}{n(n^2 - 1)}$ | [16–6] |
|---|---|---|

where:

  $d$ is the difference between the ranks for each pair.
  $n$ is the number of paired observations.

Like the coefficient of correlation, the coefficient of rank correlation can assume any value from $-1.00$ up to $1.00$. A value of $-1.00$ indicates perfect negative correlation and a value of $1.00$ perfect positive correlation among the ranks. A rank correlation of 0 indicates that there is no association among the ranks. Rank correlations of $-.84$ and $.80$ both indicate a strong association, but the former indicates an inverse relationship between the ranks and the latter a direct relationship.

**EXAMPLE**

Lorrenger Plastics, Inc. recruits management trainees at colleges and universities throughout the United States. Each trainee is given a rating by the recruiter during the on-campus interview. This rating is an expression of future potential and may range from 0 to 15, with the higher score indicating more potential. The recent college graduate then enters an in-plant training program and is given another composite rating based on tests, opinions of group leaders, training officers, and so on. The on-campus rating and the in-plant training ratings are given in Table 16–8.

TABLE 16–8  Executive Ratings and In-Plant Training Ratings for a Sample of Recent College Graduates

| Graduate | On-Campus Rating, X | Training Rating, Y | Graduate | On-Campus Rating, X | Training Rating, Y |
|---|---|---|---|---|---|
| A | 8 | 4 | G | 11 | 9 |
| B | 10 | 4 | H | 7 | 6 |
| C | 9 | 4 | I | 8 | 6 |
| D | 4 | 3 | J | 13 | 9 |
| E | 12 | 6 | K | 10 | 5 |
| F | 11 | 9 | L | 12 | 9 |

Calculate the coefficient of rank correlation. Interpret its value.

**SOLUTION**

It was decided to rank the variables from low to high. The lowest rating given by the on-campus recruiter was a 4 to graduate D, so it was ranked 1. The next lowest was a 7 to graduate H, so it was ranked 2. There were two graduates rated 8. The tie is resolved by giving each a rank of 3.5, which is the average of ranks 3 and 4. The same procedure is followed when there are more than two ratings tied. For example, note that the lowest training rating is 3, and it is given a rank of 1. Then there are three ratings of 4. The average of the three tied ranks is 3, found by (2 + 3 + 4)/3. This is illustrated along with the necessary calculations for $r_s$ in Table 16–9.

**TABLE 16–9** Calculations Needed for $r_s$

| Graduate | On-Campus Rating, X | Training Rating, Y | Rank On-Campus | Rank Training | Difference between Ranks, d | Difference Squared, $d^2$ |
|---|---|---|---|---|---|---|
| A | 8 | 4 | 3.5 | 3.0 | 0.5 | 0.25 |
| B | 10 | 4 | 6.5 | 3.0 | 3.5 | 12.25 |
| C | 9 | 4 | 5.0 | 3.0 | 2.0 | 4.00 |
| D | 4 | 3 | 1.0 | 1.0 | 0 | 0 |
| E | 12 | 6 | 10.5 | 7.0 | 3.5 | 12.25 |
| F | 11 | 9 | 8.5 | 10.5 | −2.0 | 4.00 |
| G | 11 | 9 | 8.5 | 10.5 | −2.0 | 4.00 |
| H | 7 | 6 | 2.0 | 7.0 | −5.0 | 25.00 |
| I | 8 | 6 | 3.5 | 7.0 | −3.5 | 12.25 |
| J | 13 | 9 | 12.0 | 10.5 | 1.5 | 2.25 |
| K | 10 | 5 | 6.5 | 5.0 | 1.5 | 2.25 |
| L | 12 | 9 | 10.5 | 10.5 | 0 | 0 |
|  |  |  |  |  | 0.0 | 78.50 |

$r_s$ is .726, found by:

$$r_s = 1 - \frac{6\Sigma d^2}{n(n^2 - 1)} = 1 - \frac{6(78.50)}{12(143)} = .726$$

The value of .726 indicates a strong positive association between the ratings of the on-campus recruiter and the ratings of the training staff. The graduates that received high ratings from the on-campus recruiter also tended to be the ones that received high ratings from the training staff.

## Testing the Significance of $r_s$

Testing whether correlation in the population is zero

In Chapter 13 we tested the significance of Pearson's $r$. For ranked data the question also arises whether the correlation in the population is actually zero. For instance, there were only 12 graduates sampled in the preceding example. In the solution to the example, the rank correlation coefficient of .726 indicates a rather strong relationship between the two sets of ranks. Is it possible that the correlation of .726 is due to chance and that the correlation among the ranks in the population is really 0? We will now conduct a test of significance to answer that question.

"Large" samples—10 or more

For a sample of 10 or more, the significance of $r_s$ is determined by computing $t$ using the following formula. The sampling distribution of $r_s$ follows the $t$ distribution with $n - 2$ degrees of freedom.

| HYPOTHESES TEST, RANK CORRELATION | $t = r_s \sqrt{\dfrac{n - 2}{1 - r_s^2}}$ | [16–7] |
|---|---|---|

The null and the alternate hypotheses are:

$H_0$: The rank correlation in the population is zero.
$H_1$: There is a positive association among the ranks.

The decision rule is to reject $H_0$ if the computed value of $t$ is greater than 1.812 (from Appendix F, .05 significance level, one-tailed test, and 10 degrees of freedom, found by $n - 2 = 12 - 2 = 10$).
   The computed value of $t$ is 3.338:

$$t = r_s \sqrt{\frac{n-2}{1-r_s^2}} = .726 \sqrt{\frac{12-2}{1-(.726)^2}} = 3.338$$

$H_0$ is rejected because the computed $t$ of 3.338 is greater than 1.812. $H_1$ is accepted. There is evidence of a positive correlation between the ranks given by the on-campus recruiter and the ranks assigned during training.

---

**Self-Review 16–7**

A sample of individuals applying for factory positions at Davis Enterprises revealed the following scores on an eye perception test ($X$) and a mechanical aptitude test ($Y$):

| Subject | Eye Perception | Mechanical Aptitude | Subject | Eye Perception | Mechanical Aptitude |
|---------|----------------|---------------------|---------|----------------|---------------------|
| 001 | 805 | 23 | 006 | 810 | 28 |
| 002 | 777 | 62 | 007 | 805 | 30 |
| 003 | 820 | 60 | 008 | 840 | 42 |
| 004 | 682 | 40 | 009 | 777 | 55 |
| 005 | 777 | 70 | 010 | 820 | 51 |

(a) Compute the coefficient of rank correlation.
(b) At the .05 significance level, can we conclude that the correlation in the population is different from 0?

---

# Exercises

**25.** Nielsen Media Research wants to pretest a questionnaire to be mailed to several thousand viewers. One question involves the ranking of male and female college students with respect to the popularity of programs. The composite rankings of a small group of college students are:

| Program | Ranking by Males | Ranking by Females |
|---------|------------------|--------------------|
| "Monday Night Football" | 1 | 5 |
| "Tonight Show with Jay Leno" | 4 | 1 |
| "60 Minutes" | 3 | 2 |
| "Late Show with David Letterman" | 2 | 4 |
| "Sports Center on ESPN" | 5 | 3 |

**a.** Draw a scatter diagram. Let the rankings by males be $X$.
**b.** Compute Spearman's rank-order correlation coefficient. Interpret.

**26.** Far West University offers both day and evening classes in business administration. One question in a survey of students inquires how they perceive the prestige associated with certain careers. Each student was asked to rank the careers from 1 to 8, with 1 having the most prestige and 8 the least prestige. The results were:

| Career | Ranking by Day Students | Ranking by Evening Students | Career | Ranking by Day Students | Ranking by Evening Students |
|---|---|---|---|---|---|
| Accountant | 6 | 3 | Statistician | 1 | 7 |
| Computer programmer | 7 | 2 | Marketing researcher | 4 | 8 |
| Branch bank manager | 2 | 6 | Stock analyst | 3 | 5 |
| Hospital administrator | 5 | 4 | Production manager | 8 | 1 |

Find Spearman's coefficient of rank correlation.

**27.** New representatives for the John Ford Metal and Wheel Company attend a brief training program before being assigned to a regional office. At the end of such a program, each representative was ranked with respect to future sales potential. At the end of the first sales year, their rankings were paired with their annual sales:

| Representative | Annual Sales ($ thousands) | Ranking in Training Program | Representative | Annual Sales ($ thousands) | Ranking in Training Program |
|---|---|---|---|---|---|
| Kitchen | 319 | 3 | Arden | 300 | 10 |
| Bond | 150 | 9 | Crane | 280 | 5 |
| Gross | 175 | 6 | Arthur | 200 | 2 |
| Arbuckle | 460 | 1 | Keene | 190 | 7 |
| Greene | 348 | 4 | Knopf | 300 | 8 |

**a.** Compute and interpret Spearman's rank correlation coefficient.
**b.** At the .05 significance level, can we conclude that there is a positive association between annual sales dollars and ranking in the training program?

**28.** East Texas State University has five scholarships available for the women's basketball team. The head coach provided the two assistant coaches with the names of 10 high school players with potential to play at East Texas State. Each assistant coach attended three games and then ranked the 10 players with respect to potential. To explain, the first coach ranked Norma Tidwell as the best player among the 10 scouted and Jeannie Black the worst.

| Player | Rank, by Assistant Coach Jean Cann | Rank, by Assistant Coach John Cannelli | Player | Rank, by Assistant Coach Jean Cann | Rank, by Assistant Coach John Cannelli |
|---|---|---|---|---|---|
| Cora Jean Seiple | 7 | 5 | Candy Jenkins | 3 | 1 |
| Bette Jones | 2 | 4 | Rita Rosinski | 5 | 7 |
| Jeannie Black | 10 | 10 | Anita Lockes | 4 | 2 |
| Norma Tidwell | 1 | 3 | Brenda Towne | 8 | 9 |
| Kathy Marchal | 6 | 6 | Denise Ober | 9 | 8 |

**a.** Determine Spearman's rank correlation coefficient.
**b.** At the .05 significance level, can we conclude there is a positive association between the ranks?

# Chapter Outline

**I.** The sign test.
   **A.** No assumptions need be made about the shape of the two populations.
   **B.** It is based on paired or dependent samples.
   **C.** For small samples find the number of + or − signs and refer to the binomial distribution for the critical value.

**D.** For large samples (more than 10) use the standard normal distribution and the following formula.

$$z = \frac{(X \pm .50) - .50n}{.50\sqrt{n}}$$        [16–2] [16–3]

**II.** The median test is used to test a hypothesis about a population median.
   **A.** Find $\mu$ and $\sigma$ for a binomial distribution.
   **B.** The $z$ distribution is used as the test statistic.
   **C.** The value of $z$ is computed from the following formula, where $X$ is the number of observations above or below the median.

$$z = \frac{(X \pm .50) - \mu}{\sigma}$$        [16–1]

**III.** The Wilcoxon signed-rank test.
   **A.** Data must be at least ordinal scale, and the samples must be dependent.
   **B.** The steps to conduct the test are:
      **1.** Rank absolute differences between the related observations.
      **2.** Apply the sign of the differences to the ranks.
      **3.** Sum negative ranks and positive ranks.
      **4.** The smaller of the two sums is the computed $T$ value.
      **5.** Refer to Appendix H for the critical value, and make a decision regarding $H_0$.
**IV.** The Wilcoxon rank-sum test is used to test whether two independent samples came from equal populations.
   **A.** No assumption about the shape of the population is required.
   **B.** To apply the test, the data must be at least ordinal scale.
   **C.** Each sample must contain at least eight observations.
   **D.** To determine the value of the test statistic $W$, all data values are ranked from low to high as if they were from a single population.
   **E.** The sum of ranks for each of the two samples is determined.
   **F.** $W$ is used to compute $z$, where $W$ is the sum of the ranks for population 1, from

$$z = \frac{W - \dfrac{n_1(n_1 + n_2 + 1)}{2}}{\sqrt{\dfrac{n_1 n_2(n_1 + n_2 + 1)}{12}}}$$        [16–4]

   **G.** The $z$ distribution is used as the test statistic.
**V.** The Kruskal-Wallis one-way ANOVA by ranks.
   **A.** No assumptions regarding the shape of the populations are required.
   **B.** The samples must be independent and at least ordinal scale.
   **C.** It is used to test whether several populations are the same.
   **D.** The sample observations are ranked from smallest to largest as though they were a single group.
   **E.** The test statistic follows the chi-square distribution, provided there are at least 5 observations in each sample.
   **F.** The value of the test statistic is computed from the following:

$$H = \frac{12}{n(n + 1)}\left[ \frac{(\Sigma R_1)^2}{n_1} + \frac{(\Sigma R_2)^2}{n_2} + \cdots + \frac{(\Sigma R_k)^2}{n_k} \right] - 3(n + 1)$$        [16–5]

**VI.** Spearman's coefficient of rank correlation is a measure of the association between two ordinal-scale variables.
   **A.** It can range from $-1$ up to 1.
      **1.** A value of 0 indicates there is no association between the variables.
      **2.** A value of $-1$ indicates perfect negative correlation, and 1 is perfect positive correlation.
   **B.** The value of $r_s$ is computed from the following formula.

$$r_s = 1 - \frac{6\Sigma d^2}{n(n^2 - 1)}$$        [16–6]

C. Provided the sample size is at least 10, we can conduct a test of hypothesis using the following formula:

$$t = r_s \sqrt{\frac{n-2}{1-r_s^2}}$$                                    [16–7]

1. The test statistic follows the $t$ distribution.
2. There are $n - 2$ degrees of freedom.

# Pronunciation Key

| SYMBOL | MEANING | PRONUNCIATION |
|---|---|---|
| $(\Sigma R_1)^2$ | Square of the total of the first column ranks | *Sigma R sub 1 squared* |
| $r_s$ | Spearman's coefficient of rank correlation | *r sub s* |

# Chapter Exercises

29. The Vice President of Programming at NBC is finalizing the prime-time schedule for the fall. She has decided to include a hospital drama but is unsure which of two possibilities to select. She has a pilot called "The Surgeon" and another called "Critical Care." To help her make a final decision, a sample of 20 viewers from throughout the United States was asked to watch the two pilots and indicate which show they prefer. The results were that 12 liked "The Surgeon," 7 liked "Critical Care," and one had no preference. Is there a preference for one of the two shows? Use the .10 significance level.

30. Suppose Merrill Lynch wants to award a substantial contract for fine-line pens to be used nationally in their offices. Two suppliers, Bic and Pilot, have submitted the lowest bids. To determine the preference of office employees, brokers, and others, a personal preference test is to be conducted using a randomly selected sample of 20 employees. The .05 level of significance is to be used.
    a. If the alternate hypothesis states that Bic is preferred over Pilot, is the sign test to be conducted as a one-tailed or a two-tailed test? Explain.
    b. As each of the sample members told the researchers his or her preference, a "+" was recorded if it was Bic and a "−" if it was the Pilot fine-line pen. A count of the pluses revealed that 12 employees preferred Bic, 5 preferred Pilot, and 3 were undecided. What is $n$?
    c. What is the decision rule in words?
    d. What conclusion did you reach regarding pen preference? Explain.

31. Cornwall and Hudson, a large retail department store, wants to handle just one brand of high-quality CD player. The list has been narrowed to two brands: Sony and Panasonic. To help make a decision, a panel of 16 audio experts met. A passage using Sony components (labeled A) was played. Then the same passage was played using Panasonic components (labeled B). A "+" in the following table indicates an individual's preference for the Sony components, a "−" indicates preference for Panasonic, and a 0 signifies no preference.

| Expert | | | | | | | | | | | | | | | |
|---|---|---|---|---|---|---|---|---|---|---|---|---|---|---|---|
| 1 | 2 | 3 | 4 | 5 | 6 | 7 | 8 | 9 | 10 | 11 | 12 | 13 | 14 | 15 | 16 |
| + | − | + | − | + | + | − | 0 | − | + | − | + | + | − | + | − |

Conduct a test of hypothesis at the .10 significance level to determine whether there is a difference in preference between the two brands.

32. The South Carolina Real Estate Association claims that the median rental for three-bedroom condominiums in a metropolitan area is more than $1,200 a month. To check this, a random sample of 149 units was selected. Of the 149, 5 rented for exactly $1,200 a month, and 75 rented for more than $1,200. At the .05 level can we conclude that the median rental is more than $1,200?
    a. State $H_0$ and $H_1$.
    b. Give the decision rule.
    c. Do the necessary calculations, and arrive at a decision.

33. The Citrus Council wants to find whether consumers prefer plain orange juice or juice with some orange pulp in it. A random sample of 212 consumers was selected. Each member of the sample tasted a small, unlabeled cup of one kind and then tasted the other kind. Twelve consumers said they had no preference, 40 preferred plain juice, and the remainder liked the juice with pulp better. Test at the .05 level that the preferences for plain juice and for orange juice with pulp are equal.

34. A research project involving community responsibility is to be conducted. The objective is to find whether women are more community conscious before marriage or after five years of marriage. A test to measure community consciousness was administered to a sample of women before marriage, and the same test was given to them five years after marriage. The test scores are:

| Name | Before Marriage | After Marriage | Name | Before Marriage | After Marriage |
|------|-----------------|----------------|------|-----------------|----------------|
| Beth | 110 | 114 | Carol | 186 | 196 |
| Jean | 157 | 159 | Lisa | 116 | 116 |
| Sue | 121 | 120 | Sandy | 160 | 140 |
| Cathy | 96 | 103 | Petra | 149 | 142 |
| Mary | 130 | 139 | | | |

Test at the .05 level. $H_0$ is: There is no difference in community consciousness before and after marriage. $H_1$ is: There is a difference.

35. Is there a difference in the annual divorce rates in predominantly rural counties among three geographic regions, namely, the Southwest, the Southeast, and the Northwest? Test at the .05 level. Annual divorce rates per 1,000 population for randomly selected counties are:

| | |
|---|---|
| Southwest: | 5.9, 6.2, 7.9, 8.6, 4.6 |
| Southeast: | 5.0, 6.4, 7.3, 6.2, 8.1, 5.1 |
| Northwest: | 6.7, 6.2, 4.9, 8.0, 5.5 |

36. The idle times during the eight-hour day shift and the night shift are to be compared. A time study revealed the following numbers of minutes of idle time for eight-hour periods.

| | |
|---|---|
| Day shift: | 92, 103, 116, 81, 89 |
| Night shift: | 96, 114, 80, 82, 88, 91 |

Is there a difference in the idle time between the two shifts? Test at the .05 level.

37. Social researchers studied the mobility of executives in stock exchanges, in service, in heavy construction, and in air transportation. Samples from each of these industries were selected, and the number of times an executive moved during a 10-year period was converted to an index. An index of 0 would indicate no movement, whereas 100 would indicate almost constant movement from one location to another or one firm to another. The indexes for the four groups are:

| Stock Exchange | Service | Heavy Construction | Air Transportation |
|----------------|---------|--------------------|--------------------|
| 4 | 3 | 62 | 30 |
| 17 | 12 | 40 | 38 |
| 8 | 40 | 81 | 46 |
| 20 | 17 | 96 | 40 |
| 16 | 31 | 76 | 21 |
| | 19 | | |

We cannot assume that the indexes follow the normal distribution. Thus, we must use a nonparametric test. Using the .05 level, determine whether the four populations of mobility indexes are identical.

**38.** A series of questions on sports and world events was asked of a randomly selected group of young adult naturalized citizens. The results were translated into a "knowledge" score. The scores were:

| Citizen | Sports | World Events | Citizen | Sports | World Events |
|---|---|---|---|---|---|
| J. C. McCarthy | 47 | 49 | L. M. Zaugg | 87 | 75 |
| A. N. Baker | 12 | 10 | J. B. Simon | 59 | 86 |
| B. B. Beebe | 62 | 76 | J. Goulden | 40 | 61 |
| L. D. Gaucet | 81 | 92 | A. A. Fernandez | 87 | 18 |
| C. A. Jones | 90 | 86 | A. M. Carbo | 16 | 75 |
| J. N. Lopez | 35 | 42 | A. O. Smithy | 50 | 51 |
| A. F. Nissen | 61 | 61 | J. J. Pascal | 60 | 61 |

**a.** Determine the degree of association between how the citizens ranked with respect to knowledge of sports and how they ranked on world events.
**b.** At the .05 significance level, is the rank correlation in the population greater than zero?

**39.** Early in the basketball season, 12 teams appeared to be outstanding. A panel of sportswriters and a panel of college basketball coaches were asked to rank the 12 teams. Their composite rankings were as follows.

| Team | Coaches | Sportswriters | Team | Coaches | Sportswriters |
|---|---|---|---|---|---|
| Duke | 1 | 1 | Syracuse | 7 | 10 |
| UNLV | 2 | 5 | Georgetown | 8 | 11 |
| Indiana | 3 | 4 | Villanova | 9 | 7 |
| North Carolina | 4 | 6 | LSU | 10 | 12 |
| Louisville | 5 | 3 | St. Johns | 11 | 8 |
| Ohio State | 6 | 2 | Michigan | 12 | 9 |

Determine the correlation between the rankings of the coaches and the sportswriters. At the .05 significance level, can we conclude it is different from zero?

**40.** Professor Bert Forman believes the students who complete his examinations in the shortest time receive the highest grades and those who take the longest to complete them receive the lowest grades. To verify his suspicion, he assigns a rank to the order of finish and then grades the examinations. The results are shown below:

| Student | Order of Completion | Score (50 possible) | Student | Order of Completion | Score (50 possible) |
|---|---|---|---|---|---|
| Gromney | 1 | 48 | Smythe | 7 | 39 |
| Bates | 2 | 48 | Arquette | 8 | 30 |
| MacDonald | 3 | 43 | Govito | 9 | 37 |
| Sosa | 4 | 49 | Gankowski | 10 | 35 |
| Harris | 5 | 50 | Bonfigilo | 11 | 36 |
| Cribb | 6 | 47 | Matsui | 12 | 33 |

Convert the test scores to a rank and find the coefficient of rank correlation. At the .05 significance level, can Professor Forman conclude there is a positive association between the order of finish and the test scores?

# exercises.com

**41.** Is there a correlation between the starting position in an auto race and the order of finish? To investigate, use the results of one of the major races, such as the Daytona 500 or the Indianapolis 500. You can access the results of the Indianapolis 500 by going to http://www.indy500.com. Click on **Stats,** then select **Starting Grids and Race Results,** and click on the most recent year. You will need to download the data into either Excel or MINITAB.

   **a.** Compute the coefficient of rank correlation between the starting position and the order of finish. Both of these are ordinal-scale variables. Interpret this value.
   **b.** Conduct a test of hypothesis to determine whether the rank correlation computed in part (a) is greater than zero. Interpret the result.
**42.** There is lot of information available in the online edition of the *Information Please Almanac.* For example, go to http://infoplease.com, click on **United States,** then **States,** and finally **Tabulated Data on State Governments,** and click on **Governor's salary.** There are data on the salary for the governor and the highest court for each state. You will need to download the data into Excel or MINITAB.
   **a.** Compute the coefficient of correlation between the two variables using the Pearson and Spearman methods. Comment on the amount of the difference between the two values. (Hint: to find the coefficient of rank correlation, you will need to first rank the two variables and then use the statistical software to find the Pearson coefficient of correlation *using the ranked data.*)
   **b.** Conduct a test of hypothesis to determine whether the coefficient of rank correlation is different from zero.

# Dataset Exercises

**43.** Refer to the Real Estate data which reports information on homes sold in the Denver, Colorado, area during the last year.
   **a.** Use an appropriate nonparametric test to determine whether there is a difference in the typical selling price of the homes in the several townships. Assume the selling prices are not normally distributed. Use the .05 significance level.
   **b.** Combine the homes with 6 or more bedrooms into one group and determine whether there is a difference according to the number of bedrooms in the typical selling prices of the homes. Use the .05 significance level and assume the distribution of selling prices is not normally distributed.
   **c.** Assume that the distribution of the distance from the center of the city is positively skewed. That is, the normality assumption is not reasonable. Compare the distribution of the distance from the center of the city of the homes that have a pool with those that do not have a pool. Can we conclude there is a difference in the distributions? Use the .05 significance level.
**44.** Refer to the Baseball 2002 data, which reports information on the 2002 Major League Baseball season.
   **a.** Rank the teams by the number of wins and their total team salary. Compute the coefficient of rank correlation between the two variables. At the .01 significance level, can you conclude that it is greater than zero?
   **b.** Assume that the distributions of team salaries for the American League and National League do not follow the normal distribution. Conduct a test of hypothesis to see if there is a difference in the two distributions.
**45.** Refer to the Wage data set, which reports information on annual wages for a sample of 100 workers. Also included are variables relating to industry, years of education, and gender for each worker.
   **a.** Conduct a test of hypothesis at the .05 significance level to determine if there is a difference in the median annual wages of union and nonunion members.
   **b.** Conduct a test of hypothesis at the .01 significance level to determine if there is a difference in the mean annual wages for workers in the three industries. Do not assume that the data follow a normal distribution. Compare the results with those of Exercise 47 in Chapter 12.
   **c.** Conduct a test of hypothesis at the .05 significance level to determine if there is a difference in the mean annual wages for workers in the six different occupations. Do not assume that the data follow a normal distribution.
**46.** Refer to the CIA data set, which reports demographic and economic information on 46 countries.
   **a.** Without assuming normal distributions, test at the .01 significance level whether there is a difference in the mean percent of the population over 65 years of age for countries with different levels of petroleum usage.
   **b.** Without assuming normal distributions, test at the .05 significance level whether there is a difference in the mean GDP per capita for countries with different levels of petroleum usage.

# Software Commands

1. The MegaStat for Excel commands necessary for the Wilcoxon rank-sum test on page 563 are:
   a. Enter the number of no-shows for Atlanta in column A and for Chicago in column B.
   b. Select **MegaStat, Nonparametric Tests,** and **Wilcoxon-Mann/Whitney Test,** then hit **Enter.**
   c. For Group 1 use the data on Atlanta flights (*A2:A10*) and for Group 2 use the data on Chicago flights (*B2:B9*). Click on **Correct for ties** and **one-tailed,** then click on **OK.**

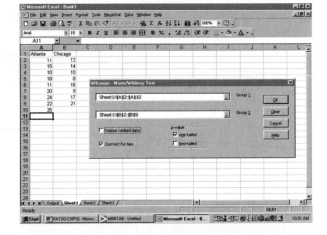

2. The MINITAB commands for the Kruskal-Wallis test on page 567 are:
   a. Enter the scores in column 1 and a code corresponding to their group in column 2. Name the variable in C1 *Scores* and the variable in C2 *Groups.*
   b. From the menu bar select **Stat, Nonparametric,** and **Kruskal-Wallis,** and hit **Enter.**
   c. Select the variables *Scores* as the **Response** variable and *Groups* as the **Factor.**

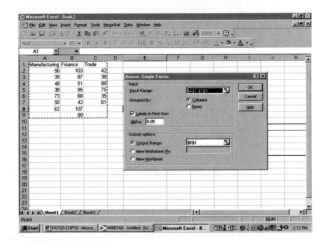

3. The Excel commands for the one-way ANOVA on page 567 are:
   a. Enter the names *Manufacturing, Finance,* and *Trade* in the first row and the data in the columns under them.
   b. Select **Tools, Data Analysis,** and **ANOVA: Single Factor,** and then click **OK.**
   c. In the dialog box the Input Range is *A1:C9,* click on **Labels in First Row,** and enter *E1* as the **Output Range,** then click **OK.**

# Chapter 16  Answers to Self-Review

**16–1  a.** Two-tailed because $H_1$ does not state a direction.

**b.**

Adding down, $.000 + .003 + .016 = .019$. This is the largest cumulative probability up to but not exceeding .050, which is half the level of significance.

**c.** Reject $H_0$; accept $H_1$. There is a preference.

**16–2  a.** $H_0: \pi \leq 0.50$, $H_1: \pi > 0.50$.

**b.** Reject $H_0$ if $z > 1.65$.

**c.** Since 80 is more than $n/2 = 100/2 = 50$, we use:

$$z = \frac{(80 - .50) - .50(100)}{.50\sqrt{100}} = \frac{29.5}{5} = 5.9$$

**d.** $H_0$ is rejected.

**e.** The screening was effective.

**16–3  a.** $H_0$: The median $\leq \$123$, $H_1$: The median is more than $123.

**b.** Reject $H_0$ if $z > 1.65$.

**c.** $z = \dfrac{(42 - .50) - 32}{.50\sqrt{64}} = \dfrac{9.5}{4} = 2.38$

**d.** Reject $H_0$.

**e.** The median amount spent is more than $123.

**16–4  a.** $n = 10$ (because there was no change for A.A.)

**b.**

| Before | After | Differ- ence | Abso- lute Differ- ence | Rank of Abso- lute Differ- ence | Nega- tive Ranks | Posi- tive Ranks |
|---|---|---|---|---|---|---|
| 17 | 18 | $-1$ | 1 | 1.5 | 1.5 | |
| 21 | 23 | $-2$ | 2 | 3.0 | 3.0 | |
| 25 | 22 | 3 | 3 | 5.0 | | 5.0 |
| 15 | 25 | $-10$ | 10 | 8.0 | 8.0 | |
| 10 | 28 | $-18$ | 18 | 10.0 | 10.0 | |
| 16 | 16 | — | — | — | — | — |
| 10 | 22 | $-12$ | 12 | 9.0 | 9.0 | |
| 20 | 19 | 1 | 1 | 1.5 | | 1.5 |
| 17 | 20 | $-3$ | 3 | 5.0 | 5.0 | |
| 24 | 30 | $-6$ | 6 | 7.0 | 7.0 | |
| 23 | 26 | $-3$ | 3 | 5.0 | 5.0 | |
| | | | | | 48.5 | 6.5 |

$H_0$: Production is the same.
$H_1$: Production has increased.

The sum of the positive signed ranks is 6.5; the negative sum is 48.5. From Appendix H, one-tailed test, $n = 10$, the critical value is 10. Since 6.5 is less than 10, reject the null hypothesis and accept the alternate. New procedures did increase production.

**16–5** $H_0$: There is no difference in the distances traveled by XL-550 and by DL-300.

$H_1$: There is a difference in the distances traveled by XL-550 and by DL-300.

Do not reject $H_0$ if the computed $z$ is between 1.96 and $-1.96$ (from Appendix D); otherwise, reject $H_0$ and accept $H_1$. $n_1 = 8$, the number of observations in the first sample.

| XL-550 | | DL-300 | |
|---|---|---|---|
| Distance | Rank | Distance | Rank |
| 252 | 4 | 262 | 9 |
| 263 | 10 | 242 | 2 |
| 279 | 15 | 256 | 5 |
| 273 | 14 | 260 | 8 |
| 271 | 13 | 258 | 7 |
| 265 | 11.5 | 243 | 3 |
| 257 | 6 | 239 | 1 |
| 280 | 16 | 265 | 11.5 |
| Total | 89.5 | | 46.5 |

$W = 89.5$

$$z = \frac{89.5 - \dfrac{8(8 + 8 + 1)}{2}}{\sqrt{\dfrac{(8)(8)(8 + 8 + 1)}{12}}}$$

$$= \frac{21.5}{9.52} = 2.26$$

Reject $H_0$: accept $H_1$. There is evidence of a difference in the distances traveled by the two golf balls.

**16–6**

| | Ranks | | |
|---|---|---|---|
| **Englewood** | **West Side** | **Great Northern** | **Sylvania** |
| 17 | 5 | 19 | 7 |
| 20 | 1 | 9.5 | 11 |
| 16 | 3 | 21 | 15 |
| 13 | 5 | 22 | 9.5 |
| 5 | 2 | 14 | 8 |
| 18 | | | 12 |

$\Sigma R_1 = 89$   $\Sigma R_2 = 16$   $\Sigma R_3 = 85.5$   $\Sigma R_4 = 62.5$

$n_1 = 6$   $n_2 = 5$   $n_3 = 5$   $n_4 = 6$

$H_0$: The population distributions are identical.
$H_1$: The population distributions are not identical.

$$H = \frac{12}{22(22 + 1)}\left[\frac{(89)^2}{6} + \frac{(16)^2}{5} + \frac{(85.5)^2}{5} + \frac{(62.5)^2}{6}\right]$$

$$- 3(22 + 1)$$

$$= 13.635$$

The critical value of chi-square for $k - 1 = 4 - 1 = 3$ degrees of freedom is 11.345. Since the computed value of 13.635 is greater than 11.345, the null hypothesis is rejected. We conclude that the turnover rates are not the same.

**16–7 a.**

| | | Rank | | | |
|---|---|---|---|---|---|
| **X** | **Y** | **X** | **Y** | **d** | **$d^2$** |
| 805 | 23 | 5.5 | 1 | 4.5 | 20.25 |
| 777 | 62 | 3.0 | 9 | −6.0 | 36.00 |
| 820 | 60 | 8.5 | 8 | 0.5 | 0.25 |
| 682 | 40 | 1.0 | 4 | −3.0 | 9.00 |
| 777 | 70 | 3.0 | 10 | −7.0 | 49.00 |
| 810 | 28 | 7.0 | 2 | 5.0 | 25.00 |
| 805 | 30 | 5.5 | 3 | 2.5 | 6.25 |
| 840 | 42 | 10.0 | 5 | 5.0 | 25.00 |
| 777 | 55 | 3.0 | 7 | −4.0 | 16.00 |
| 820 | 51 | 8.5 | 6 | 2.5 | 6.25 |
| | | | | 0 | 193.00 |

$$r_s = 1 - \frac{6(193)}{10(99)} = -.170$$

**b.** $H_0$: $\rho = 0$; $H_1$: $\rho \neq 0$. Reject $H_0$ if $t < -2.306$ or $t > 2.306$.

$$t = 0.170\sqrt{\frac{10 - 2}{1 - (-0.170)^2}} = -0.488$$

$H_0$ is not rejected. We have not shown a relationship between the two tests.

# A Review of Chapters 15 and 16

Goodness-of-fit test and contingency table analysis applicable to nominal-level data

This section is a review of the major concepts and terms introduced in Chapters 15 and 16. Chapter 15 began the study of *nonparametric,* or *distribution-free,* tests by discussing the *chi-square goodness-of-fit* test. This test compares a set of observed frequencies, $f_o$, and the corresponding set of expected frequencies, $f_e$. It involves only one characteristic possessed by an individual, such as education. If we are interested in two characteristics, such as a relationship between education level and income, the data are cross-classified into a contingency table, and the chi-square test for independence is applied. For these two tests, no assumption about the shape of the population distribution is needed; they require only that the data be nominal level.

Five tests for ordinal-level data

Chapter 16 presented five nonparametric tests of hypothesis and the coefficient of rank correlation, all of which require the ordinal level of measurement. That is, the data must be ranked from low to high. The topics discussed included: the *sign test,* the *median test,* the *Wilcoxon rank-sum test,* the *Kruskal-Wallis analysis of variance test,* the *Wilcoxon signed-rank test,* and the *Spearman's coefficient of rank correlation test.*

## Glossary

### Chapter 15

**Chi-square distribution** A distribution with these characteristics: (1) Its value can only be positive. (2) There is a family of chi-square distributions, a different one for each different degree of freedom. (3) The distributions are positively skewed, but as the number of degrees of freedom increases, the distribution approaches the normal distribution.

**Chi-square goodness-of-fit test** A test with the objective of determining how well an observed set of frequencies fits an expected set of frequencies. It is concerned with one nominal-scale variable, such as the color of a car.

**Contingency table** If two characteristics, such as gender and highest degree earned for a sample of stock brokers, are cross-classified into a table, the result is called a contingency table. The chi-square test statistic is used to investigate whether the two characteristics are related.

**Nominal level of measurement** The "lowest" level of measurement. Such data can only be classified into categories, and there is no particular order for the categories. For example, it makes no difference whether the categories "male" and "female" are listed in that order, or female first and male second. The categories are mutually exclusive—meaning, in this illustration, that a person cannot be a male and a female at the same time.

**Nonparametric or distribution-free tests** Hypothesis tests involving nominal- and ordinal-level data. No assumptions need be made about the shape of the population distribution; that is, we do not assume the population is normally distributed.

### Chapter 16

**Kruskal-Wallis one-way analysis of variance by ranks** A test used when the assumptions for the parametric analysis of variance (ANOVA) cannot be met. Its purpose is to test whether several populations are equal. The data must be at least ordinal scale.

**Sign test** A test used for dependent samples. The sign test is used to find whether there is a brand preference for two products or to determine whether performance after an experiment is greater than before the experiment. Also, the sign test is used to test a hypothesis about the median.

**Spearman's coefficient of rank correlation** A measure of the association between the ranks of two variables. It can range from $-1.00$ to $1.00$. A value of $-1.00$ indicates a perfect negative association among the ranks and a value of $1.00$ a perfect positive association among the ranks. A value of 0 indicates no association among the ranks.

**Wilcoxon matched-pair signed-rank test** A nonparametric test requiring at least ordinal-level data and dependent samples. Its purpose is to find whether there is any difference between two sets of paired (related) observations. It is used if the assumptions required for the paired $t$ test cannot be met.

**Wilcoxon rank-sum test** A nonparametric test requiring independent samples. The data must be at least ordinal level. That is, the data must be capable of being ranked. The test is used when the assumptions for the parametric Student $t$ test cannot be met. The objective of the test is to find whether two independent samples can be considered as coming from the same population.

## Exercises

### Part I—Multiple Choice

1. The degrees of freedom for a chi-square test of a contingency table with 6 rows and 3 columns is
   a. 18
   b. 15
   c. 12
   d. 10

2. When testing for a relationship between two nominal variables, which statistical technique should be used?
   a. Regression.
   b. Chi-square contingency table test.
   c. Chi-square goodness-of-fit.
   d. Spearman's coefficient of rank correlation.
3. The results of a chi-square analysis for a contingency table may not be valid when
   a. More than 20 percent of the expected frequencies are more than 5.
   b. More than 20 percent of the expected frequencies are less than 5.
   c. The significance level is .01.
   d. The expected and actual frequencies are equal.
4. In a chi-square goodness-of-fit test with 10 categories and a significance level of .05, the critical value of a chi-square statistic is
   a. 16.919
   b. 18.307
   c. 15.987
   d. 14.684
5. In a chi-square goodness-of-fit test with a chi-square test statistic equal to 0.0,
   a. The $p$-value is 1.0.
   b. The expected and observed frequencies for each cell are equal.
   c. The null hypothesis is not rejected.
   d. a, b, and c are true.
6. The nonparametric method used to test for differences between two dependent samples is
   a. The median test.
   b. Chi-square test.
   c. Wilcoxon signed-rank test.
   d. Kruskal-Wallis test.
7. Spearman's coefficient of rank correlation is best applied when
   a. The data are measured with a nominal scale.
   b. The data are measured with an ordinal scale.
   c. The data are measured with an interval scale.
   d. The data are measured with a ratio scale.
8. The Kruskal-Wallis Test
   a. Tests whether several populations are equal.
   b. Requires the nominal scale of measurement.
   c. Assumes dependent samples.
   d. None of the above.

## Part II—Problems

9. An advocate for political campaign finance reform is interested in the relationship between the amount of political contributions and political affiliation. The results of a randomized survey are in the following table.

| Political Affiliation | Amount Contributed to Campaign | | |
|---|---|---|---|
| | $1–$99 | $100–$999 | $1,000 and More |
| Republican | 170 | 120 | 180 |
| Democrat | 440 | 240 | 284 |
| Socialist | 46 | 35 | 46 |
| All others | 19 | 17 | 11 |

   a. What is the null hypothesis?
   b. What test statistic would be used to test the null hypothesis?
   c. How many degrees of freedom are there?
   d. What is the critical value? Use the .05 significance level.
   e. What conclusion can be made on the basis of the hypothesis test?
10. A consumer research firm, such as National Family Opinion (NFO), conducted a survey to find whether grocery shoppers can identify the brand name of a product if the name does not appear on the can, box, or package. For question 1, NFO deleted the name of a soup

and gave the shopper five choices: (1) Campbell's, (2) Knorr, (3) Progresso, (4) Chalet Suzanne, and (5) Heinz.

There were six similar questions, and 1,000 shoppers participated in the experiment. There is a possibility that shoppers unfamiliar with various labels and brand names would select a name at random—that is, guess the brand name. So a binomial probability distribution is generated to see what a random distribution of choices would look like. These probabilities are in column 2 of the following table; the numbers expected are in column 3. Note that we expect only 2 of the 1,000 shoppers to *guess* five of the six questions correctly. We expect practically no shoppers to guess six out of six. The actual distribution of responses is in column 4.

| 1<br>Number of<br>Correct<br>Identifications | 2<br><br><br>Probability* | 3<br><br>Expected Number<br>by Chance | 4<br><br>Actual Number<br>in Survey |
|---|---|---|---|
| 0 | .262 | 262 | 5 |
| 1 | .393 | 393 | 16 |
| 2 | .246 | 246 | 10 |
| 3 | .082 | 82 | 27 |
| 4 | .015 | 15 | 81 |
| 5 | .002 | 2 | 346 |
| 6 | .000 | 0 | 515 |
| | 1.000 | 1,000 | 1,000 |

*Probabilities from Appendix A.

**a.** State the null and alternate hypotheses.
**b.** Conduct a chi-square goodness-of-fit test. Do the data present any limitations for a chi-square goodness-of-fit test? Is so, how would you modify the data?
**c.** Test the hypothesis.
**d.** Interpret the results of the hypothesis test.

# Cases

## A. Century National Bank

Is there a relationship between the location of the branch bank and whether the customer has a debit card? Based on the information available, develop a table that shows the relationship between these two variables. At the .05 significance level, can we conclude there is a relationship between the branch location and whether the customer uses a debit card?

## B. Thomas Testing Labs

John Thomas, the owner of Thomas Testing, has for some time done contract work for insurance companies regarding drunk driving. To improve his research capabilities, he recently purchased the Rupple Driving Simulator. This device will allow a subject to take a "road test" and provide a score indicating the number of driving errors committed during the test drive. Higher scores indicate more driving errors. Driving errors would include: not coming to a complete stop at a stop sign, not using turning signals, not exercising caution on wet or snowy pavement, and so on. During the road test, problems appear at random and not all problems appear in each road test. These are major advantages to the Rupple Driving Simulator because sub-

jects do not gain any advantage by taking the test several times.

With the new driving simulator, Mr. Thomas would like to study in detail the problem of drunk driving. He begins by selecting a random sample of 25 drivers. He asks each of the selected individuals to take the test drive on the Rupple Driving Simulator. The number of errors for each driver is recorded. Next, he has each of the individuals in the group drink 3 16-ounce cans of beer in a 60-minute period and return to the Rupple Driving Simulator for another test drive. The number of driving errors after drinking the beer is also shown. The research question is: Does alcohol impair the driver's ability and, therefore, increase the number of driving errors?

Mr. Thomas believes the distribution of scores on the test drive does not follow a normal distribution and, therefore, a nonparametric test should be used. Because the observations are paired, he decides to use both the sign test and the Wilcoxon signed-rank test. Compare the results using these two procedures. Which statistical test would you suggest? What conclusion would you make regarding the effects of drunk driving? Write a brief report summarizing your findings.

| Driving Errors | | | Driving Errors | | |
| --- | --- | --- | --- | --- | --- |
| Subject | Without Alcohol | With Alcohol | Subject | Without Alcohol | With Alcohol |
| 1 | 75 | 89 | 14 | 72 | 106 |
| 2 | 78 | 83 | 15 | 83 | 89 |
| 3 | 89 | 80 | 16 | 99 | 89 |
| 4 | 100 | 90 | 17 | 75 | 77 |
| 5 | 85 | 84 | 18 | 58 | 78 |
| 6 | 70 | 68 | 19 | 93 | 108 |
| 7 | 64 | 84 | 20 | 69 | 69 |
| 8 | 79 | 104 | 21 | 86 | 84 |
| 9 | 83 | 81 | 22 | 97 | 86 |
| 10 | 82 | 88 | 23 | 65 | 92 |
| 11 | 83 | 93 | 24 | 96 | 97 |
| 12 | 84 | 92 | 25 | 85 | 94 |
| 13 | 80 | 103 | | | |

# 17

# Statistical Quality Control

A candy producer reports on the package that the calorie content is 420 per 2-ounce piece. A sample of 5 pieces from each of the last 10 days is sent for a chemical analysis of the calorie content. Based on the data in the exercise, does it appear that there are any days where the calorie count is out of control? (See Exercise 23 and Goal 2.)

# Introduction

Throughout this text we have presented many applications of hypothesis testing. In Chapter 10 we described methods for testing a hypothesis regarding a single population value. In Chapter 11 we described methods for testing a hypothesis about two populations. In this chapter we present another, somewhat different application of hypothesis testing, called **statistical process control** or **SPC**.

Statistical process control is a collection of strategies, techniques, and actions taken by an organization to ensure they are producing a quality product or providing a quality service. It begins at the product planning stage, when we specify the attributes of the product or service. It continues through the production stage. Each attribute throughout the process contributes to the overall quality of the product. To effectively use quality control, measurable attributes and specifications must be developed against which the actual attributes of the product or service can be compared.

# A Brief History of Quality Control

Prior to the 1900s U.S. industry was largely characterized by small shops making relatively simple products, such as candles or furniture. In these small shops the individual worker was generally a craftsman who was completely responsible for the quality of the work. The worker could ensure the quality through the personal selection of the materials, skillful manufacturing, and selective fitting and adjustment.

In the early 1900s factories sprang up, where people with limited training were formed into large assembly lines. Products became much more complex. The individual worker no longer had complete control over the quality of the product. A semiprofessional staff, usually called the Inspection Department, became responsible for the quality of the product. The quality responsibility was usually fulfilled by a 100 percent inspection of all the important characteristics. If there were any discrepancies noted, these problems were handled by the manufacturing department supervisor. In essence, quality was attained by "inspecting the quality into the product."

During the 1920s Dr. Walter A. Shewhart, of the Bell Telephone Laboratories, developed the concepts of statistical quality control. He introduced the concept of "controlling" the quality of a product as it was being manufactured, rather than inspecting the quality into the product after it was manufactured. For the purpose of controlling quality, Shewhart developed charting techniques for controlling in-process manufacturing operations. In addition, he introduced the concept of statistical sample inspection to estimate the quality of a product as it was being manufactured. This replaced the old method of inspecting each part after it was completed in the production operation.

Statistical quality control really came into its own during World War II. The need for mass-produced war-related items, such as bomb sights, accurate radar, and other electronic equipment, at the lowest possible cost hastened the use of statistical sampling and quality control charts. Since World War II these statistical techniques have been refined and sharpened. The use of computers in the last decade has also widened the use of these techniques.

World War II virtually destroyed the Japanese production capability. Rather than retool their old production methods, the Japanese enlisted the aid of the late Dr. W. Edwards Deming, of the United States Department of Agriculture, to help them develop an overall plan. In a series of seminars with Japanese planners he stressed a philosophy that is known today as Deming's 14 points. These 14 points are listed on the following page. He emphasized that quality originates from improving the process, not from inspection, and that quality is determined by the customers. The manufacturer must be able, via market research, to anticipate the needs of customers. Senior management has the responsibility for long-term improvement. Another of his points, and one that the Japanese strongly endorsed, is that every member of the company must contribute to the long-term improvement. To achieve this improvement, ongoing education and training are necessary.

Deming had some ideas that did not mesh with contemporary management philosophies in the United States. Two areas where Deming's ideas differed from U.S. management philosophy were with production quotas and merit ratings. He claimed these two practices, which are both common in the United States, are not productive and should be eliminated. He also pointed out that U.S. managers are mostly interested in good news. Good news, however, does not provide an opportunity for improvement. On the other hand, bad news opens the door for new products and allows for company improvement.

Listed below, in a condensed form, are Dr. Deming's 14 points. He was adamant that the 14 points needed to be adopted as a package in order to be successful. The underlying theme is cooperation, teamwork, and the belief that workers want to do their jobs in a quality fashion.

---

**DEMING'S 14 POINTS**
1. Create constancy of purpose for the continual improvement of products and service to society.
2. Adopt a philosophy that we can no longer live with commonly accepted levels of delays, mistakes, defective materials, and defective workmanship.
3. Eliminate the need for mass inspection as the way to achieve quality. Instead achieve quality by building the product correctly in the first place.
4. End the practice of awarding business solely on the basis of price. Instead, require meaningful measures of quality along with the price.
5. Improve constantly and forever every process for planning, production, and service.
6. Institute modern methods of training on the job for all employees, including managers. This will lead to better utilization of each employee.
7. Adopt and institute leadership aimed at helping people do a better job.
8. Encourage effective two-way communication and other means to drive out fear throughout the organization so that everyone may work more effectively and more productively for the company.
9. Break down barriers between departments and staff areas.
10. Eliminate the use of slogans, posters, and exhortations demanding zero defects and new levels of productivity without providing methods.
11. Eliminate work standards that prescribe quotas for the workforce and numerical goals for people in management. Substitute aids and helpful leadership in order to achieve continual improvement in quality and productivity.
12. Remove the barriers that rob hourly workers and the people in management of their right to pride of workmanship.
13. Institute a vigorous program of education and encourage self-improvement for everyone. What an organization needs is good people and people who are improving with education. Advancement to a competitive position will have its roots in knowledge.
14. Define clearly management's permanent commitment to ever-improving quality and productivity to implement all of these principles.

---

Deming's 14 points did not ignore statistical quality control, which is often abbreviated as SQC. The objective of statistical quality control is to monitor production through many stages of manufacturing. We use the tools of statistical quality control, such as $X$-bar and $R$ charts, to monitor the quality of many processes and services. Control charts allow us to identify when a process or service is "out of control," that is, when the point in time is reached where an excessive number of defective units are being produced.

## Statistics in Action

Does excellence in quality management lead to higher financial performance? Recent research compared the financial performance of companies that received the Baldrige National Quality Award to similar companies who did not receive the award. The research showed that the companies receiving the award had an average of 39% higher operating income, 26% higher sales, and were 1.22% lower in their cost per sales dollar.

Interest in quality has accelerated dramatically in the United States since the late 1980s. Turn on the television and watch the commercials sponsored by Ford, Nissan, and GM to verify the emphasis on quality control on the assembly line. It is now one of the "in" topics in all facets of business. V. Daniel Hunt, president of Technology Research Corporation, wrote in his book *Quality in America* that in the United States, 20 to 25 percent of the cost of production is currently spent finding and correcting mistakes. And, he added, the additional cost incurred in repairing or replacing faulty products in the field drives the total cost of poor quality to nearly 30 percent. In Japan, he indicates, this cost is about 3 percent!

In recent years companies have been motivated to improve quality by the challenge of being recognized for their quality achievements. The Malcolm Baldrige National Quality Award, established in 1988, is awarded annually to U.S. companies that demonstrate excellence in quality achievement and management. The award categories include manufacturing, service, small business, health care, and education. Past winners include Xerox, IBM, the University of Wisconsin-Stout, the Ritz-Carlton Hotel Corporation, Federal Express, and Cadillac. The 2002 award winners were Motorola Inc. Commercial, Government, and Industrial Solutions Sector, Schaumburg, Illinois; Branch-Smith Printing Division, Fort Worth, Texas; and SSM Health Care, a private, not-for-profit health care system based in St. Louis, Missouri. Motorola was the recipient in the manufacturing sector, Branch-Smith in the small business category, and SSM in the health care category. You can obtain more information on the 2002 winners and other winners by visiting the website: http://www.quality.nist.gov.

**Six Sigma** Six Sigma is a typical program designed to improve quality and performance throughout the company. It combines methodology, tools, software, and education to deliver a completely integrated approach to waste elimination and process capability improvement. The approach requires defining the process function, identifying, collecting, and analyzing data, creating and consolidating information into useful knowledge and the communication and application of such knowledge to reduce variation.

Six Sigma gets its name from the normal distribution. The term sigma means standard deviation, and "plus or minus" three standard deviations gives a total range of six standard deviations. So six sigma means having no more than 3.4 defects per million opportunities in any process, product, or service. Through the application of statistical thinking it uncovers the relationship between variation and its effect on waste, operating cost, cycle time, profitability, and customer satisfaction.

General Electric, Motorola, and AlliedSignal are large companies that have used six sigma methods and achieved significant quality improvement and cost savings. At Allied Signal the company saved $1.5 billion through Six Sigma, and wants to slash another $500 million. Reducing waste helps AlliedSignal raise profit margins. "Six Sigma is crucial for us," says Lawrence Bossidy, the CEO of AlliedSignal. "We're trying to broaden it outside manufacturing, and we're off to a good start. You need growth and productivity in business these days."

What is quality? There is no commonly agreed upon definition of quality. To cite a few diverse definitions: From Westinghouse, "Total quality is performance leadership in meeting the customer requirements by doing the right things right the first time." From AT&T, "Quality is meeting customer expectations." Historian Barbara W. Tuchman says, "Quality is achieving or reaching the highest standard as against being satisfied with the sloppy or fraudulent."

# Causes of Variation

No two products are *exactly* the same. There is always some variation. The weight of each McDonald's Quarter Pounder is not exactly 0.25 pounds. Some will weigh more than 0.25 pounds, others less. The standard time for the TARTA (Toledo Area Regional Transit Authority) bus run from downtown Toledo, Ohio, to Perrysburg is 25 minutes. However, each run does not take *exactly* 25 minutes. Some runs take longer. Other times the TARTA driver must wait in Perrysburg before returning to Toledo. In some cases there is a reason for the bus being late, an accident on the expressway or a snowstorm, for example. In other cases the driver may not "hit" the green lights or the traffic is unusually heavy and slow for no apparent reason. There are two general sources of variation in a process—chance and assignable.

> **CHANCE VARIATION** Variation that is random in nature. This type of variation cannot be completely eliminated unless there is a major change in the equipment or material used in the process.

Internal machine friction, slight variations in material or process conditions (such as the temperature of the mold being used to make glass bottles), atmospheric conditions (such as temperature, humidity, and the dust content of the air), and vibrations transmitted to a machine from a passing forklift are a few examples of sources of chance variation.

If the hole drilled in a piece of steel is too large due to a dull drill, the drill may be sharpened or a new drill inserted. An operator who continually sets up the machine incorrectly can be replaced or retrained. If the roll of steel to be used in the process does not have the correct tensile strength, it can be rejected. These are examples of assignable variation.

> **ASSIGNABLE VARIATION** Variation that is not random. It can be eliminated or reduced by investigating the problem and finding the cause.

There are several reasons we should be concerned with variation.

1. It will change the shape, dispersion, and central location of the distribution of the product characteristic being measured.
2. Assignable variation is usually correctable, whereas chance variation usually cannot be corrected or stabilized economically.

# Diagnostic Charts

There are a variety of diagnostic techniques available to investigate quality problems. Two of the more prominent of these techniques are *Pareto charts* and *fishbone diagrams*.

# Pareto Charts

Pareto analysis is a technique for tallying the number and type of defects that happen within a product or service. The chart is named after a nineteenth-century Italian scientist, Vilfredo Pareto. He noted that most of the "activity" in a process is caused by relatively few of the "factors." His concept, often called the 80–20 rule, is that 80 percent of the activity is caused by 20 percent of the factors. By concentrating on 20 percent of the factors, managers can attack 80 percent of the problem. For example, Emily's Family Restaurant, located at the junction of Interstates 75 and 70, is investigating "customer complaints." The five complaints heard most frequently are: discourteous service, cold food, long wait for seating, few menu choices, and unruly young children. Suppose discourteous service was mentioned most frequently and cold food second. These two factors total more than 85 percent of the complaints and hence are the two that should be addressed first because this will yield the largest reduction in complaints.

To develop a Pareto chart, we begin by tallying the type of defects. Next, we rank the defects in terms of frequency of occurrence from largest to smallest. Finally, we produce a vertical bar chart, with the height of the bars corresponding to the frequency of each defect. The following example illustrates these ideas.

**EXAMPLE**

The city manager of Grove City, Utah, is concerned with water usage, particularly in single family homes. She would like to develop a plan to reduce the water usage in Grove City. To investigate, she selects a sample of 100 homes and determines the typical daily water usage for various purposes. These sample results are as follows.

| Reasons for Water Usage | Gallons per Day |
|-------------------------|-----------------|
| Laundering              | 24.9            |
| Watering lawn           | 143.7           |
| Personal bathing        | 106.7           |
| Cooking                 | 5.1             |
| Swimming pool           | 28.3            |
| Dishwashing             | 12.3            |
| Car washing             | 10.4            |
| Drinking                | 7.9             |

What is the area of greatest usage? Where should she concentrate her efforts to reduce the water usage?

**SOLUTION**

A Pareto chart is useful for identifying the major areas of water usage and focusing on those areas where the greatest reduction can be achieved. The first step is to convert each of the activities to a percent and then to order them from largest to smallest. The total water usage per day is 339.3 gallons, found by totaling the gallons used in the eight activities. The activity with the largest use is watering lawns. It accounts for 143.7 gallons of water per day, or 42.4 percent of the amount of water used. The next largest category is personal bathing, which accounts for 31.4 percent of the water used. These two activities account for 73.8 percent of the water usage.

| Reasons for Water Usage | Gallons per Day | Percent |
|-------------------------|-----------------|---------|
| Laundering              | 24.9            | 7.3     |
| Watering lawn           | 143.7           | 42.4    |
| Personal bathing        | 106.7           | 31.4    |
| Cooking                 | 5.1             | 1.5     |
| Swimming pool usage     | 28.3            | 8.3     |
| Dishwashing             | 12.3            | 3.6     |
| Car washing             | 10.4            | 3.1     |
| Drinking                | 7.9             | 2.3     |
| Total                   | 339.3           | 100.0   |

To draw the Pareto chart, we begin by scaling the number of gallons used on the left vertical axis and the corresponding percent on the right vertical axis. Next we draw a vertical bar with the height of the bar corresponding to the activity with the largest number of occurrences. In the Grove City example, we draw a vertical bar for the activity watering lawns to a height of 143.7 gallons. (We call this the count.) We continue this procedure for the other activities, as shown in the MINITAB output in Chart 17–1.

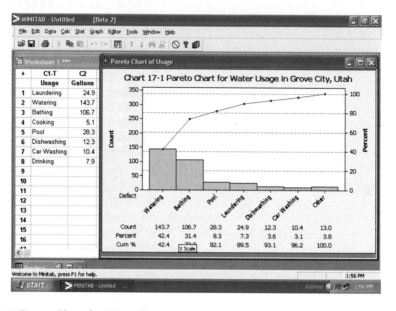

**CHART 17–1**  Pareto Chart for Water Usage in Grove City, Utah

Below the chart we list the activities, their frequency of occurrence, and the percent of the time each activity occurs. In the last row we list the cumulative percentage. This cumulative row will allow us to quickly determine which set of activities account for most of the activity. These cumulative percents are plotted above the vertical bars. In the Grove City example, the activities of watering lawn, personal bathing, and pools account for 82.1 percent of the water usage. The city manager can attain the greatest gain by looking to reduce the water usage in these three areas.

# Fishbone Diagram

Another diagnostic chart is a **cause-and-effect diagram** or a **fishbone diagram.** It is called a cause-and-effect diagram to emphasize the relationship between an effect and a set of possible causes that produce the particular effect. This diagram is useful to help organize ideas and to identify relationships. It is a tool that encourages open "brainstorming" for ideas. By identifying these relationships we can determine factors that are the cause of variability in our process. The name *fishbone* comes from the manner in which the various causes and effects are organized on the diagram. The effect is usually a particular problem, or perhaps a goal, and it is shown on the right-hand side of the diagram. The major causes are listed on the left-hand side of the diagram.

The usual approach to a fishbone diagram is to consider four problem areas, namely, methods, materials, equipment, and personnel. The problem, or the effect, is the head of the fish. See Chart 17–2.

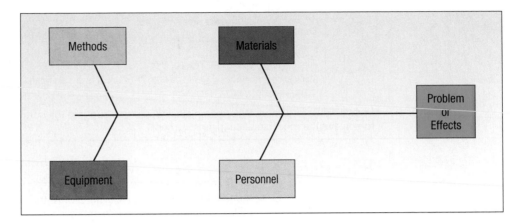

**CHART 17–2** Fishbone Diagram

Under each of the possible causes are subcauses that are identified and investigated. The subcauses are factors that may be producing the particular effect. Information is gathered about the problem and used to fill in the fishbone diagram. Each of the subcauses is investigated and those that are not important eliminated, until the real cause of the problem is identified.

Chart 17–3 illustrates the details of a fishbone diagram. Suppose a family restaurant, such as those found along an interstate highway, has recently been experiencing complaints from customers that the food being served is cold. Notice each of the subcauses are listed as assumptions. Each of these subcauses must be investigated to find the real problem regarding the cold food. In a fishbone diagram there is no weighting of the subcauses.

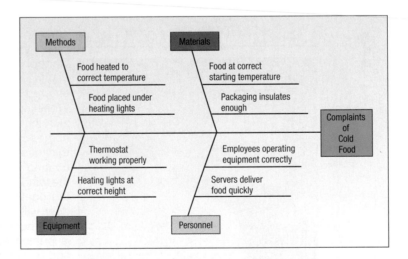

**CHART 17–3** Fishbone Diagram for a Restaurant Investigation of Cold Food Complaints

**Self-Review 17–1** The Rouse Home, located in Chicago, is a mental health facility. Recently there have been complaints regarding conditions at the home. The administrator would like to use a Pareto chart to investigate. When a patient or patient's relative has a complaint, they are asked to complete a complaint form. Listed below is a summary of the complaint forms received during the last 12 months.

| Complaint | Number | Complaint | Number |
|---|---|---|---|
| Nothing to do | 45 | Dirty conditions | 63 |
| Poor care by staff | 71 | Poor quality food | 84 |
| Medication error | 2 | Lack of respect by staff | 35 |

Develop a Pareto chart. What complaints would you suggest the administrator work on first to achieve the most significant improvement?

## Exercises

1. Tom Sharkey is the owner of Sharkey Chevy, Buick, GM. At the start of the year Tom instituted a customer opinion program to find ways to improve service. One week after the service is performed, Tom's administrative assistant calls the customer to find out whether the service was performed satisfactorily and how the service might be improved. Listed below is a summary of the complaints for the first six months. Develop a Pareto chart. What complaints would you suggest that Tom work on to improve the quality of service?

| Complaint | Frequency | Complaint | Frequency |
|---|---|---|---|
| Problem not corrected | 38 | Price too high | 23 |
| Error on invoice | 8 | Wait too long for service | 10 |
| Unfriendly atmosphere | 12 | | |

2. Out of 110 diesel engines tested, a rework and repair facility found 9 had leaky water pumps, 15 had faulty cylinders, 4 had ignition problems, 52 had oil leaks, and 30 had cracked blocks. Draw a Pareto chart to identify the key problem in the engines.

# Purpose and Types of Quality Control Charts

Control charts identify when assignable causes of variation or changes have entered the process. For example, the Wheeling Company makes vinyl-coated aluminum replacement windows for older homes. The vinyl coating must have a thickness between certain limits. If the coating becomes too thick, it will cause the windows to jam. On the other hand, if the coating becomes too thin, the window will not seal properly. The mechanism that determines how much coating is put on each window becomes worn and begins making the coating too thick. Thus, a change has occurred in the process. Control charts are useful for detecting the change in process conditions.

It is important to know when changes have entered the process, so that the cause may be identified and corrected before a large number of unacceptable items are produced.

Control charts may be compared to the scoreboard in a baseball game. By looking at the scoreboard, the fans, coaches, and players can tell which team is winning the game. However, the scoreboard can do nothing to win or lose the game. Control charts provide a similar function. These charts indicate to the workers, group leaders, quality control engineers, production supervisor, and management whether the production of the part or service is "in control" or "out of control." If the production is "out of control," the control chart will not fix the situation; it is just a piece of paper with figures and dots on it. Instead, the person responsible will adjust the machine manufacturing the part or do what is necessary to return production to "in control."

There are two types of control charts. A **variable control chart** portrays measurements, such as the amount of cola in a two liter bottle or the outside diameter of a piece of pipe. A variable control chart requires the interval or the ratio scale of measurement. An **attribute control chart** classifies a product or service as either acceptable or unacceptable. It is based on the nominal scale of measurement. The Marines stationed at Camp Lejeune are asked to rate the meals served as acceptable or unacceptable; bank loans are either repaid or they are defaulted.

## Control Charts for Variables

To develop control charts for variables, we rely on the sampling theory discussed in connection with the central limit theorem in Chapter 8. Suppose a sample of five pieces is selected each hour from the production process and the mean of each sample computed. The sample means are $\overline{X}_1$, $\overline{X}_2$, $\overline{X}_3$, and so on. The mean of these sample means is denoted as $\overline{\overline{X}}$. We use $k$ to indicate the number of sample means. The overall or grand mean is found by:

| | | |
|---|---|---|
| GRAND MEAN | $\overline{\overline{X}} = \dfrac{\Sigma \text{ of the means of the subgroups}}{\text{Number of sample means}} = \dfrac{\Sigma \overline{X}}{k}$ | [17–1] |

The standard error of the distribution of the sample means is designated by $s_{\overline{X}}$. It is found by:

| | | |
|---|---|---|
| STANDARD ERROR OF THE MEAN | $s_{\overline{X}} = \dfrac{s}{\sqrt{n}}$ | [17–2] |

These relationships allow limits to be set up around the sample means to show how much variation can be expected for a given sample size. These expected limits are called the **upper control limit** (UCL) and the **lower control limit** (LCL). An example will illustrate the use of control limits and how the limits are determined.

**EXAMPLE**

Statistical Software, Inc., offers a toll-free number where customers can call with problems involving the use of their products from 7 A.M. until 11 P.M. daily. It is impossible to have every call answered immediately by a technical representative, but it is important customers do not wait too long for a person to come on the line. Customers become upset when they hear the message "Your call is important to us. The next available representative will be with you shortly" too many times. To understand their process, Statistical Software decides to develop a control chart describing the total time from when a call is received until the representative answers the caller's question. Yesterday, for the 16 hours of operation, five calls were sampled each hour. This information is reported on the next page, in minutes until a call was answered.

| Time | Sample Number | | | | |
|------|---|---|---|---|---|
|      | **1** | **2** | **3** | **4** | **5** |
| A.M.   7 | 8 | 9 | 15 | 4 | 11 |
| 8 | 7 | 10 | 7 | 6 | 8 |
| 9 | 11 | 12 | 10 | 9 | 10 |
| 10 | 12 | 8 | 6 | 9 | 12 |
| 11 | 11 | 10 | 6 | 14 | 11 |
| P.M.  12 | 7 | 7 | 10 | 4 | 11 |
| 1 | 10 | 7 | 4 | 10 | 10 |
| 2 | 8 | 11 | 11 | 7 | 7 |
| 3 | 8 | 11 | 8 | 14 | 12 |
| 4 | 12 | 9 | 12 | 17 | 11 |
| 5 | 7 | 7 | 9 | 17 | 13 |
| 6 | 9 | 9 | 4 | 4 | 11 |
| 7 | 10 | 12 | 12 | 12 | 12 |
| 8 | 8 | 11 | 9 | 6 | 8 |
| 9 | 10 | 13 | 9 | 4 | 9 |
| 10 | 9 | 11 | 8 | 5 | 11 |

Based on this information, develop a control chart for the mean duration of the call. Does there appear to be a trend in the calling times? Is there any period in which it appears that customers wait longer than others?

A mean chart has two limits, an upper control limit (*UCL*) and a lower control limit (*LCL*). These upper and lower control limits are computed by:

| CONTROL LIMITS FOR THE MEAN | $$UCL = \bar{\bar{X}} + 3\frac{s}{\sqrt{n}} \quad \text{and} \quad LCL = \bar{\bar{X}} - 3\frac{s}{\sqrt{n}}$$ | **[17–3]** |
|---|---|---|

where *s* is an estimate of the standard deviation of the population, $\sigma$. Notice that in the calculation of the upper and lower control limits the number 3 appears. It represents the 99.74 percent confidence limits. The limits are often called the 3-sigma limits. However, other levels of confidence (such as 90 or 95 percent) can be used.

This application developed before computers were widely available and computing standard deviations was difficult. Rather than calculate the standard deviation from each sample as a measure of variation, it is easier to use the range. For fixed sized samples there is a constant relationship between the range and the standard deviation, so we can use the following formulas to determine the 99.74 percent control limits for the mean. It can be demonstrated that the term $3(s/\sqrt{n})$ from formula (17–3) is equivalent to $A_2\bar{R}$ in the following formula.

| CONTROL LIMITS FOR THE MEAN | $$UCL = \bar{\bar{X}} + A_2\bar{R} \qquad LCL = \bar{\bar{X}} - A_2\bar{R}$$ | **[17–4]** |
|---|---|---|

where:

$A_2$ is a constant used in computing the upper and the lower control limits. It is based on the average range, $\bar{R}$. The factors for various sample sizes are available in Appendix I. (Note: *n* in this table refers to the number in the sample.) A portion of Appendix I is shown below. To locate the $A_2$ factor for this problem, find the sample size for $n$ in the left margin. It is 5. Then move horizontally to the $A_2$ column, and read the factor. It is 0.577.

| $n$ | $A_2$ | $D_2$ | $D_3$ | $D_4$ |
|---|---|---|---|---|
| 2 | 1.880 | 1.128 | 0 | 3.267 |
| 3 | 1.023 | 1.693 | 0 | 2.575 |
| 4 | 0.729 | 2.059 | 0 | 2.282 |
| 5 | 0.577 | 2.326 | 0 | 2.115 |
| 6 | 0.483 | 2.534 | 0 | 2.004 |

$\overline{\overline{X}}$ is the mean of the sample means, computed by $\Sigma\overline{X}/k$, where $k$ is the number of samples selected. In this problem a sample of 5 observations is taken each hour for 16 hours, so $k = 16$.

$\overline{R}$ is the mean of the ranges of the sample. It is $\Sigma R/k$. Remember the range is the difference between the largest and the smallest value in each sample. It describes the variability occurring in that particular sample. (See Table 17–1.)

**TABLE 17–1** Duration of 16 Samples of Five Help Sessions

| Time | | 1 | 2 | 3 | 4 | 5 | Mean | Range |
|---|---|---|---|---|---|---|---|---|
| A.M. | 7 | 8 | 9 | 15 | 4 | 11 | 9.4 | 11 |
| | 8 | 7 | 10 | 7 | 6 | 8 | 7.6 | 4 |
| | 9 | 11 | 12 | 10 | 9 | 10 | 10.4 | 3 |
| | 10 | 12 | 8 | 6 | 9 | 12 | 9.4 | 6 |
| | 11 | 11 | 10 | 6 | 14 | 11 | 10.4 | 8 |
| P.M. | 12 | 7 | 7 | 10 | 4 | 11 | 7.8 | 7 |
| | 1 | 10 | 7 | 4 | 10 | 10 | 8.2 | 6 |
| | 2 | 8 | 11 | 11 | 7 | 7 | 8.8 | 4 |
| | 3 | 8 | 11 | 8 | 14 | 12 | 10.6 | 6 |
| | 4 | 12 | 9 | 12 | 17 | 11 | 12.2 | 8 |
| | 5 | 7 | 7 | 9 | 17 | 13 | 10.6 | 10 |
| | 6 | 9 | 9 | 4 | 4 | 11 | 7.4 | 7 |
| | 7 | 10 | 12 | 12 | 12 | 12 | 11.6 | 2 |
| | 8 | 8 | 11 | 9 | 6 | 8 | 8.4 | 5 |
| | 9 | 10 | 13 | 9 | 4 | 9 | 9.0 | 9 |
| | 10 | 9 | 11 | 8 | 5 | 11 | 8.8 | 6 |
| Total | | | | | | | 150.60 | 102 |

The centerline for the chart is $\overline{\overline{X}}$. It is 9.4125 minutes, found by 150.60/16. The mean of the ranges $(\overline{R})$ is 6.375 minutes, found by 102/16. Thus, the upper control limit of the $X$ bar chart is:

$$UCL = \overline{\overline{X}} + A_2\overline{R} = 9.4125 + 0.577(6.375) = 13.0909$$

The lower control limit of the $X$ bar chart is:

$$LCL = \overline{\overline{X}} - A_2\overline{R} = 9.4125 - 0.577(6.375) = 5.7341$$

$\overline{\overline{X}}$, $UCL$, and $LCL$, and the sample means are portrayed in Chart 17–4. The mean, $\overline{\overline{X}}$, is 9.4125 minutes, the upper control limit is located at 13.0909 minutes, and the lower control limit is located at 5.7341. There is some variation in the duration of the calls, but all sample means are within the control limits. Thus, based on 16 samples of 5 calls, we conclude that 99.74 percent of the time the mean length of a sample of 5 calls will be between 5.7341 minutes and 13.0909 minutes.

**CHART 17–4** Control Chart for Mean Length of Customer Calls to Statistical Software, Inc.

Because the statistical theory is based on the normality of large samples, control charts should be based on a stable process, that is, a fairly large sample, taken over a long period of time. One rule of thumb is to design the chart after at least 25 samples have been selected.

## Range Chart

In addition to the central location in a sample, we must also monitor the amount of variation from sample to sample. A **range chart** shows the variation in the sample ranges. If the points representing the ranges fall between the upper and the lower limits, it is concluded that the operation is in control. According to chance, about 997 times out of 1,000 the range of the samples will fall within the limits. If the range should fall above the limits, we conclude that an assignable cause affected the operation and an adjustment to the process is needed. Why are we not as concerned about the lower control limit of the range? For small samples the lower limit is often zero. Actually, for any sample of six or less, the lower control limit is 0. If the range is zero, then logically all the parts are the same and there is not a problem with the variability of the operation.

The upper and lower control limits of the range chart are determined from the following equations.

| CONTROL CHART FOR RANGES | $UCL = D_4\overline{R} \qquad LCL = D_3\overline{R}$ | **[17–5]** |
|---|---|---|

The values for $D_3$ and $D_4$, which reflect the usual three $\sigma$ (sigma) limits for various sample sizes, are found in Appendix I or in the table on page 726.

**EXAMPLE**

The length of time customers of Statistical Software, Inc. waited from the time their call was answered until a technical representative answered their question or solved their problem is recorded in Table 17–1. Develop a control chart for the range. Does it appear that there is any time when there is too much variation in the operation?

**SOLUTION**

The first step is to find the mean of the sample ranges. The range for the five calls sampled in the 7 A.M. hour is 11 minutes. The longest call selected from that hour was 15 minutes and the shortest 4 minutes; the difference in the lengths is 11 minutes. In the 8 A.M. hour the range is 4 minutes. The total of the 16 ranges is 102 minutes, so the average range is 6.375 minutes, found by $\overline{R} = 102/16$. Referring to Appendix I or the partial table on page 597, $D_3$ and $D_4$ are 0 and 2.115, respectively. The lower and upper control limits are 0 and 13.4831.

$$UCL = D_4\bar{R} = 2.115(6.375) = 13.4831$$
$$LCL = D_3\bar{R} = 0(6.375) = 0$$

The range chart with the 16 sample ranges plotted is shown in Chart 17–5. This chart shows all the ranges are well within the control limits. Hence, we conclude the variation in the time to service the customer's calls is within normal limits, that is, "in control." Of course, we should be determining the control limits based on one set of data and then applying them to evaluate future data, not the data we already know.

**CHART 17–5** Control Chart for Ranges of Length of Customer Calls to Statistical Software, Inc.

MINITAB will draw a control chart for the mean and the range. Following is the output for the Statistical Software example. The data are in Table 17–1. The minor differences in the control limits are due to rounding.

# Some In-Control and Out-of-Control Situations

Three illustrations of in-control and out-of-control processes follow.

1.  The mean chart and the range chart together indicate that the process is in control. Note the sample means and sample ranges are clustered close to the

centerlines. Some are above and some below the centerlines, indicating the process is quite stable. That is, there is no visible tendency for the means and ranges to move toward the out-of-control areas.

Everything OK

2.  The sample means are in control, but the ranges of the last two samples are out of control. This indicates there is considerable variation in the samples. Some sample ranges are large; others are small. An adjustment in the process is probably necessary.

Considerable variation in ranges

3.  The mean was in control for the first samples, but there is an upward trend toward *UCL*. The last two sample means were out of control. An adjustment in the process is indicated.

Mean Chart

Range Chart

Mean out of control

The above chart for the mean is an example of a control chart that offers some additional information. Note the direction of the last five observations of the mean. They are all above $\overline{\overline{X}}$ and increasing, and, in fact, the last two observations are out of control. The fact that the sample means were increasing for six consecutive observations is very improbable and another indication that the process is out of control.

**Self-Review 17–2**

The manager of River City McDonald's randomly selects four customers each hour. For these selected customers she determines the time, in minutes, between order entry and order delivery. The results are shown below.

| | Sample Times | | | |
|---|---|---|---|---|
| Time | 1 | 2 | 3 | 4 |
| 9 A.M. | 1 | 4 | 5 | 2 |
| 10 A.M. | 2 | 3 | 2 | 1 |
| 11 A.M. | 1 | 7 | 3 | 5 |

(a) Compute the mean wait, the mean range, and determine the control limits for the mean and the range.
(b) Are the measurements within the control limits? Interpret the chart.

# Exercises

3. Describe the difference between assignable variation and chance variation.
4. Describe the difference between an attribute control chart and a variable control chart.
5. Samples of size $n = 4$ are selected from a production line.
   a. What is the value of the $A_2$ factor used to determine the upper and lower control limits for the mean?
   b. What are the values of the $D_3$ and $D_4$ factors used to determine the upper and lower control limits for the range?
6. Samples of size 5 are selected from a manufacturing process. The mean of the sample ranges is .50. What is the estimate of the standard deviation of the population?

7. A new industrial oven has just been installed at the Piatt Bakery. To develop experience regarding the oven temperature, an inspector reads the temperature at four different places inside the oven each half hour. The first reading, taken at 8:00 A.M., was 340 degrees Fahrenheit. (Only the last two digits are given in the following table to make the computations easier.)

| Time | Reading 1 | 2 | 3 | 4 |
|---|---|---|---|---|
| 8:00 A.M. | 40 | 50 | 55 | 39 |
| 8:30 A.M. | 44 | 42 | 38 | 38 |
| 9:00 A.M. | 41 | 45 | 47 | 43 |
| 9:30 A.M. | 39 | 39 | 41 | 41 |
| 10:00 A.M. | 37 | 42 | 46 | 41 |
| 10:30 A.M. | 39 | 40 | 39 | 40 |

  a. On the basis of this initial experience, determine the control limits for the mean temperature. Determine the grand mean. Plot the experience on a chart.
  b. Interpret the chart. Does there seem to be a time when the temperature is out of control?
8. Refer to exercise 7.
  a. On the basis of this initial experience, determine the control limits for the range. Plot the experience on a chart.
  b. Does there seem to be a time when there is too much variation in the temperature?

# Attribute Control Charts

Often the data we collect are the result of counting rather than measuring. That is, we observe the presence or absence of some attribute. For example, the screw top on a bottle of shampoo either fits onto the bottle and does not leak (an "acceptable" condition) or does not seal and a leak results (an "unacceptable" condition), or a bank makes a loan to a customer and the loan is either repaid or it is not repaid. In other cases we are interested in the number of defects in a sample. British Airways might count the number of its flights arriving late per day at Gatwick Airport in London. In this section we discuss two types of attribute charts: the $p$-chart (percent defective) and the $c$-bar chart (number of defectives).

## Percent Defective Chart

If the item recorded is the fraction of unacceptable parts made in a larger batch of parts, the appropriate control chart is the percent defective chart. This chart is based on the binomial distribution, discussed in Chapter 6, and proportions, discussed in Chapter 9. The centerline is at $p$, the mean proportion defective. The $p$ replaces the $\overline{\overline{X}}$ of the variable control chart. The mean proportion defective is found by:

$$\text{MEAN PROPORTION DEFECTIVE} \qquad p = \frac{\text{Total number defective}}{\text{Total number of items sampled}} \qquad \textbf{[17–6]}$$

The variation in the sample proportion is described by the standard error of a proportion. It is found by:

$$\text{STANDARD ERROR OF THE SAMPLE PROPORTION} \qquad s_p = \sqrt{\frac{p(1-p)}{n}} \qquad \textbf{[17–7]}$$

Hence, the upper control limit (*UCL*) and the lower control limit (*LCL*) are computed as the mean percent defective plus or minus three times the standard error of the percents (proportions). The formula for the control limits is:

| CONTROL LIMITS FOR PROPORTIONS | $LCL, UCL = p \pm 3\sqrt{\dfrac{p(1-p)}{n}}$ | **[17–8]** |
|---|---|---|

An example will show the details of the calculations and the conclusions.

**EXAMPLE**

The Credit Department at Global National Bank is responsible for entering each transaction charged to the customer's monthly statement. Of course, accuracy is critical and errors will make the customer very unhappy! To guard against errors, each data entry clerk rekeys a sample of 1,500 of his or her batch of work a second time and a computer program checks that the numbers match. The program also prints a report of the number and size of any discrepancy. Seven people were working last hour and here are their results:

| Inspector | Number Inspected | Number Mismatched |
|---|---|---|
| Mullins | 1,500 | 4 |
| Rider | 1,500 | 6 |
| Gankowski | 1,500 | 6 |
| Smith | 1,500 | 2 |
| Reed | 1,500 | 15 |
| White | 1,500 | 4 |
| Reading | 1,500 | 4 |

Construct the percent defective chart for this process. What are the upper and the lower control limits? Interpret the results. Does it appear any of the data entry clerks are "out of control"?

**SOLUTION**

The first step is to determine the mean proportion defective *p*, using formula (17–6). It is .0039, found by 41/10,500.

| Inspector | Number Inspected | Number Mismatched | Proportion Defective |
|---|---|---|---|
| Mullins | 1,500 | 4 | .00267 |
| Rider | 1,500 | 6 | .00400 |
| Gankowski | 1,500 | 6 | .00400 |
| Smith | 1,500 | 2 | .00133 |
| Reed | 1,500 | 15 | .01000 |
| White | 1,500 | 4 | .00267 |
| Reading | 1,500 | 4 | .00267 |
| Total | 10,500 | 41 | |

The upper and lower control limits are computed by using formula (17–8).

$$LCL, UCL = p \pm 3\sqrt{\frac{p(1-p)}{n}}$$

$$= \frac{41}{10,500} \pm 3\sqrt{\frac{.0039(1-.0039)}{1,500}} = .0039 \pm .0048$$

From the above calculations, the upper control limit is .0087, found by .0039 + .0048. The lower control limit is 0. Why? The lower limit by formula is determined by .0039 − .0048, which is equal to −0.0009. A negative proportion defective is not possible, so the smallest value is 0. We set the control limit at 0. Thus, any data entry clerk whose proportion defective is between 0 and .0087 is "in control." Clerk number 5, whose name is Reed, is out of control. Her proportion defective is .01, or 1.0 percent, which is outside the upper control limit. Perhaps she should receive additional training or be transferred to another position. This information is summarized in Chart 17–6, which is output from the MINITAB system.

**CHART 17–6**  Control Chart for Proportion of Entries Defective among Data Entry Clerks at Global National Bank

## *c*-Bar Chart

The *c*-bar chart plots the number of defects or failures per unit. It is based on the Poisson distribution discussed in Chapter 6. The number of bags mishandled on a flight by Southwest Airlines might be monitored by a *c*-bar chart. The "unit" under consideration is the flight. On most flights there are no bags mishandled. On others there may be only one, on others two, and so on. The Internal Revenue Service might count and develop a control chart for the number of errors in arithmetic per tax return. Most returns will not have any errors, some returns will have a single error, others will have two, and so on. We let $\bar{c}$ be the mean number of defects per unit. Thus, $\bar{c}$ is the mean number of bags mishandled by Southwest Airlines per flight or the mean number of arithmetic errors per tax return. Recall from Chapter 6 that the standard deviation of a Poisson distribution is the square root of the mean. Thus, we can determine the 3-sigma, or 99.74 percent, limits on a *c*-bar chart by:

| CONTROL LIMITS FOR THE NUMBER OF DEFECTS PER UNIT | $LCL, UCL = \bar{c} \pm 3\sqrt{\bar{c}}$ | **[17–9]** |
|---|---|---|

**EXAMPLE**

The publisher of the *Oak Harbor Daily Telegraph* is concerned about the number of misspelled words in the daily newspaper. They do not print a paper on Saturday or Sunday. In an effort to control the problem and promote the need for correct spelling, a control chart will be used. The number of misspelled words found in the final edition of the paper for the last 10 days is: 5, 6, 3, 0, 4, 5, 1, 2, 7, and 4. Determine the appropriate control limits and interpret the chart. Were there any days during the period that the number of misspelled words was out of control?

**SOLUTION**

The sum of the number of misspelled words over the 10-day period is 37. So the mean number of defects, $\bar{c}$, is 3.7. The square root of this number is 1.924. So the upper control limit is:

$$UCL = \bar{c} + 3\sqrt{\bar{c}} = 3.7 + 3\sqrt{3.7} = 3.7 + 5.77 = 9.47$$

The computed lower control limit would be $3.7 - 3(1.924) = -2.07$. However, the number of misspelled words cannot be less than 0, so we use 0 as the lower limit. The lower control limit is 0 and the upper limit is 9.47. When we compare each of the data points to the value of 9.47, we see they are all less than the upper control limit; the number of misspelled words is "in control." Of course, newspapers are going to strive to eliminate all misspelled words, but control charting techniques offer a means of tracking daily results and determining whether there has been a change. For example, if a new proofreader was hired, her work could be compared with others. These results are summarized in Chart 17–7, which is output from the MINITAB system.

**CHART 17–7** *c*-Bar Chart for Number of Misspelled Words per Edition of the *Oak Harbor Daily Telegraph*

---

**Self-Review 17–3**

The Auto-Lite Company manufactures car batteries. At the end of each shift the Quality Assurance Department selects a sample of batteries and tests them. The number of defective batteries found over the last 12 shifts is 2, 1, 0, 2, 1, 1, 7, 1, 1, 2, 6, and 1. Construct a control chart for the process and comment on whether the process is in control.

# Exercises

9. A bicycle manufacturer randomly selects 10 frames each day and tests for defects. The number of defective frames found over the last 14 days is 3, 2, 1, 3, 2, 2, 8, 2, 0, 3, 5, 2, 0, 4. Construct a control chart for this process and comment on whether the process is "in control."

10. Scott Paper tests its toilet paper by subjecting 15 rolls to a wet stress test to see whether and how often the paper tears during the test. Following are the number of defectives found over the last 15 days: 2, 3, 1, 2, 2, 1, 3, 2, 2, 1, 2, 2, 1, 0, and 0. Construct a control chart for the process and comment on whether the process is "in control."

11. Sam's Supermarkets tests its checkout clerks by randomly examining the printout receipts for scanning errors. The following numbers are the number of errors on each receipt for October 27: 0, 1, 1, 0, 0, 1, 1, 0, 1, 1, 0. Construct a control chart for this process and comment on whether the process is "in control."

12. Dave Christi runs a car wash chain with outlets scattered throughout Chicago. He is concerned that some local managers are giving away free washes to their friends. He decides to collect data on the number of "voided" sales receipts. Of course, some of them are legitimate voids. Would the following data indicate a reasonable number of "voids" at his facilities: 3, 8, 3, 4, 6, 5, 0, 1, 2, 4? Construct a control chart for this process and comment on whether the process is "in control."

# Acceptance Sampling

The previous section was concerned with maintaining the *quality of the product as it is being produced.* In many business situations we are also concerned with the *quality of the incoming finished product.* What do the following cases have in common?

- Sims Software, Inc., purchases CDs from CDs International. The normal purchase order is for 100,000 CDs, packaged in lots of 1,000. Todd Sims, president, does not expect each CD to be perfect. In fact, he has agreed to accept lots of 1,000 with up to 10 percent defective. He would like to develop a plan to inspect incoming lots, to ensure that the quality standard is met. The purpose of the inspection procedure is to separate the acceptable from the unacceptable lots.

- Zenith Electric purchases magnetron tubes from Bono Electronics for use in their new microwave oven. The tubes are shipped to Zenith in lots of 10,000. Zenith allows the incoming lots to contain up to 5 percent defective tubes. They would like to develop a sampling plan to determine which lots meet the criterion and which do not.

- General Motors purchases windshields from many suppliers. GM insists that the windshields be in lots of 1,000. They are willing to accept 50 or fewer defects in each lot, that is, 5 percent defective. They would like to develop a sampling procedure to verify that incoming shipments meet the criterion.

The common thread in these cases is a need to verify that an incoming product meets the stipulated requirements. The situation can be likened to a screen door, which allows the warm summer air to enter the room while keeping the bugs out. Acceptance sampling lets the lots of acceptable quality into the manufacturing area and screens out lots that are not acceptable.

Of course, the situation in modern business is more complex. The buyer wants protection against accepting lots that are below the quality standard. The best pro-

**Statistics in Action**

It was reported during the late 1980s that a Canadian firm ordered some parts from a Japanese company with instructions that there should be "no more than three defective parts per one thousand." When the parts arrived, there was a note attached that said, "Your three defective parts are wrapped separately in the upper left compartment of the shipment." This is a far cry from the days when "Made in Japan" meant cheap but not reliable.

tection against inferior quality is 100 percent inspection. Unfortunately, the cost of 100 percent inspection is often prohibitive. Another problem with checking each item is that the test may be destructive. If all light bulbs were tested until burning out before they were shipped, there would be none left to sell. Also, 100 percent inspection may not lead to the identification of all defects, because boredom might cause a loss of perception on the part of the inspectors. Thus, complete inspection is rarely employed in practical situations.

The usual procedure is to screen the quality of incoming parts by using a statistical sampling plan. According to this plan, a sample of *n* units is randomly selected from the lots of *N* units (the population). This is called **acceptance sampling.** The inspection will determine the number of defects in the sample. This number is compared with a predetermined number called the **critical number** or the **acceptance number.** The acceptance number is usually designated *c.* If the number of defects in the sample of size *n* is less than or equal to *c,* the lot is accepted. If the number of defects exceeds *c,* the lot is rejected and returned to the supplier, or perhaps submitted to 100 percent inspection.

Acceptance sampling is a decision-making process. There are two possible decisions: accept or reject the lot. In addition, there are two situations under which the decision is made: the lot is good or the lot is bad. These are the states of nature. If the lot is good and the sample inspection reveals the lot to be good, or if the lot is bad and the sample inspection indicates it is bad, then a correct decision is made. However, there are two other possibilities. The lot may actually contain more defects than it should, but it is accepted. This is called **consumer's risk.** Similarly, the lot may be within the agreed-upon limits, but it is rejected during the sample inspection. This is called the **producer's risk.** The following summary table for acceptance decisions shows these possibilities. Notice how this discussion is very similar to the ideas of Type I and Type II errors presented at the beginning of Chapter 10. (See page 321.)

*Marginal notes:*
Acceptance sampling

Acceptance number

Consumer's risk

Producer's risk

|              | States of Nature |                 |
| ------------ | ---------------- | --------------- |
| **Decision** | **Good Lot**     | **Bad Lot**     |
| Accept lot   | Correct          | Consumer's risk |
| Reject lot   | Producer's risk  | Correct         |

To evaluate a sampling plan and determine that it is fair to both the producer and the consumer, the usual procedure is to develop an **operating characteristic curve,** or an **OC curve** as it is usually called. An OC curve reports the percent defective along the horizontal axis and the probability of accepting that percent defective along the vertical axis. A smooth curve is usually drawn connecting all the possible levels of quality. The binomial distribution is used to develop the probabilities for an OC curve.

*Marginal note:* OC curve

**EXAMPLE**

Sims Software, as mentioned earlier, purchases CDs from CDs International. The CDs are packaged in lots of 1,000 each. Todd Sims, president of Sims Software, has agreed to accept lots with 10 percent or fewer defective CDs. Todd has directed his inspection department to select a random sample of 20 CDs and examine them carefully. He will accept the lot if it has two or fewer defectives in the sample. Develop an OC curve for this inspection plan. What is the probability of accepting a lot that is 10 percent defective?

**SOLUTION**

This type of sampling is called **attribute sampling** because the sampled item, a CD in this case, is classified as acceptable or unacceptable. No "reading" or "measurement" is obtained on the CD. Let $\pi$ represent the actual proportion defective in the population.

The lot is good if $\pi \leq .10$.
The lot is bad if $\pi > .10$.

*Marginal note:* Attribute sampling

**Decision rule**

Let $X$ be the number of defects in the sample. The decision rule is:

Accept the lot if $X \leq 2$.
Reject the lot if $X \geq 3$.

Here the acceptable lot is one with 10 percent or fewer defective CDs. If the lot is acceptable when it has exactly 10 percent defectives, it would be even more acceptable if it contained fewer than 10 percent defectives. Hence, it is the usual practice to work with the upper limit of the percent of defectives.

The binomial distribution is used to compute the various values on the OC curve. Recall that for us to use the binomial there are four requirements:

1. There are only two possible outcomes. Here the CD is either acceptable or unacceptable.
2. There is a fixed number of trials. In this instance the number of trials is the sample size of 20.
3. There is a constant probability of success. A success is finding a defective CD. The probability of success is assumed to be .10.
4. The trials are independent. The probability of obtaining a defective CD on the third one selected is not related to the likelihood of finding a defect on the fourth CD selected.

Appendix A gives various binomial probabilities. However, the tables in Appendix A go up to only 15, that is, $n = 15$. For this problem $n = 20$, so we will use Excel to compute the various binomial probabilities. The Excel instructions for determining binomial probabilities are on page 210 in Chapter 6. The following Excel output shows the binomial probabilities for $n = 20$ when $\pi$ equal to .05, .10, .15, .20, .25, and .30.

| Number of Defects | 0.05 | 0.10 | 0.15 | 0.20 | 0.25 | 0.30 |
|---|---|---|---|---|---|---|
| | | | Incoming Lot Fraction Defective | | | |
| 0 | 0.358 | 0.122 | 0.039 | 0.012 | 0.003 | 0.001 |
| 1 | 0.377 | 0.270 | 0.137 | 0.058 | 0.021 | 0.007 |
| 2 | 0.189 | 0.285 | 0.229 | 0.137 | 0.067 | 0.028 |
| 3 | 0.060 | 0.190 | 0.243 | 0.205 | 0.134 | 0.072 |
| 4 | 0.013 | 0.090 | 0.182 | 0.218 | 0.190 | 0.130 |
| 5 | 0.002 | 0.032 | 0.103 | 0.175 | 0.202 | 0.179 |
| 6 | 0.000 | 0.009 | 0.045 | 0.109 | 0.169 | 0.192 |
| 7 | 0.000 | 0.002 | 0.016 | 0.055 | 0.112 | 0.164 |
| 8 | 0.000 | 0.000 | 0.005 | 0.022 | 0.061 | 0.114 |
| 9 | 0.000 | 0.000 | 0.001 | 0.007 | 0.027 | 0.065 |
| 10 | 0.000 | 0.000 | 0.000 | 0.002 | 0.010 | 0.031 |
| 11 | 0.000 | 0.000 | 0.000 | 0.000 | 0.003 | 0.012 |
| 12 | 0.000 | 0.000 | 0.000 | 0.000 | 0.001 | 0.004 |
| 13 | 0.000 | 0.000 | 0.000 | 0.000 | 0.000 | 0.001 |
| 14 | 0.000 | 0.000 | 0.000 | 0.000 | 0.000 | 0.000 |
| 20 | 0.000 | 0.000 | 0.000 | 0.000 | 0.000 | 0.000 |

We need to convert the terms used in Chapter 6 to acceptance sampling vocabulary. We let $\pi$ refer to the probability of finding a defect, $c$ the number of defects allowed, and $n$ the number of items sampled. In this case we will allow up to two defects, so $c = 2$. This means that we will allow 0, 1, or 2 of the 20 items sampled to be defective and still accept the incoming shipment of CDs.

To begin we determine the probability of accepting a lot that is 5 percent defective. This means that $\pi = .05$, $c = 2$, and $n = 20$. From the Excel output, the likelihood of selecting a sample of 20 items from a shipment that contained 5 percent defective and finding exactly 0 defects is .358. The likelihood of finding exactly 1 defect is .377, and finding 2 is .189. Hence the likelihood of 2 or fewer defects is .924, found by .358 + .377 + .189. This result is usually written in shorthand notation as follows (recall that bar "|" means "given that").

$$P(x \leq 2 | \pi = .05 \text{ and } n = 20) = .358 + .377 + .189 = .924$$

Continuing, the likelihood of accepting a lot that is actually 10 percent defective is .677. That is:

$$P(x \leq 2 | \pi = .10 \text{ and } n = 20) = .122 + .270 + .285 = .677$$

The complete OC curve in Chart 17–8 shows the smoothed curve for all values of $\pi$ between 0 and about 30 percent. There is no need to show values larger than 30 percent because their probability is very close to 0. The likelihood of accepting lots of selected quality levels is shown on the right-hand side of Chart 17–8. With the OC curve, management of Sims Software will be able to quickly evaluate the probabilities of various quality levels.

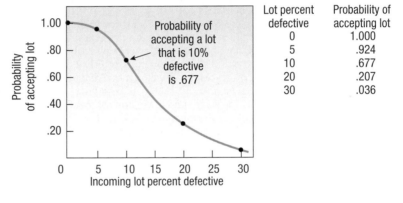

CHART 17–8 OC Curve for Sampling Plan ($n = 20, c = 2$)

**Self-Review 17–4**  Compute the probability of accepting a lot of CDs that is actually 30 percent defective, using the sampling plan for Sims Software.

# Exercises

13. Determine the probability of accepting lots that are 10 percent, 20 percent, 30 percent, and 40 percent defective using a sample of size 12 and an acceptance number of 2.
14. Determine the probability of accepting lots that are 10 percent, 20 percent, 30 percent, and 40 percent defective using a sample of size 14 and an acceptance number of 3.
15. Warren Electric manufactures fuses for many customers. To ensure the quality of the outgoing product, they test 10 fuses each hour. If no more than one fuse is defective, they package the fuses and prepare them for shipment. Develop an OC curve for this sampling plan. Compute the probabilities of accepting lots that are 10 percent, 20 percent, 30 percent, and 40 percent defective. Draw the OC curve for this sampling plan using the four quality levels.
16. Grills Radio Products purchases transistors from Mira Electronics. According to his sampling plan, Art Grills, owner of Grills Radio, will accept a shipment of transistors if three or fewer are defective in a sample of 25. Develop an OC curve for these percents defective: 10 percent, 20 percent, 30 percent, and 40 percent. You will need a statistical software package.

# Chapter Outline

**I.** The objective of statistical quality control is to monitor the quality of the product or service as it is being developed.

**II.** A Pareto chart is a technique for tallying the number and type of defects that happen within a product or service.
   **A.** This chart was named after an Italian scientist, Vilfredo Pareto.
   **B.** The concept of the chart is that 80 percent of the activity is caused by 20 percent of the factors.

**III.** A fishbone diagram emphasizes the relationship between a possible problem cause that will produce the particular effect.
   **A.** It is also called a cause-and-effect diagram.
   **B.** The usual approach is to consider four problem areas: methods, materials, equipment, and personnel.

**IV.** The purpose of a control chart is to monitor graphically the quality of a product or service.
   **A.** There are two types of control charts.
      **1.** A variable control chart is the result of a measurement.
      **2.** An attribute chart shows whether the product or service is acceptable or not acceptable.
   **B.** There are two sources of variation in the quality of a product or service.
      **1.** Chance variation is random in nature and cannot be controlled or eliminated.
      **2.** Assignable variation is not due to random causes and can be eliminated.
   **C.** Four control charts were considered in this chapter.
      **1.** A mean chart shows the mean of a variable, and a range chart shows the range of the variable.
         **a.** The upper and lower control limits are set at plus or minus 3 standard errors from the mean.
         **b.** The formulas for the upper and lower control limits for the mean are:

$$UCL = \bar{\bar{X}} + A_2\bar{R} \qquad LCL = \bar{\bar{X}} - A_2\bar{R} \qquad \text{[17–4]}$$

   **c.** The formulas for the upper and lower control limits for the range are:

$$UCL = D_4\bar{R} \qquad LCL = D_3\bar{R} \qquad \text{[17–5]}$$

      **2.** A percent defective chart is an attribute chart that shows the proportion of the product or service that does not conform to the standard.
         **a.** The mean percent defective is found by

$$p = \frac{\text{Total number defective}}{\text{Total number of items sampled}} \qquad \text{[17–6]}$$

         **b.** The control limits for the proportion defective are determined from the equation

$$LCL, UCL = p \pm 3\sqrt{\frac{p(1-p)}{n}} \qquad \text{[17–8]}$$

      **3.** A c-bar chart refers to the number of defects per unit.
         **a.** It is based on the Poisson distribution.
         **b.** The mean number of defects per unit is $\bar{c}$.
         **c.** The control limits are determined from the following equation.

$$LCL, UCL = \bar{c} \pm 3\sqrt{\bar{c}} \qquad \text{[17–9]}$$

**V.** Acceptance sampling is a method to determine whether an incoming lot of a product meets specified standards.
   **A.** It is based on random sampling techniques.
   **B.** A random sample of $n$ units is selected from a population of $N$ units.
   **C.** $c$ is the maximum number of defective units that may be found in the sample of $n$ and the lot still considered acceptable.
   **D.** An OC (operating characteristic) curve is developed using the binomial probability distribution to determine the probability of accepting lots of various quality levels.

# Pronunciation Key

| SYMBOL | MEANING | PRONUNCIATION |
|---|---|---|
| $\bar{\bar{X}}$ | Mean of the sample means | *X double bar* |

| $s_{\bar{x}}$ | Standard error of the mean | *s sub X bar* |
|---|---|---|
| $A_2$ | Constant used to determine the upper and lower control limit for the mean | *A sub 2* |
| $\bar{R}$ | Mean of the sample ranges | *R bar* |
| $D_4$ | Constant used to determine the upper control limit for the range | *D sub 4* |
| $\bar{c}$ | Mean number of defects per unit | *c bar* |

# Chapter Exercises

17. The production supervisor at Westburg Electric, Inc., noted an increase in the number of electric motors rejected at the time of final inspection. Of the last 200 motors rejected, 80 of the defects were due to poor wiring, 60 contained a short in the coil, 50 involved a defective plug, and 10 involved other defects. Develop a Pareto chart to show the major problem areas.

18. The manufacturer of athletic shoes conducted a study on its newly developed jogging shoe. Listed below are the type and frequency of the nonconformities and failures found. Develop a Pareto chart to show the major problem areas.

| Type of Nonconformity | Frequency | Type of Nonconformity | Frequency |
|---|---|---|---|
| Sole separation | 34 | Lace breakage | 14 |
| Heel separation | 98 | Eyelet failure | 10 |
| Sole penetration | 62 | Other | 16 |

19. Wendy's fills its soft drinks with an automatic machine whose operation is based on the weight of the soft drink. When the process is in control, the machine fills each cup so that the grand mean is 10.0 ounces and the mean range is 0.25 for samples of 5.
    a. Determine the upper and lower control limits for the process for both the mean and the range.
    b. The manager of the I-280 store tested five soft drinks served last hour and found that the mean was 10.16 ounces and the range was 0.35 ounces. Is the process in control? Should other action be taken?

20. A new machine has just been installed to cut and rough-shape large slugs. The slugs are then transferred to a precision grinder. One of the critical measurements is the outside diameter. The quality control inspector randomly selected five slugs each hour, measured the outside diameter, and recorded the results. The measurements (in millimeters) for the period 8:00 A.M. to 10:30 A.M. follow.

| Time | Outside Diameter (millimeters) | | | | |
|---|---|---|---|---|---|
| | 1 | 2 | 3 | 4 | 5 |
| 8:00 | 87.1 | 87.3 | 87.9 | 87.0 | 87.0 |
| 8:30 | 86.9 | 88.5 | 87.6 | 87.5 | 87.4 |
| 9:00 | 87.5 | 88.4 | 86.9 | 87.6 | 88.2 |
| 9:30 | 86.0 | 88.0 | 87.2 | 87.6 | 87.1 |
| 10:00 | 87.1 | 87.1 | 87.1 | 87.1 | 87.1 |
| 10:30 | 88.0 | 86.2 | 87.4 | 87.3 | 87.8 |

    a. Determine the control limits for the mean and the range.
    b. Plot the control limits for the mean outside diameter and the range.
    c. Are there any points on the mean or the range chart that are out of control? Comment on the chart.

21. The Long Last Tire Company, as part of its inspection process, tests its tires for tread wear under simulated road conditions. Twenty samples of three tires each were selected from different shifts over the last month of operation. The tread wear is reported below in hundredths of an inch.

| Sample | Tread Wear | | | Sample | Tread Wear | | |
|---|---|---|---|---|---|---|---|
| 1 | 44 | 41 | 19 | 11 | 11 | 33 | 34 |
| 2 | 39 | 31 | 21 | 12 | 51 | 34 | 39 |
| 3 | 38 | 16 | 25 | 13 | 30 | 16 | 30 |
| 4 | 20 | 33 | 26 | 14 | 22 | 21 | 35 |
| 5 | 34 | 33 | 36 | 15 | 11 | 28 | 38 |
| 6 | 28 | 23 | 39 | 16 | 49 | 25 | 36 |
| 7 | 40 | 15 | 34 | 17 | 20 | 31 | 33 |
| 8 | 36 | 36 | 34 | 18 | 26 | 18 | 36 |
| 9 | 32 | 29 | 30 | 19 | 26 | 47 | 26 |
| 10 | 29 | 38 | 34 | 20 | 34 | 29 | 32 |

    **a.** Determine the control limits for the mean and the range.

    **b.** Plot the control limits for the mean outside diameter and the range.

    **c.** Are there any points on the mean or the range chart that are "out of control"? Comment on the chart.

**22.** The Charter National Bank has a staff of loan officers located in its branch offices throughout the Southwest. The vice president in charge of the loan officers would like some information on the typical amount of loans and the range in the amount of the loans. A staff analyst of the vice president selected a sample of 10 loan officers and from each officer selected a sample of five loans he or she made last month. The data are reported below. Develop a control chart for the mean and the range. Do any of the officers appear to be "out of control"? Comment on your findings.

| Officer | Loan Amount ($000) | | | | | Officer | Loan Amount ($000) | | | | |
|---|---|---|---|---|---|---|---|---|---|---|---|
| | 1 | 2 | 3 | 4 | 5 | | 1 | 2 | 3 | 4 | 5 |
| Weinraub | 59 | 74 | 53 | 48 | 65 | Bowyer | 66 | 80 | 54 | 68 | 52 |
| Visser | 42 | 51 | 70 | 47 | 67 | Kuhlman | 74 | 43 | 45 | 65 | 49 |
| Moore | 52 | 42 | 53 | 87 | 85 | Ludwig | 75 | 53 | 68 | 50 | 31 |
| Brunner | 36 | 70 | 62 | 44 | 79 | Longnecker | 42 | 65 | 70 | 41 | 52 |
| Wolf | 34 | 59 | 39 | 78 | 61 | Simonetti | 43 | 38 | 10 | 19 | 47 |

**23.** The producer of a candy bar, called the "A Rod" Bar, reports on the package that the calorie content is 420 per 2-ounce bar. A sample of 5 bars from each of the last 10 days is sent for a chemical analysis of the calorie content. The results are shown below. Does it appear that there are any days where the calorie count is out of control? Develop an appropriate control chart and analyze your findings.

| Sample | Calorie Count | | | | | Sample | Calorie Count | | | | |
|---|---|---|---|---|---|---|---|---|---|---|---|
| | 1 | 2 | 3 | 4 | 5 | | 1 | 2 | 3 | 4 | 5 |
| 1 | 426 | 406 | 418 | 431 | 432 | 6 | 427 | 417 | 408 | 418 | 422 |
| 2 | 421 | 422 | 415 | 412 | 411 | 7 | 422 | 417 | 426 | 435 | 426 |
| 3 | 425 | 420 | 406 | 409 | 414 | 8 | 419 | 417 | 412 | 415 | 417 |
| 4 | 424 | 419 | 402 | 400 | 417 | 9 | 417 | 432 | 417 | 416 | 422 |
| 5 | 421 | 408 | 423 | 410 | 421 | 10 | 420 | 422 | 421 | 415 | 422 |

**24.** The Early Morning Delivery Service guarantees delivery of small packages by 10:30 A.M. Of course, some of the packages are not delivered by 10:30 A.M. For a sample of 200 packages delivered each of the last 15 working days, the following number of packages were delivered after the deadline: 9, 14, 2, 13, 9, 5, 9, 3, 4, 3, 4, 3, 3, 8, and 4.

    **a.** Determine the mean proportion of packages delivered after 10:30 A.M.

    **b.** Determine the control limits for the proportion of packages delivered after 10:30 A.M. Were any of the sampled days out of control?

    **c.** If 10 packages out of 200 in the sample were delivered after 10:30 A.M. today, is this sample within the control limits?

25. An automatic machine produces 5.0-millimeter bolts at a high rate of speed. A quality control program has been started to control the number of defectives. The quality control inspector selects 50 bolts at random and determines how many are defective. The number of defectives in the first 10 samples is 3, 5, 0, 4, 1, 2, 6, 5, 7, and 7.
    a. Design a percent defective chart. Insert the mean percent defective, *UCL,* and *LCL.*
    b. Plot the percent defective for the first 10 samples on the chart.
    c. Interpret the chart.

26. Steele Breakfast Foods, Inc. produces a popular brand of raisin bran cereal. The package indicates it contains 25.0 ounces of cereal. To ensure the product quality, the Steele Inspection Department makes hourly checks on the production process. As a part of the hourly check, 4 boxes are selected and their contents weighed. The results are reported below.

| Sample | Weights | | | |
|---|---|---|---|---|
| 1 | 26.1 | 24.4 | 25.6 | 25.2 |
| 2 | 25.2 | 25.9 | 25.1 | 24.8 |
| 3 | 25.6 | 24.5 | 25.7 | 25.1 |
| 4 | 25.5 | 26.8 | 25.1 | 25.0 |
| 5 | 25.2 | 25.2 | 26.3 | 25.7 |
| 6 | 26.6 | 24.1 | 25.5 | 24.0 |
| 7 | 27.6 | 26.0 | 24.9 | 25.3 |
| 8 | 24.5 | 23.1 | 23.9 | 24.7 |
| 9 | 24.1 | 25.0 | 23.5 | 24.9 |
| 10 | 25.8 | 25.7 | 24.3 | 27.3 |
| 11 | 22.5 | 23.0 | 23.7 | 24.0 |
| 12 | 24.5 | 24.8 | 23.2 | 24.2 |
| 13 | 24.4 | 24.5 | 25.9 | 25.5 |
| 14 | 23.1 | 23.3 | 24.4 | 24.7 |
| 15 | 24.6 | 25.1 | 24.0 | 25.3 |
| 16 | 24.4 | 24.4 | 22.8 | 23.4 |
| 17 | 25.1 | 24.1 | 23.9 | 26.2 |
| 18 | 24.5 | 24.5 | 26.0 | 26.2 |
| 19 | 25.3 | 27.5 | 24.3 | 25.5 |
| 20 | 24.6 | 25.3 | 25.5 | 24.3 |
| 21 | 24.9 | 24.4 | 25.4 | 24.8 |
| 22 | 25.7 | 24.6 | 26.8 | 26.9 |
| 23 | 24.8 | 24.3 | 25.0 | 27.2 |
| 24 | 25.4 | 25.9 | 26.6 | 24.8 |
| 25 | 26.2 | 23.5 | 23.7 | 25.0 |

Develop an appropriate control chart. What are the limits? Is the process out of control at any time?

27. An investor believes there is a 50-50 chance that a stock will increase or decrease on a particular day. To investigate this idea, for 30 consecutive trading days the investor selects a random sample of 50 stocks and counts the number that increase. The number of stocks in the sample that increased is reported below.

| | | | | | | | | | |
|---|---|---|---|---|---|---|---|---|---|
| 14 | 12 | 13 | 17 | 10 | 18 | 10 | 13 | 13 | 14 |
| 13 | 10 | 12 | 11 | 9 | 13 | 14 | 11 | 12 | 11 |
| 15 | 13 | 10 | 16 | 10 | 11 | 12 | 15 | 13 | 10 |

Develop a percent defective chart and write a brief report summarizing your findings. Based on these sample results, is it reasonable that the odds are 50-50 that a stock will increase? What percent of the stocks would need to increase in a day for the process to be "out of control"?

28. Lahey Motors specializes in selling cars to buyers with a poor credit history. Listed below is the number of cars that were repossessed from Lahey customers because they did not meet the payment obligations over the last 36 months.

| | | | | | | | | | |
|---|---|---|---|---|---|---|---|---|---|
| 6 | 5 | 8 | 20 | 11 | 10 | 9 | 3 | 9 | 9 |
| 15 | 12 | 4 | 11 | 9 | 9 | 6 | 18 | 6 | 8 |
| 9 | 7 | 13 | 7 | 11 | 8 | 11 | 13 | 6 | 14 |
| 13 | 5 | 5 | 8 | 10 | 11 | | | | |

    Develop a c-bar chart for the number repossessed. Were there any months when the number was out of control? Write a brief report summarizing your findings.

29. A process engineer is considering two sampling plans. In the first a sample of 10 will be selected and the lot accepted if 3 or fewer are found defective. In the second the sample size is 20 and the acceptance number is 5. Develop an OC curve for each. Compare the probability of acceptance for lots that are 5, 10, 20, and 30 percent defective. Which of the plans would you recommend if you were the supplier?

30. The Inter State Moving and Storage Company is setting up a control chart to monitor the proportion of residential moves that result in written complaints due to late delivery, lost items, or damaged items. A sample of 50 moves is selected for each of the last 12 months. The number of written complaints in each sample is 8, 7, 4, 8, 2, 7, 11, 6, 7, 6, 8, and 12.
    a. Design a percent defective chart. Insert the mean percent defective, *UCL,* and *LCL.*
    b. Plot the proportion of written complaints in the last 12 months.
    c. Interpret the chart. Does it appear that the number of complaints is out of control for any of the months?

31. Eric's Cookie House sells chocolate chip cookies in shopping malls. Of concern is the number of chocolate chips in each cookie. Eric, the owner and president, would like to establish a control chart for the number of chocolate chips per cookie. He selects a sample of 15 cookies from today's production and counts the number of chocolate chips in each. The results are as follows: 6, 8, 20, 12, 20, 19, 11, 23, 12, 14, 15, 16, 12, 13, and 12.
    a. Determine the centerline and the control limits.
    b. Develop a control chart and plot the number of chocolate chips per cookie.
    c. Interpret the chart. Does it appear that the number of chocolate chips is out of control in any of the cookies sampled?

32. The number of "near misses" recorded for the last 20 months at the Lima International Airport is 3, 2, 3, 2, 2, 3, 5, 1, 2, 2, 4, 4, 2, 6, 3, 5, 2, 5, 1, and 3. Develop an appropriate control chart. Determine the mean number of misses per month and the limits on the number of misses per month. Are there any months where the number of near misses is out of control?

33. The following number of robberies were reported during the last 10 days to the Robbery Division of the Metro City Police: 10, 8, 8, 7, 8, 5, 8, 5, 4, and 7. Develop an appropriate control chart. Determine the mean number of robberies reported per day and determine the control limits. Are there any days when the number of robberies reported is out of control?

34. Seiko purchases watch stems for their watches in lots of 10,000. Seiko's sampling plan calls for checking 20 stems, and if 3 or fewer stems are defective, the lot is accepted.
    a. Based on their sampling plan, what is the probability that a lot of 40 percent defective will be accepted?
    b. Design an OC curve for incoming lots that have zero, 10 percent, 20 percent, 30 percent, and 40 percent defective stems.

35. Automatic Screen Door Manufacturing Company purchases door latches from a number of vendors. The purchasing department is responsible for inspecting the incoming latches. Automatic purchases 10,000 door latches per month and inspects 20 latches selected at random. Develop an OC curve for the sampling plan if three latches can be defective and the incoming lot is still accepted.

36. At the beginning of each football season Team Sports, the local sporting goods store, purchases 5,000 footballs. A sample of 25 balls is selected, and they are inflated, tested, and then deflated. If more than two balls are found defective, the lot of 5,000 is returned to the manufacturer. Develop an OC curve for this sampling plan.
    a. What are the probabilities of accepting lots that are 10 percent, 20 percent, and 30 percent defective?

**b.** Estimate the probability of accepting a lot that is 15 percent defective.

**c.** John Brennen, owner of Team Sports, would like the probability of accepting a lot that is 5 percent defective to be more than 90 percent. Does this appear to be the case with this sampling plan?

# Software Commands

**1.** The MINITAB commands for the Pareto chart on page 592 are:

  **a.** Enter the reasons for water usage in column C1 and the gallons used in C2. Give the columns appropriate names.

  **b.** Click on **Stat, Quality Tools, Pareto Chart,** and then hit **Enter.**

  **c.** Select **Chart defects table,** indicate the location of the labels and frequencies, click on **Options** and type a chart title, and click on **OK.**

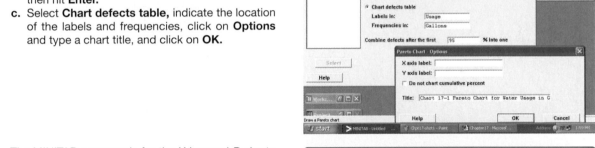

**2.** The MINITAB commands for the *X*-bar and *R* charts on page 599 are:

  **a.** Enter the information in Table 17–1 or from the CD. The file name is tbl17-1.

  **b.** Click on **Stat, Control charts, Variables Charts for Subgroups, Xbar-R,** and hit **Enter.**

  **c.** Click on the **Single column**. The **Subgroup size** is *5*. Click on **Labels,** enter the name of the chart, and then click **OK** twice.

**3.** The MINITAB commands for the percent defective chart on page 604 are:

  **a.** Enter the data on the number of mismatches from page 603.

  **b.** Click on **Stat, Control charts, Attribute Charts, P,** and hit **Enter.**

  **c.** Select the **Variable** indicating the number of mismatches, **Subgroup Size** is 1500, and enter *1500.* In the lower right click on **Labels,** type the title in the space provided, and click **OK** twice.

**4.** The MINITAB commands for the *c*-bar chart on page 605 are:

   **a.** Enter the data on the number of misspelled words from page 605.

   **b.** Click on **Stat, Control charts, Attribute, C,** and hit **Enter.**

   **c.** Select the **Variable** indicating the number of misspelled words, then click on **Labels** and type the title in the space provided, and click **OK** twice.

# Chapter 17  Answers to Self-Review

**17–1**

| Count | 84 | 71 | 63 | 45 | 35 | 2 |
| Percent | 28 | 24 | 21 | 15 | 12 | 0 |
| Cum. % | 28 | 52 | 73 | 88 | 100 | 100 |

Seventy-three percent of the complaints involve poor food, poor care, or dirty conditions. These are the factors the administrator should address.

**17–2 a.**

| Sample Times | | | | | | |
|---|---|---|---|---|---|---|
| 1 | 2 | 3 | 4 | Total | Average | Range |
| 1 | 4 | 5 | 2 | 12 | 3 | 4 |
| 2 | 3 | 2 | 1 | 8 | 2 | 2 |
| 1 | 7 | 3 | 5 | 16 | 4 | 6 |
| | | | | | 9 | 12 |

$$\bar{\bar{X}} = \frac{9}{3} = 3 \qquad \bar{R} = \frac{12}{3} = 4$$

$$UCL \text{ and } LCL = \bar{\bar{X}} \pm A_2\bar{R}$$

$$= 3 \pm 0.729(4)$$

$$UCL = 5.916 \qquad LCL = 0.084$$

$$LCL = D_3\bar{R} = 0(4) = 0$$

$$UCL = D_4\bar{R} = 2.282(4) = 9.128$$

**b.** Yes. Both the mean chart and the range chart indicate that the process is in control.

**17–3** $\bar{c} = \dfrac{25}{12} = 2.083$

$$UCL = 2.083 + 3\sqrt{2.083} = 6.413$$

$$LCL = 2.083 - 3\sqrt{2.083} = -2.247$$

Because *LCL* is a negative value, we set *LCL* = 0. The shift with 7 defects is out of control.

**17–4** $P(X \le 2 \mid \pi = .30 \text{ and } n = 20) = .036$

# Index Numbers

Johnson and Johnson's common stock is listed on the New York Stock Exchange using the symbol JNJ. This stock information is reported in their annual reports. Use the stock data to compute a simple index for domestic sales. (See Goal 1 and Exercise 17.)

# Introduction

In this chapter we will examine a useful descriptive tool called an **index.** No doubt you are familiar with indexes such as the **Consumer Price Index,** which is released monthly by the U.S. Department of Labor. There are many other indexes, such as the **Dow Jones Industrial Average (DJIA), Nasdaq, NIKKEI 225,** and **Standard & Poor's 500 Stock Average.** Indexes are published on a regular basis by the federal government, by business publications such as *Business Week* and *Forbes,* in most daily newspapers, and on the Internet.

Of what importance is an index? Why is the Consumer Price Index so important and so widely reported? As the name implies, it measures the change in the price of a large group of items consumers purchase. The Federal Reserve Board, consumer groups, unions, management, senior citizens organizations, and others in business and economics are very concerned about changes in prices. These groups closely monitor the Consumer Price Index as well as the **Producer Price Index,** which measures price fluctuations at all stages of production. To combat sharp price increases, the Federal Reserve often raises the interest rate to "cool down" the economy. Likewise, the Dow Jones Industrial Average, which is published daily, describes the overall change in common stock prices of 30 large companies during the day.

A few stock market indexes appear daily in the financial section of most newspapers. They are updated at least every 15 minutes on many websites, such as the business section of *USA Today* (http://www.usatoday.com/money/front.htm). Shown below are the Dow Jones Industrial Average, Nasdaq, and S&P 500 from the *USA Today* website.

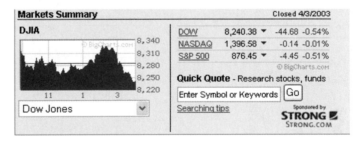

# Simple Index Numbers

What is an index number?

> **INDEX NUMBER** A number that expresses the relative change in price, quantity, or value compared to a base period.

If the index number is used to measure the relative change in just one variable, such as hourly wages in manufacturing, we refer to this as a simple index. It is the ratio of two variables and that ratio converted to a percentage. The following four examples will serve to illustrate the use of index numbers. As noted in the definition, the main use of an index number in business is to show the percent change in one or more items from one time period to another.

**EXAMPLE**

According to the Bureau of Labor Statistics, in January 1987 the average hourly earnings of production workers was $8.90. In January 2003 it was $15.07. What is the index of hourly earnings of production workers for January 2003 based on January 1987?

**SOLUTION**

It is 169.3, found by:

$$P = \frac{\text{Average hourly earnings of production workers in January 2003}}{\text{Average hourly earnings of production workers in January 1987}} (100)$$

$$= \frac{\$15.07}{\$8.90} (100) = 169.3$$

Thus, the hourly earnings in January 2003 compared to January 1987 were 169.3 percent. This means there was a 69.3 percent increase in hourly earnings during the period, found by $169.3 - 100.0 = 69.3$.

You can check the latest information on wages, the Consumer Price Indexes, and other business related values at the Bureau of Labor Statistics (BLS) website: http://www.bls.gov and click on Wages. The following chart shows some statistics from the BLS.

**Latest Numbers**

**CPI:**
-0.3% in Apr 2003

**Unemployment Rate:**
6.0% in Apr 2003

**Payroll Employment:**
-48,000(p) in Apr 2003

**Average Hourly Earnings:**
+$0.02(p) in Apr 2003

**PPI:**
-1.9%(p) in Apr 2003

**ECI:**
+1.3% in 1st Qtr of 2003

**Productivity:**
+1.9% in 1st Qtr of 2003

**U.S. Import Price Index:**
-2.7% in Apr 2003

-------
» **p**- preliminary
» **Subscribe to BLS News**
» **Publication Schedule**

**EXAMPLE**

According to ACCRA, a nonprofit research organization promoting research for economic and community development (http://www.accra.org), the mean daily cost for a private hospital room in the United States is $643.80. The mean price for a private hospital room in Las Vegas is $713.17. What is the index for Las Vegas based on the national average?

**SOLUTION**

The index is 110.8, found by:

$$P = \frac{\text{Las Vegas average cost}}{\text{U.S. average cost}} (100) = \frac{\$713.17}{\$643.80} (100) = 110.8$$

This indicates that the average cost of a private hospital room in Las Vegas is 110.8 percent of the United States average. To put it another way, the average private hospital room in Las Vegas costs 10.8 percent more than the national average $(110.8 - 100.0 = 10.8)$.

**EXAMPLE**

An index can also compare one item with another. The population of the Canadian province of British Columbia in 2002 was 4,141,272 and for Ontario it was 12,068,301. What is the population index of British Columbia compared to Ontario?

**SOLUTION**

The index of population for British Columbia is 34.3, found by:

$$P = \frac{\text{Population of British Columbia}}{\text{Population of Ontario}} (100) = \frac{4,141,272}{12,068,301} (100) = 34.3$$

This indicates that the population of British Columbia is 34.3 percent (about one-third) of the population of Ontario, or the population of British Columbia is 65.7 percent less than the population of Ontario $(100 - 34.3 = 65.7)$.

**EXAMPLE**

The following Excel output shows the number of passengers (in millions) for the five largest airports in the United States in 2002. What is the index for Atlanta, Chicago, Los Angeles, and Dallas/Ft. Worth compared to Denver?

**SOLUTION**

To find the four indexes, we divide the passengers for Atlanta, Chicago, Los Angeles, and Dallas/Ft. Worth by the number in Denver. We conclude that Atlanta had 110 percent more passengers than Denver, Chicago 85 percent more, Los Angeles 69 percent more, and Dallas/Ft. Worth 52.9 percent more.

| Airport | Passengers | Index | Found by |
|---|---|---|---|
| Atlanta, Hartsfield (ATL) | 75.8 | 210.0 | (75.8/36.1)*100 |
| Chicago, O'Hare (ORD) | 66.8 | 185.0 | (66.8/36.1)*100 |
| Los Angeles (LAX) | 61.0 | 169.0 | (61.0/36.1)*100 |
| Dallas/Ft. Worth (DFW) | 55.2 | 152.9 | (55.2/36.1)*100 |
| Denver (DEN) | 36.1 | 100.0 | (36.1/36.1)*100 |

Note from the previous discussion that:

1. The index of average hourly earnings of production workers (169.3) and the index of daily hospital costs for a private room (110.8) are actually percentages because they are based on the number 100. However, the percent symbol is usually omitted.
2. Each index has a **base period.** In the example regarding the average hourly earnings of production workers, we used January 1987 as the base period. The base period for the Consumer Price Index is 1993–95. The Parity ratio, which is the ratio of the prices received by farmers to the prices paid by farmers, still has 1910–14 as the base period. See http://agriculture.house.gov/glossary/parity_ratio.htm.
3. Most business and economic indexes are computed to the nearest whole number, such as 214 or 96, or to the nearest tenth of a percent, such as 83.4 or 118.7.

# Why Convert Data to Indexes?

Indexes allow us to express a change in price, quantity, or value as a percent.

Compiling index numbers is not a recent innovation. An Italian, G. R. Carli, is credited with originating index numbers in 1764. They were incorporated in a report he made regarding price fluctuations in Europe from 1500 to 1750. No systematic approach to collecting and reporting data in index form was evident in the United States until about 1900. The cost-of-living index (now called the Consumer Price Index) was introduced in 1913, and a long list of indexes has been compiled since then.

Why convert data to indexes? An index is a convenient way to express a change in a diverse group of items. The Consumer Price Index (CPI), for example, encompasses about 400 items—including golf balls, lawn mowers, hamburgers, funeral services, and dentists' fees. Prices are expressed in dollars per pound, box, yard, and many other different units. Only by converting the prices of these many diverse goods and services to one index number can the federal government and others concerned with inflation keep informed of the overall movement of consumer prices.

Converting data to indexes also makes it easier to assess the trend in a series composed of exceptionally large numbers. For example, the total retail sales for the month of January 2003 were $269,859,000. For January 2002, the total retail sales were $266,402,000. This increase of $3,457,000 appears significant. Yet if the January 2003 retails are expressed as an index based on January 2002 retail sales the increase is only 1.3 percent.

$$\frac{\text{January 2003 Retail Sales}}{\text{January 2002 Retail Sales}} (100) = \frac{\$269,859,000}{\$266,402,000} (100) = 101.3$$

# Construction of Index Numbers

We already discussed the construction of a simple price index. The price in a selected year (such as 2004) is divided by the price in the base year. The base-period price is designated as $p_0$, and a price other than the base period is often referred to as the *given period* or *selected period and* designated $p_t$. To calculate the simple price index $P$ using 100 as the base value for any given period use the formula:

| SIMPLE INDEX | $P = \dfrac{p_t}{p_0} \times 100$ | [18–1] |
|---|---|---|

Suppose that the price of a fall weekend package (including lodging and all means) at the Tryon Mountain Lodge in Western North Carolina in 2000 was $450. The price rose to $795 in 2004. What is the price index for 2004 using 2000 as the base period and 100 as the base value? It is 176.7, found by:

$$P = \frac{p_t}{p_0} (100) = \frac{\$795}{\$450} (100) = 176.7$$

Interpreting this result, the price of the fall weekend package increased 76.7 percent from 2000 to 2004.

The base period need not be a single year. Note in Table 18–1 that if we use 1990–91 = 100, the base price for the stapler would be $21 [found by determining the mean price of 1990 and 1991, ($20 + $22)/2 = $21]. The prices $20, $22, and $23 are averaged if 1990–92 had been selected as the base. The mean price would be $21.67. The indexes constructed using the three different base periods are presented in Table 18–1. (Note that when 1990–92 = 100, the index numbers for 1990, 1991, and 1992 average 100.0, as we would expect.) Logically, the index numbers for 2004 using the three different bases are not the same.

**TABLE 18–1** Prices of a Benson Automatic Stapler, Model 3, Converted to Indexes Using Three Different Base Periods

| Year | Price of Stapler | Price Index (1990 = 100) | Price Index (1990–91 = 100) | Price Index (1990–92 = 100) |
|------|------|------|------|------|
| 1985 | $18 | 90.0 | $\dfrac{18}{21} \times 100 = 85.7$ | $\dfrac{18}{21.67} \times 100 = 83.1$ |
| 1990 | 20 | 100.0 | $\dfrac{20}{21} \times 100 = 95.2$ | $\dfrac{20}{21.67} \times 100 = 92.3$ |
| 1991 | 22 | 110.0 | $\dfrac{22}{21} \times 100 = 104.8$ | $\dfrac{22}{21.67} \times 100 = 101.5$ |
| 1992 | 23 | 115.0 | $\dfrac{23}{21} \times 100 = 109.5$ | $\dfrac{23}{21.67} \times 100 = 106.1$ |
| 2004 | 38 | 190.0 | $\dfrac{38}{21} \times 100 = 181.0$ | $\dfrac{38}{21.67} \times 100 = 175.4$ |

**Self-Review 18–1**

1. Incomes before tax for the second quarter of 2002 for a few selected companies are:

| Company | Income ($ millions) |
|---------|---------|
| Schering-Plough | 405.0 |
| Boeing | 375.0 |
| Exxon-Mobil | 4,498.0 |
| Johnson and Johnson | 2,393.0 |
| PepsiCo, Inc. | 969.0 |

Express the income of Schering-Plough, Boeing, Exxon-Mobil, and Johnson and Johnson as an index, using PepsiCo, Inc., as the base (denominator) and 100 as the base value. Interpret.

2. The average hourly earnings of production workers for January of the selected years are given below.

| Year | Average Hourly Earnings |
|------|---------|
| 1995 | 11.27 |
| 1997 | 12.06 |
| 2000 | 13.50 |
| 2003 | 14.99 |

(a) Using 1995 as the base period and 100 as the base value, determine the indexes for the other years. Interpret the index.

(b) Use the average of 1995 and 1997 as the base and determine indexes for 2000 and 2003. Interpret the index.

# Exercises

1. PNC Bank, Inc., which has its headquarters in Pittsburgh, Pennsylvania, reported $17,446 (million) in commercial loans in 1995, $19,989 in 1997, $21,468 in 1999, $21,685 in 2000, and $15,922 in 2002. Using 1995 as the base, develop a simple index for the change in the amount of commercial loans for the years 1997, 1999, 2000, and 2002, based on 1995.
2. The table below reports the split-adjusted stock prices for Home Depot for recent years. Develop an index, with 1995 as the base, for the change in stock price over the period.

| Year | Year-end Stock Price |
|------|------|
| 1995 | $10.03 |
| 1996 | 11.00 |
| 1997 | 20.17 |
| 1998 | 40.33 |
| 1999 | 55.63 |
| 2002 | 20.90 |

3. Listed below are the net sales for Blair Corporation, a mail-order retailer located in Warren, Pennsylvania, for the years 1995 to 2002. Their website is www.blair.com. Use the mean sales for the earliest three years to determine a base and then find the index for 2001 and 2002. By how much have net sales increased from the base period?

| Year | Sales (millions) |
|------|------|
| 1995 | $560.9 |
| 1996 | 544.1 |
| 1997 | 486.6 |
| 1998 | 506.8 |
| 1999 | 522.2 |
| 2000 | 574.6 |
| 2001 | 580.7 |
| 2002 | 568.5 |

4. In January 1994 the price for a whole fresh chicken was $0.899 per pound. In March 2003 the price for the same chicken was $1.053. Use the January 1994 price as the base period and 100 as the base value to develop a simple index. By what percent has the cost of chicken increased?

# Unweighted Indexes

In many situations we wish to combine several items and develop an index to compare the cost of this aggregation of items in two different time periods. For example, we might be interested in an index for items that relate to the expense of operating and maintaining an automobile. The items in the index might include tires, oil changes, and gasoline prices. Or we might be interested in a college student index. This index might include the cost of books, tuition, housing, meals, and entertainment. There are several ways we can combine the items to determine the index.

## Simple Average of the Price Indexes

Table 18–2 reports the prices for several food items for the years 1995 and 2003. We would like to develop an index for this group of food items for 2003, using 1995 as the base. This is written in the abbreviated code 1995 = 100.

**TABLE 18–2** Computation of Index for Food Price 2003, 1995 = 100

| Item | 1995 Price | 2003 Price | Simple Index |
|---|---|---|---|
| Bread, white, cost per pound | $ 0.77 | $ 0.89 | 115.6 |
| Eggs, dozen | 1.85 | 1.84 | 99.5 |
| Milk, gallon, white | 0.88 | 1.01 | 114.8 |
| Apples, Red Delicious, 1 pound | 1.46 | 1.56 | 106.8 |
| Orange Juice, 12 oz concentrate | 1.58 | 1.70 | 107.6 |
| Coffee, 100% ground roast, 1 pound | 4.40 | 4.62 | 105.0 |
| Total | $10.94 | $11.62 | |

We could begin by computing a **simple average of the price indexes** for each item, using 1995 as the base year and 2003 as the given year. The simple index for bread is 115.6, found by using formula (18–1).

$$P = \frac{p_t}{p_0}(100) = \frac{\$0.89}{\$0.77}(100) = 115.6$$

We compute the simple index for the other items in Table 18–2 similarly. The largest price increase was for bread, 15.6 percent, and milk was a close second with 14.8 percent. The price of eggs dropped by half a percent in the period, found by 100.0 − 99.5 = 0.5. Then it would be natural to average the simple indexes. The formula is:

| SIMPLE AVERAGE OF THE PRICE RELATIVES | $P = \dfrac{\Sigma P_i}{n}$ | [18–2] |
|---|---|---|

where $P_i$ refers to the simple index for each of the items and $n$ the number of items. In our example the index is 108.2, found by:

$$P = \frac{\Sigma P_i}{n} = \frac{115.6 + \cdots + 105.0}{6} = \frac{649.3}{6} = 108.2$$

This indicates that the mean of the group of indexes increased 8.2 percent from 1995 to 2003.

A positive feature of the simple average of price indexes is that we would obtain the same value for the index regardless of the units of measure. In the above index, if apples were priced in tons, instead of pounds, the impact of apples on the combined index would not change. That is, the commodity "apples" represents one of six items in the index, so the impact of the item is not related to the units. A negative feature of this index is that it fails to consider the relative importance of the items included in the index. For example, milk and eggs receive the same weight, even though a typical family might spend far more over the year on milk than on eggs.

## Simple Aggregate Index

A second possibility is to sum the prices (rather than the indexes) for the two periods and then determine the index based on the totals. The formula is:

| SIMPLE AGGREGATE INDEX | $P = \dfrac{\Sigma p_t}{\Sigma p_0} \times 100$ | [18–3] |
|---|---|---|

This is called a **simple aggregate index.** The index for the above food items is found by summing the prices in 1995 and 2003. The sum of the prices for the base period is $10.94 and for the given period it is $11.62. The simple aggregate index is 106.2. This means that the aggregate group of prices had increased 6.2 percent in the eight-year period.

$$P = \frac{\Sigma p_t}{\Sigma p_0}(100) = \frac{\$11.62}{\$10.94}(100) = 106.2$$

Because the value of a simple aggregate index can be influenced by the units of measurement, it is not used frequently. In our example the value of the index would differ significantly if we were to report the price of apples in tons rather than pounds. Also, note the effect of coffee on the total index. For both the current year and the base year, the value of coffee is about 40 percent of the total index, so a change in the price of coffee will drive the index much more than any other item. So we need a way to appropriately "weight" the items according to their relative importance.

# Weighted Indexes

Two methods of computing a **weighted price index** are the **Laspeyres** method and the **Paasche** method. They differ only in the period used for weighting. The Laspeyres method uses *base-period weights*; that is, the original prices and quantities of the items bought are used to find the percent change over a period of time in either price or quantity consumed, depending on the problem. The Paasche method uses *current-year weights* for the denominator of the weighted index.

## Laspeyres' Price Index

Etienne Laspeyres developed a method in the latter part of the 18th century to determine a weighted index using base-period weights. Applying his method, a weighted price index is computed by:

| LASPEYRES' PRICE INDEX | $P = \dfrac{\Sigma p_t q_0}{\Sigma p_0 q_0} \times 100$ | [18–4] |
|---|---|---|

where:

$P$ is the price index.
$p_t$ is the current price.
$p_0$ is the price in the base period.
$q_0$ is the quantity used in the base period.

**EXAMPLE**

The prices for the six food items from Table 18–2 are repeated below in Table 18–3. Also included is the number of units of each consumed by a typical family in 1995 and 2003.

**TABLE 18–3** Computation of Laspeyres' and Paasche's Indexes of Food Price, 1995 = 100

| Item | 1995 Price | 1995 Quantity | 2003 Price | 2003 Quantity |
|---|---|---|---|---|
| Bread, white, cost per pound | $0.77 | 50 | $0.89 | 55 |
| Eggs, dozen | 1.85 | 26 | 1.84 | 20 |
| Milk, gallon, white | 0.88 | 102 | 1.01 | 130 |
| Apples, Red Delicious, 1 pound | 1.46 | 30 | 1.56 | 40 |
| Orange Juice, 12 oz concentrate | 1.58 | 40 | 1.70 | 41 |
| Coffee, 100% ground roast, 1 pound | 4.40 | 12 | 4.62 | 12 |

Determine a weighted price index using the Laspeyres method. Interpret the result.

SOLUTION

First we determine the total amount spent for the six items in the base period, 1995. To find this value we multiply the base period price for bread ($0.77) by the base period quantity of 50. The result is $38.50. This indicates that a total of $38.50 was spent in the base period on bread. We continue that for all items and total the results. The base period total is $336.16. The current period total is computed in a similar fashion. For the first item, bread, we multiply the quantity in 1995 by the price of bread in 2003, that is, $0.89(50). The result is $44.50. We make the same calculation for each item and total the result. The total is $365.60. Because of the repetitive nature of these calculations, a spreadsheet is effective for carrying out the calculations. Following is a copy of the Excel output.

The weighted price index for 2003 is 108.8, found by

$$P = \frac{\Sigma p_t q_0}{\Sigma p_0 q_0}(100) = \frac{\$365.60}{\$336.16}(100) = 108.8$$

Based on this analysis we conclude that the price of this group of items has increased 8.8 percent in the eight-year period. The advantage of this method over the simple aggregate index is that the weight of each of the items is considered. In the simple aggregate index coffee had about 40 percent of the weight in determining the index. In the Laspeyres index the item with the most weight is milk, because the product of the price and the units sold is the largest.

## Paasche's Price Index

The major disadvantage of the Laspeyres index is it assumes that the base-period quantities are still realistic in the given period. That is, the quantities used for the six items are about the same in 1995 as 2003. In this case notice that the quantity of eggs purchased declined by 23 percent, the quantity of milk increased by nearly 28 percent, and the number of apples increased by 33 percent.

The Paasche index is an alternative. The procedure is similar, but instead of using base period weights, we use current period weights. We use the sum of the products of the 1995 prices and the 2003 quantities. This has the advantage of using the more recent quantities. If there has been a change in the quantities consumed since the base period, such a change is reflected in the Paasche index.

| PAASCHE'S PRICE INDEX | $P = \dfrac{\Sigma p_t q_t}{\Sigma p_0 q_t} \times 100$ | [18–5] |
|---|---|---|

**EXAMPLE**

Use the information from Table 18–3 to determine the Paasche index. Discuss which of the indexes should be used.

**SOLUTION**

Again, because of the repetitive nature of the calculations, Excel is used to perform the calculations. The results are shown in the following output.

| Item | Price-95 | Quantity-03 | Price*Qty-95 | Price-03 | Quantity-03 | Price-03*Qty-95 |
|---|---|---|---|---|---|---|
| Bread | $ 0.77 | 55 | $ 42.35 | $ 0.89 | 55 | $ 48.95 |
| Eggs | $ 1.85 | 20 | $ 37.00 | $ 1.84 | 20 | $ 36.80 |
| Milk | $ 0.88 | 130 | $ 114.40 | $ 1.01 | 130 | $ 131.30 |
| Apples | $ 1.46 | 40 | $ 58.40 | $ 1.56 | 40 | $ 62.40 |
| Orange | $ 1.58 | 41 | $ 64.78 | $ 1.70 | 41 | $ 69.70 |
| Coffee | $ 4.40 | 12 | $ 52.80 | $ 4.62 | 12 | $ 55.44 |
| | | | $ 369.73 | | | $ 404.59 |

The Paasche index is 109.4, found by

$$P = \frac{\Sigma p_t q_t}{\Sigma p_0 q_t}(100) = \frac{\$404.59}{\$369.73}(100) = 109.4$$

This result indicates that there has been an increase of 9.4 percent in the price of this market basket of goods between 1995 and 2003. That is, it costs 9.4 percent more to purchase these items in 2003 than it did in 1995. All things considered, because of the change in the quantities purchased between 1995 and 2003, the Paasche index is more reflective of the current situation. It should be noted that the Laspeyres index is more widely used. The Consumer Price Index, the most widely reported index, is an example of a Laspeyres index.

How do we decide which index to use? When is Laspeyres' most appropriate and when is Paasche's the better choice?

**Laspeyres'**

Advantages — Requires quantity data from only the base period. This allows a more meaningful comparison over time. The changes in the index can be attributed to changes in the price.

Disadvantages — Does not reflect changes in buying patterns over time. Also, it may overweight goods whose prices increase.

**Paasche's**

Advantages     Because it uses quantities from the current period, it reflects current buying habits.

Disadvantages  It requires quantity data for each year, which may be difficult to obtain. Because different quantities are used each year, it is impossible to attribute changes in the index to changes in price alone. It tends to overweight the goods whose prices have declined. It requires the prices to be recomputed each year.

# Fisher's Ideal Index

As noted above, Laspeyres' index tends to overweight goods whose prices have increased. Paasche's index, on the other hand, tends to overweight goods whose prices have gone down. In an attempt to offset these shortcomings, Irving Fisher, in his book *The Making of Index Numbers,* published in 1922, proposed an index called **Fisher's ideal index.** It is the geometric mean of the Laspeyres and Paasche indexes. We described the geometric mean in Chapter 3. It is determined by taking the *k*th root of the product of *k* positive numbers.

$$\text{Fisher's ideal index} = \sqrt{(\text{Laspeyres' index})(\text{Paasche's index})} \qquad \textbf{[18–6]}$$

Fisher's index seems to be theoretically ideal because it combines the best features of both Laspeyres' and Paasche's. That is, it balances the effects of the two indexes. However, it is rarely used in practice because it has the same basic set of problems as the Paasche index. It requires that a new set of quantities be determined for each year.

**EXAMPLE**

Determine Fisher's ideal index for the data in Table 18–3.

**SOLUTION**

Fisher's ideal index is 109.1.

$$\text{Fisher's ideal index} = \sqrt{(\text{Laspeyres' index})(\text{Paasche's index})}$$
$$= \sqrt{(108.8)(109.4)} = 109.1$$

**Self-Review 18–2**

An index of clothing prices for 2004 based on 2000 is to be constructed. The clothing items considered are shoes and dresses. The information for prices and quantities for both years is given below. Use 2000 as the base period and 100 as the base value.

| Item | 2000 Price | 2000 Quantity | 2004 Price | 2004 Quantity |
|---|---|---|---|---|
| Dress (each) | $75 | 500 | $85 | 520 |
| Shoes (pair) | 40 | 1,200 | 45 | 1,300 |

(a) Determine the simple average of the price indexes.
(b) Determine the aggregate price indexes for the two years.
(c) Determine Laspeyres' price index.
(d) Determine the Paasche price index.
(e) Determine Fisher's ideal index.

# Exercises

For exercises 5–8:

a. Determine the simple price indexes.
b. Determine the simple aggregate price indexes for the two years.
c. Determine Laspeyres' price index.
d. Determine the Paasche price index.
e. Determine Fisher's ideal index.

5. Below are the prices of toothpaste (9 oz), shampoo (7 oz), cough tablets (package of 100), and antiperspirant (2 oz) for August 2000 and August 2003. Also included are the quantity purchased. Use August 2000 as the base.

| | August 2000 | | August 2003 | |
| --- | --- | --- | --- | --- |
| Item | Price | Quantity | Price | Quantity |
| Toothpaste | $2.49 | 6 | $2.69 | 6 |
| Shampoo | 3.29 | 4 | 3.59 | 5 |
| Cough tablets | 1.59 | 2 | 1.79 | 3 |
| Antiperspirant | 1.79 | 3 | 2.29 | 4 |

6. Fruit prices and the amounts consumed for 2000 and 2003 are below. Use 2000 as the base.

| | 2000 | | 2003 | |
| --- | --- | --- | --- | --- |
| Fruit | Price | Quantity | Price | Quantity |
| Bananas (pound) | $0.23 | 100 | $0.35 | 120 |
| Grapefruit (each) | 0.29 | 50 | 0.27 | 55 |
| Apples (pound) | 0.35 | 85 | 0.35 | 85 |
| Strawberries (basket) | 1.02 | 8 | 1.40 | 10 |
| Oranges (bag) | 0.89 | 6 | 0.99 | 8 |

7. The prices and the numbers of various items produced by a small machine and stamping plant are reported below. Use 2000 as the base.

| | 2000 | | 2003 | |
| --- | --- | --- | --- | --- |
| Item | Price | Quantity | Price | Quantity |
| Washer | $0.07 | 17,000 | $0.10 | 20,000 |
| Cotter pin | 0.04 | 125,000 | 0.03 | 130,000 |
| Stove bolt | 0.15 | 40,000 | 0.15 | 42,000 |
| Hex nut | 0.08 | 62,000 | 0.10 | 65,000 |

8. Following are the quantities and prices for the years 2000 and 2003 for Kinzua Valley Geriatrics. Use 2000 as the base period.

| | 2000 | | 2003 | |
| --- | --- | --- | --- | --- |
| Item | Price | Quantity | Price | Quantity |
| Syringes (dozen) | $ 6.10 | 1,500 | $ 6.50 | 2,000 |
| Thermometers | 8.10 | 10 | 8.90 | 12 |
| Advil (bottle) | 4.00 | 250 | 4.40 | 250 |
| Patient record forms (box) | 6.00 | 1,000 | 6.50 | 900 |
| Computer paper (box) | 12.00 | 30 | 13.00 | 40 |

# Value Index

Value index measures percent change in value.

A **value index** measures changes in both the price and quantities involved. A value index, such as the index of department store sales, needs the original base-year prices, the original base-year quantities, the present-year prices, and the present-year quantities for its construction. Its formula is:

| VALUE INDEX | $V = \dfrac{\Sigma p_t q_t}{\Sigma p_0 q_0} \times 100$ | [18–7] |
|---|---|---|

**EXAMPLE**

The prices and quantities sold at the Waleska Department Store for various items of apparel for May 2000 and May 2003 are:

| Item | 2000 Price, $p_0$ | 2000 Quantity Sold (thousands), $q_0$ | 2003 Price, $p_t$ | 2003 Quantity Sold (thousands), $q_t$ |
|---|---|---|---|---|
| Ties (each) | $ 1 | 1,000 | $ 2 | 900 |
| Suits (each) | 30 | 100 | 40 | 120 |
| Shoes (pair) | 10 | 500 | 8 | 500 |

What is the index of value for May 2003 using May 2000 as the base period?

**SOLUTION**

Total sales in May 2003 were $10,600,000, and the comparable figure for 2000 is $9,000,000. (See Table 18–4.) Thus, the index of value for May 2003 using 2000 = 100 is 117.8. The value of apparel sales in 2003 was 117.8 percent of the 2000 sales. To put it another way, the value of apparel sales increased 17.8 percent from May 2000 to May 2003.

$$V = \frac{\Sigma p_t q_t}{\Sigma p_0 q_0}(100) = \frac{\$10,600,000}{\$9,000,000}(100) = 117.8$$

**TABLE 18–4** Construction of a Value Index for 2003 (2000 = 100)

| Item | 2000 Price, $p_0$ | 2000 Quantity Sold (thousands), $q_0$ | $p_0 q_0$ ($ thousands) | 2003 Price, $p_t$ | 2003 Quantity Sold (thousands), $q_t$ | $p_t q_t$ ($ thousands) |
|---|---|---|---|---|---|---|
| Ties (each) | $ 1 | 1,000 | $1,000 | $ 2 | 900 | $ 1,800 |
| Suits (each) | 30 | 100 | 3,000 | 40 | 120 | 4,800 |
| Shoes (pair) | 10 | 500 | 5,000 | 8 | 500 | 4,000 |
|  |  |  | $9,000 |  |  | $10,600 |

**Self-Review 18-3** The number of items produced by Houghton Products for 1996 and 2004 and the wholesale prices for the two periods are:

| Item Produced | Price 1996 | Price 2004 | Number Produced 1996 | Number Produced 2004 |
|---|---|---|---|---|
| Shear pins (box) | $ 3 | $4 | 10,000 | 9,000 |
| Cutting compound (pound) | 1 | 5 | 600 | 200 |
| Tie rods (each) | 10 | 8 | 3,000 | 5,000 |

(a) Find the value index of production for 2004 using 1996 as the base period.
(b) Interpret the index.

# Exercises

**9.** The prices and production of grains for August 1995 and August 2003 are:

| Grain | 1995 Price | 1995 Quantity Produced (millions of bushels) | 2003 Price | 2003 Quantity Produced (millions of bushels) |
|---|---|---|---|---|
| Oats | $1.52 | 200 | $1.87 | 214 |
| Wheat | 2.10 | 565 | 2.05 | 489 |
| Corn | 1.48 | 291 | 1.48 | 203 |
| Barley | 3.05 | 87 | 3.29 | 106 |

Using 1995 as the base period, find the value index of grains produced for August 2003.

**10.** The Johnson Wholesale Company manufactures a variety of products. The prices and quantities produced for April 1994 and April 2003 are:

| Product | 1994 Price | 2003 Price | 1994 Quantity Produced | 2003 Quantity Produced |
|---|---|---|---|---|
| Small motor (each) | $23.60 | $28.80 | 1,760 | 4,259 |
| Scrubbing compound (gallon) | 2.96 | 3.08 | 86,450 | 62,949 |
| Nails (pound) | 0.40 | 0.48 | 9,460 | 22,370 |

Using April 1994 as the base period, find the index of the value of goods produced for April 2003.

# Special-Purpose Indexes

Many important indexes are prepared and published by private organizations. J. D. Power & Associates surveys automobile purchasers to determine how satisfied customers are with their vehicle after one year of ownership. This special index is called the *Consumer Satisfaction Index.* Financial institutions, utility companies, and university research centers often prepare indexes on employment, factory hours and wages, and retail sales for the regions they serve. Many trade associations prepare indexes of price and quantity that are vital to their particular area of interest. How are these special indexes prepared? An example, simplified of course, will help to explain some of the details.

**EXAMPLE**

The Seattle Chamber of Commerce wants to develop a measure of general business activity for the northwest portion of the United States. The Director of Economic Development has been assigned to develop the index. It will be called the *General Business Activity Index of the Northwest.*

**SOLUTION**

After considerable thought and research, the director has concluded that four factors should be considered: the regional department store sales (which are reported in $ millions), the regional employment index (which has a 1995 base and is reported by the State of Washington), the freight car loadings (reported in millions), and exports for the Seattle Harbor (reported in thousands of tons). Recent information on these variables is reported in Table 18–5.

**TABLE 18–5** Data for the Computation of the General Business Activity Index of the Northwest

| Year | Department Store Sales | Index of Employment | Freight Car Loadings | Exports |
|------|------------------------|---------------------|----------------------|---------|
| 1995 | 20 | 100 | 50 | 500 |
| 2000 | 41 | 110 | 30 | 900 |
| 2004 | 44 | 125 | 18 | 700 |

After review and consultation the director assigned weights of 40 percent to department store sales, 30 percent to employment, 10 percent to freight car loadings, and 20 percent to exports.

To develop the General Business Activity Index of the Northwest for 2004 using 1995 = 100, each 2004 value is expressed as a percentage, with the base-period value as the denominator. For illustration, department store sales for 2004 are converted to a percentage by ($44/$20)(100) = 220. This means that department store sales have increased 120 percent in the period. This percentage is then adjusted by the appropriate weight. For the department store sales this is (220)(.40) = 88.0. The details of the calculations for the years 2000 and 2004 are shown below.

|  | 2000 | | 2004 | |
|--|------|--|------|--|
| Department store sales | ($41/$20)(100)(.40) = | 82.0 | ($44/$20)(100)(.40) = | 88.0 |
| Employment | (110/100)(100)(.30) = | 33.0 | (125/100)(100)(.30) = | 37.5 |
| Freight car loadings | (30/50)(100)(.10) = | 6.0 | (18/50)(100)(.10) = | 3.6 |
| Exports | (900/500)(100)(.20) = | 36.0 | (700/500)(100)(.20) = | 28.0 |
| Total | | 157.0 | | 157.1 |

The General Business Activity Index of the Northwest for 2000 is 157.0 and for 2004 it is 157.1. Interpreting, business activity has increased 57.0 percent from 1995 to 2000 and 57.1 percent from the base period of 1995 to 2004.

As we stated at the start of the section, there are many special-purpose indexes. Here are a few examples.

**The Consumer Price Index** The U.S. Bureau of Labor Statistics reports this index monthly. It describes the changes in prices from one period to another for a "market basket" of goods and services. We discuss its history in detail and present some applications in the next section. You can access this information by going to www.bls.gov, going to **Prices & Living Conditions,** selecting **Consumer Price Index—All Urban Consumers, Most Requested Statistics,** and clicking on *U.S. all items 1982–84 = 100.* You may elect to include different periods. Following is a recent summary report.

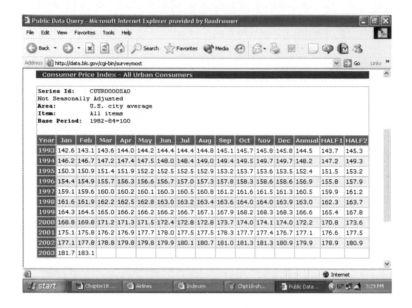

**The Producer Price Index**   Formerly called the Wholesale Price Index, it dates back to 1890 and is also published by the U.S. Bureau of Labor Statistics. It reflects the prices of over 3,400 commodities. Price data are collected from the sellers of the commodities, and it usually refers to the first large-volume transaction for each commodity. It is a Laspeyres-type index. To access this information, go to www.bls.gov, go to the Prices & Living Conditions section, select **Producer Price Index— Commodities, Most Requested Statistics,** and then select **Finished Goods.** You may select to include different periods. Below is a recent output.

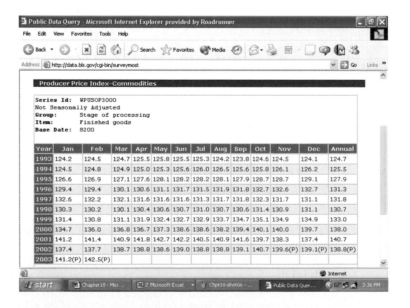

**Dow Jones Industrial Average (DJIA)**   This is an index of stock prices, but perhaps it would be better to say it is an "indicator" rather than an index. It is supposed to be the mean price of 30 specific industrial stocks. However, summing the 30 stocks and dividing by 30 does not calculate its value. This is because of stock splits, mergers, and stocks being added or dropped. When changes occur, adjustments are made in the denominator used with the average. Today the DJIA is more of a psychological indicator than a representation of the general price movement on the New York Stock Exchange. The lack of representativeness of the stocks on the DJIA is one of the reasons for the development of the **New York Stock Exchange Index.** This index was developed as an average price of *all* stocks on the New York Stock Exchange. You can find more information about the DJIA by going to the website: www.dowjones.com. You can find its current value as well as the 30 stocks that are now a part of its calculation. The chart below summarizes the DJIA for one day. It can be located at http://bigcharts.marketwatch.com.

**S&P 500 Index**  The full name of this index is the Standard and Poor's Composite Index of Stock Prices. It is an aggregate price index of 500 common stocks. It, too, is probably a better reflection of the market than is the DJIA. You can access information about the S&P 500 from the Dow Jones website. Below is a recent summary.

There are many other indexes that track business and economic behavior, such as the Nasdaq, the Russell 2000, and the Wilshire 5000.

---

**Self-Review 18–4**

As an intern in the Fulton County Economic Development Office, you have been asked to develop a special-purpose index for your county. Three economic series seem to hold promise as the basis of an index. These data are the price of cotton (per pound), the number of new automobiles sold in the county, and the rate of money turnover (published by the local bank). After discussing the project with your supervisor and the director, you decide that money turnover should have a weight of .60, the number of new automobiles sold a weight of .30, and the cotton price .10. The base period is 1995.

| Year | Cotton Price | Automobiles Sold | Money Turnover |
|------|-------------|------------------|----------------|
| 1995 | $0.20 | 1,000 | 80 |
| 2000 | 0.25 | 1,200 | 90 |
| 2004 | 0.50 | 900 | 75 |

(a) Construct the index for 2000 and 2004.
(b) Interpret the index for 2000 and 2004.

# Exercises

**11.** The index of leading economic indicators, compiled and published by the U.S. National Bureau of Economic Research, is composed of 12 time series, such as the average work hours of production in manufacturing, manufacturers' new orders, and money supply. This index and similar indexes are designed to move up or down before the economy begins to move the same way. Thus, an economist has statistical evidence to forecast future trends.

You want to construct a leading indicator for Erie County in upstate New York. The index is to be based on 2000 data. Because of the time and work involved, you decide to use only four time series. As an experiment, you select these four series: unemployment in the county, a composite index of county stock prices, County Price Index, and retail sales. Here are the figures for 2000 and 2003.

|  | 2000 | 2003 |
|---|------|------|
| Unemployment rate (percent) | 5.3 | 6.8 |
| Composite county stocks | 265.88 | 362.26 |
| County Price Index (1982 = 100) | 109.6 | 125.0 |
| Retail sales ($ millions) | 529,917.0 | 622,864.0 |

The weights you assigned are: unemployment rate 20 percent, stock prices 40 percent, County Price Index 25 percent, and retail sales 15 percent.
**a.** Using 2000 as the base period, construct a leading economic indicator for 2003.
**b.** Interpret your leading index.
**12.** You are employed by the state bureau of economic development. There is a demand for a leading economic index to review past economic activity and to forecast future economic trends in the state. You decide that several key factors should be included in the index: number of new businesses started during the year, number of business failures, state income tax receipts, college enrollment, and the state sales tax receipts. Here are the data for 2000 and 2003.

|  | 2000 | 2003 |
|---|---|---|
| New businesses | 1,088 | 1,162 |
| Business failures | 627 | 520 |
| State income tax receipts ($ millions) | 191.7 | 162.6 |
| College student enrollment | 242,119 | 290,841 |
| State sales tax ($ millions) | 41.6 | 39.9 |

**a.** Decide on the weights to be applied to each item in the leading index.
**b.** Compute the leading economic indicator for 2003.
**c.** Interpret the indexes.

# Consumer Price Index

There are two consumer price indexes.

**Statistics in Action**

Does it seem that prices only increase? The Consumer Price Index, computed and reported by the U.S. Department of Labor, is a relative measure of price changes. It shows interesting price information for categories of products and services. For example, did you know that the CPI shows a decrease from 2001 to 2002 in the relative prices of televisions, audio equipment, computers, and peripheral devices? In fact, using a base of 1982–1984 = 100, the CPI for computers and peripherals is 22.2. This means that relative prices for computers and peripherals have decreased about 78% from the prices during 1982–1984.

Frequent mention has been made of the Consumer Price Index (CPI) in the preceding pages. It measures the change in price of a fixed market basket of goods and services from one period to another. In January 1978 the Bureau of Labor Statistics began publishing CPIs for two groups of the population. One index, called the Consumer Price Index—All Urban Consumers covers about 87 percent of the total population. The other index is for urban wage earners and clerical workers and covers about 32 percent of the population.

In brief, the CPI serves several major functions. It allows consumers to determine the degree to which their purchasing power is being eroded by price increases. In that respect, it is a yardstick for revising wages, pensions, and other income payments to keep pace with changes in prices. Equally important, it is an economic indicator of the rate of inflation in the United States.

The index includes about 400 items, and about 250 agents collect price data monthly. Prices are collected from more than 21,000 retail establishments and 60,000 housing units in 91 urban areas across the country. The prices of baby cribs, bread, beer, cigars, gasoline, haircuts, mortgage interest rates, physicians' fees, taxes, and operating-room charges are just a few of the items included in what is often termed a typical "market basket" of goods and services that you purchase.

The CPI originated in 1913 and has been published regularly since 1921. The standard reference period (the base period) has been updated periodically. The current base period is 1982–84. The earlier base periods were: 1967, 1957–59, 1947–49, 1935–39, and 1925–29. Why is it necessary to change the base? Our expenditure patterns change dramatically, and these changes must be reflected in the index. The most recent revision includes consumer items, such as VCRs, home computers, and cell phones. Earlier versions of the CPI did not include these items. By changing the base, the CPI captures the most recent expenditure patterns. You may want to go to www.bls.gov, click on the **Consumer Price Index,** and read more about it.

The CPI is actually not just one index. There are Consumer Price Indexes for New York, Chicago, Seattle, and Atlanta, as well as a number of other large cities. There are also price indexes for food, apparel, medical care, and other items. A few of them are shown below, 1982–84 = 100, for September 2003.

| Item | CPI-U |
|---|---|
| All items | 185.2 |
| Food and beverage | 181.3 |
| Apparel and upkeep | 122.0 |
| Transportation | 159.4 |
| Medical care | 299.2 |
| Housing | 185.8 |

A perusal of this listing shows that a weighted index of all items has increased 85.2 percent since 1982–84; medical care has increased the most, 199.2 percent; and apparel and upkeep went up the least, 22.0 percent.

## Special Uses of the Consumer Price Index

In addition to measuring changes in the prices of goods and services, both consumer price indexes have a number of other applications. The CPI is used to determine real disposable personal income, to deflate sales or other variables, to find the purchasing power of the dollar, and to establish cost-of-living increases. We first discuss the use of the CPI in determining **real income.**

Real income

Money income

**Real Income**  As an example of the meaning and computation of *real income,* assume the Consumer Price Index is presently 200 with 1982–84 = 100. Also, assume that Ms. Watts earned $20,000 per year in the base period of 1982, 1983, and 1984. She has a current income of $40,000. Note that although her *money income* has doubled since the base period of 1982–84, the prices she paid for food, gasoline, clothing, and other items have also doubled. Thus, Ms. Watts's standard of living has remained the same from the base period to the present time. Price increases have exactly offset an increase in income, so her present buying power (real income) is still $20,000. (See Table 18–6 for computations.) In general:

| REAL INCOME | $\text{Real income} = \dfrac{\text{Money income}}{\text{CPI}} \times 100$ | [18–8] |
|---|---|---|

**TABLE 18–6**  Computation of Real Income for 1982–84 and Present Year

| Year | Annual Money Income | Consumer Price Index (1982–84 = 100) | Real Income | Computation of Real Income |
|---|---|---|---|---|
| 1982–84 | $20,000 | 100 | $20,000 | $\dfrac{\$20,000}{100}(100)$ |
| Present year | 40,000 | 200 | 20,000 | $\dfrac{\$40,000}{200}(100)$ |

Deflated income and real income are the same.

The concept of real income is sometimes called *deflated income,* and the CPI is called the *deflator.* Also, a popular term for deflated income is *income expressed in constant dollars.* Thus, in Table 18–6, to determine whether Ms. Watts's standard of living changed, her money income was converted to constant dollars. We found that her purchasing power, expressed in 1982–84 dollars (constant dollars), remained at $20,000.

**Self-Review 18–5**  The take-home pay of Jon Greene and the CPI for 2000 and 2003 are:

| Year | Take-Home Pay | CPI (1982–84 = 100) |
|---|---|---|
| 2000 | $25,000 | 170.8 |
| 2003 | 41,200 | 183.3 |

(a)  What was Jon's real income in 2000?
(b)  What was his real income in 2003?
(c)  Interpret your findings.

**Deflating Sales** A price index can also be used to "deflate" sales or similar money series. Deflated sales are determined by

Deflated sales important for showing the trend in "real" sales

| USING AN INDEX AS A DEFLATOR | $\text{Deflated sales} = \dfrac{\text{Actual sales}}{\text{An appropriate index}} \times 100$ | [18–9] |
|---|---|---|

**EXAMPLE**

The sales of Hill Enterprises, a small injection molding company in upstate New York, increased from $875,000 in 1982 to $1,482,000 in 1995, $1,491,000 in 2000, and $1,502,000 in 2004. The owner, Harry Hill, realizes that the price of raw materials used in the process has also increased over the period, so Mr. Hill wants to deflate sales to account for the increase in raw material prices. What are the deflated sales for 1995, 2000, and 2004 based on 1982 dollars? That is, what are sales for 1995, 2000, and 2004 expressed in constant 1982 dollars?

**SOLUTION**

The Producer Price Index (PPI) is an index released every month and published in the *Monthly Labor Review* and is also available at the Bureau of Labor Statistics website. The prices included in the PPI reflect the prices charged the manufacturer for the metals, rubber, and other items purchased. So the PPI seems an appropriate index to use to deflate the manufacturer's sales. The manufacturer's sales are listed in the second column of Table 18–7, and the PPI for January of each year is in the third column. The next column shows sales divided by the PPI. The right-hand column details the calculations. The results are shown in the following Excel output.

**EXCEL**

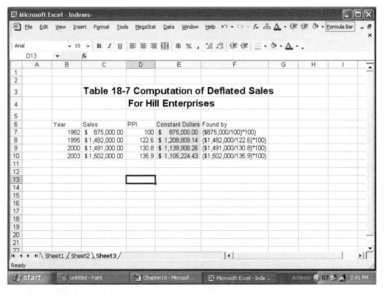

Actual sales have increased from 1995 through 2004, but if we compare the sales in constant dollars, sales declined during the period. That is, deflated sales were $1,139,908 in 2000 but declined to $1,105,224 in 2004. This is so because the prices Hill Enterprises paid for raw materials grew more rapidly than sales.

What has happened to the purchasing power of your dollar?

**Purchasing Power of the Dollar** The Consumer Price Index is also used to determine the *purchasing power of the dollar.*

| USING AN INDEX TO FIND PURCHASING POWER | $\text{Purchasing power of dollar} = \dfrac{\$1}{\text{CPI}} \times 100$ | [18–10] |
|---|---|---|

**EXAMPLE**

**SOLUTION**

Suppose the Consumer Price Index this month is 200.0 (1982–84 = 100). What is the purchasing power of the dollar?

From formula (18–10), it is 50 cents, found by:

$$\text{Purchasing power of dollar} = \frac{\$1}{200.0}\,(100) = \$0.50$$

The CPI of 200.0 indicates that prices have doubled from the years 1982–84 to this month. Thus, the purchasing power of a dollar has been cut in half. That is, a 1982–84 dollar is worth only 50 cents this month. To put it another way, if you lost $1,000 in the period 1982–84 and just found it, the $1,000 could only buy half of what it could have bought in the years 1982, 1983, and 1984.

CPI used to adjust wages, pensions, and so on.

**Cost-of-Living Adjustments** The Consumer Price Index (CPI) is also the basis for cost-of-living adjustments in many management-union contracts. The specific clause in the contract is often referred to as the "escalator clause" or COLA. About 31 million Social Security beneficiaries, 2.5 million retired military and federal civil service employees and survivors, and 600,000 postal workers have their incomes or pensions pegged to the CPI.

The CPI is also used to adjust alimony and child support payments; attorneys' fees; workers' compensation payments; rentals on apartments, homes, and office buildings; welfare payments; and so on. In brief, say a retiree receives a pension of $500 a month and the CPI increases 5 points from 165 to 170. Suppose for each point that the CPI increases the pension benefits increase 1.0 percent, so the monthly increase in benefits will be $25, found by $500 (5 points)(.01). Now the retiree will receive $525 per month.

**Self-Review 18–6**

Suppose the Consumer Price Index for the latest month is 178.6 (1982–84 = 100). What is the purchasing power of the dollar? Interpret.

## Shifting the Base

If two or more time series have the same base period, they can be compared directly. As an example, suppose we are interested in the trend in the prices of food and beverages, housing, medical care, and so on since the base period, 1982–84. Note in Table 18–8 that all of the consumer price indexes use the same base. Thus, it can be said that the price of all consumer items combined increased 78.9 percent from the base period (1982–84) to the year 2002. Likewise, housing prices increased 80.3 percent, medical care 189.3 percent, and so on.

**TABLE 18–8** Trend in Consumer Prices to 2002 (1982–84 = 100)

| Year | All Items | Food and Beverages | Housing | Apparel and Upkeep | Medical Care |
|---|---|---|---|---|---|
| 1982–84 | 100.0 | 100.0 | 100.0 | 100.0 | 100.0 |
| 1990 | 130.7 | 132.1 | 128.5 | 124.1 | 162.8 |
| 1995 | 152.4 | 148.9 | 148.5 | 132.0 | 220.5 |
| 2000 | 172.2 | 168.4 | 169.6 | 129.6 | 260.8 |
| 2002 | 178.9 | 176.5 | 180.3 | 125.1 | 289.3 |

A problem arises, however, when two or more series being compared do not have the same base period. The following example compares the two most widely reported business indexes, the DJIA and Nasdaq.

We want to compare the price changes on the Dow Jones Industrial Average with the Nasdaq. The two indexes for selected periods are as follows.

| Index | Year | | | |
|---|---|---|---|---|
| | 1995 | 1998 | 2000 | 2002 |
| Dow Jones | 5,117.12 | 9,181.43 | 10,786.85 | 8,341.43 |
| Nasdaq | 1,059.79 | 2,192.69 | 2,470.51 | 1,335.51 |

From the information given, we are not sure the base periods are the same, so a direct comparison is not appropriate. Because we want to compare the changes in the two business indexes, the logical thing to do is to let a particular year, say 1995, be the base for both periods. For the Dow Jones, 5,117.12 becomes the base, and for the Nasdaq the base becomes 1,059.79.

The calculations for the 2002 Nasdaq using 1995 = 100 are:

$$\text{Index} = \frac{1,335.51}{1,059.79}(100) = 126.02$$

The following Excel output reports the complete set of indexes.

We conclude that both indexes have increased over the period. The Dow Jones has increased more, 63.01 percent versus 26.02 percent. Both indexes declined from 2000 to 2002, with the decline in the Nasdaq much steeper.

The following chart, obtained from the financial section of Yahoo!, shows a visual comparison of the Dow Jones and the Nasdaq. The vertical axis shows the percent change from the base year of 1998 for both. From this graph we conclude that both measures have declined over the five-year period, but that the Nasdaq has declined more.

1. In the preceding example, verify that the Dow Jones price index for 2000, using 1995 as the base period, is 210.80.

2. The changes in industrial production and in the prices manufacturers paid for raw materials since 1982 are to be compared. Unfortunately, the index of industrial production, which measures changes in production, and the Producer Price Index, which measures the change in the prices of raw materials, have different base periods. The production index has a 1977 base period, and the Producer Price Index uses 1982 as the base period. Shift the base to 1982 and make the two series comparable. Interpret.

| Year | Industrial Production Index (1977 = 100) | Producer Price Index (1982 = 100) |
|---|---|---|
| 1982 | 115.3 | 100.0 |
| 1987 | 129.8 | 105.4 |
| 1994 | 142.8 | 119.2 |
| 1997 | 172.3 | 131.2 |
| 2000 | 185.6 | 138.0 |
| 2002 | 191.3 | 138.8 |

# Exercises

**13.** In February 2003 the mean salary for a nurse manager with a bachelor's degree was $82,855. The Consumer Price Index for February 2003 was 183.1 (1982–84 = 100). The mean annual salary for a nurse in the base period of 1982–84 was $19,800. What was the real income of the nurse in 2003? How much had the mean salary increased?

**14.** The Trade Union Association of Orlando, Florida, maintains indexes on the hourly wages for a number of the trades. Unfortunately, the indexes do not all have the same base periods. Listed below is information on plumbers and electricians. Shift the base periods to 2000 and compare the hourly wage increases.

| Year | Plumbers (1995 = 100) | Electricians (1998 = 100) |
|------|----------------------|---------------------------|
| 2000 | 133.8 | 126.0 |
| 2004 | 159.4 | 158.7 |

15. In 1995 the mean salary of classroom teachers in the Tinora School District was $28,650. By 2000 the mean salary increased to $33,972, and further increased in 2004 to $37,382. The American Federation of Classroom Teachers maintains information on the trends throughout the United States in classroom teacher salaries. Their index, which has a base period of 1995, was 122.5 for 2000 and 136.9 for 2004. Compare the Tinora teachers to the national trends.

16. Sam Steward is a freelance Web page designer. Listed below are his yearly wages for the years 1995 through 2004. Also included is an industry index for Web page designers that reports the rate of wage inflation in the industry. This index has a base period of 1995.

| Year | Wage ($000) | Index (1995 = 100) |
|------|-------------|--------------------|
| 2000 | 134.8 | 160.6 |
| 2001 | 145.2 | 173.6 |
| 2002 | 156.6 | 187.9 |
| 2003 | 168.8 | 203.3 |
| 2004 | 179.6 | 210.4 |

Compute Sam's real income for the period. Did his wages keep up with inflation, or did he lose ground?

# Chapter Outline

I. An index number measures the relative change from one period to another.
   A. The major characteristics of an index are:
      1. It is a percentage, but the percent sign is usually omitted.
      2. It has a base period.
      3. Most indexes are reported to the nearest tenth of a percent, such as 153.1.
      4. The base of most indexes is 100.
   B. The reasons for computing an index are:
      1. It facilitates the comparison of unlike series.
      2. If the numbers are very large, often it is easier to comprehend the change of the index than the actual numbers.
II. There are two types of price indexes, unweighted and weighted.
   A. In an unweighted index we do not consider the quantities.
      1. In a simple index we compare the base period to the given period.

$$P = \frac{p_t}{p_0} \times 100 \hspace{3cm} \text{[18–1]}$$

where $p_t$ refers to the price in the current period, and $p_0$ is the price in the base period.
      2. In the simple average of price indexes, we add the simple indexes for each item and divide by the number of items.

$$P = \frac{\Sigma P_i}{n} \hspace{3cm} \text{[18–2]}$$

      3. In a simple aggregate price index the price of the items in the group are totaled for both periods and compared.

$$P = \frac{\Sigma p_t}{\Sigma p_0} \times 100 \hspace{3cm} \text{[18–3]}$$

**B.** In a weighted index the quantities are considered.
1. In the Laspeyres method the base period quantities are used in both the base period and the given period.

$$P = \frac{\Sigma p_t q_0}{\Sigma p_0 q_0} \times 100 \qquad [18\text{--}4]$$

2. In the Paasche method current period quantities are used.

$$P = \frac{\Sigma p_t q_t}{\Sigma p_0 q_t} \times 100 \qquad [18\text{--}5]$$

3. Fisher's ideal index is the geometric mean of Laspeyres' index and Paasche's index.

$$\text{Fisher's ideal index} = \sqrt{(\text{Laspeyres' index})(\text{Paasche's index})} \qquad [18\text{--}6]$$

**C.** A value index uses both base period and current period prices and quantities.

$$V = \frac{\Sigma p_t q_t}{\Sigma p_0 q_0} \qquad [18\text{--}7]$$

**III.** The most widely reported index is the Consumer Price Index (CPI).
**A.** It is often used to show the rate of inflation in the United States.
**B.** It is reported monthly by the U.S. Bureau of Labor Statistics.
**C.** The current base period is 1982–84.
**D.** It is used by the Social Security system, so when the CPI changes, retirement benefits also change.

# Chapter Exercises

The following information was taken from Johnson and Johnson annual reports. The principal office of Johnson and Johnson is in New Brunswick, New Jersey. Their common stock is listed on the New York Stock Exchange, using the symbol JNJ.

| Year | Domestic Sales ($ million) | International Sales ($ million) | Total Sales ($ million) | Employees (thousands) |
|---|---|---|---|---|
| 1995 | 9,065 | 9,472 | 18,537 | 84.2 |
| 1996 | 10,851 | 10,536 | 21,387 | 91.5 |
| 1997 | 11,814 | 10,708 | 22,522 | 92.6 |
| 1998 | 12,901 | 10,910 | 23,811 | 96.1 |
| 1999 | 15,532 | 11,825 | 27,357 | 99.8 |
| 2000 | 17,316 | 11,856 | 29,172 | 100.9 |
| 2001 | 19,825 | 12,492 | 32,317 | 101.8 |
| 2002 | 22,455 | 13,843 | 36,298 | 108.3 |

**17.** Refer to the Johnson and Johnson data. Use 1995 as the base period and compute a simple index of domestic sales for each year from 1996 until 2002. Interpret the trend in domestic sales.
**18.** Refer to the Johnson and Johnson data. Use the period 1995–97 as the base period and compute a simple index of domestic sales for each year from 1998 to 2002.
**19.** Refer to the Johnson and Johnson data. Use 1995 as the base period and compute a simple index of international sales for each year from 1996 until 2002. Interpret the trend in international sales.
**20.** Refer to the Johnson and Johnson data. Use the period 1995–97 as the base period and compute a simple index of international sales for each year from 1998 to 2002.
**21.** Refer to the Johnson and Johnson data. Use 1995 as the base period and compute a simple index of the number of employees for each year from 1996 until 2002. Interpret the trend in the number of employees.
**22.** Refer to the Johnson and Johnson data. Use the period 1995–97 as the base period and compute a simple index of the number of employees for each year from 1998 to 2002.

The following information is from the General Electric Corporation annual report for 1998.

| Year | Revenue ($ million) | Earnings (per share) |
|------|------|------|
| 1998 | 100,469 | 0.95 |
| 1999 | 111,630 | 1.09 |
| 2000 | 129,853 | 1.29 |
| 2001 | 125,913 | 1.38 |
| 2002 | 131,698 | 1.42 |

23. Compute a simple index for the revenue of GE. Use 1998 as the base period. What can you conclude about the change in revenue over the period?
24. Compute a simple index for the revenue of GE using the period 1998–2000 as the base. What can you conclude about the change in revenue over the period?
25. Compute a simple index for earnings per share for GE. Use 1998 as the base period. What can you conclude about the change in earnings per share over the period?
26. Compute a simple index for earnings for GE using the period 1998–2000 as the base. What can you conclude about the change in earnings per share over the period?

Below is information on food items for the years 2000 and 2004.

| Item | 2000 | | 2004 | |
|------|------|------|------|------|
| | Price | Quantity | Price | Quantity |
| Margarine (pound) | $0.81 | 18 | $0.89 | 27 |
| Shortening (pound) | 0.84 | 5 | 0.94 | 9 |
| Milk (½ gallon) | 1.44 | 70 | 1.43 | 65 |
| Potato chips | 2.91 | 27 | 3.07 | 33 |

27. Compute a simple price index for each of the four items. Use 2000 as the base period.
28. Compute a simple aggregate price index. Use 2000 as the base period.
29. Compute Laspeyres' price index for 2004 using 2000 as the base period.
30. Compute Paasche's index for 2004 using 2000 as the base period.
31. Determine Fisher's ideal index using the values for the Laspeyres and Paasche indexes computed in the two previous problems.
32. Determine a value index for 2004 using 2000 as the base period.

Betts Electronics purchases three replacement parts for robotic machines used in their manufacturing process. Information on the price of the replacement parts and the quantity purchased is given below.

| Part | Price | | Quantity | |
|------|------|------|------|------|
| | 2000 | 2004 | 2000 | 2004 |
| RC-33 | $0.50 | $0.60 | 320 | 340 |
| SM-14 | 1.20 | 0.90 | 110 | 130 |
| WC50 | 0.85 | 1.00 | 230 | 250 |

33. Compute a simple price index for each of the three items. Use 2000 as the base period.
34. Compute a simple aggregate price index for 2004. Use 2000 as the base period.
35. Compute Laspeyres' price index for 2004 using 2000 as the base period.
36. Compute Paasche's index for 2004 using 2000 as the base period.
37. Determine Fisher's ideal index using the values for the Laspeyres and Paasche indexes computed in the two previous problems.
38. Determine a value index for 2004 using 2000 as the base period.

Prices for selected foods for 2000 and 2004 are given in the following table.

| Item | Price 2000 | Price 2004 | Quantity 2000 | Quantity 2004 |
|---|---|---|---|---|
| Cabbage (pound) | $0.06 | $0.05 | 2,000 | 1,500 |
| Carrots (bunch) | 0.10 | 0.12 | 200 | 200 |
| Peas (quart) | 0.20 | 0.18 | 400 | 500 |
| Endive (bunch) | 0.15 | 0.15 | 100 | 200 |

**39.** Compute a simple price index for each of the four items. Use 2000 as the base period.
**40.** Compute a simple aggregate price index. Use 2000 as the base period.
**41.** Compute Laspeyres' price index for 2004 using 2000 as the base period.
**42.** Compute Paasche's index for 2004 using 2000 as the base period.
**43.** Determine Fisher's ideal index using the values for the Laspeyres and Paasche indexes computed in the two previous problems.
**44.** Determine a value index for 2004 using 2000 as the base period.

The prices of selected items for 1980 and 2004 follow. Production figures for those two periods are also given.

| Item | Price 1980 | Price 2004 | Quantity 1980 | Quantity 2004 |
|---|---|---|---|---|
| Aluminum (cents per pound) | $ 0.287 | $ 0.76 | 1,000 | 1,200 |
| Natural gas (1,000 cu. ft.) | 0.17 | 2.50 | 5,000 | 4,000 |
| Petroleum (barrel) | 3.18 | 26.00 | 60,000 | 60,000 |
| Platinum (troy ounce) | 133.00 | 490.00 | 500 | 600 |

**45.** Compute a simple price index for each of the four items. Use 1980 as the base period.
**46.** Compute a simple aggregate price index. Use 1980 as the base period.
**47.** Compute Laspeyres' price index for 2004 using 1980 as the base period.
**48.** Compute Paasche's index for 2004 using 1980 as the base period.
**49.** Determine Fisher's ideal index using the values for the Laspeyres and Paasche indexes computed in the two previous problems.
**50.** Determine a value index for 2004 using 1980 as the base period.
**51.** A special-purpose index is to be designed to monitor the overall economy of the Southwest. Four key series were selected. After considerable deliberation it was decided to weight retail sales 20 percent, total bank deposits 10 percent, industrial production in the area 40 percent, and nonagricultural employment 30 percent. The data for 1996 and 2004 are:

| Year | Retail Sales ($ millions) | Bank Deposits ($ billions) | Industrial Production (1990 = 100) | Employment |
|---|---|---|---|---|
| 1996 | 1,159.0 | 87 | 110.6 | 1,214,000 |
| 2004 | 1,971.0 | 91 | 114.7 | 1,501,000 |

Construct a special-purpose index for 2004 using 1996 as the base period and interpret.
**52.** We are making a historical study of the American economy from 1950 to 1980. Data on prices, the labor force, productivity, and the GNP were collected. Note in the following table that the CPI has a base period of 1967, employment is in millions of persons, and so on. A direct comparison, therefore, is not feasible.
   **a.** Make whatever calculations are necessary to compare the trend in the four series from 1950 to 1980.
   **b.** Interpret.

| Year | Consumer Price Index (1967 = 100) | Total Labor Force (millions) | Index of Productivity in Manufacturing (1967 = 100) | Gross National Product ($ billions) |
|---|---|---|---|---|
| 1950 | 72.1 | 64 | 64.9 | 286.2 |
| 1967 | 100.0 | 81 | 100.0 | 789.6 |
| 1971 | 121.3 | 87 | 110.3 | 1,063.4 |
| 1975 | 161.2 | 95 | 114.9 | 1,516.3 |
| 1980 | 246.8 | 107 | 146.6 | 2,626.0 |

**53.** The management of Ingalls Super Discount stores, with several stores in the Oklahoma City area, wants to construct an index of economic activity for the metropolitan area. Management contends that if the index reveals that the economy is slowing down, inventory should be kept at a low level.

Three series seem to hold promise as predictors of economic activity—area retail sales, bank deposits, and employment. All of these data can be secured monthly from the U.S. government. Retail sales is to be weighted 40 percent, bank deposits 35 percent, and employment 25 percent. Seasonally adjusted data for the first three months of the year are:

| Month | Retail Sales ($ millions) | Bank Deposits ($ billions) | Employment (thousands) |
|---|---|---|---|
| January | 8.0 | 20 | 300 |
| February | 6.8 | 23 | 303 |
| March | 6.4 | 21 | 297 |

Construct an index of economic activity for each of the three months, using January as the base period.

**54.** The following table gives information on the Consumer Price Index and the monthly take-home pay of Bill Martin, an employee at the Jeep Corporation.

| Year | Consumer Price Index (1982–84 = 100) | Mr. Martin's Monthly Take-Home Pay |
|---|---|---|
| 1982–84 | 100.0 | $ 600 |
| 2002 | 178.9 | 2,000 |

**a.** What is the purchasing power of the dollar in 2002, based on the period 1982–84?
**b.** Determine Mr. Martin's "real" monthly income for 2002.

**55.** Suppose that the Producer Price Index and the sales of Hoskin's Wholesale Distributors for 1991 and 2002 are:

| Year | Producer Price Index | Sales |
|---|---|---|
| 1991 | 121.7 | $2,400,000 |
| 2002 | 138.8 | 3,500,000 |

What are Hoskin's real sales (also called deflated sales) for the two years?

# exercises.com

**56.** The Super Bowl is usually the TV program with the largest viewing audience each year; therefore, many companies use the Super Bowl to launch major advertising campaigns. The cost for a 30-second spot, as reported below, has increased dramatically since the first game in 1967. Also shown is the face value of a ticket to the game for the selected years.

| Year | TV Commercial | Game Ticket |
|------|---------------|-------------|
| 1967 | $   42,000 | $   8.00 |
| 1988 | 525,000 | 100.00 |
| 1999 | 1,600,000 | 325.00 |
| 2001 | 2,100,000 | 325.00 |
| 2002 | 1,900,000 | 400.00 |

Go to the Bureau of Labor Statistics website www.bls.gov/data.htm, click on **Most Requested Series,** and find the **Consumer Price Index—All Urban Consumers.** Select the base as *1967,* and find the CPI for the above years. Compare the rate of change in the Consumer Price Index to the cost of TV commercials and the cost of a game ticket. Write a brief report summarizing your findings.

**57.** Listed below are the monthly sales for the Master Chemical Company for 2002 and the first six months of 2003. Go to the U.S. Bureau of Labor Statistics (www.bls.gov/data.htm). Select **Most Requested Series,** and find the **Consumer Price Index—All Urban Consumers** (CPI-U) for the corresponding period. Select all items with the 1982–84 base and a period that includes 2002 and 2003. Adjust the CPI-U to a base of January 2002. Adjust the sales values to the same base. Write a brief report detailing the change in sales during the 18-month period in terms of constant dollars.

| Month | Year | Sales ($ million) | Month | Year | Sales ($ million) | Month | Year | Sales ($ million) |
|-------|------|-------------------|-------|------|-------------------|-------|------|-------------------|
| Jan | 2002 | 28.3 | Jul | 2002 | 44.0 | Jan | 2003 | 48.2 |
| Feb | 2002 | 38.1 | Aug | 2002 | 42.6 | Feb | 2003 | 53.5 |
| Mar | 2002 | 37.5 | Sep | 2002 | 48.3 | Mar | 2003 | 55.6 |
| Apr | 2002 | 39.0 | Oct | 2002 | 46.7 | Apr | 2003 | 54.7 |
| May | 2002 | 40.1 | Nov | 2002 | 51.3 | May | 2003 | 64.2 |
| Jun | 2002 | 41.9 | Dec | 2002 | 52.1 | Jun | 2003 | 58.3 |

# Software Commands

**1.** The Excel commands for the spreadsheet on page 627 are:

**a.** Enter the data for the prices and quantities. We entered the label *Item* in cell A4, and the item names in cells A5 through A10. The label *Price-95* was entered in B4, and the price data for 1995 in cells B5 through B10. The label *Quantity-95* was entered in cell C4, with the 1995 quantities in cells C5 through C10. Cell D4 was labeled *Price*Qty-95.*

**b.** To determine the product of the 1995 prices and quantities, highlight the cells from D5 to D10. With this group of cells still highlighted, type =*B5*C5* in cell D5 and hit **Enter.** The value 38.5 should appear. This is the product of the price of bread ($0.77) and the quantity of bread (50) sold in 1995.

**c.** With cells D5 through D10 still highlighted, select **Edit,** then **Fill,** then **Down,** and hit **Enter.** The remaining products should appear.

**d.** Move to cell D11, click on $\Sigma$ on the toolbar, and hit **Enter.** The value 336.16 will appear. This is the denominator for the Laspeyres price index. The other products and column totals are determined in a similar manner. The other Excel output in the chapter is computed similarly.

# Chapter 18  Answers to Self-Review

**18–1  1.** For Schering-Plough

$$P = (\$405.0/\$969.0)(100) = 41.8$$

For Boeing

$$P = (\$375.0/\$969.0)(100) = 38.7$$

For Exxon-Mobil

$$P = (\$4,498/\$969.0)(100) = 464.2$$

For Johnson and Johnson

$$P = (\$2,393/\$969)(100) = 247.0$$

The income for Shering-Plough and Boeing is less than for Pepsi. The income for Exxon-Mobil and Johnson and Johnson is more than Pepsi.

**2. a.** $P = (\$12.06/\$11.27)(100) = 107.0$
$P = (\$13.50/\$11.27)(100) = 119.8$
$P = (\$14.99/\$11.27)(100) = 133.0$
Hourly earnings have increased 33 percent during the period.
**b.** $x = (\$11.27 + \$12.06)/2 = 11.665$
$P = (\$13.50/\$11.665)(100) = 115.7$
$P = (\$14.99/\$11.665)(100) = 128.5$
Hourly earnings have gone up 28.5 percent.

**18–2  a.** $P_1 = (\$85/\$75)(100) = 113.3$
$P_2 = (\$45/\$40)(100) = 112.5$
$P = (113.3 + 112.5)/2 = 112.9$
**b.** $P = (\$130/\$115)(100) = 113.0$
**c.** $P = \dfrac{\$85(500) + \$45(1,200)}{\$75(500) + \$40(1,200)}(100)$
$= \dfrac{\$96,500}{85,500}(100) = 112.9$
**d.** $P = \dfrac{\$85(520) + \$45(1,300)}{\$75(520) + \$40(1,300)}(100)$
$= \dfrac{\$102,700}{\$91,000}(100) = 112.9$
**e.** $P = \sqrt{(112.9)(112.9)} = 112.9$

**18–3  a.** $P = \dfrac{\$4(9,000) + \$5(200) + \$8(5,000)}{\$3(10,000) + \$1(600) + \$10(3,000)}(100)$
$= \dfrac{\$77,000}{60,600}(100) = 127.1$
**b.** The value of sales has gone up 27.1 percent from 1996 to 2004.

**18–4  a.**

| For 2000 | |
|---|---|
| **Item** | **Weight** |
| Cotton | ($0.25/$0.20)(100)(.10) =  12.5 |
| Autos | (1,200/1,000)(100)(.30) =  36.0 |
| Money turnover | (90/80)(100)(.60) =  67.5 |
| | 116.0 |

| For 2004 | |
|---|---|
| **Item** | **Weight** |
| Cotton | ($0.50/$0.20)(100)(.10) =  25.00 |
| Autos | (900/1,000)(100)(.30) =  27.00 |
| Money turnover | (75/80)(100)(.60) =  56.25 |
| | 108.25 |

**b.** Business activity increased 16 percent from 1995 to 2000. It increased 8.25 percent from 1995 to 2004.

**18–5  a.** $14,637, found by ($25,000/170.8)(100).
**b.** $22,477, found by ($41,200/183.3)(100).
**c.** In terms of the base period, Jon's salary was $14,637 in 2000 and $22,477 in 2003. This indicates his take-home pay increased at a faster rate than the price paid for food, transportation, etc.

**18–6** $0.56, found by ($1.00/178.6)(100). Purchasing power has declined by $0.44.

**18–7  1.** 210.80, found by (10,786.85/5,117.10)(100).
**2.** With 1982 as the base period for both series:

| | Industrial Production Index | Producer Price Index |
|---|---|---|
| 1982 | 100.0 | 100.0 |
| 1987 | 112.6 | 105.4 |
| 1994 | 123.9 | 119.2 |
| 1997 | 149.4 | 131.2 |
| 2000 | 161.0 | 138.0 |
| 2002 | 165.9 | 138.8 |

From the base of 1982, industrial production increased at a faster rate (65.9 percent) than prices (38.8 percent).

# 19

# Time Series and Forecasting

Look at the selling price for a share of common stock of PepsiCo, Inc., at the close of the year. Estimate the selling price in 2006. Does this seem like a reasonable estimate based on the historical data? (See Goal 5 and Exercise 20.)

# Introduction

What is a time series?

The emphasis in this chapter is on time series analysis and forecasting. A **time series** is a collection of data recorded over a period of time—weekly, monthly, quarterly, or yearly. Two examples of time series are the sales by quarter of the Microsoft Corporation since 1985 and the annual production of sulfuric acid since 1970. The computer

image in the photo shows the volume of data traveling into the National Science Foundation network in one month. The colors represent traffic volume from zero bytes (purple) to 100 billion bytes (white).

An analysis of history—a time series—can be used by management to make current decisions and plans based on long-term forecasting. We usually assume past patterns will continue into the future. Long-term forecasts extend more than 1 year into the future; 2-, 5-, and 10-year projections are common. Long-range predictions are essential to allow sufficient time for the procurement, manufacturing, sales, finance, and other departments of a company to develop plans for possible new plants, financing, development of new products, and new methods of assembling.

Forecasting the level of sales, both short-term and long-term, is practically dictated by the very nature of business organizations in the United States. Competition for the consumer's dollar, stress on earning a profit for the stockholders, a desire to procure a larger share of the market, and the ambitions of executives are some of the prime motivating forces in business. Thus, a forecast (a statement of the goals of management) is necessary to have the raw materials, production facilities, and staff to meet the projected demand.

This chapter deals with the use of data to forecast future events. First, we look at the components of a time series. Then, we examine some of the techniques used in analyzing data. Finally, we forecast future events.

# Components of a Time Series

There are four components to a time series: the trend, the cyclical variation, the seasonal variation, and the irregular variation.

## Secular Trend

The long-term trends of sales, employment, stock prices, and other business and economic series follow various patterns. Some move steadily upward, others decline, and still others stay the same over time.

> **SECULAR TREND**  The smooth long-term direction of a time series.

The following are several examples of a secular trend.

- Home Depot was founded in 1978 and is the second largest retailer (Wal-Mart is the largest) in the United States. The following chart shows the number of employees at Home Depot, Inc. You can see this number has increased rapidly over the last 10 years. In 1993 there were just over 50,000 employees and by 2002 that number had increased to 280,900.

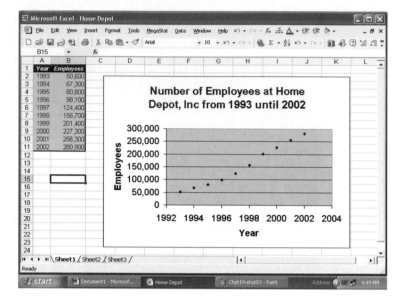

- The following chart shows the number of emergency medical service (EMS) calls in Horry County, South Carolina, since 1989. The number of calls for EMS has increased nearly 2.5 times from 12,269 in 1989 to 30,341 in 2003. Notice the number of calls increased from 1989 to 1995. From 1995 to 2000 the number of calls stayed about the same, and then in 2000 it began another increase to over 30,000. The long-run direction of the trend is increasing.

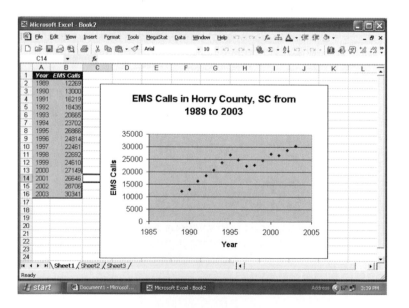

- The number of manufactured homes shipped in the United States showed a steady increase from 1990 to 1996, then remained about the same until 1999, when the number began to decline. By the year 2002 the number shipped was less than it had been in 1990. This information is shown in the following chart.

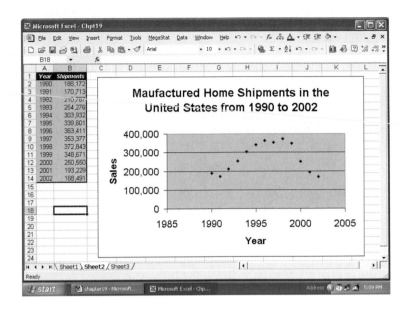

## Cyclical Variation

The second component of a time series is cyclical variation. A typical business cycle consists of a period of prosperity followed by periods of recession, depression, and then recovery. There are sizable fluctuations unfolding over more than one year in time above and below the secular trend. In a recession, for example, employment, production, the Dow Jones Industrial Average, and many other business and economic series are below the long-term trend lines. Conversely, in periods of prosperity they are above their long-term trend lines.

> **CYCLICAL VARIATION**  The rise and fall of a time series over periods longer than one year.

Chart 19–1 shows the annual unit sales of batteries sold by National Battery Retailers, Inc. from 1984 through 2003. The cyclical nature of business is highlighted. There are periods of recovery, followed by prosperity, then recession, and finally the cycle bottoms out with depression.

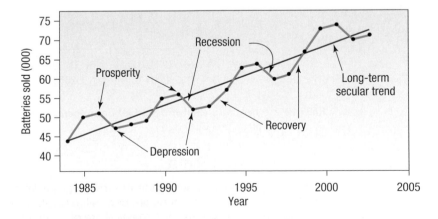

**CHART 19–1**  Batteries Sold by National Battery Retailers, Inc., from 1984 to 2003

**Statistics in Action**

Statisticians, economists, and business executives are constantly looking for variables that will forecast the country's economy. The production of crude oil, price of gold on world markets, the Dow Jones average, as well as many published government indexes are variables that have been used with some success. Variables such as the length of hemlines and the winner of the Super Bowl have also been tried. The variable that seems overall to be the most successful is the price of scrap metal. Why? Scrap metal is the beginning of the manufacturing chain. When its demand increases, this is an indication that manufacturing is also increasing.

# Seasonal Variation

The third component of a time series is the **seasonal** component. Many sales, production, and other series fluctuate with the seasons. The unit of time reported is either quarterly or monthly.

---

**SEASONAL VARIATION** Patterns of change in a time series within a year. These patterns tend to repeat themselves each year.

---

Almost all businesses tend to have recurring seasonal patterns. Men's and boy's clothing, for example, has extremely high sales just prior to Christmas and relatively low sales just after Christmas and during the summer. Toy sales is another example with an extreme seasonal pattern. More than half of the business for the year is usually done in the months of November and December. The lawn care business is seasonal in the northeast and north-central states. Many businesses try to even out the seasonal effects by engaging in an offsetting seasonal business. In the Northeast you will see the operator of a lawn care business with a snowplow on the front of the truck in an effort to earn income in the off-season. At ski resorts throughout the country, you will often find golf courses nearby. The owners of the lodges try to rent to skiers in the winter and golfers in the summer. This is an effective method of spreading their fixed costs over the entire year rather than a few months.

Chart 19–2 shows the quarterly sales, in millions of dollars, of Hercher Sporting Goods, Inc. They are a Chicago area sporting goods company that specializes in selling baseball and softball equipment to high schools, colleges, and youth leagues. They also have several retail outlets in some of the larger shopping malls. There is a distinct seasonal pattern to their business. Most of their sales are in the first and second quarters of the year, when schools and organizations are purchasing equipment for the upcoming season. During the early summer, they keep busy by selling replacement equipment. They do some business during the holidays (fourth quarter). The late summer (third quarter) is their slow season.

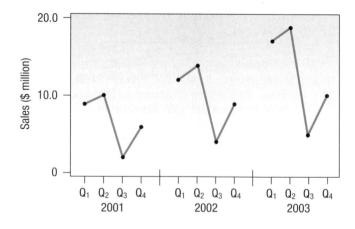

**CHART 19–2** Sales of Baseball and Softball Equipment, Hercher Sporting Goods, 2001–2003 by Quarter

# Irregular Variation

Many analysts prefer to subdivide the **irregular variation** into *episodic* and *residual* variations. Episodic fluctuations are unpredictable, but they can be identified. The initial impact on the economy of a major strike or a war can be identified, but a strike or war cannot be predicted. After the episodic fluctuations have been removed, the remaining variation is called the residual variation. The residual fluctuations, often called chance fluctuations, are unpredictable, and they cannot be identified. Of course, neither episodic nor residual variation can be projected into the future.

# The Moving-Average Method

Moving-average method
smooths out fluctuations.

The **moving-average method** is not only useful in smoothing a time series to see its trend; it is the basic method used in measuring the seasonal fluctuation, described later in the chapter. In contrast to the least squares method, which expresses the trend in terms of a mathematical equation ($Y' = a + bt$), the moving-average method merely smooths the fluctuations in the data. This is accomplished by "moving" the arithmetic mean values through the time series.

To apply the moving-average method to a time series, the data should follow a fairly linear trend and have a definite rhythmic pattern of fluctuations (repeating, say, every three years). The data in the following example have three components—trend, cycle, and irregular, abbreviated *T, C,* and *I.* There is no seasonal variation, because the data are recorded annually. What the moving-average method does, in effect, is average out *C* and *I.* The residual is trend.

If the duration of the cycles is constant, and if the amplitudes of the cycles are equal, the cyclical and irregular fluctuations can be removed entirely using the moving-average method. The result is a line. For example, in the following time series the cycle repeats itself every seven years, and the amplitude of each cycle is 4; that is, there are exactly four units from the trough (lowest time period) to the peak. The seven-year moving average, therefore, averages out the cyclical and irregular fluctuations perfectly, and the residual is a linear trend.

Compute mean
of first seven years.

The first step in computing the seven-year moving average is to determine the seven-year moving totals. The total sales for the first seven years (1978–84 inclusive) are $22 million, found by $1 + 2 + 3 + 4 + 5 + 4 + 3$. (See Table 19–1.) The total of

**TABLE 19–1** The Computations for the Seven-Year Moving Average

| Year | Sales ($ millions) | Seven-Year Moving Total | Seven-Year Moving Average |
|------|------|------|------|
| 1978 | $1 | | |
| 1979 | 2 | | |
| 1980 | 3 | | |
| 1981 | 4 | 22 | 3.143 |
| 1982 | 5 | 23 | 3.286 |
| 1983 | 4 | 24 | 3.429 |
| 1984 | 3 | 25 | 3.571 |
| 1985 | 2 | 26 | 3.714 |
| 1986 | 3 | 27 | 3.857 |
| 1987 | 4 | 28 | 4.000 |
| 1988 | 5 | 29 | 4.143 |
| 1989 | 6 | 30 | 4.286 |
| 1990 | 5 | 31 | 4.429 |
| 1991 | 4 | 32 | 4.571 |
| 1992 | 3 | 33 | 4.714 |
| 1993 | 4 | 34 | 4.857 |
| 1994 | 5 | 35 | 5.000 |
| 1995 | 6 | 36 | 5.143 |
| 1996 | 7 | 37 | 5.286 |
| 1997 | 6 | 38 | 5.429 |
| 1998 | 5 | 39 | 5.571 |
| 1999 | 4 | 40 | 5.714 |
| 2000 | 5 | 41 | 5.857 |
| 2001 | 6 | | |
| 2002 | 7 | | |
| 2003 | 8 | | |

$22 million is divided by 7 to determine the arithmetic mean sales per year. The seven-year total (22) and the seven-year mean (3.143) are positioned opposite the middle year for that group of seven, namely, 1981, as shown in Table 19–1. Then the total sales for the next seven years (1979–85 inclusive) are determined. (A convenient way of doing this is to subtract the sales for 1978 [$1 million] from the first seven-year total [$22 million] and add the sales for 1985 [$2 million], to give the new total of $23 million.) The mean of this total, $3.286 million, is positioned opposite the middle year, 1981. The sales data and seven-year moving average are shown graphically in Chart 19–3.

**CHART 19–3**  Sales and Seven-Year Moving Average

The number of data values to include in a moving average depends on the character of the data collected. If the data are quarterly, since there are four quarters in a year, then four terms might be typical. If the data are daily, since there are seven days in a week, then seven terms might be appropriate. You might also use trial and error to determine a number that best levels out the chance fluctuations.

A moving average can be easily computed in the Excel system. In fact, it requires only one command. If the original data are in locations D3 to D20 and you wish a three period moving average, you can go to position E4 and type "=(D3+D4+D5)/3" and then copy that same formula down to position E19.

A three-year and a five-year moving average for some production data are shown in Table 19–2 and depicted in Chart 19–4.

Sales, production, and other economic and business series usually do not have (1) periods of oscillation that are of equal length or (2) oscillations that have identical amplitudes. Thus, in actual practice, the application of the moving-average method to data does not result precisely in a line. For example, the production series in Table 19–2 repeats about every five years, but the amplitude of the data varies from one oscillation to another. The trend appears to be upward and somewhat linear. Both moving averages—the three-year and the five-year—seem to adequately describe the trend in production since 1985.

Determining a moving average for an even-numbered period, such as four years

Four-year, six-year, and other even-numbered-year moving averages present one minor problem regarding the centering of the moving totals and moving averages. Note in Table 19–3 that there is no center time period, so the moving totals are positioned *between* two time periods. The total for the first four years ($42) is positioned

**TABLE 19–2** A Three-Year Moving Average and a Five-Year Moving Average

| Year | Production, Y | Three-Year Moving Total | Three-Year Moving Average | Five-Year Moving Total | Five-Year Moving Average |
|---|---|---|---|---|---|
| 1985 | 5 | | | | |
| 1986 | 6 | 19 | 6.3 | | |
| 1987 | 8 | 24 | 8.0 | 34 | 6.8 |
| 1988 | 10 | 23 | 7.7 | 32 | 6.4 |
| 1989 | 5 | 18 | 6.0 | 33 | 6.6 |
| 1990 | 3 | 15 | 5.0 | 35 | 7.0 |
| 1991 | 7 | 20 | 6.7 | 37 | 7.4 |
| 1992 | 10 | 29 | 9.7 | 43 | 8.6 |
| 1993 | 12 | 33 | 11.0 | 49 | 9.8 |
| 1994 | 11 | 32 | 10.7 | 55 | 11.0 |
| 1995 | 9 | 33 | 11.0 | 60 | 12.0 |
| 1996 | 13 | 37 | 12.3 | 66 | 13.2 |
| 1997 | 15 | 46 | 15.3 | 70 | 14.0 |
| 1998 | 18 | 48 | 16.0 | 72 | 14.4 |
| 1999 | 15 | 44 | 14.7 | 73 | 14.6 |
| 2000 | 11 | 40 | 13.3 | 75 | 15.0 |
| 2001 | 14 | 42 | 14.0 | 79 | 15.8 |
| 2002 | 17 | 53 | 17.7 | | |
| 2003 | 22 | | | | |

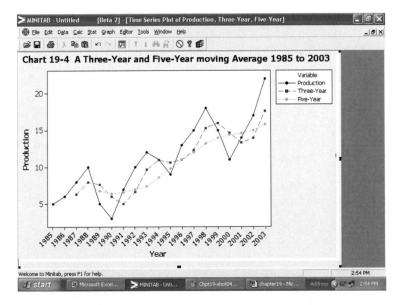

**CHART 19–4** A Three-Year and Five-Year Moving Average 1985 to 2003

between 1996 and 1997. The total for the next four years is $43. The averages of the first four years and the second four years ($10.50 and $10.75, respectively) are averaged, and the resulting figure is centered on 1997. This procedure is repeated until all possible four-year averages are computed.

**TABLE 19–3** A Four-Year Moving Average

| Year | Sales, Y | Four-Year Moving Total | Four-Year Moving Average | Centered Four-Year Moving Average |
|------|----------|------------------------|--------------------------|-----------------------------------|
| 1995 | $ 8 | | | |
| 1996 | 11 | | | |
| | | $42 (8 + 11 + 9 + 14) | $10.50 ($42 ÷ 4) | |
| 1997 | 9 | | | 10.625 |
| | | 43 (11 + 9 + 14 + 9) | 10.75 ($43 ÷ 4) | |
| 1998 | 14 | | | 10.625 |
| | | 42 | 10.50 | |
| 1999 | 9 | | | 10.625 |
| | | 43 | 10.75 | |
| 2000 | 10 | | | 10.000 |
| | | 37 | 9.25 | |
| 2001 | 10 | | | 9.625 |
| | | 40 | 10.00 | |
| 2002 | 8 | | | |
| 2003 | 12 | | | |

# Weighted Moving Average

In the moving averages method, the calculation gives the same weight or influence to each observation. For example, the three-year moving total is divided by the value 3 to yield the three-year moving average. To put it another way each data value had a weight of one-third in this case. Similarly, you can see that for the five-year moving average each data value has a weight of one-fifth.

A natural extension of the weighted mean discussed in Chapter 3 is to compute a weighted moving average. This involves selecting a possibly different weight for each data value and then computing a weighted average of the most recent $n$ values as the smoothed value. In the majority of applications we use the smoothed value as a forecast of the future. So, the most recent observation receives the most weight, and the weight decreases for older data values. Notice that for both the simple moving average and for the weighted moving average the sum of the weights is equal to 1.

Suppose for example we compute a two-year weighted moving average for the data in Table 19–3 giving twice as much weight to the most recent value. In other words give a weight of 2/3 to the last year and 1/3 to the value immediately before that. Then "forecast" sales for 1997 would be found by (1/3)($8) + (2/3)($11) = $10. The next moving average would be computed as (1/3)($11) + (2/3)($9) = $9.667. Proceeding in the same fashion, the final or 2002 weighted moving average would be (1/3)($8) + (2/3)($12) = $10.667. To summarize the technique of using moving averages, its purpose is to help identify the long-term trend in a time series (because it smooths out short-term fluctuations). It is used to reveal any cyclical and seasonal fluctuations.

**EXAMPLE**

Cedar Fair operates six amusement parks and five separately gated water parks. Their combined attendance (in thousands) for the last ten years is given in the following table. A partner asks you to study the trend in attendance. Compute a three-year moving average and a three-year weighted moving average with weights of 0.2, 0.3, and 0.5 for successive years.

| Year | Attendance |
|------|-----------|
| 1993 | 5,761 |
| 1994 | 6,148 |
| 1995 | 6,783 |
| 1996 | 7,445 |
| 1997 | 7,405 |
| 1998 | 11,450 |
| 1999 | 11,224 |
| 2000 | 11,703 |
| 2001 | 11,890 |
| 2002 | 12,380 |

**SOLUTION**

The three-year moving average is:

| Year | Attendance | Moving Average | Found by |
|------|-----------|----------------|----------|
| 1993 | 5,761 | | |
| 1994 | 6,148 | 6,231 | (5,761 + 6,148 + 6,783)/3 |
| 1995 | 6,783 | 6,792 | (6,148 + 6,783 + 7,445)/3 |
| 1996 | 7,445 | 7,211 | (6,783 + 7,445 + 7,405)/3 |
| 1997 | 7,405 | 8,767 | (7,445 + 7,405 + 11,450)/3 |
| 1998 | 11,450 | 10,026 | (7,405 + 11,450 + 11,224)/3 |
| 1999 | 11,224 | 11,459 | (11,450 + 11,224 + 11,703)/3 |
| 2000 | 11,703 | 11,606 | (11,224 + 11,703 + 11,890)/3 |
| 2001 | 11,890 | 11,991 | (11,703 + 11,890 + 12,380)/3 |
| 2002 | 12,380 | | |

The three-year weighted moving average is:

| Year | Attendance | Weighted Moving Average | Found by |
|------|-----------|--------------------------|----------|
| 1993 | 5,761 | | |
| 1994 | 6,148 | 6,388 | .2(5,761) + .3(6,148) + .5(6,783) |
| 1995 | 6,783 | 6,987 | .2(6,148) + .3(6,783) + .5(7,445) |
| 1996 | 7,445 | 7,293 | .2(6,783) + .3(7,445) + .5(7,405) |
| 1997 | 7,405 | 9,436 | .2(7,445) + .3(7,405) + .5(11,450) |
| 1998 | 11,450 | 10,528 | .2(7,405) + .3(11,450) + .5(11,224) |
| 1999 | 11,224 | 11,509 | .2(11,450) + .3(11,224) + .5(11,703) |
| 2000 | 11,703 | 11,701 | .2(11,224) + .3(11,703) + .5(11,890) |
| 2001 | 11,890 | 12,098 | .2(11,703) + .3(11,890) + .5(12,380) |
| 2002 | 12,380 | | |

Study the graph on the next page carefully. You will see that the attendance trend is evenly upwards with 360 thousand added visitors each year. However, there is a "hop" of approximately 3 million per year between 1997 and 1998. That probably reflects the fact Cedar Fair acquired Knott's Berry Farm in late 1997 leading to a one-time boost in attendance. The weighted moving average follows the data more closely than the moving average. This reflects the additional influence given to the most recent period. In other words the weighted method, where the most recent period is given the largest weight, won't be quite as smooth. However, it may be more accurate as a forecasting tool.

**Self-Review 19–1**

Determine a three-year moving average for the sales of Waccamaw Machine Tool, Inc. Plot both the original data and the moving average.

| Year | Number Produced (thousands) | Year | Number Produced (thousands) |
|------|------|------|------|
| 1998 | 2 | 2001 | 5 |
| 1999 | 6 | 2002 | 3 |
| 2000 | 4 | 2003 | 10 |

# Exercises

1. Calculate a four-quarter weighted moving average for the number of America Online (AOL) subscribers for the nine quarters of data. The data are reported in thousands. Apply weights of .1, .2, .3 and .4, respectively, for the quarters. In a few words describe the trend in the number of subscribers.

| | |
|------|------|
| 31-Mar-01 | 28,766 |
| 30-Jun-01 | 30,057 |
| 30-Sep-01 | 31,336 |
| 31-Dec-01 | 33,240 |
| 31-Mar-02 | 34,610 |
| 30-Jun-02 | 35,102 |
| 30-Sep-02 | 35,308 |
| 31-Dec-02 | 35,203 |
| 31-Mar-03 | 34,386 |

2. The yield on a 30-year treasury note at the end of each year since 1990 is recorded below. Compute a five-year weighted moving average using weights of .1, .1, .2, .3, and .3, respectively. Describe the trend in yield.

| | |
|------|------|
| 1990 | 8.61 |
| 1991 | 8.14 |
| 1992 | 7.67 |
| 1993 | 6.59 |
| 1994 | 7.37 |
| 1995 | 6.88 |
| 1996 | 6.71 |
| 1997 | 6.61 |
| 1998 | 5.58 |
| 1999 | 5.87 |
| 2000 | 5.94 |
| 2001 | 5.49 |
| 2002 | 5.43 |

# Linear Trend

The long-term trend of many business series, such as sales, exports, and production, often approximates a straight line. If so, the equation to describe this growth is:

| LINEAR TREND EQUATION | $Y' = a + bt$ | [19–1] |
|---|---|---|

where:

$Y'$ read $Y$ prime, is the projected value of the $Y$ variable for a selected value of $t$.

$a$ is the $Y$-intercept. It is the estimated value of $Y$ when $t = 0$. Another way to put it is: $a$ is the estimated value of $Y$ where the line crosses the $Y$-axis when $t$ is zero.

Slope of trend line is $b$

$b$ is the slope of the line, or the average change in $Y'$ for each increase of one unit in $t$.

$t$ is any value of time that is selected.

To illustrate the meaning of $Y'$, $a$, $b$, and $t$ in a time-series problem, a line has been drawn in Chart 19–5 to represent the typical trend of sales. Assume that this company started in business in 1995. This beginning year (1995) has been arbitrarily designated as year 1. Note that sales increased $2 million on the average every year; that is, based on the straight line drawn through the sales data, sales increased from $3 million in 1995 to $5 million in 1996, to $7 million in 1997, to $9 million in 1998, and so on. The slope, or $b$, is therefore 2. Note too that the line intercepts the $Y$-axis (when $t = 0$) at $1 million. This point is $a$. Another way of determining $b$ is to locate the starting place of the straight line in year (1). It is 3 for 1995 in this problem. Then locate the value on the straight line for the last year. It is 19 for 2003. Sales went up $19 million − $3 million, or $16 million, in eight years (1995 to 2003). Thus, 16 ÷ 8 = 2, which is the slope of the line, or $b$.

**CHART 19–5** A Straight Line Fitted to Sales Data

The equation for the line in Chart 19–5 is:

$$Y' = 1 + 2t \text{ (in millions)}$$

where:

Sales are in millions of dollars. The origin, or year 0, is 1994.
$t$ increases by one unit for each year.

In Chapter 13 we drew a line through points on a scatter diagram to approximate the regression line. We stressed, however, that this method for determining the regression equation has a serious drawback—namely, the position of the line depends on the judgment of the individual who drew the line. Three people would probably draw three different lines through the scatter plots. Likewise, the line we drew through the sales data in Chart 19–5 might not be the "best-fitting" line. Because of the subjective judgment involved, this method should be used only when a quick approximation of the straight-line equation is needed, or to check the reasonableness of the least squares line, which is discussed next.

# Least Squares Method

In the discussion of simple linear regression in Chapter 13, we show how the least squares method is used to find the best linear relationship between two variables. In forecasting methods, time is the independent variable and the value of the time series is the dependent variable. Furthermore, we often code the independent variable time to make the equations easier to interpret. In other words, we let $t$ be 1 for the first year, 2 for the second, and so on. If a time series includes the sales of General Electric for five years starting in 2000 and continuing through 2004, we would code the year 2000 as 1, 2001 as 2, and 2004 as 5.

**EXAMPLE**

The sales of Jensen Foods, a small grocery chain located in southwest Texas, since 1999 are:

| Year | Sales ($ million) |
|------|-------------------|
| 1999 | 7 |
| 2000 | 10 |
| 2001 | 9 |
| 2002 | 11 |
| 2003 | 13 |

Determine the regression equation. How much are sales increasing each year? What is the sales forecast for 2006?

**SOLUTION**

To determine the trend equation we could use formula (13–4) to find the slope, or $b$ value, and formula (13–5) to locate the intercept, or $a$ value. We would substitute $t$, the coded values for the year, for $X$ in these equations. Another approach is to use one of the software packages, such as MINITAB or Excel. Chart 19–6 is the output from MINITAB. The Year, Coded Year, Sales, and Fitted Sales values are shown in the lower left portion of the output. The upper left reports the regression output, and on the right half is a scatter plot of the data and the fitted regression line.

**CHART 19–6** Sales and Trend Line, 1999–2003

From the output the trend equation is $Y' = 6.1 + 1.3t$. How do we interpret this equation? The sales are in millions of dollars. So the value 1.3 tells us that sales increased at a rate of 1.3 million dollars per year. The value 6.1 is the estimated value of sales in the year 0. That is the estimate for 1998, which is called the base year. For example, to determine the point on the line for 2002, insert the $t$ value of 4 in the equation. Then $Y' = 6.1 + 1.3(4) = 11.3$.

If sales, production, or other data approximate a linear trend, the equation developed by the least squares technique can be used to estimate future values. It is reasonable that the sales for Jensen Foods follow a linear trend. So we can use the trend equation to forecast future sales.

See Table 19–4. The year 1999 is coded 1, the year 2001 is coded 3, and 2003 is coded 5. Logically we code 2005 as 7 and 2006 as 8. So we substitute 8 into the trend equation and solve for $Y'$.

$$Y' = 6.1 + 1.3t = 6.1 + 1.3(8) = 16.5$$

Thus, on the basis of past sales, the estimate for 2006 is $16.5 million.

**TABLE 19–4** Calculations for Determining the Points on the Least Squares Line Using the Coded Values

| Year | Sales ($ millions), $Y$ | $t$ | $Y'$ | Found by |
|------|------|------|------|------|
| 1999 | 7 | 1 | 7.4 | 6.1 + 1.3(1) |
| 2000 | 10 | 2 | 8.7 | 6.1 + 1.3(2) |
| 2001 | 9 | 3 | 10 | 6.1 + 1.3(3) |
| 2002 | 11 | 4 | 11.3 | 6.1 + 1.3(4) |
| 2003 | 13 | 5 | 12.6 | 6.1 + 1.3(5) |

In this time series example, there were five years of sales data. Based on those five sales figures, we estimated sales for 2006. Many researchers suggest that we do not project sales, production, and other business and economic series more than $n/2$

**Statistics in Action**

Investors frequently use regression analysis to study the relationship between a particular stock and the general condition of the market. The dependent variable is the monthly percentage change in the value of the stock, and the independent variable is the monthly percentage change in a market index, such as the Standard & Poor's 500 Composite Index. The value of $b$ in the regression equation is the particular stock's *beta coefficient* or just the *beta*. If $b$ is greater than 1, the implication is that the stock is sensitive to market changes. If $b$ is between 0 and 1, the implication is that the stock is not sensitive to market changes. This is the same concept that economists refer to as *elasticity*.

time periods into the future where *n* is the number of data points. If, for example, there are 10 years of data, we would make estimates only up to 5 years into the future ($n/2 = 10/2 = 5$). Others suggest the forecast may be for no longer than 2 years, especially in rapidly changing economic times.

**Self-Review 19–2**   Annual production of king-size rockers by Wood Products, Inc. since 1996 follows.

| Year | Production (thousands) | Year | Production (thousands) |
|------|-----------------------|------|-----------------------|
| 1996 | 4 | 2000 | 11 |
| 1997 | 8 | 2001 | 9 |
| 1998 | 5 | 2002 | 11 |
| 1999 | 8 | 2003 | 14 |

(a)   Plot the production data.
(b)   Determine the least squares equation using a software package.
(c)   Determine the points on the line for 1996 and 2002. Connect the two points to arrive at the line.
(d)   Based on the linear trend equation, what is the estimated production for 2006?

# Exercises

**3.**   Listed below are the net sales for Schering-Plough Corporation (a pharmaceutical company) and its subsidiaries for the six years from 1997 to 2002. The net sales are in millions of dollars.

| Year | Net Sales |
|------|-----------|
| 1997 | $ 6,714 |
| 1998 | 7,991 |
| 1999 | 9,075 |
| 2000 | 9,775 |
| 2001 | 9,762 |
| 2002 | 10,180 |

Determine the least squares equation. According to this information, what are the estimated sales for 2005?

**4.**   Listed below is the net sales in $ million for Home Depot, Inc. and its subsidiaries from 1993 to 2002.

| Year | Net Sales |
|------|-----------|
| 1993 | 9,239 |
| 1994 | 12,477 |
| 1995 | 15,470 |
| 1996 | 19,535 |
| 1997 | 24,156 |
| 1998 | 30,219 |
| 1999 | 38,434 |
| 2000 | 45,738 |
| 2001 | 53,553 |
| 2002 | 58,247 |

Determine the least squares equation. On the basis of this information, what are the estimated sales for 2005?

5. The following table lists the annual amounts of glass cullet produced by Kimble Glass Works, Inc.

| Year | Code | Scrap (tons) |
|------|------|--------------|
| 1999 | 1 | 2.0 |
| 2000 | 2 | 4.0 |
| 2001 | 3 | 3.0 |
| 2002 | 4 | 5.0 |
| 2003 | 5 | 6.0 |

Determine the least squares trend equation. Estimate the amount of scrap for the year 2005.

6. The amounts spent in vending machines in the United States, in billions of dollars, for the years 1999 through 2003 are given below. Determine the least squares trend equation, and estimate vending sales for 2005.

| Year | Code | Vending Machine Sales ($ billions) |
|------|------|-------------------------------------|
| 1999 | 1 | 17.5 |
| 2000 | 2 | 19.0 |
| 2001 | 3 | 21.0 |
| 2002 | 4 | 22.7 |
| 2003 | 5 | 24.5 |

# Nonlinear Trends

The emphasis in the previous discussion was on a time series whose growth or decline approximated a line. A linear trend equation is used to represent the time series when it is believed that the data are increasing (or decreasing) by *equal amounts,* on the average, from one period to another.

Data that increase (or decrease) by *increasing amounts* over a period of time appear *curvilinear* when plotted on paper having an arithmetic scale. To put it another way, data that increase (or decrease) by *equal percents or proportions* over a period of time appear curvilinear on arithmetic paper. (See Chart 19–7.)

The trend equation for a time series that does approximate a curvilinear trend, such as the one portrayed in Chart 19–7, may be computed by using the logarithms of the data and the least squares method. The general equation for the logarithmic trend equation is:

| LOG TREND EQUATION | $\log Y' = \log a + \log b(t)$ | [19–2] |
|---|---|---|

The logarithmic trend equation can be determined for the Gulf Shores Importers data in Chart 19–7 using Excel. The first step is to enter the data, then find the log base 10 of each year's imports. Finally, use the regression procedure to find the least squares equation. To put it another way, we take the log of each year's data then use the logs as the dependent variable and the coded year as the independent variable.

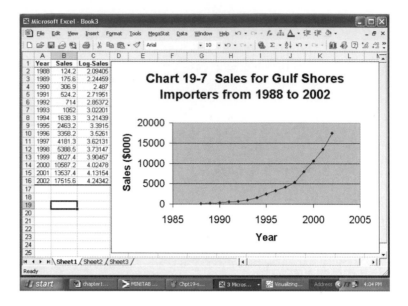

**CHART 19–7**  Sales for Gulf Shores Importers, 1988–2002

The regression equation is $Y' = 2.053807 + 0.153357t$, which is the log form. We now have a trend equation in terms of percent change. That is, the value 0.153357 is the percent change in $Y'$ for each unit increase in $t$. This value is similar to the geometric mean described in Chapter 3.

The log of $b$ is 0.153357 and its antilog or inverse is 1.423498. If we subtract 1 from this value, as we did in Chapter 3, the value 0.423498 indicates the geometric mean annual rate of increase from 1988 to 2002. We conclude that imports increased at a rate of 42.35 percent annually during the period.

We can also use the logarithmic trend equation to make estimates of future values. Suppose we want to estimate the imports in the year 2006. The first step is to determine the code for the year 2006, which is 19. How did we get 19? The year 2002 has a code of 15 and the year 2006 is four years later, so 15 + 4 = 19. The log of imports for the year 2006 is

$$Y' = 2.053807 + 0.153357t = 2.053807 + 0.153357(19) = 4.967590$$

To find the estimated imports for the year 2006, we need the antilog of 4.967590. It is 92,809. This is our estimate of the number of imports for 2006. Recall that the data were in thousands of dollars, so the estimate is $92,809,000.

---

**Self-Review 19–3**

Sales at Tomlin Manufacturing since 1999 are:

| Year | Sales ($ millions) |
|------|--------------------|
| 1999 | 2.13 |
| 2000 | 18.10 |
| 2001 | 39.80 |
| 2002 | 81.40 |
| 2003 | 112.00 |

(a)  Determine the logarithmic trend equation for the sales data.
(b)  Sales increased by what percent annually from 1999 to 2003?
(c)  What is the projected sales amount for 2004?

---

# Exercises

7. Sally's Software, Inc. is a rapidly growing supplier of computer software to the Sarasota area. Sales for the last five years are given below.

| Year | Sales ($ millions) |
|------|--------------------|
| 1999 | 1.1 |
| 2000 | 1.5 |
| 2001 | 2.0 |
| 2002 | 2.4 |
| 2003 | 3.1 |

   a. Determine the logarithmic trend equation.
   b. By what percent did sales increase, on the average, during the period?
   c. Estimates sales for the year 2006.

8. It appears that the imports of carbon black have been increasing by about 10 percent annually.

| Year | Imports of Carbon Black (thousands of tons) | Year | Imports of Carbon Black (thousands of tons) |
|------|---------------------------------------------|------|---------------------------------------------|
| 1996 | 92.0  | 2000 | 135.0 |
| 1997 | 101.0 | 2001 | 149.0 |
| 1998 | 112.0 | 2002 | 163.0 |
| 1999 | 124.0 | 2003 | 180.0 |

   a. Determine the logarithmic trend equation.
   b. By what percent did imports increase, on the average, during the period?
   c. Estimate imports for the year 2006.

# Seasonal Variation

We mentioned that *seasonal variation* is another of the components of a time series. Business series, such as automobile sales, shipments of soft-drink bottles, and residential construction, have periods of above-average and below-average activity each year.

In the area of production, one of the reasons for analyzing seasonal fluctuations is to have a sufficient supply of raw materials on hand to meet the varying seasonal demand. The glass container division of a large glass company, for example, manufactures nonreturnable beer bottles, iodine bottles, aspirin bottles, bottles for rubber cement, and so on. The production scheduling department must know how many bottles to produce and when to produce each kind. A run of too many bottles of one kind may cause a serious storage problem. Production cannot be based entirely on orders on hand, because many orders are telephoned in for immediate shipment. Since the demand for many of the bottles varies according to the season, a forecast a year or two in advance, by month, is essential to good scheduling.

An analysis of seasonal fluctuations over a period of years can also help in evaluating current sales. The typical sales of department stores in the United States, excluding mail-order sales, are expressed as indexes in Table 19–5. Each index represents the average sales for a period of several years. The actual sales for some months were above average (which is represented by an index over 100.0), and the sales for other months were below average. The index of 126.8 for December indicates that, typically, sales for December are 26.8 percent above an average month; the index of 86.0 for July indicates that department store sales for July are typically 14 percent below an average month.

**TABLE 19–5**  Typical Seasonal Indexes for U.S. Department Store Sales, Excluding Mail-Order Sales

| | | | |
|---|---|---|---|
| January | 87.0 | July | 86.0 |
| February | 83.2 | August | 99.7 |
| March | 100.5 | September | 101.4 |
| April | 106.5 | October | 105.8 |
| May | 101.6 | November | 111.9 |
| June | 89.6 | December | 126.8 |

Suppose an enterprising store manager, in an effort to stimulate sales during December, introduced a number of unique promotions, including bands of carolers strolling through the store singing holiday songs, large mechanical exhibits, and clerks dressed in Santa Claus costumes. When the index of sales was computed for that December, it was 150.0. Compared with the typical December sales of 126.8, it was concluded that the promotional program was a huge success.

## Determining a Seasonal Index

Objective: To determine a set of "typical" seasonal indexes

A typical set of monthly indexes consists of 12 indexes that are representative of the data for a 12-month period. Logically, there are four typical seasonal indexes for data reported quarterly. Each index is a percent, with the average for the year equal to 100.0; that is, each monthly index indicates the level of sales, production, or another variable in relation to the annual average of 100.0. A typical index of 96.0 for January indicates that sales (or whatever the variable is) are usually 4 percent below the average for the year. An index of 107.2 for October means that the variable is typically 7.2 percent above the annual average.

Several methods have been developed to measure the typical seasonal fluctuation in a time series. The method most commonly used to compute the typical seasonal pattern is called the **ratio-to-moving-average method.** It eliminates the trend, cyclical, and irregular components from the original data ($Y$). In the following discussion, $T$ refers to trend, $C$ to cyclical, $S$ to seasonal, and $I$ to irregular variation. The numbers that result are called the *typical seasonal index.*

We will discuss in detail the steps followed in arriving at typical seasonal indexes using the ratio-to-moving-average method. The data of interest might be monthly or quarterly. To illustrate, we have chosen the quarterly sales of Toys International. First, we will show the steps needed to arrive at a set of typical quarterly indexes. Then we use the MegaStat Excel and MINITAB software to calculate the seasonal indexes.

**EXAMPLE**

Table 19–6 shows the quarterly sales for Toys International for the years 1998 through 2003. The sales are reported in millions of dollars. Determine a quarterly seasonal index using the ratio-to-moving-average method.

**TABLE 19–6** Quarterly Sales of Toys International ($ millions)

| Year | Winter | Spring | Summer | Fall |
|------|--------|--------|--------|------|
| 1998 | 6.7 | 4.6 | 10.0 | 12.7 |
| 1999 | 6.5 | 4.6 | 9.8 | 13.6 |
| 2000 | 6.9 | 5.0 | 10.4 | 14.1 |
| 2001 | 7.0 | 5.5 | 10.8 | 15.0 |
| 2002 | 7.1 | 5.7 | 11.1 | 14.5 |
| 2003 | 8.0 | 6.2 | 11.4 | 14.9 |

**SOLUTION**

Chart 19–8 depicts the quarterly sales for Toys International over the six-year period. Notice the seasonal nature of the sales. For each year, the fourth-quarter sales are the largest and the second-quarter sales are the smallest. Also, there is a moderate

**CHART 19–8** Quarterly Sales of Toys International 1998–2003

increase in the sales from one year to the next. To observe this feature, look only at the six fourth-quarter sales values. Over the six-year period, the sales in the fourth quarter increased. If you connect these points in your mind, you can visualize fourth-quarter sales increasing for 2004.

There are six steps to determining the quarterly seasonal indexes.

**Step 1**    For the following discussion, refer to Table 19–7. The first step is to determine the four-quarter moving total for 1998. Starting with the winter

**TABLE 19–7** Computations Needed for the Specific Seasonal Indexes

| Year | Quarter | (1) Sales ($ millions) | (2) Four-Quarter Total | (3) Four-Quarter Moving Average | (4) Centered Moving Average | (5) Specific Seasonal |
|------|---------|------------------------|------------------------|--------------------------------|----------------------------|-----------------------|
| 1998 | Winter  | 6.7  |      |       |       |       |
|      | Spring  | 4.6  |      |       |       |       |
|      |         |      | 34.0 | 8.500 |       |       |
|      | Summer  | 10.0 |      |       | 8.475 | 1.180 |
|      |         |      | 33.8 | 8.450 |       |       |
|      | Fall    | 12.7 |      |       | 8.450 | 1.503 |
|      |         |      | 33.8 | 8.450 |       |       |
| 1999 | Winter  | 6.5  |      |       | 8.425 | 0.772 |
|      |         |      | 33.6 | 8.400 |       |       |
|      | Spring  | 4.6  |      |       | 8.513 | 0.540 |
|      |         |      | 34.5 | 8.625 |       |       |
|      | Summer  | 9.8  |      |       | 8.675 | 1.130 |
|      |         |      | 34.9 | 8.725 |       |       |
|      | Fall    | 13.6 |      |       | 8.775 | 1.550 |
|      |         |      | 35.3 | 8.825 |       |       |
| 2000 | Winter  | 6.9  |      |       | 8.900 | 0.775 |
|      |         |      | 35.9 | 8.975 |       |       |
|      | Spring  | 5.0  |      |       | 9.038 | 0.553 |
|      |         |      | 36.4 | 9.100 |       |       |
|      | Summer  | 10.4 |      |       | 9.113 | 1.141 |
|      |         |      | 36.5 | 9.125 |       |       |
|      | Fall    | 14.1 |      |       | 9.188 | 1.535 |
|      |         |      | 37.0 | 9.250 |       |       |
| 2001 | Winter  | 7.0  |      |       | 9.300 | 0.753 |
|      |         |      | 37.4 | 9.350 |       |       |
|      | Spring  | 5.5  |      |       | 9.463 | 0.581 |
|      |         |      | 38.3 | 9.575 |       |       |
|      | Summer  | 10.8 |      |       | 9.588 | 1.126 |
|      |         |      | 38.4 | 9.600 |       |       |
|      | Fall    | 15.0 |      |       | 9.625 | 1.558 |
|      |         |      | 38.6 | 9.650 |       |       |
| 2002 | Winter  | 7.1  |      |       | 9.688 | 0.733 |
|      |         |      | 38.9 | 9.725 |       |       |
|      | Spring  | 5.7  |      |       | 9.663 | 0.590 |
|      |         |      | 38.4 | 9.600 |       |       |
|      | Summer  | 11.1 |      |       | 9.713 | 1.143 |
|      |         |      | 39.3 | 9.825 |       |       |
|      | Fall    | 14.5 |      |       | 9.888 | 1.466 |
|      |         |      | 39.8 | 9.950 |       |       |
| 2003 | Winter  | 8.0  |      |       | 9.888 | 0.801 |
|      |         |      | 40.1 | 10.025|       |       |
|      | Spring  | 6.2  |      |       | 10.075| 0.615 |
|      |         |      | 40.5 | 10.125|       |       |
|      | Summer  | 11.4 |      |       |       |       |
|      | Fall    | 14.9 |      |       |       |       |

quarter of 1998, we add $6.7, $4.6, $10.0, and $12.7. The total is $34.0 (million). The four-quarter total is "moved along" by adding the spring, summer, and fall sales of 1998 to the winter sales of 1999. The total is $33.8 (million), found by 4.6 + 10.0 + 12.7 + 6.5. This procedure is continued for the quarterly sales for each of the six years. Column 2 of Table 19–7 shows all of the moving totals. Note that the moving total 34.0 is positioned between the spring and summer sales of 1998. The next moving total, 33.8, is positioned between sales for summer and fall of 1998, and so on. Check the totals frequently to avoid arithmetic errors.

**Step 2** Each quarterly moving total in column 2 is divided by 4 to give the four-quarter moving average. (See column 3.) All the moving averages are still positioned between the quarters. For example, the first moving average (8.500) is positioned between spring and summer of 1998.

**Step 3** The moving averages are then centered. The first centered moving average is found by (8.500 + 8.450)/2 = 8.475 and centered opposite summer 1998. The second moving average is found by (8.450 + 8.450)/2 = 8.45. The others are found similarly. Note in column 4 that a centered moving average is positioned on a particular quarter.

**Step 4** The **specific seasonal index** for each quarter is then computed by dividing the sales in column 1 by the centered moving average in column 4. The specific seasonal reports the ratio of the original time series value to the moving average. To explain further, if the time series is represented by *TSCI* and the moving average by *TC,* then, algebraically, if we compute *TSCI/TC,* the result is the specified seasonal component *SI.* The specific seasonal for the summer quarter of 1998 is 1.180, found by 10.0/8.475.

**Step 5** The specific seasonal indexes are organized in a table. (See Table 19–8.) This table will help us locate the specific seasonals for the corresponding quarters. The values 1.180, 1.130, 1.141, 1.126, and 1.143 all represent estimates of the typical seasonal index for the summer quarter. A reasonable method to find a typical seasonal index is to average these values. So we find the typical index for the summer quarter by (1.180 + 1.130 + 1.141 + 1.126 + 1.143)/5 = 1.144. We used the arithmetic mean, but the median or a modified mean can also be used.

**TABLE 19–8** Calculations Needed for Typical Quarterly Indexes

| Year | Winter | Spring | Summer | Fall | |
|------|--------|--------|--------|------|---|
| 1998 | | | 1.180 | 1.503 | |
| 1999 | 0.772 | 0.540 | 1.130 | 1.550 | |
| 2000 | 0.775 | 0.553 | 1.141 | 1.535 | |
| 2001 | 0.753 | 0.581 | 1.126 | 1.558 | |
| 2002 | 0.733 | 0.590 | 1.143 | 1.466 | |
| 2003 | 0.801 | 0.615 | | | |
| Total | 3.834 | 2.879 | 5.720 | 7.612 | |
| Mean | 0.767 | 0.576 | 1.144 | 1.522 | 4.009 |
| Adjusted | 0.765 | 0.575 | 1.141 | 1.519 | 4.000 |
| Index | 76.5 | 57.5 | 114.1 | 151.9 | |

**Step 6** The four quarterly means (0.767, 0.576, 1.144, and 1.522) should theoretically total 4.00 because the average is set at 1.0. The total of the four quarterly means may not exactly equal 4.00 due to rounding. In this problem the total of the means is 4.009. A *correction factor* is therefore applied to each of the four means to force them to total 4.00.

| CORRECTION FACTOR FOR ADJUSTING QUARTERLY MEANS | Correction factor = $\dfrac{4.00}{\text{Total of four means}}$ | [19–3] |
|---|---|---|

In this example,

$$\text{Correction factor} = \frac{4.00}{4.009} = 0.997755$$

The adjusted winter quarterly index is, therefore, .767(.997755) = .765. Each of the means is adjusted downward so that the total of the four quarterly means is 4.00. Usually indexes are reported as percentages, so each value in the last row of Table 19–8 has been multiplied by 100. So the index for the winter quarter is 76.5 and for the fall it is 151.9. How are these values interpreted? Sales for the fall quarter are 51.9 percent above the typical quarter, and for winter they are 23.5 below the typical quarter (100.0 − 76.5). These findings should not surprise you. The period prior to Christmas (the fall quarter) is when toy sales are brisk. After Christmas (the winter quarter), sales of the toys decline drastically.

As we noted earlier there is software that will perform the calculations and output the results. The MegaStat Excel output is shown below. Use of software will greatly reduce the computational time and the chance of an error in arithmetic, but you should understand the steps in the process, as outlined earlier. There can be slight differences in the answers, due to the number of digits carried in the calculations.

Centered Moving Average and Deseasonalization

| t | Year | Quarter | Sales | Centered Moving Average | Ratio to CMA | Seasonal Indexes | Sales Deseasonalized |
|---|---|---|---|---|---|---|---|
| 1 | 1998 | 1 | 6.70 | | | 0.765 | 8.759 |
| 2 | 1998 | 2 | 4.60 | | | 0.575 | 8.004 |
| 3 | 1998 | 3 | 10.00 | 8.475 | 1.180 | 1.141 | 8.761 |
| 4 | 1998 | 4 | 12.70 | 8.450 | 1.503 | 1.519 | 8.361 |
| 5 | 1999 | 1 | 6.50 | 8.425 | 0.772 | 0.765 | 8.498 |
| 6 | 1999 | 2 | 4.60 | 8.513 | 0.540 | 0.575 | 8.004 |
| 7 | 1999 | 3 | 9.80 | 8.675 | 1.130 | 1.141 | 8.586 |
| 8 | 1999 | 4 | 13.60 | 8.775 | 1.550 | 1.519 | 8.953 |
| 9 | 2000 | 1 | 6.90 | 8.900 | 0.775 | 0.765 | 9.021 |
| 10 | 2000 | 2 | 5.00 | 9.038 | 0.553 | 0.575 | 8.700 |
| 11 | 2000 | 3 | 10.40 | 9.113 | 1.141 | 1.141 | 9.112 |
| 12 | 2000 | 4 | 14.10 | 9.188 | 1.535 | 1.519 | 9.283 |
| 13 | 2001 | 1 | 7.00 | 9.300 | 0.753 | 0.765 | 9.151 |
| 14 | 2001 | 2 | 5.50 | 9.463 | 0.581 | 0.575 | 9.570 |
| 15 | 2001 | 3 | 10.80 | 9.588 | 1.126 | 1.141 | 9.462 |
| 16 | 2001 | 4 | 15.00 | 9.625 | 1.558 | 1.519 | 9.875 |
| 17 | 2002 | 1 | 7.10 | 9.688 | 0.733 | 0.765 | 9.282 |
| 18 | 2002 | 2 | 5.70 | 9.663 | 0.590 | 0.575 | 9.918 |
| 19 | 2002 | 3 | 11.10 | 9.713 | 1.143 | 1.141 | 9.725 |
| 20 | 2002 | 4 | 14.50 | 9.888 | 1.466 | 1.519 | 9.546 |
| 21 | 2003 | 1 | 8.00 | 9.988 | 0.801 | 0.765 | 10.459 |
| 22 | 2003 | 2 | 6.20 | 10.075 | 0.615 | 0.575 | 10.788 |
| 23 | 2003 | 3 | 11.40 | | | 1.141 | 9.988 |
| 24 | 2003 | 4 | 14.90 | | | 1.519 | 9.809 |

Calculation of Seasonal Indexes

| | 1 | 2 | 3 | 4 | |
|---|---|---|---|---|---|
| 1998 | | | 1.180 | 1.503 | |
| 1999 | 0.772 | 0.540 | 1.130 | 1.550 | |
| 2000 | 0.775 | 0.553 | 1.141 | 1.535 | |
| 2001 | 0.753 | 0.581 | 1.126 | 1.558 | |
| 2002 | 0.733 | 0.590 | 1.143 | 1.466 | |
| 2003 | 0.801 | 0.615 | | | |
| mean: | 0.767 | 0.576 | 1.144 | 1.522 | 4.009 |
| adjusted: | 0.765 | 0.575 | 1.141 | 1.519 | 4.000 |

Now we briefly summarize the reasoning underlying the preceding calculations. The original data in column 1 of Table 19–7 contain trend ($T$), cyclical ($C$), seasonal ($S$), and irregular ($I$) components. The ultimate objective is to remove seasonal ($S$) from the original sales valuation.

Columns 2 and 3 in Table 19–7 are concerned with deriving the centered moving average given in column 4. Basically, we "average out" the seasonal and irregular fluctuations from the original data in column 1. Thus, in column 4 we have only trend and cyclical ($TC$).

Next, we divide the sales data in column 1 ($TCSI$) by the centered fourth-quarter moving average in column 4 ($TC$) to arrive at the specific seasonals in column 5 ($SI$). In terms of letters, $TCSI/TC = SI$. We multiply $SI$ by 100.0 to express the typical seasonal in index form.

Finally, we take the mean of all the winter typical indexes, all the spring indexes, and so on. This averaging eliminates most of the irregular fluctuations from the specific seasonals, and the resulting four indexes indicate the typical seasonal sales pattern.

---

**Self-Review 19–4**

Teton Village, Wyoming, near Grand Teton Park and Yellowstone Park, contains shops, restaurants, and motels. They have two peak seasons—winter, for skiing on the 10,000-foot slopes, and summer, for tourists visiting the parks. The number of visitors (in 000) by quarter for five years follows.

|      | Quarter | | | |
| Year | Winter | Spring | Summer | Fall |
| --- | --- | --- | --- | --- |
| 1999 | 117.0 | 80.7 | 129.6 | 76.1 |
| 2000 | 118.6 | 82.5 | 121.4 | 77.0 |
| 2001 | 114.0 | 84.3 | 119.9 | 75.0 |
| 2002 | 120.7 | 79.6 | 130.7 | 69.6 |
| 2003 | 125.2 | 80.2 | 127.6 | 72.0 |

(a) Develop the typical seasonal pattern for Teton Village using the ratio-to-moving-average method.
(b) Explain the typical index for the winter season.

---

# Exercises

**9.** Victor Anderson, the owner of Anderson Belts, Inc., is studying absenteeism among his employees. His workforce is small, consisting of only five employees. For the last three years he recorded the following number of employee absences, in days, for each quarter.

|      | Quarter | | | |
| Year | I | II | III | IV |
| --- | --- | --- | --- | --- |
| 2001 | 4 | 10 | 7 | 3 |
| 2002 | 5 | 12 | 9 | 4 |
| 2003 | 6 | 16 | 12 | 4 |

Determine a typical seasonal index for each of the four quarters.

**10.** The Appliance Center sells a variety of electronic equipment and home appliances. For the last four years the following quarterly sales (in $ millions) were reported.

| Year | Quarter | | | |
|------|-----|-----|-----|-----|
|      | I | II | III | IV |
| 2000 | 5.3 | 4.1 | 6.8 | 6.7 |
| 2001 | 4.8 | 3.8 | 5.6 | 6.8 |
| 2002 | 4.3 | 3.8 | 5.7 | 6.0 |
| 2003 | 5.6 | 4.6 | 6.4 | 5.9 |

Determine a typical seasonal index for each of the four quarters.

# Deseasonalizing Data

A set of typical indexes is very useful in adjusting a sales series, for example, for seasonal fluctuations. The resulting sales series is called **deseasonalized sales** or **seasonally adjusted sales.** The reason for deseasonalizing the sales series is to remove the seasonal fluctuations so that the trend and cycle can be studied. To illustrate the procedure, the quarterly sales totals of Toys International from Table 19–6 are repeated in column 1 of Table 19–9.

**TABLE 19–9** Actual and Deseasonalized Sales for Toys International

| Year | Quarter | (1) Sales | (2) Seasonal Index | (3) Deseasonalized Sales |
|------|---------|-----------|--------------------|--------------------------|
| 1998 | Winter | 6.7 | 0.765 | 8.76 |
|      | Spring | 4.6 | 0.575 | 8.00 |
|      | Summer | 10.0 | 1.141 | 8.76 |
|      | Fall | 12.7 | 1.519 | 8.36 |
| 1999 | Winter | 6.5 | 0.765 | 8.50 |
|      | Spring | 4.6 | 0.575 | 8.00 |
|      | Summer | 9.8 | 1.141 | 8.59 |
|      | Fall | 13.6 | 1.519 | 8.95 |
| 2000 | Winter | 6.9 | 0.765 | 9.02 |
|      | Spring | 5.0 | 0.575 | 8.70 |
|      | Summer | 10.4 | 1.141 | 9.11 |
|      | Fall | 14.1 | 1.519 | 9.28 |
| 2001 | Winter | 7.0 | 0.765 | 9.15 |
|      | Spring | 5.5 | 0.575 | 9.57 |
|      | Summer | 10.8 | 1.141 | 9.47 |
|      | Fall | 15.0 | 1.519 | 9.87 |
| 2002 | Winter | 7.1 | 0.765 | 9.28 |
|      | Spring | 5.7 | 0.575 | 9.91 |
|      | Summer | 11.1 | 1.141 | 9.73 |
|      | Fall | 14.5 | 1.519 | 9.55 |
| 2003 | Winter | 8.0 | 0.765 | 10.46 |
|      | Spring | 6.2 | 0.575 | 10.79 |
|      | Summer | 11.4 | 1.141 | 9.99 |
|      | Fall | 14.9 | 1.519 | 9.81 |

To remove the effect of seasonal variation, the sales amount for each quarter (which contains trend, cyclical, irregular, and seasonal effects) is divided by the seasonal index for that quarter, that is, *TSCI/S*. For example, the actual sales for the first quarter of 1998 were $6.7 million. The seasonal index for the winter quarter is 76.5, using the MegaStat results on page 672. The index of 76.5 indicates that sales for the first quarter are typically 23.5 percent below the average for a typical quarter. By dividing the actual sales of $6.7 million by 76.5 and multiplying the result by 100, we find the *deseasonalized sales* value for the first quarter of 1998. It is $8,758,170, found by ($6,700,000/76.5)100. We continue this process for the other quarters in column 3 of Table 19–9, with the results reported in millions of dollars. Because the seasonal component has been removed (divided out) from the quarterly sales, the deseasonalized sales figure contains only the trend (*T*), cyclical (*C*), and irregular (*I*) components. Scanning the deseasonalized sales in column 3 of Table 19–9, we see that the sales of toys showed a moderate increase over the six-year period. Chart 19–9 shows both the actual sales and the deseasonalized sales. It is clear that removing the seasonal factor allows us to focus on the overall long-term trend of sales. We will also be able to determine the regression equation of the trend data and use it to forecast future sales.

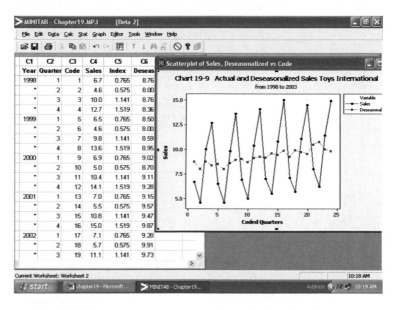

**CHART 19–9** Actual and Deseasonalized Sales for Toys International from 1998–2003

## Using Deseasonalized Data to Forecast

The procedure for identifying trend and the seasonal adjustments can be combined to yield seasonally adjusted forecasts. To identify the trend, we determine the least squares trend equation on the deseasonalized historical data. Then we project this trend into future periods, and finally we adjust these trend values to account for the seasonal factors. The following example will help to clarify.

**EXAMPLE**

Toys International would like to forecast its sales for each quarter of 2004. Use the information in Table 19–9 to determine the forecast.

**SOLUTION**

The deseasonalized data depicted in Chart 19–9 seems to follow a straight line. Hence it is reasonable to develop a linear trend equation based on these data. The deseasonalized trend equation is:

$$Y' = a + bt$$

**Statistics in Action**

Forecasts are not always correct. The reality is that a forecast may just be a best guess as to what will happen. What are the reasons forecasts are not correct? One expert lists eight common errors: (1) failure to carefully examine the assumptions, (2) limited expertise, (3) lack of imagination, (4) neglect of constraints, (5) excessive optimism, (6) reliance on mechanical extrapolation, (7) premature closure, and (8) overspecification.

where:

Y' is the estimated trend value for Toys International sales for the period t.
a is the intercept of the trend line at time 0.
b is the slope of the line.
t is the coded time period.

The winter quarter of 1998 is the first quarter, so it is coded 1, the spring quarter of 1998 is coded 2, and so on. The last quarter of 2003 is coded 24. These coded values are shown in the data section of the MINITAB output associated with Chart 19–9.

We use MINITAB to find the regression equation. The output follows. The output includes a scatter diagram of the coded time periods and the deseasonalized sales as well as the regression line.

The equation for the trend line is:

$$Y' = 8.109 + .08991t$$

The slope of the trend line is .08991. This shows that over the 24 quarters the deseasonalized sales increased at a rate of 0.08991 ($ million) per quarter, or $89,910 per quarter. The value of 8.109 is the intercept of the trend line on the Y-axis (i.e., for t = 0).

The MINITAB system also outputs the coefficient of determination. This value, called $R^2$, is 78.6 percent. It is shown in the upper right of the MINITAB output. We can use this value as an indication of the fit of the data. Because this is *not* sample information, technically we should not use $R^2$ for judging a regression equation. However, it will serve to quickly evaluate the fit of the deseasonalized sales data. In this instance because $R^2$ is rather large we conclude the deseasonalized sales of Toys International are effectively explained by a linear trend equation.

If we assume that the past 24 periods are a good indicator of future sales, we can use the trend equation to estimate future sales. For example, for the winter quarter of 2004 the value of t is 25. Therefore, the estimated sales of that period is 10.35675, found by

$$Y' = 8.109 + .08991t = 8.109 + .08991(25) = 10.35675$$

The estimated deseasonalized sales for the winter quarter of 2004 are $10,356,750. This is the sales forecast, before we consider the effects of seasonality.

We use the same procedure and an Excel spreadsheet to determine a forecast for each of the four quarters of 2004. A partial Excel output follows.

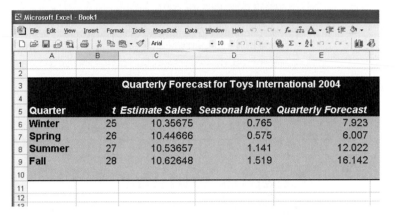

| Quarter | t | Estimate Sales | Seasonal Index | Quarterly Forecast |
|---------|---|----------------|----------------|--------------------|
| Winter | 25 | 10.35675 | 0.765 | 7.923 |
| Spring | 26 | 10.44666 | 0.575 | 6.007 |
| Summer | 27 | 10.53657 | 1.141 | 12.022 |
| Fall | 28 | 10.62648 | 1.519 | 16.142 |

*Quarterly Forecast for Toys International 2004*

Now that we have the forecasts for the four quarters of 2004, we can seasonally adjust them. The index for a winter quarter is 0.765. So we can seasonally adjust the forecast for the first quarter of 2004 by 10.35675(0.765) = 7.923. The estimates for each of the four quarters of 2004 are in the right-hand column of the Excel output. Notice how the seasonal adjustments drastically increase the sales estimates for the last two quarters of the year.

---

**Self-Review 19–5**

The Westberg Electric Company sells electric motors to customers in the Jamestown, New York, area. The monthly trend equation, based on five years of monthly data, is

$$Y' = 4.4 + 0.5t$$

The seasonal factor for the month of January is 120, and it is 95 for February. Determine the seasonally adjusted forecast for January and February of the sixth year.

# Exercises

**11.** The planning department of Padget and Kure Shoes, the manufacturer of an exclusive brand of women's shoes, developed the following trend equation, in millions of pairs, based on five years of quarterly data.

$$Y' = 3.30 + 1.75t$$

The following table gives the seasonal factors for each quarter.

|  | Quarter | | | |
|---|---|---|---|---|
|  | I | II | III | IV |
| Index | 110.0 | 120.0 | 80.0 | 90.0 |

Determine the seasonally adjusted forecast for each of the four quarters of the sixth year.

**12.** Team Sports, Inc. sells sporting goods to high schools and colleges via a nationally distributed catalog. Management at Team Sports estimates they will sell 2,000 Wilson Model A2000 catcher's mitts next year. The deseasonalized sales are projected to be the same for each of the four quarters next year. The seasonal factor for the second quarter is 145. Determine the seasonally adjusted sales for the second quarter of next year.

13. Refer to Exercise 9, regarding the absences at Anderson Belts, Inc. Use the seasonal indexes you computed to determine the deseasonalized absences. Determine the linear trend equation based on the quarterly data for the three years. Forecast the seasonally adjusted absences for 2004.

14. Refer to Exercise 10, regarding sales at the Appliance Center. Use the seasonal indexes you computed to determine the deseasonalized sales. Determine the linear trend equation based on the quarterly data for the four years. Forecast the seasonally adjusted sales for 2004.

# Chapter Outline

I. A time series is a collection of data over a period of time.
   A. The trend is the long-run direction of the time series.
   B. The cyclical component is the fluctuation above and below the long-term trend line over a longer period of time.
   C. The seasonal variation is the pattern in a time series within a year. These patterns tend to repeat themselves from year to year for most businesses.
   D. The irregular variation is divided into two components.
      1. The episodic variations are unpredictable, but they can usually be identified. A flood is an example.
      2. The residual variations are random in nature.

II. A moving average is used to smooth the trend in a time series.

III. The linear trend equation is $Y' = a + bt$, where $a$ is the $Y$-intercept, $b$ is the slope of the line, and $t$ is the coded time.
   A. The trend equation is determined using the least squares principle.
   B. If the trend is not linear, but rather the increases tend to be a constant percent, the $Y$ values are converted to logarithms, and a least squares equation is determined using the logarithms.

IV. A seasonal factor can be estimated using the ratio-to-moving-average method.
   A. The six-step procedure yields a seasonal index for each period.
      1. Seasonal factors are usually computed on a monthly or a quarterly basis.
      2. The seasonal factor is used to adjust forecasts, taking into account the effects of the season.

# Chapter Exercises

15. Refer to the following diagram.
   a. Estimate the linear trend equation for the production series by drawing a line through the data.
   b. What is the average annual decrease in production?
   c. Based on the trend equation, what is the forecast for the year 2005?

**16.** Refer to the following diagram.
- **a.** Estimate the linear trend equation for the personal income series.
- **b.** What is the average annual increase in personal income?

**17.** The asset turnovers, excluding cash and short-term investments, for the RNC Company from 1993 to 2003 are:

| 1993 | 1994 | 1995 | 1996 | 1997 | 1998 | 1999 | 2000 | 2001 | 2002 | 2003 |
|------|------|------|------|------|------|------|------|------|------|------|
| 1.11 | 1.28 | 1.17 | 1.10 | 1.06 | 1.14 | 1.24 | 1.33 | 1.38 | 1.50 | 1.65 |

- **a.** Plot the data.
- **b.** Determine the least squares trend equation.
- **c.** Calculate the points on the trend line for 1996 and 2001, and plot the line on the graph.
- **d.** Estimate the asset turnover for 2008.
- **e.** How much did the asset turnover increase per year, on the average, from 1993 to 2003?

**18.** The sales, in billions of dollars, of Keller Overhead Door, Inc. for 1998 to 2003 are:

| Year | Sales | Year | Sales |
|------|-------|------|-------|
| 1998 | 7.45 | 2001 | 7.94 |
| 1999 | 7.83 | 2002 | 7.76 |
| 2000 | 8.07 | 2003 | 7.90 |

- **a.** Plot the data.
- **b.** Determine the least squares trend equation.
- **c.** Use the trend equation to calculate the points for 2000 and 2002. Plot them on the graph and draw the regression line.
- **d.** Estimate the net sales for 2006.
- **e.** By how much have sales increased (or decreased) per year on the average during the period?

**19.** The number of employees, in thousands, of Keller Overhead Door, Inc. for the years 1998 to 2003 are:

| Year | Employees | Year | Employees |
|------|-----------|------|-----------|
| 1998 | 45.6 | 2001 | 39.3 |
| 1999 | 42.2 | 2002 | 34.0 |
| 2000 | 41.1 | 2003 | 30.0 |

- **a.** Plot the data.
- **b.** Determine the least squares trend equation.
- **c.** Use the trend equation to calculate the points for 2000 and 2002. Plot them on the graph and draw the regression line.
- **d.** Estimate the number of employees in 2006.
- **e.** By how much has the number of employees increased (or decreased) per year on the average during the period?

**20.** Listed below is the selling price for a share of PepsiCo, Inc. at the close of the year.

| Year | Price | Year | Price | Year | Price |
|------|-------|------|-------|------|-------|
| 1990 | 12.9135 | 1994 | 18.3160 | 1998 | 40.6111 |
| 1991 | 16.8250 | 1995 | 27.7538 | 1999 | 35.0230 |
| 1992 | 20.6125 | 1996 | 29.0581 | 2000 | 49.5625 |
| 1993 | 20.3024 | 1997 | 36.0155 | 2001 | 48.6800 |
|      |         |      |         | 2002 | 42.2200 |

    **a.** Plot the data.
    **b.** Determine the least squares trend equation.
    **c.** Calculate the points for the years 1993 and 1998.
    **d.** Estimate the selling price in 2006. Does this seem like a reasonable estimate based on the historical data?
    **e.** By how much has the stock price increased or decreased (per year) on average during the period?

**21.** If plotted on arithmetic paper, the following sales series would appear curvilinear. This indicates that sales are increasing at a somewhat constant annual rate (percent). To fit the sales, therefore, a logarithmic straight-line equation should be used.

| Year | Sales ($ millions) | Year | Sales ($ millions) |
|------|--------------------|------|--------------------|
| 1993 | 8.0 | 1999 | 39.4 |
| 1994 | 10.4 | 2000 | 50.5 |
| 1995 | 13.5 | 2001 | 65.0 |
| 1996 | 17.6 | 2002 | 84.1 |
| 1997 | 22.8 | 2003 | 109.0 |
| 1998 | 29.3 |      |      |

    **a.** Determine the logarithmic equation.
    **b.** Determine the coordinates of the points on the logarithmic straight line for 1992 and 2001.
    **c.** By what percent did sales increase per year, on the average, during the period from 1993 to 2003?
    **d.** Based on the equation, what are the estimated sales for 2004?

**22.** Reported below are the amounts spent on advertising ($ millions) by a large firm from 1993 to 2003.

| Year | Amount | Year | Amount |
|------|--------|------|--------|
| 1993 | 88.1 | 1999 | 132.6 |
| 1994 | 94.7 | 2000 | 141.9 |
| 1995 | 102.1 | 2001 | 150.9 |
| 1996 | 109.8 | 2002 | 157.9 |
| 1997 | 118.1 | 2003 | 162.6 |
| 1998 | 125.6 |      |      |

    **a.** Determine the logarithmic trend equation.
    **b.** Estimate the advertising expenses for 2006.
    **c.** By what percent per year did advertising expense increase during the period?

**23.** Listed below is the selling price for a share of Oracle, Inc. stock at the close of the year.

| Year | Price | Year | Price | Year | Price |
|------|-------|------|-------|------|-------|
| 1990 | 0.1944 | 1994 | 2.1790 | 1998 | 7.1875 |
| 1991 | 0.3580 | 1995 | 3.1389 | 1999 | 28.0156 |
| 1992 | 0.7006 | 1996 | 4.6388 | 2000 | 29.0625 |
| 1993 | 1.4197 | 1997 | 3.7188 | 2001 | 13.8100 |
|      |         |      |         | 2002 | 10.8000 |

a. Plot the data.
b. Determine the least squares trend equation. Use both the actual stock price and the log-arithm of the price. Which seems to yield a more accurate forecast?
c. Calculate the points for the years 1993 and 1998.
d. Estimate the selling price in 2005. Does this seem like a reasonable estimate based on the historical data?
e. By how much has the stock price increased or decreased (per year) on average during the period? Use your best answer from part (b).

24. The production of the Reliable Manufacturing Company for 1999 and part of 2000 follows.

| Month | 1999 Production (thousands) | 2000 Production (thousands) | Month | 1999 Production (thousands) | 2000 Production (thousands) |
|---|---|---|---|---|---|
| January | 6 | 7 | July | 3 | 4 |
| February | 7 | 9 | August | 5 | |
| March | 12 | 14 | September | 14 | |
| April | 8 | 9 | October | 6 | |
| May | 4 | 5 | November | 7 | |
| June | 3 | 4 | December | 6 | |

a. Using the ratio-to-moving-average method, determine the specific seasonals for July, August, and September 1999.
b. Assume that the specific seasonal indexes in the following table are correct. Insert in the table the specific seasonals you computed in part (a) for July, August, and September 1999, and determine the 12 typical seasonal indexes.

| Year | Jan. | Feb. | Mar. | Apr. | May | June | July | Aug. | Sept. | Oct. | Nov. | Dec. |
|---|---|---|---|---|---|---|---|---|---|---|---|---|
| 1999 | | | | | | | ? | ? | ? | 92.1 | 106.5 | 92.9 |
| 2000 | 88.9 | 102.9 | 178.9 | 118.2 | 60.1 | 43.1 | 44.0 | 74.0 | 200.9 | 90.0 | 101.9 | 90.9 |
| 2001 | 87.6 | 103.7 | 170.2 | 125.9 | 59.4 | 48.6 | 44.2 | 77.2 | 196.5 | 89.6 | 113.2 | 80.6 |
| 2002 | 79.8 | 105.6 | 165.8 | 124.7 | 62.1 | 41.7 | 48.2 | 72.1 | 203.6 | 80.2 | 103.0 | 94.2 |
| 2003 | 89.0 | 112.1 | 182.9 | 115.1 | 57.6 | 56.9 | | | | | | |

c. Interpret the typical seasonal index.

25. The sales of Andre's Boutique for 1999 and part of 2000 are:

| Month | 1999 Sales (thousands) | 2000 Sales (thousands) | Month | 1999 Sales (thousands) | 2000 Sales (thousands) |
|---|---|---|---|---|---|
| January | 78 | 65 | July | 81 | 65 |
| February | 72 | 60 | August | 85 | 61 |
| March | 80 | 72 | September | 90 | 75 |
| April | 110 | 97 | October | 98 | |
| May | 92 | 86 | November | 115 | |
| June | 86 | 72 | December | 130 | |

a. Using the ratio-to-moving-average method, determine the specific seasonals for July, August, September, and October 1999.
b. Assume that the specific seasonals in the following table are correct. Insert in the table the specific seasonals you computed in part (a) for July, August, September, and October 1999, and determine the 12 typical seasonal indexes.

| Year | Jan. | Feb. | Mar. | Apr. | May | June | July | Aug. | Sept. | Oct. | Nov. | Dec. |
|---|---|---|---|---|---|---|---|---|---|---|---|---|
| 1999 | | | | | | | ? | ? | ? | ? | 123.6 | 150.9 |
| 2000 | 83.9 | 77.6 | 86.1 | 118.7 | 99.7 | 92.0 | 87.0 | 91.4 | 97.3 | 105.4 | 124.9 | 140.1 |
| 2001 | 86.7 | 72.9 | 86.2 | 121.3 | 96.6 | 92.0 | 85.5 | 93.6 | 98.2 | 103.2 | 126.1 | 141.7 |
| 2002 | 85.6 | 65.8 | 89.2 | 125.6 | 99.6 | 94.4 | 88.9 | 90.2 | 100.2 | 102.7 | 121.6 | 139.6 |
| 2003 | 77.3 | 81.2 | 85.8 | 115.7 | 100.3 | 89.7 | | | | | | |

c. Interpret the typical seasonal index.

**26.** The quarterly production of pine lumber, in millions of board feet, by Northwest Lumber since 1999 is:

| Year | Winter | Spring | Summer | Fall |
|------|--------|--------|--------|------|
| | | Quarter | | |
| 1999 | 7.8 | 10.2 | 14.7 | 9.3 |
| 2000 | 6.9 | 11.6 | 17.5 | 9.3 |
| 2001 | 8.9 | 9.7 | 15.3 | 10.1 |
| 2002 | 10.7 | 12.4 | 16.8 | 10.7 |
| 2003 | 9.2 | 13.6 | 17.1 | 10.3 |

**a.** Determine the typical seasonal pattern for the production data using the ratio-to-moving-average method.
**b.** Interpret the pattern.
**c.** Deseasonalize the data and determine the linear trend equation.
**d.** Project the seasonally adjusted production for the four quarters of 2004.

**27.** Work Gloves Corp. is reviewing its quarterly sales of Toughie, the most durable glove they produce. The numbers of pairs produced (in thousands) by quarter are:

| Year | I<br>Jan.–Mar. | II<br>Apr.–June | III<br>July–Sept. | IV<br>Oct.–Dec. |
|------|-----------|-----------|------------|-----------|
| | | | Quarter | |
| 1998 | 142 | 312 | 488 | 208 |
| 1999 | 146 | 318 | 512 | 212 |
| 2000 | 160 | 330 | 602 | 187 |
| 2001 | 158 | 338 | 572 | 176 |
| 2002 | 162 | 380 | 563 | 200 |
| 2003 | 162 | 362 | 587 | 205 |

**a.** Using the ratio-to-moving-average method, determine the four typical quarterly indexes.
**b.** Interpret the typical seasonal pattern.

**28.** Sales of roof material, by quarter, since 1997 for Carolina Home Construction, Inc. are shown below (in $000).

| Year | I | II | III | IV |
|------|-----|-----|-----|-----|
| | | Quarter | | |
| 1997 | 210 | 180 | 60 | 246 |
| 1998 | 214 | 216 | 82 | 230 |
| 1999 | 246 | 228 | 91 | 280 |
| 2000 | 258 | 250 | 113 | 298 |
| 2001 | 279 | 267 | 116 | 304 |
| 2002 | 302 | 290 | 114 | 310 |
| 2003 | 321 | 291 | 120 | 320 |

**a.** Determine the typical seasonal patterns for sales using the ratio-to-moving-average method.
**b.** Deseasonalize the data and determine the trend equation.
**c.** Project the sales for 2004, and then seasonally adjust each quarter.

**29.** The inventory turnover rates for Bassett Wholesale Enterprises, by quarter, are:

| Year | I | II | III | IV |
|------|-----|-----|------|-----|
| | | Quarter | | |
| 1999 | 4.4 | 6.1 | 11.7 | 7.2 |
| 2000 | 4.1 | 6.6 | 11.1 | 8.6 |
| 2001 | 3.9 | 6.8 | 12.0 | 9.7 |
| 2002 | 5.0 | 7.1 | 12.7 | 9.0 |
| 2003 | 4.3 | 5.2 | 10.8 | 7.6 |

  **a.** Arrive at the four typical quarterly turnover rates for the Bassett company using the ratio-to-moving-average method.
  **b.** Deseasonalize the data and determine the trend equation.
  **c.** Project the turnover rates for 2004, and seasonally adjust each quarter of 2004.
**30.** The following is the number of retirees receiving benefits from the State Teachers Retirement System of Ohio from 1991 until 2002.

| Year | Service | Year | Service | Year | Service |
|------|---------|------|---------|------|---------|
| 1991 | 58,436  | 1995 | 67,989  | 1999 | 78,341  |
| 1992 | 59,994  | 1996 | 70,448  | 2000 | 81,111  |
| 1993 | 61,515  | 1997 | 72,601  | 2001 | 84,146  |
| 1994 | 63,182  | 1998 | 75,482  | 2002 | 87,206  |

  **a.** Plot the data.
  **b.** Determine the least squares trend equation. Use a linear equation.
  **c.** Calculate the points for the years 1993 and 1998.
  **d.** Estimate the number of retirees that will be receiving benefits in 2003. Does this seem like a reasonable estimate based on the historical data?
  **e.** By how much has the number of retirees increased or decreased (per year) on average during the period?
**31.** Ray Anderson, owner of the Anderson Ski Lodge in upstate New York, is interested in forecasting the number of visitors for the upcoming year. The following data are available, by quarter, since 1997. Develop a seasonal index for each quarter. How many visitors would you expect for each quarter of 2004, if Ray projects that there will be a 10 percent increase from the total number of visitors in 2003? Determine the trend equation, project the number of visitors for 2004, and seasonally adjust the forecast. Which forecast would you choose?

| Year | Quarter | Visitors | Year | Quarter | Visitors |
|------|---------|----------|------|---------|----------|
| 1997 | I       | 86       | 2001 | I       | 188      |
|      | II      | 62       |      | II      | 172      |
|      | III     | 28       |      | III     | 128      |
|      | IV      | 94       |      | IV      | 198      |
| 1998 | I       | 106      | 2002 | I       | 208      |
|      | II      | 82       |      | II      | 202      |
|      | III     | 48       |      | III     | 154      |
|      | IV      | 114      |      | IV      | 220      |
| 1999 | I       | 140      | 2003 | I       | 246      |
|      | II      | 120      |      | II      | 240      |
|      | III     | 82       |      | III     | 190      |
|      | IV      | 154      |      | IV      | 252      |
| 2000 | I       | 162      |      |         |          |
|      | II      | 140      |      |         |          |
|      | III     | 100      |      |         |          |
|      | IV      | 174      |      |         |          |

**32.** The enrollment in the College of Business at Midwestern University by quarter since 1999 is:

| Year | Quarter | | | |
|------|---------|--------|--------|-------|
|      | Winter | Spring | Summer | Fall  |
| 1999 | 2,033  | 1,871  | 714    | 2,318 |
| 2000 | 2,174  | 2,069  | 840    | 2,413 |
| 2001 | 2,370  | 2,254  | 927    | 2,704 |
| 2002 | 2,625  | 2,478  | 1,136  | 3,001 |
| 2003 | 2,803  | 2,668  | —      | —     |

Using the ratio-to-moving-average method:
**a.** Determine the four quarterly indexes.

**b.** Interpret the quarterly pattern of enrollment. Does the seasonal variation surprise you?

**c.** Compute the trend equation, and forecast the 2004 enrollment by quarter.

33. The Jamie Farr Kroger Classic is an LPGA (Women's Professional Golf) tournament played in Toledo, Ohio, each year. Listed below are the total purse and the prize for winner for the 17 years from 1987 through 2003. Develop a trend equation for both variables. Which variable is increasing at a faster rate? Project both the amount of the purse and the prize for the winner in 2005. Find the ratio of the winner's prize to the total purse. What do you find? Which variable can we estimate more accurately, the size of the purse or the winner's prize?

| Year | Purse | Prize | Year | Purse | Prize |
|------|-------|-------|------|-------|-------|
| 1987 | $225,000 | $33,750 | 1995 | $ 500,000 | $ 75,000 |
| 1988 | 275,000 | 41,250 | 1996 | 575,000 | 86,250 |
| 1989 | 275,000 | 41,250 | 1997 | 700,000 | 105,000 |
| 1990 | 325,000 | 48,750 | 1998 | 800,000 | 120,000 |
| 1991 | 350,000 | 52,500 | 1999 | 800,000 | 120,000 |
| 1992 | 400,000 | 60,000 | 2000 | 1,000,000 | 150,000 |
| 1993 | 450,000 | 67,500 | 2001 | 1,000,000 | 150,000 |
| 1994 | 500,000 | 75,000 | 2002 | 1,000,000 | 150,000 |
|      |         |        | 2003 | 1,000,000 | 150,000 |

# exercises.com

34. Go to the Bureau of Labor Statistics website, which is www.bls.gov, click on the **Consumer Price Index** option, select **Most Requested Series, Prices and Living Conditions,** and then **Consumer Price Index—All Urban Consumers (Current Series).** Ask for the yearly output for the last 10 to 20 years. Develop a regression equation for the annual Consumer Price Index for the selected period. Use both the linear and the log approach. Which do you think is best?

35. Develop a trend line for a large or well-known company, such as GM, General Electric, or Microsoft, for the last 10 years. You could go to the company website. Most companies have a section called "Financial Information." Go to that location and look for sales over the last 10 years. If you do not know the website of the company, go to the financial section of Yahoo or *USA Today,* where there is a location for "symbol look up." Type in the company name, which should then give you the symbol. Look up the company via the symbol, and you should find the information. The symbol for GM is just *GM,* the symbol for General Electric is *GE.* Comment on the trend line of the company you selected over the period. Is the trend increasing or decreasing? Does the trend follow a linear or log equation?

36. Select one of the major economic indicators, such as the Dow Jones Average, Nasdaq, or the S&P 500. Develop a trend line for the index over the last 10 years by using the value of the index at the end of the year, or for the last 30 days by selecting the closing value of the index for the last 30 days. You can locate this information in many places. For example, go to http://finance.yahoo.com, click on **Nasdaq** in the lower right corner, select **historical quotes,** and a period of time, perhaps the last 30 days, and you will find the information. You should be able to download it directly to Excel to create your trend equation. Comment on the trend line you created. Is it increasing or decreasing? Does the trend line follow a linear or log equation?

# Dataset Exercises

37. Refer to the Baseball 2002 data, which includes information on the 2002 Major League Baseball season. The data include the average player salary since 1976 and the median player salary since 1983. Plot the information and develop a linear trend equation for each. Compare the rate of increase in the median with the rate of increase for the average. Write a brief report on your findings.

# Software Commands

1. The MegaStat commands for creating the seasonal indexes on page 672 are:
   a. Enter the coded time period and the value of the time series in two columns. You may also want to include information on the years and quarters.
   b. Select **MegaStat, Time Series/Forecasting,** and **Deseasonalization,** and hit **Enter.**
   c. Input the range of the data, indicate the data are in the first quarter, and click **OK.**

# Chapter 19  Answers to Self-Review

**19–1**

| Year | Production (thousands) | Three-Year Moving Total | Three-Year Moving Average |
|------|------|------|------|
| 1998 | 2 | — | — |
| 1999 | 6 | 12 | 4 |
| 2000 | 4 | 15 | 5 |
| 2001 | 5 | 12 | 4 |
| 2002 | 3 | 18 | 6 |
| 2003 | 10 | — | — |

**19–2  a.**

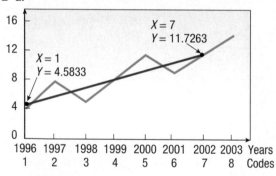

**b.** $Y' = a + bt = 3.3928 + 1.1905t$ (in thousands)

**c.** For 1996:

$$Y' = 3.3928 + 1.1905(1) = 4.5833$$

for 2002:

$$Y' = 3.3928 + 1.1905(7) = 11.7263$$

**d.** For 2006, $t = 11$, so

$$Y' = 3.3928 + 1.1905(11) = 16.4883$$

or 16,488 king-size rockers.

**19–3  a.**

| Year | Y | log Y | t |
|------|------|------|------|
| 1999 | 2.13 | 0.3284 | 1 |
| 2000 | 18.10 | 1.2577 | 2 |
| 2001 | 39.80 | 1.5999 | 3 |
| 2002 | 81.40 | 1.9106 | 4 |
| 2003 | 112.00 | 2.0492 | 5 |

$$b = 0.40945$$

$$a = 0.20081$$

**b.** About 156.7 percent. The antilog of 0.40945 is 2.567. Subtracting 1 yields 1.567.

**c.** About 454.5, found by $Y' = 0.20081 + .40945(6) = 2.65751$. The antilog of 2.64751 is 454.5.

**19–4  a.** The following values are from a software package. Due to rounding, your figures might be slightly different.

|  | Winter | Spring | Summer | Fall |
|------|------|------|------|------|
| Mean | 119.35 | 81.66 | 125.31 | 74.24 |
| Typical seasonal | 119.18 | 81.55 | 125.13 | 74.13 |

The correction factor is 0.9986.

**b.** Total sales at Teton Village for the winter season are typically 19.18 percent above the annual average.

**19–5** The forecast value for January of the sixth year is 34.9, found by

$$Y' = 4.40 + 0.5(61) = 34.9$$

Seasonally adjusting the forecast, $34.9(120)/100 = 41.88$. For February, $Y' = 4.40 + 0.50(62) = 35.4$. Then $(35.4)95/100 = 33.63$.

# An Introduction to Decision Theory

Blackbeard's Phantom Fireworks is considering introducing two new products. The company can add both to the current line, neither, or just one of the two. The success of these products depends on consumers' reactions. Refer to the data in the exercise to compute the expected monetary value for each decision. (See Goals 3, 4, and 5 and Exercise 11.)

# Introduction

A branch of statistics called **statistical decision theory** which uses probability has been developed since the early 1950s. As the name implies, the focus is on the process of making decisions and explicitly includes the payoffs that may result. In contrast, classical statistics focuses on estimating a parameter, such as the population mean, constructing a confidence interval, or conducting a hypothesis test. Classical statistics does not address the financial consequences.

Statistical decision theory is concerned with determining which decision, from a set of possible alternatives, is optimal for a particular set of conditions. Consider the following examples of decision-theory problems.

- Ford Motor Company must decide whether to purchase assembled door locks for the new model Ford F-150 truck or to manufacture and assemble the door locks

at their Sandusky, Ohio, plant. If sales of the F-150 truck continue to increase, it will be more profitable to manufacture and assemble the parts. If sales level off or decline, it will be more profitable to purchase the door locks assembled. Should they make or buy the door locks?

- Banana Republic developed a new line of summer rain jackets that are very popular in the cold-weather regions of the country. They would like to purchase commercial television time during the upcoming NCAA basketball final. If both teams that play in the game are from warm parts of the country, they estimate that only a small proportion of the viewers will be interested in the jackets. However, a match-up between two teams who come from cold climates would reach a large proportion of viewers who wear jackets. Should they purchase commercial television time?

- General Electric is considering three options regarding the prices of refrigerators for next year. GE could (1) raise the prices 5 percent, (2) raise the prices 2.5 percent, or (3) leave the prices as they are. The final decision will be based on sales estimates and on GE's knowledge of what other refrigerator manufacturers might do.

In each of these cases the decision is characterized by several alternative courses of action and several factors not under the control of the decision maker. For example, Banana Republic has no control over which teams reach the NCAA basketball final. These cases characterize the nature of decision making. Possible decision alternatives can be listed, possible future events determined, and even probabilities established, but *the decisions are made in the face of uncertainty.*

# Elements of a Decision

There are three components to any decision: (1) the choices available, or alternatives; (2) the states of nature, which are not under the control of the decision maker; and (3) the payoffs. These concepts will be explained in the following paragraphs.

The **alternatives,** or **acts,** are the choices available to the decision maker. Ford can decide to manufacture and assemble the door locks in Sandusky, or they can decide to purchase them. To simplify our presentation, we assume the decision maker can select from a rather small number of outcomes. With the help of computers, however, the decision alternatives can be expanded to a large number of possibilities.

The **states of nature** are the uncontrollable future events. The state of nature that actually happens is outside the control of the decision maker. Ford does not know whether demand will remain high for the F-150. Banana Republic cannot determine whether warm-weather or cold-weather teams will play in the NCAA basketball final.

A **payoff** is needed to compare each combination of decision alternative and state of nature. Ford may estimate that if they assemble door locks at their Sandusky plant and the demand for F-150 trucks is low, the payoff will be $40,000. Conversely, if they purchase the door locks assembled and the demand is high, the payoff is estimated to be $22,000.

The main elements of the decision under conditions of uncertainty are identified schematically:

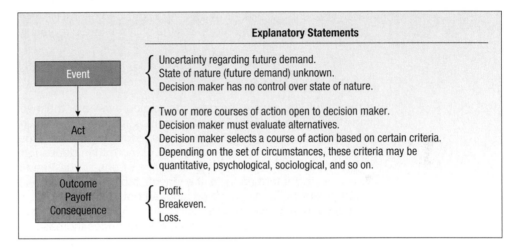

In many cases we can make better decisions if we establish probabilities for the states of nature. These probabilities may be based on historical data or subjective estimates. Ford may estimate the probability of continued high demand as .70. GE may estimate the probability to be .25 that Amana and other manufacturers will raise the prices of their refrigerators.

# A Case Involving Decision Making under Conditions of Uncertainty

At the outset it should be emphasized that this case description includes only the fundamental concepts found in decision making. The purpose of examining the case is to explain the logical procedure followed.

The first step is to set up a payoff table.

## Payoff Table

Bob Hill, a small investor, has $1,100 to invest. He has studied several common stocks and narrowed his choices to three, namely, Kayser Chemicals, Rim Homes, and Texas Electronics. He estimated that if his $1,100 were invested in Kayser Chemicals and a strong bull market developed by the end of the year (that is, stock prices increased drastically), the value of his Kayser stock would more than double, to $2,400. However, if there were a bear market (i.e., stock prices declined), the value of his Kayser stock could conceivably drop to $1,000 by the end of the year. His predictions regarding the value of his $1,100 investment for the three stocks for a bull market and for a bear market are shown in Table 20–1. This table is a **payoff table.**

TABLE 20–1  Payoff Table for Three Common Stocks under Two Market Conditions

| Purchase | Bull Market, $S_1$ | Bear Market, $S_2$ |
|---|---|---|
| Kayser Chemicals ($A_1$) | $2,400 | $1,000 |
| Rim Homes ($A_2$) | 2,200 | 1,100 |
| Texas Electronics ($A_3$) | 1,900 | 1,150 |

The various choices are called the **decision alternatives** or the **acts.** There are three in this situation. Let $A_1$ be the purchase of Kayser Chemicals, $A_2$ the purchase of Rim Homes, and $A_3$ the purchase of Texas Electronics. Whether the market turns out to be bear or bull is not under the control of Bob Hill. These uncontrolled future events are the states of nature. Let the bull market be represented by $S_1$ and the bear market by $S_2$.

## Expected Payoff

If the payoff table were the only information available, the investor might take a conservative action and buy Texas Electronics in order to be assured of at least $1,150 at the end of the year (a slight profit). A speculative venture, however, might be to buy Kayser Chemicals, with the possibility of more than doubling the $1,100 investment.

Any decision regarding the purchase of one of the three common stocks made solely on the information in the payoff table would ignore the valuable historical records kept by Moody's, Value Line, and other investment services relative to stock price movements over a long period. A study of these records, for example, revealed that during the past 10 years stock market prices increased six times and declined only four times. According to this information, the probability of a market rise is .60 and the probability of a market decline is .40.

Assuming these historical frequencies are reliable, the payoff table and the probability estimates (.60 and .40) can be combined to arrive at the **expected payoff** of buying each of the three stocks. Expected payoff is also called **expected monetary value,** shortened to EMV. It can also be described as the **mean payoff.** The calculations needed to arrive at the expected payoff for the act of purchasing Kayser Chemicals are shown in Table 20–2.

TABLE 20–2  Expected Payoff for the Act of Buying Kayser Chemicals, EMV ($A_1$)

| State of Nature | Payoff | Probability of State of Nature | Expected Value |
|---|---|---|---|
| Market rise, $S_1$ | $2,400 | .60 | $1,440 |
| Market decline, $S_2$ | 1,000 | .40 | 400 |
| | | | $1,840 |

To explain one expected monetary value calculation, note that if the investor had purchased Kayser Chemicals and the market prices declined, the value of the stock would be only $1,000 at the end of the year (from Table 20–1). Past experience, however, revealed that this event (a market decline) occurred only 40 percent of the time. In the long run, therefore, a market decline would contribute $400 to the total expected payoff from the stock, found by $1,000 × .40. Adding the $400 to the $1,440 expected under rising market conditions gives $1,840, the "expected" payoff in the long run.

These calculations are summarized as follows.

| EXPECTED MONETARY VALUE | $$EMV(A_i) = \Sigma \, [P(S_j) \times V(A_i, S_j)]$$ | [20–1] |
|---|---|---|

where:

EMV($A_i$) refers to the expected monetary value of decision alternative $i$. There may be many decisions possible. We will let 1 refer to the first decision, 2 to the second, and so on. The lower-case letter $i$ represents the entire set of decisions.

$P(S_j)$ refers to the probability of the states of nature. There can be an unlimited number, so we will let $j$ represent this possible outcome.

$V(A_i, S_j)$ refers to the value of the payoffs. Note that each payoff is the result of a combination of a decision alternative and a state of nature.

EMV($A_1$), the expected monetary value for the decision alternative of purchasing Kayser Chemicals stock, is computed by:

$$EMV(A_1) = [P(S_1) \times V(A_1, S_1)] + [P(S_2) \times V(A_1, S_2)]$$
$$= .60(\$2,400) + .40(\$1,000) = \$1,840$$

Purchasing Kayser Chemicals stock is only one possible choice. The expected payoffs for the acts of buying Kayser Chemicals, Rim Homes, and Texas Electronics are given in Table 20–3.

**TABLE 20–3** Expected Payoffs for Three Stocks

| Purchase | Expected Payoff |
|---|---|
| Kayser Chemicals | $1,840 |
| Rim Homes | 1,760 |
| Texas Electronics | 1,600 |

An analysis of the expected payoffs in Table 20–3 indicates that purchasing Kayser Chemicals would yield the greatest expected profit. This outcome is based on (1) the investor's estimated future value of the stocks and (2) historical experience with respect to the rise and decline of stock prices. It should be emphasized that although purchasing Kayser stock represents the best action under the expected-value criterion, the investor still might decide to buy Texas Electronics stock in order to minimize the risk of losing some of the $1,100 investment.

**Self-Review 20–1** Verify the conclusion, shown in Table 20–3, that the expected payoff for the act of purchasing Rim Homes stock is $1,760.

# Exercises

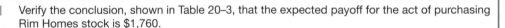

1. The following payoff table was developed. Let $P(S_1) = .30$, $P(S_2) = .50$, and $P(S_3) = .20$. Compute the expected monetary value for each of the alternatives. What decision would you recommend?

| Alternative | State of Nature | | |
|---|---|---|---|
| | $S_1$ | $S_2$ | $S_3$ |
| $A_1$ | $50 | $70 | $100 |
| $A_2$ | 90 | 40 | 80 |
| $A_3$ | 70 | 60 | 90 |

**2.** The Wilhelms Cola Company plans to market a new pineapple-flavored cola this summer. The decision is whether to package the cola in returnable or in no-return bottles. Currently, the state legislature is considering eliminating no-return bottles. Tybo Wilhelms, president of Wilhelms Cola Company, has discussed the problem with his state representative and established the probability to be .70 that no-return bottles will be eliminated. The following table shows the estimated monthly profits (in thousands of dollars) if the pineapple cola is bottled in returnable versus no-return bottles. Of course, if the law is passed and the decision is to bottle the cola in no-return bottles, all profits would be from out-of-state sales. Compute the expected profit for both bottling decisions. Which decision do you recommend?

| Alternative | Law Is Passed ($000), $S_1$ | Law Is Not Passed ($000), $S_2$ |
|---|---|---|
| Returnable bottle | 80 | 40 |
| No-return bottle | 25 | 60 |

# Opportunity Loss

Another method to analyze a decision regarding which common stock to purchase is to determine the profit that might be lost because the state of nature (the market behavior) was not known at the time the investor bought the stock. This potential loss is called **opportunity loss** or **regret.** To illustrate, suppose the investor had purchased the common stock of Rim Homes, and a bull market developed. Further, suppose the value of his Rim Homes stock increased from $1,100 to $2,200, as anticipated. But had the investor bought Kayser Chemicals stock and market values increased, the value of his Kayser stock would be $2,400 (from Table 20–1). Thus, the investor missed making an extra profit of $200 by buying Rim Homes instead of Kayser Chemicals. To put it another way, the $200 represents the opportunity loss for not knowing the correct state of nature. If market prices did increase, the investor would have *regretted* buying Rim Homes. However, had the investor bought Kayser Chemicals and market prices increased, he would have had no regret, that is, no opportunity loss.

The opportunity losses corresponding to this example are given in Table 20–4. Each amount is the outcome (opportunity loss) of a particular combination of acts and a state of nature, that is, stock purchase and market reaction.

Notice that the stock of Kayser Chemicals would be a good investment choice in a rising (bull) market, Texas Electronics would be the best buy in a declining (bear) market, and Rim Homes is somewhat of a compromise.

**TABLE 20–4** Opportunity Losses for Various Combinations of Stock Purchase and Market Movement

| Purchase | Opportunity Loss | |
|---|---|---|
| | Market Rise | Market Decline |
| Kayser Chemicals | $ 0 | $150 |
| Rim Homes | 200 | 50 |
| Texas Electronics | 500 | 0 |

**Self-Review 20–2**

Refer to Table 20–4. Verify that the opportunity loss for:
(a) Rim Homes given a market decline is $50.
(b) Texas Electronics given a market rise is $500.

# Exercises

**3.** Refer to Exercise 1. Develop an opportunity loss table. Determine the opportunity loss for each decision.
**4.** Refer to Exercise 2, involving the Wilhelms Cola Company. Develop an opportunity loss table, and determine the opportunity loss for each decision.

## Expected Opportunity Loss

The opportunity losses in Table 20–4 again ignore the historical experience of market movements. Recall that the probability of a market rise is .60 and that of a market decline .40. These probabilities and the opportunity losses can be combined to determine the **expected opportunity loss.** These calculations are shown in Table 20–5 for the decision to purchase Rim Homes. The expected opportunity loss is $140.

Interpreting, the expected opportunity loss of $140 means that, in the long run, the investor would lose the opportunity to make an additional profit of $140 if he decided to buy Rim Homes stock. This expected loss would be incurred because the investor was unable to accurately predict the trend of the stock market. In a bull market, he could earn an additional $200 by purchasing the common stock of Kayser Chemicals, but in a bear market an investor could earn an additional $50 by buying Texas Electronics stock. When weighted by the probability of the event, the expected opportunity loss is $140.

**TABLE 20–5** Expected Opportunity Loss for the Act of Buying Rim Homes Stock

| State of Nature | Opportunity Loss | Probability of State of Nature | Expected Opportunity Loss |
|---|---|---|---|
| Market rise, $S_1$ | $200 | .60 | $120 |
| Market decline, $S_2$ | 50 | .40 | 20 |
| | | | $140 |

These calculations are summarized as follows:

| EXPECTED OPPORTUNITY LOSS | $EOL(A_i) = \Sigma\ [P(S_j) \times R(A_i, S_j)]$ | [20–2] |
|---|---|---|

where:

$EOL(A_i)$ refers to the expected opportunity loss for a particular decision alternative.
$P(S_j)$ refers to the probability associated with the states of nature $j$.
$R(A_i, S_j)$ refers to the regret or loss for a particular combination of a state of nature and a decision alternative.

$EOL(A_2)$, the regret, or expected opportunity loss, for selecting Rim Homes, is computed as follows:

$$EOL(A_2) = [P(S_1) \times R(A_2, S_1)] + [P(S_2) \times R(A_2, S_2)]$$
$$= .60(\$200) + .40(\$50) = \$140$$

The expected opportunity losses for the three decision alternatives are given in Table 20–6. The lowest expected opportunity loss is $60, meaning that the investor would experience the least regret on average if he purchased Kayser Chemicals.

**TABLE 20–6** Expected Opportunity Losses for the Three Stocks

| Purchase | Expected Opportunity Loss |
|---|---|
| Kayser Chemicals | $ 60 |
| Rim Homes | 140 |
| Texas Electronics | 300 |

Incidentally, note that the decision to purchase Kayser Chemicals stock because it offers the lowest expected opportunity loss reinforces the decision made previously, that Kayser stock would ultimately result in the highest expected payoff ($1,840). These two approaches (lowest expected opportunity loss and highest expected payoff) will always lead to the same decision concerning which course of action to follow.

**Self-Review 20–3**    Referring to Table 20–6, verify that the expected opportunity loss for the act of purchasing Texas Electronics is $300.

# Exercises

**5.** Refer to Exercises 1 and 3. Compute the expected opportunity losses.
**6.** Refer to Exercises 2 and 4. Compute the expected opportunity losses.

# Maximin, Maximax, and Minimax Regret Strategies

Maximin strategy

Several financial advisors consider the purchase of Kayser Chemicals stock too risky. They note that the payoff might not be $1,840, but only $1,000 (from Table 20–1). Arguing that the stock market is too unpredictable, they urge the investor to take a more conservative position and buy Texas Electronics. This is called a **maximin strategy:** it maximizes the minimum gain. On the basis of the payoff table (Table 20–1), they reason that the investor would be assured of at least a $1,150 return, that is, a small profit. Those who subscribe to this somewhat pessimistic strategy are sometimes called **maximiners.**

Maximax strategy

At the other extreme are the optimistic *maximaxers,* who would select the stock that maximizes the maximum gain. If their **maximax strategy** were followed, the investor would purchase Kayser Chemicals stock. These optimists stress that there is a possibility of selling the stock in the future for $2,400 instead of only $1,150, as advocated by the maximiners.

Minimax strategy

Another strategy is the **minimax regret strategy.** Advisors advocating this approach would scan the opportunity losses in Table 20–4 and select the stock that minimizes the maximum regret. In this example it would be Kayser Chemicals stock, with a maximum opportunity loss of $150. Recall that you wish to *avoid* opportunity losses! The maximum regrets were $200 for Rim Homes and $500 for Texas Electronics.

# Value of Perfect Information

How much is "perfect" information worth?

Before deciding on a stock, the investor might want to consider ways of predicting the movement of the stock market. If he knew precisely what the market would do, he could maximize profit by always purchasing the correct stock. The question is: What is this advance information worth? The dollar value of this information is called the **expected value of perfect information,** written EVPI. In this example, it would mean that Bob Hill knew beforehand whether the stock market would rise or decline in the near future.

An acquaintance who is an analyst with a large brokerage firm said that he would be willing to supply Bob with information that he might find valuable in predicting market rises and declines. Of course, there would be a fee, as yet undetermined, for this information, regardless of whether the investor used it. What is the maximum amount that Bob should pay for this special service? $10? $100? $500?

The value of the information from the analyst is, in essence, the expected value of perfect information, because the investor would then be assured of buying the most profitable stock.

> **VALUE OF PERFECT INFORMATION** The difference between the maximum payoff under conditions of certainty and the maximum payoff under uncertainty.

In this example it is the difference between the maximum value of the stock at the end of the year under conditions of certainty and the value associated with the optimum decision using the expected-value criterion.

From a practical standpoint, the maximum expected value under conditions of certainty means that the investor would buy Kayser Chemicals if a market rise were predicted and Texas Electronics if a market decline were imminent. The expected payoff under conditions of certainty is $1,900. (See Table 20–7.)

**TABLE 20–7** Calculations for the Expected Payoff under Conditions of Certainty

| State of Nature | Decision | Payoff | Probability of State of Nature | Expected Payoff |
|---|---|---|---|---|
| Market rise, $S_1$ | Buy Kayser | $2,400 | .60 | $1,440 |
| Market decline, $S_2$ | Buy Texas Electronics | 1,150 | .40 | 460 |
| | | | | $1,900 |

Recall that if the actual behavior of the stock market were unknown (conditions of uncertainty), the stock to buy would be Kayser Chemicals; its expected value at the end of the period was computed to be $1,840 (from Table 20–3). The value of perfect information is, therefore, $60, found by:

$1,900   Expected value of stock purchased under conditions of certainty
−1,840   Expected value of purchase (Kayser) under conditions of uncertainty
$    60   Expected value of perfect information

In general, the expected value of perfect information is computed as follows:

**EXPECTED VALUE OF PERFECT INFORMATION**
EVPI = Expected value under conditions of certainty − Expected value under conditions of uncertainty
**[20–3]**

It would be worth up to $60 for the information the stock analyst might supply. In essence, the analyst would be "guaranteeing" a selling price on average of $1,900, and if the analyst asked $40 for the information, the investor would be assured of a

$1,860 payoff, found by $1,900 − $40. Thus, it would be worthwhile for the investor to agree to this fee ($40) because the expected outcome ($1,860) would be greater than the expected value under conditions of uncertainty ($1,840). However, if his acquaintance wanted a fee of $100 for the service, the investor would realize only $1,800 on average, found by $1,900 − $100. Logically, the service would not be worth $100, because the investor could expect $1,840 on average without agreeing to this financial arrangement. Notice that the expected value of perfect information ($60) is the same as the minimum of the expected regrets (Table 20–6). That is not an accident.

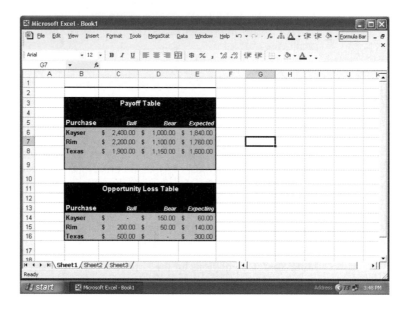

The output for the investment example using the Excel system is shown above. The expected payoff and the expected opportunity loss are the same as reported in Table 20–3 and Table 20–6. We used the Excel Formula Bar (the $f_x$ key) to find the expected values. In a larger problem this would be helpful. The calculations in the preceding investment example were kept at a minimum to emphasize the new terms and the decision-making procedures. When the number of decision alternatives and the number of states of nature become large, a computer package or spreadsheet is recommended.

# Sensitivity Analysis

**Expected payoffs are not highly sensitive.**

In the foregoing stock selection situation, the set of probabilities applied to the payoff values was derived from historical experience with similar market conditions. Objections may be voiced, however, that future market behavior may be different from past experiences. Despite these differences, *the rankings of the decision alternatives are frequently not highly sensitive to changes within a plausible range.* As an example, suppose the investor's brother believes that instead of a 60 percent chance of a market rise and a 40 percent chance of a decline, the reverse is true—that is, there is a .40 probability that the stock market will rise and a .60 probability of a decline. Further, the investor's cousin thinks the probability of a market rise is .50 and that of a decline is .50. A comparison of the original expected payoffs (left column), the expected payoffs for the set of probabilities suggested by the investor's brother (center column), and those cited by the cousin (right column) is shown in Table 20–8. The decision is the same in all three cases—purchase Kayser Chemicals.

**TABLE 20–8** Expected Payoffs for Three Sets of Probabilities

| | Expected Payoffs | | |
| --- | --- | --- | --- |
| Purchase | Historical Experience (probability of .60 rise, .40 decline) | Brother's Estimate (probability of .40 rise, .60 decline) | Cousin's Estimate (probability of .50 rise, .50 decline) |
| Kayser Chemicals | $1,840 | $1,560 | $1,700 |
| Rim Homes | 1,760 | 1,540 | 1,650 |
| Texas Electronics | 1,600 | 1,450 | 1,525 |

**Self-Review 20–4**

Referring to Table 20–8, verify that:
(a) The expected payoff for Texas Electronics for the brother's set of probabilities is $1,450.
(b) The expected payoff for Kayser Chemicals for the cousin's set of probabilities is $1,700.

A comparison of the three sets of expected payoffs in Table 20–8 reveals the best alternative would still be to purchase Kayser Chemicals. As might be expected, there are some differences in the expected future values for each of the three stocks.

If there are drastic changes in the assigned probabilities, the expected values and the optimal decision may change. As an example, suppose the prognostication for a market rise was .20 and for a market decline .80. The expected payoffs would be as shown in Table 20–9. In the long run, the best alternative would be to buy Rim Homes stock. Thus, sensitivity analysis lets you see how accurate the probability estimates need to be in order to feel comfortable with your choice.

**TABLE 20–9** Expected Values for Purchasing the Three Stocks

| Purchase | Expected Payoff |
| --- | --- |
| Kayser Chemicals | $1,280 |
| Rim Homes | 1,320 |
| Texas Electronics | 1,300 |

**Self-Review 20–5**

Is there any choice of probabilities for which the best alternative would be to purchase Texas Electronics stock? (*Hint:* This can be arrived at algebraically or by using a trial-and-error method. Try a somewhat extreme probability for a market rise.)

# Exercises

7. Refer to Exercises 1, 3, and 5. Compute the expected value of perfect information.
8. Refer to Exercises 2, 4, and 6. Compute the expected value of perfect information.
9. Refer to Exercise 1. Revise the probabilities as follows: $P(S_1) = .50$, $P(S_2) = .20$, and $P(S_3) = .30$. Does this change the decision?
10. Refer to Exercise 2. Reverse the probabilities; that is, let $P(S_1) = .30$ and $P(S_2) = .70$. Does this alter your decision?

# Decision Trees

Decision tree: A picture of all possible outcomes

An analytic tool introduced in Chapter 5 that is also useful for studying a decision situation is a *decision tree.* Basically, it is a picture of all the possible courses of action and the consequent possible outcomes. A box is used to indicate the point at which a decision must be made, and the branches going out from the box indicate the alternatives under consideration. Referring to Chart 20–1, on the left is the box with three branches radiating from it, representing the acts of purchasing Kayser Chemicals, Rim Homes, or Texas Electronics.

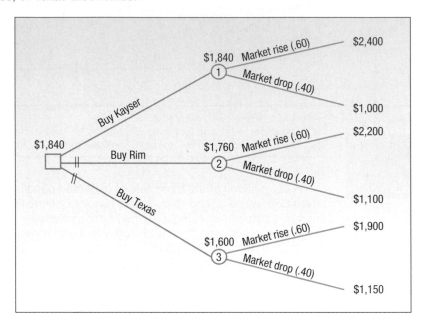

**CHART 20–1**  Decision Tree for the Investor's Decision

The three nodes, or circles, numbered 1, 2, and 3, represent the expected payoff of each of the three stocks. The branches going out to the right of the nodes show the chance events (market rise or decline) and their corresponding probabilities in parentheses. The numbers at the extreme ends of the branches are the estimated future values of ending the decision process at those points. This is sometimes called the *conditional payoff* to denote that the payoff depends on a particular choice of action and a particular chance outcome. Thus, if the investor purchased Rim Homes stock and the market rose, the conditional value of the stock would be $2,200.

After the decision tree has been constructed, the best decision strategy can be found by what is termed *backward induction.* For example, suppose the investor is considering the act of purchasing Texas Electronics. Starting at the lower right in Chart 20–1 with the anticipated payoff given a market rise ($1,900) versus a market decline ($1,150) and going backward (moving left), the appropriate probabilities are applied to give the expected payoff of $1,600 [found by .60($1,900) + .40($1,150)]. The investor would mark the expected value of $1,600 above circled node 3 as shown in Chart 20–1. Similarly, the investor would determine the expected values for Rim Homes and Kayser Chemicals.

Assuming the investor wants to maximize the expected value of his stock purchase, $1,840 would be preferred over $1,760 or $1,600. Continuing to the left toward the box, the investor would draw a double bar across branches representing the two alternatives he rejected (numbers 2 and 3, representing Rim Homes and Texas Electronics). The unmarked branch that leads to the box is clearly the best action to follow, namely, buy Kayser Chemicals stock.

The expected value under *conditions of certainty* can also be portrayed via a decision tree analysis (see Chart 20–2). Recall that under conditions of certainty the investor would know *before the stock is purchased* whether the stock market will rise or decline. Hence, he would purchase Kayser Chemicals in a rising market and Texas

Electronics in a falling market, and the expected payoff would be $1,900. Again, backward induction would be used to arrive at the expected payoff of $1,900.

If perfect information is available: Buy Kayser in rising market; buy Texas in declining market.

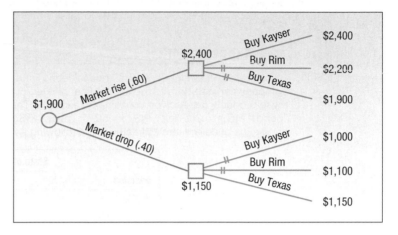

**CHART 20–2** Decision Tree Given Perfect Information

The monetary difference based on perfect information in Chart 20–2 and the decision based on imperfect information in Chart 20–1 is $60, found by $1,900 − $1,840. Recall that the $60 is the expected value of perfect information.

Decision tree analysis provides an alternative way to perform the calculations presented earlier in the chapter. Some managers find these graphic sketches help them in following the decision logic.

# Chapter Outline

I. Statistical decision theory is concerned with making decisions from a set of alternatives.
    **A.** The various courses of action are called the acts or alternatives.
    **B.** The uncontrollable future events are called the states of nature. Probabilities are usually assigned to the states of nature.
    **C.** The consequence of a particular decision alternative and state of nature is called the payoff.
    **D.** All possible combinations of decision alternatives and states of nature result in a payoff table.

II. There are several criteria for selecting the best decision alternative.
    **A.** In the expected monetary value (EMV) criterion, the expected value for each decision alternative is computed, and the optimal (largest if profits, smallest if cost) is selected.
    **B.** An opportunity loss table can be developed.
        **1.** An opportunity loss table is constructed by taking the difference between the optimal decision for each state of nature and the other decision alternatives.
        **2.** The difference between the optimal decision and any other decision is the opportunity loss or regret due to making a decision other than the optimum.
        **3.** The expected opportunity loss (EOL) is similar to the expected monetary value. The opportunity loss is combined with the probabilities of the various states of nature for each decision alternative to determine the expected opportunity loss.
    **C.** The strategy of maximizing the minimum gain is referred to as maximin.
    **D.** The strategy of maximizing the maximum gain is called maximax.
    **E.** The strategy that minimizes the maximum regret is designated minimax regret.

III. The expected value of perfect information (EVPI) is the difference between the best expected payoff under certainty and the best expected payoff under uncertainty.

**IV.** Sensitivity analysis examines the effects of various probabilities for the states of nature on the expected values.

**V.** Decision trees are useful for structuring the various alternatives. They present a picture of the various courses of action and the possible states of nature.

# Chapter Exercises

**11.** Blackbeard's Phantom Fireworks is considering introducing two new bottle rockets. The company can add both to the current line, neither, or just one of the two. The success of these products depends on consumers' reactions. These reactions can be summarized as "good," $P(S_1) = .30$; "fair," $P(S_2) = .50$; or "poor," $P(S_3) = .20$. The company's revenues, in thousands of dollars, are estimated in the following payoff table.

| Decision | State of Nature | | |
|---|---|---|---|
| | $S_1$ | $S_2$ | $S_3$ |
| Neither | 0 | 0 | 0 |
| Product 1 only | 125 | 65 | 30 |
| Product 2 only | 105 | 60 | 30 |
| Both | 220 | 110 | 40 |

**a.** Compute the expected monetary value for each decision.
**b.** What decision would you recommend?
**c.** Develop an opportunity loss table.
**d.** Compute the expected opportunity loss for each decision.
**e.** Compute the expected value of perfect information.

**12.** A financial executive for A. G. Edwards & Sons lives in Boston but frequently must travel to New York. She can go to New York by car, train, or plane. The cost for a plane ticket from Boston to New York is $100, and it is estimated that the trip takes 30 minutes in good weather and 45 minutes in bad weather. The cost for a train ticket is $50, and the trip takes an hour in good weather and two hours in bad weather. The cost to drive her own car from Boston to New York is $20, and this trip takes three hours in good weather and four in bad weather. The executive places a value of $30 per hour on her time. The weather forecast is for a 60 percent chance of bad weather tomorrow.

What decision would you recommend? (*Hint:* Set up a payoff table, and remember that you want to minimize costs.) What is the expected value of perfect information?

**13.** The Thomas Manufacturing Company has $100,000 available to invest. Doctor Thomas, the president and CEO of the company, would like to either expand his production, invest the money in stocks, or purchase a certificate of deposit from the bank. Of course, the unknown is whether the economy will continue at a high level or there will be a recession. He estimates the likelihood of a recession at .20. Whether there is a recession or not, the certificate of deposit will result in a gain of 6 percent. If there is a recession, he predicts a 10 percent loss if he expands his production and a 5 percent loss if he invests in stocks. If there is not a recession, an expansion of production will result in a 15 percent gain, and stock investment will produce a 12 percent gain.

**a.** What decision should he make if he uses the maximin strategy?
**b.** What decision should Doctor Thomas make if the maximax strategy is used?
**c.** What decision would be made if he uses the expected-monetary-value criterion?
**d.** What is the expected value of perfect information?

**14.** The quality-assurance department at Malcomb Products must either inspect each part in a lot or not inspect any of the parts. That is, there are two decision alternatives: inspect all the parts or inspect none of the parts. The proportion of parts defective in the lot, $S_j$, is known from historical data to assume the following probability distribution.

| State of Nature, $S_j$ | Probability, $P(S_j)$ |
|---|---|
| .02 | .70 |
| .04 | .20 |
| .06 | .10 |

For the decision not to inspect any parts, the cost of quality is $C = NS_jK$. For inspecting all the items in the lot, it is $C = Nk$, where:

$N = 20$ (lot size)
$K = \$18.00$ (the cost of finding a defect)
$k = \$0.50$ (the cost of sampling one item)

  **a.** Develop a payoff table.
  **b.** What decision should be made if the expected-value criterion is used?
  **c.** What is the expected value of perfect information?

**15.** Dude Ranches Incorporated was founded on the idea that many families in the eastern and southern areas of the United States do not have a sufficient amount of vacation time to drive to the dude ranches in the Southwest and Rocky Mountain areas for their vacations. Various surveys indicated, however, that there was a considerable interest in this type of family vacation, which includes horseback riding, cattle drives, swimming, fishing, and the like. Dude Ranches Incorporated bought a large farm near several eastern cities and constructed a lake, a swimming pool, and other facilities. However, to build a number of family cottages on the ranch would have required a considerable investment. Further, they reasoned that most of this investment would be lost should the ranch-farm complex be a financial failure. Instead, they decided to enter into an agreement with the Mobile Homes Manufacturing Company to supply a very attractive authentic ranch-type mobile home. Mobile Homes agreed to deliver a mobile home on Saturday for $300 a week. Mobile Homes must know early Saturday morning how many mobile homes Dude Ranches Incorporated wants for the forthcoming week. They have other customers to supply and can only deliver the homes on Saturday. This presents a problem. Dude Ranches will have some reservations by Saturday, but indications are that many families do not make them. Instead, they prefer to examine the facilities before making a decision. An analysis of the various costs involved indicated that $350 a week should be charged for a ranch home, including all privileges. The basic problem is how many mobile ranch homes to order from Mobile Homes each week. Should Dude Ranches Incorporated order 10 (considered the minimum), 11, 12, 13, or 14 (considered the maximum)?

Any decision made solely on the information in the payoff table would ignore, however, the valuable experience that Dude Ranches Incorporated has acquired in the past four years (about 200 weeks) actually operating a dude ranch in the Southwest. Their records showed that they always had nine advance reservations. Also, they never had a demand for 15 or more cottages. The occupancy of 10, 11, 12, 13, or 14 ranch cottages, in part, represented families who drove in and inspected the facilities before renting. A frequency distribution showing the number of weeks in which 10, 11, . . . , 14 ranch cottages were rented during the 200-week period is found in the following table.

| Number of Cottages Rented | Number of Weeks |
|:---:|:---:|
| 10 | 26 |
| 11 | 50 |
| 12 | 60 |
| 13 | 44 |
| 14 | 20 |
|  | 200 |

  **a.** Construct a payoff table.
  **b.** Determine the expected payoffs, and arrive at a decision.
  **c.** Set up an opportunity loss table.
  **d.** Compute the expected opportunity losses, and arrive at a decision.
  **e.** Determine the value of perfect information.

**16.** The proprietor of the newly built White Mountain Ski and Swim Lodge has been considering purchasing or leasing several snowmobiles for the use of guests. The owner found that other financial obligations made it impossible to purchase the machines. Snowmobiles Incorporated (SI) will lease a machine for $20 a week, including any needed maintenance. According to SI, the usual rental charge to the guests of the lodge is $25 a week. Gasoline and oil are extra. Snowmobiles Incorporated only leases a machine for the full season. The proprietor of Ski and Swim, knowing that leasing an excessive number of snowmobiles might cause a net loss for the lodge, investigated the records of other resort owners. The combined experience at several other lodges was found to be:

| Number of Snowmobiles Demanded by Guests | Number of Weeks |
|---|---|
| 7 | 10 |
| 8 | 25 |
| 9 | 45 |
| 10 | 20 |

a. Design a payoff table.
b. Compute the expected profits for leasing 7, 8, 9, and 10 snowmobiles based on the cost of leasing of $20, the rental charge of $25, and the experience of other lodges.
c. Which alternative is the most profitable?
d. Design an opportunity loss table.
e. Find the expected opportunity losses for leasing 7, 8, 9, and 10 snowmobiles.
f. Which act would give the least expected opportunity loss?
g. Determine the expected value of perfect information.
h. Suggest a course of action to the proprietor of the Ski and Swim Lodge. Include in your explanation the various figures, such as expected profit.

17. Casual Furniture World has had numerous inquiries regarding the availability of furniture and equipment that could be rented for large outdoor summer parties. This includes such items as folding chairs and tables, a deluxe grill, propane gas, and lights. No rental equipment of this nature is available locally, and the management of the furniture store is considering forming a subsidiary to handle rentals.

An investigation revealed that most people interested in renting wanted a complete group of party essentials (about 12 chairs, four tables, a deluxe grill, a bottle of propane gas, tongs, etc.). Management decided not to buy a large number of complete sets because of the financial risk involved. That is, if the demand for the rental groups was not as large as anticipated, a large financial loss might be incurred. Further, outright purchase would mean that the equipment would have to be stored during the off-season.

It was then discovered that a firm in Boston leased a complete party set for $560 for the summer season. This amounts to about $5 a day. In the promotional literature from the Boston firm, a rental fee of $15 was suggested. For each set rented, a profit of $10 would thus be earned. It was then decided to lease from the Boston firm, at least for the first season.

The Boston firm suggested that, based on the combined experience of similar rental firms in other cities, either 41, 42, 43, 44, 45, or 46 complete sets be leased for the season. Based on this suggestion, management must now decide on the most profitable number of complete sets to lease for the season.

The leasing firm in Boston also made available some additional information gathered from several rental firms similar to the newly formed subsidiary. Note in the following table (which is based on the experience of the other rental firms) that for 360 days of the total of 6,000 days' experience—or about 6 percent of the days—these rental firms rented out 41 complete party sets. On 10 percent of the days during a typical summer, they rented 42 complete sets, and so on.

| Number of Sets Rented | Number of Days | Number of Sets Rented | Number of Days |
|---|---|---|---|
| 40 | 0 | 44 | 2,400 |
| 41 | 360 | 45 | 1,500 |
| 42 | 600 | 46 | 300 |
| 43 | 840 | 47 | 0 |

a. Construct a payoff table. (As a check figure, for the act of having 41 complete sets available and the event of renting 41, the payoff is $410.)

    **b.** The expected daily profit for leasing 43 complete sets from the Boston firm is $426.70; for 45 sets, $431.70; and for 46 sets, $427.45. Organize these expected daily profits into a table, and complete the table by finding the expected daily profit for leasing 41, 42, and 44 sets from the Boston firm.

    **c.** On the basis of the expected daily profit, what is the most profitable action to take?

    **d.** The expected opportunity loss for leasing 43 party sets from the Boston firm is $11.60; for 45 sets, $6.60; for 46 sets, $10.85. Organize these into an expected opportunity loss table, and complete the table by computing the expected opportunity loss for 41, 42, and 44.

    **e.** According to the expected opportunity loss table, what is the most profitable course of action to take? Does this agree with your decision for part (c)?

    **f.** Determine the value of perfect information. Explain what it indicates in this problem.

**18.** Tim Waltzer owns and operates Waltzer's Wrecks, a discount car rental agency near the Cleveland Hopkins International Airport. He rents a wreck for $20 a day. He has an arrangement with Landrum Leasing to purchase used cars at $6,000 each. His cars receive only needed maintenance and, as a result, are worth only $2,000 at the end of the year of operation. Tim has decided to sell all his wrecks every year and purchase a complete set of used cars from Landrum Leasing.

    His clerk-accountant provided him with a probability distribution with respect to the number of cars rented per day.

| | Numbers of Cars Rented per Day | | | |
| --- | --- | --- | --- | --- |
| | **20** | **21** | **22** | **23** |
| Probability | .10 | .20 | .50 | .20 |

    Tim is an avid golfer and tennis player. He is either on the golf course on weekends or playing tennis indoors. Thus, his car rental agency is only open weekdays. Also, he closes for two weeks during the summer and goes on a golfing tour.

    The clerk-accountant estimated that it cost $1.50 per car rental for minimal maintenance and cleaning.

**a.** How many cars should he purchase to maximize profit?

**b.** What is the expected value of perfect information?

# Chapter 20 Answers to Self-Review

**20–1**

| Event | Payoff | Probability of Event | Expected Value |
|---|---|---|---|
| Market rise | $2,200 | .60 | $1,320 |
| Market decline | 1,100 | .40 | 440 |
| | | | $1,760 |

**20–2 a.** Suppose the investor purchased Rim Homes stock, and the value of the stock in a bear market dropped to $1,100 as anticipated (Table 20–1). Instead, had the investor purchased Texas Electronics and the market declined, the value of the Texas Electronics stock would be $1,150. The difference of $50, found by $1,150 − $1,100, represents the investor's regret for buying Rim Homes stock.

  **b.** Suppose the investor purchased Texas Electronics stock, and then a bull market developed. The stock rose to $1,900, as anticipated (Table 20–1). However, had the investor bought Kayser Chemicals stock and the market value increased to $2,400 as anticipated, the difference of $500 represents the extra profit the investor could have made by purchasing Kayser Chemicals stock.

**20–3**

| Event | Payoff | Probability of Event | Expected Opportunity Value |
|---|---|---|---|
| Market rise | $500 | .60 | $300 |
| Market decline | 0 | .40 | 0 |
| | | | $300 |

**20–4 a.**

| Event | Payoff | Probability of Event | Expected Value |
|---|---|---|---|
| Market rise | $1,900 | .40 | $ 760 |
| Market decline | 1,150 | .60 | 690 |
| | | | $1,450 |

**b.**

| Event | Payoff | Probability of Event | Expected Value |
|---|---|---|---|
| Market rise | $2,400 | .50 | $1,200 |
| Market decline | 1,000 | .50 | 500 |
| | | | $1,700 |

**20–5** For probabilities of a market rise (or decline) down to .333, Kayser Chemicals stock would provide the largest expected profit. For probabilities .333 to .143, Rim Homes would be the best buy. For .143 and below, Texas Electronics would give the largest expected profit. Algebraic solutions:

Kayser: $2,400p + (1 − p)1,000$
Rim:    $2,200p + (1 − p)1,100$

$1,400p + 1,000 = 1,100p + 1,100$
$p = .333$

Rim:    $2,200p + (1 − p)1,100$
Texas:  $1,900p + (1 − p)1,150$

$1,100p + 1,100 = 750p + 1,150$
$p = .143$

# Appendixes

# Appendix — Covariance

## Covariance Material for Chapter 6

On pages 185 and 186 we described how to compute and interpret the mean, also called the expected value, of a random variable. Recall that the mean is the long run average of a discrete probability distribution. We showed that in the long run John Ragsdale, a sales associate at Pelican Ford, could expect to sell 2.10 cars each Saturday. Next we calculated the variance and the standard deviation of the distribution of the number of cars sold. The variance and standard deviation showed the variation Mr. Ragsdale could expect in the number of cars sold.

Suppose Pelican Ford employs two sales associates. The distribution of the number of cars sold per Saturday by Bill Valiton, the other associate, follows.

| Number of cars sold | Probability |
|---|---|
| $X$ | $P(X)$ |
| 0 | .10 |
| 1 | .50 |
| 2 | .40 |

As a sales manager you are really interested in the *total* number of vehicles sold on a particular Saturday. That is, you are interested in the distribution of the total number of vehicles sold, rather than the individual distributions of Mr. Ragsdale and Mr. Valiton. We can find any linear combination of two random variables by the equation

| THE LINEAR COMBINATION OF TWO RANDOM VARIABLES | $Z = aX + bY$ |
|---|---|

where:

$X$ and $Y$   are the two random variables.
$a$ and $b$   are constants or weights.
$Z$   is the sum of the products of two random variables.

If we wish to find the expected value of the sum of two random variables and $a = b = 1$, the above equation simplifies to $E(Z) = E(X) + E(Y)$. In words, this indicates that the mean of the distribution of the sum of two random variables is the sum of the two expected values or means.

In the Pelican Ford example, the mean number of vehicles sold by Mr. Valiton is 1.30, found by

$$\mu = E(Y) = \Sigma \, Y(P(Y)) = 0(.10) + 1(.50) + 2(.40) = 1.30$$

The mean, or expected value, of the total number of vehicles sold by the two associates is

$$E(Z) = E(X) + E(Y) = 2.10 + 1.30 = 3.40.$$

This presents a solution to only part of the problem. We can reason logically about what will happen to the mean, or the expected value, of the sum of two random variables. But we are also interested in the variation of the sum of these two variables. A confounding factor is the prospect that there is an interrelationship between the two variables. In the Pelican Ford example, it is reasonable that there is an interrelationship between the sales of Mr. Ragsdale and the sales of Mr. Valiton. For example, on a very hot summer Saturday prospective buyers are not going to stand out in the hot sun, so logically the sales for both associates is likely to be low.

The **covariance** is a measure of the relationship between two random variables.

| THE COVARIANCE | $\sigma_{xy} = \Sigma (X - E(X))(Y - E(Y))P(X, Y)$ |
|---|---|

where:

$\sigma_{xy}$ is the symbol for the covariance.

$X$ and $Y$ are the outcomes of the discrete random variables.

$E(X)$ and $E(Y)$ are the expected values, or means, of the two discrete random variables.

$P(X, Y)$ is the joint probability of two random variables.

The table below shows the relationship between the sales of Mr. Ragsdale and Mr. Valiton. We observe that the probability Mr. Ragsdale sells 2 cars on a particular Saturday is .30. This value is found in the last row of the column labeled 2. The probability that Mr. Valiton sells exactly 2 cars is .40. This value is found in the rightmost column of the row labeled 2. The probability that they each sell two cars is .20, found at the intersection of the row and column. Because these sales are not independent (remember when it is a hot summer day, it is a hot summer day for both sales associates) we do not expect the special rule of multiplication to apply. That is $P(X, Y)$ does *not* equal $P(X)P(Y)$.

|  |  | Ragsdale Cars Sold (*X*) | | | | | |
|---|---|---|---|---|---|---|---|
|  |  | 0 | 1 | 2 | 3 | 4 | P(Y) |
|  | 0 | .05 | .02 | .03 | .00 | .00 | .10 |
| Valiton | 1 | .05 | .15 | .07 | .20 | .03 | .50 |
| Cars Sold (*Y*) | 2 | .00 | .03 | .20 | .10 | .07 | .40 |
|  | P(X) | .10 | .20 | .30 | .30 | .10 | 1.00 |

To determine the covariance we use

$$\sigma_{xy} = \Sigma (X - E(X))(Y - E(Y))P(X, Y)$$

where

$$\sigma_{xy} = (0 - 2.1)(0 - 1.3).05 + (1 - 2.1)(0 - 1.3).02 + \cdots + (4 - 2.1)(2 - 1.3).07$$

$$= 0.95$$

The covariance reports how the two variables move together. The 0.95 indicates that the two variables are directly related. That is, when Mr. Ragsdale sells more than his mean number of cars, the tendency is for Mr. Valiton to sell more than his mean also.

The major drawback to the covariance is we have little understanding of the magnitude of the difference. The units are "cars squared." Is 0.9500 a lot or a little? We don't know. If the covariance were a negative value, this would indicate the two distributions were inversely or indirectly related. If it were 0, then the two distributions are independent.

Because we now have information about the relationship between the two variables, we can reason about the variance of their sum. The variance of the sum of two random variables is found by

| VARIANCE OF THE SUM OF TWO RANDOM VARIABLES | $\sigma_{x+y}^2 = a^2\sigma_x^2 + b^2\sigma_y^2 + 2ab\sigma_{xy}$ |
|---|---|

The values of *a* and *b*, as before, represent the weights or constants assigned. When $a = b = 1$, the equation simplifies to

$$\sigma_{x+y}^2 = \sigma_x^2 + \sigma_y^2 + 2\sigma_{xy}$$

In words, the above equation indicates that the variance of the sum of two random variables is equal to the sum of the variances of the two random variables plus two times the covariance. This means that when we want to consider the sum of two variables, we need to account for the variation in each of the variables *plus* the interrelationship between the two variables.

To complete the question of the variability of the total number of cars sold on Saturday we need to find the variance of the distribution of the sales for Mr. Valiton. Using formula (6-2),

$$\sigma_y^2 = \Sigma(Y - \mu)^2\, P(Y) = (0 - 1.3)^2(.10) + (1 - 1.3)^2(.50) + (2 - 1.3)^2(.40) = 0.41$$

Recall that on page 186 we computed the variance of the distribution of the number of vehicles sold by Mr. Ragsdale to be 1.29. So the variance of the sum of the two random variables is

$$\sigma_{x+y}^2 = \sigma_x^2 + \sigma_y^2 + 2\sigma_{XY} = 1.29 + 0.41 + 2(0.95) = 3.60$$

To summarize, the mean number of vehicles sold each Saturday at Pelican Ford is 3.40 vehicles and the variance is 3.60. The standard deviation is 1.8974 vehicles, found by taking the square root of 3.60.

One of the most useful applications of the above relationships is in the field of financial analysis. Investors are interested in obtaining the maximum rate of return, but they are also interested in reducing the risk. In statistical terms reducing the risk means reducing the variance or the standard deviation. The following example will help to explain the details.

**EXAMPLE**

Ernie DuBrul just inherited $200,000 and will divide this inheritance into a portfolio of two investments. After some research Ernie decides to put 25 percent into American Funds World Cap and the remainder into Burger International Funds. For the American Funds World Cap the mean return is 12 percent and the standard deviation 3 percent. For the Burger International Funds the mean rate of return is 20 percent with a standard deviation of 8 percent. After some calculation, he is able to determine that the covariance between the two investments is 12. What is the expected rate of return for the portfolio? What should he conclude about the relationship between the two investments? What is the portfolio's standard deviation?

**SOLUTION**

Ernie can consider the two investments as random variables with the means of 12 percent and 20 percent, respectively. The weight of the first investment is .25 ($a = .25$) and .75 ($b = .75$) for the second. The expected amount of return for the portfolio is 18 percent, found by

$$E(Z) = E(X + Y) = a(E(X)) + b(E(Y)) = .25(12) + .75(20) = 18.0$$

The covariance of 12 suggests that there is a positive relationship between the two investments, because it is a positive number. However, the value of 12 does not give much insight into the strength of the relationship.

We can determine the variance of the portfolio as follows.

$$\sigma_{x+y}^2 = a^2\sigma_x^2 + b^2\sigma_y^2 + 2ab\sigma_{xy} = (.25)^2(3)^2 + (.75)^2(8)^2 + 2(.25)(.75)(12) = 41.0625$$

The square root of 41.0625 is 6.4 percent, which is the standard deviation of the weight sum of the two variables.

How does Ernie interpret this information? Suppose he had an opportunity to invest all $200,000 in Internet stocks, where the rate of return was the same, 18 percent, but the standard deviation of this distribution was 8.0 percent. The standard deviation of 8.0 percent indicates there is more risk in the investment of Internet stocks. Most investors want to reduce their risk; hence, the better course of action is to make the investment he originally planned.

In the above examples there was association between the two distributions; that is, the covariance was not equal to 0. Consider the following example where there is no association between the two distributions.

Suppose we are involved in a game with 2 fair coins. The coins are flipped and we count the number of heads. For each head that appears we are given $1.00 by the House; for each tail we must pay the House the same amount. We can summarize the game with the following table.

|  |  | Coin 1 | | |
|---|---|---|---|---|
|  |  | Head $1 | Tail −$1 | Total |
| **Coin 2** | Head $1 | .25 | .25 | .50 |
|  | Tail $−1 | .25 | .25 | .50 |
|  | Total | .50 | .50 | 1.00 |

The means of the two random variable are:

$$E(X) = \$1(.50) + (\$-1)(.50) = \$0.00$$

$$E(Y) = \$1(.50) + (\$-1)(.50) = \$0.00$$

The variances of the two random variable are:

$$\sigma_x^2 = (1-0)^2 \, .50 + (-1-0)^2(.50) = 1$$

$$\sigma_y^2 = (1-0)^2 \, .50 + (-1-0)^2(.50) = 1$$

The covariance of the two random variable is:

$$\sigma_{xy} = (1-0)(1-0).25 + (-1-0)(1-0).25 + (-1-0)(1-0).25 + (-1-0)(-1-0).25$$

$$\sigma_{xy} = (1).25 + (-1).25 + (-1).25 + (1).25 = 0$$

The fact that the covariance is 0 indicates that the two variables are not related. That is, the outcome of the first coin is not related to the outcome of the second coin. We already knew this from our earlier study of probability, but the fact that the covariance is 0 confirms it.

# Exercises

1. Two random variables are given by the following table.

|  | 0 | 1 | 2 | $P(y)$ |
|---|---|---|---|---|
| 0 | .3 | .1 | 0 | .4 |
| 1 | .1 | .3 | .1 | .5 |
| 2 | 0 | 0 | .1 | .1 |
| $P(x)$ | .4 | .4 | .2 | 1.00 |

a. Find the mean of the variables $x$ and $y$.
b. Find the variance of the variables $x$ and $y$.
c. Find the covariance.
d. Find the expected value of the sum of the two variables.
e. Find the variance of the sum of the two variables.

2. An analysis of two stocks indicates that the mean rate of return of the first is 8 percent with a standard deviation of 15 percent. The second has a mean rate of return of 14 percent with a standard deviation of 20 percent. Suppose we invest 40 percent in the first stock and 60 percent in the second.
   a. What is the expected rate of return on the total investment?
   b. If the two stocks are not related, what is the standard deviation of the rate of return on the total investment?
   c. Suppose the covariance between the two stocks is 150. What is the standard deviation for the rate of return?

# Covariance Material for Chapter 13

To understand the coefficient of correlation let's begin by plotting the data. Chart 13–4 on page 434 is a scatter diagram of Copier Sales of America data. Observe that as the number of sales calls increases, so does the number of copiers sold. The number of units sold is scaled on the vertical axis and the number of sales calls on the horizontal axis.

Let's compute the mean of both the sales calls ($X$) and the number of units sold ($Y$). From Table 13–2 on page 433, the mean number of sales calls is 22.0, found by 220/10. The mean number of units sold is 45, found by 450/10. So we conclude a typical sales representative for Copier Sales of America makes 22 sales calls and sells 45 copiers in a month. In Chart 13–4, we have moved the origin from the point (0, 0) to the points ($\bar{X}$, $\bar{Y}$). This will allow us to understand the association between the number of sales calls and the number of copiers sold.

At this point we can make some interpretations of the data. If the points are scattered in all four quadrants, then it is likely there is little association between the variables. A predominance of data points in Quadrants I and III indicates a positive relationship, while data points in II and IV suggest a negative relationship.

To evaluate the relationship you noted visually in Chart 13–4, compute the term $\Sigma(X - \bar{X})(Y - \bar{Y})$. Notice the thrust of this term. It is the sum of the products of the deviations between the number of sales calls and the mean number of sales calls and the number of copiers sold and the mean number of copiers sold, for each of the ten sales representatives. For a point located in the first quadrant both the $X$ and $Y$ values would be larger than their means. From Table 13–2 Soni Jones made 30 sales calls and sold 70 copiers. Both of the values are larger than the mean of 22 sales calls and 45 copiers sold. The product of these deviations $(30 - 22)(70 - 45) = 200$. Other points in the first quadrant will also have a positive result.

Points located in Quadrant IV will have a negative value. Mike Kiel, for example, made 20 sales calls and sold 50 copiers. So $(X - \bar{X})(Y - \bar{Y}) = (20 - 22)(50 - 45) = -10$.

So the value from points in Quadrant IV will offset (deduct from) those in Quadrant I. If the term $\Sigma(X - \bar{X})(Y - \bar{Y})$ is a positive value, this indicates a positive relationship between the two variables. A negative value indicates a negative relationship between the variables. The symbol $SS_{xy}$ is used to identify this term. It is computed from the following formula.

$$SS_{xy} = \Sigma(X - \bar{X})(Y - \bar{Y})$$

The term $SS_{xy}$, found by using the above formula, indicates the relationship between the $X$ and $Y$ variables. However, it is difficult to interpret because (a) the units involved will be mixed between those of $X$ and $Y$, and (b) the term could be made larger by merely increasing the sample size. To control for the sample size, the term is divided by $n - 1$, the sample size minus 1. This is the same procedure we used in determining the sample variance, described in Chapter 3. The result is called the **covariance.**

| THE SAMPLE COVARIANCE | $s_{xy} = \dfrac{SS_{xy}}{n-1}$ |
|---|---|

Returning to our Copier Sales of America problem, the covariance is 100, found by

$$s_{xy} = \frac{\Sigma(X-\bar{X})(Y-\bar{Y})}{n-1} = \frac{.900}{10-1} = 100$$

How do we interpret the covariance? Recall that the variance summarizes the variability of a single variable. The covariance summarizes the relationship *between* two variables. It differs from the variance in that it can assume negative values. A negative covariance indicates that the two variables are inversely related. The covariance is difficult to interpret, because of the units involved. In this case does a covariance of 100 indicate the variables are closely related or that they are not related at all? We cannot tell. We can only conclude that because this is a positive value, the two variables are positively related. A second difficulty involves the units of the two variables. In this example, one variable is in number of calls and the other units sold. So the units of the results are not familiar.

To remove the problem with the units, the covariance is standardized. That is, it is divided by the standard deviations of $X$ and $Y$. The result is the coefficient of correlation.

We can verify the coefficient of correlation in the Copier Sales of America example on page 434. The first step is to compute the standard deviation of the number of sales calls and the number of copiers sold. Using the data in Table 13–2 the standard deviations are:

$$s_y = \sqrt{\frac{1{,}850}{10-1}} = 14.34$$

$$s_x = \sqrt{\frac{760}{10-1}} = 9.19$$

The term $SS_{xy}$ is 900, found by

$$SS_{xy} = \Sigma(X-\bar{X})(Y-\bar{Y}) = 900$$

The covariance $s_{xy}$ is found by

$$s_{xy} = \frac{SS_{xy}}{n-1} = \frac{(900)}{9} = 100.0$$

Finally, the correlation is 0.759, the same as that determined using 13-1 on page 435.

$$r = \frac{s_{xy}}{s_x s_y} = \frac{100.0}{(9.19)(14.34)} = 0.759$$

# Exercises

3. Write a brief description of the coefficient of correlation. What is its range of values? What does it mean when it is zero? Under what conditions can it be larger than 1.00?
4. Describe what is meant by the covariance. Can it be negative? What is its range of values?
5. A phone company executive is studying the relationship between the number of telephone calls per week and the number of people in the household. A sample of twelve families is obtained.

| Calls ($Y$) | 22 | 15 | 20 | 31 | 75 | 26 | 20 | 28 | 26 | 59 | 23 | 33 |
|---|---|---|---|---|---|---|---|---|---|---|---|---|
| Family ($X$) | 4 | 5 | 4 | 3 | 7 | 5 | 6 | 5 | 5 | 7 | 2 | 5 |

Plot the information in a scatter diagram. Compute the covariance and the coefficient of correlation. Is the relationship direct or inverse, strong or weak?

6. The director of the Tampa Zoo is studying the relationship between the number of admissions, in 1,000s, and the high temperature, in degrees Fahrenheit. A sample of fifteen days is selected and the sample information is reported below.

| Admissions (1,000s) | Temperature (°F) | Admissions (1,000s) | Temperature (°F) |
|---|---|---|---|
| 2.0 | 86 | 2.2 | 84 |
| 0.6 | 71 | 2.5 | 66 |
| 2.0 | 89 | 1.3 | 76 |
| 2.1 | 73 | 3.6 | 84 |
| 2.2 | 76 | 1.0 | 75 |
| 2.1 | 75 | 1.8 | 72 |
| 0.5 | 68 | 2.1 | 76 |
| 0.3 | 72 | | |

Plot the information in a scatter diagram. Compute the covariance and the coefficient of correlation. Is the relationship direct or inverse? Would you consider the association strong or weak?

# Binomial Probability Distribution

**n = 1**

Probability

| x | 0.05 | 0.10 | 0.20 | 0.30 | 0.40 | 0.50 | 0.60 | 0.70 | 0.80 | 0.90 | 0.95 |
|---|------|------|------|------|------|------|------|------|------|------|------|
| 0 | 0.950 | 0.900 | 0.800 | 0.700 | 0.600 | 0.500 | 0.400 | 0.300 | 0.200 | 0.100 | 0.050 |
| 1 | 0.050 | 0.100 | 0.200 | 0.300 | 0.400 | 0.500 | 0.600 | 0.700 | 0.800 | 0.900 | 0.950 |

**n = 2**

Probability

| x | 0.05 | 0.10 | 0.20 | 0.30 | 0.40 | 0.50 | 0.60 | 0.70 | 0.80 | 0.90 | 0.95 |
|---|------|------|------|------|------|------|------|------|------|------|------|
| 0 | 0.903 | 0.810 | 0.640 | 0.490 | 0.360 | 0.250 | 0.160 | 0.090 | 0.040 | 0.010 | 0.003 |
| 1 | 0.095 | 0.180 | 0.320 | 0.420 | 0.480 | 0.500 | 0.480 | 0.420 | 0.320 | 0.180 | 0.095 |
| 2 | 0.003 | 0.010 | 0.040 | 0.090 | 0.160 | 0.250 | 0.360 | 0.490 | 0.640 | 0.810 | 0.903 |

**n = 3**

Probability

| x | 0.05 | 0.10 | 0.20 | 0.30 | 0.40 | 0.50 | 0.60 | 0.70 | 0.80 | 0.90 | 0.95 |
|---|------|------|------|------|------|------|------|------|------|------|------|
| 0 | 0.857 | 0.729 | 0.512 | 0.343 | 0.216 | 0.125 | 0.064 | 0.027 | 0.008 | 0.001 | 0.000 |
| 1 | 0.135 | 0.243 | 0.384 | 0.441 | 0.432 | 0.375 | 0.288 | 0.189 | 0.096 | 0.027 | 0.007 |
| 2 | 0.007 | 0.027 | 0.096 | 0.189 | 0.288 | 0.375 | 0.432 | 0.441 | 0.384 | 0.243 | 0.135 |
| 3 | 0.000 | 0.001 | 0.008 | 0.027 | 0.064 | 0.125 | 0.216 | 0.343 | 0.512 | 0.729 | 0.857 |

**n = 4**

Probability

| x | 0.05 | 0.10 | 0.20 | 0.30 | 0.40 | 0.50 | 0.60 | 0.70 | 0.80 | 0.90 | 0.95 |
|---|------|------|------|------|------|------|------|------|------|------|------|
| 0 | 0.815 | 0.656 | 0.410 | 0.240 | 0.130 | 0.063 | 0.026 | 0.008 | 0.002 | 0.000 | 0.000 |
| 1 | 0.171 | 0.292 | 0.410 | 0.412 | 0.346 | 0.250 | 0.154 | 0.076 | 0.026 | 0.004 | 0.000 |
| 2 | 0.014 | 0.049 | 0.154 | 0.265 | 0.346 | 0.375 | 0.346 | 0.265 | 0.154 | 0.049 | 0.014 |
| 3 | 0.000 | 0.004 | 0.026 | 0.076 | 0.154 | 0.250 | 0.346 | 0.412 | 0.410 | 0.292 | 0.171 |
| 4 | 0.000 | 0.000 | 0.002 | 0.008 | 0.026 | 0.063 | 0.130 | 0.240 | 0.410 | 0.656 | 0.815 |

**n = 5**

Probability

| x | 0.05 | 0.10 | 0.20 | 0.30 | 0.40 | 0.50 | 0.60 | 0.70 | 0.80 | 0.90 | 0.95 |
|---|------|------|------|------|------|------|------|------|------|------|------|
| 0 | 0.774 | 0.590 | 0.328 | 0.168 | 0.078 | 0.031 | 0.010 | 0.002 | 0.000 | 0.000 | 0.000 |
| 1 | 0.204 | 0.328 | 0.410 | 0.360 | 0.259 | 0.156 | 0.077 | 0.028 | 0.006 | 0.000 | 0.000 |
| 2 | 0.021 | 0.073 | 0.205 | 0.309 | 0.346 | 0.313 | 0.230 | 0.132 | 0.051 | 0.008 | 0.001 |
| 3 | 0.001 | 0.008 | 0.051 | 0.132 | 0.230 | 0.313 | 0.346 | 0.309 | 0.205 | 0.073 | 0.021 |
| 4 | 0.000 | 0.000 | 0.006 | 0.028 | 0.077 | 0.156 | 0.259 | 0.360 | 0.410 | 0.328 | 0.204 |
| 5 | 0.000 | 0.000 | 0.000 | 0.002 | 0.010 | 0.031 | 0.078 | 0.168 | 0.328 | 0.590 | 0.774 |

# Appendix A

## Binomial Probability Distribution (*continued*)

### n = 6

| x | \|Probability\| | | | | | | | | | | |
|---|------|------|------|------|------|------|------|------|------|------|------|
|   | 0.05 | 0.10 | 0.20 | 0.30 | 0.40 | 0.50 | 0.60 | 0.70 | 0.80 | 0.90 | 0.95 |
| 0 | 0.735 | 0.531 | 0.262 | 0.118 | 0.047 | 0.016 | 0.004 | 0.001 | 0.000 | 0.000 | 0.000 |
| 1 | 0.232 | 0.354 | 0.393 | 0.303 | 0.187 | 0.094 | 0.037 | 0.010 | 0.002 | 0.000 | 0.000 |
| 2 | 0.031 | 0.098 | 0.246 | 0.324 | 0.311 | 0.234 | 0.138 | 0.060 | 0.015 | 0.001 | 0.000 |
| 3 | 0.002 | 0.015 | 0.082 | 0.185 | 0.276 | 0.313 | 0.276 | 0.185 | 0.082 | 0.015 | 0.002 |
| 4 | 0.000 | 0.001 | 0.015 | 0.060 | 0.138 | 0.234 | 0.311 | 0.324 | 0.246 | 0.098 | 0.031 |
| 5 | 0.000 | 0.000 | 0.002 | 0.010 | 0.037 | 0.094 | 0.187 | 0.303 | 0.393 | 0.354 | 0.232 |
| 6 | 0.000 | 0.000 | 0.000 | 0.001 | 0.004 | 0.016 | 0.047 | 0.118 | 0.262 | 0.531 | 0.735 |

### n = 7

| x | \|Probability\| | | | | | | | | | | |
|---|------|------|------|------|------|------|------|------|------|------|------|
|   | 0.05 | 0.10 | 0.20 | 0.30 | 0.40 | 0.50 | 0.60 | 0.70 | 0.80 | 0.90 | 0.95 |
| 0 | 0.698 | 0.478 | 0.210 | 0.082 | 0.028 | 0.008 | 0.002 | 0.000 | 0.000 | 0.000 | 0.000 |
| 1 | 0.257 | 0.372 | 0.367 | 0.247 | 0.131 | 0.055 | 0.017 | 0.004 | 0.000 | 0.000 | 0.000 |
| 2 | 0.041 | 0.124 | 0.275 | 0.318 | 0.261 | 0.164 | 0.077 | 0.025 | 0.004 | 0.000 | 0.000 |
| 3 | 0.004 | 0.023 | 0.115 | 0.227 | 0.290 | 0.273 | 0.194 | 0.097 | 0.029 | 0.003 | 0.000 |
| 4 | 0.000 | 0.003 | 0.029 | 0.097 | 0.194 | 0.273 | 0.290 | 0.227 | 0.115 | 0.023 | 0.004 |
| 5 | 0.000 | 0.000 | 0.004 | 0.025 | 0.077 | 0.164 | 0.261 | 0.318 | 0.275 | 0.124 | 0.041 |
| 6 | 0.000 | 0.000 | 0.000 | 0.004 | 0.017 | 0.055 | 0.131 | 0.247 | 0.367 | 0.372 | 0.257 |
| 7 | 0.000 | 0.000 | 0.000 | 0.000 | 0.002 | 0.008 | 0.028 | 0.082 | 0.210 | 0.478 | 0.698 |

### n = 8

| x | \|Probability\| | | | | | | | | | | |
|---|------|------|------|------|------|------|------|------|------|------|------|
|   | 0.05 | 0.10 | 0.20 | 0.30 | 0.40 | 0.50 | 0.60 | 0.70 | 0.80 | 0.90 | 0.95 |
| 0 | 0.663 | 0.430 | 0.168 | 0.058 | 0.017 | 0.004 | 0.001 | 0.000 | 0.000 | 0.000 | 0.000 |
| 1 | 0.279 | 0.383 | 0.336 | 0.198 | 0.090 | 0.031 | 0.008 | 0.001 | 0.000 | 0.000 | 0.000 |
| 2 | 0.051 | 0.149 | 0.294 | 0.296 | 0.209 | 0.109 | 0.041 | 0.010 | 0.001 | 0.000 | 0.000 |
| 3 | 0.005 | 0.033 | 0.147 | 0.254 | 0.279 | 0.219 | 0.124 | 0.047 | 0.009 | 0.000 | 0.000 |
| 4 | 0.000 | 0.005 | 0.046 | 0.136 | 0.232 | 0.273 | 0.232 | 0.136 | 0.046 | 0.005 | 0.000 |
| 5 | 0.000 | 0.000 | 0.009 | 0.047 | 0.124 | 0.219 | 0.279 | 0.254 | 0.147 | 0.033 | 0.005 |
| 6 | 0.000 | 0.000 | 0.001 | 0.010 | 0.041 | 0.109 | 0.209 | 0.296 | 0.294 | 0.149 | 0.051 |
| 7 | 0.000 | 0.000 | 0.000 | 0.001 | 0.008 | 0.031 | 0.090 | 0.198 | 0.336 | 0.383 | 0.279 |
| 8 | 0.000 | 0.000 | 0.000 | 0.000 | 0.001 | 0.004 | 0.017 | 0.058 | 0.168 | 0.430 | 0.663 |

# Binomial Probability Distribution (*continued*)

$n = 9$

| | | | | | Probability | | | | | | |
|---|---|---|---|---|---|---|---|---|---|---|---|
| x | 0.05 | 0.10 | 0.20 | 0.30 | 0.40 | 0.50 | 0.60 | 0.70 | 0.80 | 0.90 | 0.95 |
| 0 | 0.630 | 0.387 | 0.134 | 0.040 | 0.010 | 0.002 | 0.000 | 0.000 | 0.000 | 0.000 | 0.000 |
| 1 | 0.299 | 0.387 | 0.302 | 0.156 | 0.060 | 0.018 | 0.004 | 0.000 | 0.000 | 0.000 | 0.000 |
| 2 | 0.063 | 0.172 | 0.302 | 0.267 | 0.161 | 0.070 | 0.021 | 0.004 | 0.000 | 0.000 | 0.000 |
| 3 | 0.008 | 0.045 | 0.176 | 0.267 | 0.251 | 0.164 | 0.074 | 0.021 | 0.003 | 0.000 | 0.000 |
| 4 | 0.001 | 0.007 | 0.066 | 0.172 | 0.251 | 0.246 | 0.167 | 0.074 | 0.017 | 0.001 | 0.000 |
| 5 | 0.000 | 0.001 | 0.017 | 0.074 | 0.167 | 0.246 | 0.251 | 0.172 | 0.066 | 0.007 | 0.001 |
| 6 | 0.000 | 0.000 | 0.003 | 0.021 | 0.074 | 0.164 | 0.251 | 0.267 | 0.176 | 0.045 | 0.008 |
| 7 | 0.000 | 0.000 | 0.000 | 0.004 | 0.021 | 0.070 | 0.161 | 0.267 | 0.302 | 0.172 | 0.063 |
| 8 | 0.000 | 0.000 | 0.000 | 0.000 | 0.004 | 0.018 | 0.060 | 0.156 | 0.302 | 0.387 | 0.299 |
| 9 | 0.000 | 0.000 | 0.000 | 0.000 | 0.000 | 0.002 | 0.010 | 0.040 | 0.134 | 0.387 | 0.630 |

$n = 10$

| | | | | | Probability | | | | | | |
|---|---|---|---|---|---|---|---|---|---|---|---|
| x | 0.05 | 0.10 | 0.20 | 0.30 | 0.40 | 0.50 | 0.60 | 0.70 | 0.80 | 0.90 | 0.95 |
| 0 | 0.599 | 0.349 | 0.107 | 0.028 | 0.006 | 0.001 | 0.000 | 0.000 | 0.000 | 0.000 | 0.000 |
| 1 | 0.315 | 0.387 | 0.268 | 0.121 | 0.040 | 0.010 | 0.002 | 0.000 | 0.000 | 0.000 | 0.000 |
| 2 | 0.075 | 0.194 | 0.302 | 0.233 | 0.121 | 0.044 | 0.011 | 0.001 | 0.000 | 0.000 | 0.000 |
| 3 | 0.010 | 0.057 | 0.201 | 0.267 | 0.215 | 0.117 | 0.042 | 0.009 | 0.001 | 0.000 | 0.000 |
| 4 | 0.001 | 0.011 | 0.088 | 0.200 | 0.251 | 0.205 | 0.111 | 0.037 | 0.006 | 0.000 | 0.000 |
| 5 | 0.000 | 0.001 | 0.026 | 0.103 | 0.201 | 0.246 | 0.201 | 0.103 | 0.026 | 0.001 | 0.000 |
| 6 | 0.000 | 0.000 | 0.006 | 0.037 | 0.111 | 0.205 | 0.251 | 0.200 | 0.088 | 0.011 | 0.001 |
| 7 | 0.000 | 0.000 | 0.001 | 0.009 | 0.042 | 0.117 | 0.215 | 0.267 | 0.201 | 0.057 | 0.010 |
| 8 | 0.000 | 0.000 | 0.000 | 0.001 | 0.011 | 0.044 | 0.121 | 0.233 | 0.302 | 0.194 | 0.075 |
| 9 | 0.000 | 0.000 | 0.000 | 0.000 | 0.002 | 0.010 | 0.040 | 0.121 | 0.268 | 0.387 | 0.315 |
| 10 | 0.000 | 0.000 | 0.000 | 0.000 | 0.000 | 0.001 | 0.006 | 0.028 | 0.107 | 0.349 | 0.599 |

$n = 11$

| | | | | | Probability | | | | | | |
|---|---|---|---|---|---|---|---|---|---|---|---|
| x | 0.05 | 0.10 | 0.20 | 0.30 | 0.40 | 0.50 | 0.60 | 0.70 | 0.80 | 0.90 | 0.95 |
| 0 | 0.569 | 0.314 | 0.086 | 0.020 | 0.004 | 0.000 | 0.000 | 0.000 | 0.000 | 0.000 | 0.000 |
| 1 | 0.329 | 0.384 | 0.236 | 0.093 | 0.027 | 0.005 | 0.001 | 0.000 | 0.000 | 0.000 | 0.000 |
| 2 | 0.087 | 0.213 | 0.295 | 0.200 | 0.089 | 0.027 | 0.005 | 0.001 | 0.000 | 0.000 | 0.000 |
| 3 | 0.014 | 0.071 | 0.221 | 0.257 | 0.177 | 0.081 | 0.023 | 0.004 | 0.000 | 0.000 | 0.000 |
| 4 | 0.001 | 0.016 | 0.111 | 0.220 | 0.236 | 0.161 | 0.070 | 0.017 | 0.002 | 0.000 | 0.000 |
| 5 | 0.000 | 0.002 | 0.039 | 0.132 | 0.221 | 0.226 | 0.147 | 0.057 | 0.010 | 0.000 | 0.000 |
| 6 | 0.000 | 0.000 | 0.010 | 0.057 | 0.147 | 0.226 | 0.221 | 0.132 | 0.039 | 0.002 | 0.000 |
| 7 | 0.000 | 0.000 | 0.002 | 0.017 | 0.070 | 0.161 | 0.236 | 0.220 | 0.111 | 0.016 | 0.001 |
| 8 | 0.000 | 0.000 | 0.000 | 0.004 | 0.023 | 0.081 | 0.177 | 0.257 | 0.221 | 0.071 | 0.014 |
| 9 | 0.000 | 0.000 | 0.000 | 0.001 | 0.005 | 0.027 | 0.089 | 0.200 | 0.295 | 0.213 | 0.087 |
| 10 | 0.000 | 0.000 | 0.000 | 0.000 | 0.001 | 0.005 | 0.027 | 0.093 | 0.236 | 0.384 | 0.329 |
| 11 | 0.000 | 0.000 | 0.000 | 0.000 | 0.000 | 0.000 | 0.004 | 0.020 | 0.086 | 0.314 | 0.569 |

# Appendix A

Binomial Probability Distribution (*continued*)

**n = 12**

**Probability**

| x | 0.05 | 0.10 | 0.20 | 0.30 | 0.40 | 0.50 | 0.60 | 0.70 | 0.80 | 0.90 | 0.95 |
|---|------|------|------|------|------|------|------|------|------|------|------|
| 0 | 0.540 | 0.282 | 0.069 | 0.014 | 0.002 | 0.000 | 0.000 | 0.000 | 0.000 | 0.000 | 0.000 |
| 1 | 0.341 | 0.377 | 0.206 | 0.071 | 0.017 | 0.003 | 0.000 | 0.000 | 0.000 | 0.000 | 0.000 |
| 2 | 0.099 | 0.230 | 0.283 | 0.168 | 0.064 | 0.016 | 0.002 | 0.000 | 0.000 | 0.000 | 0.000 |
| 3 | 0.017 | 0.085 | 0.236 | 0.240 | 0.142 | 0.054 | 0.012 | 0.001 | 0.000 | 0.000 | 0.000 |
| 4 | 0.002 | 0.021 | 0.133 | 0.231 | 0.213 | 0.121 | 0.042 | 0.008 | 0.001 | 0.000 | 0.000 |
| 5 | 0.000 | 0.004 | 0.053 | 0.158 | 0.227 | 0.193 | 0.101 | 0.029 | 0.003 | 0.000 | 0.000 |
| 6 | 0.000 | 0.000 | 0.016 | 0.079 | 0.177 | 0.226 | 0.177 | 0.079 | 0.016 | 0.000 | 0.000 |
| 7 | 0.000 | 0.000 | 0.003 | 0.029 | 0.101 | 0.193 | 0.227 | 0.158 | 0.053 | 0.004 | 0.000 |
| 8 | 0.000 | 0.000 | 0.001 | 0.008 | 0.042 | 0.121 | 0.213 | 0.231 | 0.133 | 0.021 | 0.002 |
| 9 | 0.000 | 0.000 | 0.000 | 0.001 | 0.012 | 0.054 | 0.142 | 0.240 | 0.236 | 0.085 | 0.017 |
| 10 | 0.000 | 0.000 | 0.000 | 0.000 | 0.002 | 0.016 | 0.064 | 0.168 | 0.283 | 0.230 | 0.099 |
| 11 | 0.000 | 0.000 | 0.000 | 0.000 | 0.000 | 0.003 | 0.017 | 0.071 | 0.206 | 0.377 | 0.341 |
| 12 | 0.000 | 0.000 | 0.000 | 0.000 | 0.000 | 0.000 | 0.002 | 0.014 | 0.069 | 0.282 | 0.540 |

**n = 13**

**Probability**

| x | 0.05 | 0.10 | 0.20 | 0.30 | 0.40 | 0.50 | 0.60 | 0.70 | 0.80 | 0.90 | 0.95 |
|---|------|------|------|------|------|------|------|------|------|------|------|
| 0 | 0.513 | 0.254 | 0.055 | 0.010 | 0.001 | 0.000 | 0.000 | 0.000 | 0.000 | 0.000 | 0.000 |
| 1 | 0.351 | 0.367 | 0.179 | 0.054 | 0.011 | 0.002 | 0.000 | 0.000 | 0.000 | 0.000 | 0.000 |
| 2 | 0.111 | 0.245 | 0.268 | 0.139 | 0.045 | 0.010 | 0.001 | 0.000 | 0.000 | 0.000 | 0.000 |
| 3 | 0.021 | 0.100 | 0.246 | 0.218 | 0.111 | 0.035 | 0.006 | 0.001 | 0.000 | 0.000 | 0.000 |
| 4 | 0.003 | 0.028 | 0.154 | 0.234 | 0.184 | 0.087 | 0.024 | 0.003 | 0.000 | 0.000 | 0.000 |
| 5 | 0.000 | 0.006 | 0.069 | 0.180 | 0.221 | 0.157 | 0.066 | 0.014 | 0.001 | 0.000 | 0.000 |
| 6 | 0.000 | 0.001 | 0.023 | 0.103 | 0.197 | 0.209 | 0.131 | 0.044 | 0.006 | 0.000 | 0.000 |
| 7 | 0.000 | 0.000 | 0.006 | 0.044 | 0.131 | 0.209 | 0.197 | 0.103 | 0.023 | 0.001 | 0.000 |
| 8 | 0.000 | 0.000 | 0.001 | 0.014 | 0.066 | 0.157 | 0.221 | 0.180 | 0.069 | 0.006 | 0.000 |
| 9 | 0.000 | 0.000 | 0.000 | 0.003 | 0.024 | 0.087 | 0.184 | 0.234 | 0.154 | 0.028 | 0.003 |
| 10 | 0.000 | 0.000 | 0.000 | 0.001 | 0.006 | 0.035 | 0.111 | 0.218 | 0.246 | 0.100 | 0.021 |
| 11 | 0.000 | 0.000 | 0.000 | 0.000 | 0.001 | 0.010 | 0.045 | 0.139 | 0.268 | 0.245 | 0.111 |
| 12 | 0.000 | 0.000 | 0.000 | 0.000 | 0.000 | 0.002 | 0.011 | 0.054 | 0.179 | 0.367 | 0.351 |
| 13 | 0.000 | 0.000 | 0.000 | 0.000 | 0.000 | 0.000 | 0.001 | 0.010 | 0.055 | 0.254 | 0.513 |

## Binomial Probability Distribution (*concluded*)

### n = 14
**Probability**

| x | 0.05 | 0.10 | 0.20 | 0.30 | 0.40 | 0.50 | 0.60 | 0.70 | 0.80 | 0.90 | 0.95 |
|---|------|------|------|------|------|------|------|------|------|------|------|
| 0 | 0.488 | 0.229 | 0.044 | 0.007 | 0.001 | 0.000 | 0.000 | 0.000 | 0.000 | 0.000 | 0.000 |
| 1 | 0.359 | 0.356 | 0.154 | 0.041 | 0.007 | 0.001 | 0.000 | 0.000 | 0.000 | 0.000 | 0.000 |
| 2 | 0.123 | 0.257 | 0.250 | 0.113 | 0.032 | 0.006 | 0.001 | 0.000 | 0.000 | 0.000 | 0.000 |
| 3 | 0.026 | 0.114 | 0.250 | 0.194 | 0.085 | 0.022 | 0.003 | 0.000 | 0.000 | 0.000 | 0.000 |
| 4 | 0.004 | 0.035 | 0.172 | 0.229 | 0.155 | 0.061 | 0.014 | 0.001 | 0.000 | 0.000 | 0.000 |
| 5 | 0.000 | 0.008 | 0.086 | 0.196 | 0.207 | 0.122 | 0.041 | 0.007 | 0.000 | 0.000 | 0.000 |
| 6 | 0.000 | 0.001 | 0.032 | 0.126 | 0.207 | 0.183 | 0.092 | 0.023 | 0.002 | 0.000 | 0.000 |
| 7 | 0.000 | 0.000 | 0.009 | 0.062 | 0.157 | 0.209 | 0.157 | 0.062 | 0.009 | 0.000 | 0.000 |
| 8 | 0.000 | 0.000 | 0.002 | 0.023 | 0.092 | 0.183 | 0.207 | 0.126 | 0.032 | 0.001 | 0.000 |
| 9 | 0.000 | 0.000 | 0.000 | 0.007 | 0.041 | 0.122 | 0.207 | 0.196 | 0.086 | 0.008 | 0.000 |
| 10 | 0.000 | 0.000 | 0.000 | 0.001 | 0.014 | 0.061 | 0.155 | 0.229 | 0.172 | 0.035 | 0.004 |
| 11 | 0.000 | 0.000 | 0.000 | 0.000 | 0.003 | 0.022 | 0.085 | 0.194 | 0.250 | 0.114 | 0.026 |
| 12 | 0.000 | 0.000 | 0.000 | 0.000 | 0.001 | 0.006 | 0.032 | 0.113 | 0.250 | 0.257 | 0.123 |
| 13 | 0.000 | 0.000 | 0.000 | 0.000 | 0.000 | 0.001 | 0.007 | 0.041 | 0.154 | 0.356 | 0.359 |
| 14 | 0.000 | 0.000 | 0.000 | 0.000 | 0.000 | 0.000 | 0.001 | 0.007 | 0.044 | 0.229 | 0.488 |

### n = 15
**Probability**

| x | 0.05 | 0.10 | 0.20 | 0.30 | 0.40 | 0.50 | 0.60 | 0.70 | 0.80 | 0.90 | 0.95 |
|---|------|------|------|------|------|------|------|------|------|------|------|
| 0 | 0.463 | 0.206 | 0.035 | 0.005 | 0.000 | 0.000 | 0.000 | 0.000 | 0.000 | 0.000 | 0.000 |
| 1 | 0.366 | 0.343 | 0.132 | 0.031 | 0.005 | 0.000 | 0.000 | 0.000 | 0.000 | 0.000 | 0.000 |
| 2 | 0.135 | 0.267 | 0.231 | 0.092 | 0.022 | 0.003 | 0.000 | 0.000 | 0.000 | 0.000 | 0.000 |
| 3 | 0.031 | 0.129 | 0.250 | 0.170 | 0.063 | 0.014 | 0.002 | 0.000 | 0.000 | 0.000 | 0.000 |
| 4 | 0.005 | 0.043 | 0.188 | 0.219 | 0.127 | 0.042 | 0.007 | 0.001 | 0.000 | 0.000 | 0.000 |
| 5 | 0.001 | 0.010 | 0.103 | 0.206 | 0.186 | 0.092 | 0.024 | 0.003 | 0.000 | 0.000 | 0.000 |
| 6 | 0.000 | 0.002 | 0.043 | 0.147 | 0.207 | 0.153 | 0.061 | 0.012 | 0.001 | 0.000 | 0.000 |
| 7 | 0.000 | 0.000 | 0.014 | 0.081 | 0.177 | 0.196 | 0.118 | 0.035 | 0.003 | 0.000 | 0.000 |
| 8 | 0.000 | 0.000 | 0.003 | 0.035 | 0.118 | 0.196 | 0.177 | 0.081 | 0.014 | 0.000 | 0.000 |
| 9 | 0.000 | 0.000 | 0.001 | 0.012 | 0.061 | 0.153 | 0.207 | 0.147 | 0.043 | 0.002 | 0.000 |
| 10 | 0.000 | 0.000 | 0.000 | 0.003 | 0.024 | 0.092 | 0.186 | 0.206 | 0.103 | 0.010 | 0.001 |
| 11 | 0.000 | 0.000 | 0.000 | 0.001 | 0.007 | 0.042 | 0.127 | 0.219 | 0.188 | 0.043 | 0.005 |
| 12 | 0.000 | 0.000 | 0.000 | 0.000 | 0.002 | 0.014 | 0.063 | 0.170 | 0.250 | 0.129 | 0.031 |
| 13 | 0.000 | 0.000 | 0.000 | 0.000 | 0.000 | 0.003 | 0.022 | 0.092 | 0.231 | 0.267 | 0.135 |
| 14 | 0.000 | 0.000 | 0.000 | 0.000 | 0.000 | 0.000 | 0.005 | 0.031 | 0.132 | 0.343 | 0.366 |
| 15 | 0.000 | 0.000 | 0.000 | 0.000 | 0.000 | 0.000 | 0.000 | 0.005 | 0.035 | 0.206 | 0.463 |

# Appendix B

## Critical Values of Chi-Square

This table contains the values of $\chi^2$ that correspond to a specific right-tail area and specific number of degrees of freedom.

Example: With 17 $df$ and a .02 area in the upper tail, $\chi^2 = 30.995$

| Degrees of Freedom, $df$ | Right-Tail Area | | | |
|---|---|---|---|---|
| | 0.10 | 0.05 | 0.02 | 0.01 |
| 1 | 2.706 | 3.841 | 5.412 | 6.635 |
| 2 | 4.605 | 5.991 | 7.824 | 9.210 |
| 3 | 6.251 | 7.815 | 9.837 | 11.345 |
| 4 | 7.779 | 9.488 | 11.668 | 13.277 |
| 5 | 9.236 | 11.070 | 13.388 | 15.086 |
| 6 | 10.645 | 12.592 | 15.033 | 16.812 |
| 7 | 12.017 | 14.067 | 16.622 | 18.475 |
| 8 | 13.362 | 15.507 | 18.168 | 20.090 |
| 9 | 14.684 | 16.919 | 19.679 | 21.666 |
| 10 | 15.987 | 18.307 | 21.161 | 23.209 |
| 11 | 17.275 | 19.675 | 22.618 | 24.725 |
| 12 | 18.549 | 21.026 | 24.054 | 26.217 |
| 13 | 19.812 | 22.362 | 25.472 | 27.688 |
| 14 | 21.064 | 23.685 | 26.873 | 29.141 |
| 15 | 22.307 | 24.996 | 28.259 | 30.578 |
| 16 | 23.542 | 26.296 | 29.633 | 32.000 |
| 17 | 24.769 | 27.587 | 30.995 | 33.409 |
| 18 | 25.989 | 28.869 | 32.346 | 34.805 |
| 19 | 27.204 | 30.144 | 33.687 | 36.191 |
| 20 | 28.412 | 31.410 | 35.020 | 37.566 |
| 21 | 29.615 | 32.671 | 36.343 | 38.932 |
| 22 | 30.813 | 33.924 | 37.659 | 40.289 |
| 23 | 32.007 | 35.172 | 38.968 | 41.638 |
| 24 | 33.196 | 36.415 | 40.270 | 42.980 |
| 25 | 34.382 | 37.652 | 41.566 | 44.314 |
| 26 | 35.563 | 38.885 | 42.856 | 45.642 |
| 27 | 36.741 | 40.113 | 44.140 | 46.963 |
| 28 | 37.916 | 41.337 | 45.419 | 48.278 |
| 29 | 39.087 | 42.557 | 46.693 | 49.588 |
| 30 | 40.256 | 43.773 | 47.962 | 50.892 |

# Appendix C

## Poisson Distribution

| | | | | | μ | | | | |
|---|---|---|---|---|---|---|---|---|---|
| x | 0.1 | 0.2 | 0.3 | 0.4 | 0.5 | 0.6 | 0.7 | 0.8 | 0.9 |
| 0 | 0.9048 | 0.8187 | 0.7408 | 0.6703 | 0.6065 | 0.5488 | 0.4966 | 0.4493 | 0.4066 |
| 1 | 0.0905 | 0.1637 | 0.2222 | 0.2681 | 0.3033 | 0.3293 | 0.3476 | 0.3595 | 0.3659 |
| 2 | 0.0045 | 0.0164 | 0.0333 | 0.0536 | 0.0758 | 0.0988 | 0.1217 | 0.1438 | 0.1647 |
| 3 | 0.0002 | 0.0011 | 0.0033 | 0.0072 | 0.0126 | 0.0198 | 0.0284 | 0.0383 | 0.0494 |
| 4 | 0.0000 | 0.0001 | 0.0003 | 0.0007 | 0.0016 | 0.0030 | 0.0050 | 0.0077 | 0.0111 |
| 5 | 0.0000 | 0.0000 | 0.0000 | 0.0001 | 0.0002 | 0.0004 | 0.0007 | 0.0012 | 0.0020 |
| 6 | 0.0000 | 0.0000 | 0.0000 | 0.0000 | 0.0000 | 0.0000 | 0.0001 | 0.0002 | 0.0003 |
| 7 | 0.0000 | 0.0000 | 0.0000 | 0.0000 | 0.0000 | 0.0000 | 0.0000 | 0.0000 | 0.0000 |

| | | | | | μ | | | | |
|---|---|---|---|---|---|---|---|---|---|
| x | 1.0 | 2.0 | 3.0 | 4.0 | 5.0 | 6.0 | 7.0 | 8.0 | 9.0 |
| 0 | 0.3679 | 0.1353 | 0.0498 | 0.0183 | 0.0067 | 0.0025 | 0.0009 | 0.0003 | 0.0001 |
| 1 | 0.3679 | 0.2707 | 0.1494 | 0.0733 | 0.0337 | 0.0149 | 0.0064 | 0.0027 | 0.0011 |
| 2 | 0.1839 | 0.2707 | 0.2240 | 0.1465 | 0.0842 | 0.0446 | 0.0223 | 0.0107 | 0.0050 |
| 3 | 0.0613 | 0.1804 | 0.2240 | 0.1954 | 0.1404 | 0.0892 | 0.0521 | 0.0286 | 0.0150 |
| 4 | 0.0153 | 0.0902 | 0.1680 | 0.1954 | 0.1755 | 0.1339 | 0.0912 | 0.0573 | 0.0337 |
| 5 | 0.0031 | 0.0361 | 0.1008 | 0.1563 | 0.1755 | 0.1606 | 0.1277 | 0.0916 | 0.0607 |
| 6 | 0.0005 | 0.0120 | 0.0504 | 0.1042 | 0.1462 | 0.1606 | 0.1490 | 0.1221 | 0.0911 |
| 7 | 0.0001 | 0.0034 | 0.0216 | 0.0595 | 0.1044 | 0.1377 | 0.1490 | 0.1396 | 0.1171 |
| 8 | 0.0000 | 0.0009 | 0.0081 | 0.0298 | 0.0653 | 0.1033 | 0.1304 | 0.1396 | 0.1318 |
| 9 | 0.0000 | 0.0002 | 0.0027 | 0.0132 | 0.0363 | 0.0688 | 0.1014 | 0.1241 | 0.1318 |
| 10 | 0.0000 | 0.0000 | 0.0008 | 0.0053 | 0.0181 | 0.0413 | 0.0710 | 0.0993 | 0.1186 |
| 11 | 0.0000 | 0.0000 | 0.0002 | 0.0019 | 0.0082 | 0.0225 | 0.0452 | 0.0722 | 0.0970 |
| 12 | 0.0000 | 0.0000 | 0.0001 | 0.0006 | 0.0034 | 0.0113 | 0.0263 | 0.0481 | 0.0728 |
| 13 | 0.0000 | 0.0000 | 0.0000 | 0.0002 | 0.0013 | 0.0052 | 0.0142 | 0.0296 | 0.0504 |
| 14 | 0.0000 | 0.0000 | 0.0000 | 0.0001 | 0.0005 | 0.0022 | 0.0071 | 0.0169 | 0.0324 |
| 15 | 0.0000 | 0.0000 | 0.0000 | 0.0000 | 0.0002 | 0.0009 | 0.0033 | 0.0090 | 0.0194 |
| 16 | 0.0000 | 0.0000 | 0.0000 | 0.0000 | 0.0000 | 0.0003 | 0.0014 | 0.0045 | 0.0109 |
| 17 | 0.0000 | 0.0000 | 0.0000 | 0.0000 | 0.0000 | 0.0001 | 0.0006 | 0.0021 | 0.0058 |
| 18 | 0.0000 | 0.0000 | 0.0000 | 0.0000 | 0.0000 | 0.0000 | 0.0002 | 0.0009 | 0.0029 |
| 19 | 0.0000 | 0.0000 | 0.0000 | 0.0000 | 0.0000 | 0.0000 | 0.0001 | 0.0004 | 0.0014 |
| 20 | 0.0000 | 0.0000 | 0.0000 | 0.0000 | 0.0000 | 0.0000 | 0.0000 | 0.0002 | 0.0006 |
| 21 | 0.0000 | 0.0000 | 0.0000 | 0.0000 | 0.0000 | 0.0000 | 0.0000 | 0.0001 | 0.0003 |
| 22 | 0.0000 | 0.0000 | 0.0000 | 0.0000 | 0.0000 | 0.0000 | 0.0000 | 0.0000 | 0.0001 |

# Appendix D

## Areas under the Normal Curve

Example:
If $z = 1.96$, then
$P(0 \text{ to } z) = 0.4750$.

0.4750

$z \longrightarrow$   0   1.96

| z | 0.00 | 0.01 | 0.02 | 0.03 | 0.04 | 0.05 | 0.06 | 0.07 | 0.08 | 0.09 |
|---|------|------|------|------|------|------|------|------|------|------|
| 0.0 | 0.0000 | 0.0040 | 0.0080 | 0.0120 | 0.0160 | 0.0199 | 0.0239 | 0.0279 | 0.0319 | 0.0359 |
| 0.1 | 0.0398 | 0.0438 | 0.0478 | 0.0517 | 0.0557 | 0.0596 | 0.0636 | 0.0675 | 0.0714 | 0.0753 |
| 0.2 | 0.0793 | 0.0832 | 0.0871 | 0.0910 | 0.0948 | 0.0987 | 0.1026 | 0.1064 | 0.1103 | 0.1141 |
| 0.3 | 0.1179 | 0.1217 | 0.1255 | 0.1293 | 0.1331 | 0.1368 | 0.1406 | 0.1443 | 0.1480 | 0.1517 |
| 0.4 | 0.1554 | 0.1591 | 0.1628 | 0.1664 | 0.1700 | 0.1736 | 0.1772 | 0.1808 | 0.1844 | 0.1879 |
| 0.5 | 0.1915 | 0.1950 | 0.1985 | 0.2019 | 0.2054 | 0.2088 | 0.2123 | 0.2157 | 0.2190 | 0.2224 |
| 0.6 | 0.2257 | 0.2291 | 0.2324 | 0.2357 | 0.2389 | 0.2422 | 0.2454 | 0.2486 | 0.2517 | 0.2549 |
| 0.7 | 0.2580 | 0.2611 | 0.2642 | 0.2673 | 0.2704 | 0.2734 | 0.2764 | 0.2794 | 0.2823 | 0.2852 |
| 0.8 | 0.2881 | 0.2910 | 0.2939 | 0.2967 | 0.2995 | 0.3023 | 0.3051 | 0.3078 | 0.3106 | 0.3133 |
| 0.9 | 0.3159 | 0.3186 | 0.3212 | 0.3238 | 0.3264 | 0.3289 | 0.3315 | 0.3340 | 0.3365 | 0.3389 |
| 1.0 | 0.3413 | 0.3438 | 0.3461 | 0.3485 | 0.3508 | 0.3531 | 0.3554 | 0.3577 | 0.3599 | 0.3621 |
| 1.1 | 0.3643 | 0.3665 | 0.3686 | 0.3708 | 0.3729 | 0.3749 | 0.3770 | 0.3790 | 0.3810 | 0.3830 |
| 1.2 | 0.3849 | 0.3869 | 0.3888 | 0.3907 | 0.3925 | 0.3944 | 0.3962 | 0.3980 | 0.3997 | 0.4015 |
| 1.3 | 0.4032 | 0.4049 | 0.4066 | 0.4082 | 0.4099 | 0.4115 | 0.4131 | 0.4147 | 0.4162 | 0.4177 |
| 1.4 | 0.4192 | 0.4207 | 0.4222 | 0.4236 | 0.4251 | 0.4265 | 0.4279 | 0.4292 | 0.4306 | 0.4319 |
| 1.5 | 0.4332 | 0.4345 | 0.4357 | 0.4370 | 0.4382 | 0.4394 | 0.4406 | 0.4418 | 0.4429 | 0.4441 |
| 1.6 | 0.4452 | 0.4463 | 0.4474 | 0.4484 | 0.4495 | 0.4505 | 0.4515 | 0.4525 | 0.4535 | 0.4545 |
| 1.7 | 0.4554 | 0.4564 | 0.4573 | 0.4582 | 0.4591 | 0.4599 | 0.4608 | 0.4616 | 0.4625 | 0.4633 |
| 1.8 | 0.4641 | 0.4649 | 0.4656 | 0.4664 | 0.4671 | 0.4678 | 0.4686 | 0.4693 | 0.4699 | 0.4706 |
| 1.9 | 0.4713 | 0.4719 | 0.4726 | 0.4732 | 0.4738 | 0.4744 | 0.4750 | 0.4756 | 0.4761 | 0.4767 |
| 2.0 | 0.4772 | 0.4778 | 0.4783 | 0.4788 | 0.4793 | 0.4798 | 0.4803 | 0.4808 | 0.4812 | 0.4817 |
| 2.1 | 0.4821 | 0.4826 | 0.4830 | 0.4834 | 0.4838 | 0.4842 | 0.4846 | 0.4850 | 0.4854 | 0.4857 |
| 2.2 | 0.4861 | 0.4864 | 0.4868 | 0.4871 | 0.4875 | 0.4878 | 0.4881 | 0.4884 | 0.4887 | 0.4890 |
| 2.3 | 0.4893 | 0.4896 | 0.4898 | 0.4901 | 0.4904 | 0.4906 | 0.4909 | 0.4911 | 0.4913 | 0.4916 |
| 2.4 | 0.4918 | 0.4920 | 0.4922 | 0.4925 | 0.4927 | 0.4929 | 0.4931 | 0.4932 | 0.4934 | 0.4936 |
| 2.5 | 0.4938 | 0.4940 | 0.4941 | 0.4943 | 0.4945 | 0.4946 | 0.4948 | 0.4949 | 0.4951 | 0.4952 |
| 2.6 | 0.4953 | 0.4955 | 0.4956 | 0.4957 | 0.4959 | 0.4960 | 0.4961 | 0.4962 | 0.4963 | 0.4964 |
| 2.7 | 0.4965 | 0.4966 | 0.4967 | 0.4968 | 0.4969 | 0.4970 | 0.4971 | 0.4972 | 0.4973 | 0.4974 |
| 2.8 | 0.4974 | 0.4975 | 0.4976 | 0.4977 | 0.4977 | 0.4978 | 0.4979 | 0.4979 | 0.4980 | 0.4981 |
| 2.9 | 0.4981 | 0.4982 | 0.4982 | 0.4983 | 0.4984 | 0.4984 | 0.4985 | 0.4985 | 0.4986 | 0.4986 |
| 3.0 | 0.4987 | 0.4987 | 0.4987 | 0.4988 | 0.4988 | 0.4989 | 0.4989 | 0.4989 | 0.4990 | 0.4990 |

# Appendix E

## Table of Random Numbers

| | | | | | | | | | |
|---|---|---|---|---|---|---|---|---|---|
| 02711 | 08182 | 75997 | 79866 | 58095 | 83319 | 80295 | 79741 | 74599 | 84379 |
| 94873 | 90935 | 31684 | 63952 | 09865 | 14491 | 99518 | 93394 | 34691 | 14985 |
| 54921 | 78680 | 06635 | 98689 | 17306 | 25170 | 65928 | 87709 | 30533 | 89736 |
| 77640 | 97636 | 37397 | 93379 | 56454 | 59818 | 45827 | 74164 | 71666 | 46977 |
| 61545 | 00835 | 93251 | 87203 | 36759 | 49197 | 85967 | 01704 | 19634 | 21898 |
| | | | | | | | | | |
| 17147 | 19519 | 22497 | 16857 | 42426 | 84822 | 92598 | 49186 | 88247 | 39967 |
| 13748 | 04742 | 92460 | 85801 | 53444 | 65626 | 58710 | 55406 | 17173 | 69776 |
| 87455 | 14813 | 50373 | 28037 | 91182 | 32786 | 65261 | 11173 | 34376 | 36408 |
| 08999 | 57409 | 91185 | 10200 | 61411 | 23392 | 47797 | 56377 | 71635 | 08601 |
| 78804 | 81333 | 53809 | 32471 | 46034 | 36306 | 22498 | 19239 | 85428 | 55721 |
| | | | | | | | | | |
| 82173 | 26921 | 28472 | 98958 | 07960 | 66124 | 89731 | 95069 | 18625 | 92405 |
| 97594 | 25168 | 89178 | 68190 | 05043 | 17407 | 48201 | 83917 | 11413 | 72920 |
| 73881 | 67176 | 93504 | 42636 | 38233 | 16154 | 96451 | 57925 | 29667 | 30859 |
| 46071 | 22912 | 90326 | 42453 | 88108 | 72064 | 58601 | 32357 | 90610 | 32921 |
| 44492 | 19686 | 12495 | 93135 | 95185 | 77799 | 52441 | 88272 | 22024 | 80631 |
| | | | | | | | | | |
| 31864 | 72170 | 37722 | 55794 | 14636 | 05148 | 54505 | 50113 | 21119 | 25228 |
| 51574 | 90692 | 43339 | 65689 | 76539 | 27909 | 05467 | 21727 | 51141 | 72949 |
| 35350 | 76132 | 92925 | 92124 | 92634 | 35681 | 43690 | 89136 | 35599 | 84138 |
| 46943 | 36502 | 01172 | 46045 | 46991 | 33804 | 80006 | 35542 | 61056 | 75666 |
| 22665 | 87226 | 33304 | 57975 | 03985 | 21566 | 65796 | 72915 | 81466 | 89205 |
| | | | | | | | | | |
| 39437 | 97957 | 11838 | 10433 | 21564 | 51570 | 73558 | 27495 | 34533 | 57808 |
| 77082 | 47784 | 40098 | 97962 | 89845 | 28392 | 78187 | 06112 | 08169 | 11261 |
| 24544 | 25649 | 43370 | 28007 | 06779 | 72402 | 62632 | 53956 | 24709 | 06978 |
| 27503 | 15558 | 37738 | 24849 | 70722 | 71859 | 83736 | 06016 | 94397 | 12529 |
| 24590 | 24545 | 06435 | 52758 | 45685 | 90151 | 46516 | 49644 | 92686 | 84870 |
| | | | | | | | | | |
| 48155 | 86226 | 40359 | 28723 | 15364 | 69125 | 12609 | 57171 | 86857 | 31702 |
| 20226 | 53752 | 90648 | 24362 | 83314 | 00014 | 19207 | 69413 | 97016 | 86290 |
| 70178 | 73444 | 38790 | 53626 | 93780 | 18629 | 68766 | 24371 | 74639 | 30782 |
| 10169 | 41465 | 51935 | 05711 | 09799 | 79077 | 88159 | 33437 | 68519 | 03040 |
| 81084 | 03701 | 28598 | 70013 | 63794 | 53169 | 97054 | 60303 | 23259 | 96196 |
| | | | | | | | | | |
| 69202 | 20777 | 21727 | 81511 | 51887 | 16175 | 53746 | 46516 | 70339 | 62727 |
| 80561 | 95787 | 89426 | 93325 | 86412 | 57479 | 54194 | 52153 | 19197 | 81877 |
| 08199 | 26703 | 95128 | 48599 | 09333 | 12584 | 24374 | 31232 | 61782 | 44032 |
| 98883 | 28220 | 39358 | 53720 | 80161 | 83371 | 15181 | 11131 | 12219 | 55920 |
| 84568 | 69286 | 76054 | 21615 | 80883 | 36797 | 82845 | 39139 | 90900 | 18172 |
| | | | | | | | | | |
| 04269 | 35173 | 95745 | 53893 | 86022 | 77722 | 52498 | 84193 | 22448 | 22571 |
| 10538 | 13124 | 36099 | 13140 | 37706 | 44562 | 57179 | 44693 | 67877 | 01549 |
| 77843 | 24955 | 25900 | 63843 | 95029 | 93859 | 93634 | 20205 | 66294 | 41218 |
| 12034 | 94636 | 49455 | 76362 | 83532 | 31062 | 69903 | 91186 | 65768 | 55949 |
| 10524 | 72829 | 47641 | 93315 | 80875 | 28090 | 97728 | 52560 | 34937 | 79548 |
| | | | | | | | | | |
| 68935 | 76632 | 46984 | 61772 | 92786 | 22651 | 07086 | 89754 | 44143 | 97687 |
| 89450 | 65665 | 29190 | 43709 | 11172 | 34481 | 95977 | 47535 | 25658 | 73898 |
| 90696 | 20451 | 24211 | 97310 | 60446 | 73530 | 62865 | 96574 | 13829 | 72226 |
| 49006 | 32047 | 93086 | 00112 | 20470 | 17136 | 28255 | 86328 | 07293 | 38809 |
| 74591 | 87025 | 52368 | 59416 | 34417 | 70557 | 86746 | 55809 | 53628 | 12000 |
| | | | | | | | | | |
| 06315 | 17012 | 77103 | 00968 | 07235 | 10728 | 42189 | 33292 | 51487 | 64443 |
| 62386 | 09184 | 62092 | 46617 | 99419 | 64230 | 95034 | 85481 | 07857 | 42510 |
| 86848 | 82122 | 04028 | 36959 | 87827 | 12813 | 08627 | 80699 | 13345 | 51695 |
| 65643 | 69480 | 46598 | 04501 | 40403 | 91408 | 32343 | 48130 | 49303 | 90689 |
| 11084 | 46534 | 78957 | 77353 | 39578 | 77868 | 22970 | 84349 | 09184 | 70603 |

# Appendix F

## Student's *t* Distribution

*c* Confidence interval

Left-tailed test

Right-tailed test

Two-tailed test

| | Confidence Intervals, *c* | | | | | |
|---|---|---|---|---|---|---|
| | 80% | 90% | 95% | 98% | 99% | 99.9% |
| | Level of Significance for One-Tailed Test, α | | | | | |
| *df* | 0.100 | 0.050 | 0.025 | 0.010 | 0.005 | 0.0005 |
| | Level of Significance for Two-Tailed Test, α | | | | | |
| | 0.20 | 0.10 | 0.05 | 0.02 | 0.01 | 0.001 |
| 1 | 3.078 | 6.314 | 12.706 | 31.821 | 63.657 | 636.619 |
| 2 | 1.886 | 2.920 | 4.303 | 6.965 | 9.925 | 31.599 |
| 3 | 1.638 | 2.353 | 3.182 | 4.541 | 5.841 | 12.924 |
| 4 | 1.533 | 2.132 | 2.776 | 3.747 | 4.604 | 8.610 |
| 5 | 1.476 | 2.015 | 2.571 | 3.365 | 4.032 | 6.869 |
| 6 | 1.440 | 1.943 | 2.447 | 3.143 | 3.707 | 5.959 |
| 7 | 1.415 | 1.895 | 2.365 | 2.998 | 3.499 | 5.408 |
| 8 | 1.397 | 1.860 | 2.306 | 2.896 | 3.355 | 5.041 |
| 9 | 1.383 | 1.833 | 2.262 | 2.821 | 3.250 | 4.781 |
| 10 | 1.372 | 1.812 | 2.228 | 2.764 | 3.169 | 4.587 |
| 11 | 1.363 | 1.796 | 2.201 | 2.718 | 3.106 | 4.437 |
| 12 | 1.356 | 1.782 | 2.179 | 2.681 | 3.055 | 4.318 |
| 13 | 1.350 | 1.771 | 2.160 | 2.650 | 3.012 | 4.221 |
| 14 | 1.345 | 1.761 | 2.145 | 2.624 | 2.977 | 4.140 |
| 15 | 1.341 | 1.753 | 2.131 | 2.602 | 2.947 | 4.073 |
| 16 | 1.337 | 1.746 | 2.120 | 2.583 | 2.921 | 4.015 |
| 17 | 1.333 | 1.740 | 2.110 | 2.567 | 2.898 | 3.965 |
| 18 | 1.330 | 1.734 | 2.101 | 2.552 | 2.878 | 3.922 |
| 19 | 1.328 | 1.729 | 2.093 | 2.539 | 2.861 | 3.883 |
| 20 | 1.325 | 1.725 | 2.086 | 2.528 | 2.845 | 3.850 |
| 21 | 1.323 | 1.721 | 2.080 | 2.518 | 2.831 | 3.819 |
| 22 | 1.321 | 1.717 | 2.074 | 2.508 | 2.819 | 3.792 |
| 23 | 1.319 | 1.714 | 2.069 | 2.500 | 2.807 | 3.768 |
| 24 | 1.318 | 1.711 | 2.064 | 2.492 | 2.797 | 3.745 |
| 25 | 1.316 | 1.708 | 2.060 | 2.485 | 2.787 | 3.725 |
| 26 | 1.315 | 1.706 | 2.056 | 2.479 | 2.779 | 3.707 |
| 27 | 1.314 | 1.703 | 2.052 | 2.473 | 2.771 | 3.690 |
| 28 | 1.313 | 1.701 | 2.048 | 2.467 | 2.763 | 3.674 |
| 29 | 1.311 | 1.699 | 2.045 | 2.462 | 2.756 | 3.659 |
| 30 | 1.310 | 1.697 | 2.042 | 2.457 | 2.750 | 3.646 |
| 40 | 1.303 | 1.684 | 2.021 | 2.423 | 2.704 | 3.551 |
| 60 | 1.296 | 1.671 | 2.000 | 2.390 | 2.660 | 3.460 |
| 120 | 1.289 | 1.658 | 1.980 | 2.358 | 2.617 | 3.373 |
| ∞ | 1.282 | 1.645 | 1.960 | 2.326 | 2.576 | 3.291 |

# Appendix G

## Critical Values of the *F* Distribution at a 5 Percent Level of Significance

| | | Degrees of Freedom for the Numerator | | | | | | | | | | | | | | |
|---|---|---|---|---|---|---|---|---|---|---|---|---|---|---|---|---|
| | | **1** | **2** | **3** | **4** | **5** | **6** | **7** | **8** | **9** | **10** | **12** | **15** | **20** | **24** | **30** | **40** |
| **Degrees of Freedom for the Denominator** | 1 | 161 | 200 | 216 | 225 | 230 | 234 | 237 | 239 | 241 | 242 | 244 | 246 | 248 | 249 | 250 | 251 |
| | 2 | 18.5 | 19.0 | 19.2 | 19.2 | 19.3 | 19.3 | 19.4 | 19.4 | 19.4 | 19.4 | 19.4 | 19.4 | 19.4 | 19.5 | 19.5 | 19.5 |
| | 3 | 10.1 | 9.55 | 9.28 | 9.12 | 9.01 | 8.94 | 8.89 | 8.85 | 8.81 | 8.79 | 8.74 | 8.70 | 8.66 | 8.64 | 8.62 | 8.59 |
| | 4 | 7.71 | 6.94 | 6.59 | 6.39 | 6.26 | 6.16 | 6.09 | 6.04 | 6.00 | 5.96 | 5.91 | 5.86 | 5.80 | 5.77 | 5.75 | 5.72 |
| | 5 | 6.61 | 5.79 | 5.41 | 5.19 | 5.05 | 4.95 | 4.88 | 4.82 | 4.77 | 4.74 | 4.68 | 4.62 | 4.56 | 4.53 | 4.50 | 4.46 |
| | 6 | 5.99 | 5.14 | 4.76 | 4.53 | 4.39 | 4.28 | 4.21 | 4.15 | 4.10 | 4.06 | 4.00 | 3.94 | 3.87 | 3.84 | 3.81 | 3.77 |
| | 7 | 5.59 | 4.74 | 4.35 | 4.12 | 3.97 | 3.87 | 3.79 | 3.73 | 3.68 | 3.64 | 3.57 | 3.51 | 3.44 | 3.41 | 3.38 | 3.34 |
| | 8 | 5.32 | 4.46 | 4.07 | 3.84 | 3.69 | 3.58 | 3.50 | 3.44 | 3.39 | 3.35 | 3.28 | 3.22 | 3.15 | 3.12 | 3.08 | 3.04 |
| | 9 | 5.12 | 4.26 | 3.86 | 3.63 | 3.48 | 3.37 | 3.29 | 3.23 | 3.18 | 3.14 | 3.07 | 3.01 | 2.94 | 2.90 | 2.86 | 2.83 |
| | 10 | 4.96 | 4.10 | 3.71 | 3.48 | 3.33 | 3.22 | 3.14 | 3.07 | 3.02 | 2.98 | 2.91 | 2.85 | 2.77 | 2.74 | 2.70 | 2.66 |
| | 11 | 4.84 | 3.98 | 3.59 | 3.36 | 3.20 | 3.09 | 3.01 | 2.95 | 2.90 | 2.85 | 2.79 | 2.72 | 2.65 | 2.61 | 2.57 | 2.53 |
| | 12 | 4.75 | 3.89 | 3.49 | 3.26 | 3.11 | 3.00 | 2.91 | 2.85 | 2.80 | 2.75 | 2.69 | 2.62 | 2.54 | 2.51 | 2.47 | 2.43 |
| | 13 | 4.67 | 3.81 | 3.41 | 3.18 | 3.03 | 2.92 | 2.83 | 2.77 | 2.71 | 2.67 | 2.60 | 2.53 | 2.46 | 2.42 | 2.38 | 2.34 |
| | 14 | 4.60 | 3.74 | 3.34 | 3.11 | 2.96 | 2.85 | 2.76 | 2.70 | 2.65 | 2.60 | 2.53 | 2.46 | 2.39 | 2.35 | 2.31 | 2.27 |
| | 15 | 4.54 | 3.68 | 3.29 | 3.06 | 2.90 | 2.79 | 2.71 | 2.64 | 2.59 | 2.54 | 2.48 | 2.40 | 2.33 | 2.29 | 2.25 | 2.20 |
| | 16 | 4.49 | 3.63 | 3.24 | 3.01 | 2.85 | 2.74 | 2.66 | 2.59 | 2.54 | 2.49 | 2.42 | 2.35 | 2.28 | 2.24 | 2.19 | 2.15 |
| | 17 | 4.45 | 3.59 | 3.20 | 2.96 | 2.81 | 2.70 | 2.61 | 2.55 | 2.49 | 2.45 | 2.38 | 2.31 | 2.23 | 2.19 | 2.15 | 2.10 |
| | 18 | 4.41 | 3.55 | 3.16 | 2.93 | 2.77 | 2.66 | 2.58 | 2.51 | 2.46 | 2.41 | 2.34 | 2.27 | 2.19 | 2.15 | 2.11 | 2.06 |
| | 19 | 4.38 | 3.52 | 3.13 | 2.90 | 2.74 | 2.63 | 2.54 | 2.48 | 2.42 | 2.38 | 2.31 | 2.23 | 2.16 | 2.11 | 2.07 | 2.03 |
| | 20 | 4.35 | 3.49 | 3.10 | 2.87 | 2.71 | 2.60 | 2.51 | 2.45 | 2.39 | 2.35 | 2.28 | 2.20 | 2.12 | 2.08 | 2.04 | 1.99 |
| | 21 | 4.32 | 3.47 | 3.07 | 2.84 | 2.68 | 2.57 | 2.49 | 2.42 | 2.37 | 2.32 | 2.25 | 2.18 | 2.10 | 2.05 | 2.01 | 1.96 |
| | 22 | 4.30 | 3.44 | 3.05 | 2.82 | 2.66 | 2.55 | 2.46 | 2.40 | 2.34 | 2.30 | 2.23 | 2.15 | 2.07 | 2.03 | 1.98 | 1.94 |
| | 23 | 4.28 | 3.42 | 3.03 | 2.80 | 2.64 | 2.53 | 2.44 | 2.37 | 2.32 | 2.27 | 2.20 | 2.13 | 2.05 | 2.01 | 1.96 | 1.91 |
| | 24 | 4.26 | 3.40 | 3.01 | 2.78 | 2.62 | 2.51 | 2.42 | 2.36 | 2.30 | 2.25 | 2.18 | 2.11 | 2.03 | 1.98 | 1.94 | 1.89 |
| | 25 | 4.24 | 3.39 | 2.99 | 2.76 | 2.60 | 2.49 | 2.40 | 2.34 | 2.28 | 2.24 | 2.16 | 2.09 | 2.01 | 1.96 | 1.92 | 1.87 |
| | 30 | 4.17 | 3.32 | 2.92 | 2.69 | 2.53 | 2.42 | 2.33 | 2.27 | 2.21 | 2.16 | 2.09 | 2.01 | 1.93 | 1.89 | 1.84 | 1.79 |
| | 40 | 4.08 | 3.23 | 2.84 | 2.61 | 2.45 | 2.34 | 2.25 | 2.18 | 2.12 | 2.08 | 2.00 | 1.92 | 1.84 | 1.79 | 1.74 | 1.69 |
| | 60 | 4.00 | 3.15 | 2.76 | 2.53 | 2.37 | 2.25 | 2.17 | 2.10 | 2.04 | 1.99 | 1.92 | 1.84 | 1.75 | 1.70 | 1.65 | 1.59 |
| | 120 | 3.92 | 3.07 | 2.68 | 2.45 | 2.29 | 2.18 | 2.09 | 2.02 | 1.96 | 1.91 | 1.83 | 1.75 | 1.66 | 1.61 | 1.55 | 1.50 |
| | ∞ | 3.84 | 3.00 | 2.60 | 2.37 | 2.21 | 2.10 | 2.01 | 1.94 | 1.88 | 1.83 | 1.75 | 1.67 | 1.57 | 1.52 | 1.46 | 1.39 |

# Appendix G

## Critical Values of the *F* Distribution at a 1 Percent Level of Significance (*concluded*)

| | | Degrees of Freedom for the Numerator | | | | | | | | | | | | | | | |
|---|---|---|---|---|---|---|---|---|---|---|---|---|---|---|---|---|---|
| | | 1 | 2 | 3 | 4 | 5 | 6 | 7 | 8 | 9 | 10 | 12 | 15 | 20 | 24 | 30 | 40 |
| **Degrees of Freedom for the Denominator** | 1 | 4052 | 5000 | 5403 | 5625 | 5764 | 5859 | 5928 | 5981 | 6022 | 6056 | 6106 | 6157 | 6209 | 6235 | 6261 | 6287 |
| | 2 | 98.5 | 99.0 | 99.2 | 99.2 | 99.3 | 99.3 | 99.4 | 99.4 | 99.4 | 99.4 | 99.4 | 99.4 | 99.4 | 99.5 | 99.5 | 99.5 |
| | 3 | 34.1 | 30.8 | 29.5 | 28.7 | 28.2 | 27.9 | 27.7 | 27.5 | 27.3 | 27.2 | 27.1 | 26.9 | 26.7 | 26.6 | 26.5 | 26.4 |
| | 4 | 21.2 | 18.0 | 16.7 | 16.0 | 15.5 | 15.2 | 15.0 | 14.8 | 14.7 | 14.5 | 14.4 | 14.2 | 14.0 | 13.9 | 13.8 | 13.7 |
| | 5 | 16.3 | 13.3 | 12.1 | 11.4 | 11.0 | 10.7 | 10.5 | 10.3 | 10.2 | 10.1 | 9.89 | 9.72 | 9.55 | 9.47 | 9.38 | 9.29 |
| | 6 | 13.7 | 10.9 | 9.78 | 9.15 | 8.75 | 8.47 | 8.26 | 8.10 | 7.98 | 7.87 | 7.72 | 7.56 | 7.40 | 7.31 | 7.23 | 7.14 |
| | 7 | 12.2 | 9.55 | 8.45 | 7.85 | 7.46 | 7.19 | 6.99 | 6.84 | 6.72 | 6.62 | 6.47 | 6.31 | 6.16 | 6.07 | 5.99 | 5.91 |
| | 8 | 11.3 | 8.65 | 7.59 | 7.01 | 6.63 | 6.37 | 6.18 | 6.03 | 5.91 | 5.81 | 5.67 | 5.52 | 5.36 | 5.28 | 5.20 | 5.12 |
| | 9 | 10.6 | 8.02 | 6.99 | 6.42 | 6.06 | 5.80 | 5.61 | 5.47 | 5.35 | 5.26 | 5.11 | 4.96 | 4.81 | 4.73 | 4.65 | 4.57 |
| | 10 | 10.0 | 7.56 | 6.55 | 5.99 | 5.64 | 5.39 | 5.20 | 5.06 | 4.94 | 4.85 | 4.71 | 4.56 | 4.41 | 4.33 | 4.25 | 4.17 |
| | 11 | 9.65 | 7.21 | 6.22 | 5.67 | 5.32 | 5.07 | 4.89 | 4.74 | 4.63 | 4.54 | 4.40 | 4.25 | 4.10 | 4.02 | 3.94 | 3.86 |
| | 12 | 9.33 | 6.93 | 5.95 | 5.41 | 5.06 | 4.82 | 4.64 | 4.50 | 4.39 | 4.30 | 4.16 | 4.01 | 3.86 | 3.78 | 3.70 | 3.62 |
| | 13 | 9.07 | 6.70 | 5.74 | 5.21 | 4.86 | 4.62 | 4.44 | 4.30 | 4.19 | 4.10 | 3.96 | 3.82 | 3.66 | 3.59 | 3.51 | 3.43 |
| | 14 | 8.86 | 6.51 | 5.56 | 5.04 | 4.69 | 4.46 | 4.28 | 4.14 | 4.03 | 3.94 | 3.80 | 3.66 | 3.51 | 3.43 | 3.35 | 3.27 |
| | 15 | 8.68 | 6.36 | 5.42 | 4.89 | 4.56 | 4.32 | 4.14 | 4.00 | 3.89 | 3.80 | 3.67 | 3.52 | 3.37 | 3.29 | 3.21 | 3.13 |
| | 16 | 8.53 | 6.23 | 5.29 | 4.77 | 4.44 | 4.20 | 4.03 | 3.89 | 3.78 | 3.69 | 3.55 | 3.41 | 3.26 | 3.18 | 3.10 | 3.02 |
| | 17 | 8.40 | 6.11 | 5.18 | 4.67 | 4.34 | 4.10 | 3.93 | 3.79 | 3.68 | 3.59 | 3.46 | 3.31 | 3.16 | 3.08 | 3.00 | 2.92 |
| | 18 | 8.29 | 6.01 | 5.09 | 4.58 | 4.25 | 4.01 | 3.84 | 3.71 | 3.60 | 3.51 | 3.37 | 3.23 | 3.08 | 3.00 | 2.92 | 2.84 |
| | 19 | 8.18 | 5.93 | 5.01 | 4.50 | 4.17 | 3.94 | 3.77 | 3.63 | 3.52 | 3.43 | 3.30 | 3.15 | 3.00 | 2.92 | 2.84 | 2.76 |
| | 20 | 8.10 | 5.85 | 4.94 | 4.43 | 4.10 | 3.87 | 3.70 | 3.56 | 3.46 | 3.37 | 3.23 | 3.09 | 2.94 | 2.86 | 2.78 | 2.69 |
| | 21 | 8.02 | 5.78 | 4.87 | 4.37 | 4.04 | 3.81 | 3.64 | 3.51 | 3.40 | 3.31 | 3.17 | 3.03 | 2.88 | 2.80 | 2.72 | 2.64 |
| | 22 | 7.95 | 5.72 | 4.82 | 4.31 | 3.99 | 3.76 | 3.59 | 3.45 | 3.35 | 3.26 | 3.12 | 2.98 | 2.83 | 2.75 | 2.67 | 2.58 |
| | 23 | 7.88 | 5.66 | 4.76 | 4.26 | 3.94 | 3.71 | 3.54 | 3.41 | 3.30 | 3.21 | 3.07 | 2.93 | 2.78 | 2.70 | 2.62 | 2.54 |
| | 24 | 7.82 | 5.61 | 4.72 | 4.22 | 3.90 | 3.67 | 3.50 | 3.36 | 3.26 | 3.17 | 3.03 | 2.89 | 2.74 | 2.66 | 2.58 | 2.49 |
| | 25 | 7.77 | 5.57 | 4.68 | 4.18 | 3.85 | 3.63 | 3.46 | 3.32 | 3.22 | 3.13 | 2.99 | 2.85 | 2.70 | 2.62 | 2.54 | 2.45 |
| | 30 | 7.56 | 5.39 | 4.51 | 4.02 | 3.70 | 3.47 | 3.30 | 3.17 | 3.07 | 2.98 | 2.84 | 2.70 | 2.55 | 2.47 | 2.39 | 2.30 |
| | 40 | 7.31 | 5.18 | 4.31 | 3.83 | 3.51 | 3.29 | 3.12 | 2.99 | 2.89 | 2.80 | 2.66 | 2.52 | 2.37 | 2.29 | 2.20 | 2.11 |
| | 60 | 7.08 | 4.98 | 4.13 | 3.65 | 3.34 | 3.12 | 2.95 | 2.82 | 2.72 | 2.63 | 2.50 | 2.35 | 2.20 | 2.12 | 2.03 | 1.94 |
| | 120 | 6.85 | 4.79 | 3.95 | 3.48 | 3.17 | 2.96 | 2.79 | 2.66 | 2.56 | 2.47 | 2.34 | 2.19 | 2.03 | 1.95 | 1.86 | 1.76 |
| | ∞ | 6.63 | 4.61 | 3.78 | 3.32 | 3.02 | 2.80 | 2.64 | 2.51 | 2.41 | 2.32 | 2.18 | 2.04 | 1.88 | 1.79 | 1.70 | 1.59 |

## Wilcoxon *T* Values

| | 2α | | | | | | |
|---|---|---|---|---|---|---|---|
| | .15 | .10 | .05 | .04 | .03 | .02 | .01 |
| | α | | | | | | |
| n | .075 | .050 | .025 | .020 | .015 | .010 | .005 |
| 4 | 0 | | | | | | |
| 5 | 1 | 0 | | | | | |
| 6 | 2 | 2 | 0 | 0 | | | |
| 7 | 4 | 3 | 2 | 1 | 0 | 0 | |
| 8 | 7 | 5 | 3 | 3 | 2 | 1 | 0 |
| 9 | 9 | 8 | 5 | 5 | 4 | 3 | 1 |
| 10 | 12 | 10 | 8 | 7 | 6 | 5 | 3 |
| 11 | 16 | 13 | 10 | 9 | 8 | 7 | 5 |
| 12 | 19 | 17 | 13 | 12 | 11 | 9 | 7 |
| 13 | 24 | 21 | 17 | 16 | 14 | 12 | 9 |
| 14 | 28 | 25 | 21 | 19 | 18 | 15 | 12 |
| 15 | 33 | 30 | 25 | 23 | 21 | 19 | 15 |
| 16 | 39 | 35 | 29 | 28 | 26 | 23 | 19 |
| 17 | 45 | 41 | 34 | 33 | 30 | 27 | 23 |
| 18 | 51 | 47 | 40 | 38 | 35 | 32 | 27 |
| 19 | 58 | 53 | 46 | 43 | 41 | 37 | 32 |
| 20 | 65 | 60 | 52 | 50 | 47 | 43 | 37 |
| 21 | 73 | 67 | 58 | 56 | 53 | 49 | 42 |
| 22 | 81 | 75 | 65 | 63 | 59 | 55 | 48 |
| 23 | 89 | 83 | 73 | 70 | 66 | 62 | 54 |
| 24 | 98 | 91 | 81 | 78 | 74 | 69 | 61 |
| 25 | 108 | 100 | 89 | 86 | 82 | 76 | 68 |
| 26 | 118 | 110 | 98 | 94 | 90 | 84 | 75 |
| 27 | 128 | 119 | 107 | 103 | 99 | 92 | 83 |
| 28 | 138 | 130 | 116 | 112 | 108 | 101 | 91 |
| 29 | 150 | 140 | 126 | 122 | 117 | 110 | 100 |
| 30 | 161 | 151 | 137 | 132 | 127 | 120 | 109 |
| 31 | 173 | 163 | 147 | 143 | 137 | 130 | 118 |
| 32 | 186 | 175 | 159 | 154 | 148 | 140 | 128 |
| 33 | 199 | 187 | 170 | 165 | 159 | 151 | 138 |
| 34 | 212 | 200 | 182 | 177 | 171 | 162 | 148 |
| 35 | 226 | 213 | 195 | 189 | 182 | 173 | 159 |
| 40 | 302 | 286 | 264 | 257 | 249 | 238 | 220 |
| 50 | 487 | 466 | 434 | 425 | 413 | 397 | 373 |
| 60 | 718 | 690 | 648 | 636 | 620 | 600 | 567 |
| 70 | 995 | 960 | 907 | 891 | 872 | 846 | 805 |
| 80 | 1,318 | 1,276 | 1,211 | 1,192 | 1,168 | 1,136 | 1,086 |
| 90 | 1,688 | 1,638 | 1,560 | 1,537 | 1,509 | 1,471 | 1,410 |
| 100 | 2,105 | 2,045 | 1,955 | 1,928 | 1,894 | 1,850 | 1,779 |

# Appendix I

## Factors for Control Charts

| Number of Items in Sample, $n$ | Chart for Averages | Chart for Ranges | | |
|---|---|---|---|---|
| | Factors for Control Limits | Factors for Central Line | Factors for Control Limits | |
| | $A_2$ | $d_2$ | $D_3$ | $D_4$ |
| 2 | 1.880 | 1.128 | 0 | 3.267 |
| 3 | 1.023 | 1.693 | 0 | 2.575 |
| 4 | .729 | 2.059 | 0 | 2.282 |
| 5 | .577 | 2.326 | 0 | 2.115 |
| 6 | .483 | 2.534 | 0 | 2.004 |
| 7 | .419 | 2.704 | .076 | 1.924 |
| 8 | .373 | 2.847 | .136 | 1.864 |
| 9 | .337 | 2.970 | .184 | 1.816 |
| 10 | .308 | 3.078 | .223 | 1.777 |
| 11 | .285 | 3.173 | .256 | 1.744 |
| 12 | .266 | 3.258 | .284 | 1.716 |
| 13 | .249 | 3.336 | .308 | 1.692 |
| 14 | .235 | 3.407 | .329 | 1.671 |
| 15 | .223 | 3.472 | .348 | 1.652 |

SOURCE: Adapted from American Society for Testing and Materials, *Manual on Quality Control of Materials,* 1951, Table B2, p. 115. For a more detailed table and explanation, see Acheson, J. Duncan, *Quality Control and Industrial Statistics,* 3d ed. (Homewood, Ill.: Richard D. Irwin, 1974), Table M, p. 927.

## Dataset 1—Real Estate

$x_1$ = Selling price in $000
$x_2$ = Number of bedrooms
$x_3$ = Size of the home in square feet
$x_4$ = Pool (1 = yes, 0 = no)
$x_5$ = Distance from the center of the city
$x_6$ = Township
$x_7$ = Garage attached (1 = yes, 0 = no)
$x_8$ = Number of bathrooms

| $x_1$ | $x_2$ | $x_3$ | $x_4$ | $x_5$ | $x_6$ | $x_7$ | $x_8$ |
|-------|-------|-------|-------|-------|-------|-------|-------|
| 263.1 | 4 | 2,300 | 1 | 17 | 5 | 1 | 2 |
| 182.4 | 4 | 2,100 | 0 | 19 | 4 | 0 | 2 |
| 242.1 | 3 | 2,300 | 0 | 12 | 3 | 0 | 2 |
| 213.6 | 2 | 2,200 | 0 | 16 | 2 | 0 | 2.5 |
| 139.9 | 2 | 2,100 | 0 | 28 | 1 | 0 | 1.5 |
| 245.4 | 2 | 2,100 | 1 | 12 | 1 | 1 | 2 |
| 327.2 | 6 | 2,500 | 0 | 15 | 3 | 1 | 2 |
| 271.8 | 2 | 2,100 | 0 | 9 | 2 | 1 | 2.5 |
| 221.1 | 3 | 2,300 | 1 | 18 | 1 | 0 | 1.5 |
| 266.6 | 4 | 2,400 | 0 | 13 | 4 | 1 | 2 |
| 292.4 | 4 | 2,100 | 0 | 14 | 3 | 1 | 2 |
| 209 | 2 | 1,700 | 0 | 8 | 4 | 1 | 1.5 |
| 270.8 | 6 | 2,500 | 0 | 7 | 4 | 1 | 2 |
| 246.1 | 4 | 2,100 | 0 | 18 | 3 | 1 | 2 |
| 194.4 | 2 | 2,300 | 0 | 11 | 3 | 0 | 2 |
| 281.3 | 3 | 2,100 | 0 | 16 | 2 | 1 | 2 |
| 172.7 | 4 | 2,200 | 1 | 16 | 3 | 0 | 2 |
| 207.5 | 5 | 2,300 | 1 | 21 | 4 | 0 | 2.5 |
| 198.9 | 3 | 2,200 | 1 | 10 | 4 | 1 | 2 |
| 209.3 | 6 | 1,900 | 1 | 15 | 4 | 1 | 2 |
| 252.3 | 4 | 2,600 | 0 | 8 | 4 | 1 | 2 |
| 192.9 | 4 | 1,900 | 1 | 14 | 2 | 1 | 2.5 |
| 209.3 | 5 | 2,100 | 0 | 20 | 5 | 0 | 1.5 |
| 345.3 | 8 | 2,600 | 0 | 9 | 4 | 1 | 2 |
| 326.3 | 6 | 2,100 | 0 | 11 | 5 | 1 | 3 |
| 173.1 | 2 | 2,200 | 1 | 21 | 5 | 1 | 1.5 |
| 187 | 2 | 1,900 | 0 | 26 | 4 | 0 | 2 |
| 257.2 | 2 | 2,100 | 0 | 9 | 4 | 1 | 2 |
| 233 | 3 | 2,200 | 0 | 14 | 3 | 1 | 1.5 |
| 180.4 | 2 | 2,000 | 0 | 11 | 5 | 0 | 2 |
| 234 | 2 | 1,700 | 0 | 19 | 3 | 1 | 2 |
| 207.1 | 2 | 2,000 | 0 | 11 | 5 | 1 | 2 |
| 247.7 | 5 | 2,400 | 0 | 16 | 2 | 1 | 2 |
| 166.2 | 3 | 2,000 | 1 | 16 | 2 | 1 | 2 |
| 177.1 | 2 | 1,900 | 0 | 10 | 5 | 1 | 2 |

# Appendix J

## Dataset 1—Real Estate (*continued*)

| $X_1$ | $X_2$ | $X_3$ | $X_4$ | $X_5$ | $X_6$ | $X_7$ | $X_8$ |
|---|---|---|---|---|---|---|---|
| 182.7 | 4 | 2,000 | 1 | 14 | 4 | 0 | 2.5 |
| 216 | 4 | 2,300 | 0 | 19 | 2 | 0 | 2 |
| 312.1 | 6 | 2,600 | 0 | 7 | 5 | 1 | 2.5 |
| 199.8 | 3 | 2,100 | 0 | 19 | 3 | 1 | 2 |
| 273.2 | 5 | 2,200 | 0 | 16 | 2 | 1 | 3 |
| 206 | 3 | 2,100 | 1 | 9 | 3 | 0 | 1.5 |
| 232.2 | 3 | 1,900 | 1 | 16 | 1 | 1 | 1.5 |
| 198.3 | 4 | 2,100 | 1 | 19 | 1 | 1 | 1.5 |
| 205.1 | 3 | 2,000 | 1 | 20 | 4 | 0 | 2 |
| 175.6 | 4 | 2,300 | 1 | 24 | 4 | 1 | 2 |
| 307.8 | 3 | 2,400 | 1 | 21 | 2 | 1 | 3 |
| 269.2 | 5 | 2,200 | 0 | 8 | 5 | 1 | 3 |
| 224.8 | 3 | 2,200 | 0 | 17 | 1 | 1 | 2.5 |
| 171.6 | 3 | 2,000 | 1 | 16 | 4 | 0 | 2 |
| 216.8 | 3 | 2,200 | 0 | 15 | 1 | 1 | 2 |
| 192.6 | 6 | 2,200 | 1 | 14 | 1 | 0 | 2 |
| 236.4 | 5 | 2,200 | 0 | 20 | 3 | 1 | 2 |
| 172.4 | 3 | 2,200 | 0 | 23 | 3 | 0 | 2 |
| 251.4 | 3 | 1,900 | 0 | 12 | 2 | 1 | 2 |
| 246 | 6 | 2,300 | 0 | 7 | 3 | 1 | 3 |
| 147.4 | 6 | 1,700 | 1 | 12 | 1 | 0 | 2 |
| 176 | 4 | 2,200 | 0 | 15 | 1 | 1 | 2 |
| 228.4 | 3 | 2,300 | 0 | 17 | 5 | 1 | 1.5 |
| 166.5 | 3 | 1,600 | 1 | 19 | 3 | 0 | 2.5 |
| 189.4 | 4 | 2,200 | 0 | 24 | 1 | 1 | 2 |
| 312.1 | 7 | 2,400 | 0 | 13 | 3 | 1 | 3 |
| 289.8 | 6 | 2,000 | 0 | 21 | 3 | 1 | 3 |
| 269.9 | 5 | 2,200 | 1 | 11 | 4 | 1 | 2.5 |
| 154.3 | 2 | 2,000 | 0 | 13 | 2 | 0 | 2 |
| 222.1 | 2 | 2,100 | 0 | 9 | 5 | 1 | 2 |
| 209.7 | 5 | 2,200 | 1 | 13 | 2 | 1 | 2 |
| 190.9 | 3 | 2,200 | 1 | 18 | 3 | 1 | 2 |
| 254.3 | 4 | 2,500 | 1 | 15 | 3 | 1 | 2 |
| 207.5 | 3 | 2,100 | 1 | 10 | 2 | 0 | 2 |
| 209.7 | 4 | 2,200 | 1 | 19 | 2 | 1 | 2 |
| 294 | 2 | 2,100 | 0 | 13 | 2 | 1 | 2.5 |
| 176.3 | 2 | 2,000 | 1 | 17 | 3 | 0 | 2 |
| 294.3 | 7 | 2,400 | 0 | 8 | 4 | 1 | 2 |
| 224 | 3 | 1,900 | 1 | 6 | 1 | 1 | 2 |
| 125 | 2 | 1,900 | 0 | 18 | 4 | 0 | 1.5 |
| 236.8 | 4 | 2,600 | 1 | 17 | 5 | 1 | 2 |
| 164.1 | 4 | 2,300 | 0 | 19 | 4 | 0 | 2 |
| 217.8 | 3 | 2,500 | 0 | 12 | 3 | 0 | 2 |
| 192.2 | 2 | 2,400 | 0 | 16 | 2 | 0 | 2.5 |
| 125.9 | 2 | 2,400 | 0 | 28 | 1 | 0 | 1.5 |

## Dataset 1—Real Estate (*concluded*)

| $X_1$ | $X_2$ | $X_3$ | $X_4$ | $X_5$ | $X_6$ | $X_7$ | $X_8$ |
|-------|-------|-------|-------|-------|-------|-------|-------|
| 220.9 | 2 | 2,300 | 1 | 12 | 1 | 1 | 2 |
| 294.5 | 6 | 2,700 | 0 | 15 | 3 | 1 | 2 |
| 244.6 | 2 | 2,300 | 0 | 9 | 2 | 1 | 2.5 |
| 199 | 3 | 2,500 | 1 | 18 | 1 | 0 | 1.5 |
| 240 | 4 | 2,600 | 0 | 13 | 4 | 1 | 2 |
| 263.2 | 4 | 2,300 | 0 | 14 | 3 | 1 | 2 |
| 188.1 | 2 | 1,900 | 0 | 8 | 4 | 1 | 1.5 |
| 243.7 | 6 | 2,700 | 0 | 7 | 4 | 1 | 2 |
| 221.5 | 4 | 2,300 | 0 | 18 | 3 | 1 | 2 |
| 175 | 2 | 2,500 | 0 | 11 | 3 | 0 | 2 |
| 253.2 | 3 | 2,300 | 0 | 16 | 2 | 1 | 2 |
| 155.4 | 4 | 2,400 | 1 | 16 | 3 | 0 | 2 |
| 186.7 | 5 | 2,500 | 1 | 21 | 4 | 0 | 2.5 |
| 179 | 3 | 2,400 | 1 | 10 | 4 | 1 | 2 |
| 188.3 | 6 | 2,100 | 1 | 15 | 4 | 1 | 2 |
| 227.1 | 4 | 2,900 | 0 | 8 | 4 | 1 | 2 |
| 173.6 | 4 | 2,100 | 1 | 14 | 2 | 1 | 2.5 |
| 188.3 | 5 | 2,300 | 0 | 20 | 5 | 0 | 1.5 |
| 310.8 | 8 | 2,900 | 0 | 9 | 4 | 1 | 2 |
| 293.7 | 6 | 2,400 | 0 | 11 | 5 | 1 | 3 |
| 179 | 3 | 2,400 | 0 | 8 | 4 | 1 | 2 |
| 188.3 | 6 | 2,100 | 1 | 14 | 2 | 1 | 2.5 |
| 227.1 | 4 | 2,900 | 0 | 20 | 5 | 0 | 1.5 |
| 173.6 | 4 | 2,100 | 0 | 9 | 4 | 1 | 2 |
| 188.3 | 5 | 2,300 | 0 | 11 | 5 | 1 | 3 |

# Appendix K

## Dataset 2—Major League Baseball

$x_1$ = Team
$x_2$ = League (American = 1, National = 0)
$x_3$ = Built (Year Stadium Was Built)
$x_4$ = Size (Stadium Capacity)
$x_5$ = Salary (Total 2002 Team Salary $ Mil)
$x_6$ = Attendance (Total 2002 Team Attendance in 000)
$x_7$ = Wins (Number of Wins in 2002)
$x_8$ = ERA (Earned Run Average)
$x_9$ = Batting (Team Batting Average)
$x_{10}$ = HR (Number of Home Runs for the Team)
$x_{11}$ = Surface (Natural = 0, Artificial = 1)
$x_{12}$ = Stolen (Stolen Bases)
$x_{13}$ = Errors (Team Errors)
$x_{14}$ = Year
$x_{15}$ = Average (Average Player Salary)
$x_{16}$ = Median (Median Player Salary)

| Team $x_1$ | League $x_2$ | Built $x_3$ | Size $x_4$ | Salary $x_5$ | Attendance $x_6$ | Wins $x_7$ | ERA $x_8$ | Batting $x_9$ | HR $x_{10}$ | Surface $x_{11}$ | Stolen $x_{12}$ | Errors $x_{13}$ | Year $x_{14}$ | Average $x_{15}$ | Median $x_{16}$ |
|---|---|---|---|---|---|---|---|---|---|---|---|---|---|---|---|
| Boston | 1 | 1912 | 33,871 | 113.795 | 2,650.86 | 93 | 3.75 | 0.277 | 177 | 0 | 80 | 104 | 1976 | 52,300 | * |
| New York Yankees | 1 | 1923 | 57,746 | 175.327 | 3,465.81 | 103 | 3.89 | 0.275 | 223 | 0 | 99 | 127 | 1977 | 74,000 | * |
| Oakland | 1 | 1966 | 43,662 | 65.878 | 2,169.81 | 103 | 3.69 | 0.261 | 205 | 0 | 46 | 102 | 1978 | 97,800 | * |
| Baltimore | 1 | 1992 | 48,262 | 72.085 | 2,682.44 | 67 | 4.46 | 0.246 | 165 | 0 | 110 | 91 | 1979 | 121,900 | * |
| Anaheim | 1 | 1966 | 45,050 | 77.184 | 2,305.55 | 99 | 3.69 | 0.282 | 152 | 0 | 116 | 87 | 1980 | 146,500 | * |
| Cleveland | 1 | 1994 | 43,368 | 90.428 | 2,616.94 | 74 | 4.91 | 0.249 | 192 | 0 | 52 | 113 | 1981 | 196,500 | * |
| Chicago White Sox | 1 | 1991 | 44,321 | 65.535 | 1,676.91 | 81 | 4.57 | 0.268 | 217 | 0 | 75 | 97 | 1982 | 245,000 | * |
| Toronto | 1 | 1989 | 50,516 | 66.698 | 1,637.90 | 78 | 4.81 | 0.261 | 187 | 1 | 71 | 107 | 1983 | 289,000 | 207,500 |
| Minnesota | 1 | 1982 | 48,678 | 53.666 | 1,924.47 | 94 | 4.12 | 0.272 | 167 | 1 | 79 | 74 | 1984 | 325,900 | 229,750 |
| Tampa Bay | 1 | 1990 | 44,027 | 43.984 | 1,065.74 | 55 | 5.29 | 0.253 | 133 | 1 | 102 | 126 | 1985 | 368,998 | 265,833 |
| Texas | 1 | 1994 | 52,000 | 130.622 | 2,352.40 | 72 | 5.16 | 0.269 | 230 | 0 | 61 | 99 | 1986 | 410,517 | 275,000 |
| Detroit | 1 | 2000 | 40,000 | 75.324 | 1,503.62 | 55 | 4.93 | 0.248 | 124 | 0 | 65 | 142 | 1987 | 402,579 | 235,000 |
| Seattle | 1 | 1999 | 45,611 | 100.045 | 3,542.94 | 93 | 4.07 | 0.275 | 152 | 0 | 137 | 88 | 1988 | 430,688 | 235,000 |
| Kansas City | 1 | 1973 | 40,529 | 58.708 | 1,323.04 | 62 | 5.22 | 0.256 | 140 | 0 | 139 | 130 | 1989 | 489,539 | 280,000 |
| Atlanta | 0 | 1993 | 50,062 | 110.770 | 2,603.48 | 101 | 3.13 | 0.260 | 164 | 0 | 76 | 114 | 1990 | 589,483 | 350,000 |
| Arizona | 0 | 1998 | 49,075 | 114.324 | 3,198.98 | 98 | 3.93 | 0.267 | 165 | 0 | 92 | 89 | 1991 | 845,383 | 412,000 |
| Houston | 0 | 2000 | 42,000 | 82.118 | 2,517.36 | 84 | 4.00 | 0.262 | 167 | 0 | 71 | 83 | 1992 | 1,012,424 | 392,500 |
| Cincinnati | 0 | 1970 | 52,953 | 62.398 | 1,855.79 | 78 | 4.29 | 0.253 | 169 | 0 | 116 | 120 | 1993 | 1,062,780 | 371,500 |
| New York Mets | 0 | 1964 | 55,775 | 109.917 | 2,804.84 | 75 | 3.91 | 0.256 | 160 | 1 | 87 | 144 | 1994 | 1,154,486 | 450,000 |
| Pittsburgh | 0 | 2001 | 38,127 | 63.701 | 1,784.99 | 72 | 4.24 | 0.244 | 142 | 0 | 86 | 115 | 1995 | 1,094,440 | 275,000 |
| Los Angeles | 0 | 1962 | 56,000 | 120.009 | 3,131.26 | 92 | 3.69 | 0.264 | 155 | 0 | 96 | 90s | 1996 | 1,101,455 | 300,000 |
| San Diego | 0 | 1967 | 53,166 | 65.677 | 2,220.60 | 66 | 4.65 | 0.253 | 136 | 0 | 71 | 128 | 1997 | 1,314,420 | 400,000 |
| Montreal | 0 | 1976 | 46,500 | 43.549 | 812.04 | 83 | 3.98 | 0.261 | 162 | 1 | 116 | 139 | 1998 | 1,384,530 | 427,500 |
| San Francisco | 0 | 2000 | 40,800 | 96.222 | 3,253.20 | 95 | 3.55 | 0.267 | 198 | 1 | 75 | 90 | 1999 | 1,567,873 | 495,000 |
| St. Louis | 0 | 1966 | 49,625 | 96.113 | 3,011.76 | 97 | 3.70 | 0.268 | 175 | 0 | 86 | 103 | 2000 | 1,983,849 | 700,000 |
| Florida | 0 | 1987 | 42,531 | 53.103 | 813.12 | 79 | 4.36 | 0.261 | 146 | 0 | 177 | 106 | 2001 | 2,138,896 | 975,000 |
| Philadelphia | 0 | 1971 | 62,411 | 72.240 | 1,618.47 | 80 | 4.17 | 0.259 | 165 | 1 | 104 | 88 | 2002 | 2,340,920 | 1,072,000 |
| Milwaukee | 0 | 2001 | 42,400 | 58.190 | 1,969.15 | 56 | 4.76 | 0.253 | 139 | 0 | 94 | 103 | | | |
| Chicago Cubs | 0 | 1914 | 38,957 | 88.838 | 2,693.10 | 67 | 4.31 | 0.246 | 200 | 0 | 63 | 114 | | | |
| Colorado | 0 | 1995 | 50,381 | 80.035 | 2,737.84 | 73 | 5.21 | 0.274 | 152 | 0 | 103 | 112 | | | |

# Appendix L

## Dataset 3—Wages and Wage Earners

$x_1$ = Annual wage in dollars
$x_2$ = Industry (1 = Manufacturing, 2 = Construction, 0 = Other)
$x_3$ = Occupation (1 = Mgmt., 2 = Sales, 3 = Clerical, 4 = Service, 5 = Prof., 0 = Other)
$x_4$ = Years of education
$x_5$ = Southern resident (1 = Yes, 0 = No)
$x_6$ = Non-white (1 = Yes, 0 = No)
$x_7$ = Hispanic (1 = Yes, 0 = No)
$x_8$ = Female (1 = Yes, 0 = No)
$x_9$ = Years of Work Experience
$x_{10}$ = Married (1 = Yes, 0 = No)
$x_{11}$ = Age in years
$x_{12}$ = Union member (1 = Yes, 0 = No)

| Row | Wage $x_1$ | Industry $x_2$ | Occupation $x_3$ | Education $x_4$ | South $x_5$ | Non-white $x_6$ | Hispanic $x_7$ |
|---|---|---|---|---|---|---|---|
| 1 | 19,388 | 1 | 0 | 6 | 1 | 0 | 0 |
| 2 | 49,898 | 2 | 0 | 12 | 0 | 0 | 0 |
| 3 | 28,219 | 0 | 3 | 12 | 1 | 0 | 0 |
| 4 | 83,601 | 0 | 5 | 17 | 0 | 0 | 1 |
| 5 | 29,736 | 0 | 4 | 8 | 0 | 0 | 1 |
| 6 | 50,235 | 1 | 0 | 16 | 0 | 0 | 0 |
| 7 | 45,976 | 0 | 2 | 12 | 0 | 0 | 0 |
| 8 | 33,411 | 1 | 2 | 12 | 1 | 0 | 0 |
| 9 | 21,716 | 0 | 5 | 12 | 0 | 0 | 0 |
| 10 | 37,664 | 0 | 5 | 18 | 0 | 0 | 0 |
| 11 | 26,820 | 0 | 5 | 18 | 0 | 0 | 0 |
| 12 | 29,977 | 0 | 4 | 16 | 0 | 1 | 0 |
| 13 | 33,959 | 0 | 5 | 17 | 0 | 0 | 0 |
| 14 | 11,780 | 0 | 2 | 11 | 0 | 0 | 0 |
| 15 | 10,997 | 0 | 4 | 14 | 0 | 1 | 0 |
| 16 | 17,626 | 0 | 3 | 12 | 0 | 0 | 0 |
| 17 | 22,133 | 0 | 5 | 16 | 0 | 0 | 0 |
| 18 | 21,994 | 0 | 1 | 12 | 0 | 0 | 0 |
| 19 | 29,390 | 0 | 0 | 13 | 0 | 0 | 0 |
| 20 | 32,138 | 0 | 4 | 14 | 0 | 0 | 0 |
| 21 | 30,006 | 1 | 3 | 16 | 0 | 0 | 0 |
| 22 | 68,573 | 0 | 5 | 16 | 1 | 0 | 0 |
| 23 | 17,694 | 0 | 4 | 8 | 0 | 0 | 0 |
| 24 | 26,795 | 0 | 0 | 7 | 1 | 0 | 0 |
| 25 | 19,981 | 0 | 4 | 4 | 0 | 0 | 0 |
| 26 | 14,476 | 0 | 5 | 12 | 0 | 0 | 0 |
| 27 | 19,452 | 0 | 4 | 13 | 0 | 1 | 0 |
| 28 | 28,168 | 1 | 0 | 13 | 0 | 0 | 0 |
| 29 | 19,306 | 0 | 5 | 9 | 1 | 1 | 0 |
| 30 | 13,318 | 1 | 0 | 11 | 1 | 0 | 0 |

# Dataset 3—Wages and Wage Earners (*continued*)

| Row | Wage $x_1$ | Industry $x_2$ | Occupation $x_3$ | Education $x_4$ | South $x_5$ | Non-white $x_6$ | Hispanic $x_7$ |
|-----|-----|-----|-----|-----|-----|-----|-----|
| 31 | 25,166 | 0 | 4 | 12 | 0 | 0 | 0 |
| 32 | 18,121 | 1 | 3 | 12 | 0 | 0 | 0 |
| 33 | 13,162 | 1 | 0 | 12 | 0 | 1 | 0 |
| 34 | 32,094 | 0 | 3 | 12 | 1 | 0 | 0 |
| 35 | 16,667 | 0 | 3 | 12 | 1 | 0 | 0 |
| 36 | 50,171 | 0 | 5 | 12 | 0 | 0 | 0 |
| 37 | 31,691 | 1 | 0 | 12 | 0 | 0 | 0 |
| 38 | 36,178 | 0 | 3 | 12 | 0 | 0 | 0 |
| 39 | 15,234 | 0 | 1 | 12 | 1 | 0 | 1 |
| 40 | 16,817 | 0 | 3 | 12 | 1 | 0 | 0 |
| 41 | 22,485 | 0 | 3 | 12 | 0 | 0 | 0 |
| 42 | 30,308 | 0 | 4 | 12 | 0 | 0 | 0 |
| 43 | 11,702 | 0 | 2 | 14 | 1 | 0 | 0 |
| 44 | 11,186 | 0 | 0 | 12 | 0 | 0 | 0 |
| 45 | 12,285 | 0 | 1 | 12 | 0 | 0 | 0 |
| 46 | 19,284 | 1 | 4 | 16 | 0 | 0 | 0 |
| 47 | 11,451 | 1 | 0 | 12 | 0 | 0 | 0 |
| 48 | 57,623 | 0 | 1 | 15 | 0 | 0 | 0 |
| 49 | 25,670 | 0 | 3 | 13 | 0 | 0 | 0 |
| 50 | 83,443 | 0 | 5 | 17 | 0 | 0 | 0 |
| 51 | 49,974 | 1 | 1 | 16 | 0 | 1 | 0 |
| 52 | 46,646 | 2 | 0 | 5 | 1 | 0 | 0 |
| 53 | 31,702 | 0 | 3 | 12 | 1 | 0 | 0 |
| 54 | 13,312 | 0 | 4 | 12 | 1 | 0 | 0 |
| 55 | 44,543 | 0 | 2 | 18 | 0 | 0 | 0 |
| 56 | 15,013 | 0 | 4 | 16 | 0 | 0 | 0 |
| 57 | 33,389 | 0 | 1 | 14 | 0 | 1 | 0 |
| 58 | 60,626 | 0 | 5 | 18 | 0 | 0 | 0 |
| 59 | 24,509 | 0 | 5 | 14 | 0 | 0 | 1 |
| 60 | 20,852 | 1 | 0 | 12 | 0 | 0 | 0 |
| 61 | 30,133 | 2 | 0 | 10 | 0 | 0 | 0 |
| 62 | 31,799 | 0 | 3 | 12 | 0 | 0 | 0 |
| 63 | 16,796 | 0 | 4 | 12 | 0 | 0 | 0 |
| 64 | 20,793 | 0 | 0 | 12 | 1 | 0 | 0 |
| 65 | 29,407 | 0 | 4 | 10 | 1 | 0 | 0 |
| 66 | 29,191 | 0 | 0 | 12 | 0 | 0 | 0 |
| 67 | 15,957 | 0 | 2 | 12 | 1 | 0 | 0 |
| 68 | 34,484 | 0 | 3 | 13 | 1 | 0 | 0 |
| 69 | 35,185 | 1 | 3 | 14 | 0 | 0 | 0 |
| 70 | 26,614 | 1 | 0 | 12 | 0 | 0 | 0 |
| 71 | 41,780 | 0 | 0 | 12 | 1 | 0 | 0 |
| 72 | 55,777 | 0 | 1 | 14 | 1 | 0 | 0 |
| 73 | 15,160 | 0 | 4 | 8 | 1 | 0 | 0 |
| 74 | 66,738 | 0 | 0 | 9 | 1 | 0 | 0 |
| 75 | 33,351 | 0 | 5 | 16 | 1 | 0 | 0 |

# Appendix L

## Dataset 3—Wages and Wage Earners (*continued*)

| Row | Wage $x_1$ | Industry $x_2$ | Occupation $x_3$ | Education $x_4$ | South $x_5$ | Non-white $x_6$ | Hispanic $x_7$ |
|-----|-----|-----|-----|-----|-----|-----|-----|
| 76 | 33,498 | 0 | 1 | 10 | 0 | 0 | 0 |
| 77 | 29,809 | 0 | 4 | 8 | 0 | 1 | 0 |
| 78 | 15,193 | 1 | 0 | 12 | 0 | 0 | 0 |
| 79 | 23,027 | 0 | 4 | 14 | 0 | 1 | 0 |
| 80 | 75,165 | 0 | 1 | 15 | 0 | 0 | 0 |
| 81 | 18,752 | 0 | 4 | 11 | 0 | 0 | 0 |
| 82 | 83,569 | 0 | 1 | 18 | 0 | 0 | 0 |
| 83 | 32,235 | 0 | 3 | 12 | 0 | 0 | 0 |
| 84 | 20,852 | 0 | 0 | 12 | 1 | 0 | 0 |
| 85 | 13,787 | 0 | 4 | 11 | 0 | 0 | 0 |
| 86 | 34,746 | 0 | 3 | 14 | 1 | 0 | 0 |
| 87 | 17,690 | 0 | 1 | 12 | 1 | 1 | 0 |
| 88 | 52,762 | 0 | 5 | 18 | 0 | 0 | 0 |
| 89 | 60,152 | 0 | 5 | 16 | 1 | 0 | 0 |
| 90 | 33,461 | 0 | 1 | 16 | 0 | 0 | 1 |
| 91 | 13,481 | 0 | 4 | 12 | 1 | 0 | 1 |
| 92 | 9,879 | 0 | 3 | 12 | 1 | 0 | 0 |
| 93 | 16,789 | 0 | 3 | 13 | 1 | 0 | 0 |
| 94 | 31,304 | 0 | 1 | 16 | 0 | 0 | 0 |
| 95 | 37,771 | 0 | 5 | 15 | 0 | 0 | 0 |
| 96 | 50,187 | 0 | 3 | 12 | 0 | 0 | 0 |
| 97 | 39,888 | 0 | 3 | 12 | 1 | 0 | 0 |
| 98 | 19,227 | 0 | 3 | 12 | 0 | 0 | 0 |
| 99 | 32,786 | 1 | 0 | 11 | 1 | 0 | 0 |
| 100 | 28,440 | 0 | 4 | 12 | 0 | 0 | 0 |

# Appendix L

## Dataset 3—Wages and Wage Earners (*concluded*)

| Row | Female $x_8$ | Experience $x_9$ | Married $x_{10}$ | Age $x_{11}$ | Union $x_{12}$ | Row | Female $x_8$ | Experience $x_9$ | Married $x_{10}$ | Age $x_{11}$ | Union $x_{12}$ |
|---|---|---|---|---|---|---|---|---|---|---|---|
| 1 | 0 | 45 | 1 | 57 | 0 | 51 | 0 | 26 | 1 | 48 | 1 |
| 2 | 0 | 33 | 1 | 51 | 1 | 52 | 0 | 44 | 1 | 55 | 0 |
| 3 | 0 | 12 | 1 | 30 | 0 | 53 | 1 | 39 | 1 | 57 | 0 |
| 4 | 0 | 18 | 1 | 41 | 0 | 54 | 1 | 9 | 1 | 27 | 0 |
| 5 | 0 | 47 | 1 | 61 | 1 | 55 | 0 | 10 | 1 | 34 | 0 |
| 6 | 0 | 12 | 1 | 34 | 0 | 56 | 0 | 21 | 1 | 43 | 0 |
| 7 | 0 | 43 | 1 | 61 | 1 | 57 | 0 | 22 | 0 | 42 | 0 |
| 8 | 0 | 20 | 1 | 38 | 0 | 58 | 0 | 7 | 1 | 31 | 0 |
| 9 | 1 | 11 | 0 | 29 | 0 | 59 | 1 | 15 | 0 | 35 | 0 |
| 10 | 0 | 19 | 1 | 43 | 0 | 60 | 1 | 38 | 1 | 56 | 0 |
| 11 | 0 | 33 | 0 | 57 | 1 | 61 | 0 | 27 | 1 | 43 | 0 |
| 12 | 1 | 6 | 1 | 28 | 0 | 62 | 1 | 25 | 0 | 43 | 0 |
| 13 | 1 | 26 | 1 | 49 | 1 | 63 | 1 | 14 | 1 | 32 | 0 |
| 14 | 1 | 33 | 1 | 50 | 0 | 64 | 1 | 6 | 0 | 24 | 0 |
| 15 | 0 | 0 | 0 | 20 | 0 | 65 | 0 | 19 | 0 | 35 | 0 |
| 16 | 1 | 45 | 1 | 63 | 0 | 66 | 0 | 9 | 0 | 27 | 0 |
| 17 | 1 | 10 | 0 | 32 | 1 | 67 | 1 | 10 | 0 | 28 | 0 |
| 18 | 1 | 24 | 1 | 42 | 0 | 68 | 1 | 28 | 0 | 47 | 0 |
| 19 | 0 | 18 | 1 | 37 | 0 | 69 | 1 | 12 | 1 | 32 | 0 |
| 20 | 0 | 22 | 1 | 42 | 1 | 70 | 1 | 19 | 1 | 37 | 0 |
| 21 | 1 | 27 | 1 | 49 | 0 | 71 | 0 | 9 | 1 | 27 | 0 |
| 22 | 0 | 14 | 1 | 36 | 1 | 72 | 0 | 21 | 1 | 41 | 0 |
| 23 | 1 | 38 | 1 | 52 | 0 | 73 | 1 | 45 | 0 | 59 | 0 |
| 24 | 0 | 44 | 1 | 57 | 0 | 74 | 0 | 29 | 1 | 44 | 0 |
| 25 | 0 | 54 | 1 | 64 | 0 | 75 | 1 | 4 | 1 | 26 | 0 |
| 26 | 1 | 3 | 1 | 21 | 0 | 76 | 0 | 20 | 1 | 36 | 0 |
| 27 | 0 | 3 | 0 | 22 | 0 | 77 | 1 | 29 | 0 | 43 | 0 |
| 28 | 0 | 17 | 0 | 36 | 0 | 78 | 1 | 15 | 0 | 33 | 0 |
| 29 | 1 | 34 | 1 | 49 | 1 | 79 | 0 | 34 | 1 | 54 | 1 |
| 30 | 1 | 25 | 1 | 42 | 1 | 80 | 0 | 12 | 1 | 33 | 0 |
| 31 | 1 | 10 | 0 | 28 | 0 | 81 | 1 | 45 | 0 | 62 | 1 |
| 32 | 1 | 18 | 1 | 36 | 0 | 82 | 0 | 29 | 1 | 53 | 0 |
| 33 | 0 | 6 | 0 | 24 | 1 | 83 | 1 | 38 | 1 | 56 | 0 |
| 34 | 1 | 14 | 1 | 32 | 0 | 84 | 0 | 1 | 0 | 19 | 0 |
| 35 | 0 | 4 | 0 | 22 | 0 | 85 | 0 | 4 | 1 | 21 | 0 |
| 36 | 0 | 39 | 1 | 57 | 1 | 86 | 1 | 15 | 1 | 35 | 0 |
| 37 | 0 | 13 | 0 | 31 | 0 | 87 | 0 | 14 | 1 | 32 | 0 |
| 38 | 1 | 40 | 1 | 58 | 0 | 88 | 0 | 7 | 1 | 31 | 0 |
| 39 | 1 | 4 | 0 | 22 | 0 | 89 | 0 | 38 | 1 | 60 | 0 |
| 40 | 1 | 26 | 0 | 44 | 0 | 90 | 0 | 7 | 1 | 29 | 1 |
| 41 | 0 | 22 | 0 | 40 | 0 | 91 | 0 | 7 | 0 | 25 | 0 |
| 42 | 0 | 10 | 1 | 28 | 0 | 92 | 1 | 28 | 1 | 46 | 0 |
| 43 | 1 | 6 | 1 | 26 | 0 | 93 | 1 | 6 | 1 | 25 | 0 |
| 44 | 0 | 0 | 0 | 18 | 0 | 94 | 0 | 26 | 1 | 48 | 0 |
| 45 | 1 | 42 | 1 | 60 | 0 | 95 | 0 | 5 | 0 | 26 | 0 |
| 46 | 0 | 3 | 0 | 25 | 0 | 96 | 1 | 24 | 1 | 42 | 0 |
| 47 | 1 | 8 | 1 | 26 | 0 | 97 | 0 | 5 | 0 | 23 | 0 |
| 48 | 0 | 31 | 1 | 52 | 0 | 98 | 1 | 15 | 1 | 33 | 0 |
| 49 | 1 | 8 | 0 | 27 | 1 | 99 | 0 | 37 | 1 | 54 | 1 |
| 50 | 1 | 5 | 0 | 28 | 0 | 100 | 1 | 24 | 1 | 42 | 0 |

# Appendix M

## Dataset 4—CIA International Economic and Demographic Data

$x_1$ = Country name
$x_2$ = Total area (square kilometers)
$x_3$ = Member of the G-20, group of industrial nations to promote international financial stability (0 = nonmember, 1 = member)
$x_4$ = Country has petroleum as a natural resource [0 = no, 1 = petroleum is a natural resource, 2 = country is a member of OPEC (Organization of Petroleum Exporting Countries)]
$x_5$ = Population (expressed in thousands)
$x_6$ = Percent of population aged 65 years and over
$x_7$ = Life expectancy at birth
$x_8$ = Literacy: percent of population age 15 or more that can read and write
$x_9$ = Gross Domestic Product per capita expressed in thousands
$x_{10}$ = Labor force (expressed in millions)
$x_{11}$ = Percent unemployment
$x_{12}$ = Exports expressed in billions of dollars
$x_{13}$ = Imports expressed in billions of dollars
$x_{14}$ = Number of mobile or cellular phones expressed in millions

| Country $x_1$ | Area (km) $x_2$ | G-20 $x_3$ | Petroleum $x_4$ | Pop (1,000s) $x_5$ | 65 & over $x_6$ | Life Expectancy $x_7$ |
|---|---|---|---|---|---|---|
| Algeria | 2,381,740 | 0 | 2 | 31,736 | 4.07 | 69.95 |
| Argentina | 2,766,890 | 1 | 1 | 37,385 | 10.42 | 75.26 |
| Australia | 7,686,850 | 1 | 1 | 19,357 | 12.5 | 79.87 |
| Austria | 83,858 | 0 | 0 | 8,150 | 15.38 | 77.84 |
| Belgium | 30,510 | 0 | 0 | 10,259 | 16.95 | 77.96 |
| Brazil | 8,511,965 | 1 | 1 | 174,469 | 5.45 | 63.24 |
| Canada | 9,976,140 | 1 | 1 | 31,592 | 12.77 | 79.56 |
| China | 9,596,960 | 1 | 1 | 1,273,111 | 7.11 | 71.62 |
| Czech Republic | 79 | 0 | 0 | 10,264 | 13.92 | 74.73 |
| Denmark | 43,094 | 0 | 1 | 5,352 | 14.85 | 76.72 |
| Finland | 337,030 | 0 | 0 | 5,175 | 15.03 | 77.58 |
| France | 547,030 | 1 | 0 | 59,551 | 16.13 | 78.9 |
| Germany | 357,021 | 1 | 0 | 83,029 | 16.61 | 77.61 |
| Greece | 131,940 | 0 | 1 | 10,623 | 17.72 | 78.59 |
| Hungary | 93,030 | 0 | 0 | 10,106 | 14.71 | 71.63 |
| Iceland | 103,000 | 0 | 0 | 278 | 11.81 | 79.52 |
| India | 3,287,590 | 1 | 1 | 1,029,991 | 4.68 | 62.68 |
| Indonesia | 1,919,440 | 1 | 2 | 228,437 | 4.63 | 68.27 |
| Iran | 1,648,000 | 0 | 2 | 66,129 | 4.65 | 69.95 |
| Iraq | 437,072 | 0 | 2 | 23,332 | 3.08 | 66.95 |
| Ireland | 70,280 | 0 | 0 | 3,840 | 11.35 | 76.99 |
| Italy | 301,230 | 1 | 0 | 57,680 | 18.35 | 79.14 |
| Japan | 377,835 | 1 | 0 | 126,771 | 17.35 | 80.8 |
| Kuwait | 17,820 | 0 | 2 | 2,041 | 2.42 | 76.27 |
| Libya | 1,759,540 | 0 | 2 | 5,240 | 3.95 | 75.65 |

## Dataset 4—CIA International Economic and Demographic Data (*continued*)

| Country $x_1$ | Area (km) $x_2$ | G-20 $x_3$ | Petroleum $x_4$ | Pop (1,000s) $x_5$ | 65 & over $x_6$ | Life Expectancy $x_7$ |
|---|---|---|---|---|---|---|
| Luxembourg | 2,586 | 0 | 0 | 443 | 14.06 | 77.3 |
| Mexico | 1,972,550 | 1 | 1 | 101,879 | 4.4 | 71.76 |
| Netherlands | 41,526 | 0 | 1 | 15,981 | 13.72 | 78.43 |
| New Zealand | 286,680 | 0 | 0 | 3,864 | 11.53 | 77.99 |
| Nigeria | 923,768 | 0 | 2 | 126,635 | 2.82 | 51.07 |
| Norway | 324,220 | 0 | 1 | 4,503 | 15.1 | 78.79 |
| Poland | 312,685 | 0 | 0 | 38,634 | 12.44 | 73.42 |
| Portugal | 92,391 | 0 | 0 | 10,066 | 15.62 | 75.94 |
| Qatar | 11,437 | 0 | 2 | 769 | 2.48 | 72.62 |
| Russia | 17,075,200 | 1 | 1 | 145,470 | 12.81 | 67.34 |
| Saudi Arabia | 1,960,582 | 1 | 2 | 22,757 | 2.68 | 68.09 |
| South Africa | 1,219,912 | 1 | 0 | 43,586 | 4.88 | 48.09 |
| South Korea | 98,480 | 1 | 0 | 47,904 | 7.27 | 74.65 |
| Spain | 504,782 | 0 | 0 | 40,038 | 17.18 | 78.93 |
| Sweden | 449,964 | 0 | 0 | 8,875 | 17.28 | 79.71 |
| Switzerland | 41,290 | 0 | 0 | 7,283 | 15.3 | 79.73 |
| Turkey | 780,580 | 1 | 0 | 66,494 | 6.13 | 71.24 |
| United Arab Emirates | 82,880 | 0 | 2 | 2,407 | 2.4 | 74.29 |
| United Kingdom | 244,820 | 1 | 1 | 59,648 | 15.7 | 77.82 |
| United States | 9,629,091 | 1 | 1 | 278,059 | 12.61 | 77.26 |
| Venezuela | 912,050 | 0 | 2 | 23,917 | 4.72 | 73.31 |

# Appendix M

## Dataset 4—CIA International Economic and Demographic Data (*concluded*)

| Country $x_1$ | Literacy % $x_8$ | GDP/cap $x_9$ | Labor force $x_{10}$ | Unemployment $x_{11}$ | Exports $x_{12}$ | Imports $x_{13}$ | Cell phones $x_{14}$ |
|---|---|---|---|---|---|---|---|
| Algeria | 61.6 | 5.5 | 9.1 | 30 | 19.6 | 9.2 | 0.034 |
| Argentina | 96.2 | 12.9 | 15 | 15 | 26.5 | 25.2 | 3 |
| Australia | 100 | 23.2 | 9.5 | 6.4 | 69 | 77 | 6.4 |
| Austria | 98 | 25 | 3.7 | 5.4 | 63.2 | 65.6 | 4.5 |
| Belgium | 98 | 25.3 | 4.34 | 8.4 | 181.4 | 166 | 1 |
| Brazil | 83.3 | 6.5 | 79 | 7.1 | 55.1 | 55.8 | 4.4 |
| Canada | 97 | 24.8 | 16.1 | 6.8 | 272.3 | 238.2 | 4.2 |
| China | 81.5 | 3.6 | 700 | 10 | 232 | 197 | 65 |
| Czech Republic | 99.9 | 12.9 | 5.2 | 8.7 | 28.3 | 31.4 | 4.3 |
| Denmark | 100 | 25.5 | 2.9 | 5.3 | 50.8 | 43.6 | 1.4 |
| Finland | 100 | 22.9 | 2.6 | 9.8 | 44.4 | 32.7 | 2.2 |
| France | 99 | 24.4 | 25 | 9.7 | 325 | 320 | 11.1 |
| Germany | 99 | 23.4 | 40.5 | 9.9 | 578 | 505 | 15.3 |
| Greece | 95 | 17.2 | 4.32 | 11.3 | 15.8 | 33.9 | 0.937 |
| Hungary | 99 | 11.2 | 4.2 | 9.4 | 25.2 | 27.6 | 1.3 |
| Iceland | 100 | 24.8 | 0.16 | 2.7 | 2 | 2.2 | 0.066 |
| India | 52 | 2.2 | * | * | 43.1 | 60.8 | 2.93 |
| Indonesia | 83.8 | 2.9 | 99 | 17.5 | 64.7 | 40.4 | 1 |
| Iran | 72.1 | 6.3 | 17.3 | 14 | 25 | 15 | 0.265 |
| Iraq | 58 | 2.5 | 4.4 | * | 21.8 | 13.8 | 0 |
| Ireland | 98 | 21.6 | 1.82 | 4.1 | 73.5 | 45.7 | 2 |
| Italy | 98 | 22.1 | 23.4 | 10.4 | 241.1 | 231.4 | 20.5 |
| Japan | 99 | 24.9 | 67.7 | 4.7 | 450 | 355 | 63.9 |
| Kuwait | 78.6 | 15 | 1.3 | 1.8 | 23.2 | 7.6 | 0.21 |
| Libya | 76.2 | 8.9 | 1.5 | 30 | 13.9 | 7.6 | 0 |
| Luxembourg | 100 | 36.4 | 0.248 | 2.7 | 7.6 | 10 | 0.215 |
| Mexico | 89.6 | 9.1 | 39.8 | 2.2 | 168 | 176 | 2 |
| Netherlands | 99 | 24.4 | 7.2 | 2.6 | 210.3 | 201.2 | 4.1 |
| New Zealand | 99 | 17.7 | 1.88 | 6.3 | 14.6 | 14.3 | 0.6 |
| Nigeria | 57.1 | 0.95 | 66 | 28 | 22.2 | 10.7 | 0.027 |
| Norway | 100 | 27.7 | 2.4 | 3 | 59.2 | 35.2 | 2 |
| Poland | 99 | 8.5 | 17.2 | 12 | 28.4 | 42.7 | 1.8 |
| Portugal | 87.4 | 15.8 | 5 | 4.3 | 26.1 | 41 | 3 |
| Qatar | 79 | 20.3 | 0.233 | * | 9.8 | 3.8 | 0.043 |
| Russia | 98 | 7.7 | 66 | 10.5 | 105.1 | 44.2 | 2.5 |
| Saudi Arabia | 62.8 | 10.5 | 7 | * | 81.2 | 30.1 | 1 |
| South Africa | 81.1 | 8.5 | 17 | 30 | 30.8 | 27.6 | 2 |
| South Korea | 98 | 16.1 | 22 | 4.1 | 172.6 | 160.5 | 27 |
| Spain | 97 | 18 | 17 | 14 | 120.5 | 153.9 | 8.4 |
| Sweden | 99 | 22.2 | 4.4 | 6 | 95.5 | 80 | 3.8 |
| Switzerland | 99 | 28.6 | 3.9 | 1.9 | 91.3 | 91.6 | 2 |
| Turkey | 85 | 6.8 | 23 | 5.6 | 26.9 | 55.7 | 12.1 |
| United Arab Emirates | 79.2 | 22.8 | 1.4 | * | 46 | 34 | 1 |
| United Kingdom | 99 | 22.8 | 29.2 | 5.5 | 282 | 324 | 13 |
| United States | 97 | 36.2 | 140.9 | 4 | 776 | 1,223 | 69 |
| Venezuela | 91.1 | 6.2 | 9.9 | 14 | 32.8 | 14.7 | 2 |

## Banking Dataset—Case

$x_1$ = Account balance in $
$x_2$ = Number of ATM transactions in the month
$x_3$ = Number of other bank services used
$x_4$ = Has a debit card (1 = yes, 0 = no)
$x_5$ = Receives interest on the account
$x_6$ = City where banking is done

| $x_1$ | $x_2$ | $x_3$ | $x_4$ | $x_5$ | $x_6$ | $x_1$ | $x_2$ | $x_3$ | $x_4$ | $x_5$ | $x_6$ |
|---|---|---|---|---|---|---|---|---|---|---|---|
| 1,756 | 13 | 4 | 0 | 1 | 2 | 1,958 | 6 | 2 | 1 | 0 | 2 |
| 748 | 9 | 2 | 1 | 0 | 1 | 634 | 2 | 7 | 1 | 0 | 4 |
| 1,501 | 10 | 1 | 0 | 0 | 1 | 580 | 4 | 1 | 0 | 0 | 1 |
| 1,831 | 10 | 4 | 0 | 1 | 3 | 1,320 | 4 | 5 | 1 | 0 | 1 |
| 1,622 | 14 | 6 | 0 | 1 | 4 | 1,675 | 6 | 7 | 1 | 0 | 2 |
| 1,886 | 17 | 3 | 0 | 1 | 1 | 789 | 8 | 4 | 0 | 0 | 4 |
| 740 | 6 | 3 | 0 | 0 | 3 | 1,735 | 12 | 7 | 0 | 1 | 3 |
| 1,593 | 10 | 8 | 1 | 0 | 1 | 1,784 | 11 | 5 | 0 | 0 | 1 |
| 1,169 | 6 | 4 | 0 | 0 | 4 | 1,326 | 16 | 8 | 0 | 0 | 3 |
| 2,125 | 18 | 6 | 0 | 0 | 2 | 2,051 | 14 | 4 | 1 | 0 | 4 |
| 1,554 | 12 | 6 | 1 | 0 | 3 | 1,044 | 7 | 5 | 1 | 0 | 1 |
| 1,474 | 12 | 7 | 1 | 0 | 1 | 1,885 | 10 | 6 | 1 | 1 | 2 |
| 1,913 | 6 | 5 | 0 | 0 | 1 | 1,790 | 11 | 4 | 0 | 1 | 3 |
| 1,218 | 10 | 3 | 1 | 0 | 1 | 765 | 4 | 3 | 0 | 0 | 4 |
| 1,006 | 12 | 4 | 0 | 0 | 1 | 1,645 | 6 | 9 | 0 | 1 | 4 |
| 2,215 | 20 | 3 | 1 | 0 | 4 | 32 | 2 | 0 | 0 | 0 | 3 |
| 137 | 7 | 2 | 0 | 0 | 3 | 1,266 | 11 | 7 | 0 | 0 | 4 |
| 167 | 5 | 4 | 0 | 0 | 4 | 890 | 7 | 1 | 0 | 1 | 1 |
| 343 | 7 | 2 | 0 | 0 | 1 | 2,204 | 14 | 5 | 0 | 0 | 2 |
| 2,557 | 20 | 7 | 1 | 0 | 4 | 2,409 | 16 | 8 | 0 | 0 | 2 |
| 2,276 | 15 | 4 | 1 | 0 | 3 | 1,338 | 14 | 4 | 1 | 0 | 2 |
| 1,494 | 11 | 2 | 0 | 1 | 1 | 2,076 | 12 | 5 | 1 | 0 | 2 |
| 2,144 | 17 | 3 | 0 | 0 | 3 | 1,708 | 13 | 3 | 1 | 0 | 1 |
| 1,995 | 10 | 7 | 0 | 0 | 2 | 2,138 | 18 | 5 | 0 | 1 | 4 |
| 1,053 | 8 | 4 | 1 | 0 | 3 | 2,375 | 12 | 4 | 0 | 0 | 2 |
| 1,526 | 8 | 4 | 0 | 1 | 2 | 1,455 | 9 | 5 | 1 | 1 | 3 |
| 1,120 | 8 | 6 | 1 | 0 | 3 | 1,487 | 8 | 4 | 1 | 0 | 4 |
| 1,838 | 7 | 5 | 1 | 1 | 3 | 1,125 | 6 | 4 | 1 | 0 | 2 |
| 1,746 | 11 | 2 | 0 | 0 | 2 | 1,989 | 12 | 3 | 0 | 1 | 2 |
| 1,616 | 10 | 4 | 1 | 1 | 2 | 2,156 | 14 | 5 | 1 | 0 | 2 |

# Appendix O

## Whitner Autoplex

$x_1$ = Selling price
$x_2$ = Selling price ($000)
$x_3$ = Age of buyer
$x_4$ = Domestic (0), Imported (1)

| Price $x_1$ | Price ($000) $x_2$ | Age $x_3$ | Type $x_4$ | Price $x_1$ | Price ($000) $x_2$ | Age $x_3$ | Type $x_4$ |
|---|---|---|---|---|---|---|---|
| 23,197 | 23.197 | 46 | 0 | 20,642 | 20.642 | 39 | 1 |
| 23,372 | 23.372 | 48 | 0 | 21,981 | 21.981 | 43 | 1 |
| 20,454 | 20.454 | 40 | 1 | 24,052 | 24.052 | 56 | 0 |
| 23,591 | 23.591 | 40 | 0 | 25,799 | 25.799 | 44 | 0 |
| 26,651 | 26.651 | 46 | 1 | 15,794 | 15.794 | 30 | 1 |
| 27,453 | 27.453 | 37 | 1 | 18,263 | 18.263 | 39 | 1 |
| 17,266 | 17.266 | 32 | 1 | 35,925 | 35.925 | 53 | 0 |
| 18,021 | 18.021 | 29 | 1 | 17,399 | 17.399 | 29 | 1 |
| 28,683 | 28.683 | 38 | 1 | 17,968 | 17.968 | 30 | 1 |
| 30,872 | 30.872 | 43 | 0 | 20,356 | 20.356 | 44 | 0 |
| 19,587 | 19.587 | 32 | 0 | 21,442 | 21.442 | 41 | 1 |
| 23,169 | 23.169 | 47 | 0 | 21,722 | 21.722 | 41 | 0 |
| 35,851 | 35.851 | 56 | 0 | 19,331 | 19.331 | 35 | 1 |
| 19,251 | 19.251 | 42 | 1 | 22,817 | 22.817 | 51 | 1 |
| 20,047 | 20.047 | 28 | 1 | 19,766 | 19.766 | 44 | 1 |
| 24,285 | 24.285 | 56 | 0 | 20,633 | 20.633 | 51 | 1 |
| 24,324 | 24.324 | 50 | 1 | 20,962 | 20.962 | 49 | 1 |
| 24,609 | 24.609 | 31 | 1 | 22,845 | 22.845 | 41 | 1 |
| 28,670 | 38.67 | 51 | 1 | 26,285 | 26.285 | 44 | 0 |
| 15,546 | 15.546 | 26 | 1 | 27,896 | 27.896 | 37 | 0 |
| 15,935 | 15.935 | 25 | 1 | 29,076 | 29.076 | 42 | 1 |
| 19,873 | 19.873 | 45 | 1 | 32,492 | 32.492 | 51 | 0 |
| 25,251 | 25.251 | 56 | 1 | 18,890 | 18.89 | 31 | 1 |
| 25,277 | 25.277 | 47 | 0 | 21,740 | 21.74 | 39 | 0 |
| 28,034 | 28.034 | 38 | 1 | 22,374 | 22.374 | 53 | 0 |
| 24,533 | 24.533 | 51 | 0 | 24,571 | 24.571 | 55 | 1 |
| 27,443 | 27.443 | 39 | 0 | 25,449 | 25.449 | 40 | 0 |
| 19,889 | 19.889 | 44 | 1 | 28,337 | 28.337 | 46 | 0 |
| 20,004 | 20.004 | 46 | 1 | 20,642 | 20.642 | 35 | 1 |
| 17,357 | 17.357 | 28 | 1 | 23,613 | 23.613 | 47 | 1 |
| 20,155 | 20.155 | 33 | 1 | 24,220 | 24.22 | 58 | 1 |
| 19,688 | 19.688 | 35 | 1 | 30,655 | 30.655 | 51 | 0 |
| 23,657 | 23.657 | 35 | 0 | 22,442 | 22.442 | 41 | 1 |
| 26,613 | 26.613 | 42 | 1 | 17,891 | 17.891 | 33 | 1 |
| 20,895 | 20.895 | 35 | 0 | 20,818 | 20.818 | 46 | 1 |
| 20,203 | 20.203 | 36 | 1 | 26,237 | 26.237 | 47 | 0 |
| 23,765 | 23.765 | 48 | 0 | 20,445 | 20.445 | 34 | 1 |
| 25,783 | 25.783 | 53 | 1 | 21,556 | 21.556 | 43 | 1 |
| 26,661 | 26.661 | 46 | 1 | 21,639 | 21.639 | 37 | 1 |
| 32,277 | 32.277 | 55 | 0 | 24,296 | 24.296 | 47 | 0 |

740

# Appendix P

## Getting Started with MegaStat*

MegaStat is an Excel add-in that performs statistical analysis within an Excel workbook. After it is installed, it appears on the Excel menu and works like any other Excel option.

## Basic Procedures

When you click on MegaStat, the main Excel menu appears (see chart above). Most of the menu options display submenus. If a menu item is followed by an ellipsis (. . .), clicking it will display the dialog box for that option.

A dialog box allows you to specify the data to be used and other inputs and options. The chart below shows a typical dialog box. After you select the data and options, click OK; the dialog box disappears and MegaStat performs the analysis.

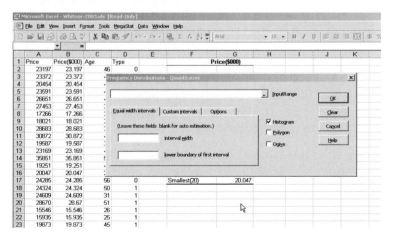

*Written by J. B. Orris, Ph.D., Butler University. MegaStat is copyrighted and is a registered trademark of J. B. Orris. This document was written for version 9.0 of MegaStat; however, most of it will be relevant for other versions.

# Buttons

Each dialog box has the four buttons down the right-hand side. See the picture on the previous page.

**OK**   This button could also be labeled "Calculate," "Go," "Execute," or "Do it." It tells MegaStat that you are done specifying inputs and you are turning control over to the software. First the software validates your input values, then disappears and performs the analysis and finally displays the output worksheet. When the dialog box disappears, it is still in memory and will contain the same inputs if it is recalled later.

**Clear**   This button removes all input values and resets any default options on the form.

**Cancel**   This button could be labeled "Never mind." It simply hides the dialog box. The dialog box is not cleared or removed from memory. Userforms do not take much memory and there is no problem with having several of them in memory. However, if you really want to unload the form, click the "X" in the upper right corner of the form.

**Help**   This button displays context sensitive help for the active userform. If you want to see the full Help System, use the Help selection on the main menu.

**Data Selection**   Most MegaStat dialog boxes have fields where you select input ranges that contain the data to be used. Input ranges can be selected four ways:

1. *Pointing and dragging with the mouse (the most common method).* Since the dialog box pops up on the screen, it may block some of your data. You can move dialog boxes around on the screen by placing the mouse pointer over the title bar (colored area at the top), clicking, and holding the left mouse button while dragging the dialog box to a new location. You can even drag it partially off the screen.
2. *Using MegaStat's AutoExpand feature.* AutoExpand allows rapid data selection without having to drag through the entire column of data. Here is how it works:

    - Make sure the input box has the focus. (Click in it or tab to it.) An input box had the focus when the insertion pointer is blinking in it.
    - Select one row of data by clicking in one cell of the column you want. If more than one column is being selected, drag the mouse across the columns.
    - Right-click over the input field or left-click the label next to the input box. The data range will expand to include all of the rows in the region where you selected one row.

3. *Typing the name of a named range.* If you have previously identified a range of cells using Excel's name box, you may use that name to specify a data range in a MegaStat userform. This method can be very useful if you are using the same data for several different statistical procedures.
4. *Typing a range address.* You may type in any valid Excel range address, e.g., B5:B43. This is the least efficient way to specify data ranges, but it certainly works.

# Data Labels

For most procedures the first cell in each input range can be a label. *If the first cell in a range is text, it is considered a label; if the first cell is a numeric value, it is considered data.* If you want to use numbers as variable labels, you must enter the numbers as text by preceding them with a single quote mark, e.g., '2. Even though Excel stores times and dates as numbers, MegaStat will recognize them as labels if they are formatted as time/date values.

If data labels are not part of the input range, the program automatically uses the cell immediately above the data range as a label if it contains a text value.

If an option can consider the entire first row (or column) of an input range as labels, any numeric value in the row will cause the entire row to be treated as data.

# Output

When you click OK on a MegaStat dialog box, it performs some statistical analysis and needs a place to put its output. It looks for a worksheet named Output. If it finds one, it goes to the end of it and appends its output; if it doesn't find an Output worksheet, it creates one. MegaStat will never make any changes to the user's worksheets; it sends output only to its Output sheet.

MegaStat makes a good attempt at formatting the output, but it is important to remember that the Output sheet is just a standard Excel worksheet and can be modified in any way by the user. You can adjust column widths and change any formatting that you think needs improvement. You can insert, delete, and modify cells. You can copy all or part of the output to another worksheet or to another application such as a word processor.

MegaStat charts get their values from cells on the Output sheet (or one of your worksheets in the case of the scatter plot). You can click a chart and select "Source Data" to see what values are being displayed.

When you click a chart, the MegaStat menu item will disappear from the main menu bar since the Chart menu becomes active. Click outside the chart to bring back the main menu that contains the MegaStat menu item.

# Repeat Last Option

Once you have performed a MegaStat option, this menu selection will allow you to redisplay the last dialog box without having to go through the menu selections. This can be handy if you need to make a change or when you need to repeat the same operation with the different data sets.

# Deactivate MegaStat

This option is used to remove the "MegaStat" item from the main menu bar. It does not delete any files or uninstall MegaStat. To restore the "MegaStat" menu item, click on Excel's main menu bar, then click on Tools and select Add-Ins. In the Add-Ins dialog box check MegaStat and click on OK.

# Uninstall MegaStat

This menu item does not actually uninstall MegaStat. It displays a dialog box prompting you on how to start the uninstallation process.

Uninstalling is the process of removing the installed MegaStat files from your system. It does not remove any data files nor does it remove the file you used to install MegaStat. You may delete the installation file (MegaStat_Setup.exe) if it is still on your system.

# Help/Information

The Help option displays the full MegaStat help program, shown below.

The "How it works (General operating procedures)" section contains all of the information in this tutorial. You can click specific topics or search for a particular item by clicking on **Index.**

# Appendix Q

## Visual Statistics

Visual Statistics, 2.0, by Doane, Mathieson, and Tracy is a package of 21 software programs and hundreds of data files and examples designed for teaching and learning basic statistics. The modules of Visual Statistics provide an interactive, highly graphical, experimental format in which to explore statistics. The software and worktext promote active learning though competency building exercises, individual and team projects, and built-in databases. Over 400 data sets are included within the package.

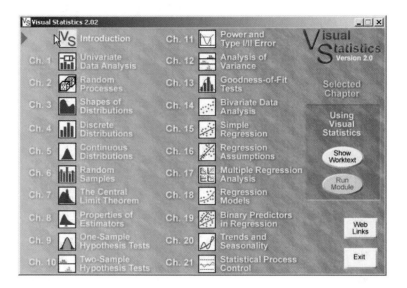

## Main Menu

To start Visual Statistics, click on the link on your student CD-ROM menu and follow the installation instructions. Open the cover and you will see a menu like the one shown above. From this menu you can: (1) view a chapter in the worktext (the Show Worktext button); (2) run a software module (the Run Module button); (3) exit Visual Statistics (the Exit button).

### Selecting a Program

To select a program, click on the chapter number or icon, then click run module. (Note: You will need to have your Student CD-ROM in the CD drive for the programs to run.)

Each program is designed to be as directly interactive as possible, with live graphics and control buttons built into the main screen for that program.

These are just a few examples.

## Selecting a Chapter

To select a chapter, click on its chapter number, its icon, or its title. When you click the chapter, a comet will streak across the screen to the Selected Chapter panel on the right, and the Show Worktext and Run Module buttons will appear in the panel. Each software module corresponds to a chapter in the worktext. The chapter's learning exercises will require that you run the corresponding software module.

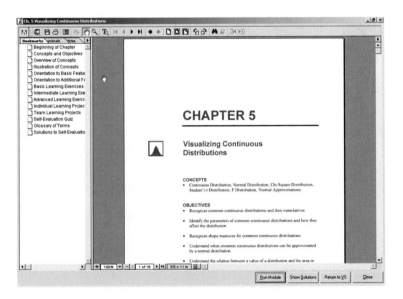

# The Worktext

The worktext has one chapter for each module. Each chapter in the worksheet contains:

- A list of concepts and learning objectives
- An overview of concepts and illustrations of concepts
- An orientation to software features
- Structured learning exercises (basic, intermediate, and advanced)
- Suggested independent projects (team, individual)
- A bank of self-test questions
- A glossary of terms
- Answers to the self-test questions

# The Notebook

Every Visual Statistics module starts with the Notebook. There is a different Notebook for each module, but they all work the same way. Click on the tabs to see each of the notebook "pages." The main purpose of the Notebook is to let you choose the type of data you want to review.

- *Examples*—examples are real data sets that have been selected to illustrate the concepts of the module.
- *Databases*—a database contains many variables. You select the ones you wish to analyze.
- *Data Editor*—lets you create your own data sets.
- *Scenarios*—allows you to experiment with the process that generates data sets.
- *Templates*—allows you to generate data conforming to a particular shape.
- *Do-It-Yourself*—gives you control over the process generating the data.

# Help

Each module has a Help section on the menu bar. Click on **Help** and an Index will appear for the topics where help is available in that module.

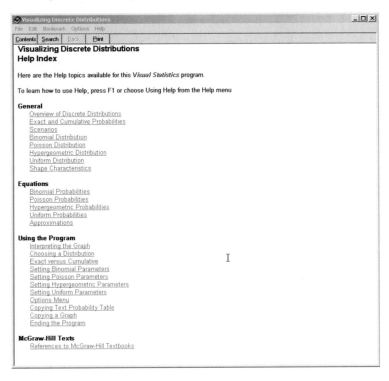

# Answers

## to Odd-Numbered Chapter Exercises

### CHAPTER 1
1. **a.** Interval
   **b.** Ratio
   **c.** Interval
   **d.** Nominal
   **e.** Ordinal
   **f.** Ratio
3. Answers will vary.
5. Qualitative data is not numerical, whereas quantitative data is numerical. Examples will vary by student.
7. Nominal, ordinal, interval, and ratio. Examples will vary.
9. A classification is exhaustive if every object appears in some category.
11. According to the sample information 120/300 or 40% would accept a job transfer.
13. Discrete variables can assume only certain values, but continuous variables can assume any values within some range. Examples will vary.
15. Answers will vary.
17. **a.** Grass or artificial turf field is a qualitative variable, the others are quantitative.
    **b.** Grass or artificial turf field is a nominal-level variable, the others are ratio-level variables.
19. **a.** All variables are quantitative except G-20 and Petroleum.
    **b.** All variables are ratio except G-20 and Petroleum.

### CHAPTER 2
1. $2^5 = 32$, $2^6 = 64$   Therefore, 6 classes.
3. $2^7 = 128$, $2^8 = 256$   Suggests 8 classes.
   $i \geq \dfrac{567 - 235}{8} = 41$   Use interval of 45.
5. **a.** $2^4 = 16$   Suggests 5 classes.
   **b.** $i \geq \dfrac{31 - 25}{5} = 1.10$   Use interval of 1.5.
   **c.** 24
   **d.**

   | Patients | f | Relative frequency |
   |---|---|---|
   | 24.0 up to 25.5 | 2 | 0.125 |
   | 25.5 up to 27.0 | 4 | 0.250 |
   | 27.0 up to 28.5 | 8 | 0.500 |
   | 28.5 up to 30.0 | 0 | 0.000 |
   | 30.0 up to 31.5 | 2 | 0.125 |
   | Total | 16 | 1.000 |

   **e.** The largest concentration is in the 27 up to 28.5 class (8).
7. **a.**

   | Number of Visits | f |
   |---|---|
   | 0 up to 3 | 9 |
   | 3 up to 6 | 21 |
   | 6 up to 9 | 13 |
   | 9 up to 12 | 4 |
   | 12 up to 15 | 3 |
   | 15 up to 18 | 1 |
   | Total | 51 |

   **b.** The largest group of shoppers (21) shop at the BiLo Supermarket 3, 4, or 5 times during a month period.

Some customers visit the store only 1 time during the month, but others shop as many as 15 times.

   **c.**

   | Number of Visits | Percent of Total |
   |---|---|
   | 0 up to 3 | 17.65 |
   | 3 up to 6 | 41.18 |
   | 6 up to 9 | 25.49 |
   | 9 up to 12 | 7.84 |
   | 12 up to 15 | 5.88 |
   | 15 up to 18 | 1.96 |
   | Total | 100.00 |

9. **a.** Histogram
   **b.** 100
   **c.** 5
   **d.** 28
   **e.** 0.28
   **f.** 12.5
   **g.** 13
11. **a.** 50
    **b.** 1.5 thousand miles, or 1,500 miles.
    **c.**

   **d.** $X = 1.5$, $Y = 5$
   **e.**

   **f.** For the 50 employees about half traveled between 6,000 and 9,000 miles. Five employees traveled less than 3,000 miles, and 2 traveled more than 12,000 miles.
13. **a.** 40
    **b.** 5
    **c.** 11 or 12
    **d.** About $18/hr
    **e.** About $9/hr
    **f.** About 75%

**15. a.** 5

**b.**

| Frequent Flier Miles | f | CF |
|---|---|---|
| 0 up to 3 | 5 | 5 |
| 3 up to 6 | 12 | 17 |
| 6 up to 9 | 23 | 40 |
| 9 up to 12 | 8 | 48 |
| 12 up to 15 | 2 | 50 |

**c.**

**d.** About 8.7 thousands of miles

**17.** Maxwell Heating & Air Conditioning far exceeds the other corporations in sales. Mancell Electric & Plumbing and Mizelle Roofing & Sheet Metal are the two corporations with the least amount of fourth quarter sales.

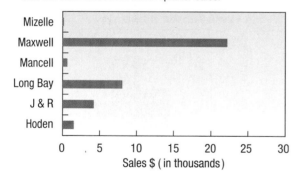

**19.** Homicides reached the highest number in 1993. They decreased steadily until 2000 and then began to increase again.

**21. Population Growth in the United States**
Population in the United States has increased steadily since 1950.

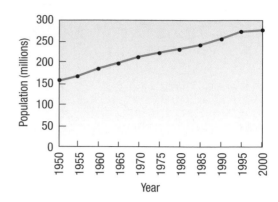

**23.** $2^6 = 64$ and $2^7 = 128$.   Suggest 7 classes.

**25. a.** 5, because $2^4 = 16 < 25$ and $2^5 = 32 > 25$.

**b.** $i \geq \dfrac{48 - 16}{5} = 6.4$   Use interval of 7.

**c.** 15

**d.**

| Class | | Frequency |
|---|---|---|
| 15 up to 22 | ||| | 3 |
| 22 up to 29 | JHf ||| | 8 |
| 29 up to 36 | JHf || | 7 |
| 36 up to 43 | JHf | 5 |
| 43 up to 50 | || | 2 |
| | | 25 |

**e.** It is fairly symmetric, with most of the values between 22 and 36.

**27. a.** 56

**b.** 10 (found by 60 − 50)

**c.** 55

**d.** 17

**29. a.** $36.60, found by ($265 − $82)/5.

**b.** $40.

**c.**

| | |
|---|---|
| $ 80 up to $120 | 8 |
| 120 up to 160 | 19 |
| 160 up to 200 | 10 |
| 200 up to 240 | 6 |
| 240 up to 280 | 1 |
| Total | 44 |

**d.** The purchases ranged from a low of about $80 to a high of about $280. The concentration is in the $120 up to $160 class.

**31.**

**33.**

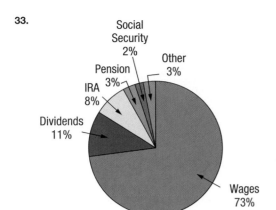

| SC Income | Percent | Cumulative |
|---|---|---|
| Wages | 73 | 73 |
| Dividends | 11 | 84 |
| IRA | 8 | 92 |
| Pensions | 3 | 95 |
| Social Security | 2 | 97 |
| Other | 3 | 100 |

By far the largest part of income in South Carolina is earned income. Almost three-fourths of the adjusted gross income comes from wages and salaries. Dividends and IRAs each contribute roughly another ten percent.

**35. a.** Since $2^6 = 64 < 70 < 128 = 2^7$, 7 classes are recommended. The interval should be at least $(1,002.2 - 3.3)/7 = 142.7$. Use 150 as a convenient value.

**b.**

**37.**

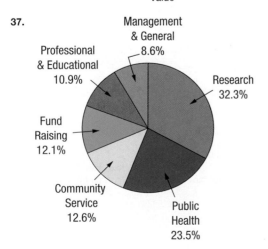

More than half of the expenses are concentrated in the categories Research and Public Health Education.

**39.**

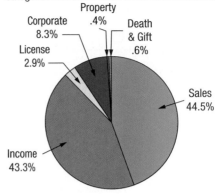

Sales tax and income tax dominate the total revenues for the state of Georgia.

**41.** There are 50 observations, so the recommended number of classes is 6. However, there are several states that have many more farms than the others, so it may be useful to have an open-ended class. One possible frequency distribution is:

| Farms in USA | Frequency |
|---|---|
| 0 up to 20 | 16 |
| 20 up to 40 | 13 |
| 40 up to 60 | 8 |
| 60 up to 80 | 6 |
| 80 up to 100 | 4 |
| 100 or more | 3 |
| Total | 50 |

Twenty-nine of the 50 states, or 58 percent, have fewer than 40,000 farms. There are three states that have more than 100,000 farms.

**43.** In 1994 the price for a Toyota Camry and a Ford Taurus was about the same, a little more than $11,000 each. Since that time the price of both cars has increased, but the rate of increase of the Camry has been larger than the Taurus. The difference in the selling price between the two cars was the largest in 2000, about $6,500. From 2000 to 2001 the selling price of the Camry decreased about $500, the only price decrease for either car during the 9-year period.

**45.** Wages paid by software companies grew from $0.4 billion to $1.65 billion per quarter between 1994 and 2002. Those paid by aerospace manufacturers remained fairly constant between $1 and $1.5 billion. Software surpassed aerospace in 1998.

**47. a.** $i \geq \dfrac{345.3 - 125.0}{7} = 31.47$.   Use interval of 35.

| Selling Price ($000) | F | CF |
|---|---|---|
| 110 up to 145 | 3 | 3 |
| 145 up to 180 | 19 | 22 |
| 180 up to 215 | 31 | 53 |
| 215 up to 250 | 25 | 78 |
| 250 up to 285 | 14 | 92 |
| 285 up to 320 | 10 | 102 |
| 320 up to 355 | 3 | 105 |

**1.** Most homes (53%) are in the 180 up to 250 range.
**2.** The largest value is near 355; the smallest, near 110.
**3.** Less than 1% of the homes sold for less than 125.

**b.**

1. About 42 homes sold for less than 200.
2. About 55% of the homes sold for less than 220. So 45% sold for more.
3. Less than 1% of the homes sold for less than 125.

**c.** The selling price ranges from about $120,000 up to about $360,000. A typical home sold for about $210,000.

**49.**

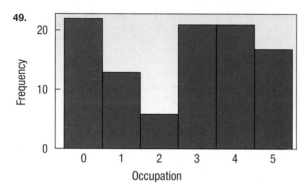

Occupational category 2 has fewer members (5 or 6), and all the others are around 19.

## CHAPTER 3

1.  $\mu = 5.4$, found by 27/5.
3.  **a.** $\bar{X} = 7.0$, found by 28/4.
    **b.** $(5-7) + (9-7) + (4-7) + (10-7) = 0$
5.  $\bar{X} = 14.58$, found by 43.74/3.
7.  **a.** 15.4, found by 154/10.
    **b.** Population parameter, since it includes all the salespersons at Midtown Ford.
9.  **a.** $54.55, found by $1,091/20.
    **b.** A sample statistic—assuming that the power company serves more than 20 customers.
11. $22.91, found by $\dfrac{300(\$20) + 400(\$25) + 400(\$23)}{300 + 400 + 400}$.
13. $17.75, found by ($400 + $750 + $2,400)/200.
15. **a.** No mode
    **b.** The given value would be the mode.
    **c.** 3 and 4 bimodal.
17. Median = 5, Mode = 5
19. **a.** Median = 2.9
    **b.** 2.9
21. **a.** $\bar{X} = 7.75$, found by 93/12.
    **b.** 7.65, found by (7.8 + 7.5)/2 and 8.6 (Jan and Dec).
    **c.** 8.6, found by 34.4/4 and 8.6. It is somewhat higher.
23. 12.8 percentage increase, found by
    $\sqrt[5]{(1.08)(1.12)(1.14)(1.26)(1.05)} = 1.128$.
25. 12.28 percentage increase, found by
    $\sqrt[5]{(1.094)(1.138)(1.117)(1.119)(1.147)} = 1.1228$.

27. 2.52%, found by $\sqrt[10]{\dfrac{179.9}{140.3}} - 1$.

29. 10.76%, found by $\sqrt[5]{\dfrac{70}{42}} - 1$.

31. **a.** 7, found by 10 − 3.
    **b.** 6, found by 30/5.
    **c.** 2.4, found by 12/5.
    **d.** The difference between the highest number sold (10) and the smallest number sold (3) is 7. On average, the number of service reps on duty deviates by 2.4 from the mean of 6.
33. **a.** 30, found by 54 − 24.
    **b.** 38, found by 380/10.
    **c.** 7.2, found by 72/10.
    **d.** The difference of 54 and 24 is 30. On average, the number of minutes required to install a door deviates 7.2 minutes from the mean of 38 minutes.
35. **a.** 15, found by 41 − 26.
    **b.** 33.9, found by 339/10.
    **c.** 4.12, found by 41.2/10.
    **d.** The ratings deviate 4.12 from the mean of 33.9 on average.
37. **a.** 5
    **b.** 4.4, found by
    $\dfrac{(8-5)^2 + (3-5)^2 + (7-5)^2 + (3-5)^2 + (4-5)^2}{5}$.
39. **a.** $2.77
    **b.** 1.26, found by
    $\dfrac{\begin{aligned}(2.68-2.77)^2 + (1.03-2.77)^2 + (2.26-2.77)^2 \\ + (4.30-2.77)^2 + (3.58-2.77)^2\end{aligned}}{5}$.
41. **a.** Range: 7.3, found by 11.6 − 4.3. Arithmetic mean: 6.94, found by 34.7/5. Variance: 6.5944, found by 32.972/5. Standard deviation: 2.568, found by $\sqrt{6.5944}$.
    **b.** Dennis has a higher mean return (11.76 > 6.94). However, Dennis has greater spread in their returns on equity (16.89 > 6.59).
43. **a.** $\bar{X} = 4$
    $$s^2 = \frac{(7-4)^2 + \cdots + (3-4)^2}{5-1} = 5.5$$
    $$s^2 = \frac{22}{5-1} = 5.50$$
    **b.** $s = 2.3452$
45. **a.** $\bar{X} = 38$
    $$s^2 = \frac{(28-38)^2 + \cdots + (42-38)^2}{10-1} = 82.6667$$
    $$s^2 = \frac{744}{10-1} = 82.6667$$
    **b.** $s = 9.0921$
47. **a.** $\bar{X} = \dfrac{951}{10} = 95.1$
    $$s^2 = \frac{(101-95.1)^2 + \cdots + (88-95.1)^2}{10-1}$$
    $$= \frac{1112.9}{9} = 123.66$$
    **b.** $s = \sqrt{123.66} = 11.12$
49. About 69%, found by $1 - 1/(1.8)^2$.
51. **a.** About 95%.
    **b.** 47.5%, 2.5%.
53. Because the exact values in a frequency distribution are not known, the midpoint is used for every member of that class.

**55.**

| Class | f | M | fM | $(M - \bar{X})$ | $f(M - \bar{X})^2$ |
|---|---|---|---|---|---|
| 20 up to 30 | 7 | 25 | 175 | −22.29 | 3,477.909 |
| 30 up to 40 | 12 | 35 | 420 | −12.29 | 1,812.529 |
| 40 up to 50 | 21 | 45 | 945 | −2.29 | 110.126 |
| 50 up to 60 | 18 | 55 | 990 | 7.71 | 1,069.994 |
| 60 up to 70 | 12 | 65 | 780 | 17.71 | 3,763.729 |
| | 70 | | 3,310 | | 10,234.287 |

$$\bar{X} = \frac{3,310}{70} = 47.29$$

$$s = \sqrt{\frac{10,234.287}{70 - 1}} = 12.18$$

**57.**

| Number of Clients | f | M | fM | $(M - \bar{X})$ | $f(M - \bar{X})^2$ |
|---|---|---|---|---|---|
| 20 up to 30 | 1 | 25 | 25 | −19.8 | 392.04 |
| 30 up to 40 | 15 | 35 | 525 | −9.8 | 1,440.60 |
| 40 up to 50 | 22 | 45 | 990 | 0.2 | 0.88 |
| 50 up to 60 | 8 | 55 | 440 | 10.2 | 832.32 |
| 60 up to 70 | 4 | 65 | 260 | 20.2 | 1,632.16 |
| | 50 | | 2,240 | | 4,298.00 |

$$\bar{X} = \frac{2,240}{50} = 44.8$$

$$s = \sqrt{\frac{4,298}{50 - 1}} = 9.37$$

**59. a.** Mean = 5, found by (6 + 4 + 3 + 7 + 5)/5. Median is 5, found by rearranging the values and selecting the middle value.
　**b.** Population, because all partners were included.
　**c.** $\Sigma(X - \mu)$ = (6 − 5) + (4 − 5) + (3 − 5) + (7 − 5) + (5 − 5) = 0.

**61.** $\bar{X} = \dfrac{545}{16} = 34.06$

　Median = 37.50

**63.** 370.08, found by 18,504/50.

**65.** $\bar{X}_W = \dfrac{\$5.00(270) + \$6.50(300) + \$8.00(100)}{270 + 300 + 100} = \$6.12$

**67.** $\bar{X}_w = \dfrac{[15,300(4.5) + 10,400(3.0) + 150,600(10.2)]}{176,300}$

　　= 9.28

**69.** GM $= \sqrt[21]{\dfrac{6,286,800}{5,164,900}} - 1 = 1.0094 - 1.0 = .0094$

**71. a.** 55, found by 72 − 17.
　**b.** 14.4, found by 144/10, where $\bar{X} = 43.2$.
　**c.** 17.6245.

**73. a.** Population.
　**b.** 183.47.

**75. a.** There were 13 flights, so all items are considered.
　**b.** $\bar{X} = \dfrac{2,259}{13} = 173.77$

　　Median = 195
　**c.** Range = 301 − 7 = 294

　　$s = \sqrt{\dfrac{133,846.3}{13}} = 101.47$

**77. a.** $\bar{X} = \dfrac{273}{30} = 9.1$, median = 9.
　**b.** Range = 18 − 4 = 14

　　$s = \sqrt{\dfrac{368.7}{30 - 1}} = 3.57$

　**c.** $2^5 = 32$, so suggest 5 classes.

　　$i = \dfrac{18 - 4}{5} = 2.8.$　　Use $i$ = 3.

| Class | M | f | fM | $M - \mu$ | $(M - \mu)^2$ | $f(M - \mu)^2$ |
|---|---|---|---|---|---|---|
| 4–6 | 5 | 10 | 50 | −4 | 16 | 160 |
| 7–9 | 8 | 6 | 48 | −1 | 1 | 6 |
| 10–12 | 11 | 9 | 99 | 2 | 4 | 36 |
| 13–15 | 14 | 4 | 56 | 5 | 25 | 100 |
| 16–18 | 17 | 1 | 17 | 8 | 64 | 64 |
| | | 270 | | | | 366 |

**d.** $\mu = \dfrac{270}{30} = 9.0$

$$s = \sqrt{\frac{366}{30 - 1}} = 3.552$$

The mean and standard deviation from grouped data are estimates of the mean and standard deviations of the actual values.

**79.**

| Distance | f | M | fM | $f(M - \bar{X})^2$ |
|---|---|---|---|---|
| 0 up to 5 | 4 | 2.5 | 10.0 | 441.00 |
| 5 up to 10 | 15 | 7.5 | 112.5 | 453.75 |
| 10 up to 15 | 27 | 12.5 | 337.5 | 6.75 |
| 15 up to 20 | 18 | 17.5 | 315.0 | 364.50 |
| 20 up to 25 | 6 | 22.5 | 135.0 | 541.50 |
| | | | 910.0 | 1,807.50 |

$$\bar{X} = \frac{910}{70} = 13$$

$$s = \sqrt{\frac{1,807.5}{70 - 1}} = 5.118$$

**81.** Answers will vary.

**83.** From statistical software:
　**a.** $n = 105$
　　$\bar{X} = 221.10$
　　$s = 47.11$
　　median = 213.60, the distribution is symmetric about $220,000.
　**b.** $n = 105$
　　$\bar{X} = 2,223.8$
　　$s = 248.7$
　　median = 2,200, the distribution is symmetric about 2,200 square feet.

**85.** From statistical software:
　**a.** $n = 46$
　　$\bar{X} = 73.81$
　　$s = 6.90$
　　median = 76.10
　**b.** $n = 46$
　　$\bar{X} = 16.58$
　　$s = 9.27$
　　median = 17.45
　　No outliers. Symmetric distribution.

## CHAPTER 4

**1.** In a histogram observations are grouped so their individual identity is lost. With a dot plot, identity of each observation is maintained.

**3. a.** Dot plot
　**b.** 15
　**c.** 1, 7
　**d.** 2 and 3

**5. a.** 620 to 629
　**b.** 5
　**c.** 621, 623, 623, 627, 629

**7. a.** 25
　**b.** One
　**c.** 38,106

**d.** 60, 61, 63, 63, 65, 65, 69
**e.** No value
**f.** 9
**g.** 9
**h.** 76
**i.** 16

**9.**

| Stem | Leaves |
|------|--------|
| 0 | 5 |
| 1 | 28 |
| 2 | |
| 3 | 0024789 |
| 4 | 12366 |
| 5 | 2 |

There were a total of 16 calls studied. The number of calls ranged from 5 to 52. Seven of the 16 subscribers received between 30 and 39 calls.

**11.** Median = 53, found by $(11 + 1)(\frac{1}{2})$ ∴ 6th value in from lowest.
$Q_1 = 49$, found by $(11 + 1)(\frac{1}{4})$ ∴ 3rd value in from lowest.
$Q_3 = 55$, found by $(11 + 1)(\frac{3}{4})$ ∴ 9th value in from lowest.

**13.** **a.** $Q_1 = 33.25$, $Q_3 = 50.25$
**b.** $D_2 = 27.8$, $D_8 = 52.6$
**c.** $P_{67} = 47$

**15.** **a.** 350
**b.** $Q_1 = 175$, $Q_3 = 930$
**c.** $930 - 175 = 755$
**d.** Less than 0, or more than about 2,060.
**e.** There are no outliers.
**f.** The distribution is positively skewed.

**17.**

```
        +----------------------------
--------                |
----|--------- | ---------|
        +----------------------------
----+---------+---------+---------+---------+---------+---
   14.0      21.0      28.0      35.0      42.0      49.0
```

The distribution is somewhat positively skewed. Note that the dashed line above 35 is longer than below 18.

**19.** 8.06%, found by (.25/3.10)(100).

**21.** **a.** Because the two series are in different units of measurement.
**b.** P.E. ratio is 16.51%. ROI 20.8%. Less spread in the P.E. ratios.

**23.** **a.** The mean is 30.8, found by 154/5. The median is 31.0, and the standard deviation is 3.96, found by

$$\sqrt{\frac{62.8}{4}}.$$

**b.** −0.15, found by $\frac{3(30.8 - 31.0)}{3.96}$.

**c.**

| Salary | $\left(\dfrac{X - \bar{X}}{s}\right)$ | $\left(\dfrac{X - \bar{X}}{s}\right)^3$ |
|--------|--------|--------|
| 36 | 1.313131 | 2.264250504 |
| 26 | −1.212121 | −1.780894343 |
| 33 | 0.555556 | 0.171467764 |
| 28 | −0.707071 | −0.353499282 |
| 31 | 0.050505 | 0.000128826 |
| | | 0.301453469 |

0.125, found by $[5/(4 \times 3)] \times 0.301$.

**25.** **a.** The mean is 21.93, found by 328.9/15. The median is 15.8, and the standard deviation is 21.18, found by

$$\sqrt{\frac{6282.9893}{14}}.$$

**b.** 0.868, found by [3(21.93 − 15.8)]/21.18.
**c.** 2.444, found by [15/(14 × 13)] × 29.658.

**27.**

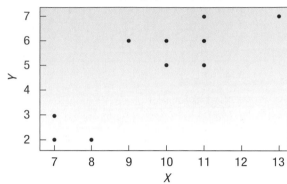

Scatterplot of Y versus X

There is a positive relationship between the variables.

**29.** **a.** Both variables are nominal scale.
**b.** Contingency table.
**c.** Men are about twice as likely to order a dessert. From the table 32% of the men ordered dessert, but only 15 percent of the women.

**31.** **a.** Dot plot
**b.** 15
**c.** 5

**33.** **a.** 70
**b.** 1
**c.** 0, 145
**d.** 30, 30, 32, 39
**e.** 24
**f.** 21
**g.** 77.5
**h.** 25

**35.** **a.** $L_{50} = (20 + 1)\frac{50}{100} = 10.50$

Median $= \dfrac{83.7 + 85.6}{2} = 84.65$

$L_{25} = (21)(.25) = 5.25$
$Q_1 = 66.6 + .25(72.9 - 66.6) = 68.175$
$L_{75} = 21(.75) = 15.75$
$Q_3 = 87.1 + .75(90.2 - 87.1) = 89.425$

**b.** $L_{26} = 21(.26) = 5.46$
$P_{26} = 66.6 + .46(72.9 - 66.6) = 69.498$
$L_{83} = 21(.83) = 17.43$
$P_{83} = 93.3 + .43(98.6 - 93.3)$
$= 95.579$

**c.**

```
              ------------------------
------------I         +        I---------------
              ------------------------
--------+---------+---------+---------+---------+--------C20
   64.0      72.0      80.0      88.0      96.0
```

**37.** **a.** $Q_1 = 26.25$, $Q_3 = 35.75$, median = 31.50.

```
              ------------------------
------------I         +        I-------------------
              ------------------------
-----+---------+---------+---------+---------+---------+
   24.5      28.0      31.5      35.0      38.5      42.0
```

**b.** $Q_1 = 33.25$, $Q_3 = 38.75$, median = 37.50.

```
        ----------------------
------I         +        I----------------------
        ----------------------
-----+---------+---------+---------+---------+---------+
   32.5      35.0      37.5      40.0      42.5      45.0
```

**c.** The median time for public transportation is about 6 minutes less. There is more variation in public transportation. The difference between $Q_1$ and $Q_3$ is

9.5 minutes for public transportation and 5.5 minutes for private transportation.

**39.** The distribution is positively skewed. The first quartile is approx. $20 and the third quartile is approx. $90. There is one outlier located at $255. The median is about $50.

**41.** $Q_1 = 44.25$, $Q_3 = 68.5$, and the median is 55.50. The distribution is approximately symmetric. The box plot is as follows.

```
--------------------|      --------------------  --------------------
                    |          +         |
--------------------|      --------------------  --------------------
---+---------+---------+---------+---------+---------+-----
   24        36        48        60        72        84 miles
```

The above results are found using MINITAB.

**43.** $sk = 0.065$ or $sk = \dfrac{3(7.7143 - 8.0)}{3.9036} = -0.22$

**45.**
### Scatterplot of Accidents versus Age

As age increases the number of accidents decreases.

**47.** 40% of the Democrats favor gun control and 36% of the Republicans favor it.

**49.** $\bar{X} = 16.216$, $s = 10.581$, $Q_1 = 7$, $Q_3 = 22.50$.
Superbowl XXIV is an outlier.

**51.**
**a.** $\bar{X} = 24.133$, $s = 24.724$, median = 14, $Q_1 = 6.25$, and $Q_3 = 36$. There are 3 outliers, Wrigley Field (Cubs), Yankee Stadium, and Fenway Park (Red Sox).
**b.** $\bar{X} = 83.550$, $s = 29.150$, $Q_1 = 63.375$, $Q_3 = 102.513$, median = 76.254. Expos are the smallest and Yankees the largest salary. The Yankees are an outlier at more than $175 million.
**c.** Positive association between wins and salary.

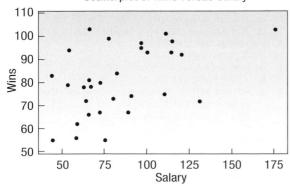
### Scatterplot of Wins versus Salary

**d.** The number of wins varies from 55 (2 teams) to 103 (2 teams).

### Dotplot of Wins

**53.**
**a.** The first quartile is 71.5 years and the third is 78.5 years. The distribution is negatively skewed with two outliers (NIgeria and South Africa at 48 and 51).
**b.** The first quartile is 8.3 and the third quartile is 24.4. The distribution is symmetric with no outliers.
**c.** Stem-and-leaf of Cell. $N = 46$, Leaf Unit = 1.0.

```
(35)  0   00000000000011111111222222222233344444
 11   0   68
  9   1   123
  6   1   5
  5   2   0
  4   2   7
  3   3
  3   3
  3   4
  3   4
  3   5
  3   5
  3   6   3
  2   6   59
```

The distribution is extremely positively skewed. The median is 2 and the mean is around 8, which is above the third quartile of about 5.

## CHAPTER 5

**1.**

| Outcome | Person 1 | Person 2 |
|---------|----------|----------|
| 1 | A | A |
| 2 | A | F |
| 3 | F | A |
| 4 | F | F |

**3.**
**a.** .176, found by $\dfrac{6}{34}$.
**b.** Empirical.

**5.**
**a.** Empirical.
**b.** Classical.
**c.** Classical.
**d.** Empirical, based on seismological data.

**7.**
**a.** The survey of 40 people about environmental issues.
**b.** 26 or more respond yes, for example.
**c.** 10/40 = .25
**d.** Empirical.
**e.** The events are not equally likely, but they are mutually exclusive.

**9.**
**a.** Answers will vary. Here are some possibilities: 123, 124, 125, 999.
**b.** $(1/10)^3$
**c.** Classical.

**11.** $P(A \text{ or } B) = P(A) + P(B) = .30 + .20 = .50$
$P(\text{neither}) = 1 - .50 = .50$.

**13.**
**a.** 102/200 = .51
**b.** .49, found by 61/200 + 37/200 = .305 + .185. Special rule of addition.

**15.** $P(\text{above } C) = .25 + .50 = .75$

**17.** $P(A \text{ or } B) = P(A) + P(B) - P(A \text{ and } B)$
$= .20 + .30 - .15 = .35$

**19.** When two events are mutually exclusive, it means that if one occurs the other event cannot occur. Therefore, the probability of their joint occurrence is zero.

**21.**
**a.** .65, found by .35 + .40 − .10.
**b.** A joint probability.
**c.** No, an executive might read more than one magazine.

**23.** $P(A \text{ and } B) = P(A) \times P(B|A) = .40 \times .30 = .12$

**25.** .90, found by (.80 + .60) − .5.
.10, found by (1 − .90).

**27.** **a.** $P(A_1) = 3/10 = .30$
   **b.** $P(B_1|A_2) = 1/3 = .33$
   **c.** $P(B_2 \text{ and } A_3) = 1/10 = .10$
**29.** **a.** A contingency table.
   **b.** .27, found by $300/500 \times 135/300$.
   **c.** The tree diagram would appear as:

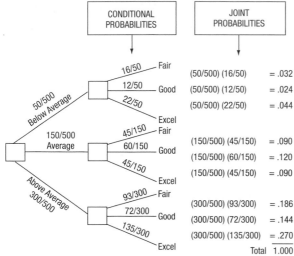

|  |  |  |
|---|---|---|
| (50/500) (16/50) | = .032 |
| (50/500) (12/50) | = .024 |
| (50/500) (22/50) | = .044 |
| (150/500) (45/150) | = .090 |
| (150/500) (60/150) | = .120 |
| (150/500) (45/150) | = .090 |
| (300/500) (93/300) | = .186 |
| (300/500) (72/300) | = .144 |
| (300/500) (135/300) | = .270 |
|  | Total 1.000 |

**31.** Probability the first presentation wins = 3/5 = .60.
   Probability the second presentation wins = (2/5)(3/4) = .30.
   Probability the third presentation wins = (2/5)(1/4)(3/3) = .10.

**33.** $P(A_1 \mid B_1) = \dfrac{P(A_1) \times P(B_1 \mid A_1)}{P(A_1) \times P(B_1 \mid A_1) + P(A_2) \times P(B_1 \mid A_2)}$

$= \dfrac{.60 \times .05}{(.60 \times .05) + (.40 \times .10)} = .4286$

**35.** $P(\text{night} \mid \text{win}) = \dfrac{P(\text{night})\, P(\text{win} \mid \text{night})}{P(\text{night})\, P(\text{win} \mid \text{night}) + P(\text{day})\, P(\text{win} \mid \text{day})}$

$= \dfrac{(.70)(.50)}{[(.70)(.50)] + [(.30)(.90)]} = .5645$

**37.** $P(\text{cash} \mid > \$50) = \dfrac{P(\text{cash})\, P(> \$50 \mid \text{cash})}{\substack{P(\text{cash})\, P(> \$50 \mid \text{cash}) \\ + P(\text{check})\, P(> \$50 \mid \text{check}) \\ + P(\text{charge})\, P(> \$50 \mid \text{charge})}}$

$= \dfrac{(.30)(.20)}{(.30)(.20) + (.30)(.90) + (.40)(.60)} = .1053$

**39.** **a.** 78,960,960
   **b.** 840, found by (7)(6)(5)(4). That is 7!/3!.
   **c.** 10, found by 5!/3!2!.
**41.** 210, found by (10)(9)(8)(7)/(4)(3)(2).
**43.** 120, found by 5!.
**45.** 10,897,286,400, found by
   $_{15}P_{10} = (15)(14)(13)(12)(11)(10)(9)(8)(7)(6)$.
**47.** **a.** Asking teenagers to compare their reactions to a newly developed soft drink.
   **b.** Answers will vary. One possibility is more than half of the respondents like it.
**49.** Subjective.
**51.** **a.** The likelihood an event will occur, assuming that another event has already occurred.
   **b.** The collection of one or more outcomes of an experiment.
   **c.** A measure of the likelihood that two or more events will happen concurrently.

**53.** **a.** .8145, found by $(.95)^4$.
   **b.** Special rule of multiplication.
   **c.** $P(A \text{ and } B \text{ and } C \text{ and } D) = P(A) \times P(B) \times P(C) \times P(D)$.
**55.** **a.** .08, found by $.80 \times .10$.
   **b.** No; 90% of females attended college, 78% of males.
   **c.**

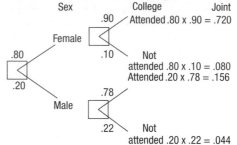

|  |  |
|---|---|
| Attended $.80 \times .90 = .720$ |
| Not attended $.80 \times .10 = .080$ |
| Attended $.20 \times .78 = .156$ |
| Not attended $.20 \times .22 = .044$ |
| Total 1.000 |

   **d.** Yes, because all the possible outcomes are shown on the tree diagram.
**57.** **a.** 0.57, found by 57/100.
   **b.** 0.97, found by (57/100) + (40/100).
   **c.** Yes, because an employee cannot be both.
   **d.** 0.03, found by $1 - 0.97$.
**59.** **a.** 0.4096, found by $(0.8)^4$.
   **b.** 0.0016, found by $(0.2)^4$.
   **c.** 0.9984, found by $1 - 0.0016$.
**61.** **a.** 0.9039, found by $(0.98)^5$.
   **b.** 0.0961, found by $1 - 0.9039$.
**63.** **a.** 0.0333, found by (4/10)(3/9)(2/8).
   **b.** 0.1667, found by (6/10)(5/9)(4/8).
   **c.** 0.8333, found by $1 - 0.1667$.
   **d.** Dependent
**65.** **a.** 0.3818, found by (9/12)(8/11)(7/10).
   **b.** 0.6182, found by $1 - 0.3818$.
**67.** **a.** 0.5467, found by 82/150.
   **b.** 0.76, found by (39/150) + (75/150).
   **c.** 0.6267, found by $82/150 + 39/150 - 27/150$.
   General rule of addition.
   **d.** 0.3293, found by 27/82.
   **e.** 0.2972, found by (82/150)(81/149).

**69.** $P(\text{poor/profit}) = \dfrac{.10(.20)}{.10(.20) + .60(.80) + .30(.60)}$

$= .0294$

**71.** **a.** $P(P \text{ or } D) = (1/50)(9/10) + (49/50)(1/10) = 0.116$
   **b.** $P(\text{No}) = (49/50)(9/10) = 0.882$
   **c.** $P(\text{No on 3}) = (0.882)^3 = 0.686$
   **d.** $P(\text{at least one prize}) = 1 - 0.686 = 0.314$
**73.** Yes. 256 is found by $2^8$.
**75.** .9744, found by $1 - (.40)^4$.
**77.** **a.** .185, found by (.15)(.95) + (.05)(.85).
   **b.** .0075, found by (.15)(.05).
**79.** **a.** $P(F \text{ and } >60) = .25$, found by solving with the general rule of multiplication:
   $P(F) \cdot P(>60|F) = (.5)(.5)$
   **b.** 0
   **c.** .3333, found by 1/3.
**81.** $26^4 = 456,976$
**83.** 1/3, 628,800
**85.** **a.** $P(D) = .20(.03) + .30(.04) + .25(.07) + .25(.065)$
   $= .05175$

   **b.** $P(\text{Tyson/defective}) = \dfrac{.20(.03)}{\substack{.20(.03) + .30(.04) \\ + .25(.07) + .25(.065)}} = .1159$

**c.**

| Supplier | Joint | Revised |
|---|---|---|
| Tyson | .00600 | .1159 |
| Fuji | .01200 | .2319 |
| Kirkpatricks | .01750 | .3382 |
| Parts | .01625 | .3140 |
| | .05175 | 1.000 |

**87.** Answers will vary.

**89. a.**

| Winning Season | Attendance | | | |
|---|---|---|---|---|
| | Low | Moderate | High | Total |
| No | 9 | 7 | 0 | 16 |
| Yes | 3 | 5 | 6 | 14 |
| | 12 | 12 | 6 | 30 |

   **1.** $P(\text{win}) = \dfrac{14}{30} = .47$

   **2.** $P(\text{win or} > 3.0) = \dfrac{14}{30} + \dfrac{6}{30} - \dfrac{6}{30} = .47$

   **3.** $P(\text{win}/> 3.0) = \dfrac{6}{6} = 1.00$

   **4.** $P(\text{win and} < 2.0) = \dfrac{9}{30} = .30$

**b.**

| Winning Season | Grass | Artificial | Total |
|---|---|---|---|
| No | 13 | 3 | 16 |
| Yes | 12 | 2 | 14 |
| | 25 | 5 | 30 |

   **1.** $P(\text{grass}) = \dfrac{25}{30} = .83$

   **2.** $P(\text{win/grass}) = \dfrac{12}{25} = .48; P(\text{w/artificial}) = \dfrac{2}{5} = .40$

      Better on grass field

   **3.** $P(\text{win or artificial}) = \dfrac{14}{30} + \dfrac{5}{30} - \dfrac{2}{30} = \dfrac{17}{30} = .57$

## CHAPTER 6

**1.** Mean = 1.3, variance = .81, found by:

$$\mu = 0(.20) + 1(.40) + 2(.30) + 3(.10) = 1.3$$

$$\sigma^2 = (0 - 1.3)^2(.2) + (1 - 1.3)^2(.4)$$

$$+ (2 - 1.3)^2(.3) + (3 - 1.3)^2(.1)$$

$$= .81$$

**3. a.** The second, or middle, one.

  **b.** .2, .4, .9

  **c.** $\mu = 14.5$, variance = 27.25, found by:

$$\mu = 5(.1) + 10(.3) + 15(.2) + 20(.4) = 14.5$$

$$\sigma^2 = (5 - 14.5)^2(.1) + (10 - 14.5)^2(.3)$$

$$+ (15 - 14.5)^2(.2) + (20 - 14.5)^2(.4)$$

$$= 27.25$$

$$\sigma = 5.22, \text{ found by } \sqrt{27.25}$$

**5.** $\mu = 0(.3) + 1(.4) + 2(.2) + 3(.1) = 1.1$

$$\sigma^2 = (0 - 1.1)^2(.3) + (1 - 1.1)^2(.4)$$

$$+ (2 - 1.1)^2(.2) + (3 - 1.1)^2(.1) = 0.89$$

$$\sigma = .943.$$

**7. a.** .20

  **b.** .55

  **c.** .95

  **d.** $\mu = 0(.45) + 10(.30) + 100(.20) + 500(.05) = 48.0$

$$\sigma^2 = (0 - 48)^2(.45) + (10 - 48)^2(.3)$$

$$+ (100 - 48)^2(.2) + (500 - 48)^2(.05) = 12{,}226$$

$$\sigma = 110.57, \text{ found by } \sqrt{12{,}226}$$

**9. a.** $P(2) = \dfrac{4!}{2!(4-2)!}(.25)^2(.75)^{4-2} = .2109$

  **b.** $P(3) = \dfrac{4!}{3!(4-3)!}(.25)^3(.75)^{4-3} = .0469$

**11. a.**

| X | P(X) |
|---|---|
| 0 | .064 |
| 1 | .288 |
| 2 | .432 |
| 3 | .216 |

  **b.** $\mu = 1.8$

$$\sigma^2 = 0.72$$

$$\sigma = \sqrt{0.72} = .8485$$

**13. a.** .2668, found by $P(2) = \dfrac{9!}{(9-2)!2!}(.3)^2(.7)^7$.

  **b.** .1715, found by $P(4) = \dfrac{9!}{(9-4)!4!}(.3)^4(.7)^5$.

  **c.** .0404, found by $P(0) = \dfrac{9!}{(9-0)!0!}(.3)^0(.7)^9$.

**15. a.** .2824, found by $P(0) = \dfrac{12!}{(12-0)!0!}(.10)^0(.9)^{12}$.

  **b.** .3765, found by $P(1) = \dfrac{12!}{(12-1)!1!}(.10)^1(.9)^{11}$.

  **c.** .2301, found by $P(2) = \dfrac{12!}{(12-2)!2!}(.10)^2(.9)^{10}$.

  **d.** $\mu = 1.2$, found by 12(.10).

$$\sigma = 1.0392, \text{ found by } \sqrt{1.08}.$$

**17. a.** 0.1858, found by $\dfrac{15!}{2!13!}(0.23)^2(0.77)^{13}$.

  **b.** 0.1416, found by $\dfrac{15!}{5!10!}(0.23)^5(0.77)^{10}$.

  **c.** 3.45, found by (0.23)(15).

**19. a.** 0.296, found by using Appendix A with $n$ of 8, $\pi$ of 0.30, and $x$ of 2.

  **b.** $P(x \le 2) = 0.058 + 0.198 + 0.296 = 0.552$

  **c.** 0.448, found by $P(x \ge 3) = 1 - P(x \le 2) = 1 - 0.552$.

**21. a.** 0.387, found from Appendix A with $n$ of 9, $\pi$ of 0.90, and $x$ of 9.

  **b.** $P(X < 5) = 0.001$

  **c.** 0.992, found by $1 - 0.008$.

  **d.** 0.947, found by $1 - 0.053$.

**23. a.** $\mu = 10.5$, found by 15(0.7) and $\sigma = \sqrt{15(0.7)(0.3)} = 1.7748$.

  **b.** 0.2061, found by $\dfrac{15!}{10!5!}(0.7)^{10}(0.3)^5$.

  **c.** 0.4247, found by 0.2061 + 0.2186.

  **d.** 0.5154, found by 0.2186 + 0.1700 + 0.0916 + 0.0305 + 0.0047.

**25.** $P(2) = \dfrac{[_6C_2][_4C_1]}{_{10}C_3} = \dfrac{15(4)}{120} = .50$

**27.** $P(0) = \dfrac{[_7C_2][_3C_0]}{[_{10}C_2]} = \dfrac{21(1)}{45} = .4667$

**29.** $P(2) = \dfrac{[_9C_3][_6C_2]}{[_{15}C_5]} = \dfrac{84(15)}{3003} = .4196$

**31. a.** .6703
   **b.** .3297
**33. a.** .0613
   **b.** .0803
**35.** $\mu = 6$
   $P(X \geq 5) = .7149$
   $= 1 - (.0025 + .0149 + .0446 + .0892 + .1339)$
**37.** A random variable is a quantitative or qualitative outcome that results from a chance experiment. A probability distribution also includes the likelihood of each possible outcome.
**39.** The binomial distribution is a discrete probability distribution for which there are only two possible outcomes. A second important part is that data collected are a result of counts. Additionally, one trial is independent from the next, and the chance for success remains the same from one trial to the next.
**41.** $\mu = 0(.1) + 1(.2) + 2(.3) + 3(.4) = 2.00$

   $\sigma^2 = (0 - 2)^2(.1) + \cdots + (3 - 2)^2(.40) = 1.0$

   $\sigma = 1$

**43.** $\mu = 0(.4) + 1(.2) + 2(.2) + 3(.1) + 4(.1) = 1.3$

   $\sigma^2 = (0 - 1.30)^2(.4) + \cdots + (4 - 1.30)^2(.1) = 1.81$

   $\sigma = 1.3454$
**45. a.** 0.001
   **b.** 0.001
**47. a.** 6, found by $0.4 \times 15$.
   **b.** 0.0245, found by $\dfrac{15!}{10!5!}(0.4)^{10}(0.6)^5$
   **c.** 0.0338, found by
      $0.0245 + 0.0074 + 0.0016 + 0.0003 + 0.0000$.
   **d.** 0.0093, found by $0.0338 - 0.0245$.
**49. a.** $\mu = 20(0.075) = 1.5$
      $\sigma = \sqrt{20(0.075)(0.925)} = 1.1779$
   **b.** 0.2103, found by $\dfrac{20!}{0!20!}(0.075)^0(0.925)^{20}$.
   **c.** 0.7897, found by $1 - 0.2103$.
**51. a.** 0.1311, found by $\dfrac{16!}{4!12!}(0.15)^4(0.85)^{12}$.
   **b.** 2.4, found by $(0.15)(16)$.
   **c.** 0.2100, found by
      $1 - 0.0743 - 0.2097 - 0.2775 - 0.2285$.
**53.** $P(2) = \dfrac{[_6C_2][_4C_2]}{[_{10}C_4]} = \dfrac{(15)(6)}{210} = 0.4286$

**55. a.**

| 0 | 0.0002 |
|---|--------|
| 1 | 0.0019 |
| 2 | 0.0116 |
| 3 | 0.0418 |
| 4 | 0.1020 |
| 5 | 0.1768 |
| 6 | 0.2234 |
| 7 | 0.2075 |
| 8 | 0.1405 |
| 9 | 0.0676 |
| 10 | 0.0220 |
| 11 | 0.0043 |
| 12 | 0.0004 |

   **b.** $\mu = 12(0.52) = 6.24$
      $\sigma = \sqrt{12(0.52)(0.48)} = 1.7307$
   **c.** 0.1768
   **d.** 0.3343, found by $0.0002 + 0.0019 + 0.0116 + 0.0418 + 0.1020 + 0.1768$.

**57. a.** $P(1) = \dfrac{[_7C_2][_3C_1]}{[_{10}C_3]} = \dfrac{(21)(3)}{120} = .5250$

   **b.** $P(0) = \dfrac{[_7C_3][_3C_0]}{[_{10}C_3]} = \dfrac{(35)(1)}{120} = .2917$

   $P(X \geq 1) = 1 - P(0) = 1 - .2917 = .7083$

**59.** $P(X = 0) = \dfrac{[_8C_4][_4C_0]}{[_{12}C_4]} = \dfrac{70}{495} = .141$

**61. a.** .0498
   **b.** .7746, found by $(1 - .0498)^5$.
**63.** $\mu = 4.0$, from Appendix C.
   **a.** .0183
   **b.** .1954
   **c.** .6289
   **d.** .5665

**65. a.** 0.1733, found by $\dfrac{(3.1)^4 \, e^{-3.1}}{4!}$.

   **b.** 0.0450, found by $\dfrac{(3.1)^0 \, e^{-3.1}}{0!}$.

   **c.** 0.9550, found by $1 - 0.0450$.
**67.** For NASA, $\mu = n\pi = 25(1/60,000) = 0.0004$

   $P(0) = \dfrac{0.0004^0 \, e^{-0.0004}}{0!} = 0.9996$

   $P(X \geq 1) = 1 - 0.9996 = 0.0004$
   For Air Force, $\mu = 25(1/35) = .7143$

   $P(0) = \dfrac{0.7143^0 \, e^{-0.7143}}{0!} = 0.4895$

   $P(X \geq 1) = 1 - .4895 = 0.5105$
   Summarizing, Air Force estimate is .5105 and NASA estimate is 0.0004.
**69.** Let $\mu = n\pi = 155(1/3709) = 0.042$

   $P(5) = \dfrac{0.042^5 \, e^{-0.042}}{5!} = 0.000000001$

   Very unlikely!

**71.** $P(2) = \dfrac{_{25}C_3 \, _5C_2}{_{30}C_5} = \dfrac{(2,300)(10)}{142,506} = .1614$

## CHAPTER 7
   **1. a.** $b = 10, a = 6$

   **b.** $\mu = \dfrac{6 + 10}{2} = 8$

c. $\sigma = \sqrt{\dfrac{(10-6)^2}{12}} = 1.1547$

d. $\text{Area} = \dfrac{1}{(10-6)} \cdot \dfrac{(10-6)}{1} = 1$

e. $P(X > 7) = \dfrac{1}{(10-6)} \cdot \dfrac{10-7}{1} = \dfrac{3}{4} = .75$

f. $P(7 \le x \le 9) = \dfrac{1}{(10-6)} \dfrac{(9-7)}{1} = \dfrac{2}{4} = .50$

3. a.

b. $\mu = \dfrac{60+70}{2} = 65$

$\sigma = \sqrt{\dfrac{(70-60)^2}{12}} = 2.8868$

$\sigma^2 = 8.3333$

c. $P(X < 68) = \dfrac{1}{(70-60)}\left(\dfrac{68-60}{1}\right) = .80$

d. $P(X > 64) = \dfrac{1}{(70-60)} \cdot \left(\dfrac{70-64}{1}\right) = .60$

5. The actual shape of a normal distribution depends on its mean and standard deviation. Thus, there is a normal distribution, and an accompanying normal curve, for a mean of 7 and a standard deviation of 2. There is another normal curve for a mean of $25,000 and a standard deviation of $1,742, and so on.

7. a. 490 and 510, found by $500 \pm 1(10)$.
   b. 480 and 520, found by $500 \pm 2(10)$.
   c. 470 and 530, found by $500 \pm 3(10)$.

9. $Z_{Rob} = \dfrac{\$50,000 - \$60,000}{\$5000} = -2$

$Z_{Rachel} = \dfrac{\$50,000 - \$35,000}{\$8000} = 1.875$

Adjusting for their industries, Rob is well below average and Rachel well above.

11. a. 1.25, found by $z = \dfrac{25-20}{4.0} = 1.25$.

   b. 0.3944, found in Appendix D.

   c. 0.3085, found by $z = \dfrac{18-20}{2.5} = -0.5$.

   Find 0.1915 in Appendix D for $z = -0.5$.
   Then $0.5000 - 0.1915 = 0.3085$.

13. a. 0.3413, found by $z = \dfrac{\$24 - \$20.50}{\$3.50} = 1.00$.
   Then find 0.3413 in Appendix D for $z = 1$.
   b. 0.1587, found by $0.5000 - 0.3413 = 0.1587$.
   c. 0.3336, found by $z = \dfrac{\$19.00 - \$20.50}{\$3.50} = -0.43$.

Find 0.1664 in Appendix D, for $z = -0.43$, then $0.5000 - 0.1664 = 0.3336$.

15. a. 0.8276: First find $z = -1.5$, found by $(44 - 50)/4$ and $z = 1.25 = (55 - 50)/4$. The area between $-1.5$ and 0 is 0.4332 and the area between 0 and 1.25 is 0.3944, both from Appendix D. Then adding the two areas we find that $0.4332 + 0.3944 = 0.8276$.
   b. 0.1056, found by $0.5000 - 0.3994$, where $z = 1.25$.
   c. 0.2029: Recall that the area for $z = 1.25$ is 0.3944, and the area for $z = 0.5$, found by $(52 - 50)/4$, is 0.1915. Then subtract $0.3944 - 0.1915$ and find 0.2029.

17. a. 0.1525, found by subtracting $0.4938 - 0.3413$, which are the areas associated with $z$ values of 2.5 and 1, respectively.
   b. 0.0062, found by $0.5000 - 0.4938$.
   c. 0.9710, found by recalling that the area of the $z$ value of 2.5 is 0.4938. Then find $z = -2.00$, found by $(6.8 - 7.0)/0.1$. Thus, $0.4938 + 0.4772 = 0.9710$.

19. a. 0.0764, found by $z = (20 - 15)/3.5 = 1.43$, then $0.5000 - 0.4236 = 0.0764$.
   b. 0.9236, found by $0.5000 + 0.4236$, where $z = 1.43$.
   c. 0.1185, found by $z = (12 - 15)/3.5 = -0.86$. The area under the curve is 0.3051, then $z = (10 - 15)/3.5 = -1.43$. The area is 0.4236. Finally, $0.4236 - 0.3051 = 0.1185$.

21. $X = 56.60$, found by adding 0.5000 (the area left of the mean) and then finding a $z$ value that forces 45 percent of the data to fall inside the curve. Solving for $X$: $1.65 = (X - 50)/4 = 56.60$.

23. 7.233: Find a $z$ value where 0.4900 of area is between 0 and $z$. That value is $z = 2.33$. Then solve for $X$: $(X - 7)/0.1$, so $X = 7.233$.

25. $1,630, found by $2,100 - 1.88($250)$.

27. a. $\mu = n\pi = 50(0.25) = 12.5$
   $\sigma^2 = n\pi(1 - \pi) = 12.5(1 - 0.25) = 9.375$
   $\sigma = \sqrt{9.375} = 3.0619$
   b. 0.2578, found by $(14.5 - 12.5)/3.0619 = 0.65$. The area is 0.2422. Then $0.5000 - 0.2422 = 0.2578$.
   c. 0.2578, found by $(10.5 - 12.5)/3.0619 = -0.65$. The area is 0.2422. Then $0.5000 - 0.2422 = 0.2578$.

29. a. 0.0192, found by $0.500 - 0.4808$.
   b. 0.0694, found by $0.500 - 0.4306$.
   c. 0.0502, found by $0.0694 - 0.0192$.

31. a. Yes. (1) There are two mutually exclusive outcomes: overweight and not overweight. (2) It is the result of counting the number of successes (overweight members). (3) Each trial is independent. (4) The probability of 0.30 remains the same for each trial.
   b. 0.0084, found by

   $\mu = 500(0.30) = 150$.

   $\sigma^2 = 500(.30)(.70) = 105$

   $\sigma = \sqrt{105} = 10.24695$

   $z = \dfrac{X - \mu}{\sigma} = \dfrac{174.5 - 150}{10.24695} = 2.39$

   The area under the curve for 2.39 is 0.4916. Then $0.5000 - 0.4916 = 0.0084$.

   c. 0.8461, found by $z = \dfrac{139.5 - 150}{10.24695} - 1.02$

   The area between 139.5 and 150 is 0.3461. Adding $0.3461 + 0.5000 = 0.8461$.

33. a. $\mu = \dfrac{11.96 + 12.05}{2} = 12.005$

   b. $\sigma = \sqrt{\dfrac{(12.05 - 11.96)^2}{12}} = .0260$

**c.** $P(X < 12) = \dfrac{1}{(12.05 - 11.96)} \dfrac{12.00 - 11.96}{1} = \dfrac{.04}{.09} = .44$

**d.** $P(X > 11.98) = \dfrac{1}{(12.05 - 11.96)} \left( \dfrac{12.05 - 11.98}{1} \right)$

$= \dfrac{.07}{.09} = .78$

**e.** All cans have more than 11.00 ounces, so the probability is 100%.

**35. a.** $\mu = \dfrac{4 + 10}{2} = 7$

**b.** $\sigma = \sqrt{\dfrac{(10 - 4)^2}{12}} = 1.732$

**c.** $P(X < 6) = \dfrac{1}{(10 - 4)} \cdot \left( \dfrac{6 - 4}{1} \right) = \dfrac{2}{6} = .33$

**d.** $P(X > 5) = \dfrac{1}{(10 - 4)} \cdot \left( \dfrac{10 - 5}{1} \right) = \dfrac{5}{6} = .83$

**37. a.** −0.4 for net sales, found by (170 − 180)/25. 2.92 for employees, found by (1,850 − 1,500)/120.

**b.** Net sales are 0.4 standard deviations below the mean. Employees is 2.92 standard deviations above the mean.

**c.** 65.54 percent of the aluminum fabricators have greater net sales compared with Clarion, found by 0.1554 + 0.5000. Only 0.18 percent have more employees than Clarion, found by 0.5000 − 0.4982.

**39. a.** 0.5000, because $z = \dfrac{30 - 490}{90} = -5.11$.

**b.** 0.2514, found by 0.5000 − 0.2486.

**c.** 0.6374, found by 0.2486 + 0.3888.

**d.** 0.3450, found by 0.3888 − 0.0438.

**41. a.** 0.3015, found by 0.5000 − 0.1985.

**b.** 0.2579, found by 0.4564 − 0.1985.

**c.** 0.0011, found by 0.5000 − 0.4989.

**d.** 1,818, found by 1,280 + 1.28(420).

**43. a.** $z = \dfrac{880 - 1,000}{50} = -0.12$

.5000 − .4974 = .0026

**b.** $z = \dfrac{1,055 - 1,000}{50} = 1.10$

.4772 − .3643 = .1129

**c.** .4974 + .3643 = .8617

**45.** About 4,099 units, found by solving for $X$. 1.65 = (X − 4,000)/60

**47. a.** 15.39%, found by (8 − 10.3)/2.25 = −1.02, then 0.5000 − 0.3461 = 0.1539.

**b.** 17.31%, found by:
$z = (12 - 10.3)/2.25 = 0.76$. Area is 0.2764.
$z = (14 - 10.3)/2.25 = 1.64$. Area is 0.4495.
The area between 12 and 14 is 0.1731, found by 0.4495 − 0.2764.

**c.** Yes, but it is rather remote. Reasoning: On 99.73 percent of the days, returns are between 3.55 and 17.05, found by 10.3 ± 3(2.25). Thus, the chance of less than 3.55 returns is rather remote.

**49. a.** 0.9678, found by:

$\mu = 60(0.64) = 38.4$.

$\sigma^2 = 60(0.64)(0.36) = 13.824$

$\sigma = \sqrt{13.824} = 3.72$

Then (31.5 − 38.4)/3.72 = −1.85, for which the area is 0.4678.
Then 0.5000 + 0.4678 = 0.9678.

**b.** 0.0853, found by (43.5 − 38.4)/3.72 = 1.37, for which the area is 0.4147. Then 0.5000 − 0.4147 = .0853.

**c.** 0.8084, found by 0.4441 + 0.3643.

**d.** 0.0348, found by 0.4495 − 0.4147.

**51.** 0.0968, found by:

$\mu = 50(0.40) = 20$

$\sigma^2 = 50(0.40)(0.60) = 12$

$\sigma = \sqrt{12} = 3.46$

$z = (24.5 - 20)/3.46 = 1.30$.

The area is 0.4032. Then, for 25 or more, 0.5000 − 0.4032 = 0.0968.

**53. a.** 1.65 = (45 − μ)/5     μ = 36.75

**b.** 1.65 = (45 − μ)/10     μ = 28.5

**c.** z = (30 − 28.5)/10 = 0.15, then 0.5000 + 0.0596 = 0.5596.

**55. a.** 21.19 percent found by z = (9.00 − 9.20)/0.25 = −0.80; so 0.5000 − 0.2881 = 0.2119.

**b.** Increase the mean. z = (9.00 − 9.25)/0.25 = −1.00; P = 0.5000 − 0.3413 = 0.1587. Reduce the standard deviation. σ = (9.00 − 9.20)/0.15 = −1.33; P = 0.5000 − 0.4082 = 0.0918. Reducing the standard deviation is better because a smaller percent of the hams will be below the limit.

**57. a.** z = (52 − 60)/5 = 1.60, so 0.5000 − 0.4452 = 0.0548.

**b.** Let z = 0.67, so 0.67 = (X − 52)/5 and X = 55.35, set mileage at 55,350.

**c.** z = (45 − 52)/5 = −1.40, so 0.5000 − 0.4192 = 0.0808.

**59.** $\dfrac{470 - \mu}{\sigma} = 0.25$    $\dfrac{500 - \mu}{\sigma} = 1.28$    σ = 29,126 and

μ = 462,718

**61.** $\mu = 150(0.15) = 22.5$    $\sigma = \sqrt{150(0.15)(0.85)} = 4.37$
$z = (29.5 - 22.5)/4.37 = 1.60$
$P(z > 1.60) = .05000 - 0.4452 = 0.0548$

**63. a.** $z = \dfrac{3,500 - 2,265.0}{753.0} = 1.64$

$P(z > 1.64) = .5000 - .4495 = .0505$
The expected number of teams is about 1.5 [found by .0505(30)]. There is one team, Seattle, with attendance greater than 3.5 million. Estimate is very good.

**b.** $z = \dfrac{50.0 - 83.55}{29.15} = -1.15$

$P(z > -1.14) = .5000 + .3749 = .8749$
The expected number of teams more than 50 is about 26. There are actually 28, so the estimate is good.

## CHAPTER 8

**1. a.** 303 Louisiana, 5155 S. Main, 3501 Monroe, 2652 W. Central

**b.** Answers will vary.

**c.** 630 Dixie Hwy, 835 S. McCord Rd, 4624 Woodville Rd

**d.** Answers will vary.

**3. a.** Bob Schmidt Chevrolet
Great Lakes Ford Nissan
Grogan Towne Chrysler
Southside Lincoln Mercury
Rouen Chrysler Jeep Eagle

**b.** Answers will vary.

**c.** York Automotive
Thayer Chevrolet Geo Toyota
Franklin Park Lincoln Mercury
Mathews Ford Oregon, Inc.
Valiton Chrysler

**5. a.**

| Sample | Values | Sum | Mean |
|--------|--------|-----|------|
| 1 | 12, 12 | 24 | 12 |
| 2 | 12, 14 | 26 | 13 |
| 3 | 12, 16 | 28 | 14 |
| 4 | 12, 14 | 26 | 13 |
| 5 | 12, 16 | 28 | 14 |
| 6 | 14, 16 | 30 | 15 |

**b.** $\mu_{\bar{x}} = (12 + 13 + 14 + 13 + 14 + 15)/6 = 13.5$
$\mu = (12 + 12 + 14 + 16)/4 = 13.5$

**c.** More dispersion with population data compared to the sample means. The sample means vary from 12 to 15, whereas the population varies from 12 to 16.

**7. a.**

| Sample | Values | Sum | Mean |
|--------|--------|-----|------|
| 1 | 12, 12, 14 | 38 | 12.66 |
| 2 | 12, 12, 15 | 39 | 13.00 |
| 3 | 12, 12, 20 | 44 | 14.66 |
| 4 | 14, 15, 20 | 49 | 16.33 |
| 5 | 12, 14, 15 | 41 | 13.66 |
| 6 | 12, 14, 15 | 41 | 13.66 |
| 7 | 12, 15, 20 | 47 | 15.66 |
| 8 | 12, 15, 20 | 47 | 15.66 |
| 9 | 12, 14, 20 | 46 | 15.33 |
| 10 | 12, 14, 20 | 46 | 15.33 |

**b.** $\mu_{\bar{x}} = \dfrac{(12.66 + \cdots + 15.33 + 15.33)}{10} = 14.6$

$\mu = (12 + 12 + 14 + 15 + 20)/5 = 14.6$

**c.** The dispersion of the population is greater than that of the sample means. The sample means vary from 12.66 to 16.33, whereas the population varies from 12 to 20.

**9. a.** 20, found by $_6C_3$

**b.**

| Sample | Cases | Sum | Mean |
|--------|-------|-----|------|
| Ruud, Wu, Sass | 3, 6, 3 | 12 | 4.00 |
| Ruud, Sass, Flores | 3, 3, 3 | 9 | 3.00 |
| ⋮ | ⋮ | ⋮ | ⋮ |
| Sass, Flores, Schueller | 3, 3, 1 | 7 | 2.33 |

**c.** $\mu_{\bar{x}} = 2.67$, found by $\dfrac{53.33}{20}$.

$\mu = 2.67$, found by $(3 + 6 + 3 + 3 + 0 + 1)/6$.

They are equal.

**d.**

**11. a.**

$$\mu = \frac{0 + 1 + \cdots + 9}{10} = 4.5$$

**b.**

| Sample | Sum | $\bar{X}$ |
|--------|-----|-----------|
| 1 | 11 | 2.2 |
| 2 | 31 | 6.2 |
| 3 | 21 | 4.2 |
| 4 | 24 | 4.8 |
| 5 | 21 | 4.2 |
| 6 | 20 | 4.0 |
| 7 | 23 | 4.6 |
| 8 | 29 | 5.8 |
| 9 | 35 | 7.0 |
| 10 | 27 | 5.4 |

Distribution of Sample Means

| Sample Mean | Number of Means | Probability |
|-------------|-----------------|-------------|
| 1.33 | 3 | .1500 |
| 2.00 | 3 | .1500 |
| 2.33 | 4 | .2000 |
| 3.00 | 4 | .2000 |
| 3.33 | 3 | .1500 |
| 4.00 | 3 | .1500 |
| | 20 | 1.0000 |

The population has more dispersion than the sample means. The sample means vary from 1.33 to 4.0. The population varies from 0 to 6.

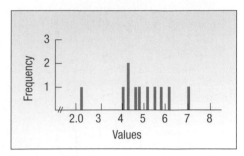

The mean of the 10 sample means is 4.84, which is close to the population mean of 4.5. The sample means range from 2.2 to 7.0, whereas the population values range from 0 to 9. From the above graph, the sample means tend to cluster between 4 and 5.

**13.** Answers will vary depending on the coins in your possession.

**15.** **a.** $z = \dfrac{63 - 60}{12/\sqrt{9}} = 0.75$

$P = .2266$, found by $.5000 - .2734$.

**b.** $z = \dfrac{56 - 60}{12/\sqrt{9}} = -1.00$

$P = .1587$, found by $.5000 - .3413$.

**c.** $P = .6147$, found by $0.3413 + 0.2734$.

**17.** $z = \dfrac{1{,}950 - 2{,}200}{250/\sqrt{50}} = -7.07$    $P = 1$, or virtually certain.

**19.** **a.** Formal Man, Summit Stationers, Bootleggers, Leather Ltd, Petries.
   **b.** Answers may vary.
   **c.** Elder-Beerman, Frederick's of Hollywood, Summit Stationers, Lion Store, Leather Ltd., Things Remembered, County Seat, Coach House Gifts, Regis Hairstylists

**21.** The difference between a sample statistic and the population parameter. Yes, the difference could be zero.

**23.** Use of either a proportional or nonproportional stratified random sample would be appropriate. For example, suppose the number of banks in Region III were as follows:

| Assets | Number | Percent of Total |
|---|---|---|
| $500 million and more | 20 | 2.0 |
| $100–$499 million | 324 | 32.4 |
| Less than $100 million | 656 | 65.6 |
|  | 1,000 | 100.0 |

For a proportional stratified sample, if the sample size is 100, then two banks with assets of $500 million would be selected, 32 medium-size banks, and 66 small banks. For a nonproportional sample, 10 or even all 20 large banks could be selected and fewer medium- and small-size banks and the sample results weighted by the appropriate percents of the total.

**25.** **a.** We selected 60, 104, 75, 72, and 48. Answers will vary.
   **b.** We selected the third observation. So the sample consists of 75, 72, 68, 82, 48. Answers will vary.
   **c.** Number the first 20 motels from 00 to 19. Randomly select three numbers. Then number the last five numbers 20 to 24. Randomly select two numbers from that group.

**27.** **a.** 15, found by $_6C_2$.
   **b.**

| Sample | Value | Sum | Mean |
|---|---|---|---|
| 1 | 79, 64 | 143 | 71.5 |
| 2 | 79, 84 | 163 | 81.5 |
| ⋮ | ⋮ | ⋮ | ⋮ |
| 15 | 92, 77 | 169 | 84.5 |
|  |  |  | 1,195.0 |

   **c.** $\mu_{\bar{x}} = 79.67$, found by $1{,}195/15$.
   $\mu = 79.67$, found by $478/6$.
   They are equal.
   **d.** No. The student is not graded on all available information. He/she is as likely to get a lower grade based on the sample as a higher grade.

**29.** **a.** 10, found by $_5C_2$.
   **b.**

| Number of Shutdowns | Mean | Number of Shutdowns | Mean |
|---|---|---|---|
| 4, 3 | 3.5 | 3, 3 | 3.0 |
| 4, 5 | 4.5 | 3, 2 | 2.5 |
| 4, 3 | 3.5 | 5, 3 | 4.0 |
| 4, 2 | 3.0 | 5, 2 | 3.5 |
| 3, 5 | 4.0 | 3, 2 | 2.5 |

| Sample Mean | Frequency | Probability |
|---|---|---|
| 2.5 | 2 | .20 |
| 3.0 | 2 | .20 |
| 3.5 | 3 | .30 |
| 4.0 | 2 | .20 |
| 4.5 | 1 | .10 |
|  | 10 | 1.00 |

   **c.** $\mu_{\bar{x}} = (3.5 + 4.5 + \cdots + 2.5)/10 = 3.4$
   $\mu = (4 + 3 + 5 + 3 + 2)/5 = 3.4$
   The two means are equal.
   **d.** The population values are relatively uniform in shape. The distribution of sample means tends toward normality.

**31.** **a.** The distribution will be normal.

   **b.** $\sigma_{\bar{x}} = \dfrac{5.5}{\sqrt{25}} = 1.1$

   **c.** $z = \dfrac{36 - 35}{5.5/\sqrt{25}} = 0.91$

   $P = 0.1814$, found by $0.5000 - 0.3186$.

   **d.** $z = \dfrac{34.5 - 35}{5.5/\sqrt{25}} = -0.45$

   $P = 0.6736$, found by $0.5000 + 0.1736$.

   **e.** 0.4922, found by $0.3186 + 0.1736$.

**33.** $z = \dfrac{\$335 - \$350}{\$45/\sqrt{40}} = -2.11$

$P = 0.9826$, found by $0.5000 + 0.4826$.

**35.** $z = \dfrac{25.1 - 24.8}{2.5/\sqrt{60}} = 0.93$

$P = 0.8238$, found by $0.5000 + 0.3238$.

**37.** Between 5,954 and 6,046, found by $6{,}000 \pm 1.96(150/\sqrt{40})$.

**39.** $z = \dfrac{900 - 947}{205/\sqrt{60}} = -1.78$

$P = 0.0375$, found by $0.5000 - 0.4625$.

**41.** **a.** Alaska, Ohio, New Jersey, Texas, Utah, Florida, Vermont, and Connecticut.
   **b.** Maine, Maryland, Michigan, Missouri, Florida, South Carolina, Oklahoma, Wyoming, and Washington.

**c.** Answers will vary depending on random numbers selected.

**43.** Answers will vary.

**45.** Answers will vary.

## CHAPTER 9

**1.** 51.314 and 58.686, found by $55 \pm 2.58(10/\sqrt{49})$.

**3.** **a.** 1.581, found by $\sigma_{\bar{x}} = 5/\sqrt{10}$.
   **b.** The population is normally distributed and the population variance is known.
   **c.** 16.901 and 23.099, found by $20 \pm 3.099$.

**5.** **a.** $20. It is our best estimate of the population mean.
   **b.** $18.60 and $21.40, found by $20 \pm 1.96(\$5/\sqrt{49})$. About 95 percent of the intervals similarly constructed will include the population mean.

**7.** **a.** 8.60 gallons.
   **b.** 7.83 and 9.37, found by $8.60 \pm 2.58(2.30/\sqrt{60})$.
   **c.** If 100 such intervals were determined, the population mean would be included in about 99 intervals.

**9.** **a.** 2.201
   **b.** 1.729
   **c.** 3.499

**11.** **a.** The population mean is unknown, but the best estimate is 20, the sample mean.
   **b.** Use the $t$ distribution as the standard deviation is unknown and the sample size is small. However, assume the population is normally distributed.
   **c.** 2.093
   **d.** Between 19.06 and 20.94, found by $20 \pm 2.093(2/\sqrt{20})$.
   **e.** Neither value is reasonable, because they are not inside the interval.

**13.** Between 95.39 and 101.81, found by $98.6 \pm 1.833(5.54/\sqrt{10})$.

**15.** **a.** 0.8, found by 80/100.
   **b.** 0.04, found by $\sqrt{\dfrac{0.8(1-0.8)}{100}}$.
   **c.** Between 0.72 and 0.88, found by $0.8 \pm 1.96\left(\sqrt{\dfrac{0.8(1-0.8)}{100}}\right)$.
   **d.** We are reasonably sure the population proportion is between 72 and 88 percent.

**17.** **a.** 0.625, found by 250/400.
   **b.** 0.0242, found by $\sqrt{\dfrac{0.625(1-0.625)}{400}}$.
   **c.** Between 0.563 and 0.687, found by $0.625 \pm 2.58\left(\sqrt{\dfrac{0.625(1-0.625)}{400}}\right)$.
   **d.** We are reasonably sure the population proportion is between 56 and 69 percent.

**19.** 33.465 and 36.535, found by $35 \pm 1.96\left(\dfrac{5}{\sqrt{36}}\right)\sqrt{\dfrac{300-36}{300-1}}$.

**21.** 1.689 up to 2.031, found by $1.86 \pm 2.58\left(\dfrac{0.50}{\sqrt{50}}\right)\sqrt{\dfrac{400-50}{400-1}}$.

**23.** 97, found by $n = \left(\dfrac{1.96 \times 10}{2}\right)^2 = 96.04$.

**25.** 196, found by $n = 0.15(0.85)\left(\dfrac{1.96}{0.05}\right)^2 = 195.9216$.

**27.** 554, found by $n = \left(\dfrac{1.96 \times 3}{0.25}\right)^2 = 553.19$.

**29.** **a.** 577, found by $n = 0.60(0.40)\left(\dfrac{1.96}{0.04}\right)^2 = 576.24$.
   **b.** 601, found by $n = 0.50(0.50)\left(\dfrac{1.96}{0.04}\right)^2 = 600.25$.

**31.** 6.14 years to 6.86 years, found by $6.5 \pm 1.96(1.7/\sqrt{85})$.

**33.** **a.** Between $1.508 and 1.530, found by $1.519 \pm 2.68\left(\dfrac{0.03}{\sqrt{50}}\right)$.
   **b.** $1.50 is not reasonable, because it is outside of the confidence interval.

**35.** **a.** Between 7.2 and 8.8, found by $8 \pm 1.68(3/\sqrt{40})$.
   **b.** 9 is not reasonable because it is outside of the confidence interval.

**37.** **a.** 65.61 up to 71.59 hours, found by $68.6 \pm 2.58(8.2/\sqrt{50})$.
   **b.** The value suggested by the NCAA is included in the confidence interval. Therefore, it is reasonable.
   **c.** Changing the confidence interval to 95 would reduce the width of the interval. The value of 2.58 would change to 1.96.

**39.** 61, found by $1.96(16/\sqrt{n}) = 4$.

**41.** Between $13,734 up to $15,028, found by $14,381 \pm 1.711(1,892/\sqrt{25})$. 15,000 is reasonable because it is inside of the confidence interval.

**43.** **a.** $62.583, found by $751/12.
   **b.** Between $60.54 and $64.63, found by $62.583 \pm 1.796(3.94/\sqrt{12})$.
   **c.** $60 is not reasonable, because it is outside of the confidence interval.

**45.** **a.** 89.4667, found by 1,342/15.
   **b.** Between 84.99 and 93.94, found by $89.4667 \pm 2.145(8.08/\sqrt{15})$.
   **c.** Yes, because even the lower limit of the confidence interval is above 80.

**47.** Between 0.648 and 0.752, found by $.7 \pm 2.58$ $\left(\sqrt{\dfrac{0.7(1-0.7)}{500}}\right)\left(\sqrt{\dfrac{20,000-500}{20,000-1}}\right)$. Yes, because even the lower limit of the confidence interval is above 0.500.

**49.** $52.56 and $55.44, found by $54.00 \pm 1.96$ $\dfrac{\$4.50}{\sqrt{35}}\sqrt{\dfrac{(500-35)}{500-1}}$.

**51.** 369, found by $n = 0.60(1-0.60)(1.96/0.05)^2$.

**53.** 97, found by $[(1.96 \times 500)/100]^2$.

**55.** **a.** 708.13, rounded up to 709, found by $0.21(1-0.21)(1.96/0.03)^2$.
   **b.** 1,068, found by $0.50(0.50)(1.96/0.03)^2$.

**57.** Between 0.573 and 0.653, found by $.613 \pm 2.58$ $\left(\sqrt{\dfrac{0.613(1-0.613)}{1,000}}\right)$. Yes, because even the lower limit of the confidence interval is above 0.500.

**59.** Between 12.69 and 14.11, found by $13.4 \pm 1.96(6.8/\sqrt{352})$.

**61.** Answers will vary.

**63.** **a.** For selling price: 212.09 up to 230.11, found by $221.1 \pm (1.96)(47.11/\sqrt{105}) = 221.1 \pm 9.01$.
   **b.** For distance: 13.697 up to 15.561, found by $14.629 \pm (1.96)(4.874/\sqrt{105}) = 14.629 \pm 0.932$.
   **c.** For garage: 0.5867 up to 0.7657, found by $0.6762 \pm (1.96)\sqrt{\dfrac{0.6762(1-0.6762)}{105}} = 0.6762 \pm 0.0895$.

**65.** **a.** $30,833 \pm 1.96\dfrac{\$16,947}{\sqrt{100}} = \$30,833 \pm 3322$, so the limits are $27,511 and $34,155. It is not reasonable that the population mean is $35,000.

**b.** $12.73 \pm 1.96 \dfrac{\$2.792}{\sqrt{100}} = \$12.73 \pm 0.55$, so the limits are 12.18 and 13.28. The population mean could be 13 years.

**c.** $39.11 \pm 1.96 \dfrac{12.57}{\sqrt{100}} = 39.11 \pm 2.46$, so the limits are 36.65 and 41.57. The mean age of the worker could be 40 years.

## CHAPTER 10

**1. a.** Two-tailed.

**b.** Reject $H_0$ and accept $H_1$ when $z$ does not fall in the region from $-1.96$ and $1.96$.

**c.** $-1.2$, found by $z = (49 - 50)/(5/\sqrt{36}) = -1.2$

**d.** Fail to reject $H_0$.

**e.** $p = .2302$, found by $2(.5000 - .3849)$. A 23.02 percent chance of finding a $z$ value this large when $H_0$ is true.

**3. a.** One-tailed.

**b.** Reject $H_0$ and accept $H_1$ when $z > 1.65$.

**c.** $1.2$, found by $z = (21 - 20)/(5/\sqrt{36}) = 1.2$

**d.** Fail to reject $H_0$ at the .05 significance level.

**e.** $p = .1151$, found by $.5000 - .3849$. An 11.51 percent chance of finding a $z$ value this large or larger.

**5. a.** $H_0: \mu = 60{,}000$ $H_1: \mu \neq 60{,}000$

**b.** Reject $H_0$ if $z < -1.96$ or $z > 1.96$.

**c.** $-0.69$, found by:

$$z = \dfrac{59{,}500 - 60{,}000}{(5{,}000/\sqrt{48})} = -0.69$$

**d.** Do not reject $H_0$.

**e.** $p = .4902$, found by $2(.5000 - .2549)$. Crosset's experience is not different from that claimed by the manufacturer. If $H_0$ is true, the probability of finding a value more extreme than this is .4902.

**7. a.** $H_0: \mu \geq 6.8$ $H_1: \mu < 6.8$

**b.** Reject $H_0$ if $z < -1.65$

**c.** $z = \dfrac{6.2 - 6.8}{0.5/\sqrt{36}} = -7.2$

**d.** $H_0$ is rejected.

**e.** $p = 0$. The mean number of DVDs watched is less than 6.8 per month. If $H_0$ is true, there is virtually no chance of getting a statistic this small.

**9. a.** $H_0$ is rejected if $z > 1.65$.

**b.** $1.09$, found by $z = (0.75 - 0.70)/\sqrt{(0.70 \times 0.30)/100}$.

**c.** $H_0$ is not rejected.

**11. a.** $H_0: \pi \leq 0.52$ $H_1: \pi > 0.52$

**b.** $H_0$ is rejected if $z > 2.33$.

**c.** $1.62$, found by $z = (.5667 - .52)/\sqrt{(0.52 \times 0.48)/300}$.

**d.** $H_0$ is not rejected. We cannot conclude that the proportion of men driving on the Ohio Turnpike is larger than 0.52.

**13. a.** $H_0: \pi \geq 0.90$ $H_1: \pi < 0.90$

**b.** $H_0$ is rejected if $z < -1.28$.

**c.** $-2.67$, found by $z = (0.82 - 0.90)/\sqrt{(0.90 \times 0.10)/100}$

**d.** $H_0$ is rejected. Fewer than 90 percent of the customers receive their orders in less than 10 minutes.

**15. a.** Reject $H_0$ when $t > 1.833$.

**b.** $t = \dfrac{12 - 10}{(3/\sqrt{10})} = 2.108$

**c.** Reject $H_0$. The mean is greater than 10.

**17.** $H_0: \mu \leq 40$ $H_1: \mu > 40$
Reject $H_0$ if $t > 1.703$.

$$t = \dfrac{42 - 40}{(2.1/\sqrt{28})} = 5.040$$

Reject $H_0$ and conclude that the mean number of calls is greater than 40 per week.

**19.** $H_0: \mu \leq 22{,}100$ $H_1: \mu > 22{,}100$
Reject $H_0$ if $t > 1.740$.

$$t = \dfrac{23{,}400 - 22{,}100}{(1{,}500/\sqrt{18})} = 3.680$$

Reject $H_0$ and conclude that the mean life of the spark plugs is greater than 22,100 miles.

**21. a.** Reject $H_0$ if $t < -3.747$.

**b.** $\bar{X} = 17$ and $s = \sqrt{\dfrac{50}{5 - 1}} = 3.536$

$$t = \dfrac{17 - 20}{(3.536/\sqrt{5})} = -1.90$$

**c.** Do not reject $H_0$. We cannot conclude the population mean is less than 20.

**d.** Between .05 and .10, about .065.

**23.** $H_0: \mu \leq 4.35$ $H_1: \mu > 4.35$
Reject $H_0$ if $t > 2.821$.

$$t = \dfrac{4.368 - 4.35}{(0.0339/\sqrt{10})} = 1.68$$

Do not reject $H_0$. The additive did not increase the mean weight of the chickens. The $p$-value is between 0.10 and 0.05.

**25.** $H_0: \mu \leq 4.0$ $H_1: \mu > 4.0$
Reject $H_0$ if $t > 1.796$.

$$t = \dfrac{4.50 - 4.0}{(2.68/\sqrt{12})} = 0.65$$

Do not reject $H_0$. The mean number of fish caught has not been shown to be greater than 4.0. The $p$-value is greater than 0.10.

**27.** $1.05$, found by $z = (9{,}922 - 9{,}880)/(400/\sqrt{100})$. Then $0.5000 - 0.3531 = 0.1469$, which is the probability of a Type II error.

**29.** $H_0: \mu \geq 10$ $H_1: \mu < 10$
Reject $H_0$ if $z < -1.65$.

$$z = \dfrac{9.0 - 10.0}{2.8/\sqrt{50}} = -2.53$$

Reject $H_0$. The mean weight loss is less than 10 pounds. $p$-value $= 0.5000 - 0.4943 = 0.0057$

**31.** $H_0: \mu \geq 7.0$ $H_1: \mu < 7.0$
Assuming a 5% significance level, reject $H_0$ if $z < -1.65$.

$$z = \dfrac{6.8 - 7.0}{0.9/\sqrt{50}} = -1.57$$

Do not reject $H_0$. West Virginia students are not sleeping less than 6 hours. $p$-value $= .5000 - .4418 = .0582$.

**33.** $H_0: \mu = \$45{,}000$ $H_1: \mu \neq \$45{,}000$
Reject $H_0$ if $z < 1.65$ or $z > 1.65$.

$$z = \dfrac{45{,}500 - 45{,}000}{\$3{,}000/\sqrt{120}} = 1.83$$

Reject $H_0$. We can conclude that the mean salary is not $45,000. $p$-value $= 0.0672$, found by $2(0.5000 - 0.4664)$.

**35.** $H_0: \mu \leq 1.50$ $H_1: \mu > 1.50$
Reject $H_0$ if $z > 1.65$.

$$z = \dfrac{\$1.52 - \$1.50}{\$0.05/\sqrt{35}} = 2.37$$

Reject $H_0$. The mean price of gasoline is greater than $1.50. The $p$-value $= 0.5000 - 0.4911 = 0.0089$.

**37.** $H_0: \pi \leq 0.60$ $H_1: \pi > 0.60$
$H_0$ is rejected if $z > 2.33$.

$$z = \frac{0.70 - 0.60}{\sqrt{(0.60 \times 0.40)/200}} = 2.89$$

$H_0$ is rejected. Ms. Dennis is correct. More than 60% of the accounts are more than 3 months old.

**39.** $H_0: \pi \leq 0.44 \qquad H_1: \pi > 0.44$
$H_0$ is rejected if $z > 1.65$.

$$z = \frac{0.480 - 0.44}{\sqrt{(0.44 \times 0.56)/1,000}} = 2.55$$

$H_0$ is rejected. We conclude that there has been an increase in the proportion of people wanting to go to Europe.

**41.** $H_0: \pi \leq 0.20 \qquad H_1: \pi > 0.20$
$H_0$ is rejected if $z > 2.33$.

$$z = \frac{(56/200) - 0.20}{\sqrt{(0.20 \times 0.80)/200}} = 2.83$$

$H_0$ is rejected. More than 20 percent of the owners move during a particular year.
$p$-value $= 0.5000 - 0.4977 = 0.0023$.

**43.** $H_0: \mu \leq 42 \qquad H_1: \mu > 42$
Reject $H_0$ if $t > 1.796$.

$$z = \frac{51 - 42}{8/\sqrt{12}} = 3.90$$

Reject $H_0$. The mean time for delivery is more than 42 days. The $p$-value is less than 0.005.

**45.** $H_0: \mu = 3.1 \qquad H_1: \mu \neq 3.1$
Reject $H_0$ if $t < -2.201$ or $t > 2.201$

$$\bar{X} = \frac{41.1}{12} = 3.425$$

$$s = \sqrt{\frac{4.0625}{12 - 1}} = .6077$$

$$t = \frac{3.425 - 3.1}{.6077/\sqrt{12}} = 1.853$$

Do not reject $H_0$. Cannot show a difference between senior citizens and the national average. $p$-value is about 0.09.

**47.** $H_0: \mu \geq 6.5 \qquad H_1: \mu < 6.5$
Reject $H_0$ if $t < -2.718$.
$X = 5.1667 \qquad s = 3.1575$

$$t = \frac{5.1667 - 6.5}{3.1575/\sqrt{12}} = -1.463$$

Do not reject $H_0$. The $p$-value is greater than 0.05.

**49.** $H_0: \mu = 0 \qquad H_1: \mu \neq 0$
Reject $H_0$ if $t < -2.110$ or $t > 2.110$.
$X = -0.2322 \qquad s = 0.3120$

$$t = \frac{-0.2322 - 0}{0.3120/\sqrt{18}} = -3.158$$

Reject $H_0$. The mean gain or loss does not equal 0. The $p$-value is less than 0.01, but greater than 0.001.

**51.** $H_0: \mu \leq 100 \qquad H_1: \mu > 100$
Reject $H_0$ if $t > 1.761$.

$$\bar{X} = \frac{1641}{15} = 109.4$$

$$s = \sqrt{\frac{1,389.6}{15 - 1}} = 9.9628$$

$$t = \frac{109.4 - 100}{9.9628/\sqrt{15}} = 3.654$$

Reject $H_0$. The mean number with the scanner is greater than 100. $p$-value is 0.001.

**53.** $H_0: \pi = 0.50 \qquad H_1: \pi \neq 0.50$
Reject $H_0$ if $z$ is not between $-1.96$ and $1.96$.

$$z = \frac{0.482 - 0.500}{\sqrt{(0.5)(0.5)/1,002}} = -1.14$$

Do not reject the null. The nation may be evenly divided.

**55. a.** $9.00 \pm 1.65(1/\sqrt{36}) = 9.00 \pm 0.275$
So the limits are 8.725 and 9.275.
**b.** $z = (8.725 - 8.900)/(1/\sqrt{36}) = -1.05$
$P(z > -1.05) = 0.5000 + 0.3531 = 0.8531$
**c.** $z = (9.275 - 9.300)/(1/\sqrt{36}) = -0.15$
$P(z < -0.15) = 0.5000 - 0.0596 = 0.4404$

**57.** $50 + 2.33 \dfrac{10}{\sqrt{n}} = 55 - .525 \dfrac{10}{\sqrt{n}} \qquad n = (5.71)^2 = 32.6$
Let $n = 33$.

**59.** $H_0: \mu \geq 8 \qquad H_1: \mu < 8$
Reject $H_0$ if $t < -1.714$.

$$t = \frac{7.5 - 8}{3.2/\sqrt{24}} = -0.77$$

Do not reject the null hypothesis. The time is not less.

**61.** Answers will vary.

**63. a.** $H_0: \mu = 80.0 \qquad H_1: \mu \neq 80$
Reject $H_0$ if $t < -2.045$ or $t > 2.045$.

$$t = \frac{83.5495 - 80.0}{29.1496/\sqrt{30}} = 0.667$$

Do not reject $H_0$. The mean could be 80.0.
**b.** $H_0: \mu \leq 2,000 \qquad H_1: \mu > 2,000$
Reject $H_0$ if $t > 1.699$.

$$t = \frac{2,264.81 - 2,000}{753.35/\sqrt{30}} = 1.925$$

Reject $H_0$. The mean attendance is greater than 2,000.

**65. a.** $H_0: \mu \leq 4.0 \qquad H_1: \mu > 4.0$
Reject $H_0$ if $z > 1.65$

$$z = \frac{8.12 - 4.0}{16.43/\sqrt{46}} = 1.70$$

Reject $H_0$. The mean number of cell phones is greater than 4.0. $p$-value $= .5000 - .4554 = .0446$
**b.** $H_0: \mu \geq 50 \qquad H_1: \mu < 50$
Reject $H_0$ if $z < -1.65$. Note there is one missing value, so $n = 45$.

$$z = \frac{36.0 - 50.0}{105.5/\sqrt{45}} = -0.89$$

Do not reject $H_0$. The mean size of the labor force is not less than 50. The $p$-value is $5000 - .3159 = .1841$.

## CHAPTER 11

**1. a.** Two-tailed test.
**b.** Reject $H_0$ if $z < -2.05$ or $z > 2.05$.
**c.** $z = \dfrac{102 - 99}{\sqrt{\dfrac{5^2}{40} + \dfrac{6^2}{50}}} = 2.59$
**d.** Reject $H_0$ and accept $H_1$.
**e.** $p$-value $= .0096$, found by $2(.5000 - .4952)$.

**3. Step 1** $H_0: \mu_1 \geq \mu_2 \qquad H_1: \mu_1 < \mu_2$
**Step 2** The .05 significance level was chosen.
**Step 3** Reject $H_0$ and accept $H_1$ if $z < -1.65$.

**Step 4** $-0.94$, found by:

$$z = \frac{7.6 - 8.1}{\sqrt{\frac{(2.3)^2}{40} + \frac{(2.9)^2}{55}}} = -0.94$$

**Step 5** Fail to reject $H_0$. Babies using the Gibbs brand did not gain less weight. $p$-value $= .1736$, found by $.5000 - .3264$.

5. Two-tailed test, because we are trying to show that a difference exists between the two means. Reject $H_0$ if $z < -2.58$ or $z > 2.58$.

$$z = \frac{31.4 - 34.9}{\sqrt{\frac{(5.1)^2}{32} + \frac{(6.7)^2}{49}}} = -2.66$$

Reject $H_0$ at the .01 level. There is a difference in the mean turnover rate. $p$-value $= 2(.5000 - .4961) = .0078$

7. **a.** $H_0$ is rejected if $z > 1.65$.
   **b.** $0.64$, found by $p_c = \frac{70 + 90}{100 + 150}$.
   **c.** $1.61$, found by

$$z = \frac{0.70 - 0.60}{\sqrt{[(0.64 \times 0.36)/100] + [(0.64 \times 0.36)/150]}}.$$

   **d.** $H_0$ is not rejected.

9. **a.** $H_0: \pi_1 = \pi_2$    $H_1: \pi_1 \neq \pi_2$
   **b.** $H_0$ is rejected if $z < -1.96$ or $z > 1.96$.
   **c.** $p_c = \frac{24 + 40}{400 + 400} = 0.08$
   **d.** $-2.09$, found by

$$z = \frac{0.06 - 0.10}{\sqrt{[(0.08 \times 0.92)/400] + [(0.08 \times 0.92)/400]}}.$$

   **e.** $H_0$ is rejected. The proportion infested is not the same in the two fields.

11. $H_0: \pi_d \leq \pi_r$    $H_1: \pi_d > \pi_r$
    $H_0$ is rejected if $z > 2.05$.

$$p_c = \frac{168 + 200}{800 + 1{,}000} = 0.2044$$

$$z = \frac{0.21 - 0.20}{\sqrt{\frac{(0.2044)(0.7956)}{800} + \frac{(0.2044)(0.7956)}{1{,}000}}} = 0.52$$

$H_0$ is not rejected. There is no difference in the proportion of Democrats and Republicans who favor lowering the standards.

13. **a.** Reject $H_0$ if $t > 2.120$ or $t < -2.120$.
    $df = 10 + 8 - 2 = 16$
   **b.** $s_p^2 = \frac{(10 - 1)(4)^2 + (8 - 1)(5)^2}{10 + 8 - 2} = 19.9375$
   **c.** $t = \frac{23 - 26}{\sqrt{19.9375\left(\frac{1}{10} + \frac{1}{8}\right)}} = -1.416$
   **d.** Do not reject $H_0$.
   **e.** $p$-value is greater than 0.10 and less than 0.20.

15. $H_0: \mu_f \leq \mu_m$    $H_1: \mu_f > \mu_m$
    $df = 9 + 7 - 2 = 14$
    Reject $H_0$ if $t > 2.624$.

$$s_p^2 = \frac{(7 - 1)(6.88)^2 + (9 - 1)(9.49)^2}{7 + 9 - 2} = 71.749$$

$$t = \frac{79 - 78}{\sqrt{71.749\left(\frac{1}{7} + \frac{1}{9}\right)}} = 0.234$$

Do not reject $H_0$. There is no difference in the mean grades.

17. $H_0: \mu_s \leq \mu_a$    $H_1: \mu_s > \mu_a$
    $df = 6 + 7 - 2 = 11$
    Reject $H_0$ if $t > 1.363$.

$$s_p^2 = \frac{(6 - 1)(12.2)^2 + (7 - 1)(15.8)^2}{6 + 7 - 2} = 203.82$$

$$t = \frac{142.5 - 130.3}{\sqrt{203.82\left(\frac{1}{6} + \frac{1}{7}\right)}} = 1.536$$

Reject $H_0$. The mean daily expenses are greater for the sales staff. The $p$-value is between 0.05 and 0.10.

19. **a.** Reject $H_0$ if $t > 2.353$.
   **b.** $\bar{d} = \frac{12}{4} = 3.00$    $s_d = \sqrt{\frac{2}{3}} = 0.816$
   **c.** $t = \frac{3.00}{0.816/\sqrt{4}} = 7.35$
   **d.** Reject $H_0$. There are more defective parts produced on the day shift.
   **e.** $p$-value is less than 0.005, but greater than 0.0005.

21. $H_0: \mu_d \leq 0$    $H_d: \mu_d > 0$
    $\bar{d} = 25.917$
    $s_d = 40.791$
    Reject $H_0$ if $t > 1.796$

$$t = \frac{25.917}{40.791/\sqrt{12}} = 2.20$$

Reject $H_0$. The incentive plan resulted in an increase in daily income. The $p$-value is about .025.

23. $H_0: \mu_M = \mu_W$    $H_1: \mu_M \neq \mu_W$
    Reject $H_0$ if $z < -2.33$ or $z > 2.33$.

$$z = \frac{24.51 - 22.69}{\sqrt{\frac{(4.48)^2}{35} + \frac{(3.86)^2}{40}}} = 1.87$$

Do not reject $H_0$. There is no difference in the number of times men and women buy take-out dinner in a month. $p$-value $= 2(.5000 - .4693) = .0614$.

25. $H_0: \mu_1 = \mu_2$    $H_1: \mu_1 \neq \mu_2$
    Reject $H_0$ if $z < -1.96$ or $z > 1.96$.

$$z = \frac{4.77 - 5.02}{\sqrt{\frac{(1.05)^2}{40} + \frac{(1.23)^2}{50}}} = -1.04$$

$H_0$ is not rejected. There is no difference in the mean number of calls. $p$-value $= 2(0.5000 - 0.3508) = 0.2984$.

27. $H_0: \mu_B \leq \mu_A$    $H_1: \mu_B > \mu_A$
    Reject $H_0$ if $z > 1.65$.

$$z = \frac{\$61{,}000 - \$57{,}000}{\sqrt{\frac{(\$7{,}100)^2}{30} + \frac{(\$9{,}200)^2}{40}}} = \frac{\$4000.00}{\$1948.42} = 2.05$$

Reject $H_0$. The mean income is larger for Plan B. The $p$-value $= .5000 - .4798 = .0202$. The skewness does not matter because of the sample sizes.

29. $H_0: \pi_1 \leq \pi_2$    $H_1: \pi_1 > \pi_2$
    Reject $H_0$ if $z > 1.65$.

$$p_c = \frac{180 + 261}{200 + 300} = 0.882$$

$$z = \frac{0.90 - 0.87}{\sqrt{\frac{0.882(0.118)}{200} + \frac{0.882(0.118)}{300}}} = 1.019$$

$H_0$ is not rejected. There is no difference in the proportions that found relief with the new and the old drugs.

**31.** $H_0: \pi_1 \leq \pi_2 \qquad H_1: \pi_1 > \pi_2$
If $z > 2.33$, reject $H_0$.

$$p_c = \frac{990 + 970}{1,500 + 1,600} = 0.63$$

$$z = \frac{.6600 - .60625}{\sqrt{\frac{.63(.37)}{1,500} + \frac{.63(.37)}{1,600}}} = 3.10$$

Reject the null hypothesis. We can conclude the proportion of men who believe the division is fair is greater.

**33.** $H_0: \mu_n = \mu_s \qquad H_1: \mu_n \neq \mu_s$
Reject $H_0$ if $t < -2.086$ or $t > 2.086$.

$$s_p^2 = \frac{(10 - 1)(10.5)^2 + (12 - 1)(14.25)^2}{10 + 12 - 2} = 161.2969$$

$$t = \frac{83.55 - 78.8}{\sqrt{161.2969\left(\frac{1}{10} + \frac{1}{12}\right)}} = 0.874$$

Do not reject $H_0$. There is no difference in the mean number of hamburgers sold at the two locations.

**35.** $H_0: \mu_1 = \mu_2 \qquad H_1: \mu_1 \neq \mu_2$
Reject $H_0$ if $t > 2.819$ or $t < -2.819$.

$$s_p^2 = \frac{(10 - 1)(2.33)^2 + (14 - 1)(2.55)^2}{10 + 14 - 2} = 6.06$$

$$t = \frac{15.87 - 18.29}{\sqrt{6.06\left(\frac{1}{10} + \frac{1}{14}\right)}} = -2.374$$

Do not reject $H_0$. There is no difference in the mean amount purchased.

**37.** $H_0: \mu_1 \leq \mu_2 \qquad H_1: \mu_1 > \mu_2$
Reject $H_0$ if $t > 2.567$.

$$s_p^2 = \frac{(8 - 1)(2.2638)^2 + (11 - 1)(2.4606)^2}{8 + 11 - 2} = 5.672$$

$$t = \frac{10.375 - 5.636}{\sqrt{5.672\left(\frac{1}{8} + \frac{1}{11}\right)}} = 4.28$$

Reject $H_0$. The mean number of transactions by the young adults is more than for the senior citizens.

**39.** $H_0: \mu_1 \leq \mu_2 \qquad H_1: \mu_1 > \mu_2$
Reject $H_0$ if $t > 2.650$.
$\bar{X}_1 = 125.125 \qquad s_1 = 15.094$
$\bar{X}_2 = 117.714 \qquad s_2 = 19.914$

$$s_p^2 = \frac{(8 - 1)(15.094)^2 + (7 - 1)(19.914)^2}{8 + 7 - 2} = 305.708$$

$$t = \frac{125.125 - 117.714}{\sqrt{305.708\left(\frac{1}{8} + \frac{1}{7}\right)}} = 0.819$$

$H_0$ is not rejected. There is no difference in the mean number sold at the regular price and the mean number sold at reduced price.

**41.** $H_0: \mu_d \leq 0 \qquad H_1: \mu_d > 0$
Reject $H_0$ if $t > 1.895$.
$\bar{d} = 1.75 \qquad s_d = 2.9155$

$$t = \frac{1.75}{2.9155/\sqrt{8}} = 1.698$$

Do not reject $H_0$. There is no difference in the mean number of absences. The $p$-value is greater than 0.05 but less than .10.

**43.** $H_0: \mu_1 = \mu_2 \qquad H_1: \mu_1 \neq \mu_2$
If $z$ is not between $-1.96$ and $1.96$, reject $H_0$.

$$z = \frac{150 - 180}{\sqrt{\frac{(40)^2}{75} + \frac{(30)^2}{120}}} = -5.59$$

Reject the null hypothesis. The population means are different.

**45.** $H_0: \mu_d \leq 0 \qquad H_1: \mu_d > 0$
Reject $H_0$ if $t > 1.895$.
$\bar{d} = 3.11 \qquad s_d = 2.91$

$$t = \frac{3.11}{2.91/\sqrt{8}} = 3.02$$

Reject $H_0$. The mean is lower.

**47.** $H_0: \mu_0 = \mu_R, H_1: \mu_0 = \mu_R$
$df = 25 + 28 - 2 = 51$
Reject $H_0$ if $t - 2.008$ or $t > 2.008$
$\bar{X}_0 = 86.24, s_0 = 23.43$
$\bar{X}_R = 92.04, s_R = 24.12$

$$s_p^2 = \frac{(25 - 1)(23.43)^2 + (28 - 1)(24.12)^2}{25 + 28 - 2} = 566.335$$

$$t = \frac{86.24 - 92.04}{\sqrt{566.335\left(\frac{1}{25} + \frac{1}{28}\right)}} = -0.886$$

Do not reject $H_0$. There is no difference in the mean number of cars in the two lots.

**49.** Answers will vary.

**51. a.** $\mu_1 = $ with pool $\qquad \mu_2 = $ without pool
$H_0: \mu_1 = \mu_2 \qquad H_1: \mu_1 \neq \mu_2$
Reject $H_0$ if $t > 2.000$ or $t < -2.000$.
$\bar{X}_1 = 202.8 \qquad s_1 = 33.7 \qquad n_1 = 38$
$\bar{X}_2 = 231.5 \qquad s_2 = 50.46 \qquad n_2 = 67$

$$s_p^2 = \frac{(38 - 1)(33.7)^2 + (67 - 1)(50.46)^2}{38 + 67 - 2} = 2,041.05$$

$$t = \frac{202.8 - 231.5}{\sqrt{2,041.05\left(\frac{1}{38} + \frac{1}{67}\right)}} = -3.12$$

Reject $H_0$. There is a difference in mean selling price for homes with and without a pool.

**b.** $\mu_1 = $ without garage $\qquad \mu_2 = $ with garage
$H_0: \mu_1 = \mu_2 \qquad H_1: \mu_1 \neq \mu_2$
Reject $H_0$ if $t > 2.000$ or $t < -2.000$.
$\alpha = 0.05 \qquad df = 34 + 71 - 2 = 103$
$\bar{X}_1 = 185.45 \qquad s_1 = 28.00$
$\bar{X}_2 = 238.18 \qquad s_2 = 44.88$

$$s_p^2 = \frac{(34 - 1)(28.00)^2 + (71 - 1)(44.88)^2}{103} = 1,620.07$$

$$t = \frac{185.45 - 238.18}{\sqrt{1,620.07\left(\frac{1}{34} + \frac{1}{71}\right)}} = -6.28$$

Reject $H_0$. There is a difference in mean selling price for homes with and without a garage.

**c.** $H_0: \mu_1 = \mu_2 \qquad H_1: \mu_1 \neq \mu_2$
Reject $H_0$ if $t > 2.036$ or $t < -2.036$.
$\bar{X}_1 = 196.91 \qquad s_1 = 35.78 \qquad n_1 = 15$
$\bar{X}_2 = 227.45 \qquad s_2 = 44.19 \qquad n_2 = 20$

$$s_p^2 = \frac{(15-1)(35.78)^2 + (20-1)(44.19)^2}{15+20-2} = 1{,}667.43$$

$$t = \frac{196.91 - 227.45}{\sqrt{1{,}667.43\left(\frac{1}{15} + \frac{1}{20}\right)}} = -2.19$$

Reject $H_0$. There is a difference in mean selling price for homes in Township 1 and Township 2.

**d.** $H_0: \pi_1 = \pi_2$     $H_1: \pi_1 \neq \pi_2$
If $z$ is not between $-1.96$ and $1.96$, reject $H_0$.

$$p_c = \frac{24+43}{52+53} = 0.64$$

$$z = \frac{0.462 - 0.811}{\sqrt{0.64 \times 0.36/52 + 0.64 \times 0.36/53}} = -3.73$$

Reject the null hypothesis. There is a difference.

**53. a.** $H_0: \mu_s = \mu_{ns}$     $H_1: \mu_s \neq \mu_{ns}$
Reject $H_0$ if $z < -1.96$ or $z > 1.96$

$$z = \frac{\$31{,}798 - \$28{,}876}{\sqrt{\frac{(17{,}403)^2}{67} + \frac{(16{,}062)^2}{33}}} = 0.83$$

Do not reject $H_0$. No difference in the mean wages.

**b.** $H_0: \mu_w = \mu_n$     $H_1: \mu_w \neq \mu_{nw}$
Note, because one sample is less than 30, use $t$ and pool variances. Also answer reported in $000.

$$s_p^2 = \frac{(90-1)(17.358)^2 + (10-1)(11.536)^2}{90+10-2} = 285.85$$

$$t = \frac{31.517 - 24.678}{\sqrt{285.85\left(\frac{1}{90} + \frac{1}{10}\right)}} = 1.214$$

Reject $H_0$ if $t < -1.99$ or $t > 1.99$.
Do not reject $H_0$. No difference in the mean wages

**c.** $H_0: \mu_h = \mu_{nh}$     $H_1: \mu_h \neq \mu_{nh}$
Reject $H_0$ if $t < -1.99$ or $t > 1.99$.
Because one sample is less than 30, use $t$. Answer reported in $000.

$$s_p^2 = \frac{(94-1)(16.413)^2 + (6-1)(25.843)^2}{94+6-2} = 289.72$$

$$t = \frac{30.674 - 33.337}{\sqrt{289.72\left(\frac{1}{96} + \frac{1}{6}\right)}} = -0.37$$

Do not reject $H_0$. No difference in the mean wages

**d.** $H_0: \mu_m = \mu_f$     $H_1: \mu_m \neq \mu_f$
Reject $H_0$ if $z < -1.96$ or $z > 1.96$

$$z = \frac{\$36{,}493 - \$24{,}452}{\sqrt{\frac{(18{,}448)^2}{53} + \frac{(12{,}446)^2}{47}}} = 3.86$$

Reject $H_0$. There is a difference in the mean wages for men and women.

**e.** $H_0: \mu_m = \mu_{nm}$     $H_1: \mu_m \neq \mu_{nm}$
Reject $H_0$ if $z < -1.96$ or $z > 1.96$

$$z = \frac{\$24{,}864 - \$33{,}773}{\sqrt{\frac{(13{,}055)^2}{33} + \frac{(17{,}933)^2}{67}}} = -2.822$$

Reject $H_0$. There is a difference in the mean wages of the two groups.

## CHAPTER 12

**1.** 9.01, from Appendix G.

**3.** Reject $H_0$ if $F > 10.5$, where degrees of freedom in the numerator are 7 and 5 in the denominator. Computed $F = 2.04$, found by:

$$F = \frac{s_1^2}{s_2^2} = \frac{(10)^2}{(7)^2} = 2.04$$

Do not reject $H_0$. There is no difference in the variations of the two populations.

**5.** $H_0: \sigma_1^2 = \sigma_2^2$     $H_1: \sigma_1^2 \neq \sigma_2^2$
Reject $H_0$ where $F > 3.10$. (3.10 is about halfway between 3.14 and 3.07.) Computed $F = 1.44$, found by:

$$F = \frac{(12)^2}{(10)^2} = 1.44$$

Do not reject $H_0$. There is no difference in the variations of the two populations.

**7. a.** $H_0: \mu_1 = \mu_2 = \mu_3$; $H_1$: Treatment means are not all the same.
**b.** Reject $H_0$ if $F > 4.26$.

**c & d.**

| Source | SS | df | MS | F |
|---|---|---|---|---|
| Treatment | 62.17 | 2 | 31.08 | 21.94 |
| Error | 12.75 | 9 | 1.42 | |
| Total | 74.92 | 11 | | |

**e.** Reject $H_0$. The treatment means are not all the same.

**9.** $H_0: \mu_1 = \mu_2 = \mu_3$; $H_1$: Treatment means are not all the same.
Reject $H_0$ if $F > 4.26$.

| Source | SS | df | MS | F |
|---|---|---|---|---|
| Treatment | 276.50 | 2 | 138.25 | 14.18 |
| Error | 87.75 | 9 | 9.75 | |

Reject $H_0$. The treatment means are not all the same.

**11. a.** $H_0: \mu_1 = \mu_2 = \mu_3$; $H_1$: Not all means are the same.
**b.** Reject $H_0$ if $F > 4.26$.
**c.** SST = 107.20, SSE = 9.47, SS total = 116.67.

**d.**

| Source | SS | df | MS | F |
|---|---|---|---|---|
| Treatment | 107.20 | 2 | 53.600 | 50.96 |
| Error | 9.47 | 9 | 1.052 | |
| Total | 116.67 | 11 | | |

**e.** Since $50.96 > 4.26$, $H_0$ is rejected. At least one of the means differs.
**f.** $(\bar{X}_1 - \bar{X}_2) \pm t \sqrt{MSE(1/n_1 + 1/n_2)}$
= $(9.667 - 2.20) \pm 2.262 \sqrt{1.052(1/3 + 1/5)}$
= $7.467 \pm 1.69$
= $[5.777, 9.157]$
Yes, we can conclude that treatments 1 and 2 have different means.

**13.** $H_0: \mu_1 = \mu_2 = \mu_3 = \mu_4$; $H_1$: Not all means are equal.
$H_0$ is rejected if $F > 3.71$.

| Source | SS | df | MS | F |
|---|---|---|---|---|
| Treatment | 32.33 | 3 | 10.77 | 2.36 |
| Error | 45.67 | 10 | 4.567 | |
| Total | 78.00 | 13 | | |

Because 2.36 is less than 3.71, $H_0$ is not rejected. There is no difference in the mean number of weeks.

**15. a.** $H_0: \mu_1 = \mu_2$; $H_1$: Not all treatment means are equal.
**b.** Reject $H_0$ if $F > 18.5$.
**c.** $H_0: \mu_1 = \mu_2 = \mu_3$; $H_1$: Not all block means are equal.
$H_0$ is rejected if $F > 19.0$.
**d.** SS total = $(46.0 - 36.5)^2 + \cdots + (35 - 35.5)^2 = 289.5$
SSE[1] = $(46 - 42.3333)^2 + \cdots + (35 - 30.6667)^2$
= $85.3333$

SST = 289.5 − 85.3333 = 204.1667
SSB = $2(38.5 − 36.5)^2 + 2(31.5 − 36.5)^2 +$
$2(39.5 − 36.5)^2 = 8 + 50 + 18 = 76$
SSE = 289.50 − 204.1667 − 76 = 9.3333

**e.**

| Source | SS | df | MS | F |
|---|---|---|---|---|
| Treatment | 204.167 | 1 | 204.167 | 43.75 |
| Blocks | 76.000 | 2 | 38.000 | 8.14 |
| Error | 9.333 | 2 | 4.667 | |
| Total | 289.5000 | 5 | | |

**f.** 43.75 > 18.5, so reject $H_0$. There is a difference in the treatments. 8.14 < 19.0, so do not reject $H_0$ for blocks. There is no difference among blocks.

**17.** For treatment:
$H_0: \mu_1 = \mu_2 = \mu_3$
$H_1$: Not all means equal
Reject if $F > 4.46$

For blocks:
$H_0: \mu_1 = \mu_2 = \mu_3 = \mu_4 = \mu_5$
$H_1$: Not all means equal
Reject if $F > 3.84$

| Source | SS | df | MS | F |
|---|---|---|---|---|
| Treatment | 62.53 | 2 | 31.2650 | 5.75 |
| Blocks | 33.73 | 4 | 8.4325 | 1.55 |
| Error | 43.47 | 8 | 5.4338 | |
| Total | 139.73 | | | |

There is a difference in shifts, but not by employee.

**19.** $H_0: \sigma_1^2 \leq \sigma_2^2; H_1: \sigma_1^2 > \sigma_2^2. df_1 = 21 − 1 = 20;$
$df_2 = 18 − 1 = 17. H_0$ is rejected if $F > 3.16$.

$$F = \frac{(45,600)^2}{(21,330)^2} = 4.57$$

Reject $H_0$. There is more variation in the selling price of oceanfront homes.

**21.** Sharkey: $n = 7$ $s_s = 14.79$
White: $n = 8$ $s_w = 22.95$

$H_0: \sigma_w^2 \leq \sigma_s^2; H_1: \sigma_w^2 > \sigma_s^2. df_s = 7 − 1 = 6;$
$df_w = 8 − 1 = 7$. Reject $H_0$ if $F > 8.26$.

$$F = \frac{(22.95)^2}{(14.79)^2} = 2.41$$

Cannot reject $H_0$. There is no difference in the variation of the monthly sales.

**23. a.** $H_0: \mu_1 = \mu_2 = \mu_3 = \mu_4$
$H_1$: Treatment means are not all equal.
**b.** $\alpha = .05$ Reject $H_0$ if $F > 3.10$.
**c.**

| Source | SS | df | MS | F |
|---|---|---|---|---|
| Treatment | 50 | 4 − 1 = 3 | 50/3 | 1.67 |
| Error | 200 | 24 − 4 = 20 | 10 | |
| Total | 250 | 24 − 1 = 23 | | |

**d.** Do not reject $H_0$.

**25.** $H_0: \mu_1 = \mu_2 = \mu_3; H_1$: Not all treatment means are equal.
$H_0$ is rejected if $F > 3.89$.

| Source | SS | df | MS | F |
|---|---|---|---|---|
| Treatment | 63.33 | 2 | 31.667 | 13.38 |
| Error | 28.40 | 12 | 2.367 | |
| Total | 91.73 | 14 | | |

$H_0$ is rejected. There is a difference in the treatment means.

**27.** $H_0: \mu_1 = \mu_2 = \mu_3 = \mu_4; H_1$: Not all means are equal.
$H_0$ is rejected if $F > 3.10$

| Source | SS | df | MS | F |
|---|---|---|---|---|
| Factor | 87.79 | 3 | 29.26 | 9.12 |
| Error | 64.17 | 20 | 3.21 | |
| Total | 151.96 | 23 | | |

Because computed $F$ of 9.12 > 3.10, the null hypothesis of no difference is rejected at the .05 level.

**29. a.** $H_0: \mu_1 = \mu_2; H_1: \mu_1 \neq \mu_2$. Critical value of $F = 4.75$.

| Source | SS | df | MS | F |
|---|---|---|---|---|
| Treatment | 219.43 | 1 | 219.43 | 23.10 |
| Error | 114.00 | 12 | 9.5 | |
| Total | 333.43 | 13 | | |

**b.** $t = \dfrac{19 − 27}{\sqrt{9.5\left(\dfrac{1}{6} + \dfrac{1}{8}\right)}} = −4.806$

Then $t^2 = F$. That is $(−4.806)^2 = 23.10$.
**c.** $H_0$ is rejected. There is a difference in the mean scores.

**31.** The null hypothesis is rejected because the $F$ statistic (8.26) is greater than the critical value (5.61) at the .01 significance level. The $p$-value (.0019) is also less than the significance level. The mean gasoline mileages are not the same.

**33. a.** The null hypothesis of equal population means is not rejected because the $F$ statistic (3.41) is less than the critical value (5.49). The $p$-value (.0478) is also greater than the significance level (0.01). The mean amounts of money withdrawn are not different.

**b.** $(82.5 − 38.2) \pm 1.703\sqrt{1,477.633\left(\dfrac{1}{10} + \dfrac{1}{10}\right)}$

This reduces to $44.3 \pm 29.3$. So there is a difference between 15.0 and 73.6.

**35.** For color, the critical value of $F$ is 4.76; for size, it is 5.14.

| Source | SS | df | MS | F |
|---|---|---|---|---|
| Treatment | 25.0 | 3 | 8.3333 | 5.88 |
| Blocks | 21.5 | 2 | 10.75 | 7.59 |
| Error | 8.5 | 6 | 1.4167 | |
| Total | 55.0 | 11 | | |

$H_0$s for both treatment and blocks (color and size) are rejected. At least one mean differs for color and at least one mean differs for size.

**37. a.** Critical value of $F$ is 3.49. Computed $F$ is .668. Do not reject $H_0$.
**b.** Critical value of $F$ is 3.26. Computed $F$ value is 100.204. Reject $H_0$ for block means.

**39.** For gasoline:
$H_0: \mu_1 = \mu_2 = \mu_3; H_1$: Mean mileage is not the same.
Reject $H_0$ if $F > 3.89$.
For automobile:
$H_0: \mu_1 = \mu_2 = \cdots = \mu_7; H_1$: Mean mileage is not the same.
Reject $H_0$ if $F > 3.00$.

| ANOVA Table | | | | |
|---|---|---|---|---|
| Source | SS | df | MS | F |
| Gasoline | 44.095 | 2 | 22.048 | 26.71 |
| Autos | 77.238 | 6 | 12.873 | 15.60 |
| Error | 9.905 | 12 | 0.825 | |
| Total | | 20 | | |

There is a difference in both autos and gasoline.

**41. a.** $H_0: \mu_1 = \mu_2 = \mu_3 = \mu_4 = \mu_5 = \mu_6$; $H_1$: The treatment means are not equal. Reject $H_0$ if $F > 2.37$.

| Source | SS | df | MS | F |
|---|---|---|---|---|
| Treatment | 0.03478 | 5 | 0.00696 | 3.86 |
| Error | 0.10439 | 58 | 0.0018 | |
| Total | 0.13917 | 63 | | |

$H_0$ is rejected. There is a difference in the mean weight of the colors.

**43.** Answers will vary.

**45. a.** $H_0: \sigma_{np}^2 = \sigma_p^2$    $H_1: \sigma_{np}^2 \neq \sigma_p^2$. Reject $H_0$ if $F > 2.05$ (estimated).
$df_1 = 67 - 1 = 66$; $df_2 = 38 - 1 = 37$.

$$F = \frac{(50.57)^2}{(33.71)^2} = 2.25$$

Reject $H_0$. There is a difference in the variance of the two selling prices.

**b.** $H_0: \sigma_g^2 = \sigma_{ng}^2$; $H_1: \sigma_g^2 \neq \sigma_{ng}^2$. Reject $H_0$ if $F > 2.21$ (estimated).

$$F = \frac{(44.88)^2}{(28.00)^2} = 2.57$$

Reject $H_0$. There is a difference in the variance of the two selling prices.

**c.** $H_0: \mu_1 = \mu_2 = \mu_3 = \mu_4 = \mu_5$; $H_1$: Not all treatment means are equal. Reject $H_0$ if $F > 2.46$.

| Source | SS | df | MS | F |
|---|---|---|---|---|
| Township | 13,263 | 4 | 3,316 | 1.52 |
| Error | 217,505 | 100 | 2,175 | |
| Total | 230,768 | 104 | | |

Do not reject $H_0$. There is no difference in the mean selling prices in the five townships.

**47. a.** $H_0: \mu_1 = \mu_2 = \mu_3$; $H_1$: Treatment means are not equal. Reject $H_0$ if $F > 3.09$. The computed value of $F$ is 1.30. We conclude there is no difference among the industries.

**b.** $H_0: \mu_1 = \mu_2 = \mu_3 = \mu_4 = \mu_5$; $H_1$: Treatment means are not equal.
Reject $H_0$ if $F > 2.31$. The computed value of $F$ is 4.85. The treatment means differ. The MINITAB output follows.

```
Level    N     Mean    StDev
0       22    28921    14517
1       13    40074    22733
2        6    27228    16101
3       21    27619     9821
4       21    21510     6946
5       17    43002    22062

Pooled St Dev = 15507

Individual 95% CIs for Mean
Based on Pooled StDev
------+---------+---------+---------+
        (------*-----)
                    (------*-----)
    (---------*--------)
      (------*-----)
  (------*-----)
                        (------*-----)
------+---------+---------+---------+
   20000     30000     40000     50000
```

From this graph the following means differ: 0 and 5, 1 and 4, 3 and 5, and 4 and 5.

**c.** $H_0: \sigma_u^2 = \sigma_{nu}^2$; $H_1: \sigma_u^2 \neq \sigma_{nu}^2$    Reject $H_0$ if $F > 1.99$. Computed $F$ is 1.36, found by $(17,413)^2/(14,940)^2$. There is no difference in the variation of union and nonunion members.

## CHAPTER 13

**1.** $\Sigma(X - \bar{X})(Y - \bar{Y}) = 10.6$, $s_x = 2.7019$, $s_y = 1.3038$

$$r = \frac{10.6}{(5 - 1)(2.7019)(1.3038)} = 0.7522$$

The 0.7522 coefficient indicates a rather strong positive correlation between $X$ and $Y$. The coefficient of determination is 0.5658, found by $(0.7522)^2$. More than 56 percent of the variation in $Y$ is accounted for by $X$.

**3. a.** Sales.
**b.**

**c.** $\Sigma(X - \bar{X})(Y - \bar{Y}) = 36$, $n = 5$, $s_x = 1.5811$, $s_y = 6.1237$

$$r = \frac{36}{(5 - 1)(1.5811)(6.1237)} = 0.9295$$

**d.** The coefficient of determination is 0.8640, found by $(0.9295)^2$.
**e.** There is a strong positive association between the variables. About 86 percent of the variation in sales is explained by the number of airings.

**5. a.** Police is the independent variable, and crime is the dependent variable.
**b.**

**c.** $n = 8$, $\Sigma(X - \bar{X})(Y - \bar{Y}) = -231.75$, $s_x = 5.8736$, $s_y = 6.4462$

$$r = \frac{-231.75}{(8 - 1)(5.8736)(6.4462)} = -0.8744$$

**d.** 0.7646, found by $(-0.8744)^2$
**e.** Strong inverse relationship. As the number of police increases, the crime decreases.

**7.** Reject $H_0$ if $t > 1.812$.

$$t = \frac{.32\sqrt{12 - 2}}{\sqrt{1 - (.32)^2}} = 1.07$$

Do not reject $H_0$.

**9.** $H_0$: $\rho \le 0$; $H_1$: $\rho > 0$. Reject $H_0$ if $t > 2.552$. $df = 18$.

$$t = \frac{.78\sqrt{20-2}}{\sqrt{1-(.78)^2}} = 5.288$$

Reject $H_0$. There is a positive correlation between gallons sold and the pump price.

**11. a.** $Y' = 3.7778 + 0.3630X$

$$b = 0.7522\left(\frac{1.3038}{2.7019}\right) = 0.3630$$

$$a = 5.8 - 0.3630(5.6) = 3.7671$$

**b.** 6.3081, found by $Y' = 3.7671 + 0.3630(7)$

**13. a.** $\Sigma(X - \bar{X})(Y - \bar{Y}) = 44.6$, $s_x = 2.726$, $s_y = 2.011$

$$r = \frac{44.6}{(10-1)(2.726)(2.011)} = .904$$

$$b = .904\left(\frac{2.011}{2.726}\right) = 0.667$$

$$a = 7.4 - .677(9.1) = 1.333$$

**b.** $Y' = 1.333 + .667(6) = 5.335$

**15. a.**

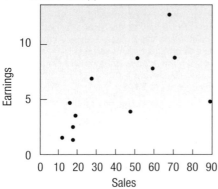

**b.** $\Sigma(X - \bar{X})(Y - \bar{Y}) = 629.64$, $s_x = 26.17$, $s_y = 3.248$

$$r = \frac{629.64}{(12-1)(26.17)(3.248)} = .6734$$

**c.** $r^2 = (0.673)^2 = 0.4529$

**d.** A strong positive association between the variables. About 45 percent of the variation in earnings is accounted for by sales.

**e.** $b = .6734\left(\frac{3.248}{26.170}\right) = 0.0836$

$$a = \frac{64.1}{12} - 0.0836\left(\frac{501.10}{12}\right) = 1.8507$$

**f.** $Y' = 1.8507 + 0.0836(50.0) = 6.0307$ ($ millions)

**17. a.** $b = -.8744\left(\frac{6.4462}{5.8736}\right) = -0.9596$

$$a = \frac{95}{8} - (-0.9596)\left(\frac{146}{8}\right) = 29.3877$$

**b.** 10.1957, found by $29.3877 - 0.9596(20)$

**c.** For each policeman added, crime goes down by almost one.

**19. a.** $\sqrt{\dfrac{2.958}{5-2}} = .993$

**b.** $Y' \pm .993$

**21. a.** $\sqrt{\dfrac{6.452}{10-2}} = .898$

**b.** $Y' \pm 1.796$

**23.** $\sqrt{\dfrac{68.4877}{8-2}} = 3.379$

**25. a.** $6.308 \pm (3.182)(.993)\sqrt{.2 + \dfrac{(7-5.6)^2}{29.2}}$
    $= 6.308 \pm 1.633$
    $= [4.675, 7.941]$

**b.** $6.308 \pm (3.182)(.993)\sqrt{1 + 1/5 + .0671}$
    $= [2.751, 9.865]$

**27. a.** [4.2939, 6.3721]

**b.** [2.9854, 7.6806]

**29.** $\bar{X} = 10$, $\bar{Y} = 6$, $\Sigma(X - \bar{X})(Y - \bar{Y}) = 40$, $s_y = 2.2361$, $s_x = 5.0$

$$r = \frac{40}{(5-1)(2.2361)(5.0)} = .8944$$

Then, $(.8944)^2 = .80$, the coefficient of determination.

**31. a.** $r^2 = 1{,}000/1{,}500 = .667$

**b.** .82, found by $\sqrt{.667}$

**c.** 6.20, found by $s_{y \cdot x} = \sqrt{\dfrac{500}{15-2}}$

**33.** The correlation between the two variables is 0.298. By squaring $X$, the correlation increases to .998.

**35.** $H_0$: $\rho \le 0$; $H_1$: $\rho > 0$. Reject $H_0$ if $t > 1.714$.

$$t = \frac{.94\sqrt{25-2}}{\sqrt{1-(.94)^2}} = 13.213$$

Reject $H_0$. There is a positive correlation between passengers and weight of luggage.

**37.** $H_0$: $\rho \le 0$; $H_1$: $\rho > 0$. Reject $H_0$ if $t > 2.764$.

$$t = \frac{.47\sqrt{12-2}}{\sqrt{1-(.47)^2}} = 1.684$$

Do not reject $H_0$. There is not a positive correlation between engine size and performance. $p$-value is greater than .05, but less than .10.

**39.** $H_0$: $\rho \ge 0$; $H_1$: $\rho < 0$. Reject $H_0$ if $t < -1.701$, $df = 28$.

$$t = \frac{-.45\sqrt{30-2}}{\sqrt{1-.2025}} = -2.67$$

Reject $H_0$. There is a negative correlation between the selling price and the number of miles driven.

**41. a.** $r = 0.589$

**b.** $r^2 = (0.589)^2 = 0.3469$

**c.** $H_0$: $\rho \le 0$; $H_1$: $\rho > 0$. Reject $H_0$ if $t > 1.860$.

$$t = \frac{0.589\sqrt{10-2}}{\sqrt{1-(.589)^2}} = 2.062$$

$H_0$ is rejected. There is a positive association between family size and the amount spent on food.

**43. a.**

There is an inverse relationship between the variables. As the months owned increase, the number of hours exercised decreases.

**b.** $r = -0.827$

**c.** $H_0$: $\rho \ge 0$; $H_1$: $\rho < 0$. Reject $H_0$ if $t < -2.896$.

$$t = \frac{-0.827\sqrt{10-2}}{\sqrt{1-(-0.827)^2}} = -4.16$$

Reject $H_0$. There is a negative association between months owned and hours exercised.

**45. a.**

| Source | SS | df | MS | F |
|---|---|---|---|---|
| Regression | 50 | 1 | 50 | 2.5556 |
| Error | 450 | 23 | 19.5652 | |
| Total | 500 | 24 | | |

**b.** $n = 25$

**c.** $s_{y \cdot x} = \sqrt{19.5652} = 4.4233$

**d.** $r^2 = \dfrac{50}{500} = 0.10$

**47. a.** $b = -0.4667, a = 11.2358$

**b.** $Y' = 11.2358 - 0.4667(7.0) = 7.9689$

**c.** $7.9689 \pm (2.160)(1.114)\sqrt{1 + \dfrac{1}{15} + \dfrac{(7 - 7.1333)^2}{73.7333}}$
$= 7.9689 \pm 2.4854$
$= [5.4835, 10.4543]$

**d.** $r^2 = 0.499$. Nearly 50 percent of the variation in the amount of the bid is explained by the number of bidders.

**49. a.**

There appears to be a relationship between the two variables. As the distance increases, so does the shipping time.

**b.** $r = 0.692$
$H_0: \rho \le 0; H_1: \rho > 0$. Reject $H_0$ if $t > 1.734$.

$$t = \dfrac{0.692\sqrt{20 - 2}}{\sqrt{1 - (0.692)^3}} = 4.067$$

$H_0$ is rejected. There is a positive association between shipping distance and shipping time.

**c.** $r^2 = 0.479$. Nearly half of the variation in shipping time is explained by shipping distance.

**d.** $s_{y \cdot x} = 1.987$

**51. a.** $b = 2.41$
$a = 26.8$
The regression equation is: Price $= 26.8 + 2.41 \times$ dividend. For each additional dollar of dividend, the price increases by $2.41.

**b.** $r^2 = \dfrac{5,057.6}{7,682.7} = 0.658$    Thus, 65.8 percent of the variation in price is explained by the dividend.

**c.** $r = \sqrt{.658} = 0.811$    $H_0: \rho \le 0$    $H_1: \rho > 0$
At the 5 percent level, reject $H_0$ when $t > 1.701$.

$$t = \dfrac{0.811\sqrt{30 - 2}}{\sqrt{1 - (0.811)^2}} = 7.34$$

Thus $H_0$ is rejected. The population correlation is positive.

**53. a.** 35

**b.** $s_{y \cdot x} = \sqrt{29,778,406} = 5456.96$

**c.** $r^2 = \dfrac{13,548,662,082}{14,531,349,474} = 0.932$

**d.** $r = \sqrt{0.932} = 0.966$

**e.** $H_0: \rho \le 0, H_1: \rho > 0$; reject $H_0$ if $t > 1.697$.

$$t = \dfrac{.966\sqrt{35 - 2}}{\sqrt{1 - (.966)^2}} = 21.46$$

Reject $H_0$. There is a direct relationship between size of the house and its market value.

**55. a.** $Y' = -1,031.0 + 1,877.3X, r^2 = .697$.

**b.** The second laptop (1.6, 1229) has a residual of $-743.64$. That is a noticeable "bargain price."

**c.** The correlation of Speed and Price is 0.835.
$H_0: \rho \le 0$    $H_1: \rho > 0$    Reject $H_0$ if $t > 1.8125$.

$$t = \dfrac{0.835\sqrt{12 - 2}}{\sqrt{1 - (0.835)^2}} = 4.799$$

Reject $H_0$. It is reasonable to say the population correlation is positive.

**57. a.** $r = .987, H_0: \rho \le 0, H_1: \rho > 0$. Reject $H_0$ if $t > 1.746$.

$$t = \dfrac{.987\sqrt{18 - 2}}{\sqrt{1 - (.987)^2}} = 24.564$$

**b.** $Y' = -29.7 + 22.93X$; an additional cup increases the dog's weight by almost 23 pounds.

**c.** Dog number 4 is an overeater.

**59. a.** Answers will vary as the number of cottages available and their prices change. At this time there are 14 cottages that meet the criteria. The correlation between the number of baths and rental price is 0.668.
$H_0: \rho \le 0$    $H_1: \rho > 0$
Reject $H_0$ if $t > 1.782$.

$$t = \dfrac{.0668\sqrt{14 - 2}}{\sqrt{1 - (0.668)^2}} = 3.11$$

Reject $H_0$. There is a positive correlation between baths and cottage price.

**b.** The regression equation is $Y' = 758 + 347X$. The weekly price increases almost $350 for each bathroom.

**c.** $H_0: \rho \le 0$    $H_1: \rho > 0$
Reject $H_0$ if $t > 1.782$.

$$t = \dfrac{0.085\sqrt{14 - 2}}{\sqrt{1 - (0.085)^2}} = .296$$

Do not reject $H_0$. We cannot conclude that there is an association between people and price.

**61. a.** The correlation between wins and salary is 0.474.
$H_0: \rho \le 0, H_1: \rho > 0$, at .05 significance level, reject $H_0$ if $t > 1.701$.

$$t = \dfrac{.474\sqrt{30 - 2}}{\sqrt{1 - (.474)^2}} = 2.848$$

Reject $H_0$: Wins and salary are related.
$Y' = 60.8 + .240X$.
An additional $5 million would increase wins by about 1.2.

**b.** The correlation between wins and ERA is $-0.824$ and between wins and batting is 0.692. The correlation between ERA and wins is stronger. The critical values are $-1.701$ for ERA and 1.701 for batting.

$$t_{ERA} = \dfrac{-0.824\sqrt{30 - 2}}{\sqrt{1 - (.824)^2}} = -7.696$$

$$t_{wins} = \dfrac{0.692\sqrt{30 - 2}}{\sqrt{1 - (.692)^2}} = 5.072$$

**c.** The correlation between wins and attendance is 0.503.

$$t = \dfrac{0.503\sqrt{30 - 2}}{\sqrt{1 - (0.503)^2}} = 3.080$$

There is a significant correlation between wins and attendance.

**63.**  **a.** The regression equation is: Unemployment = 9.558 + 0.0020 Labor force. The slope tells you one more person in the labor force will add 0.002 or 0.2% to unemployment. The predicted unemployment for UAE is 9.5608, found by 9.558 + 0.002(1.4).

    **b.** Pearson correlation of Exports and Imports = 0.948
$H_0: \rho \leq 0$      $H_1: \rho > 0$
At the 5% level, reject $H_0$ when $t > 1.680$.

$$t = \frac{0.948\sqrt{46-2}}{\sqrt{1-(0.948)^2}} = 19.758$$

Reject $H_0$. The population correlation is positive.

    **c.** Pearson correlation of 65 & over and Literacy % = 0.794
$H_0: \rho \leq 0$      $H_1: \rho > 0$
At the 5% level, reject $H_0$ when $t > 1.680$.

$$t = \frac{0.794\sqrt{46-2}}{\sqrt{1-(0.794)^2}} = 8.66$$

Reject $H_0$. The population correlation is positive.

## CHAPTER 14

**1.**  **a.** Multiple regression equation.
    **b.** The $Y$-intercept.
    **c.** $Y' = 64,100 + 0.394(796,000) + 9.6(6,940)$
$- 11,600(6.0) = \$374,748$

**3.**  **a.** 497.736, found by
$Y' = 16.24 + 0.017(18)$
$+ 0.0028(26,500) + 42(3)$
$+ 0.0012(156,000)$
$+ 0.19(141) + 26.8(2.5)$
    **b.** Two more social activities. Income added only 28 to the index; social activities added 53.6.

**5.**  **a.** 19
    **b.** 3
    **c.** .318, found by 21/66.
    **d.** 1.732, found by $\sqrt{\dfrac{45}{[19-(3+1)]}}$.

**7.**  **a.**

| Source | SS | df | MS | F |
|--------|------|----|--------|----|
| Regression | 7,500.0 | 3 | 2,500 | 18 |
| Error | 2,500.0 | 18 | 138.89 | |
| Total | 10,000.0 | 21 | | |

    **b.** $H_0: \beta_1 = \beta_2 = \beta_3 = 0$; $H_1$: Not all $\beta$s are 0. Reject $H_0$ if $F > 3.16$.
        Reject $H_0$. Not all net regression coefficients equal zero.
    **c.**

| For $X_1$: | For $X_2$: | For $X_3$: |
|-----------|-----------|-----------|
| $H_0: \beta_1 = 0$ | $H_0: \beta_2 = 0$ | $H_0: \beta_3 = 0$ |
| $H_1: \beta_1 \neq 0$ | $H_1: \beta_2 \neq 0$ | $H_1: \beta_3 \neq 0$ |
| $t = -4.00$ | $t = 1.50$ | $t = -3.00$ |

        Reject $H_0$ if $t > 2.101$ or $t < -2.101$.
        Delete variable 2, keep 1 and 3.

**9.**  **a.** $n = 40$
    **b.** 4
    **c.** $R^2 = \dfrac{750}{1250} = .60$
    **d.** $s_{y \cdot 1234} = \sqrt{500/35} = 3.7796$
    **e.** $H_0: \beta_1 = \beta_2 = \beta_3 = \beta_4 = 0$
$H_1$: Not all the $\beta$s equal zero.
$H_0$ is rejected if $F > 2.65$.

$$F = \frac{750/4}{500/35} = 13.125$$

$H_0$ is rejected. At least one $\beta_i$ does not equal zero.

**11.**  **a.** $n = 26$.
    **b.** $R^2 = 100/140 = .7143$
    **c.** 1.4142, found by $\sqrt{2}$.
    **d.** $H_0: \beta_1 = \beta_2 = \beta_3 = \beta_4 = \beta_5 = 0$
$H_1$: Not all the $\beta$s are 0.
$H_0$ is rejected if $F > 2.71$.
Computed $F = 10.0$. Reject $H_0$. At least one regression coefficient is not zero.
    **e.** $H_0$ is rejected in each case if $t < -2.086$ or $t > 2.086$. $X_1$ and $X_5$ should be dropped.

**13.**  **a.** $28,000
    **b.** $R^2 = \dfrac{\text{SSR}}{\text{SS total}} = \dfrac{3,050}{5,250} = .5809$
    **c.** 9.199, found by $\sqrt{84.62}$.
    **d.** $H_0$ is rejected if $F > 2.97$ (approximately).

$$\text{Computed } F = \frac{1,016.67}{84.62} = 12.01$$

    $H_0$ is rejected. At least one regression coefficient is not zero.
    **e.** If computed $t$ is to the left of $-2.056$ or to the right of 2.056, the null hypothesis in each of these cases is rejected. Computed $t$ for $X_2$ and $X_3$ exceed the critical value. Thus, "population" and "advertising expenses" should be retained and "number of competitors," $X_1$, dropped.

**15.**  **a.** The strongest correlation is between GPA and legal. No problem with multicollinearity.
    **b.** $R^2 = \dfrac{4.3595}{5.0631} = .8610$
    **c.** $H_0$ is rejected if $F > 5.41$.

$$F = \frac{1.4532}{0.1407} = 10.328.$$

    At least one coefficient is not zero.
    **d.** Any $H_0$ is rejected if $t < -2.571$ or $t > 2.571$. It appears that only GPA is significant. Verbal and math could be eliminated.
    **e.** $R^2 = \dfrac{4.2061}{5.0631} = .8307$.
    $R^2$ has only been reduced .0303.
    **f.** The residuals appear slightly skewed (positive), but acceptable.
    **g.** There does not seem to be a problem with the plot.

**17.**  **a.** The correlation matrix is:

|  | cars | adv | sales |
|-------|-------|-------|-------|
| adv | 0.808 | | |
| sales | 0.872 | 0.537 | |
| city | 0.639 | 0.713 | 0.389 |

    Size of sales force (0.872) has the strongest correlation with cars sold. Fairly strong relationship between location of dealership and advertising (0.713). Could be a problem.
    **b.** The regression equation is:
$Y' = 31.1328 + 2.1516adv + 5.0140sales + 5.6651city$
$Y' = 31.1328 + 2.1516(15) + 5.0140(20) + 5.6651(1)$
$= 169.352$.
    **c.** $H_0: \beta_1 = \beta_2 = \beta_3 = 0$; $H_1$: Not all $\beta$'s are 0. Reject $H_0$ if computed $F > 4.07$.

| Analysis of Variance | | | |
|---|---|---|---|
| Source | SS | df | MS |
| Regression | 5,504.4 | 3 | 1,834.8 |
| Error | 420.2 | 8 | 52.5 |
| Total | 5,924.7 | 11 | |

$F = 1{,}834.8/52.5 = 34.95$.
Reject $H_0$. At least one regression coefficient is not 0.
**d.** $H_0$ is rejected in all cases if $t < -2.306$ or if $t > 2.306$.
Advertising and sales force should be retained, city
dropped. (Note that dropping city removes the
problem with multicollinearity.)

| Predictor | Coef | StDev | t-ratio | P |
|---|---|---|---|---|
| Constant | 31.13 | 13.40 | 2.32 | 0.049 |
| adv | 2.1516 | 0.8049 | 2.67 | 0.028 |
| sales | 5.0140 | 0.9105 | 5.51 | 0.000 |
| city | 5.665 | 6.332 | 0.89 | 0.397 |

**e.** The new output is

$$Y' = 25.2952 + 2.6187adv + 5.0233sales$$

| Predictor | Coef | StDev | t-ratio |
|---|---|---|---|
| Constant | 25.30 | 11.57 | 2.19 |
| adv | 2.6187 | 0.6057 | 4.32 |
| sales | 5.0233 | 0.9003 | 5.58 |

| Analysis of Variance | | | |
|---|---|---|---|
| Source | SS | df | MS |
| Regression | 5,462.4 | 2 | 2,731.2 |
| Error | 462.3 | 9 | 51.4 |
| Total | 5,924.7 | 11 | |

**f.** Stem-and-leaf
Leaf unit = 1.0

| | | |
|---|---|---|
| 1 | −1 | 6 |
| 1 | −1 | |
| 2 | −0 | 5 |
| 5 | −0 | 110 |
| (5) | 0 | 01224 |
| 2 | 0 | 58 |

The normality assumption is reasonable.

**g.**

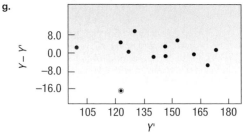

For this small sample the residual plot is acceptable.
**19. a.** The regression equation is:
$Y' = 965.3 + 2.865X_1 + 6.75X_2 + 0.2873X_3$
$Y' = \$2{,}458{,}780$

**b.**

| Analysis of Variance | | | |
|---|---|---|---|
| Source | SS | df | MS |
| Regression | 45,510,096 | 3 | 15,170,032 |
| Error | 12,215,892 | 12 | 1,017,991 |
| Total | 57,725,984 | 15 | |

$$F = \frac{15{,}170{,}032}{1{,}017{,}991} = 14.902$$

$H_0$ is rejected because computed $F$ of 14.9 is greater
than the critical value of 3.49. At least one of the
regression coefficients is not zero.
**c.** $H_0: \beta_1 = 0$    $H_0: \beta_2 = 0$    $H_0: \beta_3 = 0$
$H_1: \beta_1 \neq 0$    $H_1: \beta_2 \neq 0$    $H_1: \beta_3 \neq 0$
The $H_0$'s are rejected if $t < -2.179$ or $t > 2.179$. Both
workers and dividends are not significant variables.
Inventory is significant. Delete dividends and return
analysis.
**d.** The regression equation (if we used $X_1$ and $X_3$)

$$Y' = 1134.8 + 3.258X_1 + 0.3099X_3$$

| Predictor | Coef | StDev | t-ratio |
|---|---|---|---|
| Constant | 1134.8 | 418.6 | 2.71 |
| Workers | 3.258 | 1.434 | 2.27 |
| Inv | 0.3099 | 0.1033 | 3.00 |

| Analysis of Variance | | | | |
|---|---|---|---|---|
| Source | SS | df | MS | F |
| Regression | 45,070,624 | 2 | 22,535,312 | 23.15 |
| Error | 12,655,356 | 13 | 973,489 | |
| Total | 57,725,968 | 15 | | |

**e.**
```
Histogram of C12      N = 16
Midpoint              Count
   -1500                1      *
   -1000                3      ***
    -500                1      *
       0                6      ******
     500                2      **
    1000                2      **
    1500                0
    2000                1      *
```

The normality assumption is reasonable.
**f.**

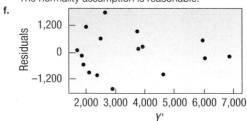

**21. a.** The correlation matrix is:

| | Salary | GPA |
|---|---|---|
| GPA | 0.902 | |
| Business | 0.911 | 0.851 |

The two independent variables are related. There may be multicollinearity.

**b.** The regression equation is: Salary = 23.447 + 2.775 GPA + 1.307 Business. As GPA increases by one point, salary increases by $2,775. The average business school graduate makes $1,307 more than a corresponding nonbusiness graduate. Estimated salary is $33,079; found by $23,447 + 2,775(3.00) + 1,307(1).

**c.** $R^2 = \dfrac{21.182}{23.857} = 0.888$

To conduct the global test: $H_0: = \beta_1 = \beta_2 = 0$;
$H_1$: Not all $\beta_i$'s = 0
At the 0.05 significance level, $H_0$ is rejected if $F > 3.89$.

| Source | SS | df | MS | F | p |
|---|---|---|---|---|---|
| Regression | 21.182 | 2 | 10.591 | 47.50 | 0.000 |
| Error | 2.676 | 12 | 0.223 | | |
| Total | 23.857 | 14 | | | |

The computed value of $F$ is 47.50, so $H_0$ is rejected. Some of the regression coefficients and $R^2$ are not zero.

**d.** Since the *p*-values are less than 0.05, there is no need to delete variables.

| Predictor | Coef | SE Coef | T | P |
|---|---|---|---|---|
| Constant | 23.447 | 3.490 | 6.72 | 0.000 |
| GPA | 2.775 | 1.107 | 2.51 | 0.028 |
| Business | 1.3071 | 0.4660 | 2.80 | 0.016 |

**e.** The residuals appear normally distributed.

Histogram of the Residuals
(response is Salary)

**f.** The variance is the same as we move from small values to large. So there is no homoscedasticity problem.

**23.** The computer output is:

| Predictor | Coef | Stdev | t-ratio | p |
|---|---|---|---|---|
| Constant | 651.9 | 345.3 | 1.89 | 0.071 |
| Service | 13.422 | 5.125 | 2.62 | 0.015 |
| Age | -6.710 | 6.349 | -1.06 | 0.301 |
| Gender | 205.65 | 90.27 | 2.28 | 0.032 |
| Job | -33.45 | 89.55 | -0.37 | 0.712 |

Analysis of Variance

| SOURCE | DF | SS | MS | F | p |
|---|---|---|---|---|---|
| Regression | 4 | 1066830 | 266708 | 4.77 | 0.005 |
| Error | 25 | 1398651 | 55946 | | |
| Total | 29 | 2465481 | | | |

**a.** $Y' = 651.9 + 13.422X_1 - 6.710X_2 + 205.65X_3 - 33.45X_4$

**b.** $R^2 = .433$, which is somewhat low for this type of study.

**c.** $H_0: \beta_1 = \beta_2 = \beta_3 = \beta_4 = 0$; $H_1$: not all $\beta$s equal zero. Reject $H_0$ if $F > 2.76$.

$$F = \dfrac{1,066,830/4}{1,398,651/25} = 4.77$$

$H_0$ is rejected. Not all the $\beta_i$s equal 0.

**d.** Using the .05 significance level, reject the hypothesis that the regression coefficient is 0 if $t < -2.060$ or $t > 2.060$. Service and gender should remain in the analyses; age and job should be dropped.

**e.** Following is the computer output using the independent variables service and gender.

| Predictor | Coef | Stdev | t-ratio | p |
|---|---|---|---|---|
| Constant | 784.2 | 316.8 | 2.48 | 0.020 |
| Service | 9.021 | 3.106 | 2.90 | 0.007 |
| Gender | 224.41 | 87.35 | 2.57 | 0.016 |

Analysis of Variance

| SOURCE | DF | SS | MS | F | p |
|---|---|---|---|---|---|
| Regression | 2 | 998779 | 499389 | 9.19 | 0.001 |
| Error | 27 | 1466703 | 54322 | | |
| Total | 29 | 2465481 | | | |

A man earns $224 more per month than a woman. The difference between technical and clerical jobs is not significant.

**25. a.** $Y' = 29.913 - 5.324X_i + 1.449X_2$

**b.** EPS is ($t = -3.26$, *p*-value = .005). Yield is not ($t = 0.81$, *p*-value = .431).

**c.** An increase of 1 in EPS results in a decline of 5.324 in *P/E*.

**d.** Stock number 2 is undervalued.

**e.** Below is a residual plot. It does *not* appear to follow the normal distribution.

Residual Histogram for P/E

Histogram of the Residuals
(response is P/E)

**f.** There does not seem to be a problem with the plot of the residuals versus the fitted values.

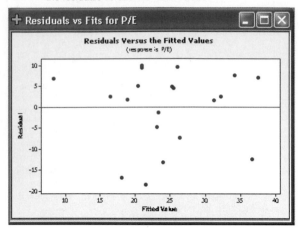

**g.**

|  | **P/E** | **EPS** |
|---|---|---|
| EPS | −0.602 | |
| Yield | .054 | .162 |

The correlation between yield and EPS is not a problem.

**27.** Answers will vary.

**29.** The computer output is as follows:

```
Predictor      Coef      SE Coef        T       P
Constant      57.03      39.99       1.43   0.157
Bedrooms       7.118      2.551      2.79   0.006
Size           0.03800    0.01468    2.59   0.011
Pool         -18.321      6.999      2.62   0.010
Distance      -0.9295     0.7279    -1.28   0.205
Garage        35.810      7.638      4.69   0.000
Baths         23.315      9.025      2.58   0.011

S = 33.21   R-Sq = 53.2%   R-Sq (adj) = 50.3%

Analysis of Variance
SOURCE             DF      SS      MS       F      P
Regression          6  122676   20446   18.54  0.000
Residual Error     98  108092    1103
Total             104  230768
```

**a.** Each additional bedroom adds about $7,000 to the selling price, a pool adds $18,300, an attached garage $35,800, and each mile the home is from the center of the city reduces the selling price by $929.

**b.** The R-square value is 0.532.

**c.** The correlation matrix is as follows:

|  | **Price** | **Bedrooms** | **Size** | **Pool** | **Distance** | **Garage** |
|---|---|---|---|---|---|---|
| Bedrooms | 0.467 | | | | | |
| Size | 0.371 | 0.383 | | | | |
| Pool | −0.294 | 0.005 | −0.201 | | | |
| Distance | −0.347 | −0.153 | −0.117 | −0.139 | | |
| Garage | 0.526 | 0.234 | 0.083 | −0.114 | −0.359 | |
| Baths | 0.382 | 0.329 | 0.024 | −0.055 | −0.195 | 0.221 |

The independent variable *garage* has the strongest correlation with price. Distance is inversely related, as expected, and there does not seem to be a problem with correlation among the independent variables.

**d.** The results of the global test suggest that some of the independent variables have net regression coefficients different from zero.

**e.** We can delete *distance*.

**f.** The new regression output follows.

```
Predictor      Coef      SE Coef        T       P
Constant      36.12      36.59       0.99   0.326
Bedrooms       7.169      2.559      2.80   0.006
Size           0.03919    0.01470    2.67   0.009
Pool         -19.110      6.994      2.73   0.007
Garage        38.847      7.281      5.34   0.000
Baths         24.624      8.995      2.74   0.007

S = 33.32   R-Sq = 52.4%   R-Sq (adj) = 50.0%

Analysis of Variance
SOURCE             DF      SS      MS       F      P
Regression          5  120877   24175   21.78  0.000
Residual Error     99  109890    1110
Total             104  230768
```

In reviewing the *p*-values for the various regression coefficients, all are less than .05. We leave all the independent variables.

**g & h.** Analysis of the residuals, not shown, indicates the normality assumption is reasonable. In addition, there is no pattern to the plots of the residuals and the fitted values of *Y*.

**31. a.** $Y' = -14,174 + 3,325X_1 - 11,675X_2 + 448X_3 - 5,355X_4$
Note age is dropped because of association with other variables. Women earn $11,675 less than men, and union members 5,355 less than nonunion workers. Wages increase $3,325 for each year of education and $448 for each year of experience.

**b.** $R^2 = .366$, which is not too good.

**c.** Education and gender have the strongest association with wages; age and experience have a nearly perfect association. Drop age.

**d.** The computed value of $F$ is 13.69, so we conclude some of the regression coefficients are not equal to zero.

**e.** Drop the union variable, $t = -1.40$.

**f.** Deleting union decreases $R^2$ to .352.

**g & h.** Analysis of the residuals, not shown, indicates the normality assumption is reasonable. In addition, there is no pattern to the plots of the residuals and the fitted values of *Y*.

## CHAPTER 15

**1. a.** 3

**b.** 7.815

**3. a.** Reject $H_0$ if $\chi^2 > 5.991$.

**b.** $\chi^2 = \dfrac{(10 - 20)^2}{20} + \dfrac{(20 - 20)^2}{20} + \dfrac{(30 - 20)^2}{20} = 10.0$

**c.** Reject $H_0$. The proportions are not equal.

**5.** $H_0$: The outcomes are the same; $H_1$: The outcomes are not the same. Reject $H_0$ if $\chi^2 > 9.236$

$$\chi^2 = \frac{(3 - 5)^2}{5} + \cdots + \frac{(7 - 5)^2}{5} = 7.60$$

Do not reject $H_0$. Cannot reject $H_0$ that outcomes are the same.

**7.** $H_0$: There is no difference in the proportions.
$H_1$: There is a difference in the proportions.
Reject $H_0$ if $\chi^2 > 15.086$.

$$\chi^2 = \frac{(47 - 40)^2}{40} + \cdots + \frac{(34 - 40)^2}{40} = 3.400$$

Do not reject $H_0$. There is no difference in the proportions.

**9.** **a.** Reject $H_0$ if $\chi^2 > 9.210$.

**b.** $\chi^2 = \dfrac{(30-24)^2}{24} + \dfrac{(20-24)^2}{24} + \dfrac{(10-12)^2}{12} = 2.50$

**c.** Do not reject $H_0$.

**11.** $H_0$: Proportions are as stated; $H_1$: Proportions are not as stated. Reject $H_0$ if $\chi^2 > 11.345$.

$$\chi^2 = \frac{(50-25)^2}{25} + \cdots + \frac{(160-275)^2}{275} = 115.22$$

Reject $H_0$. The proportions are not as stated.

**13.** $H_0$: There is no relationship between community size and section read. $H_1$: There is a relationship. Reject $H_0$ if $\chi^2 > 9.488$.

$$\chi^2 = \frac{(170-157.50)^2}{157.50} + \cdots + \frac{(88-83.62)^2}{83.62} = 7.340$$

Do not reject $H_0$. There is no relationship between community size and section read.

**15.** $H_0$: No relationship between error rates and item type. $H_1$: There is a relationship between error rates and item type. Reject $H_0$ if $\chi^2 > 9.21$.

$$\chi^2 = \frac{(20-14.1)^2}{14.1} + \cdots + \frac{(225-225.25)^2}{225.25} = 8.033$$

Do not reject $H_0$. There is not a relationship between error rates and item type.

**17.** $H_0$: $\pi_s = 0.50$, $\pi_r = \pi_e = 0.25$
$H_1$: Distribution is not as given above.
$df = 2$. Reject $H_0$ if $\chi^2 > 4.605$.

| Turn | $f_o$ | $f_e$ | $f_o - f_e$ | $(f_o - f_e)^2/f_e$ |
|------|-------|-------|-------------|---------------------|
| Straight | 112 | 100 | 12 | 1.44 |
| Right | 48 | 50 | −2 | 0.08 |
| Left | 40 | 50 | −10 | 2.00 |
| Total | 200 | 200 | | 3.52 |

$H_0$ is not rejected. The proportions are as given in the null hypothesis.

**19.** $H_0$: There is no preference with respect to TV stations. $H_1$: There is a preference with respect to TV stations. $df = 3 - 1 = 2$. $H_0$ is rejected if $\chi^2 > 5.991$.

| TV Station | $f_o$ | $f_e$ | $f_o - f_e$ | $(f_o - f_e)^2$ | $(f_o - f_e)^2/f_e$ |
|------------|-------|-------|-------------|-----------------|---------------------|
| WNAE | 53 | 50 | 3 | 9 | 0.18 |
| WRRN | 64 | 50 | 14 | 196 | 3.92 |
| WSPD | 33 | 50 | −17 | 289 | 5.78 |
| | 150 | 150 | 0 | | 9.88 |

$H_0$ is rejected. There is a preference for TV stations.

**21.** $H_0$: $\pi_n = 0.21$, $\pi_m = 0.24$, $\pi_s = 0.35$, $\pi_w = 0.20$.
$H_1$: The distribution is not as given.
Reject $H_0$ if $\chi^2 > 11.345$.

| Region | $f_o$ | $f_e$ | $f_o - f_e$ | $(f_o - f_e)^2/f_e$ |
|--------|-------|-------|-------------|---------------------|
| Northeast | 68 | 84 | −16 | 3.0476 |
| Midwest | 104 | 96 | 8 | 0.6667 |
| South | 155 | 140 | 15 | 1.6071 |
| West | 73 | 80 | −7 | 0.6125 |
| Total | 400 | 400 | 0 | 5.9339 |

$H_0$ is not rejected. The distribution of order destinations reflects the population.

**23.** $H_0$: $\pi_0 = 0.40$, $\pi_1 = 0.30$, $\pi_2 = 0.20$, $\pi_3 = 0.1$
$H_1$: The proportions are not as given. Reject $H_0$ if $\chi^2 > 7.815$.

| Accidents | $f_o$ | $f_e$ | $(f_o - f_e)^2/f_e$ |
|-----------|-------|-------|---------------------|
| 0 | 46 | 48 | 0.083 |
| 1 | 40 | 36 | 0.444 |
| 2 | 22 | 24 | 0.167 |
| 3 | 12 | 12 | 0.000 |
| Total | 120 | | 0.694 |

Do not reject $H_0$. Evidence does not show a change in the accident distribution.

**25.** $H_0$: Levels of management and concern regarding the environment are not related. $H_1$: Levels of management and concern regarding the environment are related. Reject $H_0$ if $\chi^2 > 16.812$.

$$\chi^2 = \frac{(15-14)^2}{14} + \cdots + \frac{(31-28)^2}{28} = 1.550$$

Do not reject $H_0$. Levels of management and environmental concern are not related.

**27.** $H_0$: Whether a claim is filed and age are not related. $H_1$: Whether a claim is filed and age are related. Reject $H_0$ if $\chi^2 > 7.815$.

$$\chi^2 = \frac{(170-203.33)^2}{203.33} + \cdots + \frac{(24-35.67)^2}{35.67} = 53.639$$

Reject $H_0$. Age is related to whether a claim is filed.

**29.** $H_0$: $\pi_{BL} = \pi_{BR} = \pi_Y = \pi_R = 0.2$, $\pi_G = \pi_O = 0.1$. $H_1$: The proportions are not as given. Reject $H_0$ if $\chi^2 > 11.070$.

| Color | $f_o$ | $f_e$ | $(f_o - f_e)^2/f_e$ |
|-------|-------|-------|---------------------|
| Blue | 13 | 14.4 | 0.136 |
| Brown | 17 | 14.4 | 0.469 |
| Yellow | 20 | 14.4 | 2.178 |
| Red | 7 | 14.4 | 3.803 |
| Green | 9 | 7.2 | 0.450 |
| Orange | 6 | 7.2 | 0.200 |
| Total | 72 | | 7.236 |

Do not reject $H_0$. The color distribution agrees with the manufacturer's information.

**31.** **a.** $H_0$: There is no relationship between pool and township. $H_1$: There is a relationship between pool and township. Reject $H_0$ if $\chi^2 > 9.488$.

| | | | Township | | | |
|------|----|----|----|----|----|-------|
| Pool | 1 | 2 | 3 | 4 | 5 | Total |
| Yes | 9 | 8 | 7 | 11 | 3 | 38 |
| No | 6 | 12 | 18 | 18 | 13 | 67 |
| Total | 15 | 20 | 25 | 29 | 16 | 105 |

$$\chi^2 = \frac{(9-5.43)^2}{5.43} + \cdots + \frac{(13-10.21)^2}{10.21} = 6.680$$

Do not reject $H_0$. There is no relationship between pool and township.

**b.** $H_0$: There is no relationship between attached garage and township. $H_1$: There is a relationship between attached garage and township. Reject $H_0$ if $\chi^2 > 9.488$.

| | | | Township | | | |
|--------|----|----|----|----|----|-------|
| Garage | 1 | 2 | 3 | 4 | 5 | Total |
| No | 6 | 5 | 10 | 9 | 4 | 34 |
| Yes | 9 | 15 | 15 | 20 | 12 | 71 |
| Total | 15 | 20 | 25 | 29 | 16 | 105 |

$$\chi^2 = \frac{(6 - 4.86)^2}{4.86} + \cdots + \frac{(12 - 10.82)^2}{10.82} = 1.980$$

Do not reject $H_0$. There is no relationship between attached garage and township.

33. $H_0$: Industry and gender are not related.
$H_1$: Industry and gender are related.
Note: There are only 3 observations in the industry coded 2; hence 1 and 2 are combined. There is one degree of freedom, so $H_0$ is rejected if $\chi^2 > 3.841$.

$$\chi^2 = \frac{(41 - 42.40)^2}{42.40} + \cdots + \frac{(8 - 9.40)^2}{9.40} = 0.492$$

Do not reject $H_0$. We cannot conclude gender and industry are related.

# CHAPTER 16

1. **a.** If the number of pluses (successes) in the sample is 9 or more, reject $H_0$.
   **b.** Reject $H_0$ because the cumulative probability associated with nine or more successes (.073) does not exceed the significance level (.10).
3. **a.** $H_0$: $\pi \leq .50$; $H_1$: $\pi > .50$; $n = 10$.
   **b.** $H_0$ is rejected if there are nine or more plus signs. A "+" represents a loss.
   **c.** Reject $H_0$. It is an effective program, because there were 9 people who lost weight.
5. **a.** $H_0$: $\pi \leq .50$ (There is no change in weight.)
   $H_0$: $\pi > .50$ (There is a loss of weight.)
   **b.** Reject $H_0$ if $z > 1.65$.
   **c.** $z = \dfrac{(32 - .50) - .50(45)}{.50\sqrt{45}} = 2.68$
   **d.** Reject $H_0$. The weight loss program is effective.
7. **a.** $H_0$: $\pi \leq .50$, $H_1$: $\pi > .50$. $H_0$ is rejected if $z > 2.05$.

   $$z = \frac{42.5 - 40.5}{4.5} = .44$$

   Because $.44 < 2.05$, do not reject $H_0$. No preference.
9. **a.** $H_0$: Median $\leq \$82,400$; $H_1$: Median $> \$82,400$.
   **b.** $H_0$ is rejected if $z > 1.65$.
   **c.** $z = \dfrac{170 - .5 - 100}{7.07} = 9.83$

   $H_0$ is rejected. The median income is greater than $82,400.

11.
| Couple | Difference | Rank |
|--------|-----------|------|
| 1 | 550 | 7 |
| 2 | 190 | 5 |
| 3 | 250 | 6 |
| 4 | −120 | 3 |
| 5 | −70 | 1 |
| 6 | 130 | 4 |
| 7 | 90 | 2 |

Sums: −4, +24. So $T = 4$ (the smaller of the two sums). From Appendix H, .05 level, one-tailed test, $n = 7$, the critical value is 3. Since the $T$ of $4 > 3$, do not reject $H_0$ (one-tailed test). There is no difference in square footage. Yuppies do not live in larger homes.

13. **a.** $H_0$: The production is the same for the two systems.
   $H_1$: Production using the Mump method is greater.
   **b.** $H_0$ is rejected if $T \leq 21$, $n = 13$.
   **c.** The calculations for the first three employees are:

| Employee | Old | Mump | $d$ | Rank | $R^+$ | $R^-$ |
|----------|-----|------|-----|------|-------|-------|
| A | 60 | 64 | 4 | 6 | 6 | |
| B | 40 | 52 | 12 | 12.5 | 12.5 | |
| C | 59 | 58 | −1 | 2 | | 2 |

The sum of the negative ranks is 6.5. Since 6.5 is less than 21, $H_0$ is rejected. Production using the Mump method is greater.

15. $H_0$: The distributions are the same. $H_1$: The distributions are not the same. Reject $H_0$ if $z < -1.96$ or $z > 1.96$.

| A | | B | |
|------|------|------|------|
| Score | Rank | Score | Rank |
| 38 | 4 | 26 | 1 |
| 45 | 6 | 31 | 2 |
| 56 | 9 | 35 | 3 |
| 57 | 10.5 | 42 | 5 |
| 61 | 12 | 51 | 7 |
| 69 | 14 | 52 | 8 |
| 70 | 15 | 57 | 10.5 |
| 79 | 16 | 62 | 13 |
| | 86.5 | | 49.5 |

$$z = \frac{86.5 - \dfrac{8(8 + 8 + 1)}{2}}{\sqrt{\dfrac{8(8)(8 + 8 + 1)}{12}}} = 1.943$$

$H_0$ is not rejected. There is no difference in the two populations.

17. $H_0$: The distributions are the same. $H_1$: The distribution of Country is to the right. Reject $H_0$ if $z > 1.65$.

| Country | | Rock | |
|------|------|------|------|
| Age | Rank | Age | Rank |
| 26 | 6 | 28 | 8 |
| 42 | 16.5 | 16 | 1 |
| 65 | 22 | 42 | 16.5 |
| 38 | 13 | 29 | 9.5 |
| 29 | 9.5 | 31 | 11 |
| 32 | 12 | 22 | 3 |
| 59 | 21 | 50 | 20 |
| 42 | 16.5 | 42 | 16.5 |
| 27 | 7 | 23 | 4 |
| 41 | 14 | 25 | 5 |
| 46 | 19 | | 94.5 |
| 18 | 2 | | |
| | 158.5 | | |

$$z = \frac{158.5 - \dfrac{12(12 + 10 + 1)}{2}}{\sqrt{\dfrac{12(10)(12 + 10 + 1)}{12}}} = 1.35$$

$H_0$ is not rejected. There is no difference in the distributions.

19. ANOVA requires that we have two or more populations, the data are interval or ratio-level, the populations are normally distributed, and the population standard deviations are equal. Kruskal-Wallis requires only ordinal-level data, and no assumptions are made regarding the shape of the populations.

21. **a.** $H_0$: The three population distributions are equal. $H_1$: Not all of the distributions are the same.
   **b.** Reject $H_0$ if $H > 5.991$.

**c.**

| Rank | Rank | Rank |
|---|---|---|
| 8 | 5 | 1 |
| 11 | 6.5 | 2 |
| 14.5 | 6.5 | 3 |
| 14.5 | 10 | 4 |
| 16 | 12 | 9 |
| 64 | 13 | 19 |
|  | 53 |  |

$$H = \frac{12}{16(16+1)}\left[\frac{(64)^2}{5} + \frac{(53)^2}{6} + \frac{(19)^2}{5}\right] - 3(16+1)$$

$$= 59.98 - 51 = 8.98$$

**d.** Reject $H_0$ because $8.98 > 5.991$. The three distributions are not equal.

**23.** $H_0$: The distributions of the lengths of life are the same.
$H_1$: The distributions of the lengths of life are not the same.
$H_0$ is rejected if $H > 9.210$.

| Salt | | Fresh | | Others | |
|---|---|---|---|---|---|
| **Hours** | **Rank** | **Hours** | **Rank** | **Hours** | **Rank** |
| 167.3 | 3 | 160.6 | 1 | 182.7 | 13 |
| 189.6 | 15 | 177.6 | 11 | 165.4 | 2 |
| 177.2 | 10 | 185.3 | 14 | 172.9 | 7 |
| 169.4 | 6 | 168.6 | 4 | 169.2 | 5 |
| 180.3 | 12 | 176.6 | 9 | 174.7 | 8 |
|  | 46 |  | 39 |  | 35 |

$$H = \frac{12}{15(16)}\left[\frac{(46)^2}{5} + \frac{(39)^2}{5} + \frac{(35)^2}{5}\right] - 3(16) = 0.62$$

$H_0$ is not rejected. There is no difference in the three distributions.

**25. a.**

**b.**

| Rank Males | Rank Females | $d$ | $d^2$ |
|---|---|---|---|
| 1 | 5 | −4 | 16 |
| 4 | 1 | 3 | 9 |
| 3 | 2 | 1 | 1 |
| 2 | 4 | −2 | 4 |
| 5 | 3 | 2 | 4 |
|  |  |  | 34 |

$$r_s = 1 - \frac{6(34)}{5(5^2 - 1)} = -0.7$$

Fairly strong negative correlation among the ranks.

**27.**

| Representative | Sales | Rank | Training Rank | $d$ | $d^2$ |
|---|---|---|---|---|---|
| 1 | 319 | 3 | 3 | 0 | 0 |
| 2 | 150 | 10 | 9 | 1 | 1 |
| 3 | 175 | 9 | 6 | 3 | 9 |
| 4 | 460 | 1 | 1 | 0 | 0 |
| 5 | 348 | 2 | 4 | −2 | 4 |
| 6 | 300 | 4.5 | 10 | −5.5 | 30.25 |
| 7 | 280 | 6 | 5 | 1 | 1 |
| 8 | 200 | 7 | 2 | 5 | 25 |
| 9 | 190 | 8 | 7 | 1 | 1 |
| 10 | 300 | 4.5 | 8 | −3.5 | 12.25 |
|  |  |  |  |  | 83.50 |

**a.** $r_s = 1 - \dfrac{6(83.5)}{10(10^2 - 1)} = 0.494$
A moderate positive correlation.

**b.** $H_0$: No correlation among the ranks. $H_1$: A positive correlation among the ranks. Reject $H_0$ if $t > 1.860$.

$$t = 0.494\sqrt{\frac{10-2}{1-(0.494)^2}} = 1.607$$

$H_0$ is not rejected. The correlation in population among the ranks could be 0.

**29.** $H_0$: $\pi = .50$; $H_1$: $\pi \neq .50$; $n = 19$. $H_0$ is rejected if there are either 5 or fewer "+" signs, or 14 or more. The total of 12 "+" signs falls in the acceptance region. $H_0$ is not rejected. There is no preference between the two shows.

**31.** $H_0$: $\pi = .50$   $H_1$: $\pi \neq .50$
$H_0$ is rejected if there are 12 or more or 3 or fewer plus signs. Because there are only 8 plus signs, $H_0$ is not rejected. There is no preference with respect to the two brands of components.

**33.** $H_0$: $\pi = .50$; $H_1$: $\pi \neq .50$. Reject $H_0$ if $z > 1.96$ or $z < -1.96$.

$$z = \frac{159.5 - 100}{7.071} = 8.415$$

Reject $H_0$. There is a difference in the preference for the two types of orange juice.

**35.** $H_0$: Rates are the same; $H_1$: The rates are not the same. $H_0$ is rejected if $H > 5.991$. $H = .082$. Do not reject $H_0$.

**37.** $H_0$: The populations are the same. $H_1$: The populations differ. Reject $H_0$ if $H > 7.815$. $H = 14.30$. Reject $H_0$, accept $H_1$.

**39.** $r_s = 1 - \dfrac{6(78)}{12(12^2 - 1)} = 0.727$
$H_0$: There is no correlation between the rankings of the coaches and of the sportswriters.
$H_1$: There is a positive correlation between the rankings of the coaches and of the sportswriters.
Reject $H_0$ if $t > 1.812$.

$$t = 0.727\sqrt{\frac{12-2}{1-(.727)^2}} = 3.348$$

$H_0$ is rejected. There is a positive correlation between the sportswriters and the coaches.

**41.** Answers will vary.

**43. a.** $H_0$: There is no difference in the distributions of the selling prices in the five townships. $H_1$: There is a difference in the distributions of the selling prices of the five townships. $H_0$ is rejected if $H$ is greater than 9.488. The computed value of $H$ is 4.70, so the null hypothesis is not rejected. The sample data does not suggest a difference in the distributions of selling prices.

**b.** $H_0$: There is no difference in the distributions of the selling prices depending on the number of bedrooms. $H_1$: There is a difference in the distributions of the selling prices depending on the number of bedrooms. $H_0$ is rejected if $H$ is greater than 9.448. The computed value of $H$ is 16.34, so the null hypothesis is rejected. The sample data indicate there is a difference in the distributions of selling prices based on the number of bedrooms.

c. $H_0$: There is no difference in the distributions of the distance from the center of the city depending on whether the home had a pool or not. $H_1$: There is a difference in the distributions of the distances from the center of the city depending on whether the home has a pool or not. $H_0$ is rejected if $H$ is greater than 3.84. The computed value of $H$ is 3.37, so the null hypothesis is not rejected. The sample data does not suggest a difference in the distributions of the distances.

45. a. $H_0$: Median wages the same for union and nonunion workers.
$H_1$: Median wages not the same for union and nonunion workers.
Reject $H_0$ if $z < -1.96$ or $z > 1.96$.

$$z = \frac{4037 - \dfrac{82(82 + 18 + 1)}{2}}{\sqrt{\dfrac{82(18)(82 + 18 + 1)}{12}}} = \frac{-104}{111.46} = -0.93$$

Do not reject $H_0$. There is no difference in the median wages of union and nonunion workers.

b. $H_0$: Median wages are the same for three industries.
$H_1$: Median wages are not the same for three industries.
Reject $H_0$ if $H > 9.21$.
$H = 2.97$, with a $p$-value of 0.227.
We do not reject $H_0$, the results are similar.

c. $H_0$: The wage distributions are the same in the occupations.
$H_1$: The wage distributions are not the same.
Reject $H_0$ if $\chi^2 > 11.070$.
$H = 16.75$.
Reject $H_0$. The wage distributions are not the same for the various occupations.

# CHAPTER 17

1.

| | | | | |
|---|---|---|---|---|
| Count | 38 | 23 | 12 | 10 | 8 |
| Percent | 42 | 25 | 13 | 11 | 9 |
| Cum % | 42 | 67 | 80 | 91 | 100 |

About 67% of the complaints concern the problem not being corrected and the price being too high.

3. Chance variation is random in nature; because the cause is a variety of factors, it cannot be entirely eliminated. Assignable variation is not random; it is usually due to a specific cause and can be eliminated.

5. a. The $A_2$ factor is 0.729.
b. The value for $D_3$ is 0, and for $D_4$ it is 2.282.

7. a.

| Time | $\overline{X}$, Arithmetic Means | $R$, Range |
|---|---|---|
| 8:00 A.M. | 46 | 16 |
| 8:30 A.M. | 40.5 | 6 |
| 9:00 A.M. | 44 | 6 |
| 9:30 A.M. | 40 | 2 |
| 10:00 A.M. | 41.5 | 9 |
| 10:30 A.M. | 39.5 | 1 |
| | 251.5 | 40 |

$$\overline{\overline{X}} = \frac{251.5}{6} = 41.92 \qquad \overline{R} = \frac{40}{6} = 6.67$$

$$UCL = 41.92 + 0.729(6.67) = 46.78$$

$$LCL = 41.92 - 0.729(6.67) = 37.06$$

b. Interpreting, the mean reading was 341.92 degrees Fahrenheit. If the oven continues operating as evidenced by the first six hourly readings, about 99.7 percent of the mean readings will lie between 337.06 degrees and 346.78 degrees.

9. $p = \dfrac{37}{140} = .26$

$$.26 \pm 3\sqrt{\frac{.26(.74)}{10}} = .26 \pm .42$$

The control limits are from 0 to .68. The process is out of control on the seventh day.

11. $\overline{c} = \dfrac{6}{11} = 0.545$

$0.545 \pm 3\sqrt{0.545} = 0.545 \pm 2.215$
The control limits are from 0 to 2.760, so there are no receipts out of control.

13.

| Percent Defective | Probability of Accepting Lot |
|---|---|
| 10 | .889 |
| 20 | .558 |
| 30 | .253 |
| 40 | .083 |

15. $P(X \le 1 | n = 10, \pi = .10) = .736$
$P(X \le 1 | n = 10, \pi = .20) = .375$
$P(X \le 1 | n = 10, \pi = .30) = .149$
$P(X \le 1 | n = 10, \pi = .40) = .046$

**17.**

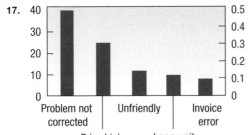

| | | | | |
|---|---|---|---|---|
| Count | 80 | 60 | 50 | 10 |
| Percent | 40 | 30 | 25 | 5 |
| Cum % | 40 | 70 | 95 | 100 |

**19. a.** $UCL = 10.0 + 0.577(0.25) = 10.0 + 0.14425$

$= 10.14425$

$LCL = 10.0 - 0.577(0.25) = 10.0 - 0.14425$

$= 9.85575$

$UCL = 2.115(0.25) = 0.52875$

$LCL = 0(0.25) = 0$

**b.** The mean is 10.16, which is above the upper control limit and is out of control. There is too much cola in the soft drinks. The process is in control for variation; an adjustment is needed.

**21. a.** $\bar{\bar{X}} = \dfrac{611.23}{20} = 30.5665$

$\bar{R} = \dfrac{312}{20} = 15.6$

$UCL = 30.5665 + (1.023)(15.6) = 46.53$

$LCL = 30.5665 - (1.023)(15.6) = 14.61$

$UCL = 2.575(15.6) = 40.17$

**b.**

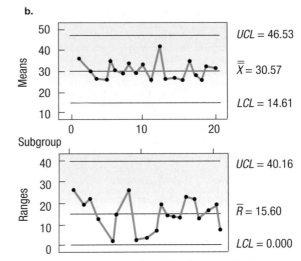

**c.** The points all seem to be within the control limits. No adjustments are necessary.

**23.** $\bar{\bar{X}} = \dfrac{4,183}{10} = 418.3$

$\bar{R} = \dfrac{162}{10} = 16.2$

$UCL = 418.3 + (0.577)(16.2) = 427.65$

$LCL = 418.3 - (0.577)(16.2) = 408.95$

$UCL = 2.115(16.2) = 34.26$

All the points are in control for both the mean and the range.

**25. a.** $p = \dfrac{40}{10(50)} = 0.08$

$3\sqrt{\dfrac{0.08(0.92)}{50}} = 0.115$

$UCL = 0.08 + 0.115 = 0.195$

$LCL = 0.08 - 0.115 = 0$

**b.**

**c.** There are no points that exceed the limits.

**27.**

P Chart for C1

$UCL = 0.4337$

$\overline{P} = 0.25$

$LCL = 0.06629$

These sample results indicate that the odds are much less than 50-50 for an increase. The percent of stocks that increase is "in control" around 0.25 or 25 percent. The control limits are 0.06629 and 0.4337.

**29.** $P(X \le 3 | n = 10, \pi = 0.05) = 0.999$
$P(X \le 3 | n = 10, \pi = 0.10) = 0.987$
$P(X \le 3 | n = 10, \pi = 0.20) = 0.878$
$P(X \le 3 | n = 10, \pi = 0.30) = 0.649$

$P(X \le 5 | n = 20, \pi = 0.05) = 0.999$
$P(X \le 5 | n = 20, \pi = 0.10) = 0.989$
$P(X \le 5 | n = 20, \pi = 0.20) = 0.805$
$P(X \le 5 | n = 20, \pi = 0.30) = 0.417$

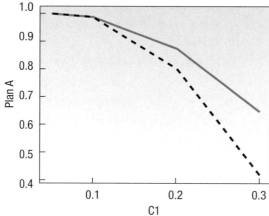

The solid line is the operating characteristic curve for the first plan, and the dashed line, the second. The supplier would prefer the first because the probability of acceptance is higher (above). However, if he is really sure of his quality, the second plan seems higher at the very low range of defect percentages and might be preferred.

**31. a.** $\overline{c} = \dfrac{213}{15} = 14.2; \; 3\sqrt{14.2} = 11.30$

$UCL = 14.2 + 11.3 = 25.5$

$LCL = 14.2 - 11.3 = 2.9$

**b.**

**c.** All the points are in control.

**33.** $\overline{c} = \dfrac{70}{10} = 7.0$

$UCL = 7.0 + 3\sqrt{7} = 14.9$

$LCL = 7.0 - 3\sqrt{7} = 0$

**35.** $P(X \le 3 | n = 20, \pi = .10) = .867$
$P(X \le 3 | n = 20, \pi = .20) = .412$
$P(X \le 3 | n = 20, \pi = .30) = .108$

**CHAPTER 18**

**1.** 114.6, found by ($19,989/$17,446)(100)
123.1, found by ($21,468/$17,446)(100)
124.3, found by ($21,685/$17,446)(100)
91.3, found by ($15,922/$17,446)(100)

**3.** 109.5, found by ($580.7/$530.53) for 2001
107.2, found by ($568.5/$530.53) for 2002

**5. a.** $P_t = \dfrac{2.69}{2.49}(100) = 108.03$  $P_s = \dfrac{3.59}{3.29}(100) = 109.12$

$P_c = \dfrac{1.79}{1.59}(100) = 112.58$  $P_a = \dfrac{2.29}{1.79}(100) = 127.93$

**b.** $P = \dfrac{10.36}{9.16}(100) = 113.1$

**c.** $P = \dfrac{\$2.69(6) + 3.59(4) + 1.79(2) + 2.29(3)}{\$2.49(6) + 3.29(4) + 1.59(2) + 1.79(3)}(100) = 111.7$

**d.** $P = \dfrac{\$2.69(6) + 3.59(5) + 1.79(3) + 2.29(4)}{\$2.49(6) + 3.29(5) + 1.59(3) + 1.79(4)}(100) = 112.2$

**e.** $I = \sqrt{112.2(111.7)} = 111.95$

**7. a.** $P_W = \dfrac{0.10}{0.07}(100) = 142.9$  $P_C = \dfrac{0.03}{0.04}(100) = 75.0$

$P_S = \dfrac{0.15}{0.15}(100) = 100$  $P_H = \dfrac{0.10}{0.08}(100) = 125.0$

**b.** $P = \dfrac{0.38}{0.34}(100) = 111.8$

**c.**

$P = \dfrac{0.10(17,000) + 0.03(125,000) + 0.15(40,000) + 0.10(62,000)}{0.07(17,000) + 0.04(125,000) + 0.15(40,000) + 0.08(62,000)}$

$(100) = 102.92$

**d.**

$P = \dfrac{0.10(20,000) + 0.03(130,000) + 0.15(42,000) + 0.10(65,000)}{0.07(20,000) + 0.04(130,000) + 0.15(42,000) + 0.08(65,000)}$

$(100) = 103.32$

**e.** $P = \sqrt{102.92(103.32)} = 103.12$

**9.** $V = \dfrac{1.87(214) + 2.05(489) + 1.48(203) + 3.29(106)}{1.52(200) + 2.10(565) + 1.48(291) + 3.05(87)}(100)$

$= 93.8$

**11. a.** $I = \dfrac{6.8}{5.3}(0.20) + \dfrac{362.26}{265.88}(0.40) + \dfrac{125.0}{109.6}(0.25) + \dfrac{622,864}{529,917}$

$(0.15) = 1.263.$
Index is 126.3.

**b.** Business activity increased 26.3 percent from 2000 to 2003.

**13.** $X = (\$82,555)/1.831 = \$45,251$
Salary increased $\$45,251 - \$19,800 = \$25,451$

**15.**

| Year | Tinora | Tinora | National Index |
|------|--------|--------|----------------|
| 1995 | $28,650 | 100.0 | 100 |
| 2000 | $33,972 | 118.6 | 122.5 |
| 2004 | $37,382 | 130.5 | 136.9 |

The Tinora teachers received smaller increases than the national average.

**17.** Index for selected years:

| Year | 1996 | 1997 | 1998 | 1999 | 2000 | 2001 | 2002 |
|------|------|------|------|------|------|------|------|
| Index | 119.7 | 130.3 | 142.3 | 171.3 | 191.0 | 218.7 | 247.7 |

**19.** Index for selected years:

| Year | 1996 | 1997 | 1998 | 1999 | 2000 | 2001 | 2002 |
|------|------|------|------|------|------|------|------|
| Index | 111.2 | 113.0 | 115.2 | 124.8 | 125.2 | 131.9 | 146.1 |

**21.** Index for selected years:

| Year | 1996 | 1997 | 1998 | 1999 | 2000 | 2001 | 2002 |
|------|------|------|------|------|------|------|------|
| Index | 108.7 | 110.0 | 114.1 | 118.5 | 119.8 | 120.9 | 128.6 |

**23.** Index for selected years:

| Year | 1999 | 2000 | 2001 | 2002 |
|------|------|------|------|------|
| Index | 111.1 | 129.2 | 125.3 | 131.1 |

**25.** Index for selected years:

| Year | 1999 | 2000 | 2001 | 2002 |
|------|------|------|------|------|
| Index | 114.7 | 135.8 | 145.3 | 149.5 |

**27.** $P_M = \dfrac{\$0.89}{\$0.81}(100) = 109.88$  $P_S = \dfrac{\$0.94}{\$0.84}(100) = 111.90$

$P_M = \dfrac{1.43}{1.44}(100) = 99.31$  $P_P = \dfrac{3.07}{2.91}(100) = 105.50$

**29.** $P = \dfrac{0.89(18) + 0.94(5) + 1.43(70) + 3.07(27)}{0.81(18) + 0.84(5) + 1.44(70) + 2.91(27)}(100) = 102.81$

**31.** $P = \sqrt{(102.81)(103.51)} = 103.16$

**33.** $P_R = \dfrac{0.60}{0.50}(100) = 120$  $P_S = \dfrac{0.90}{1.20}(100) = 75.0$

$P_W = \dfrac{1.00}{0.85}(100) = 117.65$

**35.** $P = \dfrac{0.60(320) + 0.90(110) + 1.00(230)}{0.50(320) + 1.20(110) + 0.85(230)}(100) = 106.87$

**37.** $P = \sqrt{(106.87)(106.04)} = 106.45$

**39.** $P_C = \dfrac{0.05}{0.06}(100) = 83.33$  $P_C = \dfrac{0.12}{0.10}(100) = 120$

$P_P = \dfrac{0.18}{0.20}(100) = 90$  $P_E = \dfrac{.015}{0.15}(100) = 100$

**41.** $P = \dfrac{0.05(2,000) + 0.12(200) + 1.18(400) + 0.15(100)}{0.06(2,000) + 0.10(200) + 0.20(400) + 0.15(100)}(100)$

$= 89.79$

**43.** $P = \sqrt{(89.79)(91.25)} = 90.52$

**45.** $P_A = \dfrac{0.76}{0.287}(100) = 264.8$  $P_N = \dfrac{2.50}{0.17}(100) = 1,470.59$

$P_P = \dfrac{26.00}{3.18}(100) = 817.61$  $P_P = \dfrac{490}{133}(100) = 368.42$

**47.** $P = \dfrac{0.76(1,000) + 2.50(5,000) + 26(60,000) + 490(500)}{0.287(1,000) + 0.17(5,000) + 3.18(60,000) + 133(500)}$

$(100) = 703.56$

**49.** $P = \sqrt{(703.56)(686.58)} = 695.02$

**51.** $I = 100\left[\dfrac{1,971.0}{1,159.0}(0.20) + \dfrac{91}{87}(0.10) + \dfrac{114.7}{110.6}(0.40)\right.$

$\left. + \dfrac{1,501}{1,214}(0.30)\right] = 123.05$

The economy is up 23.05 percent from 1996 to 2004.

**53.** February:  $I = 100\left[\dfrac{6.8}{8.0}(0.40) + \dfrac{23}{20}(0.35) + \dfrac{303}{300}(0.25)\right]$

$= 99.50$

March:  $I = 100\left[\dfrac{6.4}{8.0}(0.40) + \dfrac{21}{20}(0.35) + \dfrac{297}{300}(0.25)\right]$

$= 93.5$

**55.** For 1991: $1,972,062, found by $2,400,000/1.217.
For 2000: $2,521,614, found by $3,500,000/1.388.

**57.** Answers will vary.

# CHAPTER 19

1. The weighted moving averages are: 31584.8, 33088.9, 34205.4, 34899.8, 35155.0, 34887.1

3. $Y' = 6,581.87 + 666.94t$
   $Y' = 6,581.87 + 666.94(9) = 12,584.33$

5. $Y' = 1.30 + 0.90t$
   $Y' = 1.30 + 0.90 (7) = 7.6$

7. **a.** $Y' = -0.0531997 + 0.1104057t$
   **b.** 28.95%, found by $1.28945 - 1.0$
   **c.** $Y' = -0.0531997 + 0.1104057(8) = .8300459$.
   Antilog of $.8300459 = 6.76$

9.

| Quarter | Average SI Component | Seasonal Index |
|---|---|---|
| 1 | 0.6859 | 0.6911 |
| 2 | 1.6557 | 1.6682 |
| 3 | 1.1616 | 1.1704 |
| 4 | 0.4732 | 0.4768 |

11.

| t | Estimated Pairs (millions) | Seasonal Index | Quarterly Forecast (millions) |
|---|---|---|---|
| 21 | 40.05 | 110.0 | 44.055 |
| 22 | 41.80 | 120.0 | 50.160 |
| 23 | 43.55 | 80.0 | 34.840 |
| 24 | 45.30 | 90.0 | 40.770 |

13. $Y' = 5.1658 + .37805t$. The following are the sales estimates.

| Estimate | Index | Seasonally Adjusted |
|---|---|---|
| 10.080 | 0.6911 | 6.966 |
| 10.458 | 1.6682 | 17.446 |
| 10.837 | 1.1704 | 12.684 |
| 11.215 | 0.4768 | 5.343 |

15. **a.** $Y' = 18,000 - 400t$, assuming the line starts at 18,000 in 1980 and goes down to 10,000 in 2000.
    **b.** 400
    **c.** 8,000, found by $18,000 - 400(25)$.

17. **a.**

**b.** $Y' = 1.0045 + 0.04409t$, using $t = 1$ for 1993.
**c.** For 1996, $Y' = 1.18091$. For 2001 $Y' = 1.40136$.
**d.** For 2008, $Y' = 1.70999$.
**e.** Each asset turned over .044 times.

19. **a.**

**b.** $Y' = 49.140 - 2.9829t$
**c.** For 2000, $Y' = 40.1913$. For 2002 $Y' = 34.2255$.
**d.** For 2006, $Y' = 22.2939$.
**e.** The number of employees decreases at a rate of 2,983 per year.

21. **a.** Log $Y' = 0.790231 + 0.113669t$
    **b.** Log $Y' = 1.244907$, antilog is 17.575
    Log $Y' = 1.813252$, antilog is 65.05
    **c.** 29.92, which is the antilog of .113669 minus 1.
    **d.** Log $Y' = 2.154258$, antilog is 142.65

23. **a.**

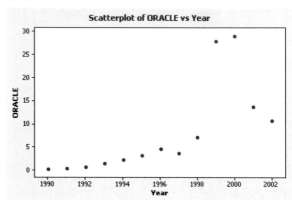

**b.** Using a linear equation,
$Y' = -4.780 + 1.8392t$, $r^2 = .518$. Using log equation,
$Y' = -0.6216 + 0.16411t$, $r^2 = .874$.
**c.** $Y' = -0.6216 + 0.16411(4) = .03484$; antilog is 1.0835.
$Y' = -0.6216 + 0.16411(9) = .85539$; antilog is 7.1679.
**d.** $Y' = -0.6216 + 0.16411(16) = 2.00416$; antilog is 100.96. This does not seem like a reasonable estimate.
**e.** Antilog of .16411 is $1.4592 - 1.00 = .4592$. This is 45.92% per year.

25. **a.** July 87.5; August 92.9; September 99.3; October 109.1.
    **b.**

| Month | Total | Mean | Corrected |
|---|---|---|---|
| July | 348.9 | 87.225 | 86.777 |
| Aug. | 368.1 | 92.025 | 91.552 |
| Sept. | 395.0 | 98.750 | 98.242 |
| Oct. | 420.4 | 105.100 | 104.560 |
| Nov. | 496.2 | 124.050 | 123.412 |
| Dec. | 572.3 | 143.075 | 142.340 |
| Jan. | 333.5 | 83.375 | 82.946 |
| Feb. | 297.5 | 74.375 | 73.993 |
| March | 347.3 | 86.825 | 86.379 |
| April | 481.3 | 120.325 | 119.707 |
| May | 396.2 | 99.050 | 98.541 |
| June | 368.1 | 92.025 | 91.552 |
| | | 1,206.200 | |

Correction $= 1,200/1,206.2 = 0.99486$
**c.** April, November, and December are periods of high sales, while February's sales are lowest.

27. **a.** Seasonal Index by Quarter

| Quarter | Average SI Component | Seasonal Index |
|---|---|---|
| 1 | 0.5014 | 0.5027 |
| 2 | 1.0909 | 1.0936 |
| 3 | 1.7709 | 1.7753 |
| 4 | 0.6354 | 0.6370 |

**b.** Production is the largest in the third quarter. It is 77.5 percent above the average quarter. The second quarter is also above average. The first and fourth quarters are well below average, with the first quarter at about 50 percent of a typical quarter.

**29. a.**      Seasonal Index by Quarter

| Quarter | Average SI Component | Seasonal Index |
|---|---|---|
| 1 | 0.5549 | 0.5577 |
| 2 | 0.8254 | 0.8296 |
| 3 | 1.5102 | 1.5178 |
| 4 | 1.0973 | 1.1029 |

**b.** $Y' = 7.667 + 0.0023t$

**c.**

| Period | Production | Index | Forecast |
|---|---|---|---|
| 21 | 7.7153 | 0.5577 | 4.3028 |
| 22 | 7.7176 | 0.8296 | 6.4025 |
| 23 | 7.7199 | 1.5178 | 11.7173 |
| 24 | 7.7222 | 1.1029 | 8.5168 |

**31.**      Seasonal Index by Quarter

| Quarter | Average SI Component | Seasonal Index |
|---|---|---|
| 1 | 1.1962 | 1.2053 |
| 2 | 1.0135 | 1.0212 |
| 3 | 0.6253 | 0.6301 |
| 4 | 1.1371 | 1.1457 |

The regression equation is: $Y' = 43.611 + 7.2153t$

| Period | Visitors | Index | Forecast |
|---|---|---|---|
| 29 | 252.86 | 1.2053 | 304.77 |
| 30 | 260.07 | 1.0212 | 265.58 |
| 31 | 267.29 | 0.6301 | 168.42 |
| 32 | 274.50 | 1.1457 | 314.50 |

In 2003 there were 928 visitors. A 10 percent increase in 2004 means there will be 1,021 visitors. The quarterly estimates are 1,021/4 = 255.25 visitors per quarter.

| Period | Visitors | Index | Forecast |
|---|---|---|---|
| Winter | 255.25 | 1.2053 | 307.65 |
| Spring | 255.25 | 1.0212 | 260.66 |
| Summer | 255.25 | 0.6301 | 160.83 |
| Fall | 255.25 | 1.1457 | 292.44 |

The regression approach is probably superior because the trend is considered.
The mean salary is increasing much faster than the median salary.
Average salary $Y' = -0.328 + .0796t$ in \$ million
Average salary is increasing at a rate of \$79,600 per year.
$r^2 = .897$.
Median salary $Y' = -0.1343 + 0.315t$ in \$ million
Median salary is increasing at a rate of \$31,500 per year.
$r^2 = .614$.

**33.** Purse: Log $Y' = 5.34 + .0434t$
Prize: Log $Y' = 4.51 + .0434t$
The slopes are identical because prize is always 15% of the purse. The projected purse for 2005 is 1.46 million, found by the antilog of $5.34 + 0.0434(19) = 6.1646$.

**35.** Answers will vary.

**37.** For Average salary $Y' = -157,578,839 + 79,620.7t$
For Median salary $Y' = -62,395,392 + 31,524.6t$

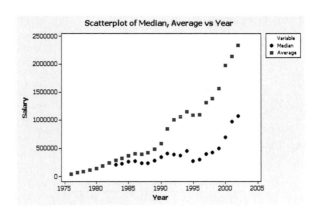

The median salary is increasing \$31,500 per year, while the average salary is increasing much more rapidly (\$79,600 per year).

## CHAPTER 20

**1.** $EMV(A_1) = .30(\$50) + .50(\$70) + .20(\$100) = \$70$

$EMV(A_2) = .30(\$90) + .50(\$40) + .20(\$80) = \$63$

$EMV(A_3) = .30(\$70) + .50(\$60) + .20(\$90) = \$69$

Decision: Choose alternative 1.

**3.**      Opportunity Loss

| | $S_1$ | $S_2$ | $S_3$ |
|---|---|---|---|
| $A_1$ | \$40 | \$ 0 | \$ 0 |
| $A_2$ | 0 | 30 | 20 |
| $A_3$ | 20 | 10 | 10 |

**5.** (Answers in \$000)

$EOL(A_1) = .30(\$40) + 50(\$0) + .20(\$0) = \$12$

$EOL(A_2) = .30(\$0) + .50(\$30) + .20(\$20) = \$19$

$EOL(A_3) = .30(\$20) + .50(\$10) + .20(\$10) = \$13$

**7.** Expected value under conditions of certainty is \$82, found by $.30(\$90) + .50(\$70) + .20(\$100) = \$82$.

$$EVPI = \$82 - \$70 = \$12$$

**9.** Yes, it changes the decision. Choose alternative 2. (Answers in \$000).

$EMV(A_1) = .50(\$50) + .20(\$70) + .30(\$100) = \$69$

$EMV(A_2) = .50(\$90) + .20(\$40) + .30(\$80) = \$77$

$EMV(A_3) = .50(\$70) + .20(\$60) + .30(\$90) = \$74$

**11. a.** (Answers in \$000)

$EMV(neither) = .30(\$0) + .50(\$0) + .20(\$0) = \$0$

$EMV(1) = .30(\$125) + .50(\$65) + .20(\$30) = \$76.00$

$EMV(2) = .30(\$105) + .50(\$60) + .20(\$30) = \$67.50$

$EMV(both) = .30(\$220) + .50(\$110) + .20(\$40) = \$129.00$

**b.** Choose both.

**c.**      Opportunity Loss

| | $S_1$ | $S_2$ | $S_3$ |
|---|---|---|---|
| Neither | \$220 | \$110 | \$40 |
| 1 | 95 | 45 | 10 |
| 2 | 115 | 50 | 10 |
| Both | 0 | 0 | 0 |

d. EOL(neither) = $129.00

   EOL(1) = $53.00

   EOL(2) = $61.50

   EOL(both) = $0

e. EVPI = $0, found by $129 − $129.

   Certainty = .30($220) + .50($110) + .20($40)

   = $129

13. The payoff table is as follows in $000.

|  | Recession, $S_1$ | No Recession, $S_2$ |
|---|---|---|
| Production | $−10.0 | $15.0 |
| Stock | −5.0 | 12.0 |
| CD | 6.0 | 6.0 |

a. Purchase a CD
b. Increase production.
c. (Answers in $000)

$$EMV(Prod.) = .2(-10) + .8(15.0) = 10.0$$

$$EMV(Stock) = .2(-5) + .8(12.0) = 8.6$$

$$EMV(CD) = .2(6) + .8(6) = 6.0$$

Expand production.

d. EVPI = [.2(6) + .8(15)] − [10.0] = 3.2

15. a.

| | | | Event | | |
|---|---|---|---|---|---|
| Act | 10 | 11 | 12 | 13 | 14 |
| 10 | $500 | $500 | $500 | $500 | $500 |
| 11 | 200 | 550 | 550 | 550 | 550 |
| 12 | −100 | 250 | 600 | 600 | 600 |
| 13 | −400 | −50 | 300 | 650 | 650 |
| 14 | −700 | −350 | 0 | 350 | 700 |

b.

| Act | Expected Profit |
|---|---|
| 10 | $500.00 |
| 11 | 504.50 |
| 12 | 421.50 |
| 13 | 233.50 |
| 14 | −31.50 |

Order 11 mobile homes because expected profit of $504.50 is the highest.

c.

| | Opportunity Loss | | | | |
|---|---|---|---|---|---|
| Supply | 10 | 11 | 12 | 13 | 14 |
| 10 | $  0 | $ 50 | $100 | $150 | $200 |
| 11 | 300 | 0 | 50 | 100 | 150 |
| 12 | 600 | 300 | 0 | 50 | 100 |
| 13 | 900 | 600 | 300 | 0 | 50 |
| 14 | 1,200 | 900 | 600 | 300 | 0 |

d.

| | Act | | | | |
|---|---|---|---|---|---|
| | 10 | 11 | 12 | 13 | 14 |
| EOL | $95.50 | $91 | $174 | $362 | $627 |

Decision: Order 11 homes because the opportunity loss of $91 is the smallest.

e. $91, found by:

   $595.50   profit under certainty

   −504.50   profit under uncertainty

   $ 91.00   value of perfect information

17. a.

| | | | Event | | | |
|---|---|---|---|---|---|---|
| Act | 41 | 42 | 43 | 44 | 45 | 46 |
| 41 | $410 | $410 | $410 | $410 | $410 | $410 |
| 42 | 405 | 420 | 420 | 420 | 420 | 420 |
| 43 | 400 | 415 | 430 | 430 | 430 | 430 |
| 44 | 395 | 410 | 425 | 440 | 440 | 440 |
| 45 | 390 | 405 | 420 | 435 | 450 | 450 |
| 46 | 385 | 400 | 415 | 430 | 445 | 460 |

b.

| Act | Expected Profit |
|---|---|
| 41 | $410.00 |
| 42 | 419.10 |
| 43 | 426.70 |
| 44 | 432.20 |
| 45 | 431.70 |
| 46 | 427.45 |

c. Order 44 because $432.20 is the largest expected profit.
d. Expected opportunity loss:

| 41 | 42 | 43 | 44 | 45 | 46 |
|---|---|---|---|---|---|
| $28.30 | $19.20 | $11.60 | $6.10 | $6.60 | $10.85 |

e. Order 44 because the opportunity loss of $6.10 is the smallest. Yes, it agrees.
f. $6.10, found by:

   $438.30   profit under certainty

   −432.20   profit under uncertainty

   $  6.10   value of perfect information

   The maximum we should pay for perfect information is $6.10.

# Answers

## to Odd-Numbered Review Exercises

### REVIEW OF CHAPTERS 1–4

**Part I—Multiple Choice**

| | | | |
|---|---|---|---|
| **1.** | B | **7.** | D |
| **3.** | D | **9.** | B |
| **5.** | A | **11.** | A |

**Part II—Problems**

**13.** **a.** Sample.
    **b.** Ratio.
    **c.** $11.60, found by $58/5.
    **d.** $11.70. Half of the employees earn below $11.70 an hour and the other half earn above $11.70 an hour.
    **e.** $s^2 = \dfrac{23.38}{5-1} = 5.845$

    **f.** $sk = \dfrac{3(11.60 - 11.70)}{2.42} = -0.124$

**15.** **a.**

| Rolls | | Frequency | |
|---|---|---|---|
| 3 up to 6 | ‖ | 2 | ‖ |
| 6 up to 9 | ЖⅠ | 6 | ЖⅠ |
| 9 up to 12 | Ж Ⅲ | 8 | Ж Ⅲ |
| 12 up to 15 | Ⅲ | 3 | Ⅲ |
| 15 up to 18 | Ⅰ | 1 | Ⅰ |

    **b.**

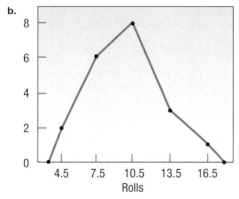

    **c.** $\bar{X} = \dfrac{186}{20} = 9.3$
    **d.** Median = 9
    **e.** 8 and 9, each occurs 4 times
    **f.** 15 using the frequency distribution, 13 using the actual data.
    **g.** $s^2 = \dfrac{1{,}762}{20-1} = 9.2737$
    **h.** $s = \sqrt{9.2737} = 3.045$
    **i.** $9.30 \pm 2(3.045)$. The limits are 3.21 up to 15.39.

**17.** **a.** 8.82%, found by 44.1/5.
    **b.** $GM = \sqrt[5]{(1.052)(1.087)(1.039)(1.068)(1.195)}$
            $= 1.0868.$
    The geometric mean increased at a rate of 8.68% per year.
    **c.** Geometric mean, because it is not highly influenced by the 19.5 percent.

**19.**

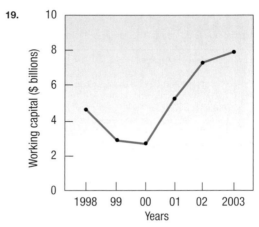

**21.** **a.** The following histogram is from MINITAB.

```
Histogram of C1    N = 50
Midpoint       Count
       0          1  *
      40          7  *******
      80          3  ***
     120          8  ********
     160         15  ***************
     200         10  **********
     240          3  ***
     280          3  ***
```

    **b and c.**

| N | MEAN | MEDIAN | TRMEAN | STDEV | SEMEAN |
|---|---|---|---|---|---|
| 50 | 147.90 | 148.50 | 146.11 | 69.24 | 9.79 |

| MIN | MAX | Q1 | Q3 |
|---|---|---|---|
| 14.00 | 299.00 | 106.00 | 186.25 |

    The distribution is fairly symmetrical because the mean ($147.90) and the median ($148.50) are quite close. The mean $\pm$ 2s indicates that the middle 95 percent of the deposits are between $147.90 \pm 2(\$69.24) = \$9.42$ and $286.38. Range = $299.00 - \$14.00 = \$285.00.

**23.** **a.** From MINITAB:

| Variable | N | Mean | Median | Tr mean | Stdev | Se mean |
|---|---|---|---|---|---|---|
| years | 85 | 15.06 | 15.00 | 14.79 | 9.63 | 1.04 |

| Variable | Min | Max | Q1 | Q3 |
|---|---|---|---|---|
| years | 0.00 | 36.00 | 6.00 | 22.50 |

    Typical length of service is about 15 years (mean or median).
    **b.** Range is 36 years, found by 36 (MAX) − 0 (MIN).
    **c.** Only slight positive skewness, because the mean of 15.06 is slightly larger than the median (15.00).

**d.** 
```
Stem-and-leaf of years      N = 85
   Leaf Unit = 1.0
      12    0  011222333444
      30    0  555555566677788999
      42    1  000133334444
     (16)   1  5555566666788899
      27    2  00001233333
      16    2  6667889
       9    3  00123344
       1    3  6
```

**25.** The typical age is 55 years. The range is 27 years.

```
Descriptive Statistics: years
Variable       N     Mean  Median  TrMean   StDev   SE Mean
years         43   54.651  55.000  54.564   6.347     0.968

Variable  Minimum  Maximum      Q1      Q3
years      42.000   69.000  50.000  58.000

Stem-and-Leaf Displays: years
Stem-and-Leaf Display: years    N = 43
Leaf Unit = 1.0

           2    4  23
           2    4
           6    4  6677
           9    4  899
          15    5  001111
          17    5  22
          (8)   5  444445555
          18    5  6667777
          11    5  8
          10    6  0111
           6    6  2
           5    6  445
           2    6
           2    6  89
```

## REVIEW OF CHAPTERS 5–7
### Part I—Multiple Choice
**1.** C      **7.** B
**3.** C      **9.** D
**5.** C     **11.** A

### Part II—Problems
**13.** **a.** .10, found by 20/200.
　　 **b.** .725, found by 145/200.
　　 **c.** .925, found by $1 - 15/200$.
**15.** **a.** .1353, found from Appendix C, where $\mu = 2.0$.
　　 **b.** 398, found by $400 - 2$.
　　 **c.** .3233, found by $1 - (.1353 + .2707 + .2707)$.
**17.** **a.** .0.523, found by 280/535.
　　 **b.** .0.526, found by 229/435.
　　 **c.** .0.903, found by 483/535.
**19.** **a.** $1.84 million, found by $0 + .64 + 1.2$.
　　 **b.** .98.
　　 **c.** .20, found by .004/.02.
　　 **d.** Yes. The $2 million premium is greater than the expected loss of $1.84 million. Thus, the expected profit is $0.16 million.

## REVIEW OF CHAPTERS 8 AND 9
### Part I—Multiple Choice
**1.** B      **5.** D      **9.** B
**3.** D      **7.** A

### Part II—Problems
**11.** $z = \dfrac{8.8 - 8.6}{2.0/\sqrt{35}} = 0.59, .5000 - 2\ .2224 = .2776$

**13.** $160 \pm 1.75\ \dfrac{20}{\sqrt{40}}$, 154.47 up to 165.53

**15.** $985.5 \pm 2.571\ \dfrac{115.5}{\sqrt{6}}$, 864.27 up to 1,106.73

**17.** $240 \pm 2.131\ \dfrac{35}{\sqrt{16}}$, 221.35 up to 258.65

Because 250 is in the interval, the evidence does *not* indicate an increase in production.

**19.** $n = \left[\dfrac{1.96(25)}{4}\right]^2 = 150$

**21.** $n = .08(.92)\left(\dfrac{2.33}{0.02}\right)^2 = 999$

**23.** $n = .4(.6)\left(\dfrac{2.33}{0.03}\right)^2 = 1{,}448$

## REVIEW OF CHAPTERS 10–12
### Part I—Multiple Choice
**1.** E      **5.** B      **9.** D
**3.** B      **7.** A

### Part II—Problems
**11.** $H_0: \mu \geq 36$; $H_1: \mu < 36$. Reject $H_0$ if $z < -1.65$.

$$z = \dfrac{35.5 - 36.0}{0.9/\sqrt{42}} = -3.60$$

Reject $H_0$. The mean height is less than 36 inches.
**13.** $H_0: \mu \leq 20$, $H_1: \mu > 20$. Reject $H_0$ if $t > 1.860$.

$$t = \dfrac{21 - 20}{6.185/\sqrt{9}} = 0.485$$

$H_0$ is not rejected. The mean amount of break time is not more than 20 minutes.
**15.** $H_0: \mu_d \leq 0$; $H_1: \mu_d > 0$. Reject $H_0$ if $t > 1.883$.

$$\bar{d} = 0.4 \qquad s_d = 6.11 \qquad t = \dfrac{0.4}{6.11/\sqrt{10}} = 0.21$$

$H_0$ is not rejected. There is no difference in the life of the paints.

## REVIEW OF CHAPTERS 13 AND 14
### Part I—Multiple Choice
**1.** D      **5.** B      **9.** A
**3.** C      **7.** D

**Part II—Problems**

**11.** **a.** Profit

  **b.** $Y' = a + b_1 X_1 + b_2 X_2 + b_3 X_3 + b_4 X_4$

  **c.** $163,200

  **d.** About 86% of the variation in net profit is explained by the four variables.

  **e.** About 68% of the net profits would be within $3,000 of the estimates; about 95% would be within 2($3,000), or $6,000, of the estimates; and virtually all would be within 3($3,000) or $9,000 of the estimates.

**13.** **a.** 0.9261

  **b.** 2.0469, found by $\sqrt{83.8/20}$

  **c.** $H_0: \beta_1 = \beta_2 = \beta_3 = \beta_4 = 0$
  $H_1:$ not all coefficients are zero
  Reject if $F > 2.87$, computed $F = 62.697$, found by 162.70/4.19.

  **d.** Could delete $X_2$ because $t$-ratio (1.29) is less than the critical $t$ value of 2.086. Otherwise reject $H_0$ for $X_1$, $X_2$, and $X_4$ because all of those $t$-ratios are greater than 2.086.

**REVIEW OF CHAPTERS 15 AND 16**

**Part I—Multiple Choice**

  **1.** D  **5.** D
  **3.** B  **7.** B

**Part II—Problems**

**9.** **a.** $H_0:$ Amount contributed and affiliation are not related
    $H_1:$ Amount contributed and affiliation are related

  **b.** Chi square

  **c.** $(3 - 1)(4 - 1) = 6$

  **d.** Reject $H_0$ if $\chi^2 > 12.592$. Computed $\chi^2$ is 19.681, so $H_0$ is rejected.

  **e.** Party affiliation and amount contributed are related.

# Photo Credits

**Chapter 1**
P1.1, Photo Courtesy of Wal-Mart Stores, Inc.; P1.2, © RF/Corbis; P1.3, © elektraVision AG/PictureQuest; P1.4, © RF/Corbis

**Chapter 2**
P2.1, Courtesy of Merrill Lynch; P2.2, Jack Star/PhotoLink/Getty Images; P2.3, PhotoDisc/Getty Images

**Chapter 3**
P3.1, This image is reproduced with permission of United Parcel Service of America, Inc. © Copyright 2003 United Parcel Service of America, Inc. All rights reserved; P3.2, RF/Corbis; P3.3, © Neil Beer/PhotoDisc/ PictureQuest; P3.4, Courtesy of Dell Inc.

**Chapter 4**
P4.1, © RF/Corbis; P4.2, The Home Depot; P4.3, © RF/Corbis; P4.4, PhotoDisc/Getty Images; P4.5, SPL/Photo Researchers, Inc.

**Chapter 5**
P5.1, AP/Wide World Photos; P5.2, AP/Wide World Photos; P5.3, Courtesy of Dean's Food; P5.4, © 2003 Busch Entertainment Corporation. All rights reserved; P5.5, © RF/Corbis

**Chapter 6**
P6.1, © elektraVision AG/PictureQuest; P6.2, © Corbis Images/PictureQuest; P6.3, © RF/Corbis; P6.4, LEGO, the LEGO logo, brick configuration and mini-figure are trademarks of the LEGO Group © 2003 The LEGO Group.The LEGO® trademarks and products are used with permission. The LEGO Group does not sponsor this publication.

**Chapter 7**
P7.1a&b, Photo Courtesy of Victoria's Secret; P7.2 © RF/Corbis; P7.3, The Good Year Tire and Rubber Company; P7.4, © RF/Corbis

**Chapter 8**
P8.1, © RF/Corbis; P8.2, Photo Disc/ Getty Images; P8.3, Terry Wild Stock, Inc. © 2003; P8.4 © BP p.l.c. 2002. All rights reserved.

**Chapter 9**
P9.1, AP/Wide World Photos; P9.2, AP/Wide World Photos; P9.3, PhotoLink/Getty Images; P9.4, AP/Wide World Photos

**Chapter 10**
P10.1, NCR Corporation; P10.2, Russell Illig/Getty Images; P10.3, Tomi/PhotoLink/Getty Images; P10.4, AP/Wide World Photos

**Chapter 11**
P11.1, Terry Wild Stock, Inc. © 2003; P11.2, © RF/Corbis; P11.3, © RF/Corbis; P11.4, David Buffington/Getty Images

**Chapter 12**
P12.1, © RF/Corbis; P12.2, Don Farrall/Getty Images; P12.3, PhotoLink/Getty Images; P12.4, Keith Brofsky/Getty Images

**Chapter 13**
P13.1, Ritz Camera Centers; P13.2, © The Coca-Cola Company; P13.3, Keith Brofsky/Getty Images

**Chapter 14**
P14.1, © RF/Corbis; P14.2, Ryan McVay/Getty Images; P14.3, Karl Weatherly/Getty Images

**Chapter 15**
P15.1, © Corbis Images/PictureQuest; P15.2, AP/Wide World Photos; P15.3, © RF/Corbis

**Chapter 16**
P16.1, PhotoLink/Getty Images; P16.2, Courtesy of Nestlé USA—Beverage Division; P16.3, © RubberBall Productions/PictureQuest; P16.4, Ryan McVay/Getty Images.

**Chapter 17**
P17.1, AP/Wide World Photos; P17.2, Courtesy of the National Institute of Standards and Technology, Office of Quality Pograms, Gaithersburg, MD; P17.3, John A. Rizzo/Getty Images; P17.4, Image by Christina Sanders; P17.5, Courtesy of ALCOA

**Chapter 18**
P18.1, © Image Ideas, Inc./PictureQuest

**Chapter 19**
P19.1, Courtesy of PepsiCo; P19.2, Copyright 1992 Donna Cox and Robert Patterson. Image produced at the National Center for Supercomputing Applications, University of Illinois at Urbana—Champaign; P19.3, PhotoLink/Getty Images.

**Chapter 20**
P20.1, Akira Kaede/Getty Images; P20.2, AP/Wide World Photos

# Index